Lecture Notes in Computer Science 3242

Commenced Publication in 1973
Founding and Former Series Editors:
Gerhard Goos, Juris Hartmanis, and Jan van Leeuwen

Editorial Board

David Hutchison
  Lancaster University, UK
Takeo Kanade
  Carnegie Mellon University, Pittsburgh, PA, USA
Josef Kittler
  University of Surrey, Guildford, UK
Jon M. Kleinberg
  Cornell University, Ithaca, NY, USA
Friedemann Mattern
  ETH Zurich, Switzerland
John C. Mitchell
  Stanford University, CA, USA
Moni Naor
  Weizmann Institute of Science, Rehovot, Israel
Oscar Nierstrasz
  University of Bern, Switzerland
C. Pandu Rangan
  Indian Institute of Technology, Madras, India
Bernhard Steffen
  University of Dortmund, Germany
Madhu Sudan
  Massachusetts Institute of Technology, MA, USA
Demetri Terzopoulos
  New York University, NY, USA
Doug Tygar
  University of California, Berkeley, CA, USA
Moshe Y. Vardi
  Rice University, Houston, TX, USA
Gerhard Weikum
  Max-Planck Institute of Computer Science, Saarbruecken, Germany

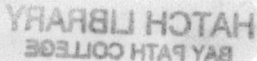

Xin Yao Edmund Burke José A. Lozano
Jim Smith Juan J. Merelo-Guervós
John A. Bullinaria Jonathan Rowe Peter Tiňo
Ata Kabán Hans-Paul Schwefel (Eds.)

Parallel Problem Solving from Nature – PPSN VIII

8th International Conference
Birmingham, UK, September 18-22, 2004
Proceedings

Volume Editors

Xin Yao, John A. Bullinaria, Jonathan Rowe, Peter Tiňo, Ata Kabán
The University of Birmingham, School of Computer Science
Edgbaston, Birmingham B15 2TT, UK
E-mail: {x.yao, j.a.bullinaria, j.e.rowe, p.tino, a.kaban}@cs.bham.ac.uk

Edmund Burke
University of Nottingham, School of Computer Science and Information Technology
Jubilee Campus, Nottingham NG8 2BB, UK
E-mail: ekb@cs.nott.ac.uk

José A. Lozano
The University of the Basque Country, Computer Science Faculty
P. Manuel de Lardizabal, 1, 20009 San Sebastian, Spain
E-mail: lozano@si.ehu.es

Jim Smith
University of the West of England
Faculty of Computing, Engineering and Mathematical Sciences
Bristol BS16 1QY, UK
E-mail: james.smith@uwe.ac.uk

Juan J. Merelo-Guervós
ETS Ingeniera Informàtica, Depto. Arquitectura y Tecnología de Computadores
C/Daniel Saucedo Aranda, s/n, 18071 Granada, Spain
E-mail: jmerelo@geneura.ugr.es

Hans-Paul Schwefel
Universität Dortmund, Fachbereich Informatik, Lehrstuhl Informatik XI
44221 Dortmund, Germany
E-mail: hps@udo.edu

Library of Congress Control Number: 2004112163

CR Subject Classification (1998): F.1-2, C.1.2, D.1-3, I.2.8, I.2.6, I.2.11, J.3

ISSN 0302-9743
ISBN 3-540-23092-0 Springer Berlin Heidelberg New York

This work is subject to copyright. All rights are reserved, whether the whole or part of the material is concerned, specifically the rights of translation, reprinting, re-use of illustrations, recitation, broadcasting, reproduction on microfilms or in any other way, and storage in data banks. Duplication of this publication or parts thereof is permitted only under the provisions of the German Copyright Law of September 9, 1965, in its current version, and permission for use must always be obtained from Springer. Violations are liable to prosecution under the German Copyright Law.

Springer is a part of Springer Science+Business Media

springeronline.com

© Springer-Verlag Berlin Heidelberg 2004
Printed in Germany

Typesetting: Camera-ready by author, data conversion by Olgun Computergrafik
Printed on acid-free paper   SPIN: 11321569   06/3142   5 4 3 2 1 0

Preface

We are very pleased to present this LNCS volume, the proceedings of the 8th International Conference on Parallel Problem Solving from Nature (PPSN VIII). PPSN is one of the most respected and highly regarded conference series in evolutionary computation and natural computing/computation. This biennial event was first held in Dortmund in 1990, and then in Brussels (1992), Jerusalem (1994), Berlin (1996), Amsterdam (1998), Paris (2000), and Granada (2002). PPSN VIII continues to be the conference of choice by researchers all over the world who value its high quality.

We received a record 358 paper submissions this year. After an extensive peer review process involving more than 1100 reviews, the programme committee selected the top 119 papers for inclusion in this volume and, of course, for presentation at the conference. This represents an acceptance rate of 33%. Please note that review reports with scores only but no textual comments were not considered in the chairs' ranking decisions.

The papers included in this volume cover a wide range of topics, from evolutionary computation to swarm intelligence and from bio-inspired computing to real-world applications. They represent some of the latest and best research in evolutionary and natural computation. Following the PPSN tradition, all papers at PPSN VIII were presented as posters. There were 7 sessions: each session consisting of around 17 papers. For each session, we covered as wide a range of topics as possible so that participants with different interests would find some relevant papers at every session.

The conference featured three distinguished keynote speakers: Mandyam Srinivasan, Benjamin Wah and Lee Giles. Their backgrounds in biology, engineering and computer science, respectively, reflect the interdisciplinary nature of PPSN VIII. Prof. Srinivasan's talk was on "Parallel Problem Solving in Honeybees: Vision, Navigation and 'Cognition'." Prof. Wah's talk was on "Constraint Partitioning and Its Applications in Parallel Problem Solving." We are very grateful to them for contributing valuable time from their busy schedules.

PPSN VIII included 8 tutorials and 6 workshops. We were extremely fortunate to have such an impressive list of internationally leading scientists from across natural computation as tutorial speakers. They provided an excellent start to the five-day event. The workshops offered an ideal opportunity for participants to explore specific topics in natural computation in an informal setting. They were sowing the seeds for the future growth of natural computation.

To encourage and reward high-quality research in the international community, PPSN VIII presented a prize of £1,100 cash plus £350 travel costs for our Best Paper Award. As far as we are aware, this is the largest prize ever awarded for a best paper at an evolutionary/natural computation conference. The prize was sponsored by the Honda Research Institute (Europe) through Dr. Bernhard Sendhoff. All accepted papers were eligible to enter the competition. A separate

Best Student Paper Award, sponsored by HP Labs via Professor David Cliff, was also given at the conference. In addition, we received generous support from Thales Research and Technology (UK) through Dr. Sophie Kain. PPSN VIII would not have been possible without the support of the Centre of Excellence for Research in Computational Intelligence and Applications (CERCIA) and the School of Computer Science at the University of Birmingham. We are very grateful to these sponsors and would like to extend our thanks to them.

The success of a conference depends on its authors, reviewers and organizers. PPSN VIII was no exception. We are grateful to all the authors for their paper submissions and to all the reviewers for their outstanding work in refereeing the papers within a very tight schedule. We relied heavily upon a team of volunteers to keep the PPSN VIII wheel turning. In particular, the following people at Birmingham contributed a significant amount of time and expertise: Jun He, Delia Sexton, Mark Roberts and Angela Richardson. We are very grateful for their efforts.

September 2004

Xin Yao
Edmund Burke
Jose A. Lozano
Jim Smith
Juan Julián Merelo Guervós
John Bullinaria
Jon Rowe
Peter Tiňo
Ata Kabán
Hans-Paul Schwefel

Organization

PPSN VIII is organised and hosted by CERCIA, School of Computer Science, University of Birmingham, UK.

PPSN VIII Conference Committee

General Chair	Xin Yao, University of Birmingham, UK
Programme Co-chairs	Edmund Burke, University of Nottingham, UK
	José A. Lozano, University of the Basque Country, Spain
	Jim Smith, University of the West of England, UK
Electronic Programme Chair	Juan J. Merelo-Guervós, University of Granada, Spain
Local Organization Chair	John Bullinaria, University of Birmingham, UK
Tutorial Chair	Jon Rowe, University of Birmingham, UK
Workshop Co-chairs	Peter Tiňo, University of Birmingham, UK
	Ata Kabán, University of Birmingham, UK
Proceedings Chair	Hans-Paul Schwefel, University of Dortmund, Germany
Publicity Co-chairs	Jun He, University of Birmingham, UK
	Shigeyoshi Tsutsui, Hannan University, Japan
	Eckart Zitzler, ETH Zurich, Switzerland
Best Paper Competition Chair	Bernhard Sendhoff, Honda Research Institute (Europe), Germany
Industrial Liaison Chair	Graham Hesketh, Rolls-Royce, UK

PPSN VIII Steering Committee

David Corne	University of Exeter, UK
Kenneth De Jong	George Mason University, USA
Gusz Eiben	Free University of Amsterdam, The Netherlands
Juan J. Merelo-Guervós	University of Granada, Spain
Marc Schoenauer	INRIA, France
Hans-Paul Schwefel	University of Dortmund, Germany
Xin Yao	University of Birmingham, UK

PPSN VIII Tutorials

Evolution in Natural and Artificial Systems
Richard Watson

Biological Applications of Evolutionary Computation
James Foster

Evolutionary Algorithms for Optimisation
Darrell Whitley

Ant Colony Optimisation and Swarm Intelligence
Marco Dorigo

Classifier Systems and Reinforcement Learning
Tim Kovacs

Market-Based Systems
Dave Cliff

Genetic Algorithm Theory
Michael Vose

Evolvable Hardware
Adrian Thompson

PPSN VIII Workshops

Workshop on Challenges in Real World Optimisation Using Evolutionary Computing
Ashutosh Tiwari and Rajkumar Roy

Workshop on Games and Emergent Behaviors in Distributed Computing Environments
Jae C. Oh

Workshop on Nature Inspired Approaches to Networks and Telecommunications
Yong Xu and Sancho Salcedo-Sanz

Workshop on Intelligence Before Training Neural Nets (IBTNN 2004)
Waseem Asrar Ahmed

Workshop on Foundations of Learning Classifier Systems
Larry Bull and Tim Kovacs

Workshop on Future Directions for Learning Classifier Systems
Will Browne

Workshop on Memetic Algorithms (WOMA-V)
William E. Hart, Natalio Krasnogor, Jim E. Smith

PPSN VIII Programme Committee

Abbass, Hussein
Aguilar-Ruiz, Jesús S.
Aickelin, Uwe
Alander, Jarmo
Alba, Enrique
Altenberg, Lee
Araujo, Lourdes
Baeck, Thomas
Bagnall, Tony
Banzhaf, Wolfgang
Barbosa, Helio
Barry, Alwyn
BenHamida, Sana
Berghe, Greet Vanden
Beyer, Hans-Georg
Blazewicz, Jacek
Blum, Christian
Bonarini, Andrea
Booker, Lashon B.
Bosman, Peter A.N.
Branke, Juergen
Braunschweig, Bertrand
Buckles, Bill
Bullinaria, John A.
Bull, Larry
Cagnoni, Stefano
Cantú-Paz, Erick
Carse, Brian
Castillo-Valdivieso, Pedro A.
Cayzer, Steve
Chan, Keith
Channon, Alastair
Cho, Sun-Bae
Coello, Carlos
Collet, Pierre
Cordon, Cordon
Corne, Dave
Costa, Ernesto
Cotta, Carlos
Darwen, Paul
Deb, Kalyanmoy
De Castro, Leandro N.

De Jong, Ken
Delahaye, Daniel
Dopico, Juan Rabuñal
Dorado, Julián
Dorigo, Marco
Dozier, Gerry V.
Droste, Stefan
Duro, Richard
Eiben, Gusz
Engelbrecht, Andries
Esparcia, Ana
Esquivel, Susana Cecilia
Fernandez, Francisco
Fleming, Peter
Floreano, Dario
Fogel, Gary
Fonlupt, Cyril
Fonseca, Carlos M.
Freisleben, Bernd
Freitas, Alex
Gallagher, Marcus
Gambardella, Luca M.
Gamez, Jose A.
Gao, Yong
Garibaldi, Jon
Garrell-Guiu, Josep M.
Gendreau, Michel
Giannakoglou, Kyriakos
González, Jesús
Gottlieb, Jens
Gustafson, Steven
Hao, Jin-Kao
Hart, Bill
Hart, Emma
Hartl, Richard
Harvey, Inman
He, Jun
Hemert, Jano van
Herdy, Michael
Herrera, Francisco
Hervás, Cesar
Hidalgo, Ignacio
Hogg, Tad

Horn, Jeff
Hughes, E.J.
Hurst, Jacob
Husbands, Phil
Iba, Hitoshi
Iglesia, Bea de la
Inza, Iñaki
Isasi, Pedro
Jansen, Thomas
Jin, Yaochu
John, Bob
Julstrom, Bryant
Kabán, Ata
Kang, Lishan
Kazarlis, Spyros
Keijzer, Maarten
Keller, Robert
Kendall, Graham
Kita, Hajime
Knowles, Joshua
Kok, Joost
Kovacs, Tim
Krasnogor, Natalio
Krink, Thiemo
Kwan, Raymond
Lanzi, Pier Luca
Larrañaga, Pedro
Lattaud, Claude
Le Riche, Rodolphe
Leung, Kwong-Sak
Liardet, Pierre
Liu, Yong
Llorá, Xavier
Lobo, Fernando
Louis, Sushil J.
Lozano, José Antonio
Lozano, Manuel
Lucas, Simon
Luo, Wenjian
Lutton, Evelyne
Marchiori, Elena
Martin, Worthy
Martí, Rafael

Matsumura, Yoshiyuki
Mattfeld, Dirk
Merz, Peter
Michalewicz, Zbigniew
Middendorf, Martin
Miller, Julian
Mohan, Chilukuri
Montana, David
Moshaiov, Amiram
Muehlenbein, Heinz
Muruzábal, Jorge
Naudts, Bart
Ochoa, Alberto
Ohkura, Kazuhiro
Osman, Ibrahim H.
Oudeyer, Pierre-Yves
Paechter, Ben
Paredis, Jan
Paton, Ray
Pelikan, Martin
Petrovic, Dobrila
Petrovic, Sanja
Pipe, Tony
Pomares, Héctor
Porto, V. William
Prugel-Bennett, Adam
Raidl, Guenther
Rasheed, Khaled
Reeves, Colin
Reynolds, Robert
Rivas, Víctor
Rizki, Mateen
Robilliard, Denis
Rojas, Ignacio
Romero, Gustavo
Rosca, Justinian
Ross, Peter
Rothlauf, Franz
Rowe, Jonathan
Roy, Rajkumar
Rudolph, Guenter
Runarsson, Thomas
Salcedo-Sanz, Sancho
Sánchez, Luciano
Santana, Roberto
Sareni, Bruno
Schaffer, David
Schmitt, Lothar M.
Schnier, Thorsten
Schwefel, Hans-Paul
Sebag, Michele
Sendhoff, Bernhard
Sen, Sandip
Shapiro, Jonathan
Smith, Alice
Smith, James
Smith, Rob
Spears, Bill
Stewart, Paul
Stützle, Thomas
Suganthan, Ponnuthurai
 Nagaratnam
Talbi, ElGhazali
Tan, Kay Chen
Tateson, Richard
Tettamanzi, Andrea
Thangiah, Sam R.
Thierens, Dirk
Thompson, Jonathan
Thomsen, Rene
Timmis, Jonathan
Tiňo, Peter
Tomassini, Marco
Tsahalis, Demosthenes
Tsang, Edward
Tsutsui, Shigeyoshi
Venturini, Gilles
Von Zuben, Fernando J.
Vose, Michael
Wang, Fang
Wang, Lipo
Watson, Jean-Paul
While, Lyndon
Whitley, Darrell
Wilson, Stewart
Wu, Annie
Wyatt, Jeremy
Yang, Shengxiang
Yao, Xin
Zalzala, Ali
Zhang, Byoung-Tak
Zhang, Qingfu
Zitzler, Eckart

Sponsoring Institutions

Centre of Excellence for Research in Computational Intelligence and Applications (CERCIA), School of Computer Science, University of Birmingham, UK

Honda Research Institute (Europe), Germany

Thales Research and Technology, UK

HP Labs Bristol, UK

Table of Contents

Theory

On the Quality Gain of $(1, \lambda)$-ES Under Fitness Noise 1
  Hans-Georg Beyer and Silja Meyer-Nieberg

Fitness Distributions and GA Hardness 11
  Yossi Borenstein and Riccardo Poli

Experimental Supplements to the Theoretical Analysis of EAs
on Problems from Combinatorial Optimization 21
  *Patrick Briest, Dimo Brockhoff, Bastian Degener, Matthias Englert,
  Christian Gunia, Oliver Heering, Thomas Jansen, Michael Leifhelm,
  Kai Plociennik, Heiko Röglin, Andrea Schweer, Dirk Sudholt,
  Stefan Tannenbaum, and Ingo Wegener*

The Ising Model: Simple Evolutionary Algorithms as Adaptation Schemes. 31
  *Patrick Briest, Dimo Brockhoff, Bastian Degener, Matthias Englert,
  Christian Gunia, Oliver Heering, Thomas Jansen, Michael Leifhelm,
  Kai Plociennik, Heiko Röglin, Andrea Schweer, Dirk Sudholt,
  Stefan Tannenbaum, and Ingo Wegener*

Evolutionary Algorithms with On-the-Fly Population Size Adjustment.... 41
  A.E. Eiben, Elena Marchiori, and V.A. Valkó

Search Space Features Underlying the Performance
of Stochastic Local Search Algorithms for MAX-SAT 51
  Holger H. Hoos, Kevin Smyth, and Thomas Stützle

Bridging the Gap Between Theory and Practice....................... 61
  Thomas Jansen and R. Paul Wiegand

A Reduced Markov Model of GAs Without the Exact Transition Matrix .. 72
  Cheah C.J. Moey and Jonathan E. Rowe

Expected Runtimes of a Simple Evolutionary Algorithm
for the Multi-objective Minimum Spanning Tree Problem 81
  Frank Neumann

On the Importance of Information Speed in Structured Populations 91
  Mike Preuss and Christian Lasarczyk

Estimating the Number of Solutions for SAT Problems 101
  Colin R. Reeves and Mériéma Aupetit-Bélaidouni

Behavior of Evolutionary Algorithms
in Chaotically Changing Fitness Landscapes 111
   Hendrik Richter

Expected Rates of Building Block Discovery, Retention and Combination
Under 1-Point and Uniform Crossover 121
   Cameron Skinner and Patricia Riddle

An Analysis of the Effectiveness of Multi-parent Crossover 131
   Chuan-Kang Ting

On the Use of a Non-redundant Encoding for Learning Bayesian Networks
from Data with a GA.. 141
   Steven van Dijk and Dirk Thierens

Phase Transition Properties of Clustered Travelling Salesman
Problem Instances Generated with Evolutionary Computation 151
   Jano I. van Hemert and Neil B. Urquhart

A Simple Two-Module Problem to Exemplify Building-Block Assembly
Under Crossover 161
   Richard A. Watson

Statistical Racing Techniques for Improved Empirical Evaluation
of Evolutionary Algorithms... 172
   Bo Yuan and Marcus Gallagher

New Algorithms

LS-CMA-ES: A Second-Order Algorithm
for Covariance Matrix Adaptation..................................... 182
   Anne Auger, Marc Schoenauer, and Nicolas Vanhaecke

Learning Probabilistic Tree Grammars for Genetic Programming......... 192
   Peter A.N. Bosman and Edwin D. de Jong

Sequential Sampling in Noisy Environments 202
   Jürgen Branke and Christian Schmidt

Evolutionary Continuous Optimization by Distribution Estimation with
Variational Bayesian Independent Component Analyzers Mixture Model .. 212
   Dong-Yeon Cho and Byoung-Tak Zhang

Spread of Vector Borne Diseases in a Population with Spatial Structure ... 222
   Dominique Chu and Jonathan Rowe

Hierarchical Genetic Algorithms 232
   Edwin D. de Jong, Dirk Thierens, and Richard A. Watson

Migration of Probability Models Instead of Individuals:
An Alternative When Applying the Island Model to EDAs 242
  Luis delaOssa, José A. Gámez, and José M. Puerta

Comparison of Steady-State and Generational Evolution Strategies
for Parallel Architectures 253
  *Razvan Enache, Bernhard Sendhoff, Markus Olhofer,
  and Martina Hasenjäger*

Control of Bloat in Genetic Programming by Means of the Island Model .. 263
  *Francisco Fernández de Vega, German Galeano Gil,
  Juan Antonio Gómez Pulido, and Jose Luis Guisado*

Saving Resources with Plagues in Genetic Algorithms 272
  *Francisco Fernández de Vega, Erik Cantú-Paz, J.I. López,
  and T. Manzano*

Evaluating the CMA Evolution Strategy on Multimodal Test Functions ... 282
  Nikolaus Hansen and Stefan Kern

Exploring the Evolutionary Details
of a Feasible-Infeasible Two-Population GA 292
  Steven Orla Kimbrough, Ming Lu, and David Harlan Wood

An Evolutionary Algorithm for the Maximum Weight Trace Formulation
of the Multiple Sequence Alignment Problem 302
  Gabriele Koller and Günther R. Raidl

A Novel Programmable Molecular Computing Method
Based on Signaling Pathways Regulated by Rho-GTPases
in Living MDCK Epithelial Mammalian Cells........................... 312
  Jian-Qin Liu and Katsunori Shimohara

Empirical Investigations on Parallelized Linkage Identification 322
  Masaharu Munetomo, Naoya Murao, and Kiyoshi Akama

The EAX Algorithm Considering Diversity Loss 332
  Yuichi Nagata

Topology-Oriented Design of Analog Circuits
Based on Evolutionary Graph Generation 342
  *Masanori Natsui, Naofumi Homma, Takafumi Aoki,
  and Tatsuo Higuchi*

A Mixed Bayesian Optimization Algorithm with Variance Adaptation 352
  *Jiri Ocenasek, Stefan Kern, Nikolaus Hansen,
  and Petros Koumoutsakos*

A Swarm Intelligence Based VLSI Multiplication-and-Add Scheme 362
Danilo Pani and Luigi Raffo

Distribution Tree-Building Real-Valued Evolutionary Algorithm 372
Petr Pošík

Optimization via Parameter Mapping with Genetic Programming 382
Joao C.F. Pujol and Riccardo Poli

Multi-cellular Development: Is There Scalability and Robustness to Gain? . 391
Daniel Roggen and Diego Federici

Constrained Evolutionary Optimization
by Approximate Ranking and Surrogate Models 401
Thomas Philip Runarsson

Robust Parallel Genetic Algorithms with Re-initialisation 411
Ivan Sekaj

Improving Evolutionary Algorithms
with Multi-representation Island Models 420
Zbigniew Skolicki and Kenneth De Jong

A Powerful New Encoding
for Tree-Based Combinatorial Optimisation Problems.................. 430
Sang-Moon Soak, David Corne, and Byung-Ha Ahn

Partially Evaluated Genetic Algorithm
Based on Fuzzy c-Means Algorithm 440
Si-Ho Yoo and Sung-Bae Cho

Applications

Metaheuristics for the Vehicle Routing Problem with Stochastic Demands . 450
Leonora Bianchi, Mauro Birattari, Marco Chiarandini, Max Manfrin, Monaldo Mastrolilli, Luis Paquete, Olivia Rossi-Doria, and Tommaso Schiavinotto

AntHocNet: An Ant-Based Hybrid Routing Algorithm
for Mobile Ad Hoc Networks 461
Gianni Di Caro, Frederick Ducatelle, and Luca Maria Gambardella

A Scatter Search Algorithm for the 3D Image Registration Problem 471
Oscar Cordón, Sergio Damas, and José Santamaría

A Hybrid GRASP –
Evolutionary Algorithm Approach to Golomb Ruler Search.............. 481
Carlos Cotta and Antonio J. Fernández

Design of an Efficient Search Algorithm for P2P Networks
Using Concepts from Natural Immune Systems 491
    Niloy Ganguly, Geoff Canright, and Andreas Deutsch

A Novel Ant Algorithm
for Solving the Minimum Broadcast Time Problem 501
    Yehudit Hasson and Moshe Sipper

Designing Multiple-Use Primer Set for Multiplex PCR
by Using Compact GAs... 511
    Yu-Cheng Huang, Han-Yu Chuang, Huai-Kuang Tsai,
    Chun-Fan Chang, and Cheng-Yan Kao

Robust Inferential Sensors Based on Ensemble of Predictors
Generated by Genetic Programming..................................... 522
    Elsa Jordaan, Arthur Kordon, Leo Chiang, and Guido Smits

Searching Transcriptional Modules Using Evolutionary Algorithms 532
    Je-Gun Joung, Sok June Oh, and Byoung-Tak Zhang

Evolution of Voronoi-Based Fuzzy Controllers 541
    Carlos Kavka and Marc Schoenauer

Analyzing Sensor States and Internal States in the Tartarus Problem
with Tree State Machines 551
    DaeEun Kim

Evolving Genetic Regulatory Networks for Hardware Fault Tolerance 561
    Arne Koopman and Daniel Roggen

Evolving Dynamics in an Artificial Regulatory Network Model........... 571
    P. Dwight Kuo, André Leier, and Wolfgang Banzhaf

The Application of Bayesian Optimization and Classifier Systems
in Nurse Scheduling 581
    Jingpeng Li and Uwe Aickelin

An Evolutionary Approach to Modeling Radial Brightness Distributions
in Elliptical Galaxies 591
    Jin Li, Xin Yao, Colin Frayn, Habib G. Khosroshahi,
    and Somak Raychaudhury

Conference Paper Assignment
Using a Combined Greedy/Evolutionary Algorithm 602
    Juan Julián Merelo-Guervós and Pedro Castillo-Valdivieso

A Primer on the Evolution of Equivalence Classes
of Bayesian-Network Structures 612
    Jorge Muruzábal and Carlos Cotta

The Infection Algorithm:
An Artificial Epidemic Approach for Dense Stereo Matching............. 622
  *Gustavo Olague, Francisco Fernández de Vega, Cynthia B. Pérez,
  and Evelyne Lutton*

Optimising Cancer Chemotherapy
Using Particle Swarm Optimisation and Genetic Algorithms............. 633
  Andrei Petrovski, Bhavani Sudha, and John McCall

An Evolutionary Algorithm for Column Generation
in Integer Programming: An Effective Approach for 2D Bin Packing...... 642
  Jakob Puchinger and Günther R. Raidl

An Improved Evaluation Function
for the Bandwidth Minimization Problem 652
  Eduardo Rodriguez-Tello, Jin-Kao Hao, and Jose Torres-Jimenez

Coupling of Evolution and Learning
to Optimize a Hierarchical Object Recognition Model.................. 662
  *Georg Schneider, Heiko Wersing, Bernhard Sendhoff,
  and Edgar Körner*

Evolution of Small-World Networks of Automata for Computation 672
  Marco Tomassini, Mario Giacobini, and Christian Darabos

Recognizing Speed Limit Sign Numbers by Evolvable Hardware 682
  Jim Torresen, Jorgen W. Bakke, and Lukas Sekanina

Dynamic Routing Problems with Fruitful Regions:
Models and Evolutionary Computation 692
  Jano I. van Hemert and J.A. La Poutré

Optimising the Performance of a Formula One Car
Using a Genetic Algorithm 702
  Krzysztof Wloch and Peter J. Bentley

Multi-objective Optimisation

An Inexpensive Cognitive Approach for Bi-objective Optimization
Using Bliss Points and Interaction................................... 712
  Hussein A. Abbass

Finding Knees in Multi-objective Optimization 722
  *Jürgen Branke, Kalyanmoy Deb, Henning Dierolf,
  and Matthias Osswald*

Multi-objective Parallel Tabu Search 732
  *Daniel Jaeggi, Chris Asselin-Miller, Geoff Parks, Timoleon Kipouros,
  Theo Bell, and John Clarkson*

SPEA2+: Improving the Performance
of the Strength Pareto Evolutionary Algorithm 2 742
  Mifa Kim, Tomoyuki Hiroyasu, Mitsunori Miki, and Shinya Watanabe

An Extension of Generalized Differential Evolution
for Multi-objective Optimization with Constraints 752
  Saku Kukkonen and Jouni Lampinen

Adaptive Weighted Particle Swarm Optimisation
for Multi-objective Optimal Design of Alloy Steels 762
  Mahdi Mahfouf, Min-You Chen, and Derek Arthur Linkens

Multi-objective Optimisation by Co-operative Co-evolution 772
  Kuntinee Maneeratana, Kittipong Boonlong, and Nachol Chaiyaratana

Sequential Process Optimisation Using Genetic Algorithms 782
  Victor Oduguwa, Ashutosh Tiwari, and Rajkumar Roy

On Test Functions for Evolutionary Multi-objective Optimization 792
  Tatsuya Okabe, Yaochu Jin, Markus Olhofer, and Bernhard Sendhoff

Multi-objective Optimization of a Composite Material Spring Design
Using an Evolutionary Algorithm 803
  *Frédéric Ratle, Benoît Lecarpentier, Richard Labib,
  and François Trochu*

Dominance Based Crossover Operator
for Evolutionary Multi-objective Algorithms 812
  Olga Rudenko and Marc Schoenauer

Evolutionary Bi-objective Controlled Elevator Group Regulates Passenger
Service Level and Minimises Energy Consumption 822
  Tapio Tyni and Jari Ylinen

Indicator-Based Selection in Multiobjective Search 832
  Eckart Zitzler and Simon Künzli

Co-evolution

Intransitivity in Coevolution 843
  Edwin D. de Jong

Group Transport of an Object to a Target
That Only Some Group Members May Sense 852
  Roderich Groß and Marco Dorigo

Hawks, Doves and Lifetime Reproductive Success 862
  Philip Hingston and Luigi Barone

Evolutionary Multi-agent Systems.................................... 872
　　Pieter J. 't Hoen and Edwin D. de Jong

Credit Assignment Among Neurons in Co-evolving Populations 882
　　Vineet R. Khare, Xin Yao, and Bernhard Sendhoff

A Visual Demonstration of Convergence Properties
of Cooperative Coevolution 892
　　Liviu Panait, R. Paul Wiegand, and Sean Luke

Cooperative Coevolution of Image Feature Construction
and Object Detection.. 902
　　Mark E. Roberts and Ela Claridge

Spatial Embedding and Loss of Gradient
in Cooperative Coevolutionary Algorithms 912
　　R. Paul Wiegand and Jayshree Sarma

A High Performance Multi-objective Evolutionary Algorithm
Based on the Principles of Thermodynamics........................... 922
　　Xiufen Zou, Minzhong Liu, Lishan Kang, and Jun He

Robotics and Multi-agent Systems

Robustness in the Long Run: Auto-teaching *vs* Anticipation
in Evolutionary Robotics.. 932
　　Nicolas Godzik, Marc Schoenauer, and Michèle Sebag

A Self-adaptive Neural Learning Classifier System with Constructivism
for Mobile Robot Control 942
　　Jacob Hurst and Larry Bull

An Approach to Evolutionary Robotics Using a Genetic Algorithm
with a Variable Mutation Rate Strategy 952
　　Yoshiaki Katada, Kazuhiro Ohkura, and Kanji Ueda

Translating the Dances of Honeybees into Resource Location 962
　　DaeEun Kim

Natural Policy Gradient Reinforcement Learning
for a CPG Control of a Biped Robot 972
　　Yutaka Nakamura, Takeshi Mori, and Shin Ishii

Evaluation of Adaptive Nature Inspired Task Allocation
Against Alternate Decentralised Multiagent Strategies 982
　　Richard Price and Peter Tiňo

A Neuroevolutionary Approach to Emergent Task Decomposition 991
　　Jekanthan Thangavelautham and Gabriele M.T. D'Eleuterio

Evolving the "Feeling" of Time Through Sensory-Motor Coordination:
A Robot Based Model 1001
    Elio Tuci, Vito Trianni, and Marco Dorigo

Learning Classifier Systems and Data Mining

An Artificial Immune System for Fuzzy-Rule Induction in Data Mining .. 1011
    *Roberto T. Alves, Myriam R. Delgado, Heitor S. Lopes,
and Alex A. Freitas*

Speeding-Up Pittsburgh Learning Classifier Systems:
Modeling Time and Accuracy 1021
    *Jaume Bacardit, David E. Goldberg, Martin V. Butz, Xavier Llorà,
and Josep M. Garrell*

A Simple Payoff-Based Learning Classifier System..................... 1032
    Larry Bull

Lookahead and Latent Learning
in a Simple Accuracy-Based Classifier System 1042
    Larry Bull

Knowledge Extraction and Problem Structure Identification in XCS 1051
    Martin V. Butz, Pier Luca Lanzi, Xavier Llorà, and David E. Goldberg

Forecasting Time Series by Means of Evolutionary Algorithms 1061
    *Cristóbal Luque del Arco-Calderón, Pedro Isasi Viñuela,
and Julio César Hernández Castro*

Detecting and Pruning Introns for Faster Decision Tree Evolution 1071
    Jeroen Eggermont, Joost N. Kok, and Walter A. Kosters

Evolutionary Multiobjective Clustering 1081
    Julia Handl and Joshua Knowles

Web Page Classification with an Ant Colony Algorithm 1092
    Nicholas Holden and Alex A. Freitas

Oneiric Processing Utilising the Anticipatory Classifier System 1103
    Julian C. Holley, Anthony G. Pipe, and Brian Carse

Self-organizing Neural Grove: Efficient Multiple Classifier System
Using Pruned Self-generating Neural Trees 1113
    Hirotaka Inoue and Hiroyuki Narihisa

Evolutionary Multiobjective Knowledge Extraction
for High-Dimensional Pattern Classification Problems 1123
    Hisao Ishibuchi and Satoshi Namba

Ensemble Learning with Evolutionary Computation:
Application to Feature Ranking 1133
    Kees Jong, Elena Marchiori, and Michèle Sebag

Fast Unsupervised Clustering with Artificial Ants 1143
    Nicolas Labroche, Christiane Guinot, and Gilles Venturini

A Novel Method of Searching the Microarray Data
for the Best Gene Subsets by Using a Genetic Algorithm 1153
    Bin Ni and Juan Liu

Using Genetic Programming for Feature Creation
with a Genetic Algorithm Feature Selector 1163
    Matthew G. Smith and Larry Bull

AgentP Model: Learning Classifier System with Associative Perception .. 1172
    Zhanna V. Zatuchna

Author Index 1183

On the Quality Gain of $(1, \lambda)$-ES Under Fitness Noise*

Hans-Georg Beyer and Silja Meyer-Nieberg

Department of Computer Science XI,
University of Dortmund,
D-44221 Dortmund, Germany
{beyer,meyer}@Ls11.cs.uni-dortmund.de

Abstract. In optimization tasks that deal with real-world applications noise is very common leading to degradation of the performance of Evolution Strategies. We will consider the quality gain of an $(1, \lambda)$-ES under noisy fitness evaluations for arbitrary fitness functions. The equation developed will be applied to several test functions to check its predictive quality.

1 Introduction

Noise is a common phenomenon in optimization tasks dealing with real-world applications. Typically, one is confronted with measurement errors, actuator vibrations, production tolerances or/and is searching for robust (i.e. insensitive) solutions.

Evolution Strategies are nature-inspired search algorithms that move through the search space by the means of variation and selection mimicking the natural evolution process. It is widely believed that they and other Evolutionary Algorithms are especially good at coping with noisy information due to the use of a population of candidate solutions (see e.g. [1], [2], [3], [4], or [5]).

However, since noise does deceive the information obtained from the objective function and thus influences the selection process, even population based algorithms are degraded in their performance. Basically, there are two negative effects that can be observed. The convergence velocity is reduced and a final steady state is reached that deviates from the real optimum.

The main focus of this paper lies on the consideration of the local performance that can be measured in the object parameter space (progress rate) or in the space of the fitness values (quality gain).

For noisy spherically symmetric quadratic and linear fitness environments, the local performance of the $(1 \stackrel{+}{,} \lambda)$-ES [6] and the (μ, λ)-ES ([5], [7]) has already been studied. We will consider the quality gain on arbitrary fitness functions. The quality gain describes the expected change of the fitness of the parent population

---

* This work was supported by the Deutsche Forschungsgemeinschaft (DFG) as part of the Collaborative Research Center (SFB) 531.

from one generation to the next. While it is a local performance measure, it can be used to gain some inside in certain steady state characteristics since the quality gain is equal to zero, once the steady state has been reached. Depending on the fitness function this property can be utilized to derive for example the so-called final fitness error, i.e. the expected difference between the fitness of the steady state and the actual optimum.

We will focus on the $(1, \lambda)$-ES with just one parent and a population of λ offsprings. Therefore, there is no recombination and only the mutation process has to be taken into account. Hence, the λ candidate solutions of the offspring population are generated by adding mutation vectors to the parental object vector. The mutations are assumed to obey a normal distribution with a constant standard deviation σ, which is called the mutation strength. After creating λ new individuals, the best of them is selected as the parent of the next generation.

This paper is organized as follows. First, we will derive an equation describing the quality gain in noisy environments. In order to evaluate the predictive power, the quality gain will then be investigated for a suite of test functions. In the concluding section an outlook will be given presenting a road map for future research.

2 The $(1, \lambda)$-Quality Gain Theory

We consider an $(1, \lambda)$-ES trying to optimize a fitness function F. Without loss of generality, we assume that the optimization task is maximization. Let us consider a parent at the position $\mathbf{y}$ in the object parameter space. An offspring is created by adding a mutation vector $\mathbf{x}$. The associated change of the fitness function is $Q(\mathbf{x}) = F(\mathbf{y} + \mathbf{x}) - F(\mathbf{y})$. Since the measurements of F are disturbed by noise, only the perceived quality $\tilde{Q}(\mathbf{x}) = Q(\mathbf{x}) + \epsilon$ can be observed. The random variable ϵ is assumed to be normally distributed with an expected value of zero and a constant standard deviation σ_ϵ, also called the noise strength.

The noise also influences the selection progress. As a consequence, the seemingly best offspring chosen to be the parent of the next generation is not necessarily the actual optimal one. We want to derive the expected value of the local quality change of this seemingly best candidate, which is called the *quality gain* $\overline{\Delta Q}_{1,\lambda} := \mathrm{E}[Q_{1,\lambda}] = \int_{-\infty}^{\hat{Q}} Q p_{1,\lambda}(Q) \, \mathrm{d}Q$, where $\hat{Q} = \max_\mathbf{x} Q(\mathbf{x})$ and $p_{1,\lambda}(Q)$ is the density function of the chosen offspring which has to be determined. Therefore, we apply the concept of noisy order statistics [8] resulting in

$$\overline{\Delta Q}_{1,\lambda} = \lambda \int_{-\infty}^{\hat{Q}} \int_{-\infty}^{\infty} Q p_Q(Q) p_\epsilon(\tilde{Q}|Q) P(\tilde{Q})^{\lambda-1} \, \mathrm{d}\tilde{Q} \, \mathrm{d}Q, \qquad (1)$$

where $p_\epsilon(\tilde{Q}|Q)$ is the conditional density function of the disturbed variable $\tilde{Q}$ given Q. Starting from (1), we develop an expression for the quality gain. First, we transform Q into the standardized variable $z = (Q - M_Q)/S_Q$, where M_Q is the expected value and S_Q the standard deviation of Q. Afterwards, we extend the upper integration limit to ∞. The quality gain splits into the sum of two integrals

$$\overline{\Delta Q}_{1,\lambda} = \underbrace{\lambda S_Q \int_{-\infty}^{\infty}\int_{-\infty}^{\infty} z p_z(z) p_\epsilon(\tilde{Q}|S_Q z + M_Q) P(\tilde{Q})^{\lambda-1} \, \mathrm{d}\tilde{Q} \, \mathrm{d}z}_{I_1} +$$

$$\underbrace{\lambda M_Q \int_{-\infty}^{\infty}\int_{-\infty}^{\infty} p_z(z) p_\epsilon(\tilde{Q}|S_Q z + M_Q) P(\tilde{Q})^{\lambda-1} \, \mathrm{d}\tilde{Q} \, \mathrm{d}z}_{I_2}. \qquad (2)$$

The solution of the second integral is easily obtained as $I_2 = M_Q$ by changing the order of integration and remembering that since $\tilde{Q} = Q + \epsilon$, its density is given as $p(\tilde{Q}) = \int_{-\infty}^{\infty} p_z(z) p_\epsilon(\tilde{Q}|S_Q z + M_Q) \, \mathrm{d}z$.

An expression for I_1 cannot be so easily obtained since expressions for $p_z(z)$ and $P(\tilde{Q})$ must be found. As a first step, we expand $p_z(z)$ into a Gram-Charlier series $p_z(z) = e^{\frac{-z^2}{2}}/\sqrt{2\pi}(1 + (\kappa_3/3!) \mathrm{He}_3(z) + ...)$, where κ_i are the cumulants and He_i is the ith Hermite polynomial, for example $\mathrm{He}_3(z) = z^3 - 3z$. Under certain conditions (see e.g. [9]) assuming an infinite dimensional search space the cumulants κ_i vanish for $i > 2$. The density function of z thus simplifies to $p_z(z) \simeq e^{-\frac{z^2}{2}}/\sqrt{2\pi}$ enabling us to derive a closed expression for the probability $P(\tilde{Q})$ by integrating $p(\tilde{Q})$ which leads to $P(\tilde{Q}) \simeq \Phi((\tilde{Q} - M_Q)/(\sigma_\epsilon \sqrt{1 + (S_Q/\sigma_\epsilon)^2}))$.

We insert the expressions for $p_z(z)$ and $P(\tilde{Q})$ into I_1 and transform $\tilde{Q}$ into $u = (\tilde{Q} - M_Q)/(\sigma_\epsilon \sqrt{1 + (S_Q/\sigma_\epsilon)^2})$. Finally changing the integration order, we get $I_1 \simeq \frac{\lambda S_Q}{\sqrt{2\pi}} \int_{-\infty}^{\infty} \sqrt{1 + (\frac{S_Q}{\sigma_\epsilon})^2} / \left(1 + (\frac{S_Q}{\sigma_\epsilon})^2\right) \left(\frac{S_Q}{\sigma_\epsilon}\right) u e^{-\frac{u^2}{2}} \Phi^{\lambda-1}(u) \, \mathrm{d}u$. Recalling the definition of the progress coefficient $c_{1,\lambda} := \lambda/\sqrt{2\pi} \int_{-\infty}^{\infty} u e^{-\frac{u^2}{2}} \Phi^{\lambda-1}(u) \, \mathrm{d}u$ [9, p.74f], which is therefore the expected value of the λth order statistics of the standard normal distribution, one obtains $I_1 \simeq c_{1,\lambda} S_Q^2/\sqrt{S_Q^2 + \sigma_\epsilon^2}$ leading to the quality gain

$$\overline{\Delta Q}_{1,\lambda} \simeq \frac{S_Q^2}{\sqrt{S_Q^2 + \sigma_\epsilon^2}} c_{1,\lambda} + M_Q. \qquad (3)$$

This expression can be used as an approximate formula for finite dimensional spaces provided that the approximation for $p_z(z)$ is still valid and that the error that stems from extending the upper integration limit of (1) when using the approximate density can be neglected.

3 Examples

The predictive quality of (3) will be examined in this section for several fitness functions. The results were obtained by performing one-generation experiments with an $(1, 20)$-ES. We will first derive the required statistical parameters S_Q^2 and M_Q for each function before discussing the results of the experiments.

Quadratic Functions. We consider quadratic functions of the form $F_1(\mathbf{y}) = \mathbf{b}^T\mathbf{y} - \mathbf{y}^T\mathbf{Q}\mathbf{y}$, where $\mathbf{b}$ and $\mathbf{y}$ are real-valued vectors and $\mathbf{Q}$ is a positive-definite matrix. The local quality is given as $Q(\mathbf{x}) = 2[\mathbf{Q}(\hat{\mathbf{y}} - \mathbf{y})]^T\mathbf{x} - \mathbf{x}^T\mathbf{Q}\mathbf{x}$, where $\hat{\mathbf{y}} = \arg\max F(\mathbf{y})$. The expected value and variance of Q are $M_Q = -\sigma^2 \text{Tr}[\mathbf{Q}]$ and $S_Q^2 = 4\sigma^2\|\mathbf{Q}(\hat{\mathbf{y}} - \mathbf{y})\|^2 + 2\sigma^4 \text{Tr}[\mathbf{Q}^2]$ (see [9, p.122f]). Assuming σ to be sufficiently small, the biquadratic term of the variance can be neglected. The quality gain (3), $\overline{\Delta Q}_{1,\lambda} = M_Q + c_{1,\lambda} S_Q^2/\sqrt{S_Q^2 + \sigma_\epsilon^2}$, thus becomes

$$\overline{\Delta Q}_{1,\lambda} \simeq \frac{4\sigma^2\|\mathbf{Q}(\hat{\mathbf{y}} - \mathbf{y})\|^2}{\sqrt{4\sigma^2\|\mathbf{Q}(\hat{\mathbf{y}} - \mathbf{y})\|^2 + \sigma_\epsilon^2}} c_{1,\lambda} - \sigma^2 \text{Tr}[\mathbf{Q}]. \tag{4}$$

To compare (4) with the result obtained in [9] for the noise-free case, we introduce the normalizations $\sigma^* = \sigma \text{Tr}[\mathbf{Q}]/\|\mathbf{Q}(\hat{\mathbf{y}} - \mathbf{y})\|$, $\sigma_\epsilon^* = \sigma_\epsilon \text{Tr}[\mathbf{Q}]/(2\|\mathbf{Q}(\hat{\mathbf{y}} - \mathbf{y})\|^2)$, and $\overline{\Delta Q}_{1,\lambda}^* = \overline{\Delta Q}_{1,\lambda} \text{Tr}[\mathbf{Q}]/(2\|\mathbf{Q}(\hat{\mathbf{y}} - \mathbf{y})\|^2)$ and get

$$\overline{\Delta Q}_{1,\lambda}^* \simeq c_{1,\lambda} \sigma^* \frac{1}{\sqrt{1 + (\frac{\sigma_\epsilon^*}{\sigma^*})^2}} - \frac{\sigma^{*2}}{2}. \tag{5}$$

As in the noise-free case with $\overline{\Delta Q}_{1,\lambda}^* \simeq c_{1,\lambda}\sigma^* - \sigma^{*2}/2$, the equation can be decomposed into a gain and a loss term. The noise only influences the gain part of the equation, an observation already made in [9] for the progress rate on the noisy sphere.

The maximum of the noisy quality gain $\overline{\Delta Q}_{1,\lambda}^*$ depends on the value of σ_ϵ^*. If the noise strength is too high, it diminishes the linear gain part such that the loss term is the deciding factor of the equation leading to a monotonically decreasing function.

The validity of (5) was tested on $F_{1.1}(\mathbf{x}) = -\sum_{i=1}^{N} i^2 x_i^2$. The experimental data were obtained by performing 1,000,000 one-generation experiments per data point. As starting vector, $\mathbf{y} = \mathbf{2}$ was chosen.

Figure 1 shows the dependence of the normalized quality gain on the noise strength σ_ϵ^* in a 10- and 100-dimensional object parameter space. As σ_ϵ^* increases, the quality gain decreases and approaches $-\sigma^{*2}/2$. The agreement between (5) and experiment in the higher dimensional space is very good, while greater deviations can be observed for $N = 10$. Here, good results for all choices of σ_ϵ^* can only be obtained for small normalized mutation strengths, e.g. $\sigma^* = 0.5$ – the lowest mutation strength examined.

Figure 2 shows the quality gain $\overline{\Delta Q}_{1,20}^*$ as a function of σ^* depicting the results obtained by (5) and the measured values for several choices of σ_ϵ^*. As before, deviations can be observed for $N = 10$ if the mutation strength is sufficiently large. If the dimensionality is increased, the predictions of (5) are very accurate. The only exception to this is the curve obtained for a noise strength of 5 for which (5) leads to an overestimation of the experimental values.

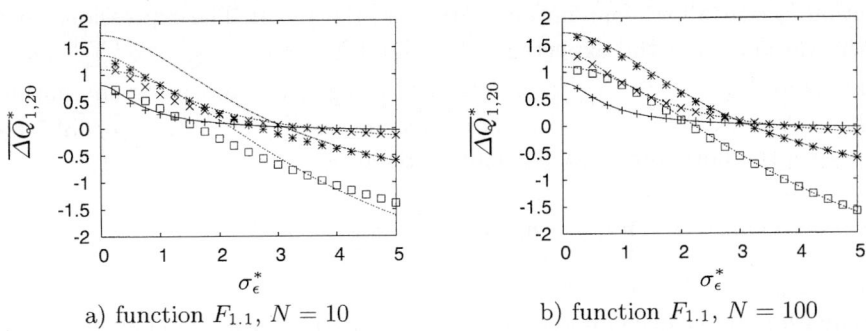

Fig. 1. Dependence of $\overline{\Delta Q}^*_{1,20}$ on the noise strength σ^*_ϵ for function $F_{1.1}$. Depicted are from top to bottom the curves for $\sigma^* = 2$, $\sigma^* = 1$, $\sigma^* = 3$, and $\sigma^* = 0.5$.

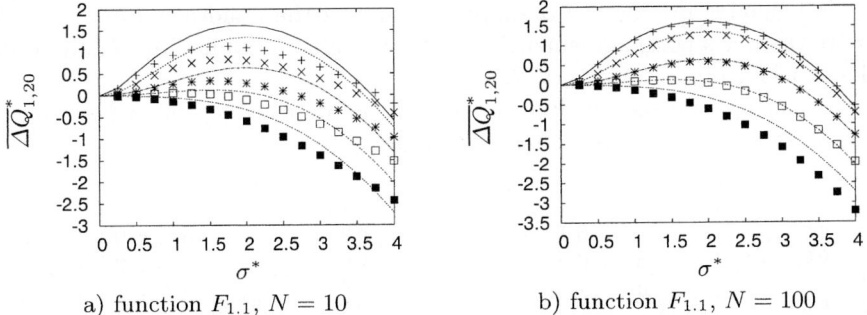

Fig. 2. Dependence of $\overline{\Delta Q}^*_{1,20}$ on the mutation strength σ^* for function $F_{1.1}$. Depicted are from top to bottom the curves for the noise strengths $\sigma^*_\epsilon = 0.5$, $\sigma^*_\epsilon = 1$, $\sigma^*_\epsilon = 2$, $\sigma^*_\epsilon = 3$, and $\sigma^*_\epsilon = 5$.

Biquadratic Functions. We will now consider functions of the form $F_2(\mathbf{y}) = \sum_{i=1}^{N} a_i y_i - c_i y_i^4$ with the local quality function $Q(\mathbf{x}) = \sum_{i=1}^{N}(a_i - 4c_i y_i^3)x_i - 6c_i y_i^2 x_i^2 - 4c_i y_i x_i^3 - c_i x_i^4$. In order to continue, we need expressions for the mean value and variance of Q which can be calculated easily as $M_Q = -3\sigma^2 \sum_{i=1}^{N} c_i(2y_i^2 + \sigma^2)$ and $S_Q^2 = \sum_{i=1}^{N} \sigma^2(a_i - 4c_i y_i^3)^2 - 24 a_i c_i y_i \sigma^4 + 168 c_i^2 y_i^4 \sigma^4 + 384 c_i^2 y_i^2 \sigma^6 + 96 c_i^2 \sigma^8$. Assuming σ to be sufficiently small, S_Q^2 simplifies to $S_Q^2 \simeq \sigma^2 \sum_{i=1}^{N}(a_i - 4c_i y_i^3)^2$. The quality gain is then obtained by inserting S_Q^2 and M_Q into (3), i.e. $\overline{\Delta Q}_{1,\lambda} = M_Q + c_{1,\lambda} S_Q^2 / \sqrt{S_Q^2 + \sigma_\epsilon^2}$, as

$$\overline{\Delta Q}_{1,\lambda} \simeq c_{1,\lambda} \sigma^2 \frac{\sum_{i=1}^{N}(a_i - 4c_i y_i^3)^2}{\sqrt{\sigma^2 \sum_{i=1}^{N}(a_i - 4c_i y_i^3)^2 + \sigma_\epsilon^2}} - 3\sigma^2 \sum_{i=1}^{N} c_i(2y_i^2 + \sigma^2). \quad (6)$$

Function F_2 only allows for a normalization of (6) if $\mathbf{y} = \mathbf{0}$. The expressions above for the variance and the expected value simplify then to $S_Q^2 = \sigma^2 \sum_{i=1}^N a_i^2 = \sigma^2 ||\mathbf{a}||^2$ and $M_Q = -3\sigma^4 \sum_{i=1}^N c_i$. Setting $c = 3 \sum_{i=1}^N c_i$ and using the normalizations $\sigma^* = \sigma \sqrt[3]{c/||\mathbf{a}||}$, $\sigma_\epsilon^* = \sigma_\epsilon \sqrt[3]{c/||\mathbf{a}||^4}$, and $\overline{\Delta Q}_{1,\lambda}^* = \overline{\Delta Q}_{1,\lambda} \sqrt[3]{c/||\mathbf{a}||^4}$ (see [9, p.134]), the normalized quality gain is given by

$$\overline{\Delta Q}_{1,\lambda}^* \simeq c_{1,\lambda} \sigma^* \frac{1}{\sqrt{1 + (\frac{\sigma_\epsilon^*}{\sigma^*})^2}} - \sigma^{*4}. \tag{7}$$

The equation can be decomposed into a approximately linear gain part influenced by the noise and a biquadratic loss part.

The predictive quality of (7) was examined using $F_{2.1}(\mathbf{y}) = \sum_{i=1}^N y_i - y_i^4$. The experimental values were obtained by averaging over 1,000,000 one-generation trials. Figure 3 shows the dependency of $\overline{\Delta Q}_{1,\lambda}^*$ on σ_ϵ^* for several choices of σ^*. The behavior we observe is similar to that of the quadratic functions. For $N = 10$, there is a good agreement between the values obtained by (7) and those of the experiments as long as σ^* is small.

This can also be seen in Fig. 4 showing the dependency of $\overline{\Delta Q}_{1,20}^*$ on the mutation strength σ^* for some noise strengths.

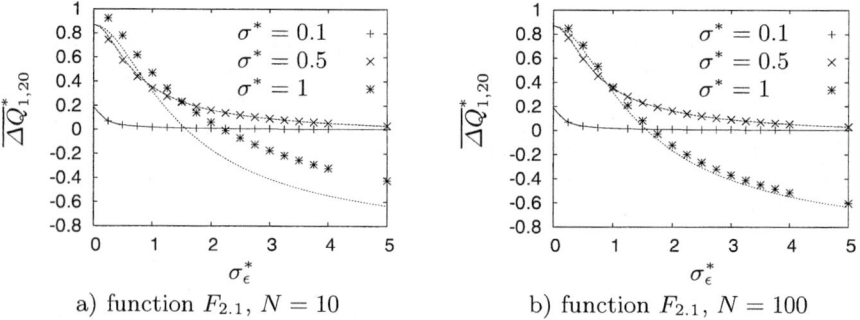

a) function $F_{2.1}$, $N = 10$ b) function $F_{2.1}$, $N = 100$

Fig. 3. Dependence of $\overline{\Delta Q}_{1,20}^*$ on the noise strength σ_ϵ^* for function $F_{2.1}$.

Sum of Absolute Values. We will now consider functions of the general form $F_3(\mathbf{y}) = c - \sum_{i=1}^N |y_i| = c - |\mathbf{y}|_1$, for which the local quality is given as $Q(\mathbf{x}) = \sum_{i=1}^N |y_i| - |y_i + x_i|$. The isometric lines of $F_3(\mathbf{y})$ form an N-dimensional rotated hypercube. As before, we have to derive the statistical parameters, assuming again the x_i to be normally distributed with variance σ^2. After some straightforward calculations, one obtains the expected value of Q as $M_Q = \sum_{i=1}^N |y_i| - y_i(2\Phi_{0,\sigma^2}(y_i) - 1) - 2\sigma^2 \phi_{0,\sigma^2}(y_i)$, where $\phi_{0,\sigma^2}(x_i) := e^{-\frac{x_i^2}{2\sigma^2}}/(\sqrt{2\pi}\sigma)$ and Φ_{0,σ^2} is the corresponding distribution function. Defining $Q(\mathbf{x}) := \sum_{i=1}^N q_i = \sum_{i=1}^N |y_i| - |y_i + x_i|$, the variance S_Q^2 can be written as $S_Q^2 = \sum_{i=1}^N \text{Var}[q_i] = \sum_{i=1}^N \text{E}[q_i^2] - \text{E}[q_i]^2$. After the calculation of the expected

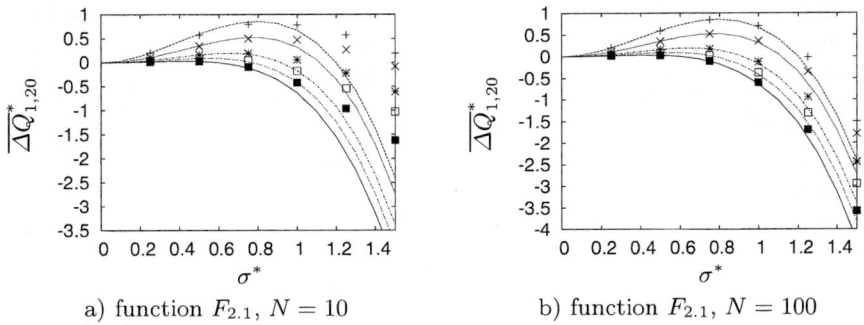

Fig. 4. Dependence of $\overline{\Delta Q}^*_{1,20}$ on the mutation strength σ^* for function $F_{2.1}$. Depicted are from bottom to top the results for $\sigma^*_\epsilon = 5$, $\sigma^*_\epsilon = 3$, $\sigma^*_\epsilon = 2$, $\sigma^*_\epsilon = 1$, and $\sigma^*_\epsilon = 0.5$.

values, we get $S_Q^2 = N\sigma^2 + 4\sum_{i=1}^N y_i^2 \Phi_{0,\sigma^2}(y_i)[1-\Phi_{0,\sigma^2}(y_i)] - 4\sigma^4 \sum_{i=1}^N \phi_{0,\sigma^2}^2(y_i)$
$-4\sigma^2 \sum_{i=1}^N \phi_{0,\sigma^2}(y_i)y_i[2\Phi_{0,\sigma^2}(y_i)-1]$. By inserting the statistical parameters into (3), $\overline{\Delta Q}_{1,\lambda} \simeq M_Q + c_{1,\lambda} S_Q^2 / \sqrt{S_Q^2 + \sigma_\epsilon^2}$, we obtain the quality gain for F_3.

Its validity was assessed by experiments conducting 500,000 one-generation experiments per data point with $\mathbf{y} = \mathbf{5}$ as starting vector and $F_{3.1}(\mathbf{y}) = -\sum_{i=1}^N |y_i|$ as test function. As can be seen in Fig. 5 and Fig. 6, the predictive quality is acceptable, which is even the case in the 10-dimensional space. For $N = 10$ and $N = 100$, the experimental values deviate from the theoretically predicted ones if the mutation strength is relatively large.

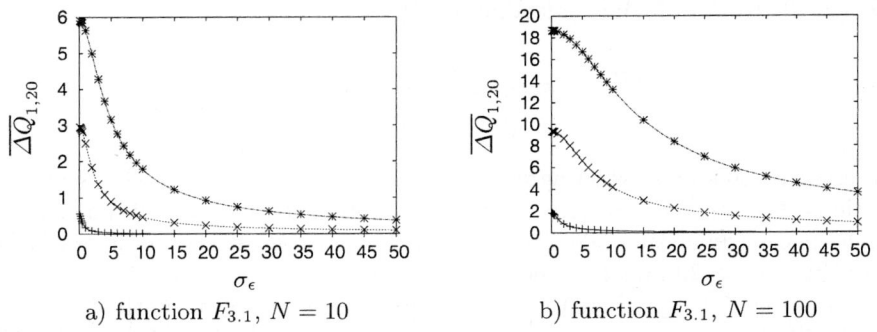

Fig. 5. $\overline{\Delta Q}_{1,20}$ as a function of the noise strength σ_ϵ for function $F_{3.1}$. Depicted are the results for $\sigma = 1$, $\sigma = 0.5$, and $\sigma = 0.1$ from top to bottom.

OneMax. The quality gain (3) was developed for continuous distributions. The discrete bit counting function OneMax $F_4(\mathbf{y}) = \sum_{i=1}^N y_i$, where $y_i \in \{0,1\}$, therefore represents an extreme test case for its applicability. For OneMax, the local quality is defined as $Q(\mathbf{x}) := F(\mathbf{x}) - F(\mathbf{y})$. If we consider strings of length N, the statistical parameters are given as (see [9, p. 128f]) $M_Q = -p_m(2F_0 - N)$ and $S_Q^2 = Np_m(1-p_m)$, where $F_0 := \sum_{i=1}^N y_i$ is the fitness value of the parental

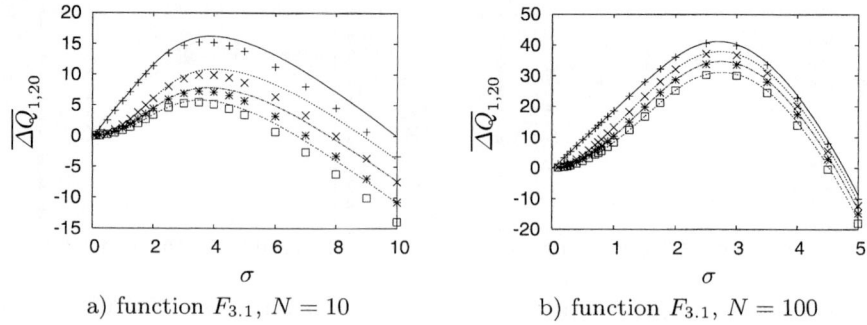

a) function $F_{3.1}$, $N = 10$ b) function $F_{3.1}$, $N = 100$

Fig. 6. Dependence of $\overline{\Delta Q}_{1,20}$ on the mutation strength σ for function $F_{3.1}$. Depicted are from top to bottom the results for $\sigma_\epsilon = 1$, $\sigma_\epsilon = 10$, $\sigma_\epsilon = 15$, and $\sigma_\epsilon = 20$.

vector and p_m is the mutation probability (mutation rate). Inserting these values into (3), the quality gain becomes

$$\overline{\Delta Q}_{1,\lambda} \simeq \frac{Np_m(1-p_m)}{\sqrt{Np_m(1-p_m)+\sigma_\epsilon^2}}c_{1,\lambda} - p_m(2F_0 - N). \qquad (8)$$

If $F_0 < N/2$, the resulting quality gain will be positive since less than half of the bit positions are occupied with ones. Equation (8) can be further simplified and normalized. Provided that $p_m \ll 1$, the influence of $(1-p_m)$ can be neglected and Np_m can be formally identified with the variance σ^2. For $F_0 > N/2$, we can introduce the normalizations $\sigma^* = 2(2F_0/N - 1)\sigma$, $\sigma_\epsilon^* = 2(2F_0/N - 1)\sigma_\epsilon$, and $\overline{\Delta Q}_{1,\lambda}^* = 2(2F_0/N - 1)\overline{\Delta Q}_{1,\lambda}$, leading finally to

$$\overline{\Delta Q}_{1,\lambda}^* \simeq \sigma^* \frac{1}{\sqrt{1+(\frac{\sigma_\epsilon^*}{\sigma^*})^2}}c_{1,\lambda} - \frac{(\sigma^*)^2}{2}. \qquad (9)$$

Interestingly, this expression agrees with the quality gain (5) of the quadratic functions. The predictive quality of (9) was examined for 30- and 100-dimensional search spaces conducting $500{,}000$ one-generation experiments. As parental fitness values, $F_0 = 20$ and $F_0 = 60$, respectively, were used. As can been seen in Fig. 8 and Fig. 7, (9) predicts the behavior up to a mutation strength of $\sigma^* = 1.5$ quite well which corresponds to mutation rates of 0.141 ($N = 100$) and 0.169 ($N = 30$). That is, using a mutation rate of $p_m = 1/N$ often recommended in literature, the corresponding σ^* is usually much smaller. Therefore, the predictive quality of (9) will in general be better than suggested by the graphs.

4 Conclusion and Outlook

We derived an equation characterizing the quality gain on arbitrary fitness functions. In order to check its predictive quality, it was applied to several test functions. Even though we used only a simple approximation, good results were

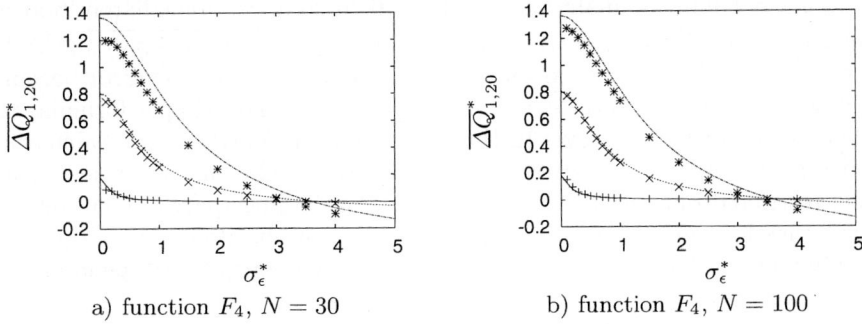

Fig. 7. Dependence of $\overline{\Delta Q}^*_{1,20}$ on the noise strength σ^*_ϵ for F_4. Depicted are from top to bottom the results for $\sigma^*_\epsilon = 0.1$, $\sigma^*_\epsilon = 0.5$, and $\sigma^*_\epsilon = 1$.

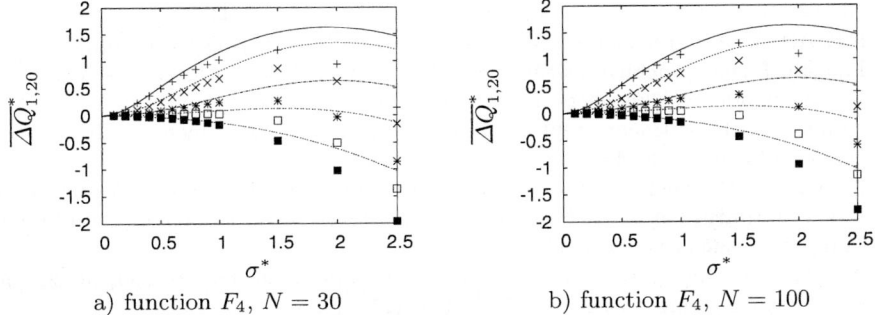

Fig. 8. Dependence of $\overline{\Delta Q}^*_{1,20}$ on the mutation strength σ^* for F_4. Depicted are from top to bottom the results for $\sigma^*_\epsilon = 0.1, \sigma^*_\epsilon = 0.5, \sigma^*_\epsilon = 1$, $\sigma^*_\epsilon = 2$, $\sigma^*_\epsilon = 3$, and $\sigma^*_\epsilon = 5$.

obtained as long as the mutation strength was sufficiently small and the search space dimensionality was sufficiently high. The quality gain can be normalized for most test functions except function F_3. Typically, the quality gain consists of two parts, a linear gain and a higher order loss term. The noise only influences the gain part of the equation.

As already mentioned in the introduction, the quality gain can be used to determine the final fitness error in the steady state which is defined as the expected value of the difference between the fitness of the steady state and the actual optimum. Since the quality gain $\overline{\Delta Q}_{1,\lambda} \simeq c_{1,\lambda} S_Q^2 / \sqrt{S_Q^2 + \sigma_\epsilon^2} + M_Q$ is equal to zero once the steady state is reached, one obtains a relationship between the mean value and the variance. Since these statistical parameters usually depend on the parental state $\mathbf{y}$, (3) can be used as a starting point for a derivation of the final fitness error. This has already been done for quadratic and some biquadratic functions [10].

As a short example, we consider the function OneMax, i.e. $F_4(\mathbf{y}) = \sum_{i=1}^{N} y_i$. The final fitness error in the steady state region is given as $E[\Delta F] = N -$

$\sum_{i=1}^{N} \mathrm{E}[y_i]$. Setting the quality gain (8) equal to zero, we immediately find for the expectation $\sum_{i=1}^{N} \mathrm{E}[y_i] = (N/2)[1 + (1-p_m)c_{1,\lambda}/\sqrt{Np_m(1-p_m) + \sigma_\epsilon^2}]$. Assuming $p_m = 1/N$ and N to be sufficiently large, the final fitness error becomes $\mathrm{E}[\Delta F] = (N/2)[1 - c_{1,\lambda}/\sqrt{1 + \sigma_\epsilon^2}]$. This is a surprisingly simple formula, the validity range of which deserves further investigations. Furthermore, calculating the final fitness error for other test function classes will be one of our next tasks.

We restricted our analysis to $(1, \lambda)$-ESs. Considering $(\mu/\mu_I, \lambda)$-variants remains a task for the future. While some of the equations already developed can be easily adopted for the $(\mu/\mu_I, \lambda)$-ES, formal derivations are still pending.

References

1. Miller, B.L.: Noise, Sampling, and Efficient Genetic Algorithms. PhD thesis, University of Illinois at Urbana-Champaign, Urbana, IL 61801 (1997) IlliGAL Report No. 97001.
2. Fitzpatrick, J., Grefenstette, J.: Genetic Algorithms in Noisy Environments. In Langley, P., ed.: Machine Learning: Special Issue on Genetic Algorithms. Volume 3. Kluwer Academic Publishers, Dordrecht (1988) 101–120
3. Branke, J.: Evolutionary Optimization in Dynamic Environments. Kluwer Academic Publishers, Dordrecht (2001)
4. Nissen, V., Propach, J.: On the Robustness of Population-Based Versus Point-Based Optimization in the Presence of Noise. IEEE Transactions on Evolutionary Computation **2** (1998) 107–119
5. Arnold, D.V., Beyer, H.G.: On the Benefits of Populations for Noisy Optimization. Evolutionary Computation **11** (2003) 111–127
6. Arnold, D.V., Beyer, H.G.: Local Performance of the $(1+1)$-ES in a Noisy Environment. IEEE Transactions on Evolutionary Computation **6** (2002) 30–41
7. Arnold, D.V., Beyer, H.G.: Investigation of the (μ, λ)-ES in the Presence of Noise. In: Proceedings of the CEC'01 Conference, Piscataway, NJ, IEEE (2001) 332–339
8. Arnold, D.V.: Noisy Optimization with Evolution Strategies. Kluwer Academic Publishers, Dordrecht (2002)
9. Beyer, H.G.: The Theory of Evolution Strategies. Natural Computing Series. Springer, Heidelberg (2001)
10. Beyer, H.G., Meyer-Nieberg, S.: Predicting the Solution Quality in Noisy Optimization. Series CI 160/04, SFB 531, University of Dortmund (2004)

Fitness Distributions and GA Hardness

Yossi Borenstein and Riccardo Poli

Department of Computer Science, University of Essex
{yboren,rpoli}@essex.ac.uk

Abstract. Considerable research effort has been spent in trying to formulate a good definition of GA-Hardness. Given an instance of a problem, the objective is to estimate the performance of a GA. Despite partial successes current definitions are still unsatisfactory. In this paper we make some steps towards a new, more powerful way of assessing problem difficulty based on the properties of a problem's fitness distribution. We present experimental results that strongly support this idea.

1 Introduction

For over a decade GA researchers have attempted to predict the behavior of a GA in different domains. The goal is to be able to classify problems as hard or easy according to the performance a GA would be expected to have on such problems, accurately and *without actually running the GA*.

The Building Block (BB) hypothesis [1] states that a GA tries to combine low, highly fit schemata. Following the BB hypothesis the notion of deception [1], [2] isolation [3] and multimodality [4] have been defined. These were able to explain a variety of phenomena. Unfortunately, they didn't succeed in giving a reliable measure of GA-hardness [5], [6].

Given the connection between GAs and theoretical genetics, some attempts to explain the behavior of GAs were inspired by biology. For example, epistasis variance [7] and epistasis correlation [8] have been defined in order to estimate the hardness of a given real world problem. NK landscapes [9], [10] use the same idea (epistasis) in order to create an artificial, arbitrary, landscape with a tunable degree of difficulty. These attempts, too, didn't succeed in giving a full explanation of the behavior of a GA [6], [11], [12].

Finally, fitness distance correlation [13] tries to measure the intrinsic hardness of a landscape, independently of the search algorithm. Despite good success, fitness distance correlation is not able to predict performance in some scenarios [14].

The partial success of these approaches is not surprising. Several difficulties present themselves when developing a general theory that explains the behavior of a GA and is able to predict how it will perform on different problems. These include:

- A GA is actually a *family* of different algorithms. Given a problem the GA designer first decides which representation (e.g. binary, multiary, permutation, real numbers) to use, then how to map the solution space into the search space, and finally which operator(s) (mutation, crossover) to use. Moreover, there are limited concrete guidelines on how to choose a representation and a genotype-phenotype

mapping. Indeed this is a very difficult task. Different genotype-phenotype representations can completely change the difficulty of a problem [15]. There have been attempts to evolve the right representation [16] and there are some general design guidelines [15], [17], [18]. However, the reality is that the responsibility of coming up with good ingredients for a GA is still entirely on the GA designer.
- According to [19] it is impossible to predict the performance of an algorithm based only on the on the *description* of the problem instance and the algorithm without actually running the algorithm.

In the absence of a good, predictive theory of GA performance, unavoidably we are only left with an experimental approach. The idea is to divide the space of real-world problems into GA hard and GA easy by finding (by experimentation and experience) a good GA (with its representation, mapping, and operators) for every specific instance (or class of instances) of a problem.

The No Free Lunch (NFL) theorem [20] states that, on average, over all possible problems, the performance of each search algorithms is equal. The basis for this claim is the observation that any prediction based on sampling a sub-space may not be valid. By studying some limitations that general knowledge of a problem might put on this observation, we introduce a new way to classify problems for GAs. In particular we explore assessing problem difficulty based on the properties of a problem's fitness distribution.

In the next sections we introduce our notation, we explain our motivation for the new classification idea, define it and give some empirical results that support it. We conclude with a discussion about possible implications and future work.

2 Definition

2.1 Notation

Following [21] we use the following notation. A **problem** is a fitness function $f : X \rightarrow Y$ that we would like to maximize (where X is the search space and Y is the ordered set of fitness values). This assigns a fitness value to each point in the search space. A **representation** is the way that we choose to represent the search space (i.e. real numbers, binary strings). We define a point in the search space as a **phenotype**, the chosen representation for it as a **genotype**, and the function that transforms the genotype into the phenotype as a **genotype-phenotype mapping**.

If we sampled the search space randomly and we recorded the fitness of the solutions sampled, different fitness values (i.e. different elements of Y) would have potentially different probabilities of occurrence. We define the **fitness distribution** $p(y)$ as the frequency of each particular $y \in Y$ for the problem of interest f. For example, the fitness distribution for a one-max problem is (assuming $X=\{0,1\}^N$):

$$p(y) = \binom{N}{y} \cdot 2^{-N} \qquad (1)$$

2.2 Problem Classification via Fitness Distribution

We suggest classifying problems according to the properties of their fitness distribution.

Traditionally, a class of problems is defined as the set of all the instances of a problem that share the same description. For example, TSP is a class of problems which share the following description: "Given a set of cities and the distances between them, find the shortest path starting from a particular city, passing through all the others and returning to the first city". Each configuration of cities and distances is an instance of a TSP.

Classifying problems based on descriptions is very useful for humans, for obvious reasons. However, this doesn't work well in a black-box scenario. The key feature of a black-box algorithm is the absence of any explicit information about the problem being solved. The information is embedded *somehow* into the landscape - it is not clear how and to what extent the landscape captures the essential features of the problem. From this point of view, the notion of a problem and a fitness distribution is closely related in the black-box paradigm. So, classifying problems according to their fitness distribution is a very natural thing to do.

2.3 Fitness Distribution and Search Performance

The performance of a search algorithm depends crucially on the fitness landscape and on the way the algorithm searches the landscape. The landscape, in turn, is a combination of a representation (genotype), a syntactic neighborhood (defined over the representation) and a genotype-phenotype mapping. The number and type of different fitness landscapes for a particular problem is dependent on the fitness distribution: for some distributions there may be only very few possible landscapes (e.g. if only one fitness value is possible then there is only one possible landscape), for others there may be many. In any case, *the fitness distribution constrains what is possible*, and so there is a strong connection between the fitness distribution and the expected performance of a search algorithm.

Let us consider the case of the simplest randomized algorithm (or black-box search algorithm): *random search*. Random search doesn't use any knowledge about the landscape, hence doesn't use any information about a problem. The fitness distribution is the only information needed in order to predict the performance of random search.

For a GA the situation is more complicated. Yet, the fitness distribution may still help predict and explain the performance of a GA. For example, let us consider two well-studied problems: the one-max, which is known to be an easy problem, and the needle-in-the-haystack (NIAH), which is a hard one. The fitness distribution of the NIAH restricts the landscape to be flat everywhere except in the needle. Therefore, irrespective of the genotype-phenotype mapping, the GA doesn't have any information to use. It is expected, therefore, to perform as random search (or worse, due to the negative effects of resampling). On the other hand, for the one-max fitness distribution, there is at least one genotype-phenotype mapping (the standard representation for the problem) that allows the GA to do better than random search by exploiting the information present in the landscape.

3 Empirical Results

At this stage we focus on a specific instance of a GA using only binary representations. We postpone the study of different representations and different types of GA to a later stage of this research.

The NFL doesn't impose any restriction on the possible problems. Using our notion of classification, we make one assumption: we restrict our attention to problems with specific fitness distributions. We make a Monte-Carlo sampling over all the possible genotype-phenotype mappings (representations). This enables us to study common characteristics of all the problems that belong to a specific class[1].

For our study we will use the fitness distribution given by the one-max and NIAH problems[2]. In all the experiments we use a generational selecto-recombinative GA, with one point crossover. The selection mechanism is a tournament of size 2. We use genotypes of length $N=12$. The population size was 50, the crossover rate was 100%, and no mutation was used. Runs were stopped when either a solution had been found or the population had fully converged.

We performed 500 experiments. In each experiment we chose, randomly with a uniform probability, a genotype-phenotype mapping. For each mapping we made 1000 runs (500,000 runs in total).

Random search is used as a reference to compare the performance of the GA. It is run for exactly the same number of fitness evaluations as the GA.

3.1 NIAH Is GA-Easier Than One-Max

We tested the performance of the GA and random search as both optimization algorithms (by looking at their ability to find the fittest individual in the search space) and approximation ones (by looking at the fittest individuals found in each run *by* any given generation).

In order to assess the performance of the GA and random search as optimization algorithms we counted, for each mapping of one-max and NIAH, the numbers of runs in which the algorithms succeeded in finding the fittest solution in the search space.

Figure 1(a) shows the average number of runs in which the GA and random search found the optimum solution. The average is taken over all the random mappings sampled. In this and the following figures the error bars represent the standard deviation. The difference between the two plots for random search is due to the fact that random search was run for exactly the same number of fitness evaluations as the GA and that the GA had different average convergence times with the two fitness distributions.

In order to measure the performance of the GA and random search as approximation algorithms we plotted the fittest individual discovered so far in each run against the generation number[3]. This is shown in Figure 1(b), which does not include the results for the NIAH fitness distribution because the notions of approximation and optimization coincide in this case.

---

[1] Alternatively and equivalently one can view this as a method to study the difficulty of a problem under all possible representations.

[2] It is important to emphasize that the one-max (NIAH) problem and the one-max (NIAH) fitness distribution are two related, but distinct things (see Sect. 2).

[3] For random search a generation is taken to mean as many samples as the GA's population size. This definition allows a direct comparison with the GA.

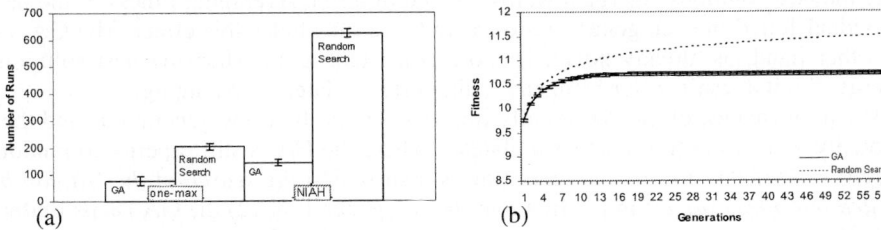

Fig. 1. (a) The average number of runs in which the GA and random search found a solution with the one-max and NIAH fitness distributions. (b) Average fitness of the fittest individual discovered by each generation.

These results are clear: firstly, random search outperforms the GA, and, secondly, rather surprisingly, the GA performs better on the NIAH fitness distribution than on the one-max fitness distribution.

The reason for the superiority of random search is that the GA resamples the same points in the search space more often than random search. This is illustrated in Figure 2(a), which shows the fitness distribution of the *distinct* solutions that were sampled by both algorithms for the one-max fitness distribution. The area beneath each curve represents the total number of distinct points in the search space that were sampled. Clearly, the GA has sampled a much smaller area. Moreover, the quality of the solutions that were sampled by the GA is no better than the quality of the solutions sampled by random search.

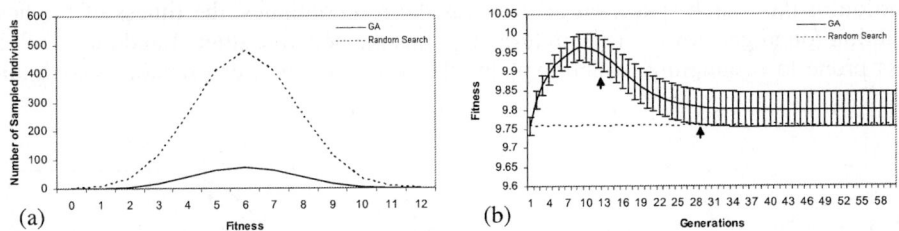

Fig. 2. (a) The histogram of the distinct points in the search space that were sampled on average during a run for the one-max fitness distribution. (b) The average (over all representations) fitness of the best individual found in each generation for the one-max fitness distribution.

3.2 Three Stages in the GA Search

In order to understand better the dynamics exhibited by the GA, in Figure 2(b), we plot for each generation the fitness of the best individual found *in that generation* for the one-max fitness distribution. The results are averaged over all the representations.

In contrast to what we observed in the previous section the GA *appears* to outperform random search. This is not a contradiction. The flat line representing the random search algorithm in Figure 2(b) is the result of averaging. With random search the best solutions found in a run can be discovered at any generation, unlike a GA where typically the best solutions emerge towards the end of a run. Averaging fitness of the best individual found in each generation over multiple runs hides this effect. The GA, on the other hand, as already noted, is more consistent as to when the best solutions emerge. So, it doesn't suffer from any hiding effect related to averaging.

The performance of the GA rapidly improves in the first few generations and then gradually worsens until it reaches a plateau (where the GA is still superior to random search). Effectively for the one-max fitness distribution *the search of the GA can be divided into three stages*: in the first one (before generation 12) the GA keeps finding new fit individuals, in the second (from generations 13 to 30) the performance drops, while in the third the population has converged. In the following sections we analyze these stages more carefully.

3.3 Stage I: Implicit Elitism

In order to check whether the GA indeed initially finds good regions of the search space, we plot the best individual found in each generation that *has not been sampled in the same run before*. This is shown on Figure 3(a). Like Figure 2(b), this plot shows three stages (with end/start points highlighted by the arrows). However, it is now clear that in the first stage the GA doesn't discover new fit individuals: the GA, to some extent, resamples the same fit individuals from previous generations. So, the GA seems to have an *implicit form of elitism*. It is important to emphasize that the negative slope shown in the plot of Figure 3(a) doesn't mean that the fittest individuals are found in the first generation. This is another averaging effect: in each generation the probability to resample the same individuals increases. Thus, the number of new discovered individuals decreases. Since we sample, each time, a smaller portion of the search space, *on average*, as the run continues, the fitness of the best solution found gets lower. This, in turn, explains the negative slope. Random search is less prone to resampling, which explains the difference between random search and the GA.

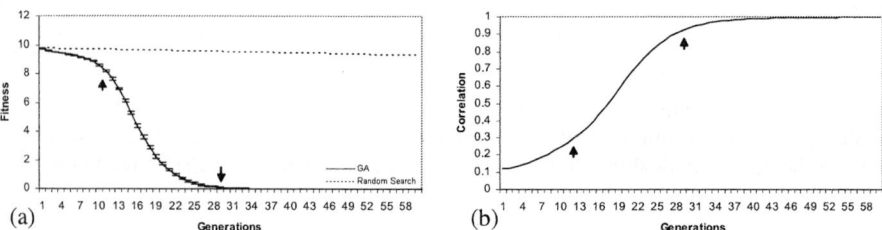

Fig. 3. (a) The average fitness of the best individuals found in each generation that haven't been sampled before for the one-max fitness distribution. (b) The correlation between the fitness of the parents and the fitness of the offspring for the one-max fitness distribution.

3.4 Stage II: Evolvability

In order to explain the second phase of the GA's search, we consider the evolvability of the population. Plotting the parents-offspring fitness correlation (Fig. 3(b)) shows that although the fitness of the best individual found in each generation decreases (see

Figure 2(b), generations 13-30) the overall evolvability as measured by the parent/offspring fitness correlation of the population increases. So, *the GA is trading fitness for evolvability*. This makes sense: when it becomes hard to increase the population fitness by discovering enough highly fit individuals, the best option is to go for areas of the landscape where the fitness of the offspring is as close as possible to the fitness of their (above average) parents.

3.5 Stage III: Convergence

Since we use no mutation in our experiments, selection and drift eventually lead the GA to converge to a population containing only copies of the same individual. This corresponds to the third phase of the GA's search shown in the previous figures.

4 Discussion

In the experiments we evaluated the performance of a GA when the representation chosen was randomly picked from the set of all possible representations. At first this procedure may seem odd, but, as we will argue below, it is not.

Firstly, one might object, in everyday practice representations are never random: they are carefully chosen by the user/designer of a GA so as to guarantee good performance. By and large this is true. However, in the presence of a new problem, for the fitness function of which no information is available, except for the information one can gather by evaluating the fitness of specific points in the search space, the designer has very little to work with to ensure the representation chosen will be a good one. In this case, one should assume that the quality of the representation chosen will be average. Finding out what exactly being "average" means for a representation is the objective of the experiments we reported above, which should clarify the value of our approach.

Secondly, one might object, if the representation is picked randomly, surely the resulting fitness landscape will include no information on the problem it originated from, and so, following NFL, one should expect equal performance in all conditions – the fact that we did not get equal performance would then suggest something was wrong in our experiments. The fallacy in this argument is assuming that no information is present in the landscape: the fitness distribution associated to a problem may induce very strong regularities in the fitness landscapes induced by the representation, even for random representations. So, it is entirely possible that on the *typical* (random) landscape induced by a certain fitness distribution a particular GA will do better than on the typical landscape induced by another fitness distribution (which is exactly what happened in our experiments with one-max and NIAH). It is therefore very important to understand what the regularities imposed by fitness distributions are and whether certain types of regularities lead to good performance (GA easiness) while others lead to bad performance (GA hardness).

Our hypothesis is that fitness distributions capture important features that make a problem GA easy or GA hard, and that grouping problems by their fitness distribution is, therefore, a very meaningful and useful way to create a *high-level* GA-hardness problem taxonomy[4].

---

[4] A complete taxonomy should consider the neighborhood structure (representation) as well.

Let us look back at our data to try and identify the fitness-distribution features that were responsible for the (unexpected) difficulties the GA hit when solving one-max-type problems. Based on our results, we can see that the GA search initially focuses on highly fit individuals. However, in the longer run, regions that contain fit, evolvable individuals are the real targets of the GA. This in turn can explain the difference in performance just mentioned.

The one-max fitness distribution spontaneously creates many evolvable, relatively fit regions. This is because, although there is only one string with maximum fitness (N), there are many strings of high fitness (e.g. there are N strings with fitness $N-1$, $N(N-1)/2$ strings with fitness $N-2$, and so on). Since the representation is random, in most cases a sub-optimal string of fitness $N-1$ will actually be an isolated local optimum. Similarly strings of fitness $N-2$ can generate many other local optima. The landscape around these local optima is also random, and so we should not expect to see any substantial regularity. However, since there are so many local optima, some of these will have more regular neighborhoods (basins of attraction) than the others. These represent highly attractive areas for the GA since individuals in such areas are both fit and evolvable. So, very likely the GA will zoom onto one such area. Once the GA zooms into a particular region of the search space it searches for new individuals only within that region. Since the landscape is random the probability that the highest fitness solution is indeed within that region is quite low. So, in the one-max case, the relatively large number of high fitness regions causes the GA to converge prematurely to one of them, rather then continue searching for the optimum, effectively making (typical) problems from the one-max fitness distribution deceptive and GA hard.

In the case of the NIAH fitness distribution, the fitness landscape is flat everywhere, except at the optimum. So, there cannot be any deceptive attractors for the GA irrespective of the representation chosen. Indeed, in our experiments the GA did not converge prematurely to such an attractor. It sampled more points in the search space and therefore performed better on the NIAH fitness distribution.

Random search is insensitive to the fitness distribution (although, naturally, it is sensitive to the frequency of the highest fitness solutions). Also, random search was observed to be less prone to resampling, and so, within the same number of fitness evaluations, it covered a larger portion of the search space. This explains why it performed better than the GA.

5 Conclusions

Different attempts to come up with a good classification for problems in relation to the performance of search algorithms, particularly GAs, have been reported in the literature. Roughly speaking, most of them firstly postulate what feature makes a problem hard for a GA, then check whether a specific problem has this feature, and finally infer the degree of GA hardness of the problem from the extent to which such a feature is present. To the best of our knowledge, this approach has so far only achieved partial success in creating meaningful and reliable problem taxonomy.

In this paper we have proposed a new way of classifying problems: grouping them on the basis of the features of their fitness distribution. As we have argued in Section 4 and empirically shown in Section 3, there are features of certain fitness distributions that induce clear regularities in the fitness landscapes of typical problems with those distributions. For example, the availability of intermediate fitness values (like in the one-max fitness distribution) can lead to landscapes (problems) with a huge number of deceptive basins of attraction, which are therefore, on average, GA hard.

Naturally, we are fully aware that more often than not the fitness distribution for a problem is not available. In these cases, the fitness distribution can be estimated. Rose, Ebeling and Asselmeyer [22] suggest the Boltzmann ensemble method as an efficient way to obtain the fitness distribution. Naudts and Landrieu [23] present a normalization technique which enables the grouping of distributions with different fitness range. The features of the estimated distribution could then be used to infer whether the problem is expected to be GA easy or hard, without actually having to run the GA. The distribution itself [23] might not be sufficient to predict the difficulty of the problem. Still, grouping problems with similar fitness distributions is meaningful. This approach could be used to check whether a particular choice of representation is reasonable. If it is not, it could suggest how to refine it (using knowledge extracted from other problems of the same group).

Our hope is that, over time, we will be able to identify which classes of representations generally work well with which types of fitness-distribution features. If this could be achieved, then the design of competent GAs would be much facilitated: one would only need to check in which fitness-distribution class a problem falls to immediately identify which representation would put the GA in good operation conditions.

References

1. D.E. Goldberg. Genetic Algorithms in Search, Optimization and Machine Learning. Morgan Kaufmann, 1989.
2. S. Forrest and M. Mitchell. Relative Building Block Fitness and the Building Block Hypothesis. In D. Whitley (ed.) Foundations of Genetic Algorithms 2. Morgan Kaufmann, San Mateo, CA, 1992.
3. D.E. Goldberg. Making genetic algorithm fly: a lesson from the Wright brothers. Advanced Technology For Developers, 2 pp.1-8, February 1993.
4. S. Rana. Examining the Role of Local Optima and Schema Processing in Genetic Search. PhD thesis, Colorado State University, 1998.
5. J.J. Grefenstette. Deception considered harmful. In Foundations of Genetic Algorithms 2, D. Whitley (Ed.), San Mateo, CA: Morgan Kaufmann, 1993.
6. T. Jansen. On Classifications of Fitness Functions. Reihe CI 76/99, SFB 531, Universität Dortmund, 1999.
7. Y. Davidor. Epistasis variance: A viewpoint on GA-hardness. In G.J.E Rawlines, editor FOGA-1,pp. 23-55. Morgan Kaufman 1991.
8. B. Naudts..Measuring GA-hardness. Ph.d thesis. UV. Of Antwerp. Belgium, 1998.
9. S.A. Kauffman. The Origins of Order: Self-Organization and Selection in Evolution. Oxford University Press, Oxford, 1993.
10. L. Altenberg. NK fitness landscapes. Handbook of Evolutionary Computation 1997b.
11. B. Naudts and L. Kallel, Comparison of summery statistics of fitness landscapes, IEEE Trans.Evol.Comp. 2000.
12. H. Guo and W.H. Hsu. GA-hardness Revisited. GECCO 2003 Poster paper.
13. T. Jones and S. Forrest. Fitness distance correlation as a measure of problem difficulty for genetic algorithms. In Larry Eshelman, editor, Proceedings of the Sixth International Conference on Genetic Algorithms, pages 184-192, San Francisco, CA, 1995.
14. L. Altenberg. Fitness Distance Correlation analysis: An instructive counter-example. ICGA, pp 57-64, 1997a.

15. F. Rothlauf. Representations for Genetic and Evolutionary Algorithms. Studies in Fuzziness and Soft Computing, Volume 104. Heidelberg: Springer, 1st edition 2002.
16. L. Altenberg. Evolving better representations through selective genome growth. Proceedings of the 1st IEEE Conference on Evolutionary Computation. Part 1, 1994.
17. A. Moraglio and R.Poli. Topological interpretation of crossover. GECCO 2004.
18. N.J. Radcliffe. Equivalence class analysis of genetic algorithms. In Foundations of Genetic Algorithms 3. Morgan Kaufmann, 1994.
19. H. Huttel. On Rice's Theorem. Aalborg University. 2001.
20. D.H. Wolpert and W.G. Macready. No free lunch theorems for optimization.IEEE Transactions on Evolutionary Computation, 4:67-82, 1997.
21. G.E. Liepins and M.D. Vose. Representational issues in genetic optimization. Journal of Experimental and Theoretical Artificial Intelligence, 2:101-115, 1990
22. H. Rose,W. Ebeling and T. Asselmeyer. The Density of States – a Measure of the Difficulty of Optimization Problems. PPSN 1996.
23. B. Naudts and I. Landrieu, Comparing population mean curves. FOGA 2000

Experimental Supplements to the Theoretical Analysis of EAs on Problems from Combinatorial Optimization

Patrick Briest, Dimo Brockhoff, Bastian Degener, Matthias Englert, Christian Gunia,
Oliver Heering, Thomas Jansen, Michael Leifhelm, Kai Plociennik, Heiko Röglin,
Andrea Schweer, Dirk Sudholt, Stefan Tannenbaum, and Ingo Wegener*

FB Informatik, LS2, Univ. Dortmund, 44221 Dortmund, Germany
{firstname.lastname}@uni-dortmund.de

Abstract. It is typical for the EA community that theory follows experiments. Most theoretical approaches use some model of the considered evolutionary algorithm (EA) but there is also some progress where the expected optimization time of EAs is analyzed rigorously. There are only three well-known problems of combinatorial optimization where such an approach has been performed for general input instances, namely minimum spanning trees, shortest paths, and maximum matchings. The theoretical results are asymptotic ones and several questions for realistic dimensions of the search space are open. We supplement the theoretical results by experimental ones. Many hypotheses are confirmed by rigorous statistical tests.

1 Introduction

Evolutionary algorithms (EAs) are heuristics with many applications to problems from combinatorial optimization. Most knowledge on EAs is based on intensive experiments but there are also theoretical results. Many of them consider artificial fitness functions in order to understand the search behavior of EAs. Moreover, one has to distinguish two types of theoretical results. Most of the results investigate "models of EAs" and the results have to be "verified" by experiments. Examples are the investigation of populations of infinite size, most results from schema theory, the assumption of populations in linkage equilibrium, and many more. In recent years, there is a growing interest in the rigorous analysis of the random variable describing the number of fitness evaluations until an optimal search point is evaluated. After a series of papers on artificial functions and typical fitness landscapes there are now three papers determining the asymptotic expected optimization time of mutation-based EAs on well-known problems from combinatorial optimization:

- minimum spanning trees (Neumann and Wegener (2004)),
- single source shortest paths (Scharnow, Tinnefeld, and Wegener (2002)),
- maximum matchings (Giel and Wegener (2003)).

No such results are known for EAs with crossover.

---
* Supported in part by the Deutsche Forschungsgemeinschaft (DFG) as part of the Collaborative Research Center "Computational Intelligence" (SFB 531).

These theoretical results give new insights into the behavior of the considered EAs and realistic problems. Nevertheless, they do not answer all questions. Asymptotic results may not describe the situation of problem dimensions considered today. Upper and lower bounds can differ and the results are concerned with the worst case and not with the typical case. For the problems listed above, we investigate properties of EAs not captured by the theoretical results and supplement the theoretical knowledge.

Section 2 introduces the investigated heuristics, mainly randomized local search (RLS) and the well-known (1+1) EA. Sections 3, 4, and 5 contain the results for the three problems and we finish with some conclusions.

The considered hypotheses have been derived from preliminary experiments which then have been tested by independent experiments. We use different statistical tests depending on the type of hypothesis under consideration. The statistical tests are carried out using the software SPSS (Version 11.5, see www.spss.com). Regression analysis is done using gnuplot (Version 3.7, see www.gnuplot.info), using the standard settings.

The statistical tests used are the Wilcoxon signed rank test (WSRT) and the Mann-Whitney test (MWT). Both are nonparametric tests to confirm the hypothesis that one random variable "systematically" produces larger values than another one. WSRT pairs the samples, takes their differences, ranks the absolute values and considers the sum of the ranks belonging to positive differences. MWT ranks all values and compares the rank sums for both samples.

Due to space limitations, we cannot present all the data (tables of data or plots). We report whether the hypotheses have been confirmed on a good significance level. More precisely, we state our results in the form "Hypothesis H has been confirmed on the significance level α" which means that the probability of producing our data if H is not true is bounded by α where α is the result of the SPSS package rounded to 3 digits. Hence, smaller values of α correspond to better results. Results are called significant, if $\alpha \leq 0.05$, very significant, if $\alpha \leq 0.01$, and highly significant, if $\alpha \leq 0.001$. Note that experiments can confirm hypotheses only for the problem dimensions n considered in the experiments and not for all n.

2 Randomized Local Search and the (1+1) EA

Most of the theoretical results for the problems listed above are for RLS and the (1+1) EA and some are for the $(1+\lambda)$ EA. Therefore, we describe these algorithms. The algorithms work with "populations" of size 1, i.e., with single individuals or search points x. The first search point x is chosen uniformly at random. Then the offspring x' is obtained from x by mutation. Selection chooses x' iff $f(x') \geq f(x)$ in the case of maximization ("$\leq$" in the case of minimization). The mutation operator of RLS chooses a position of the string x uniformly at random and replaces it with a different randomly chosen value. In the case of bit strings, the bit is flipped. In the case of strings from $\{1,\ldots,k\}^n$, one of the $k-1$ different values is chosen according to the uniform distribution. The mutation operator of the (1+1) EA changes each position independently from the others with probability $1/n$. The number of chosen positions is asymptotically Poisson distributed with $\lambda = 1$ and it is a slight variant to determine first the number of positions which will be changed according to this distribution.

RLS is a hill climber with a small neighborhood and can get stuck in local optima. Indeed, RLS in its pure form is useless for spanning trees and matchings. Therefore, we have chosen for these problems a larger neighborhood of up to two local changes. RLS_p changes one randomly chosen position with probability $1-p$ and two randomly chosen positions, otherwise. We use the notation RLS for $RLS_{1/2}$.

We assume that the reader is familiar with the basic theory on the considered problems (see Atallah (1999)).

3 Minimum Spanning Trees

Minimum spanning trees can be computed efficiently by the well-known algorithms of Kruskal and Prim. Each non-optimal spanning tree can be improved by inserting a missing edge of a minimum spanning tree and excluding a more expensive edge from the cycle created by the edge insertion. Hence, there is a sequence of at most $n-1$ "insertion plus deletion" steps which produces a minimum spanning tree with $n-1$ edges.

These steps are local in the representation by edge sets. For graphs with m edges, the search space equals $\{0,1\}^m$ and x describes the selection of all edges e_i where $x_i = 1$. The search space includes non-connected graphs and connected graphs with cycles. The fitness function has to penalize non-connected graphs. Let $c(x)$ be the number of connected components of the graph $G(x)$ consisting of the edge set described by x. Let $a(x)$ be the number of edges of $G(x)$ and $b(x)$ be the total weight of all chosen edges (weights are positive integers). We distinguish two fitness functions v and w for edge sets which are introduced by Neumann and Wegener (2004). Let

- $w(x) \leq w(x')$ iff $(c(x) < c(x'))$ or $(c(x) = c(x')$ and $(a(x) < a(x'))$ or $(c(x) = c(x'), a(x) = a(x')$, and $(b(x) \leq b(x'))$ and
- $v(x) \leq v(x')$ iff $(c(x) < c(x'))$ or $(c(x) = c(x')$ and $b(x) \leq b(x'))$.

The fitness functions force the search to create trees. Another possibility is to allow only trees. Prüfer numbers (see Raidl and Julstrom (2003)) are elements of $\{1,\ldots,n\}^{n-2}$ and a one-to-one coding of trees. The coding of T' obtained by an insertion and deletion of edges from T can be very different from the coding of T and it has been argued that Prüfer numbers are no useful coding. This is confirmed by experiments on graphs with $n = 10$ and random weights from $\{1,\ldots,2i\}, 1 \leq i \leq 25$. For each i, 10 000 random graphs have been considered. Runs with Prüfer numbers are stopped if the number of steps is by a factor of 10 larger than the average optimization time of the (1+1) EA with edge sets and fitness function v. Runs are called successful if they find a minimum spanning tree before this time bound.

Result 1 *(MWT): For $i = 1$, Prüfer numbers lead to smaller run times, for all other considered i, edge sets with fitness function v are better (highly significant). The observed success probability is less than 0.3 for $i \geq 8$.*

For $i = 1$, there are many minimum spanning trees and Prüfer numbers have the advantage to produce only trees. It has been reported in discussions (Rothlauf (2002)) that Prüfer numbers are useful if the unique minimum spanning tree is a star, i. e., all edges adjacent to vertex 1 have weight 1, all other edges have a larger weight (random values). This has been investigated for $10 \leq n \leq 15$.

Result 2 *(MWT): For all considered n and star-like minimum spanning trees, the average run time is smaller for edge sets and the median of the run times is smaller for Prüfer numbers (highly significant).*

Mean and median often yield the same kind of result. The significant differences here suggest a larger variance of run times for Prüfer numbers.

Choosing edge sets we still have the choice between the two fitness functions v and w. We have investigated the (1+1) EA on v and w for random graphs on $4i, 3 \leq i \leq 12$, vertices. Each edge exists with probability $1/2$ and the weights of existing edges are chosen randomly from $\{1, \ldots, n\}$. For each n, we have considered 500 random graphs. The average numbers of fitness evaluations do not differ much, they are smaller for v with the exception of $n = 24$ and $n = 44$. Only the result for $n = 32$ was confirmed as significant (MWT). Nevertheless, we conjecture that v is the better fitness function. We have chosen the value $n = 24$ (which was the worst for v in the first experiment) and have repeated the experiment with a larger number of approximately 25 000 random graphs.

Result 3 *(MWT): For $n = 24$ and the (1+1) EA, the number of fitness evaluations is smaller for the fitness function v (highly significant).*

After finding some spanning tree, it is typically improved by exchanging one edge in the tree with some edge currently not in the tree. Waiting for such mutations takes some time. The fitness function v allows the algorithm to add additional edges in those steps thereby increasing their probability. Removing the additional edges from the tree can be done by mutations of single bits which are found much faster. Thus, we conjecture the same result for all other values of n but corresponding experiments are time consuming. Based on these experiments, all later experiments use the fitness function v.

Neumann and Wegener (2004) have proved a bound of $O(m^2(\log n + \log w^*))$ on the worst-case expected optimization time for graphs on m edges where weights are chosen from $\{1, \ldots, w^*\}$. We have investigated the (1+1) EA for $5 \leq n \leq 40$ on random graphs where each edge exists with probability $1/2$ independently from the others and weights are chosen randomly from $\{1, \ldots, w^*\}$. We have considered six values for w^* depending on the expected number of edges $\overline{m} := n(n-1)/4$: $w^* \in \{1, 2, \log \overline{m}, \overline{m}^{1/2}, \overline{m}, \overline{m}^2\}$ where $\log \overline{m}$ and $\overline{m}^{1/2}$ are rounded. The experiments are based on 1 000 random graphs for each w^*.

Result 4 *(MWT): For all considered n, the average run time of the (1+1) EA is larger for larger values of w^* (highly significant with two exceptions, the comparison between $\log \overline{m}$ and $\overline{m}^{1/2}$ for $n \leq 15$ and the comparison between $\overline{m}$ and $\overline{m}^2$).*

The values of $\log \overline{m}$ and $\overline{m}^{1/2}$ are very close for $n \leq 12$. If there are enough weights (say $\overline{m}$) such that most edges have different weights, further possible weight values have not much influence. We conjecture that the asymptotic bound can be improved to $O(m^2 \log n)$. We have investigated by regression analysis whether the data can be represented best by functions of types $c\overline{m}^{1/2}, c\overline{m}, c\overline{m}^{3/2}, c\overline{m}^2$ or $c\overline{m}^2 \log \overline{m}$. This is indeed $c\overline{m}^2 \log \overline{m}$ for $w^* \in \{\overline{m}^{1/2}, \overline{m}, \overline{m}^2\}$ and $c\overline{m}^2$ for $w^* = \log \overline{m}$. Only the other cases are much easier than the worst-case bound, namely $c\overline{m}^{3/2}$ for $w^* = 1$ and $c\overline{m}$ for $w^* = 2$.

Theory on minimum spanning trees leads to the conjecture that 2-bit flips are essential, some 1-bit flips are necessary to obtain the correct number of edges and k-bit flips, $k \geq 3$, are almost useless. The probability of a 2-bit flip is $1/2$ for RLS and approximately $1/(2e)$ for (1+1) EA. Therefore, we expect that RLS beats the (1+1) EA by a factor of nearly $e \approx 2.7$ and $RLS_{0.99}$ beats the (1+1) EA by a factor of nearly $2e \approx 5.4$. This has been tested for 1 000 random graphs each on n vertices, $5 \leq n \leq 36$, and $w^* = n$.

Result 5 *(MWT): For all considered n, the quotient of the run times of the (1+1) EA and RLS is in $[2.4, 2.8]$ (significant for $n \geq 15$ and $n \neq 30$) and for the (1+1) EA and $RLS_{0.99}$ in $[5.2, 5.9]$ (significant for $n \geq 22$ and $n \neq 36$).*

There seem to be some special effects for small n and we have to expect some negative test results among many tests. In any case, it is highly significant (MWT) that $RLS_{0.99}$ is faster than RLS which is faster than the (1+1) EA.

Neumann and Wegener (2004) have proved that the expected number of fitness evaluations for the worst-case instance is asymptotically the same for the (1+λ) EA as long as $\lambda \leq m^2/n$. The (1+λ) EA is faster on parallel computers. Our experiments confirm that larger values of λ increase the number of fitness evaluations but the effect tends to vanish for larger n.

Result 6 *(MWT): For all considered n, the average number of fitness evaluations of the (1+1) EA is smaller than for the (1+10) EA but these differences are not significant. For $n \leq 20$, the (1+1) EA is faster than the (1+100) EA (highly significant) and for larger n, the effect gets less significant.*

An always essential question is whether a theoretical worst-case analysis captures the typical case. Neumann and Wegener (2004) present a family of graphs (with only three different weight values) where RLS and the (1+1) EA need an expected number of $\Theta(m^2 \log n)$ fitness evaluations. We have investigated the worst-case graphs on $n = 4i + 1$ vertices, $1 \leq i \leq 10$, which have $2i^2 + 4i$ edges (240 edges for the largest graph). Then we have compared 1 000 runs of the (1+1) EA for each n with 1 000 runs on random graphs with the same values of n and m and random weights from $\{1, \ldots, 1\,000\}$.

Result 7 *(MWT): For all considered n, the (1+1) EA is faster on the "asymptotic worst-case instance" than on random graphs (highly significant).*

A regression analysis proves that $cm^2 \log n$ describes the data for random graphs better than $cm, cm \log m, cm^2$ or cm^3 as is shown in Figure 1. The observable differences are in accordance with differences in mean square errors. This holds for other places where we present the results of regression analyses, too. Here, we arrive at the interesting conjecture that $\Theta(m^2 \log n)$ is the typical run time of the (1+1) EA for the computation of minimum spanning trees.

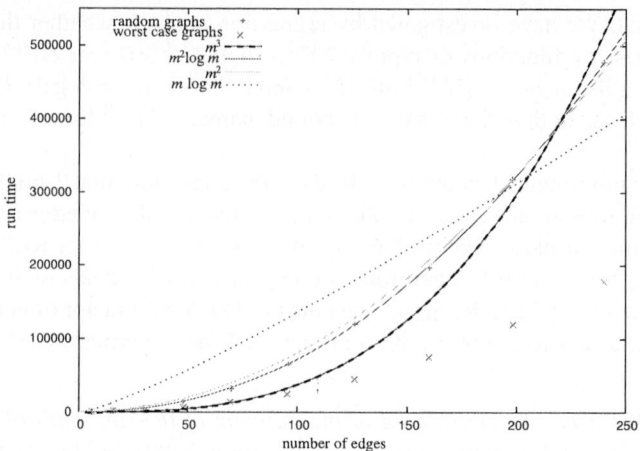

Fig. 1. Regression analysis of average run times of the (1+1) EA for the MST on random graphs.

4 Single Source Shortest Paths

The problem is to compute for a complete graph and a distinguished vertex s shortest paths from s to all other vertices. This problem is solved by Dijkstra's algorithm. Scharnow, Tinnefeld, and Wegener (2002) have investigated the search space $\{1, \ldots, n\}^{n-1}$ where x_i is the predecessor of vertex i and $s = n$. Dijkstra's algorithm computes solutions which can be described by trees rooted at n and have such a representation. The search space contains also graphs with cycles. There are two fitness functions, a single-criterion function measuring the sum of the distances of all n-i-paths and a multi-criteria function with the vector of all n-i-path lengths. Then we are interested in the unique Pareto optimal fitness vector and "$\leq$" means "$\leq$" for all vector positions. Scharnow et al. have shown that the single-criterion case contains instances with a behavior like the needle in a haystack if non-existing paths are penalized by ∞. They proved an $O(n^3)$ bound for the multi-criteria case which is tight for worst-case instances. For graphs where shortest paths do not contain too many edges, one can expect an $O(n^2 \log n)$ bound. Here, we penalize a non-existing path by a distance which is larger than the length of a longest path.

The multi-criteria fitness function contains more information but $f(x') \geq f(x)$ holds only if no n-i-path for x' is longer than for x. The question is which fitness function supports better the optimization by the (1+1) EA. We have investigated graphs on $n = 10i$ vertices, $1 \leq i \leq 15$, where the weights are chosen randomly from $\{1, \ldots, k\}, k = 2^j, 1 \leq j \leq \lfloor 2 \log n \rfloor + 1$.

Result 8 *(MWT): For all considered n and k, the (1+1) EA is faster with the single-criterion fitness function (highly significant).*

For both fitness functions, a regression analysis for functions $an^3 + bn^2 \log n + cn^2$ leads to a good fit with a-values very close to 0.

For the shortest paths problem as well as for the problem of computing minimum spanning trees, we have compared how our heuristics work on two different fitness functions. In both cases, the algorithms work better for the fitness function containing less information. This seems to be a remarkable result since it is in contrast to the plausible idea that the fitness function should contain as much information as possible.

5 Maximum Matchings

Given a graph, an edge set is a matching iff no two edges share a vertex. We use a representation by edge sets and non-matchings are penalized according to the number of conflicts, i.e., the number of edge pairs which share a vertex. Otherwise, the fitness describes the size of the matching. Matchings cannot be improved always locally but along so-called augmenting paths leading from a free vertex (not matched by the chosen edge set) to another free vertex where non-chosen and chosen edges alternate (see Figure 2). Giel and Wegener (2003) have proved that RLS and the (1+1) EA are polynomial-time randomized approximation schemes, i.e., for each constant $\varepsilon > 0$, a matching M whose size is at least $(1 - \varepsilon) \cdot |M_{\text{opt}}|$ for a maximum matching M_{opt} is obtained in expected polynomial time. However, the degree of the polynomial depends on $1/\varepsilon$. There are worst-case examples where both algorithms need on average exponential time to compute an optimal matching. Moreover, they have analyzed the expected optimization time on simple graphs. Graphs which are consisting of one path of length n are of special interest since, despite of their simpleness, one may expect to obtain augmenting paths of linear length. Based on results for the gambler's ruin problem (Feller (1968)), Giel and Wegener (2003) have proved an $O(n^4)$-bound for the expected optimization time of RLS and the (1+1) EA. This bound is tight if we obtain a search point containing an augmenting path of linear length.

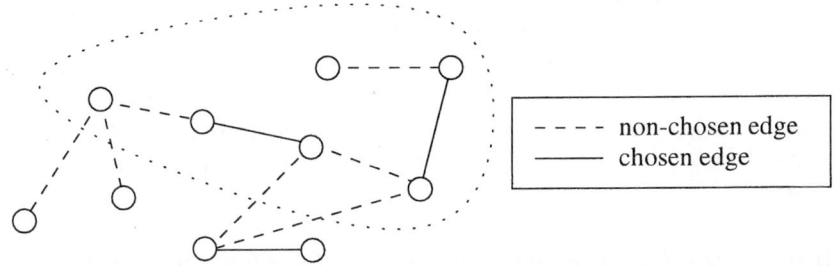

Fig. 2. An example of a graph with an augmenting path of length 5.

As in the case of minimum spanning trees, 2-bit flips seem to be the essential steps to shorten augmenting paths and 1-bit flips can improve the matching if a free edge (an edge between two free vertices) exists. Hence, we expect that RLS is better than the (1+1) EA. We have investigated paths on $10i$ vertices, $1 \leq i \leq 10$, and have performed 1 000 runs for each n.

Result 9 *(MWT): For all considered n, RLS is faster than the (1+1) EA on a path (highly significant).*

Again, we may expect a gain by a factor of approximately e. The average factor falls into $[2.3, 3.1]$ for $n \geq 30$ but the variance is too large to obtain significant results.

A regression analysis with functions $an^4 + bn^3 + cn^2 + dn$ shows that the n^4-term is necessary for a good fit. However, the n^4-term has a quite small value (as also the n^3-term). This supports the observation that there are long (linear length) augmenting paths but they are essentially shorter than n. Paths are so simple that one may conjecture that a GA with diversity-preserving methods may beat the (1+1) EA. This may be the case for two-point crossover which can replace a subpath from one individual by the corresponding subpath of another individual. However, this crossover operator is specialized to paths and not appropriate for more general graphs. Since we are not interested in this paper in problem-specific search operators, we do not discuss experiments with crossover.

Paths are special trees. Giel and Wegener (2003) have shown an $O(n^6)$ bound on the expected optimization time of RLS for finding a maximum matching on trees with n vertices but conjecture an $O(n^4)$ bound for RLS and the (1+1) EA. Trees may have a smaller diameter than paths with the same number of vertices and the size of the maximum matching typically is smaller than for paths. However, there are situations where, for trees, it is more likely to lengthen augmenting paths than to shorten them (see Figure 3). For paths, this cannot happen. Random trees can be generated by choosing randomly a Prüfer number. For $n = 10i, 1 \leq i \leq 10$, we have compared 1 000 runs of the (1+1) EA on the path with the (1+1) EA on 1 000 random trees.

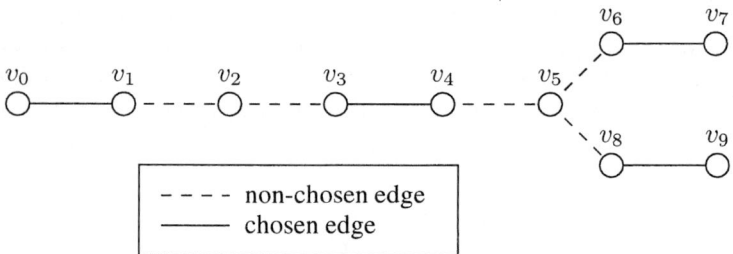

Fig. 3. An augmenting path $p = v_2, \ldots, v_5$ where RLS has at v_2 one possibility to lengthen p and one possibility to shorten p and at v_5 one possibility to shorten p and two possibilities to lengthen p.

Result 10 (*MWT*): *For all considered n, the (1+1) EA is faster on random trees than on paths (highly significant).*

It can be even confirmed that the (1+1) EA is faster on random trees on 200 vertices than on paths with 100 vertices. Regression analysis shows that the data for random trees can be well expressed by a polynomial of degree 3 while the data for paths needs an n^4-term.

Giel and Wegener (2002) have proved an $O(n^{3.5})$ bound for k-ary trees which are rooted trees of minimal depth if the number of children is k (at most k on the last two levels). Since the depth decreases with k, also the diameter and the maximal length of augmenting paths decrease with k which should lead to decreased run times. We have

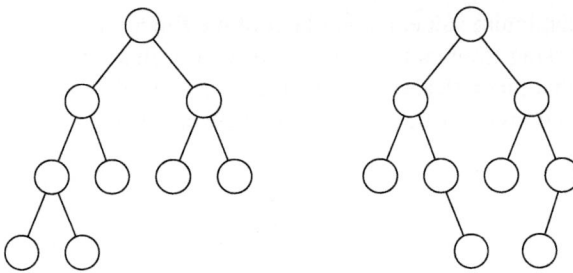

Fig. 4. Examples for the two strategies to assign the position of the leaves on the last level.

investigated random trees and k-ary trees on $10i$ vertices, $1 \leq i \leq 20$. The data confirms the following list of increasing difficulties for the (1+1) EA: 5-ary, 4-ary, ternary, binary, random. However, many comparisons were not significant. Indeed the run times for k-ary trees do not increase with n. There are significant decreases. All results depend on the positions of the leaves on the last level (see Figure 4). Assigning them from left to right leads to much smaller maximum matchings than assigning them randomly. Smaller maximum matchings can be found faster. More vertices concentrated in a small subtree may not increase the size of a maximum matching but may increase the number of maximum matchings which can simplify the optimization task. This has to be examined further and is beyond the scope of this paper.

Finally, we have followed a quite new research direction in theoretical computer science, namely the investigation of semirandom problem instances. The idea is to investigate problem instances of the following kind. First, an optimal solution is planted into the problem instance and then, randomly, further objects are added to the problem instance, see Feige and Kilian (2000) for a survey on these problem types and Feige and Krauthgamer (2000) for the problem of finding a large hidden clique in a semirandom graph.

In our case, we fix the number n of vertices and the number m of edges. Then we deterministically choose the edges of a perfect matching and, afterwards, we choose randomly $m - \lfloor n/2 \rfloor$ further edges. Since the dimension of the search space is m, we compare different values of n for fixed m. If n is large, the "planted" perfect matching typically is the only maximum one and the few further edges do not prevent an efficient search. If n is small, the many further edges produce many perfect matchings and it is easy to find one of them. Hence, it is expected, that the expected run times of the (1+1) EA are first increasing with n and decreasing after its maximal value. The experiments have considered the cases $m = 50i, 1 \leq i \leq 4$, and 100 runs for the different values of n. The differences between neighbored values of n are too small to be determined as very significant. It is convenient to compare values n and n' of small difference.

Result 11 (WSRT): *For the considered m, the average run time of the (1+1) EA on semirandom graphs is increasing with n until a maximum value is reached and then decreasing (significant, many subresults are very or even highly significant, the results are not significant close to the maximum value).*

Close to the maximum value, the gradient of the function has small absolute value and it is not surprising to obtain ambiguous results in this range. These experiments should lead to further theoretical studies in order to obtain asymptotic values for various parameter constellations described by functions between m and n, e. g., $n = m^\alpha, 1/2 < \alpha < 1$.

Conclusions

The theoretical analysis of simple heuristics on some of the best-known problems from combinatorial optimization has given a coarse picture which has been refined by our experiments. For minimum spanning trees and shortest paths, we have decided (for small dimensions of the search space) which fitness function is better suited. For many cases, we have decided which heuristic is better. In some cases, we have classified problem instances according to their difficulty for the considered heuristics. For minimum spanning trees, our experiments lead to the conjecture that worst case and typical case are asymptotically of equal difficulty. Finally, we have started experiments on semirandom problem instances, a promising research direction for experiments and theory.

References

1. Atallah, M. J. (Ed.) (1999). *Algorithms and Theory of Computation Handbook.* CRC Press.
2. Feige, U. and Kilian, J. (2000). Heuristics for semirandom graph problems. Journal of Computer and System Sciences 63, 639–671.
3. Feige, U. and Krauthgamer, R. (2000). Finding and certifying a large hidden clique in a semirandom graph. Random Structures and Algorithms 16, 195–208.
4. Feller, W. (1968). *An Introduction to Probability Theory and Its Applications.* John Wiley & Sons.
5. Giel, O. and Wegener, I. (2003). Evolutionary algorithms and the maximum matching problem. Proc. of 20th Symp. on Theoretical Aspects of Computer Science (STACS), LNCS 2607, 415–426.
6. Neumann, F. and Wegener, I. (2004). Randomized local search, evolutionary algorithms, and the minimum spanning tree problem. Proc. of Genetic and Evolutionary Computation Conference (GECCO 2004), LNCS 3102, 713–724.
7. Raidl, G. R. and Julstrom, B. A. (2003). Edge sets: an effective evolutionary coding of spanning trees. IEEE Trans. on Evolutionary Computation 7, 225–239.
8. Rothlauf, F. (2002). *Representations for Genetic and Evolutionary Algorithms.* Physica-Verlag.
9. Scharnow, J., Tinnefeld, K., and Wegener, I. (2002). Fitness landscapes based on sorting and shortest paths problems. Proc. of the 7th Conf. on Parallel Problem Solving from Nature (PPSN-VII), LNCS 2439, 54–63.

The Ising Model: Simple Evolutionary Algorithms as Adaptation Schemes

Patrick Briest, Dimo Brockhoff, Bastian Degener, Matthias Englert,
Christian Gunia, Oliver Heering, Thomas Jansen, Michael Leifhelm,
Kai Plociennik, Heiko Röglin, Andrea Schweer, Dirk Sudholt,
Stefan Tannenbaum, and Ingo Wegener[*]

FB Informatik, LS2, Univ. Dortmund, 44221 Dortmund,
Germany
{firstname.lastname}@uni-dortmund.de

Abstract. The investigation of evolutionary algorithms as adaptation schemes has a long history starting with Holland (1975). The Ising model from physics leads to a variety of different problem instances and it is interesting to investigate how simple evolutionary algorithms cope with these problems. A theoretical analysis is known only for the Ising model on the ring and partially for the Ising model on the two-dimensional torus. Here, the two-dimensional torus, the d-dimensional hypercube, and graphs consisting of two cliques connected by some bridges are investigated experimentally. Many hypotheses are confirmed by rigorous statistical tests.

1 Introduction

Holland (1975) has designed genetic algorithms (GAs) as adaptation systems. Today, evolutionary algorithms (EAs) and GAs are mainly applied as optimization algorithms. In order to understand how GAs and EAs work it makes sense to investigate their behavior on problems which are easy from the perspective of optimization but not so easy from the perspective of adaptation.

Naudts and Naudts (1998) have introduced the Ising model into this discussion. It is based on a model due to Ising (1925) to study the theory of ferromagnetism. In its most general form, the model consists of an undirected graph $G = (V, E)$ and a weight function $w \colon E \to \mathbb{R}$. Each vertex $i \in V$ has a positive or negative spin $s_i \in \{-1, +1\}$. The contribution of the edge $e = \{i, j\}$ equals $f_s(e) := s_i \cdot s_j \cdot w(e)$. The fitness $f(s)$ of the state s equals the sum of all $f_s(e), e \in E$, and has to be maximized. This general problem is NP-hard and good heuristics have been designed by Pelikan and Goldberg (2003).

Here, we are interested in the adaptation capabilities of simple EAs and consider the simple case of $w(e) = 1$ for all $e \in E$. Then it is convenient to apply an affine transformation that leads to the state space $\{0, 1\}^n$ instead of $\{-1, +1\}^n$.

---

[*] Supported in part by the Deutsche Forschungsgemeinschaft (DFG) as part of the Collaborative Research Center "Computational Intelligence" (SFB 531).

The state s describes a coloring of G by the colors 0 and 1 and the fitness function counts the number of monochromatic edges, i.e., edges $\{i,j\}$ where $s_i = s_j$. This leads to a trivial optimization problem since the monochromatic colorings 0^n and 1^n are the only optimal colorings for connected graphs. Connected monochromatic subgraphs can be considered as building blocks (schemata of high fitness). The difficulty is the property of spin-flip symmetry, i.e., $f(s) = f(\overline{s})$ for all s where $\overline{s}$ is the bitwise complement of s. This causes a problem called synchronization problem by van Hoyweghen, Goldberg, and Naudts (2002), i.e., 0-colored building blocks compete with 1-colored building blocks.

We only investigate randomized local search (RLS) and the well-known (1+1) EA. Comparisons of these two algorithms have been presented by Garnier, Kallel, and Schoenauer (1999) and Ladret (2004). These algorithms are discussed in Section 2. In Section 3, we consider graphs consisting of two cliques of equal size which are connected by some bridge edges. It is interesting to investigate how the number and the structure of the bridges help to find a monochromatic coloring. The Ising model on the ring has been analyzed intensively by Fischer and Wegener (2004) and there are some results for the two-dimensional torus by Fischer (2004). We consider the two-dimensional torus more intensively (Section 4) and investigate the torus with the smallest side length, namely the hypercube (Section 5).

Preliminary experiments have been performed to get some insight which has led to clearly formulated hypotheses. These hypotheses have been tested by independent experiments. We use different statistical tests depending on the type of hypothesis under consideration. The statistical tests are carried out using the software SPSS (Version 11.5, see www.spss.com). Regression analysis is done using gnuplot (Version 3.7, see www.gnuplot.info), using the standard settings.

The statistical tests used are the Wilcoxon signed rank test (WSRT), the Mann-Whitney test (MWT), and the binomial test. The former two tests are nonparametric tests to confirm the hypothesis that one random variable "systematically" produces larger values than another one. WSRT pairs the samples, takes their differences, ranks the absolute values and considers the sum of the ranks belonging to positive differences. MWT ranks all values and compares the rank sums for both samples. The binomial test is a test to confirm the hypothesis that the parameter p of a binomially distributed random variable is larger than some given constant p^* or that the difference of the parameters p and q of two binomially distributed random variables is larger than some given constant c.

In many cases, the hypotheses are confirmed on a good significance level. More precisely, we state our results in the form "Hypothesis H has been confirmed on the significance level α" which means that the probability of producing our data if H is not true is bounded by α using the result of the SPSS package rounded to 3 digits. Hence, smaller values of α correspond to better results. The dimension n of the search space can be arbitrarily large and, therefore, no experiment can show evidence for all n. In all cases, our results are restricted to the problem dimensions considered in the experiments. Results are called significant, if $\alpha \leq 0.05$, very significant if $\alpha \leq 0.01$, and highly significant, if $\alpha \leq 0.001$.

2 Randomized Local Search and the (1+1) EA

RLS and the (1+1) EA work on "populations" of size 1, i.e., with a single individual or search point x. The first search point x is chosen uniformly at random. Then the offspring x' is obtained from x by mutation. Selection chooses x' iff $f(x') \geq f(x)$. The mutation operator of RLS flips a single bit which is chosen uniformly at random. The mutation operator of the (1+1) EA flips each bit independently from the others with probability $1/n$.

RLS is a hill climber with a small neighborhood and can get stuck in local optima. The (1+1) EA always finds the optimum in expected finite time since each individual y has a positive probability to be produced as offspring of x. It is a matter of taste whether the (1+1) EA is considered as hill climber. No worsenings are accepted but big jumps are possible.

We restrict our investigations to these simple algorithms. One reason is that they reflect the so-called "game of life." Vertices of the graph correspond to "individuals" of some "society" and edges model relations and influences between them. The problem is to estimate the time until a stable situation is obtained and whether in this stable situation all individuals are synchronized, i.e., they have the same color. All our results imply results on independent multiple runs which seem to be more useful than larger populations without crossover where one has to ensure diversity to "approximate independency". Crossover may be helpful as shown for the ring (van Hoyweghen, Naudts, and Goldberg (2002), Fischer and Wegener (2004)). Two-point crossover is suitable on rings since it may exchange subblocks. For general graphs, only graph-specific crossover operators reflect the graph structure, e.g., exchanging rectangles for the two-dimensional torus. In this paper, we do not analyze such algorithms.

3 Partially Connected Cliques

Partially connected cliques consist of two disjoint equal-size cliques which are connected by m edges called bridges. We are interested in the success probability p of algorithm $A \in \{\text{RLS}, (1+1) \text{ EA}\}$ to find an optimal stable, i.e., a monochromatic search point before producing a stable unsynchronized search point where both cliques are monochromatic but of different colors. Theory is easy in the two extreme cases (apply the methods of Droste, Jansen, and Wegener (2002)). If $m = 0$, $p = 1/2$ and a stable situation is reached on average in $\Theta(n \log n)$ steps. If the stable search point is not an optimal one, it takes exponential time until the (1+1) EA finds an optimum. If all bridges exist, i.e., $m = n^2/4$, p is exponentially close to 1 and the expected time to produce an optimal search point is $\Theta(n \log n)$.

It seems to be obvious that many bridges are better than few bridges. Which "structure" of the bridges is useful? We distinguish three structures, namely the random choice of m bridges (r) where the set of bridges is chosen uniformly at random, the concentrated choice (c) where all bridges touch only $\lceil m^{1/2} \rceil$ vertices of each clique, and a uniform construction (u): let $v_0, \ldots, v_{n/2-1}$ be the vertices of the first clique and $w_0, \ldots, w_{n/2-1}$ the vertices of the second clique. Then structure (u) is constructed by connecting v_i with $w_i, \ldots, w_{(i+d-1) \bmod n/2}$ where $d \in \{\lfloor 2m/n \rfloor, \lceil 2m/n \rceil\}$ for all $0 \leq i \leq n/2-1$. Our results are based on 2000 runs for each scenario (n, s, q, A) where $n = 20i, 3 \leq i \leq 10$, or $n \in \{300, 400, 600\}$, $s \in \{r, u, c\}$ describes the bridge structure, $q = i/500, 0 \leq i \leq 500$, is the fraction of chosen bridges among all possible bridges, and $A \in \{\text{RLS}, (1+1) \text{ EA}\}$.

Result 1 (*WSRT*): *For all considered $n > 60$, RLS is more successful on structure u than on structure r (highly significant). This holds for the (1+1) EA only for $n \leq 100$ (significant) while the opposite is true for $n = 300$ (significant) and $n \in \{400, 600\}$ (highly significant).*

Tables and plots of the results lead to the impression that there are "obviously" no differences between the two structures. Large numbers of runs and well-chosen statistical tests can confirm small differences as highly significant. Binomial tests (for each of the 501 q-values) have confirmed (significant) that the success probabilities differ by less than 0.05. More precisely, 480 tests have confirmed this (but 4.2% outliers are expected for $\alpha = 0.05$) if $(n, A) \neq (600, (1+1) \text{ EA})$.

Result 2 (*binomial tests*): *For all cases where $(n, A) \neq (600, (1+1) \text{ EA})$ the difference between the success probability of the bridge structures r and u is less than 0.05 (significant).*

From the viewpoint of a single vertex, structure r increases the variance for the number of adjacent bridges. RLS suffers from vertices with a small number of bridges while the (1+1) EA can profit from a few vertices with many bridges in steps flipping many bits.

Result 3 (*WSRT*): *For all considered n, the success probability of the (1+1) EA on structure c is larger than on the structures r and u (highly significant).*

This can be explained as follows: The vertices with many bridges try to obtain the same color and then force the cliques to synchronize. For RLS, there is less "communication" between many vertices. For small m, the vertices with bridges have almost no influence. Moreover, if there are enough vertices without bridges, they may decide the colors of the cliques. Indeed, for each (n, q) we could decide (significant) whether RLS is better on c than on r (or u which gives the same results). Then, for fixed n and increasing q, one can observe four phases. First, RLS is better on r, then better on c, again better on r, and finally there are enough bridges to obtain a success probability close to 1 for both structures, see Figure 1.

Result 4 (*WSRT*): *For each considered n, there are values $\alpha < \beta < \gamma$ with the following properties. If $q \in (\alpha, \beta)$, RLS is more successful on c than on r, and, if $q < \alpha$ or $q \in (\beta, \gamma)$, RLS is less successful on c than on r (all statements highly significant). If $q > \gamma$, the success probability of RLS is close to 1 for both structures.*

Result 5 (*WSRT*): *For all considered (n, s), the (1+1) EA has a larger success probability than RLS (highly significant).*

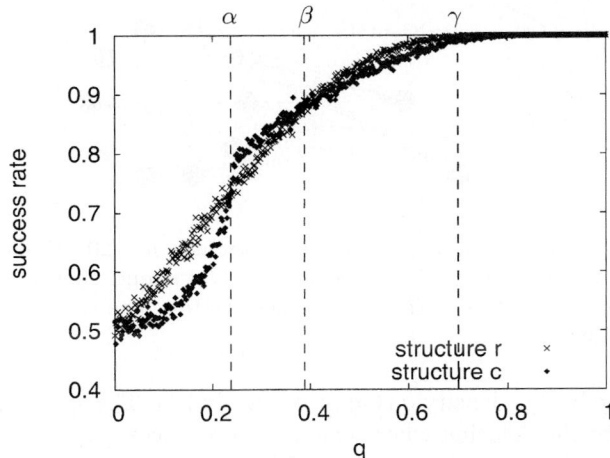

Fig. 1. The observed success rates for RLS and the two specified bridge structures and $n = 600$.

The (1+1) EA may flip a 0-vertex and a 1-vertex of the same clique. Then the bridge edges alone decide about acceptance of the new search point. This strengthens the influence of the bridges. The reader may not be surprised by the results since he or she believes that the (1+1) EA outperforms RLS almost always. However, Fischer and Wegener (2004) have proved that RLS is faster on the ring than the (1+1) EA.

Based on results of Wegener and Witt (2004) on bimodal quadratic functions one may conjecture that the very early steps decide which local optimum will be reached. This implies that, after these steps, we are able to predict whether the run is successful. We have investigated prediction rules which are applied after only $n^{3/4}$ steps, more precisely the value $n^{3/4}$ is replaced by the closest integer. Rule $R1$ predicts a success iff the majority color is given to at least $n/2 + n^{3/4}/8$ vertices while $R2$ predicts a success iff more than half of the bridges are monochromatic. The experiments are based on 1000 runs of the (1+1) EA and each pair $(n,q), n = 128i, 1 \leq i \leq 8, q = 2^{-j}, 0 \leq j \leq 9$. The results for neighbored values of n are combined.

Result 6 (*WSRT*): *For the considered n, the success probability of the prediction rules is increasing with n for each q (highly significant for $n \leq 768$, very significant for $n > 768$).*

One may conjecture that the success probabilities of the prediction rules always converge to a value close to 1.

The last issue is to investigate the expected time until a stable situation is obtained. This time equals $\Theta(n \log n)$ in the extreme cases of no bridges or all bridges. Based on all the experiments one might conjecture that this bound holds for all cases. Such a general statement cannot be confirmed by experiments. We present a bridge structure (see Figure 2) which slows down the synchronization process. Let $v_1, \ldots, v_{n/4}$ be vertices of the first clique and connect v_i to $n/2 - 2(i+1)$ bridges (which lead to arbitrary vertices of the other clique).

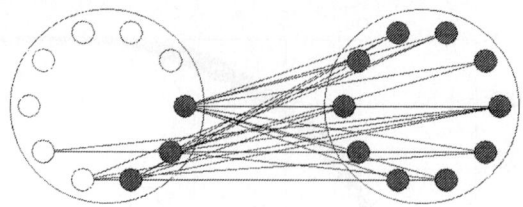

Fig. 2. An example for the specified bridge structure and $n = 20$. All clique edges are omitted to improve readability. The vertices of the first clique, shown on the left, are enumerated clockwise starting with the rightmost vertex. The coloring describes the special search point s_3.

Note that the bridge density q is approximately $1/4$. The special search point s_i corresponds to the coloring where exactly the vertices $v_1, \ldots, v_i$ and the vertices of the other clique are 0-colored, see Figure 2.

Proposition 1. *Starting with $s_i, 1 \leq i \leq n/8$, RLS and the (1+1) EA need on average $\Theta(n^2)$ steps to reach a stable situation.*

Sketch of Proof. For RLS, the only accepted step is to flip the color of v_{i+1}. This takes on average $\Theta(n)$ steps and we reach s_{i+1}. For the (1+1) EA, a step can be accepted only if $\Omega(n^{1/2})$ bits flip (this probability is exponentially small) or if v_{i+1} and only further vertices in $\{v_1, \ldots, v_{n/4}\}$ flip. Either we flip $v_{i+1}, v_{i+2}, \ldots, v_{n/4}$ one after another or we flip v_{i+1} and one of the vertices v_{i+2} and v_{i+3} in one step. The expected waiting time in both cases equals $\Theta(n^2)$. □

This proposition proves that there are situations which imply an expected waiting time of $\Theta(n^2)$. This does not disprove the conjecture since it may be very unlikely to reach such a special situation, more precisely, a search point $s_i, 1 \leq i \leq n/8$, or its bitwise complement. We have performed for each $n = 128j, 1 \leq j \leq 16$, 10000 runs of the (1+1) EA. Let p_n be the fraction of runs reaching a special situation. In our experiment, $0.1115 \leq p_n \leq 0.1278$ and there is no tendency of increasing or decreasing p_n-values. Let q_n be the true probability that a run reaches a special situation.

Result 7 (*binomial test*): *For the considered n, $0.10 \leq q_n \leq 0.14$ (highly significant).*

Hence, we should expect larger synchronization times on special partially connected cliques.

4 The Ring and the Two-Dimensional Torus

Fischer and Wegener (2004) have shown that it takes an expected number of $O(n^3)$ steps until RLS or the (1+1) EA finds the optimum of the Ising model on the ring. There are situations where this number is $\Theta(n^3)$ and experiments confirm that it is almost sure to run in such a situation. For each non-optimal search point, there are accepted 1-bit flips but they do not necessarily improve the fitness.

The two-dimensional torus T_n is defined on $n = k^2$ vertices $(i, j), 0 \leq i, j \leq k - 1$. Each vertex (i, j) has the four neighbors $(i - 1, j), (i + 1, j), (i, j - 1)$, and $(i, j + 1)$ where -1 is identified with $k - 1$ and k is identified with 0. In T_n^*, the torus with diagonals, (i, j) has four more neighbors: $(i - 1, j - 1), (i - 1, j + 1), (i + 1, j - 1)$, and $(i + 1, j + 1)$. A vertical ring of width w consists of all vertices $(i, j), i' \leq i < (i' + w), 0 \leq j \leq k - 1$. In a similar way, we can define horizontal rings. For T_n^*, diagonal rings of width w consist of all vertices (i, j) with $0 \leq i, j \leq k - 1$ such that $(i + j) \bmod k \in \{c \bmod k, \ldots, (c + w - 1) \bmod k\}$ (or $(i - j) \bmod k \in \{c \bmod k, \ldots, (c + w - 1) \bmod k\}$, resp.) holds for some fixed c (see Figure 3). Differently colored rings describe stable situations where special groups of "many" vertices have to flip for an acceptable step.

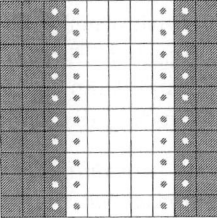 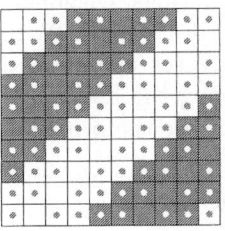

Fig. 3. Examples for vertical and diagonal rings. Vertices at the ring borders are marked with dots.

Our results are based on experiments with $k = 5i, 2 \leq i \leq 10$. The dimension of the search space is $n = k^2$ which equals 2500 for $i = 10$. Runs are stopped in stable situations. The number of runs was 2000 $(2 \leq i \leq 4)$, 1000 $(5 \leq i \leq 6)$, 500 $(i = 7)$, and 250 $(8 \leq i \leq 10)$.

One conjecture is that the probability of producing a non-optimal stable situation does not depend much on n, see Figure 4.

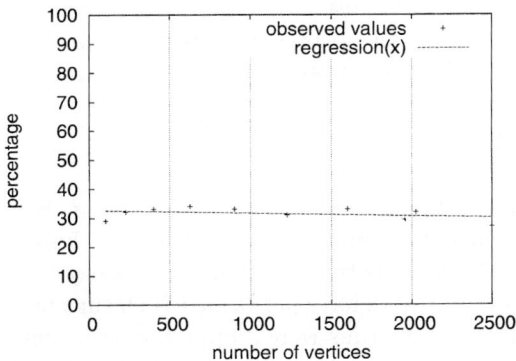

Fig. 4. The percentages of runs where the (1+1) EA reached a ring for T_n.

Result 8 (*regression analysis with functions $an+b$*): *The percentages p_n and p_n^* of runs producing a non-optimal stable situation are described best by a linear function with almost vanishing linear term, namely $a = -0.001\ldots$ and $a^* = 0.004\ldots$.*

Nevertheless, the values of p_n and p_n^* are varying with n (without clear structure). It is easier to break rings of small width than to break rings of large width. Our conjecture is that it is likely to obtain rings whose width is linear with respect to k.

Result 9 (*regression analysis with functions $ak+b$*): *If stable rings are produced, their width is best described by $0.407k - 0.108$ for T_n and $0.407k + 0.171$ for T_n^*.*

This confirms the conjecture that stable rings typically lead to very stable suboptimal solutions. By symmetry, the probability of horizontal rings is the same as for vertical rings. Diagonal rings differ from these rings. For a horizontal ring of width $w \geq 4$, there are $2k$ ring vertices with a neighbor outside the ring. This number increases to $4k$ for diagonal rings, see Figure 3. There is more information crossing the borders of diagonal rings than in the horizontal case which should decrease the probability of constructing diagonal rings.

Result 10 (*WSRT*): *For all considered n, the probability to create a diagonal ring is smaller than the probability to create a horizontal ring (highly significant).*

Fischer (2004) has proved that the expected time to create a stable situation is bounded above by $O(n^3) = O(k^6)$. It is interesting that our data leads to estimates of smaller magnitudes. Compared with the ring or the one-dimensional torus a stable situation is found more efficiently (smaller side length), but there is a non-negligible probability of producing a stable non-optimal situation.

Result 11 (*regression analysis with polynomials of degree 5*): *The time to find a stable situation for T_n is best described by*

$$-0.001k^5 + 0.123k^4 + 28k^3 - 741k^2 + 73k + 73.$$

The essential term is the $O(k^3) = O(n^{3/2})$ term. A regression with polynomials of degree 3 leads to almost the same error. Similar results hold for the two subcases of obtaining an optimal search point and of obtaining a stable non-optimal situation. It seems that the second case needs a little longer.

5 Hypercubes

One may investigate d-dimensional tori for increasing d. We investigate the extreme case of tori with the minimal side length of 2. This is equivalent to the hypercube $\{0,1\}^d$ with edges between Hamming neighbors. The dimension of the search space equals $n = 2^d$. We have performed 1000 runs for $d \in \{6,\ldots,22\}$ and RLS and the (1+1) EA. The runs were stopped in situations without 1-bit flips improving the fitness. Such search points are called stable. The first conjecture is that the (1+1) EA is better than RLS.

Result 12 (*MWT*): *For the considered d, the probability of finding an optimum as first stable search point is larger for the (1+1) EA than for RLS (highly significant).*

Result 13 (*MWT*): *Only runs not finding the optimum are considered. For the considered d, the fitness of the first stable search point is for the (1+1) EA larger than for the RLS (highly significant for odd $d \geq 9$, significant for $d = 12$, very significant for $d \in \{14, 16\}$ and highly significant for $d \in \{18, 20, 22\}$).*

However, the (1+1) EA needs more time for the better results.

Result 14 (*MWT*): *For the considered d, RLS needs less time to find a stable search point than the (1+1) EA (highly significant).*

One may conjecture that the success probability, i.e., the probability of finding an optimal search point as first stable search point, is decreasing with d. We have to be careful since there is an essential difference between odd d and even d. Each vertex has d neighbors and a flip of vertex v is accepted iff at most $d/2$ neighbors of v share their color with v. For even d, there are plateaus of constant fitness and the algorithm may finally escape from this plateau to a higher fitness level. Hence, we first compare only even values of d and only odd values of d and, afterwards, we compare odd values of d with even values of d.

Result 15 (*MWT*): *For all considered d, the probability of finding an optimal point for dimension $d + 2$ is smaller than for dimension d (highly significant for most d. For the (1+1) EA, only very significant for $d \in \{11, 12, 15\}$ and only significant for $d \in \{18, 20\}$, and not significant for $d = 6$. For RLS, only very significant for $d \in \{12, 17\}$, only significant for $d = 18$ and not significant for $d \in \{15, 16, 19, 20\}$).*

For the large values of d, the success probabilities are decreasing slower than before and it is more difficult to obtain significant results.

Another conjecture is that the algorithms produce better results for even d than for odd d. In order to check whether it is less likely to find an optimum for odd d, we compare the data for d with the union of the data for $d - 1$ and $d + 1$, which is a way to consider the mean of the average values for $d - 1$ and $d + 1$. We refer to this mean as d'.

Result 16 (*MWT*): *The success probability for odd d is smaller than for d' and for even d larger than for d' (highly significant for RLS, highly significant for the (1+1) EA for $d \leq 16$, very significant for $d \in [17, 20]$ and significant for $d = 21$).*

Similar significance levels are obtained for the following results.

Result 17 (*MWT*): *For increasing values of even d, the approximation ratio (quotient of the fitness of the first stable solution and the fitness of an optimum) is increasing. The same holds for odd d. The approximation ratio for odd d is smaller than for d' and for even d larger than for d'.*

Conclusions

The Ising model offers a variety of different scenarios to investigate a "game of life" with different relations between the individuals of the considered society. Each individual prefers to be synchronized with its "neighbors" and the question is whether the first stable situation is one where all individuals are synchronized. Even the three scenarios of partially connected cliques, the two-dimensional torus, and the hypercube lead to surprising observations. We have described and discussed those results which have been confirmed at least as significant. The tables with all the experimental data and the plots of these data contain much more information. They are not shown due to space limitations. In some situations, our statistical tests have led to results which were not observed in the tables and plots.

References

1. Droste, S., Jansen, T., and Wegener, I. (2002). On the analysis of the (1+1) evolutionary algorithm. Theoretical Computer Science 276, 51–81.
2. Fischer, S. (2004). A polynomial upper bound for a mutation-based algorithm on the two-dimensional Ising model. Proc. of the Genetic and Evolutionary Computation Conference (GECCO 2004), LNCS 3102, 1100–1112.
3. Fischer, S. and Wegener, I. (2004). The Ising model on the ring: Mutation versus recombination. Proc. of the Genetic and Evolutionary Computation Conference (GECCO 2004), LNCS 3102, 1113–1124.
4. Garnier, J., Kallel, L., and Schoenauer, M. (1999). Rigorous hitting times for binary mutations, Evolutionary Computation, Vol. 7, 173–203.
5. Holland, J. H. (1975). *Adaptation in Natural and Artificial Systems.* Univ. of Michigan, MI.
6. Ising, E. (1925). Beiträge zur Theorie des Ferromagnetismus. Z. Physik 31, 235–288.
7. Ladret, V. (2004). Asymptotic hitting time for a simple evolutionary model of protein folding. Technical report, http://arxiv.org/abs/math.PR/0308237.
8. Naudts, B. and Naudts, J. (1998). The effect of spin-flip symmetry on the performance of the simple GA. Proc. of the 5th Conf. on Parallel Problem Solving from Nature (PPSN-V), LNCS 1488, 67–76.
9. Pelikan, M. and Goldberg, D. E. (2003). Hierarchical BOA solves Ising spin glasses and MAXSAT. Proc. of the Genetic and Evolutionary Computation Conference (GECCO 2003), LNCS 2724, 1271–1282.
10. Van Hoyweghen, C., Goldberg, D. E., and Naudts, B. (2002). From twomax to the Ising model: Easy and hard symmetrical problems. Proc. of the Genetic and Evolutionary Computation Conference (GECCO 2002), 626–633. Morgan Kaufmann.
11. Van Hoyweghen, C., Naudts, B., and Goldberg, D. E. (2002). Spin-flip symmetry and synchronization. Evolutionary Computation 10, 317–344.
12. Wegener, I. and Witt, C. (2004). On the analysis of a simple evolutionary algorithm on quadratic pseudo-boolean functions. To appear in Journal of Discrete Algorithms.

Evolutionary Algorithms with On-the-Fly Population Size Adjustment

A.E. Eiben, Elena Marchiori, and V.A. Valkó

Department of Artificial Intelligence, Vrije Universiteit Amsterdam
{gusz,elena,valko}@cs.vu.nl

Abstract. In this paper we evaluate on-the-fly population (re)sizing mechanisms for evolutionary algorithms (EAs). Evaluation is done by an experimental comparison, where the contestants are various existing methods and a new mechanism, introduced here. These comparisons consider EA performance in terms of success rate, speed, and solution quality, measured on a variety of fitness landscapes. These landscapes are created by a generator that allows for gradual tuning of their characteristics. Our test suite covers a wide span of landscapes ranging from a smooth one-peak landscape to a rugged 1000-peak one. The experiments show that the population (re)sizing mechanisms exhibit significant differences in speed, measured by the number of fitness evaluations to a solution and the best EAs with adaptive population resizing outperform the traditional genetic algorithm (GA) by a large margin.

1 Introduction

The effects of setting the parameters of EAs has been the subject of extensive research by the EA community and recently there is much attention paid to self-calibrating EAs[1] that can adjust their parameters on-the-fly (see e.g., [4, 6] for a review). The most attention and most publications have been devoted to the adjustment of parameters of variation operators. Adjusting population size is much less popular, even though there are biological and experimental arguments to expect that this would be rewarding. In natural environments, population sizes of species change and tend to stabilize around appropriate values according some factors such as natural resources and carrying capacity of the ecosystem [17, 21]. Looking at it technically, population size is the most flexible parameter in natural systems: It can be adjusted much more easily than, for instance, mutation rate. In evolutionary computing, however, population size is traditionally a rigid parameter. This is not only true in the sense that for the huge majority of EAs the population size remains constant over the run, but also for the EC research community that has not spent much effort on EAs with variable population sizes. Recently, Bäck et al. [2] have provided strong indications that adjusting the population size during a run could be more rewarding than varying

---
[1] We avoid the term "self-adaptive" since the common EC terminology strongly relates it to a particular way of adjusting parameters on-line, cf. [6, Chapter 8].

the operator parameters. This forms an important motivation for the present investigation. The primary technical objective of this study is to evaluate a number of adaptive population sizing strategies on abstract fitness landscapes. The main contributions of this paper are the following:

- drawing attention to and initiating further research on varying population size in EAs
- giving a brief overview of existing approaches and introducing a new population resizing technique,
- presenting an experimental comparison for a number of these techniques,
- providing freely available Java code for these methods and our test suite, allowing reproduction of our results and further research.

The relevance of this study, and possible future efforts in this direction, lies in the potential of self-calibrating EAs. Ultimately, it would be highly desirable to utilize the inherent adaptive power of an evolutionary process for adapting *itself* to a certain problem instance, while solving that very problem instance. We believe that the extra computational overhead (i.e., solving the self-calibration problem additionally to the given technical problem) will pay off, but a solid judgment of this hypothesis requires more research.

1.1 Related Work

A few researchers provided a theoretical analysis of the optimal population size in EAs. Goldberg described two methods for optimally sizing populations in GAs. In the first one [8,9] he sized the population for optimal schema processing, in the second one [10], optimization was performed for accurate schema sampling. An overview of both methods can be found in [20]. Reeves [16] tried to specify the minimal population size for GA applications based on a theoretical background. The adopted principle was that every possible point in the search space should be reachable from the initial population by crossover only. The results show that the minimal size is depending on the alphabet cardinality and the stringlength. Specifically, for binary representations with string size of 100 the minimal size should be about 15 – 18. Hansen, Gawelczyk and Ostermeier [11] gave a theoretical analysis of sizing the populations in $(1, \lambda)$-Evolution Strategies with respect to the local progress.

There is also a number of empirical studies on population sizing. The Genetic Algorithm with Variable Population Size (GAVaPS) from Arabas [1], [15, p. 72–80] eliminates population size as an explicit parameter by introducing the age and maximum lifetime properties for individuals. The maximum lifetimes are allocated at birth depending on fitness of the newborn, while the age (initialized to 0 at birth) is incremented at each generation by one. Individuals are removed from the population when their ages reach the value of their predefined maximal lifetime. This mechanism makes survivor selection unnecessary and population size an observable, rather than a parameter. The Adaptive Population size GA (APGA) is a variant of GAVaPS where a steady-state GA is used, and the lifetime of the best individual remains unchanged when individuals grow older [2].

In [12, 14] Harik and Lobo introduce a parameter-less GA (PLGA) which evolves a number of populations of different sizes simultaneously. Smaller populations get more function evaluations, where population i is allowed to run four times more generations than the population $i + 1$. If, however, a smaller population converges, the algorithm drops it. The Random Variation of the Population Size GA (RVPS) is presented by Costa *et al.* in [3]. In this algorithm, the size of the actual population is changed every N fitness evaluations, for a given N. Hinterding, Michalewicz and Peachey [13] presented an adaptive mechanism, in which three sub-populations with different population sizes are used. The population sizes are adapted at regular intervals (*epochs*) biasing the search to maximize the performance of the group with the mid-most size. The criterion used for varying the sizes is fitness diversity. Schlierkamp-Voosen and Mühlenbein [18] use a competition scheme between sub-populations to adapt the size of the sub-populations as well as the overall population size. There is a quality criterion for each group, as well as a gain criterion, which dictates the amount of change in the group's size. The mechanism is designed in such a way that only the size of the best group can increase. A technique for dynamically adjusting the population size with respect to the probability of selection error, based on Goldberg's research [10], is presented in [19].

2 Population Resizing Mechanisms in This Comparison

For the present comparison we have selected a number of existing population resizing mechanisms to be implemented in our library. In particular, the GAVaPS from [1], the GA with adaptive population size (APGA) from [2], the parameter-less GA from [12], and three variants of the GA with Random Variation of Population Size (RVPS) from [3]. Initial testing has shown that GAVaPS was very sensitive for the *reproduction ratio* parameter and the algorithm frequently increased the size of the population over several thousand individuals, which resulted in unreliable performance. For this reason we removed it from further experimentation. Furthermore, we added a traditional genetic algorithm (TGA) as benchmark and introduced a new technique.

The new population resizing mechanism we introduce is based on improvements of the best fitness in the population. On fitness improvement the algorithm becomes more biased towards exploration increasing the population size, short term lack of improvement makes the population smaller, but stagnation over a longer period causes populations to grow again. The pseudo-code for the Population Resizing on Fitness Improvement GA (PRoFIGA) is given below. The intuition behind this algorithm is related to (a rather simplified view on) exploration and exploitation. The bigger the population size is, the more it supports explorative search. Because in early stages of an EA run fitness typically increases, population growth, hence exploration, will be more prominent in the beginning. Later on it will decrease gradually. The shrinking phase is expected to "concentrate" more on exploitation by reducing the genetic diversity in the decreasing populations. The second kind of growing is supposed to initiate re-

procedure PRoFIGA
begin
    INITIALIZE population with random individuals
    EVALUATE each individual
    while not *stop-condition* **do**
        SELECT parents from the population
        RECOMBINE pairs of parents
        MUTATE the resulting offspring
        EVALUATE each of the offspring
        REPLACE some parents by some offspring
        if *BEST_FITNESS_IMPROVED* **then**
            GROW_POPULATION_1
        elsif *NO_IMPROVEMENT_FOR_LONG_TIME* **then**
            GROW_POPULATION_2
        else
            SHRINK_POPULATION
        fi
        EVALUATE the new individuals
    od
end

newed exploration in a population stuck in local optima. Technically, PRoFIGA applies three kinds of changes in the population size:

1. If the best fitness in the population increases, the population size is increased proportionally to the improvement and the number of evaluations left until the maximum allowed. The formula used for calculating the growth rate X for GROW_POPULATION_1 is:

$$X = increaseFactor \cdot (maxEvalNum - currEvalNum) \cdot \frac{maxFitness_{new} - maxFitness_{old}}{initMaxFitness}$$

where *increaseFactor* is an external parameter from the interval $(0, 1)$, *maxEvalNum* and *currEvalNum* denote the given maximum number of fitness evaluations and the current evaluation number, $maxFitness_{new}$, $maxFitness_{old}$ and *initMaxFitness* are the best fitness values in the current generation, the same in the preceding generation and the best fitness value in the initial population. (Note that we assume the existence of *maxEvalNum*, which is very often present indeed. In case it is not given, a very large number can be used instead.)

2. The population size is increased by a factor Y if there is no improvement during the last V number of evaluations. In principle, the mechanism to increase the population size in this step can be defined independently from the previous one, but in fact we use the same growth rate X for GROW_POPULATION_2 as for GROW_POPULATION_1.

3. If neither 1. nor 2. was executed, then the population size is decreased. For the decrease factor Z in SHRINK_POPULATION a little percentage of the current population size is used, e.g. (1–5%).

The new members of the population can be chosen by different strategies, like cloning some individuals from the population, or random generation of new individuals. In this study we use cloning of good individuals that are chosen by tournament selection from the actual population.

The individuals to be replaced can be selected by, for instance, an "anti-tournament" selection. The size is not decreased further after a certain minimal population size is reached. Note that PRoFIGA uses tournament selection and delete worst replacement, together with elitism, hence the best fitness of the population cannot decrease, only stagnate.

3 Test Suite: Spears' Multimodal Problems

When choosing the test suite we deliberately avoided popular, but ad hoc collections of objective functions for reasons outlined in [5] and [6, Chapter 14]. We have chosen the multimodal problem generator of Spears [22] that has been designed to facilitate systematic studies on GA behavior. This generator creates random problems with a controllable size and degree of multi-modality. The random bit-string multi-modality problem generator constructs a number (the degree of multi-modality) of random L-bit strings, where each string represents the location of a peak in an L-dimensional space. The problem consists of identifying the location of the highest peak. The heights of the peaks can be generated using different functions: constant (all peaks have the same height), linear (the heights of peaks belong to a line), 1−square root, and logarithm-based.

The difficulty of the problem depends on the number of peaks, the height of the lowest peak (the higher it is, the more difficult the problem is), the distribution of the peak-heights (the more peaks have heights close to the global optimum, the more difficult the problems is), and the random layout of the peaks in the search space (the more isolated the peaks are, the more difficult the problem is). The first three features can be controlled externally by parameters, the distribution is created randomly in each run of the generator. To calculate the fitness of the individuals, first the nearest peak to an individual is determined: for a given string $\bar{x}$ let $Peak_{near}(\bar{x})$ be such that

$$Hamming(\bar{x}, Peak_{near}(\bar{x})) = \min_{i=1}^{\mathcal{P}}(Hamming(\bar{x}, Peak_i)),$$

in case of multiple peaks at the same distance, choose the highest neighboring peak. Then, the fitness value of a binary string chromosome in the population is determined by taking the number of bits the string has in common with the nearest peak, divided by L, and scaled by the height of the nearest peak:

$$f(\bar{x}) = \frac{L - Hamming(\bar{x}, Peak_{near}(\bar{x}))}{L} \cdot height(Peak_{near}(\bar{x})).$$

Note that the fitness assumes values between 0 and 1.

Our test suite consists of 10 different landscapes, where the height of the lowest peak is always 0.5, the distribution of the peak-heights is linear and the number of peaks ranges from 1 to 1000 through 1, 2, 5, 10, 25, 50, 100, 250, 500, and 1000.

4 Performance Measures

In order to analyze and assess the performance of the algorithms considered in our study, we perform 100 independent runs on each problem instance, and consider three statistics to measure algorithm efficiency and effectivity.

- The first effectivity measure is Success Rate (SR) that gives the percentage of runs in which the optimum (the highest peak) was found.
- The second effectivity measure is Mean Best Fitness (MBF). It is the average of the best fitness in the last population over all runs.
- Efficiency (speed) is measured by the Average number of Evaluations to a Solution (AES), which shows the number of evaluations it takes on average for the successful runs to find the optimum. If a GA has no success ($SR = 0$) then the AES measure is undefined.

5 Algorithm Setups

We use a traditional GA (TGA) as baseline algorithm for our comparison. The TGA's parameters are shown in Table 1. The population size $N = 100$ has been "optimized" through conventional hand-tuning comparing a number of different population sizes. All EAs in this comparison follow this setup, hence the algorithms differ only in the population (re)sizing mechanism they apply.

Table 1. TGA setup.

GA model	steady-state
Representation	bit-string
Chromosome length (L)	100
Population size (N)	100
Recombination	2-point crossover ($p_c = 0.9$)
Mutation	bit-flip ($p_m = 1/L$)
Selection	2-tournament
Replacement	delete worst 2
Max. no. of evals	10.000

Further details, specific for the particular algorithms, are listed below. For APGA [2] we consider the variant which assigns lifetime values according to the following bi-linear function:

$$\begin{cases} MinLT + \eta \dfrac{fitness[i] - MinFit}{AvgFit - MinFit} & if\, AvgFit \geqq fitness[i] \\ \dfrac{1}{2}(MinLT + MaxLT) + \eta \dfrac{fitness[i] - AvgFit}{MaxFit - AvgFit} & if\, AvgFit < fitness[i] \end{cases}$$

with *MinLT* and *MaxLT* equal to 1 and 11, respectively. The parameter-less GA [12] is run in parallel with the following 8 population sizes: 2, 4, 8, 16, 32, 64, 128 and 256. For RVPS (variant RW) [3] is used with insertion of randomly generated individuals and removal of the worst individuals. The minimal population size is set to 15, the maximal size to 300, the time between two resizing is 100 evaluations (the evaluation of the newly generated individuals in RVPS RW is not counted into this number). PRoFIGA (variant TMW[2]), where the population sizing mechanism uses 2-tournament selection for selecting individuals from the actual population, and where the following values are used for the other parameters of the population sizing mechanism: *increaseFactor* of 0.1, *decreaseFactor* of 0.4, *minPopSize* of 15 and *maxPopSize* 1000.

The algorithms have been implemented in PEA (Programming library for EAs), a new EA software developed for the present investigation (the Java code is available at http://www.cs.vu.nl/ci). PEA is written in Java, hence it can be run on all platforms that have a Java Runtime Environment installed.

6 Results

The results of our main experimental series are given in the graphs with a grid background in Figure 1 and the left hand side of Figure 2.

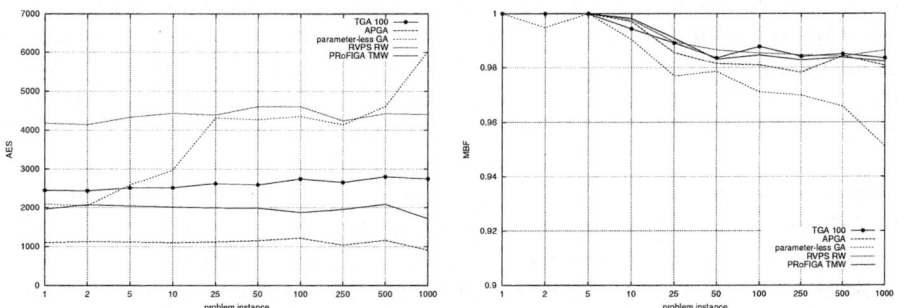

Fig. 1. AES (left) and MBF (right) of TGA, APGA, the parameter-less GA, RVPS and PRoFIGA with max-eval = 10000.

The AES plots are exhibited in Figure 1 (left). These graphs show clear differences between the algorithms. There are, however, no significant differences between the problem instances when only looking at the speed curves (except for the parameter-less GA). Apparently, finding a solution does not take more

---

[2] See [23] for details.

evaluations on a harder problem that has more peaks. (Although it should be noted that for harder problems the averages are taken over fewer runs, cf. the SR figures below, which reduces the reliability of the statistics.) This is an interesting artifact of the problem generator that needs further investigations. The increasing problem hardness, however, is clear from the decreasing average quality of the best solution found (MBF), cf. Figure 1 (right) and the decreasing probability of finding a solution (SR), cf. Figure 2 (left).

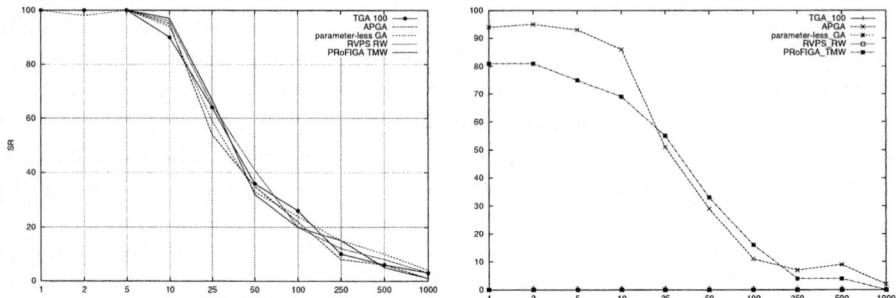

Fig. 2. SR of TGA, APGA, the parameter-less GA, RVPS and PRoFIGA with max-eval = 10000 (left) and with max-eval = 1500 (right).

We can rank the population (re)sizing methods based on the AES plots: APGA is significantly faster than the other methods, followed by PRoFIGA. The traditional GA comes third. The parameter-less GA is only competitive for easy problems and the RVPS RW is clearly inferior to the other methods.

The SR and MBF results are quite homogeneous, with only one negative outlier, the parameter-less GA. It seems that we cannot rank the algorithms by their effectivity. However, this homogeneity is a consequence of our choice of the maximum number of fitness evaluations in the termination criterion. Apparently it is "too" high allowing all contestants to reach the performance of the champions – be it slower. As a control experiment, we repeated all runs with the maximum number of fitness evaluations set to 1500. The resulting success rates are given in Figure 2 (right), showing great differences. APGA and PRoFIGA obtain somewhat worse, but comparable SR results as before, but the other algorithms never find a solution yielding SR = 0 over all peaks.

Forced by space limitations we cannot provide an analysis, nor a graphical illustration of population size dynamics for the algorithms. In summary, the experiments indicate that each algorithm has a "preferred" range of population size (except the parameter-less GA), rather independently from the hardness of the problem instance.

7 Conclusions

Looking at the results we can conclude that adapting population sizes in an EA can certainly pay off. The gains in terms of efficiency, measured by the number of fitness evaluations needed to find a solution, can be significant: the winner of our comparison (APGA) achieves the same success rate and mean best fitness as the traditional GA with less than half of the work, and even the second best (PRoFIGA) needs 20% fewer evaluations. Our second series of experiments shows that such an increase in speed can be converted into increased effectivity, depending on the termination condition. Here again, the winner is APGA, followed by PRoFIGA. It should be noted that we do not claim that on-the-fly population (re)sizing is necessarily better than traditional hand-tuning of a constant population size. Two GAs from this comparison (the parameter-less GA and RVPS RW) are much slower than the traditional GA.

Finding a sound explanation for the observed differences in algorithm behavior is a hard nut to crack. Our most plausible hypothesis is that the superior performance of APGA is due to the lifetime principle that eliminates explicit survivor selection and makes population size an observable instead of a parameter. However, it should be noted that using this idea does not mean that the number of EA parameters is reduced. In fact, it is increased in our case: instead of N in the TGA, the APGA introduces two new parameters, *MinLT* and *MaxLT*.

The present results can be naturally combined with those of Bäck *et al.* who worked on a test suite containing commonly used objective functions and found that APGA outperformed TGA and other GAs that used adaptive crossover and mutation mechanisms [2]. Our findings here amplify their conclusions on the superiority of APGA. Of course, highly general claims are still not possible about APGA. But these results together form a strong indication that incorporating on-the-fly population (re)sizing mechanisms based on the lifetime principle in EAs is a very promising design heuristic definitely worth trying and that APGA is a successful implementation of this general idea.

Acknowledgement

The authors acknowledge the valuable contribution of M. Jelasity and T. Buresch in performing the investigations reported here.

References

1. J. Arabas, Z. Michalewicz, and J. Mulawka. GAVaPS – a genetic algorithm with varying population size. In *Proceedings of the First IEEE Conference on Evolutionary Computation*, pages 73–78. IEEE Press, Piscataway, NJ, 1994.
2. T. Bäck, A.E. Eiben, and N.A.L. van der Vaart. An empirical study on GAs "without parameters". In M. Schoenauer, K. Deb, G. Rudolph, X. Yao, E. Lutton, J.J. Merelo, and H.-P. Schwefel, editors, *Proceedings of the 6th Conference on Parallel Problem Solving from Nature*, number 1917 in Lecture Notes in Computer Science, pages 315–324. Springer, Berlin, 2000.
3. J. Costa, R. Tavares, and A. Rosa. An experimental study on dynamic random variation of population size. In *Proc. IEEE Systems, Man and Cybernetics Conf.*, volume 6, pages 607–612, Tokyo, 1999. IEEE Press.

4. A.E. Eiben, R. Hinterding, and Z. Michalewicz. Parameter control in evolutionary algorithms. *IEEE Transactions on Evolutionary Computation*, 3(2):124–141, 1999.
5. A.E. Eiben and M. Jelasity. A critical note on experimental research methodology in EC. In *Proceedings of the 2002 Congress on Evolutionary Computation (CEC'2002)*, pages 582–587. IEEE Press, 2002.
6. A.E. Eiben and J.E. Smith. *Introduction to Evolutionary Computing*. Springer, 2003.
7. S. Forrest, editor. *Proceedings of the 5th International Conference on Genetic Algorithms*. Morgan Kaufmann, San Francisco, 1993.
8. D.E. Goldberg. Optimal population size for binary-coded genetic algorithms. *TCGA Report*, No. 85001, 1985.
9. D.E. Goldberg. Sizing populations for serial and parallel genetic algorithms. In J.D. Schaffer, editor, *Proceedings of the 3rd International Conference on Genetic Algorithms*, pages 70–79. Morgan Kaufmann, San Francisco, 1989.
10. D.E. Goldberg, K. Deb, and J.H. Clark. Genetic Algorithms, Noise, and the Sizing of Populations. *IlliGAL Report*, No. 91010, 1991.
11. N. Hansen, A. Gawelczyk, and A. Ostermeier. Sizing the population with respect to the local progress in $(1,\lambda)$-evolution strategies – a theoretical analysis. In *Proceedings of the 1995 IEEE Conference on Evolutionary Computation*, pages 80–85. IEEE Press, Piscataway, NJ, 1995.
12. G.R. Harik and F.G. Lobo. A parameter-less genetic algorithm. In W. Banzhaf, J. Daida, A. E. Eiben, M. H. Garzon, V. Honavar, M. Jakiela, and R. E. Smith, editors, *Proceedings of the Genetic and Evolutionary Computation Conference*, volume 1, pages 258–265, Orlando, Florida, USA, 1999. Morgan Kaufmann.
13. R. Hinterding, Z. Michalewicz, and T.C. Peachey. Self-adaptive genetic algorithm for numeric functions. In H.-M. Voigt, W. Ebeling, I. Rechenberg, and H.-P. Schwefel, editors, *Proceedings of the 4th Conference on Parallel Problem Solving from Nature*, number 1141 in Lecture Notes in Computer Science, pages 420–429. Springer, Berlin, 1996.
14. F.G. Lobo. *The parameter-less Genetic Algorithm: rational and automated parameter selection for simplified Genetic Algorithm operation*. PhD thesis, Universidade de Lisboa, 2000.
15. Z. Michalewicz. *Genetic Algorithms + Data structures = Evolution programs*. Springer, 3th edition, 1996.
16. C.R. Reeves. Using genetic algorithms with small populations. In Forrest [7], pages 92–99.
17. J. Roughgarden. *Theory of Population Genetics and Evolutionary Ecology*. Prentice-Hall, 1979.
18. D. Schlierkamp-Voosen and H. Mühlenbein. Adaptation of population sizes by competing subpopulations. In *Proceedings of the 1996 IEEE Conference on Evolutionary Computation*. IEEE Press, Piscataway, NJ, 1996.
19. R.E. Smith. Adaptively resizing populations: An algorithm and analysis. In Forrest [7].
20. R.E. Smith. *Population sizing*, pages 134–141. Institute of Physics Publishing, 2000.
21. J. Song and J. Yu. *Population system control*. Springer, 1988.
22. W.M. Spears. *Evolutionary Algorithms: the role of mutation and recombination*. Springer, 2000.
23. V.A. Valkó. Self-calibrating evolutionary algorithms: Adaptive population size. Master's thesis, Free University Amsterdam, 2003.

Search Space Features Underlying the Performance of Stochastic Local Search Algorithms for MAX-SAT

Holger H. Hoos[1,*], Kevin Smyth[1], and Thomas Stützle[2]

[1] Department of Computer Science, University of British Columbia
Vancouver, BC, V6T 1Z4, Canada
{hoos,ksmyth}@cs.ubc.ca
[2] Fachbereich Informatik, Technische Universität Darmstadt
64283 Darmstadt, Germany
stuetzle@informatik.tu-darmstadt.de

Abstract. MAX-SAT is a well-known optimisation problem that can be seen as a generalisation of the propositional satisfiability problem. In this study, we investigate how the performance of stochastic local search (SLS) algorithms – a large and prominent class of algorithms that includes, for example, Tabu Search, Evolutionary Algorithms and Simulated Annealing – depends on features of the underlying search space. We show that two well-known measures of search space structure, the autocorrelation length of random walks and the so-called fitness distance correlation, reflect complementary factors underlying instance hardness for high-performance SLS algorithms. While the autocorrelation measure is computationally cheap, the fitness distance correlation serves mainly as an *a posteriori* measure for explaining performance. We also study the dependence of SLS performance on features of the distribution of clause weights for individual instances and show that, depending on the variance of the clause weight distribution, different search strategies seem to be suited best for dealing with the structure of the respective search spaces.

1 Introduction and Background

The satisfiability problem in propositional logic (SAT) is the task to decide for a given propositional formula whether it has a model. More formally, given a set of m clauses $\{C_1, \ldots, C_m\}$ involving n Boolean variables $x_1, \ldots, x_n$, the SAT problem is to decide whether an assignment of truth values to variables exists such that all clauses are simultaneously satisfied. This problem plays a prominent role in various areas of computer science, mathematical logic and artificial intelligence, as well as in many applications [1–4].

MAX-SAT is the following optimisation variant of SAT: Given a propositional formula in conjunctive normal form (CNF), the (unweighted) MAX-SAT problem is to find a variable assignment that maximises the number of satisfied clauses. In *weighted MAX-SAT*, each clause C_i has an associated weight w_i, and the goal becomes to maximise the total weight of the satisfied clauses. Solving a given instance of a unweighted

---

* To whom correspondence should be addressed.

or weighted MAX-SAT instance corresponds to finding a global optimum of the objective function that maps each variable assignment a to the number or total weight of the clauses satisfied under a.

Both SAT and MAX-SAT are $\mathcal{NP}$-hard combinatorial problems which are mainly solved using heuristic search methods. Stochastic local search (SLS) algorithms for MAX-SAT are based on the idea of iteratively maximising the number of satisfied clauses. SLS algorithms are among the state-of-the-art methods for solving SAT, and by far the most effective methods for finding optimal or close-to-optimal solutions for large and hard instances of MAX-SAT (see, *e.g.*, [5]).

SAT and unweighted MAX-SAT can be seen as special cases of weighted MAX-SAT, and in principle, the same SLS methods can be applied to all these closely related problems. It is well-known that the performance of SLS algorithms on a given problem instance critically depends on the structure of the respective search space[1]. This raises the question whether there are substantial differences in the structure of the search spaces for SAT, unweighted MAX-SAT, and weighted MAX-SAT instances which might require different SLS methods to be used in order to find optimal solutions with minimal search cost.

In this work, we investigate the search space structure of various types of MAX-SAT instances and its impact on the performance of ILS-HSS, a high-performance SLS algorithm for MAX-SAT, whose performance we show to be highly correlated with that of state-of-the-art algorithms for the problem instances studied here. We use two well-known summary measures of search space structure: the autocorrelation length (ACL) [6–8] of random walks and the fitness distance correlation (FDC) for local optima [9]. Both measures are widely used for examining the search spaces of optimisation problems and are known to correlate with the hardness of problem instances for SLS algorithms [10–12]. While the autocorrelation measure is computationally cheap, the fitness distance correlation serves mainly as an *a posteriori* measure for explaining performance. We analyse (i) how these measures depend on the variance and the granularity of the clause weights, (ii) how these measures correlate with ILS-HSS performance between and within our test-sets and (iii) whether ACL and FDC reflect the same search space features. Our results show that ACL reflects well the differences of the instance hardness between test-sets with varying distributions of clause weights, while FDC seems to be better for explaining hardness differences within test-sets from a same instance distribution.

The remainder of this article is structured as follows. We first give a brief introduction to SLS algorithms for MAX-SAT and present ILS-HSS; next, we report the results of our ACL and FDC analyses. Finally, we discuss the implications of our findings, and we end with some concluding remarks and directions for further work.

2 SLS Algorithms for MAX-SAT

A large number of different SLS algorithms for MAX-SAT are known from the literature. Among these are SAMD (an early form of Tabu Search) and various forms of

---

[1] Following common practice, we use the the term 'search space structure' synonymously for 'search landscape structure'.

Simulated Annealing [13]; GSAT with Random Walk, a randomised iterative improvement algorithm [14]; GRASP [15]; the Discrete Lagrangian Method [16]; Guided Local Search [17]; variants of WalkSAT, one of the most successful SLS algorithms for SAT (see, *e.g.*, [18]); Ant Colony Optimisation [19]; Iterated Robust Tabu Search (IRoTS) [5]; and many others. Of these, only IRoTS, GLS and a variant of WalkSAT called Novelty$^+$ appear to reach state of the art performance on a diverse range of MAX-SAT instances [4].

In this study we use an iterated local search (ILS) algorithm for MAX-SAT that achieves excellent performance on the problem instances we considered. In general, iterated local search algorithms can be seen as performing a biased random walk in the space of the local optima encountered by an underlying local search algorithm. This walk is built by iteratively perturbing a locally optimal solution, then applying local search to obtain another locally optimal solution, and finally using an acceptance criterion for deciding from which of these solutions to continue the search. The underlying local search algorithm used in our ILS algorithm for MAX-SAT, dubbed ILS-HSS, is a tabu search algorithm with fixed tabu list length $0.12 \cdot n$. The solution perturbation is implemented by randomly flipping each variable with a probability of 0.4. If applying perturbation and subsequent local search to a solution s results in an inferior solution s', s' is accepted with a probability of 0.1; otherwise the next perturbation starts from s. In case of a tie between s and s', each is chosen with probability 0.5. The algorithm terminates when a given solution quality (*i.e.*, number or total weight of unsatisfied clauses has been reached), or a user-specified run-time limit has been exceeded, returning the best variable assignment encountered during the search. (ILS-HSS can be seen as a variant of IRoTS [5].)

3 Benchmark Sets and SLS Performance

For the computational experiments conducted in this study, we used test-sets of various types of randomly generated MAX-SAT instances. These test-sets consist of both weighted and unweighted Random 3-SAT instances with 100 instances in each set. The first of these, rnd−u, is a set of unweighted MAX-SAT instances that were sampled from the well-studied Uniform Random 3-SAT distribution [20] for 100 variables and 500 clauses, corresponding to the over-constrained region of Uniform Random-3-SAT. The other five test-sets were obtained from rnd−u by adding clause weights that were randomly generated according to truncated and discretised normal distributions. In all cases, the mean of the clause weight distribution was chosen as $\mu = 500$, and the distribution was symmetrically truncated such that all clause weights are restricted to lie in the interval $[1, 1000]$. Symmetric truncation guarantees that the actual mean is close to μ. Within this class of distributions, standard deviations σ' (before truncation) of $100, 200$ and 500 were used for generating our test-sets. For $\sigma' = 100$, test-sets for three levels of clause weight granularity were generated by discretising all weights to a grid g of size 1,10, and 100, respectively. For $\sigma' = 200$ and $\sigma' = 500$, we used test-sets with grid size one (high granularity) only. The resulting test-sets are summarised in Table 1.

For evaluating the relative performance of SLS algorithms on our test-sets, we measured run-length distributions (RLDs) for ILS-HSS on each individual problem

Table 1. Test-sets of MAX-SAT instances with different standard deviation σ' and granularity g of clause weight distributions for this study. Each test-set contains 100 instances.

Name	μ	σ'	g
rnd-u	(unweighted)		
rnd5-d100	500	100	100
rnd5-d10	500	100	10
rnd5-v100	500	100	1
rnd5-v200	500	200	1
rnd5-v500	500	500	1

instance [21]. This was done by running ILS-HSS 1 000 times on every problem instance from a given test-set, each time until a putative optimal solution for the respective instance was found. (Since for most of the MAX-SAT instances used in this study, determining provably optimal solutions using state-of-the-art complete MAX-SAT algorithms was found to be practically impossible due to prohibitively long run-times, putatively optimal solutions were determined as described in [5].) We refer to the mean of the RLD, that is, the average number of steps over the respective 1 000 runs, as the 'local search cost' (lsc) for the given MAX-SAT instance.

In preliminary experiments, we determined that for the test-sets considered here, the local search cost for ILS-HSS and other high-performance SLS algorithms for MAX-SAT, such as Robust Tabu Search, Iterated Robust Tabu Search, and Novelty$^+$/wcs+we [5,4], is relatively highly correlated (see Figure 1). Similar correlations in the performance of these algorithms are observed between our various test-sets. Nevertheless, especially for weighted MAX-SAT instances with highly variable clause weights, substantial performance differences are observed in some cases.

These observations suggest that to a large extent, the performance differences between the different test-sets as well as between different instances from the same test-set are due to search space features that affect a wide range of different SLS algorithms for MAX-SAT similarly; at the same time, there appear to be other features that have a more algorithm-specific impact. (Intuitively, this is what one would expect, given that all algorithms use the same objective function, but different search heuristics.) In the following, we focus on the former type of search space features, and investigate the fundamental question to which extent these features depend on the nature of the clause weight distributions underlying a given set of MAX-SAT instances.

4 Autocorrelation Length (ACL) Analysis

The autocorrelation length (ACL) of a random walk $y_1, \ldots, y_k$ is defined based on the autocorrelation series $\hat{\rho}(h) := c_h/c_0$, where $c_i := 1/k \cdot \sum_{j=1}^{k-i}[(y_j - \bar{y}) \cdot (y_{j+i} - \bar{y})]$ is the autocovariance function with lag i [6], and $\bar{y}$ the mean over $y_1, \ldots, y_k$. Note that $-1 \leq \hat{\rho}(i) \leq 1$. ACL is defined as the lag h for which $\hat{\rho}(h)$ falls below $1/e$. (Slightly different definitions can be found in the literature, e.g., ACL $:= -1/ln(\hat{\rho}(1))$, but for these we have observed very similar results to those reported in the following.)

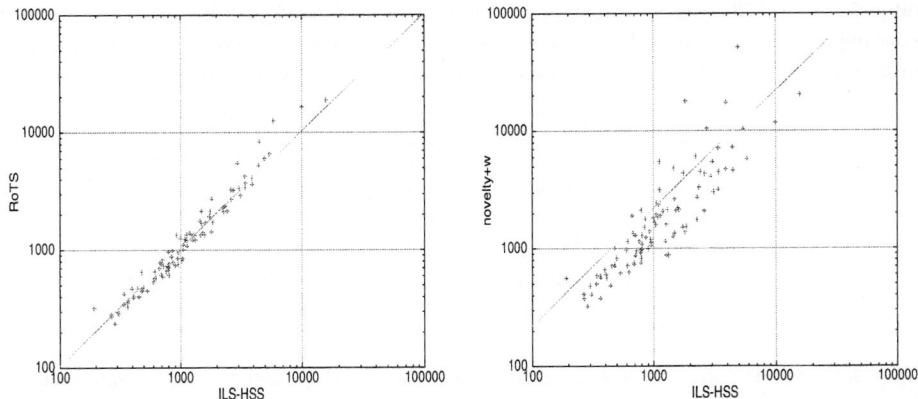

Fig. 1. Local search cost correlation between ILS-HSS and other SLS algorithms for MAX-SAT on the rnd−u (unweighted) test-set. Left: ILS-HSS *vs* RoTS. Right: ILS-HSS *vs* Novelty$^+$/wcs+we. Along the diagonal lines, the two given algorithms require equal CPU time (compensating for differences in CPU time per search step between the algorithms).

Intuitively, the ACL of a random walk through the search spaces of the given problem instances indicates how many random steps are required before the correlation between the objective function value at the current search position and the objective function value at the starting position of the walk becomes insignificant. High ACL values are an indication that search positions which are 'Hamming-close' tend to have roughly similar objective function values; this is indicative of a relatively 'smooth' search space. Conversely, low ACL values indicate that the search space is rather 'rugged' with many uncorrelated local features. The latter type of search space structure should intuitively be more difficult to deal with for SLS algorithms based on randomised improvement strategies, such as the ILS algorithm considered here.

In this section, we examine how ACL is affected by changing the variance and granularity in the clause weights, and investigate the correlation between ACL and hardness within each test-set.

ACL measurements. To generate the ACL data, we generated 100 conflict-directed random walk trajectories for each instance (that is, during each local search step, an unsatisfied clause was first selected, and then a random variable from the clause was flipped), with a length of 10 000 steps each. The ACL of each of these trajectories was calculated, and then all of the ACLs were averaged to obtain the ACL value for each instance. Table 2 shows the mean ACL over all instances in each test-set. The ACL data was also analysed for a correlation with lsc (*cf.* Table 3).

Influence of variability and granularity of clause weights on ACL. As shown in Table 2, ACL depends strongly on the variability and granularity of clause weights: average ACL decreases with increasing variability and granularity, indicating that the (weighted) objective function values over the respective search spaces tend to be most rugged for instances with high variability and fine granularity in the clause weights. Variability in clause weights appears to have a more pronounced effect on average ACL than granularity.

Table 2. Mean ACL over all instances in each test-set, compared with the mean lsc (*i.e.*, the mean number of steps required by each algorithm to find an optimal solution for a given problem instance). The column labelled $\sigma_x/\bar{x}$ shows the coefficient of variation within each test-set.

Test-Set	Mean ACL	$\sigma_x/\bar{x}$	Mean lsc (ILS-HSS)
rnd−u	41.76	0.09	1 652
rnd5-d100	40.89	0.09	3 380
rnd5−d10	40.85	0.09	4 099
rnd5−v100	40.69	0.09	4 162
rnd5−v200	38.46	0.09	8 576
rnd5−v500	36.09	0.10	13 772

Table 3. Correlation analysis of ACL vs lsc; a and b are the slope and intercept, respectively, of the regression line, r is the correlation coefficient (statistically significant if shown in bold).

Test-Set	a	b	r
rnd−u	-1.26	50.60	**-0.278**
rnd5-d100	-1.15	49.90	**-0.228**
rnd5−d10	-1.05	49.29	-0.189
rnd5−v100	-0.98	48.56	-0.181
rnd5−v200	-1.45	51.07	**-0.344**
rnd5−v500	-0.41	39.84	-0.103

Correlation of ACL and local search cost over different test-sets. As can be seen from Table 2, the variation in average ACL (where the average is over different random walks for the same problem instance) between different problem instances from the same test-set is very low. This is in contrast with the high variability in local search cost observed within these test-sets (see Figure 1). However, our ACL data suggests a inverse relationship between average ACL and average local search cost. This is consistent with the intuition that SLS algorithms based on (randomised) greedy descent strategies should have more difficulties to find optimal or high-quality solutions in rugged search spaces full of local features, most of which do not provide useful guidance [10].

Correlation of ACL and local search cost within test-sets. To investigate whether the observed correlation is solely due to the differences in the syntactical features of the respective instances (i.e., to due to the differences in their clause weights), or whether it reflects a deeper dependency between ACL and local search cost, we analysed the same correlation for the instances within each individual test-set. The results shown in Table 3 indicate a weak negative correlation between average ACL and average local search cost per instance within each test-set. Although the correlation is generally too weak to be statistically significant, it is present for all test-sets and is consistent with the negative correlation of local search cost and ACL observed over multiple test-sets[2].

---

[2] Correlations were measured using the Pearson correlation coefficient r, and their significance was assessed based on a standard test statistic for r (which, for the sample sizes used here, is approx. t-distributed); in our tables, correlations that are statistically significant at $\alpha = 0.05$ are shown in boldface.

Table 4. Mean FDC over all instances in each testset, compared with the mean lsc.

Test-Set	Mean FDC	$\sigma_x/\bar{x}$	Mean lsc (ILS-HSS)
rnd−u	0.416	0.44	1 652
rnd5-d100	0.343	0.51	3 380
rnd5−d10	0.354	0.47	4 099
rnd5−v100	0.358	0.49	4 162
rnd5−v200	0.362	0.47	8 576
rnd5−v500	0.379	0.45	13 772

5 Fitness Distance Correlation (FDC) Analysis

FDC is defined as the correlation between the 'fitness' of local minima states, and the 'distance' from those local minima states to the closest global optimum [9]. In this study, we define the fitness of a variable assignment search position as the difference between its objective function value and the optimal objective function value for the respective problem instance. We define the distance between two states as the Hamming distance between the states. The FDC coefficient is then defined as

$$\rho_{fdc}(f,d) := \frac{Cov(f,d)}{\sigma(f) \cdot \sigma(d)} = \frac{\langle f(s) \cdot d(s) \rangle - \langle f(s) \rangle \cdot \langle d(s) \rangle}{\sqrt{\langle f^2(s) \rangle - \langle f(s) \rangle^2}\sqrt{\langle d^2(s) \rangle - \langle d(s) \rangle^2}},$$

where $Cov(f,d)$ denotes the covariance of the fitness-distance pairs $(f(s), d(s))$ over all variable assignments s; $\sigma(f)$ and $\sigma(d)$ are the respective standard deviations of the fitness and the distance values for all s; and $\langle f(s) \rangle$, $\langle f^2(s) \rangle$, $\langle f(s) \cdot d(s) \rangle$ denote the averages of $f(s)$, $f^2(s)$, and $f(s) \cdot d(s)$, respectively, over all assignments s. By definition, we have that $-1 \leq \rho_{fdc}(f,d) \leq 1$. A significantly positive FDC coefficient indicates that, on average, with increasing solution quality the search is also getting closer to an optimal solution, and therefore the objective function can be expected to effectively guide the local search.

FDC measurements. FDC coefficients for each problem instance in our test-sets were determined as follows. First, we constructed a set S of putatively optimal solutions[3]. Second, we ran ILS-HSS on the given instance, recording every local minimum (LMIN) state encountered during the search along with the fitness of the state, until a putatively optimal solution was encountered. (LMIN states correspond to assignments which cannot be improved by a single variable flip.) This process was repeated until a minimum of 50 000 LMIN states had been found. We then computed the Hamming distance between each of these LMIN states and its Hamming-closest element of S, and output the respective fitness-distance pair. Finally, the FDC coefficient was calculated as the correlation coefficient over these sets of fitness-distance pairs.

Influence of variability and granularity of clause weights on FDC. The results reported in Table 4 indicate that, with the exception of our set of unweighted instances,

---

[3] Since measuring S exactly was computationally intractable for the instance types and sizes used here, we determined putatively optimal solution qualities as described in [5] and approximated S for each instance using the set of unique solutions of that quality obtained from many runs of a high-performance SLS algorithm for MAX-SAT.

Table 5. Correlation analysis of FDC *vs lsc* (left side) and of ACL *vs* FDC (right side).

Test-Set	FDC *vs lsc*			ACL *vs* FDC		
	a	b	r	a	b	r
rnd−u	-0.12	1.31	**-0.593**	0.02	-0.22	**0.319**
rnd5-d100	-0.13	1.38	**-0.553**	0.01	-0.15	**0.254**
rnd5−d10	-0.12	1.23	**-0.486**	< 0.01	0.20	0.085
rnd5−v100	-0.13	1.39	**-0.506**	0.01	0.13	0.118
rnd5−v200	-0.08	1.07	**-0.405**	< 0.01	0.20	0.087
rnd5−v500	-0.07	0.97	**-0.334**	< 0.01	0.21	0.091

there are small, but systematic differences in FDC depending on the variablity and granularity of clause weights: Mean FDC values increase monotonically with granularity and variability of clause weights. Compared to the respective ACL results, the variation of FDC values within each test-set is considerably higher (as reflected in the higher coefficient of variation). These results indicate a positive correlation between FDC values and mean local search cost – a counterintuitive finding, since we would expect that strong fitness-distance correlations (*i.e.*, high FDC values) should make a problem instance easier for an SLS algorithm such as ILS-HSS, which is essentially based on a (randomised) iterative improvement strategy. One possible explanation for this somewhat surprising result is that ruggedness effects (as captured by our ACL analysis) might dominate the impact of FDC for these test-sets.

Correlation between FDC and local search cost within test-sets. Our analysis of the correlation between FDC and mean local search cost per instance within each test-set revealed a different picture: Table 5 shows that there is a significant negative correlation, which is consistent with the previously discussed, expected impact of FDC on local search cost. This correlation seems to weaken with increasing granularity and variability of clause weights, which is probably due to the fact that for these types of instances, ILS-HSS finds significantly less high-quality local minimum states than for the much easier instances from the test-sets with low granularity and low clause weight variability. However, the correlations between FDC and mean local search cost within our test-sets are all statistically significant and much stronger than the correlations between ACL and mean local search cost within test-sets.

Correlation between ACL and FDC within test-sets. Our experimental results indicate that both ACL and FDC are correlated to some extent with mean local search cost. This raises the question whether both of these measures merely reflect the same factors underlying the hardness of a problem instance for ILS-HSS, or whether they are complementary. It seems that ACL better captures the significant differences in local search cost between test-sets, while within each test-set, search cost was much stronger correlated with FDC on a per-instance basis. This is further supported by the results of a correlation analysis between ACL and FDC within each test-set, shown in Table 5. The correlation between ACL and FDC is very weak and, except for the sets of unweighted and low granularity instances, statistically insignificant, though consistently positive for all test-sets. The latter observation is interesting, because it indicates that there appears to be a slight tendency (within the test-sets) for instances with more rugged search spaces to have a lower fitness-distance correlation. However, the weakness of this correlation and the qualitative differences in our observations regarding ACL and FDC suggests that both measures reflect different relevant aspects of search space structure.

6 Conclusions and Future Work

The results presented in this study show that autocorrelation length (ACL) and fitness-distance correlation (FDC) are useful for predicting and explaining the hardness of MAX-SAT instances for various stochastic local search algorithms. Our empirical results show that ACL and FDC capture different factors underlying local search cost. While ACL reflects the significant differences in instance hardness between test-sets with varying distributions of clause weights, FDC seems better suited for explaining the search cost differences within test-sets of instances sampled from the same distribution. ACL and FDC are also complementary in the sense that they both correlate with instance hardness, but the correlation between them is rather weak; hence, a combination of both measures has a higher predictive and explanatory power than either ACL or FDC alone. Furthermore, experimental results not included here indicate that FDC actually correlates better with local search cost than the number of optimal solutions for test-sets of instances with very high variance in the clause weights. This comes as a surprise considering the dominance of number of solutions on local search cost for unweighted SAT instances [22].

This work raises a number of interesting questions and suggests various avenues for further research. First and foremost, it would be very interesting to further explore the performance differences observed between different SLS algorithms for MAX-SAT, such as ILS-HSS, RoTS and Novelty$^+$/wcs+we, and to analyse these for possible correlations with the measures of search space structure investigated here. Secondly, it may be possible to use computationally cheap measures of search space structure, such as ACL, to predict the run-time of specific SLS algorithms for MAX-SAT, and to select the algorithm that is expected to solve a given instance most efficiently. Further directions for extending this research include an analysis of the impact of problem size (*i.e.*, number of variables and clauses) on the results reported here; an investigation of search space features of structured MAX-SAT instances (as obtained, *e.g.*, from encodings of other combinatorial problems into MAX-SAT) and their differences to those of the Random-3-SAT considered here; and a more detailed analysis of other search space characteristics (*e.g.*, the plateau and basin structure of a given search landscape) that explain some of the observed variation in local search cost that cannot be explained by global measures such as ACL and FDC.

Overall, we strongly believe that insights gained from a thorough understanding of the search space characteristics and their dependence on syntactic features of MAX-SAT instances as well as their impact on the performance of SLS algorithms for MAX-SAT will provide the key to further improving the efficiency of these algorithms, and hence the state-of-the-art in MAX-SAT solving.

References

1. Gu, J., Puri, R.: Asynchronous circuit synthesis with boolean satisfiability. IEEE Transactions on Computer–Aided Design of Integrated Circuits **14** (1995) 961–973

2. Kamath, A., Karmarkar, N., Ramakrishnan, K., Resende, M.: A continuous approach to inductive inference. Mathematical Programming **57** (1992) 215–238
3. Asirelli, P., de Santis, M., Martelli, A.: Integrity constraints in logic databases. J. of Logic Programming **3** (1985) 221–232
4. Hoos, H., Stützle, T.: Stochastic Local Search—Foundations and Applications. Morgan Kaufmann Publishers, USA (2004 (to appear))
5. Smyth, K., Hoos, H.H., Stützle, T.: Iterated robust tabu search for MAX-SAT. In Xiang, Y., Chaib-draa, B., eds.: Advances in Artificial Intelligence. Volume 2671 of LNCS., Springer Verlag, Germany (2003) 129–144
6. Weinberger, E.: Correlated and uncorrelated fitness landscapes and how to tell the difference. Biol. Cyber. **63** (1990) 325–336
7. Stadler, P.F.: Towards a theory of landscapes. In et al., R.L., ed.: Complex Systems and Binary Networks. Volume 461 of Lecture Notes in Physics., Springer Verlag, Berlin, Germany (1995) 77–163
8. Stadler, P., Happel, R.: Random field models for fitness landscapes. Journal of Mathematical Biology **38** (1999) 435–478
9. Jones, T., Forrest, S.: Fitness Distance Correlation as a Measure of Problem Difficulty for Genetic Algorithms. In: Proceedings of ICGA'95, Morgan Kauffman (1995) 184–192
10. Angel, E., Zissimopoulos, V.: On the classification of NP-complete problems in terms of their correlation coefficient. Discrete Applied Mathematics **99** (2000) 261–277
11. Merz, P., Freisleben, B.: Fitness landscapes and memetic algorithm design. In Corne, D., Dorigo, M., Glover, F., eds.: New Ideas in Optimization. McGraw-Hill (1999)
12. Merz, P., Freisleben, B.: Fitness landscape analysis and memetic algorithms for the quadratic assignment problem. IEEE Transact. on Evol. Comput. **4** (2000) 337–352
13. Hansen, P., Jaumard, B.: Algorithms for the maximum satisfiability problem. Computing **44** (1990) 279–303
14. Selman, B., Kautz, H., Cohen, B.: Noise strategies for improving local search. In: Proc. of the 12th Natl. Conf. on Artificial Intelligence, MIT Press (1994) 337–343
15. Resende, M., Pitsoulis, L., Pardalos, P.: Approximate solution of weighted MAX-SAT problems using GRASP. In Du, D., Gu, J., Pardalos, P., eds.: Satisfiability problem: Theory and Applications. Volume 35. AMS (1997) 393–405
16. Wu, Z., Wah, B.: Trap escaping strategies in discrete lagrangian methods for solving hard satisfiability and maximum satisfiability problems. In: Proc. of AAAI'99, MIT Press (1999) 673–678
17. Mills, P., Tsang, E.: Guided local search for solving SAT and weighted MAX-SAT problems. In Gent, I., van Maaren, H., Walsh, T., eds.: SAT2000 — Highlights of Satisfiability Research in the Year 2000. IOS Press (2000) 89–106
18. Jiang, Y., Kautz, H., Selman, B.: Solving problems with hard and soft constraints using a stochastic algorithm for MAX-SAT. In: Proceedings of the 1st International Joint Workshop on Artificial Intelligence and Operations Research. (1995)
19. Zlochin, M., Dorigo, M.: Model-based search for combinatorial optimization: A comparative study. In Merelo, J.J., et al., eds.: Proceedings of PPSN-VII. Volume 2439 of LNCS., Springer Verlag, Germany (2002) 651–661
20. Mitchell, D., Selman, B., Levesque, H.: Hard and easy distributions of SAT problems. In: Proc. of AAAI'92, MIT Press (1992) 459–465
21. Hoos, H., Stützle, T.: Characterising the behaviour of stochastic local search. Artificial Intelligence **112** (1999) 213–232
22. Clark, D., Frank, J., Gent, I., MacIntyre, E., Tomov, N., Walsh, T.: Local search and the number of solutions. In Freuder, E., ed.: Proc. of CP'96. Volume 1118 of LNCS., Springer Verlag, Germany (1996) 119–133

Bridging the Gap Between Theory and Practice

Thomas Jansen[1] and R. Paul Wiegand[2],*

[1] FB Informatik, LS 2, Universität Dortmund, Germany
Thomas.Jansen@udo.edu
[2] Department of Computer Science, George Mason University, Fairfax, VA 22030, USA
paul@tesseract.org

Abstract. While the gap between theory and practice is slowly closing, the evolutionary computation community needs to concentrate more heavily on the middle ground. This paper defends the position that contemporary analytical tools facilitate such a concentration. Empirical research can be improved by considering modern analytical techniques in experimental design. In addition, formal analytical extensions of empirical works are possible. We justify our position by way of a constructive example: we consider a recent empirically-based research paper and extend it using modern techniques of asymptotic analysis of run time performance of the algorithms and problems investigated in that paper. The result is a more general understanding of the performance of these algorithms for any size of input, as well as a better understanding of the underlying reasons for some of the previous results. Moreover, our example points out how important it is that empirical researchers motivate their parameter choices more clearly. We believe that providing theorists with empirical studies that are well-suited for formal analysis will help bridge the gap between theory and practice, benefitting the empiricist, the theorist, and the community at large.

1 Introduction

Historically, research in evolutionary computation (EC) has been replete with innovative refinements and augmentations to evolutionary algorithms. Analysis of improved evolutionary algorithms (EAs) has been sparse and primarily confined to empirical methods. There is a wide gap between EC theory and practice. Practitioners accuse theorists of analyzing simple algorithms and simple problems, impractical for real use and describing very little of value for real applications. Theorists are frustrated by seemingly arbitrarily engineered and poorly motivated algorithms that are difficult, if not impossible to analyze thoroughly.

Fortunately, the gap between these two sides can be made smaller. To bridge it, more attention on the middle ground between theoreticians and engineers is required. We need empiricists who are driven and guided by theory to understand the performance of these algorithms at a more fundamental level. As theorists strive to provide more advanced and applicable analytical methods, empiricists should strive to develop

---

* R. Paul Wiegand currently holds a postdoctoral position with the American Society for Engineering Education and conducts research at the Naval Research Laboratory.

experimental frameworks that provide a more fertile ground for future theoretical development, motivate their algorithmic and problem choices more carefully and thoroughly, and make use of existing theoretical results to guide and inform their research.

One way to bridge the gap is to extend empirical analysis with theoretical results. Though experimental analysis can be carried out for any EA on almost any problem, only a limited number of parameter settings can be considered. This makes it impossible to say how the performance of the algorithm scales with the size of the problem beyond the experiments actually carried out. Extending empirical research with theoretical analysis can help fill in these gaps, and provide a much stronger grasp of the "how's" and "why's" of EA performance.

Recent advances in asymptotic analyses of evolutionary algorithms has made the idea of bridging the theory-practice gap more feasible. Droste, Jansen, and Wegener [1] presented various analytical tools developed for the extremely simple (1+1) EA, a kind of randomized mutation hill-climber. Some of these methods can be extended to the use of a larger offspring population size [3]. There are also results for mutation-based evolutionary algorithms with a population size $\mu > 1$ [2, 4, 14]. Witt [15] even presented a method for proving lower bounds on the expected optimization time, which is often much harder. Additionally, though EAs using crossover are considerably more difficult to analyze [11], results on the expected running time are known for some steady-state GAs [5, 6, 12]. These results are encouraging, though admittedly contain only upper bounds; there are currently no known methods for proving lower bounds on the expected optimization time of EAs with crossover.

This paper states a firm position: not only can theory be useful for practical research, but well-designed empirical studies can both make use of theoretical results, and be extended by theoretical research. We justify this position using a constructive example taken directly from recent literature. We consider an empirical paper by Wiegand, Liles, and De Jong [13] that concentrates on the performance of a particular design aspect of a specific cooperative coevolutionary algorithm (CCEA). We provide theoretical results for the expected optimization time of this real algorithm. Our analysis is incomplete in the sense that we do not consider every experiment discussed in [13]; however, we are able to provide a surprising amount of information with contemporary analytical techniques. This shows how experimental results can be validated and generalized for larger search spaces. More generally, we uncover some interesting difficulties that are based on the specifics of empirical research and suggest changes in the presentation of empirical studies that eases the continuation of empirical research by theoretical studies.

2 An Empirical Analysis of Cooperative Coevolution

A common extension to evolutionary algorithms are coevolutionary algorithms in which fitness is a function of interactions between individuals. One common subset of such algorithms are so-called "cooperative" coevolutionary algorithms, where individuals collaborate to form complete solutions that are mutually beneficial. A very general framework for applying cooperative coevolutionary algorithms to many types of optimization problems was provided by Potter and De Jong [10]. In this framework there are multiple populations, representing problem components, and each population is evolved more or less independently with the exception of evaluation. The framework is appealing since it places no demands on the underlying EAs that are used for each population, nor on any particular kind of representation.

During evaluation, representatives (so called collaborators) from the collaborating populations must be selected to form complete solutions in order to obtain fitness. How these collaborators are chosen, and what problem properties affect this choice is a challenging issue. It has lead to a variety of work, almost all of which has been purely empirical in nature. Two representative such works are work by Bull [16] and Wiegand, Liles and De Jong [13]. We consider the latter, more recent empirical research for our example. Before we can begin, we will need to define the problems under study, as well as the specific CCEA researched.

2.1 Problem Domains for Analysis

Wiegand, Liles, and De Jong [13] consider three maximization problems in their analysis. These problems can be desribed by pseudo-Boolean functions that map bit strings of length n map to real numbers, $f\colon \{0,1\}^n \to \mathbb{R}$. All three functions are based on the well-known LEADINGONES and ONEMAX problems, investigating the influence of decomposition of the bit string on collaboration. We consider exactly the same three functions, though use a different notation that fits better within the framework of asymptotic analysis. The relation to the original notation from [13] is made explicit.

Definition 1. *For $n' \in \mathbb{N}$ let $n = 4n'$. The function $f_1\colon \{0,1\}^n \to \mathbb{R}$ is defined by*

$$f_1(x) := \left(\sum_{i=1}^{n/2} \prod_{j=1}^{i} x_j\right) + \left(\sum_{i=(n/2)+1}^{n} \prod_{j=1}^{i} x_j\right).$$

The function $f_2\colon \{0,1\}^n \to \mathbb{R}$ is defined by $f_2(x) := n \cdot f_1(x) - \text{ONEMAX}(x)$. The function $f_3\colon \{0,1\}^n \to \mathbb{R}$ is defined by

$$f_3(x) := n \cdot \left(\left(\sum_{i=1}^{n/4} \prod_{j=1}^{i} x_{2j-1} x_{2j}\right) + \left(\sum_{i=(n/4)+1}^{n/2} \prod_{j=1}^{i} x_{2j-1} x_{2j}\right)\right) - \text{ONEMAX}(x).$$

In [13] f_1 is called concatenated LEADINGONES. It can be described as LEADINGONES$(x_1 \cdots x_{n/2})$ + LEADINGONES$(x_{(n/2)+1} \cdots x_n)$. The function f_2 is called LEADINGONES − ONEMAX. The definition of f_3 corrects a misprint in [13] and is in accordance with the function used for experiments there. It is identical to the function CLOB$_{2,2}$ from [9].

2.2 A Cooperative Coevolutionary Algorithm

Wiegand, Liles, and De Jong [13] present an instantiation that uses steady-state GAs with rank-based selection, replacement of the worst, standard bit-flip mutation, and parameterized uniform crossover. In the coevolutionary framework, the strings are partitioned into components and each population is assigned the task of representing one such component. This suggests two choices: how many components (populations) will be used, and how will the bit string ($x = x_1 x_2 \cdots x_n \in \{0,1\}^n$) be decomposed among these? We use the notation k to denote the number of components (the previous study used p), and l to denote the length of a component. The pseudo-Boolean nature of the fitness functions suggests some obvious decompositions, but without intimate knowledge of the function itself engineers cannot know the most appropriate decomposition *a priori*. Two decompositions explored by the previous study are defined below.

Definition 2. *Let $l, k \in \mathbb{N}, n = lk$ be given. A bit string $x = x_1 x_2 \cdots x_n \in \{0,1\}^n$ is divided into k components $x^{(1)}, x^{(2)}, \ldots, x^{(k)}$ of equal length $l = n/k$. Regardless of the specific decomposition we write $x^{(1)} x^{(2)} \cdots x^{(k)}$ to denote the complete bit string x in its original bit ordering.*

We call this a direct decomposition *if $x^{(i)} = x_{(i-1)l+1} x_{(i-1)l+2} \cdots x_{il}$ holds for all $i \in \{1, \ldots, k\}$. We call this a* distributed decomposition *if $x^{(i)} = x_i x_{i+k} \cdots x_{i+(l-1)k}$ holds for all $i \in \{1, \ldots, k\}$.*

More precisely, we always consider the case of a direct or distributed decomposition of x into k components. There are k identical EAs, each operating on one component $x^{(i)}$. The initial population is chosen uniformly at random. The main algorithm is working in rounds, where in each round each of these k EAs is active once, i.e., each does one generation. The ordering is always $x^{(1)}, x^{(2)}, \ldots, x^{(k)}$. We consider the algorithm without stopping criterion and are interested in the first point of time when some complete bit string x is optimal under the fitness function f. This point is subtle: An optimal bit string may be constructible from the components in the k populations. However, we ask more: We require the CCEA to realize this by actually assembling such an optimal bit string for a function evaluation. We call the total number of function evaluations at this point of time the optimization time T and derive upper bounds on $E(T)$.

The steady-state GA used as underlying search heuristic in [13] has population size μ. In each generation, first two parents are selected according to the same probability distribution. Selection is done rank-based: the individuals are sorted with respect to increasing fitness values and the position within this sorted list becomes the rank. For each individual, the probability to be selected is proportional to its rank. With some probability p_c we apply parameterized uniform crossover with probability 0.2. If no crossover is performed, we copy the first parent to the offspring. In any case, standard bit-flip mutation with mutation probability $1/l$ is applied. Finally, randomly one of the individuals of the current population with minimal fitness is replaced by the offspring.

We assign a fitness value to some component $x^{(i)}$ in the following way. We select one member of the population from each EA. This can be either done uniformly at random from the whole population ($b = 0$) or uniformly at random from the individuals with maximal fitness ($b = 1$). We then assemble the complete bit string and compute the fitness value. After doing this for c times, the maximum value of the objective function values obtained is assigned as fitness to the component at hand.

We denote one such GA as $\text{GA}(\mu, p_c, c, b)$. For b we consider both values 0 and 1. Like [13] we study $c \in \{1, 2, 3\}$. For the crossover probability p_c, we are interested in the cases $p_c = 1$ (as used in [13]) and $p_c \in [\varepsilon; 1 - \varepsilon]$, where $0 < \varepsilon \leq 1/2$ is a constant. We do not fix a certain value for μ, but do our analyses for arbitrary population sizes. The reason for this is discussed below.

2.3 Poorly Motivated Empirical Choices

Empirical researchers have a variety of reasons for selecting parameter values. These include experience and intuition, but also include underlying demonstrative reasons. Unfortunately, when researchers do not state their reasoning further analysis can become difficult. The choice for μ in [13] is exactly such a parameter.

The previous study uses a constant $\mu = 10$, regardless of n and k. In that case, they fix $n = 128$ as a constant, but we are now interested in generalizing their results by looking at the asymptotic behavior of the expected optimization time $\mathrm{E}(T)$ for growing n. We might speculate that perhaps $\mu = \sqrt{n}$ is close to the value intended; but with different values of k ($k \in \{2, 4, 8, 16\}$ being used in [13]) one may argue that even $\mu = l$ would be plausible. Regardless, it is doubtful that choosing μ independent of n, i.e. $\mu = O(1)$, would be appropriate in our asymptotic setting. We avoid this by choosing not to restrict the size of μ.

Ideally, an extension such as ours should get information directly from the empirical study, but this is not always possible. Since any empirical study is necessarily restricted to a limited number of concrete parameter settings, it is tempting just to report the actual settings used. However, it is reasonable to expect some justification for these. The example of μ here makes it clear that more is needed in order to support further theoretical research: some functional correlation between the different parameters of the algorithmic system is required of the empiricist.

3 Theoretical Analyses of the CCEA

It is helpful to know something about the performance of the EA used as the underlying search heuristic in our CCEA. Therefore, we consider GA(μ, p_c, c, b) an "ordinary" GA with no decomposition. We use the notation GA(μ, p_c) since the values of b and c are only used when the GA is part of the CCEA and have no meaning here.

Theorem 1. *Let ε with $0 < \varepsilon \leq 1/2$ be some constant, $p_c \in [\varepsilon; 1-\varepsilon]$. The expected optimization time of GA(μ, p_c) on f_1 and f_2 is $O(n^2 + \mu n \ln n)$. The expected optimization time of GA(μ, p_c) on f_3 is $O(n^3 + \mu n^2 \ln n)$.*

Proof. We use a generalization of the method of fitness-based partitions [1]. Let b be the fitness of the current best individual and let n_b be the number of individuals with that fitness. Let T_i be the random variable denoting the number of function evaluations until b increased its value from i to at least $i+1$ for f_1 or from at least $n \cdot i$ to at least $n \cdot (i+1)$ for f_2 (with $i \in \{0, 1, \ldots, n-1\}$). If there is never a current best individual with fitness i, we say $T_i = 0$. Obviously, $\mathrm{E}(T_0) + \mathrm{E}(T_1) + \cdots + \mathrm{E}(T_{n-1})$ is the expected optimization time.

For f_1 and f_2 we can use the same argument. We distinguish two cases with respect to the population size μ. First, assume $\mu < n/\ln n$ holds. As long as $n_b < \mu$ holds, n_b can be increased if the GA selects a current best string as first parent (probability at least n_b/μ), does no crossover (probability $1 - p_c$), and does not flip any bit (probability $(1 - 1/n)^n$). This happens with probability at least $(n_b/\mu) \cdot (1 - p_c) \cdot (1 - 1/n)^n = \Omega(n_b/\mu)$. The expected waiting time for this event is bounded above by $O(\mu/n_b)$. Of course, n_b can take any value from $\{1, \ldots, \mu\}$ at most once. Thus, we have $O(\mu \ln \mu) = O(n)$ as upper bound on the expected waiting time until either $n_b = \mu$, or b has been increased. In the case $n_b = \mu$, we can increase b be selecting any string, doing no crossover and mutating exactly the left-most zero-bit. Such an event has probability $\Omega(1/n)$. Altogether, this yields $\mathrm{E}\,(T_i) = O(n)$ for all i. We have $O(n^2)$ as upper bound on the expected optimization time in this case. Considering the case $\mu \geq n/\ln n$, we repeat the same arguments, waiting only until $n_b \geq n/\ln n$ holds. The expected waiting time for this is $O(\mu \ln n)$. Then the probability to increase b is bounded below by $\Omega((n/(\mu \ln n)) \cdot (1/n)) = \Omega(1/(\mu \ln n))$. This implies $\mathrm{E}\,(T_i) = O(\mu \ln n)$ for all i, and we have $O(\mu n \ln n)$ as upper bound on the expected optimization time in this case.

For f_3 we can use the same arguments. We may need a mutation of two bits in order to increase b. This increases all time bounds by a factor of n. □

There is no asymptotic difference in the upper bounds for f_1 and f_2. We do not have lower bounds on $\mathrm{E}\,(T)$ since there is currently no lower bound technique known for EAs with crossover. We conjecture, however, that the similarities in the upper bound proofs reflect some common problem structure. In particular, we believe that f_2 will be slightly harder to optimize than f_1. Observe that for f_1 the bits to the right of the left-most zero-bit are all random [1]. Thus, we get about half of the bits "for free." Therefore, we speculate the observed optimization time for f_2 will be a factor of 2 longer.

The proof of Theorem 1 concentrates on the generations without crossover. Due to the steady-state replacement, generations with crossover can do no harm. If we consider $GA(\mu, 1)$, this proof technique cannot work, leading us to upper bounds that are larger by the factor $n^{2/3}/\ln n$. We do not claim that these upper bounds are sharp.

Theorem 2. *The expected optimization time of $GA(\mu, 1)$ on f_1 and f_2 is $O(n^2 + \mu n^{5/3})$. The expected optimization time of $GA(\mu, 1)$ on f_3 is $O(n^3 + \mu n^{8/3})$.*

Proof. We use the same proof technique as above. However, since we have to cope with crossover here, we concentrate on different events. Observe that the result of crossover of two bit strings with m_1 and m_2 bits set to 1 yields a bit string with at least $\min\{m_1, m_2\}$ bits set to 1 with probability $\Omega(1)$. This motivates concentration on the improvement of the worst members of the population. We estimate the time it takes to increase the function value of up to μ worst members of the population by at least 1. Doing this at most n times leaves us with at least one optimal string in the population. We can assume that non-worst individuals in the current population are improvements from the set of worst members of a previous population.

We begin with f_1 and f_2. First, assume $\mu \leq n^{1/3}$ holds. If all members of the population have the same number of leading ones, then we can increase this number for one individual by first selecting two arbitrary parents and doing crossover. With probability $\Omega(1)$ we are left with a bit string with a number of leading ones that is at least as large as its parents. Then flipping exactly the left-most bit with value 0 increases the function value. Thus, such a generation has probability $\Omega(1/n)$ and the expected waiting time is $O(n)$. If we have at least one bit string with a larger function value than the current worst, we can produce copies of this individual in the following way. We select such a current best individual as two parents (with probability $\Omega(1/\mu^2)$) and produce an offspring with a number of leadings ones that is not smaller via crossover (with probability $\Omega(1)$). Flipping no bit in mutation (with probability $\Omega(1)$) leaves us with an individual that has at least as many leading ones. For f_2 the function value may be smaller but we do not care. On average, after $O(\mu^3)$ such generations the population consists of individuals that have all the same number of leading ones, and we start over. We have do this at most n times, leading to an upper bound of $O(n^2 + n \cdot \mu^3) = O(n^2)$ for the expected optimization time in this case. In the case $\mu > n^{1/3}$ our proof is similar. Now we increase the number of leading ones in current worst individuals $\mu/n^{1/3}$ times. This increases the probability for copying one individual with a maximal number of leading ones to $\Omega(1/n^{2/3})$, leading to $O(n \cdot (n\mu)/n^{1/3} + n \cdot \mu \cdot n^{2/3}) = O(\mu n^{5/3})$.

For f_3, the proofs work in the same way but concentrate on pairs of leading ones. We distinguish the cases $\mu \leq n^{2/3}$ and $\mu > n^{2/3}$. In the latter case we increase the number of leading pairs of ones for a worst individual $\mu/n^{2/3}$ times. □

Concentrating on the worst members of the population leads to a larger upper bound that can be proven. It is not at all clear that our pessimistic analysis of the effects of crossover is realistic; however, we use the results from Theorem 1 and Theorem 2 to derive upper bounds on the expected optimization time of the cooperative coevolutionary algorithm and compare our findings with the empirical data from [13].

We begin the investigation for the case $b = 1$, i.e., a current best member of a population is selected as collaborator. This case is easier to analyze.

Theorem 3. *Let $l' \geq 1$ and $k > 1$ be two integers, $l := 2l'$, $n := l \cdot k$. We consider f_1, f_2, and f_3 on n bits with a direct decomposition into k components. Let ε with $0 < \varepsilon \leq 1/2$ be a constant, $p_c \in [\varepsilon; 1-\varepsilon]$, $c \in \{1, 2, 3\}$.*

The expected optimization time of $GA(\mu, p_c, c, 1)$ is $O(n^2 + \mu n k \log l)$ on f_1 and f_2. It is $O(n^2 l + \mu n^2 \log l)$ on f_3.

The expected optimization time of $GA(\mu, 1, c, 1)$ is $O(n^2 + \mu n^2/l^{1/3})$ on f_1 and f_2. It is $O(n^2 l + \mu n^2 l^{2/3})$ on f_3.

Proof. We start with the proof for $GA(\mu, p_c, c, 1)$ on f_1 and f_2. We consider the algorithm in rounds, where in each round each GA performs exactly one generation. Due to the steady-state selection it suffices to concentrate on improving steps for an upper bound. After an initial phase with $\Theta(\mu k)$ function evaluations, in each GA at least one sub-string that can currently be assembled into a string where it is part of the leading ones is identified if it does exist in the population. Then we concentrate in each round on a GA that contains a left-most 0 in such an assembled string. Since we have $b = 1$, the "correct" string is assembled in each round. We know from Theorem 1 that on average after $O(l^2 + \mu l \log l)$ generations this string has become all ones. We can conclude that on average after $O(kl^2 + \mu k l \log l) = O(nl + \mu n \log l)$ function evaluations this happens. This happens with probability very close to 1, and we have to wait for k GAs. This yields $O(n^2 + \mu n k \log l)$ as upper bound.

The proofs for the other statements can be done in the same way. □

Theorem 4. *Let $l' \geq 1$ and $k > 1$ be two integers, $l := 2l'$, $n := l \cdot k$. We consider f_1, f_2, and f_3 on n bits with a distributed decomposition into k components. Let ε with $0 < \varepsilon \leq 1/2$ be a constant, $p_c \in [\varepsilon; 1-\varepsilon]$, $c \in \{1, 2, 3\}$, $b \in \{0, 1\}$.*

The expected optimization time of $GA(\mu, p_c, c, 1)$ is $O(n^2 + \mu n k \log l)$ on f_1 and f_2. The $GA(\mu, p_c, c, 1)$ has no finite expected optimization time on f_3.

The expected optimization time of $GA(\mu, 1, c, 1)$ *is* $O(n^2 + \mu n^2/l^{1/3})$ *on* f_1 *and* f_2. *The* $GA(\mu, 1, c, 1)$ *has no finite expected optimization time on* f_3.

Proof. For f_1 and f_2, in the proof of Theorem 3 we concentrated on mutations of single bits. With respect to these mutations, the kind of decomposition used has no effect. Thus the same proofs are valid and the same upper bounds hold.

This is not true for f_3. There mutations of two bits may be needed: If we have $1^{2i}00\ldots$ at some point of time, changing the $(2i+1)$-th or $(2i+2)$-th bit to 1 alone will decrease the function value. Such an offspring will be inserted into the population. However, it cannot have the best function value and therefore will not be selected in the following generations as collaborator (since we have $b = 1$). Since this is already true after random initialization with positive probability, there is a non-zero probability that the global optimum will never be reached. Thus there is no finite expected optimization time. This holds regardless of the crossover probability p_c. □

When the collaborators are chosen randomly ($b = 0$), the performance is more difficult to analyze. We present much weaker upper bounds. Since we have no lower bounds, this does not prove that choosing collaborators randomly is worse for f_1, f_2, and f_3. In fact, in some ways it is even better for f_3.

Theorem 5. *Let* $l' \geq 1$ *and* $k > 1$ *be two integers,* $l := 2l'$, $n := l \cdot k$. *We consider* f_1, f_2, *and* f_3 *on* n *bits with a direct decomposition into* k *components. Let* ε *with* $0 < \varepsilon \leq 1/2$ *be a constant,* $p_c \in [\varepsilon; 1-\varepsilon]$, $c \in \{1, 2, 3\}$.

The expected optimization time of $GA(\mu, p_c, c, 0)$ *is* $O(\mu^{k-1}n^2 + \mu^k nk \log l)$ *on* f_1 *and* f_2. *It is* $O(\mu^{k-1}n^2 l + \mu^k n^2 \log l)$ *on* f_3.

The expected optimization time of $GA(\mu, 1, c, 0)$ *is* $O(\mu^{k-1}n^2 + \mu^k n^2/l^{1/3})$ *on* f_1 *and* f_2. *It is* $O(\mu^{k-1}n^2 l + \mu^k n^2 l^{2/3})$ *on* f_3.

Proof. To yield useful information, function values that are computed must be based on components carrying leading ones. Those are the best of their population and are guaranteed to become collaborators for $b = 1$. With $b = 0$ they are only selected with a small probability. We make a rough and pessimistic approximation by assuming that in each component there is only one "good" collaborator chosen with probability $1/\mu$. This can be improved to almost c/μ. It introduces an additional factor μ^{k-1} to the expected waiting time. The bounds follow directly from Theorem 3. □

Theorem 6. *Let* $l' \geq 1$ *and* $k > 1$ *be two integers,* $l := 2l'$, $n := l \cdot k$. *We consider* f_1, f_2, *and* f_3 *on* n *bits with a distributed decomposition into* k *components. Let* ε *with* $0 < \varepsilon \leq 1/2$ *be a constant,* $p_c \in [\varepsilon; 1-\varepsilon]$, $c \in \{1, 2, 3\}$, $b \in \{0, 1\}$.

The expected optimization time of $GA(\mu, p_c, c, 0)$ *is* $O(\mu^{k-1}n^2 + \mu^k nk \log l)$ *on* f_1 *and* f_2. *The expected optimization time of* $GA(\mu, p_c, c, 0)$ *is* $O(\mu^{k-1}n^2 l + \mu^k n^2 \log l)$ *on* f_3. *The expected optimization time of* $GA(\mu, 1, c, 0)$ *is* $O(\mu^{k-1}n^2 + \mu^k n^2/l^{1/3})$ *on* f_1 *and* f_2 *and it is* $O(\mu^{k-1}n^2 l + \mu^k n^2 l^{2/3})$ *on* f_3.

Proof. The proof for f_1 and f_2 follow from the Theorem 4 proof in the same way as the Theorem 5 proof follows from the Theorem 3 proof, except that things now change for f_3. As explained above, setting single bits of a pair to 1 decreases the fitness. However, such strings are generated and inserted with a positive and not too small probability.

After doing so, a bit string with such a pair of ones may be assembled due to the random choice of the collaborators. Then the increase in fitness is realized and the new pair of ones is guaranteed to remain. However, the two "lucky one bit mutations" must occur within a short time span. Otherwise, a component with a single one may be removed. We model this by concentrating on the case that these two mutation of single bits happen in a direct sequence. This has asymptotically the same probability as the joined mutation of a pair. Thus we again obtain the bounds from Theorem 5. □

Our asymptotic results are obviously not strong enough to cover all aspects of the research presented in [13], but the main observations are the same. Note that the lack of lower bounds leaves room for speculations that the true asymptotic expected optimization times may be different. But this is not supported by the empirical data in [12]. Our asymptotic analysis suggests no performance difference between f_1 and f_2, and we argue that the expected optimization time most likely differs by a factor of at most 2. This is confirmed by the experimental data from [13]. They saw no differences due to the number of collaborators. This had to be expected since the number of collaborators is restricted to a small constant. We conjecture that a number of collaborators that grows with n will have an effect that is visible within our asymptotic framework. This is supported by the data in [13]. For f_3 we can prove that with the distributed decomposition and $b = 1$ the algorithms fail to locate the global optimum. However, for the direct decomposition or $b = 0$ we can prove a polynomial upper bound on the expected optimization time. This appears to contradict that findings in [13], where f_3 seems to be very hard in any case. However, the upper bounds on the expected optimization time for f_3 are significantly larger than for f_1 and f_2. We believe that given more time the algorithms with $b = 0$ or using the direct decomposition would succeed on f_3.

4 Conclusions

Analytical extensions to experimental studies are possible. The mathematical methods for formal studies of algorithmic performance continue to improve so that increasingly more realistic algorithms may be considered. Bridging the gap between theory and practice is more attainable now than ever, but some work on the middle ground is needed by both theoreticians and empiricists. As theoretical work seeks to provide ever more flexible analytical methods, experimental scientists should begin to use existing theoretical results to guide experimental design, and offer studies that facilitate analysis by recognizing the current state of theory and motivating parameter values more clearly.

As a case in point, this paper presents an example of a theoretical extension of existing empirical study on the very same problems and algorithms used in that study [13]. Our results not only validate those discovered by experimentation, but also *generalize* them for increased search space size. Moreover, the proofs provided here offer more insights and help us understand why certain effects can be observed. The theoretical results are less concrete than the experimental results, but together they offer a much more comprehensive picture of the run time performance.

We encountered a number of difficulties when transferring the experimental setup to our analytical framework. In an asymptotic analysis one investigates the expected optimization time of an evolutionary algorithm for growing search space dimension.

Meaningful results can be obtained when parameters of the algorithm are expressed as functions of the size of the search space, but like almost all empirical studies, this is not done in [13]. This requires a careful interpretation of the chosen setup and translation into such functions. High quality empirical research should clearly present justifications for specific algorithm design choices and problem properties. They should be designed as simply as possible, while still demonstrating their points effectively, and they should consider existing theoretical results and methods while designing experiments. Only then can the work between theory and practice truly begin.

Experimental results are intrinsically restricted to the problem sizes and parameter settings that have been actually used. In order to come to results that allow meaningful statements about the expected behavior for increasing problem sizes, a theoretical analysis is needed. Asymptotic analyses are most useful in this situation. They allow for some simplifications during in the proof that makes the analysis tractable. But they still deliver rigorously proven results without unproven assumptions or simplifications with unknown consequences. Theoretical analysis can and should become an increasingly important part of research in the field of evolutionary computation.

References

1. S. Droste, T. Jansen, I. Wegener (2002): On the analysis of the (1+1) evolutionary algorithm. Theoretical Computer Science 276:51–81.
2. J. He, X. Yao (2002): From an individual to a population: an analysis of the first hitting time of population-based evolutionary algorithms. IEEE Trans. Evolutionary Computation 6(5):495-511.
3. T. Jansen, K. A. De Jong (2002): An analysis of the role of offspring population size in EAs. *Genetic and Evolutionary Computation Conf. (GECCO 2002)*, Morgan Kaufmann. 238–246.
4. T. Jansen, I. Wegener (2001): On the utility of populations. *Genetic and Evolutionary Computation Conf. (GECCO 2001)*, Morgan Kaufmann. 1034–1041.
5. T. Jansen, I. Wegener (2002): On the analysis of evolutionary algorithms – a proof that crossover really can help. Algorithmica 34(1):47–66.
6. T. Jansen, I. Wegener (2004): Real royal road – where crossover provably is essential. To appear in Discrete Applied Mathematics.
7. T. Jansen, R. P. Wiegand (2003): Exploring the explorative advantage of the cooperative coevolutionary (1+1) EA. *Genetic and Evolutionary Computation Conf. (GECCO 2003)*, LNCS 2724, Springer. 310–321.
8. T. Jansen, R. P. Wiegand (2003): Sequential versus parallel cooperative coevolutionary (1+1) EAs. In *Congress on Evolutionary Computation (CEC 2003)*, IEEE Press. 30–37.
9. T. Jansen, R. P. Wiegand (2004): The cooperative coevolutionary (1+1) EA. Accepted for *Evolutionary Computation*.
10. M. A. Potter, K. A. De Jong (1994): A cooperative coevolutionary approach to function optimization. *Parallel Problem Solving from Nature (PPSN III)*, LNCS 866, Springer. 249–257.
11. Y. Rabani, Y. Rabinovich, A. Sinclair (1998): A computational view of population genetics. Random Structures and Algorithms 12(4):313–334.
12. T. Storch, I. Wegener (2003): Real royal road functions for constant population size. *Genetic and Evolutionary Computation Conf. (GECCO 2003)*, LNCS 2724, Springer. 1406–1417.
13. R. P. Wiegand, B. Liles, K. A. De Jong (2002): The effects of cross-population epistasis on collaboration methods in cooperative coevolution. *Parallel Problem Solving from Nature (PPSN VII)*. LNCS 2439, Springer. 257–270.

14. C. Witt (2003): Population size vs. runtime of a simple EA. *Congress on Evolutionary Computation (CEC 2003)*, IEEE Press. 1996–2003.
15. C. Witt (2004): An analysis of the $(\mu+1)$ EA on simple pseudo-boolean functions. Accepted for GECCO 2004.
16. L. Bull (1997): Evolutionary Computing in Multi-agent Environments: Partners. *Int'l Conf. on Genetic Algorithms (ICGA 1997)*, Morgan Kaufmann. 370–377.

A Reduced Markov Model of GAs Without the Exact Transition Matrix

Cheah C.J. Moey and Jonathan E. Rowe

School of Computer Science,
University of Birmingham,
Birmingham B15 2TT, Great Britain
{ccm,jer}@cs.bham.ac.uk

Abstract. Modelling a finite population genetic algorithm (GA) as a Markov chain can quickly become unmanageable since the number of population states increases rapidly with the population size and search space size. One approach to resolving this issue is to "lump" similar states together, so that a tractable Markov chain can be produced. A paper by Spears and De Jong in [1] presents an algorithm that can be used to lump states together, thus compressing the probability transition matrix. However, to obtain a lumped model, one needs to calculate the exact transition matrix before the algorithm can be applied to it. In this paper, we explore the possibility of producing a reduced Markov model without the need to first produce the exact model. We illustrate this approach using the Vose model and Spears lumping algorithm on the Onemax problem with a selection-mutation GA.

1 Introduction

A Markov process is a stochastic process, in which the current state is determined through some random events, and is dependent on what happened in the previous time step. Therefore, the genetic algorithm is a Markov process because the state of the current population is determined through a series of evolutionary events such as selection, crossover and mutation acting upon the previous population. Markov chain models of GAs have been widely used by Davis and Principe [2], De Jong et al. [3], He and Yao [4], Nijssen and Bäck [5], Rees and Koehler [6], and Wright and Zhao [7] to analyse GAs. Although it is possible to derive some general conclusions about GAs from this work, it is often impractical to perform any calculations with these models, since the number of possible populations (and thus states of the system) grows enormously with the population size and string length. If the population size is N and the string length is ℓ, then the number of distinct populations is

$$\binom{N + 2^\ell - 1}{N}. \qquad (1)$$

Therefore, if we are using a standard binary encoded string length of 8 and a population size of 10, we will have an order of 10^{17} different possible population states. Obviously, trying to perform calculations with such a large number of states will be impractical.

Fortunately, there has been some interest in finding ways to reduce the number of states in Markov chain models, by "lumping" similar states together. This allows the transition matrix of Markov chain models to become more tractable, by greatly reducing its dimensionality. In this paper, we consider a lumping technique proposed by Spears and De Jong in [1] and [8]. Naturally, this cannot typically be done without loss of information, and so, only approximate results can be obtained from such simplified models. Spears and De Jong present empirical evidence that their method can produce good approximate results, though this has not been proven analytically.

Even though it is possible to have a low dimensionality Markov chain models, we will still need to calculate the exact transition matrix first, before the compression algorithm proposed by Spears can be applied. So, if we are to model a GA, say with a string length of 8 and a population size of 10, we will still need to calculate a matrix of $10^{17} \times 10^{17}$ dimension before Spears' compression algorithm can be used. Therefore, it is desirable if we can somehow obtain the compressed transition matrix directly without the need to calculate the exact transition matrix beforehand.

In this paper, we will explore a possible way of obtaining the compressed transition matrix of a Markov chain model of a GA without the need to calculate the exact transition matrix.

2 Modelling Work

2.1 Notations and Terminology

Let ℓ denote the string length. If a fixed-length standard binary encoded string is used, then the number of possible strings in the search space is $n = 2^\ell$. A finite population of size N can be represented using an *incidence vector*. If the number of possible strings is n, the vector $v \in \mathbb{N}^n$ represents a population in which v_k is the number of copies of string k. So, we require $\sum_k v_k = N$.

For the infinite population model, the representation of a population vector will be independent of the population size N. A population vector $p \in \mathbb{R}^n$ represents a population in which p_k is the proportion of string k. Hence p_k can be in the range of $[0, 1]$. Clearly, we require $\sum_k p_k = 1$. Throughout this paper, the symbols p, q will represent population vectors, and u, v will represent incidence vectors. Given an incidence vector v we can calculate the corresponding population vector by setting $p = v/N$.

The set of all possible vectors, whose components sum to 1 is known as the *simplex* or (the n-simplex) and is denoted by

$$\Lambda = \left\{ p \in \mathbb{R}^n : \forall k, p_k \geq 0, \sum_{i=0}^{n-1} p_i = 1 \right\}. \qquad (2)$$

Obviously, all real populations correspond to points within the simplex. However, not all points in the simplex correspond to finite populations, since components in the corresponding population vectors must be rational numbers.

2.2 The Vose Infinite Population Model

In this paper, we will consider a selection-mutation only GA with fitness proportional selection and bitwise mutation (no crossover). In the Vose infinite population model, the random heuristic map $\mathcal{G}$ is an operator that is composed of genetic operators such as selection and mutation that maps a point in the simplex to another point in the simplex. For a mutation and selection only GA, the random heuristic map is defined as $\mathcal{G} = \mathcal{U} \circ \mathcal{F}$, where $\mathcal{U} : \Lambda \to \Lambda$ describes mutation and $\mathcal{F} : \Lambda \to \Lambda$ describes selection. According to theory of infinite population GA by Vose in [9], a mutation and selection only GA has a fixed point in the simplex. The action of $\mathcal{G}$ is is given by

$$\mathcal{G}(p) = \mathcal{U} \circ \mathcal{F}(p) = \mathcal{U}(\mathcal{F}(p)) = \frac{U\,\mathbf{diag}[f]p}{f^T p} \tag{3}$$

where p is the population vector. The fitness proportional selection operator $\mathcal{F}(p)$ is given by

$$\mathcal{F}(p) = \frac{\mathbf{diag}[f]p}{f^T p}$$

where f is the fitness function (expressed as a vector, $f_k = f(k)$), $\mathbf{diag}[f]$ is the diagonal matrix of f and $f^T p$ is the average fitness of the population p. The operator $\mathcal{U}$ is given by

$$\mathcal{U}(p) = Up$$

where U is the mutation matrix, with $U_{i,j}$ being the probability that item j mutates to item i. The sequence of $p, \mathcal{G}p, \mathcal{G}^2 p, \ldots, \mathcal{G}^t p$ as $t \to \infty$ will converge to a fixed point in the simplex. If q is the fixed point of $\mathcal{G}$ then

$$\mathcal{G}q = \frac{U\,\mathbf{diag}[f]q}{f^T q} = q$$

$$U\,\mathbf{diag}[f]q = (f^T q)q \tag{4}$$

where q is the eigenvector of the matrix $U\mathbf{diag}[f]$ and $(f^T q)$ is the average fitness of the population q. By the Perron-Frobenius theorem, there is exactly one eigenvector in the simplex and it corresponds to the leading eigenvalue. We therefore refer to this as the "leading fixed point" of $\mathcal{G}$.

Although $\mathcal{G}$ gives the expected next population distribution in the infinite population limit, it can be extended to calculate the transition matrix of a Markov chain for finite populations [10]. It is known that for the simple genetic algorithm, the transition matrix is calculated by the multinomial distribution sampling on $\mathcal{G}(p)$, as described by Vose in [9]. The probability of transiting to a state $u = N\mathcal{G}(p)$ in the next generation given a current population $v = Np$, is given by

$$\Pr[u|v] = N! \prod_i \frac{\Pr[i|v]^{u_i}}{u_i!} \tag{5}$$

where $\Pr[i|v]$ is the probability that string i is generated in the next generation (that is, $\Pr[i|v] = \mathcal{G}(p)_i$), and the product is over all strings[1]. For a selection-mutation GA, we have

$$\Pr[i|v] = \frac{\sum_j U_{i,j} v_j f(j)}{\sum_j v_j f(j)} \qquad (6)$$

where $U_{i,j}$ is the probability that string j mutates to i, and $f(j)$ is the fitness of string j. From the preceding sections, we know that the transition matrix Q, where $Q_{u,v} = \Pr[u|v]$ will become intractable as N and n increase in size. Therefore, it is desirable to reduce Q using a much smaller set of states. The following section will describe a method of reducing Q using an algorithm from Spears and De Jong in [1].

2.3 The Spears Aggregated Markov Model

Assume we have a finite set E of states, and it is partitioned into a disjoint union of sets. We have a transition matrix Q for the Markov process on E. We attempt to define a transition matrix on the sets of the partition, which will approximate Q. Given aggregates $A, B \subset E$, we would like to define $\Pr[A|B]$.

Let us begin by assuming that the value $\Pr[a|b]$ is constant for all $b \in B$. Then it is relatively easy to calculate the probability that we end up in the subset A, since it is only the sum of probabilities of ending up in any state contained in A and is given by

$$\Pr[A|B] = \sum_{a \in A} \Pr[a|B] . \qquad (7)$$

This equation is exact. However, in general, it is impossible to assign a consistent value to $\Pr[a|B]$, since the probability of ending up in a state $a \in E$ will depend on which state in B we are currently in. This is where we need an approximation. A first approximation would be to simply average all the probabilities over the set B. Nevertheless, this will not work well in general, due to the fact that some states in B may be much more likely to occur than others. Therefore, following Spears and De Jong, we use a weighted average on those states. We estimate the likelihood of being in a given state $b \in B$ by looking at the probability of ending up in b given a random previous state. That is, set the weight of state b to be

$$w_b = \sum_{e \in E} \Pr[b|e] . \qquad (8)$$

Consequently, we can now estimate $\Pr[a|B]$ by setting

$$\Pr[a|B] = \frac{\sum_{b \in B} w_b \Pr[a|b]}{\sum_{b \in B} w_b} . \qquad (9)$$

---

[1] One of the reviewers has pointed out that the Nix and Vose formalism of equation 5 is also known in the Mathematical Biology community as the Wright-Fisher model in [11] and [12].

Putting everything together, we can now estimate the transition between aggregated states A and B as

$$\Pr[A|B] = \frac{\sum_{b \in B} w_b \sum_{a \in A} \Pr[a|b]}{\sum_{b \in B} w_b}. \tag{10}$$

Finally, we need to decide on how to create the aggregated states, so that the exact transition matrix Q can be compressed. Spears and De Jong in [1] only allow states to be lumped together if the corresponding columns of the transition matrix Q are similar (that is, are close, when considered as vectors). Hence, in order to obtain the compressed matrix, they first generate the entire exact transition matrix and then compare similarities between its columns.

2.4 Calculating the Aggregated Markov Model Directly

In [13] by Moey and Rowe, we know that it is possible to aggregate population states based on GA semantics such as average fitness and best fitness, and still being able to get a good reduction in the number of states with a reasonable loss in accuracy. However, the exact transition matrix Q will still need to be generated first before any aggregating strategy in [13] can be applied to it. This is the same problem that is encountered in [1] by Spears and De Jong. In this paper, we will use a similar approach in aggregation that is shown in [13] but instead of aggregating based on GA semantics, we will attempt to aggregate based on the fixed-points of the Vose infinite population model. We show that by using this approach, we are able to aggregate finite population states into a reduced Markov chain model using the lumping algorithm by Spears and De Jong without the need to calculate the exact transition matrix, Q.

The idea is based on the hypothesis that a finite population GA will spend most of its time in the vicinity of a fixed-point of $\mathcal{G}$ (see [9]). We will accordingly focus our attention on populations that are within a given distance of the leading fixed-point. Those populations that are not within the specified radius of this fixed-point (the majority) will all be lumped together into a state called "Rest". The reduced model therefore has $(\alpha + 1)$ states, where α is the number of states that are within the given distance of the leading infinite population fixed point (IPFP) and all others that are not within that radius are lumped together, in the Rest state. If the hypothesis is correct, then the GA will spend only a little time in this lumped state, and so the errors that are introduced should not be significant.

Let p be the leading IPFP of a selection-mutation GA. We generate a finite set E of all possible population states and calculate the distance between each state in E from p. The distance between any two vectors is given by,

$$D(x,y) = \frac{\sqrt{\sum_i |x_i - y_i|^2}}{\sqrt{2}} \tag{11}$$

where $D(x,y)$ is the (normalised) distance between any two vectors. The algorithm for modelling a GA using the $(\alpha + 1)$-state Markov model above is given by,

1. Generate a set E of all possible populations.
2. Identify populations x that are near p, using $D(x,p) < \epsilon$.
3. All populations not near p are in a state called $Rest$.
4. Exactly calculate the transition probabilities of those states near p.
5. Exactly calculate $\Pr[Rest|i]$ by making sure the column sum is 1, where i is a state near p.
6. Allocate an array w, which is of size $|Rest|$.
7. Let $Denominator = 0$.
8. For each state b in $Rest$,
   a) Let $w_b = 0$.
   b) For each e in E,
      $w_b = w_b + Pr[b|e]$.
   c) $Denominator = Denominator + w_b$.
9. For each i near p,
   a) Let $Numerator = 0$.
   b) For each b in $Rest$,
      $Numerator = Numerator + (w_b \times \Pr[i|b])$.
   c) Calculate $\Pr[i|Rest] = Numerator/Denominator$.
10. Calculate $\Pr[Rest|Rest]$ by making sure the column sum is 1.

3 Results

We show results of our approach using a Onemax problem. The fitness function is defined as,

$$f(x) = 1 + \sum_i [x_i = 1]$$

where x is a bit string and $[expr]$ is an expression operator that evaluates to 1, if $expr$ is true. The mutation matrix U whose entries give the probabilities that a string with j ones mutates to a string with i ones, is given by,

$$U_{i,j} = \sum_{k=0}^{n-j} \sum_{l=0}^{j} [j+k-l=i] \binom{n-j}{k} \binom{j}{l} \mu^{k+l}(1-\mu)^{n-k-l}$$

where μ is the mutation probability and is described further in [14]. The modelling error is measured by comparing the leading eigenvector of the lumped model with an average of 30 GA runs, and is calculated using equation 11.

We show examples of modelling the Onemax problem described in the previous paragraphs using different parameters such as string length and population size. The reason for using an Onemax problem is because of the fact that we can dramatically reduce the size of our search space from $n = 2^\ell$ to $n = \ell + 1$, which further helps us to reduce the size of our finite population state space. This has been suggested in [15]. Figure 1 shows results of modelling an Onemax problem with a string length of 2 and a mutation rate of 0.1 (i.e. $\approx 1/4\ell$), and figure 2 shows results with a string length of 4 and a mutation rate of 0.06.

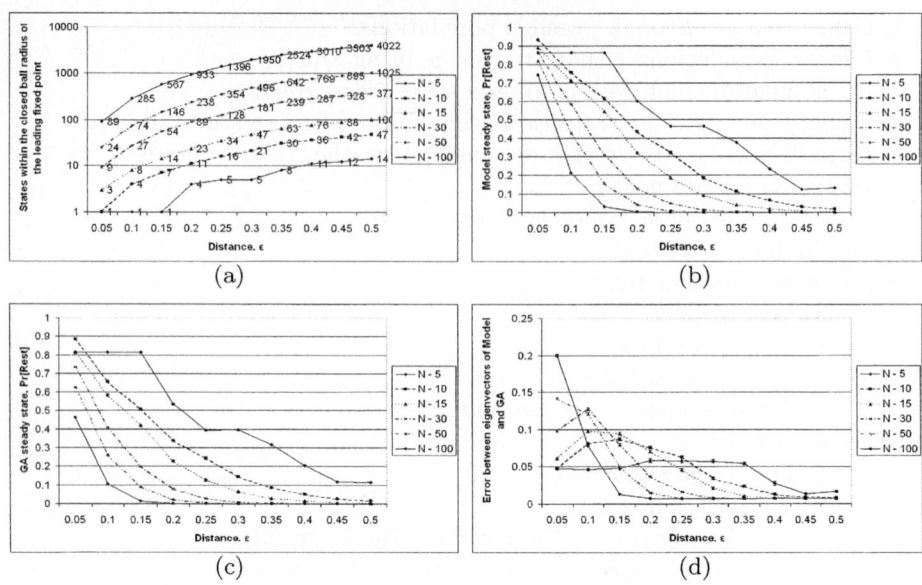

Fig. 1. Onemax with $\ell = 2$ and $\mu = 0.1$.

For comparison purposes, we calculate the steady state probability of being in the Rest-state and we record the number of occurences of such state once its corresponding real GA has reached its steady state behaviour. In this paper, all real GAs have a run length of 10 000 generations and we assume they will reach their steady state behaviour after 200 generations. Data points in figures 1(c) and 2(c) are recorded from an average GA run of 30 runs. Figures 1(a) and 2(a) show the number of states that are near p as a function of ϵ for various population sizes. Finally, figures 1(d) and 2(d) show the error between the model and its corresponding real GA. The error bars are shown where appropriate.

4 Conclusion

In this paper, we have shown an interesting way to aggregate the states of a finite population GA based on the fixed point of the infinite population model. The method rests fundamentally on two hypotheses:

1. That the finite population GA spends most of its time near a fixed-point of the operator $\mathcal{G}$.
2. That the Spears and De Jong lumping algorithm produces a reduced transition matrix which is a good approximation to the original.

Our method enables us to calculate a reduced Markov model without having to calculate the exact transition matrix. Although we have a reduced model of $(\alpha + 1)$ states, α will still increase as a function N, ℓ and ϵ (i.e. the radius). Therefore, it may be assumed that we are able to lump all population states

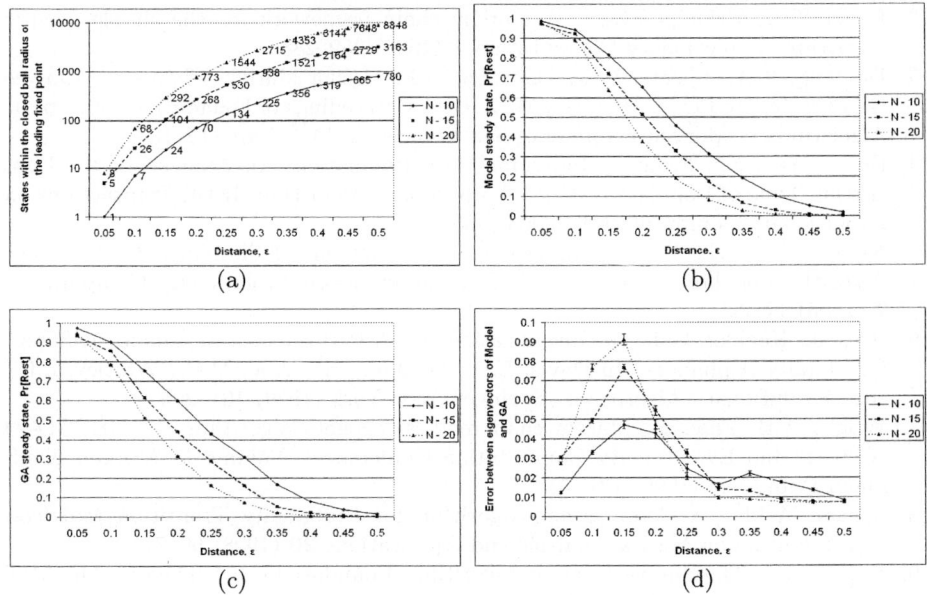

Fig. 2. Onemax with $\ell = 4$ and $\mu = 0.06$.

into a two-state Markov model consisting of a Near-state and a Rest-state, where Near-state contains population states that are within the closed ball radius of the fixed point of the GA. We have done so but at a cost of obtaining somewhat larger errors.

From Figure 1 and Figure 2, we can see that Pr[Rest] decreases for fixed radii when the population size increases. This is interesting because the emerging picture is when the population size increases, the long-term behaviour of the GA shown in this paper will spend less of its time in the Rest-state and more of its time within the closed ball radius of the fixed point. In the infinite population limit, the GA will converge to this fixed point.

Further work will attempt to model a selection-mutation only GA using fixed points as "states" of Markov models as suggested in [9] by Vose. For problems such as trap functions and Royal Road functions, the fixed-points outside the simplex will also come into play.

Acknowledgements

The authors would like to thank the anonymous reviewers for their many useful comments that were helpful in improving the paper.

References

1. Spears, W.M., De Jong, K.A.: Analyzing GAs using Markov Chains with Semantically Ordered and Lumped States. In: Proceedings of Foundations of Genetic Algorithms, Morgan Kaufmann Publishers (1996)

2. Davis, T.E., Principe, J.C.: A markov chain framework for the simple genetic algorithm. Evolutionary Computation **1** (1993) 269–288
3. De Jong, K.A., Spears, W.M., Gordon, D.F.: Using Markov Chains to Analyze GAFOs. In Whitley, L.D., Vose, M.D., eds.: Proceedings of Foundations of Genetic Algorithms 3. Morgan Kaufmann, San Francisco, CA (1995) 115–137
4. He, J., Yao, X.: From an Individual to a Population: An Analysis of the First Hitting Time of Population-Based Evolutionary Algorithm. IEEE Transactions on Evolutionary Computation **6** (2003) 495–511
5. Nijssen, S., Bäck, T.: An Analysis of the Behaviour of Simplified Evolutionary Algorithms on Trap Functions. IEEE Transactions on Evolutionary Computation **7** (2003) 11–22
6. Rees, J., Koehler, G.J.: An Investigation of GA Performance Results for Different Cardinality Alphabets. In Davis, L.D., De Jong, K., Vose, M.D., Whitley, L.D., eds.: Evolutionary Algorithms. Springer, New York (1999) 191–206
7. Wright, A.H., Zhao, Y.: Markov chain models of genetic algorithms. In: GECCO-99 (Genetic and Evolutionary Computation Conference). Volume 1., Morgan Kaufmann Publishers (1999) 734–741
8. Spears, W.M.: A Compression Algorithm for Probability Transition Matrices. SIAM Journal on Matrix Analysis and Applications **20** (1998) 60–77
9. Vose, M.D.: The Simple Genetic Algorithm: Foundations and Theory. The MIT Press, Cambridge, MA (1999)
10. Nix, A.E., Vose, M.D.: Modelling genetic algorithms with Markov chains. Annals of Mathematics and Artificial Intelligence **5** (1992) 79–88
11. Wright, S.: Evolution in Mandelian populations. Genetics **16** (1931) 97–159
12. Fisher, R.A.: The genetical theory of natural selection. Oxford: Clarendon Press (1930)
13. Moey, C.C.J., Rowe, J.E.: Population Aggregation Based on Fitness. Natural Computing **3** (2004) 5–19
14. Rowe, J.E.: Population fixed-points for functions of unitation. In Reeves, C., Banzhaf, W., eds.: In Foundations of Genetic Algorithms. Volume 5. Morgan Kaufmann Publishers (1998)
15. Spears, W.M.: Aggregating Models of Evolutionary Algorithms. In Angeline, P.J., Michalewicz, Z., Schoenauer, M., Yao, X., Zalzala, A., eds.: Proceedings of the Congress on Evolutionary Computation. Volume 1., IEEE Press (1999) 631–638

Expected Runtimes of a Simple Evolutionary Algorithm for the Multi-objective Minimum Spanning Tree Problem

Frank Neumann

Institut für Informatik und Praktische Mathematik,
Christian-Albrechts-Univ. zu Kiel, 24098 Kiel, Germany
fne@informatik.uni-kiel.de

Abstract. Evolutionary algorithms are applied to problems that are not well understood as well as to problems in combinatorial optimization. The analysis of these search heuristics has been started for some well-known polynomial solvable problems. Such analyses are starting points for the analysis of evolutionary algorithms of difficult problems. We consider the NP-hard multi-objective minimum spanning tree problem and give upper bounds on the expected time until a simple evolutionary algorithm has produced a population including for each extremal point of the Pareto Front a corresponding spanning tree.

1 Introduction

Evolutionary algorithms (EAs) are randomized search heuristics which have found many applications in solving real world problems as well as generating good solutions for NP-hard combinatorial optimization problems. In the last years, a lot of progress has been made in the analysis of such algorithms with respect to the expected runtime and the probability to find an optimum after a fixed number of steps (see Droste, Jansen, Wegener [1] for an overview).

The analysis of evolutionary algorithms for combinatorial optimization problems has been started for some well-known problems. There are results on sorting and shortest path problems (Scharnow, Tinnefeld and Wegener [2]), on maximum matchings (Giel and Wegener [3]), on Eulerian cycles (Neumann [4]), and on minimum spanning trees (Neumann and Wegener [5]). All these mentioned problems can be solved in polynomial time by deterministic algorithms. An analysis of evolutionary algorithms of problems belonging to the complexity class P is necessary to understand how evolutionary algorithms work on NP-hard problems as well as to develop better algorithms for such problems.

There are only a few results on the expected runtimes of multi-objective evolutionary algorithms. Laumanns et al. [6] have analyzed two local search algorithms (SEMO and FEMO) for a problem with conflicting objectives. Giel [7] has investigated a simple multi-objective evolutionary algorithm that searches globally (Global SEMO). He has presented bounds on the expected runtime and success probability for simple pseudo boolean functions.

The aim of this paper is to start the analysis of evolutionary algorithms for NP-hard combinatorial optimization problems as well as to start the analysis of EAs for multi-objective combinatorial optimization problems. This is indeed the first paper analyzing a multi-objective EA with respect to the expected runtime on a NP-hard combinatorial optimization problem.

We consider the multi-objective minimum spanning tree problem. Many successful evolutionary algorithms have been proposed for this problem (see e.g Zhou and Gen [8] or Knowles and Corne [9]). Recently, Neumann and Wegener [5] have shown that randomized search heuristics are able to compute minimum spanning trees in expected polynomial time. Their analysis is based on the investigation of the expected multiplicative weight decrease (with respect to the difference of the weight of the current graph and the weight of a minimum spanning tree) and serves as a starting point for our analysis.

After having given a motivation for our work we introduce in Section 2 the basic concepts of Pareto optimality and our model of the multi-objective minimum spanning tree problem. In Section 3, we present the multi-objective evolutionary algorithm which we will consider in this paper. In Section 4, we analyze the algorithm with respect to the expected time until the algorithm has produced a population that includes for each extremal point of the Pareto Front a corresponding spanning tree. We finish with concluding remarks.

2 Multi-objective Minimum Spanning Trees

In the scenario of multi-objective optimization k, often conflicting, objectives have to be optimized at the same time. The aim is to find solutions such that an improvement of one objective can only be achieved at the expense of another objective. These ideas lead to the following definition of Pareto optimality.

Definition 1. *Given a minimization problem in a search space S and a function $f = (f_1, \ldots, f_k), f : S \to F, F \subseteq \mathbb{R}^k$. A search point $x^* \in S$ is called Pareto optimal if there is no search point $x \in S$ which dominates x^*. x dominates x^* ($x \prec x^*$), if $f_i(x) \leq f_i(x^*)$ holds for $i = 1 \ldots k$ and $f_i(x) < f_i(x^*)$ holds for at least one i. The set of all Pareto optimal decision vectors X^* is called the Pareto set. $F = f(X^*)$ is the set of all Pareto optimal objective vectors and is called the Pareto-Front. The aim is to find for each $q \in F$ an object $x^* \in X^*$.*

The problem to compute multi-objective minimum spanning trees can be stated as follows. Given an undirected connected graph $G = (V, E)$ on n vertices and m edges and for each edge $e \in E$ k positive integer weights $w_1(e), \ldots, w_k(e)$. Find for each $q \in F$ a spanning tree with vector q. In the case of at least two weight functions the problem is NP-hard (see e.g. Ehrgott [10]). In the rest of this paper we consider the case $k = 2$.

Raidl and Julstrom [11] have examined different encodings of spanning trees and pointed out that one should work with so-called "edge sets". The search space equals $S = \{0, 1\}^m$ where each position corresponds to one edge. A search point s corresponds to the choice of all edges e_j, $1 \leq j \leq m$ where $s_j = 1$ holds.

Let w_i^{max} be the maximum weight of w_i, $w_i^{ub} = (n-1)w_i^{max}$, $w_{max} = \max w_i^{max}$, and $w_{min} = \min w_i^{max}$. The fitness of one individual s is described by a vector $w(s) = (w_1(s), \ldots w_k(s))$ with

$$w_i(s) := (c(s) - 1)(w_i^{ub})^2 + (e(s) - (n-1))w_i^{ub} + \sum_{j \mid s_j = 1} w_i^j$$

where w_i^j is the value of edge e_j with respect to the function w_i, $c(s)$ is the number of connected components of the graph described by s and $e(s)$ is the number of edges in this graph. The most important issue is to decrease $c(s)$ until we have graphs connecting all vertices. The next issue is to decrease $e(s)$ under the condition that s describes a connected graph. Finally, we look for Pareto optimal spanning trees.

The fitness function w penalizes the number of connected components as well as the extra connections. This is not necessary since breaking a cycle decreases the fitness value. Therefore we are also interested in the fitness function $w'(s) = (w_1'(s), \ldots w_k'(s))$ with

$$w_i'(s) := (c(s) - 1)w_i^{ub} + \sum_{j \mid s_j = 1} w_i^j.$$

Note that the fitness functions w and w' compute the same objective vector if s describes a spanning tree.

Considering a spanning tree S we can create another spanning tree S' by integrating an edge $e \in E \setminus S$ into S and removing one edge of the created cycle $Cyc(S, e)$. Using such local changes we can transform a spanning tree S into another spanning tree T. We state some properties of local changes for the minimum spanning tree problem with one single weight function w. The following result has been proven by Kano [12] using an existence proof and Mayr and Plaxton [13] presenting an explicit construction procedure.

Theorem 1. *Let T be a minimum spanning tree and S be an arbitrary spanning tree of a given weighted graph $G = (V, E)$. Then there exists a bijection Φ from $T \setminus S$ to $S \setminus T$ such that for every edge $e \in T \setminus S$, $\Phi(e) \in Cyc(S, e)$ and $w(\Phi(e)) \geq w(e)$.*

We will use Theorem 1 to get a Pareto optimal minimum spanning tree with respect to one single weight function as well as to analyze how transform one spanning tree of $conv(F)$ into another spanning tree of $conv(F)$, where $conv(F)$ denotes the convex hull of the Pareto Front F.

Neumann and Wegener [5] have analyzed randomized local search (RLS) and the (1+1) EA using the fitness functions defined above for the minimum spanning tree problem with one single weight function and achieved the following result.

Theorem 2. *The expected time until RLS or the (1+1) EA working on the fitness function w or w' constructs a minimum spanning tree is bounded by $O(m^2(\log n + \log w_{max}))$.*

Their proof is based on the following observation. If the current solution is not optimal and describes a spanning tree in the case of w resp. a connected graph in the case of w', there are either many local changes which decrease $w(s)$ by an amount which is not too small or there are a few local changes, which on the average, cause a larger weight decrease.

3 The Algorithm

We consider the algorithm called Global SEMO (Simple Evolutionary Multi-objective Optimizer) which has already been discussed by Giel [7] applying it to pseudo boolean functions. The algorithm starts with a population P consisting of one randomly chosen individual x. In each generation an individual x of P is chosen uniformly at random to produce one child x' by mutation. In the mutation step each bit of x is flipped independently of the others with probability $1/m$. After that x' is added to the population if each individual in P is either incomparable to x' or dominated by x'. If x' is added to P all individuals of P that are dominated by x' are removed from P. We can describe Global SEMO as follows.

Algorithm 1 *Global SEMO*

1. *Choose $x \in \{0,1\}^m$ uniformly at random.*
2. *Determine $f(x)$.*
3. *$P \leftarrow \{x\}$.*
4. *Repeat*
   - *Choose $x \in P$ uniformly at random.*
   - *Create x' by flipping each bit of x with probability $1/m$.*
   - *Determine $f(x')$.*
   - *If $\forall z \in P : x' \not\succeq_f z$ then $P \leftarrow \{z \in P \mid z \not\succeq_f x'\} \cup \{x'\}$*

In applications, we need a stopping criterion. Here we are interested in the expected number of fitness evaluations until the algorithm has produced a population including for each extremal point of the Pareto Front a corresponding spanning tree. This is called the expected time until Global SEMO has found the desired solutions.

4 Analysis of Global SEMO

Let F be the Pareto Front of a given instance. If we consider the bi-objective problem $conv(F)$ is a piecewise linear function. Note that for each spanning tree T on the convex hull there is a $\lambda \in [0,1]$ such that T is a minimum with respect to the single weight function $\lambda w_1 + (1-\lambda) w_2$ (see e.g. Knowles and Corne [9]). We will use this to transform one arbitrary spanning tree into a desired Pareto optimal spanning tree T on $conv(F)$ using Theorem 1.

Let q_1 and q_r be the Pareto optimal vectors with minimal weight with respect to w_1 resp. w_2. We denote by g_i, $1 \leq i \leq r-1$, the linear functions with gradients m_i describing $conv(F)$. $i < j$ holds for two linear functions g_i and g_j iff $m_i < m_j$. Hence, the linear functions are ordered with respect to increasing gradients. Let q_i, $2 \le i \le r-1$, be the intersecting point of g_{i-1} and g_i. Our aim is to analyze the expected time until Global SEMO has found for each vector of $F' = \{q_1, q_2, \ldots, q_r\}$ a spanning tree. We call the vectors of F' the extremal points of the Pareto Front.

Lemma 1. *Global SEMO working on the fitness function w or w' constructs a population consisting of connected graphs in expected time $O(m \log n)$.*

Proof. Due to the fitness functions no steps increasing the number of connected components are accepted. The current population P consists at each time of solutions having the same number of connected components. If P consists of search points with l components there are for each search point in P at least $l-1$ edges whose inclusion decreases the number of connected components. The probability of a step decreasing the number of connected components is therefore at least $\frac{1}{e} \cdot \frac{l-1}{m}$. After we have decreased the number of connected components for one solution, all solutions with more connected components are deleted from the population. Hence, the expected time until the population consists only of solutions describing connected graphs is upper bounded by

$$em\left(1 + \ldots + \frac{1}{n-1}\right) = O(m \log n).$$

□

Lemma 2. *Global SEMO working on the fitness function w constructs a population, which includes for each of the vectors q_1 and q_r a spanning tree, in expected time $O(m^2 n w_{min}(\log n + \log w_{max}))$.*

Using Lemma 1, we work under the assumption that P consists of individuals describing connected graphs. In this case, all individuals of P consist of the same number of edges. If there are N edges in each solution there are $N - (n-1)$ edges whose exclusion decreases the number of edges without increasing the number of connected components. Hence, the probability to decrease the number of edges is at least $\frac{1}{e} \cdot \frac{N-(n-1)}{m}$ and we can bound the expected time to create a population consisting of spanning trees by

$$em\left(1 + \ldots + \frac{1}{m-(n-1)}\right) = O(m \log(m-n+1)) = O(m \log n).$$

If P consists of spanning trees the population size is bounded by $(n-1)w_{min}$ because there is only one spanning tree for each value of one single function in the population. We show an upper bound on the expected time to create a population consisting of a spanning tree with vector q_1. The expected optimization time of the (1+1) EA in the case of one cost function is bounded by $O(m^2(\log n + w_{max}))$ see Theorem 2. We are working with a population of size $O(nw_{min})$ and consider in each step the individual with the smallest weight with respect to the function

w_1. In each step this individual is chosen with probability at least $\frac{1}{(n-1)w_{min}}$. Following the ideas in the proof of Theorem 2, we can upper bound the expected time until P includes a spanning tree having minimal weight with respect to w_1 by $O(m^2 n w_{min}(\log n + \log w_1^{max}))$.

It remains to bound the expected time to create from a population with a minimal spanning tree S with respect to w_1, a population with a spanning tree T which is minimal with respect to w_1 and also Pareto optimal. If $|S \setminus T| = k$ holds we can consider pairs of edges s_i, t_i with $s_i \in S \setminus T$ and $t_i \in T \setminus S$ due to Theorem 1. As S and T are both minimum spanning trees with respect to w_1, $w_1(s_i) = w_1(t_i)$ holds for $i = 1, \ldots k$, because otherwise we are able to improve T or S with respect to w_1. This contradicts the assumption that S and T are both minimum spanning trees with respect to w_1. $w_2(t_i) \leq w_2(s_i)$ holds for $i = 1, \ldots, k$, because otherwise we are able to improve T with respect to w_2 without changing the value of w_1. A contradiction to the assumption that T is Pareto optimal. Hence, there are k exchange operations which turn S into T and the expected time to create T from S is bounded by $O(m^2 n w_{min}(\log n + \log w_2^{max}))$ using the ideas in the proof of Theorem 2.

Altogether we obtain an upper bound of $O(m^2 n w_{min}(\log n + \log w_1^{max} + \log w_2^{max})) = O(m^2 n w_{min}(\log n + \log w_{max}))$ to contruct a spanning with vector q_1. After we have constructed a population including a spanning tree for q_1, we can upper bound the expected time to create a population including for each of the vectors q_1 and q_r a spanning tree by $O(m^2 n w_{min}(\log n + \log w_{max}))$ using the same arguments as before and this proves the lemma. □

Lemma 3. *Global SEMO working on the fitness function w' constructs a population, which includes for each of the vectors q_1 and q_r a spanning tree, in expected time $O(m^3 w_{min}(\log n + \log w_{max}))$.*

Proof. We consider the expected time to create a spanning tree with vector q_1. At each time the population size is bounded by $m w_{min}$, because there is only one search point for each value of one single function in the population. We consider in each step the connected graph with the minimal weight with respect to w_1 in P. Using the ideas of Lemma 2 a connected subgraph with minimal costs with respect to w_1 is constructed in expected time $O(m^3 w_{min}(\log n + \log w_1^{max}))$. This is a spanning tree, because otherwise the weight of w_1 can be decreased. After that we consider the spanning tree with minimal weight with respect to w_1 in P. We are in the situation to minimize the weight of this spanning tree with respect to w_2 and this can be done in expected time $O(m^3 w_{min}(\log n + \log w_2^{max}))$ using the ideas of Lemma 2. The expected time to create a spanning tree with vector q_r can be bounded in the same way. □

In the following we work under the assumption that $F = F'$. In this case we call the Pareto Front strongly convex. Let $d(T, T') = |T \setminus T'|$ denote the distance of two spanning trees T and T' which equals the minimal number of exchanges of two edges to construct T' from T.

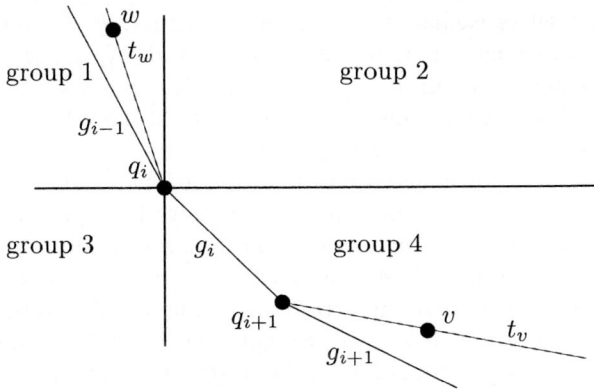

Fig. 1. The strongly convex Pareto Front and the classification of exchange operations creating a spanning tree T' with vector q_{i+1} from a spanning tree T with vector q_i.

Lemma 4. *Assume that the Pareto-Front F is strongly convex. For each spanning tree T with $w(T) = q_i$, $1 \leq i \leq r-1$ there is a spanning tree T' with $w(T') = q_{i+1}$ and $d(T, T') = 1$.*

Proof. As T and T' are different $d(T, T') > 0$ holds. We assume that T' is a spanning tree with vector q_{i+1} which has minimal distance to T. We work under the assumption that $d(T, T') > 1$ holds for all spanning trees T' with vector q_{i+1} and show a contradiction. We can apply Theorem 1 because for each spanning tree T' of $conv(F)$ there is a $\lambda \in [0, 1]$ such that T' is a minimum spanning tree for the single weight function $\lambda w_1 + (1-\lambda)w_2$. We partition the exchange operations $exchange(e, e')$ inserting e and deleting e' and chosen due to Theorem 1 into 4 groups (see figure 1). Let $d = exchange(e, e')$ and $w(d) = (w_1(e) - w_1(e'), w_2(e) - w_2(e'))$ be the vector describing the weight changes of this operation. d belongs to group 1, if $w_1(d) < 0 \land w_2(d) > 0$, to group 2, if $w_1(d) \geq 0 \land w_2(d) \geq 0$, to group 3, if $w_1(d) < 0 \land w_2(d) < 0$, and to group 4, if $w_1(d) > 0 \land w_2(d) < 0$.

There is no exchange operation d with $w(d) = (0, 0)$, because otherwise T' is not a spanning tree with vector q_{i+1} and minimal distance to T. All other operations belonging to group 2 are not possible because the remaining operations applied to T would construct a spanning tree dominating T'. A contradiction to the assumption that T' is Pareto optimal. Operations belonging to group 3 are not possible because they would construct a spanning tree dominating T. Let $q_i = (x_i, y_i)$, $1 \leq i \leq r$. There is no exchange operation belonging to group 4 which constructs a spanning tree T'' with value $x_i < w_1(T'') < x_{i+1}$, because q_{i+1} lexicographically follows q_i in the Pareto Front. There is also no operation belonging to group 4 constructing a spanning tree with value $w_1(T'') \geq x_{i+1}$ and $w_2(T'') \geq y_{i+1}$, because otherwise the remaining operations applied to T construct a spanning tree which dominates T'. A contradiction to the fact that T' is Pareto optimal.

Let M be the set of exchange operations constructing T' from T, $M_1 \subseteq M$ be the set of operations belonging to group 4, and $M_2 \subset M$ be the subset of operations belonging to group 1. Note that $M_1 \cup M_2 = M$ holds due to previous observations. We assume that M consists of more than one operation. As $x_{i+1} > x_i$ holds, M_1 is not empty. Let $v = (v_x, v_y)$ be the vector of the spanning tree which is constructed when all operations of M_1 are applied to T. $v_x > x_{i+1}$ and $v_y < y_{i+1}$ holds, because otherwise we have produced a spanning tree with vector q_{i+1} by one single operation (a contradiction to $d(T, T') > 1$), have constructed a spanning tree dominating T', or the remaining operations applied to T construct a spanning tree dominating T'. We consider the linear function t_v with the gradient m_v intersecting the points q_{i+1} and v. As F is strongly convex $m_v \geq m_i > m_{i-1}$ holds. To construct a spanning tree with vector q_{i+1} M_2 can not be empty. Let $w = (w_x, w_y)$ be the vector of the spanning tree which is constructed when the operations of M_2 are applied to T and let t_w be the linear function with gradient m_w intersecting q_i and w. As F is strongly convex $m_w \leq m_{i-1}$ holds which implies $m_v > m_w$. Let $z = (z_x, z_y)$, $z_x < 0, z_y > 0$, be the vector such that $q_i + v + z = q_{i+1}$. As the operations of M applied to T construct T' with vector q_{i+1}, $w_x = z_x$ must hold. Taking the gradient m_w into account, we can compute the value of the second component by $v_y + m_w \cdot z_x > v_y + m_v \cdot z_x = y_{i+1}$. A contradiction to the assumption that the operations of M applied to T construct a spanning tree T' with vector q_{i+1}. Hence, T' has to be constructed from T by one single operation belonging to group 4. □

Let $|F|$ be number of Pareto optimal vectors. Note that $|F| \leq (n-1)w_{min}$ holds. In the following, we show an upper bound on the expected time until the population P includes for each vector of F a corresponding spanning tree.

Theorem 3. *The expected time until Global SEMO working on the fitness function w or w' has constructed a population, which includes a spanning tree for each vector of a strongly convex Pareto Front F, is bounded by $O(m^2 n w_{min}(|F| + \log n + \log w_{max})$ resp. $O(m^3 w_{min}(|F| + \log n + \log w_{max})$.*

Proof. We consider the fitness function w. Due to Lemma 2 the expected time to create a population consisting of spanning trees for the Pareto optimal vectors q_1 and q_r is bounded by $O(m^2 n w_{min}(\log n + \log w_{max}))$. We assume that the population includes a spanning tree for each q_j, $1 \leq j \leq i$. For each spanning tree T with vector q_i there exists a spanning tree T' with vector q_{i+1} and $d(T, T') = 1$. The probability to choose the individual representing T in the next mutation step is at least $\frac{1}{(n-1)w_{min}}$, because the population size is bounded by $(n-1)w_{min}$. As $d(T, T') = 1$ holds for at least one spanning tree T' with vector q_{i+1}, the probability to construct such a T', after having chosen the individual x describing T, is at least $\frac{1}{m^2}\left(1 - \frac{1}{m}\right)^{m-2} \geq \frac{1}{em^2}$. Hence, the expected time to create a spanning tree with vector q_{i+1} is bounded by $O(m^2 n w_{min})$. As there are $|F|$ Pareto optimal vectors the expected time until Global SEMO constructs a spanning tree for each Pareto optimal vector of a strongly convex Pareto Front is bounded by $O(m^2 n w_{min}(|F| + \log n + \log w_{max}))$. The ideas can be easily adapted to w' using Lemma 3 and the upper bound $m w_{min}$ on the population size. □

We consider the general case now and give an upper bound on the expected time until Global SEMO has constructed a population including a spanning tree for each extremal point $q \in F'$. Let $C = |conv(F)|$ be the number of optimal objective vectors on the convex hull of F.

Theorem 4. *The expected time until Global SEMO working on the fitness function w or w' has constructed a population, which includes a spanning tree for each vector $q \in F'$, is bounded by $O(m^2 n w_{min}(C + \log n + \log w_{max}))$ resp. $O(m^3 w_{min}(C + \log n + \log w_{max}))$.*

Proof. Again we consider the fitness function w and adapt the ideas to achieve the upper bound for w'. By Lemma 2 the population P includes spanning trees for the vectors q_1 and q_r after an expected number of $O(m^2 n w_{min}(\log n + \log w_{max}))$ steps. To transform a spanning tree of $conv(F)$ into another spanning tree of $conv(F)$ we use the set of exchange operations described by Theorem 1. Let T be a spanning tree with vector q_i, $1 \leq i \leq r-2$ and suppose that T' is a spanning tree with vector q_{i+1} and minimal distance to T. Let M be the set of exchanges operations that construct T' from T. Using the arguments in the proof of lemma 4 there are no exchanges belonging to group 2 or 3 in M. We show that each subset of M applied to T constructs a spanning tree on g_i. Suppose that a subset $M' \subseteq M$ of the operations constructs a spanning with a vector v not lying on g_i. This vector has to lie above g_i because otherwise it is outside of $conv(F)$. To construct a spanning tree with vector q_{i+1} on g_i the operations of $M'' = M \setminus M'$ have to construct a spanning lying below g_i. A contradiction to the assumption that g_i is part of $conv(F)$.

We consider the spanning tree T'' with the lexicographic greatest vector $v = (v_x, v_y)$ on g_i in the population. If $v \neq q_{i+1}$ T' can be constructed from T'' by a sequence of exchanges of two edges, where each single exchange operation executed on T'' yields a spanning tree with vector on g_i. As $v_x < x_{i+1}$ holds there is at least one operation in this sequence which constructs a spanning tree on g_i with vector $s = (s_x, s_y)$ where $v_x < s_x \leq x_{i+1}$ holds. Such a spanning tree is a spanning of $conv(F)$. We assume that g_i, $1 \leq i \leq r-2$, consists of C_i Pareto optimal vectors excluding the lexicographic smallest vector and including the lexicographic greatest vector. The expected time to construct from a population P having spanning trees for the vectors of $\{q_1, \ldots, q_i, q_r\}$, $1 \leq i \leq r-2$, a population consisting of spanning trees for the vectors of $\{q_1, \ldots q_i, q_{i+1}, q_r\}$ is therefore upper bounded by $O(m^2 n w_{min}|C_i|)$.

As $\sum_{i=1}^{r-2} C_i < C$ holds, the expected time, starting with a population including spanning trees for q_1 and q_r, to construct a population including a spanning tree for each vector of F' is bounded by $O(m^2 n w_{min}|C|)$. Together with Lemma 2 we obtain the proposed bound.

To prove the upper bound for w' we use Lemma 3 and the upper bound of $m w_{min}$ on the population size. Together with previous ideas we obtain an upper bound of $O(m^3 w_{min}|C|)$ after having constructed a population which includes spanning trees for q_1 and q_r and this proves the theorem. □

5 Conclusions

The multi-objective minimum spanning tree problem is one of the best-known multi-objective combinatorial optimization problems. For the first time evolutionary algorithms have been analyzed with respect to the expected time until they produce solutions of the Pareto Front. In the case of a strongly convex Pareto Front, we have achieved a pseudopolynomial bound on the expected time until the population includes for each Pareto optimal objective vector a corresponding spanning tree. For an arbitrary Pareto Front similar upper bounds have been achieved until the population includes a solution for each extremal point.

Acknowledgements

Thanks to Ingo Wegener for proofreading and helpful discussions during the preparation of this work.

References

1. Droste, S., Jansen, T., and Wegener, I. (2002). On the analysis of the (1+1) evolutionary algorithm. Theoretical Computer Science 276, 51–81.
2. Scharnow, J., Tinnefeld, K., and Wegener, I. (2002). Fitness landscapes based on sorting and shortest paths problems. Proc. of Parallel Problem Solving from Nature – PPSN VII. LNCS 2939, 54–63.
3. Giel, O. and Wegener, I. (2003). Evolutionary algorithms and the maximum matching problem. Proc. of 20th STACS. LNCS 2607, 415–426.
4. Neumann, F. (2004). Expected Runtimes of evolutionary algorithms for the Eulerian cycle problem. Accepted for CEC 2004.
5. Neumann, F., and Wegener, I. (2004). Randomized local search, evolutionary algorithms, and the minimum spanning tree problem. Accepted for GECCO 2004.
6. Laumanns, M., Thiele, L., Zitzler, E., Welzl, E., and Deb, K. (2002). Running time analysis of multi-objective evolutionary algorithms on a simple discrete optimization problem. Proc. of Parallel Problem Solving from Nature – PPSN VII. LNCS 2939, 44–53.
7. Giel, O. (2003). Expected Runtimes of a Simple Multi-objective Evolutionary Algorithm. In Proceedings of the 2003 Congress on Evolutionary Computation (CEC 2003), pp. 1918-1925.
8. Zhou, G. and Gen, M. (1999). Genetic algorithm approach on multi-criteria minimum spanning tree problem. European Journal of Operational Research 114, 141–152.
9. Knowles, J.D. and Corne, D.W. (2001). A comparison of encodings and algorithms for multiobjective minimum spanning tree problems. CEC 2001.
10. Ehrgott, M. (2000). Multicriteria Optimization. Berlin, Springer.
11. Raidl, G.R. and Julstrom, B.A. (2003). Edge sets: an effective evolutionary coding of spanning trees. IEEE Trans. on Evolutionary Computation 7, 225–239.
12. Kano, M. (1987). Maximum and kth maximal spanning trees of a weighted graph. Combinatorica 7, 205–214.
13. Mayr, E.W. and Plaxton, C.G. (1992). On the spanning trees of weighted graphs. Combinatorica 12, 433–447.

On the Importance of Information Speed in Structured Populations

Mike Preuss and Christian Lasarczyk[*]

University of Dortmund,
D-44221 Dortmund, Germany
{mike.preuss,christian.lasarczyk}@cs.uni-dortmund.de

Abstract. A radius-based separation of selection and recombination spheres in diffusion model EAs is introduced, enabling a new taxonomy, oriented towards information flow analysis. It also contains parallel hillclimbers, panmictic EA and an unexplored area. Experiments are performed systematically on five complex binary and real coded problems in search of the best performing variants w.r.t. available optimization time. Additionally, information flow through recombination and selection is emulated by means of a simple model, that produces qualitative similar results.

1 Introduction

It is a generally agreed on opinion that for successfully performing evolutionary search on multimodal and epistatic optimization problems, population diversity maintenance plays an important role. To prevent an evolutionary algorithm (EA) from concentrating on a small search space area, many different operators and structures based on local interaction have been introduced. In contrast to panmictic population models, they deliberately slow down the information flow.

Aranging individuals in topologies and and selecting offspring from local neighborhoods obviously exerts a certain influence on the information flow. This selection type severely limits the distance covered by the offspring as an information carrier. A second influence arises in connection with recombination: Local selection can lead to subpopulations in terms of sets of individuals with low diversity, resulting in high parent-offspring-fitness correlation.

As opposed to this, subpopulation boundaries often reveal incompatibilities with respect to recombination where individuals from different areas usually only bear offspring of much lower fitness than their parents. Fig. 1(a) shows this phenomenon for an exemplary ring topology EA run. Population separation in search space may lead to undesired effects: Subpopulations can get stuck far away from well known optima whereas others get extinct despite being located in promising areas. This happens e.g. if one out of two adjacent subpopulations is able to populate the common border position instead of bad individuals resulting from cross subpopulation recombination.

---

[*] Authors appear in random order.

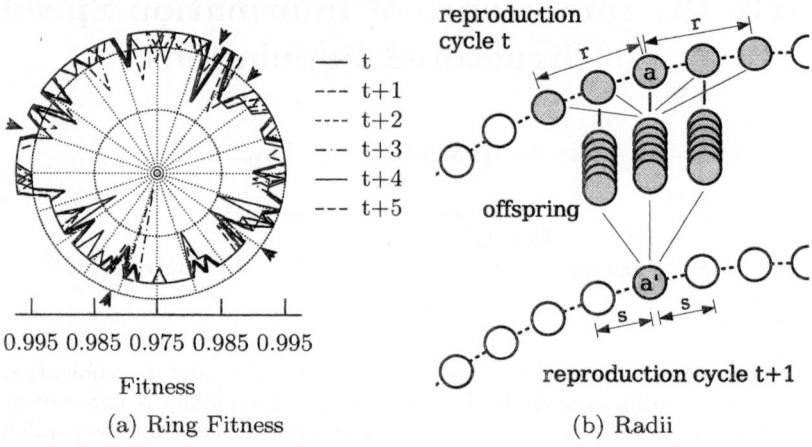

Fig. 1. Left hand: This plot uses radial coordinates to show the individuals fitness against their ring position, presenting six successive generations. Several connected areas exist, seperated by ring postions always showing fitness worse than their neighbors. These permanent fitness slumps indicate, that genomes of adajcent individuals could not be recombined successfully. Right hand: Offspring is generated by a central individual and mating partners from recombination radius r; selection accepts the best individual from the offspring pools within selection radius s.

In this paper, we consider the information flow induced into structured populations by the two ubiquitous non-unary evolutionary operators, recombination (sexual reproduction) and selection. Our aim is to separately observe their influence systematically under different local interaction radii in order to get insight into the mechanisms leading to relatively good or bad optimization performance on multimodal problems.

2 Generalized Local Selection in Structured Populations

Once originating from parallelization efforts, evolutionary algorithms employing structured populations are nowadays regarded as an approach to implicitly preserve diversity and thus prevent premature convergence to a non-optimal solution in case of a complex optimization task [2]. If explicit mechanisms (such as crowding [3], fitness sharing [4], species conservation [5], guided local search [6] or topology based selection in genetic programming [7]) are not considered, mainly two classes of algorithms remain, representing different control and communication methodologies: island model and diffusion model EAs [8]. As the former introduce additional operators like migration, we concentrate on the latter and investigate their relations to multi-hillclimber strategies on the one hand and algorithms using structureless, panmictic populations on the other hand.

Topology issues like size and shape of local neighborhoods in diffusion model EAs have been subject to extensive research (e.g. [9], [10]). Definition of overlapping demes containing all parents available for mating is strictly oriented towards the needs of the recombination operator. Parent replacement is directly linked with the production of new offspring and usually happens either at the center or a random position of the actual deme.

However, in absence of expensive communication on a parallel hardware, nothing prevents us from copying an accepted individual to another location that belongs to different deme. In analogy to the specification of a recombination range, we may also define a selection range. For each parent individual, it would contain the locations a replacing offspring can originate from during selection. Going to the extremes, the selection range could include the whole population or just one individual. The former would correspond to global selection, the latter is local selection where only direct descendants are allowed to replace a parent. This scheme enables systematic empiric testing of different recombination and selection ranges.

A concrete instantiation of the previously suggested selection range depends on definition of an underlying topology. As we target optimization of very difficult multimodal and epistatic problems, it may be beneficial to slow down information distribution to a minimum and thus keep diversity high for a long period of time. We therefore restrict ourselves to mapping the parent population onto a ring topology. This provides us with maximum characteristic path length and indistinguishable local conditions (2 direct neighbors) for each individual.

We can now define a distance between individuals in algorithmic space, independent from their distance in search space. Distance between two individuals is ascertained by counting edges between them, distance of individuals to themselves is zero. For any arbitrarily chosen center individual, this enables constructing a neighborhood from all individuals found within a certain radius, a method also used in [10]. The whole population is included at radius $\mu/2$ if μ denotes the population size.

Consequently, we introduce two radii for determining recombination and selection ranges. As we want to model speed of information flow rather than analyze the impact of specific concrete operators, we idealize recombination as method that takes two parent individuals and generates one offspring. Likewise, idealized selection is a process that takes a number of offspring individuals and replaces a parent with the best one. Recombination radius r defines the maximum distance of individuals available for mating. As an individual is contained in its own recombination radius for any $r \geq 0$, we always permit selfing, which results in cloning the parent for individuals of constant length. Produced offspring is stored in sets assigned to their first parents until selection.

The distance between this set and the parent individual an offspring may possibly replace is called selection radius s. During selection we process each member of the parent population in random order and detect the best not yet assigned offspring individual from the union of all sets contained in s (see also fig. 1(b)). The chosen offspring always replaces the considered parent individual, resulting in a comma selection. In contrast to other local selection schemes, this allows for individuals being replaced by offspring from outside their recombination radius if $s > r$.

In the following, we refer to EA variants determined by concrete recombination and selection radii as *strategies*. Exploring their taxonomy given by r and s (see fig. 2(a)), we identify several well-known strategies: $(r = 0, s = 0)$, in short $(0, 0)$, corresponds to μ independent $(1, \lambda/\mu)$-hillclimbers. The two arrows in fig. 2(a) represent diffusion models: $(r, 0)$ means replacement of the central individual of a deme, whether for $r = s$ strategies, replacement is randomly done within the recombination radius. Note that the $(\mu/2, \mu/2)$ strategy is very similar to a panmictic population structure with global selection, the only difference lies in the enforced minimum offspring number of λ/μ per parent. To our knowledge, EAs with $s > r$ are yet unexplored.

3 EA-Systems and Experiments

The previously described radius approach matches well with environmental selection driven by a birth surplus. Therefore, in all our experiments $\mu = 100$ parents bear $\lambda = 500$ offspring. To enable local selection, strict mating is enforced, so that each parent generates λ/μ offspring with randomly chosen mates from its recombination range. The following paragraphs describe the remaining settings of the utilized evolutionary algorithms and tested problems. Note that we use problem generators ([11]) instead of hand chosen problem instances wherever applicable, to obtain increased predictive power of the experimental results.

3.1 Experiments on Real-Valued Problems

For the real-valued problems, we use an EA instance containing mutation and recombination operators from standard evolution strategies [1]: self-adaptation of one mutation strength for gaussian mutations and dominant (discrete) or intermediary recombination with two parents.

Significance tests yielded that a maximum mutation strength of 1.0, a learning factor $\tau = 0.05$ and dominant recombination for the object parameters are robust settings for all three problems. All three continuous problems are formulated for minimization.

Rastrigin Function. The highly multimodal but strictly symmetrical Rastrigin function has originally been considered as difficult testbed for EA, especially when using small population sizes. However, more recent studies (e.g. [10]) demonstrated that it is efficiently solvable given that the population size exceeds a certain threshold. We use the function in a generalized form mentioned in [1] and generate problem instances by drawing random numbers for the waviness $B \in [2, 7]$, keeping the number of dimensions constant at 50. Search for good strategy parameters yielded dominant mutation strength recombination, low initial mutation strength (0.5) and low minimum mutation strength (10^{-30}). Each run is allowed 10^6 function evaluations and the object parameters are initialized at $5.0 + N(0, 1)$.

Continuous n-Peak Problem. This function generator serves as flexible tool in producing multimodal problem instances of configurable complexity. Its basic concept is to buildup fitness landscapes by combining several peaks of different height and structure as suggested in [12]. We use 100 problem instances with 8 randomly distributed optima in a $d = 10$ dimensional search space. For each peak we also define a dependency matrix to ensure non-separability of the resulting problem, a method inspired by [13]. Equations below summarize fitness computation for an object parameter vector $\mathbf{x}$. Herein, $f(\mathbf{x})$ stands for the fitness function, $g(\mathbf{x}, \mathbf{p})$ is the evaluation result of $\mathbf{x}$ for peak $\mathbf{p}$, $dist(\mathbf{x},\mathbf{p})$ is the modified euclidean distance, and $dep(\mathbf{x},\mathbf{p})$ calculates a dependencies term. The parameters s_p, h_p, and r_p denote peak shape, height and radius, respectively. All peaks are distributed in the space bounded by $x_i \in [0, 20]$, with $s_p \in [2, 3]$ and $r_p \in [10, 20]$. Peak heights of local optima are randomly chosen in between 0.7 and 0.9, such that fitness values below 0.1 originate only from search points on the peak containing the global optimum, with $h_p = 1.0$.

$$f(\mathbf{x}) = \min_{\forall p}(g(\mathbf{x}, \mathbf{p})), \quad g(\mathbf{x}, \mathbf{p}) = h_p \left(\sqrt[s_p]{\max\left(0, \frac{\text{dist}(\mathbf{x},\mathbf{p})}{r_p}\right)} - 1 \right) + 1$$

$$\text{dist}(\mathbf{x}, \mathbf{p}) = \sqrt{\sum (x_i - p_i)^2 + \text{dep}(\mathbf{x}, \mathbf{p})}$$

$$\text{dep}(\mathbf{x}, \mathbf{p}) = \sum_{j=1}^{d} \sum_{k=j+1}^{d} (x_j - p_j)(x_k - p_k) D_{pjk}, \quad D_{pjk} := \frac{\text{random}(-0.5, 0.5)}{d-1-j}$$

On this problem class, dominant mutation strength recombination, low initial mutation strength (0.5) and low minimum mutation strength value (10^{-30}) prevail against all other tested strategy parameter combinations, as for the Rastrigin function. Also, an observation period of 10^6 function evaluations seems sufficient. Object parameters of initial individuals are randomly distributed, $x_i \in [0, 20]$.

Keane's Bump Function. Keane introduced this function [14] as test problem with several local optima occurring very near to constraint boundaries. For this problem we use the same problem instance with 20 dimensions for all runs. Strategy parameters chosen for this function are: low initial 0.5 mutation strength, high minimum mutation strength 10^{-4}, and dominant mutation strength recombination. A quadratic penalty function ensures strong attraction towards valid function regions. Runs start with object parameters randomly distributed in the valid interval $0 < x_i < 10$ and end after $2 * 10^6$ function evaluations.

3.2 Experiments on Boolean Coded Problems

Normally genetic algorithms (GA) use mating selection, so this is the most important point in which we differ from classic GA. Most other utilized settings are comparable to a standard configuration. We use 1-point-crossover to recombine two individuals and bit-flipping for mutation. Each bit is mutated with equal probability. This probability is equal to the reciprocal value of the individuals length.

NK Fitness Landscapes. Using NK models, every gene locus contributes to fitness. More precisely, its contribution does not only depend on its binary value, but also on the value of K other (adjacent) loci. Each gene of a genome can thus contribute to 2^{K+1} different values. Theses values are drawn randomly with uniform distribution out of $[0,1]$ and managed in N different tables. The mean value of the $N = 48$ loci is the individuals fitness, which is to be maximized.

L-SAT, a Boolean Satisfiablity Problem. Boolean satisfiablity problems are frequently used as representatives of the class of NP-complete problems. The task is to find an assignment of boolean values to V variables, so that a boolean expression becomes true.

Mitchell et al.[15] presented the random L-SAT problem generator, which creates expressions in conjunctive normal form using three parameters. These expressions consist of C clauses of length L. The L variables are drawn randomly out of a set of V variables, and each of them is negated with a probability of 0.5. When optimized with GAs, fitness of a candidate solution is typically measured by the proportion of satisfied clauses. Here we use $V = 100$ variables and each clause is composed of $C = 3$ (possibly negated) variables.

4 Results

Our experimental design focuses on the influence of different combinations of selection and recombination radius. We thus consider 36 different *strategies* as defined in sec.2, resulting from $r \times s$ with $r, s \in [0, 1, 2, 5, 16, 50]$. We chose this logarithmic distribution of measuring points, because test runs showed promising results in the range of low radii. For each tackled problem class and strategy combination we carry out 100 runs. On the same problem the set of instances is equal for all strategies.

First we want to investigate how effectiveness of strategies depends on the number of objective function evaluations. We call a strategy dominant if its populations show best average best ever fitness. Fig. 2(b) plots the sequence of parameters of dominant strategies at each time step.

The strategy-time-trajectories show consistent gradients for most problems. On short runs, strategies using high radii usually perform best. However, at a later point in time, strategies with lower selection radii start to dominate. These allow for mating with distant individuals, but only offspring at central and neighboring positions can get selected. Figure 3 plots the average best ever fitness progression of selected strategies. Ring-strategies ($r = 1, s = 0$) with minimal deme size show best results from around 10^5 evaluations on most problems. On the long run, multi-hillclimber strategies with ($r = 0, s = 1$) and without ($r = 0, s = 0$) individual "migration by selection" also perform well, the latter starting faster, but stagnating earlier. The former eventually take the lead at nearly 10^6 evaluations for the n-Peak and the two L-Sat problems. Both strategies are not allowed to use sexual reproduction (apart from selfing) and thus have no means to mix genetic information of two individuals. Nevertheless, recombination seems

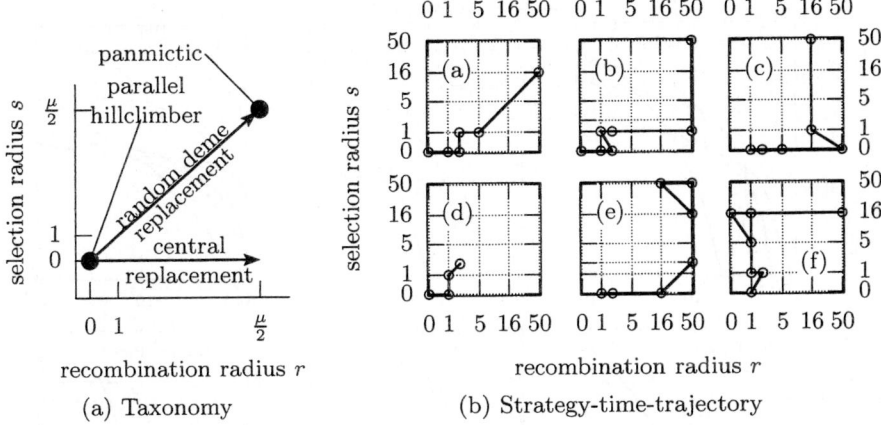

Fig. 2. Left hand: Taxonomy of population models using selection and recombination radius, with the positions of well-known EA variants. Right hand: Strategy-time-trajectory of considered problems. For each measuring point in time, we plot the strategy displaying best average best ever fitness. At first, high radii dominate, but later on strategies with low radii take the lead. (a) L-Sat ($C = 400$), (b) L-Sat ($C = 1200$), (c) NK, (d) n-Peak, (e) Rastrigin, (f) Keane's Bump.

to be crucial for solving Keane's bump and Rastrigin problems and at least important for the "NK" problem where ring-strategies stay dominant.

Figure 2(b) first suggests that strategies with high selection and low recombination radius are medium-term advantageous on Keane's Bump function. However, fig. 3 shows that this part of the strategy-time-trajectory corresponds to the early stages of the optimization, where most strategies achieve similar results. This is true until the ($r = 1, s = 1$)-strategy starts to dominate. In our opinion, the short dominance of strategies with low recombination and high selection radius is not statistically significant. Choosing radii that comply with $s > r$ does not seem to make sense in general. For these strategies recombination and selection radii are effectively equal, because an individual chosen for mating within a small neighborhood may just have been transferred into it from a far away position during the previous reproduction cycle.

5 Radius Dependent Information Speed Model

The previously identified qualitatively similar relations between strategies raise the question, whether these results are reproducible by means of a simple simulation model. Such a model shall only take information transfer via recombination and selection into account, ignoring mutation. We thus suggest to consider each position on the ring topology as host of an information carrier, representing an amount of information with a single real value $x \in [0, 1]$. Initially we deposit information quantity 1 at one position and set all other positions to value 0.

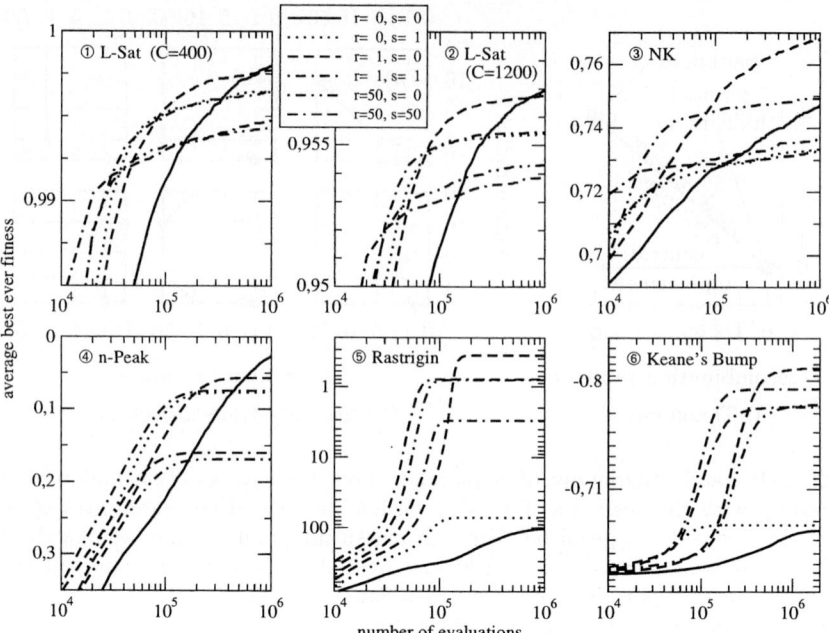

Fig. 3. Time dependent average best ever fitness on considered problems for a small subset of analyzed strategies, scaled differently to stress important fitness ranges. Higher curves show better fitness.

We then measure how fast this information is transferred to the opposite ring position. We assume neutral fitness, i.e. we only model the genetic drift effect.

Each simulation time step consists of randomly determining a position and replacing its information carrier. Therefore, we randomly select an other information carrier a within its selection radius s and chose a random mating partner b out of the recombination radius r of a. Assigned information quantity $I(o)$ of offspring o depends on information quantities of its parents and their diversity. It is drawn randomly from a normal distribution $N((I(a)+I(b))/2, |I(a)-I(b)|/2)$, with values outside $[0, 1]$ adjusted to the limits.

Fig. 4 plots the average amount of information transfered to the opposite position for different (r,s) configurations, averaged from 1000 replicates. Settings using recombination radius $r = 0$ are only capable of transferring information as a whole by selection and thus always yield discrete values zero or one at the opposite position. Setting $(r = 0, s = 0)$ prohibits information transfer completely and always leads to zero values at the opposite position.

The ring-strategy $(r = 1, s = 0)$ shows desirable behavior in this simple model, too. Note that it yields high information quantities despite an expectedly deferred start.

Further comparison with fitness plots of fig. 3 reveals, that high radii lead to a fast increase of information quantity in the beginning but also favor early

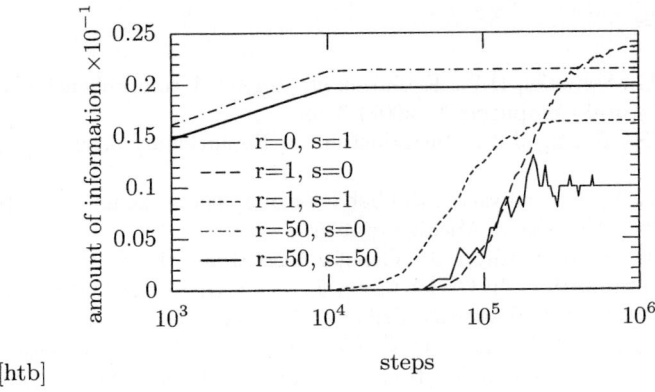

Fig. 4. Amount of information at the opposite ring position using a simple model of information transfer by means of recombination and selection.

stagnation. Low radii settings need much more time to start information transfer, but show progress for longer periods of time. Again, recombination seems to be important, enabling transfer of parts of information in contrast to the "all or nothing"-principle of pure selection.

6 Conclusion and Outlook

An improved success rate by increased diversity on the one hand and a loss of computing time on non-promising regions of search space on the other hand are the two conflicting effects of local recombination and selection. These effects are adjustable by the degree of locality, controlled by selection and recombination radii, which have to be chosen with respect to the available optimization time.

Using the radius based approach we identified three important strategies for optimizing complex problems with an EA: Panmictic population structures provide early results whereas for long runs, we suggest use of a local-selection EA with minimal recombination radius $(1, 0)$. Alternatively, a multi-hillclimber approach may be worthwhile although it seemingly fails on some problems like NK landscapes, Keane's Bump or the Rastrigin function. This can be due to bad parameterization (e.g. mutation strength) or the inability to aggregate matching building blocks.

In the presented approach, we explicitly modelled the speed of information flow in EAs. Beside rings we considered other topologies as small-world networks [16] that are well known as topologies of natural systems. Thus, we shortened average path lengths by adding shortcuts instead of increasing radii. As those shortcuts connect very diverse subpopulations, we again met the problem of unsuccessful recombination.

In our opinion, investigation and control of information flow is a promising approach to improve and better understand the dynamics of EAs. Nevertheless, research on this area shall be guided by examination of recombineability.

References

1. Beyer, H.G., Schwefel, H.P.: Evolution strategies: A comprehensive introduction. Journal Natural Computing **1** (2002) 3–52
2. Eiben, A.E., Smith, J.E.: Introduction to Evolutionary Computing. Springer (2003)
3. De Jong, K.A.: An analysis of the behavior of a class of genetic adaptive systems. PhD thesis, University of Michigan (1975)
4. Goldberg, D.E., Richardson, J.: Genetic algorithms with sharing for multimodal function optimization. In Grefenstette, J., ed.: Genetic Algorithms and their Applications (ICGA'87), Lawrence Erlbaum Associates (1987) 41–49
5. Li, J.P., Balazs, M.E., Parks, G.T., Clarkson, P.J.: A species conserving genetic algorithm for multimodal function optimization. Evolutionary Computation **10** (2002) 207–234
6. Voudouris, C.: Guided local search – an illustrative example in function optimisation. BT Technology Journal **16** (1998) 46–50
7. Lasarczyk, C.W.G., Dittrich, P., Banzhaf, W.: Dynamic subset selection based on a fitness case topology. Evolutionary Computation **12** (2004) in print.
8. Alba, E., Tomassini, M.: Parallelism and evolutionary algorithms. IEEE Transactions on Evolutionary Computation **6** (2002) 443–462
9. Sarma, J., De Jong, K.: An analysis of the effects of neighborhood size and shape on local selection algorithms. In Voigt, H., Ebeling, W., Rechenberg, I., eds.: Parallel Problem Solving from Nature – PPSN IV, Berlin, Springer (1996) 236–244
10. Sprave, J.: Linear neighborhood evolution strategy. In Sebald, A.V., Fogel, L.J., eds.: Proc. EP'94, Singapore, World Scientific (1994) 42–51
11. De Jong, K.A., Potter, M.A., Spears, W.M.: Using problem generators to explore the effects of epistasis. In Bäck, T., ed.: ICGA, San Francisco, CA, Morgan Kaufmann (1997) 338–345
12. De Jong, K.A., Spears, W.M.: An analysis of the interacting roles of population size and crossover in genetic algorithms. In Schwefel, H.P., Männer, R., eds.: Proceedings PPSN I, Springer-Verlag (1990) 38–47
13. Salomon, R.: Re-evaluating genetic algorithm performance under coordinate rotation of benchmark functions: A survey of some theoretical and practical aspects of genetic algorithms. BioSystems **39** (1996) 263–278
14. Keane, A.J.: Experiences with optimizers in structural design. In Parmee, I.C., ed.: Proc. Adaptive Computing in Engineering Design and Control 94, Plymouth, UK. (1994) 14–27
15. Mitchell, D., Selman, B., Levesque, H.: Hard and easy distributions of SAT problems. In: Proceedings of AAAI-92, San Jose, California, AAAI Press, Menlo Park, California, USA (1992) 459–465
16. Watts, D.J., Strogatz, S.H.: Collective dynamics of 'small-world' networks. Nature **393** (1998) 440–442

Estimating the Number of Solutions for SAT Problems

Colin R. Reeves and Mériéma Aupetit-Bélaidouni

School of Mathematical and Information Sciences
Coventry University
Coventry, UK

Abstract. The study of fitness landscapes is important for increasing our understanding of local-search based heuristics and evolutionary algorithms. The number of acceptable solutions in the landscape is a crucial factor in measuring the difficulty of combinatorial optimization and decision problems. This paper estimates this number from statistics on the number of repetitions in the sample history of a search. The approach is applied to the problem of counting the number of satisfying solutions in random and structured SAT instances.

1 Introduction

The need to solve a combinatorial optimization problem (COP) or decision problem (CDP) is common in almost many areas of business and technology. The solution of such problems consists of finding a solution in a very large but finite set of alternative combinations. However, they are usually very hard to solve exactly because of their complexity and their size.

For this reason, solutions can often be found only with the help of approximate or heuristic methods, often based on the idea of local search (LS), and applications of techniques such as simulated annealing (SA), tabu search (TS) and the genetic algorithm (GA).

2 SAT Problems

The satisfiability (SAT) problem is one of the most fundamental of all combinatorial problems. At its most general, it assumes a set of variables $\{x_i\}$ taking values from a domain $\mathcal{D}_i$, and a set of constraints upon subsets of those variables. In many applications it is posed for the case where x_i is a Boolean variable, (i.e., $\mathcal{D}_i = \{0, 1\} \ \forall i$), and the constraints or *clauses* are disjunctions of the variables or their complements. The requirement is to find an assignment of values to the variables such that all clauses are true.

For example, suppose we have a SAT instance comprising 4 variables and 5 clauses

$$(x_1 \vee x_2) \wedge (\bar{x}_2 \vee \bar{x}_3) \wedge (x_1 \vee \bar{x}_2 \vee x_3) \wedge (\bar{x}_1 \vee x_3 \vee x_4) \wedge (x_2 \vee x_3 \vee \bar{x}_4)$$

where $\bar{x}$ means 'not-x', and $\vee, \wedge$ mean 'or', 'and' respectively. An assignment such as $(1, 0, 1, 0)$ to the 4 variables makes all clauses true according to Boolean logic, and thus this problem is 'satisfiable'. In cases that are not satisfiable, a related problem (MAXSAT) is to find assignments that satisfy as many clauses as possible. It is well known that the SAT decision problem is NP-complete in general [1], and remains so even if we restrict the size of a clause to just 3 variables (3-SAT).

In applications, it may be important to have alternative solutions to a particular problem instance. The total *number* of satisfying assignments thus becomes a relevant issue in practice. It is also relevant from a theoretical viewpoint since, *ceteris paribus*, SAT instances with few solutions are likely to be harder to solve (i.e., to find any solution at all) than those with a large number of solutions. Complexity theorists have defined a class #P that relates to questions of counting solutions (see [1] for details). The #SAT problem is defined as the problem of counting the number of satisfying assignments of a SAT problem (its value is this number), and it can be shown to be #P-complete. Even approximating this number is NP-hard [2], and unless P=NP computing the value of #SAT is likely to be intractable in general.

In practice, as hinted above, the number of solutions to an instance of a SAT problem can vary greatly. Instances can be categorized by the values of n_c and n_v – the numbers of clauses and variables, respectively. Experiments have shown that there is a marked *phase transition* as the ratio $\rho = n_c/n_v$ increases. For small values of ρ, there are many solutions; for large values there are few, or even none. The transition occurs very rapidly at a value around $\rho = 4.3$, and it is instances in this region that are typically the hardest to solve.

3 Local Search

Local search (LS) is a rather simple idea: we start with a solution to a problem instance and evaluate a *neighbour* of this solution with a view to its possible installation as the new solution to the instance. The diversity of local search techniques comes about by varying strategies for

- the definition of a neighbourhood;
- the method for selection of a neighbour;
- the criterion for acceptance or rejection of the candidate neighbour;
- the choice of additional parameters to control some or all of the above.

In the case of Boolean SAT problems, a typical choice of neighbourhood is that obtained by changing the value of a single variable. For example, the neighbours of a solution $(1, 0, 0, 1)$ are $\{(0, 0, 0, 1), (1, 1, 0, 1), (1, 0, 1, 1), (1, 0, 0, 0)\}$. In some cases a neighbour is chosen uniformly at random from the list; sometimes the list is searched in some pre-determined order. In the popular approach of *steepest descent*, all neighbours are evaluated and one of the neighbours with the best value of some objective function is chosen.

4 Landscapes

In parallel with the development of new and better performing variants of LS, there has been some activity in researching theoretical aspects of LS methods. The most successful and fruitful theoretical concept of a general nature in this work is that of a *landscape* [3–6], which is induced by each particular implementation of LS. Certain properties of the landscape of a problem instance can be measured, such as the autocorrelation coefficient (AC) associated with a random walk on the underlying search landscape.

Most LS methods generate data as the search progresses, but surprisingly, very little useful information is normally gleaned. Several variants of LS methods use data-driven approaches to guide the search itself [7], but this information could also be used to investigate properties of the landscape.

Perhaps the simplest LS method is merely to repeat the search many times from different random initial configurations. Recent work [8–10] has shown that the results of such a restart process lead to estimates *for the specific instance* of the number of local optima; by extension they can also provide probabilistic guarantees and/or principled termination rules.

Counting the number of local optima in an optimisation problem is clearly very similar to counting the number of solutions in a decision problem, and suggests that the methodology developed in [8–10] could be used for the #SAT problem. Indeed, the principle (although not the methodology) has been suggested before [11].

4.1 The Metropolis Algorithm

An obvious alternative to repeated restarts is to use the Metropolis algorithm. This is the basis for the well-known *simulated annealing* algorithm, and it has also been used previously to investigate properties such as the 'density of states' of COPs [12, 13].

The Metropolis algorithm was developed in statistical mechanics [14] for simulating physical systems. It is basically local search in which a neighbour is chosen at random, and accepted if either (a) it has lower energy than the initial point, or (b) [if it has higher energy] with a probability that depends on the energy difference between the two points. If the temperature of the system is T and the energy difference is ΔE, the acceptance probability is $\exp\left(-\Delta E/T\right)$, which is realised in practice by drawing a uniform random number $R \in [0, 1]$ and applying the stochastic rule

$$\text{accept if } R \leq \exp\left(-\Delta E/T\right) \qquad (1)$$

In the context of combinatorial problems, 'energy' is replaced by an objective function, which for SAT problems is the number of unsatisfied clauses (i.e., we try to optimize the equivalent MAXSAT problem). In principle, the choice of T is important. If it is small, few inferior neighbours will be accepted, and the walk will stagnate for long periods. On the other hand, if it is too large, the algorithm becomes pure random search. While this is a serious issue for COPs whose range of functional values is unknown, it is a relatively minor question for MAXSAT, where we know the possible values range from zero to n_c and can choose T accordingly.

The Metropolis process is a realisation of a Markov chain describing a walk in the space $\{0,1\}^{n_v}$. Provided the walk lasts 'long enough', and given a suitable value for T, it can be shown that the stationary distribution of this chain is the overall density of states.

4.2 Sampling Protocol

The results of a Metropolis run on a SAT instance consists of a sequence of points, some of which are solutions (i.e., all clauses satisfied), and others not.

In [10], several methods are described whereby an estimate of the total number of entities in a population can be estimated by counting the number of times a given entity is resampled in a scenario where repeated sampling takes place with replacement. The most important quantity is k – the number of *distinct* points sampled in r independent draws from the population. In [8, 9], these methods were experimentally compared on instances of a range of COPs where the entities in question were local optima. Four methods seemed worth further development and testing, of which two were chosen for the experiments reported in this paper, where we count the frequency of occurrence of solutions rather than local optima. (Solutions are of course global optima to the MAXSAT problem.)

Given the Metropolis mechanism, it is obvious that successive points on the walk are correlated, and this may cause a problem in our estimation procedure. Thus for a walk on the landscape of a (MAX)SAT instance, the correlations are seen in that (not infrequently) the re-occurrence of a previously sampled point is almost immediate. This merely reflects the fact that a 'deleterious' step was made last time under the stochastic rule (1), followed by an immediate retreat to the previous solution. Thus the number of distinct solutions found may well be inflated relative to the value for independent sampling. For this reason we introduced a 'dead-time' rule for sampling from the Metropolis sequence: a reoccurrence of a previously visited solution is only counted if at least D steps have been made since its last occurrence. Theoretical considerations [15] suggest a reasonable choice for D is

$$D \approx \exp\left(\overline{\Delta E}/T\right)$$

where $\overline{\Delta E}$ is the expected difference between a solution and a non-solution, which we can estimate from experimental data. Experiments with D centred on this value showed considerable robustness in the variability of observed values of k, and it is likely that the actual value of D is not critical.

4.3 Maximum Likelihood Approach

It is assumed that there are ν solutions, each of which has its own 'basin of attraction': the set of points from which the final solution will be reached. In the case of local optima and steepest descent, it is possible to define the idea of a basin quite precisely [10] so that every point has its own unique attractor (local optimum). However, in the case of SAT instances, the landscape will consist of many plateaux at uniform 'heights', and the idea of a unique attractor for a given point cannot really be sustained. However, this may be an advantage in applying the method to this problem.

In the case of a uniform basin size, the probability distribution of K, the random variable describing the number of *distinct* points sampled in r draws from the population is given by

$$P[K = k] = \frac{\nu!}{(\nu - k)!} \frac{S(r, k)}{\nu^r}, \quad 1 \leq k \leq \min(r, \nu),$$

where $S(r, k)$ is the Stirling number of the second kind[16]. From this the maximum likelihood estimate of ν is obtained by solving the equation

$$r \log(1 - 1/\nu) - \log(1 - k/\nu) = 0$$

The value of $\kappa = k/r$ is important in determining the approach to be used for solving this equation. For small values of κ ($\kappa \leq 0.3$) it was found that the best estimate of ν is actually k – i.e., with such small values it is likely that all solutions have been found. (The probability of finding all solutions can also be found – details are given in [10]). For larger values ($\kappa \geq 0.8$) a Newton-Raphson method is useful; otherwise a binary search is quite efficient. As $\kappa \to 1$, estimation becomes increasingly unstable.

Experiments reported in [8] showed that the estimates based on this approach were good for landscapes with uniform basin sizes, but have a negative bias when basin sizes are not identical.

4.4 Jack-Knife Method

In principle, a better estimate should be obtained by using a non-parametric approach to correct for the bias. One such estimator is the jack-knife [17], which starts from the obviously biased estimator $\hat{\nu} = k$ (i.e., the actual number of distinct solutions found), and assumes that the bias decreases with increasing r. By leaving out one point of the original sample at a time, we obtain r 're-samples' of the original data, and thus r estimates of ν, which can be combined to give a new estimate

$$\hat{\nu}_{(r-1)} = k - \frac{\beta_1}{r}$$

where β_j is the number of solutions seen exactly j times. Finally, the jack-knife estimate is found by using this to correct the estimate $\hat{\nu} = k$; it reduces to

$$\hat{\nu}^{JK} = k + \frac{r-1}{r} \beta_1.$$

Burnham and Overton [17] provide appropriate $\{a_{j,s}\}$ values for a generalized jack-knife estimator of the form $\hat{\nu}_s^{JK} = \sum_{j=1}^{r} a_{j,s} \beta_j$, assuming we leave out $s > 1$ observations at a time, and suggest a test for finding the best value of s.

The jack-knife estimate was found to be somewhat inconsistent in [9], but its does have the merit of a simple closed-form computation, which would be a considerable advantage if it could be applied routinely.

5 Experiments

Another important factor in the difficulty of solving a SAT instance is its *backbone size* n_b. The backbone [18] is defined as the set of variables whose values remain the same in all solutions. The benchmark library SATLIB [19] contains many instances categorized by n_c, n_v and n_b. We investigated some of these problem instances of 3-SAT with $n_v = 100$ and $n_c = 429$ (which are in the phase transition region) at different backbone sizes. From each group we selected 100 instances at random, and in all cases the exact number of solutions has been determined by an implicit enumeration method. We used a Metropolis walk until 10^6 points had been accepted, recording k and r, and applied both methods in order to compare the estimated values for ν with the actual values.

The graphs in Figs. (1–3) display the exact values, the Metropolis value (i.e, k) and the maximum likelihood and jack-knife estimates for backbone sizes of 90, 50 and 10 respectively.

It is clear that the number of solutions increases substantially as the backbone size decreases, and that the value of k falls further and further below the true value of ν. However, it can also be seen that the maximum likelihood estimate is rather successful in removing the bias in k, except in the very extreme cases at the far right-hand end of Fig. (3). However, the jack-knife estimate is very inconsistent; it shows a tendency to provide a substantial overestimate in case of (relatively) small ν (Fig. (1)), and a severe underestimate for large ν (Fig. (3)), but otherwise its performance is fairly arbitrary.

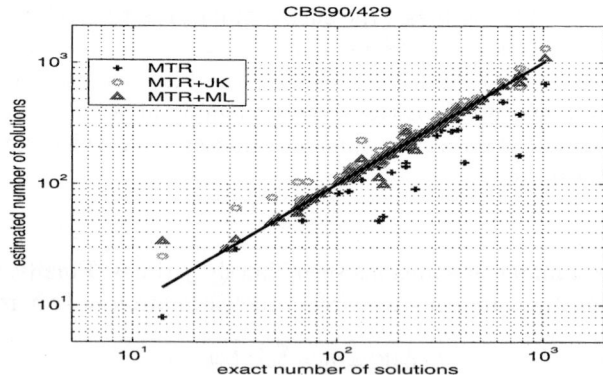

Fig. 1. CBS90. Plot of the exact number of solutions against k (MTR), $\hat{\nu}^{ML}$ (MTR+ML), and $\hat{\nu}^{JK}$ (MTR+JK) for $n_b = 90$. The continuous line shows the case where the estimate would be exact. Note the log scale on both axes.

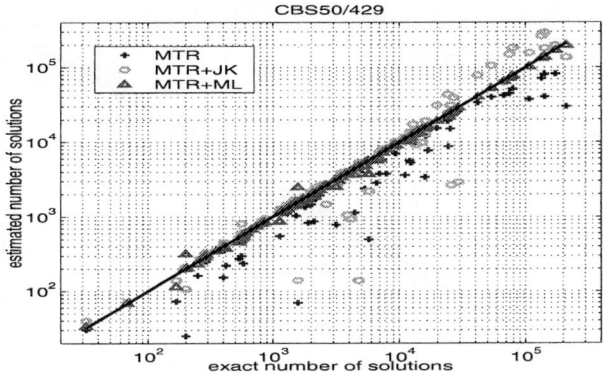

Fig. 2. CBS50. Plot of the exact number of solutions against k (MTR), $\hat{\nu}^{ML}$ (MTR+ML), and $\hat{\nu}^{JK}$ (MTR+JK) for $n_b = 50$. The continuous line shows the case where the estimate would be exact. Note the log scale on both axes.

Alongside these general conclusions, plots of relative error for the various estimates can be made, which show that despite generally good performance, quite large errors (up to 50%) can be made even with the maximum likelihood approach. (Lack of space forbids the display of these graphs here.)

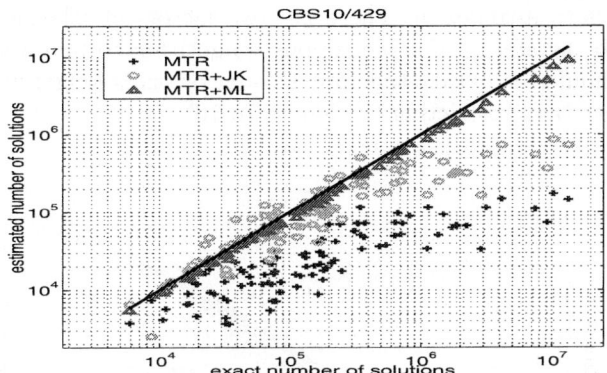

Fig. 3. CBS10. Plot of the exact number of solutions against k (MTR), $\hat{\nu}^{ML}$ (MTR+ML), and $\hat{\nu}^{JK}$ (MTR+JK) for $n_b = 10$. The continuous line shows the case where the estimate would be exact. Note the log scale on both axes.

For a comparison, we also investigated some of the 'flat' graph colouring problem instances in SATLIB. These are SAT instances with a special form, unlike the randomly generated ones used previously. Figs. (4) and (5) show the results of these experiments – in the case of the FGC50 instances, we have used a random selection of 100 from the 1000 instances in SATLIB. Again, the ML

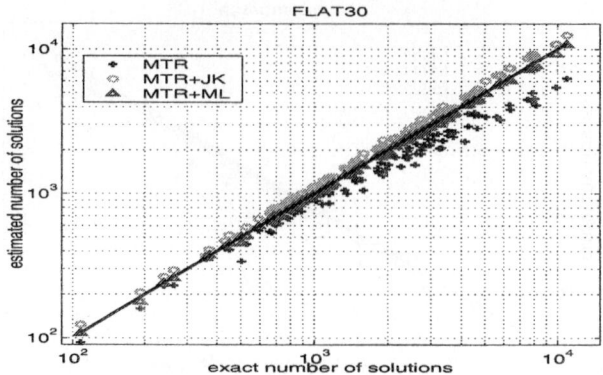

Fig. 4. FGC30. Plot of the exact number of solutions against k (MTR), $\hat{\nu}^{ML}$ (MTR+ML), and $\hat{\nu}^{JK}$ (MTR+JK) for graph colouring instances with 30 vertices. The continuous line shows the case where the estimate would be exact. Note the log scale on both axes.

estimate performs rather well, even for large values of ν, while the jack-knife also does well for the FGC30 cases, even if there is a tendency to a positive bias. However, for large values of ν, the performance of the jack-knife once more starts to fall away.

In general, the larger the problem instance, and the smaller the backbone, the harder it is to estimate ν. There are two factors of relevance: firstly, this correlates with the ability of a Metropolis walgorithm to find a solution at all; secondly, we should really take this into account by using longer walks for harder problems rather than restricting the length to 10^6.

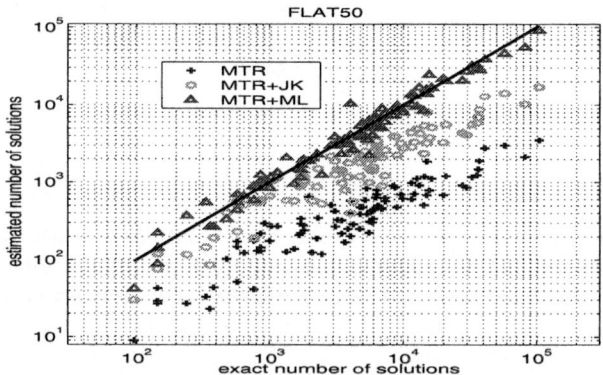

Fig. 5. FGC50. Plot of the exact number of solutions against k (MTR), $\hat{\nu}^{ML}$ (MTR+ML), and $\hat{\nu}^{JK}$ (MTR+JK) for graph colouring instances with 50 vertices. The continuous line shows the case where the estimate would be exact. Note the log scale on both axes.

6 Conclusions

We have presented experimental data concerning the usefulness of estimates of the number of solutions in SAT problem instances, extending earlier work on local optima in combinatorial landscapes. The maximum likelihood estimate appears to be fairly reliable, although it may occasionally provide a rather poor estimate. Still, for a sample size that is typically less than a 10^{-24} fraction of the search space, this is not bad. Unfortunately, although the jack-knife is an easier technique to apply, its consistency and reliability make it much less useful as a means of estimating the value of a #SAT problem instance.

The work can easily be extended to consider different estimators: in [10] several other possibilities are described, although they tend to require more computation than either of the two methods used here. We also need to examine further the question of a suitable sample size – the value of 10^6 accepted points in the Metropolis walk was arrived at somewhat arbitrarily, and it should be possible to use an adaptive approach where the walk is curtailed (or extended) in response to the observations made as it progresses. Finally, the question of the 'dead-time' rule needs further investigation; it could be argued that the good performance of the ML estimator in particular suggests our simple approach is about right, but more work can still be done. In this connection, it would also be interesting to compare the Metropolis approach with the independent restarts used for COPs in [10], although it is likely that the latter would be more difficult to apply in the case of decision problems like #SAT. We conjecture that Metropolis would be more generally applicable, if we can assure ourselves of the statistical independence of the solutions used.

Another interesting question is raised by a comparison of this problem with that of estimating the number of local optima in a COP. Previous research [8] found that maximum likelihood approach produced a strong negative bias, which is readily traced to the non-uniform basins of attraction that usually obtain in such landscapes. However, for SAT instances the ML approach has worked rather well. There are two (not mutually exclusive) possible explanations: perhaps the assumption of uniform basins reflects something about the nature of MAXSAT landscapes; alternatively, the use of Metropolis sampling has the effect of 'softening' the demarcation of basins to the point where it becomes unimportant. It is intended to pursue these investigations further.

Acknowledgement

We would like to thank Olivier Bailleux for helpful information and Roberto Bayardo for his computer program to enumerate the solutions for SAT instances.

References

1. M.R.Garey and D.S.Johnson (1979) *Computers and Intractability: A Guide to the Theory of NP-Completeness*, W.H.Freeman, San Francisco, CA.

2. D.Roth (1996) On the hardness of approximate reasoning. *Artificial Intelligence*, **82**, 273-302.
3. T.C.Jones (1995) *Evolutionary Algorithms, Fitness Landscapes and Search*, Doctoral dissertation, University of New Mexico, Albuquerque, NM.
4. P.F.Stadler (1995) *Towards a Theory of Landscapes*. In R.Lopéz-Peña, R.Capovilla, R.García-Pelayo, H.Waelbroeck and F.Zertuche (Eds.) *Complex Systems and Binary Networks*, Springer-Verlag, Berlin, 77-163.
5. C.R.Reeves (1999) Landscapes, operators and heuristic search. *Annals of Operations Research*, **86**, 473-490.
6. C.M.Reidys and P.F.Stadler (2002) Combinatorial landscapes. *SIAM Review*, **44**, 3-54.
7. C.R.Reeves and T.Yamada (1998) Genetic algorithms, path relinking and the flowshop sequencing problem. *Evolutionary Computation*, **6**, 45-60.
8. A.Eremeev and C.R.Reeves (2002) Non-parametric estimation of properties of combinatorial landscapes. In S.Cagnoni, J.Gottlieb, E.Hart, M.Middendorf and G.Raidl (Eds.) (2002) *Applications of Evolutionary Computing*, LNCS2279, Springer-Verlag, Berlin, 31-40.
9. A.V.Eremeev and C.R.Reeves (2003) On confidence intervals for the number of local optima. In G.Raidl et al. (Eds.) *Applications of Evolutionary Computing*, LNCS2611, Springer-Verlag, Berlin, 224-235.
10. C.R.Reeves and A.V.Eremeev (2004) Statistical analysis of local search landscapes. *Journal of the Operational Research Society*, **55**, 687-693.
11. O.Bailleux (1998) Local search for statistical counting. *Proceedings of AAAI-98*, AAAI Press, Menlo Park, CA, 386-391.
12. T.Asselmeyer, W.Ebeling and H.Rosé (1996) Smoothing representation of fitness landscapes – the genotype-phenotype map of evolution. *BioSystems*, **39**,63-76.
13. Mériéma Bélaidouni and Jin-Kao Hao (2001) SAT, local search dynamics and density of states. In P.Collet, C.Fonlupt, J-K. Hao, E.Lutton and M.Schoenauer (Eds.) *Artificial Evolution, Proceedings of the Fifth International Conference, Evolution Artificielle (EA 2001)*, LNCS2310, Springer-Verlag, Berlin, 192-204.
14. N.Metropolis, A.W.Rosenbluth, M.N.Rosenbluth, A.H.Teller and E.Teller (1953) Equation of state calculation by fast computing machines. *J.of Chem. Phys.*, **21**, 1087-1091.
15. P.J.M.Van Laarhoven and E.H.L.Aarts (1988) *Simulated Annealing: Theory and Applications*. Kluwer, Dordrecht.
16. N.L.Johnson and S.Kotz (1969) *Discrete distributions*, Wiley, New York.
17. K.P.Burnham and W.S.Overton (1978) Estimation of the size of a closed population when capture probabilities vary between animals. *Biometrika*, **65**, 625-633.
18. J.Singer, I.Gent and A.Smaill (2000) Backbone fragility and the local search cost peak. *J.Artificial Intelligence Research*, **12**, 235-270.
19. H.H.Hoos and T.Stützle (2000) SATLIB: An online resource for research on SAT. In I.P.Gent, H.v.Maaren and T.Walsh (Eds.) *SAT 2000*, IOS Press, 283-292. Available online at http://www.satlib.org/ (last accessed April 15, 2004).

Behavior of Evolutionary Algorithms in Chaotically Changing Fitness Landscapes

Hendrik Richter

HTWK Leipzig, Fachbereich Elektrotechnik und Informationstechnik,
Institut Mess-, Steuerungs- und Regelungstechnik,
Postfach 30 11 66, D–04125 Leipzig, Germany
richter@fbeit.htwk-leipzig.de

Abstract. We study an evolutionary algorithm used for optimizing in a chaotically changing dynamic environment. The corresponding chaotic non-stationary fitness landscape can be characterized by quantifiers of the underlying dynamics-generating system. We give experimental results about how these quantifiers, namely the Lyapunov exponents, together with the environmental change period of the landscape influence performance measures of the evolutionary algorithm used for tracking optima.

1 Introduction

Starting with the work of Goldberg and Smith [8], evolutionary algorithms fit to perform in dynamic environments became a topic of increasing interest, see [6, 7, 10, 17] for recent examples. In dynamic optimization the morphological features of the fitness landscape are assumed to be moving with time, which may include changing coordinates and magnitudes of the optima. Such a fitness landscape that changes with time can be considered as a (spatial) dynamical system. A dynamical system may be specified by its governing equations and further characterized by certain quantifiers, for instance by its Lyapunov exponents, see e.g. [15], p.129. To characterize dynamic fitness landscapes by the quantifiers of the dynamics-generating system is one major content of the paper.

Apart from the problem which morphological feature of the fitness landscape is changing with time, we are also interested in the mode in which the change takes place. So far, three different modes of dynamics in dynamic fitness landscapes have been widely considered: linear (translatory), circular (cyclic), and random, see e.g. [1, 2, 4, 6]. Another typical mode of dynamical behavior is chaotic movement. Chaos is a deterministic behavior of a nonlinear dynamical system, which is characterized by a time evolution that is non-periodic oscillatory and extremely sensitive to perturbations of the system's initial conditions and parameters. This sensitivity results in long-term unpredictability of chaotic movements. Because of the non-periodic oscillations and the limitation in predicting the time evolution, chaos appears to be similar to realizations of random processes. However, in chaos, unpredictable fluctuation arises from a deterministic dynamical system for which the governing equations and the Lyapunov exponents are known. Hence, considering chaotic dynamics for driving a nonstationary fitness landscape offers to study "random-like" movements that are generated by deterministic rules and quantified by numerical values.

The goal of the paper is to study evolutionary algorithms used for tracking optima in a dynamic environment that changes in a chaotic way. Therefore, we examine the dependency between the Lyapunov exponents, the environmental change period (that defines the speed of the change, compared to the evolutionary algorithm), and performance measures of the evolutionary algorithm. We provide experimental results about how with increasing chaoticity (and hence, increasing unpredictability) of the movement of the fitness landscape, the algorithm's ability to track optima reaches limits.

The paper is organized as follows. In Sect. 2 we review nonlinear dynamical systems and discuss how Lyapunov exponents can be used to characterize their behavior. In Sect. 3 the dynamic fitness landscape is given and it is shown how a chaotic nonlinear system can be employed to move the landscape chaotically. The evolutionary algorithm to optimize in the chaotically moving fitness landscape is described in Sect. 4, where also methods that measure the performance of the algorithm are recalled and numerical results are presented. Finally, in Sect. 5 the findings are summarized and conclusions are drawn.

2 Nonlinear Dynamics and Lyapunov Exponents

We consider a discrete-time dynamical system

$$x(k+1) = f(x(k), \alpha), \tag{1}$$

where $x \in \mathbb{R}^n$ is the state vector, $\alpha \in \mathbb{R}$ is a parameter, $f : \mathbb{R}^n \times \mathbb{R} \to \mathbb{R}^n$, and $k \in \mathbb{N}_0$. With the initial conditions $x(0) = x_0$, the system evolves with time and generates the trajectory $x(0), x(1), x(2), \ldots$. Depending on the parameter values and the initial conditions, the system can exhibit different modes of dynamics, that is movement to a steady state or cyclic motion or chaotic behavior.

In essence, the differences between the modes of dynamical behavior are differences in the way nearby trajectories behave to each other. Therefore, to distinguish between modes of dynamics, we study neighboring trajectories, which leads us to the concept of Lyapunov exponents. We consider an infinitesimal displacement $\Delta x(k)$ from a trajectory and determine how this displacement evolves with time:

$$\Delta x(k+1) = J(x(k)) \cdot \Delta x(k), \tag{2}$$

where $J(x(k)) = \left.\frac{\partial f}{\partial x}\right|_{x=x(k)}$ is the Jacobian along the trajectory. The initial displacement is $\Delta x(0) = \Delta x_0$. The direction of the displacement is $\frac{\Delta x(k)}{\|\Delta x(k)\|}$ and $\frac{\|\Delta x(k)\|}{\|\Delta x_0\|}$ is the factor by which the displacement grows or shrinks. With the transition matrix $\Phi(k)$ a solution of the (time-variant) linear system (2) can be expressed as

$$\Delta x(k+1) = \Phi(k) \cdot \Delta x_0. \tag{3}$$

The growing and shrinking rates for the time evolution of the displacement in orthogonal directions of the state space can be obtained by studying the mapping of all initial states Δx_0 situated on a unit sphere by Eq. (3). By this mapping, the unit sphere is deformed to a hyperellipsoid $E = \{x \in \mathbb{R}^n | \|\Delta x(k)\| = 1\}$ with $\|\Delta x(k)\|^2 = \Delta x(k)^T \Delta x(k) = \Delta x_0^T \Phi(k-1)^T \Phi(k-1) \Delta x_0 = 1$. The lengths of its principal axis scale to the growing and shrinking rates for the time evolution of the displacement in orthogonal directions. These rates can be obtained by the singular values $\sigma_i(\Phi(k))$, $\sigma_i \in \mathbb{R}$, $\sigma_i \geq 0$, $i = 1, 2, \ldots, n$, of the transition matrix $\Phi(k)$. So, the n Lyapunov exponents λ_i, $\lambda_i \in \mathbb{R}$, of a dynamical system (1) can be defined by [9, 19]:

$$\lambda_i = \lim_{k \to \infty} \frac{1}{k} \ln \sigma_i(\Phi(k)) \qquad i = 1, 2, \ldots, n. \tag{4}$$

Based on this definition, the behavior of a dynamical system can be distinguished by its Lyapunov exponents (4) using: (i) their sign pattern, and (ii) their magnitudes, e.g. [15], p.132. A dynamical system is chaotic if at least one Lyapunov exponent is positive. The magnitude of the largest (positive) Lyapunov exponent indicates the degree of chaoticity. By contrast, translatory and cyclic behavior is characterized by negative Lyapunov exponents.

In the numerical experiments, we use the Generalized Hénon map (GHM) as nonlinear driving function for dynamic fitness landscapes. The GHM is

$$\begin{pmatrix} x_1(k+1) \\ x_j(k+1) \end{pmatrix} = f(x(k), \alpha) = \begin{pmatrix} \alpha - x_{n-1}(k)^2 - 0.1 x_n(k) \\ x_{j-1}(k) \end{pmatrix}, \tag{5}$$

where $j = 2, 3, \ldots, n$, $\alpha > 0$, and $x \in \mathbb{R}^n$ (see [5, 16] for detailed studies). It is a map of given dimension, which shows chaotic and hyperchaotic behavior for certain parameter values and initial conditions. The map possesses the property that its largest Lyapunov exponent scales with the map's dimension n, that is

$$\lambda_1(n) = \frac{c}{n}, \tag{6}$$

where $c > 0$ is a constant [16]. Hence, using the GHM as nonlinear driving function allows to chaotify the dynamic fitness landscape in a quantified and convenient way by selecting the dimension n of the GHM.

3 Modelling Chaotically Changing Fitness Landscapes

In the previous section, we have considered nonlinear dynamical systems, which may exhibit chaotic behavior for certain parameter values and initial conditions. We have further shown that the dynamics of a given system can be distinguished by its Lyapunov exponents. In particular, the largest Lyapunov exponent λ_1 identifies the mode of behavior (translatory, cyclic or chaotic) by its sign and in addition it provides a measure for the strength of the mode of behavior by its magnitude. In terms of chaotic movements, the larger the Lyapunov exponent is, the more chaotic is the system.

We now apply these results to dynamically changing fitness landscapes. To this end, we use a framework for generating dynamic fitness landscapes proposed in [12]. Within this framework the dynamic fitness landscape consists of two components: a static fitness function specifying the general morphology of the landscape and a discrete-time dynamical system employed as driving function. This driving function adds dynamics to the landscape by providing a rule for changing certain variables of the static fitness function with time.

As static fitness function $F(X) : \mathbb{R}^m \to \mathbb{R}$, we employ an m-dimensional "field of cones on a zero plane", where the cones have randomly chosen heights and slopes and are initially distributed across the landscape. So, we write

$$F(X) = \max\left\{0, \max_{1 \leq i \leq N}[h_i - s_i\|X - X_i\|]\right\}, \qquad (7)$$

where N is the number of cones in the landscape, X_i are the coordinates of the i-th cone, and h_i, s_i specifies its height and slope. Hence, the static optimization problem becomes

$$\max_{X \in \mathbb{R}^m} F(X) = \max\left\{0, \max_{1 \leq i \leq N}[h_i - s_i\|X - X_i\|]\right\}. \qquad (8)$$

As driving function we use a nonlinear dynamical system (1), specified by the GHM (5), and move the locations X_i by

$$X_i(k) = g_i(x_j(k)), \qquad (9)$$

where the functions $g_i : \mathbb{R}^n \to \mathbb{R}^m$, $i = 1, 2, ..., N$, depend on time through components x_j of the state vector of the GHM (5). So, dynamical properties of the system are transferred to the dynamic fitness landscape. For the functions g_i being bijective smooth mappings, Eq. (9) preserves the Lyapunov exponents. It was mentioned before that the values of the heights h_i and slopes s_i are randomly initialized at $k = 0$ and remain constant as the fitness landscape changes with time. Chaotically changing heights and/or slopes of the fitness landscape can be treated within the same framework by changing these quantities through a driving system. Such changes are not the topic of this paper and should be studied in future research.

By combining the Eqs. (7) and (9), the dynamic fitness function can be written:

$$F(X, k) = \max\left\{0, \max_{1 \leq i \leq N}[h_i - s_i\|X - g_i(x_j(k))\|]\right\}. \qquad (10)$$

Hence, the dynamic optimization problem is

$$\max_{X \in \mathbb{R}^m} F(X, k) = \max\left\{0, \max_{1 \leq i \leq N}[h_i - s_i\|X - g_i(x_j(k))\|]\right\}, \quad k \geq 0, \qquad (11)$$

whose solution

$$X_s(k) = \arg\max\left\{0, \max_{1 \leq i \leq N}[h_i - s_i\|X - g_i(x_j(k))\|]\right\} \qquad (12)$$

forms a solution trajectory in the search space $\mathbb{R}^m$.

The optimization problem (11) can be solved by an evolutionary algorithm with real number representation and μ individuals $a \in \mathbb{R}^m$, which form the population $P \in \mathbb{R}^{m \times \mu}$. Such an evolutionary algorithm can be described by the generation transition function $\Psi : \mathbb{R}^{m \times \mu} \to \mathbb{R}^{m \times \mu}$ (see e.g. [3], p.64–65). By this generation transition function a population at generation $t \in \mathbb{N}_0$ is transformed into a population at generation $t + 1$,

$$P(t+1) = \Psi(P(t)), \quad t \geq 0. \quad (13)$$

Starting from an initial population $P(0)$, the population sequence $P(0)$, $P(1)$, $P(2), \ldots$ represents the movement of the population with time. Typically, the generation transition function depends on deterministic and probabilistic operators, namely selection, recombination and mutation. Hence, the evolutionary algorithm generating the movement of the population within the fitness landscape can be viewed as a dynamical system depending on random variables.

The dynamic fitness function $F(X, k)$ and the individuals a of the population P described by the population transition function $\Psi(P(t))$ move in the same space $x \in \mathbb{R}^m$, but they might have different speeds. This difference in speed can be specified by the environmental change period $\gamma \in \mathbb{N}$ (cf. [13]). Between the speed of the evolutionary algorithm and the speed of the fitness landscape change, we find

$$t = \gamma k. \quad (14)$$

Apparently, if $\gamma = 1$, then the dynamic fitness landscape and the evolutionary algorithm have the same speed, resulting in the landscape changing every generation. For $\gamma > 1$, the fitness landscape changes every γ generations, which offers to study the performance of the evolutionary algorithm depending on the frequency in which the dynamic fitness landscape changes. It should be noted that in principle the environmental change period γ could also be defined as $\gamma \in \mathbb{R}_+$, which allows to model changes in the dynamic fitness landscape between generations. But as fitness evaluation usually takes place just once in a generation, these changes would probably not come into effect before the next generation, that is the next integer following any $\gamma \in \mathbb{R}_+$. Therefore, we consider $\gamma \in \mathbb{N}$.

In [13], experiments have been reported in order to establish a relationship between γ and certain design parameters of the evolutionary algorithm, namely the hypermutation rates. In the numerical experiments given in Sect. 4, we will similarly look for a relationship between γ and the Lyapunov exponent λ_1 characterizing the chaoticity of the dynamics of the fitness landscape.

4 Experimental Results

4.1 Performance Measurement

As optimization in dynamic fitness landscapes does not merely mean to find the optimum but rather to track its movement, specific quantities for measuring the performance of the evolutionary algorithm are required, see [14, 18] for

Table 1. Settings of the evolutionary algorithm, the fitness landscape and the numerical experiments.

Design parameter	Symbol	Value	Setting	Symbol	Value
Population size	μ	50	Dimension of landscape	m	2
Generations in a run	T	150	Number of cones	N	10
Initial population width	ω^2	5	Driving function (9), (5)	$g_i(x_j)$	$0.3x_j(k)$ $+f_j(x_j(k))$
Base mutation rate	bm	0.1			
Hypermutation rate	hm	30	GHM (5)	α	1.76
			Number of considered runs	R	100

a discussion of features, advantages and disadvantages of various performance measures for dynamic environments. A common measurement is to give averages of the fitness values of the best-of-generation across a sufficient large number of algorithm runs over run-time. Although this measure provides a good overview about the dynamics of the fitness landscape and the evolutionary algorithm, the obtained curves are difficult to use for interpreting the performance of the algorithm across the entire range of the moving fitness landscape. Therefore, other types of averages have been suggested [13, 14], which we will adopt for presenting numerical results.

In the experiments carried out, we assume that the values of the moving optimum $F(X_s, k)$ are known. Hence, we can compute the Mean Fitness Error (MFE) by

$$MFE = \frac{1}{R}\sum_{r=1}^{R}\left[\frac{1}{T}\sum_{t=1}^{T}\left(F\left(X_s, t/\gamma\right) - \max_{a \in P} F\left(a, t/\gamma\right)\right)\right], \quad (15)$$

where $F(X_s, t/\gamma)$ is the maximum fitness value at generation t, $\max_{a \in P} F(a, t/\gamma)$ is the fitness value of the best individual $a \in P$ at generation t, T is the number of generations used in the run, and R is the number of consecutive runs of the evolutionary algorithm taken into consideration in the experiments. Note that $F(X_s, t/\gamma)$ and $\max_{a \in P} F(a, t/\gamma)$ change according to Eq. (10) every γ generations. In addition to the MFE, the long-term behavior of the performance can be quantified by the Collective Mean Fitness (CMF) [14]

$$CMF = \frac{1}{R}\sum_{r=1}^{R}\left[\frac{1}{T}\sum_{t=1}^{T}\max_{a \in P} F\left(a, t/\gamma\right)\right], \quad (16)$$

where $\max_{a \in P} F(a, t/\gamma)$, T, and R are defined as in Eq. (15). Note that this measure can also be used if the value of the maximum fitness is not known.

4.2 Experimental Setup

In the following, we report numerical results in tracking chaotically changing optima by an evolutionary algorithm. The algorithm uses real number representation, fixed population size, tournament selection with tournament size 2 and

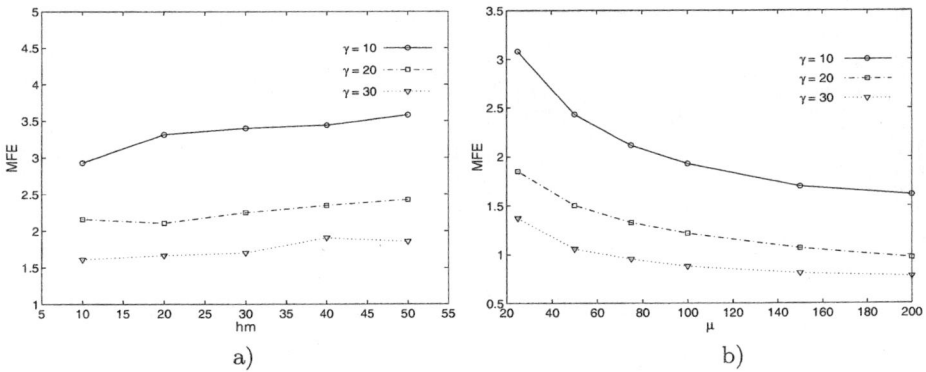

Fig. 1. Performance specified by the MFE with $N = 10$ and $n = 4$ for different γ versus: a) hypermutation rate hm for $\mu = 15$, b) population size μ for $hm = 30$.

fitness-based recombination. The initial population is created by realizations of a random variable normally distributed on $[0, \omega^2]$. In order to cope with the changing landscape, in addition to standard mutation with base mutation rate bm, triggered hypermutation [13] is employed. This triggered hypermutation relies on a triggering that detects changes in the fitness landscape. It initiates the hypermutation if the moving average of the fitness of the best-of-generation calculated over five generations decreases. Then the base mutation rate bm is multiplied by the hypermutation rate hm.

In a first numerical investigation we look at how some basic design parameters of the evolutionary algorithm scale with the MFE (15), see Fig. 1. This figure shows the relationship between the MFE and the hypermutation rate hm (Fig. 1a) and between the MFE and the population size μ (Fig. 1b) for different environmental change periods γ. We observed a light increasing MFE for hm getting larger. These results can be interpreted as a lower hypermutation rate outperforming higher ones, particularly at higher γ. Also, it can be seen that the MFE gets gradually smaller for an increasing population size, which indicates that tracking the optimum gets easier for larger populations. For both experiments, the leading factor in the performance of the algorithm is γ. In general, the more frequent the change of the landscape takes place (that is, the smaller γ), the larger is the MFE. This means that following the optimum successfully becomes harder with increasing frequency of the landscape changes, which agrees with previous studies [13, 17]. Interpreting these results, we chose $hm = 30$ and $\mu = 50$. Tab. 1 summarizes the design parameter of the algorithm together with settings of the dynamic fitness landscape and the given numerical experiments.

4.3 Discussion of Results

Next, results of optimum tracking in chaotically changing fitness landscapes are given. Fig. 2 shows the time evolution of the fitness for the best-of-generation for different γ. The algorithm responds rapidly to the changes in the fitness land-

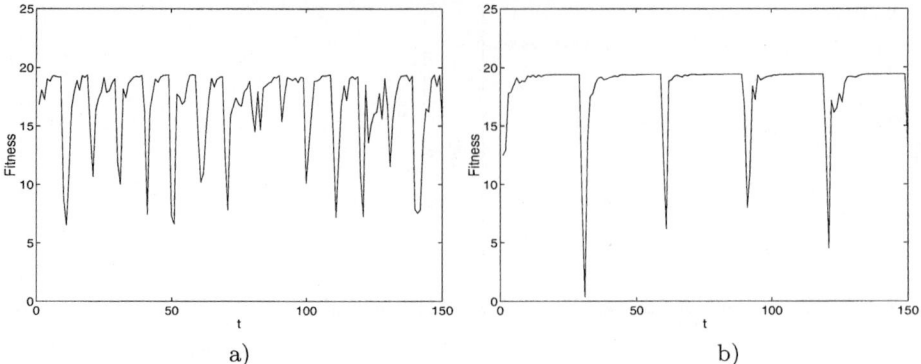

Fig. 2. Fitness of the best-of-generation $\max\limits_{a \in P} F(a, t/\gamma)$ for $n = 4$ versus generation t for $\mu = 50$ and $N = 10$: a) $\gamma = 10$, b) $\gamma = 30$.

scape. In Fig. 3, the performance measures CMF (16) and MFE (15) are given as a function of the dimension n and the largest Lyapunov exponent λ_1 specifying the chaotic driving function (5), depicted on semi-logarithmic scale. Both quantities represent the chaoticity of the chaotically changing fitness landscape (10). It can be seen that for a constant environmental change period γ the CMF increases with the dimension n of the driving system, Fig. 3a,b. On the other hand, the CMF falls for higher Lyapunov exponents λ_1. An inverse relationship can be obtained for the performance measure MFE, Fig. 3c,d. As given in Eq. (6), the largest Lyapunov exponent and the dimension are reciprocal for the used driving function (5). For the dimension getting smaller and therefore the Lyapunov exponent becoming larger, the driving function and hence the chaotically changing fitness landscape increases in chaoticity. Higher chaoticity means changes of the fitness landscape being more unpredictable. From the obtained performance measure given in Fig. 3, it can be concluded that the more unpredictable the movement of the optimum is, the more difficult is tracking it with an evolutionary algorithm. In addition, this relationship is only given for a certain range of λ_1. For a chaoticity under a certain threshold, we obtain constant performance measures.

5 Conclusions

We have studied an evolutionary algorithm used for optimization in a chaotic dynamic environment. It has been shown by numerical experiments that the tracking performance of the algorithm diminishes with increasing Lyapunov exponents. The largest Lyapunov exponent expresses the degree of chaoticity (and hence unpredictability) of the changing fitness landscape. So, we have found evidence for a relationship between the predictability of the changes of the fitness landscape and the algorithm's performance. A possible interpretation of these results is that larger predictability of the movement of the fitness landscape makes it easier for the evolutionary algorithm to learn from tracking the optimum and hence to improve its performance.

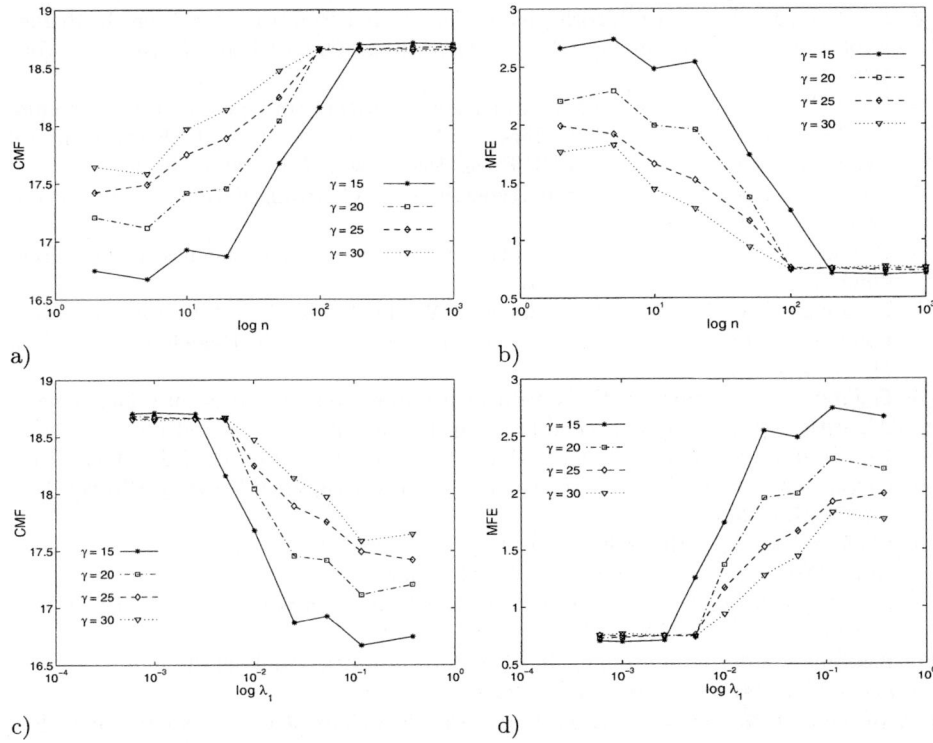

Fig. 3. Performance specified by the CMF and the MFE as functions of quantifiers of the dynamics fitness landscape's driving function (5) on semi-logarithmic scale: a),b) dimension n, c),d) the largest Lyapunov exponent λ_1.

Finally, another aspect of optimization in chaotically moving fitness landscapes should be mentioned. Evolving and self-organizing systems are generally understood to have fitness landscapes whose movements poise between order and chaos, e.g. [11], Ch. 6. Organisms together with the chaotically changing fitness landscape which they populate, form a coevolving ecosystem in which adaptation and self-organization may take place. Analysis and design of evolutionary algorithms fit to perform in chaotic environments might offer clues for further insight into such complex adapting and coevolving structures.

References

1. Angeline, P.J.: Tracking Extrema in Dynamic Environments. In: Angeline, P.J., Reynolds, R.G., McDonnell, J.R., Eberhart, R. (eds.): Evolutionary Programming VI. Springer-Verlag, Berlin Heidelberg New York (1997) 335–345
2. Arnold, D.V., Beyer, H.G.: Random Dynamics Optimum Tracking with Evolution Strategies. In: Merelo Guervós, J.J., Panagiotis, A., Beyer, H.G., Fernández Villácañas, J.L., Schwefel, H.P. (eds.): Parallel Problem Solving from Nature-PPSN VII. Springer-Verlag, Berlin Heidelberg New York (2002) 3–12

3. Bäck, T.: Evolutionary Algorithms in Theory and Practice: Evolution Strategies, Evolutionary Programming, Genetic Algorithms. Oxford Univ. Press, New York (1996)
4. Bäck, T.: On the Behavior of Evolutionary Algorithms in Dynamic Environments. In: Fogel, D.B., Schwefel, H.P., Bäck, T., Yao, X. (eds.): Proc. IEEE Int. Conf. on Evolutionary Computation, IEEE Press, Piscataway, NJ (1998) 446–451
5. Baier, G., Klein, M.: Maximum Hyperchaos in Generalized Hénon Maps. Phys. Lett. A151 (1990) 281–284
6. Branke, J.: Evolutionary Optimization in Dynamic Environments. Kluwer Academic Publishers, Dordrecht (2001)
7. De Jong, K.A.: Evolving in a Changing World. In: Raś, Z., Skowron, A. (eds.): Foundations of Intelligent Systems. Springer-Verlag, Berlin Heidelberg New York (1999) 513–519
8. Goldberg, D.E., Smith, R.E.: Nonstationary Function Optimization Using Genetic Algorithms with Dominance and Diploidy. In: Grefenstette, J.J. (ed.): Proc. Second Int. Conf. on Genetic Algorithms. Lawrence Erlbaum, Hillsdale, NJ (1987) 59–68
9. Green, J.M., Kim, J.S.: The Calculation of the Lyapunov Spectra. Physica D24 (1987) 213–225
10. Grefenstette, J.J.: Evolvability in Dynamic Fitness Landscapes: A Genetic Algorithm Approach. In: Angeline, P.J., Michalewicz, Z., Schoenauer, M., Yao, X., Zalzala, A. (eds.): Proc. Congress of Evolutionary Computation. IEEE Press, Piscataway, NJ (1999) 2031–2038
11. Kauffman, S.A.: The Origin of Order: Self–Organization and Selection in Evolution. Oxford Univ. Press, New York (1993)
12. Morrison, R.W., De Jong, K.A.: A Test Problem Generator for Non-stationary Environments. In: Angeline, P.J., Michalewicz, Z., Schoenauer, M., Yao, X., Zalzala, A. (eds.): Proc. Congress of Evolutionary Computation. IEEE Press, Piscataway, NJ (1999) 2047–2053
13. Morrison, R.W., De Jong, K.A.: Triggered Hypermutation Revisited. In: Zalzala, A., Fonseca, C., Kim, J.H., Smith, A., Yao, X. (eds.): Proc. Congress of Evolutionary Computation. IEEE Press, Piscataway, NJ (2000) 1025–1032
14. Morrison, R.W.: Performance Measurement in Dynamic Environments. In: Barry, A.M. (ed.): Proc. GECCO 2003: Workshops, Genetic and Evolutionary Computation Conference. AAAI Press, Menlo Park, CA (2003) 99–102
15. Ott, E.: Chaos in Dynamical Systems. Cambridge Univ. Press, Cambridge (1993)
16. Richter, H.: The Generalized Hénon Maps: Examples for Higher-dimensional Chaos. Int. J. Bifurcation and Chaos 12 (2002) 1371–1384
17. Weicker, K., Weicker, N.: On Evolution Strategy Optimization in Dynamic Environments. In: Angeline, P.J., Michalewicz, Z., Schoenauer, M., Yao, X., Zalzala, A. (eds.): Proc. Congress of Evolutionary Computation. IEEE Press, Piscataway, NJ (1999) 2039–2046
18. Weicker, K.: Performance Measures for Dynamic Environments. In: Merelo Guervós, J.J., Panagiotis, A., Beyer, H.G., Fernández Villácañas, J.L., Schwefel, H.P. (eds.): Parallel Problem Solving from Nature-PPSN VII. Springer-Verlag, Berlin Heidelberg New York (2002) 64–73
19. Wolf, A., Swift, J.B., Swinney, H.L., Vastano, J.A.: Determining the Lyapunov Exponents from a Time Series. Physica D16 (1985) 285–313

Expected Rates of Building Block Discovery, Retention and Combination Under 1-Point and Uniform Crossover

Cameron Skinner and Patricia Riddle

Department of Computer Science
The University of Auckland

Abstract. Choosing the right crossover operator for the problem at hand is a difficult problem. We describe an experiment that shows a surprising result when comparing 1-point and uniform crossover on the Royal Road problem and derive equations for calculating the expected rates of building block discovery, retention and combination. These equations provide an explanation for the surprising results and suggest several directions for future research into hybrid operators.

1 Introduction

It is widely known in the Genetic Algorithm (GA) community that crossover works by combining low order partial solutions into higher order solutions – this is the "building block hypothesis" [1]. It is also widely accepted that the choice of crossover operator (1-point, n-point, uniform or some other flavour) is vital to the success of the algorithm.

The GA attempts this approach by making certain assumptions about the problems it is used to solve. In order for the building block hypothesis to hold we must assume first that the problem at hand does in fact contain seperable partial solutions that can be combined by crossover, and we also assume that our genetic operators are capable of combining those partial solutions once they are found. In general, however, we cannot know *a priori* which operators will, in fact, be capable of discovering and combining building blocks.

We describe an experiment that investigates the effect of different forms of crossover on two variants of the Royal Road problem [2]. We expected that 1-point crossover would perform well on the standard version of the Royal Road problem (i.e. a problem with *tight linkage*), and poorly on a version where the bits of each building block are spread out over the string (i.e. a problem with *loose linkage*). We also expected that uniform crossover would perform better than 1-point crossover on the loose linkage problem. We obtained a surprising result that proved these expectations to be incorrect. After closer analysis, however, it was shown that this behaviour is to be expected – we had made assumptions about the behaviour of the two operators that were incorrect, leading to incorrect expectations about their performance. The structure of this paper is as follows. Section 2 illustrates related work in the field. Section 3 describes the surprising results obtained on the Royal Road problem, followed by the derivation of a theory for calculating the expected rates of building block discovery, retention and combination for 1-point and uniform crossover in Section 4. This theory is then validated by experimental results in Section 5. We conclude in Section 6 with some directions for future research.

2 Related Work

Choosing the right operators has been a popular topic almost from the beginning of the GA literature. It is widely accepted that the "right" operators will be ones that somehow match the problem, but this is not easy. Many publications have investigated different forms of operators, for example [3, 4], and the general conclusion seems to be that each operator works well in certain situations, and poorly otherwise.

Mutation, n-point crossover and uniform crossover have all been discussed in terms of disruption and construction potential [5–7]. This paper extends those analyses and provides more meaningful calculations of discovery and combination. Other works consider cases where a child has a block as a successful discovery irrespective of whether either of the parents already had the block. In this work we make a distinction between discovery and retention.

This work is similar in some respects to the literature on *mixing* [8], however we consider not only the ability of the algorithm to combine (mix) different blocks, but also its ability to discover new blocks.

Spears and De Jong [6] reached the important conclusion that "if one operator is better than another for survival, it is worse for recombination". In other words, no one operator will be better than another at both exploration (recombination in Spears and De Jong's words) and exploitation (survival).

Crossover usually comes in one of two flavours: *1-point* (or n-point) and *uniform*. 1-point crossover cuts the parents in one place and generates a child by combining the first part of the first parent with the second part of the second parent. This form of crossover has a high positional bias – adjacent locations on the genome are likely to be copied together. Uniform crossover selects a value for each locus randomly from each parent, thus there is no positional bias.

The major difference between 1-point crossover and uniform crossover is this different positional bias. If the solution to our problem has groups of dependent bits (i.e. building blocks with a short defining length) then, by the building block hypothesis [1], a crossover operator with a high positional bias is likely to perform better as it will be more able to preserve those blocks of bits. Conversely, if the building blocks are spread throughout the string then uniform crossover is likely to perform better as it can select bits from throughout the string and copy them to the child genome intact [1, 9]. Unfortunately this hypothesis only holds in certain circumstances [6]. In Section 5 we will explain why this wisdom sometimes does not hold even when it appears that it should.

3 Experiments

Consider two versions of the Royal Road problem: Version one (V_1) is the classic problem R_1 described by Forrest, Mitchell and Holland [2]. Version two (V_2) is essentially the same as V_1 but with one important difference: instead of each block consisting of a continuous set of bits they are now spread evenly over the genome. The schemata making up function V_2 are shown in Figure 1.

```
s1 = 1******* 1******* 1******* 1******* 1******* 1******* 1******* 1*******   c1 = 8
s2 = *1****** *1****** *1****** *1****** *1****** *1****** *1****** *1******   c2 = 8
s3 = **1***** **1***** **1***** **1***** **1***** **1***** **1***** **1*****   c3 = 8
s4 = ***1**** ***1**** ***1**** ***1**** ***1**** ***1**** ***1**** ***1****   c4 = 8
s5 = ****1*** ****1*** ****1*** ****1*** ****1*** ****1*** ****1*** ****1***   c5 = 8
s6 = *****1** *****1** *****1** *****1** *****1** *****1** *****1** *****1**   c6 = 8
s7 = ******1* ******1* ******1* ******1* ******1* ******1* ******1* ******1*   c7 = 8
s8 = *******1 *******1 *******1 *******1 *******1 *******1 *******1 *******1   c8 = 8
```

Fig. 1. Royal Road Function V_2.

A series of experiments were conducted using V_1 and V_2, each with either 1-point or uniform crossover. The intent of these experiments was to demonstrate the effect of the positional bias on the ability of the GA to solve the problem. It was expected that 1-point crossover would perform well on V_1 and poorly on V_2, and that 1-point crossover would outperform uniform crossover on V_1. Four such experiments were conducted using the four combinations of fitness function and crossover operator on $8 \times n$-bit block problems, where $n = \{8, 9, 10, 11, 12\}$. We used 5-tournament selection, a population size of 128 and mutation rate of 0.01 per bit. Each experiment was repeated 100 times.

After analysing the results (Table 1) both predictions turned out to be incorrect. When we changed the problem from V_1 to V_2 1-point crossover performed better in most cases, not worse. Changing the crossover operator from 1-point to uniform on problem V_1 also resulted in better performance in most cases.

What is causing this strange behaviour? We measured the number of building blocks created each generation for each of the four experiments (results not shown). Those measurements clearly show that 1-point crossover creates more blocks on problem V_2 than on problem V_1, and uniform crossover creates more blocks than 1-point crossover on V_1. Perhaps this increase in block construction rates is driving the algorithm to success? Does 1-point crossover actually combine blocks more often on problem V_1 than on V_2? What we need is a theory of building block construction, retention and combination.

4 A Wee Bit of Mathematics

We are interested in three aspects of building block behaviour under crossover. First, what is the probability that we will discover a particular block given that neither parent has the block? Second, if one parent has the block and the other parent does not, what is the probability that the child will successfully inherit

Table 1. Average number of generations before a solution is found. Standard deviations are in brackets. Bold entries are the surprising results when compared with 1-point crossover on problem V_1.

Block length	1-point, V_1	1-point, V_2	Uniform, V_1
8	158.45 (78.63)	185.07 (65.07)	**118.08 (54.95)**
9	275.63 (129.89)	**266.83 (104.23)**	**214.01 (96.39)**
10	517.36 (261.16)	**398.30 (150.06)**	**344.49 (170.18)**
11	815.87 (414.22)	**675.72 (312.19)**	**693.54 (263.19)**
12	1380.92 (611.87)	**1146.67 (541.97)**	1421.3 (653.32)

that block? Finally, if one parent has block 1 but not block 2 and the other parent has block 2 but not block 1, what is the probability that the child contains both?

Consider a Royal Road problem consisting of n non-overlapping blocks[1] $\{B_1, B_2, ..., B_n\}$ each of order k_i in a string of length l. Note that a building block is exactly equivalent to a single schemata. Each block has a defining length d_i and there are $l-1$ possible crossover points. We say, without loss of generality, that a bit is "correct" if it has a value of one and "incorrect" otherwise. We assume that if an individual does not have an entire block correct[2] then the bits of that block have random values[3].

We will use the following notation in the equations that follow. Parents are denoted as A and B and the child is C. If we refer to an individual X that has block i then we use the notation X_i, if it does not have block i then we use $\neg X_i$. The probability that an individual X contains block i is given by $p(X_i)$. If we consider a crossover point to be at index j then we mean that the crossover occurs between bits j and $j+1$. When a crossover occurs we denote the relevant bits of block i that come from parent A as a_i, and those from parent B as b_i. We also define $left(x,i)$ as the number of defined bits in block i that are to the left of crossover point x, and $right(x,i)$ as the number of bits to the right. Subscripts are ommitted where there is no ambiguity. Note that we consider a form of crossover that produces only one child.

4.1 Discovery

Suppose we take two parents that have no blocks correct. If we know the number of relevant bits taken from each parent, a and b respectively, then we need to derive the probabilities that those bits have the correct value. This is independent of the form of crossover used, and obviously $k = a + b$. There are 2^k possible strings for each parent. We have assumed that strings containing all k bits correct are not present, thus there are $2^k - 1$ possible strings for each parent. Parent 1 needs to have a correct bits – there are $k - a$ other bits and therefore $2^{k-a} - 1$

---
[1] Two blocks are non-overlapping if and only if they do not share any defined bits.
[2] We consider an individual to have a block correct if and only if the bitstring represented by the individual is an instance of the schemata represented by the block.
[3] With the obvious exception that it is not the case that all bits in the block are one.

such strings possible. This gives a probability that parent 1 has a correct bits, but not k correct, of $\frac{2^{k-a}-1}{2^k-1}$. Similarly for parent 2 there is a success probability of $\frac{2^{k-b}-1}{2^k-1}$. We multiply these to obtain the probability that the child inherits all k correct bits, shown in Equation 1.

We can now easily derive the probabilities of discovery for both 1-point and uniform crossover. For 1-point crossover we can simply sum the probabilities over all possible crossover points, giving Equation 2. Obviously a and b depend on the particular value of x.

Uniform crossover is similar except that we sum over different values of a. There are $\binom{k}{a}$ ways of choosing a relevant bits from parent A out of 2^k possible uniform crossovers. Thus, Equation 1 becomes Equation 3. Note that if $a=0$ or $a=k$ then $p_{discovery}=0$ so we only need to sum a over the range $[1..k-1]$.

$$p_{discovery}(k,a,b) = f(k,a,b) = \frac{2^{k-a}-1}{2^k-1} \times \frac{2^{k-b}-1}{2^k-1} \qquad (1)$$

$$p_{1-point}(C_i|\neg A_i, \neg B_i) = \frac{1}{l-1} \times \sum_{x=1}^{l-1} f(k, left(x,i), right(x,i)) \qquad (2)$$

$$p_{uniform}(C_i|\neg A_i, \neg B_i) = \sum_{a=1}^{k-1} \frac{\binom{k}{a}}{2^k} \times f(k, a, k-a) \qquad (3)$$

4.2 Retention

If parent A has block i and B does not, then what is the probability that C will contain i? This is a more specific version of the discovery calculation, except that we know that one of the parents contains all correct bits in the block of interest. We merely need to drop a term from Equation 1 to obtain Equation 4 – we know that parent A has all bits correct and we only need to consider the probability that parent B has b bits correct. Equations 5 and 6 follow for 1-point crossover and uniform crossover respectively. For uniform crossover we now sum over possible values of b. We can ignore the case where $b=k$, but not $b=0$.

$$p_{retention}(k,b) = g(k,b) = \frac{2^{k-b}-1}{2^k-1} \qquad (4)$$

$$p_{1-point}(C_i|A_i, \neg B_i) = \frac{1}{l-1} \times \sum_{x=1}^{l-1} g(k, right(x,i)); \qquad (5)$$

$$p_{uniform}(C_i|A_i, \neg B_i) = \sum_{b=0}^{k-1} \frac{\binom{k}{b}}{2^k} \times g(k,b) \qquad (6)$$

4.3 Combination

Finally, if parent A has block i and parent B has block j then what is the probability of the child having both blocks? This case is essentially an extension of the retention case and is shown in Equation 7. It is as simple as requiring retention of block i and retention of block j, but with the constraint that we use the same crossover operation for both retention tests.

For any given crossover operation we take a_i bits from parent A relevant to block i and a_j bits relevant to block j. Similarly we take b_i and b_j bits from parent B. Parent A must have a_j bits correct, giving $2^{k_j-a_j}-1$ possibilities out of $2^{k_j}-1$. The probability of the child having block i present is therefore $\frac{2^{k_j-a_j}-1}{2^{k_j}-1}$. Similarly, the probability of the child having block j present is $\frac{2^{k_i-b_i}-1}{2^{k_i}-1}$.

We sum over all crossover points for 1-point crossover to obtain Equation 8. For uniform crossover we observe that there are $\binom{k_j}{a_j} \times \binom{k_i}{b_i}$ ways of choosing a_j and b_i relevant bits for the child out of $2^{k_i+k_j}$ possible uniform crossovers, resulting in Equation 9.

$$p_{combination}(k_i, k_j, a_j, b_i) = h(k_i, k_j, a_j, b_i) = \frac{2^{k_j-a_j}-1}{2^{k_j}-1} \times \frac{2^{k_i-b_i}-1}{2^{k_i}-1} \quad (7)$$

$$p_{1-point}(C_i, C_j | A_i, B_j, \neg A_j, \neg B_i) = \frac{1}{l-1} \times \sum_{x=1}^{l-1} h(k_i, k_j, left(x,j), right(x,i)) \quad (8)$$

$$p_{uniform}(C_i, C_j | A_i, B_j, \neg A_j, \neg B_i) = \sum_{a_j=0}^{k_j-1} \sum_{b_i=0}^{k_i-1} \left[\frac{\binom{k_i}{b_i} \times \binom{k_j}{a_j}}{2^{k_i+k_j}} \times h(k_i, k_j, a_j, b_i) \right] \quad (9)$$

5 Explaining the Anomaly

We can now calculate the probabilities of generating, retaining and combining building blocks under 1-point and uniform crossover and relate them to the experiments described in Section 3. In these experiments we consider 8 10-bit blocks, so $n = 8$, $k_i = 10$ and $l = 80$. For problem V_1 we have $d_i = 10$, for V_2 $d_i = 71$. Mutation is disallowed. The probabilities of discovery, retention and combination for each operator on each problem are shown in Table 2.

5.1 Predictions

We can now make three predictions about the relative behaviour of 1-point and uniform crossover on each of the two problems.

Table 2. Discovery, retention and combination probabilities.

Operator	Problem	Discovery	Retention	Combination
1-point	V_1	8.7×10^{-5}	0.46	0.15
1-point	V_2	6.9×10^{-4}	0.14	7.9×10^{-4}
Uniform	Both	9.8×10^{-4}	0.055	0.003

1-Point Crossover vs Uniform Crossover on V_1 When we change the crossover operator from 1-point to uniform on problem V_1 we expect the following changes:

1. We expect uniform crossover to be more than 11 times better at discovery.
2. We expect 1-point crossover to be 8 times better at retention.
3. We expect 1-point crossover to be nearly 50 times better at combination.

1-Point Crossover on V_1 vs 1-Point Crossover on V_2 When we change from problem V_1 to V_2 with 1-point crossover we expect the following changes:

1. We expect the rate of discovery to increase by a factor of 8.
2. We expect the rate of retention to decrease by a factor of 3.
3. We expect the successful combinations to decrease by a factor of 190.

These predicted rates of discovery, retention and combination explain the anomalous results obtained in Section 3. While 1-point crossover is indeed better at combining blocks on problem V_1 than uniform crossover, the much higher discovery rate of uniform crossover swamps this effect. The fact that 1-point crossover is 50 times better at combination on V_1 is of little consequence because it is so bad at discovering blocks that most of the time there is nothing that *can* be combined. If we had a good external source of raw building blocks (negating uniform crossover's only advantage) then 1-point crossover should outperform uniform crossover on problem V_1. When changing from problem V_1 to V_2 with 1-point crossover the higher discovery rate outweighs the poor retention and combination performance for the same reason.

5.2 More Experiments

A series of experiments were conducted using the same parameters as described in Section 3, but with mutation turned off, to measure the real rates of discovery, retention and combination. Table 3 shows the proportion of successful discoveries, blocks retained and combinations in the first new generation averaged over 1000 repeats. Standard deviations are shown in brackets. Successful combinations are detected by looking at any pair of blocks i and j such that $i \neq j, A_i, \neg A_j, B_j, \neg B_i$. If we find that the child has both blocks then we have had a successful combination[4].

---

[4] Note that because of this pairwise comparison we would treat the situation where parent A has two blocks and parent B has two different blocks producing a child containing all four blocks as 4 successful combinations.

We must note that the variances in all the results are extremely high[5] – in most cases the standard deviation of the result is larger than the result itself. We must therefore not read too much into these results, however we can observe that on the first generation the experimental results appear to agree with the theory.

Unfortunately only 1-point crossover on problem V_1 had any successful combinations in the first generation. Looking at subsequent generations (not shown) we observed standard deviations on the other two columns that are all *an order of magnitude* larger than the averages themselves, making the combination results extremely unreliable. Nevertheless, the relative rates of combination are generally consistent with those predicted.

5.3 Anomalous No More

We now have a reasonable explanation for the strange results obtained in Section 3. While 1-point crossover does combine blocks more often on problem V_1 than V_2, as expected, this effect is swamped by the huge difference in the discovery rate. It becomes easier for the algorithm to just discover the blocks one by one in a single individual than to find each block simultaneously and combine them. Similarly when changing to uniform crossover on V_1 the higher discovery rate simply outweighs the poor combination performance.

Clearly when we design a genetic algorithm we need to take these effects into account. For example, if we know that we are using 1-point crossover then we want a selection scheme that complements this. We know that 1-point crossover is good at combination but poor at discovery, so we should make sure that when choosing parents for crossover we pick ones that are likely to contain different blocks, and we might use a higher mutation rate to compensate for 1-point crossover's poor discovery performance. How best to do this is an open question.

Finally, we must consider the problem size. The discovery, retention and combination rates all decay exponentially with problem size, except for 1-point crossover's retention rates and 1-point crossover's combination rates on V_1, which appear almost linear. Interestingly, when we change down to 8-bit blocks the "anomalous" behaviour observed in Section 3 disappears. As the problem size gets smaller 1-point crossover is less affected by its poor discovery performance because of the relative ease of discovery of the smaller blocks. As the problem gets larger it becomes more important to retain blocks because of the difficulty of rediscovering a block once it is lost.

---

[5] It is not clear why the variance is so high. Running 1000 repeats instead of 100 had no effect. It is possible that the high variance stems from the fact that most of the time any given generation produces zero discoveries, and only occasionally does one of the repeats have a non-zero discovery rate. Using a higher population might alleviate this, as each generation will be more likely to have more than zero successful discoveries.

Table 3. Discovery, Retention and Combination rates for the first generation. Standard deviations are in brackets, combination results are averaged over the first 5 generations.

Feature	1-Point, V_1		1-Point, V_2		Uniform, V_1	
	Predicted	Actual	Predicted	Actual	Predicted	Actual
Discovery $\times 10^{-4}$	0.87	0.76 (2.74)	6.9	6.6 (8.5)	9.8	8.9 (9.3)
Retention	0.46	0.46 (0.24)	0.14	0.15 (0.18)	0.055	0.051 (0.118)
Combination	0.15	0.20 (0.37)	0.00079	0 (0)	0.003	0 (0)

6 Conclusions

We have seen that choosing the "right" crossover operator is not a trivial task. On the surface, after running experiments on the Royal Road problems with 1-point and uniform crossover, the results were surprising. We expected 1-point crossover to outperform uniform crossover on tightly linked building blocks, and we expected 1-point crossover to perform better on tightly linked blocks than loosely linked ones. Both these predictions were incorrect.

After analysing the mechanisms of the two operators these results turned out to be not so surprising after all – the assumptions we had made about the behaviour of the two operators were incorrect, leading us to incorrect expectations of their performance. Clearly, more care needs to be taken when designing operators in order to construct an algorithm that properly takes advantage of the dynamics of those operators. For example, if we want to use 1-point crossover to maximise block combination then we need a good source of raw building blocks to compensate for 1-point crossovers poor discovery.

The theory presented here can be expanded trivially to consider arbitrary cardinality alphabets, and not so trivially to consider cases where allele values are not randomly distributed. The theory can also be used to develop predictions of the set of blocks contained by any particular individual given two parents and a crossover operator which can be further extended to derive a probability distribution over sets of blocks for the next generation, given the current generation and a selection mechanism. This is the focus of ongoing work.

Development of hybrid operators could be extended to make use of these theoretical results, for example if the algorithm detects that many blocks are being rediscovered then it could change to 1-point crossover to promote combination of blocks. If it detects that few blocks are being discovered then uniform crossover might be preferred, along with a suitable selection scheme for maintaining blocks once they are found.

References

1. Goldberg, D.E.: Genetic Algorithms in Search, Optimization and Machine Learning. Addison-Wesley (1989)
2. Mitchell, M., Forrest, S., Holland, J.H.: The Royal Road for Genetic Algorithms: Fitness Landscapes and GA Performance. In Varela, F.J., Bourgine, P., eds.: Towards a Practice of Autonomous Systems: Proceedings of the First European Conference on Artificial Life, 1991, MIT Press (1992) 245–254

3. Pollack, J.B., Watson, R.A.: Recombination Without Respect: Schema Combination and Disruption in Genetic Algorithm Crossover. In et al, D.W., ed.: Proc. GECCO-2000, Morgan Kaufmann (2000) 112–119
4. Watson, R.A., Pollack, J.B.: Symbiotic Combination as an Alternative to Sexual Recombination in Genetic Algorithms. In Schwefel, H.P., Schoenauer, M., Deb, K., Rudolph, G., Yao, X., Lutton, E., Merelo, J.J., eds.: Parallel Problem Solving from Nature VI, Springer Verlag (2000)
5. Spears, W.M.: Crossover or Mutation? In Whitley, L.D., ed.: Foundations of Genetic Algorithms 2. Morgan Kaufmann (1993) 221–237
6. Spears, W.M., Jong, K.A.D.: On the Virtues of Parameterized Uniform Crossover. In Belew, R., Booker, L., eds.: Proceedings of the Fourth International Conference on Genetic Algorithms, Morgan Kaufman (1991) 230–236
7. Skinner, C.: Selection, Mutation and the Discovery of Lowest-Level Building Blocks. In Barry, A.M., ed.: GECCO 2003: Proceedings of the Bird of a Feather Workshops, Genetic and Evolutionary Computation Conference, AAAI (2003)
8. Sastry, K., Goldberb, D.E.: Analysis of Mixing in Genetic Algorithms: A Survey. Technical Report 2002012, Illinois Genetic Algorithms Laboratory (IlliGAL) (2002)
9. Holland, J.H.: Adaptation in Natural and Artificial Systems. The University of Michigan Press (1975)

An Analysis of the Effectiveness of Multi-parent Crossover

Chuan-Kang Ting

International Graduate School of Dynamic Intelligent Systems
University Paderborn, 33098 Paderborn, Germany
ckting@upb.de

Abstract. Multi-parent crossovers have shown their superiority over classic two-parent crossovers in several problems. However, they still lack theoretical foundation to support the advantages of using more than two parents. In this paper we propose a uniform population model that helps analyze the behavior of crossover beyond the influence of selection process and the number of parents. An analysis of the probability for multi-parent diagonal crossover to obtain the optimal solution is derived accordingly. Analytical results demonstrate the advantage and limitation of multi-parent crossovers over two-parent crossover.

1 Introduction

Genetic algorithms (GAs) have been validated by their outstanding performance in a variety of optimization problems. The basic idea of GAs is to simulate the mechanisms of natural evolution such as selection, crossover, and mutation [1]. Crossover is one of the most salient features in GAs. It reproduces offspring by exchanging and recombining genetic information from selected parents.

GAs traditionally perform crossover with two parents. This is reasonable because, to the best of our knowledge, all sexual organisms on earth adopt two parents to reproduce their offspring. However, it is possible for GAs to break through this limitation. Beyond two parents, Eiben et al. proposed scanning crossover [4] and diagonal crossover [5, 6] as generalization of uniform crossover and one-point crossover, respectively. In addition, Mühlenbein et al. [8, 14] introduced the concept of global recombination, a common recombination used in evolutionary strategies [9], into GAs as a gene pool recombination (GPR). Instead of only two parents, GPR samples the genes for recombination from the gene pool consisting of several pre-selected parents. Tsutsui and Jain [12] further proposed multi-cut crossover (MX) and seed crossover (SX). Multi-cut crossover generalizes the classic two-point crossover. In terms of real-coded GAs, Tsutsui and Ghosh [10, 11] presented a series of multi-parent crossovers: the center of mass crossover (CMX), multi-parent feature-wise crossover (MFX), and seed crossover (SX). Furthermore, simplex crossover (SPX) [13] was proposed to reproduce by sampling a simplex formed from multiple parents. Kita et al. [7] introduced the concept of multiple parents into the unimodal normal distribution crossover (UNDX) to improve its performance. These multi-parent crossovers successfully demonstrate the power of using more parents [2, 3]. However, the effectiveness of them is examined empirically. It still lacks theoretical analysis to validate the advantage of multiple parents.

This work proposes a probability model to analyze the effectiveness of diagonal crossover – a multi-parent generalization of the classic one-point crossover. First, a uniform population model is proposed to analyze the effectiveness of crossover beyond the influence of selection process and the number of parents. Second, we analyze the probability for multi-parent diagonal crossover to obtain the optimal solution. Analytical results of this proposed probability model show its capability of explaining the superiority and limitation of multi-parent crossover over the classic 2-parent crossover.

The rest of this paper is organized as follows. Section 2 presents the uniform population model. In Section 3 a description and formal definition of diagonal crossover is given. Section 4 describes the proposed probability model for the effectiveness of multi-parent diagonal crossover. Analytical results are presented in Section 4 as well. Finally, conclusions are drawn in Section 5.

2 Uniform Population

In this paper, we present the *uniform population* as the basis for analyzing the effectiveness of crossover. Crossover is an operator used to recombine and exchange the genetic material of selected parents. However, the outcome of crossover depends upon the composition of population and the selected parents. For this, we propose the uniform population model to focus on the effectiveness of crossover beyond the effects of population composition and selection process.

We start with the formal definition of components in GAs.

Definition 1 (Chromosome and Population)
(a) A chromosome $\vec{c}$ is encoded as an l-bit string: $\vec{c} := (c_1, \ldots, c_l) \in \{0,1\}^l$, where $c_i \in \{0,1\}$ denotes a gene and l is called chromosome length.
(b) A population P is a set of chromosomes[1]: $P = \{\vec{c}_1, \ldots, \vec{c}_m \mid \vec{c}_i \in \{0,1\}^l\}$. The cardinality m is called population size.

A population is defined to be *uniform* if each chromosome in this population has a distance from the optimal solution[2] by k genes. In other words, the hamming distance between the optimal solution and any chromosome in uniform population is exactly k. Here the value k is called the *order* of uniform population.

Definition 2 (k-Order Uniform Population)
Let $\vec{c}^*$ be the only optimal solution for the given problem. A k-order uniform population, denoted as $P_{(k)}$, is defined by

$$P_{(k)} = \{\vec{c}_1, \ldots, \vec{c}_m \mid \vec{c}_i \in \{0,1\}^l \text{ and } H(\vec{c}_i, \vec{c}^*) = k\}, \tag{1}$$

where H is the hamming distance function.

---

[1] In this paper, the population is assumed to contain no duplicate chromosomes; that is, $\forall \vec{c}_i, \vec{c}_j \in P : \vec{c}_i \neq \vec{c}_j$ for $i \neq j$.
[2] We assume there is only one optimal solution for the given problem.

Example. Without loss of generality we assume the optimal solution is '000...000', i.e. l number of zeros. A 1-order uniform population $P_{(1)}$, consisting m chromosomes, is illustrated in Fig. 1. △

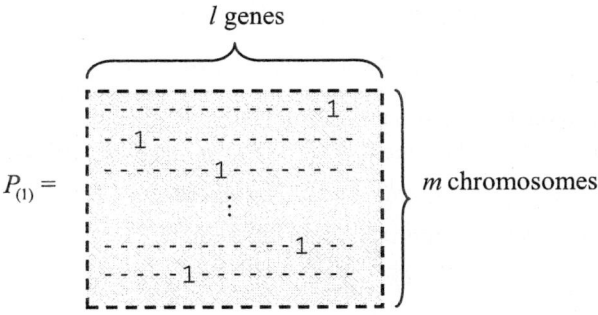

Fig. 1. A 1-order uniform population ('1' represents the bit 1, and '-' represents the bit 0).

Remark 1 *From a k-order uniform population the set of selected parents[3] forms a k-order uniform population as well.*

This characteristic helps to analyze crossover without concerning the composition and the number of selected parents.

3 Diagonal Crossover

Diagonal crossover was first proposed by Eiben [5] as a generalization of the classic one-point crossover. For n parents, diagonal crossover cuts each parent into n segments by $(n-1)$ cutting points. Thereafter the crossover picks one segment from each parent in a diagonal way and recombines these segments into complete offspring. This manner of picking segments gives the name 'diagonal' crossover. Figure 2 illustrates a 4-parent diagonal crossover. Clearly diagonal crossover with 2 parents will coincide with one-point crossover; that is, diagonal crossover generalizes one-point crossover.

The formal definitions about one-point crossover and diagonal crossover are given as follows.

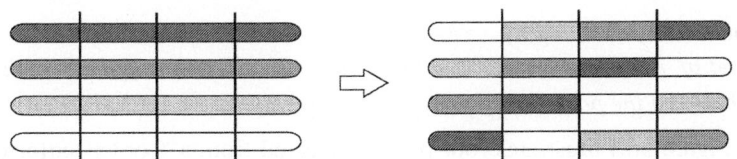

Fig. 2. Diagonal crossover.

---

[3] *This paper assumes there is no duplicate in the set of selected parents.*

Definition 3 (One-point Crossover)
Let $(\vec{p}_1, \vec{p}_2) = (\vec{c}_u, \vec{c}_v) \in P$ be a pair of parents selected from population P and $\vec{c}_u \neq \vec{c}_v$. Given a crossover position $\chi \in \{1, \ldots, l-1\}$, this cutting point χ separates the parent $\vec{p}_i$ into two segments $\vec{p}_{i,1}$ and $\vec{p}_{i,2}$, e.g. $\vec{p}_{1,1} = (c_{u_1}, \ldots, c_{u_\chi})$ and $\vec{p}_{1,2} = (c_{u_{\chi+1}}, \ldots, c_{u_l})$. The offspring $\vec{c}'$ is then reproduced by

$$\vec{c}' = (\vec{p}_{1,1}, \vec{p}_{2,2}) = (c_{u_1}, \ldots, c_{u_\chi}, c_{v_{\chi+1}}, \ldots, c_{v_l}). \tag{2}$$

Definition 4 (Diagonal Crossover)
Let $(\vec{p}_1, \ldots, \vec{p}_n) \in P$ be n parents and $\vec{p}_i \neq \vec{p}_j$ for any $i \neq j$. Given $(n-1)$ cutting points $\chi_1, \ldots, \chi_{n-1} \in \{1, \ldots, l-1\}$, they cut parent $\vec{p}_i$ into n segments $\vec{p}_{i,1}, \vec{p}_{i,2}, \ldots, \vec{p}_{i,n}$. The diagonal crossover then reproduces the offspring $\vec{c}'$ by

$$\vec{c}' = (\vec{p}_{1,1}, \vec{p}_{2,2}, \ldots, \vec{p}_{n,n}). \tag{3}$$

Remark 2 Diagonal crossover generalizes one-point crossover.
Proof Given two parents $(\vec{p}_1, \vec{p}_2)$, the offspring reproduced by diagonal crossover can be represented as

$$\vec{c}' = (\vec{p}_{1,1}, \vec{p}_{2,2}), \tag{4}$$

which coincides with one-point crossover in (2). Therefore diagonal crossover generalizes one-point crossover. □

4 Analysis of Effectiveness

In this paper, we analyze the effectiveness of crossover under 1-order uniform population $P_{(1)}$. By the definition each chromosome in the 1-order uniform population has a hamming distance of 1 gene from the optimal solution. This 1-order uniform population can be viewed as a population in the final stage of evolution, i.e. next to the convergence of evolution. The related definitions of 1-order uniform population and the criterion for the effectiveness of crossover are stated as follows.

Definition 5 (Distinct gene)
Given a parent $\vec{p} \in P_{(1)}$, the distinct gene of $\vec{p}$, denoted as d, is the only different gene between the chromosome $\vec{p}$ and the optimal solution $\vec{c}^*$.

Definition 6 (Distinct Length)
Given a set of n distinct genes $D = \{d_1, \ldots, d_n\}$, the distinct length δ is the longest distance between the positions of these distinct genes.

Example Figure 3(a) illustrates four parents selected from a 1-order uniform population ($l = 7$). Here the optimal solution is still assumed as '0000000'. Then the parents can be represented in the form of distinct genes as shown in Fig. 3(b), where the symbol 'd' denotes the distinct gene while the symbol '−' denotes the same genes with the optimal solution. The distinct length of parents in Fig. 3 is the distance between the distinct genes of parent 1 and 2; thus $\delta = 6 - 2 = 4$. △

```
p1: 0100000              -d-----
p2: 0000010              -----d-
p3: 0000100              ----d--
p4: 0010000              --d----
     (a)                    (b)
```

Fig. 3. Examples of (a) parents selected from uniform population $P_{(1)}$, (b) the corresponding distinct genes.

Definition 7 (Effectiveness of Crossover)
Let $\vec{c}^*$ be the optimal solution and $\vec{c}'$ be the offspring reproduced by crossover $\mathcal{X}$, i.e. $\vec{c}' \leftarrow \mathcal{X}(\vec{p}_1, \ldots, \vec{p}_n)$, where $\vec{p}_i \in P_{(k)}$. The effectiveness of crossover is defined:

$$\mathcal{X} \text{ is effective} \Leftrightarrow H(\vec{c}', \vec{c}^*) = 0. \tag{5}$$

A crossover operation $\mathcal{X}$ is classified *effective* if it can yield the optimal solution with the selected parents. For example, in Fig. 3, a crossover is classified *effective* if it can reproduce offspring without any distinct gene 'd' (or gene '1'), i.e. the optimal solution '0000000'.

4.1 Probability of Effectiveness

This section formulates the probability of effectiveness for multi-parent crossover. Selecting n parents from 1-order uniform population $P_{(1)}$, there will be n distinct genes participating in the crossover operation. According to the definition, a crossover is effective if it can reproduce the offspring without distinct genes, i.e. the optimal solution. Let D denote the set of distinct genes in the offspring and $|D|$ denote the cardinality of D. Given n distinct genes, the probability (p_d) that a crossover reproduces an offspring with no distinct genes is

$$p_d = \mathcal{P}(|D|=0) = 1 - \mathcal{P}(|D|=1,2,\ldots,n) = 1 - \mathcal{P}\left(\bigcup_{i=1}^{n} d_i\right). \tag{6}$$

Given n distinct genes, the probability to select a certain distinct gene d_i is $\mathcal{P}(d_i) = \frac{1}{n}$. Thus the probability of reproducing no distinct genes can be derived:

$$\begin{aligned}
p_d &= 1 - \mathcal{P}\left(\bigcup_{i=1}^{n} d_i\right) \\
&= 1 - \left[\sum_{1}^{n} \mathcal{P}(d_i) - \sum_{i<j} \mathcal{P}(d_i \cap d_j) + \sum_{i<j<k} \mathcal{P}(d_i \cap d_j \cap d_k) + \cdots \right. \\
&\quad \left. + (-1)^{n+1} \sum \mathcal{P}(d_1 \cap d_2 \cap \ldots \cap d_n)\right] \\
&= 1 - \left[\binom{n}{1}\frac{1}{n} - \binom{n}{2}\frac{1}{n}\frac{1}{n-1} + \binom{n}{3}\frac{1}{n}\frac{1}{n-1}\frac{1}{n-2} + \cdots + (-1)^{n+1}\binom{n}{n}\frac{1}{n!}\right]
\end{aligned} \tag{7}$$

$$= 1 - \left[1 - \frac{1}{2!} + \frac{1}{3!} - \frac{1}{4!} + \cdots + (-1)^{(n+1)}\left(\frac{1}{n!}\right)\right] = \sum_{i=0}^{n} \frac{(-1)^i}{i!} .$$

It is worthy to note that the probability p_d will approach the constant $e^{-1} \approx 0.367879$ when n is large enough.

Equation (7) cannot directly represent the probability of effectiveness because the positions of cutting points should be taken into account. Depending on the definition of diagonal crossover, an n-parent diagonal crossover will result in $(n-1)$ cutting points. An effective crossover, however, needs at least one cutting point existing inside the range of distinct genes: the distinct length δ is used to describe this range.

Given the chromosome length L, the number of possible cutting positions l_χ is $l_\chi = l - 1$. Let $|X|$ denote the number of cutting points inside the distinct length, for 2-parent diagonal crossover the probability that there exits one (exact one) cutting point inside the distinct length is

$$P(|X| = 1) = \frac{\delta}{l_\chi} = 1 - \frac{l_\chi - \delta}{l_\chi} . \quad (8)$$

Extending (8) to more parents, the probability (p_χ) that there exists at least one cutting points inside the distinct length for n-parent crossover can be generalized:

$$\begin{aligned} p_\chi(\delta) &= P(|X| \geq 1) \\ &= 1 - P(|X| = 0) \\ &= 1 - \binom{l_\chi - \delta}{n-1} / \binom{l_\chi}{n-1} = 1 - \frac{(l-1-\delta)_{n-1}}{(l-1)_{n-1}} , \end{aligned} \quad (9)$$

where $(x)_n$ denotes the falling factorial of x.

The probability of effectiveness can then be obtained by multiplying the independent probability p_d and p_χ:

$$\begin{aligned} p_E^*(\delta) &= P(\mathcal{X} \text{ is effective}) \\ &= p_d \cdot p_\chi(\delta) . \end{aligned} \quad (10)$$

Theorem 1 *Given n parents selected from $P_{(1)}$ and the consequent distinct length δ, the probability of effectiveness for n-parent diagonal crossover, p_E^*, is:*

$$p_E^*(\delta) = \left(\sum_{i=0}^{n} \frac{(-1)^i}{i!}\right)\left[1 - \frac{(l-1-\delta)_{n-1}}{(l-1)_{n-1}}\right] . \quad (11)$$

Proof The steps of proof have been demonstrated in the above text. □

Next, we examine the expectation of the probability of effectiveness. To obtain the expectation of $p_E^*(\delta)$, we need the probability distribution of distinct length δ. For 2 parents, the distinct length is the distance between two loci of distinct genes. Assume the probability distribution of distinct gene on each locus is uniform; the probability distribution of distinct length δ for 2 parents is

$$\mathcal{P}(\delta) = (l-\delta) \Big/ \binom{l}{2}, \quad \delta \in \{1,\ldots,l-1\}. \tag{12}$$

The increase of parents means that there are more distinct genes. With more distinct genes between these 2 loci, the number of combinations is $C(\delta-1, n-2)$. This gives the probability mass function (p_δ) of distinct length for n parents:

$$\begin{aligned}
p_\delta &= (l-\delta) \binom{\delta-1}{n-2} \Big/ \binom{l}{n} \\
&= (l-\delta) \frac{n(n-1)\cdot(\delta-1)_{n-2}}{(l)_n}.
\end{aligned} \tag{13}$$

Thus, the expected value can be derived:

$$\mathrm{E}\!\left[p_E^*\right] = \sum_{\delta=1}^{l-1} p_E^*(\delta) \cdot p_\delta. \tag{14}$$

Theorem 2 *Given n parents selected from 1-order uniform population $P_{(1)}$, the expectation of effectiveness for n-parent diagonal crossover is:*

$$\mathrm{E}\!\left[p_E^*\right] = \left(\sum_{i=0}^{n} \frac{(-1)^i}{i!}\right) \cdot \sum_{\delta=1}^{l-1}\left[1 - \frac{(l-1-\delta)_{n-1}}{(l-1)_{n-1}}\right] \cdot (l-\delta) \cdot n(n-1) \cdot \frac{(\delta-1)_{n-2}}{(l)_n}. \tag{15}$$

Proof The steps of proof have been demonstrated in the above text. □

4.2 Analytical Results

In this section we examine the effectiveness of multi-parent diagonal crossover according to the derived probability equations. First we check the probability of effectiveness p_E^*. Figure 4 plots the probabilities p_E^* of different number of parents in terms of chromosome length $l = 100$. For $n \geq 4$, the probability increases with the number of parents in the distinct length shorter than 70 genes. This outcome demonstrates multi-parent diagonal crossover ($n \geq 4$) can achieve satisfying probability of effectiveness even though distinct genes locate close to each other, whereas the classic 2-parent diagonal crossover cannot perform comparably in such a condition. On the other hand, when the distinct length is longer than 70 genes, the probability for different numbers of parents, except for 2 and 3 parents, does not make a significant difference. In addition, the result in Fig. 4 demonstrates that probability p_E^* approaches to the value $e^{-1} \approx 0.367879$ when n increases. The 2-parent crossover, nevertheless, breaks through this bound and achieves a higher probability at 0.5. It implies 2-parent crossover can outperform multi-parent crossover in the case of $\delta > 70$. However, this probability of effectiveness p_E^* is dependent upon the distinct length. The probability distribution of distinct length, therefore, should be further taken into account.

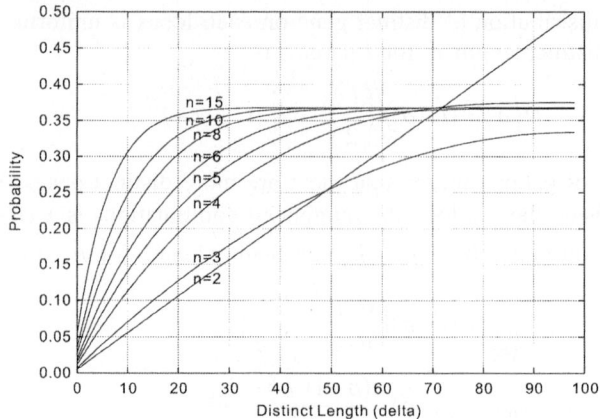

Fig. 4. Probability of effectiveness (p_E^*) in $l = 100$.

Figure 5 illustrates the probability distribution of distinct length, p_δ, in terms of the number of parents selected from 1-order uniform population. This figure shows that the probability of distinct length for 2 parents decreases linearly with the value of distinct length. This characteristic diminishes the advantage of 2-parent crossover in the higher effectiveness of $\delta > 70$. Additionally, as the number of parents n increases ($n > 2$), the longer distinct lengths ($\delta > 70$) account for higher probabilities.

The expectation of effectiveness based on (15) is presented in Fig. 6 in terms of different chromosomes lengths (l) and different numbers of parents (n). Obviously, the expectation of effectiveness augments as the number of parents increases. The diagonal crossover with 5 parents achieves a probability nearly 2 times the probability of effectiveness of 2-parent diagonal crossover. However, this improvement in effectiveness is not unlimited: the expectation will converge to the value $e^{-1} \approx 0.367879$ when the number of parents $n > 5$. It reveals that the increase of parents will not always cause a further enhancement. Specifically, the improvement in effectiveness nearly halts for $n > 5$ according to the results in Fig. 6.

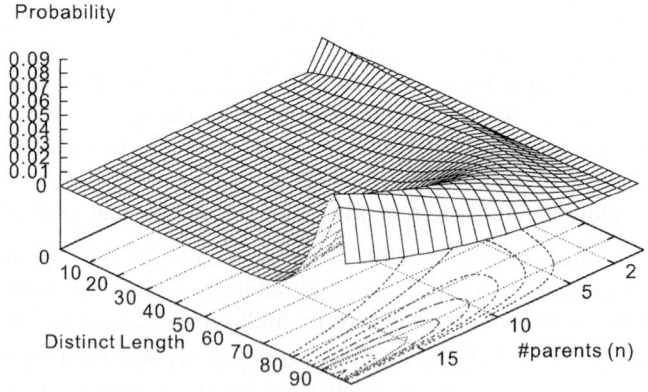

Fig. 5. Probability distribution of distinct length (p_δ) in $l = 100$.

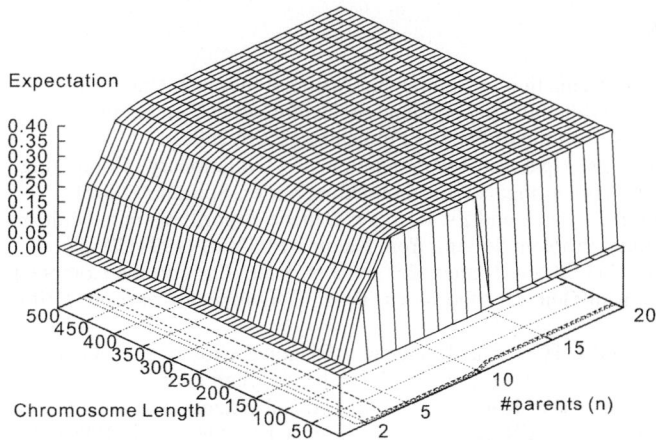

Fig. 6. Expectation of effectiveness of n-parent diagonal crossover ($E\left[p_E^*\right]$).

5 Conclusions

This work analyzes the effectiveness of multi-parent crossover under the 1-order uniform population. The proposed uniform population model helps to analyze the behavior of multi-parent crossover beyond the influence of selection process and the number of parents. Based on this uniform population, a model analyzing the probability that a diagonal crossover can yield the optimal solution is derived.

The analytical results from the proposed probability model demonstrate that multi-parent diagonal crossover can achieve a higher probability of effectiveness than its 2-parent version, namely one-point crossover. Specifically, 5-parent diagonal crossover achieves a probability nearly 2 times the probability of effectiveness of 2-parent diagonal crossover. In addition, the proposed probability model shows that increasing the number of parents does not always lead to an improvement in effecttiveness. Our analysis reveals that the probability of effectiveness will converge to the constant $e^{-1} \approx 0.367879$ as the number of parents increases.

Even though 1-order uniform population represents a specific population condition, it can be viewed as a population in the final stage of evolution. The proposed probability model, therefore, provides an insight into the scenarios of multi-parent crossover as the evolution approaches convergence. Furthermore, this work establishes a theoretical foundation to analyze the effectiveness of crossover. Currently we are extending this analysis to a k-order ($k>1$) uniform population for a more realistic prediction of the effectiveness of multi-parent crossover. Analysis of other crossovers through this method is also underway.

Acknowledgements

The author would like to thank Prof. Hans Kleine Büning, Klaus Brinker, and the anonymous referees for their helpful suggestions and comments on earlier drafts.

References

1. J.H. Holland: Adaptation in Natural and Artificial Systems. Univ. Michigan (1975)
2. A.E. Eiben: Multiparent Recombination. Evolutionary Computation 1: Basic Algorithms and Operators, Institute of Physics Publishing (2000) 289-307
3. A.E. Eiben: Multiparent Recombination in Evolutionary Computing. Advances in Evolutionary Computing, Natural Computing Series, Springer (2002)
4. A.E. Eiben, P-E. Raué, and Zs. Ruttkay: Genetic Algorithms with Multi-parent Recombination. Parallel Problem Solving from Nature - PPSN III (1994) 78-87
5. A.E. Eiben, C.H.M. van Kemenade, and J.N. Kolk: Orgy in the Computer: Multi- parent Reproduction in Genetic Algorithms. Proc. 3rd European Conf. on Artificial Life (1995) 934-945
6. A.E. Eiben and C.H.M. van Kemenade: Diagonal Crossover in Genetic Algorithms for Numerical Optimization. Journal of Control and Cybernetics, vol. 26(3) (1997) 447-465
7. H. Kita, I. Ono, and S. Kobayashi: Multi-parental Extension of the Unimodal Normal Distribution Crossover for Real-coded GAs. Proc. CEC1999, vol. 2 (1999) 1581-1588
8. H. Mühlenbein, M. Schomisch, and J. Born: The Parallel Genetic Algorithm as Function Optimizer. Parallel Computing, vol. 17 (1991) 619-632
9. H.-P. Schwefel: Evolution and Optimum Seeking. Wiley, New York (1995)
10. S. Tsutsui: Multi-parent Recombination in Genetic Algorithms with Search Space Boundary Extension by Mirroring. PPSN V (1998) 428-437
11. S. Tsutsui and A. Ghosh: A Study on the Effect of Multi-parent Recombination in Real Coded Genetic Algorithms. Proc. IEEE Conf. on Evolutionary Comp. (1998) 828-833
12. S. Tsutsui and L.C. Jain: On the Effect of Multi-parents Recombination in Binary Coded GAs. Proc. 2nd. Knowledge-based Intelligent Electronic Systems (1998) 155-160
13. S. Tsutsui, M. Yamamura, and T. Higuchi: Multi-parent Recombination with Simplex Crossover in Real Coded Genetic Algorithms. Proc. GECCO1999. (1999) 657-664
14. H.-M. Voigt and H. Mühlenbein: Gene Pool Recombination and Utilization of Covariances for the Breeder GA. Proc. 2nd Conf. on Evolutionary Computation (1995) 172-177

On the Use of a Non-redundant Encoding for Learning Bayesian Networks from Data with a GA

Steven van Dijk and Dirk Thierens

Institute of Information and Computing Sciences, Utrecht University
P.O.Box 80.089, 3508 TB Utrecht, The Netherlands
{steven,dirk}@cs.uu.nl

Abstract. We study the impact of the choice of search space for a GA that learns Bayesian networks from data. The most convenient search space is redundant and therefore allows for multiple representations of the same solution and possibly disruption during crossover. An alternative search space eliminates this redundancy, and potentially allows a more efficient search to be conducted. On the other hand, a non-redundant encoding requires a more complicated implementation. We experimentally compare several plausible approaches (GAs) to study the impact of this and other design decisions.

1 Introduction

Bayesian Networks (BNs) are probabilistic graphical models that capture a joint probability distribution by explicitly modelling the independences between the statistical variables in a directed acyclic graph (DAG). BNs are widely used as powerful tools for reasoning with uncertainty. One of the drawbacks of BNs is that the construction of the model is very labour-intensive. As a result, much research has been done on algorithms for learning a Bayesian Network from a given database that provides statistical information. The learning problem is NP-hard [1], but various heuristic approaches have been able to find acceptable results.

The learning problem is suitable for solving with a GA since the structure of the problem is easily discernible. A connection between two nodes in the goal network indicates the corresponding variables are dependent. Therefore we can make an assessment of the linkage by identifying in a preprocessing step variables which are dependent. In previous work [2], an undirected graph called the *skeleton* was built that effectively acted as a template for constructing DAGs (by deleting or orienting edges). The assessment of the linkage, as represented by the skeleton, was used in the design of a GA to constrain the search space and to build efficient operators.

To keep the implementation of the GA simple, it used DAGs for its representation. Most probability distributions can be represented with several DAGs. One possible problem that can occur with using DAGs is disruption during crossover. Even when both parents represent the same distribution, they can do so in different ways. Therefore, it will be more difficult for the child to inherit building blocks, a key requirement for many GAs to perform well. A non-redundant representation, therefore, has the potential to allow a more efficient search. In addition, recent theoretical results [3] have shown that the non-redundant search space is more tractable. An optimal solution can be found in the limiting case of very large databases using a simple greedy algorithm [4]. Another potential advantage is that search can become more efficient because no time is wasted on evaluating different solutions that represent the same distribution. Therefore, it is worthwhile to study the impact of the representation on the search process.

Our contributions are as follows. Firstly, we studied the feasibility of using a non-redundant representation for a GA for structure learning of Bayesian networks. Secondly, we investigated the effect of different choices for several crucial design parameters: choice of crossover, choice of representation, and the amount of local search performed on the children after crossover. We used several predictive measures to study the effect of these choices on the search mechanism employed by the GA.

This paper is organised as follows. In Section 2 we discuss related work. Some preliminaries are handled in Section 3. The design of the various GAs are explained in Section 4. A thorough comparison of the algorithms is presented in Section 5. We conclude with a discussion.

2 Related Work

Early work on score-based learning of Bayesian networks from data [5–7] considered only search in the search space of DAGs. As will be explained more fully in the next section, a DAG is a redundant encoding because multiple DAGs can represent the same distribution. A search algorithm based on non-redundant *partial DAGs* (PDAGs) called Greedy Equivalence Search (GES), was proposed by Spirtes and Meek [8]. Chickering [9] described efficient operators to traverse PDAG-space and proved [4] that GES can find the optimal result, provided that the database is large enough. For realistically sized databases, greedy algorithms may still find a local optimum. A variant of GES was introduced by Nielsen et al. [10] that included a tunable stochastic element in the choice of the next graph from the neighbourhood. The algorithm by Castelo and Kočka [3] kept the search in DAG-space, but an additional operator was used to ensure that the representation did not constrain the neighbourhood. Acid and de Campos [11] considered a representation that is more constrained than a PDAG, but is still able to represent multiple DAGs.

The analysis of the search process of GAs and predicting their success has received considerable attention in the literature. Fitness distance correlation was proposed by Jones and Forrest [12] as a single measure that expresses the difficulty of a problem. The measure was found useful under certain circumstances but requires knowledge of the global optimum to be used. In addition, Altenberg [13] showed that it is possible that the measure gives counterintuitive results. He proposed a measure called the *evolvability* of the search process or operator, which is essentially the probability that the output of a certain operator will be better than its input. This approach was generalised to the notion of *fitness evolvability portraits* by Smith et al. [14]. A measure that tries to capture the amount of heritability was proposed by Manderick et al. [15]. They calculate the correlation coefficient of a set of input-output pairs. For crossover, the average fitness of the parents and that of the children can be compared. Low coefficients correspond with disruptive crossover operators, in which the children are not very similar to their parents. A study by Thierens [16] showed that for the problem of training neural networks, a more efficient GA did indeed achieve a higher coefficient. Naudts and Kallel [17] compared several predictive measures such as epistasis measures and autocorrelation, and concluded that any single measure can never be an accurate predictor for all problems. Rothlauf and Goldberg [18] performed an analysis of the use of redundancy in genetic search and concluded that a beneficial effect can only be found if the building block is over-represented. Note that there is no reason to believe that this is the case for DAGs and PDAGs.

To analyse the search mechanisms of the various GAs that we will develop, we will use three measures to study the effect of crossover: the correlation coefficient, the average difference in fitness between parents and children, and the probability that the application of crossover produces fitter children.

3 Preliminaries

A Bayesian Network consists of two components, a directed acyclic graph (DAG) and a set of probability tables associated with the nodes. Each statistical variable is represented by a node in the graph, and we will use both terms interchangeably. The probability table of a node expresses the influences between the node and its parents. A BN has the property that it expresses the joint probability over all variables by a factorisation over the nodes. That is, $P(X_1,\ldots,X_N) = \prod_{i=1}^{n} P_i(X_i \mid \Pi(X_i))$, where $P_i(\cdot)$ is the probability table of node X_i and $\Pi(\cdot)$ yields the parents of a node.

(In)dependences can be read off the graph by a criterion called *d-separation* [19]: two variables X and Y are independent given a set of variables Z if the nodes X and Y are d-separated by Z. Two nodes are d-separated when every path between them (ignoring the directions of the arcs) is *blocked*. The role of so-called v-structures plays an important role in d-separation. If there are three nodes p,q,r, where q has parents p,r and no arc between p and r exists, they are called a *v-structure*. A path can be blocked by Z if it includes the sequence $\ldots p - q - r \ldots$ and one of two conditions holds:

1. The nodes p,q,r do *not* form a v-structure and q is included in Z.
2. The nodes p,q,r form a v-structure and neither q nor any descendant of q is included in Z.

Consider Figure 1 in which a little network with four nodes is shown. Nodes p and r are not separated by $Z = \{\}$ but are by $Z = \{q\}$. With $Z = \{\}$, nodes q and s are separated because q,r,s forms a v-structure. However, if $r \in Z$, q and s are not d-separated.

Now consider the four networks from Figure 2 (left). For the top three networks, using the d-separation criterion reads off the same independence statements. However, the fourth network represents different independences because it consists of a v-structure.

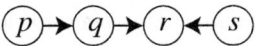

Fig. 1. Example of d-separation. Nodes p and r are d-separated by $Z = \{q\}$. Nodes q and s are d-separated in the v-structure $q \rightarrow r \leftarrow s$ with $Z = \{\}$, but not if $Z = \{r\}$.

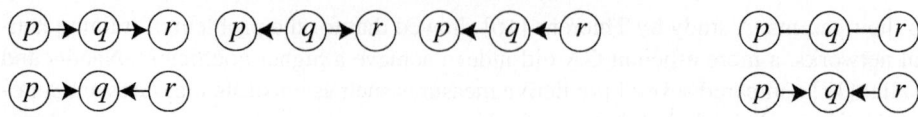

Fig. 2. Left: four DAGs of which the three above are equivalent. Right: PDAG representations.

Consequently, the first three networks are *equivalent:* they can represent exactly the same distributions. The equivalence relation yields a division in equivalence classes. Each such class can be uniquely represented by a graph consisting of arcs to represent v-structures, and edges for other connections. Each DAG in the class can be constructed by orienting the edges without creating new v-structures or cycles. The representation of an equivalence class is called a *partial DAG* (PDAG). Figure 2 (right) shows the PDAG representations of the example DAGs from the figure.

4 GAs for Learning BNs from Data

In previous work [2, 20], we proposed a GA for learning Bayesian networks from data that uses a preprocessing step to rule out implausible dependences between variables. By using only 0- and 1-order dependence tests, an undirected graph called the *skeleton* is built in which each node corresponds to a variable and each edge indicates a plausible dependence between the variables. The GA only searches among DAGs that can be constructed by either replacing the edges in the skeleton with arcs, or removing them. A further study confirmed that the skeleton provides for a careful balance between accuracy and a tractable search space [20]. The GA uses for its representation a string of genes. Each gene correspond to an edge in the skeleton and can be set to the following values: ARCFROM, ARCTO, NONE. The two possible orientations of an arc are indicated with ARCFROM and ARCTO, whereas NONE indicates its removal.

Another characteristic of the GA was that it was built according to principled design rules [21]. Consequently, the crossover operator was constructed with the goals of good mixing and minimal disruption in mind. The structure of the skeleton graph translates directly into an assessment of the linkage: a building block is assumed to be the optimal setting for all edges adjacent to a node in the skeleton. To transfer a building block whole from a parent to a child, crossover is done by repeatedly choosing a node and marking all adjacent edges. When approximately half the edges are marked, they are transfered together from a parent to a child, and the other half is taken from the other parent. We will call this crossover operator *linkage-respecting*. Since building blocks can overlap, a limited amount of local search is performed after crossover to repair possibly disrupted building blocks. Only edges corresponding to possibly disrupted building blocks are considered, and they can be improved only once. The amount of local search is kept minimal to keep children similar to their parents.

Since initialisation and crossover can introduce cycles, an additional operator is applied to the solutions they generate. This operator identifies all cycles and builds a list of connections. From this list a random connection is chosen which is reversed, or deleted if thereby a new cycle is introduced. After the cycle is broken, the list is updated. New connections are chosen from cycles until all cycles are broken.

For the fitness function, any quality measure can be taken. In the original paper [2], the MDL measure was used. Here, we will minimise the BDeu measure as defined by Chickering [9]. This will allow us to compare against the hillclimbing variant as proposed by Chickering. The selection scheme used is the incremental elitist recombination scheme. Crossover is always performed, and no random mutation is used.

PDAG representation. To allow searching in the space of PDAGs, we extend the representation with a possible value (EDGE, denoting an undirected edge) and ensure all operators keep solutions valid PDAGs. Initialisation is done by generating a random DAG (constrained by the connections of the skeleton), and subsequently reducing it to a PDAG. To calculate the fitness of a solution, we temporarily extend it to a DAG. Crossover is done as before. After crossover, single arcs (resulting from a v-structure that was split over two children) are turned into edges. However, breaking cycles and local search are performed in DAG space. Finally, the solution is turned into a PDAG.

Switching back and forth from DAG to PDAG is computationally expensive. However, it does not affect the number of fitness evaluations, which we will use to examine the efficiency of the search. It is possible to avoid switching representations by using only operators that guarantee that the solution remains a valid PDAG [9]. However, this requires a more complicated implementation and is only of practical interest.

GAs. We can now consider several variants of the GA for learning Bayesian networks from data, depending on the choices for representation, crossover, and whether we perform local search. We will compare twelve GAs, by varying three design choices:

1. Representation: we consider the DAG and PDAG representation.
2. Crossover: we consider uniform crossover and our linkage-respecting crossover.
3. Local search: after crossover, local search can be applied on the children. In addition to no optimisation, we considered the local optimisation described above, which we will call *building-block repair*, and a so-called *memetic* approach in which hillclimbing is performed until a local optimum is found.

5 Experiments

To compare the GAs, we conducted experiments based on three real networks. The Alarm network (37 nodes, 46 arcs) is well-known in the learning literature as a de facto benchmark. The Oesoca network [22] (42 nodes, 59 arcs) was built to aid gastroenterologists in assessing the stage of oesophageal cancer and predicting treatment outcome. The VSD network [23] (38 nodes, 52 arcs), was developed for treatment planning for a congenital heart disease. From these networks we generated databases of 500 and 5000 records by logic sampling. We then used the algorithms to learn back the network. All GAs used a population size of 150. Results for the GAs were averaged from five separate runs with different seeds for the random-number generator.

The results are shown in Table 1. For the sake of comparison, results for a DAG-based hillclimber and a PDAG-based hillclimber [4] are provided too. Both hillclimbers can connect any two nodes and start with an empty graph. Results where the hillclimbers are constrained by the same skeleton that the GAs used are provided as well.

All algorithms perform well. Note that most results are scored better than the network from which the data was originally sampled. Among the algorithms, the ones that perform a local search step after crossover slightly outperform the others. The small differences among the algorithms with local search seem insignificant. The use of a non-redundant representation does not seem to incur any benefits. Of particular interest is the result of the hillclimbers on the Oesoca-500 and VSD-500 databases, where they outperform all GAs. This indicates an overly restrictive skeleton.

Table 1. Relative BDeu scores of results. The score of the best result is subtracted from all other scores. Scores closer to zero are better.

	500 records	ALARM	OESOCA	VSD
	Absolute score of best	−7268.78	−9935.01	−9246.84
	Relative score of original	−1535.55	−2601.91	−3119.82
GA	DAG uniform	$-49.25^{25.22}$	$-151.87^{20.45}$	$-53.78^{24.87}$
GA	PDAG uniform	$-60.06^{29.94}$	$-58.50^{17.40}$	$-42.40^{9.89}$
GA	DAG link resp	$-49.80^{25.57}$	$-112.14^{34.66}$	$-47.08^{11.51}$
GA	PDAG link resp	$-65.28^{21.58}$	$-77.71^{29.75}$	$-44.67^{11.87}$
GA	DAG uniform loc srch	$-0.62^{0.76}$	$-11.81^{6.83}$	$-34.14^{0.00}$
GA	PDAG uniform loc srch	$-53.27^{25.15}$	$-8.40^{0.00}$	$-34.14^{0.00}$
GA	DAG link resp loc srch	$-0.31^{0.62}$	$-8.54^{0.27}$	$-34.14^{0.00}$
GA	PDAG link resp loc srch	$-10.80^{12.01}$	$-8.40^{0.00}$	$-34.14^{0.00}$
GA	DAG uniform meme	$0.00^{0.00}$	$-8.40^{0.00}$	$-34.14^{0.00}$
GA	PDAG uniform meme	$0.00^{0.00}$	$-8.40^{0.00}$	$-34.14^{0.00}$
GA	DAG link resp meme	$0.00^{0.00}$	$-8.40^{0.00}$	$-34.14^{0.00}$
GA	PDAG link resp meme	$0.00^{0.00}$	$-8.40^{0.00}$	$-34.14^{0.00}$
HC	DAG	−45.92	−90.96	0.00
HC	PDAG	−123.68	0.00	0.00
HC w. skel	DAG	−110.40	−131.04	−34.14
HC w. skel	PDAG	−138.00	−8.40	−34.14
	5000 records	ALARM	OESOCA	VSD
	Absolute score of best	−50713.37	−76715.90	−74590.96
	Relative score of original	−465.65	−1480.91	−2207.23
GA	DAG uniform	$-642.88^{76.94}$	$-435.59^{94.47}$	$-588.78^{307.64}$
GA	PDAG uniform	$-864.40^{218.32}$	$-372.08^{134.35}$	$-82.74^{64.06}$
GA	DAG link resp	$-728.69^{173.85}$	$-366.65^{198.41}$	$-423.28^{290.45}$
GA	PDAG link resp	$-634.90^{161.89}$	$-200.84^{134.34}$	$-54.87^{9.09}$
GA	DAG uniform loc srch	$-53.01^{28.27}$	$-8.09^{12.49}$	$-0.35^{0.69}$
GA	PDAG uniform loc srch	$-755.70^{44.34}$	$-74.66^{33.37}$	$-32.75^{24.76}$
GA	DAG link resp loc srch	$-21.07^{17.20}$	$-0.76^{1.51}$	$0.00^{0.00}$
GA	PDAG link resp loc srch	$-366.68^{213.07}$	$-47.53^{39.01}$	$-21.56^{25.03}$
GA	DAG uniform meme	$0.00^{0.00}$	$0.00^{0.00}$	$0.00^{0.00}$
GA	PDAG uniform meme	$0.00^{0.00}$	$0.00^{0.00}$	$-1.74^{0.00}$
GA	DAG link resp meme	$0.00^{0.00}$	$0.00^{0.00}$	$-0.35^{0.69}$
GA	PDAG link resp meme	$0.00^{0.00}$	$0.00^{0.00}$	$-1.04^{0.85}$
HC	DAG	−1113.37	−559.54	−101.89
HC	PDAG	−944.23	−1709.90	−5.04
HC w. skel	DAG	−1024.00	−1580.86	−779.71
HC w. skel	PDAG	−4552.28	−1904.14	−5.04

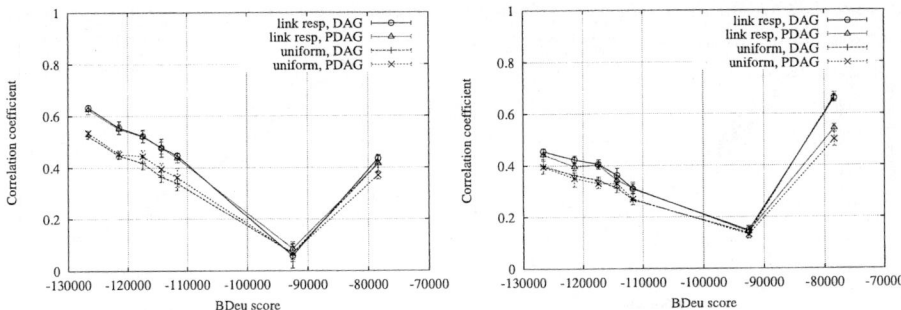

Fig. 3. Heritability of crossover for different slices of the search space for the OESOCA-5000 database. Left/right: without/with BB repair.

Correlation coefficient. We employed three predictive measures to study whether the different variants used different search mechanisms to find their solutions. The first measure calculated the correlation coefficient of the relation between the average fitness of the parents and the average fitness of the children after crossover. For each GA, we generated parents and performed crossover to obtain the children. After 1000 crossovers, we calculated the correlation coefficient . This was done four times, and the coefficients were averaged. Figure 3 shows the results for the Oesoca-5000 dataset. Other datasets showed similar results. To cover the whole search space, parents were obtained by holding tournaments of 1,2,4,8 and 16 randomly-generated individuals. In addition, parents were generated by hillclimbing to a local optimum, or until a specified goal half-way through was reached.

The correlation coefficient is useful for estimating the heritability of the crossover operator. That is, if the GA finds good solutions by combining building blocks in a single individual, children have to inherit the parts of the parents that contributed to the quality of the parents. Recall that the linkage-respecting crossover was constructed to minimise disruption and mix building blocks properly. This expectation is confirmed by the results, in which the GAs that use linkage-respecting crossover have higher coefficients than the GAs that use uniform crossover. Note that there is no difference between GAs that use different representations, except with parents that are the result of hillclimbing to the local optimum. In an actual GA run, a population will be largely converged before parents achieve fitness values that high. However, the difference could be relevant for a memetic algorithm, which always keeps all individuals locally optimised.

Average improvement. Next, we study the average improvement in fitness for different slices of the search space. Figure 4 shows the results for the Oesoca-5000 dataset, which are typical for all datasets considered. There is no significant difference between the two representations. A small difference can be observed between the two crossover operators. At the start of the run, the average improvement in fitness is larger for uniform crossover compared to the linkage-respecting crossover. Further on in the search, fitnesses of the parents will be higher and the results show that uniform crossover will, on average, produce less fit children than the linkage-respecting crossover. This matches our expectations: uniform mixes harder but is also more disruptive. Note that the disruptive disadvantage of uniform crossover disappears when building-block repair is applied to the children.

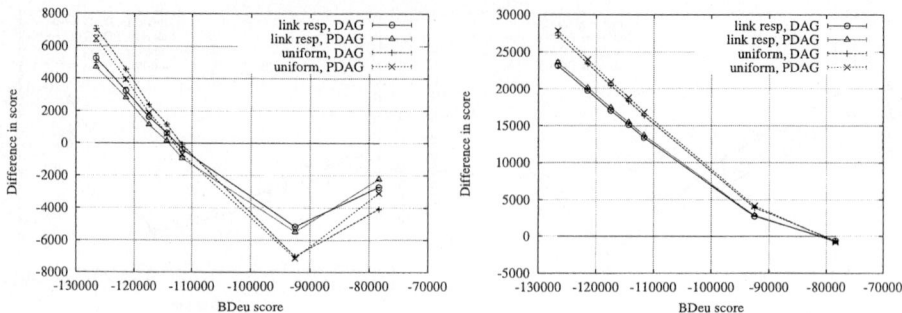

Fig. 4. Change in amount of improvement for Oesoca-5000. Left/right: without/with BB repair.

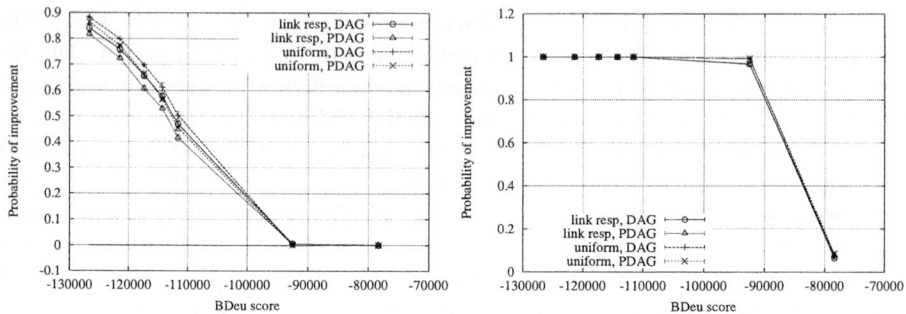

Fig. 5. Change in probability of improvement for Oesoca-5000. Left/right: without/with BB repair.

Probability of improvement. Figure 4 showed that for runs without building-block repair, the children have an average fitness that is lower than their parents fairly quickly. The fraction of children that have higher fitness is shown in Figure 5. We found no significant differences among the algorithms.

Running times. A comparison of running times is shown in Figure 6. Note that we count the number of crossover operations that are performed by the algorithms. This gives us an indication of the number of steps taken by the algorithm to reach its final solution, even though the actual clock time may be much larger. Results for the Oesoca network are shown for both database sizes. The results for Alarm and VSD were comparable. Generally speaking, a division of the algorithms in three groups can be made. The first group contains the memetic algorithms, which took the least number of steps. The second group contains algorithms that employed building-block repair, and the third group used no local search at all. Second-group algorithms took less steps than those of the third group. The use of the non-redundant representation did not improve the efficiency of the search, and may even worsen it. Between both crossovers (uniform and linkage-respecting), no significant differences can be found.

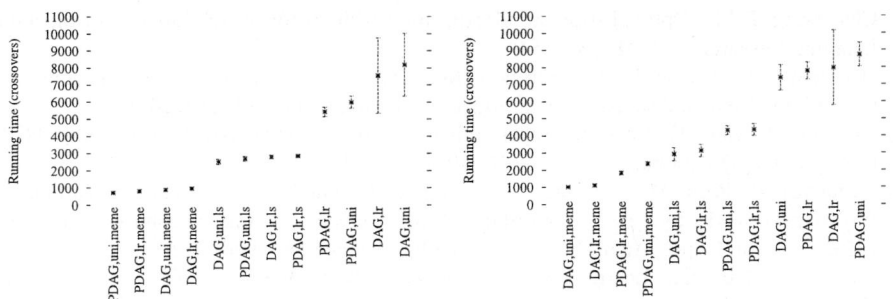

Fig. 6. Comparison of number of crossovers for Oesoca databases. Left/right: 500/5000 cases.

6 Discussion

In this paper, we examined the impact of the choice of representation and other design choices for the problem of learning Bayesian networks from data with a GA. Contrary to expectations, the use of a non-redundant representation does not incur any significant benefit for most variants of the GAs we examined. The only algorithm for which any indication was found that it could benefit was the memetic algorithm, where heritability of the crossover operator was improved by using the PDAG representation.

Our study of the search processes of the GAs found several differences. Firstly, there is a clear benefit in using some form of local search to combat disruption after crossover. It is noteworthy that a minimal amount of local search (as done by the building-block repair) is equally beneficial as a complete jump to the nearest local optimum that the memetic algorithm employs. Secondly, the use of a linkage-respecting crossover does indeed cause less disruption than uniform crossover, as indicated by the higher correlation coefficient. Thirdly, algorithms using a form of local search required less steps to find their solution. Of course, a trade-off is made with the run time of local search itself.

On the whole, there was remarkably little difference in the results of the algorithms tested. Of particular note are the results by the hillclimber, which were shown to be competitive with the genetic algorithms. This suggests that either the GAs failed to find the best solutions, or there was simply not much room for improvement. It seems unlikely that among all GAs tested, no variant would find a close-to-optimal solution. The other possibility, however, is equally surprising, given the long history of research on the learning problem. We intend to resolve this issue in future research.

References

1. Chickering, D.M., Meek, C., Heckerman, D.: Large-sample learning of Bayesian networks is NP-hard. [24] 124–133
2. van Dijk, S., Thierens, D., van der Gaag, L.C.: Building a GA from design principles for learning Bayesian networks. In Cantú-Paz, E., et al., eds.: GECCO. Volume 2723 of Lecture Notes in Computer Science., Springer (2003) 886–897
3. Castelo, R., Kočka, T.: On inclusion-driven learning of Bayesian networks. Journal of Machine Learning Research **4** (2003) 527–574

4. Chickering, D.M.: Optimal structure identification with greedy search. Journal of Machine Learning Research **3** (2002) 507–554
5. Heckerman, D., Geiger, D., Chickering, D.M.: Learning Bayesian networks: The combination of knowledge and statistical data. Machine Learning **20** (1995) 197–243
6. Lam, W., Bacchus, F.: Learning Bayesian belief networks. an approach based on the MDL principle. Computational Intelligence **10** (1994) 269–293
7. Larrañaga, P., Poza, M., Yurramendi, Y., Murga, R., Kuijpers, C.: Structure learning of Bayesian networks by genetic algorithms: A performance analysis of control parameters. IEEE Trans. on Pattern Analysis and Machine Intelligence **18** (1996) 912–926
8. Spirtes, P., Meek, C.: Learning Bayesian networks with discrete variables from data. In Fayyad, U.M., Uthurusamy, R., eds.: Proc. of the First Int. Conf. on Knowledge Discovery and Data Mining, AAAI Press (1995) 294–299
9. Chickering, D.M.: Learning equivalence classes of Bayesian-network structures. Journal of Machine Learning Research **2** (2002) 445–498
10. Nielsen, J.D., Kocka, T., Pena, J.M.: On local optima in learning Bayesian networks. [24]
11. Acid, S., de Campos, L.M.: Searching for Bayesian network structures in the space of restricted acyclic partially directed graphs. Journal of Artificial Intelligence Research **18** (2003) 445–490
12. Jones, T., Forrest, S.: Fitness distance correlation as a measure of problem difficulty for genetic algorithms. In Eshelman, L.J., ed.: Proc. of the 6th Int. Conf. on Genetic Algorithms, Morgan-Kaufmann (1995) 184–192
13. Altenberg, L.: Fitness distance correlation analysis: An instructive counterexample. In Bäck, T., ed.: Proc. of the 7th Int. Conf. on Genetic Algorithms, Morgan-Kaufmann (1997) 57–64
14. Smith, T., Husbands, P., Layzell, P., O'Shea, M.: Fitness landscapes and evolvability. Evolutionary Computation **10** (2002) 1–34
15. Manderick, B., de Weger, M., Spiessens, P.: The genetic algorithm and the structure of the fitness landscape. In Belew, R., Booker, L., eds.: Proc. of the Fourth Int. Conf. on Genetic Algorithms and their Applications, Morgan-Kaufmann (1991)
16. Thierens, D.: Non-redundant genetic coding of neural networks. In: Proc. of the IEEE Int. Conf. on Evolutionary Computation, IEEE Press (1996) 571–575
17. Naudts, B., Kallel, L.: A comparison of predictive measures of problem difficulty in evolutionary algorithms. IEEE Trans. on Evolutionary Computation **4** (2000) 1
18. Rothlauf, F., Goldberg, D.E.: Redundant representations in evolutionary computation. Evolutionary Computation **11** (2003) 381–415
19. Pearl, J.: Probabilistic Reasoning in Intelligent Systems: Networks of Plausible Inference. Morgan Kaufmann (1988)
20. van Dijk, S., van der Gaag, L.C., Thierens, D.: A skeleton-based approach to learning Bayesian networks from data. In Lavrač, N., et al., eds.: PKDD. Volume 2838 of Lecture Notes in Computer Science., Springer (2003) 132–143
21. van Dijk, S., Thierens, D., de Berg, M.: On the design and analysis of competent selectorecombinative GAs. Evolutionary Computation **12** (2004)
22. van der Gaag, L.C., Renooij, S., Witteman, C., Aleman, B., Taal, B.: Probabilities for a probabilistic network: A case-study in oesophageal cancer. Artificial Intelligence in Medicine **25** (2002) 123–148
23. Peek, N., Ottenkamp, J.: Developing a decision-theoretic network for a congenital heart disease. In Keravnou, E., et al., eds.: Proc. of the 6th European Conf. on Artificial Intelligence in Medicine, Springer (1997) 157–168
24. Meek, C., Kjærulff, U., eds.: Proc. of the 19th Conf. on Uncertainty in Artificial Intelligence. In Meek, C., Kjærulff, U., eds.: Proc. of the 19th Conf. on Uncertainty in Artificial Intelligence, Morgan-Kaufmann (2003)

Phase Transition Properties of Clustered Travelling Salesman Problem Instances Generated with Evolutionary Computation

Jano I. van Hemert[1] and Neil B. Urquhart[2]

[1] National Institute for Mathematics and Computer Science, Amsterdam (CWI)
jvhemert@cwi.nl
[2] School of Computing, Napier University, Edinburgh
n.urquhart@napier.ac.uk

Abstract. This paper introduces a generator that creates problem instances for the Euclidean symmetric travelling salesman problem. To fit real world problems, we look at maps consisting of clustered nodes. Uniform random sampling methods do not result in maps where the nodes are spread out to form identifiable clusters. To improve upon this, we propose an evolutionary algorithm that uses the layout of nodes on a map as its genotype. By optimising the spread until a set of constraints is satisfied, we are able to produce better clustered maps, in a more robust way. When varying the number of clusters in these maps and, when solving the Euclidean symmetric travelling salesman person using Chained Lin-Kernighan, we observe a phase transition in the form of an easy-hard-easy pattern.

1 Introduction

During the development of new algorithms for solving combinatorial optimisation problems, it is important to discover the limits within which each algorithm operates successfully. Accepted practice has often been to test new techniques on problem instances used in previous studies. Such problem instances include those published by Solomon [1] or those available via OR-LIB [2]. A disadvantage with such an approach is that the techniques developed may become somewhat fitted to the problem instances, in a similar way as classification techniques can be overfitted to data [3]. This phenomenon is well known in the field of neural networks, where is under study since the late eighties [4]. Contrary to benchmark suites, parameterized problem generators provide customisable problem instances, which may involve specific constraints to which each instance must adhere. Furthermore, the investigator may produce instances that differ only in a very specific manner, thus allowing the influence of a particular aspect of the problem to be investigated thereby focusing on the weak or strong points of a technique.

Solomon [1] originally published 56 instances of the vehicle routing problem in 1983, each containing 100 customers, these instances have been extensively used in the literature, in studies on both the vehicle routing problem [5, 6] and the travelling salesman problem TSP [7]. Backer et al. [8] have transformed these instances into a static set of problem instances that can be used for studies on dynamic vehicle routing. A various number of problem instances relating to various vehicle routing problems are available on-line from OR-LIB [2]. The upside of these problem instances is that benchmark results are easy accessible. However, the downside to that this has led to many publications that contribute new techniques which only provide an improvement over previous techniques on these instances without showing the weak and strong points in relation to the problem class itself. Braun and Buhmann [9] provide evidence of what the effect can be of performance studies on a fixed set of Euclidean TSP instances. In their study they attempt to improve their algorithm by learning the underlying common structural properties of problem instances and using it to guide the search. This led to an overfitting effect as soon as the algorithm learned from optimal solutions.

Beck et al. [10] use a simple problem generator to produce specialist vehicle routing problems. The locations for possible delivery point layout are determined from a file containing the (x, y) coordinates of postal codes within the City of Glasgow, distances between them being calculated as Manhattan distances. The remaining items, such as job length, were set using user defined parameters. This makes it a kind of hybrid approach where reality is mixed with artificial data. In this study we shall use a map generator to produce layouts of locations in an artificial way while keeping a link with real routing problem by focusing on a property often observed in real routing problems, that of clustered locations. This may help us to identify what structure in a map would make solving a routing problem more difficult. Instead of working with full routing problems, we simplify our analysis here by focusing on the Euclidean symmetric travelling salesman problem (TSP). The objective in the Euclidean symmetric TSP is to find the shortest Hamiltonian path through all the nodes. These nodes lie in a 2-dimensional space and the distance to travel between two of them is defined as the Euclidean distance. The TSPLIB [11] problem instances repository contains 112 problem instances of this type. It makes a nice starting point for testing new algorithms, as it also contains optimal and best known results. However, besides the aforementioned problem of overfitting, it also contains insufficient problem instances for current research purposes. The total number of instances in this study lies over 27 000.

The work of Cheeseman at al. [12] was the first of many studies on the phenomena of phase transitions in constraint satisfaction and constrained optimisation problems. A phase transition occurs in many NP-complete problems, when one or more order parameters are varied. The system that is created this way moves through an easy-hard-easy pattern. For example, in graph k-colouring, when one tries to solve different problem instances where the ratio of edges in the graph is varied, at a certain point the average effort required to solve problem instances with that ratio of edges, will be the highest. For a while, the consensus was that no such phase transition occurs in the travelling salesman problem.

This changed with the work of Gent and Walsh [13], wherein it was shown that, although no phase transition occurs in the optimisation problem, it does occur in the equivalent decision problem with either the tour length or the number of nodes as the order parameter. Here we will show that another order parameter exists, which reveals a phase transition in the optimisation problem of TSP. By varying the number of clusters in generated Euclidean symmetric TSP instances, an easy-hard-easy patter can be identified. Furthermore, a preliminary estimation is given of the location of the, on average, most difficult to solve problem instances.

The general outline of the paper is as follows. First, we shall introduce the concept of generating maps. Then in Section 3, we introduce an evolutionary algorithm that makes layouts of maps with clustered nodes. The tools used in the experiments are discussed in Section 4. Section 5.1 presents a robust set of parameters to be used in the objective function of the evolutionary algorithm. These parameter settings are used in further experiments. In Section 5.2 we compare maps created by two different methods. In Section 5.3 we show that, when the ratio of clusters is varied, a phase transition occurs in the difficulty of solving travelling salesman problems with Chained Lin-Kernighan. We draw conclusions in Section 6.

2 Generating 2-Dimensional Maps

The evolutionary algorithm discussed in the next section is part of a larger software package, which will facilitate in creating routing problems. It is incorporated in a map generator that can distribute a given number of nodes onto a 2-dimensional plane with a given size. This can be done using uniform sampling or using the evolutionary algorithm. When a number of clusters is supplied it will first create the centres of these clusters, and then, distribute the nodes equally over these clusters. For uniform sampling, the amount of space to which a cluster is confined is equal to a rectangular area defined by the maximum width and height, both divided by the number of clusters. The evolutionary algorithm restricts the size and spread of clusters by trying to satisfy two constraints; first, the maximum distance between nodes and second, the minimum distance between nodes.

Attempting to satisfy both constraints is in many cases impossible, for instance as the minimum distance is increased, it becomes more difficult to fit larger numbers of nodes into smaller maps. As the minimum and maximum distance constraints move closer together so the number of feasible solutions becomes less. A similar relationship exists between the numbers of locations that may be placed within a given area with respect to the maximum distance constraint.

3 Evolutionary Algorithm for Generating Maps

The representation of each individual takes the form of a list of points each representing one node point on the map. The evolutionary algorithm employs a steady-state evolutionary model with 2-tournament selection [14, Part C2.3] to determine the pool of parents, and to determine the replacement. A population size of 20 is used, where 10 new individuals are created at each generation. Two-point crossover is used with a recombination rate of 0.5 [14, Part C3.3.1.2]. The offspring not created by the recombination of two parents are directly cloned from one parent. Mutation is applied to all offspring. A mutation is defined as the translation of a node by a small, randomly chosen, amount j. Initially, all nodes are set to the origin which is located at the centre of the map. At the start, the translations are performed using a random amount in the range $(0, \ldots, j \times 2)$. If, after a translation, a node will be of the map or on top of another node, other translations are tried until this is resolved. The value j is initially set to the maximum inner cluster distance. After 100 generations have passed without an improvement, j is reduced by 10%. This is repeated over the run of the algorithm. Thus the amount of adjustment made to the positions of nodes decreases as the algorithm progresses. This cooling down is a familiar process in evolutionary computation [14, Part E1.2.3]. When either $j = 0$, a solution is found, or 5 000 generations are past the evolutionary algorithm is terminated.

To compute the fitness of an individual we first calculate the Euclidean distance between all of nodes, during which the smallest distance (min) and the largest distance (max) is noted. The fitness is then computed as follows:

fitness $= 0$
if min $<$ *minimum-distance* **then**
    fitness $=$ *fitness* $+$ *minimum-distance* $-$ min
if max $>$ *maximum-distance* **then**
    fitness $=$ *fitness* $+$ max $-$ *maximum-distance*

This fitness needs to be minimised, where *fitness* $= 0$ means a solution is found and the algorithm will terminate.

4 Tools

Here we discuss two tools, which will be used in the experiments. First, the clustering algorithm GDBSCAN and second, the Chained Lin-Kernighan algorithm for solving travelling salesman problems.

4.1 Density-Based Clustering Method Based on Connected Regions with Sufficiently High Density

To measure how well maps are clustered we use the clustering algorithm GDBSCAN [15]. This algorithm uses no stochastic process, assumes no shape of clusters, and works without a predefined number of clusters. This makes it an ideal candidate to cluster 2-dimensional spatial data, as the methods suffers the least amount of bias possible. It works by using an arbitrary neighbourhood function, which in this case is the minimum Euclidean distance. It determines clusters based on their density by first seeding clusters and then iteratively collecting objects that adhere to the neighbourhood function. The neighbourhood function here is a spatial index, which results in a run-time complexity of $O(n \log n)$. This method relies on the way nodes are spread solely in terms of distance, which is our reason for using it to test whether the maps generated contain the number of clusters we have requested. The settings for the minimum Euclidean distance will be set in the experimental setups.

4.2 Chained Lin-Kernighan

To determine the difficulty of problem instances, expressed in how much time is required to get a good solution, we employ the well known Lin-Kernighan [16] algorithm. Here we use Chained Lin-Kernighan with the implementation from the Concorde system [17]. This latter algorithm performs multiple runs of Lin-Kernighan, where for each next run the initial tour is the result of the previous run after a slight perturbation. The number of runs of Lin-Kernighan depends on the size of the input, it equals to the number of cities. The authors have shown that it is an efficient method, with a high probability of achieving optimal routes, even on very large problem instances.

The stochastic nature of Chained Lin-Kernighan requires multiple runs. For each map in a test, we let it perform 50 independent runs. During a run we count the number of elementary steps performed. As opposed to measuring processor time usage, this measure is independent of hardware, software, and programming specifics. The elementary step of Lin-Kernighan, which makes up for more than 99% of the execution time, consists of flipping a segment in the tour.

5 Experiments

In all the experiments we fix the size of a map to 500×500. In this section we shall first determine a robust parameter setting for the constraints in the fitness function of the evolutionary algorithm. Then, we will show the improvement of the EA over uniform sampling. Finally, we shall provide evidence for the occurrence of a phase transition with varying amounts of clusters.

5.1 Finding Robust Parameter Settings

The number of nodes is set to 100 and the number of clusters to 10. Because of the maximum size of the map, the maximum distance constraint of the evolutionary algorithm is set to 500 to make sure the whole area will be used. This leaves us with finding a good value for the minimum distance constraint. As the setting of this parameter determines the spread of the nodes within clusters, it is mostly responsible for the quality of the map. To determine a robust value we try different settings and assess the quality of each setting using GDBSCAN. We vary the minimum distance from 5 to 120, with steps of 5. For each setting we generate 50 maps, and run GDBSCAN with a minimum Euclidean distance of 50. Figure 1

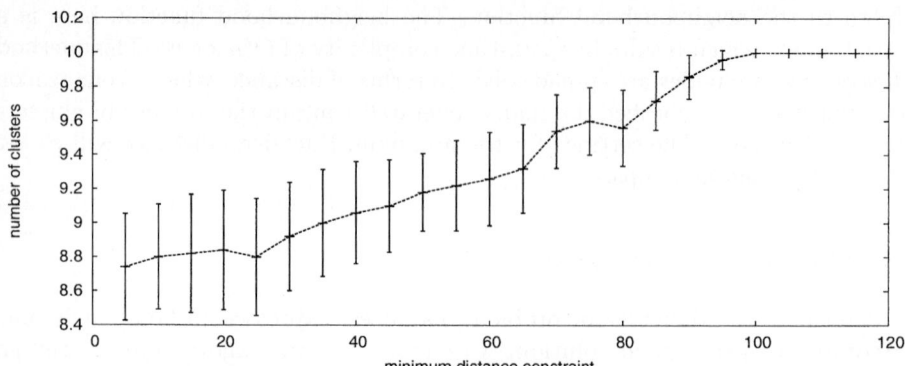

Fig. 1. The effect of the minimum distance constraint on the forming of clusters measured by the average number of clusters found by the GDBSCAN clustering algorithm. Confidence intervals of 95% are shown where for each setting of the minimum distance constraint 50 maps were generated.

shows the average number of clusters found by GDBSCAN in these maps together with 95% confidence intervals.

At a setting of 100 the confidence intervals only maps with 10 clusters are generated. The almost monotone-increasing plot, together with the decrease of the confidence intervals, make this a save setting for further experiments. Higher values will result in sparser clusters, and eventually, overlapping clusters, which is not what we are interested in.

5.2 Comparison with Uniform Randomly Generated

We compare the maps generated with the evolutionary algorithm to maps created uniform randomly as explained in Section 2. First, in Figure 2 we give a visual presentation of a map created with both the evolutionary algorithm and uniform random method. These maps contain 100 nodes and 10 clusters. Generally speaking, the clusters of the map created with the evolutionary algorithm show less deformations than the ones in a map generated uniform randomly. Also, the map created uniform randomly suffers from the size restriction on the map, which is apparent from the cluster at $(500, 125)$. This cluster is squashed against the edge of the map.

Although visual presentations help identify the problems in maps, they do not provide scientific evidence that the evolutionary algorithm creates better maps in a more robust way. To show how well the maps are laid out we use again the GDBSCAN clustering algorithm. Every clustering algorithm needs a definition of what makes a cluster, and such definitions always involve a parameter. In the case of GDBSCAN this parameter is the neighbourhood function, which is defined here as the minimum Euclidean distance. By varying this parameter we get an idea of the sensitivity of the clustering algorithm to the given clustering problems.

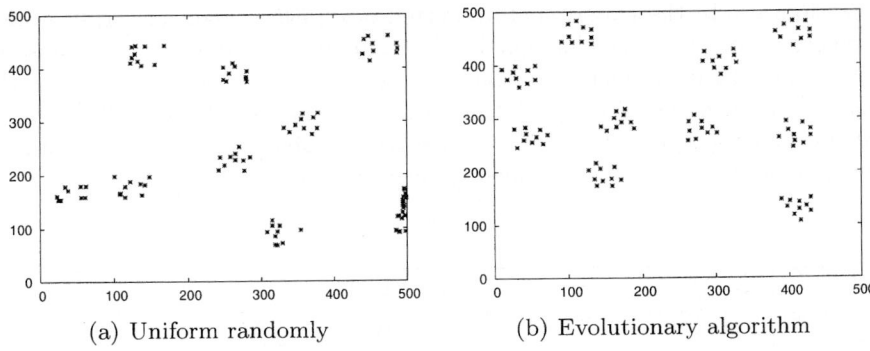

(a) Uniform randomly   (b) Evolutionary algorithm

Fig. 2. Examples of maps with ten clusters.

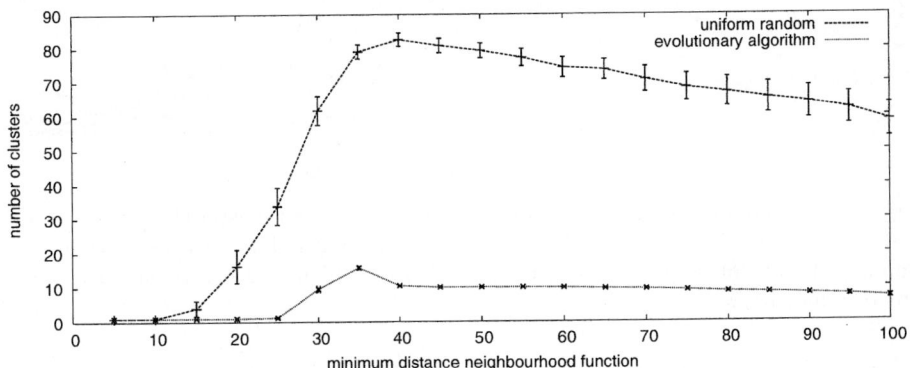

Fig. 3. Analysing the sensitivity of both the evolutionary algorithm and the uniform random method to the clustering parameter. For every setting we generated 50 maps. 95% confidence intervals included.

In Figure 3, we show the sensitivity of the GDBSCAN algorithm to the minimum Euclidean distance parameter when clustering maps from both the evolutionary algorithm and the uniform random method. For very small distances, GDBSCAN is not able to find a clustering. Where maps of the evolutionary algorithm are concerned, from 40 onwards GDBSCAN starts finding the correct number of clusters. It does this with a very low variance, visible from the small confidence intervals. For maps created uniform randomly, only at one setting, which is at approximately 18, the correct number of clusters may be identified. For larger settings, a much too high number of clusters is identified, which shows that the clusters in those maps are not spread in a satisfactory way.

5.3 Phase Transition

We investigate the difficulty of solving the Euclidean symmetric travelling salesman problem, where the problem instances are based on clustered maps generated by the evolutionary algorithm with the robust parameter settings described in Section 5.1. In the experiments reported next, every map, i.e., TSP problem instance, is solved using Chained Lin-Kernighan in 50 independent runs. For each setting of the number of clusters, 50 problem instances are generated, thus making 2500 runs per setting. We perform the same test for 50, 100, 150, and 200 nodes. To measure the difficulty of solving problem instances we count the average amount of Lin-Kernighan steps needed to reach good solutions.

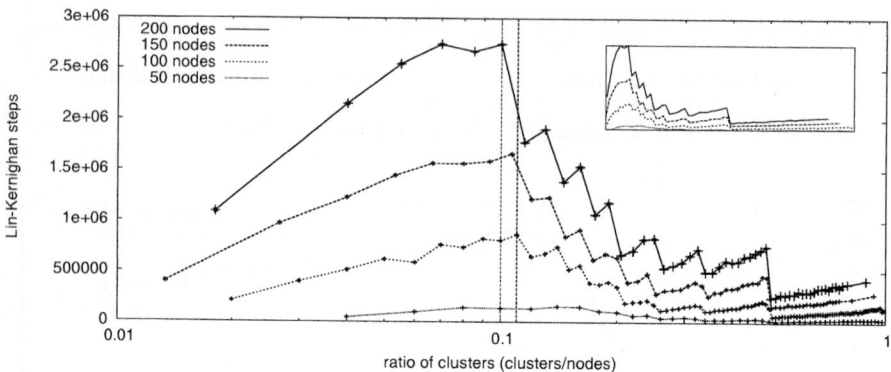

Fig. 4. The difficulty of solving Euclidean symmetric TSP for clustered maps of 50, 100, 150, and 200 nodes, generated with the evolutionary algorithm. At each setting of the number of clusters, 50 maps are generated. 95% confidence intervals included, which are very narrow.

Figure 4 shows the four plots corresponding to the different settings of the number of nodes. As the number of nodes differ for each of the settings, we take as the x-axis the ratio of clusters, i.e., the number of clusters divided by the number of nodes. With increasing ratio of clusters the average difficulty increases to, up until a highest point, after which it decreases with a pattern of short increases and sharp drops. In the easy-hard-easy pattern that appears, we clearly see that the problem instances that are on average the most difficult to solve are found when this ratio lies approximately in the interval $(0.10, 0.11)$.

The pattern of short increases and sharp drops after the peak is related to how nodes are distributed over the clusters. When the number of clusters increases, the difficulty increases until a point is reached when $0 = nodes(\mod clusters)$. By adding one more cluster, the difficulty drops sharply. Thus, an evenly distributed set of loads seems to lead to more difficult to solve problem instances. Note that as the ratio of clusters approaches one, we are essentially creating random problem instances, where most clusters contain only one, and sometimes two, nodes. Such problem instances are much easier to solve than those found near the peak of the phase transition. On average, problem instances at the peak are approximately 5.9 times as difficult as randomly distributed ones, with a standard deviation of 0.6.

6 Conclusions

We have shown that the proposed evolutionary algorithm to layout nodes in a 2-dimensional space is able to create well clustered maps in a robust way. The quality of the spread of nodes in clusters is measured by using GDBSCAN, a clustering algorithm that makes no assumptions about the shape of clusters and the total number of clusters. The resulting maps are of a better quality than those generated using random uniform sampling.

The maps created using the evolutionary algorithm also represent Euclidean symmetric travelling salesman problem instances. Through the use of the Chained Lin-Kernighan algorithm we can show how hard it is to solve these instances, measured in time complexity. When varying the number of clusters a typical phase transition appears, where we get an easy-hard-easy pattern. For the values used in the experiments presented here, i.e., 50, 100, 150, and 200 nodes on a 500 × 500 map, the most difficult to solve instances occur when *clusters/nodes* lies in $(0.10, 0.11)$. This suggests that the position of the phase transition depends only on the ratio of clusters. Moreover, it seems that the distribution of nodes over the clusters has a large impact on the difficulty of solving travelling salesman using the Lin-Kernighan algorithm, where more evenly distributed maps are more difficult to solve.

Future research will be on vehicle routing problems, where clustering is an essential part of the problem. The knowledge gained here will be used to create appropriate maps that will form the basis for non-trivially solved routing problems. Furthermore, research on the travelling salesman problem continues whereby focusing on the difference between using uniform and evolutionary methods as well as by observing larger problem instances.

Acknowledgements

This work is supported by DEAL (Distributed Engine for Advanced Logistics) as project EETK01141 under the Dutch EET programme.

References

1. Solomon, M.M.: Algorithms for the vehicle routing and scheduling problems with time window constraints. Operations Research **35** (1987) 254–264
2. Beasley, J.E.: OR-library: distributing test problems by electronic mail. Journal of the Operational Research Society **41** (1990) 1069–1072
3. Ng, A.Y.: Preventing "overfitting" of cross-validation data. In: Machine Learning: Proceedings of the Fourteenth International Conference. (1997) 245–253
4. Baum, E., Haussler, D.: What size net gives valid generalization? Neural Computation **1** (1989) 151–160
5. Golden, B., Assad, A.: Vehicle Routing: methods and studies. Elsevier Science Publishers B.V. (1988)
6. Toth, P., Vigo, D.: The Vehicle Routing Problem Discrete Math. Society for Industrial and Applied Mathematic (2001)

7. Lawler, E.L., Lenstra, J.K., Rinnooy Kan, A.H.G., Shmoys, D.B.: The Traveling Salesman Problem. John Wiley & Sons, Chichester (1985)
8. Backer, B., Furnon, V., Kilby, P., Prosser, P., Shaw, P.: Solving vehicle routing problems using constraint programming and metaheuristics. Journal of Heuristics **6** (2000)
9. Braun, M.L., Buhmann, J.M.: The noisy euclidean traveling salesman problem and learning. In Dietterich, T.G., Becker, S., Ghahramani, Z., eds.: Advances in Neural Information Processing Systems 14, Cambridge, MA, MIT Press (2002)
10. Beck, J.C., Prosser, P., Selensky, E.: Vehicle routing and job shop scheduling: What's the difference? In: To appear in Proc. of the 13th International Conference on Automated Planning and Scheduling (ICAPS'03). (2003)
11. Reinelt, G.: Tsplib, a library of sample instances for the tsp (and related problems) from various sources and of various types (2002) Available at http://www.iwr.uni-heidelberg.de/groups/comopt/software/TSPLIB95/.
12. Cheeseman, P., Kenefsky, B., Taylor, W.M.: Where the really hard problems are. In: Proceedings of the IJCAI'91. (1991) 331–337
13. Gent, I., Walsh, T.: The TSP phase transition. Artificial Intelligence **88** (1996) 349–358
14. Bäck, T., Fogel, D., Michalewicz, Z., eds.: Handbook of Evolutionary Computation. Institute of Physics Publishing Ltd, Bristol and Oxford University Press, New York (1997)
15. Sander, J., Ester, M., Kriegel, H.P., Xu, X.: Density-based clustering in spatial databases: The algorithm GDBSCAN and its applications. In Data Mining and Knowledge Discovery **2** (1998) 169–194
16. Lin, S., Kernighan, B.W.: An effective heuristic algorithm for the travelling salesman problem. Operations Research **21** (1973) 498–516
17. Applegate, D., Bixby, R., Chvátal, V., Cook, W.: On the solution of traveling salesman problems. Documenta Mathematica Extra Volume Proceedings ICM III (1998) 645–656

A Simple Two-Module Problem to Exemplify Building-Block Assembly Under Crossover

Richard A. Watson

Harvard University, Organismic and Evolutionary Biology,
Cambridge, MA 02138, USA
rwatson@oeb.harvard.edu

Abstract. Theoretically and empirically it is clear that a genetic algorithm with crossover will outperform a genetic algorithm without crossover in some fitness landscapes, and vice versa in other landscapes. Despite an extensive literature on the subject, and recent proofs of a principled distinction in the abilities of crossover and non-crossover algorithms for a particular theoretical landscape, building general intuitions about when and why crossover performs well when it does is a different matter. In particular, the proposal that crossover might enable the assembly of good building-blocks has been difficult to verify despite many attempts at idealized building-block landscapes. Here we show the first example of a two-module problem that shows a principled advantage for crossover. This allows us to understand building-block assembly under crossover quite straightforwardly and build intuition about more general landscape classes favoring crossover or disfavoring it.

1 Introduction

Theoretically and empirically it is clear that a genetic algorithm [1] with crossover will outperform a genetic algorithm without crossover in some fitness landscapes, and vice versa in other landscapes [2]. Historically, there has been much debate about when crossover will perform well, [3],[4],[5],[6], and, in particular, there has been some difficulty, [7],[8], in defining landscapes that exemplify the notion of building-block assembly, as per the building-block hypothesis [1],[9],[10],[11]. However, some analytic results showing a strong advantage for crossover on particular landscapes have been derived, [12], and recently, a proof has been provided that, on a particular landscape, a crossover algorithm is expected to discover fit genotypes in time polynomial in the number of problem variables whereas a mutation hill-climber will require exponential time [13]. This distinction has also been shown in a hierarchical building-block landscape [14],[15],[16]. However, Jansen's example [13] is not designed to exemplify the intuitive assembly of building-blocks, and the hierarchical building-block example [14] is rather complex. There is still much work required to build intuition about when and why crossover might work well when it does, and to understand better how to maximize the possibility of the polynomial versus exponential advantage of crossover in cases where it might be available.

In this paper we introduce a simple abstract fitness landscape that shows a principled advantage for crossover. More importantly, this landscape is the first to show a case where building-block assembly of just two building-blocks is possible under crossover but not possible for a mutation-only method. This example enables us to see a general principle where parallel discovery of high-fitness schemata is easy but sequential discovery of the same schemata is difficult – thus preventing a hill-climber-like process from succeeding. This landscape includes strong fitness interactions within building-blocks (when compared to the interactions between building-blocks) which corresponds well with the intuitions proposed by the building-block hypothesis. It should be noted however, that the parallel discovery of high-fitness schemata requires suitable methods for maintaining population diversity. In [13] Jansen systematically removed duplicate genotypes, and our prior work [16] used deterministic crowding [17] – both methods assume that genotypic diversity was meaningful for maintaining diversity. In this paper we use a simple multi-deme island model [18] to maintain diversity.

The following sections describe our model landscape, algorithms, and simulation results.

2 A Two-Module Fitness Landscape

We assume a genotype is a vector of $2n$ binary variables, $G=<g_1,g_2,...,g_{2n}>$, and define the fitness of a genotype, $f(G)$, as follows:

$$f(G)=R_{(i,j)}(2^i+2^j) \qquad (1)$$

where i is the number of 1s in the first half of the genotype, (i.e. $\{g_1,g_2,...,g_n\}$), and j is the number of 1s in the second half of the genotype (i.e. $\{g_{n+1},g_{n+2},...,g_{2n}\}$), and $R_{(i,j)}$ returns a value drawn uniformly in the range (0.5,1] for each pair i and j – (these values may be re-drawn to create different instances of the problem, but remain fixed throughout a given simulation run). This function can be interpreted as a function over the number of 'good mutations' in each of two genes each consisting of n nucleotide sites. The 'good mutations' being the 1s at each site, and the two genes corresponding to the left and right halves of the genotype (Fig. 1.).

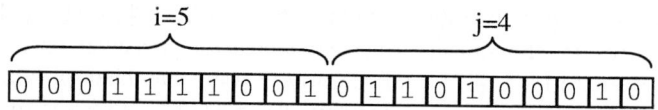

Fig. 1. A genotype is divided into two genes, left and right, and the number of 1s in each half is counted.

The good 'alleles' for each gene then are the all-1s configurations for the corresponding half of the genotype. The terms 2^i and 2^j simply create a landscape that has very strong synergy between sites within genes and additive fitness effects for sites in different genes. The effect of these two terms is depicted in Fig. 2. (left). $R_{(i,j)}$ then defines a fixed array of 'noise' (Fig. 2. center). The product of these components, as defined by Equation 1, creates the landscape depicted in Fig. 2. (right).

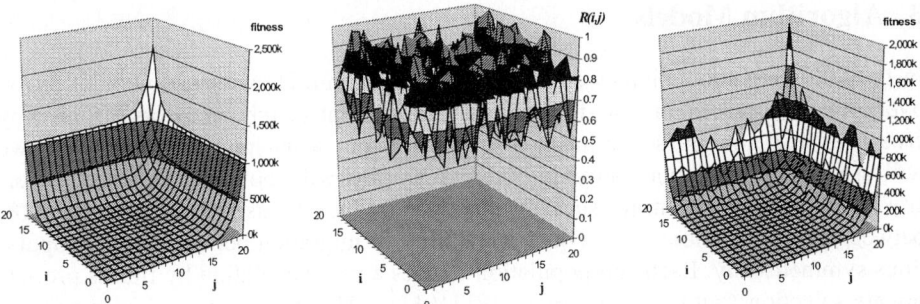

Fig. 2. Landscape defined by Eq. 1 and its component terms. Left) 2^i+2^j. Center) $R_{(i,j)}$. Right) $R_{(i,j)}(2^i+2^j)$.

2.1 Motivations

The motivation for this function is as follows. It defines two obvious building-blocks – the all-1 alleles of each gene – where each building-block is easy to find starting from a random genotype. This is true because 1-mutations are strongly rewarded within each gene and these fitness contributions are strong enough to overcome the random noise in the landscape. However, having found a good allele for one gene it becomes difficult to find the good allele for the other gene as the noise in the fitness function prevents progress along the ridges. This prevents an optimization process from accumulating the good alleles for the two genes *sequentially*. A hill-climbing process, for example, will become stuck on some local peak on either of the two ridges shown in Fig. 2 (right) (although the $i=j$ diagonal is monotonically increasing in fitness, the stronger fitness gradients pull the search process away from the diagonal toward the ridges). In contrast, a process that can find good alleles *in parallel* would be able to find both alleles easily – and subsequent crossover between an individual having the good allele for gene 1 with an individual having the good allele for gene 2 may create a single individual that has the good alleles for both genes. Such a cross creates a new individual at the intersection of these two ridges, and this intersection necessarily corresponds to the highest fitness genotypes because this is where both additive components, i.e. 2^i and 2^j, are maximized.

As mentioned, the only additional complication concerns maintenance of diversity in the population so as to allow a reasonable likelihood that some individuals can find the good allele for gene 1 whilst some other individuals can find the good allele for gene 2. For this purpose we utilize a multi-deme, or subdivided, population model described in the next section. It is fitting that some requirement for diversity, as seen in prior models also, should be part of our requirements to see a benefit for crossover. Without significant diversity in the population, variation from crossover is not interestingly different from variation from spontaneous point mutations, as we will discuss.

3 Algorithm Models

In the following simulations we use a genetic algorithm [1] with and without crossover, or sexual recombination, to illustrate the different search behaviors afforded by crossover and non-crossover mechanisms. To afford a meaningful comparison we will use a subdivided population in both cases – this will show that increased diversity alone is not sufficient for success in this landscape. We use island migration [18] between sub-populations – i.e. equal probability of migration between all subpopulations symmetrically. Each sub-population creates a new generation by fitness proportionate selection (with replacement), [18],[19],[1]. The crossover method uses one-point crossover, where for each pair of parents an inter-local position is chosen at random and the sites to the left of this position are copied from parent one, and the sites to the right are copied from parent two. In both the crossover and non-crossover methods, new individuals are subject to a small amount of point mutation – assigning a new random allele at each site with a small probability. For our purposes here we are not interested in the complications arising from loss of fit genotypes through genetic drift. Accordingly we use a small amount of elitism – i.e. we retain one copy of the fittest individual in each deme from the prior generation without modification. This is not essential to see the effect shown – it is merely used so that we know that the effect applies even when populations have no problem retaining high-fitness genotypes under mutation and stochastic selection, even when the populations are small. The use of elitism ensures that each deme performs at least as well as a mutation hill-climber (with a small overhead for the size of the deme). In fact, in the simulations that follow each deme behaves very much like a hill-climber, having a highly converged population, and algorithmically, could logically be replaced by a hill-climber. Crossover between individuals in the same deme is therefore more or less redundant, and it is crossover between a migrant and the individuals of another deme that does the interesting variation in the search process.

4 Simulations and Results

We used a total population of 400 individuals, subdivided into 20 demes of 20 individuals each. Migration between demes was such that one individual in each new generation in each deme was a migrant from some other randomly selected deme. Each individual in each deme is initialized to a random binary string of length $2n$. Mutation was applied at a rate of $1/2n$ per site. In the crossover method, one-point crossover was applied to all reproduction events. In the following experiments we varied n, the number of sites in each gene, and recorded the number of generations until the first occurrence of the fittest genotype. Each data point is the average of 30 runs of the simulation.

In Fig. 3 we see that the time for the crossover method to find the fittest genotype remains low even for large n. Whereas in contrast, the time for the non-crossover method increases dramatically with n. Runs that fail to find the peak in the evaluation limit of 2000 generations are not plotted. In Figure 3 (right) we can see that this in-

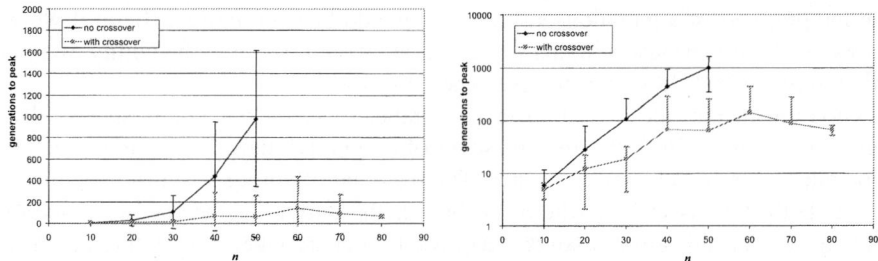

Fig. 3. Left) Results of simulations for a subdivided-population genetic algorithm, on the fitness function defined in Equation 1, with and without crossover. Each point is the mean time to reach the peak of the fitness function averaged over 30 independent runs. Error bars show +/- one standard deviation. Right) as (left) but shown with log scale on vertical axis.

crease for the non-crossover method is approximately exponential in n, as indicated by an approximately straight line on a l og scale. (The last point on this curve falls off from an exponential increase – this is possibly due to the fact that some runs do not succeed in 2000 generations with $n=50$ – the average of those runs that do succeed thus appears low since it does not include the evaluations used by runs that failed.)

4.1 Mutation Rates, Crossover Rates, and the Genetic Map

We should not be so much interested in the quantitative times shown in these simulation results – they should be taken merely as an illustration of the qualitative effect that is quite expected from the design of the fitness function. Simulations using larger and smaller numbers of sub-populations and larger and smaller numbers of individuals per sub-populations showed qualitatively similar results. However, if the number of populations was reduced too much then occasionally all demes would happen to find the high-fitness allele of the same gene – subsequent crossing of migrants among these demes thus had no significant effect and the run would fail. Similarly, if the migration rate between demes is increased too far then fit migrants from one deme will invade other demes and cause the population as a whole to converge before alleles for both genes and successful crossing can occur.

Consideration of higher mutation rates is more interesting. Clearly a population that is 'stuck' on some local optimum on the ridges of the landscape (corresponding to a fit allele for one gene and an arbitrary allele for the other) could escape to the highest fitness genotypes through a fortunate combination of point mutations. However, it should be clear that the expected time for this fortuitous mutation to occur is at least exponential in the number of sites that must be modified. An appropriately tuned mutation rate may be able to minimize this waiting time. However, since the expected distance of a local optimum to the global optimum increases linearly with n, a method relying on fortuitous mutations will still show the exponential increase in time to the peak observed above for increasing n. Exploratory simulations with larger mutation rates agree with this reasoning – for $n=60$ we found no mutation rate that could find the peak of the function in the evaluation limit of 2000 generations. Note that the progress of a mutation-only method would be even more difficult if we were not using elitism because a higher mutation rate would decrease the ability of a population to retain high-fitness genotypes when discovered.

Variation in the rate of crossover or number of crossover points should also be considered. Fig. 5. illustrates the crossover of two individuals, P1 and P2, which have good alleles for complementary genes. The resultant offspring, C, must have the same bits as both parents at loci where the bits in the parents agree (before mutation is applied). Under uniform crossover, [20], where loci are taken from either parent with equal probability independently, the loci where the parents disagree may take either 0 or 1 with 0.5 probability, as indicated by "?"s in Fig. 4. The chances of a recombinant offspring produced by uniform crossover having all-1^s therefore decreases exponentially with the number of loci where the parents disagree. Since this increases approximately linearly with n, the expected time for a successful cross under uniform crossover increases approximately exponentially with n.

```
P1   11111111110101001010
P2   00010100101111111111
C    ???1?1??1??1?1??1?1?
```

Fig. 4. Crossover of two individuals, P1 and P2, produces some offspring genotype C.

This can also be understood geometrically. Fig. 5. shows the state of all the demes in the subdivided population for no crossover, one-point crossover, and uniform crossover. We see that all demes are clustered close to one ridge or the other in the left frame (mutation only, no crossover). In Fig. 5. (center) using one-point crossover we see that in addition to some demes scattered along the ridges, some demes have recombinant individuals that are at the top-right corner of the frame – corresponding to the fittest genotypes. In contrast, Fig. 5. (right) using uniform crossover shows a few demes that have recombinants produced by crossing individuals from one ridge with individuals from the other ridge, but these recombinant genotypes are very unlikely to be at the peak. Although a cross that produces the all-1s genotype is possible under uniform crossover, this is only one of a very large number of possible recombinants, increasing exponentially with the number of loci where the parents disagree. Accordingly, recombinants that land on the peak are exponentially unlikely, and most recombinants land somewhere on the straight line between the two demes of the parents in the $i \times j$ space. Fig. 5. (right) shows a couple of demes having approximately half the good mutations from P1 and half the good mutations from P2. These geometric considerations illustrate well the principles explained in [21] and [22] with respect to the distribution of offspring under crossover.

Of course, this is again as expected. The benefit of crossover in this model is entirely dependent on the correspondence of the epistatic dependencies and the genetic map (the ordering of sites on the chromosome). This agrees with the intuitive notion of a building-block as Holland [1] conceived it – i.e. a schema of above average fitness and short defining length (distance between first and last loci of the schema). Simulation runs with a randomized genetic map – i.e. where the subsets of loci used to define i and j are random disjoint sets of n sites each, rather than the left and right

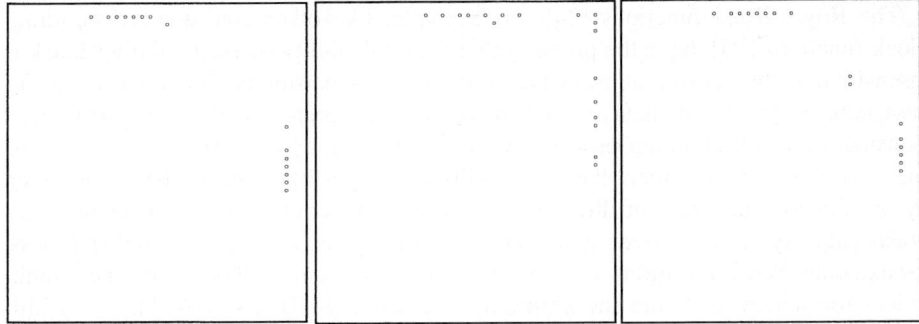

Fig. 5. Snap-shot of the demes at around 200 generations for three different crossover models. In each frame, the horizontal axis is the number of 1s in the first gene and the vertical axis is the number of 1s in the second gene – i.e. these axes correspond to i and j in Equation 1, and the horizontal plane used in Fig. 2. Each small circle within each frame indicates the genotypes of a deme – specifically, it shows the i,j pair for the fittest individual in that deme. Left) A run with no crossover. Center) A run with one-point crossover. Right) A run with uniform crossover.

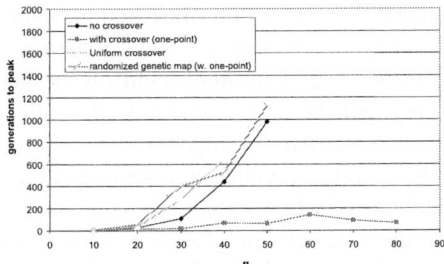

Fig. 6. Simulation results for control experiments using uniform crossover and also for one-point crossover but with a randomized genetic map. Curves for "no crossover" and "with crossover (one-point)" are as per Fig. 4. (left) for comparison.

halves of the genotype – show performance similar to that of the non-crossover method (Fig. 6.). Similarly, simulations using uniform crossover also show performance similar to that of the non-crossover method, as expected (Fig. 6.).

5 Discussion

These results should not be overstated. We have not shown a general benefit for crossover in genetic algorithms (which would not be a sensible goal in any case [2]), but rather a benefit specific to this kind of basic modular or building-block structure. This is intended to provide a simple illustration of reasoning that is already well-known (albeit controversial [23]) in the field. However, although the intuition for this kind of building-block assembly is straightforward it is worth discussing why it has been difficult to illustrate in previous simple building-block models.

The Royal Road functions [24], for example, like other concatenated building-block functions [25], have the property that the evolvability of each building-block is insensitive to the configuration of bits in other block partitions. Specifically, the fitness rank-order of schemata in each partition is independent of other partitions... Considering a hill-climbing process to start with, we may discard fitness-scaling issues. For a hill-climber then, the evolvability of a high-fitness genotype is controlled by the fitness rank-order of different genotypes. This controls the number of mutational pathways from a given genotype to another given genotype of higher fitness, for example. When partitions are separable, in this sense of independent fitness rank-orders for schemata within the partition, it means that: If it is possible for a hill-climber to find a high-fitness schema in *some* genetic background then it is possible for it to find that high-fitness schema in *any* genetic background. Accordingly, the evolvability of high-fitness schemata in each partition is independent of the configurations in other partitions. This means that there is nothing to prevent an optimization process from accumulating beneficial schemata sequentially. Accordingly, if a hill-climber can find high-fitness schemata in each partition, it can find the fittest genotypes (having high-fitness schemata in all partitions). In such naïve building-block functions the action of crossover is thus not required to find high-fitness genotypes.

In contrast, in the function we have described here, and in prior functions such as Jansen's 'gap function', [13], and Watson's 'HIFF' function [14], the evolvability of a fit schema in one partition is strongly dependent on the genetic background. Specifically, in [13] the fittest genotype consists only of 1-alleles, and from a random (low-fitness) genotype, increasing the number of 1-alleles is easy because they are individually rewarded. However, when the number of 1-alleles on background loci is high, increasing the number of 1-alleles on subsequent loci is not rewarded. Accordingly, it is not possible for a hill-climbing algorithm to accumulate all the 1-alleles sequentially. In [14] the situation is a little different. Here the fittest configuration for one building-block is equally either all-1^s or all-0^s given a random genetic background at a neighboring block. However, when the neighboring block is well-optimized, one of these fit configurations becomes fitter than the other depending on how the neighboring block was solved. This can still be understood as a function that prevents sequential accumulation of good schemata by using epistasis such that the discovery of the fittest schemata becomes more difficult as other partitions become well-optimized.

The landscape introduced in this paper works via this principle but illustrates the idea straightforwardly using two obvious building-blocks. It is the random noise component, $R(i,j)$, that prevents the sequential evolution of good schemata: When neither gene is well-optimized, the fitness contributions of 1^s in either gene are strong enough to overcome these random fluctuations in the landscape; But when one of the genes is already optimized, the fitness contributions of 1^s in the other gene are individually relatively insignificant compared to the random fluctuations. This is easily seen using the two cross-sections of the fitness landscape shown in Fig. 7. When $i=0$ the fitness coefficients for mutations that increase j are reliably informative in leading search towards the all-1^s allele (although they may be low in magnitude sometimes). In contrast, when $i=20$ increasing j is not reliably correlated with increasing fitness.

It should be clear that the possibility of combining good building-blocks together is available in prior simple building-block landscapes such as [24] and [25]. However, this operation of crossover is not necessary for finding fit genotypes when it is possible to accumulate building-blocks sequentially. This is the observation provided by Jones [8] when he applied macro-mutation hill-climbers to concatenated sub-function problems. It is the relatively subtle manner in which the evolvability of a building-block changes with genetic background that is important in the design of the function we have shown here. Specifically, the salient properties of this function are that there are relatively independent fitness contributions provided for each of the building-blocks (with epistasis and the genetic map in good correspondence), but additionally, the other important feature is that the discovery of good alleles for these partitions becomes more difficult as more partitions become well-optimized. This seems not unreasonable in some circumstances – for example, as the number of functioning modules increases, the number of dependencies affecting the evolution of subsequent modules also increases, thus making them less evolvable – but it is not our intent here to argue for this in general.

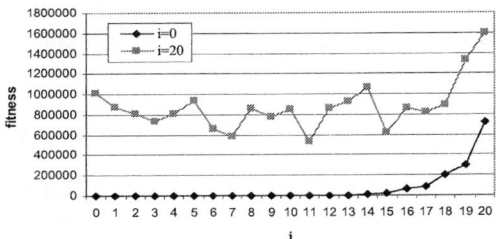

Fig. 7. Two cross sections through the landscape defined by Equation 1. One curve shows the fitness for different values of j when $i=0$, the other for different values of j when $i=20$.

6 Conclusions

In this paper we have provided a simple two-module building-block function that illustrates a principled advantage for crossover. It is deliberately designed to be easy for crossover whilst being difficult for a hill-climber, in a manner that makes the simulations easy to predict and understand. In particular, this model exemplifies the advantage of crossover from the assembly of individually fit building-blocks as per the building-block hypothesis [1],[9],[10],[11]. However, an important characteristic of this model is that the sequential discovery of fit building-blocks is prevented – in this case, by arbitrary epistatic noise that becomes more important as other genes are optimized. This characteristic is analogous to some properties of prior models, [13],[14], but notably, it is not part of the original intuition of the building-block hypothesis.

This result helps us to better understand some of the general properties of landscapes that may make them amenable to solution by genetic algorithms using crossover. It also provides a simple illustration of the dependencies of this advantage on the properties of epistatic structure and the genetic map. It is notable that the simple form of modularity used here (Fig.1), where genes are constituted by a large number of nucleotide sites that are grouped both functionally (with epistasis) and physically (by location), is also seen in natural systems where the nucleotides of a gene are grouped functionally and physically by virtue of the transcription and translation machinery.

References

1. Holland, JH, 1975, *Adaptation in Natural and Artificial Systems*, Ann Arbor, MI: The University of Michigan Press.
2. Wolpert, D, & Macready, W, 1997, "No Free Lunch Theorems for Optimization", *IEEE Transactions on Evolutionary Computation*, 1(1):67-82, 1997.
3. Mitchell, M, Holland, JH, & Forrest, S, 1995 "When will a Genetic Algorithm Outperform Hill-climbing?" *Advances in Neural Information Processing Systems*, 6:51--58, Morgan Kaufmann, CA.
4. Culberson, JC, 1995, "Mutation-Crossover Isomorphisms and the Construction of Discriminating Functions", *Evolutionary Computation*, 2, pp. 279-311.
5. Muhlenbein, H, 1992, "How genetic algorithms really work: I. mutation and hill-climbing." In *Parallel Problem Solving from Nature 2*, Manner, R & Manderick, B, (eds), pp. 15--25. Elsevier.
6. Spears, WM, 1992, "Crossover or Mutation?", in *Foundations of Genetic Algorithms-2*, Whitley, D, (ed.). 221-237.
7. Forrest, S, & Mitchell, M, 1993b, "What makes a problem hard for a Genetic Algorithm? Some anomalous results and their explanation" *Machine Learning 13*, pp.285-319.
8. Jones, T, 1995, *Evolutionary Algorithms, Fitness Landscapes and Search*, PhD dissertation, 95-05-048, University of New Mexico, Albuquerque.
9. Holland, JH, 2000, "Building Blocks, Cohort Genetic Algorithms, and Hyperplane-Defined Functions", *Evolutionary Computation* 8(4): 373-391.
10. Goldberg, DE, 1989, *Genetic Algorithms in Search, Optimization and Machine Learning*, Reading Massachusetts, Addison-Wesley.
11. Forrest, S, & Mitchell, M, 1993a, "Relative Building block fitness and the Building block Hypothesis", in *Foundations of Genetic Algorithms 2*, Whitley, D, ed., Morgan Kaufmann, San Mateo, CA.
12. Rogers, A, & Prügel-Bennett, A, 2001, "A Solvable Model Of A Hard Optimisation Problem", in *Procs. of Theoretical Aspects of Evolutionary Computing*, eds. Kallel, L, et.al., pp. 207-221.
13. Jansen T., & Wegener, I. (2001) Real Royal Road Functions - Where Crossover Provably is Essential, in Procs. *of Genetic and Evolutionary Computation Conference*, eds. Spector, L., et. al. (Morgan Kaufmann, San Francisco, CA.), pp. 374-382.
14. Watson, RA, Hornby, GS, & Pollack, JB, 1998, "Modeling Building block Interdependency", *Procs. of Parallel Problem Solving from Nature V*, eds.Eiben, et. al., Springer. pp. 97-106.
15. Watson, RA, 2001, "Analysis of Recombinative Algorithms on a Non-Separable Building block Problem", *Foundations of Genetic Algorithms VI*, (2000), eds., Martin WN & Spears WM, Morgan Kaufmann, pp. 69-89.

16. Watson, RA, 2002, *Compositional Evolution: Interdisciplinary Investigations in Evolvability, Modularity, and Symbiosis, in Natural and Artificial Evolution*, PhD dissertation, Brandeis University, May 2002.
17. Mahfoud, S, 1995, *Niching Methods for Genetic Algorithms*, PhD thesis, University of Illinois. (also IlliGAl Report No. 95001)
18. Wright, S. (1931) Evolution in Mendelian populations, *Genetics*. 16, 97-159.
19. Fisher, R.A. (1930) *The genetical theory of natural selection* (Clarendon Press, Oxford).
20. Syswerda, G, 1989, "Uniform Crossover in Genetic Algorithms", in *Proc. Third International Conference on Genetic Algorithms*, Schaffer, J. (ed.), Morgan Kaufmann Publishers, Los Altos, CA, pp. 2-9, 1989.
21. Stadler, P.F., & Wagner, G.P. (1998) "Algebraic theory of recombination spaces", *Evolutionary Computation, 5*, 241-275.
22. Gitchoff, P, and Wagner, GP, 1996, "Recombination induced hypergraphs: a new approach to mutation-recombination isomorphism", *Complexity 2*: pp. 37-43.
23. Vose, MD, *The Simple Genetic Algorithm: Foundations and Theory*, 1999, Bradford Books.
24. Mitchell, M, Forrest, S, and Holland, JH, 1992, "The royal road for genetic algorithms: Fitness landscapes and GA performance", in *Toward a practice of autonomous systems, Proceedings of the First European Conference on Artificial Life*. Cambridge, MA: Bradford Books, pp. 245-54.
25. Deb, K, & Goldberg, DE, 1992a, "Analyzing Deception in Trap Functions", in Whitley, D, ed., *Foundations of Genetic Algorithms 2*, Morgan Kaufmann, San Mateo, CA. pp. 93-108.

Statistical Racing Techniques for Improved Empirical Evaluation of Evolutionary Algorithms

Bo Yuan and Marcus Gallagher

School of Information Technology and Electrical Engineering,
University of Queensland, QLD 4072, Australia
{boyuan,marcusg}@itee.uq.edu.au

Abstract. In empirical studies of Evolutionary Algorithms, it is usually desirable to evaluate and compare algorithms using as many different parameter settings and test problems as possible, in order to have a clear and detailed picture of their performance. Unfortunately, the total number of experiments required may be very large, which often makes such research computationally prohibitive. In this paper, the application of a statistical method called racing is proposed as a general-purpose tool to reduce the computational requirements of large-scale experimental studies in evolutionary algorithms. Experimental results are presented that show that racing typically requires only a small fraction of the cost of an exhaustive experimental study.

1 Introduction

Metaheuristic optimization methods such as Evolutionary Algorithms (EAs) are commonly evaluated and compared using empirical methods, due to the complexity of the dynamics and the problems to which they are applied. Due to many constraints, researchers often perform limited empirical studies where candidate algorithms with hand-tuned parameters are tested on a small set of benchmark problems. The shortcomings of this kind of methodology have been pointed out [1-3]. For example, parameter settings may often have significant influence on the performance of EAs and finding good parameter values can itself be a difficult optimization problem. Also, benchmark problems are often selected arbitrarily, and since there is typically no relationship between these problems, it is dangerous to make general conclusions about performance on the basis of such results.

A more principled way to evaluate EAs empirically is to systematically explore a well-defined experimental space over algorithm parameter values and problems of interest. Unfortunately, an exhaustive or brute force approach quickly becomes computationally prohibitive, typically as the result of an explosion in the size of the space when experiments are scaled up. In this paper, a statistical technique called racing [4, 5] is proposed as one tool that can be applied to allow researchers to expand their empirical studies, by significantly reducing the computational requirements over a large experimental space.

The content of this paper is structured as follows. The next section presents the framework of racing and some details of the statistical tests. Section 3 specifies algorithms and problems that create the experimental space to be investigated. A set of racing experiments are conducted in Section 4 to justify the usefulness of racing. Section 5 concludes our work and points out some directions of further work.

2 Racing

2.1 An Overview

Racing algorithms [4, 5] have recently been proposed to solve the model selection problem in Machine Learning: given a set of data points and a number of candidate lazy learning algorithms (which could include multiple versions of some algorithm with different, specified parameter values), which algorithm yields the minimum prediction error based on leave-one-out cross validation? In contrast to a brute force method, which is to sequentially evaluate all algorithms on all available data points and choose the best performing algorithm, the racing method investigates all algorithms in parallel. In each step, all algorithms are tested on a single independently selected data point and their prediction errors on that point are calculated. The mean predication error of each algorithm on data points that have already been seen is also maintained. This error, E_{est}, is an estimation of the true prediction error E_{true} over the entire data set. As the algorithms are tested on more and more data points, E_{est} approaches E_{true}. The fundamental mechanism of racing attempts to identify and eliminate weak candidates on the basis of E_{est} as early as possible to minimize the number of unnecessary predication queries. Candidates compete with each other for computational resources and only promising candidates survive to undertake further testing. There are several possible ways of deciding if and when a candidate should be eliminated, based on statistical tests.

2.2 Statistical Tests in Racing

In Hoeffding races [4], the upper and lower boundaries of E_{true}, called the worst possible error and the best possible error respectively, which specify the confidence intervals of E_{true}, are estimated at each step based on E_{est}, the number of data points that have been seen, the confidence level and the greatest possible error [6]. If at some stage, the best possible error of any algorithm is worse than the worst possible error of the current best algorithm, this algorithm will be eliminated. The advantage of Hoeffding races is that no assumptions are made about the distribution of the data, which makes it applicable to a wide range of situations.

Candidate algorithms can be eliminated more quickly and/or more reliably if the data is approximately normally distributed [5]. In this case, each candidate has a population of errors and statistical methods such as ANOVA (Analysis of Variance) can be utilized to determine if the means of these populations are significantly different. In the meantime, since there is often some kind of correspondence relationship among different groups of data, it is also possible to use methods like the Friedman test [7], which employs a block design [8] to eliminate unwanted sources of variability. The data set in the Friedman test is a $b \times k$ matrix where b is the number of blocks and k is the number of candidates. Each block contains the experimental results of all candidates on a single test instance and each column contains the experimental results of a single candidate on all test instances. The framework of racing algorithms based on ANOVA or the Friedman test is given in Table 1.

Table 1. The framework of racing algorithms based on ANOVA or the Friedman test.

Repeat following steps until only one candidate left or no more unseen instance
• Randomly select an unseen instance and test all remaining candidates on it
• Store results in corresponding performance populations
• If no difference in the means of performance populations is detected by ANOVA or the Friedman test, continue
• Conduct multiple comparison of means and delete candidates if they are significantly worse than others at predefined significance level

2.3 Racing Evolutionary Algorithms

There is a similarity between the model selection problem in Machine Learning and the task of parameter tuning in EAs. In each case, the user is faced with a meta-optimization problem: to find values for all of the adjustable parameters of the model (algorithm) in order to produce the best results when the algorithm is applied to the original problem. Since racing methods only utilize the statistics of the results generated by sets of algorithms, they should also be applicable to parameter tuning in EAs. In fact the set of algorithms to be raced need not to be different instances of the same algorithm. Racing can be used in quite a general sense in an attempt to reduce the experimental effort required, when a comparison is required over a range of experimental configurations.

We are aware of only one application of racing to the experimental evaluation of EAs [9]. Birattari et al employ a racing algorithm to find a parameter configuration of an Ant Colony Optimization (ACO) algorithm that performs as well as possible on a set of instances of the Traveling Salesman Problem (TSP). The TSP instances were randomly generated, which can be regarded as a set of test points drawn from a specific problem space. The parameters of the algorithm were systematically varied to create a set of fully-specified candidate algorithm instances. A racing algorithm called F-race based on the Friedman test was employed to find an as good as possible algorithm instance within a limited amount of time. The experimental results show that F-race outperformed two other racing algorithms based on the paired t-test. Also, there was no significant difference between the results produced by F-race and results produced by a limited brute-force method.

In this paper we aim to clarify the use of racing algorithms in a more general experimental scenario, and to show some different ways in which racing can be applied (e.g., across random restarts of algorithms, or to select for problems instead of algorithms). We also provide a comparison between the racing algorithms and an exhaustive method in each case, and examine the influence of various experimental factors on the effectiveness of racing.

3 Algorithms and Problems

3.1 Algorithm Framework

The algorithm presented below is within the framework of Estimation of Distribution Algorithms (EDAs) [10]. The basic idea of EDAs is to estimate the probability distribution of a few selected individuals in each generation and all new individuals are generated by sampling from this probability distribution.

A Gaussian Kernel EDA

Step 1: Initialize population P by randomly generating N individuals
Step 2: Evaluate all individuals
Step 3: Chose M best individuals as kernels
Step 4: Create P' by sampling N individuals from the kernel density estimator
Step 5: Evaluate all new individuals in P'
Step 6: Combine P and P' to create a new population
Step 7: Go to Step 3 until Stop

The general form of the kernel density estimator is given by Eq. 1:

$$p(x) = \frac{1}{M}\sum_{i=1}^{M} K(x, x_i) \tag{1}$$

In this paper, we use a spherical Gaussian kernel function K and the probability distribution is estimated by a Gaussian kernel density estimator, with kernels placed over the selected individuals themselves (i.e., x_i). In this model, the value of the standard deviation σ, which is a smoothing parameter, plays an important role in the model's performance [11]. If the value is too small, the model may tend to overfit the data and a very smooth estimation may be generated with a very large value, which may not be able to reveal some structure details. The value of M is another important parameter to determine, which controls the trade off between exploration and exploitation and is usually set based on some kind of rule of thumb. In fact, this algorithm can be regarded as an ES with truncation selection and when M is equal to N, it will work as a standard $(\mu+\lambda)$ ES(See [12] for an analysis of the connection between EDAs and ESs).

3.2 Landscape Generator

For some of the experiments in the following section we use a continuous problem/fitness landscape generator as a source of test problems [13]. The landscape generator provides a source from which a large number of (randomized) problem instances (i.e., to be maximized) can be produced. It is based on a sum of Gaussian functions and is parameterized by a small number of parameters such as the number of Gaussians, their locations and covariance structure. These parameters have a direct influence on the structure of the fitness landscapes generated, and several interesting properties of the landscapes (e.g., the values of local and global optima, the number and distribution of optima) can be controlled and smoothly varied via the parameters.

For results presented below, the parameters of the landscape generator are set to the fixed values specified, to produce a set of multimodal functions.

4 Experiments

4.1 Racing Multiple Algorithms on a Single Problem

In this section we apply racing to the task of running a set of specified algorithms on a single test problem. The performance of most EAs is stochastic and depends on their initialization. In empirical studies, this is normally accounted for by running an algorithm repeatedly from different initial conditions. Racing can be applied to reduce the total number of algorithms in this scenario. For this purpose, we chose a well-known benchmark problem: Rastrigin's Function, which is a minimization problem.

$$F(x,y) = 20 + x^2 + y^2 - 10 \cdot (\cos 2\pi \cdot x + \cos 2\pi \cdot y) \qquad x, y \in [-5, 5] \qquad (2)$$

Fifty instances of the Gaussian kernel algorithm were tested with varying values for two of the algorithm parameters: δ from 0.2 to 2.0 with step size 0.2 and the value of M from 10 to 50 with step size 10. To evaluate the performance of the racing algorithms, an exhaustive set of experiments was conducted. Each algorithm was run on the problem for 50 trials (i.e., population size=50, maximum number of generations=100) and the best solution found in each trial was recorded. The performance of all algorithms (in terms of this best solution fitness value) is summarized using boxplots with the horizontal axis nominally representing algorithms and the vertical axis representing performance distributions among restarts (Fig.1). It is possible to inspect these results visually and determine, for example which algorithms were able to reliably find a good solution value.

Using racing, we aim to make a similar observation at a fraction of the computational effort required for the above exhaustive experiment. The procedure operates here by eliminating poor performing algorithms on the basis of a smaller number of random restarts. Two racing algorithms called F-races and A-races based on the Friedman test and ANOVA respectively were applied at the significance level α=0.05. Since the sequence of test instances may have more or less influence on the performance of racing, in this paper, each racing algorithm was run for 10 trials with random sequences. The average number of remaining algorithms during racing is shown in Fig. 2 from which it is clear that both methods eliminated a large number of algorithms after around 15 restarts. The efficiency of racing corresponds to the ratio between the area below the curve and the area of the whole rectangular area in the figure. From a quantitative point of view, the average costs of F-races and A-races were 13.98% and 20.43% of the cost of the brute force method. Note that the single best algorithm in terms of mean performance from the exhaustive experiment (No.2) was always among the remaining algorithms at the end of racing.

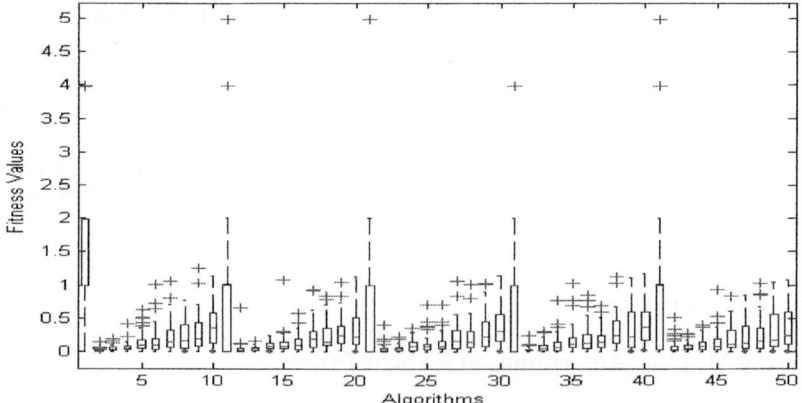

Fig. 1. Performance distributions of 50 algorithms on Rastrigin's Function.

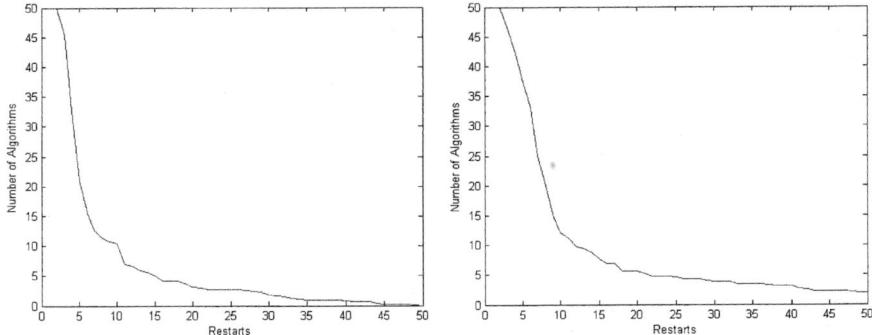

Fig. 2. Number of remaining algorithms vs. restarts: F-races (left) and A-races (right).

4.2 Racing a Single Algorithm on Multiple Problems

Researchers are often interested in qualifying the performance of a single algorithm on a variety of test problems. In this section we demonstrate how racing algorithms can be used to efficiently identify (for example) which problems from a given set are more difficult for a single algorithm. We selected arbitrarily a Gaussian kernel-based algorithm from above with $\delta=0.2$ and $M=20$. The landscape generator described in Section 3.2 was used to generate fifty 5-D random landscapes. Each landscape contained 10 Gaussians, which generally corresponds to 10 optima (though this may vary due to overlaps in the random locations of the components of the landscape). The global optimum in each landscape had fitness value 1.0 and the fitness values of other local optima were randomly generated between 0 and 0.8. The algorithm was first run exhaustively on each landscape for 50 trials (population size=50, maximum number of generations=50) and the best solution found in each trial was recorded (Fig. 3).

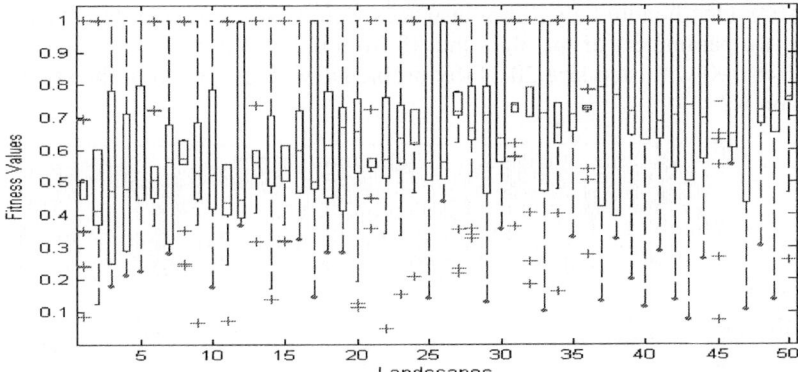

Fig. 3. Difficulty distributions of 50 problems on one algorithm (sorted based on mean values).

The racing algorithms (F-races and A-races) were again applied to this task (attempting to remove problems from experimentation iterating over restarts of the algorithm) and the results are shown in Fig. 4. Note that at the end of the experiment, the problems that have not been eliminated during racing correspond to a much smaller

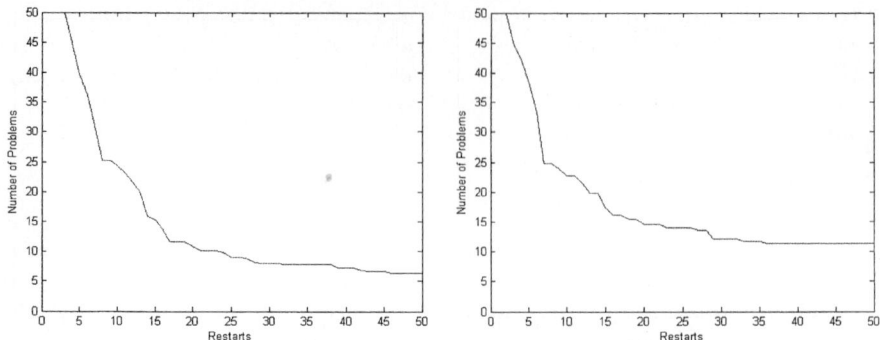

Fig. 4. Number of remaining problems vs. restarts: F-races (left) and. A-races (right).

set of problems that are seemingly difficult for this algorithm to perform well on. The average costs of F-races and A-races were 30.63% and 36.00% respectively compared to the brute force method (Fig. 4). The most difficult problem(No.1) was among the remaining problems by the end of racing in 9 out of 10 trials.

4.3 Racing Multiple Algorithms on Multiple Problems

Finally, racing was applied to identifying the best performing algorithms for a set of problems and to identifying the most difficult problems for a set of algorithms. Note that in the experiments in Sections 4.1 and 4.2 racing was carried out with respect to restarts of an algorithm on a problem. In order to carry out racing with respect to different algorithms or problems, the performance of the algorithm across restarts must be summarized. Birattari et. al appear to conduct racing by running each algorithm only once on a problem – this may lead to sensitive or unrepresentative results in general. In the following experiments, each algorithm was run on each problem for 10 trials and the average value was recorded (population size=200, number of generations=100). One hundred algorithm instances were generated by systematically varying the two parameters of the algorithm (δ from 0.2 to 4.0 with step size 0.2 and M from 20 to 100 with step size 20). Fifty problems were generated in the same way as in Section 4.2.

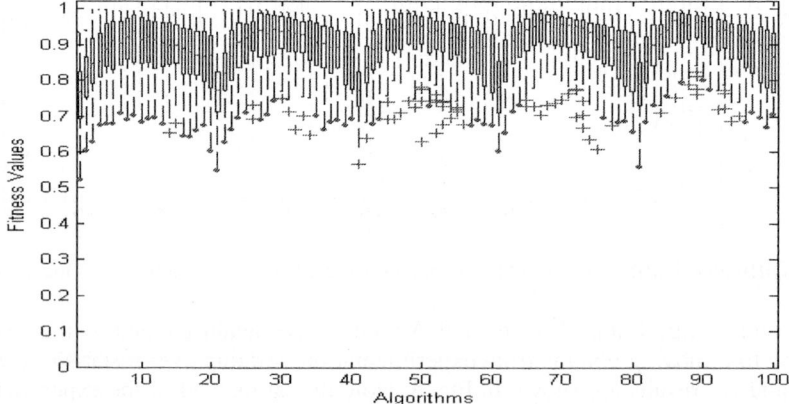

Fig. 5. Performance distributions of 100 algorithms on 50 landscapes.

The results of the exhaustive experiments are shown in Figs. 5&6 over algorithms and problems respectively. The average costs of F-races and A-races in finding the best algorithm were 13.68% and 45.76% respectively (Fig. 7) and the average costs in finding the most difficult problem were 3.58% and 3.05% respectively (Fig. 8), compared to the brute force method. Again, the best algorithm (No. 86) and the most difficult problem (No.1) were never eliminated.

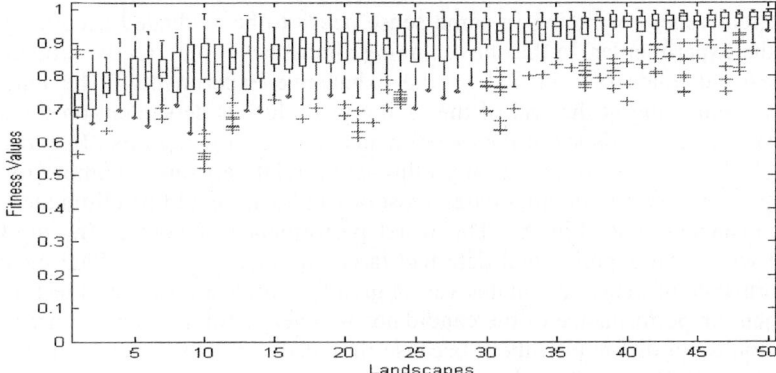

Fig. 6. Difficulty distributions of 50 problems on 100 algorithms (sorted based on mean values).

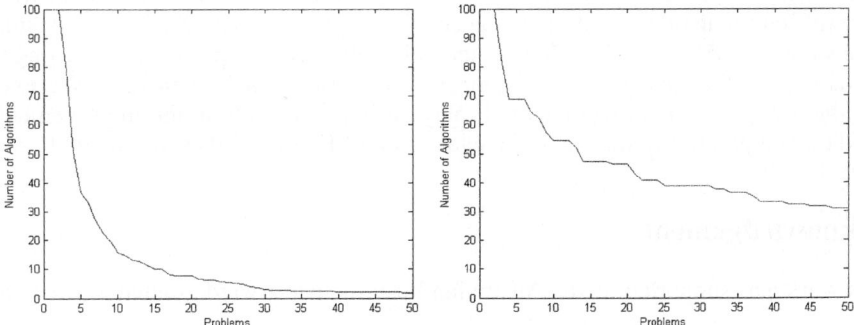

Fig. 7. Number of remaining algorithms vs. problems: F-races (left) and A-races (right).

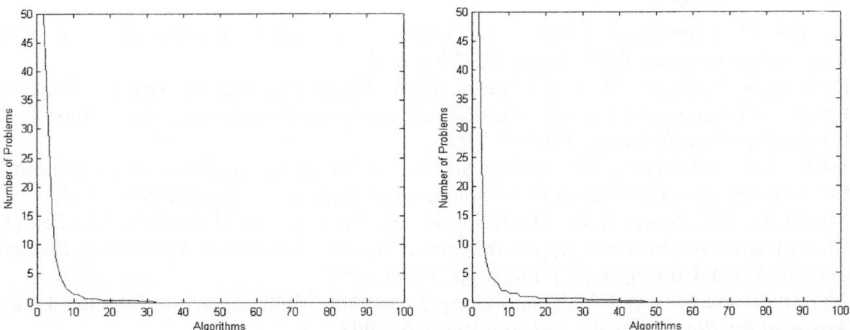

Fig. 8. Number of remaining problems vs. algorithms: F-races (left) and A-races (right).

5 Conclusion

It is clear that for each of our experiments, racing provides significant computational benefit over an exhaustive set of experiments. The F-races algorithm was observed to be more effective at eliminating candidates from experimentation than A-races. Note however that the F-races method is based on ranks instead of raw fitness values, which means that it actually works on a different performance measure.

The effectiveness of racing in some sense needs to be evaluated according to the aims of the experimenter. In the above, racing almost never incorrectly eliminated the single best candidate (as verified by the exhaustive experiments). The number of candidates remaining at the end of the racing procedure is dependent on the significance level (α), the statistics of the experiments and the stopping time. In some of the experiments above, racing could only eliminate a relatively small number of candidates (e.g., Fig. 4) while in other cases most of candidates could be eliminated after a few test instances (e.g., Fig. 8). The worst performance of both racing algorithms occurred where the experimental data had large variance (Fig. 3), which means that the performance of many candidates varied greatly from test instance to test instance. Also, when the performance of the candidates was very similar to each other (Fig. 5), A-races could not distinguish them because they had very close mean values (Fig. 7 right). However, F-races (based on the block design and ranks) showed much better performance in the same situation (Fig. 7 left). As a contrast, in the final set of experiments (Fig. 8) both racing algorithms worked extremely well. Examination of the experimental data set (Fig. 6) shows that the most difficult problem was significantly more difficult than others and the variance of each group of data was relatively small.

In summary, this paper has shown that racing algorithms represent a promising tool for increasing the capacity and efficiency of empirical research in EAs. We expect that the use of statistical methods will play an important role in the improvement of standard and practice in the empirical evaluation of EAs and other metaheuristics.

Acknowledgement

This work was supported by the Australian Postgraduate Award granted to Bo Yuan.

References

1. Whitley, D., Mathias, K., Rana, S. and Dzubera, J.: Evaluating Evolutionary Algorithms. *Artificial Intelligence*, **85**(1-2): pp. 245-276, 1996.
2. De Jong, K.A., Potter, M.A. and Spears, W.M.: Using Problem Generators to Explore the Effects of Epistasis. In *Seventh International Conference on Genetic Algorithms*, T. Bäck Ed., Morgan Kauffman, pp. 338-345, 1997.
3. Eiben, A.E. and Jelasity, M.: A Critical Note on Experimental Research Methodology in EC. In *Congress on Evolutionary Computation*, Hawaii, IEEE, pp. 582-587, 2002.
4. Maron, O. and Moore, A.W.: Hoeffding Races: Accelerating Model Selection Search for Classification and Function Approximation. In *Advances in Neural Information Processing Systems 6*, J.D. Cowan, et al., Editors, pp. 59-66, 1994.
5. Maron, O. and Moore, A.W.: The Racing Algorithm: Model Selection for Lazy Learners. *Artificial Intelligence Review*, **11**: pp. 193-225, 1997.

6. Hoeffding, W.: Probability Inequalities for Sums of Bounded Random Variables. *Journal of the American Statistical Association*, **58**(301): pp. 13-30, 1963.
7. Conover, W.J.: Practical Nonparametric Statistics. 3rd ed, John Wiley & Sons, Inc., 1999.
8. Box, G.E.P., Hunter, W.G. and Hunter, J.S.: Statistics for Experimenters. Wiley, 1978.
9. Birattari, M., Stutzle, T., Paquete, L. and Varrentrapp, K.: A Racing Algorithm for Configuring Metaheuristics. In *Genetic and Evolutionary Computation Conference (GECCO 2002)*, pp. 11-18, 2002.
10. Mühlenbein, H. and Paaß, G.: From Recombination of Genes to the Estimation of Distributions: I. Binary Parameters. In *Parallel Problem Solving from Nature IV*, H.-M. Voigt, et al. Eds., pp. 178-187, 1996.
11. Bishop, C.M.: Neural Networks for Pattern Recognition. Oxford University Press, 1995.
12. Gallagher, M.: Multi-Layer Perceptron Error Surfaces: Visualization, Structure and Modelling. PhD Thesis, The University of Queensland, 2000.
13. Yuan, B. and Gallagher, M.: On Building a Principled Framework for Evaluating and Testing Evolutionary Algorithms: A Continuous Landscape Generator. In *the 2003 Congress on Evolutionary Computation*, pp. 451-458, 2003.

LS-CMA-ES: A Second-Order Algorithm for Covariance Matrix Adaptation

Anne Auger[1], Marc Schoenauer[1], and Nicolas Vanhaecke[2]

[1] TAO team, INRIA Futurs
LRI, Bât. 490, Université Paris-Sud
91405 Orsay Cedex, France
{anne.auger,Marc.Schoenauer}@inria.fr
[2] Molecular Physics Department
Fritz-Haber-Institut der Max-Planck-Gesellschaft
Faradayweg 4-6, 14195 Berlin, Germany
vanhaeck@fhi-berlin.mpg.de

Abstract. Evolution Strategies, a class of Evolutionary Algorithms based on Gaussian mutation and deterministic selection, are today considered the best choice as far as parameter optimization is concerned. However, there are multiple ways to tune the covariance matrix of the Gaussian mutation. After reviewing the state of the art in covariance matrix adaptation, a new approach is proposed, in which the update of the covariance matrix is based on a quadratic approximation of the target function, obtained by some Least-Square minimization. A dynamic criterion is designed to detect situations where the approximation is not accurate enough, and original Covariance Matrix Adaptation (CMA) should rather be directly used. The resulting algorithm is experimentally validated on benchmark functions, outperforming CMA-ES on a large class of problems.

1 Introduction

Among the class of Evolutionary Algorithms (EAs), Evolution Strategies (ESs), based on the so-called Gaussian mutations, are today considered the state-of-the-art in parameter optimization, *i.e.*, optimization of a function defined on $\mathbb{R}^n$ for some $n \geq 1$ [4]. Basic ESs generate λ offspring by mutating the μ parents (without selection), and then deterministically replace the parents by the μ best individuals either from the offspring (this variant is then called the (μ, λ)–ES), or from the merge of parents and offspring (and it is then called the $(\mu+\lambda)$–ES). The Gaussian mutation operator for this class of algorithms consists in adding some Gaussian random noise to the parent, and can be formally written as

$$\mu_{\sigma,C} : X_0 \mapsto X_0 + \sigma N(0, C). \tag{1}$$

where $N(0, C)$ represents one realization of a multivariate Gaussian distribution with mean 0 and *covariance matrix* C, a symmetric positive definite matrix, and σ is a positive real value called the *step-size*. This distinction can seem arbitrary (the actual covariance matrix is $\sigma^2 C$), but it is often convenient to consider that C is somehow normalized, giving the "direction" in which sampling should occur, while σ indicates how far the mutation should go in that "direction".

The performance of the EA is of course highly dependent on the choices of C and σ, that have to be tuned not only to the problem at hand, but also to the current state of the evolution process. Several techniques have been proposed, from the self-adaptation of the mutation parameters in Evolution Strategies (SA-ES) [11] to the Covariance Matrix Adaptation (CMA-ES) [7] where the covariance matrix C is deterministically adapted from the last move of the algorithm. Some Estimation of Distribution Algorithms [8] can also be considered as pertaining to the same category of algorithms that repeatedly sample some Gaussian distribution to generate next test points.

However, we argue in this paper (Section 2) that none of those algorithms does make an optimal use of all previously sampled points. We then discuss, in section 3, what the optimal covariance matrix should be, based on the case of elliptic functions. In Section 4 we propose the LS-CMA-ES algorithm, an ES-like algorithm that updates the covariance matrix by learning some curvature information of the fitness function. Finally, Section 5 presents experimental results on several benchmark functions from the literature, and discusses the limitations of the present algorithm and possible directions to overcome them.

2 State of the Art in Covariance Matrix Learning

Since the early work of Rechenberg and Schwefel, who first used Gaussian mutations to evolve real-valued parameters (see, *e.g.*, [3,4] for a detailed history of the field), it has been clear that the most critical issue of ESs was the tuning of the mutation parameters. Initial works were concerned mainly with the step-size: Rechenberg's one-fifth rule [9], derived from theoretical considerations on the progress rate, as well as Schwefel's first self-adaptive ES [11] were only concerned with the optimal step-size, *i.e.*, considered the covariance matrix to be the identity matrix. However, Schwefel soon proposed to self-adapt one step-size per variable, *i.e.*, to use a covariance matrix that is diagonal with positive diagonal terms, and further extended the self-adapted parameters to the so-called *correlated mutations*, corresponding to the general case of Equation 1 where all parameters of the covariance matrix C are self-adapted [11].

The basic idea of self-adaptation for correlated mutations is to rely on mutations of the mutation parameters themselves to adjust the covariance matrix $\sigma^2 C$. Whereas this clever idea removed the need for manual tuning, it does not take into account the history of evolution to direct the search – as did the one-fifth rule for the step-size. Therefrom, Hansen and Ostermeier designed the Covariance Matrix Adaptation-ES (CMA-ES) algorithm [7], later made more computationally efficient in [6]. The basic idea of CMA-ES is to deterministically use the most recent descent-direction, *i.e.*, the direction between the best parents at two consecutive generations: the covariance matrix C is gradually updated with rank-one matrices whose unique non-zero eigenvalue has the last descent direction as eigenvector (see the complete equations at lines 8 and 10 of

Table 1). In some sense, whereas CMA-ES has been thought as a derandomized correlated mutation from the ES point of view, it could also be viewed as a randomized steepest-descent algorithm from the point of view of standard numerical optimization. Note that the complete CMA-ES algorithm also includes some derandomized step-size adaptation. However, it has been shown (see, *e.g.*, [10]) that this step-size adaptation is not crucial on the sphere function.

Estimation of Distribution Algorithms (EDAs) is a recent paradigm using similar ideas – at least in the continuous case (see [8] for a survey of the whole field). EDAs evolve a probability distribution over the search space. The main loop of an EDA first samples that distribution, then selects some of the samples according to their fitness, and finally updates the distribution from those selected individuals. Hopefully, the distribution will gradually concentrate on the optima of the fitness function. Of course, the update step depends on the model that has been chosen for the distribution. A typical EDA for parameter optimization is the EMNA family [8], where the distribution is sought as a multi-variate Gaussian distribution: the sampling phase of EMNA using such a distribution is then equivalent to the birth of offspring using Equation 1, and EMNA does adapt a covariance matrix, similarly to the ES algorithms described above.

On the one hand, EMNA uses many points to refine the covariance matrix – and hence one could think that it will get a better approximation of the "optimal" covariance matrix, if such a thing exists (see Section 3). However, the selection phase of EMNA (and of most EDAs) is merely binary: if for instance the best half of the population is selected, individuals get selected without any reference to their respective fitness. Moreover, in the case where a completely new covariance matrix is generated from the selected samples, using some Maximum Likelihood principle, such a covariance matrix only tries to "explain" the distribution of sample at hand, without paying any attention to other parts of the search space, even those that have been visited before. And this situation is only slightly improved if the covariance matrix is updated from the previous one at each generation.

Experiments have shown that the best-performing EAs for parameter optimization is clearly the CMA-ES algorithm (see [7] for comparison of SA-ES and CMA-ES, and [10] for a comparison of CMA-ES with some EDAs) – and the reason for that seems to be that it provides the best adaptation of the covariance matrix to the fitness landscape. The purpose of this paper is to try to make a better use of all the points that have been sampled by the algorithm, and to update the covariance matrix with the help of some information on the local curvature of the target function. But before that, we need to clarify what could be the ideal covariance matrix within an algorithm using Gaussian sampling.

3 Rationale

The simplest problem, on which the behavior of optimization algorithm can be studied in great detail, is the sphere model, where the goal is to minimize the function f_S defined by $f_S(x) = x^T x$.

It has been shown numerically [4] that the optimal covariance matrix in that case is the identity matrix I_n. Moreover, some theoretical studies have proved the convergence of the $(1, \lambda)$-ES, either with a dynamic step-size [2] or in the case of self-adaptive step-size [1]. From those results, plus the naive consideration of the isotropy of the fitness function itself, we shall from now on suppose that indeed I_n is a good, if not optimal, covariance matrix when optimizing the sphere function.

But suppose that we now want to minimize the elliptic function $f_E = \frac{1}{2}x^T H x$ where H is a symmetric positive definite matrix. The choice of the optimal covariance matrix to solve that problem with Evolution Strategies becomes obvious after a change of variables that will turn this problem into a sphere problem. Consider the eigen decomposition of H in an orthonormal basis: $H = P^T \Delta\Delta P$ where P is an orthonormal matrix $(P^{-1} = P^T)$ and Δ a diagonal matrix whose diagonal terms are the square roots of the eigenvalues of H. Now let $W = \Delta^{-1} P X$. Simple calculations show that $f_E(X) = f_S(W)$ and that the mutation operator given by equation (1) with $C = (\frac{1}{2}H)^{-1}$ transforms W_0 into $W_0 + \sigma N(0, I_n)$. Hence, if we consider that I_n is the best choice for the covariance matrix for the sphere problem, then $(\frac{1}{2}H)^{-1}$ is the best choice for the covariance matrix for the elliptic problem.

On the other hand, thanks to Taylor expansion, any regular function can be locally approximated by an elliptic function:

$$f(X) = f(X_0) + (X - X_0)^T \nabla f(X_0) + \frac{1}{2}(X - X_0)^T H(X_0)(X - X_0) + o(||X - X_0||^2) \quad (2)$$

where $\nabla f(X_0)$ denotes the gradient of f at point X_0 and $H(X_0)$ the Hessian matrix of f at point X_0 (its second derivatives). Hence, it makes sense to try to use within ESs an approximation of the Hessian matrix of the fitness function to compute what would be the optimal covariance matrix of the mutation operator if the fitness were elliptic.

4 The LS-CMA-ES Algorithm

The goal of this section is to detail the LS-CMA-ES algorithm that builds on the ideas developped in the two previous sections: it will first compute an approximation $\hat{H}$ of the Hessian of the fitness from available evaluated points, and then use $(\frac{1}{2}\hat{H})^{-1}$ as the covariance matrix of its mutation.

However, whereas such strategy is optimal for elliptic functions, it can fail on functions that are far from ellipticity, because the quadratic approximation then becomes very inaccurate. Hence we shall design a criterion to detect such situations, in order to then rather use the CMA-ES update for the covariance matrix.

4.1 Approximating the Hessian Matrix

This step of the proposed algorithm aims at learning the local Hessian matrix of the target function. Suppose that we have N sample points $(X_k, k \in [1, N])$

together with their actual fitness $f(X_k)$, located "not too far" from a given point X_0. Starting from the Taylor expansion, Equation 2, some approximations g and H for both $\nabla f(X_0)$ and $H(X_0)$ can be easily obtained by solving the linear least-square minimization problem:

$$\min_{g \in \mathbb{R}^d, H \in \mathcal{S}(\mathbb{R}^d)} \sum_{k=1}^{N} \left(f(X_k) - f(X_0) - (X_k - X_0)^T g - \frac{1}{2}(X_k - X_0)^T H (X_k - X_0) \right)^2 \quad (3)$$

The unknowns of this problem are g (n unknown parameters), and H ($n(n+1)/2$ unknown parameters). Hence, as soon as more than $n(n+3)/2$ sample points are available, the linear system corresponding to equation 3 is overdetermined, and its solution can be found by evaluating its pseudo-inverse. Note that the cost of the direct computation of such pseudo-inverse by standard numerical methods (*e.g.*, directly available in Matlab) scales as n^6.[1]

If the function f is elliptic, the solution of problem 3 is exactly given by $\nabla f(X_0)$ and $H(X_0)$, and the least-square value reaches 0. However, in the general case, denoting by $\hat{g}$ and $\hat{H}$ the solutions of problem 3, the minimum is not 0, and a measure of the quality of the approximation of the gradient and the Hessian matrix is given by

$$\sum_{k=1}^{N} \left(f(X_k) - f(X_0) - (X_k - X_0)^T \hat{g} - \frac{1}{2}(X_k - X_0)^T \hat{H} (X_k - X_0) \right)^2.$$

Normalizing this measure so that it becomes invariant under any dilatation or offset of the target function f leads to a criterion to detect the cases of poor approximations where the matrix $\hat{H}$ should not be used in the mutation:

$$Q = \frac{1}{N} \sum_{k=1}^{N} \left(\frac{f(X_k) - f(X_0) - (X_k - X_0)^T \hat{g} - \frac{1}{2}(X_k - X_0)^T \hat{H} (X_k - X_0)}{f(X_k) - f(X_0) - (X_k - X_0)^T \hat{g}} \right)^2.$$

(4)

4.2 Gathering Examples

The approximation method described above requires at least $n(n+3)/2$ samples (*i.e.*, points of the search space together with their actual fitnesses). Those samples will of course be gathered from the points used during evolution. A trade-off has to be found, however, between the accuracy of the approximation and the computational effort, as drawing exactly $n(n+3)/2$ points at every generation would obviously be far too costly. Hence only points that need to be evaluated during the normal course of the algorithm will be used, and the approximation will be based on the most recent visited points. The approximation could nevertheless be computed at every generation, using some sliding window of recent points. But again, this has a cost, and another trade-off has to be made, computing a new approximation only at given times, using the same covariance matrix in between.

---

[1] Typically the numerical method is a QR decomposition which scales as $(n(n+3)/2)^3$, *i.e.*, scales as n^6.

4.3 Adapting the Step-Size

So far, we have only discussed the covariance matrix of the Gaussian mutation described by Equation 1. However, even with the optimal covariance matrix, an ES algorithm will never work properly if the step-size is not correctly adapted too. As mentioned in section 2, CMA-ES has a deterministic update rule for its step-size, but this step-size adaptation is not crucial in the case of the sphere function. Since the basic idea of LS-CMA-ES is to turn an elliptic problem into a sphere problem, it was thus decided to use standard self-adaptive rule of ES algorithms for the step-size.

4.4 The $(1, \lambda)$-LS-CMA-ES

The first complete algorithm based on the ideas developed above is the $(1, \lambda)$-LS-CMA-ES algorithm, whose pseudo-code is given in Table 1, where g is the generation counter, $x^{(g)}$ the current parent, $\sigma^{(g)}$ the current step-size, and $C^{(g)}$ the current covariance matrix. *Mode* is a boolean flag indicating whether the approximate Hessian should be used for mutation, or whether the algorithm should use standard CMA-ES update rule. We shall now discuss the different steps in turn.

A $(1, \lambda)$-SA-ES. The basis of the LS-CMA algorithm is a standard self-adaptive Evolution Strategy. Line 4 of Table 1 is the generation of λ offspring using the Gaussian mutation of equation 1 where the step-size is a log-normal mutation of the step-size of the parent. Lines 5 and 6 are the usual evaluation and selection steps of $(1, \lambda)$-ESs.

Covariance matrix update. Lines 8 and 10 are the standard covariance matrix adaptation of the CMA method [6]. However, the computation of the steepest direction p_c must be performed even in LS mode to be accurate when mode switches to CMA. In LS mode, the covariance matrix of the mutation is unchanged (line 9).

Quadratic approximation. Every n_{upd} generations (line 11), the approximation of the Hessian is computed from equation 3 (line 12). The sample points have been gathered along evolution (line 7).

If the error on the approximation is below the threshold, then the new approximation replaces the old one, whether it came from CMA or LS modes, and mode is turned to LS (line 13). Otherwise, mode is turned to CMA (line 14), and the main loop resumes (line 16).

The parameters. The values of some parameters of the LS-CMA-ES algorithm have to be manually fixed. The following values, either from [11] or [6] when relevant, or adjusted by trial-and-error during preliminary runs, have been used in all experiments of Section 5. The number of offspring λ was set to 10 for the LS-CMA-ES and to $4 + \lfloor 3 * \log(N) \rfloor$ for the CMA algorithm, c_c and c_{cov}, the relaxation parameters, to respectively $\frac{4}{n+4}$ and $\frac{2}{(n+\sqrt{2})^2}$ [6]. The update parameter of the self-adaptive log-normal mutation of the step-size, τ, was set to $\frac{1}{\sqrt{n}}$ [11]. The threshold $\mathcal{Q}_{th}$ on the approximation error for the Hessian matrix

Table 1. Pseudo code for the $(1, \lambda)$-LS-CMA-ES algorithm.

Initialization: $x^{(0)} \leftarrow x_0$; $\sigma^{(0)} \leftarrow \sigma_0$; $C^{(0)} \leftarrow I_n$; $p_c^{(0)} \leftarrow 0$; archive $\leftarrow \emptyset$; Mode $\leftarrow$ LS 1
while (not stopping condition) **do** 2
   $g \leftarrow g + 1$ 3
   Create λ offspring: $x_j^{(g+1)} \leftarrow x^{(g)} + \sigma^{(g)} \exp(\tau \tilde{N}_j(0,1)) N_j(0, C^{(g)})$, $j \in [1, \lambda]$ 4
   Evaluate offspring: Compute $f(x_j^{(g+1)})$ for all $1 \leq j \leq \lambda$ 5
   Select best offspring $x^{(b)}$: $x^{(g+1)} \leftarrow x_b^{(g+1)}$; $\sigma^{(g+1)} \leftarrow \sigma^{(g)} \exp(\tau \tilde{N}_b(0,1))$ 6
   Store offspring in archive 7
   $p_c^{(g+1)} \leftarrow (1 - c_c) p_c^{(g)} + \frac{\sqrt{c_c(2-c_c)}}{\sigma^{(g)}} (x^{(g+1)} - x^{(g)})$ 8
   if in LS mode $C^{(g+1)} \leftarrow C^{(g)}$ 9
   else (CMA mode) $C^{(g+1)} \leftarrow (1 - c_{cov}) C^{(g)} + c_{cov} p_c^{(g+1)} (p_c^{(g+1)})^T$ 10
   if (g mod n_{upd} =0) 11
      Compute $\hat{g}_{x^{(g)}}, \hat{H}_{x^{(g)}}$ from n^2 recent archived samples solving Eq. 3 12
      if $\mathcal{Q}(\hat{g}_{x^{(g)}}, \hat{H}_{x^{(g)}}) < \mathcal{Q}_{th}$ Mode $\leftarrow$ LS; $C^{(g+1)} \leftarrow (\frac{1}{2}\hat{H}_{x^{(g)}})^{-1}$ 13
      else   Mode $\leftarrow$ CMA 14
   end if 15
end while 16

that will decide to switch back and forth between LS mode and pure CMA mode, was set to 10^{-3}, after intensive monitoring on the elliptic and Rosenbrock functions. Finally, n_{upd} was set to 100 with of course a possibly delay in the first update in order to have n^2 samples available for the first update.

5 Experimental Results

This section presents the first results obtained using the $(1, \lambda)$-LS-CMA-ES algorithm. It will be compared to the best-performing to-date algorithm in the class of ES-like algorithms, the original CMA-ES algorithm, as described in [6], using the original implementation that the first author kindly makes available [5]. Two variants of CMA-ES are used, the best performing CMA-ES, that uses $\lfloor \frac{\lambda}{2} \rfloor$ parents as default value, and a $(1, \lambda)$-CMA-ES, for a fair comparison. The analytical form of all test functions is given in Table 2. All tests have been performed 100 times independently, from the same initial position $(5, 5, \ldots, 5)$. At each generation, the minimum, median and maximum values out of the 100 runs have been gathered.

First experiments. The elliptic function f_{elli} and the Rosenbrock function f_{Ros} have been intensively tested. *A priori*, if our hypothesis of section 3 about the optimality of $(\frac{1}{2}H)^{-1}$ as covariance matrix is correct, the LS-CMA-ES method should perform very well on the elliptic function. Rosenbrock function, on the other hand, is quite different, and behaves more like $|x|^6$ close to the optimum. The approximation error $\mathcal{Q}$ defined in Equation 4 should hence be larger.

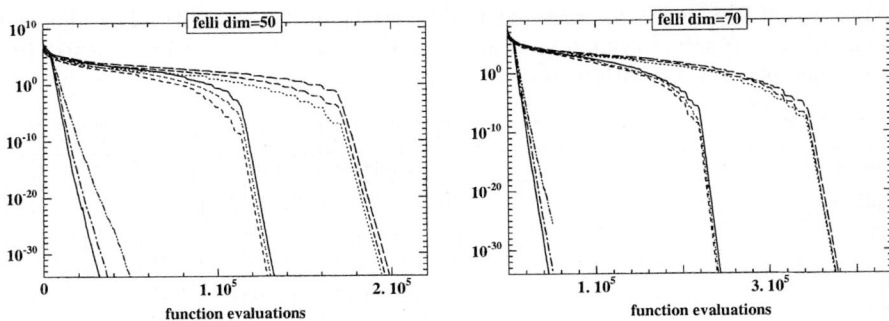

Fig. 1. Comparative on-line results for the elliptic function in dimensions 50 and 70.

Elliptic. The results for f_{elli} (Figure 1) are very clear, and match our expectations: the three groups of three different lines, from left to right are respectively the min, median and max for LS-CMA-ES, then the min, median and max for pure CMA-ES and finally the min, median and max for $(1, \lambda)$-CMA-ES. The variance is very small for all three algorithms. For both CMA-ES algorithms, the flat plateau before actually diving toward 0 is the time that is necessary to learn the correct covariance matrix – while LS-CMA-ES has it all right from the beginning, whatever the dimension (only the minimum number of sample points before the first matrix can be learned makes a small difference). Note, however, that such plateaus can result in a huge difference of actual results in practice, when the stopping criterion is likely to be driven by the computational cost when the actual value of the minimum is unknown.

Rosenbrock. The picture is somewhat different with the Rosenbrock function: this function is not unimodal, and furthermore has a very flat region between the local optimum and the global optimum. For this function LS is not active and LS-CMA-ES behaves like CMA-ES, the differences that can be observed in Table 2 come from the difference in the step-size adaptation which is self-adaptive for LS-CMA-ES and derandomized for CMA-ES. Note that since the function is multi-modal, some runs did not converged.

Other functions. Several other functions, also used in [7, 6] (except for f_{exp}), have been investigated to further validate those first conclusions. Some off-line results are summarized in Table 2. The tendencies observed on the elliptic and Rosenbrock functions are indeed confirmed: f_{cigar}, f_{tablet} and f_{cigtab} are elliptic functions, on which LS-CMA-ES definitely outperforms even the complete CMA-ES; On the other hand, $f_{diff-pow}$ is and f_{exp} are not elliptic, f_{exp} is even "infinitely flat" (all derivatives are 0 at the minimum), and the results are similar to those on the Rosenbrock function. However, as these functions are unimodal, no premature convergence takes place.

Discussion. Those experimental results show an outstanding improvement of performance for LS-CMA-ES over pure CMA-ES on elliptic functions. This

Table 2. Off-line results for different test functions in dimension 20. The figures are the number of function evaluations (unit $= 10^4$) before the algorithm reached 10^{-10} (or – when it never did within 10^5 evaluations).

Function	LS-CMA-ES			CMA-ES			$(1,\lambda)$-CMA		
	min	med	max	min	med	max	min	med	max
$f_{elli} = \sum_{i=1}^{n}(10^6)^{\frac{i-1}{n-1}}x_i^2$	0.51	0.57	0.72	2.05	2.15	2.26	2.9	3.0	3.1
$f_{Ros} = \sum_{i=1}^{n-1}100(x_i^2-x_{i+1})^2+(x_i-1)^2$	0.98	6.03	–	1.4	2.3	–	1.4	3.1	–
$f_{cigtab} = x_1^2 + \sum_{2}^{n-1}10^4 x_i^2 + 10^8 x_n^2$	0.53	0.61	0.70	1.45	1.52	1.58	2.36	2.47	2.57
$f_{tablet} = 10^6 x_1^2 + \sum_{2}^{n}x_i^2$	0.42	0.50	0.56	1.61	1.71	1.78	3.4	3.7	3.9
$f_{cigar} = x_1^2 + \sum_{2}^{n}10^6 x_i^2$	0.45	0.51	0.57	0.90	0.95	1.01	1.04	1.08	1.1
$f_{diff-pow} = \sum_{1}^{n}|x_i|^{2+10\frac{i-1}{n-1}}$	1.53	2.14	3.66	1.18	1.36	1.58	1.53	2.14	2.66
$f_{exp} = \exp(\|x\|^2) - 1$	0.22	0.29	0.31	0.27	0.29	0.32	0.35	0.40	0.45

should not be too surprising if referring to classical methods of numerical optimization: Whereas the CMA-ES can be seen as a steepest descent technique, where the covariance matrix is updated using the previous descent direction (see Section 2), the LS-CMA-ES can be considered similar to second-order quasi-Newton techniques, *i.e.*, relying on local curvature information to find out next points to sample.

Yet, the improvement has only be demonstrated on unimodal or quasi-unimodal functions while the niche for Evolutionary Algorithms is rather global optimization in multi-modal context. However, the exploitation phase of an EA is important too, and many refinements of ES algorithms have concentrated on that phase. As for exploration, it is generally emphasized in the early generations, when the step-sizes are still large enough, by using more than one parent.

We have set up a $(\mu \backslash \mu_I, \lambda)$–LS-CMA-ES in order to optimize multi-modal-functions. The first tests are promising and have to be continued.

One possible drawback of the LS-CMA-ES that cannot be grasped from the results is its computational cost: as mentioned in Section 4.1, direct solution of the least-square linear system theoretically scales like n^6. Thanks to Matlab efficient implementation, it was nevertheless possible to go up to dimension 70 (overhead costs for one approximation on a 3.0GHz Pentium roughly take 1, 280 and 1320 seconds for dimensions 20, 50 and 70). A first remark is that in high dimensions, this additional cost could be greatly reduced by using an iterative method to solve Equation 3. Furthermore, when solving very costly real-world problems, *e.g.*, in CFD domain, where the computation of a single fitness value can take up to a few hours, the approximation overhead will be negligible compared to the gain of a few fitness computation.

6 Conclusion

This paper has introduced LS-CMA-ES, the first second-order evolutionary algorithm for parameter optimization. Initial results have demonstrated the efficiency of this algorithm on a large class of (quasi-)unimodal functions, where the best

CMA-ES algorithm is outperformed by several orders of magnitude on elliptic problems. Moreover, a dynamic criterion allows the algorithm to switch back to CMA when the second-order approximation is poor, resulting in better results than the one-parent CMA-ES on "more flat" functions, as far as the best runs are concerned.

There remains a lot of room for improvement of the proposed algorithm, starting by further experimenting the multi-membered version of the algorithm especially on multi-modal case. Next all parameters (*e.g.*, the number of offspring) needs to be fine-tuned and especially their dependence on the dimension has to be considered. Then noisy problems have to be considered too.

We do believe that this algorithm is a significant step forward in Evolutionary Parameter Optimization, and will be able with some additional work to combine the accuracy of the best deterministic methods with the global search capabilities of Evolutionary Algorithms.

References

1. A. Auger. Convergence Results for $(1,\lambda)$-SA-ES using the Theory of φ-irreducible Markov Chains. In Th. Bäck and M. Schoenauer, editors, *Wokshop on Evolutionary Algorithms – ICALP 2003*, Eindhoven, The Netherlands, July 2003.
2. A. Auger, C. Le Bris, and M. Schoenauer. Dimension-independent Convergence Rate for Non-isotropic $(1,\lambda)-$ES. In E. Cantu-Paz et al., editor, *Proceedings of the Genetic and Evolutionary Conference 2003*, pages 512–524. LNCS 2723 and 2724, Springer Verlag, 2003.
3. T. Bäck, F. Hoffmeister, and H.-P. Schwefel. A survey of Evolution Strategies. In R. K. Belew and L. B. Booker, editors, *Proceedings of the 4th International Conference on Genetic Algorithms*, pages 2–9. Morgan Kaufmann, 1991.
4. Th. Bäck and H.-P. Schwefel. An Overview of Evolutionary Algorithms for Parameter Optimization. *Evolutionary Computation*, 1(1):1–23, 1993.
5. N. Hansen. CMA-ES for Noisy Optimization: Implementations in Matlab. http://www.bionik.tu-berlin.de/user/niko/cmaes_inmatlab.html.
6. N. Hansen, S. Müller, and P. Koumoutsakos. Reducing the Time Complexity of the Derandomized Evolution Strategy with Covariance Matrix Adaptation (CMA-ES). *Evolutionary Computation*, 11(1):1–18, 2003.
7. N. Hansen and A. Ostermeier. Completely Derandomized Self-Adaptation in Evolution Strategies. *Evolutionary Computation*, 9(2):159–195, 2001.
8. P. Larranaga and J. A. Lozano. *Estimation of Distribution Algorithms. A New Tool for Evolutionary Computation*. Kluwer Academic Publishers, 2001.
9. I. Rechenberg. *Evolutionstrategie: Optimierung Technisher Systeme nach Prinzipien des Biologischen Evolution*. Fromman-Hozlboog Verlag, Stuttgart, 1973.
10. N. Hansen D. Büche J. Ocenasek S. Kern, S.D. Müller and P. Koumoutsakos. Learning Probability Distributions in Continuous Evolutionary Algorithms - A Comparative Review. In Th. Bäck and M. Schoenauer, editors, *Wokshop on Evolutionary Algorithms – ICALP 2003*, Eindhoven, The Netherlands, July 2003.
11. H.-P. Schwefel. *Numerical Optimization of Computer Models*. John Wiley & Sons, New-York, 1981. 1995 – 2nd edition.

Learning Probabilistic Tree Grammars for Genetic Programming

Peter A.N. Bosman and Edwin D. de Jong

Institute of Information and Computing Sciences, Utrecht University,
P.O. Box 80.089, 3508 TB Utrecht, The Netherlands
{Peter.Bosman,dejong}@cs.uu.nl

Abstract. Genetic Programming (GP) provides evolutionary methods for problems with tree representations. A recent development in Genetic Algorithms (GAs) has led to principled algorithms called Estimation-of-Distribution Algorithms (EDAs). EDAs identify and exploit structural features of a problem's structure during optimization. Here, we investigate the use of a specific EDA for GP. We develop a probabilistic model that employs transformations of production rules in a context-free grammar to represent local structures. The results of performing experiments on two benchmark problems demonstrate the feasibility of the approach.

1 Introduction

GP [1, 2] offers algorithms to search highly expressive classes of functions, and has been applied to a diverse range of problems including circuit design, symbolic regression, and control. Most GP methods employ the subtree-crossover operator, which exchanges randomly selected subtrees between individuals. Due to the particular structure of trees, subtrees (rather than e.g. any combination of nodes and arcs) appear a reasonable choice as the form of the partial solutions that will be exchanged since the functionality of a subtree is independent of its place within the tree. However, basic GP does not make informed choices as to *which* partial solutions will be exchanged; both the size of the removed subtree and the position where it will be inserted are chosen randomly.

Several subtree encapsulation methods exist that make more specific choices as to which partial solutions are selected to be further propagated, e.g. GLiB [3], ADFs [4], and ARL [5]. Subtree encapsulation methods have been found to substantially improve performance on a variety of problems. Yet, the criteria for the selection of partial solutions they employ are still heuristic; typically, either the fitness of the tree in which a subtree occurs is used as an indication of its value, or the partial solution is itself subject to evolution.

Here, we explore whether a more principled approach to the selection of partial solutions and their recombination is possible. If the distribution of high-fitness trees can be estimated, this would directly specify which combinations of elements are to be maintained in the creation of new individuals and thus which combinations of partial solutions may be fruitfully explored. We investigate how the principle of distribution estimation may be employed in the context of tree-based problems. In GAs, the development of EDAs and other linkage learning techniques has yielded a better insight into the design of competent GAs by rendering the assumptions implicitly made by algorithms explicit. Our aim is that the application of distribution estimation techniques to tree-based problems may likewise clarify the design of principled methods for GP. This paper represents a first step in that direction.

To estimate distributions over the space of trees, a representation must be chosen. In Probabilistic Incremental Program Evolution (PIPE) [6], trees are matched on a fixed-size template, such that the nodes becomes uniquely identifiable variables. The size of the template may increase over time however as trees grow larger. Using this representation, all nodes are treated equally. While this permits the encapsulation of any combination of nodes, it does not exploit the particular non-fixed-size and variable-child-arity structure of trees. The complexity of such an algorithm is determined by the maximally allowed shape for the trees, which must be chosen in advance. In PIPE the distribution is the same for each node, which corresponds to a univariately factorized probability distribution over all nodes. In Extended Compact Genetic Programming (ECGP) [7], trees are represented in the same way as in PIPE. However, the probability distribution that is estimated is a marginal-product factorization that allows the modelling of dependencies between multiple nodes that are located anywhere in the fixed-size template. Moreover, the size of the template is fixed beforehand in ECGP and does not increase over time. In this paper, a method will be employed that estimates the distribution of trees based on the subtrees that actually occur. The representation specifies a set of rules whose expansion leads to trees. The rules capture local information, thereby offering a potential to exploit the specific structure of trees, while at the same time their use in an EDA offers a potential for generalization that is not provided by using fixed-size templates. Shan et al. [8] use a similar approach (based on stochastic grammars). The main difference is that their approach starts from an explicit description of a specific set of trees and then generalizes the description to represent common subtrees. In our approach we do the reverse. Our approach starts from a description of all possible trees and then tunes it to more specifically describe the set of trees.

The remainder of this paper is organized as follows. In Section 2 we introduce basic notation and terminology. In Section 3 we define the probability distribution over trees that we work with. We also show how to draw new samples from the distribution and how the distribution is estimated from data. In Section 4 we perform experiments on two benchmark problems and compare the performance of standard GP and an EDA based on the proposed distribution. We present our conclusions and a discussion of future research in Section 5.

2 Terminology

A grammar G is a vector of l_r production rules $R_j, j \in \{0, 1, \ldots, l_r - 1\}$, that is, $G = (R_0, R_1, \ldots, R_{l_r-1})$.

A production rule is denoted by $R_j : S_k \to E_j$, where S_k is a symbol that can be replaced with the expansion E_j of the production rule. Let K be the number of available symbols, then $k \in \{0, 1, \ldots, K-1\}$. We will use only one symbol and allow ourselves to write S instead of S_k.

An expansion E_j of production rule R_j is a tree. We will therefore generally call E_j an expansion tree. The internal nodes of an expansion tree are functions with at least one argument. The leaves are either symbols, constants or input variables. An example of an expansion tree is $E_j = +(\sin(S), (-(\log(S), \cos(S))))$ which, in common mathematical notation, represents $\sin(S) + (\log(S) - \cos(S))$.

A sentence is obtained from a grammar if a production rule is chosen to replace a symbol repeatedly until all symbols have disappeared. Sentences can therefore be seen as trees. We denote a sentence by s. We will denote a subtree of a sentence by t and call it a sentence subtree.

A sentence subtree t is said to be matched by an expansion tree E_j, denoted $t \in E_j$ if and only if all nodes of E_j coincide with nodes found in t following the same trails, with the exception of symbol nodes, which may be matched to any non-empty sentence subtree.

The following grammar $\boldsymbol{G} = (R_0, R_1, \ldots, R_{5+n})$ with $l_r = 6+n$ is an example of a grammar that describes certain n-dimensional real-valued functions:

$$R_0 : S \to c \text{ (a constant} \in \mathbb{R})$$
$$R_1 : S \to i_0 \text{ (input variable 0)}$$
$$\vdots$$
$$R_n : S \to i_{n-1} \text{ (input variable n-1)}$$

$$R_{n+1} : S \to +(S, S)$$
$$R_{n+2} : S \to \cdot(S, S)$$
$$R_{n+4} : S \to \sin(S)$$
$$R_{n+5} : S \to \cos(S)$$

3 Probability Distribution

3.1 Definition

To construct a probability distribution over sentences, we introduce a random variable S that represents a sentence and a random variable T that represents a sentence subtree. Because sentence subtrees are recursive structures we define a probability distribution for sentence subtrees recursively. To do so, we must know where the tree terminates. This information can be obtained by taking the depth of a sentence subtree into account. Let $P^{\boldsymbol{G}}(T = t|D = d)$ be a probability distribution over all sentence subtrees t that occur at depth d in a sentence. Now, we define the probability distribution over sentences s by:

$$P^{\boldsymbol{G}}(S = s) = P^{\boldsymbol{G}}(T = s|D = 0) \tag{1}$$

Since sentence subtrees are constructed using production rules, we can define $P^{\boldsymbol{G}}(T = t|D = d)$ using the production rules. Since there is only one symbol, we can also focus on the expansion trees. Although depth can be used to model the probability of terminating a sentence at some node in the tree, sentences can be described more precisely if depth is also used to model the probability of occurrence of functions at specific depths. Preliminary experiments indicated that this use of depth information leads to better results.

We define $P_j^E(J = j|D = d)$ to be a discrete conditional probability distribution that models the probability of choosing expansion tree E_j, $j \in \{0, 1, \ldots, l_r\}$ at depth d when constructing a new sentence.

We assume that the values of the constants and the indices of the input variables in an expansion tree are not dependent on the depth. Conforming to this assumption we define $2l_r$ multivariate probability distributions that allow us to model the use of constants and inputs inside production rules other than the standard rules $\mathcal{S} \to c$ and $\mathcal{S} \to i_k$, $k \in \{0, 1, \ldots, n-1\}$:

- $P_j^C(\boldsymbol{C}_j)$, $j \in \{0, 1, \ldots, l_r - 1\}$, a probability distribution over all constants in expansion tree E_j, where $\boldsymbol{C}_j = (C_{j0}, C_{j1}, \ldots, C_{j(n_{C_j}-1)})$. Each C_{jk} is a random variable that represents a constant in E_j.
- $P_j^I(\boldsymbol{I}_j)$, $j \in \{0, 1, \ldots, l_r - 1\}$, a probability distribution over all inputs in expansion tree E_j, where $\boldsymbol{I}_j = (I_{j0}, I_{j1}, \ldots, I_{j(n_{I_j}-1)})$. Each I_{jk} is a random variable that represents all input variables, i.e. $I_{jk} \in \{0, 1, \ldots, n-1\}$.

The above definition of $P_j^I(\boldsymbol{I}_j)$ enforces a single production rule $\mathcal{S} \to i$, where i represents all input variables, instead of n production rules $\mathcal{S} \to i_j$, $j \in \{0, 1, \ldots, n-1\}$. This reduces the required computational complexity for estimating the probability distribution, especially if n is large. However, it prohibits the introduction of production rules that make use of specific input variables.

We will enforce that any sentence subtree t can be matched by only one expansion tree E_j. The probability distribution over all sentence subtrees at some given depth $D = d$ is then the product of the probability of matching the sentence subtree with some expansion tree E_j and the product of all (recursive) probabilities of the sentence subtrees located at the symbol-leaf nodes in E_j.

Let $\mathcal{S}_{jk}$ be the k-th symbol in expansion tree E_j, $k \in \{0, 1, \ldots, n_{\mathcal{S}_j} - 1\}$. Let $stree(\mathcal{S}_{jk}, t)$ be the sentence subtree of sentence subtree t at the same location where $\mathcal{S}_{jk}$ is located in the expansion tree E_j that matches t. Let $depth(\mathcal{S}_{jk})$ be the depth of $\mathcal{S}_{jk}$ in expansion tree E_j. Finally, let $match(t)$ be the index of the matched expansion tree, i.e. $match(t) = j \Leftrightarrow t \in E_j$. We then have:

$$P^{\boldsymbol{G}}(T = t|D = d) = \quad (2)$$

$$P^E(J = j|D = d) P_j^C(\boldsymbol{C}_j) P_j^I(\boldsymbol{I}_j) \prod_{k=0}^{n_{\mathcal{S}_j}-1} P^{\boldsymbol{G}}(T = stree(\mathcal{S}_{jk}, t)|D = d + depth(\mathcal{S}_{jk}))$$

where $j = match(t)$

Summarizing, formulating a probability distribution for sentences requires:

- $P^E(J|D)$; a univariate discrete conditional probability distribution over all possible production rules, conditioned on the depth of occurrence.
- $P_j^C(\boldsymbol{C}_j)$; l_r multivariate probability distributions over n_{C_j} variables.
- $P_j^I(\boldsymbol{I}_j)$; l_r multivariate probability distributions over n_{I_j} variables.

3.2 Estimation from Data

General Greedy Approach. We choose a greedy approach to estimate $P^G(S)$ from a set $\mathcal{S}$ of sentences. Greedy approaches have been used in most EDAs so far and have led to good results [9–12]. The algorithm starts from a given initial grammar. Using transformations, the grammar is made more involved. A transformation results in a set of candidate grammars, each slightly different and each more involved than the current grammar. The goodness of each candidate grammar is then evaluated and the best one is accepted if it is better than the current one. If there is no better grammar, the greedy algorithm terminates.

Transformations. The only transformation that we allow is the substitution of one symbol of an expansion tree with one expansion tree from the base grammar. The base grammar is the grammar that is initially provided. To ensure that after a transformation any sentence subtree can be matched by only one expansion tree we assume that the base grammar has this property. To transform the grammar we only allow to substitute symbols with expansion trees of the base grammar. Here is an example of expanding the base grammar (first column) using a single expansion (second column):

Base grammar	Single expansion	Full expansion
$R_0 : \mathcal{S} \to c$	$R_0 : \mathcal{S} \to c$	$R_0 : \mathcal{S} \to c$
$R_1 : \mathcal{S} \to i$	$R_1 : \mathcal{S} \to i$	$R_1 : \mathcal{S} \to i$
$R_2 : \mathcal{S} \to f(\mathcal{S}, \mathcal{S})$	$R_2 : \mathcal{S} \to f(\mathcal{S}, \mathcal{S})$	$R_2 : \mathcal{S} \to f(\mathcal{S}, \mathcal{S})$
$R_3 : \mathcal{S} \to g(\mathcal{S}, \mathcal{S})$	$R_3 : \mathcal{S} \to g(\mathcal{S}, \mathcal{S})$	$R_3 : \mathcal{S} \to g(c, \mathcal{S})$
	$R_4 : \mathcal{S} \to g(f(\mathcal{S}, \mathcal{S}), \mathcal{S})$	$R_4 : \mathcal{S} \to g(i, \mathcal{S})$
		$R_5 : \mathcal{S} \to g(f(\mathcal{S}, \mathcal{S}), \mathcal{S})$
		$R_6 : \mathcal{S} \to g(g(\mathcal{S}, \mathcal{S}), \mathcal{S})$

Note that the set of expansion trees can now no longer be matched uniquely to all sentence trees. For instance, sentence $g(f(c,c),c)$ can at the top level now be matched by expansion trees 3 and 4. To ensure only a single match, we could expand every expansion tree from the base grammar into a production rule and subsequently remove the original production rule that has now been expanded (third column in the example above). However, this rapidly increases the number of production rules in the grammar and may introduce additional rules that aren't specifically interesting for modelling the data at hand. To be able to only introduce the rules that are interesting, we equip the symbols with a list of indices that indicate which of the production rules in the base grammar may be matched to that symbol. Once a substitution occurs, the symbol that was instantiated may no longer match with the expansion tree that was inserted into it. For example:

Base grammar	Expanded grammar
$R_0 : \mathcal{S} \to c$	$R_0 : \mathcal{S} \to c$
$R_1 : \mathcal{S} \to i$	$R_1 : \mathcal{S} \to i$
$R_2 : \mathcal{S} \to f(\mathcal{S}^{0,1,2,3}, \mathcal{S}^{0,1,2,3})$	$R_2 : \mathcal{S} \to f(\mathcal{S}^{0,1,2,3}, \mathcal{S}^{0,1,2,3})$
$R_3 : \mathcal{S} \to g(\mathcal{S}^{0,1,2,3}, \mathcal{S}^{0,1,2,3})$	$R_3 : \mathcal{S} \to g(\mathcal{S}^{0,1,3}, \mathcal{S}^{0,1,2,3})$
	$R_4 : \mathcal{S} \to g(f(\mathcal{S}^{0,1,2,3}, \mathcal{S}^{0,1,2,3}), \mathcal{S}^{0,1,2,3})$

A sentence can now be preprocessed bottom-up in $\mathcal{O}(n)$ time to indicate for each node which expansion tree matches that node, where n is the number of nodes in the tree. The sentence can then be traversed top-down to perform the frequency count for the expansion trees. It should be noted that this approach means that if a symbol list does not contain all indices of the base grammar, then it represents only the set of the indicated rules from the base grammar. In the above example for instance $\mathcal{S}^{0,1,3}$ represents $\mathcal{S} \to c$, $\mathcal{S} \to i$ and $\mathcal{S} \to g(\mathcal{S}^{0,1,2,3}, \mathcal{S}^{0,1,2,3})$. Therefore, the probability associated with this particular symbol is not the recursive application of the distribution in equation 2, but is uniform over the indicated alternatives. This is comparable to the approach of default tables for discrete random variables in which instead of indicating a probability for all possible combinations of values for the random variables, only a subset of them is explicitly indicated. All remaining combinations are assigned an equal probability such that the distribution sums to 1 over all possible values.

Goodness Measure. The goodness of a grammar is determined using its associated probability distribution. This distribution can be estimated by traversing each sentence and by computing the proportions of occurrence for the expansion trees at each depth. Probability distributions $P_j^C(\boldsymbol{C}_j)$ and $P_j^I(\boldsymbol{I}_j)$ can be estimated after filtering the sentences to obtain for each expansion tree a set of sets of constants and a set of sets of variables (one set of constants or variables for each match of the expansion tree). From these sets, the distributions $P_j^C(\boldsymbol{C}_j)$ and $P_j^I(\boldsymbol{I}_j)$ can be estimated using well-known density estimation techniques (such as proportion estimates for the discrete input variable indices).

Once all parameters have been estimated, the probability-distribution value of each sentence in the data can be computed to obtain the likelihood (or the negative log-likelihood). The goodness measure that we ultimately use to distinguish between probability distributions is the MDL metric [13], which is a form of likelihood penalization, also known as the extended likelihood principle [14]:

$$\mathrm{MDL}\left(P^{\boldsymbol{G}}(S)\right) = -\sum_{i=0}^{|\boldsymbol{S}|-1} \ln\left(P^{\boldsymbol{G}}(S = \boldsymbol{S}_i)\right) + \frac{1}{2}\ln(|\boldsymbol{S}|)|\boldsymbol{\theta}| + \zeta \qquad (3)$$

where $|\boldsymbol{\theta}|$ denotes the number of parameters that need to be estimated in probability distribution $P^{\boldsymbol{G}}(T)$ and ζ denotes the expected additional number of bits required to store the probability distribution. In our case, $|\boldsymbol{\theta}|$ equals:

$$|\boldsymbol{\theta}| = 2d_{\max} + l_r - 4 + \left(\sum_{j=0}^{l_r-1} |\boldsymbol{\theta}| \leftarrow P_j^C(\boldsymbol{C}_j)\right) + \left(\sum_{j=0}^{l_r-1} n^{n_{I_j}} - 1\right) \qquad (4)$$

Since in the latter case, the number of parameters grows exponentially with the number of input variables in an expansion tree, this is likely to be a strong restriction on the number of input variables that the greedy algorithm will allow into any expansion tree. As an alternative, independence can be enforced between input variables. The resulting distribution can then no longer model correlation between multiple input variables in one expansion tree. The number of parameters to be estimated reduces drastically however and this in turn will allow more input variables to be incorporated into the expansion trees. Effectively, we thus enforce $P_j^I(\boldsymbol{I}_j) = \prod_{k=0}^{n_{I_j}-1} P_j^I(I_{jk})$, which changes the last term in the number of parameters $|\boldsymbol{\theta}|$ into $\sum_{j=0}^{l_r-1}(n-1)n_{I_j}$.

The expected additionally required number of bits ζ in our case come from the production rules. The more production rules, the more bits are required. Moreover, longer production rules require more bits. The number of bits required to store a production rule is $\ln(l_{r_{base}})$ times the number of internal nodes in the expansion tree where $l_{r_{base}}$ is the number of production rules in the base grammar. Finally, symbols have lists of production-rule indices. To store one such list, the number of required bits equals $\ln(l_{r_{base}})$ times the length of that list. The value of ζ equals the sum of these two terms over all production rules.

3.3 Sampling

1. Initialize the sentence tree of the new sentence: a single symbol as the root.
2. Set $d = 0$.
3. Visit the symbol at the root.
4. Draw an integer $j \in \{0, 1, \ldots, l_r - 1\}$ randomly from $P^E(J|D = d)$ if the list of production-rule indices associated with the visited symbol is complete, or draw a random integer from the list otherwise.
5. Make a copy of expansion tree E_j.
6. Draw all constants in the copied tree randomly from $P_j^C(\boldsymbol{C}_j)$.
7. Draw all input indices in the copied tree randomly from $P_j^I(\boldsymbol{I}_j)$.
8. Expand the current sentence tree by replacing the symbol that is being visited with the copied tree.
9. Extract the symbols from the copied tree and their relative depths.
10. Recursively visit each symbol in the copied tree after setting the depth d properly (current depth plus relative symbol depth).

4 Experiments

We have performed experiments with the probability distribution from Section 3 by using it in an EDA. We compared the performance of the resulting EDA with a standard GP algorithm that only uses subtree-swapping crossover. Both algorithms select 50% of the population and apply recombination (i.e. either distribution estimation and sampling or crossover) to obtain new solutions that replace the remaining 50% of the population. We applied the algorithms to two GP-benchmarking problems, namely the royal tree problem by Punch, Zongker and Goodman [15] and the tunable benchmark problem by Korkmaz and Üçoluk [16], which we will refer to as the binary-functions problem. A more detailed description of these problems may be found in the aforementioned references or in related work [17]. Both problems are non-functional, which means that fitness is defined in terms of the structure of the sentence and input variables have an empty domain. The binary-functions problem is harder because it contains a higher order of dependency and it has multiple (sub)optima.

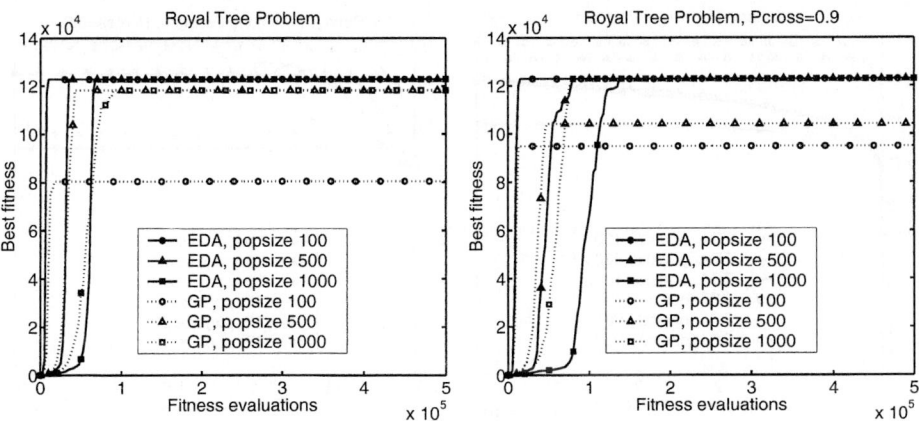

Fig. 1. Results for the Royal Tree problem.

For both problems, we have computed convergence graphs for both algorithms and three different population sizes. The curves in the graphs are averaged over 25 runs. For the Royal Tree problem (see Fig. 1, left), GP achieves reasonable results for population sizes 500 and 1000, but does not reliably find the optimum. The EDA algorithm identifies the optimal solution in every single run and for all population sizes. The Royal Tree problem is a benchmark problem for GP that features a depth-wise layered structure. Clearly, the use of depth information therefore renders the EDA particularly appropriate for problems of this kind. Still, this result demonstrates the feasibility of our EDA to GP. Figure 1 (right) shows the results when recombination is performed in only 90% of the cases, and copying a random parent is performed in the remaining 10%. Although GP is in this case also able to reliably find the optimum this is only the case for a population size of 1000 whereas the EDA is still able to reliably find the optimum for all population sizes. Although lowering the probability of recombination normally speeds up convergence, in this case the EDA is only hampered by it because the distribution can perfectly describe the optimum and therefore using the distribution more frequently will improve performance. Moreover, copying introduces spurious dependencies that are estimated in the distribution and will additionally hamper optimization.

Figure 2 shows the results for the binary-functions problem (maximum fitness is 16). This problem has dependencies that are much harder for the distribution to adequately represent and reliably reproduce. Very large subfunctions are required to this end. Moreover, the multiple (sub)optima slow down convergence for the EDA as can be seen in Figure. 2 on the left. Crossover in GP is much more likely to reproduce large parts of parents. Hence, crossover automatically biases the search towards one of these solutions, allowing for faster convergence. The use of copying leads to faster convergence of the EDA. However, the deficiency of the distribution with respect to the dependencies in the problem still hamper the performance of the EDA enough to not be able to improve over standard GP. Additional enhancements may be required to make the distribu-

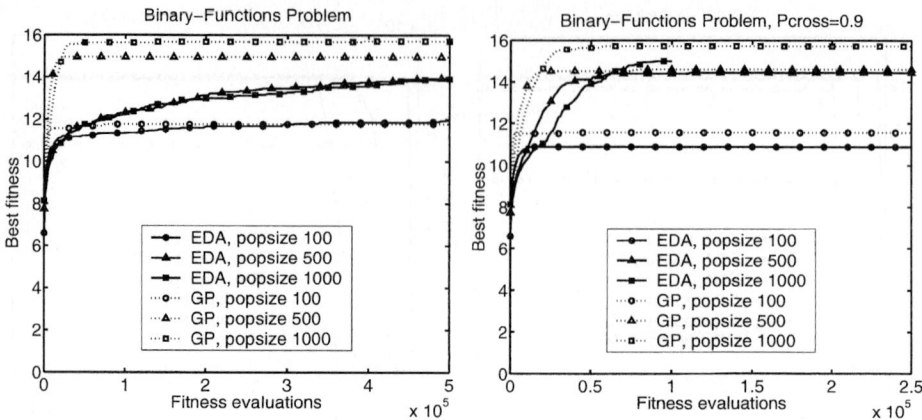

Fig. 2. Results for the binary-functions problem.

tion used more suited to cope with dependencies such as those encountered in the binary-functions problem, after which an improvement over standard GP may be expected similar to the improvement seen for the Royal Tree problem.

5 Discussion and Conclusions

In this paper we have proposed a probability distribution over trees to be used in an EDA for GP. The distribution basically associates a probability with each production rule in a context-free grammar. More involved production rules or subfunctions can be introduced using transformations in which one production rule is expanded into another production rule. This allows the probability distribution to become more specific and to express a higher order of dependency. We have performed experiments on two benchmark problems from the literature. The results indicate that our EDA for GP is feasible. It should be noted however that learning advanced production rules using the greedy algorithm proposed in this paper can take up a lot of time, especially if the number of production rules and the arity of the subfunctions increase. To speed up this greedy process, only a single rule can be randomly selected into which to expand each production rule from the base grammar instead of expanding each production rule from the base grammar into each currently available production rule. Although this significantly reduces the number of candidate distributions in the greedy algorithm, it also significantly improves the running time. Moreover, since the greedy algorithm is iterative and the probability distribution is estimated anew each generation, the most important subfunctions are still expected to emerge.

Because our approach to estimating probability distributions over trees does not fix or bound the tree structure beforehand, our approach can be seen as a more principled way of identifying abitrarily-sized important subfunctions than by constructing subfunctions randomly (e.g. GLiB [3]) or by evolving them (e.g. ADFs [4] and ARL [5]). As such, this paper may provide one of the first steps in a new and interesting direction for GP that allows to detect and exploit substructures in a more principled manner for enhanced optimization performance.

References

1. Cramer, N.L.: A representation for the adaptive generation of simple sequential programs. In Grefenstette, J.J., ed.: Proceedings of the First International Conference on Genetic Algorithms and their Applications, Hillsdale, NJ, Carnegie-Mellon University, Lawrence Erlbaum Associates (1985) 183–187
2. Koza, J.R.: Genetic Programming. The MIT Press, Cambridge, MA (1992)
3. Angeline, P.J., Pollack, J.B.: The evolutionary induction of subroutines. In: Proceedings of the Fourteenth Annual Conference of the Cognitive Science Society, Hillsdale, NJ, Lawrence Erlbaum Associates (1992) 236–241
4. Koza, J.R.: Genetic Programming II: Automatic Discovery of Reusable Programs. The MIT Press, Cambridge, MA (1994)
5. Rosca, J.P., Ballard, D.H.: Discovery of subroutines in genetic programming. In Angeline, P., Kinnear, Jr., K.E., eds.: Advances in Genetic Programming 2. The MIT Press, Cambridge, MA (1996) 177–202
6. Salustowicz, R.P., Schmidhuber, J.: Probabilistic incremental program evolution. Evolutionary Computation **5** (1997) 123–141
7. Sastry, K., Goldberg, D.E.: Probabilistic model building and competent genetic programming. In Riolo, R.L., Worzel, B., eds.: Genetic Programming Theory and Practise. Kluwer (2003) 205–220
8. Shan, Y., McKay, R., Baxter, R., Abbass, H., Essam, D., Nguyen, H.: Grammar model-based program evolution. In: Proceedings of the 2004 Congress on Evolutionary Computation – CEC2004, Piscataway, New Jersey, IEEE Press (2004)
9. Bosman, P.A.N.: Design and Application of Iterated Density-Estimation Evolutionary Algorithms. PhD thesis, Utrecht Univ., Utrecht, the Netherlands (2003)
10. Larrañaga, P., Lozano, J.A.: Estimation of Distribution Algorithms. A New Tool for Evolutionary Computation. Kluwer Academic, London (2001)
11. Pelikan, M.: Bayesian optimization algorithm: From single level to hierarchy. PhD thesis, University of Illinois at Urbana-Champaign, Urbana, Illinois (2002)
12. Pelikan, M., Goldberg, D.E., Lobo, F.G.: A survey of optimization by building and using probabilistic models. Computational Optimization and Applications **21** (2002) 5–20
13. Rissanen, J.: Hypothesis selection and testing by the MDL principle. The Computer Journal **42** (1999) 260–269
14. Buntine, W.: A guide to the literature on learning probabilistic networks from data. IEEE Transactions On Knowledge And Data Engineering **8** (1996) 195–210
15. Punch, W.F., Zongker, D., Goodman, E.D.: The royal tree problem, a benchmark for single and multiple population genetic programming. In Angeline, P.J., Kinnear, Jr., K.E., eds.: Advances in Genetic Programming 2. The MIT Press, Cambridge, MA, USA (1996) 299–316
16. Korkmaz, E.E., Üçoluk, G.: Design and usage of a new benchmark problem for genetic programming. In: Proceedings of the 18th International Symposium on Computer and Information Sciences ISCIS–2003, Berlin, Springer-Verlag (2003) 561–567
17. Bosman, P.A.N., de Jong, E.D.: Grammar transformations in an EDA for genetic programming. In Pelikan, M., et al., eds.: Proceedings of the Optimization by Building and Using Probabilistic Models OBUPM Workshop at the Genetic and Evolutionary Computation Conference GECCO–2004, Berlin, Springer-Verlag (2004)

Sequential Sampling in Noisy Environments

Jürgen Branke and Christian Schmidt

Institute AIFB, University of Karlsruhe, Germany
{branke,csc}@aifb.uni-karlsruhe.de

Abstract. In an environment where fitness evaluations are disturbed by noise, the selection operator is prone to errors, occasionally and intendedly selecting the worse individual. A common method to reduce the noise is to sample an individual's fitness several times, and use the average as an estimate of the true fitness. Unfortunately, such a noise reduction is computationally rather expensive. Sequential sampling does not fix the number of samples in advance for all individuals, but instead selects samples one at a time, until a certain level of confidence is achieved. This allows to reduce the number of samples, because individuals with very different true fitness values can be compared on the basis of only few samples (as the signal-to-noise ratio is rather high in this case) while very similar individuals are evaluated often enough to guarantee the desired level of confidence. In this paper, for the case of tournament selection, we show that the use of a state-of-the-art sequential sampling procedure may save a significant portion of the fitness evaluations, without increasing the selection error. Furthermore, we design a new sequential sampling procedure and show that it saves an even larger portion of the fitness evaluations. Finally, we compare the three methods also empirically on a simple onemax function.

1 Introduction

Many real-world optimization problems involve noise, i.e. a solution's quality (and thus the fitness function) is a random variable. Examples include all applications where the fitness is determined by a stochastic computer simulation, or where fitness is measured physically and prone to measuring error.

Already many years ago, researchers have argued that evolutionary algorithms (EAs) should be relatively robust against noise (see e.g. [1]), and recently a number of publications have appeared which support that claim at least partially [2–5].

For most noisy optimization problems, the uncertainty in fitness evaluation can be reduced by sampling an individual's fitness n times and using the average as estimate for the true fitness. Unfortunately, sampling n times reduces the standard deviation of the noise only by a factor of $\sqrt{n}$, thus an effective noise reduction is computationally quite expensive, and may actually be computationally prohibitive. There seems to be a fundamental trade-off: either one can use relatively exact estimates but only evaluate a small number of individuals (because a single estimate requires many evaluations), or one can let the algorithm work with relatively crude fitness estimates, but allow for more individuals to be evaluated (as each estimate requires less effort).

In a previous paper [6], we have suggested two ways out of this dilemma in the context of stochastic tournament selection (a selection mechanism which randomly chooses two individuals from the population and selects the better one with probability $1-\gamma$, where γ is a parameter to tune the selection pressure):

1. to adapt the selection mechanism to take the noise into account, and
2. to vary the number of samples depending on the observed fitness difference.

As we have shown, these two methods allow to drastically reduce the number of samples required, and thus to significantly save computation time. However, the method in [6] to vary the number of samples was very ad hoc and rather primitive. The goal of this paper is to elaborate on the sampling procedure by looking at the state of the art and designing an even better methodology.

The paper is structured as follows: In the following section, we discuss some related work. Section 3 describes the sampling procedures considered in this paper. These are compared empirically in Section 4. The paper concludes with a summary and some ideas for future work.

2 Related Work

Several people have looked at the trade-off between the number of fitness samples per individual and the population size, with contradictory results. Fitzpatrick and Grefenstette [1] conclude that for the genetic algorithm studied, it is better to increase the population size than to increase the sample size. On the other hand, Beyer [7] shows that for a $(1,\lambda)$ evolution strategy on a simple sphere, one should increase the sample size rather than λ. Hammel and Bäck [8] confirm these results and empirically show that it also doesn't help to increase the parent population size μ. Finally, Arnold and Beyer [2, 3] show analytically on the simple sphere that increasing the parent population size μ is helpful in combination with intermediate multi-recombination. Miller and Goldberg [9, 5] have developed some simplified theoretical models which allow to simultaneously optimize the population size and the sample size. A good overview of theoretical work on EAs applied to noisy optimization problems can be found in [10, 11].

All papers mentioned so far assume that the sample size is fix for all individuals. Aizawa and Wah [12] were probably the first to suggest that the sample size could be adapted during the run, and suggested two adaptation schemes: increasing the sample size with the generation number, and using a higher sample size for individuals with higher estimated variance or higher quality. Albert and Goldberg [13] look at a slightly different problem, but also conclude that the sample size should increase over the run. For (μ,λ) or $(\mu+\lambda)$ selection, Stagge [14] has suggested to base the sample size on an individual's probability to be among the μ best (and thus should survive to the next generation).

Branke et al. [15, 16] and Sano and Kita [17, 18] propose to take the fitness estimates of neighboring individuals into account when estimating an individual's fitness. This also improves the estimation without requiring additional samples.

As has already been noted in the introduction, the present papers is based heavily on one of the authors' previous publications [6], with a particular focus on improving the sequential sampling procedure.

Finally, another related subject is that of searching for robust solutions, where instead of a noisy fitness function the decision variables are disturbed (cf. [19, 15, 20]).

3 Sequential Sampling Procedures

Sequential sampling is a well studied problem in statistics. In the following, we present two sequential sampling procedures with the aim to determine the better of two individuals in a tournament with a given confidence. While the first sampling procedure is taken from a recent publication, the second has been generated by means of binary search and simulation.

In this paper, we use the following basic notation: Let us denote the two individuals to be compared in a tournament as x and y. If the fitness is noisy, the fitness of individual x resp. y is a random variable F_x resp. F_y with $F_x \sim \mathcal{N}(\mu_x, \sigma_x^2)$ resp. $F_y \sim \mathcal{N}(\mu_y, \sigma_y^2)$.[1] If $\mu_x > \mu_y$, we would like to select individual x with probability $P(S = x) = (1 - \gamma)$ and vice versa. However, μ_x and μ_y are unknown, we can only estimate them by sampling each individual's fitness a number of n_x resp. n_y times and using the averages $\bar{f}_x$ and $\bar{f}_y$ as estimators for the fitnesses, and the sample variances s_x^2 and s_y^2 as estimators for the true variances.

If the actual fitness difference between the two individuals is denoted as $\delta = \mu_x - \mu_y$, the observed fitness difference is a random variable and is denoted by $d = \bar{f}_x - \bar{f}_y$. The variance of d depends on the number of samples drawn from each individual, n_x and n_y, and can be calculated as $\sigma_d^2 = \sigma_x^2/n_x + \sigma_y^2/n_y$. We define $\delta^* = \delta/\sqrt{\sigma_x^2 + \sigma_y^2}$ as the standardized fitness difference. Correspondingly, $d^* = (\bar{f}_x - \bar{f}_y)/\sqrt{s_x^2 + s_y^2}$ is the standardized observed fitness difference.

The general outline of both sampling procedures discussed here is described in Algorithm 1: New samples are generated until the observed fitness difference between the two individuals, d or d^*, exceeds a threshold ε_k, where k is an index for the iteration. The methods differ in the way they determine appropriate ε_k and in the basis of the comparison.

3.1 Kim and Nelson's Indifference Zone Procedure

One of the recent publications on sequential sampling is that of Kim and Nelson [21]. Their method takes as input a minimal fitness difference δ_r considered relevant, and a maximal allowed error probability α. The method then guarantees an error probability of at most α for a true fitness difference greater than δ_r. When the fitness difference between the two individuals is smaller than δ_r, the two solutions are considered equivalent, and no bounds on the error probability are maintained. This is particularly suitable to be used in combination with the idea from [6] to adjust the selection probability to the noise present in the problem, as this method can tolerate an error probability less

---

[1] Note that it will be sufficient to assume that the average difference obtained from sampling the individuals' fitnesses n times is normally distributed. This is certainly valid if each individual's fitness is normally distributed, but also independent of the actual fitness distributions for large enough n (central limit theorem).

Algorithm 1 General sequential sampling with at most K stages.

Sample each individual n_0 times
Determine standardized fitness difference d^*
FOR $k = 1$ TO $K - 1$ {
    IF $|d^*| > \varepsilon_k$
        RETURN better individual   /* decision possible */
    Generate one additional sample for each individual
    Update d^*
}
Sample each individual n_K times
RETURN better individual   /* decision enforced */

than γ. The procedure by Kim and Nelson is outlined in Algorithm 2. It should be noted that the original algorithm in [21] is more general in that it may be used to find the best out of a larger set of candidates.

Algorithm 2 Kim and Nelson's Indifference Zone Procedure.

Sample each individual $n_0 = 4$ times
Determine fitness difference d and common variance $s^2 = s_x^2 + s_y^2$
REPEAT {
    Calculate $\varepsilon = \max\left\{0, \frac{\delta_r}{2n}\left(\frac{3((2\alpha)^{-2/3}-1)s^2}{\delta_r^2} - n\right)\right\}$
    IF $|d| > \varepsilon$
        RETURN better individual
    Generate one additional sample for each individual
    Update d and s^2
}

The drawback with this procedure is, that it is based on d and δ_r instead of d^* and δ_r^*. So to apply the procedure we have to set $\delta_r = \delta_r^* \sqrt{\sigma_x^2 + \sigma_y^2}$, which affords that the common variance is known.

3.2 Equal Error on Each Stage

Kim and Nelson's procedure has been derived analytically, based on some simplifying assumptions. While the error bounds are guaranteed, the procedure is not necessarily minimal in the number of samples used. Here, we design a sequential sampling procedure based on the assumption that the actual error probability in each iteration should be a constant α_c. Note that because the procedure may stop in any iteration due to a large observed fitness difference, the underlying probability distributions are truncated and become rather skewed with an increasing number of iterations. Therefore, we determine the thresholds ε_k and the total actual error probability (which also depends on the probability to make a decision in stage k) empirically by simulation. This method is described as Algorithm 3, where $\Phi_{\delta^*,k}(x)$ denotes the cumulative probability distribution for the observed standardized fitness difference in stage k, based on a true fitness difference δ^*. The total number of stages is at most K.

We use binary search to find a per-stage error probability α_c which yields a total error probability of α at δ_r^*. Note that the procedure to determine the ε_k is computationally more demanding than Kim and Nelson's method. However, this effort has to be spent only once for a given indifference threshold δ_r^* and error probability α, and could in principle be provided by tables.

Algorithm 3 Determining thresholds and total error probability.

Input: constant error per stage α_c
Generate a large number of pairs of individuals with standardized fitness difference δ_r^*
Sample each individual $n_0 = 4$ times
Estimate $\Phi_{\delta_r^*,0}$ from the observed d^* of all pairs of individuals
FOR $k = 0$ TO $K - 1$ DO {
    $\varepsilon_k = \max\{0, -\Phi_{\delta_r^*,k}^{-1}(\alpha_c)\}$
    Determine probability $p_k^{\delta_r^*}$ to go to next stage based on ε_k and $\Phi_{\delta_r^*,k}$
    Estimate $\Phi_{\delta_r^*,k+1}$ by truncating at ε_k, $-\varepsilon_k$, and resampling remaining individuals
}
RETURN total error probability $A = \alpha_c + \sum_{k=1}^{K} \alpha_c \prod_{i=0}^{k-1} p_i^{\delta_r^*}$ and thresholds ε_k

---

4 Experiments

We present two kinds of experiments. In all cases, we assume the use of stochastic tournament selection, where two individuals are chosen randomly, and the better individual is to be chosen with probability $1 - \gamma = 80\%$. In the first set of experiments, we compare the error probabilities of different methods for a single tournament, depending on the (standardized) true fitness difference. In the second set, we test the approaches on a simple 1000 bit onemax problem, and compare the obtained fitness based on the total number of evaluations. For the optimization runs, we assume a simple GA with generational reproduction, population size of 20, one-point crossover with probability 0.6, and bit-flip mutation with mutation probability 1/(chromosome length). Unless stated otherwise, we assume a Gaussian noise with mean 0 and standard deviation $\sigma = 2$.

We compare the different methods based on the *average* population fitness, as the true best is generally unknown in a stochastic environment. Results are averaged over 40 runs.

4.1 Selection Error

The smallest observable fitness difference possible for the onemax problem is 1 (solutions differ in only 1 bit). Given a Gaussian noise with standard deviation σ, the standardized fitness difference between two such individuals is $\delta_{min}^* = 1/\sqrt{2\sigma^2}$. If we want to eliminate the effect of noise, we thus require that the selection error is close to zero for $\delta^* > \delta_{min}^*$.

Let us first consider the case of standard stochastic tournament selection, where the observed better individual is accepted with $(1 - \gamma) = 80\%$ probability. For the assumed

Table 1. Actual selection probability for better individual P(S), depending on the number of samples per individual n and assuming a true standardized fitness difference of 0.35.

n	1	10	20	30	40	50
$P(S)$	0.582	0.720	0.765	0.784	0.792	0.796

Gaussian noise with $\sigma = 2$, we get $\delta^*_{min} \approx 0.35$. Table 1 then shows the actual probability of selecting the truly better individual if the true standardized fitness difference is equal to 0.35, depending on the number of samples used per individual. Any deviation from the desired 80% is due to the noise.

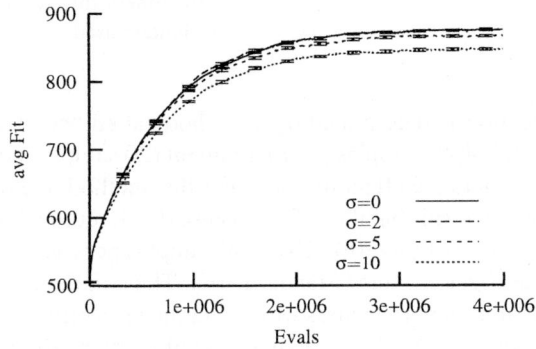

Fig. 1. Average fitness of population for different levels of noise, with error bars.

As can be seen, about 40 samples per individual are required to reduce the effect of noise to less than 1% deviation. Figure 1 confirms that indeed this is sufficient to eliminate the effect of noise. It shows the average fitness of the population over time, for different levels of noise, assuming 80 samples per tournament (40 per individual). As expected, a noise of $\sigma = 2$ has basically no effect (the lines for $\sigma = 2$ and $\sigma = 0$ are indistinguishable), while larger noise leads to inferior performance (see $\sigma = 5$ or $\sigma = 10$).

As this example shows, the effect of noise can be eliminated by multiple sampling. However, it also demonstrates the excessive computational burden (80 samples per tournament instead of 2 if the environment would be deterministic). In the following, we show how this computational burden can be reduced dramatically.

First of all, in [6], we have proposed to modify the selection probability of stochastic tournament selection to take the noise into account. This method, which we will denote as noise-adjusted tournament selection (NATS) in the following, allowed to reduce the number of samples required by approximately 50%, without incurring extra computational efforts. Due to space limitations, we can not describe that method here in more detail, but the general idea is to use a probability of selection for the better individual which depends on the observed standardized fitness difference d^*, and not to simply select the observed better individual with 80% probability. The appropriate

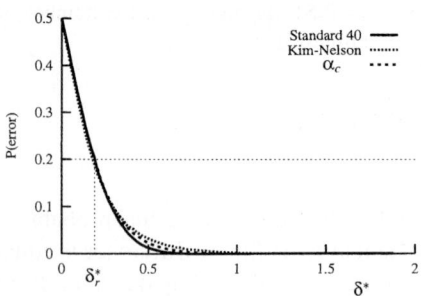
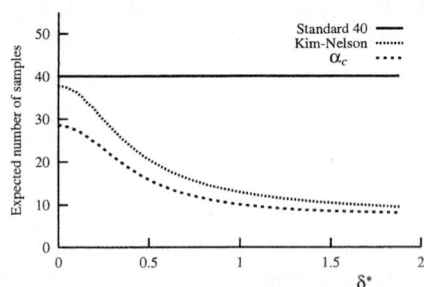

Fig. 2. Error probability curves for different sampling techniques.

Fig. 3. Average number of samples taken per tournament, depending on the true standardized fitness difference δ^* and the sampling technique used.

probability of selection is determined by a method called "bootstrapping". Assuming we use NATS, a total of 40 samples per tournament (20 samples per individual) should be sufficient to eliminate the effect of noise. For this method, the only relevant issue is when the selection error (probability of observing $d < 0$ although $\delta > 0$ or vice versa) falls below the threshold of $\gamma = 20\%$. Using 40 samples per tournament, this is the case for $\delta_r^* = 0.188$ (see Figure 2, line "Standard 40"). Thus, in the following, we are looking for sequential sampling procedures which guarantee an error probability of less than $\alpha = 20\%$ for $\delta^* > \delta_r^* = 0.188$, because these sampling plans should allow us to obtain a selection behavior very close to standard tournament selection based on 80 samples per tournament (and thus complete elimination of noise).

Using Kim and Nelson's procedure and our new proposed sequential sampling procedure with constant α_c. For the given $\delta_r^* = 0.35$ and $\alpha = 0.2$, we observe the error probabilities depicted in Figure 2. As can be seen, the error bounds are observed in all three cases. For $\delta^* > \delta_r^*$, Kim and Nelson's procedure results in a slightly higher error probability than the standard method. Our sampling procedure is better than Kim and Nelson's, but the error is still higher than when the constant sample size is used. This small increase in error might slightly impact the optimization if the sampling method were used in isolation. In our case, however, it is of no importance, because we use it in combination with NATS, which is capable of completely compensating an error of less than $\gamma = 20\%$.

On the other hand, the savings in terms of samples required are depicted in Figure 3. As can be seen, savings are dramatic for both sequential sampling methods, in particular if the true standardized fitness difference δ^* is large. Our method significantly outperforms Kim and Nelson's procedure, yielding savings of about 14-24% of the samples and lower error probabilities. Therefore in the rest of the paper we only use our sequential sampling method α_c.

As has been stated above, all methods can now be combined with NATS as suggested in [6]. Figure 4 compares the actual selection probability of the better individual depending on the actual standardized fitness difference δ^*, for the following three configurations:

1. the standard stochastic tournament selection with 80 samples per tournament
2. the tournament selection probabilities modified according to [6] (NATS) and 40 samples per tournament
3. our sequential sampling procedure with constant error α_c per stage and selection probabilities modified by NATS

As can be seen, all curves look more or less identical. Overall, this means that in order to eliminate the effect of noise, instead of 80 samples per tournament, we only need between 8 and 29 samples (depending on the actual fitness difference of the individuals) by using our new sequential sampling mechanism together with NATS proposed in [6].

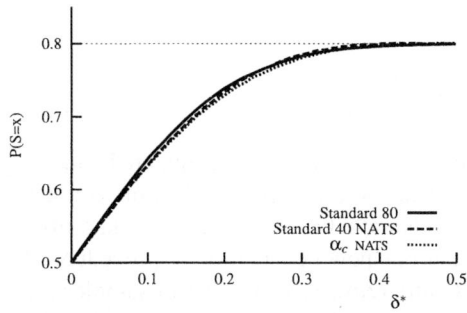

Fig. 4. Resulting selection probability depending on the true standardized fitness difference δ^* for the standard approach with 80 samples per tournament, the standard approach with 40 samples and NATS, and NATS combined with the α_c sequential sampling scheme.

4.2 Behavior During Optimization

In the previous section, it has been shown that by using appropriate sampling techniques, it is possible to avoid the effect of noise with a much smaller number of samples than if each individual would just be sampled the same number of times. To show that these considerations also hold during optimization, Figure 5 empirically compares the convergence curves of the different sampling techniques on the 1000 bit onemax problem. They are all virtually identical to the deterministic case without noise. The corresponding numbers of evaluations per generation are shown in Figure 6 Naturally, the standard approaches sample the same number of times independent of the generation. Surprisingly, the number of samples is also quite constant for the sequential sampling procedure. Only in the very beginning, the number of samples is significantly smaller than later in the run. For our constant α_c method, the sampling effort is never more than 19% of the standard approach, i.e. by integrating the noise into the selection process, we save approximately 81 % of the samples.

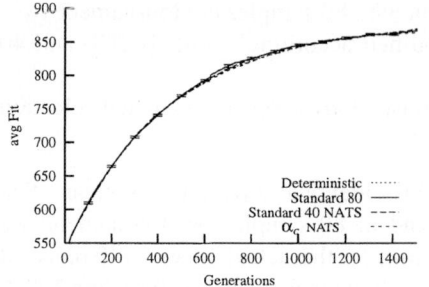 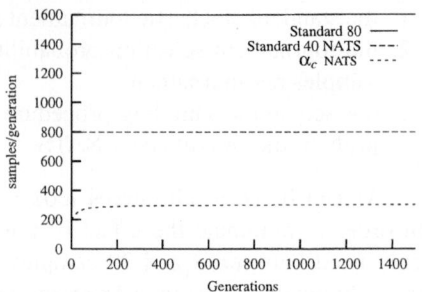

Fig. 5. Fitness over generations, for different sampling techniques, with error bars. For comparison, the GA's behavior in a deterministic environment is also shown.

Fig. 6. Average number of samples required per generation, relative to the deterministic case, for different sampling techniques used.

5 Conclusion

In this paper, we have considered different sequential sampling techniques to reduce the selection error of stochastic tournament selection in noisy environments. Two sequential sampling methods have been compared: a state-of-the-art Indifference Zone Selection procedure, and our new constant-error procedure. As we have shown, both methods allow to drastically reduce the number of samples required to guarantee a desired maximal selection error, with our method performing best. Furthermore, we have demonstrated that either sampling method can be favorably combined with the idea to adjust the selection probabilities to account for the noise which we have presented in [6]. At the example of a simple onemax problem, we have shown that the proposed methods allow to completely eliminate the effect of noise, using only 19% of the samples that are required for the standard selection method.

Future work will include additional improvements resulting from sampling only one individual at a time (instead of both individuals participating in a tournament), and from re-using samples for individuals participating in several tournaments. Sequential sampling procedures can easily be applied to other selection schemes like (μ, λ) or $(\mu + \lambda)$ strategies.

One further direction of our research is the integration of appropiate population sizing, as it may be crucial to the success of a GA in noisy environments.

References

1. Fitzpatrick, J.M., Grefenstette, J.J.: Genetic algorithms in noisy environments. Machine Learning **3** (1988) 101–120
2. Arnold, D.V., Beyer, H.G.: Efficiency and mutation strength adaptation of the $(\mu/\mu_i, \lambda)$-ES in a noisy environment. [22] 39–48
3. Arnold, D.V., Beyer, H.G.: Local performance of the $(\mu/\mu_i, \lambda)$-ES in a noisy environment. In Martin, W., Spears, W., eds.: Foundations of Genetic Algorithms, Morgan Kaufmann (2000) 127–142

4. Arnold, D.V., Beyer, H.G.: A comparison of evolution strategies with other direct search methods in the presence of noise. Computational Optimization and Applications **24** (2003) 135–159
5. Miller, B.L., Goldberg, D.E.: Genetic algorithms, selection schemes, and the varying effects of noise. Evolutionary Computation **4** (1996) 113–131
6. Branke, J., Schmidt, C.: Selection in the presence of noise. In Cantu-Paz, E., ed.: Genetic and Evolutionary Computation Conference. Volume 2723 of LNCS., Springer (2003) 766–777
7. Beyer, H.G.: Toward a theory of evolution strategies: Some asymptotical results from the $(1 \stackrel{+}{,} \lambda)$-theory. Evolutionary Computation **1** (1993) 165–188
8. Hammel, U., Bäck, T.: Evolution strategies on noisy functions, how to improve convergence properties. In Davidor, Y., Schwefel, H.P., Männer, R., eds.: Parallel Problem Solving from Nature. Volume 866 of LNCS., Springer (1994)
9. Miller, B.L.: Noise, Sampling, and Efficient Genetic Algorithms. PhD thesis, Dept. of Computer Science, University of Illinois at Urbana-Champaign (1997) available as TR 97001.
10. Arnold, D.V.: Noisy Optimization with Evolution Strategies. Kluwer (2002)
11. Beyer, H.G.: Evolutionary algorithms in noisy environments: Theoretical issues and guidelines for practice. Computer methods in applied mechanics and engineering **186** (2000) 239–267
12. Aizawa, A.N., Wah, B.W.: Scheduling of genetic algorithms in a noisy environment. Evolutionary Computation (1994) 97–122
13. Albert, L.A., Goldberg, D.E.: Efficient evaluation genetic algorithms under integrated fitness functions. Technical Report 2001024, Illinois Genetic Algorithms Laboratory, Urbana-Champaign, USA (2001)
14. Stagge, P.: Averaging efficiently in the presence of noise. In Eiben, A.E., Bäck, T., Schoenauer, M., Schwefel, H.P., eds.: Parallel Problem Solving from Nature V. Volume 1498 of LNCS., Springer (1998) 188–197
15. Branke, J.: Creating robust solutions by means of an evolutionary algorithm. In Eiben, A.E., Bäck, T., Schoenauer, M., Schwefel, H.P., eds.: Parallel Problem Solving from Nature. Volume 1498 of LNCS., Springer (1998) 119–128
16. Branke, J., Schmidt, C., Schmeck, H.: Efficient fitness estimation in noisy environments. In Spector, L., Goodman, E.D., Wu, A., Langdon, W.B., Voigt, H.M., Gen, M., Sen, S., Dorigo, M., Pezeshk, S., Garzon, M.H.., Burke, E., eds.: Genetic and Evolutionary Computation Conference, Morgan Kaufmann (2001) 243–250
17. Sano, Y., Kita, H.: Optimization of noisy fitness functions by means of genetic algorithms using history of search. [22] 571–580
18. Sano, Y., Kita, H., Kamihira, I., Yamaguchi, M.: Online optimization of an engine controller by means of a genetic algorithm using history of search. In: Asia-Pacific Conference on Simulated Evolution and Learning, Springer (2000) 2929–2934
19. Tsutsui, S., Ghosh, A.: Genetic algorithms with a robust solution searching scheme. IEEE Transactions on Evolutionary Computation **1** (1997) 201–208
20. Branke, J.: Evolutionary Optimization in Dynamic Environments. Kluwer (2001)
21. Kim, S.H., Nelson, B.: A fully sequential procedure for indifference-zone selection in simulation. ACM Transactions on Modelin and Computer Simulation **11** (2001) 251–273
22. Schoenauer, M., Deb, K., Rudolph, G., Yao, X., Lutton, E., Merelo, J.J., Schwefel, H.P., eds. Parallel Problem Solving from Nature. Volume 1917 of LNCS., Springer (2000)

Evolutionary Continuous Optimization by Distribution Estimation with Variational Bayesian Independent Component Analyzers Mixture Model

Dong-Yeon Cho and Byoung-Tak Zhang

Biointelligence Labratory
School of Computer Science and Engineering
Seoul National University
Seoul 151-742, Korea
{dycho,btzhang}@bi.snu.ac.kr
http://bi.snu.ac.kr

Abstract. In evolutionary continuous optimization by building and using probabilistic models, the multivariate Gaussian distribution and their variants or extensions such as the mixture of Gaussians have been used popularly. However, this Gaussian assumption is often violated in many real problems. In this paper, we propose a new continuous estimation of distribution algorithms (EDAs) with the variational Bayesian independent component analyzers mixture model (vbICA-MM) for allowing any distribution to be modeled. We examine how this sophisticated density estimation technique has influence on the performance of the optimization by employing the same selection and population alternation schemes used in the previous EDAs. Our experimental results support that the presented EDAs achieve better performance than previous EDAs with ICA and Gaussian mixture- or kernel-based approaches.

1 Introduction

In the variation operators, particularly mutations of the continuous evolutionary algorithms such as evolution strategy, probability distributions have been used to generate new offspring. Although one of the most popular distributions is Gaussian in continuous cases, we have no prior knowledge of which type of the probability distributions is suitable for the given problem and how the parameter values of the distributions are determined to guide further searches toward the optimal point. This is the reason why we study the effective methods to estimate the probability distributions of the good solutions in the current population. For the last decade, many researchers developed this kind of evolutionary optimization techniques called estimation of distribution algorithms (EDAs) [1] for both discrete and continuous cases. Detailed reviews of existing EDAs can be found in [2] and [3].

For the continuous cases, most of the previous EDAs are based on the multivariate Gaussian distribution and their variants or extensions although there are a few exceptions such as marginal histogram models [4]. In spite of the wide usage of the Gaussian distribution, we suffer from the size of covariance matrix as the dimensionality of the problem increases. This can be alleviated by ignoring the covariance structure (i.e., employing diagonal covariance matrix). In fact, this is assumed in the simplest version of EDAs. However, it extremely cuts down the flexibility of the model.

The conditional factorization of a multivariate joint probability with conditional dependence assumptions can reduce the number of required parameters to define the probability distribution. It can also explicitly represent the conditional dependencies among the variables of the problem by an acyclic directed graph. Larrañaga *et al.* [5] used a probabilistic graphical model called Gaussian network which can be considered as a factorization tool. It decomposes the probability distribution of the given problem into various factors or conditional probabilities. Bosman and Thierens [6] present continuous IDEA instances which also exploit the fact that every multivariate joint probability distribution can be written as a conditional factorization.

We can readily implement this factorization by introducing latent or hidden variables. Latent variable model provides a powerful approach to probabilistic model-building by supplementing a set of directly observed variables with additional latent variables [7]. By defining a joint distribution over visible and latent variables, the corresponding distribution of the observed variables is then obtained by marginalization. This allows relatively complex distributions to be expressed in terms of more tractable joint distributions over the expanded variable space. In addition, it is easy to sample new data from the estimated distribution since latent variable models are generative. More comprehensive explanation and experimental results for our continuous EDAs based on latent variable models can be found in [8] and [9].

Since the data often have the intricate structure which is difficult to capture by a high-order-dependency model such as the Gaussian network, we should consider more complicated probability models. Clustering techniques can be an useful solution to alleviate these difficulties. After making some groups of similar data, we are able to use the existing probability models to obtain an appropriate interpretation for each cluster. Mixture models provide a natural way to handle these clusters in EDAs. They can also build very complex distributions through a proper choice of its components to represent accurately the local areas of support of the true distribution. For continuous cases, the Gaussian mixture models have been successfully applied to the function optimization in [10] and [11]. We also presented a mixture version of continuous EDAs with latent variable models which are corresponding to Gaussian mixtures [12].

As an extreme case of the mixture models, Gaussian Kernels are used in the IDEA frameworks [13]. The localized aspect of the kernel method is better than that of the normal distribution since there is a density function for each data point. However, it completely misses the linkage information and tends to quickly overfit the data. Therefore, the performance of the optimization is seriously affected by the density of sample points and kernel variances. To overcome these difficulties, the mixed Bayesian optimization algorithm (MBOA) uses a Bayesian network with decision trees whose leaf nodes are one-dimensional Gaussian kernel estimators [14]. MBOA is an extension of hierarchical Bayesian Optimization Algorithm (hBOA) [15] from binary to continuous domain. Actually, MBOA can solve both the discrete and continuous problems, but we concentrate on the continuous cases in this paper.

One of the drawbacks in these Gaussian mixture- or kernel-based approaches is that each component or separated domain should be Gaussian. However, this cannot hold in many real cases. In this paper, we propose a new continuous EDAs with the variational Bayesian independent component analyzers mixture model (vbICA-MM) [16]. It can not only model non-Gaussian, separated clusters by incorporating a very flexible ICA model, but also automatically determine the local dimensionality of each cluster by employing recent developments in variational Bayesian inference. We examine how this sophisticated density estimation technique has influence on the performance of the optimization by using the same population alternation schemes as the mixture version of iterated density estimation evolutionary algorithm (MIDEA) and MBOA.

The paper is organized as follows. In Section 2, the basic concept of vbICA-MM is explained. Section 3 presents the EDAs with vbICA-MM for the continuous domain. Then, Section 4 reports the experimental results and their analysis on some benchmark functions. Finally, conclusions of this study are drawn in Section 5.

2 Theoretical Background for vbICA-MM

2.1 Independent Component Analysis Model

Independent component analysis (ICA) tries to model an observed S-dimensional data vector x as a linear combination of statistically independent sources (latent variables) s of dimension L with added Gaussian noise

$$x = As + y + e,$$

where y is an S-dimensional bias vector, A is the $S \times L$ mixing matrix, and e is S-dimensional additive noise which is assumed to be zero-mean Gaussian and isotropic with precision λI. Then, the conditional probability of observing a data vector x^n is given by

$$p(x^n|A, s^n, y, \lambda) = \left(\frac{\lambda}{2\pi}\right)^{\frac{S}{2}} \exp\left\{-\frac{\lambda}{2}(x^n - As - y)^T(x^n - As - y)\right\}.$$

Since the sources $s = \{s_1, s_2, \ldots, s_L\}$ are mutually independent by definition and a mixture of only 1-dimensional Gaussians with m_i components per source is adopted, the distribution over s for data point n can be written as

$$p(s^n|\varphi) = \prod_{i=1}^{L} \sum_{q_i=1}^{m_i} \pi_{i,q_i} \mathcal{N}(s_i^n; \mu_{i,q_i}, \beta_{i,q_i}),$$

where μ_{i,q_i} and β_{i,q_i} are the mean and precision of Gaussian q_i in source i respectively. The mixture proportions π_{i,q_i} are the prior probabilities of choosing component q_i of the ith source. The parameters of source i are $\varphi_i = \{\pi_i, \mu_i, \beta_i\}$ and the complete parameter set of the source model is $\varphi = \{\varphi_1, \varphi_2, \ldots, \varphi_L\}$. This mixture of Gaussian source model allows any distribution to be modeled [17].

The complete collection of possible source states is denoted $\boldsymbol{q} = \{\boldsymbol{q}_1, \boldsymbol{q}_2, \ldots, \boldsymbol{q}_m\}$ and runs over all $m = \prod_i m_i$ possible combinations of source states. By integrating and summing over the hidden variables, $\{\boldsymbol{s}, \boldsymbol{q}\}$, the likelihood of the IID data $\boldsymbol{X} = \{\boldsymbol{x}^1, \boldsymbol{x}^2, \ldots, \boldsymbol{x}^N\}$ given the model parameters $\Theta = \{\boldsymbol{A}, \boldsymbol{y}, \lambda, \varphi\}$ can now be written as

$$p(\boldsymbol{X}|\Theta) = \prod_{n=1}^{N} \sum_{q=1}^{m} \int p(\boldsymbol{x}^n, \boldsymbol{s}^n, \boldsymbol{q}^n|\Theta) d\boldsymbol{s}, \qquad (1)$$

where $d\boldsymbol{s} = \prod_i ds_i$.

2.2 ICA Mixture Model

We suppose that a data vector $\boldsymbol{x}^n$ is generated from a C-component mixture model given assumptions $\mathcal{M}$. Then, the probability can be written in the form

$$p(\boldsymbol{x}^n|\mathcal{M}) = \sum_{c=1}^{C} p(c|\mathcal{M}_0) p(\boldsymbol{x}^n|\mathcal{M}_c, c), \qquad (2)$$

where $\mathcal{M} = \{\mathcal{M}_0, \mathcal{M}_1, \ldots, \mathcal{M}_C\}$ is the vector of assumptions about the mixture process, $\mathcal{M}_0$, and component model assumptions, $\mathcal{M}_c$. The variable c indicates which component of the mixture model is chosen to generate a given data vector.

For the ICA mixture model, we specify a form for $p(c|\mathcal{M}_0)$ and substitute (1) into (2). Then, we can quantifies the likelihood of the observed data under the ICA mixture model as follows

$$p(\boldsymbol{x}^n|\mathcal{M}) = \sum_{c=1}^{C} p(c|\boldsymbol{\kappa}) p(\boldsymbol{X}|\Theta_c, c),$$

where $p(c|\boldsymbol{\kappa}) = \{p(c=1) = \kappa_1, p(c=2) = \kappa_2, \ldots, p(c=C) = \kappa_C\}$ and Θ_c is the parameters for the cth ICA model. We can obtain the maximum likelihood (ML) estimation for these parameters as well as the values of the latent variables by using gradient descent or the EM algorithm. However, the ML methods can easily get caught in local maxima and fail to determine the best model structure since there is no consideration of model complexity.

2.3 Variational Bayesian Learning for vbICA-MM

Bayesian approaches overcome the weakness of ML methods by integrating out the parameters $\{\boldsymbol{\kappa}, \Theta_c\}$ and hidden variables $\{\boldsymbol{s}_c, \boldsymbol{q}_c\}$ and penalizing more complex models which can lead to overfitting. For this purpose, the prior distributions over the model parameters and hidden variables are properly chosen to be conjugate to allow the tractability. A detailed statement for the priors over the ICA mixture models can be found in [16].

Although Bayesian inference has the ability to handle the overfitting and select the best model structure, it is often computationally intensive and analytically intractable in practice. One of the useful tools for Bayesian integration is the variational approximation. We consider the log evidence for data $\boldsymbol{X}$ and form a lower bound on it using Jensen's inequality:

$$\log p(\boldsymbol{X}) = \log \int d\boldsymbol{W} p(\boldsymbol{X}, \boldsymbol{W}) \geq \int d\boldsymbol{W} p'(\boldsymbol{W}) \log \frac{p(\boldsymbol{X}, \boldsymbol{W})}{p'(\boldsymbol{W})} \equiv F[\boldsymbol{W}], \quad (3)$$

where $\boldsymbol{W}$ is the vector of all hidden variables and unknown parameters, and $p'(\boldsymbol{W})$ is a tractable approximation to the posterior $p(\boldsymbol{W}|\boldsymbol{X})$. We can compare various models by calculating F for each model as well as implicitly integrate out the unknowns $\boldsymbol{W}$ by maximizing F.

For the tractable Bayesian learning of the ICA mixture model, the following factorization of the distribution of the parameters and hidden variables is used:

$$p'(\boldsymbol{W}) = p'(c)p'(\boldsymbol{s}_c|\boldsymbol{q}_c, c)p'(\boldsymbol{q}_c|, c)p'(\boldsymbol{\kappa})p'(\boldsymbol{y})p'(\boldsymbol{\lambda})p'(\boldsymbol{A})p'(\boldsymbol{\alpha})p'(\boldsymbol{\varphi}), \quad (4)$$

where $p'(\boldsymbol{\varphi}) = p'(\boldsymbol{\pi})p'(\boldsymbol{\mu})p'(\boldsymbol{\beta})$, $p'(a|b)$ is the approximating density of $p'(a|b, \boldsymbol{X})$, and $\boldsymbol{\alpha}$ is the precision vector for each column of mixing matrix $\boldsymbol{A}$ whose elements have a zero-mean Gaussian as the prior distribution. The posteriors over the sources also factorize such that

$$p'(\boldsymbol{s}_c|\boldsymbol{q}_c, c) = \prod_{i=1}^{L_c} p'(q_i|c)p'(s_{c,i}|q_i, c).$$

This additional factorization allows efficient scaling of computation with the number of latent variables. By substituting $p(\boldsymbol{X}, \boldsymbol{W})$ and (4) into (3), we obtain expressions for the bound, F, to the ICA mixture model. In order to know how the measure F is maximized, that is, how the vbICA-MM algorithm is implemented in detail, see [16].

3 Continuous EDAs with vbICA-MM

3.1 Distribution Estimation by vbICA-MM

Most evolutionary algorithms for continuous optimization problems maintain a population of real vectors to search for an optimal point. The vbICA-MM can put similar individuals together in a group and estimate the density for each group simultaneously. This means that vbICA-MM implicitly divides the current population into C sub-populations and finds the values of latent variables and parameters to build a corresponding density model for each sub-population by variational Bayesian learning. Unlike the mixture of Gaussian or other Gaussian-based latent variable models, each cluster can have a non-Gaussian distribution in the vbICA-MM. This is because the source model can enclose the distributions with positive and negative kurtosis and complex multimodal distributions.

We first select the good candidates from the current population as the data used in the density estimation step. Both selection schemes of MIDEA and MBOA were tried in our experiments. MIDEA adopts the truncation selection where the best $\lfloor \tau N \rfloor$ $(0 < \tau < 1)$ vectors are taken. In MBOA, $\lfloor \tau N \rfloor$ vectors are chosen by repeating the tournament selection (where the tournament size is two).

To estimate the probability distribution of the selected population, we use the MATLAB vbICA-MM software from Choudrey[1]. Although we can determine which model is preferred, that is, what is the best value for C by monitoring F according to the number of mixtures, we just fix the value of C in our experiments for the fast estimation. We also utilize the maximum number of sources, which means that the source vector has the same dimensions as the data ($L = S$). However, the relevance of each source may be automatically determined. Column i of the mixing matrix $\boldsymbol{A}_c$ will be close to zero if the precision α_i for the column is large, indicating source i is irrelevant. The ICA mixture model is trained until F changed by less than 0.01 or the number of iterations reached 10.

3.2 Generating a New Population

To create a new individual $\tilde{\boldsymbol{x}}^n$ from the trained model, we first have to determine which component density c is responsible for the randomly chosen parent $\boldsymbol{x}^n$ from the selected vectors as the data. According to a probability proportional to the estimated component posterior probability, the component c is selected. Then, we can sample easily the new individual $\tilde{\boldsymbol{x}}^n$ from the conditional distribution given the corresponding latent variable $\boldsymbol{s}_c^n$ defined to be the Gaussian distribution $\mathcal{N}(\boldsymbol{A}_c \boldsymbol{s}_c^n + \boldsymbol{y}_c, \lambda_c \boldsymbol{I})$. This sampling task is trivial since we can have the reconstructed values of hidden variables and parameters from the trained model and the noise is assumed to be zero-mean Gaussian and isotropic. As mentioned earlier, however, the source distribution is not a simple Gaussian but the factorized mixture of Gaussians, which makes the vbICA-MM more flexible than Gaussian mixtures and the mixture version of other latent variable models. This sampling procedure is repeated until $(N - \lfloor \tau N \rfloor)$ vectors are obtained.

Besides the way to estimate the density, a population alternation method is also important. We tried both schemes of MIDEA and MBOA with vbICA-MM. The new sampled vectors replace the worst $(N - \lfloor \tau N \rfloor)$ vectors in MIDEA. To ensure an effective niching, MBOA employs restricted tournament replacement (RTR) proposed originally in [18]. RTR selects a subset of the original population for each new sampled offspring. The size of these subsets is fixed to some constant, called the window size. Then, the new offspring competes with the most similar member of the subset. If the new one is better, it replaces the corresponding individual; otherwise, the new one is discarded.

---

[1] [online] http://www.robots.ox.ac.uk/~riz/Code/vbICA1_0.tar.gz

4 Experimental Results

To evaluate the quality of the proposed EDA with vbICA-MM, we compare our EDAs with three evolutionary optimization algorithms based on the learning of probability distribution. For fair experiments, each selection and population alternation schemes of three previous algorithms is incorporated into the EDA with vbICA-MM, respectively.

4.1 UMDA/ICA

As a first attempt to combine EDAs with ICA, Zhang et al. [19] proposed univariate marginal distribution algorithm with independent component analysis (UMDA/ICA). This algorithm applies ICA to the points in the selected parent set before the density is estimated. Since this preprocessing via ICA eliminates some nonlinear interrelations among the variables, we can prevent a bad approximation of the density by using UMDA [1] which assumes all variables are independent.

To compare our EDAs with UMDA/ICA, we used same test function as [19]:

$$f(x_1, x_2, x_3, x_4) = \sum_{i=1}^{3} \sum_{j=i+1}^{4} \{100(x_i^2 - x_j)^2 + (1 - x_1)^2\}, \quad |x_i| \leq 2.048.$$

In this function, each variable interacts with every other variable. The smallest function value is 0 at point $(1,1,1,1)$. The population size N in all experiments were 3,000. All algorithms were stopped if the number of generation is equal to 120. We used 2-tournament selection like UMDA/ICA. The population is divided into 1,500 groups of 2 points, and the point with lower function value in each group is selected. All selected points are directly entered into the next generation and the half of the population is filled with the new sampled points from the estimated probability density. For vbICA-MM, we set three components per source mixture of Gaussian and the number of mixtures C for data vectors is 4. As shown in Table 1, our EDAs with vbICA-MM has a better performance and stability than UMDA/ICA.

Table 1. Comparative results with UMDA/ICA. The objective function values are averaged over 10 independent runs. Here, the results for UMDA and UMDA/ICA came from [19]. ([†]We have no idea about what the precision is.)

Algorithm	Objective function value		
	Mean ± Stdev	Best	Worst
UMDA	4.6247 ± 0.537	3.528	5.189
UMDA/ICA	2.499 ± 1.650	0[†]	4.704
EDA with vbICA-MM	4.316 ×10^{-6} ± 2.617 × 10^{-6}	1.002 ×10^{-6}	9.740 ×10^{-6}

4.2 MIDEA

To compare our EDAs with MIDEA, we use two benchmark functions. One of them is a ten-dimensional Rosenbrock function,

$$f_{Ro}(\boldsymbol{x}) = \sum_{i=2}^{10}(100(x_i - x_{i-1}^2)^2 + (1 - x_{i-1})^2).$$

Although this function is unimodal, there are non-linear dependencies between variables. It has parabolic valleys along the curves $x_i = x_{i-1}^2$ in the search interval $|x_i| \leq 5.12$ with the minimum 0 at point (1,...,1). The other is a ten-dimensional Fletcher-Powell function,

$$f_{FP}(\boldsymbol{x}) = \sum_{i=1}^{10}(\sum_{j=1}^{10}(a_{ij}\sin\alpha_j + b_{ij}\cos\alpha_j) - \sum_{j=1}^{10}(a_{ij}\sin x_j + b_{ij}\cos x_j))^2,$$

where a_{ij} and b_{ij} are random integers in the range [-100, 100]. Obviously the minimum value is 0 at $x_j = \alpha_j \in [-\pi, \pi]$. This function is highly multimodal and not symmetric. We used the same values for a_{ij}, b_{ij} and α_j published in [20].

The parameter setting for MIDEA is as follow. The maximum amount of clusters is 8 and the threshold of the BEND leader algorithm used for clustering in MIDEA is 0.3 (which is determined to make 8 clusters in almost every generation). We also allowed the maximum number of parents for any variable in the Gaussian networks. The portion τ of the selected individuals to build the probabilistic model is 0.3. To choose the best population size for MIDEA, we used the testing sequence $N = [200, 400, 800, 1600, 3200, 6400]$ performing 20 runs for each size. From these tests, we obtained the best average fitness when N is 6400 for both functions. Same parameter values are applied to our EDAs with vbICA-MM. All algorithms are terminated when the number of function evaluation is 10^6.

Table 2 shows the comparative results. Although we fail to obtain the optimum value of the Rosenbrock function for both methods, our EDAs with vbICA-MM has a little better performance than MIDEA. However, our methods outperform MIDEA for the Fletcher-Powell function while consuming more time than MIDEA.

4.3 Fletcher-Powell Function

With the above testing sequence, we set the population size for MBOA. The best mean fitness values are shown when N is 3200 for Rosenbrock function and 800 for Fletcher-Powell function. These population sizes are also used in our methods. The window size in RTR is $N/20$ and the number of mixtures C for vbICA-MM is 8. All algorithms are allowed 10^6 function evaluations.

For Rosenbrock function, there is no significant difference of the performance. However, this function can be optimized more efficiently by EDAs with vbICA-MM than MBOA. Our EDAs are better than MBOA for Fletcher-Powell function with respect to the performance and stability while our methods are more time-consuming than MBOA for this multimodal case (Table 3).

Table 2. Comparative results with MIDEA. Mean fitness values with standard deviations and relative time (RT) averaged on 20 runs.

	Rosenbrock		Fletcher-Powell	
Algorithm	Mean ± Stdev	RT	Mean ± Stdev	RT
MIDEA	7.538 ± 0.049	6.888	103.861 ± 31.404	0.255
EDA with vbICA-MM	3.954 ± 1.501	51.302	$6.417 \times 10^{-3} \pm 0.010$	47.284

Table 3. Comparative results with MBOA. Mean fitness values with standard deviations and relative time (RT) averaged on 20 runs.

	Rosenbrock		Fletcher-Powell	
Algorithm	Mean ± Stdev	RT	Mean ± Stdev	RT
MBOA	$2.886 \times 10^{-2} \pm 0.0314$	5135.15	$4.243 \times 10^{-1} \pm 1.272$	7.573
EDA with vbICA-MM	$1.693 \times 10^{-2} \pm 0.0307$	500.53	$2.320 \times 10^{-2} \pm 0.007$	378.65

5 Conclusions

We presented a new estimation of distribution algorithm based on the variational Bayesian independent component analyzers mixture model. The influence of this novel density estimation technique on the optimization performance is analyzed by adopting the same selection and population alternation schemes used in the previous EDAs. Experimental results show that EDAs with vbICA-MM outperform the ICA-combined UMDA. They are also better than EDAs with Gaussian mixture- or kernel-based approaches for two benchmark functions. This superiority is more evident in the multimodal case than unimodal one.

Acknowledgments

This research was supported by the Ministry of Commerce, Industry and Energy through the MEC project, the Ministry of Science and Technology through National Research Lab (NRL), and the Ministry of Education and Human Resources Development under the BK21-IT Program. The ICT at Seoul National University provided research facilities for this study.

References

1. Mühlenbein, H., Paaß, G.: From Recombination of Genes to the Estimation of Distribution I. Binary Parameters. In: Voigt, H.-M. et al. (eds.): *Parallel Problem Solving from Nature IV.* Lecture Notes in Computer Science, Vol. 1141. Springer (1996) 178-187
2. Larrañaga, P.: A Review on Estimation of Distribution Algorithms. In: Larrañaga, P., Lozano, J.A. (eds.), *Estimation of Distribution Algorithms: A New Tools for Evolutionary Computation.* Kluwer Academic Publishers (2001) 57-100

3. Pelikan, M., Goldberg, D.E., Lobo, F.G.: A Survey of Optimization by Building and Using Probabilistic Models. *Computational Optimization and Applications* **21** (2002) 5-20
4. Tsutsui, S., Pelikan, M., Goldberg, D.E.: Evolutionary Algorithm using Marginal Histogram in Continuous Domain. In *Proceedings of the GECCO-2001 Workshop Program*. (2001) 230-233
5. Larrañaga, P., Etxeberria, R., Lozano, J.A., Peña, J.M.: Optimization in Continuous Domains by Learning and Simulation of Gaussian Networks. In *Proceedings of the GECCO-2000 Workshop Program*. (2000) 201-204
6. Bosman, P., Thierens, D.: Expanding from Discrete to Continuous Estimation of Distribution Algorithms: The IDEA. In: Schoenauer, M. et al. (eds.): *Parallel Problem Solving from Nature VI*. Lecture Notes in Computer Science, Vol. 1917. Springer (2000) 767-776
7. Bishop, C.M.: Latent Variable Models. In: Jordan, M.I. (ed.), *Learning in Graphical Models*. The MIT Press (1999) 371-403
8. Shin, S.-Y., Zhang, B.-T.: Bayesian Evolutionary Algorithms for Continuous Function Optimization. In *Proceedings of 2001 Congress on Evolutionary Computation*, Vol. 1. (2001) 508-515
9. Cho, D.-Y., Zhang, B.-T.: Continuous Estimation of Distribution Algorithms with Probabilistic Principal Component Analysis. In *Proceedings of 2001 Congress on Evolutionary Computation*, Vol. 1. (2001) 521-526
10. Gallagher, M., Frean, M., Downs, T.: Real-Valued Evolutionary Optimization Using a Flexible Probability Density Estimator. In: *Proceedings of 1999 Genetic and Evolutionary Computation Conference*, Vol. 1. (1999) 840-846
11. Bosman, P., Thierens, D.: Advancing Continuous IDEAs with Mixture Distributions and Factorization Selection Metrics. In *Proceedings of the GECCO-2001 Workshop Program*. (2001) 208-212
12. Cho, D.-Y., Zhang, B.-T.: Evolutionary Optimization by Distribution Estimation with Mixtures of Factor Analyzers. In *Proceedings of 2002 Congress on Evolutionary Computation*, Vol. 2. (2002) 1396-1401
13. Bosman, P., Thierens, D.: IDEAs Based on the Normal Kernels Probability Density Function. Technical Report, UU-CS-2000-11. Utrecht University (2002)
14. Ocenasek, J., Schwarz, J.: Estimation of Distribution Algorithm for Mixed Continuous-Discrete Optimization. In *Proceedings of the 2nd Euro-International Symposium on Computational Intelligence*. (2002) 227-232
15. Pelikan, M., Goldberg, D.E.: Escaping Hierarchical Traps with Competent Genetic Algorithms. In: Spector, L. et al. (eds.): *Proceedings of 2001 Genetic and Evolutionary Computation Conference*. (2001) 511-518
16. Choudrey, R.A., Roberts, S.J.: Variational Mixture of Bayesian Independent Component Analyzers. *Neural Computation* **15** (2003) 213-252
17. Attias, H.: Independent Factor Analysis. *Neural Computation* **11** (1999) 803-851
18. Harik, G.R.: Finding Multimodal Solutions Using Restricted Tournament Selection. In: Eshelman, L.J. (ed.): *Proceedings of the sixth International Conference on Genetic Algorithms*. (1995) 24-31
19. Zhang, Q., Allinson, N.M., Yin, H.: Population Opimization Algorithm Based on ICA. In: Yao, X. and Fogel, D. B. (eds.): *Proceedings of the First IEEE Symposium on Combinations of Evolutionary Computation and Neural Networks*. (2000) 33-36
20. Bäck, T.: *Evolutionary Algorithms in Theory and Practice*. Oxford University Press (1996)

Spread of Vector Borne Diseases in a Population with Spatial Structure

Dominique Chu and Jonathan E. Rowe

School of Computer Science, University of Birmingham
Birmingham B15 2TT, UK
{dxc,jer}@cs.bham.ac.uk
http://www.cs.bham.ac.uk

Abstract. Mathematical modelling of the spread of infectious diseases is a well established field with high practical importance. Underlying most analytical approaches is the assumption of "perfect mixing", that is the idea that the spatial structure of the population can be neglected. This assumption is crucial to the solvability of the models, but can be dropped when using computational models instead of analytical approaches. Using methods from Artificial Life, we investigate under which conditions the perfect mixing assumption becomes a good approximation to describe the spread of vector borne disease in a population with spatial structure.

1 Introduction

Understanding the spread of vector borne diseases is of great importance. Despite a global AIDS crisis, vector borne diseases (i.e. infections that are transmitted by an intermediate agent (vector) that is usually not affected by the infection itself. One important example of such a disease is Malaria) remain an important cause of premature deaths in tropical countries. Beside the human tragedy, premature deaths do of course also have economic implications. It is therefore of great interest for governments to set measures to eradicate or at least minimise the spread of these diseases.

Mathematical and computational modelling[1–3] of the spread of these diseases can help gain an understanding of which measures might be effective before they are actually implemented (thus saving costs). A great advantage of mathematical (i.e. equation based) approaches is their great versatility and generality. Particularly analytic solutions to those models lead to an understanding of the various dynamical regimes of the system. However, analytical solutions are typically only possible under rather restrictive assumptions. In the context of infectious disease modelling, it is usually assumed that the spatial structure of the population can be ignored, that is that all participants of the system interact with one another. This assumption is usually referred to as "perfect mixing."

An important methodological tool of Artificial Life is agent-based modelling (ABM)[4–6]. ABMs allow for an easy representation of populations with spatial structure. At the same time they allow the precision of the control of assumptions as other formal modelling approaches; a drawback of ABMs is their lack of generality. In principle for every set of parameters, a simulation needs to be run. In practise however, this is not necessary. A coarse grained exploration of the parameter space is usually sufficient, but might nevertheless necessitate a very large number of simulations.

One way to integrate equation and agent-based models is to use the latter as validation test-beds to guide the development of the former[7, 8]. In the present context of vector borne diseases, ABMs are particularly useful as test-beds that help create an understanding of the scope of the perfect mixing assumption. It is quite obvious that in the real world the perfect mixing assumption is probably never fulfilled exactly; an important question is thus to understand under which conditions a system starts to behave as though it was perfectly mixed.

2   Description of the Model

The model we describe in this article is not meant to be realistic with respect to the behaviour of any real system. The main emphasis of the model is to maximise the simplicity, which then allows us to maximise the understanding of its dynamics. Once this basic understanding is reached, it will be possible to add effects to the model in order to make it more realistic.

ABMs are best described in order of their major components:

- Environment
- Agents
- Interactions

The environment of the model is a 2 dimensional continuous space of size $2L \times 2L$, where L is measured in some unit. The environment has no features other than that it provides a topology for the agents.

There are two types of agents in the model, "vectors" and "people". Those agents are mainly distinguished by their infection period, movement rules, and mode of infection transmission. An infection can only be transmitted between agents of different type. The number of agents of each type is held constant during a simulation run. Agents are thus characterised by their position in the environment and by their internal state, which can be either "infected" or "healthy".

At each time-step the agents take a random position within a square of linear size *StepSize* centred around their current position. *StepSize* is a parameter of the model and set independently for people and vectors. Movement is always subject to the constraint that the agents stay within the boundaries of the environment. A parameter of the model s called the *shrink factor* allows to restrict the space of the people agents to a square of size $2Ls \times 2Ls$ in the centre of the world. Vectors continue to occupy the entire world. This enables us to vary the population density of the people agents.

The only form of interaction between agents is transmission of an infection. At each time-step vectors interact simultaneously with all people that are at most one unit away from it. If the vector is infected then all agents it interacts with will also be infected from the following time-step on. If the vector is not infected, but at least one of the people is infected, then the vector will be infected from the next time-step on. Throughout all simulations presented here, vectors keep their infection for two time-steps and people keep their infection for 40 time-steps. However, the model has re-infection, that is whenever an agent interacts with another infected agent, while it is already infected, then its remaining infection period is reset to its full value. So, for example, if a people agent is re-infected 39 time-steps after it has been infected the last time, then it will still have to wait for 40 more time-steps until it loses its infection again.

3 Analysis of the Perfect Mixing Case

In this particular model, each agent is associated with a bite area, that is a circle of radius one centred around it. Vectors and people agents will only interact with one another if they are within each other's bite area. This bite area models spatial proximity of the agents. If the area of the world is $W = 4L^2$, then the possibly overlapping bite areas b of n agents in the system will occupy a fraction $q(n)$ of the entire space.

$$q(n, s) = 1 - s^2 \exp(-bn/(s^2 W)) \tag{1}$$

The additional variable s allows to take into account that people agents might be restricted to a particular fraction s^2 of the overall space (the shrink factor – see below).

If P and p are the total number of people agents and the number of infected agents respectively, and M and m are the analogous values for vectors, then we can write down a set of equations describing the behaviour of the people and vector population in equilibrium.

Assume R_m and R_p are the number of time-steps necessary for the vectors and people agents to recover. According to eq. 1, in perfect mixing the probability for a particular people agent not to be within the bite area of a vector is given by $1 - q(m, 1)$. People agents are not infected if they have not been within the bite area of an infected vector during the last R_p time-steps. A similar reasoning holds for vectors, with the additional complication that we also want to account for the case that people are restricted to a fraction s of the overall space. In this case we have to take into account that the density of people agents within their area is increase (because they are crammed into smaller space), but the probability for a vector to land within the space of occupied by the agents is only s^2.

The fraction of infected people (vector) agents is then given by the probability that the people (vector) agent has been within the bite area of a vector (people agent) within the last R_p (R_m) time-steps at least once.

$$\frac{m}{M} = 1 - \left(1 - s^2 q(p, s)\right)^{R_m}$$
$$\frac{p}{P} = 1 - \left(1 - q(m, 1)\right)^{R_p} \tag{2}$$

Table 1. Meaning of the variables used in the model of section 3.

M	total number of vectors
P	total number of people
m	number of infected vectors
p	number of infected people
R_m	time for vector to recover
R_p	time for person to recover
b	biting area of a vector
W	world size (area)

We could not find an analytical solution for this set of equations; instead we obtain all theoretical predictions reported in this article by numerically solving the equations for m and p.

An approximation to eqn. 2 allows us to find the minimal system size at which the infection will be sustained within the population. Suppose the system is at time-step t. Again, a people agent will not be infected at the next time-step if it has not been bitten for the last R_p time-steps. So similar to eqn. 1 we write:

$$\frac{p(t+1)}{P} = 1 - \exp\left(\frac{-m(t)bR_p}{W}\right) \qquad (3)$$

A vector is not infected at time $t+1$ if they have not bitten an infected person for the last R_m steps. Assume that the density of agents is not very high, such that the overlapping between the bite areas can be ignored. If a vector is dropped into the area occupied by people agents, then the probability of landing within the bite area of a people agent is $b/(s^2W)$; in order to obtain the correct result, this probability needs to be multiplied with the probability of actually being dropped into the occupied area s^2. Altogether the fraction of infected vectors at time $t+1$ equals the fraction probability that a vector has been bitten at least once during the previous R_m time-steps by any of the infected people agents. Assuming that the system is close to or at equilibrium, we can write

$$\frac{m(t+1)}{M} = 1 - \prod_{i=t-R_m}^{t}\left(1 - s^2\frac{b}{s^2W}\right)^{p(t)}$$

$$= 1 - \left(1 - s^2\frac{b}{s^2W}\right)^{p(t)R_m} \approx \frac{bR_m p(t)}{W} \qquad (4)$$

where the approximation is good if b is much smaller than W. Because we are at equilibrium, $m(t+1) = m(t) = m$. Combining those results gives

$$p(t+1) = P - P\exp\left(-\frac{MR_m R_p b^2 p(t)}{W^2}\right)$$

One solution is $p = 0$. This corresponds to all people agents being uninfected. To find when this is stable, we proceed as follows: Write

$$G(p) = P - P\exp\left(-\frac{MR_m R_p b^2 p}{W^2}\right)$$

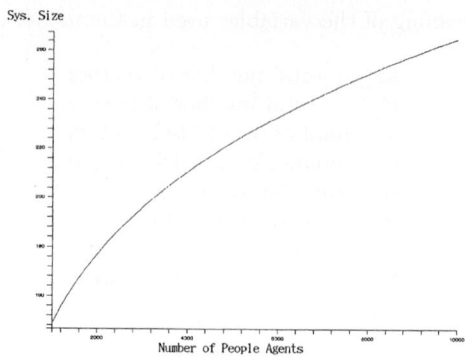

Fig. 1. Assuming a fixed vector population of 10000, this graph shows the points at which the infection gains foothold in a system according to equation 5.

so that $p(t+1) = G(p)$ at equilibrium. Then the state $p = 0$ is stable if $|dG/dp| < 1$ when $p = 0$.

$$\frac{dG}{dp} = \frac{PMR_m R_p b^2}{W^2} \exp\left(-\frac{MR_m R_p b^2 p}{W^2}\right)$$

At $p = 0$ we have

$$\frac{dG}{dp}\bigg|_{p=0} = \frac{PMR_m R_p b^2}{W^2}$$

So the equilibrium is stable if

$$\frac{PMR_m R_p b^2}{W^2} < 1$$

or, alternatively,

$$\frac{b}{W} < \frac{1}{\sqrt{MPR_m R_p}} \tag{5}$$

This equation enables us to predict the minimal world-size for which the infection gets established in the system (see figure 1). Note that equation 5 predicts that the shrink factor does not seem to influence the minimal world size.

4 Results

In all simulation runs presented in this article, the infection period for vectors and people agents is kept constant at 2 and 40 respectively. This choice is to a large degree arbitrary, but reflects the idea that the life-time of the vectors is shorter than the infection period of the people. In all simulations shown, we varied the linear size L of the system in discrete steps of 10 from 10 to 400; this corresponds to system of area between 400 and 640000 square units. For each linear system size setting we simulated the system for 5000 time-steps and recorded the fraction of the infected people and vector agents averaged over the

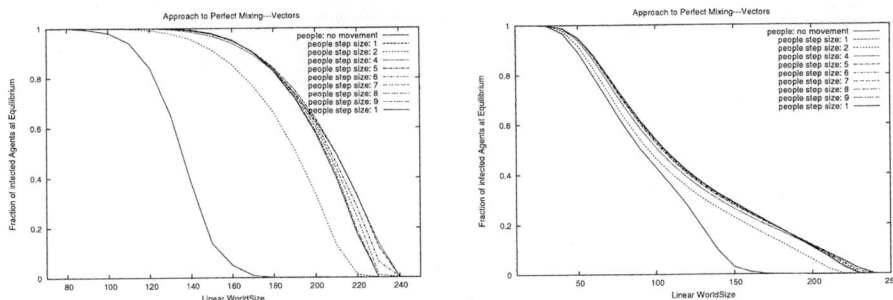

Fig. 2. The left (right) graph shows the fraction of infected people agents (vectors) versus the linear system size. The recorded data points are not shown here, but replaced by connecting line segments for better viewing. Increasing the mobility of people initially has a dramatic effect on the infection levels in the population, but further increases show less dramatic increases.

last 1000 time-steps. At this time the system has reached its steady state. For all simulations presented here we keep the number of agents and vectors in the system at 5000 and 10000 respectively.

In the first series of simulations we kept the step-size of the vectors constant at one, whereas the step-size of the people agents steps varied from 0 to 9. The results of those simulations are summarised in figure 2. The graphs show clearly that already a slight increase of the movement leads to a dramatic change of the behaviour of the system. When the step-size is zero (no movement for people) the infection gets established at a linear system size of 180. However, in the case of a step-size of 1, the infection can establish itself at considerably lower densities, namely at a linear system size of about 230. The graph shows clearly that this is already the same density as in the case of a step-size of 9. Note that for intermediate step-sizes the infection is actually slightly more severe, (i.e. higher infection rates at similar densities) than for the large step-sizes.

Figure 3 shows a comparison between the theoretical prediction for the perfect mixing case and experimental results from an implementation of the perfect mixing scenario. This graph shows that when the people agents' step-size is nine, then the model behaves like in perfect mixing, even if the vectors' step-size is only 1.

In the next set of experiments the people agents are distributed on a smaller area than the vectors. In the specific simulations we performed, the agents are distributed on a square in the centre of the environment. The linear size of the square is half the size of entire world. Equation 5 predicts that the shrinkage of the agent area does not have any influence on the minimal world size where the infection gets established in the world. Theoretical predictions (that is numerical solutions of eqn. 2) could confirm this for a number of example simulations (data not shown); furthermore, this result is also confirmed by actual simulation of the system as can be seen in figure 4. The $s < 1$ case is a good approximation for the symmetric case, when the total area of the world is large, but still supports the

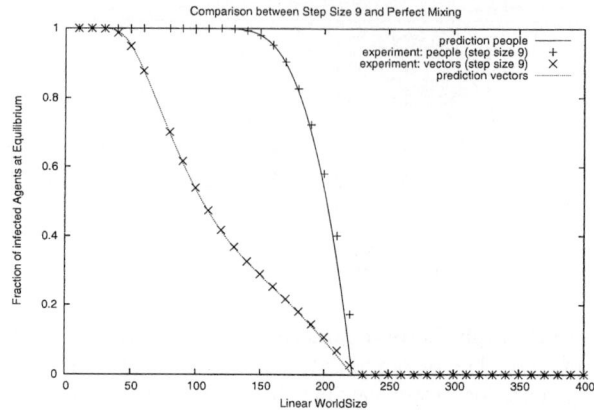

Fig. 3. This graph compares the predicted behaviour of a perfect mixing model with the actual simulation results obtained from a simulations of people with step-size nine and vectors with a step-size of 1.

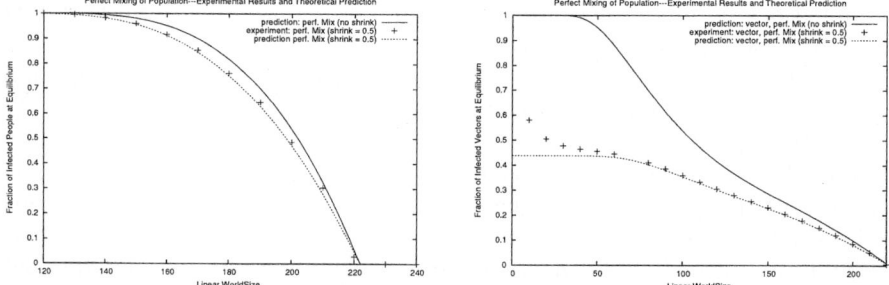

Fig. 4. Those graphs show a comparison of the perfect mixing case with and without shrinkage of the agent-area. The lhs shows the infection levels in the people population; the rhs analogous results for the vector agent population.

infection. This approximation becomes progressively worse, as the linear size of the world L and s decrease. Figure 5 shows that the approximation is only good for the people agent population, whereas the vector populations has infection levels very different from the $s = 1$ case.

As shown above, when $s = 1$ then increasing the step-size of people agents quickly approximates the perfect mixing case, even though the agents retain a maximal step-size. Simulations show that this is not the case any more when $s < 1$. Figure 5 shows that agent movement can not approximate the perfect mixing case of the population any more, if the people agents are restricted to a shrunk area. Instead the people population seems to approximate the behaviour of an $s = 1$ system with the same density of agents. This is only true for the people agents; for not too small world-sizes, the vector population has s^2 times the infection level of the scaled-up system.

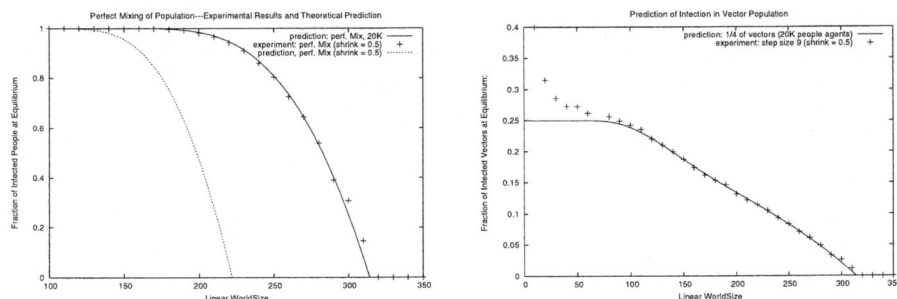

Fig. 5. When only the people agents are allowed to move, then this does not lead to perfect mixing any more. The crosses represent data points won from the actual simulation. The dotted curve is the theoretical prediction for the perfect mixing case of the shrunk population. The solid curve is the theoretical prediction for an $s = 1$ system, but with the same people density as the shrunk system in the shrunk area; in this case this is 20K people agents.

5 Discussion

An extreme case of spatial structure in the population is reached when the step-size of people agents is zero. In this case it is useful to think the system as consisting of a number of separated clusters. A cluster is defined as a group of connected people agents. Two such agents are connected if there exists a possibility that a vector can catch an infection from one agent and infect the second one. By this definition it is thus impossible to have cross-infection between agents of two separate clusters.

An important factor for the understanding of the dynamics of infections in clusters is that an infection might not be very stable in small clusters if the density of vectors is low. In order to sustain the infection within one cluster it is necessary that at least once every 40 time-steps a vector infects itself from a people agent and either re-infects this people agent or carries the infection to another agent in the cluster. Clearly, there are a number of important factors influencing whether or not an infection will be sustained. Shape and density of the clusters have an important influence on the likelihood of cross-infection between agents. Similarly, the density of vectors across every cluster is a crucial factor and can be assumed to be approximate well the average density M/W.

If we assume that the internal structure of clusters of a given size tend to be similar to each other, then the vector density is the crucial factor. At small densities (i.e. large W) small clusters will tend to lose their infection within relatively short times through random fluctuation of vector densities. We can thus assume that only clusters of a minimum size A will contribute to the overall infection rate., where A is a function of the vector density.

Once the people agents start to move around, the clustering effect disappears. The agents can move around thus increasing contact between agents and facilitation infection across larger areas of the world. The speed of agent movement (the step-size) still causes temporal clusters: The maximum distance between people agents so that an infection can be transmitted from one to the other is 83 units if the step-size is 1. This number increases with the step-size. The simulations indicate for a step-size of 2 (163 units maximal distance between people) perfect mixing is very well approximated, particularly for smaller linear system sizes. At a step-size of 9 the system behaves like the perfect mixing case over all linear system sizes.

If we restrict the linear size of the agent area to a fraction s of the overall area, then, the density of agents within this area will increase by s^2. Thus whenever a vector is within the area populated by people, then it will have a dramatically increased chance of actually being near an agent and catching/transmitting an infection. However, at every time-step the probability of actually being within the populated area is only s^2. Figure 4 shows that in the perfect mixing case $s = 1$ system is well approximated by the $s = 1/2$ system. Further decreasing the factor will result in increasingly bad approximations.

The situation is very different for vectors. While in the shrunk case people agents still behave similarly to the $s = 1$ case (if the shrinkage factor is not too large), the infection levels in the vector population remain consistently lower in the shrunk case than in the $s = 1$ case. This effect is easily explained if one considers that the vectors will only have a chance to interact with people no more than every s^2-th time-step. Thus in the limit of a very densely populated people area, the probability for a vector being infected is equal to $2(1 - \frac{1}{s^2})\frac{1}{s^2} + (\frac{1}{s^2})^2$. For the shown case of $s = (1/2)$ this yields an infection level for the vectors of .4375. This theoretical prediction is only partially confirmed by the simulation in figure 4, however, where the fraction of the infected vector population seems to converge to 1 as the world size gets smaller. This discrepancy is easily explained by considering that while the people are restricted to the shrunk area, a vector can still catch an infection if it is outside this area, but still within 1 unit of an agent. As W decreases this edge effect becomes increasingly important and in the limit of very small systems every part of the world will be within 1 unit of a people agent.

In the case of the $s = 1$ system, perfect mixing is reached if the agents' step-size is sufficiently large, even though the step-size of the vectors is not. In the case of $s < 1$ this is no longer the case. The dynamics in this case can be easily understood by considering that the vector population splits up into two weakly connected sub-populations, those vectors inside the people agents' area and the one outside. One characteristic of perfect mixing is that the internal state of the system at time t is nearly independent of the system state at time $t - 1$. If $s = 1$ a sufficiently large step-size of agents can ensure that the correlation between system states at various times become quickly un-correlated. If on the other hand the space occupied by people agents is smaller than the space occupied by vectors, then perfect mixing requires two things to hold. Firstly, within the area occupied by the people agent, people agents need to mix well with vectors. Secondly, there needs to be rapid mixing between the two vector sub-populations inside and outside the people agent area.

6 Conclusions

We have used agent-based simulations and corresponding mathematical analysis to help understand the conditions under which a perfect mixing assumption is a good approximation to the dynamics of a vector-borne disease in a spatially distributed population. We find that perfect mixing is a reasonable approximation under the following conditions:

- People and vectors spread over same area, with modest movement for all agents. Perfect mixing is a good approximation for both vectors and people.
- People distributed over a restricted area, with modest movement for all agents. Perfect mixing (with the same *density* of agents) is a good approximation for the people, but not for the vectors.

However, if the movement of people is very small compared to the world size, then the population breaks up into clusters, which require a critical density to be able to maintain the infection. This seems to be a reasonable model of large-scale population distributions (for example, consider across whole countries or continents), whereas the perfect mixing model may better approximate the disease dynamics in a smaller area (e.g. a cities or isolated rural area).

References

1. M. A. Janssen and W. J. M. Martens. Modeling malaria as a complex adaptive system. *Artificial Life*, 3(3):213–236, 1997.
2. I. Kleinschmidt. *Spatial statistical analysis, modelling and mapping of malaria in Africa*. PhD thesis, University Basel, 2001.
3. Who Study Group on Malaria. Vector control for malaria and other mosquito borne diseases. Technical Report 857, World Health Organisation, 1995.
4. J. Casti. *Would-Be Worlds*. John Wiley & Sons, New York, 1997.
5. J. Holland. *Hidden Order*. Addison-Weseley, Reading, 1995.
6. J. Holland. *Emergence*. Oxford University Press, Oxford, 1998.
7. D. Gross. *Agent-Based Modelling: An Interdisciplinary Approach*. PhD thesis, University of Bergen, 2000.
8. D. Gross and R. Strand. Can Agent-Based Models Assist Decisions on Large-Scale Practical Problems? A Philosophical Analysis. *Complexity*, 5(5):26–33, 2000.

Hierarchical Genetic Algorithms

Edwin D. de Jong[1], Dirk Thierens[1], and Richard A. Watson[2]

[1] Universiteit Utrecht
Decision Support Systems Group
The Netherlands
{dejong,dirk}@cs.uu.nl
[2] Harvard University
Dept. of Organismic and Evolutionary Biology
Cambridge, MA 02138
rwatson@oeb.harvard.edu

Abstract. Current Genetic Algorithms can efficiently address order-k separable problems, in which the order of the linkage is restricted to a low value k. Outside this class, there exist hierarchical problems that cannot be addressed by current genetic algorithms, yet can be addressed efficiently in principle by exploiting hierarchy. We delineate the class of hierarchical problems, and describe a framework for Hierarchical Genetic Algorithms. Based on this outline for algorithms, we investigate under what conditions hierarchical problems may be solved efficiently. Sufficient conditions are provided under which hierarchical problems can be addressed in polynomial time. The analysis points to the importance of efficient sampling techniques that assess the quality of module settings.

1 Introduction

Linkage learning employs the concept of dependencies to describe Genetic Algorithm problems. Two variables are *independent* of one another if the contribution of each variable to the fitness of the individual is independent of the setting of the other variable. If a variable never depends on more than $k-1$ other variables, the linkage is said to be limited to order k.

Competent Genetic Algorithms [1] can efficiently address problems in which the order of the linkage is limited to some small number k, called order-k separable problems. The class of problems with high-order linkage can not be addressed efficiently in general. However, specific subclasses of this class *can* be addressed efficiently if there is some form of structure that can be exploited. A prominent case is given by the class of *hierarchical problems*.

By using small partial solutions to construct larger partial solutions in a recursive fashion, hierarchy offers a potential to achieve scalability and address large problems efficiently. Simon's parable of the two watchmakers Tempus and Hora [2] is an early source pointing out the large potential for efficiency improvement afforded by the use of hierarchy.

While several examples of hierarchical problems exist, such as H-IFF [3] and H-TRAP [4], the class of hierarchical problems has so far not been precisely

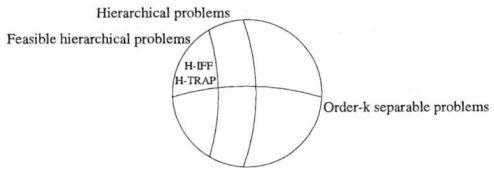

Fig. 1. A classification of problems. Order-k separability divides the class of problems in two. Hierarchy makes an orthogonal distinction. The subclass of *feasible* hierarchical problems contains for example the H-IFF and H-TRAP problems.

delineated. Two generators exist that can produce hierarchical problems [3, 5], but these are not limited to producing hierarchical problems. Based on Watson's notion of *decomposability* [6], we define the notion of *modularity*. Based on the modularity definition, we delineate the class of hierarchical problems.

Several algorithms currently exist that can exploit hierarchy. One approach to hierarchical problem solving, on which we will focus here, is to form explicit representations of modules [7, 8]. Another successful approach is the use of Estimation of Distribution algorithms [4]. We reserve the term Hierarchical Genetic Algorithm (H-GA) for algorithms that are able to exploit the structure present in hierarchical problems to achieve efficiency improvements. The term 'hierarchical' has also been used for genetic algorithms that are not aimed at addressing hierarchical problems in general, but feature some other hierarchical aspect, including the use of a fitness-based hierarchy of populations [9], problem-specific subdivision of an algorithm into multiple levels [10], and the use of a hierarchical representation by using control genes that regulate other genes [11].

To make precise how the structure present in hierarchical problems may be exploited, we describe a general framework for *Hierarchical Genetic Algorithms*. While H-GAs can be applied to any hierarchical problem, not all hierarchical problems can be addressed efficiently. Therefore, our main aim is to investigate under what conditions hierarchical problems can be addressed efficiently. Such problems will be called *feasible* hierarchical problems. Figure 1 depicts the relations between the problem classes of order-k separable problems, hierarchical problems, and feasible hierarchical problems.

The structure of the article is as follows. Section 2 provides definitions of the notions of modularity and hierarchy. Section 3 describes an algorithm outline for H-GAs. Section 4 analyzes the computational requirements of H-GAs, and discusses factors that determine the feasibility of hierarchical problems. The paper ends with conclusions.

2 Defining Modularity and Hierarchy

The principles behind the modularity and hierarchy notions that will be detailed below are as follows. A module is a subset of variables for which only *part* of the settings are near-optimal in some context. This permits a reduction of the parts of the search space that must be visited to find a global optimum. Hierarchy applies the same principle recursively and thereby permits such reductions at all scales. This affords a potential to address certain problems with high order linkage in a scalable manner.

Definition (**Individual**): An individual x is a sequence of n elements chosen from an alphabet $\mathcal{A}$: $x \in \mathcal{A}^n$. The ith element of an individual is denoted x_i.

Definition (**Position-Value Pair**): A position-value pair (i, v) specifies that the ith element x_i of an individual x equals v, where $i \in I$, the set of allowed positions (indices) $I = \{i | 1 \leq i \leq n\}$, and $v \in \mathcal{A}$.

Definition (**Partition**): A partition P is a set of indices, where each index represents a position on the genotype of individuals: $P \subseteq I$.

The possible settings for a partition P are:
$V(P) = \{\bigcup_{i \in P} \{(i, a)\} | (i, a) \in \{i\} \times A\}$

Definition (**Context**): The context $C(P)$ of a partition P is its complement, i.e. the set of indices not contained in the partition: $C(P) = I \setminus P$. The context $C(M)$ of a module M is the context of the partition represented by the module.

Modules are defined as particular kinds of partitions. Two types of modules exist: *primitive modules* and *composite modules*. We proceed to define these.

Definition (**Primitive Module**): The primitive modules in a problem are simply given by the variables in the problem:
$\mathcal{M}_p = \{M_p^i | 1 \leq i \leq n\}$
The *values* of a primitive module are its possible settings:
$V(M_p^i) = \{i\} \times \mathcal{A}$
The ϵ-optimal settings of a module in a context are those module settings that maximize the fitness of the whole given the setting for the context, up to a small factor ϵ:
$V^*(M, V_C) = \{V_M \in V(M) | \max_{V'_M \in V(M)} F(V'_M \cup V_C) - F(V_M \cup V_C) < \epsilon\}$
Using this, we can define the ϵ-context-optimal settings of a module as those settings that are ϵ-optimal in *some* context:
$V^*(M) = \{V_M \in V(M) | \exists V_C \in V(C(M)) : V_M \in V^*(M, V_C)\}$
Given the notions of the settings and ϵ-context-optimal settings of a module, we can now define composite modules. To this end, we first define the notion of a module combination as any combination of up to k existing modules:
$M_{combi} = \{M_1, M_2, \ldots M_k\}$
where $M_i \in \mathcal{M}$ is a module. The values of a module combination are limited to the ϵ-context-optimal settings of its constituents; since any module setting that is part of an ϵ-optimal solution must by definition be ϵ-context-optimal, we can safely disregard all other settings. This is what makes the identification of modules beneficial. Thus, the possible settings of a module combination M_{combi} are:
$V(M_{combi}) = \{\bigcup_i V_i | \forall i, 1 \leq i \leq k : V_i \in V^*(M_i)\}$
Watson [6] defines *decomposability* as the property that the number of ϵ-optimal settings of a module is lower than its total number of settings, and provides

an extensive discussion of this and related ideas. Based on this criterion, the following definition of a composite module can be given.

Definition (**Composite Module**): A module combination M_{combi} is a *composite module* if and only if its number of ϵ-context-optimal settings is lower than its total number of settings, and no subset of the module combination establishes such a reduction:
$$|V^*(M_{combi})| < |V(M_{combi})| \text{ and } \nexists M'_c \subset M_c : |V^*(M'_c)| < |V(M'_c)|$$
The set of all composite modules is written as $\mathcal{M}_c$. Finally, we can define our notion of a module as the union of primitive and composite modules:

Definition (**Module**): The set of modules for a problem is given by the union of the primitive and composite modules in the problem: $\mathcal{M} = \mathcal{M}_p \cup \mathcal{M}_c$. We study fitness functions for which modules do not partially overlap, i.e. the partition specified by a module must either be a strict subset or a strict superset of any other module:
$$\forall M_i, M_j \in \mathcal{M} : \quad M_i \subset M_j \quad \vee \quad M_j \subset M_i$$

Definition (**Modularity**): A problem is called *modular* if it contains at least one composite module, i.e. if $|\mathcal{M}_c| > 0$

Definition (**Hierarchy**): A problem is called *hierarchical* if there is at least one composite module that contains another composite module, i.e. if $\exists M \cdot \exists M' \in M \cdot |M'| > 1$. A problem is called *fully hierarchical* if there exists a single module that covers all indices, and whose settings thus specify complete individuals.

This definition delineates the class of *Hierarchical Problems*. The motivation for these specific modularity and hierarchy definitions is that these notions, when present in a problem, permit a reduction of the required search effort. The following sections will discuss how this potential for efficiency improvement may be exploited by hierarchical genetic algorithms.

Two constructions exist that can generate different hierarchical problems given different parameters, and which are therefore valuable as generators of hierarchical problems. Watson et al. [3] define a tree whose nodes represent subsets of the variables in a problem, and a base function that is applied to these nodes to provide a fitness function. Pelikan and Goldberg [5] offer a construction that allows for blocks of variable size, and permits blocks with different base functions. Both constructions only yield hierarchical problems for certain parameter choices. Thus, the constructions do not delineate classes of hierarchical problems.

3 The Class of Hierarchical Genetic Algorithms

The notions of modularity and hierarchy have been defined. In the following, we describe a general form for algorithms exploiting modularity and hierarchy.

An individual in a hierarchical GA consists of a set of modules and corresponding module settings. In a valid individual of length n, each index $1 \leq i \leq n$ is a member of precisely one module. The crossover and mutation operators employed by a hierarchical GA respect the modules that have been identified. For crossover, an offspring must be a combination of modules from the parents, where the setting of each module is that of one the parents. Thus, the settings of the variables inside a module are not disrupted during crossover. This feature is required to achieve scalability in genetic algorithms [12, 13]. Mutation replaces the setting of a randomly chosen module by another ϵ-optimal setting for that module.

H-GA()

1. init_mods($\mathcal{M}$)
2. Pop:=init_pop($\mathcal{M}$)
3. done=false
4. **while** ($\neg$ done)
5.   Evolve_Pop(Pop, $\mathcal{M}$, n_c)
6. $\mathcal{M}'$=Module_Formation($\mathcal{M}$, Pop)
7.   **if** $\mathcal{M}'$=$\mathcal{M}$
8.   done=true
9.   **else**
10. $\mathcal{M}:=\mathcal{M}'$
11.   Replace_Modules($\mathcal{M}$, Pop)
12. **end**
13. Construct_Solution($\mathcal{M}$)

Fig. 2. An algorithm outline for Hierarchical Genetic Algorithms (H-GAs); see text.

Init_mods($\mathcal{M}$) initializes the module set as $\mathcal{M} := (M^1, M^2, \ldots M^n)$, $M^i = \{i\}$, and determines the possible settings for these modules: $\forall i, 1 \le i \le n : V[M^i] = \{V_{M^i} \in V(M^i) | \exists V_C \in Sample(V(C(M^i))) : V_{M^i} \in V^*(M^i, V_C)\}$ where $Sample(V)$ returns a sample of the settings in V, $V^*(M, V_C) = \{V_M \in V(M) \mid \max_{V'_M \in V(M)} F(V'_M \cup V_C) - F(V_M \cup V_C) < \epsilon\}$, and $V(M^i) = \{i\} \times \mathcal{A}$.

Init_pop creates a population where each individual is a random combination of module settings. Replace_Modules ensures that for any module combination that forms a composite module, occurrences in the population are replaced by the composite module. The replacement is only carried out if the setting of the modules corresponds to an ϵ-optimal setting for the composite module.

At the heart of an H-GA is the module formation step. For combinations M of up to k existing modules, this procedure determines whether M is a module. A difference with the module definition is that rather than considering all possible context settings, a *sample* of the context settings occurring in the population is used. This leads to the following algorithm for module formation:

$Sample(Pop, P)$ returns a sample of settings for partition P. The sample may simply be a subset of the settings of the partition occurring in the population, but may also be independent of the population.

module_formation($\mathcal{M}$, Pop)

1. $k' := 2$
2.   while $k' \leq k$
3.   for $M \in \mathcal{M}^{k'}$
4.   if $\not\exists M' \in \mathcal{M} : |M'| > 1 \wedge M' \subset M$
5.   S=Sample(Pop, C(M))
6.   if $|V^*(M,S)| < |V(M)|$
7. $\mathcal{M} := \mathcal{M} \cup M$
8. $V[M] := V^*(M,S)$
9.   return $\mathcal{M}$
10.   end
11.   end
12.   end
13. $k' := k' + 1$
14.   end
15. return $\mathcal{M}$

Fig. 3.

$V^*(M,S)$ is determined as $\{V_M \in V(M) | \exists V_C \in S : \max_{V'_M \in V(M)} F(V'_M \cup V_C) - F(V_M \cup V_C) < \epsilon\}$, and this completes the discussion of the module formation step.

The cycle of the H-GA is repeated until the module formation step no longer results in new modules. The step of the algorithm that evolves the population should run long enough to provide an appropriate sampling distribution (see below). The final step in the H-GA is Construct_Solution($\mathcal{M}$). This step selects a set of modules that together yield a complete specification of an individual: $M = \{M_i \in \mathcal{M}\}$ such that $\forall i, j : M_i \cap M_j = \emptyset$ and $\cup_i M_i = I$. For efficiency reasons, the choice of M may be made such that the resulting number of combinations of allowed settings, $\prod_i |V[M_i]|$, is minimized. Next, all combinations of the allowed settings $V[M_i]$ for the modules M_i are considered, and from the resulting individuals a maximum-fitness solution is selected.

4 Feasibility of Hierarchical Problem Solving

An H-GA can address certain problems with high-order dependencies efficiently. Two questions are under which conditions an optimal solution can be found, and what amount of computational effort is required to do so. In the following, we address these questions.

4.1 Correctness

First, to permit finding a global optimum, it must be ensured that module formation does not exclude global optima.

Proposition (**Correctness**): For any problem, the H-GA can avoid the exclusion of global optima with a probability arbitrarily close to 1.

Excluding ϵ-context-optimal settings can be avoided by choosing a sufficiently large sample size; in the limit of considering all possible context settings, no ϵ-optimal module setting will be excluded, and the solution-construction step is guaranteed to identify an optimal solution. The number of possible context settings can be very large however, and a question of practical importance therefore is whether ϵ-optimal solutions can be found with high probability.

Let p_m denote the probability that a module setting that is ϵ-optimal in *some* context maximizes fitness for a sampled context, where the sampling method is defined as part of the algorithm. Then the probability that the ϵ-optimality of this module setting remains undiscovered for a sample of size $|S|$ is $q^{|S|}$, where $q = 1 - p_m$. Thus, to discover the ϵ-optimality of a setting at the α confidence level, $|S| = \lceil \frac{ln(\alpha)}{ln(q)} \rceil$ samples are required. Example: if a module setting achieves the maximum fitness attainable for a context setting for one in a hundred context settings, i.e. $p_m = 0.01$, then to ensure the identification of such a context at a confidence level of one percent ($\alpha = 0.01$), $|S| = \lceil \frac{ln(0.01)}{ln(0.99)} \rceil = 459$ samples are required.

A given ϵ-optimal setting will be identified as such with probability $1 - \alpha$. Thus, *all* ϵ-optimal module settings out of n_s possible settings, including the truly optimal ones ($\epsilon = 0$), will be identified correctly with probability $(1-\alpha)^{n_s}$. If this occurs, an optimal solution can be constructed. For any desired probability $P < 1$, we can therefore choose α as $\lfloor 1 - p_m^{\frac{1}{n_s}} \rfloor$ and set the sample size accordingly to ensure that the probability of finding an optimal solution is at least P.

4.2 Computational Effort

If no global optima are excluded, the presence of global optima among the remaining possible module settings is guaranteed. The remaining question therefore is how much search effort is required to identify the ϵ-context-optimal module settings and consider all combinations thereof.

The computational effort for an H-GA is determined by the module formation step (line 6 in Fig. 2), and the construction of a solution from the modules that have been identified. The complexity of the module formation step is as follows. The algorithm (lines 2,3) considers combinations of up to k existing modules. A convenient upper bound for the number of such combinations is $k n_m^k$, where n_m is the total number of modules present in a problem. Since each module may occur only once, this number can be reduced to $k \binom{n_m}{k}$ combinations. A further reduction is possible by avoiding overlapping module combinations.

For each module combination M, all settings are considered in all contexts from the sample $|S|$ in line 3. If the highest number of ϵ-optimal settings for a module is named m, this requires $m^k |S|$ operations.

Together, this leads to $k n_m^k m^k |S|$ operations for the module formation procedure. Assuming m and k are constant, the complexity of the module formation procedure is therefore $\mathcal{O}(n_m^k |S|)$.

The module formation step is executed n_m times, including the less expensive module initialization procedure. Next, an optimal solution is constructed from the final set of modules. If the number of modules required to specify an individual completely is written n_c, this requires m^{n_c} operations. Thus, the total complexity of the H-GA is $\mathcal{O}(n_m{}^{(k+1)}|S|+m^{n_c})$. For a fully hierarchical problem, i.e. a problem for which a single module M_{n_m} exists that specifies a complete solution, any of the ϵ-optimal settings $V*(M_{n_m})$ for this module are global optima. For these problems, the complexity therefore reduces to $\mathcal{O}(n_m{}^{(k+1)}|S|)$.

We consider under which conditions a hierarchical problem can be efficiently solved by an H-GA. This is the case when the above complexity is polynomial. We will call such problems *feasible hierarchical problems*, and proceed by detailing this class of problems. First, it was assumed that m and k are constant. Assuming the problem satisfies this condition, a further requirement is that the three terms in the complexity of the algorithm must all be polynomial: $n_m{}^{(k+1)}$, m^{n_c}, and $|S|$.

The first term requires that the number of modules n_m must be polynomial in the problem size, which is given by the number of variables n. This is the case for any hierarchical problem, as the maximum number of modules in a problem is $2n-1$, obtained for the case of full binary tree.

The second term (m^{n_c}) is polynomial only if the number of modules required to specify a complete solution, n_c, is at most logarithmic in n.

This can be achieved as follows. Let a forest F be a set of k module trees. Each node in a tree represents a module consisting of up to k constituent modules. If the ith tree has $n_{l,i}$ leaves, F represents a hierarchical problem of size $n = \prod_1^k n_{l,i}$. Given F, we can construct a problem of size kn as follows. First, combine the root modules of the k trees in F into a single new composite module M. Next, the resulting module tree M is copied $k-1$ times, yielding a new forest F' that contains k n-variable trees. The optimal settings for each copy of M must be chosen such that M has at most m ϵ-context-optimal settings. While F' represents a hierarchical problem of size kn, the number of modules n_c required to specify a complete solution still equals k. Thus, the above procedure provide a way to transform a given hierarchical problem into a larger hierarchical problem with the same n_c, so that n_c is constant (independent of n), thereby satisfying the above constraint. The procedure may be repeated recursively to produce a family of increasingly large feasible hierarchical problems given some initial hierarchical problem. A fully hierarchical problem may be obtained by selecting the tree M before it is copied to yield a new forest.

The final condition that must be satisfied in order for a hierarchical problem to be efficiently addressed concerns the sample size $|S|$. We expect this to be the most important issue in constructing practical hierarchical algorithms. The question is whether sampling methods can be identified for which p_m (see previous section) is sufficiently large to permit a practical sample size.

An important idea employed by SEAM [7] is to construct the contexts in the sample from the ϵ-context-optimal settings of the context variables, rather than selecting the settings of these variables randomly. Since the goal is to identify a global optimum, module settings that are ϵ-context-optimal in non-ϵ-optimal context settings only may be safely disregarded. This principle can greatly reduce the required sample size.

A more specific characterization of required sample sizes would be valuable, and forms an important objective for further research. This may be undertaken for example by means of empirical investigation of the p_m quantity achieved by different sampling methods.

Many problems in design feature hierarchical structure [2], and we believe that the development of H-GAs can therefore have a significant practical impact, but practical applications of H-GAs will have to show whether this is indeed the case.

A final practical question for hierarchical algorithms is how k, the maximum number of modules considered for combination, may be chosen. Since this number greatly influences the computational complexity of an H-GA, it is essential to avoid overestimating k. A simple procedure that guarantees this is to change k incrementally, analogous to iterative deepening search.

5 Conclusions

The notions of modularity and hierarchy have been defined. By exploiting hierarchy, certain problems that are not order-k separable can be addressed efficiently, thus extending the range of problems that evolutionary computation can efficiently address.

A general form for Hierarchical Genetic Algorithm (H-GAs) has been provided. H-GAs incrementally form a set of modules that are used to adapt the representation of the search, and can thereby gradually restrict the search space without excluding optimal solutions. Conditions are provided under which H-GAs can efficiently solve hierarchical problems. These conditions define a class of feasible hierarchical problems.

The H-GA framework can be instantiated to yield various specific H-GAs by choosing a particular sampling method or population evolution method, or by adapting the module formation procedure. It is found that the identification of effective sampling methods is an important factor in the development of efficient hierarchical algorithms.

References

1. Goldberg, D.E.: The design of innovation. Lessons from and for competent genetic algorithms. Kluwer Academic Publishers (2002)
2. Simon, H.A.: The Sciences of the Artificial. The MIT Press, Cambridge, MA (1968)
3. Watson, R.A., Hornby, G.S., Pollack, J.B.: Modeling building-block interdependency. In Eiben, A., Bäck, T., Schoenauer, M., Schwefel, H.P., eds.: Parallel Problem Solving from Nature, PPSN-V. Volume 1498 of LNCS., Berlin, Springer (1998) 97–106

4. Pelikan, M., Goldberg, D.E.: Escaping hierarchical traps with competent genetic algorithms. In Spector et al., L., ed.: Proceedings of the Genetic and Evolutionary Computation Conference, GECCO-01, Morgan Kaufmann (2001) 511–518
5. Pelikan, M., Goldberg, D.E.: Hierarchical problem solving by the bayesian optimization algorithm. In Whitley et al., D., ed.: Proceedings of the Genetic and Evolutionary Computation Conference (GECCO-2000), Las Vegas, Nevada, USA, Morgan Kaufmann (2000) 267–274
6. Watson, R.A.: Compositional Evolution: Interdisciplinary Investigations in Evolvability, Modularity, and Symbiosis. PhD thesis, Brandeis University (2002)
7. Watson, R.A., Pollack, J.B.: A computational model of symbiotic composition in evolutionary transitions. Biosystems **69** (2003) 187–209 Special Issue on Evolvability, ed. Nehaniv.
8. De Jong, E.D., Thierens, D.: Exploiting modularity, hierarchy, and repetition in variable-length problems. In: Proceedings of the Genetic and Evolutionary Computation Conference, GECCO-04. (2004)
9. Hu, J., Goodman, E.D.: The hierarchical fair competition (HFC) model for parallel evolutionary algorithms. In Fogel, D.B., El-Sharkawi, M.A., Yao, X., Greenwood, G., Iba, H., Marrow, P., Shackleton, M., eds.: Proceedings of the 2002 Congress on Evolutionary Computation CEC2002, IEEE Press (2002) 49–54
10. Gulsen, M., Smith, A.E.: A hierarchical genetic algorithm for system identification and curve fitting with a supercomputer implementation. In Davis et al., L.D., ed.: Evolutionary Algorithms. Springer, New York (1999) 111–137
11. Tang, K., Man, K., Istepanian, R.: Teleoperation controller design using hierarical genetic algorithms. In: Proceedings of the IEEE International conference on Industrial Technology. (2000) 707–711
12. Thierens, D., Goldberg, D.: Mixing in genetic algorithms. In: Proceedings of the Fifth International Conference on Genetic Algorithms, Morgan Kaufmann (1993) 38–45
13. Thierens, D.: Scalability problems of simple genetic algorithms. Evolutionary Computation **7** (1999) 331–352

Migration of Probability Models Instead of Individuals: An Alternative When Applying the Island Model to EDAs

Luis delaOssa, José A. Gámez, and José M. Puerta

Departamento de Informática / i^3A
Universidad de Castilla-La Mancha
Campus Universitario s/n,
Albacete, 02071
{ldelaossa,jgamez,jpuerta}@info-ab.uclm.es

Abstract. In this work we experiment with the application of island models to Estimation of Distribution Algorithms (EDAs) in the field of combinatorial optimization. This study is motivated by the success obtained by these models when applied to other meta-heuristics (such as genetic algorithms, simulated annealing or VNS) and by the use of a compact representation of the population that make EDAs through probability distributions. This fact can be exploited during information interchange among islands. In this work we experiment with two types of island-based EDAs: (1) migration of individuals, and (2) migration of probability models. Also, two alternatives are studied for the phase of model combinations: assigning constant weights to inner and incoming models or assigning adaptive weights based-on their fitness. The proposed algorithms are tested over a suite of four combinatorial optimization problems.

1 Introduction

Due to the nature of genetic algorithms and their use in solving problems which became increasingly harder, first attempts to parallelize them soon emerged. Thus, searches were intended to perform faster by taking advantage of computing power of parallel machines. These first attempts lead the development of new models of algorithms that, in some cases, differed from sequential models. As reported in [1] parallel genetic algorithms often lead to superior numerical performance (speedup and solution quality) even when the algorithms run on a single processor, the use of a structured population (many times in the form of a set of islands or demes) being the responsible for such numerical benefits.

Multideme Parallel Evolutionary Algorithms (PEAs) or Island models appeared as one of the ways to carry out this parallelization. They basically consist of considering a set of subpopulations (islands or demes) which evolve independently and occasionally exchange individuals among them. This kind of PEA is very popular, it is the class of PEA which is most difficult to understand because

(1) the effects of migration are not fully understood and (2) the large set of parameters involved in their design [3]. Besides genetic algorithms, island models have been tested successfully with other meta heuristics.

This work concerns the application of the island model to a recent family of evolutionary algorithms: *Estimation of Distribution Algorithms* (EDAs). Our proposal here is twofold: first, as an alternative to the classical migration of individuals we propose to migrate a compact representation of the population of each island, its probability model; then, we make an empirical comparison between the two alternatives over a set of well known combinatorial optimization problems.

In order to do this, the paper is organized into six sections besides this introduction. Section 2 briefly describes EDAs and concretely the univariate algorithm used in this work: UMDA. Next, in Section 3 basic ideas about parallel evolutionary algorithms based on the islands model are given. Sections 4 and 5 are the kernel of the paper and describe the kind of migration we propose and the design of the proposal islands-based EDAs. Section 6 is devoted to experiments and to the analysis of the obtained results, and finally, in Section 7 we present our conclusions and some possiblities for future research.

2 Estimation of Distribution Algorithms: EDAs

EDAs [8] are a family of evolutionary algorithms where the transition from one population to another is made by estimating the probability distribution from better individuals and sampling it. In the case of combinatorial optimization (there are extensions to deal with numerical optimization), discrete EDAs are used, that is, each variable x_i can take a finite number of states $\{x_i^1, \ldots, x_i^k\}$ and a multinomial distribution is used to model the joint probability $P(x_1, \ldots, x_n)$.

The pseudo code of a canonical EDA is as follows:

1. $D_0 \leftarrow$ Generate initial population (m individuals)
2. Evaluate population D_0
3. $k = 1$
4. Repeat until stop condition
    (a) $D_{k-1}^{S_e} \leftarrow$ Select $n \leq m$ individuals from D_{k-1}
    (b) Estimate a new probabilistic model $\mathcal{M}$ from $D_{k-1}^{S_e}$
    (c) $D_{k-1}^m \leftarrow$ Sample m individuals from $\mathcal{M}$
    (d) Evaluate D_{k-1}^m
    (e) $D_k \leftarrow$ Select m individuals from $D_{k-1} \cup D_{k-1}^m$
    (f) $k = k + 1$

One of the advantages of EDAs is their ability to represent the existing interrelations among the variables involved in individuals through joint probability distribution (JPD). Since in real problems it is very hard to deal with JPD (increase in number of parameters and overfitting problem), the idea is to estimate a probabilistic model $\mathcal{M}$ which will be a simplification of such distribution. The more complex $\mathcal{M}$ is the richer it becomes, but it also increases the complexity of model estimation. Thus, three main groups of EDAs are usually considered [8]: univariate models, which assume that variables are marginally independent; bivariate models, which accept dependences between pairs of variables; and multivariate models where the degree of dependence is not limited.

In this initial approach we limit our study to the use of univariate models, and concretely to the Univariate Marginal Distribution Algorithm (UMDA, [12]). UMDA is (probably) the simplest EDA. It is based on the assumption of marginal independence among variables, which gives rise to the following factorization of the JPD:

$$P(x_1, x_2, \ldots, x_N) = \prod_{i=1}^{N} P(x_i)$$

This fact simplifies the calculus because no structural learning is required and we only have to estimate unidimensional probability distributions. Although considering the frequencies (maximum likelihood estimation) of each pair (variable, value) would be enough to estimate marginal probabilities, it is very common to use a smoothing technique such as m-estimation or Laplace correction [6]. Of course, the drawback of this approach is that we do not take into account the possible dependences existing among variables of the problem. However, as happens with other techniques that use very strong assumptions (such as Naive Bayes on classification problems) the results obtained by this algorithm are really competitive.

3 Coarse-Grained PEAs: The Islands Model

In literature, we can find several ways to parallelize evolutionary algorithms, going from a simple distribution of individuals evaluation among different processors to complex mechanisms which make a very intensive use of communication [4]. As has been mentioned before, of the different types of PEAs coarse-grained parallel algorithms are the most popular. These algorithms, also known as island based (or multi-deme) parallel algorithms, consist of multiple sub-populations which evolve independently and, occasionally, exchange information (individuals) among them.

When designing an island-based algorithm, apart from the parameter setting required to specify the evolutionary algorithm which will be used to define evolution whithin each island (population size, ...), it becomes necessary to specify parameters which determine interaction among the islands. These are the main ones:

- Number of islands (#islands). When real parallelism is used, this parameter is constrained by the available hardware, but when parallelism is simulated, this is a tunable parameter.
- Number of individuals (#migrated) which migrate from one island to another.

- Migration policies. The most common option consist of fixing the number of generations (#epoch) elapsed in an island before individuals are received or sent from/to others.
- Topology. Islands and migrations must be defined by some interconnection topology (star, ring, etc).
- Replacement policies. It is necessary to define how population inside an island is formed after a migration is carried out.

4   Migration of Individuals vs Migration of Models

Cooperation among islands is carried out by interchanging *information* among them. In most cases this *information* is reduced to a set of individuals which is *migrated* from the population contained in each island, to other island/s. In this work we investigate the interchange of a different kind of *information*: the probabilistic model which accounts for the population in an island.

Without any doubt, the main characteristic of an EDA algorithm is the probabilistic model used to codify the best individuals in the population. In this sense, isolated individuals do not play as important a role as in GAs, where they give rise directly to new individuals by means of selection, crossover and mutation. In EDAs new individuals are sampled from the probabilistic model, that is, from a compact representation of a subset of the whole population. Because of this, we believe that it could be of interest to exploit this different behaviour when applying the island model to EDAs. Thus, what we propose is to migrate this compact representation of the population, the probabilistic model, instead of a subset of the population individuals. Moreover, this alternative opens the possibility of reducing the communication cost in real hardware implementations by exchanging just one vector instead of a set of them, although this is a point which needs to be studied.

The next point to discuss is how to combine the incoming model with the one currently active in a concrete island. As this process can be viewed as a refinement of the inner model in a given island and we are dealing with univariate models involving only marginal distributions, we propose to use a convex combination (as in PBIL [12] or IUMDA [2] algorithms) controlled by a parameter β. Concretely, if $\mathcal{M}_i$ is the inner model on island i and $\mathcal{M}_r$ is the incoming model, the new model $\mathcal{M}'_i$ is obtained as follows:

$$\mathcal{M}'_i(X_j) = \beta \mathcal{M}_i(X_j) + (1-\beta)\mathcal{M}_r(X_j)$$

We have considered two different strategies to select the value of β:
- *Constant value.* In our initial experiments we have tried with different values for β getting the best results with a rather conservative value ($\beta = 0.9$).
- *Adaptive value.* In this case we take into account the goodness of the incoming model with respect to to the inner one when adjusting the value of β. In this way, an island i sends/receives a pair $(\mathcal{M}, f)$ where $\mathcal{M}$ is a probabilistic model and f is its associated fitness, which is computed as the fitness average of the

$V\%$ best individuals of population in island i. Thus, f_j can be viewed as the goodness of population/model in island j. Finally,

$$\beta = \begin{cases} \frac{f_i}{f_i+f_r} & \text{if } f_r \geq f_i \\ 0.9 & \text{otherwise} \end{cases},$$

where f_i is the fitness associated to the inner model and f_r is the fitness associated to the incoming model.

5 Islands-Based EDAs

In literature we can find some works related to application of parallelism to EDAs. In some of them [9, 10] complex probabilistic models (Bayesian networks) are considered, and the goal is to parallelize the process of model induction. Other works [13] are devoted to solving concrete problems by using classical island models applied to EDAs (basically ring topology and migration of individuals). Finally, in some papers ([14,5]) migration of probability vectors is outlined, although the replacement policy is based on populations and not on the combination of the probabilistic models.

In this section we specify the design criteria we have considered in order to completely specify the proposed islands-based EDAs. Apart from migrating individuals or models and considering constant or adaptive values for beta, we have tried with different topologies: ring, star and broadcast. Thus, we get eight different islands-based EDAs:

- Ring.i: The topology used is a ring (figure 1.b). Each island sends individuals to the next through a unidirectional ring. Concerning replacement policy, elitism is used, that is, incoming individuals substitute those with worst fitness in the island population.

- Star.i: The topology used is a star (figure 1.a). A specialized processor or bridge is used in order to receive the information from all the islands, process it and return the result to all of them. In this model, the islands send individuals to the bridge, and it generates a pool with the union of all the received individuals. Afterward, the bridge selects (by fitness) the best subset from the pool and sends it to every island. There is not BCast.i algorithm because its behaviour is practically the same that Star.i, except that it is the island which receives the individuals who select the best subset.

- Ring.m.f: The topology used is a ring (figure 1.b). Each island sends the pair $(\mathcal{M}_i, f_i)$ to the next through a unidirectional ring. Models are combined by using adaptive computation for β.

- Ring.m.09: Same algorithm as above but with $\beta = 0.9$.

- Star.m.f: The topology used is a star (figure 1.a). Each island sends the pair $(\mathcal{M}_i, f_i)$ to the bridge. The bridge returns the pair $(\mathcal{M}_j, f_j)$ to all the islands, where $j = \arg\max_i f_i$. Models are combined by using adaptive computation for β.

- Star.m.09: Same algorithm as above but with $\beta = 0.9$.

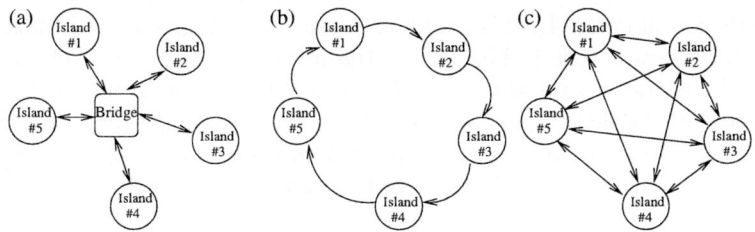

Fig. 1. Topologies considered.

- BCast.m.f: The topology used is a fully connected graph (figure 1.c). Each island broadcasts the pair $(\mathcal{M}_i, f_i)$ to the rest of the islands in the topology. Then, if $\{(\mathcal{M}_k, f_k); k \neq i\}$ is the set of incoming pairs received by island i, the incoming pair to be considered during model combination is computed as the following weighted average:

$$\mathcal{M}_r(X_j) = \sum_{k; f_k > f_i} \frac{f_k}{F} \mathcal{M}_k(X_j) \quad \text{with} \quad F = \sum_{k; f_k > f_i} f_k$$

and f_r is the arithmetic mean of the fitness involved in the computation of $\mathcal{M}_r$. Finally, models are combined by using adaptive computation for β.
- BCast.m.09: Same algorithm as above but finally, models are combined by using $\beta = 0.9$.

For the remaining design criteria we have chosen a set of values that can be considered as typical. Thus, the UMDA running on each island has a population of 256, the best 128 individuals are used to learn the probabilistic model, and D_k is obtained by selecting the m fittest individuals from $D_{k-1} \cup D_{k-1}^m$. With respect to parameters concerning the parallel model we have set #migrated=10%, V=10%, #islands=8, #epoch=10, and the maximum number of generations is 300, but the algorithm stops if there is no improvement in 100 generations. In our experiments, this second condition is the one that usually stops the search.

6 Experimentation

6.1 Cases of Study

For our study we have chosen four different combinatorial optimization problems. The first is described in [11] and the others have been used in the literature to evaluate different EDA models e.g. [7]. In all of them we represent the individuals as a binary vector, however, we have tried to find different features:

- Colville function. Consists of the optimization of the following function.

$$F_c(x_1, x_2, x_3, x_4) = 100(x_2 - x_1^2)^2 + (1 - x_1)^2 + 90(x_4 - x_3^2)^2 + (1 - x_3)^2 \\ + 10.1((x_2 - 1)^2 + (x_4 - 1)^2) + 19.8(x_2 - 1)(x_4 - 1)$$

Where $-10 \leq x_i \leq 10$. In our setting, an individual is represented by 60 binary positions/variables. The minimum value for F_c is 0.

- **CheckerBoard function.** In this problem, a $s \times s$ grid is given. Each point of the grid can take a value 0 or 1. The goal of the problem is to create a checkerboard pattern of 0's and 1's on the grid. The evaluation counts, for each position except the corners, how many of the bits in the four basic directions has the opposite value to it. If we consider the grid as a matrix $x = [x_{ij}]_{i,j=1,\ldots,s}$ and interpret $\delta(a,b)$ as the Kronecker's delta function, the checkerboard function can be written as:

$$F_{cb}(x) = 4(s-2)^2 - \sum_{i=2}^{s-1}\sum_{j=2}^{s-1}\{\delta(x_{ij}, x_{i-1j}) + \delta(x_{ij}, x_{i+1j}) + \delta(x_{ij}, x_{ij-1}) + \delta(x_{ij}, x_{ij+1})\}.$$

The maximum value is $4(s-2)^2$. We use $s = 10$, so dimension is 100.

- **EqualProducts function.** Given a set of n random real numbers $a_1, a_2, \ldots, a_n$ from an interval $[0, k]$, a subset of them is selected. The aim of the problem is to minimize the difference between the products of the selected and unselected numbers. It can be written as follows:

$$F_{ep}(x) = abs\left(\prod_{i=1}^{n} h(x_i, a_i) - \prod_{i=1}^{n} h(1-x_i, a_i)\right) \text{ with } h(x, a) = \begin{cases} 1 & if\, x = 0 \\ 0 & if\, x = 1 \end{cases}$$

We have taken dimension to be 50. The numbers have been generated randomly from a uniform distribution in $[0, 4]$, therefore, we don't know the optimum for this problem. However, values close to zero are better.

- **SixPeaks function.** This problem can be defined mathematically as:

$$F_{sp}(x, t) = max\{tail(0, x), head(1, x), tail(1, x), head(0, x)\} + R(x, t)$$

$$\text{with } \begin{cases} tail(b, x) = \text{number of trailing b's in } x. \\ head(b, x) = \text{number of leading b's in } x \\ R(x, t) = \begin{cases} n & \text{if } tail(0, x) > t \text{ and } head(1, x) > t \text{ or} \\ & tail(1, x) > t \text{ and } head(0, x) > t \\ 0 & \text{otherwise} \end{cases} \end{cases}$$

We have taken dimension (n) to be 100 and t to be 30. This problem is characterized because it has 4 global and 2 local optima. In our setting the optimum value is 169.

6.2 Experiments

In order to have a baseline for comparison, our first experiment was to run the sequential version of UMDA over the four problems. One hundred independent runs were carried out for each problem. Table 1 shows the results (mean ± standard dev.) for fitness (first row) and number of evaluations (second row).

In our second experiment each of the eight islands-based algorithms described in section 5 was run over the four problems. Again, one hundred independent runs were carried out for each problem. Table 2 shows the results).

Table 1. Results of sequential UMDA (population size = 1024).

CheckerBoard	Colville	SixPeaks	Equal Products
243.3±9.22	-3.15±2.08	102.2±15.82	-0.81±0.83
46900.0±7745.3	56450.0±65391.5	100700.0±9392.6	67200.0±44610.1

Table 2. Results for the islands-based algorithms.

	CheckerBoard	Colville	SixPeaks	Equal Products
Star.i	245.91±8.83 96153.60±27857.51	-0.70±1.11 201011.20±44196.30	148.76±30.28 196710.40±52905.60	-0.45±0.45 **134860.80±8924.88**
Ring.i	251.32±6.52 124006.40±75473.40	-0.34±0.79 343040.00±121530.41	150.26±27.99 236748.80±78419.17	**-0.32±0.31** 170393.60±96107.10
Star.m.f	251.74±6.20 **90931.20±27272.00**	-0.47±0.87 153804.80±89991.93	99.05±3.68 197120.00±19033.11	-0.39±0.38 138752.00±66114.19
Star.m.09	252.46±5.43 106496.00±68772.50	-0.43±0.74 **131891.20±71342.97**	160.58±9.71 290099.20±70917.39	-0.42±0.38 150425.60±69761.36
Ring.m.f	252.22±5.70 125747.20±103573.50	-0.46±0.85 142028.80±71411.99	118.67±27.54 199987.20±39454.34	-0.35±0.31 164659.20±90423.01
Ring.m.09	**252.74±5.54** 124723.20±94956.08	**-0.34±0.70** 146739.20±71744.73	**165.31±11.11** 340377.60±101354.40	-0.38±0.41 151961.60±74982.04
BCast.m.f	252.32±5.68 98918.40±46850.73	-0.40±0.77 146841.60±76340.07	103.60±14.32 **170598.40±71439.51**	-0.35±0.34 174387.20±90809.99
BCast.m.09	251.83±5.56 122265.60±90181.91	-0.45±0.86 148992.00±72252.93	154.78±25.93 348160.00±120419.73	-0.42±0.45 156262.40±75769.19

	CheckerBoard	Colville	SixPeaks	EqualProducts	
1	Ring.m.09	Ring.m.09	Ring.m.09	Ring.i	
2	Star.m.09	Ring.i	Star.m.09	◇ BCast.m.f	
3	BCast.m.f	BCast.m.f	BCast.m.09	◇ Ring.m.f	
4	Ring.m.f	Star.m.09	Ring.i	◇ Ring.m.09	
5	BCast.m.09	BCast.m.09	Star.i	◇ Star.m.f	◇
6	Star.m.f	Ring.m.f	Ring.m.f	◇ BCast.m.09	◇
7	Ring.i	◇ Star.m.f	BCast.m.f	◇ Star.m.09	◇
8	Star.i	◇ Star.i	◇ Star.m.f	◇ Star.i	◇

Fig. 2. Results of the statistical tests (fitness).

6.3 Results Analysis

From these results we can clearly obtain the following conclusion: Island-based algorithms perform better (with respect to fitness) than the sequential version, no matter whether models or individuals are migrated, however, they carried out more evaluations.

When analyzing island-based algorithms, things are not so clear, therefore we have analyzed whether there are any statistically significant differences among them by using t-tests. In figure 2 the algorithms have been ranked (descending order) according to their fitness mean. Algorithms marked with a ◇ are those which have a statistical difference (significance level $\alpha = 0.05$) with respect to the algorithm in the first position. From this statistical analysis, we can conclude that the behaviour of the algorithms depends on the problem, although some general conclusions can be drawn:

Table 3. Results for the islands-based algorithms.

CheckerBoard		Colville		SixPeaks		Equal Products	
M09	252.34±5.51	M09	-0.40±0.76	M09	160.21±17.72	MF	-0.36±0.34
MF	252.09±5.86	MF	-0.44±0.82	IN ⋄	149.51±29.12	IN	-0.38±0.39
IN ⋄	248.61±8.20	IN ▷	-0.51±0.97	MF ⋄	107.10±19.87	M09 ⋄	-0.40±0.41

(a) Type of migration

CheckerBoard		Colville		SixPeaks		Equal Products	
Ring	252.09±5.95	Ring	-0.37±0.78	Ring	144.74±30.52	Ring	-0.35±0.34
BCast	252.07±5.62	BCast	-0.42±0.81	Star ⋄	136.12±32.43	BCast	-0.38±0.39
Star ⋄	250.04±7.55	Star ⋄	-0.53±0.92	BCast ⋄	129.19±33.07	Star ⋄	-0.42±0.40

(b) Topology

- Algorithm Ring.m.09 is always in the first group, that is, it is either the algorithm with the best mean or there is no statistical difference between it and the algorithm with the best mean.
- When migrating individuals Star.i seems to be the worst option, because it is never in the first group. Moreover, in three of the four cases it is the algorithm with the worse mean.

In order to get more insight into the comparison between migration of individuals or models, we have grouped the results obtained in three series: individuals (IN), models weighted by fitness (MF) and models using $\beta = 0.9$ (M09). Table 3.a shows the results (mean±sd) for the three series. As in figure 2 we have ranked the series by mean, and t-tests have been carried out. The following conclusions can be drawn:

- In F_{cb} and F_{cv}, M09 is ranked as the best algorithm having a statistically significant difference[1] with IN but not with MF.
- In F_{sp}, M09 is again the best algorithm, showing in this case statistical difference with respect to the other two series IN and MF. A point to note in this case is the bad behaviour shown by MF (there is also statistical difference between IN and MF). This fact can be of interest because F_{sp} belongs to the class of deceptive problems. Notice that in MF when the incoming model has a better fitness that the resident one, then $\alpha < 0.5$, so the model obtained from the convex combination is really influenced by the incoming model. In this function it is quite probable that models driving the search to local optima appear quickly and dominate those islands exploring other regions (notice the considerably smaller number of evaluations carried out by these algorithms). This behaviour is avoided by the *conservative policy* used in M09.
- In F_{ep} the result is different, MF being the best algorithm having statistical difference with M09 although not with respect to IN, furthermore no statistical difference is found between IN and M09.
- To summarise, it seems that migration of models behaves better than migration of individuals, and that on average it is better to use a conservative policy in favour of the resident model (M09).

---

[1] In F_{cv} we use the mark ▷ instead of ⋄ because there is no statistical difference with $\alpha = 0.05$, but the p-value obtained shows that significant difference is obtained with a slightly higher α, e.g. 0.07.

The same study has been carried out by grouping the algorithms by topology (table 3.b). In this case, Ring appears to be best, though no statistical difference is found wit respect to BCast in three of the four cases.

Finally, with respect to the number of evaluations carried out by the algorithms, we do not reproduce the statistical analysis here because of lack of space, but as a general conclusion we can say that those algorithms obtaining the best fitness are, in general, those requiring more evaluations.

7 Conclusions and Future Work

In this paper we have studied some aspects of island-based EDAs. The attention has been focused on an alternative to the classical migration of individuals: migration of probability models. In this first approach the simplest EDA has been used: UMDA, because model combinations can be done in a simple way (we proposed using a convex combination, although combinations based on crossover operators can be used). Although there are many parameters to take into account in the design of an island-based algorithm, in this paper we have taken common choices for all of them, restricting ourselves to experimenting with the type of migration (individuals or models), the topology (ring, star or broadcast) and the parameter β used in the convex combination.

From the results, we can conclude that migration of models obtains, in general, better results than migration of individuals. Besides, migration of models appear as a natural way to parallelize EDAs, and more research in this topic is needed to establish sound conclusions. For the future we plan to work on two different lines: (1) to experiment with more problems and parameter in order to get more insight into what is happening when models are migrated instead of individuals; and (2), to extend our study to bivariate and multivariate EDAs, where the way of combining the models is not easy.

Acknowledgments

This work has been partially supported by the Consejería de Ciencia y Tecnología (JCCM) under project PBC-02-002.

References

1. E. Alba and J.M. Troya. A Survey of Parallel Distributed Genetic Algorithms. *Complexity*, 4:303–346, 1999.
2. S. Baluja. Population-based incremental learning: A method for integrating genetic search based function optimization and competitive learning. Tech. Rep. CMU-CS-94-163, Computer Science Dpt., CMU, 1994.
3. E. Cantú-Paz. A survey of parallel genetic algorithms. Tech. Rep. IlliGAL 97003. University of Illinois at Urbana-Champaign. 1997.
4. E. Cantú-Paz. *Efficient and Accurate Parallel Genetic Algorithms*. Kluwer, 2001.

5. D.E. Goldberg. *Genetic algorithms in search, optimization, and machine learning.* Addison-Wesley, New York, 1989.
6. I.J. Good. *The Estimation of Probabilities.* MIT Press, Cambridge, 1965.
7. P. Larrañaga, R. Etxeberria, J.A. Lozano, and J.M. Peña. Optimization by learning and simulation of Bayesian and Gaussian networks. Tech. Rep. EHU-KZAA-IK-4-99, EHU, 1999.
8. P. Larrañaga and J.A. Lozano. *Estimation of distribution algorithms. A new tool for evolutionary computation.* Kluwer Academic Publishers, 2001.
9. J.A. Lozano, R. Sagarna, and P. Larrañaga. *Estimation of Distribution Algorithms. A new tool for evolutionary computation*, chapter Paralell estimation of distribution algorithms, pages 0–1. Kluwer Academic Publishers, 2001.
10. A. Mendiburu, E. Bengoetxea, and J. Miguel. Paralelización de algoritmos de estimación de distribuciones. In *XIII Jornadas de Paralelismo*, pages 37–41, 2002.
11. Z. Michalewicz. *Genetic Algorithms + Data Structures = Evolution Programs.* Springer-Verlag, 1996.
12. H. Mühlenbein. The equation for response to selection and its use for prediction. *Evolutionary Computation*, 5:303–346, 1998.
13. V. Robles, M.S. Pérez, J.M. Peña, V. Herves, and P. Larrañaga. Parallel interval estimation naïve Bayes. In *XIV Jornadas de Paralelismo*, pages 349–353, 2003.
14. M. Schmidt, K. Kristensen, and T.R. Jensen. Adding genetics to the standard PBIL algorithm. In *Congress of Evolutionary Computation*, pages 1527–1534, 1999.

Comparison of Steady-State and Generational Evolution Strategies for Parallel Architectures

Razvan Enache[1], Bernhard Sendhoff[2],
Markus Olhofer[2], and Martina Hasenjäger[2]

[1] École Nationale Supérieure de Télécommunications
46 rue Barrault, 75013 Paris, France
[2] Honda Research Institute Europe
Carl-Legien-Strasse 30, 63073
Offenbach am Main, Germany

Abstract. Steady-state and generational selection methods with evolution strategies were compared on several test functions with respect to their performance and efficiency. The evaluation was carried out for a parallel computing environment with a particular focus on heterogeneous calculation times for the assessment of the individual fitness. This set-up was motivated by typical tasks in design optimization. Our results show that steady-state methods outperform classical generational selection for highly variable evaluation time or for small degrees of parallelism. The 2D turbine blade optimization results did not allow a clear conclusion about the advantage of steady-state selection, however this is coherent with the above findings.

1 Introduction

Evolution strategies (ES) are a class of evolutionary algorithms designed for real-valued parameter optimization that are known to show very good performance on high-dimensional and multi-modal problems. Evolution strategies have been used successfully on design problems such as turbine blade optimization [4, 7]. Since the computation time needed to evaluate an individual in real world applications can be very long, evolution strategies are often parallelized on multi-computer clusters. The "basic" parallelization of evolution strategies is very simple if one processor can be reserved for each individual. If the evaluation of each individual takes about the same time, this type of parallelization is maximally efficient. However, if one of the two constraints is not fulfilled, efficiency can degrade rapidly. When every processor but one waits for the last evaluation, the cluster's efficiency deteriorates to that of a single processor. There are two main reasons why in practical applications this breakdown of efficiency occurs frequently. First, even if a sufficient number of processors is available, computing power has often to be shared with other projects. Second, the evaluation times often vary drastically between individuals. For example, computational fluid-dynamics (CFD) calculations work iteratively until a convergence criterion is satisfied. However, the number of iterations can vary between designs. Furthermore, design optimization is often used in conjunction with meta-models [3]. In this case, the evaluation time of individuals for which the meta-model is used is of orders of magnitude smaller than the evaluation time of the ones for which the CFD tool is used (milliseconds compared to hours).

Therefore, there is a need to explore possibilities to replace generational selection methods in evolution strategies by steady-state type selection algorithms, which integrate a newly evaluated individual directly in the population without waiting for the evaluation results of the whole generation. The overall target is to achieve parallelization without a break-down of efficiency if individual evaluation times vary drastically.

The first steady-state ES, the $(\mu+1)$, was proposed by Rechenberg [5]. More recently two steady-state selection methods have been proposed, which claim to be compatible with the self-adaptation principle of evolution strategies: median selection [8, 9] and continuous selection [6]. Both are non-elitist selection mechanisms.

On a single processor, these steady-state ESs have already been shown to perform better on many test functions than the typically used generational (μ, λ) or $(\mu + \lambda)$ methods. However, the performance and the efficiency on parallel architectures have not been evaluated yet to the extent necessary to be able to replace generational selection with steady-state selection in a practical application of optimization, like in the design optimization of turbine blades.

This comparison is the target of this paper. We test the performance of all three selection methods for varying degrees of parallelism and for different distributions of the evaluation time in Sec. 4. Before we do so, we will recall the steady-state selection methods for ES in the next section and define our experimental set-up in Sec. 3. In Sec. 5, we will extend our comparison to include a real optimization case, the design of the 2D cross-section of a turbine blade. In Sec. 6 we will conclude this paper.

2 Selection Methods in Evolution Strategies

The idea of steady-state selection is not new to evolutionary strategies. Indeed, the first type of multi-membered ES proposed by Rechenberg, the $(\mu+1)$-ES, was a steady-state algorithm! However, it turned out that due to a tendency to reduce the mutation strength one of the key features of ES – the self-adaptation of the strategy parameters – could not be realized with this algorithm [1], hence this direction of research was abandoned for the time being in favor of the study of $(\mu \dagger \lambda)$ strategies. Recently interest in steady-state ESs has revived again and with median selection [9, 8] and continuous selection [6] two algorithms have been proposed that take different courses in tackling the problem of endowing steady state ESs with self-adaptation.

In generational selection the problem of self-adaptation is solved by introducing an offspring population of λ individuals from which μ individuals are selected to become the parent population of the next generation. We consider the case of comma selection where in each generation the complete parent population is replaced by newly created individuals.

In steady-state ES, we cannot rely on an offspring population since only one newly evaluated individual is available at a time. Thus we have to exploit information that is available from previously evaluated individuals.

Median selection [9, 8] does this by observing that in generational selection only the best offspring individuals have the chance to be selected at all for generating the next parent population. This defines a fitness threshold that separates individuals which can be discarded immediately from those that may be selected. In the same spirit median selection only accepts individuals to the parent population whose rank with respect to the fitness of the last n_m evaluated individuals exceeds a certain threshold rank. In order to avoid elitism and the related disadvantages always the oldest parent is replaced when a new individual is admitted to the parent population. Note that, similarly to generational selection, median selection handles two populations: a parent population containing the last μ selected individuals and a history buffer containing the last n_m evaluated individuals.

Continuous selection [6] proceeds differently. Here the basic idea is that each individual has a limited reproduction capacity, i.e. it is only able to produce a finite number of offspring. Practically, continuous selection maintains a pool of n_c previously evaluated individuals from which the best μ have the chance to produce new offspring. Either the offspring individuals are fitter than the parent, in which case the parent will eventually be replaced, or the parent fails to produce fitter offspring within a reasonable time span which means that it should be discarded anyhow. The selection mechanism is controlled by a replacement strategy that replaces the worst individual in the pool unless the reproduction capacity of the parent expires. In this case the parent is replaced.

Note that median selection was proposed for derandomized ESs while continuous selection was proposed for the general case. For use with derandomized ESs, the latter can easily be modified by omitting steps that aim at suppressing random fluctuations in the strategy parameters.

3 Experimental Setup

3.1 Parameters of the Evolution Strategy

In order to cope with the long computation times for design optimization tasks, usually small population sizes are chosen. Since the results of our comparison of the three selection methods discussed above shall carry over to this kind of application, we also used small population sizes for the test functions.

For the generational selection method, we used $\mu = 5$ parents and $\lambda = 20$ offspring. The free parameters of the steady-state selection were chosen as similar as possible to their equivalent in generational selection. Thus for median selection the parent population also consisted of $\mu = 5$ parents and for determining the fitness threshold the last $n_m = \lambda = 20$ evaluated individuals were taken into account. The threshold rank was given by $\theta = n_m \frac{\mu}{\lambda} = 5$. In continuous selection the selection pool consisted of $n_c = \lambda = 20$ individuals. The reproduction capacity was $\gamma = \frac{\lambda}{\mu} = 4$. This is equal to the average number of times an individual reproduces in generational selection.

For all three selection algorithms we used a derandomized self-adaptation method, the covariance matrix adaptation [2], with default parameters, as recommended in [2]. The damping factor for the adaptation of the global step size was $d_\sigma = 1 + \frac{1 - \frac{N}{T}}{c_\sigma} = 26.35$, for $T = 12000$ evaluations. The maximal condition value of the covariance matrix was 10^{14} and the minimal effective step size 10^{-15}.

The strategy parameters, i.e. the covariance matrix, the evolution path, and the global step size were associated with each individual. Therefore, every individual had an associated search distribution which was the result of the adaptation to the series of mutations that created that individual's genotype. We did not use any type of recombination operator in this study.

The objective variables of the initial population were initialized with random numbers uniformly distributed in the interval $[x_{min}, x_{max}]$ and the initial global step size was given by the values for σ in Tab. 1.

We conducted experiments with a large number of widely used test functions that are listed in Tab. 1. The test functions were evaluated in dimension $N = 100$. Note, that the optimization target was minimization.

Table 1. Test functions and initialization parameters.

Name	x_{min}	x_{max}	σ	Target	Formula
Sphere	-5.12	5.12	1	1e-10	$\sum_{i=1}^{N} x_i^2$
Ellipsoid	-5.12	5.12	1	1e-10	$\sum_{i=1}^{N} 10^{6\frac{i-1}{N-1}} x_i^2$
Cigar	-5.12	5.12	1	1e-10	$x_1^2 + \sum_{i=2}^{N} 10^6 x_i^2$
Tablet	-5.12	5.12	1	1e-10	$10^6 x_1^2 + \sum_{i=2}^{N} x_i^2$
Cigar-Tablet	-5.12	5.12	1	1e-10	$x_1^2 + \sum_{i=2}^{N-1} x_i^2 + 10^8 x_N^2$
Two axes	-5.12	5.12	1	1e-10	$\sum_{i=1}^{\lfloor N/2 \rfloor} 10^6 x_i^2 + \sum_{i=\lfloor N/2 \rfloor}^{N} x_i^2$
Weighted sphere	-5.12	5.12	1	1e-10	$\sum_{i=1}^{N} i x_i^2$
Different powers	-5.12	5.12	0.1	1e-15	$\sum_{i=1}^{N} |x_i|^{2+10\frac{i-1}{N-1}}$
Rosenbrock	-5.12	5.12	0.1	1e-10	$\sum_{i=1}^{N-1} (100(x_i^2 - x_{i+1})^2 + (x_i - 1)^2)$
Rastrigin	-5.12	5.12	100	1e-10	$10N + \sum_{i=1}^{N} x_i^2 - 10\cos(\omega x_i)$
Parabolic ridge	0	0	1	-1e10	$-x_1 + 100 \sum_{i=2}^{N} x_i^2$
Sharp ridge	0	0	1	-1e10	$-x_1 + 100 \sqrt{\sum_{i=2}^{N} x_i^2}$
Ackley	-32.7	32.7	1	1e-10	see below
Schwefel	-65.5	65.5	1	1e-10	$\sum_{i=1}^{N} \left(\sum_{j=1}^{i} x_j \right)^2$

Ackley function : $-a \cdot \exp\left(-b \sqrt{\frac{1}{N} \sum_{i=1}^{N} x_i^2} \right) - \exp\left(\frac{1}{N} \cdot \sum_{i=1}^{N} \cos(c x_i) \right)$

3.2 Evaluation Time and Computing Resources

The test functions require a very small and constant evaluation time. To study the effect of parallelism in a context closer to real world applications, we simulated two different types of variable evaluation times:

A. The evaluation time of an individual was considered to be a random variable drawn from a normal distribution $\mathcal{N}(\mu, \sigma^2)$ with $\mu = 90s$ and $\sigma = 10s$, where s denotes seconds. This setting corresponds to a situation with only small variations in the fitness function evaluation times.
B. The evaluation time of an individual was considered to be a random variable drawn from an exponential distribution $\mathcal{E}(x) = \lambda \exp(-\lambda x)$ with $\lambda = 90$. In this case the fitness function evaluation time varies largely.

In both sets of experiments we varied the degree of parallelization starting with only one processor up to the case where the number of processors was identical to λ, the number of offspring in the generational selection method.

3.3 Performance Measure

In order to achieve a fair comparison, we limited the duration T of every run so that the *computing power* $P = p \cdot T$ was constant for any number of processors p. This allows taking into account the differences in the computational efficiency of the ESs, see Fig. 1.

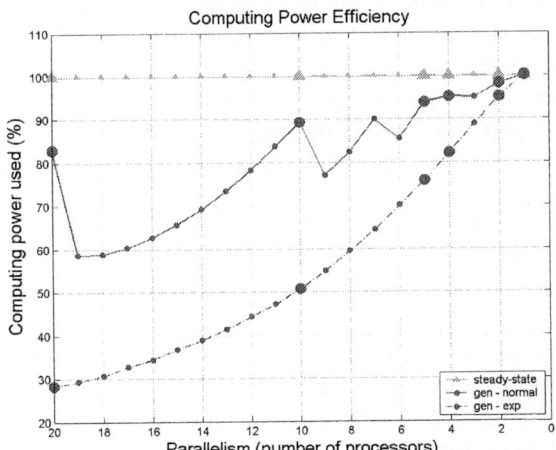

Fig. 1. Usage of the computing power by generational selection for normally (gen-normal) and exponentially (gen-exp) distributed evaluation times and by steady-state selection (steady-state). For steady-state selection the curve is independent from the time distribution. On the contrary generational selection is very sensitive to the distribution of the evaluation time. In any case efficiency is lower for generational selection.

The measure used to characterize the performance of an ES was the fitness value reached by using the given computing power. The simulations were performed for two values of the computing power, $P_1 = 100$ processor-hours and $P_2 = 300$ processor-hours. If we consider the above mentioned average of 90 seconds per fitness function evaluation, this is equivalent to a maximally efficient algorithm with 4000 and 12000 fitness function evaluations, respectively. However, the number of evaluations performed depends on the efficiency of the ES.

All performance values are averages $\bar{m}$ of the best fitness values over 20 independent runs. For a more complete image, the corresponding standard deviations $\bar{\sigma}$ are also given.

4 Results

As stated in Sec. 3.2, two sets of experiments were conducted, corresponding to normally and exponentially distributed evaluation times (set A and set B, respectively).

For the set A of experiments, represented by solid curves in Fig. 2, we observe that with one exception both steady-state methods outperformed the generational selection algorithm for all degrees of parallelization. The exception was the maximally efficient parallelization with generational selection, i.e., the number of processors was equal to the number of offspring, in our case $\lambda = 20$.

The set B of experiments is represented by dashed curves in Fig. 2. We see that for any degree of parallelization both steady-state methods performed similarly irrespective of the probability distribution of the evaluation times. Thus, whether there was a large or a small variation in evaluation times among individuals had no impact on the performance of steady-state methods. This was very different for the generational selection algorithm. We observe a sharp decrease in the performance for large variations (exponential distribution) in particular for the 20 processor case.

Fig. 2 shows the results of both sets of experiments for the special case of the Schwefel test function, cf. Tab. 1. However, for most of the other test functions the curves look qualitatively similar (not shown here). Moreover, similar results were obtained for different computing powers (Fig. 3).

The average relative performance of the steady state selection methods with respect to generational selection is shown for all test functions in Fig. 4 for the case of 20 processors and $P_2 = 300$ processor-hours.

For all test functions represented in the lower left quadrant of the plot steady-state selection showed better results than generational selection: both means and standard deviations were smaller than for generational selection. As expected, for small variations in the evaluation time generational selection outperformed steady-state selection methods (note that the case for $p = \lambda$ processors is shown), see Fig. 4 (right). However, for the exponentially distributed evaluation times, which result in large differences, the situation is reversed. On nearly all test

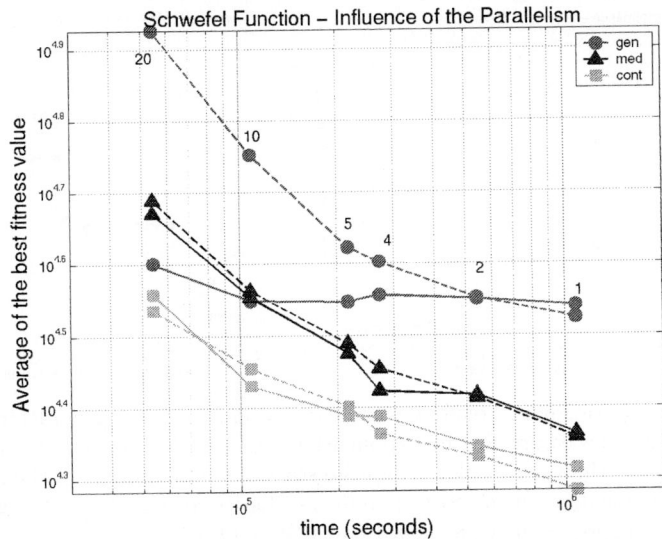

Fig. 2. Comparison of normally (solid curves) and exponentially (dashed curves) distributed evaluation times for the Schwefel function. The points on each curve correspond, from left to right, to 20, 10, 5, 4, 2 and 1 processor(s), respectively. Here gen/med/cont refer to generational/median/continuous selection.

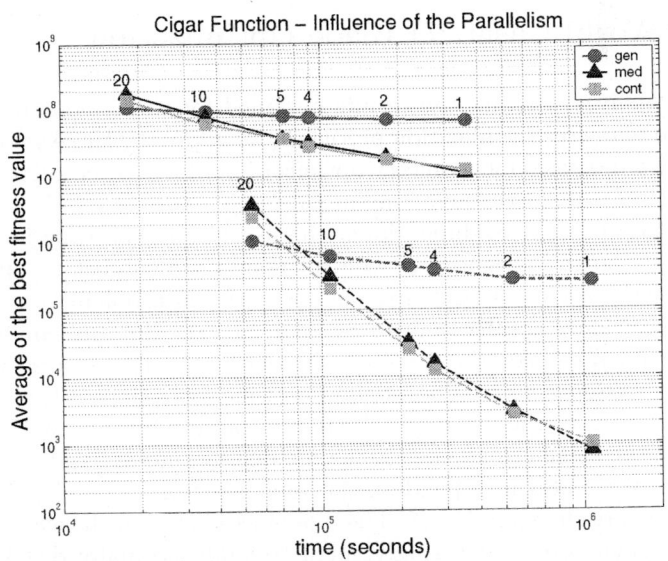

Fig. 3. The influence of parallelism on the cigar function. The lower (dashed) curves correspond to $P_2 = 300$ processor-hours and the upper (solid) curves correspond to $P_1 = 100$ processor-hours. The points on each curve correspond, from left to right, to 20, 10, 5, 4, 2 and 1 processor(s), respectively. Here gen/med/cont refer to generational/median/continuous selection.

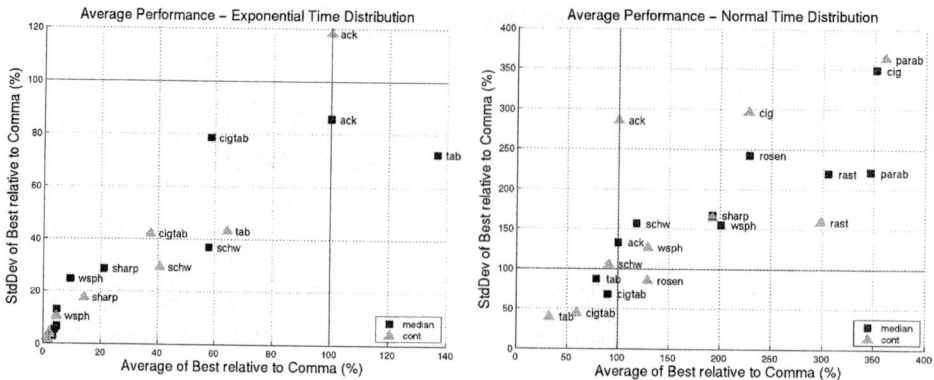

Fig. 4. Average performance of steady state selection relative to generational selection for $p = \lambda = 20$ processors for an exponential time distribution (left) and a normal time distribution (right). The plot shows the statistics $\bar{m}_{ss}$ and $\bar{\sigma}_{ss}$ of the steady-state methods as a percentage of the corresponding statistics $\bar{m}_c$ and $\bar{\sigma}_c$ for the generational selection, i.e., the points have the coordinates $\frac{\bar{\sigma}_{ss}}{\bar{\sigma}_c}$ and $\frac{\bar{m}_{ss}}{\bar{m}_c}$.

functions steady-state selection shows better performance than generational selection, see Fig. 4 (left).

5 Real World Case: 2D Blade Optimization

In order to analyze whether the results obtained for the various test functions carry over to real-world application problems, we apply the three selection methods to the two-dimensional geometry optimization of an outlet guide vane in the turbine stage of a small turbofan engine.

The contour of the two-dimensional cross-section of the vane is represented by a 3rd B-spline curve, whose 22 control points are subject to optimization. Thus, we have to solve a 44 dimensional optimization problem.

The fitness values are determined by analyzing the fluid dynamic properties of the proposed vane geometries using a Navier-Stokes flow solver, see [7, 4] for details of the system set-up. The calculation time for a single fitness evaluation for this problem is of the order of 3-5 minutes on an Opteron 2GHz processor. Variations in the calculation time are mainly due to different starting conditions of the flow solver and also depend on the vane geometry.

The results are shown in Fig. 5. The differences between the evaluation times in this experiment were surprisingly small (roughly normally distributed with mean $\mu = 257s$ and standard deviation $\sigma = 42s$). As expected from the previous results on the test functions, we observe in Fig. 5 a behavior which is similar to the set A of experiments. Therefore, steady-state selection did not significantly improve the optimization. Indeed the curves for all three selection methods look very similar. In order to give a clear recommendation for steady-state selection for the design optimization application additional investigations are necessary. We will come back to this point in the last section.

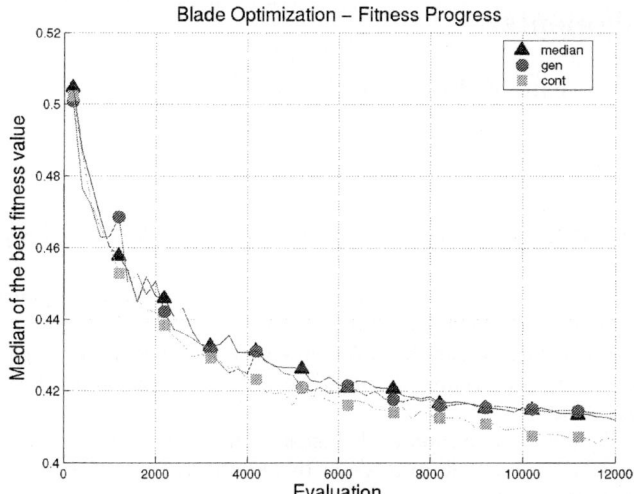

Fig. 5. Average performance of steady state selection relative to generational selection on the blade optimization problem. The median of the best fitness value is plotted against the evaluation number for median, generational and continuous selection.

6 Conclusions

This paper is concerned with the performance evaluation and the comparison of three different types of selection methods for evolution strategies. Two steady-state methods have been analyzed and compared to the standard generational selection algorithm for different distributions of the evaluation time and for degrees of parallelism ranging from a single processor to the maximally efficient parallelization for generational selection, i.e. with $p = \lambda$ processors.

From the two sets of experiments – one with normally and one with exponentially distributed evaluation times – we observe that steady-state selection methods outperform generational selection in all but one case. This case, which we termed "maximally efficient" parallelization, is realized if the number of processors equals the number of individuals and if the evaluation times are fairly similar between individuals. As we argued already in the introduction, these two criteria will not always be met in applications. Therefore, steady-state selection methods present a more flexible alternative to generational selection. Furthermore, they are more efficient and in most cases also show higher performance.

Unfortunately, the first results for the design optimization task in a "real-world" optimization environment, do not provide a picture as clear as for the test functions. The main reason is that the variations of the evaluation time between individuals were smaller than what we recorded for previous design optimization tasks. Therefore, we can only conclude that steady-state selection methods perform similarly as generational selection. In order to verify their advantage, additional experiments are necessary. We are currently using our meta-model assisted design optimization environment [3] as a test bed. Furthermore, we plan to run additional experiments for a smaller number of processors.

Acknowledgments

We would like to thank E. Körner for his support.

References

1. H.-G. Beyer and H.-P. Schwefel. Evolution strategies. *Natural Computing*, 1:3–52, 2002.
2. N. Hansen and A. Ostermeier. Completely derandomized self-adapatation in evolution strategies. *Evolutionary Computation*, 9(2):159–195, 2001.
3. Y. Jin, M. Olhofer, and B. Sendhoff. A framework for evolutionary optimization with approximate fitness functions. *IEEE Transactions on Evolutionary Computation*, 6(5):481–494, 2002.
4. M. Olhofer, T. Arima, T. Sonoda, M. Fischer, and B. Sendhoff. Aerodynamic shape optimisation using evolution strategies. In *Optimisation in Industry III*, pages 83–94. Springer, 2001.
5. I. Rechenberg. *Evolutionstrategie '94*. Frommann-Holzboog, Stuttgart, 1994.
6. T. Runarsson and X. Yao. Continuous selection and self-adaptive evolution strategies. In *Proceedings of the 2002 Congress on Evolutionary Computation (CEC)*, pages 279–284. IEEE Press, 2002.
7. T. Sonoda, Y. Yamaguchi, T. Arima, M. Olhofer, B. Sendhoff, and H. A. Schreiber. Advanced high turning compressor airfoils for low reynolds number condition, Part 1: Design and optimization. *Journal of Turbomachinery*, 2004. In press.
8. J. Wakunda and A. Zell. Median-selection for parallel steady-state evolution strategies. In *Proceedings of the 6th International Conference Parallel Problem Solving from Nature (PPSN VI)*, pages 405–414. Springer, 2000.
9. J. Wakunda and A. Zell. A new selection scheme for steady-state evolution strategies. In *Proceedings of the Genetic and Evolutionary Computation Conference (GECCO)*, pages 794–801. Morgan Kaufmann, 2000.

Control of Bloat in Genetic Programming by Means of the Island Model

Francisco Fernández de Vega[1], German Galeano Gil[1],
Juan Antonio Gómez Pulido[2], and Jose Luis Guisado[1]

[1] Centro Universitario de Mérida, University of Extremadura
C/ Calvario, s/n. 06800 Mérida, Spain
{fcofdez,ggaleano}@unex.es
[2] Escuela Politécnica, University of Extremadura,
Cáceres, Spain
jangomez@unex.es
http://atc.unex.es/pacof

Abstract. This paper presents a new proposal for reducing bloat in Genetic Programming. This proposal is based in a well-known parallel evolutionary model: the island model. We firstly describe the theoretical motivation for this new approach to the bloat problem, and then we present a set of experiments that gives us evidence of the findings extracted from the theory. The experiments have been performed on a representative problem extracted from the GP field: the even parity 5 problem. We analyse the evolution of bloat employing different settings for the parameters employed. The conclusion is that the Island Model helps to prevent the bloat phenomenon.

1 Introduction

When an evolutionary algorithm is applied to a difficult problem, a large number of individuals is usually required for making up the population, and very frequently, a large number of generations have to be computed in order to find a successful solution for the problem. Therefore, the computational effort required for solving difficult problems is sometimes prohibitive.

It is also well known that in Genetic Programming (GP) – one of the members of EAs' family – individuals tend to increase their size as population evolves. This growth is not necessarily correlated with increases in the fitness of the evolved programs, and many times individuals increase their size while fitness doesn't improve. The problem is that individuals require computing time to be evaluated; and given that individuals undergo the problem of increasing their size as they are evolved, generations will take progressively longer time to be computed, which is a big concern for GP researchers.

The above describe problem is usually known as the bloat phenomenon, and has been frequently studied during the last few years [3, 4, 5, 6, 13, 14]. As said above, bloat has a large impact in the search process.

Besides presenting several studies that aims at offering reasons for the bloat [13, 14], researchers try to offer alternatives for controlling that problem. In [3] some of these proposals are described: firstly, by placing a universal upper limit either on tree depth or program length; secondly, by incorporating a penalty which is proportional to program size; and finally, tailoring the genetic operations.

On the other hand, given that any EA requires long time for solving difficult problems, some approaches taken from parallel computing field have also been applied to alleviate the problem. These approaches try to apply some degree of parallelization to the basic algorithm. There are important differences in the way it can be done, and the kind of EA employed. For instance, Cantú-Paz [10] studied how to apply parallelism to Genetic Algorithms (Gas), and also presented some theoretical results involved in the parallel version of the algorithm. Also Fernández et al [7, 8, 9] have studied Parallel GP, and the importance of some key parameters that are only employed in the parallel algorithm, such as synchrony, migration frequency, granularity and so on.

All of the above referred studies employ the well-known Island model for the parallel algorithm. The idea behind this model is simple: Divide the entire population of individuals into smaller ones, so that each sub-population is computed in a different processor. Populations may sometimes exchange good individuals. The results have shown that the Island Model improves fitness quality of individuals while also saves computing time because of the use of several processors [7, 8, 10].

Nevertheless, for the time being, the Island model has always been analysed with the idea of improving quality of solutions and for saving computing time, and only once a report on the evolution of bloat when using the model for GP has been presented [9], although no hypothesis for the reason of the behaviour observed was provided.

In this paper we continue the study on the bloat phenomenon, employing this non-traditional point of view: Instead of focusing on the kind of genetic code that causes bloat (such as non-operating instructions in programs, subprograms functionally equivalent to instructions, etc. [14]) we show that the island based algorithm can also help to prevent the bloat of individuals in GP, while we also provide a reason for this behaviour. The island models could be thus considered as a new technique for preventing bloat when looking for solutions by means of GP.

A set of experiments is presented for supporting the theoretical motivation that describes the advantages of the Island Model.

This paper is structured in the following way: Section 2 describes the theoretical motivation that justify why Island Models are of interest when fighting bloat. Section 3 briefly describes the problem studied, while Section 4 shows the results we have obtained in a set of experiments. Finally, section 5 presents our conclusions and future work.

2 Motivation

Langdon and Poli have established that programs size increases on average at less than $O(time^{\alpha})$ with $\alpha \in [1.2,2]$, and it will approach a square power law, $O(t^2)$, as the programs get bigger (see [5,6]) In this section, for simplicity, we assume the later $O(t^2)$ for the increase of programs size (although other α values within the range will not change the main conclusion). We also consider that programs sizes are measured be counting the number of nodes contained in the tree.

When a generational evolutionary algorithm is employed, time can be measured by means of the number of generations computed, so that time and generations have similar meanings. When generations are computed time runs. Therefore, we could formulate $O(g^2)$ as an equivalent expression to $O(t^2)$ (g being generation computed). We can then write:

$$O(t^2)=O(g^2) \tag{1}$$

'=' sign according to big-Oh notation.

We also know that individuals grow when crossover and mutation operators are applied. A GP algorithm lacking both operands -that only apply selection and copy of individuals- will evolve to a population of identical individuals, all of them copies of any of the individuals making up the initial population. This is because no variation operator is employed. In this condition, the bloat phenomenon is not present, because individuals can not change their size (the only difference between the size of individuals at the end of the algorithm is due to the difference between the individual that has dominated the population and the remaining ones). Nevertheless this cannot be considered bloat.

Therefore, bloat only exists when variation operators are applied to produce new individuals, and may thus appear larger ones. The more new individuals we produce (crossover and mutation operators are then applied), the more opportunities for bloat. We could thus say that bloat approach $O(i^2)$ i being the number of new individuals produced per generation, and according to equation (1):

$$O(t^2)=O(g^2)= O(i^2) \tag{2}$$

If the number of individuals created per generation is proportional to the number of individuals in the population, which is usually the case, we could instead employ the expression $O(n^2)$ -n being the number of individuals in the population- for the limit on bloat growth. This can only be stated if mutation and crossover are applied a number of times proportional to the size of populations. Summarising we have the following expression:

$$\text{Bloat}(n) = O(t^2) = O(g^2) = O(i^2) = O(n^2) \tag{3}$$

The first idea obtained from the above expression is that different population sizes should produce different bloat values.

By analysing these results and those presented for the island model in [9], and considering that $bloat(n)= O(n^2)$, being n the size of the population, we can ask the following question: what would happen if we distribute all of the individuals among several subpopulations? If we employ x subpopulations, we would have n/x individuals per subpopulation. What we will try to analyse now is whether such distribution change the bloat evolution.

The big-Oh notation from equation 3 tells us that the bloat equation for a population with n individuals is a second degree polynomial function:

$$bloat(n) = O(n^2) \Rightarrow bloat(n) = an^2 + bn + c \tag{4}$$

By $bloat(n)$ we mean a function that measure the number of nodes obtained with a population of size n on a given problem. If the number of individuals in the population n is not very small, then we can write:

$$bloat(n) \approx an^2 + bn \tag{5}$$

We are studying the bloat evolution when individuals are distributed among a set of populations, so that the total number of individuals n remains unaltered, but we employ n/x individuals in each of the x populations. The total bloat for each of the subpopulations is *bloat(n/x);* if we consider that the bloat phenomenon occurs similarly in every subpopulation, employing equation 5 we can add up to obtain the total bloat:

$$\sum_{i=1}^{x} bloat(\tfrac{n}{x}) = x \cdot bloat(\tfrac{n}{x}) \tag{6}$$

Let's now make an assumption, and then we will try to check if it can be satisfied. Let's consider that the island model does not affect the evolution of bloat, i.e. the total bloat obtained when adding the bloat for each of the subpopulation correspond with the bloat obtained when using only one population. If this is true, the following expression must be true:

$$x \cdot bloat(\tfrac{n}{x}) = bloat(n) \tag{7}$$

But, if we substitute in both terms of the expression employing equation 5, we obtain:

$$x\left(a\frac{n^2}{x^2} + b\frac{n}{x}\right) = an^2 + bn \tag{8}$$

and equivalently:

$$\frac{an^2}{x} = an^2 \tag{9}$$

And this can only be true for $x=1$ i.e. employing the panmictic model. Nevertheless we first stated that we employ the island model, so that $x>1$. So, the left part of expression (9) will become smaller as new populations are added to the model. Given this contradiction, we infer that the initial assumption of an equivalent global rate of bloat in the Island Model is false.

Once we have seen that bloat rate is different when using the Island Model, and given the left part of equation (9), we conclude that as more subpopulations we use, a smaller bloat we will obtain. This statement is in agreement with results obtained in [9], in which the Island Model was applied to study bloat, although no clue for the behaviour observed was provided.

In the following sections we revisit the Island Model, for analysing again bloat evolution in a very well-know problem employed in GP studies: the even parity 5 problem. We try to see if the predictions from the theory confirmed by experimentation.

3 Experiments

We have employed a well-known GP problem, the even parity 5 problem [2], with several settings in order to make comparisons. The goal in the even parity 5 problem is to generate a Boolean function that gives us the parity of a set of 5 bits. The Parallel GP tool employed is described in [12].

Experiments have been performed in a cluster of PCs running a distribution of Linux specially suited for clusters [1]. We show the averages values obtained over 50 runs for each of the experiments.

Table 1 shows the setting used in the experiments with the evenp-5 problem. The maximum depths have been established identically in all of the experiments, so that differences we may found will not be due to differences in this parameter. On the other hand, Table 2 provides the parameter specifically employed when using the Island Model (See [7] for a whole description of the model). The number of subpopulations is different for each of the experiments performed, and this information is provided within the graphs.

Table 1. Parameters for the Evenp Problem.

Crossover Probability	98.0
Creation Probability	1.0
Max. Depth For Creation	6
Max. Depth For Crossover	17
Swap Mutation Probability	1.0
Selection	10 individuals per Tournament

Table 2. Parameters for the Island Model.

Generations between Migration	10
% of the population that migrate	10%
Synchrony	Asynchronous model

4 Results

4.1 Panmictic Model

Before analysing results obtained with the Island Model, we have performed a couple of experiments to check the validity of Equation (3). The equation tell us that the bloat phenomenon must change with the size of the population, so we have firstly performed an experiment employing different population sizes when using the evenp-5 problem and the panmictic model.

Figure 1 presents the results that we have obtained for the evenp-5 problem. We have performed 50 experiments for each of the curve, and then we have computed the average length per generation. We notice that when we increase the size of the population, the average length is larger. So, the first idea extracted from equation (3) is confirmed by results obtained.

The second idea that can be extracted from equation (3) is simple: if we change the number of genetic operations applied per generation, or equivalently, the number of new individuals created per generation, we may change the bloat rate. We have thus performed another experiment that helps us to confirm this idea for the panmictic model.

The experiment is simple: suppose we don't create each generation a number of new individuals proportional to the size of the population n, but we create instead a number of new ones proportional to $n/2$ or proportional to $n/4$. Equation (3) tell us that bloat obtained is proportional to the number of new individuals created, and this time, this value would not be equivalent to the size of the population.

Figure 2 shows the evolution of the average length of individuals that have been obtained in experiments following the idea described above. Each curve corresponds to an experiment in which a number of new individuals are created (a percentage of the size of the population). We can easily observe that bloat is smaller when the number of new individuals created reduces (a smaller number of crossover and mutation operations are applied). Its interesting to see that bloat is not present when no individuals are created, as we could expect (curve labelled as "without evolution"). Several population sizes have been employed with similar results.

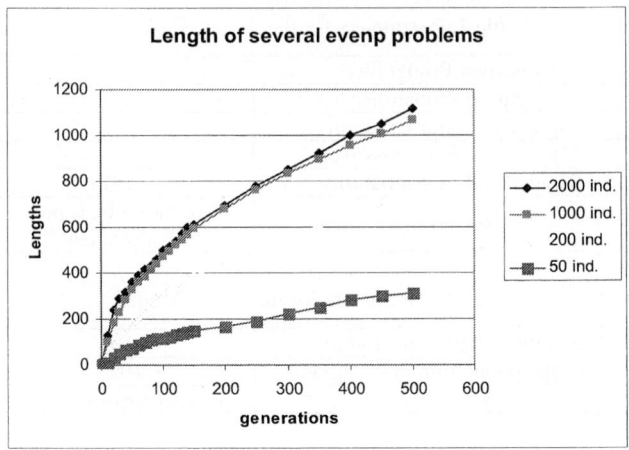

Fig. 1. Length Evolution in the even parity 5 problem, with different populations' sizes. The bigger population, the larger bloat.

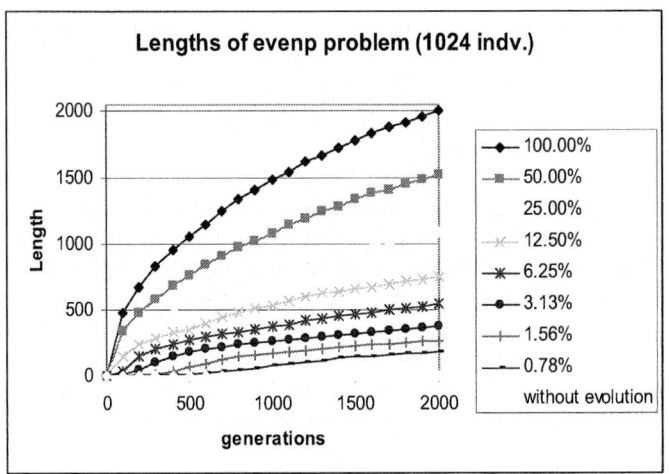

Fig. 2. Length Evolution in the evenp-5 problem Size of population= 1024. Percentage values means the number of new individuals over the size of the population created each generation.

Table 3, numerically shows the average size of individuals in different number of generations. These results numerically show the same results provided in figures 1 and 2. Nevertheless, they help to verify quantitatively how different rates of creation of individuals change the rate of bloat. We can notice that no bloat occurs when no new individuals are created.

Table 3. Length evolution in the evenp problem.

% new in-div.	Generations			
	2000	1000	500	100
100.00%	2002.4	1483.8	1057.5	474.6
50.00%	1514.8	1074.9	760.1	335.2
25.00%	1091.2	789.6	548.1	258.5
12.50%	746.5	533.8	353.1	148.4
6.25%	541.0	374.2	270.6	38.2
3.13%	368.3	262.4	179.3	7.4
1.56%	263.6	169.4	64.0	5.1
0.78%	180.4	75.6	11.8	5.0
0.39%	65.1	10.4	5.3	5.0
0.00%	5.0	5.0	5.0	5.0

4.2 Island Model

The next step was to analyse the island model. We want to maintain the classical setting, by generating a number of new individuals per generation proportional to the size of the population. We want to compare bloat evolution with that observed within the panmictic model.

Several experiments have been performed for the evenp-5 problem, employing different population sizes for both the panmictic model, and also employing the Island Model and 2, 4, 10 and 20 subpopulations (equally distributing all of the individuals among the subpopulations employed in each experiment). Figure 3 shows the average length value obtained over 50 runs in a couple of experiment that employs 100 individuals, while figure 4 has been obtained employing 2500 individuals. We can see that bloat reduces as a larger number of subpopulations are employed to distribute the global population.

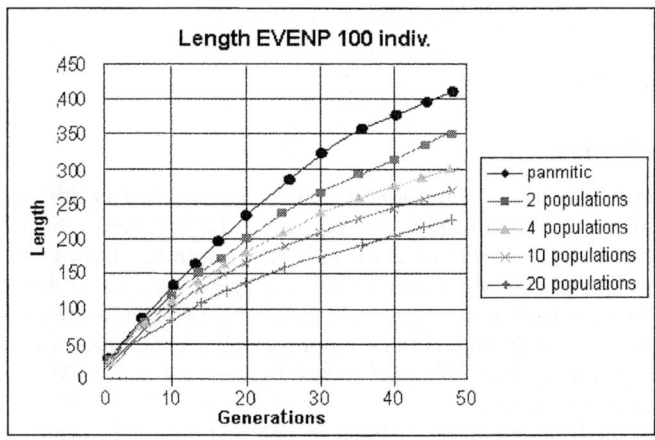

Fig. 3. Length evolution in the evenp-5 problem when using the Island Model.

We have not tried to study in this paper which is the best number of island to be employed in a given experiment. This problem has been addressed before, and no perfect recipes exist [7]. Nevertheless, the above presented results make evident a new advantage of the Island Model that to our best knowledge has not been presented for GP before.

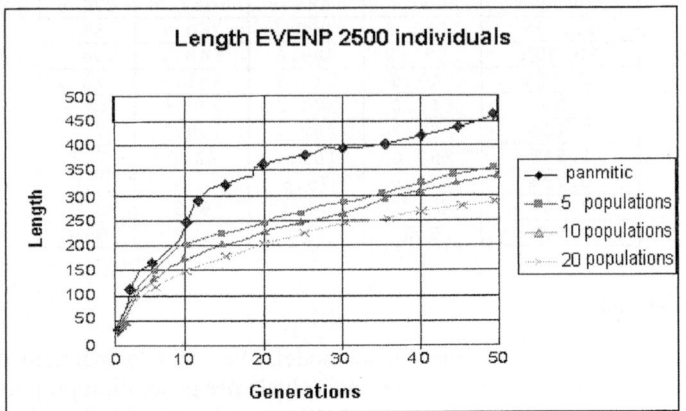

Fig. 4. Length evolution in the ant problem when using the Island Model.

The results obtained with the Island Model in the problem, confirms the prediction of the theoretical model employed in section 2: the bloat rate reduces when individuals are distributed among a set of subpopulations. This is a new advantage for the Island Model: Not only it find better fitness quality, but also reduces the bloat phenomenon.

The above mentioned advantage of the Island Models is now added to another important feature of island-based GP: it can be easily computed on multiprocessor systems: we just have to distribute populations among processors, and both advantages helps together to save computing effort when GP is applied to solve optimization problems.

5 Conclusions

A new approach for reducing the bloat problem is presented in this paper. We have first employed a theoretical model that predicted the different rate of code growth when the island model is employed in Genetic Programming. The model suggests that distributing individuals among a number of subpopulation will reduce the bloat phenomenon, and this reduction is larger when more subpopulations are employed.

The even partiy 5 problem has been employed as a benchmark for experimenting the evolution of code growth. We also shown that results obtained are coherent with those predicted by the model.

We have studied the evolution of bloat in panmictic models, when the number of genetic operations applied each generation (and also the number of new individuals created) is not the same as the size of the population. By means of this experiments we have presented evidences that make us to be confident about the predictions of the theory on the Island Model.

Finally, the study has focussed on the Island Model. We have first seen that bloat depends on the size of the subpopulations, and then we have performed several tests employing the Island Model, that have experimentally shown in a well-known GP problem that distributing a population into several ones of smaller size helps to prevent the bloat phenomenon.

In the future, we will present a larger report including a wider set of both test and real-life problems corroborating conclusions presented in this paper.

References

1. Philip M. Papadopoulos, Mason J. Katz, and Greg Bruno, *NPACI Rocks: Tools and Techniques for Easily Deploying Manageable Linux Clusters* ,. Concurrency and Computation: Practice and Experience. Volume 15, Issue 7-8, Date: June - July 2003, Pages: 707-725.
2. J.R. Koza: "Genetic Programming. On the programming of computers by means of natural selection". Cambridge MA: The MIT Press. 1992.
3. W. Langdom and R. Poli. *"Fitness causes bloat"*. In P.K. Chawdhry et. Al., editors. Soft Computing in Engineering Design and Manufacturing, pp 13-22. Springer London, 1997.
4. W. Banzhaf, W. B. Langdon, *"Some Considerations on the Reason for Bloat"*, In Genetic Programming and Evolvable Machines, 3, 81-1, 2002.
5. W.B. Langdom, Riccardo Poli. *Foundations of Genetic Programming*. Ed. Springer, 2001. "Convergence and *bloat*". Pp 193-217
6. W. B. Langdon, *"Quadratic Bloat in Genetic Programming"*, In proceedings of the 2000 Genetic and Evolutionary Computation Conference. 2000.
7. F. Fernández, "Parallel and Distributed Genetic Programming models, with application to logic synthesis on FPGAs", PhD Thesis. Universidad de Extremadura, February 2001.
8. F. Fernández, M. Tomassini, L. Vanneschi, "*An Empirical Study of Multipopulation Genetic Programming*", . Genetic Programming and Evolvable Machines, Vol. 4. 2003. pp. 21-51. Kluwer Academic Publishers.
9. G. Galeano, F. Fernández, M. Tomassini, L. Vanneschi, *"Studying the Influence of Synchronous and Asynchronous Parallel GP on Programs Length Evolution"*. In Proceedings of Conference on Evolutionary Computation 2002.
10. Erick Cantú-Paz. "Efficient and Accurate Parallel Genetic Algorithms ". Kluwer Academic PublishersISBN 0-7923-7221-2. Volume 1 of the Book Series on Genetic Algorithms and Evolutionary Computation
11. W.F. Punch: "How effective are multiple populations in Genetic Programming". Genetic Programming 1998: Proceedings of the Third Annual Conference, J. R. Koza, W. Banzhaf, K. Chellapilla, K. Deb, M. Dorigo, D. B. Fogel, M. Garzon, D. Goldberg, H. Iba and R. L. Riolo (Eds),Morgan Kaufmann, San Francisco, CA, 308-313, 1998.
12. M. Tomassini, F. Fernández, L. Vanneschi, L. Bucher, *"An MPI-Based Tool for Distributed Genetic Programming"*. In Proceedings of IEEE International Conference on Cluster Computing CLUSTER2000, IEEE Computer Society. Pp.209-216. 2000.
13. T. Soule, *Exons and code growth in genetic programming,* In J. A. Foster et al (eds.) LNCS 2278. pp. 142-151. Aril 2002.
14. S. Luke « Modification Point Depth and Genome Growth in Genetic Programming ». Evolutionary Computation. Spring 2003. Vol 11, Num 1. pp 67.

Saving Resources with Plagues in Genetic Algorithms

Francisco Fernández de Vega[1], Erik Cantú-Paz[2], J.I. López[1], and T. Manzano[1]

[1] Artificial Evolution Group, Centro Universitario de Mérida,
Universidad de Extremadura, Spain
fcofdez@unex.es
[2] Center for Applied Scientific Computing
Lawrence Livermore National Laboratory

Abstract. The population size of genetic algorithms (GAs) affects the quality of the solutions and the time required to find them. While progress has been made in estimating the population sizes required to reach a desired solution quality for certain problems, in practice the sizing of populations is still usually performed by trial and error. These trials might lead to find a population that is large enough to reach a satisfactory solution, but there may still be opportunities to optimize the computational cost by reducing the size of the population. This paper presents a technique called plague that periodically removes a number of individuals from the population as the GA executes. Recently, the usefulness of the plague has been demonstrated for genetic programming. The objective of this paper is to extend the study of plagues to genetic algorithms. We experiment with deceptive trap functions, a tunable difficult problem for GAs, and the experiments show that plagues can save computational time while maintaining solution quality and reliability.

1 Introduction

When researchers apply evolutionary algorithms (EAs), one of the first parameters to be chosen is the size of the population. Usually, difficult problems require a large population, while easier problems can be solved with a small population [1, 2]. A large number of individuals requires a large amount of computing resources, both memory space and computing power for the fitness evaluations. Recently, a technique called plague that dynamically reduces the population size was demonstrated to improve the performance of genetic programming without sacrificing solution quality [3, 4]. In this paper, we demonstrate that plagues can also be successfully applied to genetic algorithms.

Plagues work by periodically removing a number of individuals from the population. Several policies may be employed for selecting individuals to be deleted. For instance, individuals may be removed at random or they can be removed according to some criteria, such as their fitness value, size (in the case of GP), or similarity to other individuals in the population. Plagues can be applied with arbitrary fixed frequencies or they can be triggered by some measure of the progress of the run, such as a measure of population diversity.

In this paper we show, by means of a series of experiments, that plagues may help GAs solve difficult problems in shorter times. The experiments consider a classic tunable problem usually employed to test GAs. As a first study of the application of plagues in GAs, this paper reports results using plagues in every generation, removing a fixed number of individuals per generation, and choosing the worst individuals for removal. We experiment varying the number of individuals removed. Other options of frequency and removal policies are left for future studies. The results suggest that plagues can reduce the computational effort required to reach the global optimum with some certainty.

This paper is structured as follows: section 2 presents a summary of the research related to the plague operator and also some arguments supporting its usefulness. Section 3 describes the way we measure results and the problem employed as a benchmark, while section 4 presents some results obtained using plagues and GAs. Finally we offer our conclusions in section 5.

2 Previous Work

A number of researchers have focused on the study of population size, because of its importance for obtaining solutions of high quality. One of the first studies of population sizing is by Goldberg [6]. His objective was to find the population size that maximizes the rate of schema processing, and found that this rate is maximized with small populations when fitness is evaluated serially and with large populations with parallel evaluations. Goldberg et al. [7] proposed a population sizing estimate based on the variance of fitness. This estimate directly tied population size to solution quality. Goldberg et al. [1] refined the model and obtained a conservative bound on the convergence quality of GAs. Their model is based on the probability of choosing correctly between the best building block and its closest competitor. Later, Harik et al. [8, 2] used some of Goldberg's results to obtain a model that, for some problems, relates accurately the population size to the quality of the solution of a GA.

A few authors have addressed the idea of populations of variable size in GAs. For instance, Kirley applied the concept of "disasters" when using cellular GA [9], where the population is laid on a lattice and individuals interact only with their neighbors. Kirley's idea was to suppress all the individuals in a randomly chosen portion of the lattice. Eventually, the area that suffered the disaster is repopulated with offspring from the individuals that border the disaster area. Since disasters have the effect of fragmenting the population into isolated groups of individuals, it is possible to preserve lesser individuals that would be suppressed quickly in the original population. This mechanism helps maintain diversity in the population that might be useful in later stages of the algorithm.

Smith and Smuda [10] adapted the population size using Goldberg et al.'s population sizing theory [1]. Smith and Smuda employed a dynamic estimate of the variance of building blocks. Tan et al. [11], employ an EA with dynamic population size for discovering the tradeoff surface when solving a multi-objective optimization problem. They modify the size of populations according to distribution of solutions on the search space.

However, all these proposals differ with the concept of plague described above, because plagues do not take into account the structure of the population (as in Kirley's work) nor the distribution of solutions (as in Smith's and Tan's work).

In genetic programming (GP), people have been even more concerned with deciding the size of populations, because of the well-known problem of bloat [12], which consists of the growth of individuals as the search progresses. Since the total effort depends on the size of the individuals and the population size, deciding the size of the population is important for reducing the computing effort that will be required.

During the last year, the first attempts to directly change the size of the population while the evolutionary process is working were presented in GP. Plagues were first described by Fernández [3] as a new operator acting on the population, and were described in more detail in [5] and [4].

Similar proposals were also described by Monsieurs [13] and Luke [14] later. Luke et al. [14] performed a few experiments to extend the concept of plague to GAs. Their results, however, did not show statistically significant differences in the final fitness values obtained by a fixed-size GA and one with a plague on three optimization problems. Our results differ from Luke's. We not only study mean best fitness values obtained from a set of runs, but also the number of runs that reach the optimum, and these are the curves that better show the advantage of the reduction of population size.

3 Methods

3.1 Computing Effort

In EAs studies, results are commonly presented by comparing a measure of quality (e.g., number of successes in a set of runs, average fitness value) to the number of generations employed. But this comparison is correct only when the computational effort required for computing each of the generations is the same. When conditions change from generation to generation, this way of presenting results is misleading. This is usually the case in GP, when individuals grow as a run progresses. In our case, since plagues reduce the size of populations each generation, the computing power required to evaluate each generation decreases progressively. In [15] and [16] a new way of measuring results under these conditions was presented for GP. Here, we adapt that measure for GA.

We use the *effort of computation* defined as the total number of individuals evaluated for a given number of generations. To calculate this strictly increasing measure, we must first compute the partial effort at a given generation (that we will denote as PE_g) defined as the number of individuals evaluated ($PE_g = i$, i is the number of individuals in the population at generation g). Then, we calculate the effort of computation E_g, at generation g, as

$$E_g = PE_g + PE_{g-1} + PE_{g-2} + \ldots + PE_0.$$

Thus the effort of computation for generation g is the total number of individuals that have been evaluated before generation $g + 1$. Clearly, this measure is problem-specific but it is useful for comparing different solutions and different settings of experiments for the same problem.

It was not our intention here to compare execution times. Our intention is to track the convergence process itself, without directly taking into account actual execution time. However, a reduced effort of computation will imply a reduction in the computation time, regardless of the computer employed.

3.2 Experiments

The experiments used deceptive trap functions, which are used in numerous studies of genetic algorithms because they have known properties and their difficulty can be regulated easily [17]. The values of the deceptive functions depend on the number, u, of bits set to one in their k-bit input substring. The fitness increases with more bits set to zero until it reaches a local optimum, but the global maximum is at the opposite extreme where all the bits in the input are set to one. The order-k traps are defined as

$$f_k(u) = \begin{cases} k - u - d & \text{if } u < k, \\ k & \text{if } u = k, \end{cases} \quad (1)$$

where d is the fitness difference of the two peaks, which in our case is always set to one. The trap functions become more difficult by increasing the number of bits k in the basin of the deceptive optimum and by reducing d.

In the experiments, we varied k from 4 to 8. The fitness functions are formed by concatenating fully-deceptive trap functions and adding their individual contributions. We set the length of the individuals to $l = 20 * k$ bits. For example, for the 6-bit trap problem, the individuals are $l = 120$ bits long and their fitness is calculated as $\sum_{i=0}^{20} f_6(u_{6i})$, where u_{6i} denotes the number of ones in the substring that starts at position $6i$.

We follow previous studies that used deceptive trap functions [2, 19] and set the mutation probability to zero and use pairwise (binary) tournament selection. Although in [19] two-point crossover is used for avoiding excessive disruption on the longer BBs, we used uniform crossover with probability 1. We wanted to make the problem more difficult so that experiments with larger populations are of interest.

Plagues remove a fixed number of individuals every generation. The number of individuals to be removed is a parameter of the operator, and is specified below for each experiment as well as the initial population sizes. When plague is applied, we always remove the worst individuals from the population, according to their fitness value. As we mentioned above, other removal strategies based on fitness or similarity to other individuals are possible, but their study is outside the scope of this paper. Each run was terminated after 50 generations or until the population was empty.

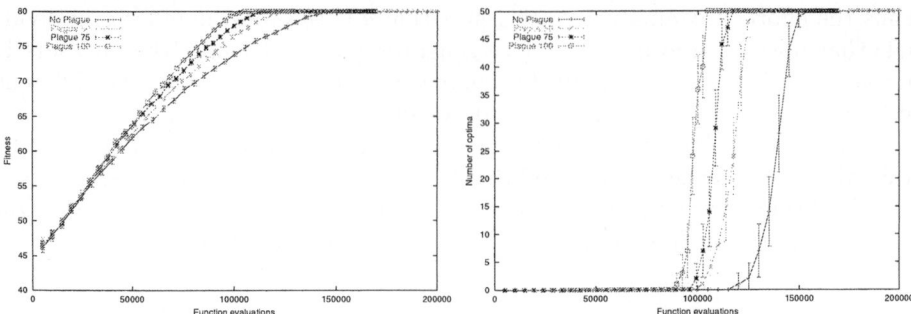

Fig. 1. Fitness (left) and number of times the experiment reached the global optimum out of 50 experiments (right) for different plagues. The initial population size was $N = 5000$ individuals and $k = 4$. The error bars denote 95% confidence intervals.

The experiments consider 50 independent runs for each of the parameter settings. The graphs present the number of times that the GAs reached the global solution or the mean fitness values vs. the number of fitness evaluations.

The experiments were carried out using GALib [18]. Only small modifications to the source code were necessary to include the plague operation.

4 Experimental Results

We begun the experiments using the fitness function formed with 20 copies of a $k = 4$ deceptive trap. Figure 1 shows average best fitness vs. the effort of computation and the number of runs that have reached the maximum fitness value for each effort level. In these experiments, the initial population was set to 5000 individuals and the plague was applied every generation removing 50, 75, and 100 individuals. The figure clearly shows that as more individuals are removed, fewer functions evaluations are required to reach a specific fitness level or a number of optima.

The initial population sizes used in the previous experiments are large enough to allow the GAs to find the global solution every time, with and without plagues. This observation suggests that although the plagues saved considerable computational effort, it may be possible to obtain further savings by using smaller initial populations. However, we expect that smaller populations (with or without plague) will result in lower reliability of the GAs and the global optimum will be found less often than with large populations. The next series of experiments examine the effect of plagues on much smaller populations.

Figures 2 and 3 show results obtained when comparing GAs with fixed populations and GAs with plagues. The initial number of individuals in the populations varies from 1250 to 500 individuals, and we experimented with plagues of 5 and 10 individuals. The general trend of these experiments is consistent with the previous experiments with very large initial populations: for a similar effort, the GAs reach the optimum more often with plagues than without plagues and

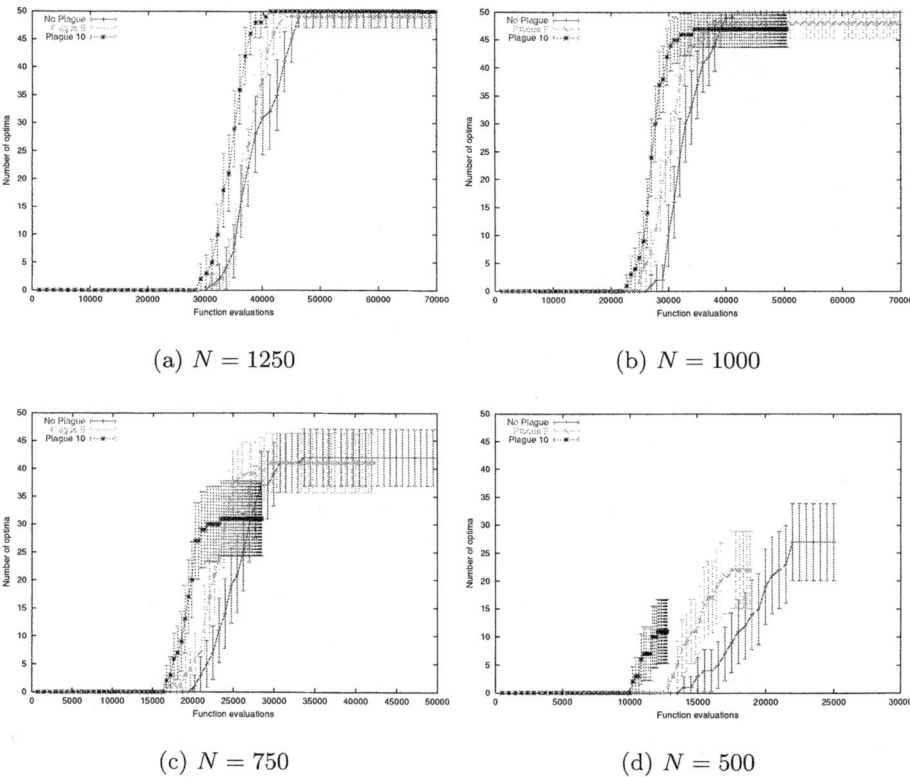

Fig. 2. Number of times that the maximum fitness is reached in 50 runs with and without plagues. In these experiments, $k = 4$ and plagues that remove 5 and 10 individuals per generation were used. Error bars denote 95% confidence intervals.

there are only small differences when the fitness is compared. For $N = 1250$ and $N = 1000$, the plagues save time and maintain the same reliability of the GA without plagues. But as smaller populations are used, the GA has difficulties locating the global optimum consistently. For $N = 1000$, the GA without plagues misses the global about 20% of the time, which is about the same reliability of the GA with a plague that removes 5 individuals. Removing more individuals or using smaller initial populations results in even more failures to locate the global (e.g., see the graph for $N = 500$).

These failures are caused by using populations that are too small to reliably solve the problem in the first place (the GA with $N = 500$ fails about half the time without plagues) and by the plagues emptying these populations quickly. Possible remedies include using smaller plagues or restricting the final population size to a fraction of the original size (instead of zero individuals). In any case, we emphasize that this set of experiments was intended to study when and how the plagues would fail.

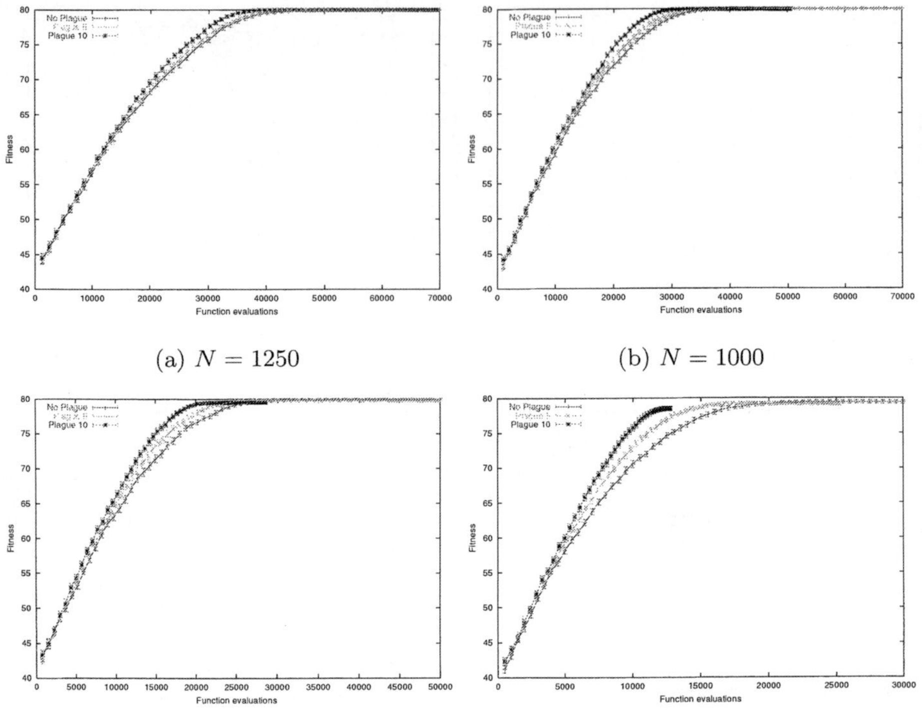

(a) $N = 1250$ (b) $N = 1000$

(c) $N = 750$ (d) $N = 500$

Fig. 3. Mean fitness vs. computational effort for $k = 4$ and plagues that remove 5 and 10 individuals per generation. Error bars denote 95% confidence intervals.

Next, we study how plagues scale up to more difficult problems. We increased the problem difficulty by increasing k to 5 and 6. Given the increase in the difficulty of the problem, the initial size for the population has been also increased to $N = 5000$ individuals. Given the large initial size of the populations, we also enlarged the size of the plagues, removing 50, 75, and 100 individuals per generation. The effect of smaller plagues would be negligible. Figure 4 presents the results of these experiments. As in the case of $k = 4$, removing more individuals seems beneficial. However, the graph for $k = 6$ shows that a few of the experiments did not reach the global optima and that as more individuals are removed, the reliability of the algorithm decreases. This behavior is expected, because as problems become more difficult larger populations are required to solve them and aggressive plagues might delete too many individuals or might delete them too fast (emptying the population before it has enough time to reach the global optimum).

Figure 5 shows results with $k = 8$. We experimented with initial population sizes of 12000 and 14000 individuals and plagues that remove 50 and 75 individuals per generation. In all cases, the plagues resulted in computational savings.

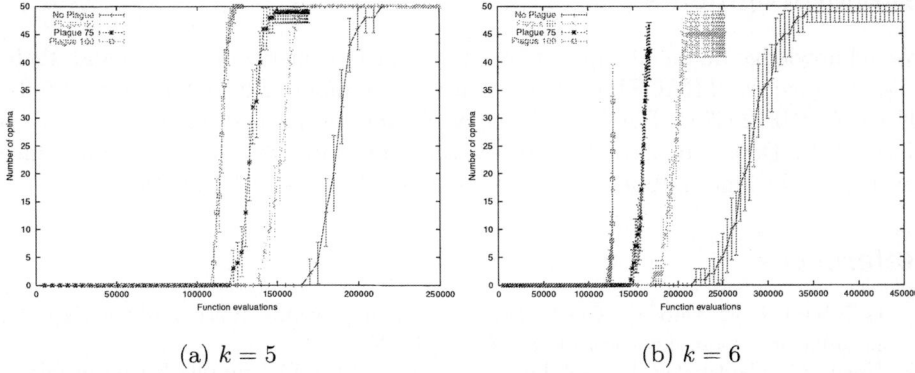

(a) $k = 5$ (b) $k = 6$

Fig. 4. Mean number of times the experiment reached the global optimum out of 50 experiments. The initial population size was $n = 5000$ individuals. The error bars denote 95% confidence intervals.

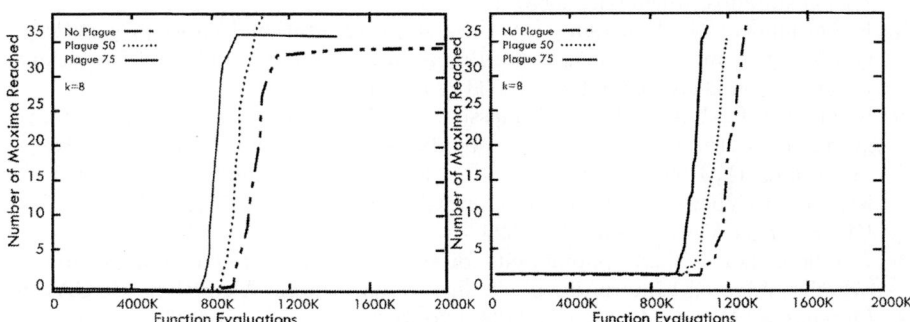

Fig. 5. Number of times that the maximum fitness is reached in 50 runs with and without plagues. $k = 8$.

5 Conclusions

This paper introduced the use of plagues to reduce the population size in genetic algorithms. By means of experiments with a tunable problem, we have shown that plagues help GAs to find solutions of a given quality using smaller efforts than the classic fixed-size algorithm.

Although we have employed only a plain version of the plague that removes a fixed number of the worst individuals in each generation, other elimination techniques should be tested in the future. Experiments varying the frequency and size of plagues are also necessary to verify the sensitivity of the GA to these parameters.

Acknowledgments

We acknowledge financial support by the Spanish Ministry of Science and Technology (project TRACER) under contract number TIC2002-04498-C05-01. UCRL-CONF-204742. Portions of this work were performed under the auspices of the U.S. Department of Energy by the University of California, Lawrence Livermore National Laboratory under contract No. W-7405-Eng-48.

References

1. Goldberg, D.E., Deb, K., Clark, J.H.: Genetic algorithms, noise, and the sizing of populations. Complex Systems **6** (1992) 333–362
2. Harik, G., Cantú-Paz, E., Goldberg, D., Miller, B.L.: The gambler's ruin problem, genetic algorithms, and the sizing of populations. Evolutionary Computation **7** (1999) 231–253
3. Fernandez, F.: Estudio de poblaciones de tamaño variable en programacion genetica. In: Actas del 2° Congreso Español obre Metaheuristicas, Algoritmos Evolutivos y Bioinspirados, Maeb 03. (2003) 424–428
4. F. Fernandez, M. Tomassini, L.V.: Saving computational effort in genetic programming by means of plagues. In: Proceeding of the Conference on Evolutionary Computation 2003, IEEE Press (2003) 2042–2049
5. Fernandez, F., Vanneschi, L., Tomassini, M.: The effect of plagues in genetic programming:a study of variable-size populations. In Ryan, C., Soule, T., Keijzer, M., Tsang, E., Poli, R., Costa, E., eds.: Proceedings of the Sixth European Conference on Genetic Programming (EuroGP-2003). Volume 2610 of LNCS., Essex, UK, Springer Verlag (2003) 317–326
6. Goldberg, D.E.: Sizing populations for serial and parallel genetic algorithms. In Schaffer, J.D., ed.: International Conference on Genetic Algorithms (ICGA), San Mateo, CA, Morgan Kaufmann (1989) 70–79
7. Goldberg, D.E., Rudnick, M.: Genetic algorithms and the variance of fitness. Complex Systems **5** (1991) 265–278
8. Harik, G., Cantú-Paz, E., Goldberg, D.E., Miller, B.L.: The gambler's ruin problem, genetic algorithms, and the sizing of populations. In: International Conference on Evolutionary Computation, Piscataway, NJ, IEEE (1997) 7–12
9. Kirley, M., Li, X., Green, D.G.: Investigation of a cellular genetic algorithm that mimics landscape ecology. In McKay, B., Yao, X., Newton, C.S., Kim, J.H., Furuhashi, T., eds.: Proceedings of the 2nd Asia-Pacific Conference on Simulated Evolution and Learning (SEAL-98). Volume 1585 of LNAI., Berlin, Springer (1999) 90–97
10. Smith, R.E., Smuda, E.: Adaptively resizing populations: Algorithm, analysis, and first results. Complex Systems **9** (1995) 47–72
11. Tan, K., Lee, T., Khor, E.: Evolutionary Algorithms with Dynamic Population Size and Local Exploration for Multiobjective Optimization. IEEE Transactions on Evolutionary Computation **5** (2001) 565–588
12. Banzhaf, W., Langdon, W.B.: Some considerations on the reason for bloat. Genetic Programming and Evolvable Machines **3** (2002) 81–91
13. Monsieurs, P., Flerackers, E.: Reducing population size while maintaining diversity. In Ryan, C., Soule, T., Keijzer, M., Tsang, E., Poli, R., Costa, E., eds.: Proceedings of the Sixth European Conference on Genetic Programming (EuroGP-2003). Volume 2610 of LNCS., Essex, UK, Springer Verlag (2003) 142–152

14. Luke, S., Balan, G.C., Panait, L.: Population implosion in genetic programming. In et al., E.C.P., ed.: Genetic and Evolutionary Computation – GECCO-2003. Volume 2724 of LNCS., Berlin, Springer-Verlag (2003) 1729–1739
15. Fernandez de Vega, F.: Distributed Genetic Programming Models with Application to Logic Synthesis on FPGAs. PhD thesis, University of Extremadura (2001)
16. Fernandez, F., Tomassini, M., Vanneschi, L.: An empirical study of multipopulation genetic programming. Genetic Programming and Evolvable Machines 4 (2003) 21–51
17. Deb, K., Goldberg, D.E.: Analyzing deception in trap functions. In Whitley, L.D., ed.: Foundations of Genetic Algorithms 2, San Mateo, CA, Morgan Kaufmann (1993) 93–108
18. Wall, M.: Galib 2.3.2 (1995)
19. Cantú-Paz, E.: Efficient and Accurate Parallel Genetic Algorithms. Kluwer Accademic Publishers (2000)

Evaluating the CMA Evolution Strategy on Multimodal Test Functions

Nikolaus Hansen and Stefan Kern

Computational Science and Engineering Laboratory (CSE Lab),
Swiss Federal Institute of Technology (ETH) Zurich, Switzerland
{nikolaus.hansen,skern}@inf.ethz.ch
http://www.icos.ethz.ch/cse/

Abstract. In this paper the performance of the CMA evolution strategy with rank-μ-update and weighted recombination is empirically investigated on eight multimodal test functions. In particular the effect of the population size λ on the performance is investigated. Increasing the population size remarkably improves the performance on six of the eight test functions. The optimal population size takes a wide range of values, but, with one exception, scales sub-linearly with the problem dimension. The global optimum can be located in all but one function. The performance for locating the global optimum scales between linear and cubic with the problem dimension. In a comparison to state-of-the-art global search strategies the CMA evolution strategy achieves superior performance on multimodal, non-separable test functions without intricate parameter tuning.

1 Introduction

The derandomized Evolution Strategy (ES) with Covariance Matrix Adaptation (CMA) [1] adapts the complete covariance matrix of the normal mutation (search) distribution. The CMA-ES exhibits several invariances. Hereunder are (a) invariance against order preserving (i.e. strictly monotonic) transformations of the objective function value; (b) invariance against angle preserving transformations of the search space (rotation, reflection, and translation) if the initial search point is transformed accordingly; (c) scale invariance if the initial scaling is chosen accordingly. Invariances are highly desirable: they imply uniform behavior on classes of functions and therefore generalizability of empirical results.

Originally designed for small population sizes, the CMA-ES was interpreted as a robust local search strategy [2]. It efficiently minimizes unimodal test functions [1] and in particular is superior on ill-conditioned and non-separable problems. It was successfully applied to a considerable number of real world problems[1]. In [3, 4] the CMA-ES was expanded by the so-called rank-μ-update. The

---

[1] See www.icos.ethz.ch/software/evolutionary_computation/cmaapplications.pdf for a list of references.

rank-μ-update exploits the information contained in large populations more effectively without affecting the performance[2] for small population sizes. It can reduce the time complexity of the strategy (i.e. the number *of generations* to reach a certain function value) from quadratic to linear [4]. A recent study [5] showed a surprisingly good performance of this CMA-ES on the multimodal Rastrigin function. Large populations and rank-μ-update were the prerequisites for this observation. Therefore, we empirically investigate the effect of the population size λ on the global search performance of the CMA-ES.

The remainder is organized as follows: In Sect. 2 we describe the CMA-ES using weighted recombination and rank-μ-update. In Sect. 3 test functions and methodology for the performance study are outlined. Section 4 examines the performance depending on the population size and compares the CMA-ES with other global search strategies. Sect. 5 gives a summary and conclusion.

2 The CMA-ES with Rank-μ-Update and Weighted Recombination

We thoroughly define the CMA-ES combining weighted recombination [1] and rank-μ-update of the covariance matrix [3,4]. In this (μ_W, λ)-CMA-ES the λ individuals (candidate solutions) of generation $g+1$ are generated according to

$$\boldsymbol{x}_k^{(g+1)} \sim \mathcal{N}\left(\langle\boldsymbol{x}\rangle_\mathrm{w}^{(g)}, \sigma^{(g)^2} \boldsymbol{C}^{(g)}\right), \quad k = 1, \ldots, \lambda, \qquad (1)$$

where $\mathcal{N}(\boldsymbol{m}, \boldsymbol{C})$ denotes a normally distributed random vector with mean $\boldsymbol{m}$ and covariance matrix $\boldsymbol{C}$.[3]

The recombination point $\langle\boldsymbol{x}\rangle_\mathrm{w}^{(g)} = \sum_{i=1}^\mu w_i \boldsymbol{x}_{i:\lambda}^{(g)}$ is the weighted mean of the selected individuals, $w_i > 0$ for all $i = 1 \ldots \mu$ and $\sum_{i=1}^\mu w_i = 1$. The index $i:\lambda$ denotes the i-th best individual. Setting all w_i to $1/\mu$ is equivalent to intermediate (multi-)recombination. The adaptation of the mutation parameters consists of two parts: (i) adaptation of the covariance matrix $\boldsymbol{C}^{(g)}$, and (ii) adaptation of the global step size $\sigma^{(g)}$. The covariance matrix $\boldsymbol{C}^{(g)}$ is adapted by the evolution path $\boldsymbol{p}_c^{(g+1)}$ and by the μ *weighted* difference vectors between the recent parents and $\langle\boldsymbol{x}\rangle_\mathrm{w}^{(g)}$:

$$\boldsymbol{p}_c^{(g+1)} = (1 - c_c) \cdot \boldsymbol{p}_c^{(g)} + H_\sigma^{(g+1)} \sqrt{c_c(2 - c_c)} \cdot \frac{\sqrt{\mu_\mathrm{eff}}}{\sigma^{(g)}} \left(\langle\boldsymbol{x}\rangle_\mathrm{w}^{(g+1)} - \langle\boldsymbol{x}\rangle_\mathrm{w}^{(g)}\right) \qquad (2)$$

$$\boldsymbol{C}^{(g+1)} = (1 - c_\mathrm{cov}) \cdot \boldsymbol{C}^{(g)} + c_\mathrm{cov} \frac{1}{\mu_\mathrm{cov}} \boldsymbol{p}_c^{(g+1)} \left(\boldsymbol{p}_c^{(g+1)}\right)^\mathrm{T} \qquad (3)$$

$$+ c_\mathrm{cov} \cdot \left(1 - \frac{1}{\mu_\mathrm{cov}}\right) \sum_{i=1}^\mu \frac{w_i}{\sigma^{(g)^2}} \left(\boldsymbol{x}_{i:\lambda}^{(g+1)} - \langle\boldsymbol{x}\rangle_\mathrm{w}^{(g)}\right) \left(\boldsymbol{x}_{i:\lambda}^{(g+1)} - \langle\boldsymbol{x}\rangle_\mathrm{w}^{(g)}\right)^\mathrm{T},$$

---

[2] We define performance as the number of function evaluations needed to reach a certain function value.

[3] Note that $\mathcal{N}\left(\langle\boldsymbol{x}\rangle_\mathrm{w}^{(g)}, \sigma^{(g)^2} \boldsymbol{C}^{(g)}\right) \sim \langle\boldsymbol{x}\rangle_\mathrm{w}^{(g)} + \sigma^{(g)} \boldsymbol{B}^{(g)} \boldsymbol{D}^{(g)} \mathcal{N}(\boldsymbol{0}, \boldsymbol{I})$, see below.

where $H_\sigma^{(g+1)} = 1$ if $\frac{\|p_\sigma^{(g+1)}\|}{\sqrt{1-(1-c_\sigma)^{2(g+1)}}} < (1.5 + \frac{1}{n-0.5})\mathrm{E}(\|\mathcal{N}(0, I)\|)$, and 0 otherwise. $\mu_\text{eff} = 1/\sum_{i=1}^\mu w_i^2$ denotes the "variance effective selection mass" and $\mu_\text{eff} = \mu$ if $w_i = 1/\mu$. The weights w_i are used for the summation term in (3), a matrix with rank $\min(\mu, n)$. Parameter $c_\text{cov} \approx \min(1, 2\mu_\text{eff}/n^2)$ determines the learning rate for the covariance matrix C. The adaptation of the global step size $\sigma^{(g+1)}$ is based on a "conjugate" evolution path $p_\sigma^{(g+1)}$:

$$p_\sigma^{(g+1)} = (1 - c_\sigma) \cdot p_\sigma^{(g)} \qquad (4)$$
$$+ \sqrt{c_\sigma(2 - c_\sigma)} \cdot B^{(g)} D^{(g)^{-1}} B^{(g)^T} \cdot \frac{\sqrt{\mu_\text{eff}}}{\sigma^{(g)}} \left(\langle x \rangle_\text{w}^{(g+1)} - \langle x \rangle_\text{w}^{(g)} \right).$$

The orthogonal matrix $B^{(g)}$ and the diagonal matrix $D^{(g)}$ are obtained through a principal component analysis of $C^{(g)}$; $C^{(g)} = B^{(g)} D^{(g)^2} B^{(g)^T}$ (cf. [1]). The global step size $\sigma^{(g+1)}$ obeys

$$\sigma^{(g+1)} = \sigma^{(g)} \cdot \exp\left(\frac{c_\sigma}{d_\sigma} \left(\frac{\|p_\sigma^{(g+1)}\|}{\mathrm{E}(\|\mathcal{N}(0, I)\|)} - 1 \right) \right), \qquad (5)$$

where $\mathrm{E}(\|\mathcal{N}(0, I)\|) = \sqrt{2}\Gamma(\frac{n+1}{2})/\Gamma(\frac{n}{2}) \approx \sqrt{n}\left(1 - \frac{1}{4n} + \frac{1}{21n^2}\right)$ is the expected length of p_σ under random selection.

Initial values are $p_\sigma^{(0)} = p_c^{(0)} = 0$ and $C^{(0)} = I$, while $x^{(0)}$ and $\sigma^{(0)}$ are problem dependent. Default strategy parameter values are

$$\lambda = 4 + \lfloor 3 \cdot \ln(n) \rfloor, \quad \mu = \lfloor \lambda/2 \rfloor, \quad w_{i=1\ldots\mu} = \frac{\ln(\mu+1) - \ln(i)}{\sum_{j=1}^\mu \ln(\mu+1) - \ln(j)}, \qquad (6)$$

$$c_\sigma = \frac{\mu_\text{eff} + 2}{n + \mu_\text{eff} + 3}, \quad d_\sigma = 1 + 2\max\left(0, \sqrt{\frac{\mu_\text{eff} - 1}{n+1}} - 1\right) + c_\sigma, \quad c_c = \frac{4}{n+4}, \qquad (7)$$

$$\mu_\text{cov} = \mu_\text{eff}, \quad c_\text{cov} = \frac{1}{\mu_\text{cov}} \frac{2}{(n+\sqrt{2})^2} + \left(1 - \frac{1}{\mu_\text{cov}}\right) \min\left(1, \frac{2\mu_\text{eff} - 1}{(n+2)^2 + \mu_\text{eff}}\right). \qquad (8)$$

While $1/c_\sigma$, and $1/c_c$ can be interpreted as memory time constants, d_σ is a damping parameter. Parameters from (7) and (8) are not meant to be in the users choice. A profound discussion of the strategy parameters is given in [1].

We consider weighted recombination to be more natural than intermediate recombination, because the ranking of all $\lambda/2$ best individuals is fully regarded[4]. Nevertheless, to our experience weighted recombination, where $\mu \approx \lambda/2$, only slightly outperforms intermediate recombination, where $\mu \approx \lambda/4$.

3 Test Functions and Experimental Procedure

3.1 Test Functions

The unconstrained multimodal test problems are summarized in Table 1.

---

[4] Even the mating success in nature is not well described by two possible outcomes.

Table 1. Test functions to be minimized and initialization regions.

Name	Function	Init
Ackley	$f_{\text{Ackley}}(\boldsymbol{x}) = 20 - 20 \cdot \exp\left(-0.2\sqrt{\frac{1}{n}\sum_{i=1}^{n} x_i^2}\right)$ $+ \text{e} - \exp\left(\frac{1}{n}\sum_{i=1}^{n} \cos(2\pi x_i)\right)$	$[1, 30]^n$
Bohachevsky	$f_{\text{Bohachevsky}}(\boldsymbol{x}) = \sum_{i=1}^{n-1} \left(x_i^2 + 2x_{i+1}^2\right.$ $\left. - 0.3\cos(3\pi x_i) - 0.4\cos(4\pi x_{i+1}) + 0.7\right)$	$[1, 15]^n$
Griewank	$f_{\text{Griewank}}(\boldsymbol{x}) = \frac{1}{4000}\sum_{i=1}^{n} x_i^2 - \prod_{i=1}^{n} \cos\left(\frac{x_i}{\sqrt{i}}\right) + 1$	$[10, 600]^n$
Rastrigin	$f_{\text{Rastrigin}}(\boldsymbol{x}) = 10n + \sum_{i=1}^{n}\left(x_i^2 - 10\cos(2\pi x_i)\right)$	$[1, 5]^n$
Scaled Rastrigin	$f_{\text{RastScaled}}(\boldsymbol{x}) = 10n + \sum_{i=1}^{n}\left((10^{\frac{i-1}{n-1}} x_i)^2\right.$ $\left. - 10\cos(2\pi 10^{\frac{i-1}{n-1}} x_i)\right)$	$[1, 5]^n$
Skew Rastrigin	$f_{\text{RastSkew}}(\boldsymbol{x}) = 10n + \sum_{i=1}^{n}\left(y_i^2 - 10\cos(2\pi y_i)\right)$, with $y_i = \begin{cases} 10 \cdot x_i & \text{if } x_i > 0, \\ x_i & \text{otherwise} \end{cases}$	$[1, 5]^n$
Schaffer	$f_{\text{Schaffer}}(\boldsymbol{x}) = \sum_{i=1}^{n-1}(x_i^2 + x_{i+1}^2)^{0.25}$ $\cdot \left[\sin^2\left(50 \cdot (x_i^2 + x_{i+1}^2)^{0.1}\right) + 1.0\right]$	$[10, 100]^n$
Schwefel	$f_{\text{Schwefel}}(\boldsymbol{x}) = 418.9828872724339 \cdot n$ $- \sum_{i=1}^{n} x_i \cdot \sin(\sqrt{|x_i|})$	$[-500, 300]^n$

All considered functions have a high number of local optima, are scalable in the problem dimension, and have a minimal function value of 0. The known global minimum is located at $\boldsymbol{x} = \boldsymbol{0}$, except for the Schwefel function, where the global minimum within $[-500, 500]^n$ equals 420.96874636 in each coordinate. Additional bounds are implemented for f_{Schwefel} (in $[-500, 500]^n$) and f_{Ackley} (in $[-30, 30]^n$) by adding a quadratic penalty term. E.g., $f_{\text{Schwefel}}(\boldsymbol{x}) + 10^4 \cdot \sum_{i=1}^{n} \theta(|x_i| - 500)x_i^2$ is minimized, where $\theta(.)$ is the Heaviside function. The skew Rastrigin function was proposed by [6] to be deceptive for the CMA-ES.

Besides f_{RastSkew} and f_{Schwefel}, the functions are point symmetrical around the global optimum. To avoid an easy exploitation of the symmetry, we suggest non-symmetrical initialization intervals, see Table 1. The Rastrigin functions and f_{Schwefel} are additively separable, while f_{Ackley} and $f_{\text{Bohachevsky}}$ are separable, in that the global optimum can be located by optimizing each variable independently. Recall, that both is not exploited by the CMA-ES, because *all results of the CMA-ES are invariant under orthogonal transformations (rotations) of the coordinate system, given accordingly transformed initial intervals.*

3.2 Experimental Procedure

The performance of the CMA-ES is tested for dimensions $n = [2, 5, 10, 20, 40, 80]$.[5] All runs are performed with the default strategy parameter setting given in Sect. 2, except for the population size λ.[6] Starting from $\lambda = 5$, the population

---
[5] For simulations we used the MATLAB code cmaes.m, Version 2.24, available from http://www.icos.ethz.ch/software/evolutionary_computation/cma.
[6] Note that μ is chosen dependently on λ and further parameters depend on μ.

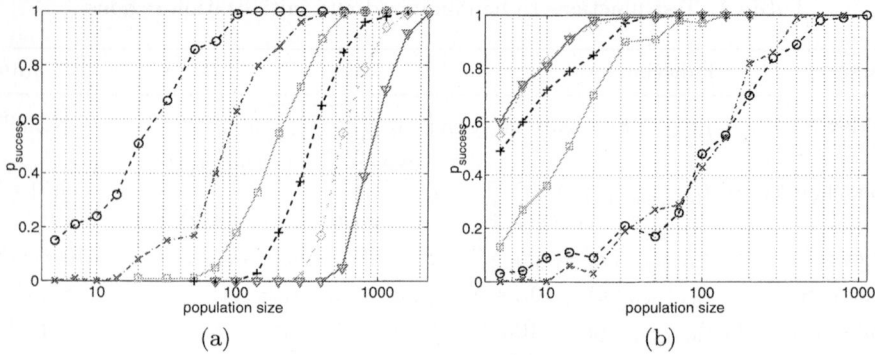

Fig. 1. Success rate to reach $f_{\text{stop}} = 10^{-10}$ versus population size for (a) Rastrigin function (b) Griewank function for dimensions $n = 2$ ('$--\bigcirc--$'), $n = 5$ ('$-\cdot-\times-\cdot-$'), $n = 10$ ('$-\square-$'), $n = 20$ ('$--+--$'), $n = 40$ ('$-\cdot-\diamond-\cdot-$'), and $n = 80$ ('$-\triangledown-$').

size is increased repeatedly in the sequence 5, 7, 10, 14, 20, 32, 50, $\lfloor 50\sqrt{2} \rfloor$, 100, $\lfloor 100\sqrt{2} \rfloor$, 200, ..., and for each setting 100 runs are conducted. The starting point $x^{(0)}$ is sampled uniformly within the initialization intervals given in Table 1. The initial step size $\sigma^{(0)}$ is set to half of the initialization interval. Too small initial step sizes have a considerable impact on the performance on multimodal functions. Each run is stopped and regarded as successful, when the function value is smaller than $f_{\text{stop}} = 10^{-10}$. Additionally, the run is stopped after 10^7 function evaluations, or when the condition number of the covariance matrix C exceeds 10^{14}, or by the option TolX, set to 10^{-15} (for f_{Schaffer} 10^{-30}).

4 Simulation Results

The success rate to reach f_{stop} depends strongly on the population size, see Fig. 1, where exemplary results are shown for (a) $f_{\text{Rastrigin}}$ and (b) f_{Griewank}. The Rastrigin function (Fig. 1a) represents the typical picture. The graphs have a sigmoidal shape and larger dimensions require larger population sizes to approach 100% success rate. We observe two exceptions from this behavior. First, on f_{RastSkew} the success rates are low with any population size, and, except for very low dimensions, f_{RastSkew} is not solvable for the CMA-ES. The second exception is shown in Fig. 1b: on f_{Griewank} smaller dimensions require larger population sizes, but success rates of 100% can be achieved in all dimensions.

Figures 2a and 3a show the scaling of the (minimal) population size w.r.t. the problem dimension to achieve success rates of (at least) 5, 25, 50, 75, 95%. Graphs for $f_{\text{RastScaled}}$ are almost identical with $f_{\text{Rastrigin}}$ and therefore omitted. Except for f_{RastSkew} (not shown), larger success rates require larger population sizes. The figures are sorted from (i.a) to (vi.a) by increasing slopes that indicate the scaling. The steepest slope (f_{Schwefel}) is slightly above linear. For all other functions the slope is sub-linear.

Figures 2b and 3b show performance versus population size. Performance is measured as mean number of function evaluations for successful runs, divided by

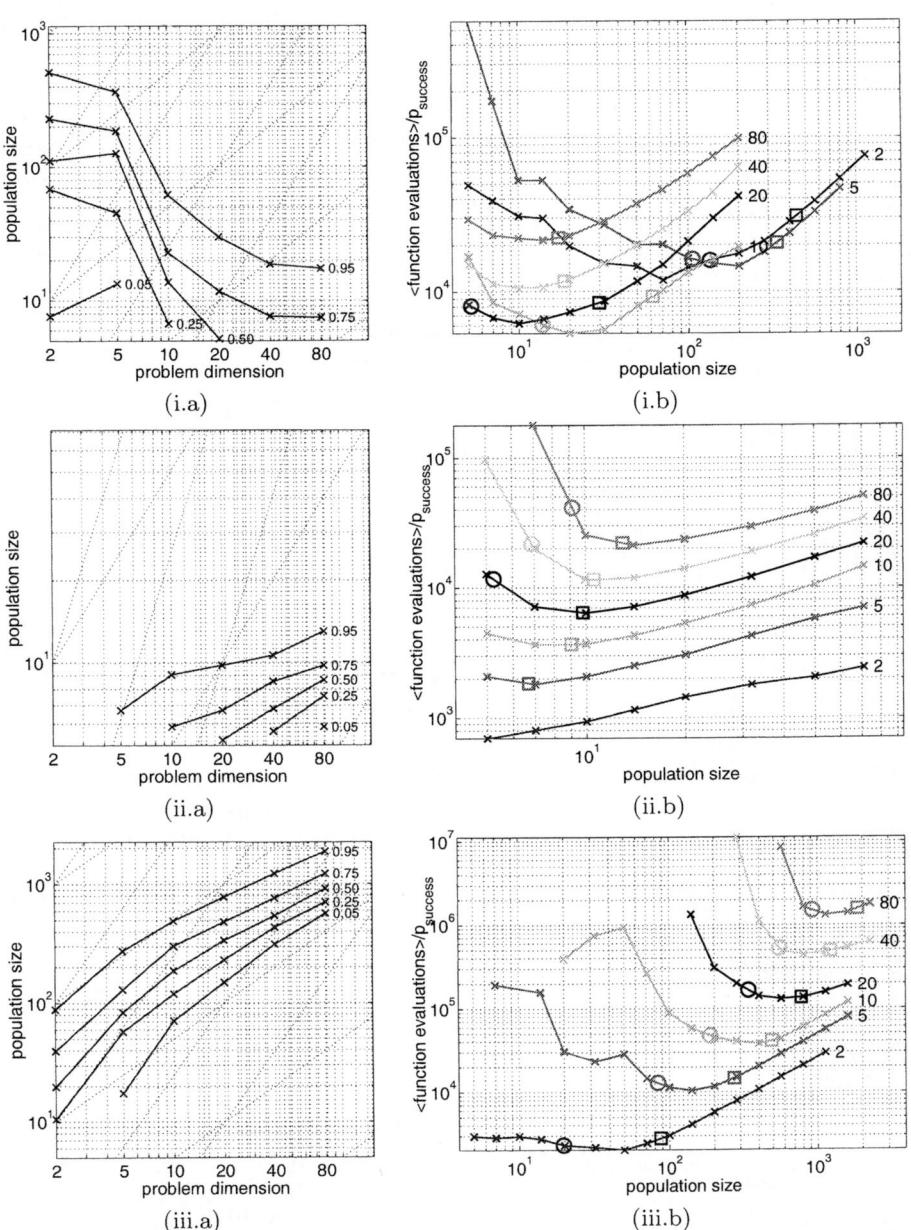

Fig. 2. (i) Griewank function, (ii) Ackley function, (iii) Rastrigin function. (a) population size to reach success rates of 0.05, 0.25, 0.5, 0.75, and 0.95 versus problem dimension n. The sloping grid indicates linear and quadratic dependency. (b) average number of function evaluations to reach $f_{\text{stop}} = 10^{-10}$ divided by the success rate, versus population size for problem dimensions $n = 2, 5, 10, 20, 40, 80$. The symbols $\bigcirc$ and $\square$ indicate success rates of 50% and 95%, respectively. Missing points on the left side of a graph indicate that no run (out of 100 runs) was successful.

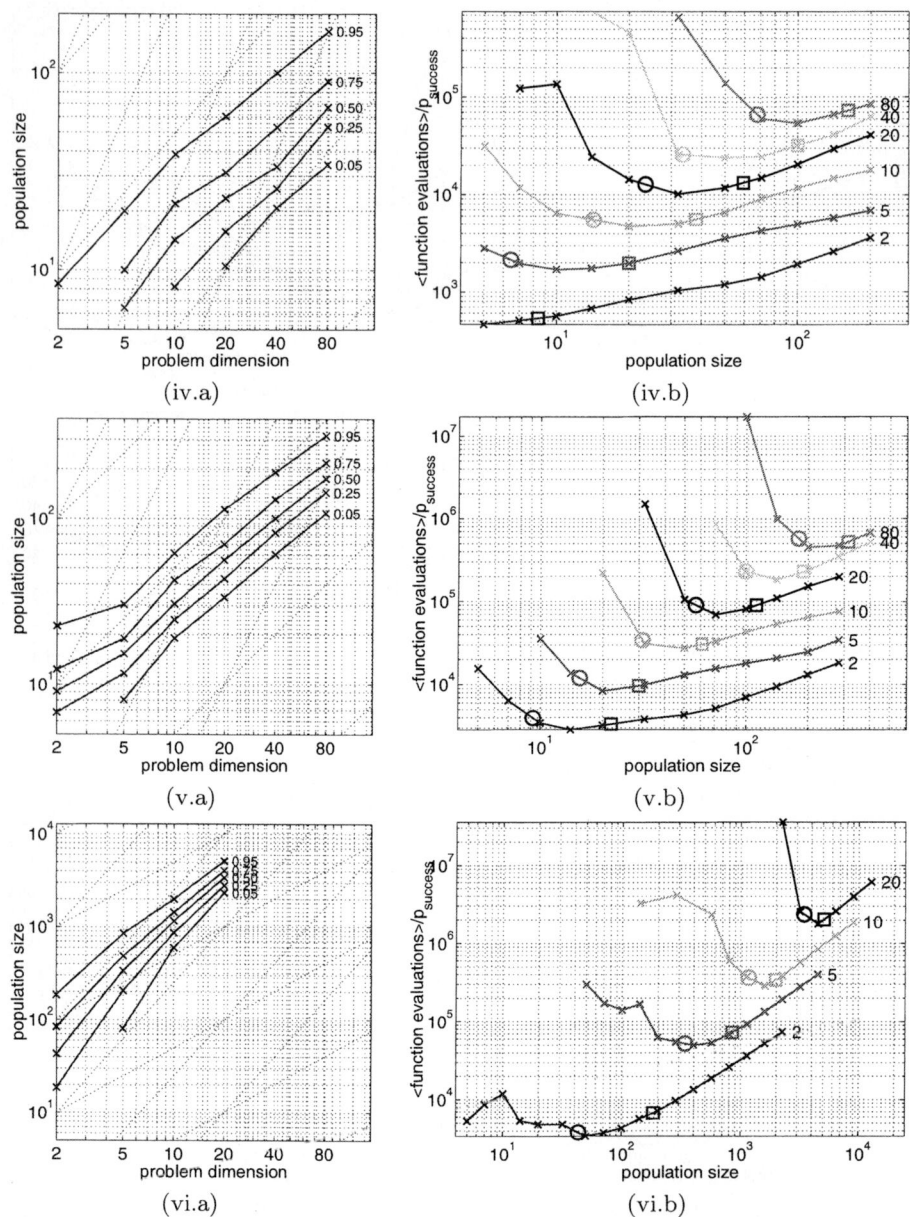

Fig. 3. (iv) Bohachevsky function, (v) Schaffer function, (vi) Schwefel function. (a) population size to reach success rates of 0.05, 0.25, 0.5, 0.75, and 0.95 versus problem dimension n. The sloping grid indicates linear and quadratic dependency. (b) average number of function evaluations to reach $f_{\text{stop}} = 10^{-10}$ divided by the success rate, versus population size for problem dimensions $n = 2, 5, 10, 20, 40, 80$. The symbols ◯ and □ indicate success rates of 50% and 95%, respectively. Missing points on the left side of a graph indicate that no run (out of 100 runs) was successful.

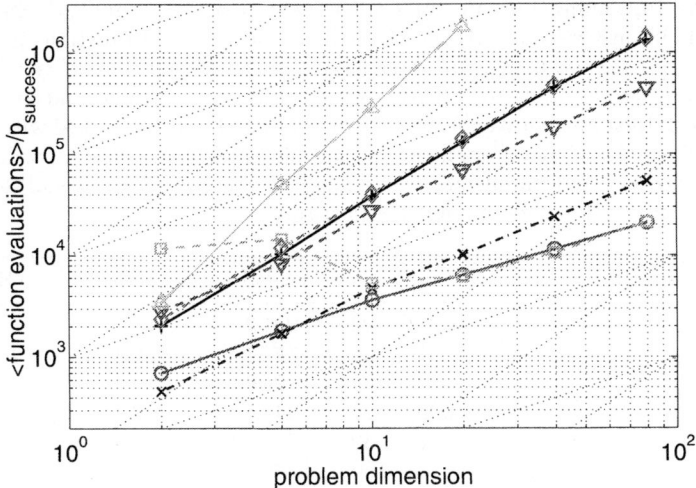

Fig. 4. Mean number of function evaluations to reach f_stop versus problem dimension n for CMA-ES on Ackley ('—○—'), Bohachevsky ('—·—×—·—'), Griewank ('——□——'), Rastrigin ('—+—'), Scaled Rastrigin ('— · — ◇ — ·—'), Schaffer ('— — ▽ — —'), and Schwefel ('—△—') function.

the success rate. This performance measure assumes the same expected number of function evaluations for successful and for unsuccessful runs. The best performance is usually achieved for success rates between 50% and 95%. The impact of a smaller than optimal population size can be high. With increasing population size the performance decreases at most linearly.

Figure 4 shows the scaleup of the performance with optimal population size. The scaleup with n, put in order, appears to be at most linear for f_Ackley and f_Griewank, between linear and quadratic for $f_\text{Bohachevsky}$, f_Schaffer, $f_\text{Rastrigin}$, and $f_\text{RastScaled}$, and slightly below cubic for f_Schwefel.

Table 2 compares the performance of the CMA-ES with optimal population size to the performance of Differential Evolution (DE) [7], the Robust Evolution Strategy (RES) [8], and a Local Optima Smoothing (LOS) [9] restart BFGS algorithm. For each function the results with the best parameter tuning were taken from the respective publication and additional experiments were performed with DE and BFGS[7]. Only on the additively separable functions $f_\text{Rastrigin}$ and f_Schwefel, DE outperforms the CMA-ES by a factor of five to 50. Otherwise, the CMA-ES outperforms DE by a factor of at least three, while DE even fails to find the global optimum on the non-separable $f_\text{Rastrigin}(\boldsymbol{Ax})$, where an orthogo-

---

[7] In [9] the results for LOS are stated as numbers of necessary local searches to hit the global optimum. The average number of function evaluations for a local search using BFGS is simulated with MATLAB's `fminunc` with `MaxFunEvals = 500n` and `TolX = TolFun = 10⁻³` (0.9 for $f_\text{Rastrigin}$). A *random* restart strategy performs much worse than LOS.

Table 2. Average number of function evaluations to reach f_stop of CMA-ES versus DE, RES, and LOS on Griewank, Ackley, Rastrigin, and Schwefel function. If f_stop is not reached the *best function value/number of function evaluations* are stated. The initialization regions do not apply to CMA-ES for which the more difficult intervals from Table 1 are used. Results are taken from [7–9], except for the cases marked with * obtained using the DE code available from http://www.icsi.berkeley.edu/~storn/code.html. The matrix $A = [o_1, \ldots, o_n]^T$ implements an angle-preserving (i.e. orthogonal) linear transformation of x (cf. [1]), chosen anew for each run.

Function	f_stop	init	n	CMA-ES	DE	RES	LOS
$f_\text{Ackley}(x)$	1e-3	$[-30, 30]^n$	20	**2667**	.	.	6.0e4
			30	**3701**	12481	1.1e5	9.3e4
			100	**11900**	36801	.	.
$f_\text{Griewank}(x)$	1e-3	$[-600, 600]^n$	20	**3111**	8691	.	.
			30	**4455**	11410 *	8.5e-3/2e5	.
			100	**12796**	31796	.	.
$f_\text{Rastrigin}(x)$	0.9	$[-5.12, 5.12]^n$	20	68586	**12971**	.	9.2e4
		DE: $[-600, 600]^n$	30	147416	**20150** *	1.0e5	2.3e5
			100	1010989	**73620**	.	.
$f_\text{Rastrigin}(Ax)$	0.9	$[-5.12, 5.12]^n$	30	**152000**	171/1.25e6 *	.	.
			100	**1011556**	944/1.25e6 *	.	.
$f_\text{Schwefel}(x)$	1e-3	$[-500, 500]^n$	5	43810	**2567** *	.	7.4e4
			10	240899	**5522** *	.	5.6e5

nal transformation A of the search space is applied, and performes much worse on $f_\text{Schwefel}(Ax)$ (not shown)[8]. This supports our hypothesis that DE strongly exploits the separability of the function. The RES too exploits separability by sampling Cauchy distributions which strongly favor steps in coordinate directions. Even so, on the separable $f_\text{Rastrigin}$ RES outperforms CMA-ES only by a factor of 1.5, while on f_Ackley and f_Griewank it performs worse by a factor of 30 or more. The LOS performs between a factor 1.5 (on $f_\text{Rastrigin}$) and a factor of 25 (on f_Ackley) worse than the CMA-ES[9].

5 Summary and Conclusion

The CMA-ES with rank-μ-update is investigated on a suit of eight highly multimodal test functions for problem dimensions between 2 and 80. Tuning (that is increasing) the population size considerably improves the performance on six

---
[8] On $f_\text{Rastrigin}$, the parent number equals 20 in DE. Increasing the parent number improves the performance on $f_\text{Rastrigin}(Ax)$. However, even with 500 parents for $n = 10$, the minimum function value reached does not drop below 2 after 10^7 function evaluations. Choosing the recombination parameter CR = 1, DE becomes invariant against orthogonal transformations, but performs even worse on $f_\text{Rastrigin}$.
[9] Two parameters of LOS, r and K, see [9], are chosen to be optimal for each entry. In particular r has a considerable impact on the performance.

of the functions, compared to the performance with default population size. On seven of the eight functions, the CMA-ES can precisely locate the global optimum. If the local optima can be interpreted as pertubations of an underlying unimodal function, the CMA-ES with a large population size can "detect" the global topology. Then, the global optimum is located within $300n$ and $500n^2$ function evaluations. A strong asymmetry of the underlying function jeopardizes a successful detection and can lead to a failure (as on f_{RastSkew}). The optimal population size usually scales sub-linearly with the problem dimension n, but significantly depends on the test function considered.

The results were compared with other global search strategies, stated to achieve superior results in earlier investigations. Surprisingly, the CMA-ES outperforms these global searchers, typically by a factor of three, with the following exception. Only if the function is *additively separable*, Differential Evolution strongly outperforms the CMA-ES. If the search space is rotated, the performance of the CMA-ES is unchanged, however Differential Evolution massively degrades in performance or even fails to locate the global optimum with a reasonable probablity. For the CMA-ES the population size was tuned, while for the compared algorithms up to three parameters had to be tuned to the given objective function. In our opinion, tuning the population size in the CMA-ES is comparatively unproblematic. The results suggest that a CMA-ES restart strategy with a successively increased population size (by a factor of three, initialized with the default population size) constitutes a highly competitive, quasi parameter free global optimization algorithm for non-separable objective functions.

References

1. Hansen, N., Ostermeier, A.: Completely derandomized self-adaptation in evolution strategies. Evol. Comput. **9** (2001) 159–195
2. Hansen, N., Ostermeier, A.: Adapting arbitrary normal mutation distributions in evolution strategies: The covariance matrix adaptation. In: Proceedings of the 1996 IEEE Conference on Evolutionary Computation (ICEC '96). (1996) 312–317
3. Müller, S.D., Hansen, N., Koumoutsakos, P.: Increasing the serial and the parallel performance of the CMA-evolution stategy with large populations. In: Parallel Problem Solving from Nature (PPSN). (2002)
4. Hansen, N., Müller, S.D., Koumoutsakos, P.: Reducing the time complexity of the derandomized evolution strategy with covariance matrix adaptation (CMA-ES). Evol. Comput. **11** (2003) 1–18
5. Kern, S., Müller, S.D., Hansen, N., Büche, D., Ocenasek, J., Koumoutsakos, P.: Learning probability distributions in continuous evolutionary algorithms – a comparative review. Natural Computing **3** (2004) 77–112
6. Büche, D.: Personal communication (2003)
7. Storn, R., Price, K.: Differential evolution: A simple and efficient heuristic for global optimization over continuous spaces. J. Glob. Opt. **11** (1997) 341–359
8. Ohkura, K., Matsumura, Y., Ueda, K.: Robust evolution strategies. Lect. Notes Comput. Sc. **1585** (1999) 10–17
9. Addis, B., Locatelli, M., Schoen, F.: Local optima smoothing for global optimization. Technical report dsi 5–2003, Dipartimento di Sistemi e Informatica, Università degli Studi di Firenze (2003)

Exploring the Evolutionary Details of a Feasible-Infeasible Two-Population GA

Steven Orla Kimbrough[1], Ming Lu[1], and David Harlan Wood[2]

[1] University of Pennsylvania
{kimbrough,milu}@wharton.upenn.edu
[2] University of Delaware
wood@cis.udel.edu

Abstract. A two-population Genetic Algorithm for constrained optimization is exercised and analyzed. One population consists of feasible candidate solutions evolving toward optimality. Their infeasible but promising offspring are transferred to a second, infeasible population. Four striking features are illustrated by executing challenge problems from the literature. First, both populations evolve essentially optimal solutions. Second, both populations actively exchange offspring. Third, beneficial genetic materials may originate in either population, and typically diffuse into both populations. Fourth, optimization vs. constraint tradeoffs are revealed by the infeasible population.

1 Introduction

Constrained optimization problems (COPs) are ubiquitous. It is well known that people are poor at finding good solutions to even quite small constrained optimization problems. What is more, modern problems often contain tens of thousands of decision variables and hence are beyond direct comprehension by humans. Automated computational and algorithmic support is necessary. In spite of enormous progress in algorithmic theory and computerization, the need for solutions to COPs far outstrips the state-of-the-art in exact solution technique. And the situation is getting worse, because new applications for complex COPs continue to arise in bioinformatics, logistics, data mining, and other areas. The difficulty is fundamental; with few exceptions COPs are known to be NP-hard. So, approximating metaheuristics would seem to be a profitable approach.

Genetic algorithms (GAs) have much to recommend them as metaheuristics for constrained optimization, and are used routinely to attempt to maximize or minimize an objective function of a number of decision variables. Because GAs are general-purpose procedures they can be used even in computationally challenging cases in which the objective function and/or constraints are nonlinear, and/or the decision variables are integers or mixtures of integers and reals. When the objective function is constrained, however, use of GAs is problematic. Considerable attention has been paid to incorporating constraints (see [1–5] for excellent reviews), but no consensus approach has emerged. A natural – and the most often used – approach is to penalize a solution in proportion to the size of its constraint violations. A feasible solution is not penalized; an infeasible solution is penalized as a function of the magnitude of the violation(s) of the constraint(s). This is the general form of a maximization constrained optimization problem:

$$\max_{x_i} z = Z(x), \text{subject to } E(x) \geq a, F(x) \leq b, G(x) = c, x_i \in S_i \qquad (1)$$

Here, $Z(x)$ is the objective function value produced by the candidate solution x.[1] E, F and G each yield zero or more constraint inequalities or equalities. As functions, Z, E, F, G can be any functions at all (on x). S_i is the set of permitted values for the x_i (the components of the vector x), which are called the *decision variables* for the problem. S_i may include reals, integers, or a mixture. The purpose of a penalty function formulation is to produce a representation of the problem that can be directly and naturally encoded as a GA. To indicate a penalty function representation, let x be a (candidate) solution to a maximization constrained optimization problem. Its absolute fitness, $W(x)$, in the presence of penalties for constraint violation is $Z(x) - P(x)$ and the COP is defined as:

$$\max_{x_i} z = W(x) = Z(x) - P(x), \qquad (2)$$

where $P(x)$ is some total penalty associated with constraint violations at x. Problems representable as in expression (2) are directly and naturally encoded as GAs. Typically, and by design, the penalty imposed on an infeasible solution will severely reduce the net fitness of the solution in question, leading to quick elimination of the solution from the population. This may be undesirable, since infeasible solutions may carry valuable information and may be useful in searching for optimal values.

We focus here on a feasible-infeasible two-population (FI-2Pop) GA deployed for constrained optimization problems (COPs). In this way of organizing an evolutionary process, two populations of solutions are maintained and evolved: the feasible population (consisting only of feasible solutions) and the infeasible population (consisting only of infeasible solutions). Genetic operations are applied to the two populations sequentially. Offspring are placed in one of the two populations, depending only on whether they are feasible or not. Thus, feasible parents may produce infeasible children and infeasible parents may produce feasible children. It is evident from prior work, [6–8], and from new results reported here, that the FI-2Pop GA has considerable merits. We wish to understand why. To this end, there are three main issues we wish to address: (a) What are the characteristic properties of this search process? (b) How does the infeasible population contribute to the search process? and (c) How might information in the infeasible population be exploited for decision making? Our approach will be an empirical

---

[1] By *candidate solution* or just *solution* we mean any instance of x. The components of x are called the *decision variables* for the problem; any solution method seeks optimal values for these variables. Some candidate solutions are feasible and some not. An optimal solution is a candidate solution, which is feasible and no feasible candidate solution yields a better value of $Z(x)$.

one, in which we follow the details of the evolutionary process under the FI-2Pop GA. We have been impressed by analogous studies of biological systems, e.g., [9–11], and we note that some of these scientists have turned to digital agents and computational systems in order to examine the microstructure of evolutionary processes, e.g. [12]. What works in nature should work in management science.

We next discuss the first (of four) optimization problems, newly treated here with the FI-2Pop GA. Following that, we report briefly on the remaining three challenge problems, each of which is nonlinear and can be solved by Genocop III, a standard and generally excellent GA solver [13]. See Table 2 for a comparison of the two-population GA solutions to those obtained by Genocop III. In general agreement with previously-published results [7], the two-population GA outperforms Genocop III both in best solution found and in the standard deviation (and mean) of the best solution found, across a sample of runs[2].

2 Four Problems

Yuan, our first problem, is discussed in [16, page 266] and was originated in [17]. The model is nonlinear (quadratic and logarithmic) in the objective function and quadratic in the constraints. Moreover, it is a mixed-integer model, with three continuous variables and four binary variables. The constraints for all four of our models are inequalities. Genocop III is unable to handle models of this sort [13]. As reported by [16, page 266] and [17], at optimality the (minimizing) value of the objective function is $z^* = 4.5796$, with the decision variables set at $\mathbf{x}^* = (0.2, 0.8, 1.908)^T$ and $\mathbf{y}^* = (1, 1, 0, 1)^T$.

We describe now results from one quite typical run of the two-population GA on the Yuan problem. At the end of 5,000 generations of alternating feasible and infeasible genetic exploration (equivalent to 10,000 generations in an ordinary GA), z^+, the objective function value of the best solution found, is 4.579588292413069. The variable settings in this solution are $\mathbf{y}^T = (1, 1, 0, 1)$, $x_1 = 0.199998178908325$, $x_2 = 0.799999776184869$, $x_3 = 1.90787728616851$.

Feasible Population Converges as Variance Minimizes. The feasible population finds solutions within 0.5% of optimal by generation 136. Table 1 shows a subsequent slow, steady improvement in z^+, on the average. The variance of the feasible population appears to stabilize (Table 1, column 7), but cannot go

---

[2] There is insufficient space to describe fully our FI-2Pop GA. For details see [14], also [8]. In brief, all parameters were set *ex ante*, were not tuned for any of the problems, and were set identically for all problems. We used fitness-proportional selection of parents, single-point crossover (probability 0.4), and mutation (at probability 0.4, non-uniform mutation for floating point alleles, with degrees (*b* in Michalewicz's formula [15, pages 103, 111]) equal to 2). We note that the results reported in Table 2 for the two-population GA relied on uncollected random number seeds determined by reading the system clock. For close comparison with GENOCOP, the feasible and infeasible populations were sized at 50 each. A run of the FI-2Pop GA consisted of 5,000 feasible generations and 5,000 infeasible generations, alternating. The comparison runs of GENOCOP were for 10,000 generations on populations of 50.

Table 1. Yuan Results: Averages over 100 generations. Violation= $-1 \cdot$sum of absolute violations of constraints (averaged over each solution for 100 generations). InF→Fea = number of feasible offspring from the infeasible population (by generation, averaged over 100 generations). Fea→InF = number of infeasible offspring from the feasible population (by generation, averaged over 100 generations). z^+ = best objective function value found in the feasible population (by generation, averaged over 100 generations). medz_{InF} = median objective function value in the infeasible population (by generation, averaged over 100 generations). $\sigma^2 z_{\text{Fea}}$ = variance of objective function values in the feasible population (averaged over all solutions in 100 generations). $\sigma^2 z_{\text{InF}}$ = variance of objective function values in the infeasible population (averaged over all solutions in 100 generations).

Generations	Violation	InF→Fea	Fea→InF	z^+	medz_{InF}	$\sigma^2 z_{\text{Fea}}$	$\sigma^2 z_{\text{InF}}$
0–99	-0.2824	3.5400	7.3000	5.222503	7.123	2.302	6.839
900–999	-0.2005	3.4100	6.6200	4.594130	6.577	0.840	8.928
1900–1999	-0.0453	3.3100	6.4000	4.581232	9.468	1.015	7.713
2900–2999	-0.0858	3.0400	6.4800	4.579938	5.926	0.426	3.302
3900–3999	-0.0501	2.7000	6.3300	4.579845	5.103	0.251	1.775
4900–4999	-0.0126	3.2900	4.8200	4.579653	5.245	0.253	0.948

to zero because of mutation and continuing immigration. In any event, the two-population GA evidences excellent performance on this problem.

Infeasible Population Converges towards Feasibility as Its Variation Decreases. As seen in Table 1, the average infeasibility (Violation, column 2 of Table 1) of solutions in the infeasible population becomes closer to 0 as the run progresses. In the run under display here, the average infeasible solution reduced its Violation by more than an order of magnitude during the run.

The infeasible solutions are not subjected to selection with regard to the z (objective function) values. Most interestingly, the z values for the infeasible population nevertheless clearly move towards z^+ (or z^*) as the run progresses. In the end, the best of these z values are not far from the optimal value, z^*. Compare the rightmost two columns of Table 1. Note that there is an overall reduction in the variance in z for the infeasible population as the generations progress. This is in contrast to the variance in z for the feasible population, which appears to stabilize during the last 1000 generations.

Mixing Between the Feasible and Infeasible Populations. The infeasible population can produce offspring that are feasible. Although this might seem to be unlikely, our example data show the infeasible population was steadily producing feasible solutions. See the InF→Fea column in Table 1. We also note some indication of modestly declining migration as the run progressed. Column Fea→InF in Table 1 shows the feasible population produced infeasible offspring at roughly double the rate InF→Fea of the infeasible population. Fea→InF, however, may be declining more rapidly than InF→Fea .

These data support a clear and consistent picture of what is happening in the two-population GA data in this typical run for this problem (but in our

Table 2. Comparison of the Two-Population GA with Genocop III.

problem	Best known	Genocop III Best of 10	Std.	Two-population GA Best of 10	Std.
Hesse (min)	-310	-306.972	16.185309	-309.9907	0.044785738
Pooling (max)	450	433.6981	37.02992564	444.157	15.08449889
Colville (min)	10122.69643	10126.6504	108.3765361	10122.8412	0.715469975

experience it is representative). Selection is driving the feasible population closer and closer to the boundary of the feasible region. Not only is there improvement in z^+ over time; there is steady but fluctuating improvement in the average z each generation. Similarly, selection is driving the infeasible population closer to the boundary separating the feasible and infeasible regions[3].

Genetic Benefits of Immigration. The flow of offspring from one population to the other offers two benefits. First, maintaining infeasible solutions can preserve useful genetic materials, in contrast to a one-population GA. Second, useful genetic materials tend to diffuse into both populations. Detailed examination of the run reveals that alleles and patterns of alleles (building blocks) will often arise in one population, quickly move to the other, and then be maintained indefinitely in both populations.

Information on Potentially Profitable Tradeoffs Automatically Generated. There is potentially valuable information among the infeasible solutions. Constraints may often be relaxed, for sufficient gain. These are opportunities where relaxing one or a few constraints 'legalizes' a known improvement. For example, at generation 236, there appears an infeasible solution for which $z = 4.47002605609438$, which is much better (smaller) than z^+, the best feasible solution found during the run, and z^*. This infeasible solution is at: $x_1 = 0.195462908809646, x_2 = 0.795752247026746, x_3 = 1.96768190221611, y_1 = y_2 = y_4 = 1, y_3 = 0$. The variable values in this solution, except x_3, are close to those of near-optimal solutions in z^+ (and z^*). Further, only one constraint is violated, $(y_2^2 + x_3^2 \leq 4.64)$, which comes in at 4.871772068. This infeasible solution at generation 236 provides a specific measure of the *shadow price* for constraint $(y_2^2 + x_3^2 \leq 4.64)$. If the cost of relaxing this constraint is not too much, the decision maker has been presented with an opportunity discovered by the algorithm. Many such opportunities occur in practice[4].

Problem: Hesse. Our second problem is discussed in [16, page 24] and originated in [20]. It is quadratic in the objective function and in two constraints. The variables are continuous, and the best reported solution, $z^* = -310$, is at $\mathbf{x}^T =$

---

[3] We use elite selection, which copies the best-of-generation solution into the next generation. Also, we use non-uniform mutation [15, pages 103, 111], in which the expected step size change from mutation of a floating point allele is a decreasing function of the number percentage of generations elapsed. This by itself will have the effect of reducing emigration between the populations as the run progresses.

[4] This concept has been explored in the context of a conventional GA [18, 19].

Table 3. Hesse Results: Averages over 100 generations. See Table 1 for legend.

Generations	Violation	InF→Fea	Fea→InF	z^+	medz_{InF}	$\sigma^2 z_{\text{Fea}}$	$\sigma^2 z_{\text{InF}}$
0–99	-0.6650	1.5000	6.5400	-275.883824	-250.401	1284.434	13446.196
900–999	-0.4406	1.5500	6.5300	-292.164230	-288.285	331.403	3170.694
1900–1999	-0.2420	2.1000	6.6700	-306.323098	-241.333	230.956	5167.766
2900–2999	-0.1088	1.6900	6.3200	-306.606229	-284.745	43.058	413.583
3900–3999	-0.0342	1.9300	6.4900	-308.839796	-298.533	4.607	151.386
4900–4999	-0.0001	2.1400	5.1700	-309.969180	-309.930	0.000248	0.001351

(5, 1, 5, 0, 5, 10). The two-population GA found its z^+ at -309.99141652481194. For this solution, $x_1 = 4.999949615359374$, $x_3 = 5.0$, $x_4 = 4.3379483053785203E-5$, $x_2 = 1.0000502743019608$, $x_5 = 4.9999277165343345$, $x_6 = 10.0$.[5]

Table 3, for the Hesse problem, corresponds to Table 1 for the Yuan problem. The comments previously made about the Yuan problem and the patterns in evolution noticed there apply to the Hesse problem without much qualification. In this run of the Hesse problem we see an even stronger movement (than in Table 1) by the infeasible population towards feasibility. As shown in Table 3 the *average* infeasibility of the infeasible solutions during the last 100 generations of the run is -0.0001. During the last generation the average is $-3.99733965164017e-07$.

Mixing Between the Feasible and Infeasible Populations. As with Yuan, notice that both populations continue to export throughout the run, the feasible population at a somewhat higher rate. Again, the median z values in the infeasible population approach z^+ even though selection in the infeasible population is not directed at z. Finally, although the overall pattern is similar, the z variances in Hesse decline over time much more rapidly than they do in Yuan.

Information on Potentially Profitable Tradeoffs Automatically Generated. On the uses of the infeasible population for automatically identifying constraint reconsiderations, we note that at generation 20 there appears in the infeasible population the solution $\mathbf{x}^T = (5.30504506985872, 1.09360041810019, 4.03893111661352, 4.74281156868017, 4.86902458174934, 9.62832716285562)$ with $z = -330.33892227141$ and infeasibility of -0.42288930351706. Only two constraints are violated: one constraint is violated by amount -0.024243816 and the other is violated by amount -0.398645488, for a total violation of -0.422889304. Further, the sum of slacks in the constraints is 21.5538596235044, so there is considerable room to tighten other constraints, e.g., by selling capacity. For example, a third constraint comes in at 13.12158005, well above its minimum of 4. This leaves more than 9 units of slack capacity, for which there may be other uses. As in the Yuan problem, the infeasible population contains many solutions such as this one, which may be used by managers profitably.

Problem: Pooling. Our third problem is discussed in [16, pages 38–9] and was originated in [21]. It is multiplicative in both the objective function and

---

[5] This is a better solution than reported in Table 2. The random number seed used for this run, 2, just happens to produce a better result. The run is not atypical.

Table 4. Variable settings at z^+ for the Pooling run under discussion.

2-pop variable	2-pop value at z^+	z^* value
x_1	0.00307775542406007E4	0
x_2	0.49999973531965175	0.5
x_3	2.4252327646072726E-27	0
x_4	100.61930243127915	100
x_5	4.06847097629025E-30	0
x_6	99.3805723645953	100

Table 5. Pooling Results: Averages over 100 generations. See Table 1 for legend.

Generations	Violation	InF→Fea	Fea→InF	z^+	medz_{InF}	$\sigma^2 z_{\text{Fea}}$	$\sigma^2 z_{\text{InF}}$
0–99	-11.6311	1.40	9.68	396.665205	26.172	12734.450	80033.132
900–999	-10.0925	1.83	11.32	439.451911	369.936	1341.593	17441.671
1900–1999	-5.3936	1.26	10.98	447.986872	417.019	379.998	3812.274
2900–2999	-2.4942	1.36	10.46	449.080888	432.793	120.450	927.995
3900–3999	-0.6229	1.56	10.09	449.090581	441.848	6.935	89.803
4900–4999	-0.0015	2.01	7.78	449.330277	449.273	0.002987	0.008043

the constraints. All variables are continuous. The reported optimal solution is $z^* = 450$, at $q_{11} = 0$, $q_{21} = 0.5$, $q_{41} = 0.5$, $y_{11} = 0$, $y_{12} = 100$, $z_{31} = 0$, and $z_{32} = 100$.

We map the problem variables as follows: $y_{11} \mapsto x_3$, $y_{12} \mapsto x_4$, $q_{11} \mapsto x_1$, $q_{21} \mapsto x_2$, $q_{41} \mapsto 1 - x_1 - x_2$, $z_{31} \mapsto x_5$, $z_{32} \mapsto x_6$. This eliminates the equality constraint and yields a mathematically equivalent problem. In the run to be discussed here we obtained $z^+ = 449.3803716736962$ with a random seed of 1. (This random seed was not used in the data for Table 2, which used seeds based on the system clock.) Table 4 shows the value of $\mathbf{x}^{+T}$ and its correspondence to the settings of the original variables at z^*.

Information on Potentially Profitable Tradeoffs Automatically Generated. Again we see that important managerial information is algorithmically extractable from the infeasible population. We note that in generation 4187 of the infeasible population a solution with $z = 453.692728740051$ was found, but then immediately lost. It has an infeasibility of -0.948398970709817, with the decision variables set to $\mathbf{x}^T = (0.00751253130969082, 0.499665249936584, 3.06696077041$-$692e - 27, 100.552108603048, 4.6473502896556e - 30, 99.4273030879242)$. In this solution, only one constraint is violated. If the right-hand side could cheaply be raised from 0 to at least 0.948398970709817, this solution would become profitable and feasible. Also, there is extra slack associated with this solution: 100.959097265662. At z^+ the slack is 100.49712706071. There are many other examples of possible tradeoffs in this run.

Problem: Colville. Our fourth problem is discussed in [16, pages 92–3] and originated in [22]. It is multiplicative and quadratic in the objective function and

Table 6. Colville Results: Averages over 100 generations. See Table 1 for legend.

Generations	Violation	InF→Fea	Fea→InF	z^+	medz_{InF}	$\sigma^2 z_{\text{Fea}}$	$\sigma^2 z_{\text{InF}}$
0–99	-7.6055	2.5700	9.5700	10510.09	10105.056	439324.262	619808.371
900–999	-5.2850	2.0000	11.6800	10125.22	9900.066	53933.498	194832.518
1900–1999	-3.0104	1.7300	11.6800	10124.72	9962.886	17250.181	146940.068
2900–2999	-1.3644	1.9600	12.0600	10124.72	10059.269	3709.520	13635.974
3900–3999	-0.3630	1.6100	11.5900	10123.61	10093.688	184.869	1625.862
4900–4999	-0.0006	2.5600	8.7300	10123.47	10123.412	0.00364	0.03279

multiplicative in the constraints. The variables are continuous. The reported optimal value is $z^* = 10122.69643^6$ with $\mathbf{t}^{*T} = (78, 33, 29.998, 45, 36.7673)$. In the run we shall consider here, $z^+ = 10123.464905030838$ and $\mathbf{t}^{+T} = (78.00000321918812, 33.01144193119939, 30.001941327255274, 44.99999999924409, 36.75964862060901)$.

The patterns to be seen in the summary data for Colville, in Table 6, are the familiar ones, given above for Yuan and Hesse.

Information on Potentially Profitable Tradeoffs Automatically Generated. Again, and there are many other examples in this run, we see that important managerial information about constraints is contained in the infeasible population. We observe that in generation 4908 of the infeasible population a solution with $z = 10122.6441615269$ was found and retained for some time. It has a low infeasibility, -0.000226063887148076, with the decision variables set to $\mathbf{t}^T = (78, 33.0114452272884, 30.0001612811051, 44.9999999992441, 36.7558397945725)$. Also, there is considerable slack associated with this solution: 2007.93820179402. At z^+ the slack is 2007.7787830732.

3 Discussion and Conclusion

We have newly examined four constrained optimization problems, recognized as difficult in the literature. We report results confirming – and extending to more difficult problems – previous work on the two-population GA: it works very well. We have discerned a number of characteristic properties of this search process, which are summarized in Tables 1, 3, 5, and 6. On four rather different problems a common, untuned FI-2Pop GA (parameters were set *ex ante*) produced excellent results in each case *and* produced similar patterns of behavior. Further, we picked these four problems for this study based only on their independent interest. Specifically: we are not withholding any unfavorable results on unreported cases.

Interpreting these results broadly, it appears that the FI-2Pop GA is successful because the infeasible population maintains genetic variation that would otherwise be destroyed. The genetic material so preserved is available, perhaps much later, to combine with newly-arisen improvements. Much, however, remains to

---

[6] We note an error in [16, page 93], where it is reported as 1.1436. Plugging in the variable values they give yields $z^* = 10122.69643$.

be investigated. We note in this regard that there are other – rather different – varieties of two-population GAs. SGGA maintains two violation-penalized populations, using different penalty functions, and crossbreeds between them [23, 24]. GENOCOP III is based on repair and maintains two populations; both are feasible throughout. See [25] for a review of both systems. Chu & Beasley [26, 27] have explored a single-population GA in which each solution receives two fitness scores, one on the objective function (or 'fitness'), one on infeasibility (or 'unfitness'). Parents are selected for breeding based only their 'fitness' values; individuals are removed from the population in order of their 'unfitness' values. Yuchi & Kim [28] report success with a two-population scheme in which a portion of the infeasible solutions are probabilistically accepted for breeding each generation, based on their objective function values. Systematic comparison of these approaches must await future research.

References

1. Bäck, T.: Evolutionary Algorithms in Theory and Practice: Evolution Strategies, Evolutionary Programming, Genetic Algorithms. Oxford University Press, New York, NY (1996)
2. Bäck, T., Fogel, D., Michalewicz, Z., eds.: Advanced Algorithms and Operators. Institute of Physics Publishing, Bristol, UK (2000)
3. Coello, C.A.: A survey of constraint handling techniques used with evolutionary algorithms. Technical report Lania-RI-99-04, Laboratorio Nacional de Informática Avanzada, Veracruz, México (1999) http://www.lania.mx/~ccoello/constraint.html.
4. Bäck, T., Fogel, D., Michalewicz, Z., eds.: Handbook of Evolutionary Computation. Institute of Physics Publishing, http://www.iop.org/Books/CIL/HEC/index.htm (1997–2003)
5. Coello, C.A.: List of references on constraint-handling techniques used with evolutionary algorithms. World Wide Web (Accessed January 2003) http://www.cs.cinvestav.mx/~constraint/index.html.
6. Kimbrough, S.O., Lu, M., Wood, D.H., Wu, D.J.: Exploring a two-market genetic algorithm. In Langdon, W.B., Cantú-Paz, E., et al., eds.: Proceedings of the Genetic and Evolutionary Computation Conference (GECCO 2002), San Francisco, CA, Morgan Kaufmann (2002) 415–21
7. Kimbrough, S.O., Lu, M., Wood, D.H., Wu, D.J.: Exploring a two-population genetic algorithm. In Cantú-Paz, E., et al., eds.: Genetic and Evolutionary Computation (GECCO 2003). LNCS 2723, Berlin, Germany, Springer (2003) 1148–1159
8. Kimbrough, S.O., Lu, M., Safavi, S.M.: Exploring a financial product model with a two-population genetic algorithm. In: Proceedings of the 2004 Congress on Evolutionary Computation, Piscataway, NJ, IEEE Neural Network Society, IEEE Service Center (June 19–23, 2004) 855–862
9. Cooper, T.F., Rozen, D.E., Lenski, R.E.: Parallel changes in gene expression after 20,000 generations of evolution in *e. coli*. Proceedings of the National Academy of Sciences **100** (2003) 1072–1077
10. Taddei, F., Radman, M., Maynard-Smith, J., Toupance, B., Gouyon, P.H., Goodelle, B.: Role of mutator alleles in adaptive evolution. Nature **387** (1997) 700–703

11. Lenski, R.E., Mongold, J.A., Sniegowski, P.D., Travisano, M., Vasi, F., Gerrish, P.J., Schmidt, T.M.: Evolution of competitive fitness in experimental populations of E. coli: what makes one genotype a better competitor than another? Antonie van Leeuwenhoek **73** (1998) 35–47
12. Wilke, C.O., Wang, J., Ofria, C., Lenski, R.E., Adami, C.: Evolution of digital organisms at high mutation rate leads to survival of the flattest. Nature **412** (2003) 331–333
13. Michalewicz, Z.: Genocop – optimization via genetic algorithms. World Wide Web (Accessed January 2003) http://www.cs.sunysb.edu/~algorith/implement/genocop/implement.shtml.
14. Kimbrough, S.O., Lu, M., Wood, D.H.: Exploring the evolutionary details of a feasible-infeasible two-population genetic algorithm in the context of constrained optimization. Working paper, University of Pennsylvania, Department of Operations and Information Management, Philadelphia, PA (2004) Posted at http://opim-sun.wharton.upenn.edu/~sok/comprats/.
15. Michalewicz, Z.: Genetic Algorithms + Data Structures = Evolution Programs. Third edn. Springer, Berlin, Germany (1996)
16. Floudas, C.A., Pardalos, P.M., et al.: Handbook of Test Problems in Local and Global Optimization. Kluwer Academic Publishers, Dordrecht, The Netherlands (1999)
17. Yuan, X., Zhang, S., Pibouleau, L.: A mixed-integer nonlinear-programming method for process design. RAIRO - Recherche Opérationnelle-Operations Research **22** (1988) 331–346
18. Kimbrough, S.O., Oliver, J.R., Pritchett, C.W.: On post-evaluation analysis: Candle-lighting and surrogate models. Interfaces **23** (May-June 1993) 17–28
19. Branley, B., Fradin, R., Kimbrough, S.O., Shafer, T.: On heuristic mapping of decision surfaces for post-evaluation analysis. In Sprague, Jr., R.H., ed.: Proceedings of the Thirtieth Annual Hawaii International Conference on System Sciences, Los Alamitos, CA, IEEE Press (1997)
20. Hesse, R.: A heuristic search procedure for estimating a global solution of nonconvex programming problems. Operations Research **21** (1973) 1267
21. Ben-Tal, A., Eiger, G., Gershovitz, V.: Global minimization by reducing the duality gap. Mathematical Programming **63** (1994) 193–212
22. Rijckaert, M., Martens, X.: Comparision of generalized geometric programming algorithms. Journal of Optimization Theory and Applications. **26** (1978) 205
23. Le Riche, R., Haftka, R.T.: Improved genetic algorithm for minimum thickness composite laminate design. Composites Engineering **3** (1995) 121–139
24. Le Riche, R., Knopf-Lenoir, C., Haftka, R.T.: A segregated genetic algorithm for constrained structural optimization. In: Proceedings of the Sixth International Conference on Genetic Algorithms, Morgan Kaufmann (1995) 558–565
25. Michalewicz, Z., Dasgupta, D., Le Riche, R., Schoenauer, M.: Evolutionary algorithms for constrained engineering problems. Computers & Industrial Engineering Journal **30** (1996) 851–870
26. Chu, P.C., Beasley, J.E.: A genetic algorithm for the generalized assignment problem. Computers and Operations Research **24** (1997) 17–23
27. Chu, P.C., Beasley, J.E.: A genetic algorithm for the multidimensional knapsack problem. Journal of Heuristics **4** (1998) 63–86
28. Yuchi, M., Kim, J.H.: Grouping-based evolutionary algorithm: Seeking balance between feasible and infeasible individuals of contrained optimization problems. In: Proceedings of the 2004 Congress on Evolutionary Computation, Piscataway, NJ, IEEE Neural Network Society, IEEE Service Center (June 19–23, 2004) 280–7

An Evolutionary Algorithm for the Maximum Weight Trace Formulation of the Multiple Sequence Alignment Problem[*]

Gabriele Koller and Günther R. Raidl

Institute of Computer Graphics and Algorithms,
Vienna University of Technology, Vienna, Austria
{koller,raidl}@ads.tuwien.ac.at

Abstract. The multiple sequence alignment problem (MSA) can be reformulated as the problem of finding a maximum weight trace in an alignment graph, which is derived from all pairwise alignments. We improve the alignment graph by adding more global information. A new construction heuristic and an evolutionary algorithm with specialized operators are proposed and compared to three other algorithms for the MSA, indicating the competitiveness of the new approaches.

1 Introduction

Multiple sequence alignments are of great practical interest in the area of molecular biology. For example, they are essential for the prediction of secondary and tertiary structures of protein sequences and for finding conserved motifs in a group of related proteins [2]. As a DNA or protein sequence can be represented by a string over a finite alphabet Σ, the multiple sequence alignment problem (MSA) can be defined as follows.

Given a set of $k > 2$ strings $S = \{S_1, \ldots, S_k\}$, where each string S_a, $a = 1, \ldots, k$, consists of characters $s_{a,1}, \ldots, s_{a,l_a} \in \Sigma$, find a multiple sequence alignment $\hat{S} = \{\hat{S}_1, \ldots, \hat{S}_k\}$ over the alphabet $\hat{\Sigma} = \Sigma \cup \{\text{``-''}\}$ which minimizes a given scoring function and has the following properties: (1) all strings in $\hat{S}$ have the same length l with $\max_{a=1\ldots k}(l_a) \leq l \leq \sum_{a=1}^{k} l_a$, (2) ignoring dashes, $\hat{S}_a$ is identical with S_a, $\forall a = 1, \ldots, k$, (3) no column of $\hat{S}$ only contains dashes. In the alignment, a dash represents a space between characters of the original sequences. Fig. 1a gives an example for the MSA.

To score an alignment, the weighted sum-of-pairs (SP) function with affine gap penalties is most widely used [2]. Optimal pairwise alignments ($k = 2$) can be found in time $O(l^2)$ by dynamic programming [6]. For the general case $k > 2$ the time complexity of exact methods with SP-score increases exponentially with k. Thus, exact methods can in practice only be applied to instances with few, rather short sequences. For larger instances, various heuristics have been developed.

Heuristic methods for the MSA fall into different categories, see [7] for an extensive survey. The majority of them follow the progressive approach, in which

---

[*] This work is supported by the Austrian Science Fund (FWF) under grant P16263-N04.

an alignment is built by repeatedly aligning two sequences or multiple alignments of subsets of the sequences by a pairwise alignment method. A widely used algorithm of this category is ClustalW [12]. While it is usually fast and yields acceptable solutions, it may produce sub-optimal alignments due to the preservation of gaps of the pairwise alignments. T-Coffee [9] is also based on the progressive method, but tries to avoid such drawbacks by using a tree-based consistency objective function called COFFEE [10]. A library containing all pairwise alignments replaces the usual substitution matrix for the evaluation of aligned characters. To incorporate more global information, the library is extended by transitive relationships for all character triples from different sequences.

Iterative algorithms try to overcome the drawbacks of progressive methods by refining an initial alignment, generated randomly or by some other method, via local improvement and/or random variation. Evolutionary algorithms such as SAGA [8] fall into this category. SAGA was one of the first attempts to apply a evolutionary algorithm (EA) to the MSA with SP-score. It uses a 2D array to represent the alignment and includes a variety of crossover and mutation operators. The EA of Zhang et al. [13] focuses on identifying fully matched columns. The evolutionary programming approach by [1] uses a different objective function; it maximizes a score for matched characters minus a gap penalty.

In our work we focus on the maximum weight trace formulation, which maps the MSA to a graph problem [3]. This formulation is described in Sect. 2. Two novel strategies for improving the information in the underlying alignment graph are presented in Sect. 3. In Sect. 4, a construction heuristic for deriving a trace from an alignment graph is described. Sect. 5 presents an EA with specific operators based on the construction heuristic. The algorithms are experimentally compared to ClustalW, T-Coffee, and SAGA in Sect. 6.

2 The Maximum Weight Trace Formulation of the MSA

The problem of aligning multiple sequences can be transformed into the maximum weight trace problem (MWT), which has been introduced by Kececioglu [3] as a natural formulation of merging partial alignments to form multiple alignments. Like MSA, MWT is NP-hard. It is based on the concept of the *alignment graph* $G = (V, E)$, whose nodes V correspond to the characters of the k input sequences and are labeled correspondingly, and whose edges E represent desirable alignments of character pairs. Each edge $e \in E$ is assigned a weight $w(e) > 0$ corresponding to the desirability of the pairwise character alignment. For convenience, G is extended to a mixed graph $\hat{G} = (V, E, H)$ by adding directed arcs H connecting all successive nodes of each sequence, see Fig. 1b. A *trace* $T \subseteq E$ is a subset of edges that can be realized in a multiple alignment, i.e., each pair of characters connected by an edge appears in the multiple alignment in the same column. A set of edges forms a trace iff the arc-extended subgraph $\hat{G}_T = (V, T, H)$ does not contain any cycle including an arc, see Fig. 2. Given a weighted alignment graph G, the MWT is to find a trace T with maximum total weight $w(T) = \sum_{e \in T} w(e)$.

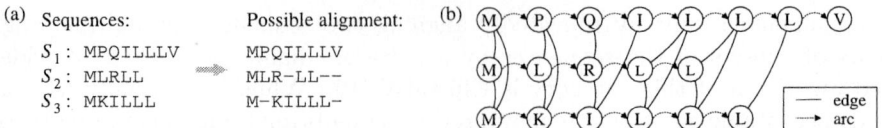

Fig. 1. Examples for (a) a multiple sequence alignment and (b) an arc-extended alignment graph for three sequences (edge weights are omitted).

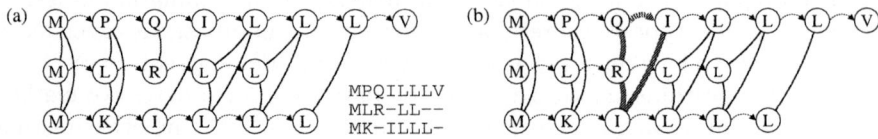

Fig. 2. Examples for traces for the alignment graph in Fig. 1b: (a) a trace and a corresponding alignment (note that edge (R,I) is not in the trace), (b) an edge set violating the trace property since it contains a cycle including an arc: characters Q and I of row 1 cannot simultaneously be aligned with character I of row 3.

A shortest possible multiple alignment can be derived from a given trace column by column by aligning characters connected by an edge in the trace. For each column, the algorithm considers in each sequence the left-most character not yet included in the alignment – the *front* – and adds it to the current column if it is not connected by an edge to a character to the right of the front.

A branch-and-bound algorithm [3] and a polyhedral approach [4] have been proposed to solve small to moderately sized instances of the MWT exactly. In these approaches, the alignment graph is constructed by calculating all pairwise alignments and including corresponding edges. Edge weights are simply assigned according to an appropriate substitution matrix.

3 Improvements on the Alignment Graph

Obviously, the edges of the alignment graph and their weights are crucial for the success of any method applied to the MWT formulation of the MSA. So far, finding appropriate edges and weights has received only little attention. We propose two concepts to better reflect some of the global information contained in all pairwise alignments: a neighborhood-dependant weighting scheme for calculating edge weights and an edge extension.

We first obtain a preliminary edge set E from all pairwise sequence alignments which are computed using dynamic programming. For each pair of aligned characters $s_{a,i}$ and $s_{b,j}$, we add an edge $e = (s_{a,i}, s_{b,j})$. The purpose of the new weighting scheme is to take the neighborhood of an edge into consideration and to reward edges in regions of higher similarity with higher weights. The edge weight $w(e)$ is calculated as a weighted sum of the value from ClustalW's substitution matrix for the pairwise alignment of $s_{a,i}$ and $s_{b,j}$ and the values for up to b consecutively aligned character pairs to the right and to the left of e. The value of a neighbor with distance Δ to e in terms of columns is scaled by the

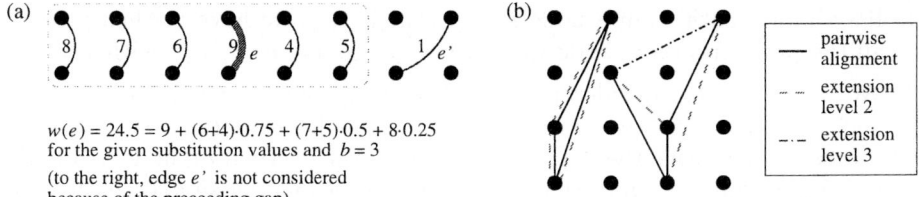

$w(e) = 24.5 = 9 + (6+4) \cdot 0.75 + (7+5) \cdot 0.5 + 8 \cdot 0.25$
for the given substitution values and $b = 3$
(to the right, edge e' is not considered
because of the preceeding gap)

Fig. 3. Examples for (a) the computation of an edge weight and (b) the alignment graph extension by adding transitive edges up to level $d_{\max=3}$.

factor $1 - \frac{\Delta}{b+1}$. The block of considered character pairs is limited by the first gap or by b. An example is given in Fig. 3a.

Furthermore, we extend the edge set E by transitive edges up to a level $d_{\max}$. This extension can be viewed as a generalization of the concept of the extended library [9] where only transitive edges of level 2 are considered. An edge $e_t = (s_{a,i}, s_{b,j})$ is called a *transitive edge* of level $d \geq 2$ if there exists a path of d edges between $s_{a,i}$ and $s_{b,j}$, where only one character per sequence may be involved, see Fig. 3b. The weight of a transitive edge depends on the minimum edge weight $w_{\min}$ on the path and on the level: $w(e_t) = w_{\min}/(d-1)$. If e_t already exists, then its weight is increased by $w(e_t)$. The addition or update of all transitive edges of level $d = 2, \ldots, d_{\max}$ for k sequences of maximum length l can be performed in time $O(l \cdot k^{d_{\max}+1})$ using a recursive depth-first search algorithm. Experiments indicate that $d_{\max} = 3$ is a good choice in practice [5].

4 The Repeated Edge-Insertion Construction Heuristic

This section describes a new heuristic for deriving a feasible trace from a given weighted alignment graph, which we call *repeated edge-insertion construction heuristic* (REICH). The basic idea follows Kruskal's greedy algorithm for finding a minimum spanning tree of an undirected graph. Initially, trace T is the empty set, and all edges are sorted according to decreasing weight; ties are broken randomly. In its main part, the algorithm considers each edge in the predetermined order and adds it to the trace if this does not violate the feasibility of the trace. Otherwise, the edge is discarded.

As discussed in Sect. 2, a set of edges represents a trace as long as the arc-extended subgraph does not contain any cycle including an arc. When we consider an edge $(s_{a,i}, s_{b,j}) \in E$ for inclusion in the trace, we therefore check if a path from $s_{a,i}$ to $s_{b,j}$ or a path from $s_{b,j}$ to $s_{a,i}$ already exists in the arc-extended trace. We can safely add edge $(s_{a,i}, s_{b,j})$ to T if no such path exists or the found path does not contain any arcs.

Since the alignment graph usually contains many edges, the running time of the path-search procedure is critical. We make the following observations and later exploit them in an efficient algorithm. For convenience, we say *a path enters/leaves a sequence* if it contains an edge leading to a node of this sequence or an edge leading away from a node of this sequence, respectively.

1. If we find a path from a node $s_{a,i}$ to a node $s_{b,j}$, we have implicitly found all the paths from any node $s_{a,i'}$ with $i' \leq i$ to any node $s_{b,j'}$ with $j' \geq j$.

2. We only have to consider paths which enter/leave any sequence at most once. Furthermore, the path must not enter the sequence containing the source node or leave the sequence containing the destination node. All paths visiting a sequence more than once have corresponding simpler paths that use arcs of this sequence as shortcuts.

3. It follows that we only have to consider paths containing at most $k-1$ edges (plus the arcs, whose number is not limited by k).

4. Let $s_{a,i}$ be the source node. If we have identified the edge $(s_{a,m}, s_{c,n})$ with minimum $m \geq i$ from all the edges connecting nodes of sequences a and c, we do not have to consider any further edge inbetween these two sequences. For any subsequent edge $(s_{a,m'}, s_{c,n'})$ with $m' > m$, $n' > n$ must hold (otherwise, the trace would be infeasible), and, due to observation (1), only a subset of the nodes already reachable via edge $(s_{a,m}, s_{c,n})$ is reachable via the edge $(s_{a,m'}, s_{c,n'})$. More generally, there even cannot exist any path from $s_{a,m'}$, $m' > m$, to any node $s_{c,n''}$ with $n'' \leq n$. However, a path from $s_{a,m''}$ with $m'' < m$ to a node $s_{c,n''}$, $n'' < n$, may exist.

A simple depth-first search in the arc-extended trace for identifying a path from $s_{a,i}$ to $s_{b,j}$ would clearly be inefficient. Instead, we perform a breadth-first search starting from $s_{a,i}$ and consider the above observations for pruning the search tree. Global variables $M_1, \ldots, M_k$ are used to store for each sequence the minimum indices of the nodes which are reachable via the already considered edges/paths; initially, $M_a = i$ and $M_c = \infty$, $\forall c \neq a$. At any iteration of the breadth-first search, at most $k-1$ different *active paths* exist, which have last improved the values M_c, $\forall c \neq a$. The path we consider next for an extension with a new edge is always the one with the minimum number of edges; if two or more paths with the same minimum number of edges exist, we choose the path involving the smallest number of arcs.

To optimally support this breadth-first search, the trace is implemented as a special data structure. For each pair of sequences $c = 1, \ldots, k$ and $d = 1, \ldots, k$, $c \neq d$, we maintain a balanced tree $A_{c,d}$ which stores references to all edges connecting nodes of sequences c and d, sorted by the index of the node in sequence c. In this way, we can efficiently identify the "next" edge leading from a certain position in sequence c to sequence d, i.e., the edge $(s_{c,m'}, s_{d,n})$ with minimum $m' \geq m$ for given m, c, and d. The balanced trees allow this operation in time $O(\log \hat{l})$, with $\hat{l} = \max\{l_1, \ldots, l_k\}$, and need $O(k^2 + |T|)$ space.

When using this data structure, the total running time of REICH is bounded above by $O(|E| \log |E| + |E| k^3 \log \hat{l})$, where the first term represents the initial sorting of edges and the factor $O(k^3 \log \hat{l})$ of the second term comes from the breadth-first search[1].

---

[1] The depth of the breath-first search is bounded by $k-1$. In depth t, $0 < t < k$, a maximum of $k-1-t$ possible extensions must be further considered for each of the $\leq k-1$ active paths. Considering the time $O(\log \hat{l})$ for finding an edge for a possible extension, we get the total time complexity $O(k^3 \log \hat{l})$ for one call of the search.

The running time of the described algorithm can be further improved to a worst case complexity of $O(|E|\log|E| + |T|k^2 \log \hat{l} + |E|\log \hat{l})$. For this purpose, we additionally store two kinds of auxiliary edges in the trace data structure: (a) An *alias-edge* $(s_{c,m}, s_{d,n})$ is stored if the two incident nodes are already connected by a path containing no arcs. (b) A *directed path-edge* $(s_{c,m}, s_{d,n})$ is stored if a path including at least one arc exists from node $s_{c,m}$ to node $s_{d,n}$, and we are so far not aware of any node $s_{d,n''}$ with $n'' < n$ that is reachable from $s_{c,m}$. Keeping the trace data structure up-to-date with these auxiliary edges needs additional bookkeeping, but it turns out to be worthwhile, since some effective additional conditions for further pruning the breadth-first search can now be efficiently checked.

5 The Maximum Trace Evolutionary Algorithm (MTEA)

The evolutionary algorithm described in this section is the first one that makes use of the MWT formulation of the MSA problem. In combines and enhances ideas of REICH and previous genetic algorithms for MSA.

5.1 Representation and Initialization

Candidate alignments are primarily represented in the most direct form as two-dimensional array $\hat{S}$. When needed, the trace data structure is additionally created and stored.

To create promising initial candidate solutions and to ensure diversity at the same time, a randomized version of REICH is used: A random number $|D| \in \{\lfloor k \cdot \hat{l}/2 \rfloor, \ldots, \lfloor k \cdot (k-1) \cdot \hat{l}/2 \rfloor\}$ is picked; a list $D \subseteq E$ of the $|D|$ edges with highest weights is determined and randomly permuted. Then, REICH is performed on this list to obtain a trace, which is finally decoded into a multiple alignment. To achieve higher diversity, we keep track of the edges from D that could not be included in the trace. When creating the next solution, these edges are forced to be included in D before all other edges. Additionally, REICH is applied once to the whole list of edges.

5.2 Variation Operators

We apply the following five variation operators. They were carefully chosen or designed with their specific strengths and computational efforts in mind in order to achieve highest possible synergy. The first three operators are relatively simple and fast; they are traditionally working directly on the multiple alignments. In contrast, the latter two operators focus on the MWT formulation and make active use of the trace data structure and the alignment graph; they are more powerful, however, computationally also more expensive.

One-point crossover has been used in several previous EAs for MSA including [8, 13]. The first parent alignment is cut straight after a randomly chosen column.

The whole left part is copied to the offspring. The right part is adopted from the second parent alignment which is tailored accordingly so that it can be appended while keeping the characters' order of the original sequences. Any void space appearing at the junction point is filled with gaps.

Block shuffling mutation has also previously been used [8]. From one sequence a block of consecutive characters being bounded left or right by one or more gaps is randomly chosen. This block is then shifted over the neighboring gaps. When there is more than one neighboring gap, we either check them all and keep the best position or determine the target position randomly; the actually applied strategy is decided at random. To limit the changes and the computational effort, we apply this operator only to blocks of a maximum length of 9 and consider at most 9 neighboring new positions.

Best consistent cut crossover. Columns of two alignments are called *consistent*, when for each sequence their characters (or gaps) are identical with respect to the corresponding positions in the original sequence. Blocks inbetween consistent columns can be directly exchanged among parent alignments [8]. For the alignment of many protein sequences, however, such consistent columns are rare, and the operator can therefore not often be applied. We relax the requirements by introducing *consistent cuts*: A cut of the first parent alignment after some column is said to be consistent if no right-most symbol of the left part is aligned with a symbol of the right part in the second parent alignment. In this case, the second parent can also be cut straight at the corresponding position and the right part of the second parent can simply be concatenated to the left part of the first parent. In our crossover, we determine all possible consistent cuts and choose the one yielding the highest total weight. Since the weights can be calculated incrementally, only one sweep over the parent alignments is necessary, and the operator can be implemented in time $O(k^2 \hat{l})$.

Edge insertion mutation selects an edge from the alignment graph and includes it in the alignment. The selection is performed by determining a uniform random value $u \in [0, 1)$, calculating an exponentially distributed rank $r = \lfloor \rho \log(1 - u) \rfloor \mod |E| + 1$ from it, and using this rank as an index into an array containing references to all edges E sorted according to decreasing weight. The strategy parameter ρ is set according to theoretical and experimental investigations described in [5]. If an edge is selected that already exists in the trace of the current alignment, the edge-selection is repeated.

In order to feasibly include the selected edge e, it is usually necessary to remove several other edges from the alignment's trace. All edges of the original alignment's trace realized in the alignment in columns to the left or the right of both end-nodes of edge e will remain unchanged. All other edges of the trace, thus, the edges representing alignments of symbols in the alignment-block $\hat{B}$ delimited to the left and right by the columns containing the characters to be aligned when including e, are temporarily removed and stored in a list R. The new edge e can now safely be added to the trace. Then, REICH is used to process R in order of decreasing weight and re-insert as many of the edges as possible.

Finally, as local improvement, we determine all edges from E being incident to a character in block $\hat{B}$ and not contained in R. These edges are also considered in decreasing weight order for insertion in the trace by applying REICH.

Path relinking uses two parent alignments $\hat{A}$ and $\hat{B}$ and transforms $\hat{A}$ step by step into $\hat{B}$. Thus, we consider all solutions lying in the search space on a path connecting the two parents. The best intermediate solution is kept as offspring.

We transform $\hat{A}$ into $\hat{B}$ column by column from left to right. Let $\hat{I}_i$ be the ith intermediate solution, with $\hat{I}_0 = \hat{A}$ and $\hat{I}_z = \hat{B}$. The first i columns of alignment $\hat{I}_i$ always correspond to those in parent $\hat{B}$. We determine $\hat{I}_{i+1}$ from $\hat{I}_i$ for $i = 0, \ldots, z-1$ as follows. Let X be the characters appearing in column $i+1$ of $\hat{B}$. This column will be realized in $\hat{I}_{i+1}$ in a locally optimal way.

Let Y denote the set of all characters appearing in $\hat{B}$ to the right of X, and let $Y^C \subseteq Y$ be the subset of characters connected with a character of X in the trace of I_i. In order to align the characters of X, the edges connecting X and Y^C cannot be retained, and they are therefore deleted from the trace. All edges from E connecting two nodes from X are then realized and added to the trace; the characters in X are actually aligned. Finally, we check if the performed removal of edges allows for an inclusion of new edges from E at the right side of X: All edges from $(a, b) \in E$ with $a \in Y^C$ and $b \in Y$ are considered, and if they do not yet appear in the trace they are tried to be included by using the edge-insertion algorithm of REICH. The corresponding alignment I_{i+1} is updated accordingly. In this way, all intermediate solutions determined by path relinking are locally optimal in the sense that no further edges from E can be realized in the trace without removing others.

5.3 General Structure of the Algorithm

We use an island model as basic structure for the EA. Each island follows the steady-state concept by always only creating a single new solution candidate per iteration. If this offspring is a duplicate of another solution of the island, it is discarded. Otherwise, it replaces the worst solution. Within each island, an offspring is always created by performing either one-point crossover or best consistent cut crossover (each with 50% probability) followed by the block shuffling mutation. The more complex and time-demanding path relinking and edge insertion mutation are applied with relatively low probabilities as inter-island operators. Parents are randomly chosen among the best solutions of all islands, and the offspring is incorporated into another randomly chosen island. Additionally, traditional migration is performed: With a certain probability, the best solution of a randomly chosen island is copied into another island.

6 Experimental Results

We experimentally compare REICH and MTEA to ClustalW 1.82, T-Coffee, and SAGA using 130 instances of the BAliBASE 1.0 benchmark library [11]

Table 1. Average results of ClustalW, T-Coffee, SAGA, REICH, and MTEA on the five benchmark classes: annotated SPS-values, total edge weights $w(T)$ for REICH and MTEA and corresponding average standard deviations σ for the 10 runs of MTEA.

	ClustalW	T-Coffee	SAGA	REICH		MTEA		
	SPS	SPS	SPS	$w(T)$	SPS	$w(T)$	σ	SPS
Ref 1	0.857	0.850	0.780	1090	0.872	1097	0.7	**0.874**
Ref 2	0.877	0.849	0.762	26945	0.900	26952	3.1	**0.901**
Ref 3	**0.863**	0.795	0.716	21629	0.839	21676	5.8	0.846
Ref 4	0.760	0.764	0.522	4772	0.775	4785	2.5	**0.777**
Ref 5	0.850	**0.894**	0.705	5207	0.877	5211	1.2	0.875
Total avg.	0.849	0.839	0.746	5339	0.863	5348	1.5	**0.865**

for protein sequence alignment. These instances are grouped into five classes: equidistant sequences of similar length (Ref 1), a related family with divergent, orphan sequences (Ref 2), families of related distances (Ref 3), sequences with N/C-terminal extensions (Ref 4), and sequences with internal insertions (Ref 5).

The alignment graph for REICH and MTEA was built using the weighting scheme with $b = 10$ and extension level $d_{\max} = 3$. Appropriate parameters for MTEA were obtained in preliminary tests: The population size was 100, divided into four equally sized islands. Migration was performed with probability 0.1%, path relinking with 2%, and insert edge mutation with 10% per iteration. A run was terminated when no new best solution had been found for 1 000 iterations or after a total of 10 000 iterations. The EAs were run 10 times on each instance. ClustalW, T-Coffee, and SAGA were performed using standard parameter settings. All experiments were performed on a single Pentium 4/1.9 GHz PC.

The resulting alignments were evaluated using the annotated SPS-values of [11], which indicate the proportion of correctly aligned character pairs of an alignment with respect to the manually refined BAliBASE reference alignment considering only trusted blocks. A value of 1 means that the computed alignment is identical to the reference alignment, whereas 0 signifies that no character pair has been correctly aligned. Table 1 shows average results for each algorithm on each of the five classes of instances. With respect to the SPS-values, REICH and MTEA performed on most test instances as good as or better than ClustalW and T-Coffee. SAGA was outperformed on almost all instances by all the other algorithms. In detail, the best known solutions were obtained by MTEA and REICH for 67% of all instances compared to 45% by ClustalW and 26% by SAGA. For instance classes 1, 2, and 4, MTEA also yielded the best average results. ClustalW was only significantly better on class 3, and T-Coffee exhibited slightly better average results on class 5. MTEA performed slightly better than REICH on all five classes on average, however, quality differences are in general not significant. See [5] for details.

Running times strongly depend on the individual instances. In general, ClustalW was fastest, but also T-Coffee and REICH took only about one minute on the largest instances. SAGA and MTEA needed up to 107 minutes.

7 Conclusion

The maximum weight trace formulation of the MSA is a well-suited model for finding accurate multiple alignments. The proposed calculation of edge weights and the extension of the alignment graph by transitive edges enhance the model by the inclusion of more global information. The construction heuristic REICH is fast and yields high quality alignments which are often superior to those obtained by ClustalW, T-Coffee, and SAGA. If longer running times are acceptable, the proposed EA sometimes finds slightly better solutions.

References

1. K. Chellapilla and G. B. Fogel. Multiple sequence alignment using evolutionary programming. In P. J. Angeline et al., editors, *Proceedings of the 1999 IEEE Congress on Evolutionary Computation*, pages 445–452. IEEE Press, 1999.
2. D. Gusfield. *Algorithms on Strings, Trees, and Sequences*. Cambridge University Press, 1997.
3. J. D. Kececioglu. The maximum weight trace problem in multiple sequence alignment. In *Proceedings of the 4th Symposium on Combinatorial Pattern Matching*, number 684 in LNCS, pages 106–119. Springer, 1993.
4. J. D. Kececioglu, H.-P. Lenhof, K. Mehlhorn, P. Mutzel, K. Reinert, and M. Vingron. A polyhedral approach to sequence alignment problems. *Discrete Applied Mathematics*, 104:143–186, 2000.
5. S. Leopold. An alignment graph based evolutionary algorithm for the multiple sequence alignment problem. Master's thesis, Vienna University of Technology, Vienna, Austria, February 2004.
6. S. Needleman and C. Wunsch. A general method applicable to the search for similarities in the amino acid sequence of two proteins. *J. Mol. Biol.*, 48:443–453, 1970.
7. C. Notredame. Recent progresses in multiple sequence alignment: A survey. *Pharmacogenomics*, 3(1):131–144, 2002.
8. C. Notredame and D. G. Higgins. SAGA: Sequence alignment by genetic algorithm. *Nucleic Acids Research*, 24(8):1515–1524, 1996.
9. C. Notredame, D. G. Higgins, and J. Heringa. T-COFFEE: A novel method for fast and accurate multiple sequence alignment. *J. Mol. Biol.*, 392:205–217, 2000.
10. C. Notredame, L. Holm, and D. G. Higgins. COFFEE: An objective function for multiple sequence alignment. *Bioinformatics*, 14(5):407–422, 1998.
11. J. Thompson, F. Plewniak, and O. Poch. BAliBASE: A benchmark alignments database for the evaluation of multiple sequence alignment programs. *Bioinformatics*, 15:87–88, 1999.
12. J. D. Thompson, D. G. Higgins, and T. J. Gibson. CLUSTAL W: Improving the sensitivity of progressive multiple sequence alignment through sequence weighting, position specific gap penalties and weight matrix choice. *Nucleic Acids Research*, 22(22):4673–4680, 1994.
13. C. Zhang and A. K. C. Wong. A genetic algorithm for multiple molecular sequence alignment. *CABIOS*, 13(6):565–581, 1997.

A Novel Programmable Molecular Computing Method Based on Signaling Pathways Regulated by Rho-GTPases in Living MDCK Epithelial Mammalian Cells

Jian-Qin Liu and Katsunori Shimohara

ATR Network Informatics Laboratories, 2-2-2 Hikaridai, "Keihanna Science City",
Kyoto, 619-0288, Japan
{jqliu,katsu}@atr.jp

Abstract. In this paper, we propose a new biomolecular computing method based on the crosstalked pathways of living cells and the corresponding kinase-phosphatase networks under the regulation of Rho family GTPases. Owing to their merits of efficient regulation in controlled pathway complexity and low cost in implementation, we propose a feasible protocol (the algorithm) for kinase-and-phosphatase-based computers (called kinase computers for short) and the materials and methods for their implementation. In order to obtain high programmability in molecular computation, we have successfully designed pathway regulation schemes for computation. Here we report our latest simulation results on a designed controllable crosstalk mechanism and efficient schemes for engineered GTPase-based signaling communications for stable kinase computing under the dynamical environment of a cell culture assay. This is significant for the application of molecular computing to medical nano-bioinformatics and also provides a testbed for new and unconventional computing paradigms inspired by nature.

1 Introduction

Using nanobiomaterials to build unconventional computers is one of the most promising ways to achieve the central goal of "parallel problem solving from nature" [1], because nanobiomachines can provide various types of moleware architecture at the nano-meter level from the viewpoint of material science. Our research project at ATR [2] is aimed at using the functional proteins involved in the signal transduction of living cells to build nanobiomachines for computing purposes. The ultimate goal in building this kind of molecular computer is to apply computational wetware to proteomic analysis. This would be highly effective for biomedical applications of nano-biocomputers, because the signal transduction of Rho family GTPases affects the major neural behaviors of the cells and functionally acts as the kernel signaling mechanism of the cells [3~7]. The proteomic analysis of the signaling pathways of Rho family GTPases may, for example, lead to the discovery of entirely new medicines for neurodegeneration diseases.

In this paper, we propose a new programmable method for designing scalable biomolecular computers built by the related signaling pathways of cells with crosstalks and present our latest research results, in which sustainable computation can be provided through well designed cell cultures in engineering. Our method is different from L. Landweber and L. Kari's method based on the gene mechanism of evolution in the bacterium mechanism of ciliates [8], A. Ehrenfeucht et al.'s computation model of micronuclear genes in ciliate [9], R. Weiss and T. Knight's amorphous computing [10], G. Păun's P-systems or "membrane computing" [11], A. Regev and E. Shapiro's work in [12], and M. O. Magansco's model based on chemical kinetics [13]. The difference is that we propose using the signaling pathways of living cells for building biomolecular computers, whereby the efficiency of control can be guaranteed and low-cost implementation can be obtained. Feasible architecture designs for scalable biomolecular computers are the most crucial prerequisites for testing an autonomous cell-based molecular computer in an engineered way. In our research, the signaling pathways of phosphorylation and dephosphorylation regulated by kinases and phosphatases under the activation of Rho family GTPases are employed to design a new biomolecular computer. Because the signaling mechanism of pathways in cells is adaptive, to design and control the engineered pathways of cells for the purpose of molecular computing is therefore become possible. Under the condition of well-designed architecture and proper control schemes of the related pathways, to build a computational nanobiomachine by cellular pathways can be reasonably expected.

Compared with our previous work, programmable cross-talk mechanisms of signaling pathways have been introduced into kinase computing in this paper so that efficiency of related computing processes can be obtained. The protein interaction network of Rho GTPases with 10×10 size is constructed. The corresponding architecture with 100 PEs (Processing Elements) is designed based on pathway controllers. Pathway stability is calculated according to normalized Hill coefficient n'_H. Kinase computers built by cross-talked pathways of cells will be beneficial to the development of a new generation of nanobiomachines for medical applications in terms of natural computation.

2 Implementation of a Kinase Computer: Materials and Methods

In this paper, the kernel units of biomolecular computers based on the engineered signal transduction of Rho family GTPases are signaling pathways that carry out the required computing tasks and are implemented in biochemical reactions with interactions. Here, "engineered pathways" refer to controlled signaling pathways of living cells that can carry out biochemical reactions under the condition of related enzymes. We call the engineered pathways EPs for short (also Cf. Fig.6). The word "engineered" mentioned here is used to show that the controlled pathways behave differently compared with the natural existing pathways of living cells (For more details, Cf. [20]). Programming here refers to the controlling process of the kinase-phosphatase sequences within cells for computing purpose. The information of the computing processes is encoded as the form of phosphorylation and dephosphorylation. Here the phosphorylation state represents 1 and the dephosphorylation state represents 0. The regulation functions are used to activate the Rho family GTPases by

GEFs (Guanine nucleotide Exchange Factors). The words of programs for biomolecular computers are monitored by the regulation of the related upstream pathways of Rho family GTPases and corresponding GEFs. The set of Rho family GTPases and the set of GEFs are activated initially by thrombin through cell membranes. The significance here is in the crosstalk mechanism of cellular signaling, which is the key to the cell communications and other major aspects of cells [3~7].

The kinase computing prototype we are building consists of three parts: (a) phosphorylation-dephosphorylation encoding for granularity in information, (b) kinase-and-phosphatase based pathway operators for data flow in the underlying system when computation is carried out, and (c) Readout by immunofluorescence analysis. Based on the encoding scheme of phosphorylation and dephosphorylation, we summarize the operations of biomolecular computing as a set of {input, activate, compute, output} as shown in Figure 1.

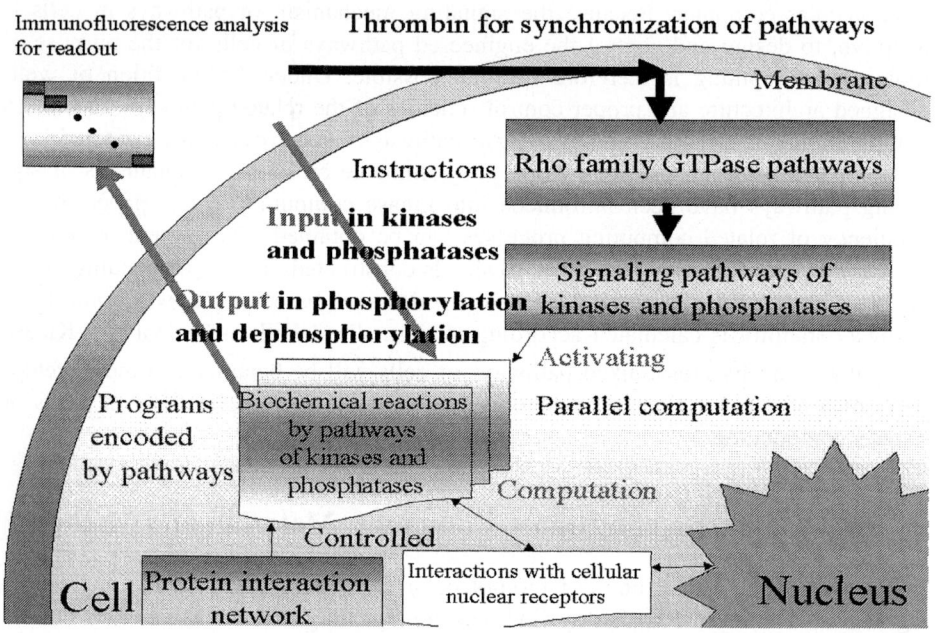

Fig. 1. The structure of a kinase computer.

The pathway architecture of the nanobiomachine, which we are constructing to demonstrate computational performance, consists of three major units: (a) the signaling pathways of the Rho family GTPases that regulate the activation of the Rho family GTPases and act as the switches in the cycle between the active state of GTP-bound conformation and the inactive state of GDP-bound conformation, (b) the pathways of activation of mammalian target proteins/effectors by Rho-GTP (Rho associated GTP), and (c) the pathways of reversible protein phosphorylation and dephosphorylation by protein kinases and phosphatases. Here, GEFs and GAPs switch the states of GTP and GDP in two different directions of the cycle. The stabilization of Rho-GDP can be achieved by using GDIs (guanine nucleotide exchange inhibitors) [3]. With the signaling mechanism constructed by using pathways in cells, the engineered pathways under the regulation of Rho family GTPases are used to construct a bio-molecular computer. Compared with the basic design for the architecture of kinase computers in [2], the architecture of kinase computing we have made improvement recently is the cross-talked mechanism of cellular signaling and program-oriented controller of related engineered pathways. The interactions among the signaling pathways under the necessary controls can help us to obtain an autonomous architecture of nanobiomachines for nature-inspired computing.

2.1 Materials

Compared with the material of Rho family GTPases we suggest in [2], the main technological improvement for materials in this paper is that we use the set of GTPases that includes {Ras, Rho, Rab, Arf, Ran}, i.e., the superfamily of Rho family GTPases for the cell communication mechanism between the upstream pathways and downstream pathways. The upstream pathways refer to the pathways of Rho GEFs/GAPs that are used to control GTP/GDP switches. The downstream pathway refers to the pathways of the related target molecules. So, the available number of the GTPases and related signaling molecules is bigger than the number suggested in [2]. So, the performance of kinase computing in scalability and information capacity is improved. In mammalian cells, the related techniques are mature and practical in laboratories of molecular biology and biochemistry [14, 4] and can guarantee the necessary accuracy of the computation achieved by biochemical reactions in living cells.

2.2 Feasible Operations by Using Signaling Pathways of In Vitro Cells

In the kinase computer, the four major operators in this set are defined as follows: (1) *input:* to activate the target molecules, such as kinases and phosphatases, in the cells/cell culture; (2) *activate:* to activate the related signaling pathways that encode the constraint (e.g., clauses in a 3-SAT problem [2]) in cells in the computing processes in which the signaling molecules involved are labeled; (3) *compute:* to carry out the computing tasks in the form of biochemical reactions among the signaling molecules by the related pathway; and (4) *output:* to detect and readout the result of the computation process given above. The major related signaling mechanisms include (1) Phosphorylation and dephosphorylation processes controlled by kinases and phosphatases, (2) GTP/GDP switching mechanism controlled by Rho family GTPases, and (3) The signaling processes of functional protein interacted with nuclear receptors in cells. The interactions between the pathways guided by Rho GTPases and nuclear receptors may cause feedback on the related pathways. So, the quantity of the related enzymes for different pathways needs to be adjusted.

2.3 Programmable Logic Units of Signaling Pathways of Cells

Programs of kinase computers are carried out in the form of primitives defined by the biochemical operators and are assigned with the corresponding parameters obtained from experiments that make the stability of the engineered pathways feasible. The kernel of the kinase computer we are designing is reflected in the following protocol.

The Protocol of Kinase Computers. The protocol of kinase computers is summarized as follows:

1. Preparing the MDCK cells, Rho GTPases and antibodies for the corresponding signaling molecules;
2. Growing the MDCK cells with other related molecules in a cell culture environment;
3. Activating the engineered pathways in cells and carrying out phosphorylation assay;
4. Catalyzing the biochemical reactions between the products of the phosphorylation assay and corresponding antibodies;
5. Detection of phosphorylation-dephosphorylation states by immunofluorescence analysis and readout in terms of transducers from the fluorescence signals into readable electrical signals.

In the cell culture of above-mentioned processes of kinase computing, epithelial MDCK (Madin-Darby canine kidney) cells, ERM family proteins (ezrin/radixin/moesin), PKC (protein kinase C), Botulinum for ATP, and TRITC (tetramethylrhodamine B isothiocyanate) [14] will be included.

3 Experimental Results and Discussion

The feasibility of implementation of kinase computers and their experimental faithfulness have been studied (Cf. [2]). When applying the method of kinase computing in 3-SAT problem solving, the linear order of control-space complexity can be obtained. So, the number of signaling molecules that need to be controlled is with the linear order. The signaling crosstalk mechanism [15~19] is the major foundation for efficiently designing pathways of cells for molecular computers according to the schemes proposed in this paper. By using the entire cell to design the moleware (molecular-ware) architecture, we can expect to make the best use of cells that exist in nature [21], by which the difficulties of manufacturing individual molecules will be avoided. Its significance is obvious in its application to nano-bioinformatics for medicine. Of course, the regulation and control of corresponding engineered pathways are necessary.

Based on the quantitative measure that we suggested – normalized n_H coefficient, i.e., n'_H (here n_H refers to the Hill coefficient for describing the sensitivity of biochemical reactions) – is proposed to map the range of n_H: $(0, +\infty)$ into the range of n'_H: $(0, 1)$. After n'_H is introduced into the measurement of engineered signaling pathways, we can quantitatively observe the activity of the related enzymes and

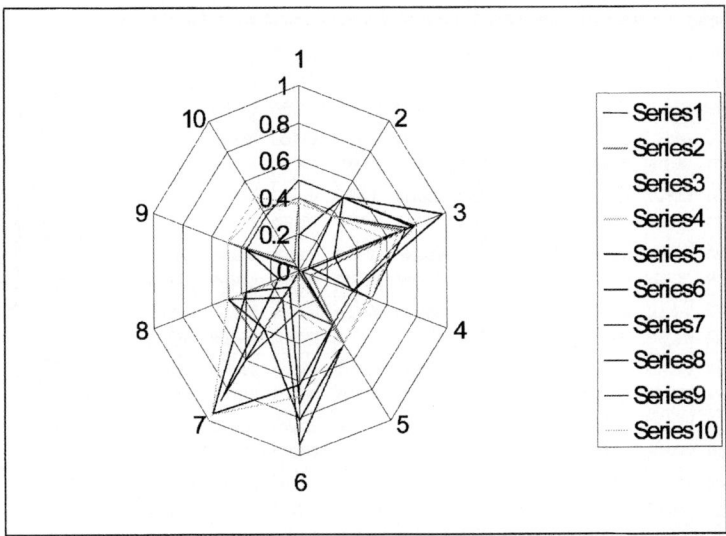

Fig. 2. The crosstalk links among the protein interaction network by 100 kinases/phosphatases.

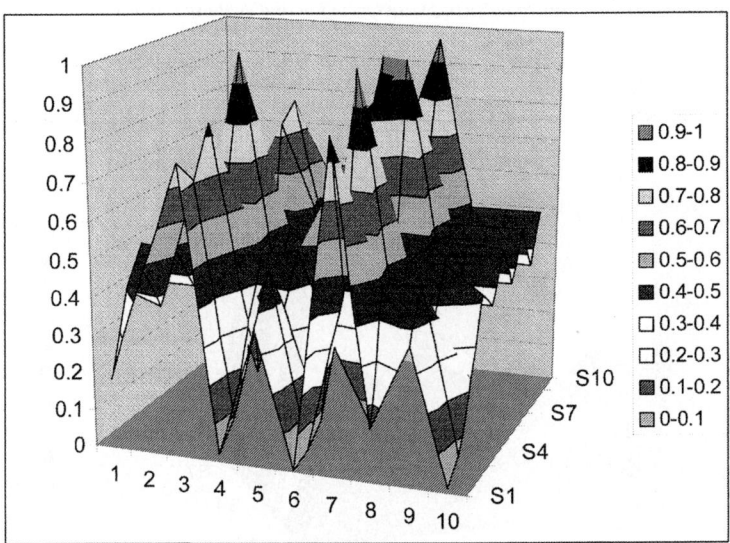

Fig. 3. The normalized n_H coefficient distribution.

therefore control the related signaling mechanism so that feasibility of the designed stable pathways can be guaranteed. Fig. 2 describes the crosstalk links among the protein interaction network by 100 kinases/phosphatases, in which series refers to the cluster of 10 proteins and total 100 proteins are given. In Fig. 3, the normalized n_H coefficient distribution of enzyme activity is given. The series in Fig. 3 correspond to the series in Fig. 2. The GAP/GDP switches in Fig. 5 are controlled to regulate the

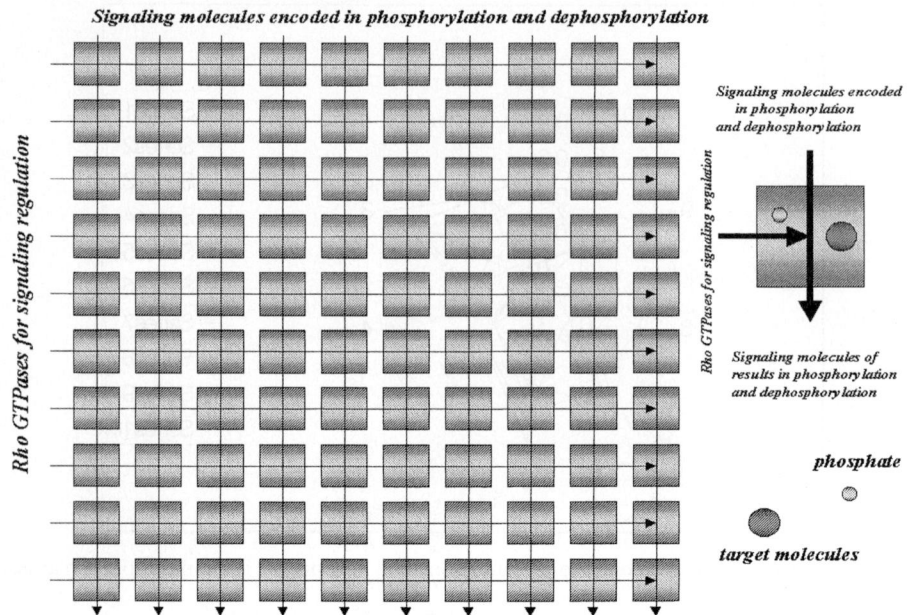

Fig. 4. The architecture of a kinase computer.

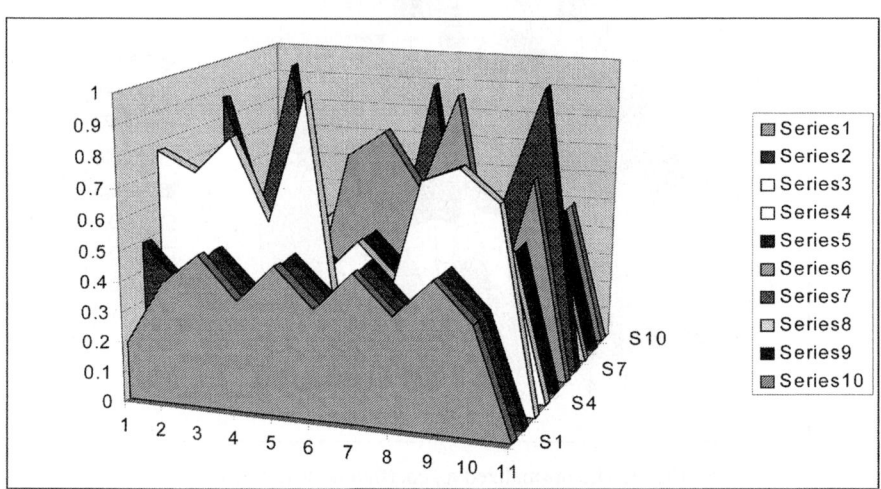

Fig. 5. The quantitative level of GAPs/GDPs in activation.

crosstalks in Fig. 4 of the 100 EPs according to the detection of n_H. Verification of massive parallelism in biomolecular computation is thus realized. Based on kinases and phosphatases, which are available with the current experimental tools, we are able to control the interactome (genome-wide protein interaction) network of cellular pathways by Rho family GTPases, where transcriptome (genome-wide transcription) for intracellular pathways interacted with cellular nuclear receptors and interlogs among cell culture (samples) from different species (GAPs/GDPs and kinases and phosphatases are from mammalian cells, GTPases are from Arabidopsis thaliana for low cost). In Fig. 6, an example of the related interaction is illustrated using nine kinases/phosphatases from the families of Rho, Rac and Cdc42. MBS and MLC (that belong to the Rho family) are crosstalked. PI3-kinase and S6-kinase (that belong to the set of Rac family) and IQGAP (that belongs to the Cdc42 family) are crosstalked. For the crosstalk between MBS and MLC, MBS needs to be controlled to decouple its dephosphorylation effect on MLC [14]. In Fig. 2, Fig. 3, Fig. 5 and Fig. 6, the interaction relationship among the signaling molecules is illustrated. In Fig. 4, an example of the architecture of kinase computing is given.

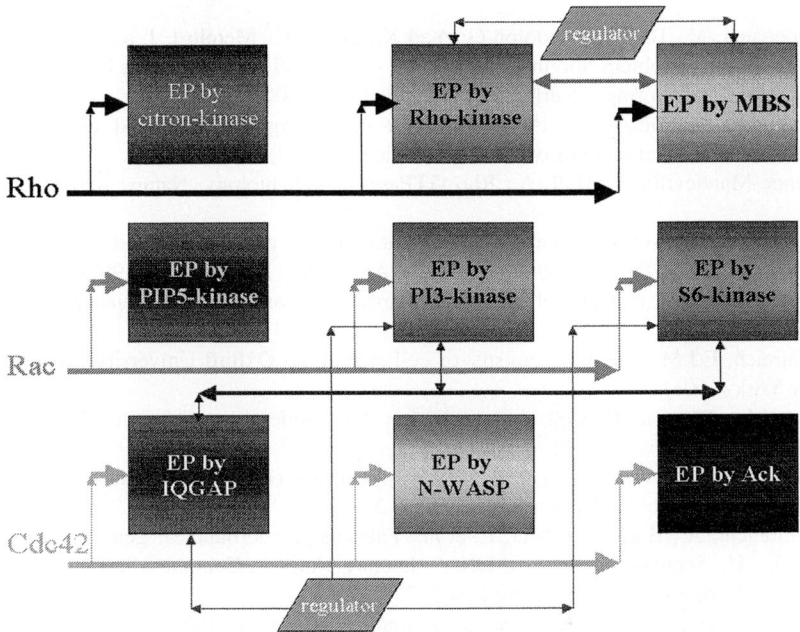

Fig. 6. The interactions of pathways and their control.

4 Conclusion

In the viewpoint of biological faithfulness, we have presented programmable schemes of kinase computing and studied the quantitative measurement and control structure for cross-talked signaling mechanism of kinase computing. The simulation result shows that cross-talked pathways can be conditionally used for parallel molecular computing. This is important for further studies on constructing a massively parallel kinase computer.

Acknowledgement

This research was conducted as part of 'Research on Human Communication' with funding from the National Institute of Information and Communications Technology. The authors sincerely thank Prof. Kozo Kaibuchi, Dr. Shinya Kuroda and Dr. Mutsuki Amano for their advice, discussion and academic help on the signal transduction of cells and molecular biology, Prof. Xin Yao and Prof. Shigeyoshi Tsutsui for their advice and kind academic help on natural computation, and anonymous referees for their advice on improving this manuscript.

References

1. Schoenauer, M., Deb, K., Rudolph G., Yao X., Lutton E., Merelo J. J. and Schwefel H.-P. (eds.): Parallel Problem Solving from Nature – PPSN VI. Lecture Notes in Computer Science, Vol. 1917. Springer-Verlag, Berlin Heidelberg (2000).
2. Liu, J.-Q., Shimohara, K.: A biomolecular computing method based on Rho family GTPases. IEEE Transactions on Nanobioscience. 2 (2003) 58-62.
3. Etienne-Manneville, S., Hall, A.: Rho GTPases in cell biology. Nature. 420 (2002) 629-635.
4. Kaibuchi, K., Kuroda S., Amano, M., Regulation of the cytoskeleton and cell adhesion by the Rho family GTPases in mammalian cells, Annu. Rev. Biochem. 68 (1999) 459-486.
5. Hafen, E.: Kinase and phosphatases – a marriage is consummated. Science. 280 (1998) 1212-1213.
6. Helmreich, E.J.M.: The biochemistry of cell signalling. Oxford University Press, Oxford, New York (2001).
7. Scott, J.D., Pawson, T.: Cell communication: the inside story, Scientific American, 282 (2000) 54-61.
8. Landweber, L.F., Kari, L.: The evolution of cellular computing: nature's solution to a computational problem. BioSystem 52 (1999) 3–13.
9. Ehrenfeucht, A., Harju, T., Peter, I., et al.: Patterns of micronuclear genes in ciliates. In: Jonoska, H., Seeman, N.C. (eds.): DNA7. Lecture Notes in Computer Science, Vol. 2340. Springer-Verlag, Berlin Heidelberg (2002) 279–289.
10. Weiss, R., Knight, T.F.Jr.: Engineered communications for microbial robotics, in: Condon, A., Rozenberg, G. (eds.): DNA6. Lecture Notes in Computer Science Vol. 2054. Springer-Verlag, Berlin Heidelberg (2001) 1–16.
11. Păun, G.: From cells to computers: computing with membranes (P systems). BioSystem 59 (2001) 139–158.
12. Regev, A., Shapiro, E.: Cellular abstractions: cells as computation. Nature 419 (2002) 343.
13. Magansco, M. O.: Chemical kinetics is Turing universal. Phys. Rev. Let. 78 (1997) 1190–1193.
14. Kawano, Y., Fukata, Y., Oshiro, N., et al.: Phosphorylation of myosin-binding subunit (MBS) of myosin phosphatase by Rho-kinase in vivo. The Journal of Cell Biology. 147 (1999) 1023-1037.
15. Liu, F., Wan, Q., Pristupa, Z.B., et al.: Direct protein-protein coupling enables cross-talk between dopamine D5 and γ-aminobutyric acid A receptors. Nature. 403 (2000) 274-280.
16. Tarricone, C., Xiao, B., Justin, N., et al.: The structural basis of Arfaptin-mediated crosstalk between Rac and Arf signalling pathways. Nature 411 (2001) 215-219.

17. Digicaylioglu, M., Lipton, S.A.: Erythropoietin-mediated neuroprotection involves crosstalk between Jak2 and NF-κB signaling cascades. Nature 412 (2001) 641-647.
18. Katoh, H., Negishi, M.: RhoG activates Rac1 by direct interaction with the Dock180-binding protein Elmo. Nature 424 (2003) 461-464.
19. Yoo, A.S., Bais, C., Greenwald, I.: Crosstalk between the EGFR and LIN-12/Notch pathways in C. elegans vulval development. Science 303 (2004) 663-666.
20. Masip, L., Pan, J.L., Haldar, S., et al.: An engineered pathway for the formation of protein disulfide bonds. Science. 303 (2004) 1185-1189.
21. Stix, G.: Little big science. Scientific American 285 (2001) 32-37.

Empirical Investigations on Parallelized Linkage Identification

Masaharu Munetomo[1], Naoya Murao[2], and Kiyoshi Akama[1]

[1] Information Initiative Center
Hokkaido University, Sapporo 060-0811, Japan
[2] Graduate School of Engineering,
Hokkaido University, Sapporo 060-0811, Japan

Abstract. To solve GA-difficult problems in which we cannot ensure tight linkage in their encoding, advanced methods such as linkage identification techniques and estimation of distribution algorithms work effectively although they need some additional computational cost. The computation time can be reduced by employing parallel computers and several approaches have been proposed for their parallelized algorithms. This paper presents empirical results on parallelization of the linkage identification compared to that of an estimation of distribution algorithm.

1 Introduction

Among a series of advanced methods in genetic and evolutionary computations, linkage identification/learning techniques and estimation of distribution algorithms (EDAs) are considered two major approaches to realize effective mixing of building blocks even when tight linkage is not ensured. In linkage identification techniques such as the linkage identification by nonlinearity check (LINC)[3, 2, 4], a linkage group – a set of loci tightly linked to form a building block (BB) – can be detected by checking nonlinearity with perturbations on a pair of loci. Effective mixing is realized by applying crossovers based on the identified linkage groups. In order to obtain accurate solutions with less computational time, several approaches have been proposed for their parallelization. In parallel linkage identification originally proposed by Munetomo et. al.[5], calculation of linkage identification for each pair of loci is highly independent each other and therefore, it is easy to parallelize. In numerical simulations comparing the number of fitness evaluations, the parallelized linkage identification achieves quasi-linear speedup that exceeds conventional parallel GAs such as island models. They also show that overall performance of the parallel linkage identification exceeds conventional methods not only when we cannot ensure tight linkage, but also when fitness contribution of BBs is largely different each other.

On the other hand, estimation of distribution algorithms (EDAs) such as the Bayesian optimization algorithm (BOA)[6, 7] estimate probability distribution of strings after applying selections to generate proper candidates of BBs in the next generation. The model building process in BOA by constructing Bayesian networks needs extensive computational cost, which should be parallelized. In the distributed BOA (DBOA) proposed in Ocenasek's doctoral thesis[1], each processor generates its subpopulation independently and model-building process is also parallelized by assigning nodes that represent probabilistic variables of a Bayesian network to processors.

In this paper, we perform empirical investigations on parallel linkage identification in comparison to the parallelized BOA. This is because these two approaches can solve difficult problems where we cannot ensure tight linkage in advance, whereas, other conventional PGAs such as with master-slave and island models cannot solve loosely-linked difficult problems even when we employ a number of parallel processors. (In the original paper of parallel linkage identification[5], results of numerical simulations on tightly encoded easier problems are presented in comparison to the conventional PGAs.)

The experiments are performed on an actual parallel architecture not by numerical simulations, because comparisons based only on the number of fitness evaluations do not reflect actual performance, especially for the Bayesian optimization algorithm whose majority of overheads lie in its model-building process which does not need explicit fitness evaluations.

2 Parallel Linkage Identification

Linkage identification by nonlinearity check (LINC) [3, 2, 4] is a first step toward identifying linkage groups – sets of loci tightly linked – only by bit-wise perturbations. In the LINC, linkage groups are identified by applying perturbations for pairs of loci to detect nonlinear interactions in fitness changes. In order-k delinearble functions – the sum of nonlinear sub-functions whose maximum order is k, nonlinear interactions exist only inside the sub-functions. When we assume that the objective function of the problem is a strict or loose order-k delinearble function, we can identify bit-positions for each sub-function by detecting nonlinearity by the perturbations. The nonlinearity detection must be performed on all the strings in a properly-sized population because even in a GA-difficult nonlinear sub-function, some linear attractors might be existent.

Therefore, the LINC calculates the following values for each pair of loci (i,j) and for all the strings s in a randomly initialized population that has $O(c2^k)$ strings where $c = \log(1-r)$ is a constant determined by the allowable probability r of detection failure, and k is the maximum order of linkage groups:

$$\begin{aligned}
\Delta f_i(s) &= f(..\bar{s}_i.....) - f(..s_i.....) \\
\Delta f_j(s) &= f(.....\bar{s}_j..) - f(.....s_j..) \\
\Delta f_{ij}(s) &= f(..\bar{s}_i.\bar{s}_j..) - f(..s_i.s_j...),
\end{aligned} \quad (1)$$

where $f(s)$ is a fitness functions of a string s and $\bar{s}_i = 1 - s_i$ is a bitwise perturbation ($0 \to 1$ or $1 \to 0$) at the i-th locus of s.

If $\Delta f_{ij}(s) \neq \Delta f_i(s) + \Delta f_j(s)$, then s_i and s_j are considered to belong to a same linkage group – we add i to the linkage group of locus j, and add j to the linkage group of i. Otherwise, s_i and s_j may not be a member of a linkage group, or they are linked but linearity exists in the current context. The LINC checks the nonlinearity condition for all the string s in a population. When the nonlinearity condition is satisfied for at least one string s, the pair (i,j) should be considered tightly linked. The LINC is performed according to the following algorithm[3]:

1. Randomly initialize a population of $O(c2^k)$ binary strings
2. For each string in the population, performs the following
3. For each pair of loci (i, j), performs the following
4. Calculate $\Delta f_{ij}(s)$, $\Delta f_i(s)$, and $\Delta f_j(s)$ by bit-wise perturbations
5. If $\Delta f_{ij}(s) \neq \Delta f_i(s) + \Delta f_j(s)$, locus i is included in the linkage group of j and locus j is included in the linkage group of i

The underlying assumption of the LINC is that fitness functions can be represented as the sum of nonlinear sub-functions whose optimal sub-solutions are building blocks. Strict nonlinearity condition cannot be applicable to real-world problems, therefore, we have introduced an allowable error ε for the condition and modified the above nonlinearity as follows: if $|\Delta f_{ij}(s) - (\Delta f_i(s) + \Delta f_j(s))| > \varepsilon$ then loci i and j is considered tightly linked.

The computational cost of the LINC is $O(nl^2)$ where n is the population size of $O(c2^k)$ (k : maximum order of building blocks) and l is the string length. The nonlinearity check for each pair of loci can easily be parallelized because there is no interdependency among their calculations. Employing P processors, we can reduce its computation time to $O(nl^2/P)$.

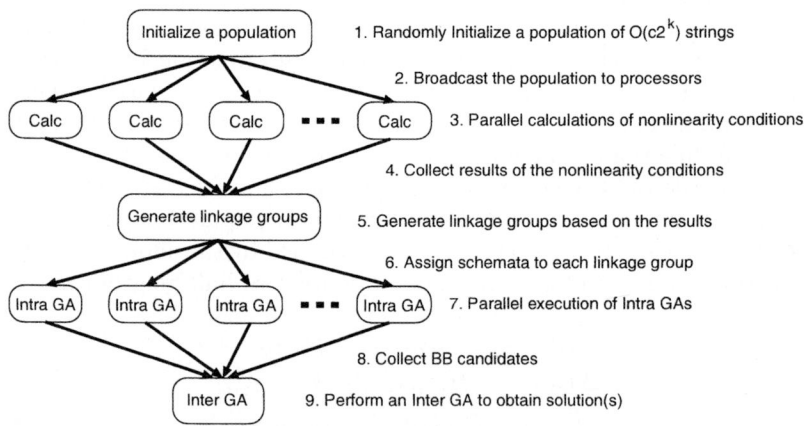

Fig. 1. PGA based on linkage identification[5].

The parallelized LINC (pLINC) is performed on a master-slave parallel computer consisting of a master processor and slave processors as follows:

1. A master processor randomly initializes a population of $n = O(c2^k)$ strings and broadcasts them to all the slave processors. (Therefore, all the processors have the same initial populations.)
2. Each slave processor calculates its assigned nonlinearity conditions for each pair of loci.
3. Results of the condition are collected from slave processors to the master processor.
4. The master generates linkage groups based on the collected results.
5. The master processor divides strings into schemata according to the obtained linkage groups and assigns them to the slave processors.
6. Each slave processor performs Intra GA that is performed inside a linkage group to search building block candidates concerning the assigned linkage group.
7. The master collects building block candidates obtained in slave processors.
8. The master performs Inter GA for the candidates to obtain solutions.

The Intra GAs and the Inter GA were originally introduced in a GA based on linkage identification[2]. For Intra GA, initial strings are divided into schemata based on the obtained linkage groups. Figure 2 (left) illustrates this decomposition process.

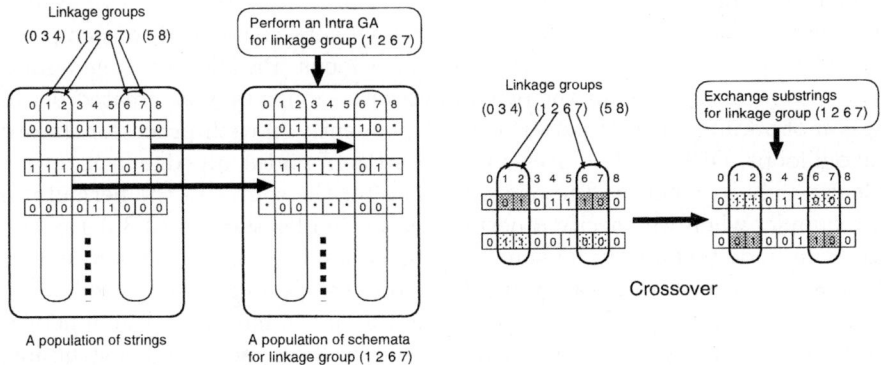

Fig. 2. Division of strings into schemata based on linkage groups (left) and Crossover operator of the Inter GA (right) [2].

The Intra GA performs a SGA with ranking selections, uniform crossovers and simple mutations inside a linkage group. To evaluate schemata, a template based on the current best string is employed, which is similar to competitive templates originally introduced in messy GA[8]. After the Intra GAs, we select a limited number of well-performed schemata as BB candidates in each linkage group.

The Inter GA applies ranking selections and crossovers based on the linkage groups that mix the BB candidates. Figure 2 (right) illustrates the crossover operator employed in the Inter GA.

3 Parallel Bayesian Optimization Algorithm

Estimation of distribution algorithms (EDAs) estimate probabilistic distributions of alleles for promising strings survived after applying selections, which is employed to make offsprings for the next generations. The early EDA models such as the PBIL (Population-Based Incremental Learning) estimates probability of 1's occurrence in each locus and generates offsprings based on the probabilities. A series of EDA methods have been proposed such as the UMDA (Univariate Marginal Distribution Algorithm), the BMDA (Bivariate Marginal Distribution Algorithm), and so on. The Bayesian optimization algorithm (BOA) proposed by Pelikan et. al[6, 7] is considered one of the most sophisticated algorithm among the EDA methods, which builds probabilistic models employing Bayesian networks. As for computational complexity of BOA, its network construction – searching an optimal network that minimizes the Bayesian-Dirichlet (BD) metric – tends to dominate its computational overhead, which should be parallelized. Computational complexity for searching network structure of BOA is $O(k2^k l^2 N + kl^3)$ where k is the maximum degree of nodes (maximum number of links connected to a node) and N is the number of instances.

Distributed BOA (DBOA)[1] parallelizes processes of generating strings and constructing Bayesian networks. Parallelization of the strings generation is simple: each node generates its assigned subpopulation of strings based on the conditional probabilities determined by Bayesian networks. In order to parallelize construction of the networks, each node of a network is assigned to each processor, which represents a random variable for a locus. Parallelized edge addition may cause inconsistency for the overall network – loops may be created because decision of adding edges is performed independently in each processor. In order to avoid loops, DBOA introduces a permutation of nodes: an edge from a source node can only be connected to one which is after the source in the permutation. For example, when we specify a permutation of nodes such as (2 3 6 1 5 4), an edge from node 6 can only be connected to nodes 1, 5, and 4. This mechanism restricts search space of the network; therefore, the permutation is randomly regenerated in each stage of the network construction to have an optimal network. The time complexity of the parallelized version of the network construction is approximated by $O((k2^k l^2 N + kl^3)/P)$ where P is the number of processors.

4 Empirical Results

In order to compare the parallel LINC (pLINC) and the Distributed BOA (DBOA), numerical experiments comparing the number of fitness evaluations are not considered appropriate because they differ in their major source of computational overheads. The computational overheads of pLINC come from $O(l^2)$ fitness evaluations and those of DBOA come from $O(l^3)$ network construction that does not need fitness evaluations. To compare overall computational overheads, we need to observe those for fitness evaluations and for network construction in actual situations. Therefore, we perform experiments on an actual parallel architecture. In the following experiments, we employ a parallel computer SGI Onix 300 consisting of MIPS R14000/600MHz × 32 CPUs with 16GB shared memory connected via NUMAflex^{TM} high-speed network. For communications among processors, Message Passing Interface (MPI) is employed.

We employ an one-max function and the sum of k-bit trap functions defined as follows as our test functions.

$$f(s) = \sum_{i=1}^{L} f_i(u_i). \qquad (2)$$

where f_i is a k-bit trap sub-function defined as follows:

$$f_i(u_i) = \begin{cases} k - u_i - 1 & \text{if } 0 \leq u_i \leq k-1 \\ k & \text{if } u_i = k \end{cases} \qquad (3)$$

where u_i is the number of 1's occurrence in a k-bit substring s_i ($s = s_1 s_2 \cdots s_L$).

We employ one-max, 3-bit trap, and 5-bit trap functions in the following experiments in order to control difficulty of the test problems. The string length of the problems is fixed to $l = 105$ ($L = 35$ for the 3-bit trap function and $L = 21$ for the 5-bit trap function). We observe time to obtain optimal solutions changing the number of processors $P = 1, 2, 4, 8, 16$. Population size and other parameters of the algorithms are optimized for each experiment in order to minimize the time to obtain optimal solutions, and we perform 20 experiments and plot their average in the following figures.

4.1 Comparison of Speedups

Figure 3 shows a comparison of speedups by pLINC and DBOA for the 5-bit trap test function. In the figure, the x-axis shows the number of processors employed and the y-axis is the speedup factor $S = T_s/T_p$ where T_s is execution time for a serial processor (when $P = 1$) and T_p is that for the parallel machine.

This illustrates pLINC achieves better results compared to DBOA in the speedup factors. This is because parallel calculation of nonlinearity condition for each pair of loci is highly independent and communication is necessary only when the master processor distributes an initial population and collects the results. On the other hand, parallel network construction in DBOA needs more frequent communications among processors during its search for an optimal network that minimizes the BD metric. This figure shows that pLINC is more preferable than DBOA in parallel computing environment for this problem. We have obtained similar results for one-max and 3-bit trap test functions. Since comparisons only by speedup factors are not enough to compare parallel algorithms – an inefficient algorithm by serial processing may achieve high speedup factors because its T_s is large, we perform comparisons for time to obtain optimal solutions in the following.

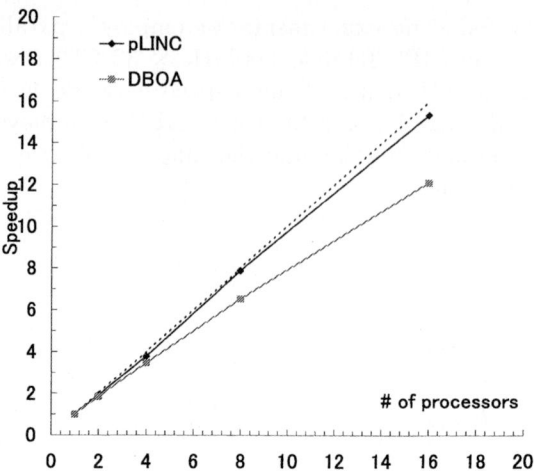

Fig. 3. Comparison of speedups between pLINC and DBOA.

4.2 Time for Linkage Identification vs. Model Building

Figure 4 shows comparisons of execution time for the one-max problem. In the figure, the x-axis is the number of processors employed and the y-axis shows execution time to obtain optimal solutions. For pLINC, time to evaluate fitness values dominates its computational cost. This is because it needs $O(l^2)$ fitness evaluations. On the other hand, for DBOA, model-building dominates its computational overheads. Comparing overall computation time, pLINC needs less than one-third of time for DBOA.

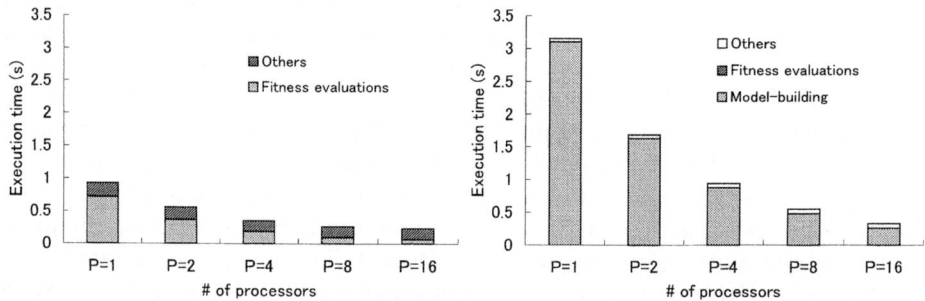

Fig. 4. Comparison of execution time to obtain optimal solutions between pLINC(left) and DBOA(right) for the one-max problem.

Figure 5 is the experimental results for the 3-bit trap function and figure 6 is for the 5-bit trap function. These results are similar to that for the one-max function. For more difficult 5-bit trap function, DBOA needs much more computational time than that of pLINC because computational overheads in

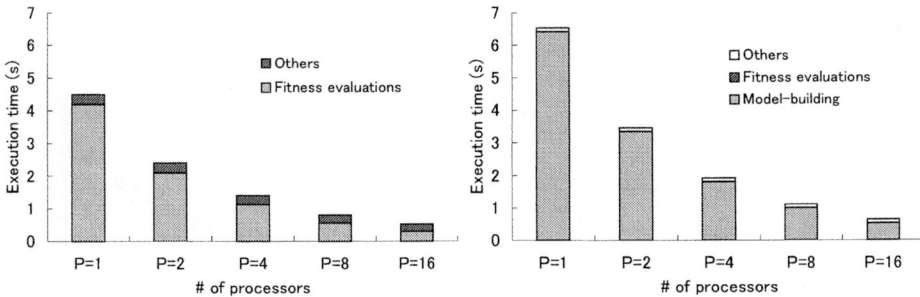

Fig. 5. Comparison of execution time to obtain optimal solutions between pLINC(left) and DBOA(right) for the 3-bit trap function.

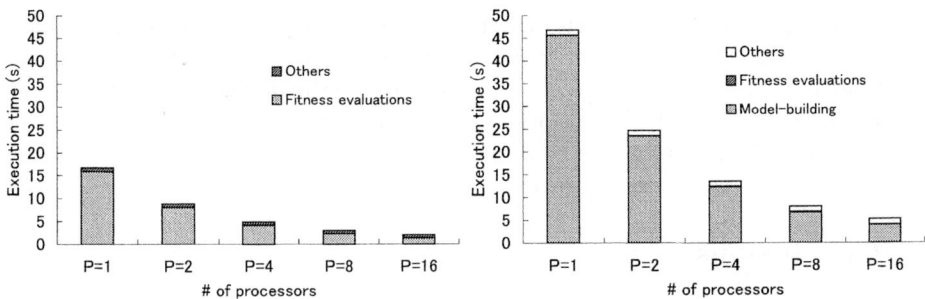

Fig. 6. Comparison of execution time to obtain optimal solutions between pLINC(left) and DBOA(right) for the 5-bit trap function.

its model-building process increase rapidly when problem difficulty increases concerning the order of BBs.

As expected from the previous results on speedups, fitness evaluations in pLINC and model-building in DBOA can be parallelized effectively – their computation time can greatly be reduced by employing parallel processors.

4.3 Effects of Fitness Evaluation Overheads

The major source of computational overheads for pLINC comes from its $O(l^2)$ fitness evaluations and that for DBOA comes from its network construction in model-building process. Therefore, it is expected that pLINC needs more computational time when time to evaluate a fitness value increases. In figure 7, we compare overall execution time employing 16 processors ($P = 16$) changing time to evaluate a fitness value by inserting wait in each evaluation. The 5-bit trap function is employed for this experiment.

From this result, computation time of the pLINC increases more rapidly compared with the DBOA along the wait increases. When wait equals to 1,000 micro-seconds = 1 milli-second, their computation time becomes about the same. This means we should employ pLINC when time to evaluate a fitness value is less

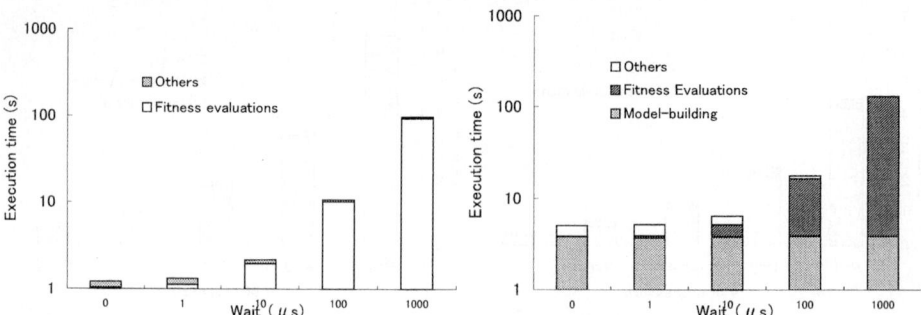

Fig. 7. Comparison of execution time varying waits for fitness evaluation time between LINC(left) and BOA(right) for the 5-bit trap function.

than 1 milli-second and otherwise we should employ DBOA in this experimental setting. A CPU of the parallel machine can perform around 500,000 floating-point calculations in 1 milli-second since a rough performance estimation of the R14000 is around 500MFLOPS (for a matrix calculation). This means that unless we need to perform exhaustive computations for a fitness evaluation, we should employ parallel linkage identifications.

5 Conclusions

Through empirical investigations performed on an actual parallel architecture, we show the effectiveness of the parallelized linkage identification compared with a parallel BOA. The result shows that pLINC achieves effective speedups compared to DBOA unless we need exhaustive computational overheads in evaluating a fitness value. In our experimental setting, the time border whether we should employ pLINC or DBOA is around 1 milli-second per evaluation, where we can perform about half million floating-point calculations for the processor we used.

We can consider the following source of GA-difficulties: (1) search space is extremely large such as in combinatorial optimization problems, (2) maximum order of building blocks is large – building block search becomes difficult and we need to have large initial populations, and (3) fitness evaluations are costly that require much computational overheads. The parallelized linkage identification is considered an effective approach that solves difficulties of the first and the second situations. For future works, we need to make theoretical models of relations between the source of problem difficulties and parallel algorithms to be employed.

References

1. Ocenasek Jiri. *Parallel Estimation of Distribution Algorithms*. PhD thesis, Brno University of Technology, 2002.
2. Masaharu Munetomo and David E. Goldberg. Designing a genetic algorithm using the linkage identification by nonlinearity check. Technical Report IlliGAL Report No.98014, University of Illinois at Urbana-Champaign, 1998.

3. Masaharu Munetomo and David E. Goldberg. Identifying linkage by nonlinearity check. Technical Report IlliGAL Report No.98012, University of Illinois at Urbana-Champaign, 1998.
4. Masaharu Munetomo and David E. Goldberg. Identifying linkage groups by nonlinearity/non-monotonicity detection. In *Proceedings of the 1999 Genetic and Evolutionary Computation Conference*, 1999.
5. Masaharu Munetomo, Naoya Murao, and Kiyoshi Akama. A parallel genetic algorithm based on linkage identification. In *Proceedings of the 2003 Genetic and Evolutionary Computation Conference, Part-1, LLNCS-2723*, pages 1222–1233, 2003.
6. M. Pelikan, D. E. Goldberg, and E. Cantú-Paz. BOA: The Bayesian optimization algorithm. IlliGAL Report No. 99003, Urbana, IL, 1999.
7. Martin Pelikan, David E. Goldberg, and Kumara Sastry. Bayesian optimization algorithm, decision graphs, and occam's razor. In *Proceedings of the Genetic and Evolutionary Computation Conference (GECCO-2001)*, pages 519–526. Morgan Kaufmann, 2001.
8. David E. Goldberg, Kalyanmoy Deb, and Bradley Korb. Messy genetic algorithms revisited: Studies in mixed size and scale. *Complex Systems*, 4:415–444, 1990.

The EAX Algorithm Considering Diversity Loss

Yuichi Nagata

Graduate School of Information Sciences,
Japan Advanced Institute of Science and Technology
nagatay@jaist.ac.jp

Abstract. The edge assembly crossover (EAX) is considered the best available crossover for traveling salesman problems (TSPs). In this paper, a modified EAX algorithm is proposed. The key idea is to maintain population diversity by eliminating any exchanges of edges by the crossover that does not contribute to an improved evaluation value. The proposed method is applied to several benchmark problems up to 4461 cities. Experimental results shows that the proposed method works better than other genetic algorithms using other improvements of the EAX. The proposed method can reach optimal solutions in most benchmark problems up to 2392 cities with probabilities higher than 90%. For the fnl4461 problem, this method can reach the optimal solution with a 60% probability for a population size of 300 – an extremely small population compared to that needed in previous studies.

1 Introduction

The traveling salesman problem (TSP) is a widely cited NP-hard optimization problem. Let $G = (V, E, w)$ be a weighted complete graph with n vertices, where V, E and w are the set of vertices, the set of edges, and the weights of edges, respectively. The optimal solution is defined as the Hamilton cycle (tour) having the shortest tour length, where the tour length is the sum of the weights of the edges included in the tour. When we want to find an optimal solution or near optimal solutions for a given TSP, genetic algorithms (GAs) are an effective type of approximate optimization algorithm [1] [2]. Many researchers have developed GAs to try to find solution candidates having the shortest possible tour length and to try to minimize the computational cost [1] [2] [3] [4].

When applying GAs for a particular problem, we must design crossover operators, mutation operators, and alternation-generation methods. Because the performance of a GA is highly dependent on the design of crossovers, much effort has gone into designing effective crossovers suitable for such problems. Several crossovers for TSPs have been proposed – EX [3] EXX [8], EAX [1], and so on. Many researchers [1] [4] [9] have found that EAX works particularly well, and several analyses have been done to explain why EAX works well [5] [6]. There have also been extensions of EAX aimed at improving performance by making minor changes to the EAX algorithm [4] [7] [9].

Many alternation-generation models have been proposed and applied experimentally. The alternation-generation model mainly consists of a *selection for mating* function which determines how parents are selected to generate children from the population, and a *selection for survival* function that determines which children survive. The model should be designed to take into account the trade-off between exploitation and exploration; that is, to maintain population diversity. Mutation operators are used to introduce diversity into the population. Huai et al. [4] proposed the use of a neighbor-join (NJ) operator as a mutation operator, and demonstrated that the EAX GA performance can be improved by incorporating this operator.

In this paper, we propose a modified EAX algorithm which can adjust the population diversity through its crossover procedure. The key modification is to restrict the exchange of edges by EAX under some set of criteria. If a child is generated from parents by EAX and then one of the parents is replaced by the child, then the two remaining individuals tend to be more similar to each other than was the case for the parents. This cause a loss of diversity in the population. If the gain in the evaluation value (the tour length) by the replacement is the same, the loss of the diversity between two individuals should be made as small as possible to maintain population diversity. The crossover proposed here is thus aimed at eliminating any exchange of edges that does not increase the evaluation value. Though maintaining the population diversity is usually the role of the alternation-generation model and the mutation, the proposed crossover plays this role in the procedure for the EAX algorithm.

Experimental results show that a GA using the proposed crossover with a population of 300 can reach optimal solutions in most TSP benchmark problems up to 2392 cities with probabilities higher than 90%. For the fnl4461 problem, the GA can reach the optimal solution with a 60% probability with a population of 300– an extremely small population compared to that needed in previous papers [9] [4].

The reminder of this paper is organized as follows. Section 2 look at existing work related to EAX, and Section 3 describes the proposed method. The experiments and results are described in Section 4. Section 5 provides a conclusion.

2 Related Work

In this section, we will briefly introduce related works of this paper. First we describe the algorithm of EAX and then introduce some extensions of EAX which have been improvements of EAX.

2.1 EAX

The EAX was proposed by Nagata et al. [1] as a crossover for TSPs. The EAX algorithm is briefly explained below and illustrated in Fig. 1. The details of the algorithm are available elsewhere [1]. In the paper, a *E-set* is constructed by randomly selecting *AB-cycles* with a probability of 0.5 in step 3 of the EAX algorithm. We call this *EAX-Rand*.

[EAX algorithm]

1. A pair of parents are denoted as tour-A and tour-B, and G_{AB} is defined as the complete graph constructed by merging tour-A and tour-B.
2. Divide edges on G_{AB} into *AB-cycles*, where an *AB-cycle* is defined as a closed loop on G_{AB} that can be generated by alternately tracing edges of tour-A and tour-B.
3. Construct an *E-set* by selecting *AB-cycles* according to a given rule.
4. Generate an intermediate solution by applying the *E-set* to tour-A; *i.e.* by removing tour-A's edges in the *E-set* from tour-A and adding tour-B's edges in the *E-set* to tour-A.
5. Modify the intermediate solution to create a valid tour by connecting its sub-tours. Two sub-tours are connected by deleting a single edge from each sub-tour and adding two edges to connect them. Which sub-tours are connected and which edges are reconnected are determined heuristically.

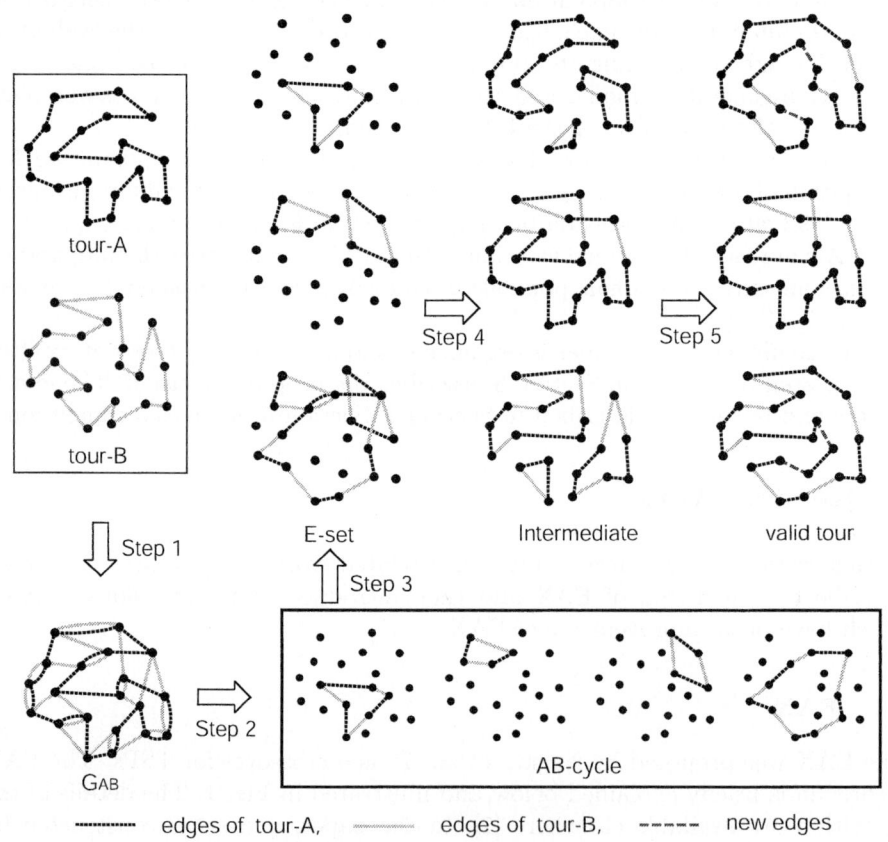

Fig. 1. The algorithm of EAX.

2.2 Some Extensions of EAX

EAX-Rand constructs an *E-set* by randomly selecting *AB-cycles*. Other selection methods and extensions have been proposed.

EAX-1AB. Another selection method where an *E-set* is constructed from a single *AB-cycle* was proposed in Nagata's doctoral thesis [7]. The intermediate solution is thus produced around tour-A; that is, the children are produced by removing a small number of edges from tour-A and adding the same number of edges from tour-B. We call this *EAX-1AB*. The experimental results in Section 4.2 show that the performance of the GA using *EAX-1AB* is better than that when using *EAX-Rand*. The same results are shown in [7] [9].

dMSXF. Ikeda et al. [9] proposed an extension of *EAX-1AB*. Specifically, they proposed a deterministic version of multi-step crossover fusion [10] and applied it to the *EAX-1AB*. This algorithm uses *EAX-1AB* iteratively to produce children from a pair of parents. The procedure is as follows.

1. Let A and B be parents. Set $A_1 = A$ and $k = 1$.
2. Generate μ children from parents A_k and B using *EAX-1AB*.
3. Select the best solution from among the μ children.
4. Let A_{k+1} be the best child selected in step 3, increment k, and goto step 2 until k reaches k_{max} or A_{k+1} equals B.

This crossover is called *EAX-dMSXF*. $k_{max} \times \mu$ children are generated from a pair of parents. They showed that the performance of a GA using *EAX-dMSXF* exceeded that of one using *EAX-Rand* or *EAX-1AB*, where (k_{max}, μ) was set to $(4, 6)$ or $(5, 8)$.

3 Proposed Methods

3.1 Motivation

Assume that the following alternation-generation model [9] is used.
[Alternation-Generation Model I]

(0) Set N_{pop} and N_{cross} as the population size and the number of children generated from a pair of parents, respectively.
(1) Set $t = 0$. Randomly generate N_{pop} solution candidates $x_1, x_2, \ldots, x_{N_{pop}}$.
(2) Shuffle the population randomly; *i.e.* the index is randomly assigned.
(3) For $i = 1, \ldots, N_{pop}$, x_i and x_{i+1} are selected as a pair of parents.
(4) For each pair of parents, generate N_{cross} children. The best individual among x_i and the children is added to the population instead of x_i.
(5) If no improvement in shortest tour length of the population is observed over 20 generations (the loop from (2) to (4)), then stop; else increment t and go to (2).

Let the parents x_i and x_{i+1} be denoted as A and B, respectively, at step (3). Also, let the distance $d(A,B)$ be defined by the number of different edges between A and B. When using *EAX-Rand*, the children C are constructed from A and B by randomly assembling A's edges and B's edges under the condition that the intermediate solution holds its restrictions. Of course, new edges are included in the children in step 5 of the EAX algorithm, but the ratio of the new edges is usually less than 2% [6]. Thus, the sum of $d(C,A)$ and $d(C,B)$ is close to $d(A,B)$, and $d(C,A)$ and $d(C,B)$ are almost equal. Then the distance $d(C,B)$ becomes half of $d(A,B)$ on average. Because A is replaced with C in step (3), the replacement tend to decrease the distance $d(x_i, x_{i+1})$ and course the loss of population diversity. Let $L(X)$ be defined as the tour length of a individual X. If a gain in the tour length caused by the replacement; *i.e.* $L(A)-L(C)$, is the same, the reduction of the distance between the two individuals; *i.e.* $d(A,B)-d(C,B)$, should be small for the purpose of preserving population diversity. On the other hand, if the reduction is the same, the gain should be large. Fig. 2 shows an example of this relation, where the horizontal axis represents the distance $d(C,B)$ and the vertical axis represents the gain from A to C. In this figure, A and B having tour lengths of 6834 and 6823, respectively and having $d(A,B)$ of 91 are sampled. The instance is rat575 (optimum is 6773). By applying the EAX algorithm, 29 *AB-cycles* are formed from these parents. In the figure, the cross-shaped points represent A and B. 100 children are generated by *EAX-Rand* which correspond to the triangular points. The twenty-four square points correspond to the children of *EAX-1AB*, where 29 children are generated, some of which are same as each other. The twenty-one black-diamond points correspond to the children of *EAX-dMSXF*, where 24 children $((k_{max}, \mu) = (4,6))$ were generated.

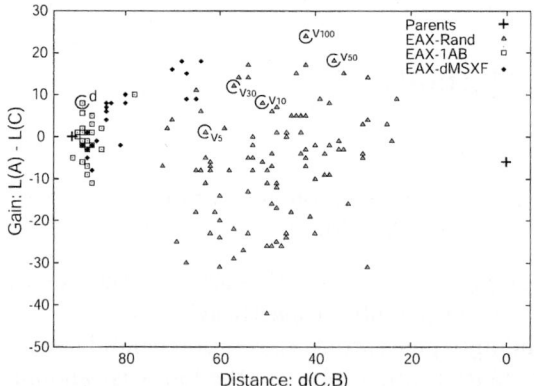

Fig. 2. The relation between the gain and the distance.

As shown in the figure, the points which correspond to the children of *EAX-Rand* appear in the middle between A and B along the horizontal axis. If we want to reduce the distance loss caused by the replacement, children should be generated around the parents A; that is, child C should be constructed from the large number of A's edges and the small number of B's edges. One simple method to do so is using *EAX-1AB*. Also in the figure, the points corresponding to *EAX-1AB* appear around A with few close to B. When choosing the child having the shortest tour length among the children generated by each of crossover, the gain with *EAX-Rand* is generally greater than that with *EAX-1AB*. On the other hand, the loss of distance with *EAX-Rand* between the two individuals is generally greater than that with *EAX-1AB*. *EAX-dMSXF* has intermediate characteristics between *EAX-Rand* and *EAX-1AB*. So there is a trade-off between the gain in tour length and the distance reduction, where four points are Pareto optimal solutions in Fig. 2. Though we cannot know appropriate trade-off in advance, we can expect a GA using *EAX* to improve its performance by evaluating children considering this trade-off.

3.2 Preliminary Experiments

One simple method to improve the performance of a GA using *EAX-Rand* with regard to the motivation given above is to increase the number of children for each pair of parents, which is denoted by N_{cross} in generation-alternation model I. In the Fig. 2, the points $v_n, (n = 5, \ldots, 100)$ are the best children among the first n children of 100 children generated by *EAX-Rand*. According to alternation-generation model I, n corresponds to N_{cross}, and v_n corresponds to the best child in step (4). As shown, the large number of n produce large gains, while the reductions in the distance caused by the replacement is independent of n. Therefore, we can expect the quality of the solution obtained by *EAX-Rand* to be improved by simply increasing N_{cross}. Although increasing N_{cross} raises the computational cost, at present we just want to justify the argument given in the motivation. Table 1 shows the results when N_{cross} was 5, 10, 30, 50, or 100, where N_{pop} was set to 300, and att532 and rat575 were used as the instances. Fifty trials are executed for each value of N_{cross}. As shown in the table, a larger N_{cross} raises the probability of obtaining optimal solutions.

Fig. 3 shows the population diversity against the average tour length in the population with various N_{corss}. The diversity is defined by the distance between two individuals average over all possible pair of parents in the population. These curves were averaged data over the fifty runs. As shown, the population diversity can be maintained by increasing N_{cross}. A curve corresponding N_{corss} of 100 is omitted because it closely overlap with that of 50. And then the performance cannot be improved by increasing N_{cross} from 50 to 100, that is shown in table 1.

3.3 Proposed Crossover

Though we cannot determine the appropriate trade-off between the gain and the distance reduction, we can establish criteria to determine which child should be selected to replace parent A. The first criterion we propose for evaluating children is the amount of gain achieved for a unit reduction in the distance. A child C generated from parents A and B is evaluated as follows:

Table 1. Comparison of the performance of the GA with varius N_{corss}. The meaning of each column is in Table 2.

	Npop	Ncross	opt.	err.(%)	gen.	time(s)		Npop	Ncross	opt.	err.(%)	gen.	time(s)
	300	5	8	0.035	26.4	6.1		300	5	0	0.033	28.9	8.3
	300	10	14	0.021	21.2	7.7		300	10	2	0.024	23.1	10.4
att532	300	30	16	0.014	15.9	12.8	rat575	300	30	8	0.018	18.1	18.4
	300	50	33	0.009	14.6	19.7		300	50	17	0.014	16.6	26.5
	300	100	34	0.008	13.1	32.8		300	100	18	0.012	15.1	45.2

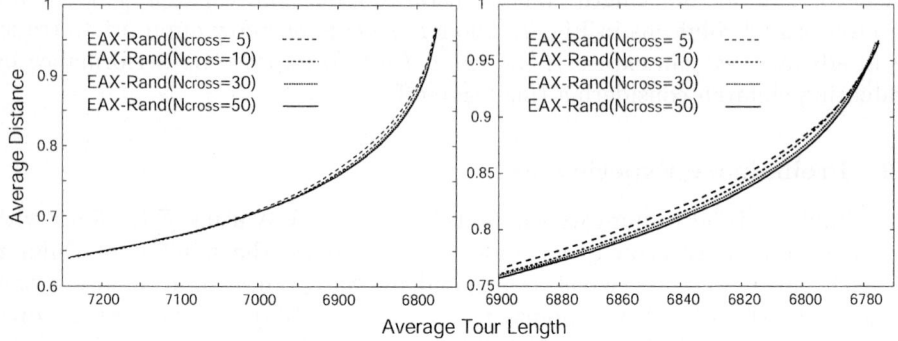

Fig. 3. The diversity against the average tour length of the population, where the instance rat575 was used. The right-hand graph is enlargement.

$$eval(C) = \frac{L(A) - L(C)}{d(A,B) - d(C,B)}$$

The individual having the highest evaluation value is selected as the best one in step (4) of alternation-generation model I. If the denominator is equal or less than zero, $eval(C)$ is given a value of zero. Though $d(A,B) - d(C,B)$ represents the number of B's edges introduced into the parent A to produce a child C, we use the number of B's edges in an *E-set* instead of $d(A,B) - d(C,B)$ to reduce the computational cost. Note that the number of B's edges in an *E-set* is equal to the number of B's edges introduced into tour-A to form an intermediate solution in step 4 of the EAX algorithm. Though this number is not exactly equal to $d(A,B) - d(C,B)$ because of the modification in step 5 of EAX algorithm, the difference is small.

When we consider three crossovers – *EAX-Rand, EAX-1AB*, and *EAX-dMSXF* – the most highly evaluated child tends to be generated by *EAX-1AB*. Fig. 2 illustrates this case, where point d is the most highly evaluated child. Therefore, we use *EAX-1AB* to generate children and evaluate them by the evaluation function defined above. We call this crossover *EAX-Dis*.

4 Experiments

4.1 The Detail of the Experiments

We applied the GA using *EAX-Dis* to several benchmark problems from the TSP library [11], and compared the performance with those of GAs using *EAX-Rand*, *EAX-1AB*, or *EAX-dMSXF*. The GAs were implemented in C++, and executed using 1.7 GHz Xeon processors. Alternation-generation model I was used. Fifty trials were executed for each instance. The population size N_{pop} was set to 300, and N_{cross} and (k_{max}, μ) were set to appropriate values for each crossovers, that are shown in the table 2. For large instances, N_{pop} was also set to 1000.

According to alternation-generation model I, if no improvement of the shortest tour length in the population is observed over 20 generations, a single trial will terminate. However, the GAs using *EAX-1AB* or *EAX-Dis* cannot converge upon the terminating condition because these crossovers cannot generate many children from a pair of parents for a lack of *AB-cycles* at the final stage of a run. So once the termination condition was satisfied, *AB-rand* was used instead of *EAX-1AB* or *EAX-Dis* and the search process continued until the population converged. The initial population was generated by a 2-opt local search to reduce the computational cost.

4.2 Results and Discussion

Table 2 shows the performance of the GA when using each of the four crossovers. Fig. 4 shows the population diversity against the average tour length in the population with the GA using each of four crossovers. As shown, the crossover that maintain the population diversity can reach optimal solutions with high probabilites. Especially, the average diversity of the GA using *EAX-Dis* is smallest than others. As a comparison of the column gen., the GA using *EAX-Dis* reaches best solutions slower than the others; nevertheless the computational cost is not much higher than the others because this crossover creates children less than N_{cross} in most case; *i.e.* the number of *AB-cycles* is less than N_{cross}. Therefore, the GA using *EAX-Dis* outperforms the GAs using other EAX-based crossovers.

Table 2 shows that the GA using the proposed crossover with a population size of 300 can reach optimal solutions in the TSP benchmark problems ecept for u1432 instance up to 2392 cities with probabilities higher than 90%. For fnl4461 problem, the GA can reach the optimal solution with a 60% probability with a population size of 300 This population size is extremely small compared to that needed in previous studies [4] [9] [7]. When a population size of 1000 was used for the pcb3038 and fnl4461 problems, the GA could find optimal solutions 49 and 50 times, respectively, over 50 trials.

5 Conclusion

In this paper, we have proposed a new crossover named *EAX-Dis* for solving TSPs. This crossover is the result of a minor change to EAX. The proposed

Table 2. Comparisons of the performance of the GAs using four crossovers. The column headed opt. shows the number of trials that can reach optimal solutions. The err. shows the average excess from the optimal tour length. The gen. shows the average generation(the loop from step (2) to (4) in Model I) required to reach the best individual in each trial. The time shows the avearged execution time required for a run, where all GAs were implemented in C++ and executed using 1.7 GHz Xeon processors.

instance	Npop	Ncross	opt.	err.(%)	gen.	time(s)	instance	Npop	Ncross	opt.	err.(%)	gen.	time(s)
att532	300	50	33	0.0097	14.6	19	att532	300	30	26	0.0152	35.1	12
rat575	300	50	17	0.0141	16.6	26	rat575	300	30	35	0.0047	42.3	17
u724	300	50	45	0.0026	15.3	40	u724	300	30	45	0.0022	35.7	19
mv1084	300	50	11	0.0099	19.0	67	mv1084	300	30	24	0.0083	49.3	56
pcb1173	300	50	35	0.0033	21.3	72	pcb1173	300	30	37	0.0020	63.3	48
u1432	300	50	12	0.0259	20.6	212	u1432	300	30	12	0.0283	81.8	89
mv1748	300	50	23	0.0224	24.3	323	mv1748	300	30	18	0.0308	88.7	200
pr2392	300	50	29	0.0043	27.3	413	pr2392	300	30	40	0.0015	117.1	328
pcb3038	300	50	0	0.0165	38.6	622	pcb3038	300	30	8	0.0077	182.8	794
	1000	50	0	0.0095	35.7	1859		1000	30	12	0.0047	177.6	2321
fnl4461	300	50	0	0.0546	66.0	2637	fnl4461	300	30	2	0.0065	347.3	3095
	1000	50	0	0.0237	58.8	7064		1000	30	4	0.0021	313.8	8742

instance	Npop	k_{max}	opt.	err.(%)	gen.	time(s)	instance	Npop	Ncross	opt.	err.(%)	gen.	time(s)
att532	300	4, 6	31	0.0103	20.1	21	att532	300	30	48	0.0010	49.5	17
rat575	300	4, 6	45	0.0014	25.2	25	rat575	300	30	50	0.0000	61.6	24
u724	300	4, 6	46	0.0016	20.0	28	u724	300	30	50	0.0000	54.0	29
mv1084	300	4, 6	23	0.0095	24.4	66	mv1084	300	30	47	0.0011	62.2	77
pcb1173	300	4, 6	28	0.0031	35.3	93	pcb1173	300	30	49	0.0000	85.1	70
u1432	300	5, 8	22	0.0200	45.3	140	u1432	300	30	26	0.0105	110.8	150
mv1748	300	5, 8	36	0.0072	32.3	211	mv1748	300	30	50	0.0000	96.7	253
pr2392	300	5, 8	42	0.0019	39.8	302	pr2392	300	30	50	0.0000	164.2	464
pcb3038	300	5, 8	4	0.0090	70.2	691	pcb3038	300	30	34	0.0013	262.1	1129
	1000	5, 8	20	0.0027	72.0	2146		1000	30	49	0.0000	252.9	3074
fnl4461	300	5, 8	2	0.0820	217.1	3387	fnl4461	300	30	29	0.0013	535.3	4730
	1000	5, 8	9	0.0019	194.6	10369		1000	30	50	0.0000	527.8	11843

method is based on particular observations regarding the replacement of parents with children and the resulting trade-off between the gain and the reduction of distance. For a child to replace a parent there should be a large gain and the resulting reduction of distance between the two individuals should be small. Based on these requirements, we have proposed a method that generates children through *EAX-1AB* and evaluates the children based on the gain for a unit reduction in the distance. Experimental results have shown that a GA using the proposed crossover outperforms a GA using other crossovers that also present minor changes to EAX. When using a population size of 300, the GA using *EAX-Dis* reached optimal solutions in most TSP benchmark problems up to 2392 cities with probabilities higher than 90%. For fnl4461 problem, the GA reached the optimal solution with a 60% probability with a population size of 300; this is much smaller population than needed in previous studies.

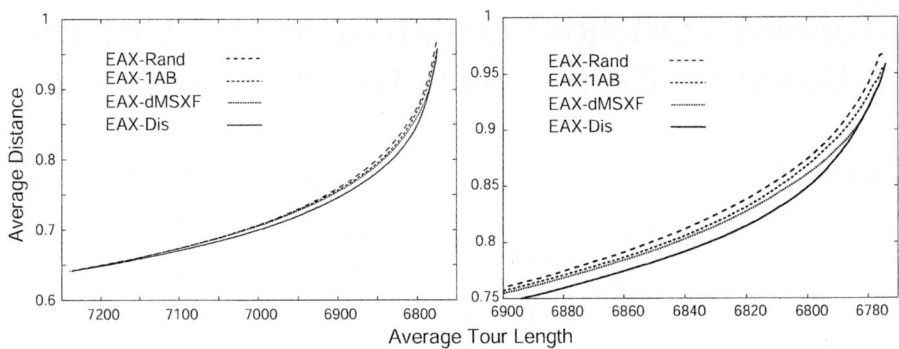

Fig. 4. The diversity against the average tour length of the population, where the instance rat575 was used. The right-hand graph is enlargement.

References

1. Y. Nagata and S. Kobayashi, Edge Assembly Crossover: A High-power Genetic Algorithm for the Traveling Salesman Problem, Proc. of the 7th Int. Conference on Genetic Algorithms, pp. 450-457, 1997.
2. P. Merz and B. Freisleben: Genetic Local Search for the TSP: New Results, Proc. of the 1997 IEEE Int. Conf. on Evolutionary Computation, pp.159-163 (1997).
3. D. Whitley, T. Starkweather, and D. Fuquay, Scheduling Problems and Traveling Salesman: The Genetic Edge Recombination Operator, Proc. of the 3rd Int. Conference on Genetic Algorithms, pp. 133-140, 1989.
4. H.K. Tsai, J.M. Yang, and C.Y. Kao, Solving Traveling Salesman Problems by Combining Global and Local Search Mechanisms, Proc. of the the 2002 Congress on Evolutionary Computation, pp. 12920-1295, 2002.
5. J. Watson, C. Poss D. Whitley and so on, The Traveling Salesrep Problem, Edge Assembly Crossover, and 2-opt, Proc. of the fifth Int. Conference on Parallel Probrem Solving from Nature, pp. 823-833, 2000.
6. Y. Nagata, Criteria for designing crossovers for TSP, Proc. of the 2004 Congress on Evolutionary Computation, , (to be appeared), 2004.
7. Y. Nagata, Genetic Algorithm for Traveling Salesman Problem using Edge Assembly Crossover: its Proposal and Analysis, Doctoral thesis, 2000.
8. K. Maekawa, N. Mori, H. Kita, and H.Nishikawa, A Genetic Solution for the Traveling Salesman Problem by Means of a Thermodynamical Selection Rule, Proc. 1996 IEEE Int. Conference on Evolutionary Computation, pp. 529-534, 1996.
9. K. Ideda and S. Kobayashi, Deterministic Multi-step Crossover Fusion: A Handy Crossover Composition for GAs, Proc. of the seventh Int. Conference on Parallel Probrem Solving from Nature, pp. 162-171, 2002.
10. T. Yamada and N. Ryohei, Scheduling by Genetic Local Search with Multi-Step Crossover, Proc. of the fourth Int. Conference on Parallel Probrem Solving from Nature, 1996.
11. TSPLIB95, http://www.iwr.uni-heidelberg.de/iwr/compt/soft/TSPLIB95/TSPLIB.html.

Topology-Oriented Design of Analog Circuits Based on Evolutionary Graph Generation

Masanori Natsui[1], Naofumi Homma[1,*], Takafumi Aoki[1], and Tatsuo Higuchi[2]

[1] Graduate School of Information Sciences, Tohoku University
Aoba-yama 05, Sendai 980-8579, Japan
[2] Faculty of Engineering, Tohoku Institute of Technology
Sendai 982-8577, Japan

Abstract. This paper presents an efficient graph-based evolutionary optimization technique called Evolutionary Graph Generation (EGG), and its application to the topology-oriented design of analog circuit structures. An important feature of EGG is its capability to optimize general graph structures directly instead of encoding the structures into indirect representations, such as bit strings and trees. The potential of the proposed approach is demonstrated through the experimental design of MOS current mirrors.

1 Introduction

Electronic design automation (EDA) has matured as a technology to be universally accepted for producing highly integrated VLSI systems. However, there still remain many difficult design problems to be addressed in the advanced SoC (System on Chip) era. For example, further research and development are needed to establish systematic automated techniques for synthesizing high-level processor architectures, high-performance arithmetic datapath circuits, transistor-level circuits for high-performance logic, analog circuits and analog/digital-mixed circuits, etc. Design of these structures still requires the knowledge and experience of the experts who had trained in a particular way to understand basic characteristics of hardware algorithms and circuit/device technologies.

We have proposed a new approach to designing circuit structures using an evolutionary optimization technique called Evolutionary Graph Generation (EGG) (see [1–3] for earlier discussions on this topic). Key features of the proposed EGG system are to employ general graph structures as individuals and to introduce new evolutionary operations for manipulating the individual graph structures directly without encoding them into other indirect representations, such as bit strings used in Genetic Algorithm (GA)[4] and trees used in Genetic Programming (GP)[5]. The potential of EGG has already been investigated through the design of digital circuits, such as high-performance parallel multipliers [3], pipelined datapaths [6].

---

* The author is also with PRESTO, JST 4-1-8 Honcho Kawaguchi, Saitama, Japan.

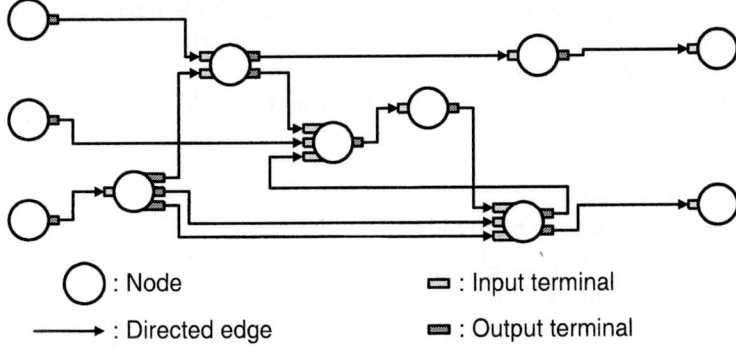

Fig. 1. Circuit graph.

In this paper, we present an application of EGG to analog circuit design. It is well known that an analog circuit inherently involves trade-off among a large number of performance metrics and the performance is determined by the complex and nonlinear nature of the relations between the topology and parameter values (e.g. device sizes) of a circuit. Therefore, the analog circuit design often requires simultaneous optimization of circuit topology and parameter values. This is the major motivation to introduce evolutionary optimization techniques for the design automation.

There are already some approaches to the evolutionary design of analog circuit structures [5,7]. The reference [5] describes various analog circuit design including analog filters and amplifiers by means of Genetic Programming. Also, the reference [7] proposes a method of representing electronic circuit structures by "linear representation" and its application to analog circuit synthesis using Genetic Algorithm. These approaches appear to perform both topology and parameter optimization equally. Our approach, on the other hand, performs topology-oriented optimization for pruning the search space of analog circuits. In the EGG system, we employ a set of functional nodes with parameter values (e.g. aspect ratio of a transistor), considering a limited search for parameter values. The performance of the EGG system is demonstrated through an experimental synthesis of nMOS current mirrors. The experimental result shows that our approach successfully generates better circuit structures depending on the target characteristics.

2 Basic Concept of EGG

The EGG system has been designed to generate *circuit graphs* as individuals, where each individual represents a specific circuit structure. A circuit graph consists of nodes and directed edges as shown in Fig. 1. Every node has its own name, the function type and input/output terminals. We assume that every directed edge must connect one output terminal (of a node) and one input terminal (of another node), and that each terminal has one edge connection at most.

A circuit graph is said to be *complete* if all the terminals have an edge connection. In order to guarantee valid circuit structures, all the circuit graphs used in the EGG system are complete circuit graphs.

More precisely, a circuit graph is defined as $G = (N^G, T_O^G, T_I^G, \nu_O^G, \nu_I^G, \epsilon^G)$, where

N^G : the set of nodes,
T_O^G : the set of output terminals,
T_I^G : the set of input terminals,
ν_O^G : mapping from T_O^G to N^G;
   $n = \nu_O^G(u)$ means that the output terminal u ($\in T_O^G$) belongs to the node n ($\in N^G$),
ν_I^G : mapping from T_I^G to N^G;
   $n = \nu_I^G(v)$ means that the input terminal v ($\in T_I^G$) belongs to the node n ($\in N^G$),
ϵ^G : bijection from S_O^G to S_I^G, where $S_O^G \subseteq T_O^G$, $S_I^G \subseteq T_I^G$ and $|S_O^G| = |S_I^G|$;
   $v = \epsilon^G(u)$ means that the output terminal u ($\in S_O^G$) and the input terminal v ($\in S_I^G$) have a directed edge connection.

Note here that S_O^G (or S_I^G) is the set of output (or input) terminals having edge connections. The circuit graph G is said to be complete if and only if $S_O^G = T_O^G$ and $S_I^G = T_I^G$, where S_O^G and S_I^G are the domain and the range of ϵ^G, respectively.

Figure 2 shows the overall procedure of the EGG system. At first, the system generates embryonic circuit graphs randomly to form the initial population $P(0)$. After generating the initial population, the system evaluates their fitness of the circuit graphs in terms of behavior or characteristics. Then the circuit graphs having higher scores are selected to perform the evolutionary operations of *crossover* and *mutation*. The offsprings generated by the evolutionary operations form the populations $C(t)$ and $M(t)$, where $C(t)$ and $M(t)$ are obtained from crossovers and mutations, respectively. The crossover, illustrated in Fig. 3 (a), recombines two parent graphs into two new graphs. The mutation, on the other hand, selects the subgraph randomly and replaces it with a randomly generated subgraph that is compatible with the original subgraph as shown in Fig. 3 (b). Note that the system is designed to preserve the completeness property during these variation operations. The individuals for the next generation $P(t+1)$ are selected from the current population $P(t)$, $C(t)$ and $M(t)$. This evaluation-and-reproduction cycle is repeated for a specified number of generations.

We develop a generic object-oriented framework for EGG system, which can be systematically modified for different design problems by inheriting the framework class templates. The current version of EGG framework used in this paper is open to the public at http://www.aoki.ecei.tohoku.ac.jp/egg/.

```
program EGG_System_Flow
  begin
    t := 0;   { t: number of generations }
    initialize(P(t));   { P(t): population }
    evaluate(P(t));
    while t ≤ max. num. of generations do
      begin
        C(t) := crossover(P(t));   { C(t): offsprings generated by crossover }
        M(t) := mutation(P(t));    { M(t): offsprings generated by mutation}
        evaluate(C(t) ∪ M(t));
        P(t + 1) := select(C(t) ∪ M(t) ∪ P(t));
        t := t + 1
      end
end.
```

Fig. 2. EGG system flow.

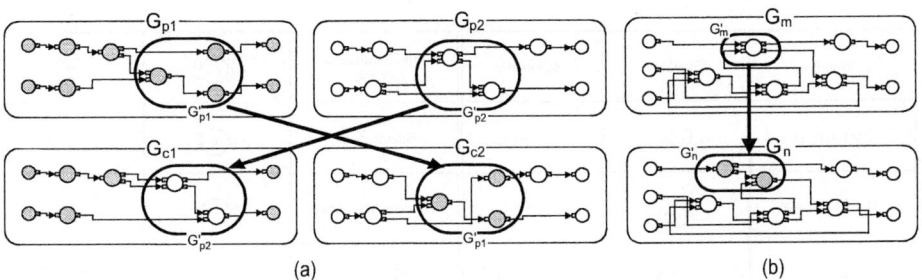

Fig. 3. Examples of evolutionary operations: (a) crossover, (b) mutation.

3   Transistor-Level Circuit Design of Current Mirrors

This section presents the experimental synthesis of analog circuits using EGG. The design specification considered here is a nMOS current mirror. A current mirror is one of the fundamental building blocks of analog circuits including operational amplifiers, operational transconductance amplifiers and biasing networks. Thus, the realization of a high performance current mirror plays an important part in the successful design of analog circuits. The main function of current mirrors is to produce an output current equal to the input current. Desirable characteristics of current mirrors are: (i) small DC voltage drop at the input, (ii) high output impedance, (iii) low output saturation voltage, (iv) good frequency response and (v) linear current transfer ratio. Due to the trade-offs among these characteristics, there are various possible choices for the current mirror structure as shown in Fig. 4.

In this experiment, the EGG system can be implemented mainly by setting the following items: (i) functional nodes contained in circuit graphs, (ii) methods for generating initial circuit graphs, (iii) fitness function for evaluating the electrical behavior of circuit graphs and (iv) system parameter values. Each item is determined as follows in this experiment.

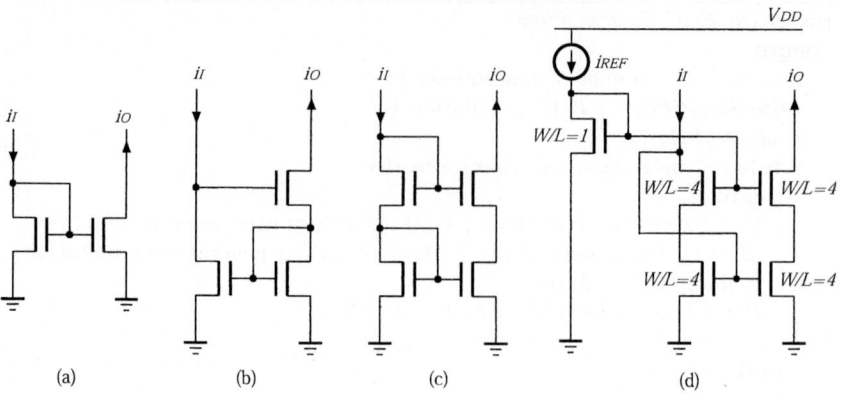

Fig. 4. Current mirrors: (a) a simple current mirror, (b) a Wilson current mirror, (c) a cascode current mirror and (d) a wide-swing cascode current mirror.

Name	Symbol	Schematic			
Operand input	X_1 (IN) Y_1	X_1 —— Y_1	Branch node	X_1 (B) Y_1/Y_2	X_1 ⊣ Y_1/Y_2
Operand output	X_1 (OUT) Y_1	X_1 —— Y_1	Connection node	X_1/X_2 (C) Y_1	X_1/X_2 ⊢ Y_1
Ground	X_1 (GND)	X_1 ⏚	Current source node	(I) Y_1	V_{DD} / Y_1
nMOS transistor node	X_1/X_2 (n) Y_1	X_2 ⊣ Y_1 / X_1	Bias voltage node	(V) Y_1	V_{DD} / Y_1

(first row of schematic column): nMOS transistor pair node — $X_1/X_2/X_3$ (2-n) Y_1/Y_2 — $X_1/X_2/X_3$ ⊢ Y_1/Y_2

Fig. 5. Functional nodes.

We have determined a set of functional nodes shown in Fig. 5 for transistor-level synthesis of various current mirrors. We assume that each transistor in the nMOS transistor node, nMOS transistor pair node, current source node and bias voltage node has the aspect ratio W/L as a design parameter. For limited parameter optimization, W/L takes one of the quantized values from 1, 2, 3, 4 and 5 with $L = 0.6 \mu m$ in our design.

At the initialization stage, the system creates the embryonic circuit graphs consisting of functional nodes shown in Fig. 5. The generation process can be done by the following three steps: (i) select an initial set of functional nodes randomly, (ii) add another set of nodes to the initial set for adjusting the number of terminals so as to satisfy the completeness property, and (iii) make random edge connections among these terminals. The generated circuit graph is translated into the corresponding SPICE netlist, which is simulated to analyze its electrical behavior and characteristics.

During the evolution process, the EGG system sometimes generates invalid circuit structures that cannot be simulated by SPICE. It is difficult not to generate such invalid structures since the system is designed to search for a wide variety of circuit structures. Using the domain specific knowledge about the target structures, we can eliminate invalid structures, which may have some adverse effects on the evolution process. In this experiment, the EGG system assigns the worst value of fitness to an individual without the SPICE simulation if the individual has any of the following topological characteristics: (i) a direct connection between the gate of a nMOS transistor and the ground, and (ii) a closed loop between the source of a nMOS transistor and the drain of itself. That makes possible to reduce the total computation time.

The individuals are evaluated by a combination of four different evaluation metrics: (i) i_I-i_O characteristic, (ii) v_O-i_O characteristic, (iii) transient response, and (iv) circuit area. We define the synthetic evaluation function F as follows:

$$F = \sum_{i=1}^{4} w_i F_i,$$

where F_1 evaluates the accuracy of i_I-i_O characteristic in comparison with the ideal characteristic, F_2 evaluates the output saturation voltage investigated through the DC transfer analysis, F_3 evaluates the settling time obtained from the transient response of $i_O(t)$ to a step input $i_I(t)$, F_4 evaluates the area efficiency of evolved circuits, and w_i is a weighting coefficient for F_i. Each F_i takes a value between 0 and 1. The value of 1 shows that the evolved circuit has an acceptable performance in terms of F_i. We give the detailed explanation for each function in the following.

The function F_1 aims to minimize the error between the obtained and ideal i_I-i_O characteristics. The i_I-i_O characteristic is obtained by a DC transfer analysis, in which the input current i_I is swept from the minimum to the maximum current at n sampling points. F_1 is defined as

$$F_1 = \frac{1}{1+E}, \qquad (1)$$

where E (≥ 0) indicates the average error over the whole sampling points. E is given by

$$E = \frac{C_1}{n} \sum_{k=1}^{n} max(0, S(k) - T(k)), \qquad (2)$$

where n is the number of sampling points, $S(k) = |\tilde{i}_O(k) - i_O(k)|$ is the absolute value of the error between the obtained and ideal output currents at a sampling point k, $T(k) = \epsilon^{accept}|i_O(k)|$ is the acceptable error range at a sampling point k, C_1 is a constant which determines a sensitivity of F_1 to E, and ϵ^{accept} is a constant which determines the acceptable error range. In our experiment, $C_1 = 10^7$ and $\epsilon^{accept} = 10^{-2}$. F_1 is equal to 1 if $S(k) \leq T(k)$ at any sampling point k.

The function F_2 aims to minimize the output saturation voltage $\tilde{v}_O$, which is obtained by a DC transfer analysis over the range of $0[V]$ to $v_O^{max}[V]$. F_2 is

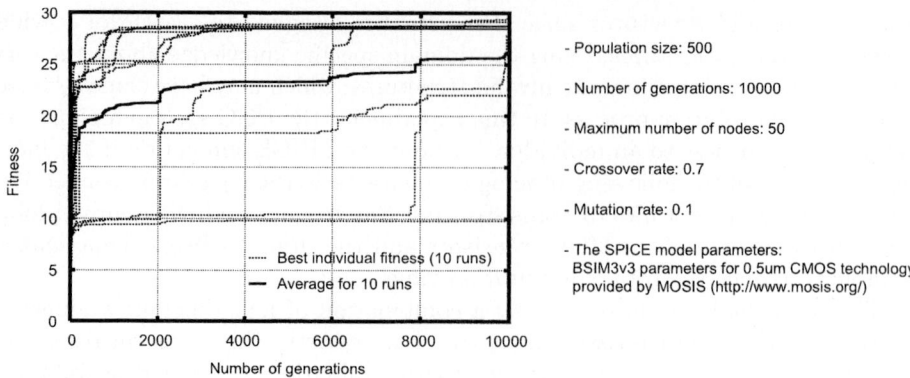

Fig. 6. Fitness transition.

defined as

$$F_2 = min(1, \frac{v_O^{max} - \tilde{v}_O}{v_O^{max} - v_O^{accept}}), \tag{3}$$

where v_O^{accept} is the acceptable value of $\tilde{v}_O$. In our experiment, $v_O^{accept} = 0.5$.

The function F_3 evaluates the settling time of an evolved circuit $\tilde{t}$, which is obtained by a trangent analysis over the range of 0[s] to t^{max}[s]. The function F_3 is defined as

$$F_3 = min(1, \frac{t^{max} - \tilde{t}}{t^{max} - t^{accept}}), \tag{4}$$

where t^{accept} is the acceptable value of $\tilde{t}$. In our experiment, $t^{accept} = 0$.

The function F_4 is defined as

$$F_4 = \frac{1}{A}, \tag{5}$$

where A is the circuit area roughly estimated from the sum of all transistor sizes.

Using a set of coefficients $(w_1, w_2, w_3, w_4) = (10, 10, 10, 1)$, we have performed 10 distinct evolutionary runs. The experimental condition indicates that we emphsize the importance of I/O characteristics in the generated current mirrors. Figure 6 shows the transition of the best individual fitness. Figure 7 shows a current mirror generated by the EGG system. We observe that the current mirror is composed of a wide-swing cascode current mirror and its compensation circuit for improving low voltage operation. Figure 8 illustrates the characteristics of the evolved current mirror and those of conventional current mirrors shown in Fig. 4. Note that parameter values of each conventional current mirror are optimized by an automatic sizing software called *NeoCircuit* of Neolinear, Inc.. Compared with the conventional current mirrors, the evolved current mirror has better DC characteristic, lower output saturation voltage and faster transient response under the experimental condition. The experimental result indicates that the

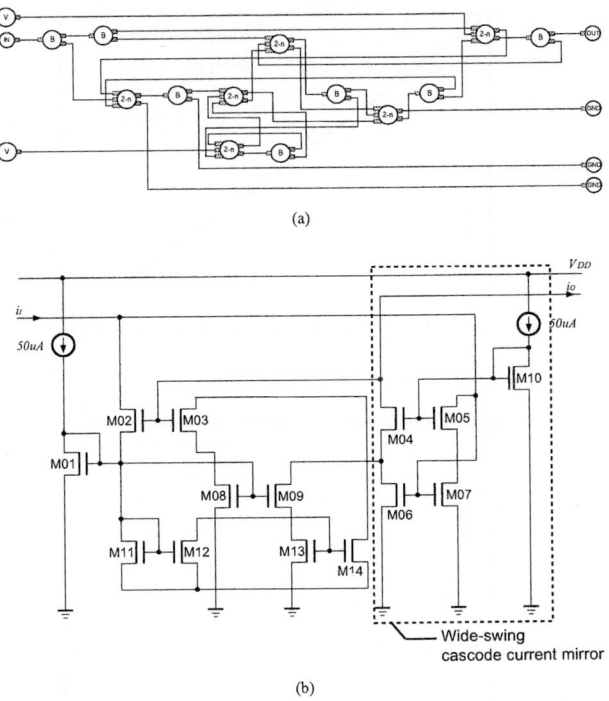

Fig. 7. Solution generated by the EGG system with four evaluation metrics: (a) generated circuit graph, (b) circuit structure corresponding to the graph (a).

topology-oriented optimization can generate higher-performance circuits than the conventional ones having optimal transistor sizes.

The performance of the obtained circuit can be enhanced using a commercially available software such as NeoCircuit. Table 1 shows a set of aspect ratios in evolved current mirror and one optimized by NeoCircuit. Note that NeoCircuit explores a search space with twice the precision of EGG, that is, an aspect ratio W/L takes one of the quantized values between 1 and 10 with a step of 1 ($L = 0.3\mu m$). Table 2 shows the performance of the current mirrors described above. As shown in Tab.2, the performance of the evolved current mirror can be further improved by the appropriate transistor sizing. Thus, the two-stage optimization approach can be effective in applying evolutionary optimization techniques to the design problems of analog circuits.

Table 1. Aspect ratios of two current mirrors: (a) the evolved current mirror by EGG and (b) parameter optimized design by NeoCircuit.

	M01	M02	M03	M04	M05	M06	M07	M08	M09	M10	M11	M12	M13	M14
(a)	2	3	3	5	5	5	5	5	5	2	3	3	4	4
(b)	2	1.5	1.5	5	5	5	5	5	5	2	2	2	4	4

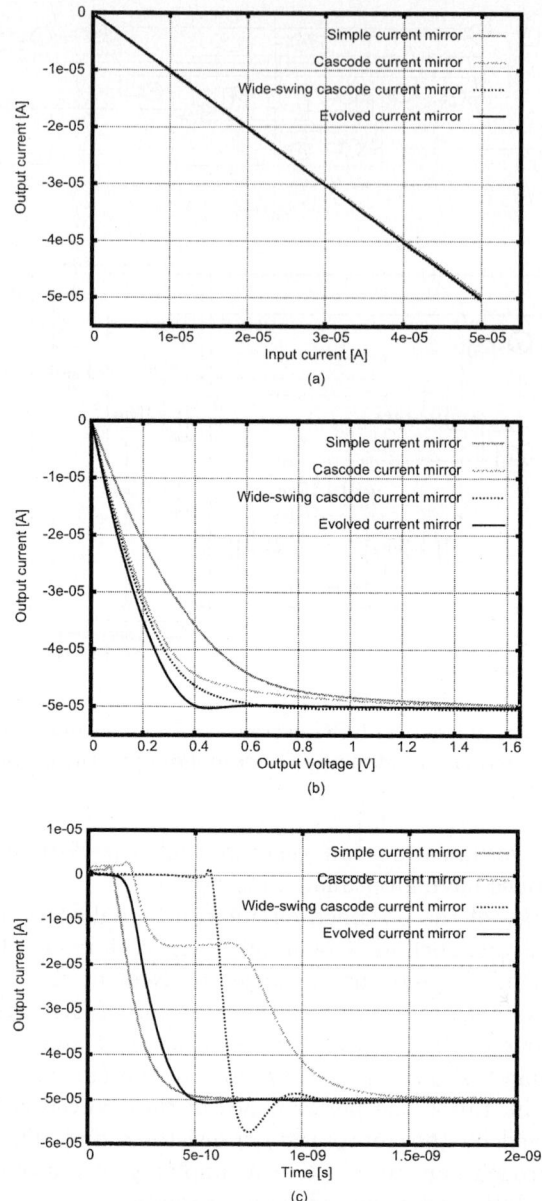

Fig. 8. Characteristics of various current mirrors: (a) i_I-i_O characteristic, (b) v_O-i_O characteristic and (c) transient response.

4 Conclusion

In this paper, we have presented an efficient graph-based evolutionary optimization technique called Evolutionary Graph Generation (EGG), and its application

Table 2. Comparison between (a) the performance of the evolved current mirror and (b) that of a parameter optimized design.

	Mean error[A]	Output saturation voltage[V]	Settling time[s]	Circuit area
(a)	2.02E-07	0.391	4.67E-10	58.7
(b)	2.20E-08	0.396	4.80E-10	52.7

to the synthesis of analog circuits using transistor-level components. The experimental result show that the topology-oriented optimization can be effective for the transistor-level design of current mirrors. For more practical applications, we need to introduce a systematic way of determining the degree of search for parameter values in the EGG system. Further investigations are now being conducted to develop the new type of EGG system in cooperation with analog circuit sizing techniques in the near future.

References

1. T. Aoki, N. Homma, and T. Higuchi, "Evolutionary design of arithmetic circuits," *IEICE Trans. Fundamentals*, Vol. E82-A, No. 5, pp. 798–806, May 1999.
2. N. Homma, T. Aoki, and T. Higuchi, "Evolutionary synthesis of fast constant-coefficient multipliers," *IEICE Trans. Fundamentals*, Vol. E83-A, No. 9, pp. 1767–1777, September 2000.
3. N. Homma, T. Aoki, and T. Higuchi, "Evolutionary graph generation system with transmigration capability and its application to arithmetic circuit synthesis," *IEE Proc. Circuits Devices Syst.*, Vol. 149, No. 2, pp. 97–104, April 2002.
4. F. J. Miller, P. Thomson, and T. Fogarty, "Designing electronic circuits using evolutionary algorithms. Arithmetic circuits: A case study," *Genetic Algorithms and Evolution Strategies in Engineering and Computer Science*, pp. 105–131, September 1997.
5. R. J. Koza, H. F. III, Bennett, D. Andre, A. M. Keane, and F. Dunlap, "Automated synthesis of analog electrical circuits by means of genetic programming," *IEEE Trans. Evolutionary Computation*, Vol. 1, No. 2, pp. 109–128, July 1997.
6. M. Motegi, N. Homma, T. Aoki, and T. Higuchi, "Evolutionary graph generation system and its application to bit-serial arithmetic circuit synthesis," *Parallel Problem Solving from Nature - PPSN VII, Lecture Notes in Computer Science 2439*, Springer-Verlag, pp. 831–840, September 2002.
7. D. J. Lohn and S. P. Colombano, "A circuit representation technique for automated circuit design", *IEEE Trans. Evolutionary Computation*, Vol. 3, No. 3, pp. 205–219, September 1999.

A Mixed Bayesian Optimization Algorithm with Variance Adaptation

Jiri Ocenasek[1], Stefan Kern[2], Nikolaus Hansen[2], and Petros Koumoutsakos[1,2]

[1] Computational Laboratory (CoLab), Swiss Federal Institute of Technology ETH
[2] Institute of Computational Science, Swiss Federal Institute of Technology ETH
Hirschengraben 84, 8092 Zürich, Switzerland
{jirio,skern,hansenn,petros}@inf.ethz.ch

Abstract. This paper presents a hybrid evolutionary optimization strategy combining the Mixed Bayesian Optimization Algorithm (MBOA) with variance adaptation as implemented in Evolution Strategies. This new approach is intended to circumvent some of the deficiences of MBOA with unimodal functions and to enhance its adaptivity. The Adaptive MBOA algorithm – AMBOA – is compared with the Covariance Matrix Adaptation Evolution Strategy (CMA-ES). The comparison shows that, in continuous domains, AMBOA is more efficient than the original MBOA algorithm and its performance on separable unimodal functions is comparable to that of CMA-ES.

1 Introduction

A class of Evolutionary Algorithms (EAs) implement probability distributions to identify the underlying relationship of the objective function with its parameters in order to accelerate the convergence rate of the algorithms. Estimation of Distribution Algorithms (EDAs) [1–3] sample a probability distribution learned from the fittest solutions. A class of EDAs use a Bayesian network with a local structure in the form of a decision graph to model the relationship between discrete parameters on a global level. In addition to that, the Mixed Bayesian Optimization Algorithm (MBOA) [4] is able to deal with discrete and continuous parameters simultaneously by using a Gaussian kernel model to capture the local distribution of the continuous parameters.

MBOA has been shown to perform successfully for several combinatorial problems [5]. However, on certain continuous benchmarks – including unimodal functions – MBOA is outperformed [6] by Evolution Strategies, like Covariance Matrix Adaptation ES (CMA-ES) [7, 8]. The reason for this is attributed to the relative deficiency of MBOA in adapting the variance of the search distribution. In order to overcome this deficiency we propose a new variance adaptation mechanism which significantly increases the efficiency of MBOA in continuous domains.

Section 2 introduces the principles of the MBOA algorithm. In Section 3 we analyze the main difference between the estimation of variance in MBOA and in CMA-ES and propose an improved algorithm, AMBOA, with robust adaptation of the estimated variance. In Section 4 we present experimental results that demonstrate the successful design of AMBOA.

2 Mixed Bayesian Optimization Algorithm (MBOA)

2.1 Main Principles of MBOA

MBOA belongs to the class of Estimation of Distribution Algorithms (EDAs) that explore the search space by sampling a probability distribution that is developed during the optimization. MBOA works with a population of N candidate solutions. Each generation, typically the $N/2$ fittest individuals are used for the model building and $N/2$ new solutions are generated from the model. These offspring individuals are evaluated and incorporated into the original population, replacing some of the old ones. This process is repeated until the termination criteria are met.

A Bayesian network (BN) is one of the general models to express discrete probability distributions. The underlying probability distribution $p(\boldsymbol{X})$ is approximated as the product of conditional probability distributions of each parameter X_i given $\boldsymbol{\Pi}_i$ – the variables that influence X_i

$$p(X_0, ..., X_{n-1}) = \prod_{i=0}^{n-1} p(X_i|\boldsymbol{\Pi}_i). \qquad (1)$$

We use upper case symbols X_i to denote the i-th design parameter (or the i-th gene in EA terminology or the i-th random variable in mathematical terminology) whereas lower-case symbols x_i denote a realization of this parameter. Boldface symbols distinguish vectors from scalars. $\boldsymbol{x}_j^{(g)}$ denotes the j-th individual in generation number g.

The construction of an optimal BN from the population of candidate solutions is itself an NP hard problem [9], and EDAs usually use either an incremental or a greedy version of the learning algorithm to accelerate the BN construction. MBOA uses the latter approach.

MBOA can be formulated for continuous and discrete domains. In binary domain it performs similarly to the hierarchical Bayesian Optimization Algorithm [10], but it employs a different model building algorithm which ensures efficient parallelization. In continuous domains, MBOA searches for a decomposition of the search space into partitions where the parameters seem to be mutually independent. This decomposition is captured globally by the Bayesian network model and Gaussian kernel distributions are used locally to approximate the values in each resulting partition.

2.2 Construction of the Continuous Probabilistic Model in MBOA

MBOA attempts to capture the local conditional probability density functions of the continuous parameters $f(X_i|\boldsymbol{\Pi}_i)$. Each $f(X_i|\boldsymbol{\Pi}_i)$ is captured in the form of a decision tree [11], which is more efficient than the traditional way of keeping $\boldsymbol{\Pi}_i$ explicitly in the form of a dependency graph and using tabular representations for local conditional distributions.

We will describe how the decision tree for a concrete parameter X_i is constructed from the population D. In particular, for each parameter X_i the set of influencing variables $\boldsymbol{\Pi}_i$ has to be determined. Since it is computationally expensive to test independence directly in the continuous domain MBOA recursively transforms the problem into binary domain.

First, X_i and all continuous parameters that are available as the potential candidates to form $\boldsymbol{\Pi}_i$ are temporarily converted into new binary variables by defining continuous split boundaries on them. The method for finding the boundaries is presented in [4]. As soon as all variables are discrete, the Bayesian-Dirichlet metrics with likelihood equivalence (BDe) [12] is used to determine the variable that influences X_i the most. The chosen variable is then used for splitting the population D and the construction is recursively repeated for both branches of the new split. The recursion stops when for all variables the BDe score (decreased by the complexity penalty term) returns a negative value.

This results in a decomposition of the $f(X_i|\boldsymbol{\Pi}_i)$ domain into axis-parallel partitions where X_i is assumed to be decorrelated from the variables in $\boldsymbol{\Pi}_i$ and can be approximated by univariate probability density functions. The Gaussian kernel distribution of a parameter X_i in a concrete leaf j given a concrete π_i (the realization of $\boldsymbol{\Pi}_i$) can be expressed as:

$$f(X_i|\pi_i \in \{\pi_i\}_j) = \frac{1}{|\{x_i\}_j|} \sum_{\forall m \in \{x_i\}_j} \mathcal{N}(m, \sigma_{ij}^2) \qquad i = 0, ..., n-1, \quad (2)$$

where $\{\pi_i\}_j$ denotes the set of all possible realizations of $\boldsymbol{\Pi}_i$ traversing to the j-th leaf, $\{x_i\}_j \subset \mathbb{R}$ denotes the set of realizations of variable X_i among the individuals from population D that traverse to j-th leaf, and $|\{x_i\}_j|$ denotes the size of this set. All the kernels in the same leaf have the same height $1/|\{x_i\}_j|$ and the same width σ_{ij}. In our experiments we set σ_{ij} equal to

$$\sigma_{ij} = \frac{\max\{x_i\}_j - \min\{x_i\}_j}{r}, \quad (3)$$

where the default setting for the scaling factor r in MBOA is $r = |\{x_i\}_j| - 1$.

The newly generated offspring population is used to replace some part of the former population. For effective diversity preservation, MBOA uses the so-called Restricted Tournament Replacement (RTR). In RTR, each offspring competes with the closest individual selected from a random subset of the former population. This subset comprises 5% of the population in our experiments.

3 Adaptive MBOA – AMBOA

3.1 Motivation

We investigated the susceptibility of the original MBOA to premature convergence and compared it to the Evolution Strategy with Covariance Matrix Adap-

Table 1. Test functions to be minimized and the corresponding stopping criterion. The initial solutions were generated uniformly using the initialization region $[0.5, 1.5]^n$ for f_{plane} and $[-3, 7]^n$ for the other functions, the global step size $\sigma^{(g)}$ of CMA-ES was initialized to 1.0 for f_{plane} and 5.0 for the other functions.

Name	Function	Stop. criterion
Plane	$f_{\text{plane}} = -x_0$	-10^{10}
Sphere	$f_{\text{sphere}} = \sum_{i=0}^{n-1} x_i^2$	10^{-10}
Ellipsoid	$f_{\text{elli}} = \sum_{i=0}^{n-1} 10^{4\frac{i}{n-1}} x_i^2$	10^{-10}
Rastrigin	$f_{\text{Rastrigin}} = 10n + \sum_{i=0}^{n-1}(x_i^2 - 10\cos(2\pi x_i))$	10^{-10}

tation [7, 8]. We used the (μ, λ)-CMA-ES as described in [13], where the covariance matrix $\boldsymbol{C}$ is updated by μ ranked parents selected from the λ individuals.

The ability to enlarge the overall population variance can be tested using the plane function f_{plane} (see Tab. 1). Within a small enough neighborhood, a linear function is a good approximation for any smooth function. Therefore, f_{plane} is a good test case for a situation where the population variance is (far) too small. Fig. 1a shows the function value versus the number of function evaluations for both methods. It can be seen that CMA-ES reaches the termination criteria of f_{plane} fast, using a population of only 10 individuals. On the other hand, MBOA is slower by 3 orders of magnitude. The reason is that MBOA – unlike CMA-ES – has no effective mechanism to increase the variance. Up to large population sizes ($N < 3200$ for $n = 10$ on f_{plane}), MBOA is not able to divert the solutions to fulfill the stopping criterion. We observed that the variance shrinks faster than the mean of the distribution moves. With $N \geq 3200$, the Restricted Tournament Replacement (RTR) is able to reduce shrinking, but at the expense of slow convergence.

Subsequently, we tested MBOA on the sphere function (see Tab. 1) and increased the population size according to the sequence 10, 20, 50, 100, 200, 400, 800, 1600, 3200 until the optimum was found in all 20 runs. In Fig. 1b it is shown that population size $N=100$ is needed by MBOA to solve the 10-dimensional f_{sphere} benchmark. With lower population size some of MBOA runs were not able to reach the precision 10^{-10}.

Consequently, we identified that MBOA performance is harmed in case of low population size. This can be explained by the large deviation present in the estimated parameters. These deviations are further propagated by iterated sampling and re-estimation. In contrast, CMA-ES adjusts the variance robustly and needs only very small populations. Moreover, the model parameters in CMA-ES are updated incrementally, which makes them less susceptible to deviations.

3.2 Design of AMBOA

Based on the above observations, we aimed at improving MBOA. To prevent variance from premature shrinking, we experimented with the width of Gaussian kernel σ_{ij} by setting the factor r (in Eq. (3)) as $r = \sqrt{|\{x_i\}_j|}$ or even $r = 1$.

However, different benchmarks required different settings to perform efficiently. Therefore, we introduce an overall scaling factor, η, to control the kernel width of the marginal distributions adaptively:

$$f(X_i|\pi_i \in \{\pi_i\}_j) = \frac{1}{|\{x_i\}_j|} \sum_{\forall m \in \{x_i\}_j} \mathcal{N}(m, \eta^{(g)^2}\sigma_{ij}^2). \tag{4}$$

Compared to eq. (2) one can see that the factor η is used to scale the width of each kernel. Inspired by the well-known 1/5-success rule for ESs [14], the factor is adjusted according to the success rate of RTR. In our implementation the information about success or failure of each individual is immediately accumulated into the step size. In case of success the factor is multiplied by α, otherwise it is multiplied by $\alpha^{\frac{p}{p-1}}$. For $N/2$ offspring individuals (with N_{succ} successes and N_{fail} failures), the total change of factor in the g-th generation can be expressed as

$$\eta^{(g+1)} = \eta^{(g)} \alpha^{N_{succ}} \alpha^{N_{fail}\frac{p}{p-1}}, \tag{5}$$

where p denotes the desired success rate (for $N_{succ}/(N_{succ}+N_{fail}) = p$ it holds $\eta^{(g+1)} = \eta^{(g)}$). The choice of α determines how fast the desired success rate is achieved. For increasing α the adaptation is faster, but also more sensitive to oscillations. Our experiments with f_{sphere} and $f_{\text{Rastrigin}}$ indicate that the choice of α does not depend significantly on the problem size n, but it depends on the population size N. To limit the maximal change of $\eta^{(g+1)}$ per generation, we choose $\alpha = e^{4/N}$. If all the offspring individuals are accepted - which is very unlikely – then it holds $\eta^{(g+1)} = e^2 \eta^{(g)}$. We also performed a number of experiments to determine the optimal choice of p. For unimodal functions the choice of p is not critical (2a) and the Rechenberg's rule $p = 1/5$ could have been used. For several multimodal functions the optimal p is decreasing with problem size. This is demonstrated in Fig. 2b for $f_{\text{Rastrigin}}$. As the trade-off between speed of solving unimodal test functions and robustness of solving multimodal test functions, we choose $p = 0.05 + \frac{0.3}{\sqrt{n}}$. Detailed analysis of the proper choice of a success rate for deceptive functions and the role of RTR during the adaptation will be a subject of future research.

4 Experimental Results

We compare the performance of the newly proposed AMBOA to the original MBOA and to CMA-ES. The benchmark functions are summarized in Tab. 1. All functions are separable, and only $f_{\text{Rastrigin}}$ is multimodal. In Fig. 1, 3, and 4 the bold lines are the median values of 20 runs, whereas thin lines show the minimum and maximum values. The five symbols per each measurement represent maximum, 75-percentile, median, 25-percentile, and minimum function values. The plots show results for the minimal population size for which all 20 runs converged. We start each experiment with population size $N = \lambda = 10$. If any of 20 runs do not reach the convergence criterion, the population size is increased

A Mixed Bayesian Optimization Algorithm with Variance Adaptation   357

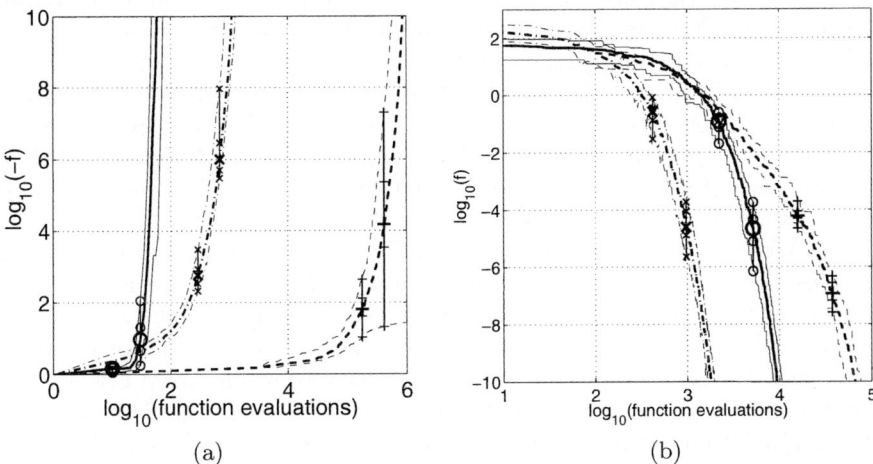

Fig. 1. Function value versus the number of function evaluations for MBOA (dashed line,'+'), CMA-ES (dot-and-dashed line,'×') and AMBOA (solid line,'∘') on 10-dimensional f_{plane} (a) and f_{sphere} (b). Population sizes (a): $\lambda = 10$ for CMA-ES, $N = 3200$ for MBOA and $N = 10$ for AMBOA. Population sizes (b): $\lambda = 10$ for CMA-ES, $N = 100$ for MBOA, $N = 10$ for AMBOA. The five symbols per each measurement represent maximum, 75-percentile, median, 25-percentile, and minimum function values of 20 runs.

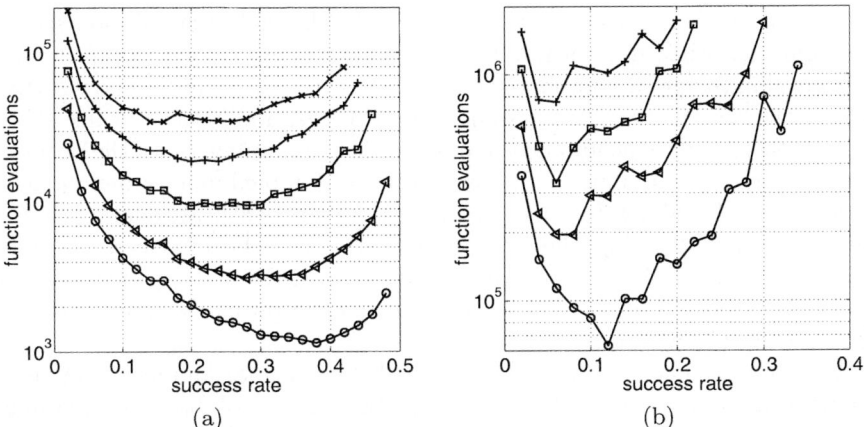

Fig. 2. (a) The influence of chosen success rate p on the number of evaluations MBOA needs to solve 5-dimensional ('∘'), 10-dimensional ('◁'), 20-dimensional ('□'), 30-dimensional ('+') , and 40-dimensional ('×') f_{sphere}. (b) The influence of chosen success rate p on the number of evaluations MBOA needs to solve 15-dimensional ('∘'), 25-dimensional ('◁'), 35-dimensional ('□'), and 45-dimensional ('+') $f_{\text{Rastrigin}}$. The success rates from $p = 0.02$ to $p = 0.48$ in 0.02 steps were examined. Median values out of 20 runs are shown for success rates where MBOA converged within less than $2e10^6$ fitness evaluations in at least 50% cases. Population size (a) $N = 10$, (b) $N = 100$.

according to the sequence 10,20,50,100,200,400,800,1600,3200 until the method converges in all 20 runs. The maximum population size tested was 3200.

We test AMBOA on f_{plane}, and f_{sphere}. In Section 3.1 these functions appeared to be difficult for MBOA. AMBOA effectively increases the variance on the 10-dimensional f_{plane} as shown in Fig. 1a. In addition, it requires a significantly smaller population size of $N = 10$ compared to $N = 3200$ for MBOA and it even requires less fitness evaluations than CMA-ES. AMBOA needs only a population size of $N = 10$ to reliably optimize the 10-dimensional f_{sphere} function, whereas MBOA needs $N = 100$ (Fig. 1b). The variance adaptation mechanism decreases the minimal required population size. This results in lower number of fitness evaluations, proportionally to the decrease of N. The same type of AMBOA behaviour is evident from Fig. 3, where the results of optimizing the 10-dimensional f_{elli} are depicted. The comparison of results from Fig. 1b and 3 indicates that AMBOA performs similarly on f_{sphere} and f_{elli}. The adaptation of the scaling factor η plays the same role in both cases, whereas the relative scaling of the individual coordinates is estimated empirically. In contrast, for CMA-ES it is much easier to adapt on the sphere function, because it starts with the spherically shaped distribution (so it is sufficient to adapt the mean and scaling factor only), whereas for the f_{elli} it has to estimate the complete covariance matrix.

We compare AMBOA, MBOA and CMA-ES on the 10-dimensional Rastrigin function (Fig. 4). The Rastrigin function is multimodal but its underlying model is a hyper-paraboloid. With a large population size $\lambda = 800$ CMA-ES is able to discover this underlying model in all 20 runs. AMBOA needs a population size of $N = 100$ whereas MBOA needs $N = 200$. With smaller population sizes the algorithms get stuck in a local optimum. Since AMBOA does not approximate the fitness landscape by a unimodal density, there is a different way how AMBOA explores the search space. We assume that AMBOA and MBOA utilize RTR to keep samples from the neighborhood of several local minima. Since the problem is separable, the local minima in all dimensions are sampled independently to form new solutions. Provided that in each dimension there is at least one solution that contains the proper value, the global optimum is reached after a small number of trials. The slope of the convergence curve of AMBOA is steeper than that of MBOA. This indicates that the variance adaptation plays a role in the local improvement of new solutions.

We investigate how AMBOA and CMA-ES behave for an increasing number of dimensions on f_{elli} (Fig. 5). We measure the number of fitness evaluations to achieve the given fitness in 2, 5, 10 and 20 dimensions, with $\lambda = 10$ for CMA-ES and $N = 10$ for AMBOA. The medians of 20 runs are shown. We observe that CMA requires less fitness evaluations to evolve high precision solutions, but the differences between AMBOA and CMA-ES decreases with increasing number of dimensions.

The proposed mechanism for variance adaptation allows MBOA to solve separable unimodal benchmarks with relatively small population sizes. With low population sizes the RTR behaves like the usual tournament replacement, so its

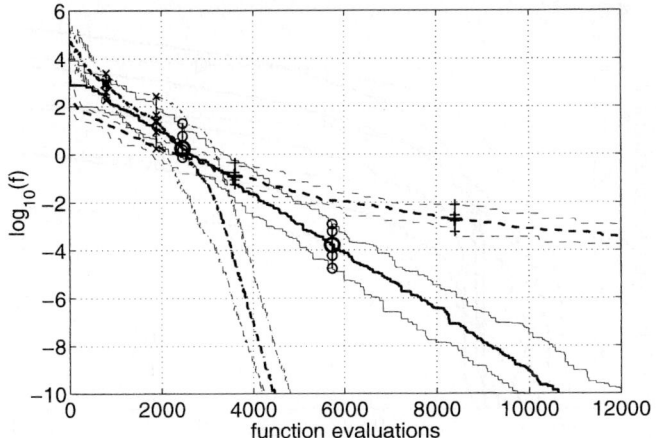

Fig. 3. AMBOA (solid line,'o'), CMA-ES (dot-and-dashed line,'×'), and MBOA (dashed line,'+') on 10-dimensional f_{elli}. Population sizes: $\lambda = 10$ for CMA-ES, $N = 10$ for AMBOA and $N = 100$ for MBOA. The median of the number of required fitness evaluations to reach 10^{-10} precision was 4450 for CMA-ES, 5885 for AMBOA and 65650 for MBOA.

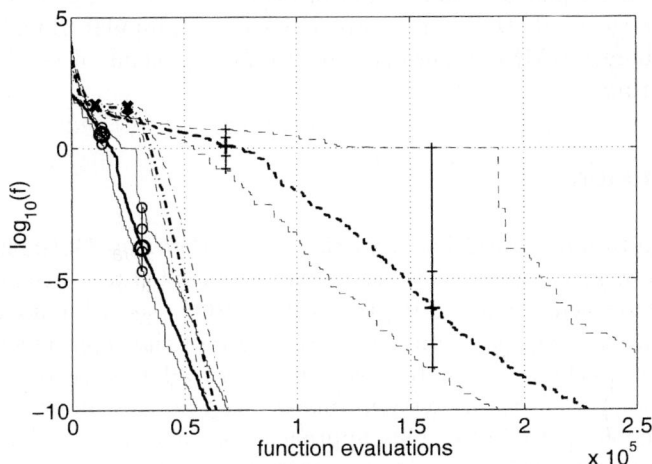

Fig. 4. AMBOA (solid line,'o'), CMA-ES (dot-and-dashed line,'×') and MBOA (dashed line, '+') on 10-dimensional $f_{Rastrigin}$. Population sizes: $\lambda = 800$ for CMA-ES, $N = 100$ for AMBOA and $N = 200$ for MBOA. The median of the number of required fitness evaluations to reach 10^{-10} precision was 38550 for AMBOA, 64000 for CMA-ES and 227900 for MBOA.

niching effect is eliminated. Additionally, in case of small populations, MBOA penalizes most of the discovered dependencies and does not incorporate them into the model, thus imposing the separability of the optimized problem.

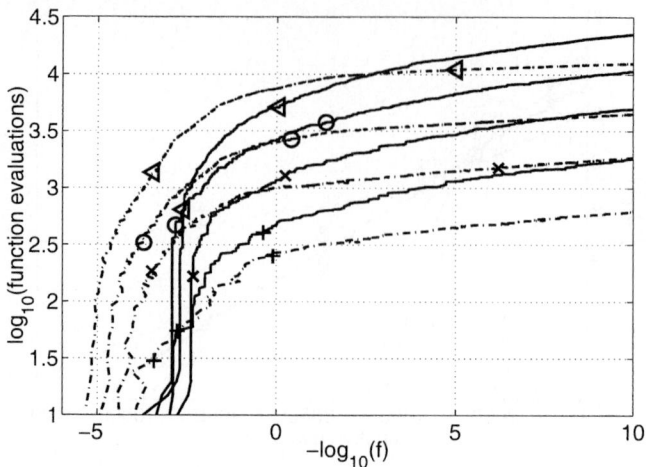

Fig. 5. Comparison of AMBOA (solid line) and CMA-ES (dashed line) behavior on 2-dimensional ('+'), 5-dimensional ('×'), 10-dimensional ('o') and 20-dimensional ('◁') function f_{elli}. Population sizes: $\lambda = 10$ for CMA-ES and $N = 10$ for AMBOA.

In case of nonseparable multimodal problems, our first experiments indicate that CMA performs better if the problem has a unimodal global underlying attractor, whereas AMBOA performs better for problems of combinatorial or deceptive nature.

5 Conclusion

Variance-adaptation is introduced to the Mixed Bayesian Optimization Algorithm as a necessary ingredient for the reliable and efficient solving of unimodal optimization problems. The newly proposed AMBOA algorithm uses a variance-adaptation mechanism based on the success rate of the replacement operator. The proposed mechanism can be also seen as an adaptation of Rechenberg's success rule for kernel-based distributions and can be used in general, not only within the scope of AMBOA. This approach does not rely on the assumption of unimodality and can be used together with the elitistic selection and replacement. On the examples of the separable test functions – plane, sphere, ellipsoid, and Rastrigin – we showed that the improved AMBOA performs comparably to Covariance Matrix Adaptation Evolution Strategy and requires a much lower population size and a much lower number of fitness evaluations than the original MBOA.

Most of the existing Estimation of Distribution Algorithms – for example the Iterated Density Estimation Evolutionary Algorithm [15] – do not have the means to effectively adjust the variance. The usefulness of the variance adaptation for the EDA framework and for non separable functions is a subject of future research.

References

1. Mühlenbein, H., Paass, G.: 1996, 'From Recombination of Genes to the Estimation of Distributions: I. Binary Parameters'. *Lecture Notes in Computer Science* **1141**, pp. 178–187, 1996.
2. Pelikan, M., Goldberg, D. E., Lobo, F.: 'A Survey of Optimization by Building and Using Probabilistic Models'. *IlliGAL Report No. 99018*, Illinois Genetic Algorithms Laboratory, University of Illinois at Urbana-Champaign, Urbana, IL, 1999.
3. Larrañaga, P.: 'A Review on Estimation of Distribution Algorithms'. In: P. Larrañaga and J. A. Lozano (eds.): *Estimation of Distribution Algorithms.* pp. 80–90, Kluwer Academic Publishers, 2002.
4. Ocenasek, J., Schwarz, J.: 'Estimation of Distribution Algorithm for mixed continuous- discrete optimization problems'. In: *2nd Euro-International Symposium on Computational Intelligance.* pp. 227–232, IOS Press, Kosice, Slowakia, 2002.
5. Schwarz, J., Ocenasek, J.: 'Bayes-Dirichlet BDD as a probabilistic model for logic function and evolutionary circuit decomposer'. In: *Proceedings of the 8th International Mendel Conference on Soft Computing, Mendel 2002*, Brno University of Technology, Brno, Czech Rep., pp. 117–124, 2002.
6. Kern, S., Hansen, N., Müller, S., Büche, D., Ocenasek, J., Koumoutsakos, P.: 'Learning Probability Distributions in Continuous Evolutionary Algorithms – Review and Comparison.' Natural Computing, **3** (1), pp. 77–112, 2004.
7. Hansen, N., Ostermeier, A.: 2001, 'Completely Derandomized Self-Adaptation in Evolution Strategies'. *Evolutionary Computation* **9**(2), pp. 159–195, 2001.
8. Hansen, N., Müller, S. D., Koumoutsakos, P.: 'Reducing the Time Complexity of the Derandomized Evolution Strategy with Covariance Matrix Adaptation (CMA-ES)'. *Evolutionary Computation* **11**(1), pp. 1–18, 2003.
9. Chickering, D.M., Geiger, D., Heckerman, D.E.: 'Learning Bayesian networks is NP-hard', *Technical Report MSR-TR-94-17*, Microsoft Research, Redmond, WA, 1995.
10. Pelikan, M., Goldberg, D. E., Sastry, K.: 'Bayesian Optimization Algorithm, Decision Graphs, and Occam's Razor', *IlliGAL Report No. 2000020*, University of Illinois at Urbana-Champaign, Illinois Genetic Algorithms Laboratory, Urbana, IL, 2000.
11. Friedman, N., Goldszmidt, M.: 'Learning Bayesian Networks with Local Structure', In: M. I. Jordan ed. *Learning and Inference in Graphical Models*, 1998.
12. Heckerman, D., Geiger, D., Chickering, M.: 'Learning Bayesian networks: The combination of knowledge and statistical data'. *Technical Report MSR-TR-94-09*, Microsoft Research, Redmond, WA, 1994.
13. Hansen, N., Kern, S.: 'Evaluating the CMA Evolution Strategy on Multimodal Test Functions'. *Parallel Problem Solving from Nature PPSN VIII*, Springer, Birmingham, 2004, accepted.
14. Rechenberg, I.: 'Evolutionsstrategie: Optimierung technischer System nach Prinzipien der biologischen Evolution,' Fromann-Holzboog, Stuttgart, 1973.
15. Bosman, P.A.N., Thierens, D.: Expanding from discrete to continuous estimation of distribution algorithms: The IDEA. *Parallel Problem Solving from Nature PPSN VI*, pp. 760–776, Springer, 2000.

A Swarm Intelligence Based VLSI Multiplication-and-Add Scheme

Danilo Pani and Luigi Raffo

DIEE – Department of Electrical and Electronic Engineering, University of Cagliari,
P.zza d'Armi, 09123, Cagliari, Italy
{pani,luigi}@diee.unica.it

Abstract. Starting from the observation of natural systems, bio-inspired collaborative schemes exploit the power of a fully decentralized control to perform complex tasks. Currently this approach concerns software and robotic systems. In this paper we apply a such approach to the VLSI implementation of the basic task in DSP systems: the summation of products. We analyze such operation in terms of parallel distributed computation, showing how such reformulation can take advantages from the cooperation between cells of a small colony. The interaction among cells, based on simple social rules, leads to a full exploitation of cells computational capabilities obtaining a more efficient usage of their computational resources in a so important task. A preliminary VLSI implementation and theoretical results are presented to show the feasibility of this approach.

1 Introduction

A great number of bio-inspired systems derive from observation of social animals: the interactions among individuals determine the capability to perform complex tasks without a centralized control. One of these approach is Swarm Intelligence, which derives from observation of swarms, large sets of simple individuals that can perform complex tasks taking advantages by cooperation among themselves. Advantages of cooperation can be in task acceleration or in making a too onerous task possible. As a result of cooperation in many kind of micro-scale behavior, macro-scale complex behavior seems to emerge without any central or hierarchical control [1]. In this sense ant, wasp and others social insects colonies exhibit a self-organizing behavior. The self-organization theory simply tells that *at some level of description* it is possible to explain complex behavior by assuming that it is the result of the activities of simple interacting entities [2].

At the moment the application of such approaches has mainly concerned developing of computer programs to implement optimization and problem solving algorithms like the Travelling Salesman Problem (TSP) and other computational-intensive problems [3, 4]; the particular filed of swarm robotic has conducted to the creation of simple little robots realizing real world operative tasks [5, 6]. Adaptive routing algorithms for communication networks have been developed starting from Swarm Intelligence approaches [7, 8].

In this scenario we collocate our work, that applies the concepts of Swarm Intelligence and cooperative systems to the VLSI implementation of a typical Digital Signal Processing (DSP) task: the multiply-and-add operation. In this work we present a preliminary VLSI implementation of a system composed by 8 cells that cooperate by means of simple rules to perform the sum of 8 products. Products are generated using a partial reformulation of the sequential Modified Booth Algorithm (MBA) which exploit intensively the hardware resources. The overall system has been described in Verilog HDL, and synthesized using Synopsys Design Compiler on a CMOS 0.18μm standard cell technology.

It should be clear that the goal of this research is not to develop a new multiplier, but just to explore possible alternatives to the traditional approaches exploiting the Swarm Intelligence approach.

In Section 2 we introduce the chosen multiplication algorithm. In Section 3 we explore data complexity, a central issue in this work, whereas in Section 4 we illustrate the adopted collaborative scheme. Section 5 shows the proposed architecture, whose implementation and performances evaluation are exposed in section 6. Conclusions are presented in Section 7.

2 Sequential VLSI Multiplication

Linear algebra applications, matrix manipulation and DSP algorithms have a common denominator: in general almost all the operations involved in them can be decomposed into elementary summations of products. In DSP, typical examples are digital filters, i.e. Finite Impulse Response (FIR) filters, where the relationship between input and output takes exactly this form.

Software routines and hardware implementation of such algorithms are the two possible existing alternatives. When a such system has to be implemented on silicon, it should be carefully considered the impact of a single multiplier in terms of silicon area and critical path length. With respect to their implementation, multipliers can be divided into sequential (multi-step) and combinatorial (single-step) ones. Sequential multipliers can be optimized to find the best solution for area and performance. There are many approaches to sequential multiplication implementation. The traditional Booth algorithm spends N steps with N-bit operands, because it examines one multiplier bit at a time, whereas the MBA examines two or more multiplier bits at a time, reducing the overall latency. In particular we focus on the MBA with multiplier partitioning into 3-bit groups with one bit overlap.

2.1 The Modified Booth Algorithm

Take a binary 2's complement number α, and let us consider α composed by triplets β of bits, with one bit overlap between adjacent triplets:

$$\beta_i = \{\alpha_{2i+1}, \alpha_{2i}, \alpha_{2i-1}\}, \qquad 0 < i < \frac{\omega_\alpha}{2} - 1 \qquad (1)$$

Every triplet in the number α has an associated weight the original weight of its α_{2i} bit in positional binary notation), whereas the bits of the triplet have relative weights $w = \{-2, 1, 1\}$.

The decimal interpretation of α can be written like in (2), taking $\alpha_{-1} = 0$.

$$\alpha = \sum_{i=0}^{\frac{\omega_\alpha}{2}-1} (-2\alpha_{2i+1} + \alpha_{2i} + \alpha_{2i-1}) \cdot 2^{2i} \qquad (2)$$

The term between brackets can take only the values listed below, functions of $\{\alpha_{2i+1}, \alpha_{2i}, \alpha_{2i-1}\}$:

- 0 for $\{0,0,0\}$ or $\{1,1,1\}$
- 1 for $\{0,1,0\}$ or $\{0,0,1\}$
- -1 for $\{1,1,0\}$ or $\{1,0,1\}$
- 2 for $\{0,1,1\}$
- -2 for $\{1,0,0\}$

and, excluding the zero, they are all power of two.

If we coded using the above coding scheme the multiplier α in a multiplication between α and another number γ, the result may be obtained calculating only $\omega_\alpha/2$ partial products and then summating them. In a sequential scheme the summation is performed step-by-step in form of accumulation, and take $\omega_\alpha/2$ cycles. The result is:

$$\gamma \times \alpha = \sum_{i=0}^{\frac{\omega_\alpha}{2}-1} (-2\alpha_{2i+1} + \alpha_{2i} + \alpha_{2i-1}) \cdot 2^{2i} \cdot \gamma \qquad (3)$$

Because all factors in the summation, with the only exception of the number γ, are powers of two, the partial products are simple left-shifted replicas of γ, and the shift amount corresponds to the exponent of two.

3 Speculative Data Analysis

The data carry with itself natively the concept of complexity, but in terms of VLSI design this aspect is often ignored because the overall system is build on the worst case. In some cases input data value is an interesting design variable: among them we can comprise those systems that speculate on the distance between subsequent data or coefficients (i.e. in digital filters), adopting differential approaches (DCM [9], DCIM [10], DECOR [11], etc.). Nevertheless they exploit characteristics proper of a *data sequence* and not of *single data inputs*.

The proposed approach is completely different, assuming that in some cases the value of *each* bit forming the data word is relevant for computational latency reduction, that is the number of clock cycles required to accomplish the computation. Consider an operation decomposable into elementary steps whose number varies depending on data complexity: a Swarm Intelligence approach can conduce to a faster achievement of the result exploiting the collective effort of colony members in the specific task.

3.1 Data Complexity in the Modified Booth Algorithm

We can introduce the notion of *complexity* in the context of MBA, limitedly to the multiplier, as follows:

Definition 1. *Given a ω_α-bit binary number α, described like an ordered set of triplets β_i, we define complexity of α the number $\mathbf{C}$ of triplets β_i that differ from $\{0,0,0\}$ and $\{1,1,1\}$.*

Take a 2's complement number made up of many $\{0,0,0\}$ and $\{1,1,1\}$ triplets (in the following named *null triplets*) as multiplier, and another number as multiplicand. Implementing the system we find out that every time a *null triplet* is encountered the system wastes a cycle making nothing useful to obtain the result. It follows that the effective number of steps needed could be equal to the number of non-*null triplets* composing the multiplier, that is its *complexity*. For a 32-bit wide binary number the *complexity* is $0 \leq C \leq 16$. An immediate outcome is that if the VLSI multiplier could perform an overall number of steps equal to its multiplicand complexity C, it should operate like a traditional system in the worst case, but statistically it could obtain a percentage clock cycles reduction exploiting data complexity fluctuations, which obviously are random.

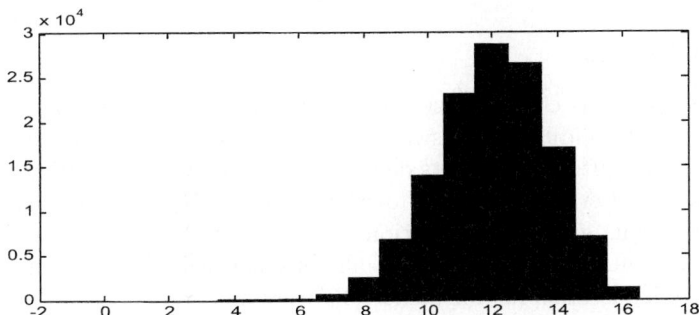

Fig. 1. Histogram of data complexity for a 128,000 random numbers dataset. The average value is 12.00.

The histogram of data *complexity* for a dataset of 128,000 random numbers is depicted in Fig. 1 (in this example the average value is 12.00). The same shape can be obtained with arbitrarily large datasets. This result suggests that if the VLSI multiplier is able to skip *null triplets*, on the average it should spend 12 rather than 16 cycles to complete the operation, with a percentage reduction of 25% in latency.

4 Computational Density and Cooperation Strategies

For the multiply-and-add task, we can conceive that every *cell* in the colony is a kind of multiplier that potentially can perform a simple multiplication on its own. The algorithm we want to execute is this:

$$y = \sum_{k=0}^{M-1} \gamma_k \alpha_k = \sum_{k=0}^{M-1} \sum_{i=0}^{\frac{\omega_\alpha}{2}-1} (-2\alpha_{2i+1} + \alpha_{2i} + \alpha_{2i-1}) \cdot 2^{2i} \cdot \gamma_k \qquad (4)$$

If we have a small colony of cell (i.e. 8) that are able to perform multiplications using the MBA and skipping *null triplets*, and we allow that when a cell terminate its own operation could help another cell accumulating partial products on its register, and at the end the final summation could take place, we have created a cooperative multiply-and-add. In this manner we obtain a *dense* computation.

Consider loading into an 8-cells system 8 data with complexities 4, 8, 6, 4, 1, 5, 1, and 0. Without cooperation among cells, even if our MBA multipliers skip *null triplets*, the overall latency equals the worst cell latency, that is 8. However the average complexity is 3.625, not 8, and one cell is never used, two cells are used only for one step, and so on. We are wasting computational resources and time too. If we define *computational density* the sum over all cells of activity instants with respect to the sum of activity and inactivity instants, we obtain a density of 45% for the example above. A collaborative approach should potentially achieve a latency of 4 steps, with a computational density of 90% (that implies a good usage of hardware).

4.1 Social Rules

Swarm Intelligence is characterized by simple social rules that govern the interactions among individuals. The swarm's goal is to execute all the simple operations (obtainable after the triplets decomposition of every multiplier) as soon as possible, each cell starting with its own input data. If data complexities for all cells are the same, and no cooperation can take place, then every cell performs a multiply operation, and at the end all cells perform the final summation. If data complexity is different for some cells they can cooperate by means of the following simple rules:

- if a cell is working and its residual complexity differs from zero, than it asks for collaboration spreading a help request: the request will be served during the next cycle if this cell is the most priority cell requesting. We'll call a such cell a *H* cell;
- if a cell residual complexity goes to zero, the cell indicates its availability to help other cells of the swarm, and it becomes bus slave if it is the most priority cell available. We'll call such cell a *D* cell;
- if a *H* cell receives an availability signal, it propagates its multiplicand and shift factor to the *D* cell (helper), and decreases its own residual complexity monitor;
- if a *D* cell receives an help request, it processes the incoming data storing the result in its own register;
- when all cells declare to have finished the elaboration, they organize themselves to perform the last summation, at the end of which they indicate the end of elaboration (the elaboration time is complexity-dependent).

5 The Proposed Architecture

The architecture of the proposed Swarm Multiply-and-Add (SM&A) consists of 8 undifferentiated cells that form a colony of interacting *hardware agents* able to perform an operation of multiply-and-add based on a partial reformulation of the sequential MBA.

To work with reasonable number complexities the input data size has been chosen equal to 32 bits, whereas the output size (full precision) is 67 bits (64 plus 3 guard bits for cells results accumulation). During an algorithm steps (which corresponds to 4 clock cycles) 3 time-slots are available for interactions among cells.

5.1 Hardware Agents and Decentralized Control

Swarms are composed by mobile elements. About cell mobility, with respect to software agents systems or robots, the *hardware agent* is constrained by physical hardware communication channels, dedicated or shared. The highest flexibility is guaranteed by point-to-point connections but this should cause a connectivity explosion. It is possible to limit the problem allowing the non-simultaneous usage of a shared resource.

In our system, communications take place by means of buses which transport multiplicand and shift amount from the H cell to the D cell. This architectural choice allows interactions between any couple of cells. Since every cell could be (in different moments) an H or a D cell, cells access the bus bi-directionally. This implies that cells need to adopt a bus arbitrage to avoid collisions. We have chosen a fully decentralized arbitrage based on a priority scheme that establishes a cells rank starting from a cell-ID assigned to cells at synthesis time. Knowing the cell-ID, every arbiter can resolve by itself if it can or cannot access the data buses. If a cell can't access the buses for a help request, simply the arbiter masks to its cell any availability from other cells, and if a cell is not enough priority to help another cell, than its arbiter masks the help request from the requesting cell.

A such distributed arbitrage scheme involves replication of logical blocks but it ensures the total absence of a centralized control system.

5.2 Cell Architecture

The cell architecture is based on the empirical observation that the control structure, implemented by means of a Finite State Machine (FSM), should be much faster than the datapath structure. Starting from this observation we can allow cooperation during an operative step of the algorithm, using a single clock structure and a synchronous traditional approach (more useful for results comparisons but probably less efficient than other possible approaches).

Cell structure is divisible in layers. Mainly we can distinguish between 4 layers: the elaboration layer, the source layer, the interconnection layer and the control layer, the latest controlling the others.

The *Elaboration Layer* accommodates the datapath, which taking as input the multiplicand and the shift amount, produces the partial result. This operation requires 4 clock cycles (an algorithm step corresponds to 4 clock cycles), during which the cell can't elaborate other data. This layer is controlled from the control layer in terms of control points and register enables. The flexibility of this layer allows to reuse structural resources by means of run-time reconfiguration of the datapath, decided autonomously by each cell without a centralized controller.

The *Source Layer* of a cell implements the data source for that cell and for other cells during computation. If we intend cells like agents consuming spread resources, the source layer is the resources container. It consists of triplets decoding systems that allow *null triplets* skipping during elaboration. The control layer of its own cell controls it, even if another cell is sourcing from it. The layer exports towards the other layers only multiplicand, shift amount for the actual triplet, and a signal that indicate data unavailable (when the number of non-*null triplet* not yet processed reaches zero).

The *Interconnection Layer* allows communications among cells, and it passes data from source layer towards elaboration layer. The bus arbitrage is fully decentralized, and by means of this layer every cell knows if it can or cannot access the bus (like a bus master or slave). This layer operates without the explicit control of the control layer.

The *Control Layer* has been implemented by means of a FSM, optimised to obtain the highest performances allowable. This is the core element of the cell, and operates passing through 4 modes: load mode, internal elaboration mode, helping mode and accumulation mode. The controller operates complying with the social rules exposed above.

- During load mode the controller governs only the source layer to load the operands and initialize the pipeline stages.
- During the internal elaboration mode, the cell executes its own single step of operation, during which other cells can help it. In this condition the controller govern the elaboration layer, and the source layer too if one or more cells are available for helping.
- During the helping mode a cell that consumed its data executes partial products of other cells, accumulating the result into its own output register. In this mode the controller governs only the elaboration layer.
- Finally, in accumulation mode, the controller sets up its elaboration layer to perform the final summation. This operation is conducted using an algorithm that permits the exploitation of a pipelined structure of the adders/subtracters included in the elaboration layer.

6 Experimental Results and Analysis

The overall system composed by 8 cells, with 32-bit input data and 67-bit output result, has been synthesized using Synopsys Design Compiler v2001.08 on standard cell CMOS technology (UMC18μ1P6M).

To adapt a theoretically fully asynchronous system to a synchronous implementation we have chosen multicycle solutions for datapath implementation, preserving the synchrony property for implementation comparisons. In this first version we set at 3 the number of interactions allowable during an algorithm step. This choice reduced the complexity of the system but its performances too. In fact an increase in the number of allowable interactions implies better performances algorithmically, but it influences negatively the system's performances in terms of area/latency for this synchronous implementation. In Fig. 2 we can appreciate the difference in terms of algorithm cycles for the SM&A proposed and the same system without cooperation (but always skipping *null triplets*).

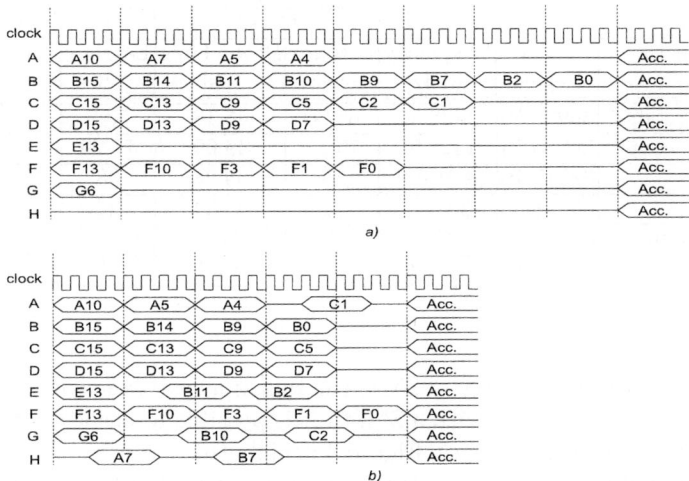

Fig. 2. The example in Sect. 4 for *a)* MBA+*null triplets* skipping and *b)* SM&A. A, B, ..., H are the cells (in descending order of priority), horizontal lines indicate no activity, *Acc.* stands for the final summation phase. For each cell's activity instant there is an alphanumerical label where the letter indicates the owner of the triplet-multiplicand pair in process, and the number indicates the triplet number.

In Tab. 1 we compare the results of the simulations for different architectures. Simulations for SM&A have been conducted on many datasets, obtaining comparable results. Hence results in Tab. 1 have been obtained from a single dataset. In the first row our approach with a cooperative effort 3 (three interaction per algorithm step) is presented. The effect of cooperation is evidenced by the comparison with row 2 where the cooperative effort is reduced to 0. The improvement is more relevant when the dataset is characterized by a reduced complexity (C=8). Row 3 and 4 report standard sequential implementation (Booth and MBA), we can see how performances are independent from the complexity of the data and lower than the SM&A's ones. Areas (i.e. hardware complexity) are in the same order of magnitude. The last two rows report two top (combinatorial and order 2 pipelined) implementations from Synopsys DesignWare Library, in which no area constraint is considered and only the throughput is considered. Beyond the consideration that these are two non-sequential architectures, the difference with respect to the others is also in their implementation: these are very regular gate-level HDL descriptions whereas the others are RTL level HDL architectures (less optimized).

Table 1. Comparison of performances for different architectures. The first dataset (C=12) has been obtained generating absolutely random number, the second generating numbers staring from a dataset of random complexity values. Datasets consists of 32,000 multiplier values.

			C=12		C=8	
Architecture	Area eq.gate	Frequency [MHz]	Latency cycles	Proc. Time [ps]	Latency cycles	Proc. Time [ps]
SM&A coop3	36985.56	1428.57	65.96	46.18	53.9	37.73
SM&A coop0	36985.56	1428.57	70.13	49.09	71.29	49.9
Booth	32817.16	641.03	38	59.28	38	59.28
MBA	35731.65	507.61	22	43.34	22	43.34
Combinatorial	64526.47	84.75	1	11.8	1	11.8
DW_2_stages	81322.16	510.2	2	3.92	2	3.92

A very important property of SM&A is that if a system needs to deal with a broad range of data widths, with a SM&A it is possible to use the same architecture with the best performances. Figure 3 depicts the comparison between the 4 sequential architecture in Tab. 1 for 6 datasets with different data width (data are sign-extended to obtain 32-bit values) and hence for different complexities.

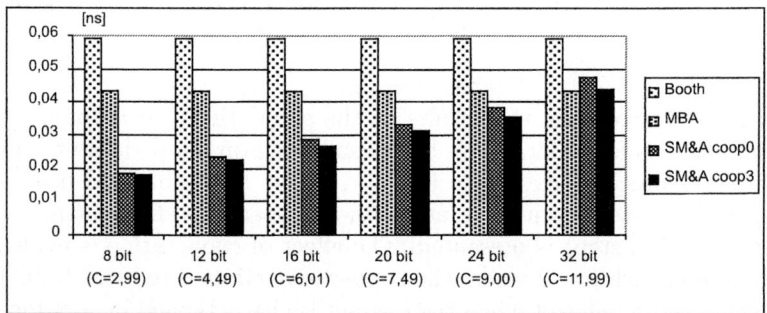

Fig. 3. Processing time for the 4 sequential architecture in Tab. 1, on different complexity datasets.

7 Conclusions

In this paper we have presented an efficient multiply-and-add architecture in which the computation is assigned to a number of simple units that recursively (on each operation) and parallely (on different data) perform the task. The control of such units is distributed, and the overall system expose a self-organizing behavior. We have shown how introducing cooperation rules typical of Swarm Intelligence the performances of the system can be improved, in particular when complexity (according to a proper definition of it) of the data stream is limited. It should be noted that reduced complexity of dataset is typical of stream processing. The core of the system described has been implemented and synthesized on standard CMOS technology. Results of simulations show the potentiality of the approach. Better results could be obtained with custom implementation of some modules of the system and self-timed/asynchronous approaches.

References

1. Kawamura, H., Yamamoto, M.: Multiple Ant Colonies Algorithm Based on Colony Level Interactions. IEICE Trans. Fundamentals **E83-A** (2000) No.2, 371–379
2. Bonabeau, E., Dorigo, M., Theraulaz, G. : Swarm Intelligence, From Natural To Artificial Systems. Oxford University Press (1999)
3. Dorigo, M., Gambardella, L. M.: Ant Colonies for the Traveling Salesman Problem. BioSystems **43** (1997) 73–81
4. Dorigo, M., Maniezzo, V., Colorni, A.: The Ant System: Optimization by a Colony of Cooperating Agents. IEEE Trans. on Systems, Men and Cybernetics - B **26** (1996) 29–41
5. Kube, C. R.: Collective Robotics: From Local Perception to Global Action. Ph.D. Thesis, University of Alberta (1997)
6. Martinoli, A. Yamamoto, M., Mondada, F.: On the Modelling of Bio-Inspired Collective Experiments with Real Robots. Proc. of the Fourth European Conference on Artificial Life (ECAL 97) Brighton, UK (1997)
7. Schoonderwoerd, R., Holland, O., Bruten, J., Rothkrantz, L.: Ant-Based Load Balancing in Telecommunications Networks. Adaptive Behavior **5** (1996) 169–207
8. Di Caro, G., Dorigo, M. AntNet: Distributed Stigmergetic Control for Communications Networks. Journal of Artificial Intelligence Research **9** (1998) 317–365
9. Sankarayya, N., Roy, K., Bhattacharya, D.: Algorithm for Low Power and High Speed FIR Filter Realization Using Differential Coefficients. IEEE Transactions on Circuits and Systems - II **44** (1997) 488–497
10. Chang, T. S., Chu, Y. H., Jen, C. W.: Low Power FIR Filter Realization with Differential Coefficients and Inputs. IEEE Transactions On Circuits and Systems - II **47** (2000) No. 2, 137–145
11. Ramprasad, S., Shanbhag, N. R., Hajj, I. N.: Decorrelating (DECOR) Transformations for Low-Power Digital Filters. IEEE Transactions On Circuits and Systems - II **46** (1999), No. 6, 776–788

Distribution Tree-Building Real-Valued Evolutionary Algorithm

Petr Pošík

Faculty of Electrical Engineering, Department of Cybernetics
Czech Technical University in Prague
Technická 2, 166 27 Prague 6, Czech Republic
posik@labe.felk.cvut.cz

Abstract. This article describes a new model of probability density function and its use in estimation of distribution algorithms. The new model, the distribution tree, has interesting properties and can form a solid basis for further improvements which will make it even more competitive. Several comparative experiments on continuous real-valued optimization problems were carried out and the results are promising. It outperformed the genetic algorithm using the traditional crossover operator several times, in the majority of the remaining experiments it was comparable to the genetic algorithm performance.

1 Introduction

This article addresses the problem of the real-valued optimization with box constraints. The stochastic genetic and evolutionary algorithms (GAs, EAs) are often considered to be a very flexible tool for searching the space of potential solutions. Due to the dependencies among the problem variables the ordinary GEAs are often not able to solve the task at hand reliably. One possible solution of this *linkage problem* is presented by the so-called estimation of distribution algorithms (EDAs).

In EDAs, new individuals are not created by means of traditional crossover operators, rather each generation a probabilistic model describing the distribution of good individuals in the search space is created and new individuals are sampled from it. We can view the model-building-and-sampling as a generalized multi-parent crossover operator. The characteristics of the resulting EDA are mainly determined by the probabilistic model used during the evolution. If the model is flexible enough, the algorithm can use the dependencies among the problem variables to guide the search more efficiently than just the plain selection (which guides the search in ordinary EAs). The structure of an EDA is depicted in Fig. 1. The EDA framework emerged in the field of GAs (see e.g. [4], [6] for surveys). In the real-valued optimization we can find 'continuous counterparts' of the algorithms developed originally for the bit strings, some approaches which assume the independence of individual variables (the univariate marginal distribution algorithm, UMDA, see e.g. [7], [8]), and on the other side of the spectra there are approaches which use very general kinds of models like the

	EDAStructure
1	Initialize and evaluate the population
2	Repeat
3	Select individuals which should serve as a basis for model creation
4	Create a probabilistic model of distribution of selected individuals
5	Sample new individuals from created model
6	Insert new individuals into population
7	Mutate some individuals in population (not a typical part of EDA)
8	Evaluate new and modified individuals
9	Until a termination condition is met

Fig. 1. Structure of the estimation of distribution algorithm.

finite mixtures of multivariate normal distributions (see e.g. [3], [1]) or bayesian networks (see [5]) that are able to cover very complex kinds of interactions.

The following sections include the first examination of EDA using the distribution tree model. In section 2, the way of distribution tree construction is described. Section 3 includes the description of carried out experiments along with their results. Finally, in section 4 you will find a short summary and conclusions.

2 Distribution Trees

The ideal probabilistic model for EDAs should have the following features:

- *Easy and fast to build.* The model is built every generation; a fast way to create it must exist.
- *Generative.* We need to create new population members in accordance with the distribution encoded in the model. If we do not know how to sample from the model, we are not able to create new individuals.
- *Flexible enough.* The model must be able to cover the interactions between variables (at least to some extent). It should also be able to decompose or factorize the problem if possible.

The distribution tree (DiT[1]) is an attempt to construct such kind of model. It is based mainly on the Classification and Regression Trees (CART) framework introduced by Breiman [2], but it differs from CART in several important aspects.

On the contrary to CART, the primary objective of DiT is not to present a model to classify or predict new, previously unseen data points, but rather to generate new individuals so that the distribution of them in the search space is very similar to that of the original data points.

When presented with the training set of data (the population members selected for mating), the distribution tree is built by recursively searching for the

---

[1] In this article for the distribution tree model the abbreviation 'DiT' is used in order to prevent messing it with the 'DT' abbrev. commonly used for the decision trees.

'best' axis-parallel split. The leaf nodes of DiT present a complete partitioning of the search space. The shape of each partition can be described as a multi-dimensional hyper-rectangle whose edges are aligned with the coordinate axes. Thus, the final model forms a mixture of multivariate uniform distributions.

When compared to other structure-building algorithms, e.g. the Ocenasek's MBOA [5], the DiT is much simpler model. The tree here is a kind of temporary structure; after the model is created we can forget the tree, only the leaf nodes are important because they form a mixture of uniform distributions. The structure in MBOA plays much more important role as it captures the dependency structure of individual variables. The DiT algorithm is able to cover some kind of interactions but only as a side-effect.

2.1 Growing the Distribution Tree

Let us denote the set of data points at hand (the population) as $\mathbb{P} = \{x^i\}_{i=1}^{N}$, N is the population size, $x^i = (x_1^i, x_2^i, \ldots, x_D^i)$ is the i-th individual, D is the dimensionality of the search space. Further, there are three parameters of the algorithm: $minToSplit$, describing the minimal node size[2] allowed to be split, $minInNode$, the minimal number of data points that must remain in the left and right part of the node after splitting, and $maxPValue$, the maximal p-value for which we consider the split statistically significant.

The tree building algorithm is very simple (see Fig. 2). The algorithm parameters are assigned to the steps where they apply (written in parentheses).

Function SplitNode	
1	If there are not enough data points in the node ($minToSplit$) then exit
2	Find best split among all possible splits ($minInNode$)
3	If there is a 'good-enough' split ($maxPValue$),
3.1	Divide the data points into left and right node
3.2	Apply the SplitNode function recursivelly on left and right node
3	Return the just realized node split

Fig. 2. Procedure for splitting the node.

The heart of this procedure is constituted by the way we search for the best split. We can place the split between each pair of the successive data points in each dimension. If we have N D-dimensional data points in the node, we have $D \times (N-1)$ possible splits. Each of these candidate splits is evaluated via hypothesis testing. We assume that in each leaf node the data points should have approximately the uniform distribution. This assumption is tested via the χ^2-test. Eventually, the split 'which gives us the least similarity between the

---
[2] To prevent misunderstanding, let me point out that 'size of node' or 'node size' refers to the number of data points which belong to the respective node. When I describe the 'physical size' of node in DiT I use the term 'node volume'.

uniform and the observed distribution' is selected, if the test says 'there is a sufficiently high probability of big difference between the uniform and the observed distribution'. Otherwise we have no reason to split this node even if it has a large size.

Function FindBestSplit
1   For all dimensions
1.1   Compute the density of individuals in this node
1.2   Build a list of candidate split points
1.3   For all candidate split points
1.3.1   Determine expected frequencies in left and right subnode
1.3.2   Determine observed frequencies in left and right subnode
1.3.3   Compute the test statistic
1.3.4   Carry out the χ^2-test, determine the p-value
1.3.5   If the best split so far was found, remember it
2   Return the best split

Fig. 3. Procedure for searching the best split.

For each particular candidate split we can count the points in the left and the right subnode which are the observed sizes, N_L^{obs} and N_R^{obs}. For both subnodes we can also directly compute the expected sizes, N_L^{exp} and N_R^{exp}, knowing the size of node as a whole and the relative volumes of the left and right subnodes. The χ^2-test allows us to compare the observed sizes with the expected ones. First, we compute the test statistic

$$Chi^2 = \frac{(N_L^{exp} - N_L^{obs})^2}{N_L^{exp}} + \frac{(N_R^{exp} - N_R^{obs})^2}{N_R^{exp}} . \quad (1)$$

The Chi^2 is a random variable with χ^2 distribution with 1 degree of freedom. It describes to what extent the observed and expected frequencies differ from each other. Thus, we can compute the probability of observing this or greater Chi^2 assuming the uniform distribution in the node as 1 minus the value of the cumulative distribution function of χ^2 distribution with 1 degree of freedom at point Chi^2.

$$p = 1 - CDF\chi^2(1, Chi^2) \quad (2)$$

This way we can select the split that gives us the highest discrimination from the uniform distribution with a sufficiently high probability, i.e. among all candidate splits we select the one with the lowest p-value, and we realize the split if the p-value is lower than $maxPValue$.

2.2 Sampling from the Distribution Tree

The process of creating new individuals, i.e. sampling from the distribution tree, is very straightforward. The leaf nodes of the tree fully cover the whole search space. New individuals are sampled this way: each leaf has a certain number of 'parent' individuals which belong to that node after the DiT creation; the same number of 'offsprings' is created in each leaf just by several calls to the uniform random number generator. Since an empty leaf node is not possible, this ensures that the search will not stop in any area of the search space.

3 Experiments

The carried out experiments compared the DiT evolutionary algorithm to several other evolutionary techniques. For all experiments, I used the evolutionary model of Tsutsui et al. [8]. Let the population size be N. Each iteration consists of the following phases:

1. Based on the current population, create N new individuals (i.e. build a probabilistic model and sample from it in case of EDAs, or use the crossover to create N offsprings in case of GAs) and evaluate them.
2. Join the old and the new population to get a data pool of size $2N$.
3. Use the truncation selection to select the better half of data points (returning the population size back to N).

These phases were repeated until the number of evaluations exceeded 50,000.

3.1 Test Suite

For the performance evaluation of the EA using DiT several reference optimization problems were used. The test functions were selected to show some of the strengths and weaknesses of the DiT-EA and are listed in Table 1.

Table 1. Test functions and related parameters. The f function can be described as a polyline going through points $(0,0)$, $(1,5)$, $(2,0)$, $(7,4)$, $(12,0)$.

Function	Expression	Domain
2D Two Peaks	$F = 10 - \sum_{i=1}^{2} f(x_i)$	$\langle 0, 12 \rangle^2$
20D Two Peaks	$F = 100 - \sum_{i=1}^{20} f(x_i)$	$\langle 0, 12 \rangle^{20}$
2D Griewangk	$F = 1 + \sum_{i=1}^{2} \frac{x_i^2}{4000} - \prod_{i=1}^{2} \cos \frac{x_i}{\sqrt{i}}$	$\langle -5, 5 \rangle^2$
10D Griewangk	$F = 1 + \sum_{i=1}^{10} \frac{x_i^2}{4000} - \prod_{i=1}^{10} \cos \frac{x_i}{\sqrt{i}}$	$\langle -5, 5 \rangle^{10}$
2D Rosenbrock	$F = 100 \times (x_1^2 - x_2)^2 + (1 - x_1)^2$	$\langle -2.048, 2.048 \rangle^2$
10D Rosenbrock	$F = \sum_{i=1}^{5} (100 \times (x_{2i-1}^2 - x_{2i})^2 + (1 - x_{2i-1})^2)$	$\langle -2.048, 2.048 \rangle^{10}$

The Two Peaks function was used in the work of Tsutsui et al. [8]. The number of its local optima grows exponentially with the dimensionality, on the other hand it is completely separable function. The global optimum lies in the point $(1, 1, \ldots, 1)$ and the optimal value is 0. Algorithm which is not able to decompose this problem to a set of 1D problems has a very small chance to find the global optimum.

The Griewangk function is an example of a non-separable function. It has one global optimum in the origin of the coordinate system and several (the exact number depends on the dimensionality) local optima surrounding (and hiding) the global one. Many evolutionary algorithms fall in trouble with this function.

The Rosenbrock (a.k.a. Banana) function has a high degree of dependency between the variables. It is very hard to optimize using ordinary evolutionary algorithms. The basic form of this function is two-dimensional. The optimal value of this function is 0 for point $(1, 1)$.

3.2 Involved Evolutionary Techniques

The distribution tree evolutionary algorithm (DiT-EA) is compared to the genetic algorithm (with a low and a high resolution), to the histogram UMDA, to the random search and to the line search heuristic.

Sampling individuals one by one with the uniform distribution on the whole search space – that is the simple *random search*. In order to give some indication of how complex the test problems are, I tried to optimize them also with the so-called *line search* (LS) method [9] which is a heuristic very efficient for separable problems. The discretization step for the LS was set to 0.01. This means that for Two Peaks function the LS algorithm evaluates 1201 data points for each dimension. If the LS gets stuck (no further improvement possible), it is restarted from another randomly generated point.

Further I compared the DiT-EA to 2 instantiations of GAs. It is very hard to compare a GA to an EDA in the continuous domain. While the EDA searches the space of real numbers (or rational numbers when evolving *in silico*), the GA evolves binary strings and searches a discretized space, and thus solves a different, much easier task. The resolution can deteriorate the GA performance e.g. due to insufficient precision. Thus, in experiments I used two GAs – one with a low resolution (allowing the GA to find such a solution the distance of which from the global optimum is not larger than 0.001), and second with a high resolution (allowing the GA to find such a solution the distance of which from the global optimum is not larger than 2.22^{-16}). The actual settings for individual test functions can be found in Table 2.

Table 2. Summary of settings of several algorithms involved in the study.

Algorithm		Function					
		Two Peaks		Griewangk		Rosenbrock	
GA-low	Crossover:	Uniform, 100%					
	Resolution:		14 bits	Resolution:	14 bits	Resolution:	12 bits
GA-high	Crossover:	Uniform, 100%					
	Resolution:		56 bits	Resolution:	56 bits	Resolution:	55 bits
Hist-UMDA	Histogram type:	Equi-height					
	Number of Bins:	120		Number of Bins:	100	Number of Bins:	41

The univariate marginal distribution algorithm (UMDA) with the equi-height histogram model was described e.g. in [7, 8]. The number of bins for each histogram is set in such a way that if all the bins had equal width, none of them would be larger than 0.1 (see Table 2).

The distribution tree, its construction and sampling is described in section 2. The only parameters to be set are the minimal number of individuals that must remain in each node ($minInNode$ set to 3), the minimal node size allowing the split in the node ($minToSplit$ set to 5), and the maximal p-value for which we consider a split statistically significant ($maxPValue$ set to 0.001).

In all experiments, no mutation was used. The study is aimed at generalized crossover operators and the mutation would introduce a noise which would make it impossible to distinguish the effects of mutation and crossover. Moreover, typical mutation operators for binary and real chromosomes are incomparable.

3.3 Results and Discussion

The overall results for all problems are shown in Table 3. For population based algorithms experiments with population sizes of 20, 50, 100, 200, 400, 600, and 800 were carried out. Each experiment was repeated 20 times, and the average best fitness and its standard deviation based on all 20 runs was measured. The population size which resulted in the best average score after 50,000 evaluations was selected to be included in the table.

Table 3. Results of experiments on all test functions. The first row in each cell shows the best fitness averaged over 20 runs and its standard deviation in parentheses. The second row shows the population size for which the results are reported.

Func	Algorithm					
	Random	Line Search	GA low res.	GA high res.	Hist UMDA	DiT EA
2D Two Peaks	0,1788 (0,0752)	0 (0)	0,0018 (0)	2,5e-11 (3,9e-11)	0 (0)	4,8e-13 (2,3e-13)
			400	600	200	600
2D Griewangk	2,1e-4 (2,5e-4)	0 (0)	2,3e-5 (8,7e-5)	1,3e-7 (5,1e-7)	0,0024 (0,0026)	0 (0)
			600	600	800	400
2D Rosenbrock	0,0012 (0,0021)	0,0051 (0,0053)	5,3e-5 (1,4e-4)	9e-7 (3,1e-6)	0,0044 (0,0042)	5e-5 (9,6e-5)
			800	800	800	600
20D Two Peaks	35,3914 (1,8198)	0 (0)	0,8168 (0,7827)	0,9627 (0,6612)	0,0027 (0,0059)	27,1593 (2,7677)
			400	400	400	100
10D Griewangk	0,4874 (0,0874)	0,2975 (0,3412)	0,0063 (0,0031)	0,0083 (0,0057)	0,0033 (0,002)	2,5e-4 (4,9e-4)
			400	400	800	600
10D Rosenbrock	27,0552 (10,418)	1,168 (0,4596)	1,9947 (1,3471)	2,2752 (0,9745)	0,6373 (0,1714)	1,8554 (0,6581)
			400	400	400	600

As expected, the Hist-UMDA was very efficient when solving separable problems, i.e. the 2D and 20D Two Peaks function, and the 10D Rosenbrock function as well. Although the variables in the basic 2D Rosenbrock function are not independent, due to the way the 10D version was constructed, each pair of variables in the 10D Rosenbrock function is independent of the rest.

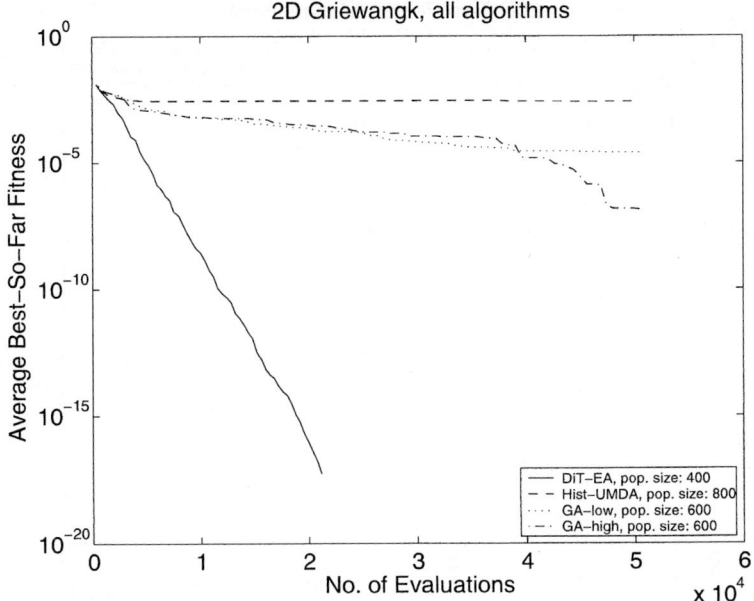

Fig. 4. Evolution of the involved algorithms on the test problem for which the DiT-EA performed best.

The DiT-EA was the best competitor when solving both variants of the Griewangk function (see Fig. 4 for an illustration). In both cases it was able to find a solution of significantly better quality. In the majority of the rest of the involved test problems, its efficiency was better or comparable to that of GAs. The 20D Two Peaks function is the only exception (see Fig. 5). The DiT-EA was able to find solutions only slightly better than those obtained by random search. I hypothesize that this poor behavior is caused by the great number of local optima of this function (to be precise, the 20D Two Peaks function has 2^{20} local optima). To capture the problem structure, the DiT-EA would need a huge population. Hundreds of individuals allow the algorithm to make only limited number of leaf nodes with 'almost the same' density.

For the 2D functions, the GA-high found better solutions than the GA-low. GA with low resolution suffered from the insufficient bit string length. For the multidimensional functions, however, the difference between the two GAs vanished and they performed almost identically along the whole evolution when compared by a human eye.

4 Summary, Conclusions and Future Work

The article described an estimation of distribution algorithm using the distribution tree model. The model is developed here and to the best of the author's

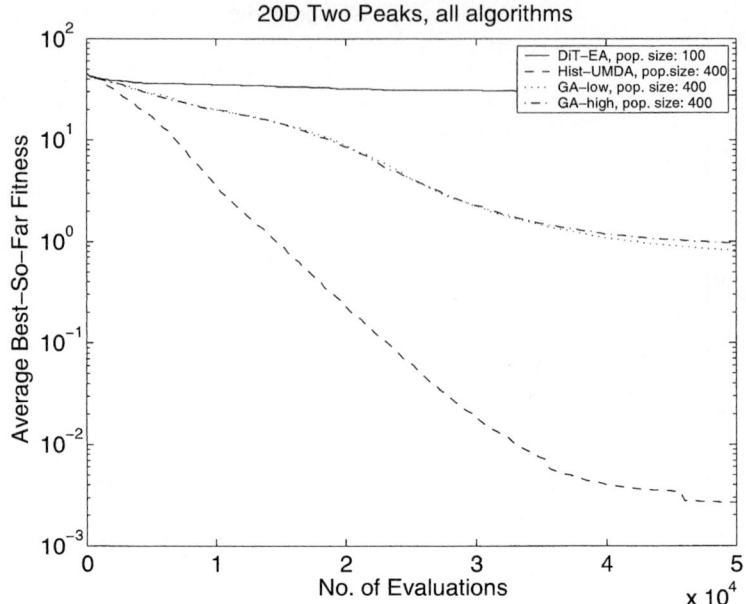

Fig. 5. Evolution of the involved algorithms on the test problem for which the DiT-EA performed worst.

knowledge it is original and has not been used anywhere else yet. The DiT-EA was compared to other search algorithms on several test functions and it showed up to be a strong competitor in the field of the real-valued optimization with box constraints. The experiments showed that the members of EDA class of algorithms (histogram UMDA and DiT-EA) in almost all cases outperformed the GAs – they were able to find more precise solutions with less time needed.

It can be stated that the DiT-EA is very efficient when solving problems with several well-distinguished local optima. The population members after selection then form clusters in the search space and the DiT-EA seems to be able to identify them and to use this information in evolution (the DiT model tries to identify rectangular areas of the search space with significantly different densities). Furthermore, the DiT presents a model built on the basis of rigid statistical testing which is not rather common in the field of EAs.

The DiT has its own bottlenecks, of course. First, it is able to create only axis-parallel splits of the search space which can result in a limited ability to search the promising areas of the space if they look like valleys which are not parallel to the coordinate axes. This drawback can be reduced by employing a kind of coordinate transformations in the node. The Independent Component Analysis seems to be very suitable method for making the DiT model rotationally invariant.

Second, the presented version of the algorithm is not able to decompose the task at hand as was shown on the 20D Two Peaks function. Using some technique of independency detection in each node would allow the algorithm to hierarchically decompose the problem into a set of problems of lower dimensionality. Such a model would be comparable to models capturing the dependency structure of variables, e.g. the MBOA. In that case the model deserves much thorougher analysis, e.g. in the scalability area.

Another possibility for future work is the fact that the model building algorithm allows very simple generalization for discrete variables. Only the procedure for creating the set of candidate splits would have to be changed.

Acknowledgments

This research was supervised by Doc. Ing. Jiří Lažanský, CSc. and was supported by the Grant agency of the Czech Republic with the grant No. GACR 102/02/0132 entitled "Use of Genetic Principles in Evolutionary Algorithms".

References

1. Peter A.N. Bosman and Dirk Thierens. Continuous iterated density estimation evolutionary algorithms within the IDEA framework. In *Workshop Proceedings of the Genetic and Evolutionary Computation Conference (GECCO-2000)*, pages 197–200, 2000.
2. Leo Breiman, Jerome Friedman, Charles J. Stone, and R. A. Olshen. *Classification and Regression Trees*. Kluwer Academic Publishers, January 1984.
3. Marcus R. Gallagher, Marcus Frean, and Tom Downs. Real-valued evolutionary optimization using a flexible probability density estimator. In *Genetic and Evolutionary Computation Conference (GECCO-1999)*.
4. Pedro Larrañaga and Jose A. Lozano, editors. *Estimation of Distribution Algorithms*. GENA. Kluwer Academic Publishers, 2002.
5. Jiří Očenášek and Jiří Schwarz. Estimation of Distribution Algorithm for Mixed Continuous-Discrete Optimization Problems. In *2nd Euro-International Symposium on Computational Intelligence*, IOS Press, Kosice, Slovakia, 2002, pages 227–232. ISBN 3-540-444139-5, ISSN 0302-9743.
6. Martin Pelikan, David E. Goldberg, and Fernando Lobo. A survey of optimization by building and using probabilistic models. Technical Report IlliGAL Report No. 98018, University of Illinois, Urbana-Champaign, September 1999.
7. Petr Pošík. Comparing various marginal probability models in evolutionary algorithms. In Pavel Ošmera, editor, *MENDEL 2003*, volume 1, pages 59–64, Brno, 2003. Brno University. ISBN 80-214-2411-7.
8. Shigeyoshi Tsutsui, Martin Pelikan, and David E. Goldberg. Evolutionary algorithm using marginal histogram models in continuous domain. Technical Report IlliGAL Report No. 2001019, University of Illinois, Urbana-Champaign, March 2001.
9. D. Whitley, K. Mathias, S. Rana, and J. Dzubera. Evaluating evolutionary algorithms. *Artificial Intelligence*, 85:245–276, 1996.

Optimization via Parameter Mapping with Genetic Programming

Joao C.F. Pujol[1] and Riccardo Poli[2]

[1] CDTN, Rua Prof. Mario Werneck s/n,
30123 970, Belo Horizonte, Brazil
pujol@cdtn.br
[2] University of Essex, Wivenhoe Park, CO4 3SQ, Colchester, UK
rpoli@essex.ac.uk

Abstract. This paper describes a new approach for parameter optimization that uses a novel representation for the parameters to be optimized. By using genetic programming, the new method evolves functions that transform initial random values for the parameters into optimal ones. This new representation allows the incorporation of knowledge about the problem being solved. Moreover, the new approach addresses the scalability problem by using a representation that, in principle, is independent of the size of the problem being addressed. Promising results are reported, comparing the new method with differential evolution and particle swarm optimization on a test suite of benchmark problems.

1 Introduction

Parameter Optimization (*POPT*) problems present themselves in a variety of important domains ranging from engineering to *AI*, from mathematics to biological sciences, in areas such as function optimization, system identification, *AI* search, control, machine learning, design and many others. In order to solve *POPT* problems using computers, one has to specify a *representation* for the parameters of a system and then an *algorithm* that will perform the optimization of these parameters.

A lot of research has gone into search, learning and optimization algorithms, but by no means it can be claimed that a clear understanding of the space of all such algorithms has been achieved. Also, insufficient research has been devoted to the question of choosing a good parameter representation for a system. Indeed, most of the methods of parameter optimization proposed in the literature use simple arrays of numbers as a representation for the system's parameters. Overall performance differences are then the result of algorithms' differences/improvements only. This is not satisfactory because major speedup is often attainable through a change in representation of the solutions rather than in the search algorithm.

In the area of evolutionary computation there has been some interest in different ways of representing parameters. In most cases the research focus has been the so-called genotype/phenotype mapping [1, 2, 9], but rarely has this research considered real-valued mappings.

An issue that also plagues optimization methods is the so called scalability problem. As the number of parameters to be optimized increases, the size of the search space increases exponentially, making the problem intractable. To avoid the exponential growth of the search space, one can impose constraints on the parameters. However this is not always possible nor desirable.

In this work a new approach for parameter optimization based on Genetic Programming (GP) [4, 5] is described. The new method introduces a new parameter representation that is independent of the number of parameters to be optimized. Moreover, the new algorithm allows the incorporation of information about the problem being dealt with. In Section 2, the new approach is described. In Section 3, results of experiments are reported. Section 4 concludes with suggestions for further research.

2 Parameter Mapping Approach

The basic idea behind the *parameter mapping approach* (PMA) is to use computer programs to represent both the optimization algorithms and the parameters to be optimized at the same time, and to evolve such programs using GP. In PMA a population of GP programs represents a set of trial mapping functions which transform initial sets of parameter values into adapted ones. Under the guidance of an appropriate performance measure, GP iteratively improves such functions, until a mapping function is evolved which can satisfactorily transform a given initial set of parameter values into a good set of values. The method is illustrated in Figure 1. In the *initialisation block*, random values are assigned to each parameter being optimized. These initial values do not change in the course of the evolutionary process. They are random constants initialized once and for all.

It is interesting to note that, as the same scalar GP function is used to map each parameter, the result of the evolutionary process performed in PMA can

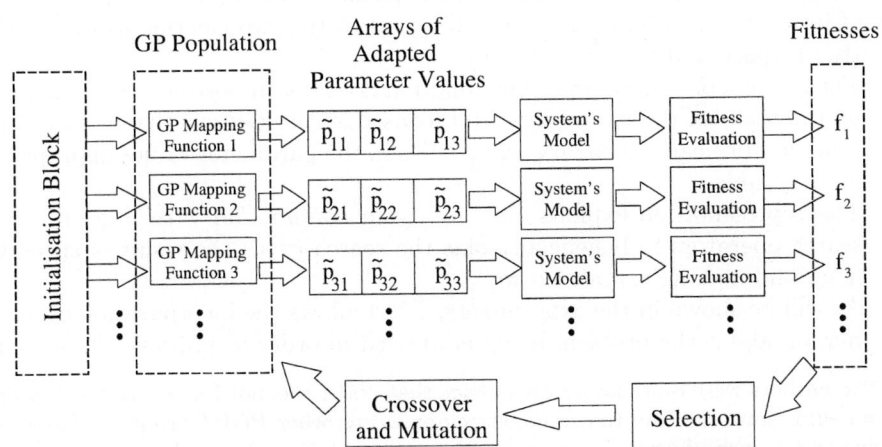

Fig. 1. PMA applied to a system with three parameters

be interpreted as a non-iterative *POPT* algorithm that, given the initial set of random parameters, is able to map it into the target set in one pass. A second interpretation is to consider the fact that in one way or another the scalar *GP* function is a representation for a whole set of parameter values since, given as input, each component of the initial set of random values produces as output a corresponding optimum value.

So, in the first interpretation the evolutionary process performed in *PMA* is searching the space of possible non-iterative *POPT* methods for a perfect direct parameter optimization algorithm. In the second interpretation, the evolutionary process performed in *PMA* is searching for a holistic representation for the target set of parameter values. Naturally, these two viewpoints are equivalent.

In previous research [6, 8], an early version of *PMA* was applied to the training of neural networks (*NNs*). This was inspired by the observation that the process of training the weights of *NNs* is simply a (usually iterative) transformation from a set of initial (typically random) raw weights to a set of trained weights, and that that transformation does not have to be necessarily implemented in the iterative gradient-descent way of typical *NNs* learning rules. If the trained weights were known in advance, it would be a simple task to build a training set of pairs (initial-random-weight/trained-weight), and then fit a function to them by error minimization. However, as the target values are usually unknown, Genetic Programming was used to evolve a function by using the output error of the neural network as fitness function. The evolved function was then used to compute the trained weights by using the initial random weights as input. The experiments revealed that *PMA* was more effective than more traditional approaches[1].

The original version of *PMA* has the following important features that presumably will also be shared by more general forms of *PMA*:

1. Within each individual the parameters to be optimized are not individually encoded: they are represented by a single function. Consequently, the representation does not necessarily grow quickly with the size of the problem of interest (which unavoidably would lead to the exponential growth of the search space and poor scalability).
2. The use of a parameter mapping function does not impose strong constraints on the value of the parameters and, consequently, *GP* can discover and use arbitrary or nearly arbitrary regularities in the parameter values appropriate for a system.
3. The representation exploits this ability in conjunction with a good set of search operators to beneficially bias the search (with the result of speeding it up and making it scale up well).
4. As will be shown in the experiments, *PMA* allows the incorporation of information about the problem being addressed in order to improve the search.

---

[1] The authors were quite aware of the fact that *PMA* was not limited to the training of neural networks, and that it could be applied to other *POPT* problems. However, due to the lack of financial support, further research could not be carried out. As funding has now become available, the exploration of *PMA* was resumed.

3 Experiments

3.1 GP Implementation

To carry out the experiments a steady state form of *GP* was used, with standard subtree crossover and tournament selection (tournament size=2). Mutation was implemented as a replacement of nodes by random nodes of the same arity. An elitist strategy was also implemented, by performing crossover with the best individual of the population. In all experiments, 50% of the offspring were created by crossover. The other 50% were generated by mutation. The offspring is inserted in the population, if it is superior to at least one of the parents. Replacement is carried out by negative tournament.

The *GP* function set included the arithmetic operators of *addition*, *subtraction*, *multiplication* and *protected division* (which returns the numerator if the denominator is zero).

The terminal set included a variable representing the parameter to be optimized. In some of the experiments (identified in the text) the terminal set was extended to include other variables, to convey information about the problem being tackled, and also random constants.

3.2 Test Functions

To explore the potential of the new method, it was applied to minimize a set of benchmark functions, the well-known De Jong set. This set of functions was chosen because it has been extensively used as a test suite for optimization algorithms. In addition, it includes functions of varying degrees of difficulty, so that one can compare the performance of different optmization methods. Two other functions taken from [13] were also included. The whole test suite is as follows:

1) First De Jong function. $F1(\mathbf{x}) = \sum_{j=1}^{3} x_j^2$, where $x_j \in [-5.12, 5.12]$. Minimum *is* $F1(0) = 0$.
2) Second De Jong function. $F2(\mathbf{x}) = 100 \times (x_1^2 - x_2)^2 + (1 - x_1)^2$, where $x_j \in [-2.48, 2.48]$. Minimum *is* $F2(1) = 0$.
3) Third De Jong function. $F3(\mathbf{x}) = 30 + \sum_{j=1}^{5} \lfloor x_j \rfloor$, where $x_j \in [-5.12, 5.12]$. Minimum *is* $F3(-5.12 \leq x_j < -5) = 0$.
4) Fourth De Jong function modified according to [13]. $F4(\mathbf{x}) = \sum_{j=1}^{30} (x_j^4 \times j + \nu)$, where $x_j \in [-1.28, 1.28]$. Minimum is $F4(0) \leq 30 \times \overline{\nu} = 15$, where $\nu \in [0, 1)$ is a random variable with a uniform distribution, and $\overline{\nu} = 0.5$ is its expected value.
5) Fifth De Jong function.

$$F5(\mathbf{x}) = \frac{1}{0.002 + \sum_{i=1}^{25} \frac{1}{i+(x_1-a_{i1})^6+(x_2-a_{i2})^6}},$$

where $x_j \in [-65.536, 65.536]$
$a_{i1} = [-32, -16, 0, 16, 32, -32, -16, \ldots, 0, 16, 32]$

$a_{i2} = [-32, -32, -32, -32, -32, -16, -16, \ldots, 32, 32, 32]$
Minimum is $F5(-32, -32) \approx 1$.

6) Corona's parabola [13]. $F6(\mathbf{x}) = \sum_{j=1}^{4} f_j$,
where $f_j = 0.15 \times (z_j - 0.05 \times sign(z_j))^2 \times d_j$, if $\|x_j - z_j\| < 0.05$
$otherwise f_j = d_j \times x_j^2$; $x_j \in [-1000, 1000]$
with $z_j = \lfloor \|\frac{x_j}{0.2}\| + 0.49999 \rfloor \times sign(x_j) \times 0.2$ and $d_j = \{1, 1000, 10, 100\}$
Minimum is $F6(\mathbf{x})=0$, with $\|x_j - z_j\| < 0.05$.

7) Griewangk's function [13]. $F7(\mathbf{x}) = \sum_{j=1}^{10} \frac{x_j^2}{4000} - \prod_{j=1}^{10} \cos(\frac{x_j}{\sqrt{j+1}}) + 1$,
where $x_j \in [-400, 400]$. Minimum is $F7(\mathbf{0})=0$.

The performance of the *PMA* approach was tested on these function, and the results were compared to two other methods: Differential Evolution (*DE*) and Particle Swarm Optimization (*PSO*), as described in [11, 12].

In all experiments, when the value of a parameter generated by *GP* or the other methods, exceeded the boundaries defined for the function being optimized, the closest boundary value was assigned to the parameter.

The results of these experiments are discussed in the next section.

3.3 Experimental Results

To evaluate the performance of the three methods, 100 independent runs were carried out. The 100 runs were divided into 10 batches of 10 runs each. For each batch, average values for the number of successful optimizations and for the number of fitness evaluations to achieve that result were obtained. The results for the 10 batches were then used to compute standard deviations.

First Set of Experiments. In the first set of experiments, only a single variable representing the parameter to be optimized was used in the *GP* terminal set. The results of this set of experiments are summarized in Table 1a.

In terms of number of fitness evaluations (*NFE*) to find a solution, *PMA* considerably outperformed both *DE* and *PSO*, with the exception of functions *F3* and *F5*. Although outstanding, these results should not lead one to jump to conclusions. For most of the functions optimized, the minimum values are either *0* or *1*, and these values are extremely easy to generate by using the *PMA* representation. For example, a *GP* tree encoding the algebraic expression *x-x*, will always produce *0* as a result. Similarly, the algebraic expression *x/x* will always produce *1*, provided that x is greater than zero. This effect becomes clear on the optimization of functions *F3* and *F5*, where the minimum is neither *0* nor *1*, *PMA* was outperformed by both *DE* and *PSO*. Actually, *PMA* behaved surprisingly well for these two functions, since no constants (random or otherwise) were included in the *GP* terminal set to help build the solutions.

The three methods converged to a solution in almost all runs. However, their performance varied considerably for some of the functions. As expected, for function *F5*, *PMA* performed poorly as compared to the other two methods. On the other hand, for function *F4*, *PMA* was successful in 63% of the cases, as compared to 22% and 1% yielded by *DE* and *PSO*, respectively. Moreover, for functions *F6* and *F7*, *PSO* did not converge to any solution at all. These results seem to indicate that *PMA* is more robust than *DE* and *PSO*.

Second Set of Experiments. In the second set of experiments, the degree of difficulty was increased by introducing a random shift in each dimension of the function $F(x)$ being optimized. The same random shift was applied to each dimension. So that the functions are now $F(x_1 - r, \ldots, x_i - r, \ldots, x_N - r)$, where r is a random constant in the range (-1,1), generated by using a uniform distribution. As a consequence, the optimal values are not *0s* and *1s* anymore, but are shifted by the amount provided by the random constant. The boundaries constraining the search were also shifted by the same amount.

For this set of experiments the *GP* terminal set was expanded to include three other variables: one to represent the random shift r, and two others to represent the boundaries. By using these additional variables, one is actually taking advantage of available information about the problem being addressed. Table 1b shows the results of this set of experiments.

In terms of number of fitness evaluations to find a solution, the situation was even better than in the first set of experiments, as *PMA* was only outperformed by the other two methods to find a solution for function *F5*. In terms of number of successful runs for this function, *PMA* was still outperformed by *DE* and *PSO*, but its rate of success increased to 73%. This gain in performance is a consequence of the use of available information about the problem to improve the search.

Third Set of Experiments. In a third set of experiments, the situation was made even harder by introducing a different random shift in each dimension of the function $F(x)$ being optimized. Except for the variable representing the parameter to be optimized, no additional variables to convey information about the problem, were included in the terminal set this time. That means, the functions to be optimized were supposed to be black boxes. In this case, no information neither about the random shifts nor the boundaries is available and, consequently, was not given as input. Instead, random constants in the (-1,+1) were added to the *GP* terminal set to allow the evolutionary process to build appropriate numerical constants. Table 1c summarizes the results for this set of experiments.

As expected, things were much harder for *PMA* this time. In terms of fitness evaluations it was outperformed by *DE*, except on functions *F3* and *F4*. As compared to *PSO*, *PMA* was superior on functions *F4*, *F6* and *F7*. As for the number of successful runs, although *PMA* has not converged to a solution all the time, it has clearly outperformed *DE* and *PSO* on function *F4*. Once again, *PSO* failed to produce any solution to functions *F6* and *F7*.

Although slower, *PMA* proved to be quite robust, achieving the optimum in at least 40% of the runs, irrespective of the problem, while for *DE* and *PSO*, there were problems where the performance dropped very significantly. This is particularly true if one uses a constant setup for *DE* and *PSO*. Actually, for many settings *DE* and *PSO* simply failed to converge.

Table 1. (a) Results for the first set of experiments. (b) Results for the second set of experiments. (c) Results for the third set of experiments. NFE represents the average number of fitness evaluations. HITS is equal to the average number of successful runs. SF is the scaling factor, and CP is the crossover probability. MS is the maximum speed. Standard deviations are in brackets

F_i			DE			PSO		PMA	
i	SF	CP	NFE	HITS	MS	NFE	HITS	NFE	HITS
1	0.5	0.3	937(23)	10(0)	0.01	4,378(251)	10(0)	10(3)	10(0)
2	0.9	0.5	961(64)	10(0)	0.01	6,193(604)	10(0)	24(5.7)	10(0)
3	0.8	0.3	157(13)	10(0)	10	49(2.9)	10(0)	238(66)	10(0)
4	0.2	0.2	892,622(93,531)	2.2(1.8)	0.01	99,291 (2,128)	0.1(0.3)	94,514(17,980)	6.3(1.2)
5	0.9	0.3	2,097(121)	10(0)	1.0	2,638(224)	10(0)	32,438(6,577)	1.4(0.8)
6	0.4	0.2	2,413(39)	10(0)	0.01-5	2,000,000(0)	no hit	12(4.2)	10(0)
7	0.2	0.2	62,875(2,451)	10(0)	0.01-5	2,000,000(0)	no hit	9(3.4)	10(0)

(a)

F_i			DE			PSO		PMA	
i	SF	CP	NFE	HITS	MS	NFE	HITS	NFE	HITS
1	0.5	0.3	481(10)	10(0)	0.01	4,335(217)	10(0)	44(8)	10(0)
2	0.9	0.5	1,021(64)	10(0)	0.01	6,175(586)	10(0)	469(158)	10(0)
3	0.8	0.3	160(12)	10(0)	10	50(3)	10(0)	20(7)	10(0)
4	0.2	0.2	473,027(20,807)	1.3(0.8)	0.01	97,153 (3,095)	0.8(0.8)	52,010(18,752)	8.1(1.0)
5	0.9	0.3	2,112(125)	10(0)	1.0	2,741(306)	10(0)	9,970(1,970)	7.3(1.3)
6	0.4	0.2	2,442(38)	10(0)	0.01-5	2,000,000(0)	no hit	42(9)	10(0)
7	0.2	0.2	32,947(1,366)	10(0)	0.01-5	2,000,000(0)	no hit	44(6)	10(0)

(b)

F_i			DE			PSO		PMA	
i	SF	CP	NFE	HITS	MS	NFE	HITS	NFE	HITS
1	0.5	0.3	500(29)	10(0)	0.01	4,083(339)	10(0)	60,757(10,306)	9.7(0.5)
2	0.9	0.5	902(44)	10(0)	0.01	5,828(556)	10(0)	50,794(7,110)	9.2(1)
3	0.8	0.3	142(11)	10(0)	10	49(3.4)	10(0)	110(34)	10(0)
4	0.2	0.2	902,137(69,548)	1.9(0.8)	0.01	95,186 (3,349)	1.1(0.5)	134,062(52,689)	8.6(1.2)
5	0.9	0.3	1,309(61)	10(0)	1.0	2,733(230)	10(0)	59,473(21,340)	8.6(1.2)
6	0.4	0.2	3,613(42)	10(0)	0.01-5	2,000,000(0)	no hit	281,183(41,306)	6(1.3)
7	0.2	0.2	63,153(1,930)	10(0)	0.01-5	2,000,000(0)	no hit	1,332,880(106,524)	4(1.9)

(c)

4 Conclusion and Further Research

In this paper a new approach for parameter optimization has been presented. The results of the experiments have shown that the new paradigm can be more robust than other methods. It has been also shown how the new approach can take advantage of information about the problem being addressed, in order to improve performance. It should be pointed out, that the ideas presented here should be further explored. For example:

1. Instead of using random-valued variables as input to the *GP* trees, one can use integers that identify the parameters to be optimized. So that the *GP* tree would actually operate as an addressed-by-integers memory that returns the target values of the parameters.
2. The *GP* function set may include functions that affect particular parameters but not others. This may help the evolutionary process to reduce or increase the interaction between parameters, as necessary.
3. Context information can be provided to the mapping function so that the value of the updated parameter can be made sensitive to context information, such as the value of neighboring or otherwise related parameters. In conventional learning methods a similar strategy is beneficially used. For example, for training neural networks, where the updating of a particular weight depends on the value of the others.

In any case, the parameter mapping approach need to be better understood and positioned in terms of other *POPT* algorithms. This can be achieved through comparative experimentation involving a range of optimization algorithms applied to a variety of interesting test problems, exhibiting various levels of complexity.

References

1. L. Altenberg. *Genome growth and the evolution of the genotype-phenotype map.* In W. Banzhaf and F. H. Eeckman, editors, *Evolution as a Computational Process*, pages 205–259. Springer-Verlag, Berlin, Germany,1995.
2. W. Banzhaf. *Genotype-phenotype-mapping and neutral variation – A case study in genetic programming.* In Y. Davidor et al., editors, *Parallel Problem Solving from Nature III*, volume 866 of *LNCS*, pages 322–332, Jerusalem, 9-14 Oct. 1994. Springer-Verlag.
3. D. Fogel and A. Ghozeil. *A note on representations and variation operators. IEEE Trans. on Evolutionary Computation*, 1(2):159–161, 1997.
4. J. Koza. *Genetic Programming: On the Programming of Computers by Means of Natural Selection.* MIT Press, Cambridge, MA, USA, 1992.
5. W. B. Langdon and R. Poli. *Foundations of Genetic Programming.* Springer, 2002.
6. J. Pujol. *Evolution of Artificial Neural Networks Using a Two-dimensional Representation.* PhD thesis, School of Computer Science, University of Birmingham, UK, Apr. 1999. (Available from http://www.cdtn.br/~pujol/tese19.ps)
7. J. Pujol and R. Poli. *Evolution of neural networks using a two-dimensional aproach.* In L. C. Jain, editor, *Evolution of Engineering and Information Systems and Their Applications*, CSC Press international series on computational intelligence. CRC Press, Boca Raton, Florida, USA, 1999.
8. J. Pujol and R. Poli. *Evolution of neural networks using weight mapping.* In W. Banzhaf et al., editors, *Proceedings of the Genetic and Evolutionary Computation Conference*, volume 2, pages 1170–1177, Orlando, Florida, USA, 13-17 July 1999. Morgan Kaufmann. (Available from
http://cswww.essex.ac.uk/staff/poli/papers/Pujol-GECC01999.pdf)

9. M. Shackleton, R. Shipman, and M. Ebner. *An investigation of redundant genotype-phenotype mappings and their role in evolutionary search.* In *Proceedings of the 2000 Congress on Evolutionary Computation CEC00*, pages 493–500, La Jolla Marriott Hotel La Jolla, California, USA, 6-9 July 2000. IEEE Press.
10. D. Wolpert and W. Macready. *No free lunch theorems for optimization.* IEEE Transactions on Evolutionary Computation, 1(1):67–82, Apr. 1997.
11. J. Kennedy and R. Eberhart. *The Particle Swarm: Social Adaptation in Information-Processing Systems.* In D. Corne et. al, editors. *New Ideas in Optimization*, pages 379-387, McGraw-Hill Publishing Company,1999.
12. K. Price. *An Introduction to Differential Evolution.* In D. Corne et. al, editors. *New Ideas in Optimization*, pages 379-387, McGraw-Hill Publishing Company,1999.
13. R. Storn and K. Price. *Differential Evolution - A simple and efficient adaptive scheme for global optimization over continuous spaces.* TR-95-012,International Computer Science Institute, Berkeley, USA,1995.

Multi-cellular Development:
Is There Scalability and Robustness to Gain?

Daniel Roggen[1] and Diego Federici[2]

[1] Autonomous Systems Laboratory, EPFL, Lausanne, Switzerland
daniel.roggen@epfl.ch
http://asl.epfl.ch
[2] Norwegian University of Science and Technology, Trondheim, Norway
federici@idi.ntnu.no
http://www.idi.ntnu.no/~federici

Abstract. Evolving large phenotypes remains nowadays a problem due to the combinatorial explosion of the search space. Seeking better scalability and inspired by the development of biological systems several indirect genetic encodings have been proposed. Here two different developmental mechanisms are compared. The first, developed for hardware implementations, relies on simple mechanisms inspired upon gene regulation and cell differentiation. The second, inspired by Cellular Automata, is an Artificial Embryogeny system based on cell-chemistry. This paper analyses the scalability and robustness to phenotypic faults of these two systems, with a direct encoding strategy used for comparison.
Results show that, while for direct encoding scalability is limited by the size of the search space, developmental systems performance appears to be related to the amount of regularity that they can extract from the phenotype. Finally the importance of comparing different genetic encodings is stressed, in particular to evaluate which key characteristics are necessary for better scalability or fault-tolerance. The lack of standard tests or benchmarks is highlighted and some characterisations are proposed.

1 Introduction

The evolution of large phenotypes is one of the most serious problems in the field of evolutionary computation. With each characteristic of the phenotype encoded by a single gene, the increase of the phenotypic size imposes for direct encoding strategies a combinatorial explosion of the search space.

On the other hand, biological systems develop into mature organisms with a complex process of embryogeny. Embryogeny is mediated by the interaction of DNA, RNA and proteins to produce the cell regulatory system. This sort of interaction does not permit a one to one map from gene to phenotypic trait (phene), since each gene influences several aspects of the phenotype (pleiotropy).

Motivated by the development of biological systems, several authors have proposed indirected encoding schemes. With indirect encoding, each phenotype is developed by a process in which genes are reused several times.

In this case, development is de facto a decompression of the genotype. But since compression is generally higher for regular targets, a serious question is how much these methods will prove viable for the evolution of arbitrarily complex phenotypes. For example, the correlation between genotype and phenotype space may decrease as the complexity of the target increases [1].

In other words, when looking at system evolvability, it appears that there is a tradeoff between the combinatorial gain achieved by searching in a restricted genotypic space and hindrances of a more complex fitness landscape caused by gene reuse.

Additionally, the restriction on the search space implies that a part of the solution space becomes unreachable, and some targets (such as those of high regularity) might be more viable than others.

These considerations imply that in the analysis of such systems, performance benchmarks play a fundamental role. Still, there is little agreement on a set of evolutionary targets that can be used for assessing their quality. On the contrary, it appears that the tasks are often selected ad hoc to highlight the strengths of a particular model.

In this paper we want to compare two different developmental models, the first used in the POEtic circuit [2, 3], the latter an Artificial Embryogeny system [4] based on cell chemistry [5, 6]. The comparison is carried out for varying phenotypic sizes, against a direct encoding strategy in a task that should favour the latter.

The intention is to investigate the viability of these two indirect encoding methods without leaving doubts about the generality of the results.

To this end, we have tried to set up a 'worst case scenario' for developmental systems, pushing for results that do not depend on particular features of the targets.

The selected task is the evolution of specific 2D patterns of various complexity (figures 3 and 4) and sizes (from 8x8 to 128x128), with fitness being proportional to the resemblance to the target. In the case of the direct encoding strategy, with a gene representing a single pixel, the fitness landscape is a simple unimodal function. On the contrary, in the case of development, gene reuse may imply a multimodal deceptive fitness landscape. Thus, the comparison of the methods will allow to address the influence of search space and pleiotropy on evolvability.

Development systems also provide internal dynamics which are absent in direct encoding strategies. These dynamics may provide a way to withstand phenotypic injuries. This aspect is explored by comparing the tolerance to faults of both systems with the linear deterioration typical of direct encodings.

The rest of this paper is organized as follows. Section 2 gives an overview of the development systems, section 3 describes the evolutionary task, section 4 presents the results on fault resistance and section 5 concludes.

2 Multi-cellular Growth and Differentiation Mechanisms

2.1 Morphogenetic System (MS)

The morphogenetic system [3] (**MS**) is a developmental model designed for multi-cellular systems and focusing on simplicity and compact hardware implementation, initially developed for the POEtic circuit [2]. It uses signalling and expression mechanisms which are remotely inspired by the gene expression and cell differentiation of living organisms [7], notably by the fact that concentrations of proteins and inter-cellular chemical signalling regulate the functionality of cells. Related works include the use of L-Systems [8] and various cell-based developmental processes [9, 10], and biologically plausible development models [11].

The **MS** assigns a functionality to each cell of the circuit from a set of predefined functionalities. Here functionalities are the colours necessary to draw the patterns. It operates in two phases: a *signalling phase* and an *expression phase*.

The signalling phase uses inter-cellular communication to exchange signals among adjacent cells to implement a diffusion-like process. A signal is a simple numerical value (signal intensity) that a cell owns. Special cells, called *diffusers*, own a signal of maximum intensity and start the diffusion process. Diffusion rules rely on the four neighbours of a cell to generate signal intensities which decrease linearly with the Manhattan distance from the diffuser. They do so by taking the smallest value for which the signal gradient with all the initialized neighbours is -1, 0 or 1. Figure 1 shows an example of the signalling phase in the case of a single type of signal, with two diffusers placed in the cellular circuit.

The expression phase finds the functionality to be expressed in each cell by matching the signal intensities in each cell with a corresponding functionality stored in an expression table.

The genetic code contains the content of the expression table and the position of the diffusers. A genetic algorithm is used for evolution. 16 diffusers and 4 functionalities (colours) are used. The population is composed of 400 individuals, selection is rank selection of the 300 best individuals, the mutation rate is 0.5% per bit, one-point crossover rate is 20% and elitism is used by copying best individuals without modifications into the new generation.

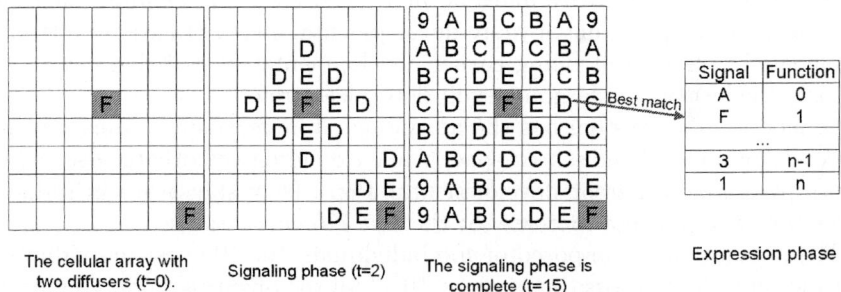

Fig. 1. The arrays on the left are snapshots of the signalling phase with one type of signal and two diffusers (gray cells) at the start of the signalling phase, after two time steps, and when the signalling is complete. The number inside the cells indicates the intensity of the signal in hexadecimal. The expression table used in the expression phase is shown on the right. The signal D matches the second entry of the table with signal F (smallest Hamming distance), thus expressing function F_1.

2.2 Embryogeny Model Based on Cell Chemistry

Introduction. Another way to develop the phenotype is to proceed with a recursive process of rewriting, which starts from a single egg cell to produce the mature organism. Among these Artificial Embryogeny (AE) systems [4], there are two main approaches.

The first is aimed at the evolution of a grammar which is repeatedly applied to the phenotype. Examples include the Matrix Rewriting scheme [12], the Cellular Encoding [10], Edge Encoding [13] and the GenRe system [14].

The second evolves the regulatory system of a cell with its metabolism and its ability to duplicate. Ontogeny results of the emergent interaction of neighboring cells and the chemical concentrations in the environment.

The model used in this paper belongs to this second category, and is an extension of the one presented in [6]. An extensive description on the model can be found in [5].

Description. Phenotypes are developed starting from a single egg (zygote) placed in the center of a fixed size 2D grid. Morphogenesis proceeds in discrete developmental steps, during which the growth program is executed for each cell, one cell at a time.

Cells are characterized by internal and external variables. Two internal variables (cell type and internal chemical concentration) define the cell state and move with it, while the external one belongs to the environment and follows a simple conservative diffusion law.

At each developmental step, any existing cell can release a chemical to the environment, change its own type, alter its internal metabolism and produce new cells in the cardinal directions North, West, South and East.

The growth program is governed by a feedforward Artificial Neural Networks (Morphers) without hidden layers. Each Morpher is specified by 144 genes (floating values), one for each of the 8 inputs, 16 outputs and bias weights (see figure 2).

Ontogeny is governed by multiple morphers, each one defining an Embryonic Stage which spans one or more developmental steps. Stages are introduced incrementally, those controlling earlier developmental steps being evolved first and only the last one undergoing evolution (please refer to [5] for the full details of the model). This system has the advantage of increasingly adding resolution to promising areas of the search space while excluding the others, also reducing pleiotropy among different developmental steps. New stages are introduced if the performance did not increase for the last 100 generations.

The population is composed of 400 individuals, the 100 best individuals survive and reproduce. Crossover is set at 10%. All the offspring undergo mutation: each of the weights of the evolving Morpher being changed with a .01 probability by adding Gaussian noise with .035 variance.

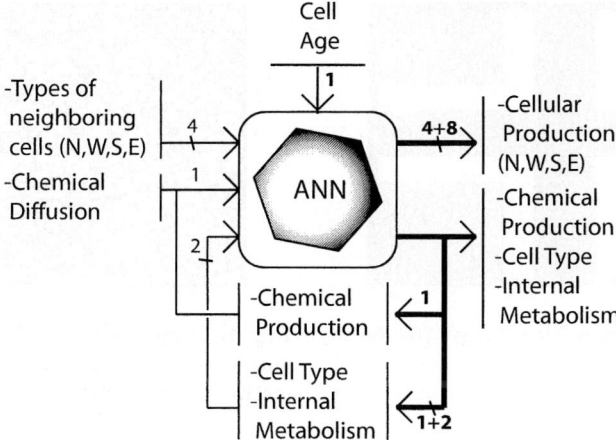

Fig. 2. The growth program (Morpher) input and output lines with their respective sizes. Each line is a floating point value $\in [-1, 1]$. The Morpher is implemented by a feedforward ANN, even though each cell internal variables (cell type and metabolism), implement a direct feedback pathway. Chemical production and diffusion offer a channel for inter-cell communication.

3 Evolution of Patterns and Scalability

The evolutionary task consists in evolving phenotypes resembling specific 2D patterns of increasing size. This type of problem has been selected in order to simplify the analysis of the results and avoid that the developmental models might benefit from embedded "*tricks*", which will not be applicable in other settings.

The targets are 8x8, 12x12, 16x16, 32x32, 64x64, 96x96 and 128x128 multi-cellular arrays. Each cell can take one of four possible types (colours). Two different typologies of targets are considered. The first one is a more regular 'Norwegian flag' pattern (figure 3) which presents a high degree of symmetry that should be exploitable by developmental systems. The latter, is a very complex pattern generated from a Cellular Automata using Wolfram's rule 90 and starting from random initial conditions (figure 4). Wolfram's rule 90 has been selected because it steadily produces patterns of high complexity, which are supposedly very difficult targets of developmental systems. In the case of direct encoding, the target patterns have equivalent difficulty.

Fitness is proportional to the resemblance of the individual to the target. In order to avoid premature convergence, individuals with rare phenotypic traits (pixels) are rewarded (please refer to [5] for further details).

The experiments were conducted 20 times for each target size. The population is composed of 400 individuals, undergoing elitism selection for 2000 generations. Model specific GA parameters are listed in section 2. For direct coding, the GA parameters are 10% single point crossover, mutation rate of 0.5% per gene, and each gene represents one of the 4 possible colors.

Fig. 3. Norwegian Flag Target (64x64).

Fig. 4. Target generated using a cellular-automata with rule 90 of Wolfram starting from a random initial line (64x64).

The genotype dimension for the various encodings and target sizes are listed in table 1. The size of the genetic code with the **MS** scales with the logarithm of the size of the array because the number of bits used to encode the position of the diffusers depends on the size of the array. The size of the genetic code using the embryogeny model remains constant because the morpher neural network relies only on the state of immediate neighboring cells to update the state of the current cell and hence needs no information about the size of the array. Size of direct encoding scales with the size of the array.

Table 1. Search space size of the 3 encoding methods presented for each target size. Genes, in the Direct Encoding determine the color at a given position, in the Indirect Encodings regulate the ontogeny of the phenotype. In the **MS** each gene is a bit, in the Embryogeny model is a floating point number in the range $[-1, 1]$.

Encoding	Search space by target dimension						
	8x8	12x12	16x16	32x32	64x64	96x96	128x128
Direct coding	64	144	256	1024	4096	9216	16384
MS	192	224	224	256	288	320	320
AES	144	144	144	144	144	144	144

Scalability is shown in figure 5 for the Norwegian flag and the CA-generated pattern. Direct encoding steadily reaches 100% fitness for arrays up to size 32x32. For larger targets, the explosion of the search space limits the overall performance.

Both development approaches perform similarly for small target sizes where they tend to get high fitness scores. Larger targets show a reduced performance which tends to stabilize around a certain level. In the case of the Norwegian flag, this level is determined by the complexity of the target pattern, which is constant with its size. In the case of the CA-generated target, complexity increases with size and solutions tend to exploit more the spatial frequency of the colours than their exact position.

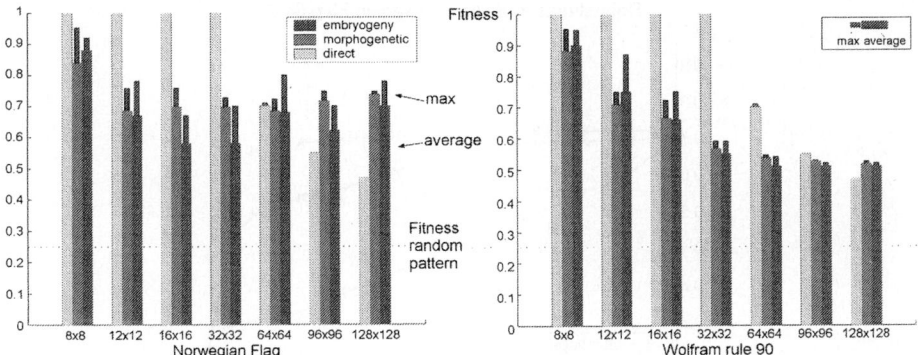

Fig. 5. Scalability for the morphogenetic system (**MS**), embryonic model (**AES**) and direct encoding on evolution of the Norwegian flag and CA-generated pattern.

Figure 6 shows the best evolved solutions for 64x64 targets with the different encoding schemes. Notice that the solutions generated by development systems show artifacts, due to their decoding scheme (diamond-shaped patterns for the **MS** and regular repetitions for the **AES**). On the other hand, direct encoding exhibits Salt and Pepper noise.

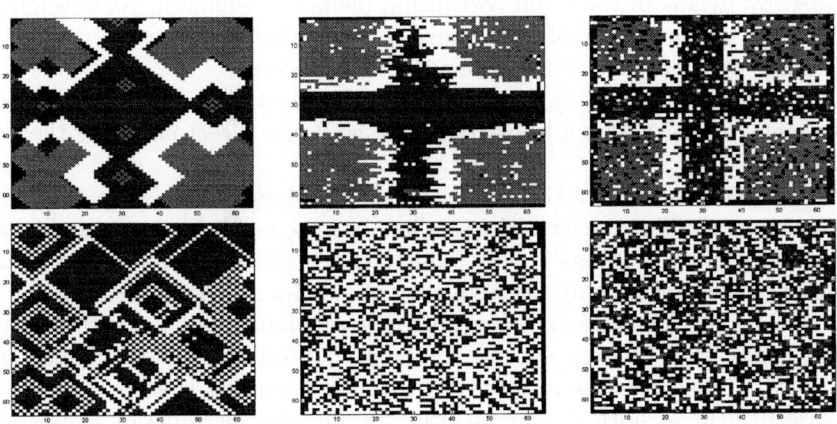

Fig. 6. Best evolved 64x64 solutions using, from left to right, **MS**, **AES** and direct coding. Norwegian flag above, CA-generated pattern below. Please refer to figures 3 and 4 for the actual targets.

4 Robustness

Natural organisms exhibit recovery capabilities, for example in case of injuries. In this section, we explore how these models behave when subjected to faults.

In order to have a meaningful deterioration mechanism for both developmental models, we consider here transient events which damage the state of the

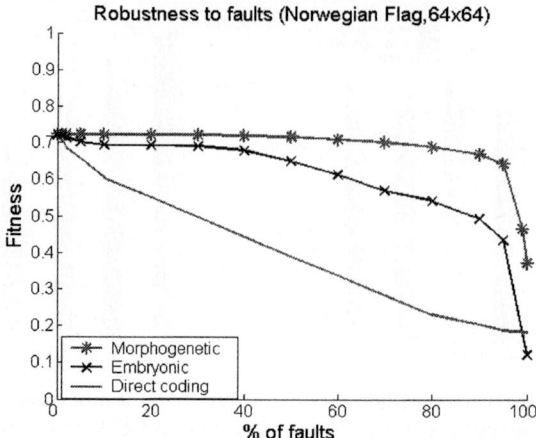

Fig. 7. Robustness of the **MS**, the **AES** and the direct coding on the Norwegian flag (size 64x64). Average over 100 tests. The fitness with 0% faults, is the one of the evolved solutions (.72 for development systems, .71 for direct encoding). Phenotypes with similar fitness scores were selected for better comparison. Fault recovery was not selected for.

cell (e.g. by means of radiation corrupting memory elements). As development continues to operate normally, cell functionality could be recovered. Notice that individuals were not selected for their fault resistance.

In the case of the **MS**, faults modify the chemical content of a cell[1]. For the embryogeny model, faults kill selected cells, while for direct encoding they alter their colour.

Robustness is tested on the best evolved phenotype of the Norwegian flag on the 64x64 array. This pattern and size has been selected because the fitness of the three genetic encodings is very similar and higher than the trivial solution consisting of exploiting only the frequency of colours as is the case with the CA-generated target. The damage rate (percentage of faulty cells) is varied between 0% and 100%. The damage process is repeated 100 times for each damage rate.

Figure 7 illustrates the results. While direct encoding is subject to a linear decrease in fitness, both developmental systems show a superior resistance to faults.

The **MS** benefits from the fact that chemical concentrations vary with continuity, and can be reconstructed with little effort. Also, evolution assigned the most frequent colour in the target to the default cell type, which explains the fitness value with 100% of faults.

In the case of the **AES**, fault recovery is a byproduct of ontogeny. These results are in support to what was previously observed in [6, 5].

---

[1] It is assumed that no faults occur in the expression table, since in any case it can be recovered from neighboring cells with a majority voting scheme.

5 Conclusions

We have tested the scalability of two developmental and one direct encoding strategy on a minimal task involving the evolution of specific target phenotypes.

Results show that the selected task, which was intended to be favorable to the direct encoding scheme, is easily solvable by the latter only for reasonably small target sizes. In these cases direct encoding greatly outperforms the developmental systems. Direct encoding benefits from the fact that each gene contributes independently to the fitness and therefore its landscape is both unimodal and non-deceptive.

On the other side, developmental systems suffer from the pleiotropy introduced by gene reuse. Also, as there is a single optimal solution, this utterly complicates the evolutionary task, since it is not guaranteed to fall within the space of expressible phenotypes.

In any case, with bigger targets, development systems can take advantage of their reduced search spaces, and this is reflected in their performance levels starting at the 64x64 Norwegian flag and 96x96 CA-generated targets.

Developmental systems seem 'smarter' at finding exploitable regularities in the targets, such as shape and most frequent cell types. On the other side, this is impossible for direct encodings, so that errors in the evolved phenotypes must take the shape of high frequency noise. This gives a different 'psychological' perception of incomplete phenotypes and seems to affect performance for larger targets.

Finally, both developmental systems behave very well against phenotypic faults and are capable of recovering from significant amount of damage, even if the tested individuals were not selected for this characteristic.

As a last remark, we want to stress the lack of standard tasks usable for benchmarking developmental systems. In [4] the authors suggest 4 different tasks: evolution of pure symmetry, of specific shapes, of specific connectivity patterns and of a simple controller.

We believe that some of these, albeit interesting to demonstrate capabilities of a model in principle, leave doubts about the generality of the results. For example, the evolution of a controller is a task that imposes complex fitness landscapes with usually many optimal and suboptimal solutions, and therefore is difficult to analyse in relation to system evolvability.

On the other side, testing a developmental model against targets of various phenotypic complexity[2], from pure symmetry to total lack of it, may offer a good indication of the system strengths and weaknesses in more general settings.

Acknowledgments

Daniel Roggen is funded by the Future and Emerging Technologies programme (IST-FET) of the European Community, under grant IST-2000-28027 (POETIC).

---

[2] Possibly calculating phenotypic complexity as its compressibility with standard algorithms.

The information provided is the sole responsibility of the authors and does not reflect the Community's opinion. The Community is not responsible for any use that might be made of data appearing in this publication. The Swiss participants to this project are funded by the Swiss government grant 00.0529-1.

References

1. Lehre, P., Haddow, P.C.: Developmental mappings and phenotypic complexity. Proceeding of CEC 2003, 62–68 (2003)
2. Tyrrell, A.M., Sanchez, E., Floreano, D., Tempesti, G., Mange, D., Moreno, J.M., Rosenberg, J., Villa, A.: POEtic Tissue: An Integrated Architecture for Bio-Inspired Hardware. In Tyrrell, A.M., et al., eds.: Proc. of the 5th Int. Conf. on Evolvable Systems (ICES 2003), Berlin, Springer (2003) 129–140
3. Roggen, D., Floreano, D., Mattiussi, C.: A Morphogenetic Evolutionary System: Phylogenesis of the POEtic Tissue. In Tyrrell, A.M., et al., eds.: Proc. of the 5th Int. Conf. on Evolvable Systems (ICES 2003), Berlin, Springer (2003) 153–164
4. Stanley, K., Miikulainen, R.: A taxonomy for artificial embryogeny. Artificial Life 9(2):93–130 (2003)
5. Federici, D.: Using embryonic stages to increase the evolvability of development. to appear in proceedings of WORLDS workshop at GECCO 2004 (2004)
6. Miller, J.: Evolving developmental programs for adaptation, morphogenesys, and self-repair. Proceeding of ECAL 2003, 256–265 (2003)
7. Coen, E.: The art of genes. Oxford University Press, New York (1999)
8. Haddow, P.C., Tufte, G., van Remortel, P.: Shrinking the Genotype: L-systems for EHW? In Liu, Y., et al., eds.: Proc. of the 4th Int. Conf. on Evolvable Systems (ICES 2001), Berlin, Springer (2001) 128–139
9. Eggenberger, P.: Cell interactions as a control tool of developmental processes for evolutionary robotics. In Maes, et. al., eds.: From Animals to Animats 4: Proceedings of the Fourth International Conference on Simulation of Adaptive Behavior, Cambridge, MA, MIT Press-Bradford Books (1996) 440–448
10. Gruau, F.: Automatic definition of modular neural networks. Adaptive Behavior **3** (1994) 151–183
11. Kumar, S., Bentley, P.J.: Biologically inspired evolutionary development. In Tyrrell, A.M., et al., eds.: Proc. of the 5th Int. Conf. on Evolvable Systems (ICES 2003), Berlin, Springer (2003) 57–68
12. Kitano, H.: Designing neural networks using genetic algorithms with graph generation system. Complex Systems, 4(4):461–476 (1990)
13. Luke, S., Spector, L.: Evolving graphs and networks with edge encoding: Preliminary report. In Koza, J.R., ed.: Late Breaking Papers GP-96. (1996) 117–124
14. Hornby, G.S., Pollack, J.B.: The advantages of generative grammatical encodings for physical design. In: Proceedings of CEC 2001, 600–607. (2001)

Constrained Evolutionary Optimization by Approximate Ranking and Surrogate Models

Thomas Philip Runarsson

Science Institute, University of Iceland
tpr@hi.is

Abstract. The paper describes an evolutionary algorithm for the general nonlinear programming problem using a surrogate model. Surrogate models are used in optimization when model evaluation is expensive. Two surrogate models are implemented, one for the objective function and another for a penalty function based on the constraint violations. The proposed method uses a sequential technique for updating these models. The quality of the surrogate models is determined by their consistency in ranking the population rather than their statistical accuracy. The technique is evaluated on a number of standard test problems.

1 Introduction

In engineering design optimization expensive mathematical or physical models are common. Surrogate models are numerical or physical simplifications of these models, respectively. These simplifications are essentially inexpensive models. Surrogate models have been used in optimization [11], also known as approximate models [1] and meta-models [9]. In optimization surrogate models are based on scarce samples of the expensive model.

In evolutionary optimization there is an increased interest in applying surrogate models in place of expensive fitness models. A recent survey of fitness approximation in evolutionary computation is presented in [2] and a framework for evolutionary optimization established in [3]. Engineering design optimization problems commonly include constraints which are often more costly to evaluate than the objective. The handling of general nonlinear constraints in evolutionary optimization using surrogate models has not received much attention. This problem is tackled here by introducing two surrogate models: one for the objective function and another for a penalty function based on the constraint violations. The proposed method uses a sequential technique for updating these models. The quality of the surrogate models are determined by their consistency in ranking the population rather than their statistical accuracy or confidence. At each generation the surrogate models are updated and at least one expensive model evaluation is performed. The key new idea here is to evaluate the accuracy of the model by observing how it changes the behavior of the evolutionary algorithm (EA). That is, how does the surrogate model influence selection?

The paper is organized as follows. In section 2 an effective EA for the general nonlinear programming problem is described. In section 3 the surrogate models implemented are presented. The performance of these models is evaluated on the sphere model. In section 4 the most effective way of sampling an expensive model is investigated. In section 5 the heuristic method of approximate ranking is described which will help determine how often the expensive model needs to be sampled. This is followed by a detailed experimental study of the proposed method on 13 benchmark functions in section 6. The paper concludes with a discussion and summary.

2 Constrained Evolutionary Optimization

Consider the general nonlinear programming problem formulated as

$$\text{minimize} \quad f(\mathbf{x}), \quad \mathbf{x} = (x_1, \ldots, x_n) \in \mathcal{R}^n, \tag{1}$$

where $f(\mathbf{x})$ is the objective function, $\mathbf{x} \in \mathcal{S} \cap \mathcal{F}$, $\mathcal{S} \subseteq \mathcal{R}^n$ defines the search space bounded by the parametric constraints $\underline{x}_i \leq x_i \leq \overline{x}_i$, and the feasible region $\mathcal{F}$ is defined by

$$\mathcal{F} = \{\mathbf{x} \in \mathcal{R}^n \mid g_j(\mathbf{x}) \leq 0 \ \forall \ j\}, \tag{2}$$

where $g_j(\mathbf{x})$, $j = 1, \ldots, m$, are inequality constraints (equality constraints may be approximated by inequality constraints). Using a penalty function approach the constraint violations are treated as a single function,

$$\phi(\mathbf{x}) = \sum_{j=1}^{m} \max[0, g_j(\mathbf{x})]^2. \tag{3}$$

In [7] an effective algorithm for solving nonlinear programming problems was introduced. This algorithm is described by the pseudocode in fig. 1. The algorithm is essentially an improved version of the (μ, λ) evolution strategy (ES) using stochastic ranking presented in [6]. The algorithm in fig. 1 also uses stochastic ranking, which balances the influence of the penalty and objective function in determining the overall ranking of the population. In particular the population of individuals, of size λ, are ranked from best to worst, denoted $(\mathbf{x}_{1;\lambda}, \ldots, \mathbf{x}_{\mu;\lambda}, \ldots, \mathbf{x}_{\lambda;\lambda})$, and only the best μ are selected. The further modification, presented here, is simply the attempt to replace both $\phi(\mathbf{x})$ and $f(\mathbf{x})$ by surrogate models. The surrogate models only influence the ranking, the remainder of the algorithm is unchanged.

3 Nearest Neighborhood Regression

Deciding on a general surrogate model for optimization, especially when taking the no-free lunch theorems [10] into consideration, is difficult. Commonly used surrogate models include, among others, Kriging, polynomial regression and radial basis function [2]. Perhaps the most simple and transparent surrogate model is the nearest neighbor (NN) regression model, that is

$$\hat{h}(\mathbf{x}_i) = h(\mathbf{y}_j) \text{ where } j = \underset{k=1,\ldots,\ell}{\text{argmin}} \|\mathbf{x}_i - \mathbf{y}_k\| \tag{4}$$

1 *Initialize:* $\sigma'_k = (\bar{\mathbf{x}}_k - \underline{\mathbf{x}}_k)/\sqrt{n},\ \mathbf{x}'_k = \underline{\mathbf{x}}_k + (\bar{\mathbf{x}}_k - \underline{\mathbf{x}}_k)\mathbf{U}_k(0,1),\ k = 1,\ldots,\lambda$
2 **for** $t := 1$ **to** T **do** *(generational loop)*
3   *evaluate:* $f(\mathbf{x}'_k),\ \phi(\mathbf{x}'_k), k = 1\ldots,\lambda$
4   *rank the* λ *points and copy the best* μ *in their ranked order:*
5     $(\mathbf{x}_i, \sigma_i) \leftarrow (\mathbf{x}'_{i;\lambda}, \sigma'_{i;\lambda}),\ i = 1,\ldots,\mu$
6   **for** $k := 1$ **to** λ **do** *(replication)*
7       $i \leftarrow \mod(k-1,\mu) + 1$ *(cycle through the best* μ *points)*
8   **if** $(k < \mu)$ **do** *(differential variation)*
9          $\sigma'_k \leftarrow \sigma_i$
10         $\mathbf{x}'_k \leftarrow \mathbf{x}_i + \gamma(\mathbf{x}_1 - \mathbf{x}_{i+1})$ *(if out of bounds retry using standard mutation)*
11   **else** *(standard mutation)*
12         $\sigma'_{k,j} \leftarrow \sigma_{i,j}\exp\left(\tau' N(0,1) + \tau N_j(0,1)\right),\ j = 1,\ldots,n$
13         $\mathbf{x}'_k \leftarrow \mathbf{x}_i + \sigma'_k \mathbf{N}(0,1)$ *(if out of parametric bounds then retry)*
14         $\sigma'_k \leftarrow \sigma_i + \alpha(\sigma'_k - \sigma_i)$ *(exponential smoothing [5])*
15   **od**
16   **od**
17 **od**

Fig. 1. The improved (μ,λ) ES using the differential variation (lines 8 – 11) performed once for each of the best $\mu-1$ points ($\gamma \approx 0.8$). $U(0,1)$ is a uniform random number in $[0,1]$ and $N(0,1)$ is normally distributed with zero mean and variance one. $\tau' \propto 1/\sqrt{2n}$, $\tau \propto 1/\sqrt{2\sqrt{n}}$ and $\alpha \approx 0.2$, see also [5,7].

where $\mathbf{Y} \equiv \{\mathbf{y}\}_{j=1}^{\ell}$ are the set of points which have been evaluated using the expensive model $h(\mathbf{y})$. The approximate model passes exactly through the function values at the given points $\mathbf{Y}$. For this reason points evaluated using either the surrogate or expensive model may be compared directly. An obvious refinement of the nearest neighbor regression model is to weight the contribution of κ neighbors according to their distance to the query point $\mathbf{x}_i$. This is achieved by calculating the weighted average of the κ nearest neighbors,

$$\hat{h}(\mathbf{x}_i) = \frac{\sum_{j=1}^{\kappa} v_i h(\mathbf{y}_j)}{\sum_{j=1}^{\kappa} v_j} \qquad (5)$$

where $v_j = 1/\|\mathbf{x}_i - \mathbf{y}_j\|^2$ is the distance-weighted contribution of the κ nearest neighbors. If there exists a neighbor j where $\|\mathbf{x}_i - \mathbf{y}_j\| < \varepsilon$ (a small value), then $\hat{h}(\mathbf{x}_i)$ is assigned $h(\mathbf{y}_j)$, that is, use (4).

The convenience in using nearest neighborhood regression is that learning consists of simply storing points, evaluated using the expensive model, in $\mathbf{Y}$. Each time a point is added the model is improved. If all the points are used, $\kappa = \ell$ in (5), the surrogate is called a *global model* and if only the nearest points are used a *local model*. Determining which model is most appropriate is problem dependent. For example, consider the case when the expensive model is the sphere model ($h(\mathbf{x}) = \sum_{k=1}^{n} x_k^2, n = 100$) and one is interested in the surrogate model resulting in the greatest rate of progress [8] towards the optimum. The progress rate may be simulated as follows: sample the expensive model space ℓ times, construct a surrogate model, and compute the progress. The experiment

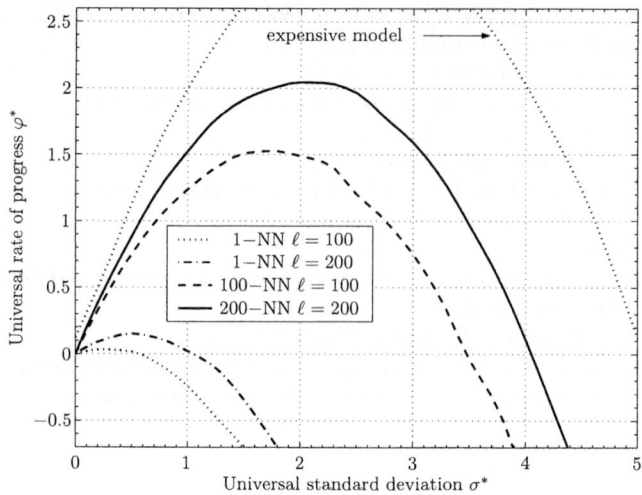

Fig. 2. The simulated progress rates for the local and global nearest neighbor regression models for the sphere model using a $(1, 100)$ evolution strategy.

is repeated 10.000 times and the expectation taken. The progress rates for a $(1, 100)$ ES using the surrogate models (4) and (5) for $\kappa = \ell$ is given in fig. 2. For the sphere model the weighted average of all nearest neighbors is the better surrogate model. Furthermore, it is clear that as the design space is sampled more densely, $\ell = 200$ rather than $\ell = 100$, the better the approximation and hence the progress. However, expensive models prohibit such an approach and so a sequential strategy, which regularly refines the surrogate model, is more suitable. Evolutionary algorithms are sequential (or generational) in nature and so this approach can be readily adapted.

4 Sampling Strategy

In this section an attempt is made to answer the following question. Given λ offspring which should be evaluated using the expensive model so that progress toward the optimum is maximized? As in the previous section the answer is sought via simulation. First of all, the individuals from previous generations are in $\mathbf{Y}$. For the $(1, \lambda)$ progress rate simulation this implies that initially $\mathbf{Y} = \mathbf{x}_o$. Three different sampling strategies are investigated for selecting the offspring, $\mathbf{x}_i \notin \mathbf{Y}$, to add to the set $\mathbf{Y}$. The first simply selects the best individual according to the surrogate model, the second selects an individual at random, and the third strategy is to select the offspring that is the furthest distance from its closest neighbor in $\mathbf{Y}$. The last strategy is motivated by the fact that the individual furthest from its nearest neighbor in $\mathbf{Y}$ is the worst approximated. The algorithm used to perform this progress rate simulation is presented in fig. 3. The progress rate simulations using $\lambda = 2\ell$ are presented in fig. 4 using the three different sampling strategies and various values of ℓ ($\lambda = 2\ell$) on the sphere model ($n =$

1 *Initialize*: $\sigma = \sigma^*(r/n)$, $r = \|\mathbf{x}^* - \mathbf{x}_o\|$
2 **for** $j := 1$ to M **do** *(Monte Carlo Simulation)*
3    $\mathbf{Y} = \mathbf{x}_o$, $\mathbf{x}_i = \mathbf{x}_o + \mathbf{N}_i(0, \sigma^2)$, $i = 1\ldots, \lambda$
4   **for** $k := 2$ to $(\ell + 1)$ **do** *sample points*
5   compute $\hat{h}(\mathbf{x}_i)$ using (5), $i = 1\ldots, \lambda$
6      $\mathbf{y}_k = \mathbf{x}_i$, $\mathbf{x}_i \notin \mathbf{Y}$ and i sampled according to a strategy
7   evaluate $h(\mathbf{y}_k)$ *(expensive model)*
8   **od**
9    $\varphi_j = r - \|\mathbf{x}^* - \mathbf{x}_{1:\lambda}\|$
10 **od**
11 Return *expectation*: $\varphi^* = (n/r) \sum_{j=1}^{M} \varphi_j / M$

Fig. 3. Computer simulation used to estimate the progress rates for the different sampling strategies. $M = 10.000$ and $\mathbf{x}^*$ is the optimum.

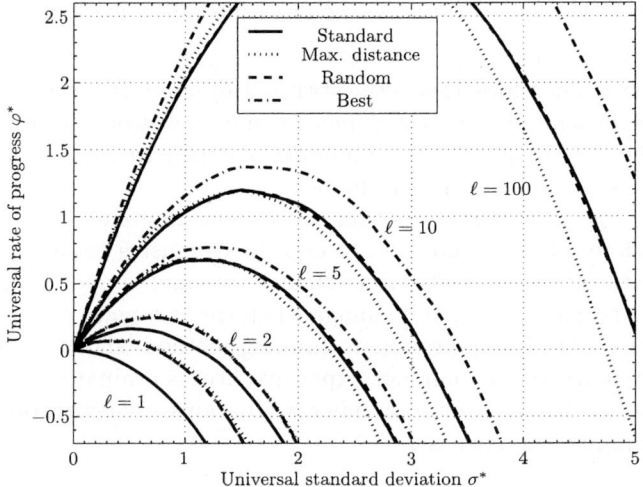

Fig. 4. $(1, 2\ell)$ progress rate for the three different sampling strategies, compared with standard method $(1, \ell)$, and different values of ℓ. $M = 10.000$.

100). Furthermore, the standard progress rate is given for the $(1, \ell)$ strategy using the expensive model directly. For small values of ℓ and λ all sampling strategies result in a greater progress than the standard method. However, as ℓ and λ increase sampling the best point, according to the surrogate, is the only sampling strategy which results in greater progress than the standard approach.

5   Approximate Ranking

In the previous section different sampling strategies were investigated. The results suggest that it would be most beneficial, in terms of progress, to evaluate the

```
1  approximate: $\hat{f}(\mathbf{x}'_k), \hat{\phi}(\mathbf{x}'_k), k = 1 \ldots, \lambda$
2  rank and determine the parent set $\mathbf{X}_1 \equiv \{\mathbf{x}'_{i:\lambda}\}_{i=1}^{\mu}$
3  $\mathbf{y}_j \leftarrow \mathrm{argmin}_{\mathbf{x}'_{i:\lambda}} i$ for $\mathbf{x}'_{i:\lambda} \notin \mathbf{Y}, j \leftarrow j+1$ (approximated best point)
4  evaluate: $f(\mathbf{y}_j), \phi(\mathbf{y}_j)$ (expensive model evaluation)
5  for $i := 2$ to $\lambda$ do
6      approximate: $\hat{f}(\mathbf{x}'_k), \hat{\phi}(\mathbf{x}'_k), k = 1 \ldots, \lambda$
7      determine new parent set $\mathbf{X}_i \equiv \{\mathbf{x}'_{i:\lambda}\}_{i=1}^{\mu}$
8      if $\mathbf{X}_{i-1} \neq \mathbf{X}_i$ do (the parent set has changed)
9          $\mathbf{y}_j \leftarrow \mathrm{argmin}_{\mathbf{x}'_{i:\lambda}} i$ for $\mathbf{x}'_{i:\lambda} \notin \mathbf{Y}, j \leftarrow j+1$
10         evaluate: $f(\mathbf{y}_j), \phi(\mathbf{y}_j)$
11     else (parent set remains unchanged)
12         break (exit for loop)
13     od
14 od
```

Fig. 5. The *approximate ranking* procedure where initially $Y \neq \emptyset$.

best individuals. Therefore, this is the strategy adopted. However, the number of samples to be evaluated using the expensive model was not established. Clearly one would like to minimize the total number of expensive model evaluations and yet retain a good quality surrogate model.

From the EA's perspective as long as a good approximate estimate of the parent set is found there is no need to call the expensive model. Therefore, the simple heuristic proposed is that the surrogate model is approximately correct as long as the parent set does not change when the surrogate model is improved. As a result the following approximate ranking method, shown in fig. 5, is used to determine indirectly the number expensive fitness evaluations needed at any given generation. The maximum number evaluations per generation is therefore λ and the minimum number is 1.

6 Experimental Study

In the following experiment 13 nonlinear programming problems from the literature [6,7] are studied. The improved ES in fig 1, denoted ιES, is compared with a surrogate version of the same algorithm, denoted $\hat{\iota}$ES. In the surrogate version lines 3–4 in fig. 1 are replace with the approximate ranking described in fig. 5. The only additional modification is that the set $\mathbf{Y}$ has a fixed size ℓ so that any new point added to the set automatically overwrites the oldest point. The idea here is that the old points are furthest away from the current population. The set $\mathbf{Y}$ should, however, be large enough to accept all new point at any given generation, that is $\ell \geq \lambda$. Clearly, the smaller ℓ becomes the faster the surrogate model is evaluated. There exist also a number of fast implementations of the NN algorithm, see for example [4].

The experimental setup is the same as in [6,7] where all experiments are run for a fixed number of generations, $T = 350000/\lambda$ with the exception of problem g12 which is run for $T = 35000/\lambda$ generations. As a first experiment the improved $(15, 100)\iota\text{ES}$ is compared with its surrogate counterpart using $\ell = 100$ and $\ell = 200$ respectively. In table 1 the results, for 30 independent runs, using the simple nearest neighbor regression (4) as the surrogate model is given. The quality of solutions found by surrogate version are similar to the one using the expensive model evaluations. The mean number of expensive model evaluations needed to locate the best solution may be found in the column labeled `feval` along with its standard deviation. The number of expensive model evaluation has been reduced for all problems, but only significantly for functions g01, g08, g09 and g12. Using a set size of $\ell = \lambda$ is also sufficiently large.

It is interesting to observe how the number of expensive fitness evaluations changes per generation due to the approximate ranking. This is shown in fig. 6 for two test functions based on an average of 100 independent runs. Also shown is the corresponding mean best objective value. For g01 the entire population must be evaluated using the expensive model at the beginning of the run. The number is reduced once the population enters the feasible region, then remains constant for some time at 40% of the population and then falls again toward the end of the run. For g02 the number of expensive function evaluations increases towards the end of the run.

When using the surrogate model (5) with $\kappa = \ell$ a poor global search performance is observed. For this reason it is decided to use $\kappa = 10$ and the entire experiment is repeated. This result is given in table 2. Using the 10-NN regression reduces the number of expensive function evaluations for test function g12 even further but now there are some difficulties in locating feasible solutions for test function g10 where only 18/30 and 26/30 feasible solutions are found for $\ell = 100$ and 200 respectively. In general there is no improvement over using just the simple nearest neighbor regression, i.e. 1-NN.

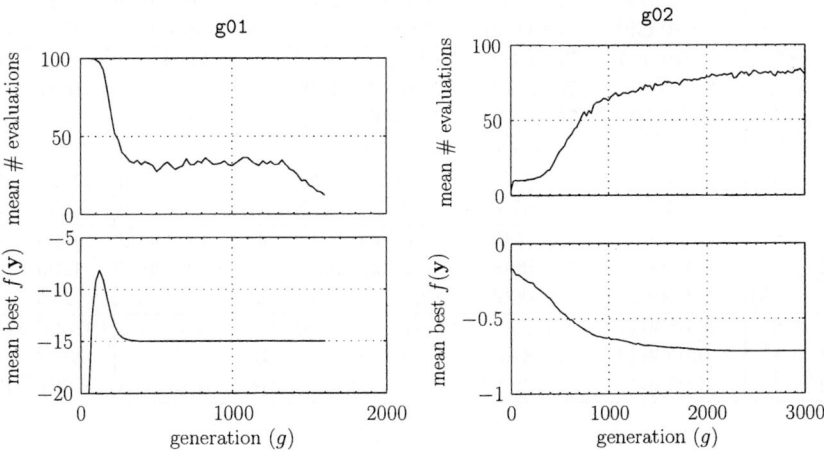

Fig. 6. Top plots shows the mean number of expensive model evaluation per generation and the bottom the corresponding mean best objective function value.

Table 1. Statistics for 30 independent runs using a $(15, 100)$ ES and its surrogate version using 1−NN.

	objective					feval	
	best	median	mean	st. dev.	worst	mean	std
g01 − ιES	−15.000	−15.000	−15.000	3.6E−16	−15.000	122163	5062
iES$(\ell = \lambda)$	−15.000	−15.000	−15.000	0.0E+00	−15.000	67341	6116
iES$(\ell = 2\lambda)$	−15.000	−15.000	−15.000	3.2E−16	−15.000	61783	7283
g02 − ιES	−0.803619	−0.760456	−0.753209	3.7E−02	−0.609330	348606	2578
iES$(\ell = \lambda)$	−0.803617	−0.708854	−0.707586	5.7E−02	−0.570960	209416	36582
iES$(\ell = 2\lambda)$	−0.803619	−0.744804	−0.731058	6.4E−02	−0.527944	211497	37225
g03 − ιES	−1.001	−1.001	−1.001	1.7E−05	−1.001	324206	27783
iES$(\ell = \lambda)$	−1.001	−1.001	−1.001	3.2E−06	−1.001	275094	7661
iES$(\ell = 2\lambda)$	−1.001	−1.001	−1.001	5.7E−07	−1.001	278894	6373
g04 − ιES	−30665.539	−30665.539	−30665.539	2.2E−11	−30665.539	68023	6004
iES$(\ell = \lambda)$	−30665.539	−30665.539	−30665.539	7.3E−12	−30665.539	53815	2669
iES$(\ell = 2\lambda)$	−30665.539	−30665.539	−30665.539	7.3E−12	−30665.539	53216	2479
g05 − ιES	5126.497	5126.497	5126.497	5.8E−12	5126.497	62976	3388
iES$(\ell = \lambda)$	5126.497	5126.497	5126.497	2.0E−12	5126.497	60844	3174
iES$(\ell = 2\lambda)$	5126.497	5126.497	5126.497	1.4E−07	5126.497	62814	3783
g06 − ιES	−6961.814	−6961.814	−6961.814	6.4E−12	−6961.814	55203	2900
iES$(\ell = \lambda)$	−6961.814	−6961.814	−6961.814	3.6E−12	−6961.814	46524	3349
iES$(\ell = 2\lambda)$	−6961.814	−6961.814	−6961.814	3.6E−12	−6961.814	46424	2305
g07 − ιES	24.306	24.323	24.337	4.1E−02	24.635	347393	12789
iES$(\ell = \lambda)$	24.308	24.336	24.375	7.6E−02	24.591	237195	41850
iES$(\ell = 2\lambda)$	24.307	24.326	24.337	3.5E−02	24.450	231089	44286
g08 − ιES	−0.095825	−0.095825	−0.095825	4.2E−17	−0.095825	64863	41349
iES$(\ell = \lambda)$	−0.095825	−0.095825	−0.095825	8.8E−18	−0.095825	2504	1957
iES$(\ell = 2\lambda)$	−0.095825	−0.095825	−0.095825	7.6E−18	−0.095825	2634	1766
g09 − ιES	680.630	680.630	680.630	7.4E−04	680.635	264120	82602
iES$(\ell = \lambda)$	680.630	680.631	680.632	2.4E−03	680.638	145955	23840
iES$(\ell = 2\lambda)$	680.630	680.630	680.631	1.8E−03	680.637	133523	17545
g10 − ιES	7049.404	7064.109	7082.227	4.2E+01	7258.540	304066	86127
iES$(\ell = \lambda)$	7050.290	7071.520	7086.310	4.0E+01	7191.870	283637	75378
iES$(\ell = 2\lambda)$	7049.620	7099.250	7118.900	7.1E+01	7367.780	295030	65746
g11 − ιES	0.750	0.750	0.750	1.8E−15	0.750	47046	2968
iES$(\ell = \lambda)$	0.750	0.750	0.750	1.1E−16	0.750	39289	2453
iES$(\ell = 2\lambda)$	0.750	0.750	0.750	1.1E−16	0.750	38566	3004
g12 − ιES	−1.000000	−1.000000	−1.000000	0.0E+00	−1.000000	19726	1462
iES$(\ell = \lambda)$	−1.000000	−1.000000	−1.000000	0.0E+00	−1.000000	4200	900
iES$(\ell = 2\lambda)$	−1.000000	−1.000000	−1.000000	0.0E+00	−1.000000	4216	921
g13 − ιES	0.053942	0.053942	0.111671	1.4E−01	0.438804	197606	117774
iES$(\ell = \lambda)$	0.053942	0.053942	0.143746	1.6E−01	0.438902	93302	14605
iES$(\ell = 2\lambda)$	0.053942	0.053942	0.182229	1.8E−01	0.181425	90768	12624

7 Summary

A new approach using surrogate models for global optimization has been presented and tested on some general nonlinear programming problems. A simple

Table 2. Statistics for 30 independent runs using a $(15, 100)$ ES and its surrogate version using 10−NN.

	objective					feval	
	best	median	mean	st. dev.	worst	mean	std
g01 − ιES	−15.000	−15.000	−15.000	3.6E−16	−15.000	122163	5062
ιES($\ell = \lambda$)	−15.000	−15.000	−15.000	0.0E+00	−15.000	64320	6219
ιES($\ell = 2\lambda$)	−15.000	−15.000	−15.000	3.2E−16	−15.000	60522	7030
g02 − ιES	−0.803619	−0.760456	−0.753209	3.7E−02	−0.609330	348606	2578
ιES($\ell = \lambda$)	−0.792608	−0.731221	−0.706970	6.8E−02	−0.552092	254828	9817
ιES($\ell = 2\lambda$)	−0.785266	−0.679370	−0.679007	5.6E−02	−0.564173	257185	8281
g03 − ιES	−1.001	−1.001	−1.001	1.7E−05	−1.001	324206	27783
ιES($\ell = \lambda$)	−1.000	−1.001	−1.001	6.8E−05	−1.001	259112	19095
ιES($\ell = 2\lambda$)	−1.000	−1.001	−1.001	1.1E−04	−1.001	257262	15739
g04 − ιES	−30665.539	−30665.539	−30665.539	2.2E−11	−30665.539	68023	6004
ιES($\ell = \lambda$)	−30665.539	−30665.539	−30665.539	7.3E−12	−30665.539	51369	3354
ιES($\ell = 2\lambda$)	−30665.539	−30665.539	−30665.539	7.2E−12	−30665.539	50733	3361
g05 − ιES	5126.497	5126.497	5126.497	5.8E−12	5126.497	62976	3388
ιES($\ell = \lambda$)	5126.497	5126.497	5126.497	8.8E−08	5126.497	59657	2555
ιES($\ell = 2\lambda$)	5126.497	5126.497	5126.497	5.6E−12	5126.497	58923	3288
g06 − ιES	−6961.814	−6961.814	−6961.814	6.4E−12	−6961.814	55203	2900
ιES($\ell = \lambda$)	−6961.814	−6961.814	−6961.814	3.6E−12	−6961.814	41787	2773
ιES($\ell = 2\lambda$)	−6961.814	−6961.814	−6961.814	3.6E−12	−6961.814	43462	2574
g07 − ιES	24.306	24.323	24.337	4.1E−02	24.635	347393	12789
ιES($\ell = \lambda$)	24.308	24.334	24.358	6.2E−02	24.531	234441	50231
ιES($\ell = 2\lambda$)	24.307	24.325	24.331	3.0E−02	24.476	209696	43488
g08 − ιES	−0.095825	−0.095825	−0.095825	4.2E−17	−0.095825	64863	41349
ιES($\ell = \lambda$)	−0.095825	−0.095825	−0.095825	1.3E−17	−0.095825	18801	17018
ιES($\ell = 2\lambda$)	−0.095825	−0.095825	−0.095825	1.1E−17	−0.095825	14188	12716
g09 − ιES	680.630	680.630	680.630	7.4E−04	680.635	264120	82602
ιES($\ell = \lambda$)	680.630	680.630	680.630	8.1E−04	680.634	124675	15821
ιES($\ell = 2\lambda$)	680.630	680.630	680.631	2.3E−03	680.643	122770	16603
g10 − ιES	7049.404	7064.109	7082.227	4.2E+01	7258.540	304066	86127
ιES($\ell = \lambda$)	7054.928	7952.319	7697.312	9.1E+02	10282.820	170499	76428
ιES($\ell = 2\lambda$)	7119.248	7545.843	7373.358	5.2E+01	8909.700	160202	64015
g11 − ιES	0.750	0.750	0.750	1.8E−15	0.750	47046	2968
ιES($\ell = \lambda$)	0.750	0.750	0.750	1.1E−16	0.750	39148	2469
ιES($\ell = 2\lambda$)	0.750	0.750	0.750	1.1E−16	0.750	39894	2493
g12 − ιES	−1.000000	−1.000000	−1.000000	0.0E+00	−1.000000	19726	1462
ιES($\ell = \lambda$)	−1.000000	−1.000000	−1.000000	0.0E+00	−1.000000	2742	598
ιES($\ell = 2\lambda$)	−1.000000	−1.000000	−1.000000	0.0E+00	−1.000000	2536	477
g13 − ιES	0.053942	0.053942	0.111671	1.4E−01	0.438804	197606	117774
ιES($\ell = \lambda$)	0.053942	0.053942	0.18223	1.8E−01	0.438836	102921	31912
ιES($\ell = 2\lambda$)	0.053942	0.053942	0.20789	1.9E−01	0.438809	93012	13840

heuristic is proposed where the surrogate model is said to be sufficiently accurate if any improvement in the surrogate does not change the parent set $\{\mathbf{x}'_{i;\lambda}\}_{i=1}^{\mu}$ at any given generation.

It is clear that the best surrogate model will depend on the properties of the expensive model. For the sphere model the distance-weighted NN regression model is more appropriate than a simple nearest-neighbor model. However, for the general nonlinear programming problems the 1−NN model seems more appropriate. The sampling methods also influence search performance. It was found that expensive model evaluation of the best approximated points was the best strategy for the sphere model. This is not necessarily the best strategy for other surrogate and expensive models. The idea of using approximate ranking is, however, equally applicable to other surrogate models and sampling strategies. This and applications to real world problems will be the topic of future research.

References

1. J.-F. M. Barthelemy and R.T. Haftka. Approximation concepts for optimum structural design – A review. *Stuctural Optimization*, 5:129–144, 1993.
2. Y. Jin. A comprehensive survey of fitness approximation in evolutionary computation. *Soft Computing*, 2003.
3. Y. Jin, M. Olhofer, and B. Sendhoff. A framework for evolutionary optimization with approximate fitness functions. *IEEE Transactions on Evolutionary Computation*, 6(5), October 2002.
4. J. McNames. A fast neartest neighbor algorithm based on a principle axis search tree. *IEEE Transactions on Pattern Analysis and Machine Intelligence*, 23(9), September 2001.
5. T. P. Runarsson. Reducing random fluctuations in mutative self-adaptation. In *Parallel Problem Solving from Nature VII (PPSN-2002)*, volume 2439 of *LNCS*, pages 194–203, Granada, Spain, 2002. Springer Verlag.
6. T. P. Runarsson and X. Yao. Stochastic ranking for constrained evolutionary optimization. *IEEE Transactions on Evolutionary Computation*, 4(3):284–294, September 2000.
7. T. P. Runarsson and X. Yao. Search biases in constrained evolutionary optimization. *IEEE Transactions on System, Man, and Cybernetics: Part C*, (to appear, see http://www.hi.is/~ tpr), 2004.
8. H.-P. Schwefel. *Evolution and Optimum Seeking*. Wiley, New-York, 1995.
9. T. W. Simpson, J. Peplinski, P. N. Koch, and J. K. Allen. On the use of statistics in design and the implications for deterministic computer experiments. In *Design Theory and Methodology - DTM'97*, number DETC97/DTM-3881, Sacramento, CA, 1997. ASME.
10. D. H. Wolpert and W. G. Macready. No free lunch theorems for optimization. *IEEE Transactions on Evolutionary Computation*, 1(1):67–82, 1997.
11. S. Yesilyurt and A. T. Patera. Surrogates for numerical simulations; optimization of eddy-promoter heat exchangers. *Comp. Methods Appl. Mech. Engr.*, 121:231–257, 1995.

Robust Parallel Genetic Algorithms with Re-initialisation

Ivan Sekaj

Department of Automatic Control Systems
Faculty of Electrical Engineering and Information Technology
Slovak University of Technology, Ilkovičova 3, 812 19 Bratislava, Slovak Republic
sekaj@kasr.elf.stuba.sk

Abstract. The influence of different parallel genetic algorithm (PGA) architectures on the GA convergence properties is analysed. Next, two proposed versions of these PGA architectures are compared – homogenous and heterogeneous. Finally the effect of re-initialisation in some partial populations on the PGA convergence has been analysed. The proposed PGA modifications are useful mainly in case of non-smooth cost function optimisation.

1 Introduction

Important factors, which influence the convergence properties of the genetic algorithm (GA) are the selective pressure and population diversity [10],[1],[6]. Selective pressure is a measure of preferring currently better individuals from the population of a particular GA for the currently worse ones. Algorithms with a high selective pressure are characterized by fast convergence, but generally to some local optimum. The population diversity is a measure of gene dissimilarity and with its increase it is possible to unbend the algorithm from the current local optimum and redirect it to better solutions, if possible to the global optimum. A too low diversity, but on the other hand also a too high one can slow down the convergence rate. Increase of the selective pressure can be influenced using such selection methods, which prefer highly fit individuals. Opposite to this, population diversity can be increased by such selection methods, which contain more randomness, regardless of fitness considering. Other important factor, which increases diversity, is the increasing effect of operators modifying the current individuals in the population (e.g. mutation).

In the GA's with a simple population, the selective pressure and population diversity act against each another. For a good GA convergence it is important to find equilibrium between the selective pressure and the population diversity. Note, that the equilibrium depends on the solved problem. This equilibrium can change by introducing multiple populations in parallel genetic algorithms (PGA). By this way it is possible to increase the selective pressure in some populations and simultaneously to increase the population diversity in other populations. In the presented contribution the influence of using various PGA architectures, various genetic operations and population re-initialisation on the PGA convergence are analysed.

2 Parallel GA Architectures

In the literature, different PGA architecture types and also different viewpoints of their classification can be found [3],[5]. Some authors are using the division to fine-grained and coarse-grained PGA's [2].

For our analysis 6 representative PGA architectures have been selected, each with 9 populations (Fig.1A-F). In all cases a periodical migration of one individual from each population into other populations has been considered. That means that in each migration period (say each n/10 or n/100 generations, n is the generation number) the best individual of each of the 9 populations is selected and its copy is sent to the specified populations according to the defined migration structure. In the architecture types A and B a grid PGA structure with the communication of the neighbour population has been used. The type C is a hierarchical structure with 8 low-level nodes and 1 upper-level node. In the case D the ring architecture has been used. The cases E and F have three level hierarchical structures with different linkage between the low and middle levels. Additionally, the types A and B are using a bi-directional migration while C, D, E and F use only a unidirectional one.

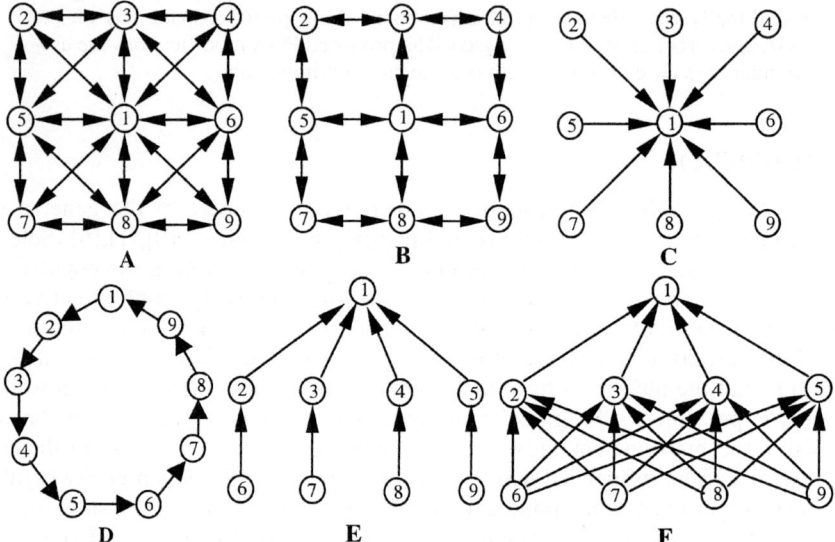

Fig. 1. Different PGA architecture types.

The GA scheme, which has been used in our experiments in each population of the PGA with some modifications (which will be explained later) and also in the simple population GA (SGA), is as follows:

1. Initialisation of the population (randomly) and fitness calculation.
2. Selection of best individuals (one or more), which are without any change copied into the new population – Pop1. Random selection of a group of individuals, which are copied without any change, into the new population – Pop2.
3. Selection of parents, which will be modified by genetic operations crossover and mutation – Pop3.
4. Mutation of the group Pop3.
5. Crossover of the group Pop3.
6. Completion of the new population by unification of the groups Pop1, Pop2 and Pop3.
7. New population fitness calculation. Test of terminating condition, if not fulfilled, then jump to the step 2.

In our analysis, the above scheme has been used, with following modifications. From the selection method in the step 3 the tournament selection [4],[7],[8] the linear ranking selection and the random selection (random selection of strings, without considering fitness) have been used. Next, two mutation versions have been used. In the global mutation the mutated gene is replaced by a random (real) value from the entire search space with uniform probability distribution. In the local mutation there are small random real numbers added to (or subtracted from) the original gene values. The used size of random changes was between 1% and 20 % of the entire search space, with a uniform distribution and a zero mean value. In case of crossover, a simple one-point crossover or an intermediate crossover known from Evolution strategies [9],[6] have been used. The size of each population was set to 20 strings and real coding of strings has been used. More details about the used operations will be specified in Section 2.2.

In order to demonstrate the analysis results, let us use the following test functions. The first function f_1 consists of three partial functions – quadratic, Schwefel function and 3 Gauss peaks (holes)

$$f_1(x) = x_1^2 + x_2^2 + x_3^2 \quad \text{if} \quad -500 > x_i > 500; \quad i=1,2,3$$

otherwise

$$f_1(x) = \frac{1}{2}\sum_{i=1}^{3}\left(-x_i \sin\left(\sqrt{|x_i|}\right)\right) - 800\exp\left(-\frac{x_1^2}{1500} - \frac{x_2^2}{1500} - \frac{x_3^2}{1500}\right) -$$
$$-400\exp\left(-\frac{(x_1^2 - 200)}{1500} - \frac{(x_2^2 - 200)}{1500} - \frac{(x_3^2 - 200)}{1500}\right) -$$
$$-300\exp\left(-\frac{(x_1^2 + 300)}{1500} - \frac{(x_2^2 + 300)}{1500} - \frac{(x_3^2 + 300)}{1500}\right)$$

The global minimum is $f_1(x_1,x_2,x_3) = -800$; $x_1=x_2=x_3=0$. This function belongs to the category of "deceptive functions", where the search for the global optimum is not an easy problem, because of the "unexpected" position of the global optimum. Graph of f_1 for the two variable case is in Fig.2.

The second test function is the "Egg holder function"

$$f_2(X) = \sum_{i=1}^{n-1}\left(-x_i \sin\left(\sqrt{|x_i - (x_{i+1} + 47)|}\right) - (x_{i+1} + 47)\sin\left(\sqrt{\left|x_{i+1} + 47 + \frac{x_i}{2}\right|}\right)\right)$$

A graph for the two variable case $f_2(x_1,x_2)$ is in Fig.3. It is a multi-modal function. The global minimum for the used 10 variable case is near the value $f_2(x) = -8247$; x=[440 455 470 426 441 455 471 426 442 456].

The last used test function is the Griewangk function

$$f_3(x) = \sum_{i=1}^{n}\frac{x_i^2}{4000} - \prod_{i=1}^{n}\cos\left(\frac{x_i}{\sqrt{i}}\right) + 1; \quad -600 > x_i > 600; \quad i=1,2,\ldots,7$$

with the global minimum $x_i^* = 0$; $i=1,2,\ldots,n$ and the value $f_3(x^*) = 0$.

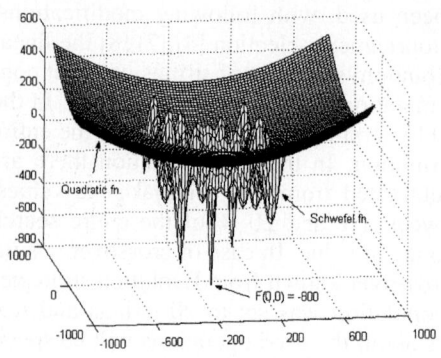

Fig. 2. Graph of function f_1. **Fig. 3.** Graph of function f_2 – "Egg holder".

Let us consider four different situations, which will be analysed in more detail:
1. The GA's in all 9 partial populations are identical, identical GA operations and parameters are used – "homogenous PGA".
2. In different populations different GA operations and parameters are applied – "heterogeneous PGA".
3. Like in case 1, but some populations are periodically re-initialised.
4. Like in case 2, but some populations are periodically re-initialised.

2.1 Homogenous PGA

In each of the 9 populations the identical GA with the above mentioned structure has been used with the following specification: selection of 1 best string into Pop1, tournament selection for Pop3, probability of local and global mutation of a gene is 0.05, the step size of additive mutation is limited to 5% from the entire space, conventional one point crossover. In Fig.4 convergence graphs for all 6 types of PGA architectures with homogenous structure are compared on the $f_1(x)$ minimization example. Next, the convergence of a single population GA is depicted. The size of this population is equal to the number of all populations of the PGA 9 x 20 = 180, the specification is the same as mentioned above for all partial populations in the PGA. Note, that the convergence graph is the dependence of the best fitness value of all populations of the PGA, on the generation number. Each graph (also in next experiments) represents the average of 25 PGA runs. The graphs are marked A1, B1, C1, D1, E1 and F1 according the Fig.1A-F, index 1 belongs to homogenous PGA. SGA is the single population GA. Due to the use of parallel structures the convergence rate is better than for the SGA, which is characterized by a premature convergence. The first advantage of PGA's is, that in more relatively independent populations there is a better chance to find the direction to the global optimum, without any influence of some currently better local optima. Note, if the migration structure has a "high density" (too many migration connections) or/and the migration period is too short, the PGA behaviour can be similar to the SGA one and it can lead to a premature convergence.

2.2 Heterogeneous PGA

In the heterogeneous PGA, opposite to the homogenous case, the partial GA's in populations 1 to 9 are not identical. The aim is to introduce a diversity of search properties into the PGA. Let us consider following GA modifications in particular populations:

Population 1 and 5: the same GA as in the Section 2.1.

Population 2-4: The local (additive) mutation uses different mutation ranges (mutation step limitation) of 1%, 5%, 10% and 20% respectively from the entire search space.

Population 6: "Super elitist" algorithm, where 4 copies of the best string, 3 copies of the second best string, 2 copies of the third best string and one copy of the fourth best string are selected for the "reproduction group" (Pop3). The remaining strings are selected randomly. The rest is similar as in the Section 2.1.

Population 7: The strings for the reproduction group are selected only randomly.

Population 8: Similar to the population 1, but the mutation probability (global and local) is 0.2 (0.05 in population 1).

Population 9: Similar to the population 1, but instead of a conventional crossover the intermediate crossover is used.

In some populations, the heterogeneous PGA enables to increase the gene diversity, for instance with a high mutation probability, using random selection etc. and in other populations to increase the selection pressure with high elitism, without violating the overall PGA operation. For example, in the hierarchical PGA architectures E and F it is advantageous to keep a high diversity measure in populations in the lower hierarchical level (populations 6-9), to increase the local search performance using high local mutation probability in combination with high selective pressure in the middle level (populations 2-5) and to concentrate the best solutions and to finalize the evolution at the upper level (population 1). In Fig.5 convergence of all 6 PGA architecture types has been compared using the example of $f_i(x)$ minimization (the index 2 belongs to heterogeneous PGA). The difference between the homogenous and heterogeneous version is more transparent, when the GA in the homogenous version is not well adjusted (parameterised) for the particular solved problem. The heterogeneous PGA structures can be more robust and adaptable to various practical problems.

2.3 PGA with Re-initialisation

Last two modifications will extend the PGA with a periodic re-initialisation of just some populations. In our case, this re-initialisation is implemented after each migration period, which appeared in our experiments after each 100 generations and represents the exchange of the current population by a completely new, randomly generated population. The re-initialisation has been applied in the 6 architecture types in following populations:

    A (Fig.1A): in population 3,5,6,8
    B (Fig.1B): in population 3,5,6,8
    C (Fig.1C): in populations 2-9

D (Fig.1D): in all populations, but before the re-initialisation the best individual of the PGA is saved for the next generation
E (Fig.1E): in populations 6-9
F (Fig.1F): in populations 6-9

In Fig.6 and 7 there are the results of a similar experiments as in the last two cases, but with the re-initialisation. Here, the index 3 denotes the homogenous PGA type and the index 4 the heterogeneous one. Next, the architecture types C and E for both homogenous and heterogeneous PGA's, without and with re-initialisation for each test function have been compared (C1-homogenous, C2-heterogeneous, C3-homogenous with re-initialisation, C4-heterogeneous with re-initialisation and the same for the type E). Results of the $f_1(x)$ minimization are depicted in Fig.8, Fig.9 is for the $f_2(x)$ and Fig.10 for the $f_3(x)$ case (f_3 is a relatively smooth cost function).

From the analysis it is evident, that the re-initialisation has a positive influence on the GA convergence properties. This effect is most visible in case of such functions or optimisation problems, which cost functions are non-smooth, non-ordinary, with "unexpected" global optimum position (deceptive functions, like f_1). Sometimes the re-initialisation is able to remove differences between homogenous and heterogeneous PGA's.

The re-initialisation is able to increase the population diversity, because it is producing new perspective search directions and in connection with a sufficiently high selective pressure (in other populations of the PGA) it is an effective way for the global optimum search.

3 Re-initialisation Types

Finally, different re-initialisation mechanisms have been proposed and tested. The simplest way was already mentioned in Section 2.3 - the periodical use, without any other conditions. Additionally two other methods have been proposed. In the first, the algorithm after some number of generations compares the best individuals of each population. If there are some similar (or even identical) individuals (in terms of the Euclidian distance), the population which representative has the inferior fitness will be completely re-initialised. In the second method, n fittest strings of each population have been selected, where n was set to 1/4 of the population size. Let this subpopulation be in form of a matrix

$$B = \left[b_{sg}\right]_{g=1...m}^{s=1...n}$$

where the rows s represent strings and the columns g are their genes. Let δ be a population diversity measure in the form

$$\delta = \sum_{g=1}^{m}\left(\frac{1}{n}\sum_{s=1}^{n}\left|b_{sg} - \overline{b}_g\right|\right) \quad (1)$$

The expression in the brackets is the mean absolute deviation, $\overline{b}_g$ is the mean value of the g-th column. If δ will decrease under a small defined value $\delta<\varepsilon$, we can assume, that the population is close to an optimum and it will no more change significantly. Such population can be re-initialised (the best individual migrates before the re-initialisation).

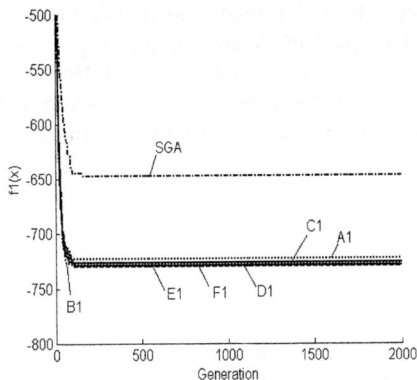

Fig. 4. Homogenous PGA's, $f_1(x)$.

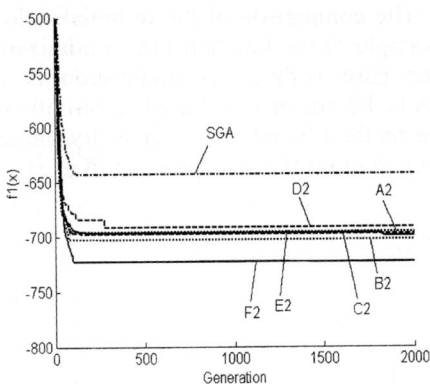

Fig. 5. Heterogeneous PGA's, $f_1(x)$.

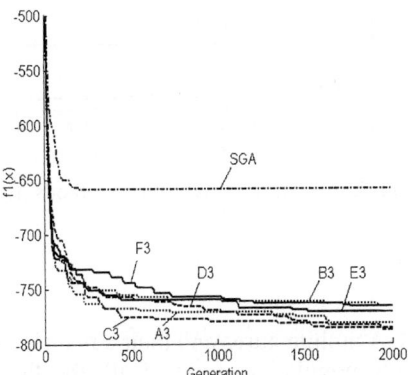

Fig. 6. Homogenous PGA's with re-initialisation, $f_1(x)$.

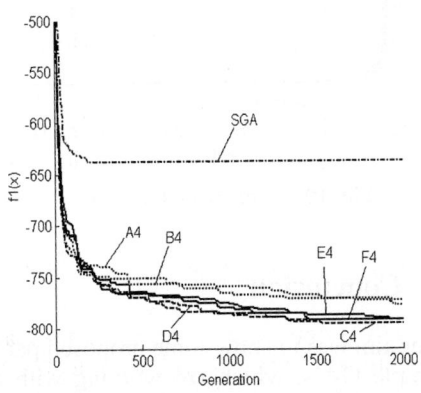

Fig. 7. Heterogeneous PGA's with re-initialisation, $f_1(x)$.

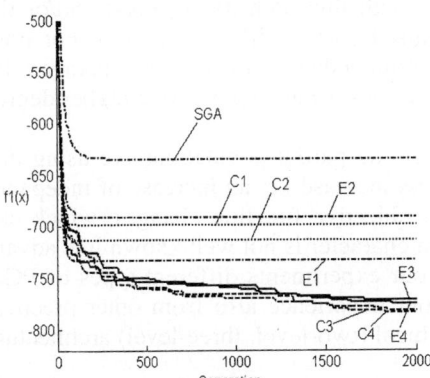

Fig. 8. Comparison for $f_1(x)$.

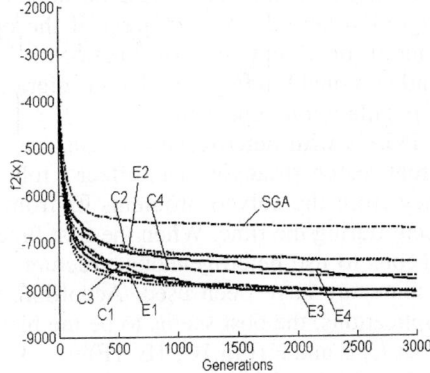

Fig. 9. Comparison for $f_2(x)$.

The comparison of the re-initialisation methods is demonstrated in Fig.11 on the example of the function $f_1(x)$ minimization. The used PGA architecture type was C. The case without re-initialisation is marked 1, the periodic re-initialisation is marked 2, the method based on re-initialisation of similar populations is marked 3 and the method based on the diversity measure according (1) is marked 4 (remark, that each graph is the average of 25 PGA runs).

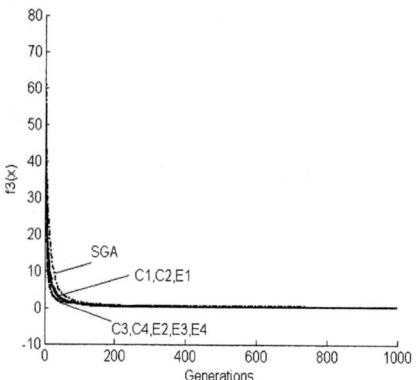

Fig. 10. Comparison for $f_3(x)$.   **Fig. 11.** Different re-initialisation methods, $f_1(x)$.

4 Conclusion

Our aim was to show some proposed parallel GA architectures and their advantages to simple GA's, which are working with a single population. First of all, the PGA's bring about the benefit of multiple independent search directions. This form of parallelism is slightly different from the parallelism in a single-population GA. In this paper different PGA architectures with different migration structures are presented. The migration linkage should be numerous (with high density of links) and/or the migration period not very large if the optimised cost function is smooth. For non-smooth (or deceptive) cost functions it is recommended to use a scarce linkage with unidirectional bindings and larger migration periods, so as to preserve a higher degree of population independency.

PGA's with heterogeneous structure, where the partial populations are using different search strategies, can effect a robustness increase i.e. an increase of independency from the solved problems or from the objective function changes, which can occur during the time. When the cost function character is not well known it is advantageous to use heterogeneous structures. In our experiments different types of PGA architecture have been used. According to our experience also from other practical applications, the best seems to be the hierarchical (two-level, three-level) architecture types C, E and F (Fig.1C, 1E, 1F).

An additional improvement in case of optimisation problems, which have "highly non-smooth" cost function can be caused by the re-initialisation of some populations of the PGA. Another observation is, that the re-initialisation is able to remove differences between homogenous and heterogeneous PGA's or between different PGA architecture types respectively. However, all the presented PGA modifications can speed up the search process and prevent the search algorithm from a premature convergence.

Acknowledgement

This work has been supported from the grants of the Slovak grant agency VEGA 1/0155/03 and 1/0158/03.

References

1. Bäck T.: Selective pressure in evolutionary algorithms: A characterization of selection mechanisms. ICEC-94, 57-62, (1994)
2. Cantú-Paz, E.: A summary of research on parallel genetic algorithms. IlliGAL Report No. 95007, Illinois Genetic Algorithms Laboratory, University of Illinois at Urbana-Champaign, (1995)
3. Chipperfield, A.J., Fleming, P.J.: Parallel genetic algorithms: A survey. ACSE Research Report No.518, University of Sheffield, (1994)
4. Goldberg, D.E., Deb, K.: A comparative analysis of selection schemes used in genetic algorithms. In G.Rawlins, ed., Foundation of Genetic Algorithms, Morgan Kaufmann, (1991)
5. Man, K.F., Tang K.S, Kwong, S.: Genetic Algorithms, Concepts and Deigns. Springer (2001)
6. Michalewicz, Z.: Genetic Algorithms + Data Structures = Evolution Programs. 3rd edn. Springer-Verlag, Berlin Heidelberg New York (1996)
7. Mitchell, M.: An introduction to Genetic Algorithms, MIT Press, (1996)
8. Oei C.K., Goldberg D.E., Chang S.J.: Tournament selection, niching, and the preservation of diversity. Technical Report 91011, University of Illinois Genetic algorithm laboratory, (1991)
9. Schwefel, H.P.: Numerische Optimierung von Computer-Modellen mittels der Evolutionsstrategie. Birkhäuser, Basel, (1977)
10. Whitley, D.: The GENITOR Algorithm and Selection Pressure.: Why Rank-based Allocation of Reproductive Trials is Best. In Proceedings of the Conf. of Genetic Algorithms, Morgan Kaufmann Publ., San Mateo, CA, (1989), 116-121

Improving Evolutionary Algorithms with Multi-representation Island Models

Zbigniew Skolicki and Kenneth De Jong

George Mason University, 4400 University Drive, Fairfax, VA 22031, USA
{zskolick,kdejong}@gmu.edu

Abstract. We present an island model that uses different representations in each island. The model transforms individuals from one representation to another during migrations. We show that such a model helps the evolutionary algorithm to escape from local optima and to solve problems that are difficult for single representation EAs. We illustrate this approach with a two population island model in which one island uses a standard binary encoding and the other island uses a standard reflective Gray code. We compare the performance of this multi-representation island model with single population EAs using only binary or Gray codes. We show that, on a variety of difficult multi-modal test functions, the multi-representation island model does no worse than a standard EA on all of the functions, and produces significant improvements on a subset of them.

1 Introduction

The continuing successes of EA applications have resulted in exploring their use on new and more challenging problems. As the complexity of these new applications increases, there is a corresponding need for more sophisticated evolutionary algorithms. One direction that is being explored is the use of island models to increase the problem-solving capabilities of EAs. The research described in this paper is in this area and presents some preliminary results on the advantages of using island models in which different islands use different representations. Specifically we show that by using a two-island model, each with a different representation, and allowing for migrations between them, we are able to effectively solve problems that are difficult to solve with single representation EAs.

In section 2 we present a short background on island models and on using several different representations. In section 3 we describe our multi-representation island model with transforming migrations and verify our suppositions with some initial experiments. In section 4 we present the results of a more systematic set of experiments, and we finish with conclusions in section 5.

2 Island Models and Multiple Representations

Separating individuals spatially from each other results in a qualitative change in the behavior of evolutionary algorithms. The two most well known approaches to separating individuals is to either group them into populations (*island models*) [1–3] or put them on a grid and restrict their interaction to some neighborhood (*neighborhood models*) [4, 5].

The first most obvious outcome of separating individuals is the slowing down of the information flow between individuals [6]. The results of this may be twofold. On one hand it may be undesirable – it can prevent successful mixing, which would lead to constructing a novel solution. On the other hand, the results may be positive – it may stop individual solutions from dominating the population and allow different building blocks to be discovered in separated regions.

In island models the exchange of information is carried out by migrating individuals between populations. Migrations are characterized by several parameters such as size, frequency and migration policy [7]. Although initially people used island models simply for the purpose of distributing computations on many machines, often island models produce better qualitative results [8].

In island models different algorithms and/or representations can be used in the same time inside populations. Seemingly useless redundancy of different representations may lead to different evolvability characteristics, and ultimately to a more effective search – as suggested by the neutrality theory [9, 10]. One of the problems of search algorithms, including evolutionary algorithms, is getting locked in a local optimum. A local optimum is defined as a solution, whose all direct neighbors are worse in terms of fitness. However, switching representation changes the exploration distribution around a given solution, and opens a possibility for genetic operators to discover new regions of the search space. Therefore a local optimum in one representation may not necessarily be so in another. Also, basins of attraction of local optima change. A simple example of such situation is shown in Figure 1. Circles represent solutions, lines represent neighborhood relation and the numbers are fitness values. The search space on the left hand side has two local optima, but the search space on the right hand side has only one (filled circles).

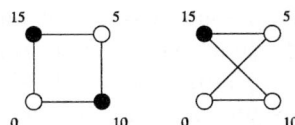

Fig. 1. Changing representation (or operators) affects neighborhood relation. Solution which is a local optimum in one representation may belong to a basin of attraction of another optimum in a different representation.

A well known implementation of island model with different representations is the injection island model [11]. In this model there are several islands with different precisions of representation and different fitnesses. Some islands have simpler representations and faster fitness evaluation. Their task is to evolve the first, coarse approximations of the final solution. The best solutions migrate to the islands with more detailed representations and more expensive evaluations.

There might be several levels of islands and the final solution is taken from the most complex one.

Another interesting approach to dynamically switching representations was proposed in [12, 13]. This algorithm uses single population and changes the representation for all the individuals, when it gets trapped in a minimum. The representations used are Gray encodings and the method switches from one Gray code to another by "rotating" the encoding, which is called *shifting*. By doing so the authors are often able to make two local minima become neighbors and thus "collapse" the worse of them. The usefulness of the method was experimentally confirmed. More information on shifting and properties of both binary and Gray encodings is included in [14] and [15].

3 Transforming Migrations

The model that we propose in this paper is an island model in which we transform individuals from one representation to another during migrations. Such a model allows for changing representations in either direction, as opposed to injection islands, where the flow of individuals is one-directional, from coarser to more precise representations. In other approaches (like shifting) the representation changes for all individuals in the same time. Again, our model is more flexible, because it allows for having different representations simultaneously, and the control of representation is more at the individual level than at the whole population level. The general model we just described doesn't make any assumptions about the sort of representations used, or number of populations.

For every problem there exist better and worse representations. Some of them may create deceptive regions, whereas others will result in an easy landscape. In many cases it is impossible to decide *a priori* what representation to choose for a given problem. It may even happen that all the representations we are trying produce a deceptive landscape. However, even then, a local optimum in one representation need not be a local optimum in the other representation. Therefore by switching representations in some cases we should be able to escape from such situations. Optimally, if a function is easy for some representation in places where it is difficult for others, the island model using multiple representations should behave better on this function than a standard single population EA using any of those representations.

In this paper we try to support these intuitions by analyzing a particular example of the described model. We will use two populations. Migrations will be occurring at the same time from the first population to the second and vice versa and their parameters will be the same throughout any single experiment. We will use two relatively simple encodings: a standard binary encoding and a standard reflected Gray encoding. For those representations we will show a function F which has the characteristics of the problem described above, and we will show that the multi-representation island model indeed behaves better than standard EAs.

3.1 Exemplary Function

We will construct a function F representing a minimization problem. Let us denote the solution search space by Ω and by G_n denote a graph, in which nodes are binary strings of length n and the edges represent the neighborhood relation (for a more formal definition and discussion see [14]). An encoding f is a function $f : \Omega \to G_n$. We will denote the binary and Gray encodings by $binary : \Omega \to G_n$ and $gray : \Omega \to G_n$.

To construct our function we first define two functions from G_n to $\mathbb{N}$.

Let us define a function $easy : G_n \to \mathbb{N}$ by

$$easy(a) = hamming(a, 0^n)/4$$

where the function $hamming$ returns the number of bits by which its two arguments differ and 0^n denotes a string of length n consisting of 0's. It is easy to see that it is a simple unimodal function with one global optimum equal to 0^n.

Let us also define a function $deceptive : G_n \to \mathbb{N}$ by

$$deceptive(a) = \begin{cases} 3 * hamming(a, 0^n) & \text{if } hamming(a, 0^n) < \frac{1}{4}n \\ n - hamming(a, 0^n) & \text{otherwise} \end{cases}$$

The function has two optima. One is global (0^n), and the other one is local (1^n) and has a bigger basin of attraction. Therefore the function is deceptive – it is easy for EA to get stuck in the local minimum.

We further define a function $F_1 : \Omega \to \mathbb{N}$ by

$$F_1(x) = deceptive(gray(x)) + easy(binary(x))$$

The second component ($easy$) of the function is usually smaller and thus has a smaller impact when using the Gray encoding. However, it influences the trajectory of EA when using binary encoding. F_1 is difficult for Gray encoding and relatively easy for binary encoding.

Similarly, we define a function $F_2 : \Omega \to \mathbb{N}$ by

$$F_2(x) = deceptive(binary(x)) + easy(gray(x))$$

Analogously, F_2 is difficult for binary and relatively easy for Gray encoding.

Finally we can construct the function F to be

$$F(x) = min(F_1(x), F_2(x))$$

The function inherits both local minima from F_1 and F_2 and has one global optimum at 0^n with value 0. It is a difficult function when using only binary or only Gray encoding, but turns out to be much easier when switching between representation is allowed.

3.2 Initial Observations

To verify our assumptions about the behavior of the model and the properties of the function F, we start with analyzing single runs of EA. Not surprisingly, single populations using just one encoding usually fail to find the global optimum. A typical run for the binary encoding is shown in Figure 2. and a typical run for Gray encoding is shown in Figure 3. We plot the best fitness of the population. The length of genomes was $n = 100$. In both cases the EA was trapped in local optima, which are neighborhoods of respectively $binary^{-1}(1^n)$ and $gray^{-1}(1^n)$.

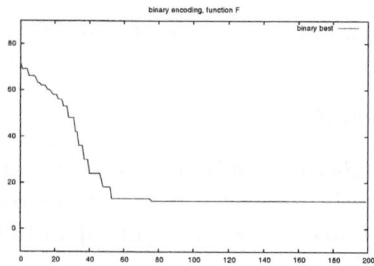
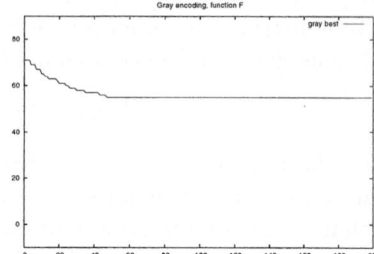

Fig. 2. A typical single run with binary encoding on function F. EA got trapped in a local minimum.

Fig. 3. A typical single run with Gray encoding on function F. EA got trapped in a local minimum.

The situation changes when we allow for the island model with both representations in the same time. On Figure 4. we show an analog run with two representations. A careful inspection of the figure shows that the representations "help each other", not allowing each other to get stuck in local minima. One may notice that it is the binary representation that is leading in the beginning but it is the Gray representation that plays an important role towards the end. Vertical changes in best fitness correspond to migrations from the other population. The influence of such migrations is very distinct in generations 20–35 for the Gray encoding and in generations 55–65 for the binary encoding.

To make the influence of migrations even more visible, we have run a set of experiments in which migrations occur very rarely (every 50 generations). Again, a single run is shown in Figure 5. One can clearly see the initial leading role of the population with binary representation. By generation 50 the Gray encoding population is already stuck at its local minimum. A migration helps it escape from this minimum. Later the roles of the populations get reversed and it is the Gray encoding population that helps the binary encoding population escape from its local minimum, by means of migrations at generations 100 and 150.

4 Experiments

We have conducted several sets of experiments, the statistical results of which we report in this section. Firstly, we changed EA parameters to study the robustness of the model. Then we explored the influence of migration level. Finally, we ran experiments on different functions known in the literature to confirm the

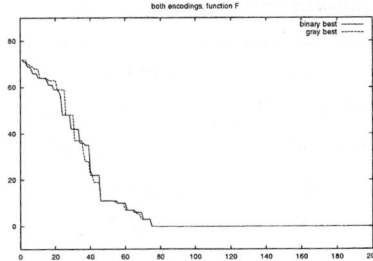 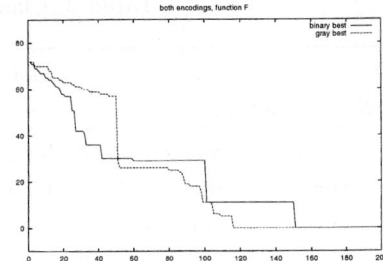

Fig. 4. A single run with both encodings on function F. EA found the global optimum.

Fig. 5. A single run with both encodings and rare migrations, on function F. Mutual influence of populations by means of migrations is very visible in generations 50, 100 and 150.

Table 1. Parameters used.

Parameter	Value
mutation rate	$1/n$
recombination type	two-point
recombination rate	1.0
selection strategy	ranked with elitism
population size	100 (binary), 100 (Gray) and 50+50 (binary+Gray)
migration policy	copy best - replace random
migration size	10%
generations between migrations	5
total number of generations	500
number of runs	50

applicability of the model to a wider set of problems. Unless explicitly stated otherwise, for each experiment we used the parameters given in Table 1.

4.1 Changing EA Parameters

We have tested the model using two crossover types (two-point and uniform) and two selection strategies (ranked with elitism and binary tournament). The island model performed better because it was the only one to find the global optimum and it was either statistically better or comparable in terms of average fitness of the best optimum. For experiment 2 the island model found the global optimum every time. In experiment 3 the binary encoding EA was finding optima with values 55 and 11, whereas island model EA was finding optima of 55 and 0. Therefore the averages are not significantly different. The results of experiments are presented in Table 2. The confidence interval ($\alpha = 0.05$) is given for reference only, as the calculations assume normal distribution and the distribution of local optima of the function is probably very different.

Table 2. Changing EA parameters.

No	Description	Binary Average	%Opt	Gray Average	%Opt	Island Model Average	%Opt
1	two-point, ranked	21.08±4.99	0%	55.00±0.00	0%	22.00±7.54	60%
2	uniform, ranked	12.00±0.00	0%	55.00±0.00	0%	0.00±0.00	100%
3	two-point, b.tourn.	25.38±5.76	0%	55.00±0.00	0%	27.50±7.70	50%
4	uniform, b.tourn.	12.00±0.00	0%	55.00±0.00	0%	3.48±2.16	38%

4.2 Changing Migrations Parameters

Similar analysis was performed for different levels of migration. Experiments 1, 5 and 6 maintained the same total number of individuals exchanged (changing migration size and frequency). Experiments 1, 7 and 8 maintained the same migration size, but different frequencies (and thus changed the total number of exchanged solutions). The results are given in Table 3. Again, because the EAs converge to several very different optima, the averages and confidence intervals don't tell us much. In all experiments the global optimum was found relatively often. Although we cannot state it with statistical significance, there is an interesting observation about experiments 7 and 8. Frequent migrations resulted in lower average optimum found, but the global optimum was found less often. This means that EAs converged to good, but suboptimal solutions. On the other hand, infrequent migrations resulted in higher average optimum, but the the global optimum was found more often.

Table 3. Changing migration parameters.

No	Description	Average	%Opt
1	10 %, 5 gen.	22.0±7.54	60%
5	2 %, 1 gen.	20.9±7.48	38%
6	40 %, 20 gen.	18.7±7.3	34%
7	10 %, 1 gen.	17.6±7.19	32%
8	10 %, 20 gen.	30.8±7.65	56%

4.3 Changing Fitness Functions

The last experiments were aimed at verifying the applicability of the model for functions other than the one presented so far. Therefore a set of 4 functions which are well-known in the literature, was taken. The functions are multi-modal test functions, known as Rosenbrock, Schwefel, Rastrigin and Griewangk (see Table 4). A 10-dimensional versions of each of them were used and each parameter was represented with 12 bits. To maintain the mutation rate of $\frac{1}{n}$, it was set to 0.0083. The Figures 6 – 9 show the results (confidence with α=0.05).

Table 4. Test functions.

Name	Formula
Rosenbrock	$f(x_1,\ldots,x_n) = \sum_{i=2}^{n}(100(x_i - x_{i-1}^2)^2 + (1 - x_{i-1})^2)$
Schwefel	$f(x_1,\ldots,x_n) = \sum_{i=1}^{n} -x_i sin(\sqrt{|x_i|})$
Rastrigin	$f(x_1,\ldots,x_n) = 10n + \sum_{i=1}^{n}(x_i^2 - 10cos(2\pi x_i))$
Griewangk	$f(x_1,\ldots,x_n) = 1 + \sum_{i=1}^{n} \frac{x_i^2}{4000} - \prod_{i=1}^{n} cos(\frac{x_i}{\sqrt{i}})$

For the Rosenbrock function the proposed model doesn't differ significantly from the single-population single-representation models. Its performance seems to be slightly better than that of binary representation and comparable with Gray representation. However the differences are within a statistical error.

For Schwefel function the performance of the multi-representation model looks better. It is significantly better than both that of binary as well as of Gray representation for short term runs (around generation 200) and at the end, when it converges to very low minimum of value around 0.015.

The model behaves well on Rastrigin function, again with most visible advantage in short runs. After 500 generations the Gray encoding model becomes

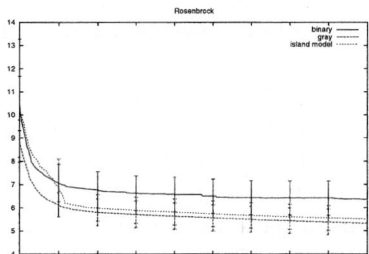

Fig. 6. Average results from 50 runs for Rosenbrock function, from generation 50.

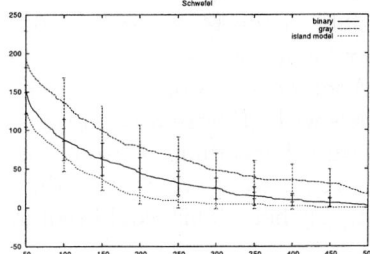

Fig. 7. Average results from 50 runs for Schwefel function, from generation 50.

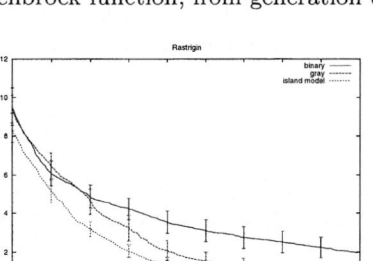

Fig. 8. Average results from 50 runs for Rastrigin function, from generation 50.

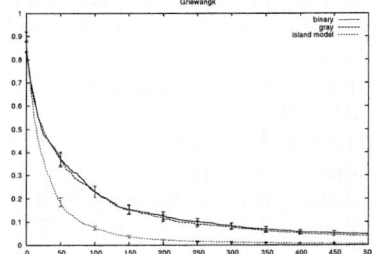

Fig. 9. Average results from 50 runs for Griewangk function, all generations.

statistically in-differentiable from the island model while the binary encoding model occurs significantly worse.

Finally, for Griewangk function, we observe a huge advantage of using the multi-representation island model. It not only converges faster but also finds a better optimum.

We are currently analyzing these landscapes in more detail in order to understand more precisely what causes the island model to behave better on certain functions than on others, and hope to present those results in a later paper.

5 Conclusions

The results presented in this paper suggest that island models with different representations and transforming migrations may behave better than standard EAs for difficult, deceptive and multi-modal problems. What is interesting is that they often behaved better than EAs using either of the two representations. This suggests that representations with dynamically changing neighborhood can be in general better than any static-neighborhood representation. Of course, the No Free Lunch theorem states that they cannot be better for any function – but they may be better for commonly used test and real-life problems.

The observations from single runs convinces us that the multi-representation island models produce better results because the representations "help each other" by means of migrations. A further investigation into this process and possibly making it dependent on some population-based feedback would definitely be an interesting area for future work.

Another area worth exploring is the behavior of multi-representation island models with other representations than presented in the paper, for example with real valued encodings. It would be also interesting to see how the model behaves when representations are very different and some solutions are representable only in one of them. This would require special transformation procedures.

References

1. Wright, S.: The roles of mutation, inbreeding, crossbreeding and selection in evolution. In Jones, D.F., ed.: Proceedings of the Sixth International Conference of Genetics, Brooklyn Botanic Garden (1932) 356–366
2. Grosso, P.: Computer Simulations of Genetic Adaptation: Parallel Subcomponent Interaction in a Multilocus Model. PhD thesis, University of Michigan, Ann Arbor, MI (1985)
3. Gordon, V., Whitley, D., Bohn, A.: Dataflow parallelism in genetic algorithms. In Manner, R., Manderick, B., eds.: Parallel Problem Solving from Nature 2, Amsterdam, Elsevier Science (1992) 553–542
4. Manderick, B., Spiessens, P.: Fine-grained parallel genetic algorithms. In Schaffer, J.D., ed.: Proceedings of the Third Int. Conf. on Genetic Algorithms, Morgan Kauffman (1989) 428
5. Mühlenbein, H.: Parallel genetic algorithms, population genetic and combinatorial optimization. In Schaffer, J., ed.: Proceedings on the Third International Conference on Genetic Algorithms, Morgan Kaufmann (1989) 416–421

6. Sarma, J.: An Analysis of Decentralized and Spatially Distributed Genetic Algorithms. PhD thesis, George Mason University, Fairfax, VA (1998)
7. Cantú-Paz, E.: Migration policies, selection pressure, and parallel evolutionary algorithms. Journal of Heuristics **7** (2001) 311 – 334
8. Whitley, D., Rana, S., Heckendorn, R.B.: The island model genetic algorithm: On separability, population size and convergence. Journal of Computing and Information Technology **7** (1999) 33–47
9. Toussaint, M.: Self-adaptive exploration in evolutionary search. Technical Report IRINI-2001-05, Institute for Neuroinformatics, Ruhr-University Bochum (2001)
10. Toussaint, M., Igel, C.: Neutrality: A necessity for self-adaptation. In: Proceedings of the IEEE Congress on Evolutionary Computation (CEC 2002). (2002) 1354–1359
11. Eby, D., Averill, R., Goodman, E., Punch, W.: The optimization of flywheels using an injection island genetic algorithm. In Bentley, P., ed.: Evolutionary Design by Computers. Morgan Kaufmann, San Francisco (1999) 167–190
12. Rana, S., Whitley, L.: Bit representation with a twist. In: Proceedings of the Seventh International Conference on Genetic Algorithms (ICGA-97), Morgan Kaufmann (1997)
13. Barbulescu, L., Watson, J.P., Whitley, D.: Dynamic representations and escaping local optima: Improving genetic algorithms and local search. In: AAAI/IAAI. (2000) 879–884
14. Rowe, J., Whitley, D., Barbulescu, L., Watson, J.P.: Properties of gray and binary representations. Evolutionary Computation **12** (2004) 47–76
15. Whitley, D.L., Rana, S., Heckendorn, R.B.: Representation issues in neighborhood search and evolutionary algorithms. In Quagliarelli, D., Periaux, J., Poloni, C., Winter, G., eds.: Genetic Algorithms in Engineering and Computer Science. John Wiley & Sons Ltd., Chichester (1997) 39–57

A Powerful New Encoding for Tree-Based Combinatorial Optimisation Problems

Sang-Moon Soak[1], David Corne[2], and Byung-Ha Ahn[1]

[1] Dept. of Mechatronics, Gwang-ju Institute of Sci. and Tech., Republic of Korea
{soakbong,bayhay}@gist.ac.kr
[2] Department of Computer Science, University of Exeter, UK
D.W.Corne@exeter.ac.uk

Abstract. We describe a new encoding scheme and associated operators for tree structures on graphs and test it in the context of an evolutionary algorithm applied to the degree-constrained minimum spanning tree problem (DC-MST). The new encoding is relatively simple and easily copes with degree constraints. We compare with three existing encoding schemes, including *edge-set*, which represents the current state of the art on the DC-MST. The new encoding demonstrates superior performance on the larger instances of the well-used 'Structured Hard' DC-MST problems, and similar performance on the smaller instances. We conclude that the new encoding is a recommended method for the DC-MST.

1 Introduction

Consider an *undirected complete graph* $G = (V, E)$, where $V = \{1, 2, ..., N\}$ is the set of N nodes and $E = 1, 2, ..., M$ is the set of M edges, each with a given distance (or cost). The degree-constrained minimum spanning tree (DC-MST) problem on a graph is the problem of generating a minimum spanning tree satisfying degree constraints on the number of edges that can be incident to nodes on the tree. Unlike the MST, the DC-MST cannot, in general, be found using a polynomial time algorithm, and in fact it is a well-known NP-hard problem of importance in communications network design, road network design and other network-related problems [5].

Following seminal work on the DC-MST by Narula and Ho [13], recent years have seen much interest, primarily using evolutionary algorithms (EAs) in addressing realistically sized instances. Much of the conceptual effort in this has been the design of novel encodings (and associated operators) [1,2,6–10,14, 17–20]. Most encodings investigated suffer from poor locality and inheritance properties; i.e. neighbouring genomes in the encoding tend to express quite different phenotypes, hence undermining the basis for *exploiting* good solutions by trying to find better solutions in the locality. Meanwhile, several of these encodings require a repair process, since either an encoded tree or a mutant (or child of crossover) will often not map into a valid tree.

We propose a new tree encoding scheme which avoids these common disadvantages, and also turns out to perform very well. The main idea is to encode a *subgraph* in a simple way, and then transform this subgraph reliably into a spanning tree. Section 2 provides full details of the encoding, while section 3 describes the specialised crossover operator designed for use with it, as well as a new EA selection/reproduction strategy which we use in some of the experiments. In section 4 we compare the new encoding scheme with the Prüfer number encoding [6] (known to have poor performance, hence used as a baseline), the Network Random Keys (which we call NetKeys) encoding [18, 19], and the state of the art Edge Set encoding [16, 17]. We conclude in section 5, summarising our findings and considering future work.

2 A New Encoding for Trees

In the context of needing to encode candidate spanning trees over a complete graph, our new encoding hybridises a direct encoding of a subgraph with a tree-construction algorithm. Consider the tree in Fig. 1. This consists of the 'edge set': $EdgeSet\{(1,2),(1,3),(1,4),(1,5),(1,6),(1,7),(1,8),(1,9)\}$. Now make a linear string to connect all of these edges, simply by reading nodes from the edge set from left to right. The string becomes (1, 2, 1, 3, 1, 4, 1, 5, 1, 6, 1, 7, 1, 8, 1, 9). This encodes a subgraph as follows. Move a window of length two along the string, one step at a time. Initially the subgraph is empty. The window then first sees '1 2', so we add this edge to our developing subgraph. The window then sees '2 1', then '1 3', and so on. We successively consider the edges indicated by each window, and include them or not according to the particular tree construction rule in place (see later this section). Herein, we only consider undirected graphs, so (1 2) is equivalent to (2 1). Hence, in the previous example, when '2 1' is seen, it will not be included, since it is already present. In more general and formal terms, our encoding works with a string of L node identifiers $(i_1, i_2, ..., i_L)$, where all $i_j \in 1, ..., N$ and which in general may have $i_j = i_k$ for distinct j,k. Abstractly, this string is interpreted in two steps. First, we extract an ordered set of unique edges from this string. Second, we use a Tree Construction Rule (TCR) to generate a spanning tree from these edges. A TCR may or may not work with the given ordering of edges, and the two steps may be interleaved for convenience. Herein, the first step always proceeds in the same way, as illustrated by the example above, retaining only the unique edges. Note that this set of edges is a subgraph (it may contain cycles). Also, we ignore edges of the form (i_k, i_k).

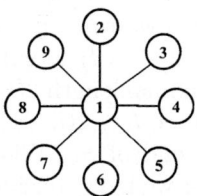

Fig. 1. A spanning tree.

We now need to clarify the required length of the string, and any constraints on its contents. It will be useful to first present our straightforward Cycle Free TCR (CF-TCR), and then we will return to this question.

2.1 The Cycle-Free Tree Construction Rule

Derived from Prim's algorithm [15], CF-TCR builds a tree by continually adding edges which link a new node to an existing selected node in a growing subtree, ensure there are no cycles, and continued until every node is connected. To illustrate, consider the chromosome (1, 3, 1, 2, 4, 5, 5, 3). First, set $SelNode\{\phi\}$ and $EdgeSet\{\phi\}$ where these are the sets of selected nodes and selected edges respectively. We start with the leftmost two genes, (1, 3), which populate the node and edge sets to leave us with: $EdgeSet\{(1,3)\}$ and $SelNode\{1,3\}$. Moving our two-node window left to right, the next *new* edge to consider is (1, 2). Node 2 has not been selected, so use this edge, giving $EdgeSet\{(1,3),(1,2)\}$ and $SelNode\{1,3,2\}$. Next we consider (2, 4). Node 4 is not yet selected, so we use this edge, giving us: $EdgeSet\{(1,3),(1,2),(2,4)\}$ and $SelNode\{1,3,2,4\}$. Finally we check edge (4, 5). Node 5 has not been selected, so we connect nodes 4 and 5, and the final result is $EdgeSet\{(1,3),(1,2),(2,4),(4,5)\}$ and $SelNode\{1, 3, 2, 4, 5\}$. CF-TCR terminates now since the number of selected edges is $N - 1$. Given space limitations and the similarity with the well-known Prim's algorithm, we omit the pseudo code for CF-TCR.

It turns out that, using the basic CF-TCR, in order to encode all possible spanning trees of an N node graph, a string needs to be of length $2 \times (N - 1)$. We prove this in the following theorem.

Theorem 1: When CF-TCR used, any spanning tree on $N \geq 2$ nodes can be encoded by a sequence of at most $2(N - 1)$ node identifiers.

Proof: We prove this by induction on N. First, consider the case $N = 2$. There is only one possible string which satisfies the given constraints, and that is: (1, 2). This single edge is also the only possible spanning tree on a 2-node graph. Hence we have proved the case for $N = 2$. We now need to show the inductive case; that is, we need to prove that if the theorem statement is true for $N = k$ then it is also true for $N = k + 1$.

To this end, assume the theorem is true for $N = k$. First we show that any spanning tree on $k+1$ nodes can be encoded by a string of at most $2((k+1)-1)$ node identifiers. Consider any such tree. We can remove an arbitrary leaf, leaving a spanning tree on k nodes, which we will call T_k, and an unconnected node, u, which had previously been connected to T_k at c. By assumption, we know that T_k can be encoded by a string of maximal length $2(k-1)$. Assume '$S_k = (n_1, ..., n_L)$' is such a string, encoding T_k, where $L \leq 2(k-1)$. Now, consider the string S_{k+1} formed by adding (c, u) to the end of S_k. When we interpret this using CF-TCR, then (by assumption) after we have considered the node-pair '(n_{L-1}, n_L)', we have already built the tree T_k. Next we consider the node-pair '(n_L, c)'; CF-TCR will ignore this potential edge and move on, since it contains two nodes (or perhaps two copies of the same node) already in *SelNode*. Finally, CF-TCR will consider the node-pair (c, u); since u is not in *SelNode* at this point, it will be added, and the edge (c, u) will be incorporated, producing our original 'arbitrary' tree on $k + 1$ nodes. Also, the length of S_{k+1} is $L + 2$, and clearly $(L + 2) <= (2(k - 1) + 2) <= 2((k + 1) - 1)$. By induction, it follows that the statement of theorem 1 is true for all $N \geq 2$.

We have yet to prove that every string that satisfies this length constraint actually encodes a valid spanning tree. The next theorem covers this.

Theorem 2: When CF-TCR used, every sequence which contains every node identifier at least once, and is no longer than $2(N - 1)$, encodes a valid spanning tree on $N \geq 2$ nodes.

Proof: We prove this by appeal to the operation of CF-TCR. As CF-TCR proceeds, it considers edges (n_1, n_2), (n_2, n_3), and so on, up to (n_{L-1}, n_L), where $N \leq L \leq 2(N - 1)$, building *SelNode*, which contains all nodes contained so far in the developing tree. Consider the first time a given node n appears in the string. If we have $n = n_1$ or $n = n_2$, then n will be seen in the first iteration and immediately become part of the developing tree. Otherwise, and in general, we will first see n in the context of a window (n_i, n) for some i, with $1 \leq i < L$. There are two cases: either n_i is already in *SelNode*, or it is *not*. In the first case, CF-TCR will clearly add (n_i, n) to the developing tree. The second case can only happen in the first iteration of CF-TCR, which we have already covered. So, node n will always be added to the tree. It follows that every node appearing in the string must also appear in the tree. Given that we ensure every node appears at least once in the sequence, and that the CF-TCR guarantees to maintain a tree with no cycles, it is clear that any string satisfying the given constraints will encode, via CF-TCR, a valid spanning tree on N nodes.

It turns out that we can naturally and easily handle degree-constraints by simply ensuring that, if a node has a maximum allowed degree of d, then that node appears at most $d - 1$ times in the sequence. It is straightforward to see that this works by appealing again to the operation of CF-TCR; however, to save space, we omit that argument here.

2.2 The d-Kruskal Tree Construction Rule

Kruskal's algorithm [11] works by first sorting all edges of a graph in ascending order of cost, and then building a spanning tree by including edges (following this ordering), maintaining a set of partial trees as it proceeds, discarding any edges which introduce a cycle. Kruskal's algorithm is a common inspiration in recent encodings for tree problems [16–19].

In d-K-TCR, following step 1 (extraction of the edges encoded in the string), we apply a version of Kruskal's algorithm to the resulting subgraph as follows. First d-K-TCR enumerates all edges in the encoded subgraph and then sorts these in ascending order of cost. It then repeatedly adds the shortest edge in the subgraph to a set of growing partial trees, so long as this shortest edge does not result in a cycle or a degree constraint violation. When *N-1* edges are gathered, the process is terminated.

With *d*-K-TCR, as with CF-TCR, every chromosome is a string of $2(N-1)$ node identifiers, with each node appearing at least once, and at most $d-1$ times. However, the operation of *d*-K-TCR as described does not guarantee to obtain a valid tree (since partway through it may discard an edge necessary to any valid tree in the subgraph). We have not yet designed an efficient way to address this, and in this paper we simply choose a random valid edge when necessary, and ensure that the choice is recorded if necessary to recover a best-so-far solution. This enables us to maintain *consistency* in the encoding, although in a non-ideal way. In the experiments reported next, this random choice occurs less than 0.1 times per chromosome. We are investigating improved methods, but meanwhile the low incidence seems to us to be acceptable.

3 Details of the Evolutionary Algorithm and Operators

All experiments using the new encoding use a chromosome comprising a sequence of $2(N-1)$ node identifiers in which each node appears at least once and at most $d-1$ times, where N is the number of nodes in the particular DC-MST problem under study, and d is the uniform degree constraint. We used a fixed length of $2(N-1)$ for convenience. As proven, this is sufficient to encode all spanning trees over N nodes, however we note that many such trees could also be encoded with fewer nodes. In the $2(N-1)$-length encoding, this just corresponds to termination of the TCR before it has reached the end of the string. Note that this means the encoding does not have the ideal *uniqueness* property (a 1-1 map between genotype and phenotype) and it also does not possess uniformity (where each phenotype is encoded by the same number of genotypes); however there seems to be a clear tradeoff in the area of tree-encodings between such properties and others such as locality and inheritance.

We use simple *swap* mutation, in which we randomly select two positions and swap the genes at those positions. This is used in our experiments on the new, Prüfer and NetKeys encodings, following observations in preliminary work that it was at least as effective as alternative operators.

Our crossover operator for the new encoding, which we call "Common Gene Preservation Crossover" (CGPX) is designed to focus on the inheritability of common genetic information [4], as well as exploit edge-cost information. CPGX produces two children, O^1 and O^2, from two parents, P^1 and P^2, as follows:

We use P_i^k (or O_i^k) to denote the node at position i in individual k. To produce O^1, we first set $O_1^1 = P_1^1$. Then, working from left to right (i.e. from $i = 2$ to $i = 2(N-1)$), we compare P_i^1 and P_i^2. Whenever these are the same, i.e. $P_i^1 = P_i^2 = n$ we make $O_i^1 = n$, unless this would mean more than $d-1$ ns appearing in O^1. If that is the case, then a random choice of node is made from those with fewer than $d-1$ occurrences in the string so far. When $P_i^1 \neq P_i^2$, we compare the costs of the edges (O_{i-1}^1, P_i^1) and (O_{i-1}^1, P_i^2), and make $O_i^1 = P_i^l$, where $l = 1$ or $l = 2$, whichever corresponds to the lower cost of these two edges. However, if one of $l = 1$ or $l = 2$ violates the degree constraint, then we use the other; if both would violate the degree constraint, then we make a random valid choice for O_i^1. We use precisely the same process to generate O^2, except that we begin with $O_1^2 = P_1^2$.

Finally, we note that we are investigating a novel selection/reproduction strategy which we call "Real World Tournament Selection" (RWTS). RWTS is a way of producing an entire intermediate population. Operators are then later applied to the intermediate population to produce the next generation. The intermediate population is produced by a series of two-chromosome tournaments. First, all chromosomes in the population are paired to produce *pop_size*/2 tournaments; the winner of each of these *level* 1 tournaments enters the intermediate generation. This process is repeated with the *level 1* winners, and so on recursively, until the intermediate population is complete with *pop_size* members.

4 Experiments

In these experiments, we evaluate the new encoding by comparing it with the state of the art Edge Set encoding [17], the highly effective Network Random Keys (NetKeys) encoding [18, 19], and, as a baseline measure, the well known Prüfer number encoding [6, 20]. Space limitations prevent us from explaining the comparative encoding schemes, however the associated references at the end of this article include URLs from which interested readers can freely obtain such details.

The new encoding uses CGPX, the Prüfer number experiments use two-point crossover, the NetKeys experiments use uniform crossover and the edge-set representation uses the heuristic crossover operator described in [17]. The edge-set experiments also use the heuristic mutation and heuristic initialisation methods described in [17]. The other encodings all use standard swap mutation (as described above) and only use random initialisation of the population. The EA was a standard generational EA with population 100. Crossover and mutation rates were both 0.6 when the new, Prüfer number and NetKey encodings were used, and both 0.8 when edge-set was used (following [17]). Experiments continue for a maximum of 50,000 evaluations (all methods appeared to converge well before this limit), and each trial is repeated 10 times with different random seeds.

This represents an attempt to compare different encodings in a maximally fair way. Hence, each encoding is used with its published specialised or chosen operators, but we have not used aspects of previous published work which does not seem essential to the encoding. In particular, we do not use the simple diversity-preservation method in our EA which is used by [16, 17]. But we feel this would have only a minor effect, and we note that if it would improve the edge-set results it would likely also improve the results for the other encodings. As noted, however, we *do* use heuristic initialisation of the population when the edge-set encoding is used (since this is a prominent aspect of the description of the edge-set approach), but not when other encodings are used. Our basic selection method is standard binary tournament selection [12] (which we call GTS – Goldberg's tournament selection); on similar problems, this has been found to outperform $(\mu+\lambda)$ selection [18]. As part of our investigation of RWTS (described above), a set of ten trials of every experiment is also done with RWTS.

Finally, we note that our benchmark problems are the structured hard DC-MST problems (SHRD problems) described by Krishnamoorthy [10]. We generated such structured hard DCMST instances using Krishnamoorthy's method, producing problems with 30, 40 and 50 nodes respectively, each leading to three DC-MSTs, one for each of the degree constraints 3, 4 and 5.

Table 1. Experiment Results.

		Prüfer	NetKey	Edge Set			New Method				
							C-F TCR			d-K-TCR		
N	d	Avg.	Avg.	Worst	Avg.	Best	Worst	Avg.	Best	Worst	Avg.	Best.
SHRD30	3	2.25	3.49	3.74	3.81	3.89	1.54	3.14	3.74	3.80	**3.86**	3.89
		(-4.98)	(3.10)	(3.67)	(3.84)	(3.89)	(-0.92)	(0.77)	(1.67)	(2.34)	(2.54)	(2.76)
	4	4.85	4.93	5.86	6.03	6.09	5.29	5.62	5.86	6.05	**6.06**	6.09
		(-2.09)	(4.46)	(5.94)	(6.04)	(6.09)	(-3.03)	(-0.67)	(2.52)	(4.00)	(4.79)	(5.25)
	5	1.81	3.76	4.69	4.72	4.78	3.59	4.43	4.69	4.74	**4.76**	4.78
		(-3.01)	(2.74)	(4.69)	(4.75)	(4.78)	(-5.62)	(-3.23)	(-0.42)	(1.97)	(2.92)	(3.63)
SHRD40	3	5.58	6.23	6.52	6.59	6.69	5.89	6.16	6.47	6.64	**6.71**	6.76
		(-3.31)	(-4.15)	(6.37)	(6.58)	(6.67)	(0.11)	(2.51)	(4.04)	(5.52)	(5.67)	(5.97)
	4	2.79	3.67	4.93	5.10	5.19	4.42	4.71	4.99	5.13	**5.17**	5.21
		(-3.83)	(3.00)	(4.95)	(5.05)	(5.13)	(-10.79)	(-5.28)	(-1.38)	(2.08)	(3.21)	(3.85)
	5	2.95	2.51	4.95	4.80	4.95	3.79	4.42	4.76	4.73	**4.89**	4.95
		(-3.64)	(1.94)	(4.87)	(4.69)	(4.60)	(-12.78)	(-7.94)	(-3.36)	(0.02)	(1.22)	(1.97)
SHRD50	3	18.92	18.41	19.75	19.65	19.56	19.10	19.40	19.65	19.75	**19.80**	19.85
		(9.80)	(18.37)	(19.62)	(19.71)	(19.80)	(11.77)	(14.59)	(16.06)	(18.26)	(18.50)	(18.78)
	4	13.03	12.80	14.25	14.42	14.61	13.84	14.26	14.50	14.62	**14.67**	14.72
		(4.37)	(11.74)	(14.35)	(14.53)	(14.66)	(-0.34)	(3.30)	(7.17)	(9.98)	(11.59)	(13.42)
	5	10.31	8.98	11.94	12.13	12.23	10.77	11.90	12.08	12.21	**12.28**	12.32
		(3.03)	(8.29)	(12.19)	(12.11)	(11.98)	(4.58)	(-4.47)	(9.36)	(4.47)	(6.42)	(7.98)

Note: "()" indicates results using GTS; N is the number of nodes; d is the degree constraint.

Table 1 summarises all our experimental results on the test SHRD instances. In it, a table entry gives the relative difference between the mean (over the ten trials) solution C for the algorithm, and the mean solution for ten trial runs of d-Prim (C_{d-Prim})[1] as follows:

$$Gains = (C_{d-Prim} - C)/C_{d-Prim} \times 100\% \qquad (1)$$

Bold indicates the best result over all algorithms for a particular problem.

RWTS vs. Standard Tournament Selection. We first analyse the performance of RWTS, which then helps narrow down the statistical comparisons

---

[1] d-Prim is a version of Prim's algorithm commonly used to quickly generate low-cost DC-MSTs; it is simply Prim's, modified to maintain degree constraints. In our work, one trial of d-Prim's consists of running it 20 times with randomly chosen starting node each time, and returning the best of those 20 results.

which need to be done to analyse the relative performance of the encodings. To this end, we compared the two schemes for each specific problem/encoding pair, using *randomization testing* [3] as our statistical tool. This is a relatively sensitive but assumption-free method (e.g. we do not need to assume that results come from a Gaussian distribution, or that results from separate algorithms share the same variance), and we obtained p-values for a comparison via examination of 100,000 random permutations of the data involved.

Table 2. Summary of statistical analysis of RWTS reproduction scheme vs generational reproduction and tournament selection (GTS).

nodes/d	Prüfer	Netkeys	Edge-set	CF-TCR	d-K-TCR
30/3	R ($< 10^{-5}$)	R (< 0.008)	inc.	R ($< 10^{-5}$)	inc.
30/4	R ($< 10^{-5}$)	inc.	GTS (< 0.06)	R ($< 10^{-5}$)	R ($< 10^{-4}$)
30/5	R ($< 10^{-5}$)	R (< 0.015)	inc.	R ($< 10^{-5}$)	R ($< 10^{-5}$)
40/3	R ($< 10^{-5}$)	R (< 0.0015)	inc.	R ($< 10^{-5}$)	inc.
40/4	R ($< 10^{-5}$)	R (< 0.07)	inc.	R ($< 10^{-5}$)	R ($< 10^{-4}$)
40/5	R (< 0.0004)	R (< 0.004)	GTS (< 0.06)	R ($< 10^{-5}$)	R ($< 10^{-5}$)
50/3	R ($< 10^{-5}$)	R ($< 10^{-5}$)	inc.	R ($< 10^{-5}$)	R ($< 10^{-5}$)
50/4	R ($< 10^{-5}$)	R (< 0.004)	R (< 0.058)	R ($< 10^{-5}$)	R ($< 10^{-5}$)
50/5	R ($< 10^{-5}$)	R (< 0.061)	R (< 0.019)	R ($< 10^{-5}$)	R ($< 10^{-5}$)

One-tailed randomisation tests comparing RWTS with standard tournament selection and generational reproduction are summarised in Table 2. E.g. if we look at the "40/4" row, this concerns experiments on the 40-node SHRD instance with degree constraint 4. On this problem, when Prüfer was used, RWTS was found significantly better than GTS, with a p-value of below 10^{-5}; RWTS was found significantly better than GTS in the case of the other encodings too, except for Edge-set, where the result was inconclusive (as indicated by "inc." in the table), with a p-value no smaller than 0.1. RWTS is clearly more effective than GTS overall, especially as the problem size increases. With edge-set, the difference appears generally to be insignificant, until we get to larger problem instances. We refrain from further comment on the comparison between RWTS and GTS since a far more thorough comparison with other EA designs need to be done to make clear claims for RWTS. However further comparisons below are now be restricted to sets of trials which used RWTS, except for the two edge-set cases where GTS appeared statistically better.

The Edge-Set Encoding vs. the New Encoding. First, we simply report that, when the new encoding is used, d-K-TCR always statistically outperformed CF-TCR (in all 9 problem/degree scenarios, - p-value 0.02 on the 30/3 problem, and < 0.0001 in all other cases). Therefore, confining comparison between d-K-TCR and edge-set, we have Table 3.

Edge-set was never statistically better than the new encoding in these nine cases, and hence the table indicates either that no statistical difference was found

Table 3. Summary of statistical analysis of d-K-TCR *versus* Edge-Set.

30/3	30/4	30/5	40/3	40/4	40/5	50/3	50/4	50/5
inc.	inc.	inc.	$p < 0.011$	inc.	inc.	$p < 0.0002$	$p < 0.014$	$p < 0.012$

(e.g. the 30-node problems), or, when a *p*-value is given, it indicates that the new encoding was found to outperform edge-set with confidence at least $(1-p)$.

We mention some additional observations on the raw data from all trials. To simplify the discussion, we define best(n/d) to be the best result from all trials of every algorithm on the problem with n nodes and degree-constraint d. Also, let best$(n/d, M)$ be the best result among the ten trials of method M, with worst$(n/d,M)$ defined analogously. In *every* problem/degree-constraint case, best$(n/d,$ *new-encoding*$)$ was the same as best(n/d). Further, it was always the case that worst$(n/d,$ *new-encoding*$)$ was better than worst$(n/d,$ *edge-set*$)$. Finally, best$(n/d,$ *new-encoding*$)$ was better than best$(n/d,$ *edge-set*$)$ for $n = 50$ and $d = 3, 4, 5$. Each of edge-set and the new encoding was statistically superior to both NetKeys and the Prüfer encoding with very high confidence, while all methods were superior to the Prüfer encoding with very high confidence.

5 Conclusions

The DC-MST is an NP-hard combinatorial optimization problem which is important in practice. In this paper we have introduced a new encoding, which combines simplicity with flexibility, and which has been shown to outperform (at least on the standard testbed studied) the edge-set encoding for this problem, which is currently the state of the art in the published literature on the DC-MST. The results also appeared to show a trend towards the superiority of the new encoding as problem instances increased in size.

Our results have therefore shown great promise for the new encoding, in particular when used in conjunction with the d-K-TCR method, and we recommend it for further research and also for use in the context of other tree-oriented problems (we are currently testing it for the Optimal Communication Spanning Tree Problem and preliminary results look very encouraging), although a full evaluation awaits comparative testing on real-world examples of the DC-MST. Here we have used Krishnamoorthy's SHRD problems, which were designed with realism in mind and are the commonly used benchmarks. It seems fair to claim that the new encoding (using the d-K-TCR method), in conjunction with a good EA, represents the best-so-far approach to large DC-MST problems which are of similar structure to the testbed studied.

We have also presented a novel reproduction scheme (RWTS) and found it to perform well, however this method was far from fully evaluated here.

References

1. F.N. Abuali, R.L. Wainwright and D.A. Schoenefeld, Determinant Factorization: A New Encoding Scheme for Spanning Trees Applied to the Probabilistic Minimum Spanning Tree Problem, in Proc. of the Sixth International Conference on Genetic Algorithms, Larry J. Eshelman, Ed. (1995) 470–477.
2. B. Dengiz, F. Altiparmak, and A.E. Smith, Local Search Genetic Algorithm for Optimal Design of Reliable Networks, IEEE Transactions on Evolutionary Computation, Vol. 1, No. 3, (1997) 179–188.
3. E. Edgington : *Randomization Tests*, Marcel Dekker Inc.,New York (1980).
4. B. Freisleben, P. Merz, A Genetic Local Search Algorithm for Solving Symmetric and Asymmetric Traveling Salesmen Problems. IEEE Int. CEC, (1996) 616–621.
5. M.R. Garey and D.S. Johnson, Computers and Intractability, A Guide to the Theory of NP-Completeness, San Francisco, Freeman, (1979).
6. M. Gen and R. Chen, *Genetic Algorithms and Engineering Design*, Wiley, (1997). Also see (for Prüfer encoding): http://www.ads.tuwien.ac.at/publications/bib/pdf/gottlieb-01.pdf.
7. B. Julstrom and G. Raidl, Initialization is Robust in Evolutionary Algorithms that Encode Spanning Trees as Sets of Edges, *ACM Symp. on Applied Computing*, (2002).
8. C. Palmer and A. Kershenbaum, An Approach to a Problem in Network Design Using Genetic Algorithms, *Networks*,**26**:151–163, (1995).
9. Knowles, J., Corne, D. A new evolutionary approach to the degree-constrained minimum spanning tree problem, *IEEE Trans. on Evolutionary Computation*, **4**(2):125–134, (2000).
10. M. Krishnamoorthy, A. Ernst and Y. Sharaiha, Comparison of Algorithms for the DC-MST, *Journal of Heuristics*,**7**, 587–611, (2001).
11. J. B. Kruskal, On the shortest spanning tree of a graph and the travelling salesman problem, *Proc. of the American Mathematical Society*, **7** (1):48–50, (1956).
12. Z. Michalewicz, Genetic Algorithms+Data Structures=Evolution Programs, Springer, (1992).
13. S.C. Narula and C.A. Ho, Degree-constrained minimum spanning tree, *Computer and Operations Research*,**7**:239–249, (1980).
14. P. Piggott and F. Suraweera. Encoding graphs for genetic algorithms: An investigation using the minimum spanning tree problem. *Progress in Evolutionary Computation* LNAI 956, 305–314 Springer, (1995).
15. R. Prim, Shortest connection networks and some generalisations, *Bell Systems Technical Journal*,**36**, 1389–1401, (1957).
16. G. R. Raidl, An Effecient Evolutionary Algorithm for the Degree-Constrained Minimum Spanning Tree Problem, *Proc.IEEE CEC*, 104–111, (2000).
17. G.R. Raidl and B. Julstrom : Edge-Sets: An Effective Evolutionary Coding of Spanning Trees, *IEEE Trans. on Evolutionary Computation*, **7**(3), 225–239, (2003). Also see http://citeseer.ist.psu.edu/547892.html.
18. F. Rothlauf, D. Goldberg and A. Heinzl, Network Random Keys - A Tree Network Representation Scheme for Genetic and Evolutionary Algorithms, *Evolutionary Computation*,**10**(1):75–97, (2002).Also see http://www.uni-mannheim.de/i3v/00068900/18198591.htm
19. B. Schindler, F. Rothlauf and H. Pesch, Evolution Strategies, Network Random Keys, and the One-Max Tree Problem, *Evoworkshops*, Springer, 143–52, (2002).
20. G. Zhou and M. Gen : An Effective GA Approach to The Quadratic Minimum Spanning Tree Problem, *Computers in Operations Research*, **25**(3):229–237, (1998).

Partially Evaluated Genetic Algorithm Based on Fuzzy c-Means Algorithm*

Si-Ho Yoo and Sung-Bae Cho

Dept. of Computer Science, Yonsei University
134 Shinchon-dong, Sudaemoon-ku, Seoul 120-749, Korea
bonanza@sclab.yonsei.ac.kr, sbcho@cs.yonsei.ac.kr

Abstract. To find the optimal solution with genetic algorithm, it is desirable to maintain the population size as large as possible. In some cases, however, the cost to evaluate each individual is relatively high and it is difficult to maintain large population. To solve this problem we propose a partially evaluated GA based on fuzzy clustering, which considerably reduces evaluation cost without any loss of its performance by evaluating only one representative for each cluster. The fitness values of other individuals are estimated from the representative fitness values indirectly. We have used fuzzy c-means algorithm and distributed the fitness according to membership matrix. The results with nine benchmark functions are compared to six hard clustering algorithms with Euclidean distance and Pearson correlation coefficients for measuring the similarity between the representative and its members in fitness distribution.

1 Introduction

Genetic algorithm (GA) is an efficient method for machine learning, optimization and classification, based on evolution mechanisms such as biological genetics and natural selection [1]. It is required to make the population size of evolution as large as possible because GA approach evolves the population spread over the search space. However, in some domains where the cost of evaluation is relatively high, it is difficult to maintain large number of individuals in a population. Smaller population causes several negative effects such as genetic drift.

One example that cannot help utilizing only smaller population is interactive genetic algorithm (IGA) application [2]. IGA is a technique that performs optimization based on human evaluation. A human operator can obtain what he wants through repeated interaction with computer. It has a special advantage, which is to adopt user's choice as fitness, when fitness function cannot be explicitly defined. This property allows IGA to be applied to artistic domains such as music and design, which are almost impossible to be solved with simple GA [2]. Also, there is the difficulty of high cost in solving the inverse problem with simple GA [3]. It is impossible to maintain large population size to search for the optimal solution in such domains.

---

* This paper was supported in part by Biometrics Engineering Research Center, KOSEF, and Brain Science and Engineering Research Program sponsored by Korean Ministry of Science and Technology in Korea.

To cope with this shortcoming an efficient GA where some parts of population are evaluated by human and remaining part by computer was proposed [4]. GA that evaluates only a few individual directly and evaluates the rest of individuals by their similarity to the selected individuals was also proposed [5]. Also, the hybrid GA based on clustering which considerably reduces the number of evaluations by evaluating only one representative of each cluster's center after clustering individuals in population was presented [6]. However, distributing fitness values of individuals linearly with only one representative does not provide precise fitness values if the hybrid GA could not form the ideal cluster partition.

In this paper, we propose a partially evaluated GA based on fuzzy clustering algorithm to solve this problem. At first, we make N clusters of individuals in a population by fuzzy c-means algorithm and calculate the fitness values of the representative in each cluster. Remaining individuals in each cluster get their fitness estimated by their membership values which indicate individuals' degree of belongness to the clusters. The fitness value of an individual that belongs to multiple clusters is estimated by all the relevant cluster representatives. Nine benchmark functions [7] have used to test the proposed method and the results are compared to six hard clustering algorithms with Euclidean distance and Pearson correlation coefficient for fitness estimation.

2 Clustering Algorithms

Clustering refers to the process of grouping samples in order to be similar within group [8]. These groups are called clusters. There are three general categories of clustering techniques: Hierarchical clustering, partitional clustering, and overlapping clustering.

2.1 Hierarchical Clustering

Hierarchical clustering algorithm constructs a structure of clusters. In this structure a cluster can have several substructures which are composed of other clusters. There are several hierarchical clustering algorithms such as single linkage algorithm, complete linkage algorithm, and average linkage algorithm [9]. Single linkage algorithm defines inter-cluster distance as the closest distance between two samples belonging to two different clusters. Complete linkage algorithm uses the distance between the most remote samples belonging to two different clusters as inter-cluster distance. Average linkage algorithm measures the average distance between all of the samples belonging to two different clusters for inter-cluster distance.

2.2 Partitional Clustering

Different from hierarchical clustering which creates a series of nested clusters, partitional clustering usually creates one set of clusters that partition the data into groups. Samples close to one another are assumed to be similar and the goal of the partitional clustering algorithm is to group data to be close together. k-means algorithm and hard c-means algorithm are good examples of partitional clustering. The k-means algorithm, one of the most widely used ones, attempts to solve the clustering problem by optimizing a given objective function [9].

$$J(X,V) = \sum_{i=1}^{c} \sum_{x \in C_i} d(x, v_i) \qquad (1)$$

where v_i is the ith cluster's center and $d(x,v_i)$ is the Euclidean distance between x and v_i. k-means algorithm puts each individual to its closest cluster by minimizing intra-cluster distance. Hard c-means algorithm uses different objective function [9].

$$J(X,U,V) = \sum_{i=1}^{c} \sum_{j=1}^{n} u_{ij} d^2(x_j, v_i) \qquad (2)$$

Here, u_{ij} represents the belongness of the ith individual to the jth cluster. When the individual belongs to the cluster the value of u_{ij} is 1 and if not, the value is 0. $d^2(x_j,v_i)$ is the squared Euclidean distance between x_j and v_i. Like k-means algorithm, hard c-means algorithm optimizes its objective function by minimizing its values.

2.3 Overlapping Clustering

Overlapping clustering algorithm has no hierarchical structure between clusters, similar to partitional clustering. In overlapping clustering, each cluster can be overlapped partially with others. According to the similarity of an individual to each cluster, the degree of belongness of the individual is calculated. For many real-world problems, overlapping clustering method is more realistic than general hard partitioning clustering algorithms [10].

3 Method

Partially evaluated GA groups individuals in population and evaluates only one representative for each group. The fitness values of other individuals are estimated indirectly from the representative's fitness values. This method consists of two main parts: (1) It conducts clustering of individuals by their similarity and (2) distributes representative's fitness to its members according to the similarity between the center of cluster and the individual. The overview of the proposed method is shown in Fig 1. In the first part, we have used fuzzy c-means algorithm for clustering, making N groups of individuals. Only N evaluations are conducted on each cluster center and the fitness of the remaining individuals is estimated from membership matrix which indicates their belongness to all the clusters.

3.1 Fuzzy Clustering

The most widely used fuzzy clustering algorithm is fuzzy c-means algorithm proposed by Bezdeck [11]. It generates a fuzzy partition providing a degree of membership of each data to a given cluster. The values of the membership lie between 0 and 1. Values close to 0 indicate the absence of a strong association to the corresponding cluster. Similarly, values close to 1 indicates the strong association to the cluster. The procedure of the algorithm is shown in Fig 2.

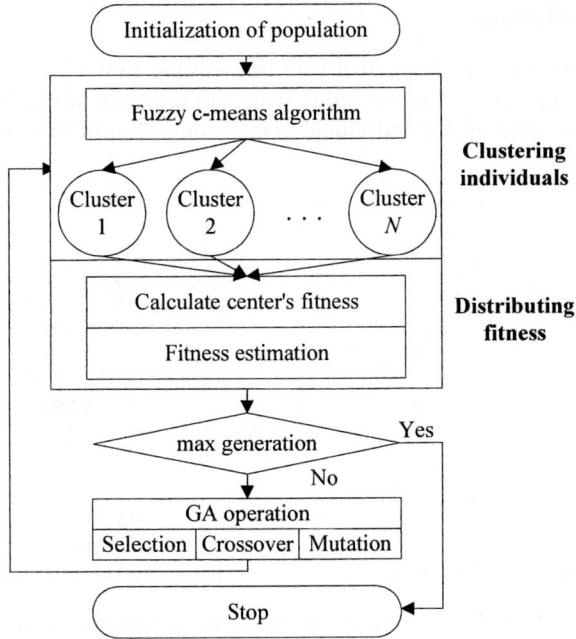

Fig. 1. An overview of the proposed method of partially evaluated GA based on fuzzy clustering.

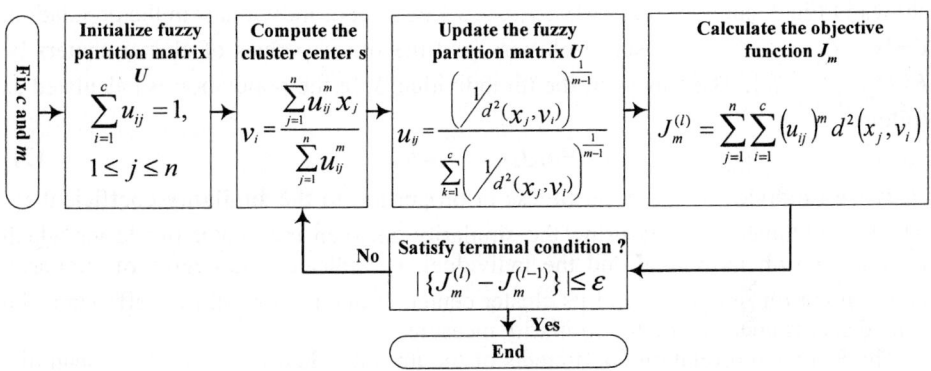

Fig. 2. Process of fuzzy c-means algorithm.

The objective of this algorithm is to minimize the objective function J_m to get the optimal fuzzy partition for a given dataset $X=\{x_1, x_2, \ldots, x_n\}$, where m is a real-valued number which controls the 'fuzziness' of the resulting clusters and u_{ij} is the membership degree of data x_j to a cluster i, an element of a ($c \times n$) pattern matrix $U=[u_{ij}]$. $d^2(x_j,v_i)$ corresponds to the square value of the Euclidean distance between a data x_j and the cluster center v_i [12].

3.2 Fitness Distribution

Fitness distribution plays an important role in evolving individuals. If an individual could not obtain appropriate fitness value from the representative, the evaluation of this missed fitness value of the individual goes wrong, diminishing the efficiency of the proposed method.

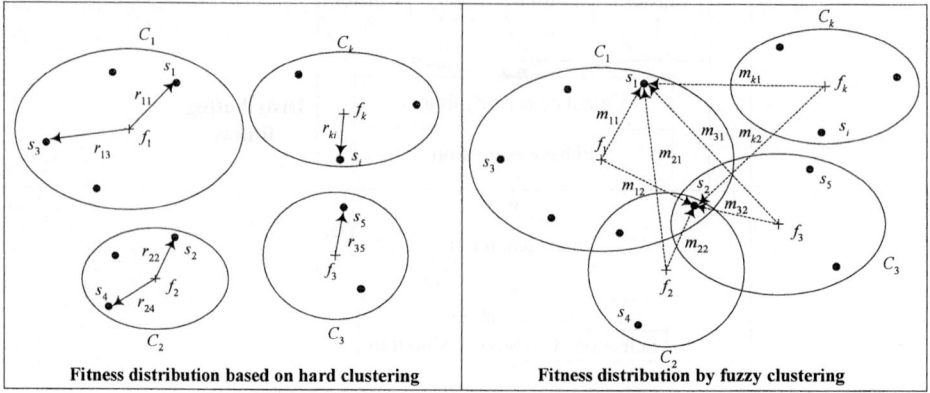

Fitness distribution based on hard clustering | **Fitness distribution by fuzzy clustering**

Fig. 3. Comparison between fitness distribution based on similarity measure and membership matrix.

In hard clustering, the fitnesses of the individuals are distributed based on the similarity between the center of a cluster and the individual belonging to that cluster. As shown in Fig 3, suppose that $S=\{s_1, s_2, \ldots, s_i\}$ be a set of individuals in the population, $C=\{C_1, C_2, \ldots, C_k\}$ be a set of clusters, and the fitness values of cluster centers be $F=\{f_1, f_2, \ldots, f_k\}$. The fitness of the ith individual s_i in the population is calculated as follow:

$$s_i = r_{ki} f_k, \quad s_i \in C_k \qquad (3)$$

The ith individual s_i gets its fitness in proportion to the similarity coefficient r_{ki}, which is obtained by measuring the similarity between the center of cluster which includes the ith individual and the individual. r_{ki} indicates the degree of similarity between the ith individual and its cluster center. Pearson correlation coefficients and Euclidean distance can be for similarity measure.

The Pearson correlation coefficients of the ith individual (PC_i) and Euclidean distance of the ith individual s_i to its cluster center (ED_i) are calculated as follows:

$$PC_i = \frac{\sum s_i c_k - \frac{\sum s_i \times \sum c_k}{D}}{\sqrt{\left(\sum s_i^2 - \frac{(\sum s_i)^2}{D}\right) - \left(\sum c_k^2 - \frac{(\sum c_k)^2}{D}\right)}}, \quad s_i \in C_k, \; r_{ki} = \alpha \bullet PC_i \qquad (4)$$

$$ED_i = \sqrt{\sum_{i=1}^{P} (c_k - s_i)^2}, \quad s_i \in C_k, \; r_{ki} = \alpha \bullet \frac{1}{ED_i} \qquad (5)$$

s_i belongs to the kth cluster C_k and c_k means the center of C_k. D is the dimension of the individual and P is the size of population. Since the larger value of PC and the smaller value of ED indicate strong similarity between the individual and its cluster center, we have calculated r_{ki} proportion to each individual's PC value and inverse proportion to their ED value. Both PC and ED are used for hard clustering method as similarity measures in fitness distribution, based on assumption that an individual only belongs to one cluster. It cannot be hardly expected that they get precise fitness values from representatives, since each individual gets fitness value linearly from its representatives.

In this paper, we propose a new fitness distribution method using membership matrix. Fig. 3 shows the fitness distribution method based on fuzzy clustering. This method distributes the fitness value of each cluster center to the individuals that are located in the cluster by their membership values. m_{ki} is the membership value of the ith individual to the kth cluster which represents the degree of belongness to the kth cluster. The distributed fitness value of the ith individual s_i is as follow:

$$s_i = \sum_{k=1}^{K} m_{ki} \times f_k \tag{6}$$

s_i gets its fitness value from the centers of all the clusters in proportion to their membership values. In Fig. 3, dashed line indicates the relation between the cluster center and the individual belonging to multiple clusters and solid line indicates the relation between the cluster center and the individual which belongs to only one cluster. An individual like s_2 belongs to c_1, c_2, and c_3 simultaneously and could not get its correct distributed fitness value from only one of three belonging clusters. However, the proposed method distributes the fitness value from all the clusters reflecting the individual's characteristics in the population.

4 Experiments

4.1 Experimental Environments

To prove the efficiency of the proposed method, we have conducted several benchmark tests. Nine benchmark functions have been used to compare several genetic algorithms including the proposed partially evaluated GA. Nine benchmark functions are DeJong function 1(EF1: 3 variables), DeJong function 2(EF2: 2 variables), DeJong function 3(EF3: 5 variables), DeJong function 4(EF4, 30 variables), DeJong function 5(EF5: 2 variables), Rastrigin function (EF6: 20 variables), Schwefel function (EF7: 10 variables), Griewangk function (EF8: 10 variables), and Ackley function (EF9: 30 variables). Simple GAs with population size of 100 (Pop100) and population size of 10 (Pop10), partially evaluated GA (Cluster10) with hard clustering algorithms using Euclidean distance and Pearson correlation coefficients, and the proposed method (Cluster10) with fuzzy clustering using membership matrix are compared. We have chosen the number of cluster N to be 10. All the experiments are conducted 10 times and the average values are represented as results. The length of chromosome is 30*(# of x), since we have used 30 bit binary representation for each x in benchmark functions. Crossover rate and mutation rate are 0.9 and 0.001 respectively. Roulette wheel method is employed to as a selection strategy. Fuzziness parameter and terminal condition for fuzzy c-means algorithm are 1.2 and 10^{-7} respectively.

4.2 Results Analysis

Performance comparison between the partially evaluated GA with Pearson correlation coefficient (PC) and Euclidean distance (ED) as a fitness distribution method and the proposed method (FCM) is shown in Table 1. For each evaluation function, the sum of difference between each individual's real fitness value and distributed fitness value from its representative in a whole population is calculated. Except De Jong function 4, the results of FCM are smaller than PC and ED which means that FCM distributes fitness value of each representative to its members more accurately than the other methods.

Table 1. Difference between real fitness values and distributed fitness values by PC, ED, and FCM.

	PC	ED	FCM
EF 1	11.263	9.226	**9.074**
EF 2	299.696	247.037	**240.107**
EF 3	3.096	2.744	**2.618**
EF 4	250.104	**249.889**	250.043
EF 5	0.00150	0.00114	**0.00114**
EF 6	178.888	134.572	**134.040**
EF 7	1463.260	648.380	**622.800**
EF 8	214.815	173.414	**172.322**
EF 9	20.132	13.267	**13.331**

Table 2 shows the best fitness values of nine benchmark functions from six hard clustering algorithms which use PC for fitness distribution and the proposed method (FCM). Six hard clustering algorithms are S-L (single-linkage), C-L (complete-linkage), A-L (average-linkage), Ward, HCM (hard c-means), and KM (k-means). Except EF6, EF8, and EF9, FCM shows the best performance for all cases. The best fitness values of six hard clustering algorithms with ED and the proposed method (FCM) are shown in Table 3. Pop10 shows the worst performance on all the evaluation functions for all cases and Pop100 outperforms FCM in EF6. Only in EF 8, Cluster10 with ED and PC have higher fitness values than the proposed method. The proposed method performs as well as Pop100, superior to PC and ED in most of evaluation functions.

Table 4 shows the t-test result of Pop100 and FCM. Average fitness values (Avg.) and standard deviation (SD) for each benchmark function is shown in Table 4. Except EF 1, EF 6, and EF 9, hypothesis that the average fitness of FCM is equal to the average fitness of Pop100 is significant at =0.05 by a one tailed test. This proves that the partial evaluation makes almost the same performance as simple GA which evaluates much more times than the proposed partially evaluated GA.

Table 2. Best fitness values of Pop100, Pop10, and Cluster10 (six hard clustering algorithms using PC and FCM).

	Pop 100	Pop 10	Cluster 10						
			S-L	C-L	A-L	Ward	HCM	KM	FCM
EF 1	75.15	71.59	74.11	73.15	74.70	73.92	74.11	75.05	**75.43**
EF 2	3835.3	3732.4	3825.8	3811.7	3827.3	3813.6	3811.5	3829.1	**3849.0**
EF 3	18.40	13.90	18.40	18.10	18.10	16.83	17.37	17.00	**20.70**
EF 4	569.89	542.83	592.04	571.79	577.08	586.60	560.90	498.30	**594.98**
EF 5	0.84	0.49	0.77	0.71	0.72	0.55	0.60	0.74	**0.95**
EF 6	**380.53**	352.28	377.80	378.69	369.15	375.60	376.23	360.46	379.92
EF 7	6445.0	6135.8	6368.5	6379.7	6381.2	6365.4	6422.4	6259.6	**6555.4**
EF 8	648.39	617.66	**660.39**	654.84	652.46	649.04	640.57	603.47	642.99
EF 9	21.68	21.61	**21.70**	21.68	21.69	21.68	21.68	21.61	21.69

Table 3. Best fitness values of Pop100, Pop10, Cluster10 (six hard clustering algorithms using ED and FCM).

	Pop 100	Pop 10	Cluster 10						
			S-L	C-L	A-L	Ward	HCM	KM	FCM
EF 1	75.15	71.59	74.41	75.13	**75.44**	74.76	73.99	74.57	75.43
EF 2	3835.3	3732.4	3818.2	3826.3	3825.4	3825.5	3795.8	3820.5	**3849.0**
EF 3	18.40	13.90	18.10	17.27	16.9	18.17	17.27	17.43	**20.70**
EF 4	569.89	542.83	572.81	557.72	554.21	565.12	553.75	508.14	**594.98**
EF 5	0.8358	0.4942	0.6872	0.6695	0.7098	0.6777	0.6193	0.6654	**0.9468**
EF 6	**380.53**	352.28	372.33	370.38	375.24	372.57	372.99	374.17	379.92
EF 7	6445.0	6135.8	6332.2	6446.2	6493.0	6416.6	6422.9	6408.9	**6555.4**
EF 8	648.39	617.66	647.94	649.21	644.81	626.37	646.39	**651.90**	642.99
EF 9	21.68	21.61	21.68	**21.69**	21.68	21.68	**21.69**	**21.69**	**21.69**

Table 4. T-test results of pop100 and FCM.

	Pop 100		FCM		t-test
	Avg.	SD	Avg.	SD	
EF1	45.245	11.951	31.659	14.048	7.365
EF2	1649.42	811.311	1600.34	1127.07	0.352
EF3	10.3	4.9316	12.1	4.239	-2.737
EF4	248.230	54.005	293.949	111.136	-3.699
EF5	0.109	0.812	0.660	0.4347	-12.03
EF6	288.509	31.601	221.370	35.7431	14.072
EF7	4426.47	516.488	4249.8	588.768	2.254
EF8	338.72	63.857	396.391	77.729	-5.732
EF9	21.151	0.2053	20.838	0.2770	9.070

Fig 4 shows the evolution process for four evaluation functions for which the FCM was the best. De Jong function 2 shows not much difference between the methods, only performing slightly better. The reason why FCM outperforms all the other methods in De Jong function 3 is that it has many local optima and deviation between the individuals is very small: Fuzzy clustering method is more appropriate for grouping these kinds of population rather than general hard clustering algorithms.

In De Jong function 4, FCM converges very fast in the beginning of the evolution and finds the optimal solution. The proposed method outperforms the other methods and even Pop100 for this evaluation function. Evolution process of De Jong function 5 is quite different. Since the landscape of this function has 25 significant holes within a plane, there exist several local optima before reaching the global optimum. Also the speed of convergence is slower than other evaluation functions. Pop100 reaches optimal solution faster than any other methods, but at last FCM outperforms it when the iteration number exceeds 180. Other hard clustering methods and Pop10 stuck at local optima.

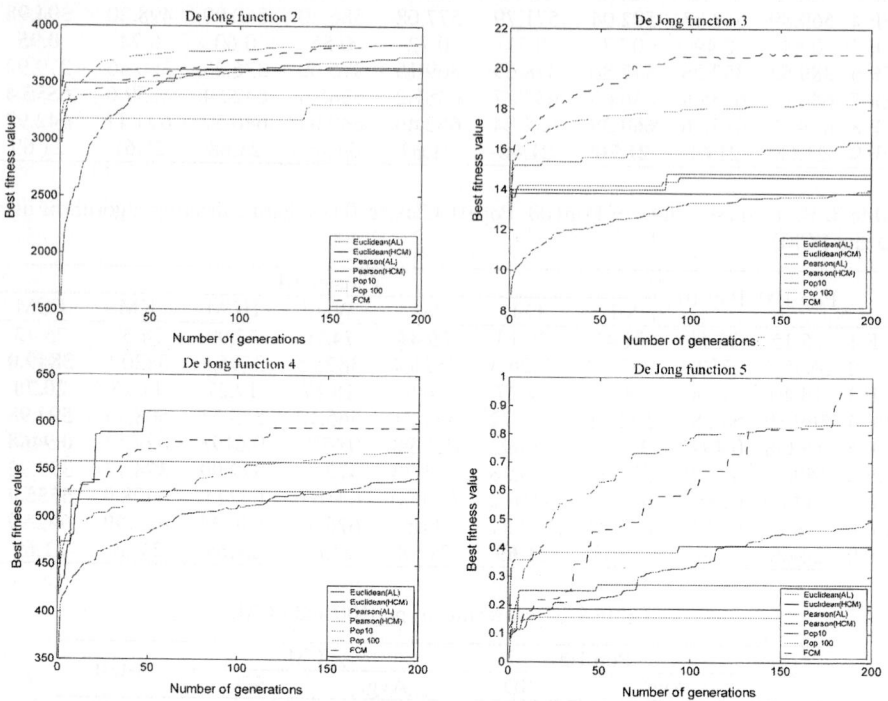

Fig. 4. Evolution process of De Jong function2, De Jong function3, De Jong function4, and De Jong function5.

In other evaluation functions, the proposed method also has showed better performance than Euclidean distance and Pearson correlation coefficient as a fitness distribution method. FCM distributes fitness value of each representative efficiently to the individuals in the population.

5 Concluding Remarks

We have proposed an efficient genetic algorithm with less fitness evaluation by fuzzy clustering. It divides the whole population into several clusters, and evaluates one individual for each cluster. The fitness values of other individuals are estimated from the representative fitness values indirectly by their membership values. This partially evaluated GA with fuzzy clustering can efficiently reduces the evaluation number without any loss of the performance. The results from several benchmark problems show that the algorithm has almost same performance to conventional GA that evaluates far more times than the proposed partially evaluated GA. Also, distributing fitness values by fuzzy membership matrix has worked well on the individuals with multiple clusters, outperforming Euclidean distance and Pearson correlation coefficient for fitness distribution.

References

1. L. Chamber, Practical Handbook of Genetic Algorithm, CRC Press, 1995.
2. H. Takagi, "Interactive evolutionary computation: Fusion of the capabilities of EC optimization and human evaluation," Proc. of the IEEE, vol. 89, no. 9, pp. 1275-1296, 2001.
3. M. V. Mannino and M. V. Koushik, "The cost minimizing inverse classification problem: A genetic algorithm approach," Decision Support Systems, vol. 29, pp. 283-300, October 2000.
4. M. Shibuya, H. Kita, and S. Kobayashi, "Integration of multi-objective and interactive genetic algorithms and its application to animation design," Proc. 99' Int'l Conf. on Systems, Man, and Cybernetics, vol. 3, pp. 646-651, 1999.
5. F. Sugimoto, and M. Yoneyama, "Hybrid fitness assignment strategy in IGA," Proc. IEEE Workshop on Multimedia Siganl Processing, pp. 284-287, Dec. 2002.
6. H.-S. Kim and S.-B. Cho, "An efficient genetic algorithm with less fitness evaluation by clustering," Proc. 2001 IEEE Congress on Evolutionary Computation, pp. 887-894, May 2001.
7. X. Yao, Y. Liu and G. Lin, "Evolutionary programming made faster," IEEE Trans. Evolutionary Computation, vol. 3, no. 2, pp. 82-102, July 1999.
8. B. K. Lavine, "Clustering and classification of analytical data," Encyclopedia of Analytical Chemistry, October 2000.
9. R. O. Duda, P. E. Hart and D. G. Stock, Pattern Classification, Wiley-Interscience Publication, 2001.
10. I. Gath and A.B. Geva, "Unsupervised optimal fuzzy clustering," IEEE Trans. Pattern Analysis and Machine Intelligence, vol. 11, no. 7, pp. 773-781, 1989.
11. J. C. Bezdek, Pattern Recognition with Fuzzy Objective Function Algorithms, Plenum Press, 1981.
12. F. Höppner, F. Klawonn, R. Kruse and T. Runkler, Fuzzy Cluster Analysis, Wiley, 2000

Metaheuristics for the Vehicle Routing Problem with Stochastic Demands

Leonora Bianchi[1], Mauro Birattari[2], Marco Chiarandini[3],
Max Manfrin[2], Monaldo Mastrolilli[1], Luis Paquete[3],
Olivia Rossi-Doria[4], and Tommaso Schiavinotto[3]

[1] IDSIA, USI-SUPSI, Switzerland
`leonora@idsia.ch`
[2] IRIDIA, Université Libre de Bruxelles, Belgium
[3] Intellectics Group, TU Darmstadt, Germany
[4] School of Computing, Napier University, UK

Abstract. In the vehicle routing problem with stochastic demands a vehicle has to serve a set of customers whose exact demand is known only upon arrival at the customer's location. The objective is to find a permutation of the customers (an a priori tour) that minimizes the expected distance traveled by the vehicle. Since the objective function is computationally demanding, effective approximations of it could improve the algorithms' performance. We show that a good choice is using the length of the a priori tour as a fast approximation of the objective, to be used in the local search of the several metaheuristics analyzed. We also show that for the instances tested, our metaheuristics find better solutions with respect to a known effective heuristic and with respect to solving the problem as two related deterministic problems.

1 Introduction

The Vehicle Routing Problem with Stochastic Demands (VRPSD) is defined on a complete graph $G = (V, A, D)$, where $V = \{0, 1, ..., n\}$ is a set of nodes (customers) with node 0 denoting the depot, $A = \{(i,j) : i,j \in V, i \neq j\}$ is the set of arcs joining the nodes, and $D = \{d_{ij} : i,j \in V, i \neq j\}$ are the travel costs (distances) between nodes. The cost matrix D is symmetric and satisfies the triangular inequality. One vehicle with capacity Q has to deliver goods to the customers according to their demands, minimizing the total expected distance traveled, and given that the following assumptions are made. Customers' demands are stochastic variables ξ_i, $i = 1, ..., n$ independently distributed with known distributions. The actual demand of each customer is only known when the vehicle arrives at the customer location. It is also assumed that ξ_i does not exceed the vehicle's capacity Q, and follows a discrete probability distribution $p_{ik} = \text{Prob}(\xi_i = k)$, $k = 0, 1, 2, ..., K \leq Q$. A feasible solution to the VRPSD is a permutation of the customers $s = (s(1), s(2), \ldots, s(n))$ starting at the depot (that is, $s(1) = 0$), and it is called a priori tour. The vehicle visits the customers in the order given by the a priori tour, and it has to choose, according to the actual customer's demand, whether to proceed to the next customer or to go to depot for restocking. Sometimes the choice of restocking is the best one, even if the vehicle is not empty, or if its capacity is bigger than the expected demand of the next scheduled customer, this action is called 'preventive restocking'. The goal of preventive restocking is to avoid the bad situation when the vehicle has not enough load to serve a customer and thus it has to perform a back-and-forth trip to the depot for completing the delivery at the customer. In the VRPSD, the objective is to find an a priori tour that minimizes the expected distance traveled by the vehicle, which is computed as follows. Let $s = (0, 1, \ldots, n)$ be an a priori tour. After the service completion at customer j, suppose the vehicle has a remaining load q, and let $f_j(q)$ denote the total expected cost from node j onward. With this notation, the expected cost of the a priori tour is $f_0(Q)$. If L_j represents the set of all possible loads that a vehicle can have after service completion at customer j, then, $f_j(q)$ for $q \in L_j$ satisfies $f_j(q) = \text{Minimum}\{f_j^p(q), f_j^r(q)\}$, where

$$f_j^p(q) = d_{j,j+1} + \sum_{k:k \leq q} f_{j+1}(q-k)p_{j+1,k} + \sum_{k:k>q}[2d_{j+1,0} + f_{j+1}(q+Q-k)]p_{j+1,k}, \quad (1)$$

$$f_j^r(q) = d_{j,0} + d_{0,j+1} + \sum_{k=1}^{K} f_{j+1}(Q-k)p_{j+1,k}, \quad (2)$$

with the boundary condition $f_n(q) = d_{n,0}$, $q \in L_n$. In (1-2), $f_j^p(q)$ is the expected cost corresponding to the choice of proceeding directly to the next customer, while $f_j^r(q)$ is the expected cost in case preventive restocking is chosen. As shown in [1], the optimal choice is of threshold type: given the a priori tour, for each customer j there is a load threshold h_j such that, if the residual load after serving j is greater than or equal to h_j, then it is better to proceed to the next planned customer, otherwise it is better to go back to the depot for preventive restocking. The computation of $f_0(Q)$ runs in $O(nKQ)$ time; the memory required is $O(nQ)$, if one is interested in memorizing all intermediate values $f_j(q)$, for $j = 1, 2, \ldots, n$ and $q = 0, 1, \ldots, Q$, and $O(Q)$ otherwise.

The preventive restocking strategy for the VRPSD has been applied in [2] and [1]. In [2], a simple but effective heuristic called cyclic heuristic is studied. [1] focuses on the single and multiple-vehicle VRPSD. The authors analyze several heuristics and compare them with an exact branch-and-bound approach for small instances up to 15 customers. They also adapt to the stochastic case the local search due to Or [3], by proposing a fast approximation computation for the change in the objective function when performing a local search move. Approaches different from the restocking policy exist in the VRPSD literature, for references and a brief review see [4].

In this paper we focus on an important aspect of designing metaheuristics for the VRPSD (and for stochastic combinatorial optimization problems in general): the objective function is computationally demanding, and effective approximations of it should be employed. Due to the analogies between the VRPSD and the traveling salesman problem (TSP), a natural approximation of the objective function is the length of the a priori tour. In fact, if the vehicle has infinite capacity, the consequent VRPSD can be seen as a TSP. In this paper we consider basic implementations of five metaheuristics: iterated local search (ILS), tabu search (TS), simulated annealing (SA), ant colony optimization (ACO) and evolutionary algorithms (EA). Our main goal is to test the impact on the metaheuristics performance of using the TSP length of the a priori tour as fast approximation of the VRPSD objective function. The solution quality of our metaheuristics are also compared with the cyclic heuristic and with a priori tours obtained by solving the problems as a TSP and as a deterministic VRP where the demand is assumed to be equal to the average demand of the VRPSD.

The remainder of the paper is organized as follows. Section 2 describes the metaheuristics, pointing out the common elements and the way the VRPSD objective function has been approximated. Section 3 reports on computational experiments, and section 4 summarizes the conclusions that can be drawn from the experimental results.

2 The Metaheuristics

As already stated in the introduction, the main goal of this study was to see whether approximating the exact but computationally demanding objective with the fast computing length of the a priori tour is convenient or not. Our hypothesis was that the speedup due to the use of a fast approximation of the objective would be an advantage especially during the phase of local search, when many potential moves must be evaluated before one is chosen. In fact, the exact cost of a local search move is the expected cost difference between the a priori tour after the move and before the move; however, this computation takes $O(nKQ)$ time. Hence, we consider two different approximation schemes for the move cost: i) *VRPSDlike*, that was suggested in [1], and requires $O(KQ)$ time, and ii) *TSPlike*, that requires $O(1)$ time. Given that all metaheuristics use the same local search, we consider two versions for each metaheuristic according to the type of local search approximation scheme. In the remainder of the paper, when we want to specify a version of a metaheuristic, we add to its name the -VRPSDlike or -TSPlike label (as, for example, ILS-VRPSDlike or ILS-TSPlike). Notice also that, depending on the metaheuristic, the local search may be used either as a black-box, or not. In particular, ACO, EA and ILS use the local search as a black-box, but TS and SA do employ their own strategy for examining the neighborhood of a solution. In the following, we describe in more detail the local search with its two approximation schemes, the initialization criterion of metaheuristics, the metaheuristics, and the other algorithms that took part at the experimental comparisons.

The OrOpt Local Search. We chose the *OrOpt insertion* as suggested in [1]. Given a starting tour, sets S_k of k consecutive customers with $k \in \{1, 2, 3\}$ are moved from one position to another in the tour. In the following we describe the two types of approximation schemes used for the computation of the move cost.

VRPSDlike approach. The move cost may be computed in two stages: i) compute the saving from extracting the set of costumers from the tour; ii) compute the cost of inserting it back somewhere else in the tour. Let i and $i+k+1$ be the nodes immediately preceding, respectively following, S_k in the tour, and let j be the node immediately after which S_k is to be inserted. Here, we assume that j is *after* i in the a priori tour. Let $f_i(q)$ and $f_{i+k+1}(q)$ be the expected cost-to-go from nodes i, respectively $i+k+1$ onward before the extraction of S_k. Apply one dynamic programming recursion step starting with cost vector $f_{i+k+1}(\cdot)$ at node $i+k+1$ back to node i, without considering the sequence S_k. Let $f'_i(\cdot)$ be the resulting cost vector at node i, that is, after extracting S_k from the tour. Then, define the approximate extraction saving as a simple average over q of $f'_i(q) - f_i(q)$. The computation of the approximate insertion cost of S_k between nodes j and $j+1$ in the tour, is done analogously, if we assume that the insertion point (node j) is after the extraction point (node i). Let $f_j(q)$ be the cost-to-go at node j before inserting S_k, and $f''_j(q)$ be the cost-to-go at node j after inserting the S_k. The total approximate cost of an OrOpt move is computed by subtracting the approximate extraction saving form the approximate insertion cost, as follows

$$VRPSDlike\text{-}move\text{-}cost = \frac{\sum_{q=0}^{Q}[(f''_j(q) - f_j(q)) - (f'_i(q) - f_i(q))]}{Q+1}. \quad (3)$$

Note that the cost vectors are assumed to be already available from the computation of the expected cost for the starting tour, thus, they do not need to be computed when evaluating eq. (3). The only computations that must be done here are the evaluation of cost vectors $f'_{i+1}(\cdot)$ and $f''_j(\cdot)$, requiring $O(KQ)$ time, and the average of eq.(3), requiring $O(Q)$ time. Therefore, with the proposed *VRPSDlike* approximation, the cost of an OrOpt move can be computed in $O(KQ)$ time. Although it is possible that tours which are worsening with respect to the evaluation function are accepted because recognized as improving by the approximate evaluation, in practice this approximation scheme behave quite well. For a deeper discussion on the issues related with this scheme we refer the reader to the original paper [1].

TSPlike approach. In the *TSPlike* approach the cost of an OrOpt move coincides with the difference between the length of the tour before the move and after the move:

$$TSPlike\text{-}move\text{-}cost = d_{i,i+k+1} + d_{j,i+1} + d_{i+k,j+1} - d_{i,i+1} - d_{i+k,i+k+1} - d_{j,j+1}, \quad (4)$$

where, as before, i and j are the extraction, respectively insertion point of a string of k consecutive customers. Clearly, eq. (4) is computable in constant time.

The OrOpt neighborhood examination follows the same scheme proposed in [1]. Briefly, all possible sequences of length $k \in \{1,2,3\}$ are considered for insertion in a random position of the tour after the extraction point. Then, only the 'best' move among those of length k is chosen. The 'best' move is the move corresponding to the most negative move cost, which is computed by eq. (3) in the *VRPSDlike* approach and by eq. (4) in the *TSPlike* approach.

Randomized Farthest Insertion. The Farthest Insertion is a tour construction heuristic originally designed for the TSP; it builds a tour by choosing as next customer the not-yet-visited customer which is furthest from the current one, of course the final solution depends on the starting customer. Here, we consider the Randomized Farthest Insertion heuristic (FR), that picks randomly the first customer, and after the tour has been completed, the starting customer is shifted to the depot. Like in all our metaheuristics, after the tour is built, the OrOpt local search is applied for further improving it. All metaheuristics use FR for generating a starting solution (ILS, TS, SA), or a set of starting solutions (ACO, EA).

Simulated Annealing. The SA metaheuristic [5] uses the local search operators described before, but also accepts non improving neighbors according to a function of a temperature parameter which depends on the deterioration in the cost function. The initial temperature is given by the average cost (*VRPSDlike* or *TSPlike*) of a sample of 100 tours of the initial tour multiplied by a given factor μ. Every $TL = \psi \cdot n$ iterations the temperature is updated as $T_{n+1} = \alpha \times T_n$ (standard geometric cooling). After $\rho \cdot TL$ without improvement in the approximate cost of a tour the temperature is increased by adding T_i to the current value. The tour considered for checking improvements is the best since the last re-heating. From preliminary experiments we set: $\mu = 0.05$, $\alpha = 0.98$, $\psi = 1$ and $\rho = 20$.

Tabu Search. The TS metaheuristic [6] is based on the idea of accepting also worsening neighbors during local search but controlling cycles by avoiding the repetition of visited tours. For the VRPSD, we defined the tabu mechanism as follows. After an Or-opt move on the current tour S (extracting the sub-sequence S_k for a given size k from position i and re-inserting it at position j) the moves that become tabu are all insertions such that: i) a customer at position $i+1$ of S becomes again the successor of customer at position i of S; or ii) a customer at position $i+k+1$ of S becomes again the successor of customer at position $i+k$ of S. The tabu tenure is randomly chosen in the interval $[0.8(n-k-1), (n-k-1)]$. We consider a probabilistic acceptance criterion as follows: if a move is non tabu its cost is evaluated with a probability of 0.8 and selected if it leads to an improving tour. If the move is tabu its cost is evaluated with a probability of 0.3 and the move is selected in spite of its tabu status if it leads to the best tour found so far.

In TS-VRPSDlike the selection and acceptance of a move is done according to the *VRPSDlike* approximation scheme. The exact cost of the new tour obtained is then computed. In TS-TSPlike, the selection depends on the *TSPlike* approximation scheme, but the selected move is performed only if it leads to a real improvement of the exact cost of the tour. If the move selected does not lead to a real improvement no move is performed and the search continues with a different k.

Iterated Local Search. The ILS metaheuristic is based on the idea of improving the local search procedure by providing new starting tour obtained from a perturbation of the current solution [7]. In our implementation the *perturbation* consists in a sampling of n neighboring tours according to the 2-opt exchange neighborhood [8]. Each new tour is evaluated with the exact cost function and if a tour is found that has cost smaller than the best tour found so far plus ε, the sampling ends. $\varepsilon = \frac{n}{10}$ was empirically the best value found on some preliminary runs. Otherwise, the best perturbed tour is returned.

The local search uses respectively the *VRPSDlike* or the *TSPlike* approximation scheme. Finally, the *acceptance criterion* evaluates each new local optima found with the exact VRPSD cost function and accept it as current solution if it is the best tour found so far.

Ant Colony Optimization. In the ACO metaheuristic, a set of agents (ants) build solutions to the given problem cooperating through pheromone-mediated indirect and global communication. Here, we consider the Ant Colony System (ACS), an ACO variant proposed in [9]. At each iteration, m ants construct a tour by building a complete sequence of customers using information stored in a "pheromone matrix" $\tau: V \times V \to \Re_{\geq 0}$. The pheromone values $\tau_{i,j}$ estimate of the utility of going from a customer i to a customer j in the a-priori tour. An ant which is at customer i chooses a not-yet-visited customer j as next customer with probability proportional to $\tau_{i,j}$. After each construction step a *local update rule* is applied to the element $\tau_{i,j}$ corresponding to the chosen customer pair: $\tau_{i,j} = (1 - \psi) \cdot \tau_{i,j} + \psi \cdot \tau_0$, with $\psi \in [0,1]$. After all the m ants have built their tours, the local search is applied to each of them. Then, the best tour S_{best} found since the beginning of the run according to the exact VRPSD cost function is determined, and it is used in the *global update rule* to change all the entries in the pheromone matrix as follows: if $(i,j) \in S_{best}$, $\tau_{i,j} = (1-\rho) \cdot \tau_{i,j} + \rho \cdot \frac{q}{f(S_{best})}$, otherwise $\tau_{i,j} = (1-\rho) \cdot \tau_{i,j}$, where $q, \rho \in [0,1]$ are parameters. Pheromone is initialized in the following way. First, all pheromone values are set to τ_0, and S_{best} is initialized with the best among m tours generated by the FR heuristic refined by the OrOpt local search. Then, the global update rule is applied r times to the pheromone matrix. In our ACS implementation, heuristic information is only used by FR in the initialization phase, but not in the ants' tour construction process. From preliminary experiments the set of parameters that was chosen is: $m = 5$, $\tau_0 = 0.5$, $\psi = 0.3$, $\rho = 0.1$, $q = 10^7$, $r = 100$. In ACS every tour outside the local search is evaluated with the exact cost function. The *VRPSDlike* and *TSPlike* approximation schemes are only used in the local search.

Evolutionary Algorithm. EA metaheuristics are based on the essence of natural evolution processes, which involve the reproduction, random variation, competition, and selection of contending individuals in a population [10]. Here, the population is initialized with solutions produced by the FR heuristic. At each iteration two parent solutions are chosen among the best ones to generate a new child solution through the recombination operator. After some preliminary experiments, we chose the Edge Recombination operator [11]. It tries to build a child tour exclusively from the edges present in both parent tours, whenever possible. A mutation operator, consisting of swapping adjacent customers without considering the depot, is applied with probability 0.5. Then, local search is used to improve the solution. Finally, the improved solution replaces the worst solution in the population. We use a population of size 10. As for ACS, in EA the only difference between the *VRPSDlike* version and the *TSPlike* version is in the local search they use.

Other Algorithms. In order to better understand the influence of the stochasticity in the problem, two state of the art algorithms to solve the VRPSD as a TSP [12] and as a capacitated VRP (CVRP) [13] have also been included in our study. In the first case, the coordinates of all customers (depot included) are used to define a corresponding TSP instance; the instance is solved by the state of the art TSP algorithm and the solution found is then shifted so to start with the depot. In the second case, the coordinates, average customers' demands and vehicle capacity are used to define a corresponding CVRP instance. A CVRP solution in general is not a single a priori tour visiting the depot once, but it is composed by a set of tours visiting different sets of customers (apart from the depot). Such a solution is transformed into an a priori tour by keeping the same order in which customers are visited and by deleting the intermediate multiple visits to the depot. In both cases (TSP and CVRP) the final solution, once transformed into a VRPSD a priori tour, is finally evaluated with the exact cost function of the VRPSD.

For comparison with the existing literature about the VRPSD, we have also implemented the simple but effective cyclic heuristic [2]. Following the description of [2], the cycle heuristic works as follows. First, heuristically solve a TSP over the n customers (depot excluded). Then, for each of the n cyclic permutations of the tour found, use the 2-opt local search to obtain a new tour. Evaluate with the VRPSD objective function the $2n$ tours obtained, and choose the best one. The computational experience in [2] suggests that the cyclic heuristic provides good quality solutions for instances with 50 to 100 customers, uniformly distributed on the unit square, and it is therefore an example of the effectiveness of the TSP analogy.

3 Experimental Comparisons

Instances and Experimental Setup. In the literature there is no commonly used benchmark for the VRPSD, therefore we have generated our own testbed. We have tried to consider instances which are 'interesting' from different points of view. First of all, the position of customers was not chosen uniformly at random, but randomly with normal distributions around two centers (so customers are grouped in two clusters). This is done in order to consider instances nearer to the real world situations, where customers may be located for instance in two different cities. The clusters' centers have coordinate in [0,99], and customers' coordinates are all different. We considered a total of 120 instances, of these, 75 instances have 50 customers, 40 instances have 100 customers, and 5 instances have 200 customers.

As it emerged from [14], an important factor that influences the 'difficulty' of a VRPSD instance is the ratio between the total (average) demand of customers and the vehicle's capacity. The bigger the ratio, the more 'difficult' the instance. Here, the vehicle capacity Q was chosen as $Q = \lceil \frac{\text{total average demand} \cdot r}{n} \rceil$, where the parameter r may be approximately interpreted as the average number of served customers before restocking. In our testbed, we have generated instances with $r = 4$, which corresponds to demand over capacity ratios from about 12 to 50, which is a much higher value than the values used in the VRPSD literature (typical values are below 3).

Each customer's demand is an integer stochastic variable uniformly distributed on an interval. The demand interval for each customer i was generated using two parameters: the average demand D_i, and the spread S_i, so that the possible demand values for customer i are the $2S_i + 1$ integers in the interval $[D_i - S_i, D_i + S_i]$. Average demands were chosen so that for each customer i, $D_i \in [1, 49]$ with probability $1/2$, and $D_i \in [50, 100]$ with probability $1/2$. Spreads were chosen so that for each customer i, $S_i \in \{1, 5\}$ with equal probability.

Each algorithm was tested once on each instance for a time equal to 60, 600 or 6000 seconds for instances respectively with 50, 100 or 200 customers. All algorithms, except the cyclic heuristic and the TSP state of the art algorithm, used all the available time for the computation. FR was restarted from a newly generated solution each time that the local search stopped in a local optimum. Experiments were performed on a cluster of 6 PCs with Athlon CPUs 1400MHz running GNU/Linux Debian OS, and all algorithms were coded in C++.

Results. Results are summarized in the boxplots of Fig. 1. Each row of a boxplot shows the distribution of the quantity on the horizontal axis obtained by each metaheuristic on all the tested instances. The left plot of Fig. 1 reports on the horizontal axis the expected cost of the solutions found, normalized with respect to the range of improvement found by FR. So, for a given instance and a given metaheuristic MH, the normalized value reported on the boxplot is (MH $_{\text{final value}}$ − FR $_{\text{final value}}$)/(FR $_{\text{starting value}}$ − FR $_{\text{final value}}$). The right plot of Fig. 1 shows the ranking of metaheuristics; the results of all executions on the same instance are ordered by quality of the solution (VRPSD expected cost) to determine the rank.

For the interpretation of the results, one could consider the performance of FR like a sort of minimal requirement for a metaheuristic. In fact, FR does essentially the simple iteration of the same local search for different starting solutions, until the available computation time is not over. Therefore, it is reasonable to request that a good algorithm for the VRPSD perform significantly better than FR. From Fig. 1, it seems that only ILS, EA and TS perform significantly better than FR. This observation is confirmed by the one-tailed paired Wilcoxon test, confidence level 95% with Holmes corrections for multiple tests , that we have done for each couple MH-FR (with the same type of approximation scheme).

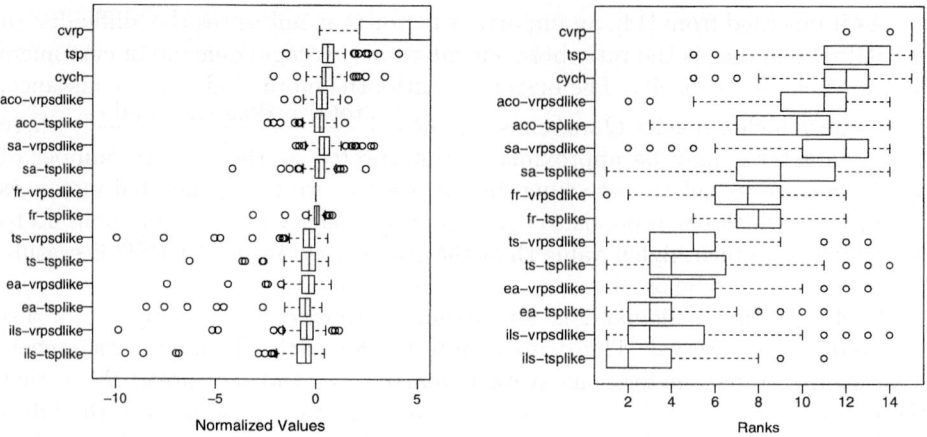

Fig. 1. Results over the 120 tested instances.

We have also verified if the TSPlike version of the metaheuristics is significantly better than the VRPSDlike version, and the answer is positive. We refer the reader interested in the details of the performed statistical tests to the webpage http://iridia.ulb.ac.be/vrpsd.ppsn8/experiments.html.

Another point to note is that the cyclic heuristic performs worse than all metaheuristics. This is an interesting results, since the cyclic heuristic was performing very well [2] for different types of instances (customers uniformly distributed on the unit square and low demand over capacity ratio). The worst algorithms in our tests are the two state of the art heuristics for the TSP, respectively CVRP; this is a point which encourages the development of VRPSD problem-specific algorithms, and let us conclude that, for the type of tested instances, the stochasticity of the problem is not negligible.

4 Conclusions

Our main goal in this paper was to test the impact on the metaheuristics' performance of using the length of the a priori tour as fast approximation of the exact but computationally demanding objective function. For this porpuse, we have considered two different approximation schemes for evaluating the cost of a local search move: the *VRPSDlike* approximation (as also suggested in [1]) and the *TSPlike* approximation. We show experimentally that using the *TSPlike* approximation leads to better performing metaheuristics with respect to using the *VRPSDlike* approximation. We also show that for the tested instances, our metaheuristics find better solutions with respect to the cyclic heuristic (which is known from the literature to perform well on different types of instances) and with respect to solving the problem as a traveling salesman problem and as a capacitated vehicle routing problem, which are related classical deterministic problems. Additionally, we remark that the test instances for which we obtained the above results are characterized by high demand over capacity ratios. This feature makes our instances nearer to many real-world vehicle routing problem instances.

Acknowledgments

This work was supported by the *Metaheuristics Network*, a Research Training Network funded by the IHP programme of the EC, grant HPRN-CT-1999-00106. M. Manfrin also acknowledges support by "COMP2SYS", a Marie Curie Early Stage Training Site, funded by the the EC through the HRM programme. The information provided is the sole responsibility of the authors and does not reflect the EC's opinion. The EC is not responsible for any use that might be made of data appearing in this publication. This research was also funded by the "ANTS" project, an "Action de Recherche Concertée" funded by the Scientific Research Directorate of the French Community of Belgium.

References

1. W. Yang, K. Mathur, and R. H. Ballou. Stochastic vehicle routing problem with restocking. *Transportation Science*, 34(1):99–112, 2000.
2. D. J. Bertsimas, P. Chervi, and M. Peterson. Computational approaches to stochastic vehicle routing problems. *Transportation Science*, 29(4):342–352, 1995.
3. I. Or. *Traveling salesman-type combinatorial problems and their relation to the logistics of blood banking*. PhD thesis, Department of Industrial Engineering and Management Sciences, Nortwestern University, Evanston, IL, 1976.
4. L. Bianchi, M. Birattari, M. Manfrin, M. Mastrolilli, L. Paquete, O. Rossi-Doria, and T. Schiavinotto. Metaheuristics for the vehicle routing problem with stochastic demands. Technical Report IDSIA-06-04, IDSIA, April 2004.
5. S. Kirkpatrick, C. D. Gelatt, and M. P. Vecchi. Optimization by simulated annealing. *Science*, (4598):671–680, 1983.
6. F. Glover. Tabu search - Part I. *ORSA Journal on Computing*, 1(3):190–206, 1989.
7. H.R. Lourenço, O. Martin, and T. Stützle. In F. Glover and G. Kochenberger, editors, *Handbook of Metaheuristics*, volume 57 of *International Series in Operations Research & Management*, chapter Iterated Local Search, pages 321–353. Kluwer Academic Publishers, Boston, U.S.A., 2002.
8. D. S. Johnson and L. A. McGeoch. The travelling salesman problem: A case study in local optimization. In E. H. L. Aarts and J. K. Lenstra, editors, *Local Search in Combinatorial Optimization*, pages 215–310. John Wiley and Sons, Ltd., New York, U.S.A., 1997.
9. M. Dorigo and L. M. Gambardella. Ant Colony System: A cooperative learning approach to the travelling salesman problem. *IEEE Transactions On Evolutionary Computation*, 1(1):53–66, 1997.
10. T. Baeck, D. Fogel, and Z. Michalewicz, editors. *Evolutionary Computation 1: Basic Algorithms and Operators*. Institute of Physics Publishing, Bristol, UK, 2000.

11. D. Whitley, T. Starkweather, and D. Shaner. The travelling salesman and sequence scheduling: Quality solutions using genetic edge recombination. In L. Davis, editor, *Handbook of Genetic Algorithms*, pages 350–372. Van Nostrand Reinhold, New York, U.S.A., 1991.
12. T. Stützle and H. Hoos. In P. Hansen and C. Ribeiro, editors, *Essays and Surveys on Metaheuristics*, chapter Analyzing the Run-time Behaviour of Iterated Local Search for the TSP, pages 589–612. Kluwer Academic Publishers, Boston, U.S.A., 2002.
13. L. M. Gambardella, E. Taillard, and G. Agazzi. MACS-VRPTW: A multiple ant colony system for vehicle routing problems with time windows. In D. Corne, M. Dorigo, and F. Glover, editors, *New Ideas in Optimization*. McGraw-Hill, 1999.
14. M. Gendreau, G. Laporte, and R. Séguin. An exact algorithm for the vehicle routing problem with stochastic demands and customers. *Transportation Sciences*, 29(2):143–155, 1995.

AntHocNet: An Ant-Based Hybrid Routing Algorithm for Mobile Ad Hoc Networks

Gianni Di Caro*, Frederick Ducatelle, and Luca Maria Gambardella

Istituto Dalle Molle sull'Intelligenza Artificiale (IDSIA)
Galleria 2, CH-6928 Manno-Lugano, Switzerland
{gianni,frederick,luca}@idsia.ch

Abstract. In this paper we present AntHocNet, a new algorithm for routing in mobile ad hoc networks. Due to the ever changing topology and limited bandwidth it is very hard to establish and maintain good routes in such networks. Especially reliability and efficiency are important concerns. AntHocNet is based on ideas from Ant Colony Optimization. It consists of both reactive and proactive components. In a reactive path setup phase, multiple paths are set up between the source and destination of a data session, and during the course of the communication session, ants proactively test existing paths and explore new ones. In simulation tests we show that AntHocNet can outperform AODV, one of the most important current state-of-the-art algorithms, both in terms of end-to-end delay and packet delivery ratio.

1 Introduction

In recent years there has been an increasing interest in Mobile Ad Hoc Networks (MANETs) [13]. In this kind of networks, all nodes are mobile, and they communicate with each other via wireless connections. There is no fixed infrastructure. All nodes are equal and there is no centralized control or overview. There are no designated routers: all nodes can serve as routers for each other, and data packets are forwarded from node to node in a multi-hop fashion.

Routing is the task of directing data flow from source to destination maximizing network performance. This is particularly difficult in MANETs. Due to the mobility of the nodes, the topology of the network changes constantly, and paths which were initially efficient can quickly become inefficient or even infeasible. This means that routing information should be updated more regularly than in wired networks, so that in principle more routing control packets are needed. However, this is a problem in MANETs, since the bandwidth of the wireless medium is very limited, and the medium is shared: nodes can only send or receive data if no other node is sending in their neighborhood. The access

---

* Corresponding author. This work was partially supported by the Future & Emerging Technologies unit of the European Commission through project "BISON: Biology-Inspired techniques for Self Organization in dynamic Networks" (IST-2001-38923) and by the Hasler Foundation through grant DICS-1830.

to the shared channel is controlled by protocols at the Medium Access Control layer (MAC), such as ANSI/IEEE 802.11 DCF [7] (the most commonly used in MANETs), which in their turn create extra overhead.

In this work we propose *AntHocNet*, a new MANET routing algorithm based on ideas from ant-based routing. For wired networks, a number of successful ant-based routing algorithms exist (eg. ABC [14] and AntNet [3]). They are based on the pheromone trail laying-following behavior of real ants and the related framework of ant colony optimization (ACO) [4]. The main idea is to continuously sample possible paths with ant-like agents, and to indicate the quality of paths by means of artificial pheromone variables. Multiple paths are made available this way, and data packets are stochastically spread over them following the pheromone values. Ant-based routing algorithms exhibit a number of desirable properties for MANET routing: they work in a distributed way, are highly adaptive, are robust, and provide automatic load balancing.

In this paper, we aim to propose an algorithm which can work efficiently in MANETs, while still maintaining those properties which make ant-based algorithms so appealing. The rest of this paper is organized as follows. In section 2 we describe related work in MANET and ant-based routing. Section 3 contains the description of our algorithm and in section 4 we present simulation results.

2 Related Work: MANET Routing and Ant-Based Routing

The specific challenges and possible applications of MANETs have made this a very popular research area, and a lot of routing algorithms have been proposed. People traditionally classify these algorithms as either *proactive* or *reactive*. In purely proactive protocols (e.g., DSDV [11]) nodes try to maintain at all times routes to all other nodes. This means that they need to keep track of all topology changes, which can become difficult if there are a lot of nodes or if they are very mobile. Therefore, reactive protocols (e.g., AODV [12] or DSR [8]) are in general more scalable (see [2]). In these protocols, nodes only gather routing information on demand: only when they have data for a certain destination they construct a path, and only when the path becomes infeasible they search a new path. In this way they greatly reduce the routing overhead, but they can suffer from oscillations in performance since they are never prepared for disruptive events. *Hybrid algorithms* like ZRP [6] have both a proactive and a reactive component, in order to try to combine the best of both worlds.

Most of the algorithms are single path: at any time, they use only one path between source and destination. Multipath routing (see [10] for an overview) offers an interesting alternative in terms of link failure robustness and load balancing. Some algorithms create multiple paths at path setup time, and use the best of these until it fails, after which they switch to the second best and so on (e.g., AODV-BR [9]). A problem with this way of working is that alternative paths are often infeasible by the time they need to be used. Moreover, when only the best path is used, one looses the opportunity to spread data packets over the different paths, a practice which can improve the network throughput.

The first ant-based routing algorithms were ABC [14] and AntNet [3]. Both algorithms follow a similar general strategy. Nodes send ant agents out at regular intervals to randomly chosen destinations. The main aim of the ants is to sample the paths, assign a quality to them, and use this information to update the routing tables in the nodes they pass. These routing tables contain an entry for each destination and each neighbor, indicating the goodness of going over this neighbor on the way to the destination. This goodness value is called pheromone. This pheromone information is used for the routing of both ants and data packets: all packets are routed stochastically, choosing with a higher probability those links with higher pheromone values. If enough ants are sent to the different destinations, nodes keep up-to-date information about the best paths, and automatically adapt their data load spreading to this.

Ant-based routing algorithms have a number of properties which are desirable in MANETs: they are highly adaptive to network changes, use active path sampling, are robust to agent failures, provide multipath routing, and take care of data load spreading. However, the fact that they crucially rely on repeated path sampling can cause significant overhead if not dealt with carefully. There have been a number of attempts to design ant-based routing algorithms for MANETs. Examples are ARA [5] and PERA [1]. However, these algorithms loose much of the proactive sampling and exploratory behavior of the original ant-based algorithms in their attempt to limit the overhead caused by the ants.

3   AntHocNet

AntHocNet is a hybrid multipath algorithm. When a data session is started at node s with destination d, s checks whether it has up-to-date routing information for d. If not, it reactively sends out ant-like agents, called *reactive forward ants*, to look for paths to d. These ants gather information about the quality of the path they followed, and at their arrival in d they become *backward ants* which trace back the path and update routing tables. The routing table $\mathcal{T}^i$ in node i contains for each destination d and each possible next hop n a value $\mathcal{T}^i_{nd} \in \mathcal{R}$. $\mathcal{T}^i_{nd}$ is an estimate of the goodness of the path over n to d, which we call pheromone. In this way, pheromone tables in different nodes indicate multiple paths between s and d, and data packets can be routed from node to node as datagrams. They are stochastically spread over the paths: in each node they select the next hop with a probability proportional to its pheromone value. Once paths are set up and the data session is running, s starts to send *proactive forward ants* to d. These ants follow the pheromone values similarly to data packets. In this way they can monitor the quality of the paths in use. Moreover, they have a small probability of being broadcasted, so that they can also explore new paths. In case of link failures, nodes either try to locally repair paths, or send a warning to their neighbors such that these can update their routing tables. In the rest of this section we describe each of these functions in detail.

3.1 Reactive Path Setup

Reactive forward ants looking for a destination d are either broadcasted or unicasted, according to whether or not the node they are currently in has routing information for d. Due to the broadcasting, ants can proliferate quickly over the network, following different paths to the destination. When a node receives several ants of the same generation (i.e., they started as the same original forward ant at the source), it will compare the path travelled by the ant to that of the previously received ants of this generation: only if its number of hops and travel time are both within a certain factor (a parameter which we empirically set to 1.5) of that of the best ant of the generation, it will forward the ant. Using this policy, overhead is limited by removing ants which follow bad paths, while the possibility to find multiple good paths is not hindered.

The main task of the reactive forward ant is to find a path connecting s and d. It keeps a list $\mathcal{P}$ of the nodes $[1, \ldots, n]$ it has visited. Upon arrival at the destination d, the forward ant is converted into a *backward ant*, which travels back to the source retracing $\mathcal{P}$. The backward ant incrementally computes an estimate $\hat{T}_\mathcal{P}$ of the time it would take a data packet to travel over $\mathcal{P}$ towards the destination, which is used to update routing tables. $\hat{T}_\mathcal{P}$ is the sum of local estimates $\hat{T}_{i \to i+1}$ in each node $i \in \mathcal{P}$ of the time to reach the next hop $i+1$: $\hat{T}_\mathcal{P} = \sum_{i=1}^{n-1} \hat{T}_{i \to i+1}$. The value of $\hat{T}_{i \to i+1}$ is defined as $(Q_{mac}^i + 1)\hat{T}_{mac}^i$: the product of the estimate of the average time to send one packet, $\hat{T}_{mac}^i$, times the current number of packets in queue (plus one) to be sent at the MAC layer, Q_{mac}^i. $\hat{T}_{mac}^i$ is calculated as a running average of the time elapsed between the arrival of a packet at the MAC layer and the end of a successful transmission. So if t_{mac}^i is the time it took to send a packet from node i, then node i updates its estimate as follows: $\hat{T}_{mac}^i = \alpha \hat{T}_{mac}^i + (1-\alpha) t_{mac}^i$ with $\alpha \in [0,1]$. Since $\hat{T}_{mac}^i$ is calculated at the MAC layer it includes channel access activities, so it takes into account local congestion of the shared medium. Forward ants calculate a similar time estimate, which is used for filtering the ants, as mentioned above.

At each intermediate node $i \in \mathcal{P}$, the backward ant virtually sets up a path towards the destination d, creating or updating routing table entries T_{nd}^i. Upon arrival in a node i from its neighbor n, the ant creates an entry in the routing table $\mathcal{T}^i$, indicating n as next hop to take from this node in order to reach d. The entry will contain a pheromone value T_{nd}^i, which is an indication of the goodness of the path going to destination d over next hop n. The pheromone value represents an average of the inverse of the cost, in terms of both estimated time and number of hops, to travel to d through n. If $\hat{T}_{i \to d}$ is the travelling time estimated by the ant, and h is the number of hops, the pheromone value is defined as: $\tau_{id} = \left((\hat{T}_{s \to d} + h T_{hop})/2 \right)^{-1}$, where T_{hop} is a fixed value representing the time of taking one hop in unloaded conditions. Taking this average is a way to avoid possibly large oscillations in the time estimates gathered by the ants (e.g., due to local bursts of traffic) and to take into account both end-to-end delay and number of hops. If there was already an entry T_{nd}^i in $\mathcal{T}^i$, its value is updated using a weighted average: $T_{nd}^i = \gamma T_{nd}^i + (1-\gamma)\tau_{id}$, $\gamma \in [0,1]$ (γ and α were set to 0.7 in the experiments).

3.2 Stochastic Data Routing

The path setup phase described above creates a number of good paths between source and destination, indicated in the routing tables of the nodes. Data can then be forwarded between nodes according to the values of the pheromone entries. Nodes in AntHocNet forward data stochastically. When a node has multiple next hops for the destination d of the data, it will randomly select one of them, with the probability P_{nd} of a next hop n assigned as the square of its pheromone: $P_{nd} = \frac{T_{nd}^2}{\sum_{i \in \mathcal{N}_d} T_{id}^2}$. We take the square in order to be more greedy with respect to the better paths. According to this strategy, we do not have to choose a priori how many paths to use: their number will be automatically selected in function of their quality.

The probabilistic routing strategy leads to data load spreading with consequent *automatic load balancing*. When a path is clearly worse than others, it will be avoided, and its congestion will be relieved. Other paths will get more traffic, leading to higher congestion, which will make their end-to-end delay increase. By continuously adapting the data traffic, the nodes try to spread the data load evenly over the network. This is quite important in MANETs, because the bandwidth of the wireless channel is very limited. Of course, to do this properly, it is important to frequently monitor the quality of the different paths. To this end we use the proactive ants.

3.3 Proactive Path Maintenance and Exploration

While a data session is running, the source node sends out proactive forward ants according to the data sending rate (one ant every n^{th} data packet). They follow the pheromone values in the same way as the data (although the pheromone values are not squared, so that they sample the paths more evenly), but have a small probability at each node of being broadcasted. In this way they serve two purposes. If a forward ant reaches the destination without a single broadcast it simply samples an existing path. It gathers up-to-date quality estimates of this path, and updates the pheromone values along the path from source to destination. A backward ant does the same for the direction from the destination back to the source. If on the other hand the ant got broadcasted at any point, it will leave the currently known pheromone trails, and explore new paths.

After a broadcast the ant will arrive in all the neighbors of the broadcasting node. It is possible that in this neighbor it does not find pheromone pointing towards the destination, so that it will need to be broadcasted again. The ant will then quickly proliferate and flood the network, like a reactive forward ant does. In order to avoid this, we limit the number of broadcasts to two. If the proactive ant does not find routing information within two hops, it will be deleted. The effect of this mechanism is that the search for new paths is concentrated around the current paths, so that we are looking for path improvements and variations.

In order to guide the forward ants a bit better, we use *hello messages*[1]: using these messages, nodes know about their immediate neighbors and have pheromone information about them in their routing table. So when an ant arrives in a neighbor of the destination, it can go straight to its goal. Looking back at the ant colony inspiration of our model, this can be seen as pheromone diffusion: pheromone deposited on the ground diffuses, and can be detected also by ants further away. In future work we will extend this concept, to give better guidance to the exploration by the proactive ants. Hello messages also serve another purpose: they allow to detect broken links. This allow nodes to clean up stale pheromone entries from their routing tables.

3.4 Link Failures

Nodes can detect link failures (e.g., a neighbor has moved far away) when unicast transmissions (of data packets or ants) fail, or when expected hello messages were not received. When a link fails, a node might loose a path to one or more destinations. If the node has other next hop alternatives to the same destination, or if the lost destination was not used regularly by data, this loss is not so important, and the node will just update its routing table and send a notification of the update to its neighbors. On the other hand, if the destination was regularly used for data traffic, and it was the node's only alternative for this destination, the loss is important and the node should try to *repair the path*. This is the strategy followed in AntHocNet, with the restriction that a node only repairs the path if the link loss was discovered with a failed data packet transmission.

After the link failure, the node broadcasts a *route repair ant* that travels to the involved destination like a reactive forward ant: it follows available routing information when it can, and is broadcasted otherwise. One important difference is that it has a maximum number of broadcasts (which we set to 2 in our experiments), so that its proliferation is limited. The node waits for a certain time (empirically set to 5 times the estimated end-to-end of the lost path), and if no backward repair ant is received, it concludes that it was not possible to find an alternative path to the destination which is removed from the routing table.

In the case the node still has other entries for the destination(s) involved in a link failure, but the lost next hop was its best alternative for the destination, or if the link failure was due to an ant packet, the node will only send a *notification* to its neighbors. Also in the case of a failed path repair it will send a similar notification. The notification contains a list of the destinations it lost a path to, and the new best estimated end-to-end delay and number of hops to this destination (if it still has entries for the destination). All its neighbors receive the notification and update their pheromone table using the new estimates. If

---

[1] Hello messages are short messages broadcasted every t_{hello} seconds (e.g., $t_{hello} = 1 sec$) by the nodes. If a node receives a hello message from a new node n, it will add n as a new destination in its routing table. After that it expects to receive a hello from n every t_{hello} seconds. After missing a certain number of expected hello's (2 in our case), n will be removed.

they in turn lost their best or their only path to a destination due to the failure, they will broadcast the notification further, until all nodes along the different paths are notified of the new situation.

4 Simulation Experiments

We evaluate our algorithm in a number of simulation tests. We compare its performance with AODV [12] (with route repair), a state-of-the-art MANET routing algorithm and a de facto standard. In 4.1 we describe the simulation environment and the test scenarios, and in 4.2 we show and discuss the results.

4.1 Simulation Environment

As simulation software we used Qualnet, a discrete-event simulator developed by Scalable Networks as a follow-up of GloMoSim, which was designed by UCLA. Qualnet is specifically optimized to simulate large-scale MANETs, and comes with correct implementations of the most important routing protocols.

All our simulation scenarios are derived from the base scenario used in [2], which is an important reference. In this base scenario 50 nodes are randomly placed in an area of 1500×300 m^2. The area is rectangular in order to have more long paths. Within this area, the nodes move according to the random waypoint model [8]: each node randomly chooses a destination point and a speed, and moves to this point with the chosen speed. After that it stops for a certain pause time and then chooses a new destination and speed. The maximum speed in the scenario is $20m/s$ and the pause time is 30 seconds. The total length of the simulation is 900 seconds. Data traffic is generated by 20 constant bit rate (CBR) sources sending one 64-byte packet per second. Each source starts sending at a random time between 0 and 180 seconds after the start of the simulation, and keeps sending until the end. At the physical layer we use a two-ray signal propagation model. The transmission range is 300 meters, and the data rate is $2Mbit/s$. At the MAC layer we use the popular 802.11 DCF protocol.

The different test scenarios used below were derived from the base scenario by changing some of the parameters. In particular, we varied the pause time, the area dimensions and the number of nodes. For each new scenario, 5 different problems were created, by choosing different initial placements of the nodes and different movement patterns. The reported results are averaged over 5 different runs (to account for stochastic elements, both in the algorithms and in the physical and MAC layers) on each of the 5 problems.

4.2 Simulation Results

In a first set of experiments we progressively extended the long side of the simulation area. This has a double effect: paths become longer and the network becomes sparser. The results are shown in figure 1. In the base scenario, AntHocNet has a better delivery ratio than AODV, but a higher average delay.

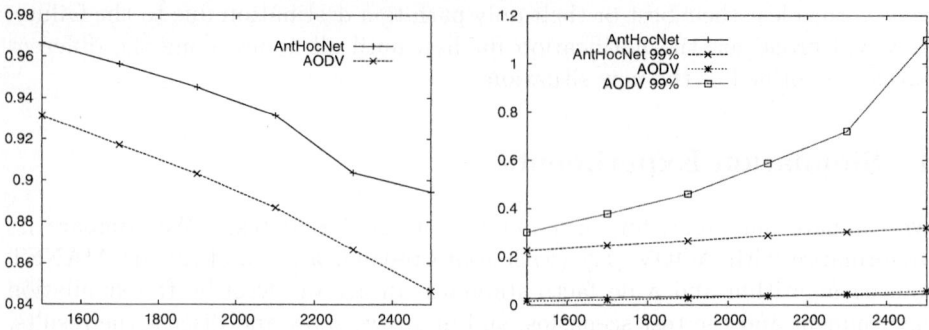

Fig. 1. On the left the delivery ratio (the fraction of sent packets which actually arrives at their destination) and on the right the average and the 99th percentile of the delay per packet. On x-axis the long edge of the area: starting from the base scenario of $1500 \times 300\ m^2$, and ending at $2500 \times 300\ m^2$.

For the longer areas, the difference in delivery ratio becomes bigger, and AODV also looses its advantage in delay. If we take a look at the 99th percentile of the delay, we can see that the decrease in performance of AODV is mainly due to a small number of packets with very high delay. This means that AODV delivers packets with a very high delay jitter, a crucial problem in terms of quality of service (QoS). The jitter could be reduced by removing these packets with very high delay, but that would mean an even worse delivery ratio for AODV. Next we changed the mobility of the nodes, varying the pause time between 0 seconds (all nodes move constantly) and 900 seconds (all nodes are static). The area dimensions were kept on $2500 \times 300\ m^2$, like at the end of the previous experiment (results for $1500 \times 300\ m^2$ were similar but less pronounced). In figure 2 we can see a similar trend as in the previous experiment. For easy situations (long pause times, hardly any mobility), AntHocNet has a higher delivery ratio, while AODV has lower delay. As the environment becomes more difficult (high mobility), the difference in delivery ratio becomes bigger, while the average delay of AntHocNet becomes better than that of AODV. Again, the 99th percentile of AODV shows that this algorithm delivers some packets with a very high delay. Also AntHocNet has some packets with a high delay (since the average is above the 99th percentile), but this number is less than 1% of the packets. In a last experiment we increased the scale of the problem. Starting from 50 nodes in a $1500 \times 500\ m^2$ area, we multiply both terrain edges by a scaling factor and the number of nodes by the square of this factor, up to 200 nodes in a $3000 \times 1000\ m^2$ area. The results, presented in figure 3, show again the same trend: as the problem gets more difficult, the advantage of AntHocNet in terms of delivery ratio increases, while the advantage of AODV in terms of average delay becomes a disadvantage. Again this is due to a number of packets with a very high delay.

The experiments described above show that AntHocNet has some clear advantages over AODV. First of all, AntHocNet gave a better delivery ratio than AODV in all scenarios. The construction of multiple paths at route setup, and

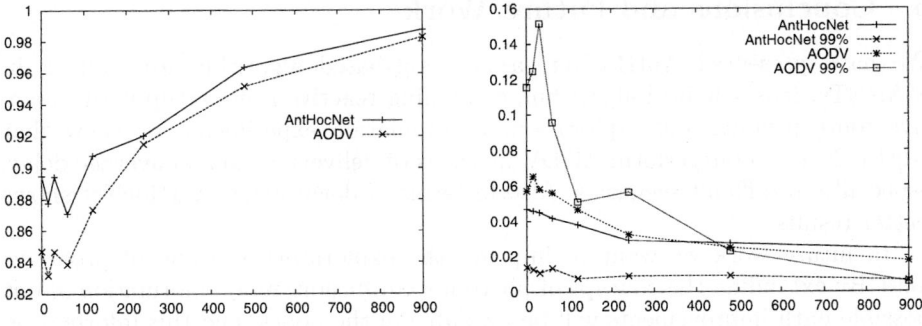

Fig. 2. On the left the delivery ratio and on the right the average and 99th percentile of the delay. On the x-axis the node pause time in seconds.

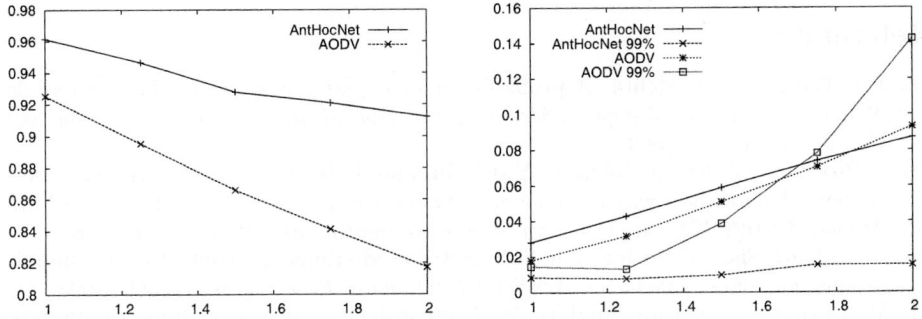

Fig. 3. On the left the delivery ratio and on the right the average and 99th percentile of the delay. On the x-axis the scaling factor for the problem.

the continuous search for new paths with proactive ants ensures that there are often alternative paths available in case of route failures, resulting in less packet loss. Second, AntHocNet has a higher average delay than AODV for the simpler scenarios, but a lower average delay for the more difficult ones. The average delay of AODV increases sharply in each of the difficult scenarios, and the 99th percentile figures indicate that this is mainly due to a fraction of packets which is delivered with an abnormally high delay. Moreover, the 95th percentile (not shown in the figures) is usually lower for AODV than for AntHocNet, indicating that AODV still delivers most of its packets faster than AntHocNet. This is in line with the multipath nature of AntHocNet: since it uses different paths simultaneously, not all packets are sent over the shortest path, and so the average delay will be slightly higher. On the other hand, since AODV relies on just one path, delays can become very bad when this path becomes inefficient or invalid. This is especially likely to happen in difficult scenarios, with longer paths, lower node density or higher mobility, rather than in the dense and relatively easy base scenario. Delivering packets with low variability and low maximum delay is an important factor in QoS routing.

5 Conclusions and Future Work

We have presented AntHocNet, a new ant-based algorithm for routing in MANETs. It is a hybrid algorithm, combining reactive route setup with proactive route probing and exploration. In simulation experiments we show that AntHocNet can outperform AODV in terms of delivery ratio and average delay, especially in difficult scenarios. Also in terms of delay jitter, AntHocNet shows better results.

In future work we want to improve the exploratory working of proactive ants. By extending the concept of pheromone diffusion, more information about possible path improvements will be available in the nodes, and this information can guide proactive ants. This should lead to better results with less overhead. Also, we would like to try out a virtual circuit based approach. This could result in better control over paths, so that data delivery can be made more reliable.

References

1. J. S. Baras and H. Mehta. A probabilistic emergent routing algorithm for mobile ad hoc networks. In *WiOpt03: Modeling and Optimization in Mobile, Ad Hoc and Wireless Networks*, 2003.
2. J. Broch, D. Maltz, D. Johnson, Y.-C. Hu, and J. Jetcheva. A performance comparison of multi-hop wireless ad hoc network routing protocols. In *Proc. of 4th Annual ACM/IEEE Int. Conf. on Mobile Computing and Networking*, 1998.
3. G. Di Caro and M. Dorigo. AntNet: Distributed stigmergic control for communications networks. *Journal of Artificial Intelligence Research*, 9:317–365, 1998.
4. M. Dorigo, G. Di Caro, and L. M. Gambardella. Ant algorithms for discrete optimization. *Artificial Life*, 5(2):137–172, 1999.
5. M. Günes, U. Sorges, and I. Bouazizi. ARA - the ant-colony based routing algorithm for manets. In *Proc. of 2002 ICPP Workshop on Ad Hoc Networks*, 2002.
6. Z. J. Haas. A new routing protocol for the reconfigurable wireless networks. In *Proc. of the IEEE Int. Conf. on Universal Personal Communications*, 1997.
7. IEEE 802.11 working group. ANSI/IEEE std. 802.11, 1999 edition: Wireless LAN medium access control (MAC) and physical layer (PHY) specifications. Technical report, ANSI/IEEE, 1999.
8. D. B. Johnson and D. A. Maltz. *Mobile Computing*, chapter Dynamic Source Routing in Ad Hoc Wireless Networks, pages 153–181. Kluwer, 1996.
9. S.-J. Lee and M. Gerla. Aodv-br: Backup routing in ad hoc networks. In *Proceedings of IEEE WCNC 2000*, 2000.
10. S. Mueller, R. Tsang, and D. Ghosal. Multipath routing in mobile ad hoc networks: Issues and challenges. In *Performance Tools and Applications to Networked Systems*, volume 2965 of *Lecture Notes in Computer Science*. Springer-Verlag, 2004.
11. C. Perkins and P. Bhagwat. Highly dynamic destination-sequenced distance-vector routing (DSDV) for mobile computers. In *ACM SIGCOMM'94 Conference on Communications Architectures, Protocols and Applications*, 1994.
12. C. Perkins and E. Royer. Ad-hoc on-demand distance vector routing. In *Proc. of 2nd IEEE Workshop on Mobile Computing Systems and Applications*, 1999.
13. E. M. Royer and C.-K. Toh. A review of current routing protocols for ad hoc mobile wireless networks. *IEEE Personal Communications*, 1999.
14. R. Schoonderwoerd, O. Holland, J. Bruten, and L. Rothkrantz. Ant-based load balancing in telecommunications networks. *Adaptive Behavior*, (2):169–207, 1996.

A Scatter Search Algorithm for the 3D Image Registration Problem*

Oscar Cordón[1], Sergio Damas[2], and José Santamaría[3]

[1] Dept. of Computer Science and A.I., University of Granada
ocordon@decsai.ugr.es
[2] Dept. of Software Engineering, University of Granada
sdamas@ugr.es
[3] Faculty of Odontology, University of Granada
jsantam@ugr.es

Abstract. Image registration has been a very active research area in the computer vision community. In the last few years, there is an increasing interest on the application of Evolutionary Computation in this field and several evolutionary approaches have been proposed obtaining promising results. In this contribution we introduce the use of an advanced evolutionary algorithm, *Scatter Search*, to solve the 3D image registration problem. The new proposal will be validated using two different shapes (both synthetic and MRI), considering three different transformations for each of them, and testing its performance with a *Basic Memetic Algorithm* and the classical, problem-specific *ICP* algorithm.

1 Introduction

Image registration (IR) is a fundamental task in computer vision used to finding a correspondence (or transformation) among two or more pictures taken under different conditions: at different times, using different sensors, from different viewpoints, or a combination of them [2].

In the last few years, there is an increasing interest on applying *Evolutionary Computation* (EC) fundamentals to IR [12, 8, 3]. In this work, we try to exploit the benefits of applying *Scatter Search* (SS) [9] to solve the IR problem and our contributions are related to the fact of jointly solving matching and transformation estimation problems in 3D using curvature derived information, which has been proved to return good quality solutions [5]. We consider this information in order to reduce the number of meaningful points and to obtain a good topological characterization of the shape, therefore enabling a better matching.

The performance of the SS algorithm proposed is tested against a *Basic Memetic Algorithm* (BMA) in order to check the influence of the evolutionary approach in the problem solving. Besides, a classical IR technique is also considered as a baseline for both evolutionary approaches.

---

* This work was partially supported by the Spanish Ministerio de Ciencia y Tecnologia under project TIC2003-00877 (including FEDER fundings) and under Network HEUR TIC2002-10866-E.

To do so, in Section 2 we give some IR basics while the image information we will take advantage of to solve the IR problem is described in Section 3. Section 4 is devoted to introduce the common components of the BMA and SS, while Sections 5 and 6 show their specific characteristics. Section 7 includes the experiments developed (and the corresponding analysis) to test our proposal with a number of transformations and two different images (one sintetic and one from a magnetic resonance). Finally, Section 8 presents some concluding remarks and several open lines for future research.

2 Image Registration

IR can be defined as a mapping between two images (I_1 and I_2, called scene and model, respectively) both spatially and with respect to intensity: $I_2(x, y, z, t) = g(I_1(f(x, y, z, t)))$. The goal will be finding out the transformation that must be applied to the scene image in order to reach the model one. Therefore, we will match every pixel intensity value in I_2 (located in (x,y,z) at time t) with a pixel intensity value in I_1. Such a value will be obtained after applying a geometric transformation f to (x, y, z, t) and then a second intensity-based transformation g to the new location given by f.

We can usually find situations where intensity difference is inherent to scene changes, and thus intensity transformation estimation given by g is not necessary. In this contribution, we will consider both that the latter is the case (so no estimation of g is tackled) and that f represents a similarity transformation. Therefore, there are seven parameters of f to be estimated for 3D IR: traslation (t_x, t_y, t_z), rotation $(\alpha_x, \alpha_y, \alpha_z)$ and uniform scaling (s).

The problem we are facing is specially hard as the amount of data to be managed is huge. *Feature-based* registration methods solve this drawback by matching only the most relevant geometric primitives (points, lines, triangles, etc.) in both images. These primitives are the result of a preprocessing step of the intensity values of the pixels in the scene and the model images. Only the most significant data is to be studied, therefore reducing the problem complexity.

Although the final registration problem solution consists of the right values for the parameters which determine f, two different solving approaches arise, each of them working in a different solution space: i) to search for the optimal geometric primitive correspondence in the matching space and then identify the appropriate transformation parameters – using numerical methods such as least square estimation – to overlay the scene and the model considering such matching ([1,5,4]), and ii) to directly search in the parameter space (usually by means of evolutionary algorithms), computing the matching between scene and model geometric primitives to validate the estimated transformation once it has been applied ([8, 12, 3]). While the former involves determining which of the scene primitives matches each model one, the latter deals with the estimation of the registration transformation causing this model-scene overlapping.

Among the different algorithms based on the former approach (search in the matching space), the *Iterative Closest Point* (ICP) [1, 5] is the most known. It applies on an iterative loop where the current transformation f is applied on the scene image primitives, each of these primitives is matched against the closest model image primitive, and the parameters of f are newly estimated by least squares until a registration error threshold is overcome. As said, ICP will be considered as a baseline in the experimentation developed in this work.

3 Shape-Derived Heuristic Information for 3D Image Registration

This section is devoted to introduce the information that can be derived from the shapes included in the images to be registered in order to better solve the IR problem. To do so, let us first define the iso-intensity surface of a 3D image, which will be called simply the iso-surface in the rest of this paper. For any continuous function $C(x, y, z)$ of $\mathbb{R}^3$, any value I of $\mathbb{R}$ (called the iso-value) defines a continuous, not self-intersecting surface, without hole, which is called the iso-intensity surface of C [10]. A non ambiguous way to define the iso-surface is to consider it as being the surface which separates the space regions where the intensity of C is greater or equal to I from these regions whose intensity is strictly lower than I. Wheter such an iso-surface corresponds to the boundary of the scanned object is another problem, that will not be considered in the current contribution. Because of their good topological properties, iso-surface techniques are the most widely used segmentation methods for 3D medical images.

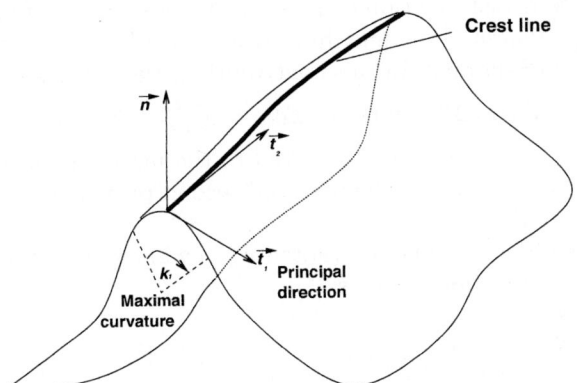

Fig. 1. Differential characteristics of surfaces.

Let us see now some properties of the iso-surfaces (see Figure 1). At each point p of those surfaces, there is an infinite number of curvatures but, for each direction t in the tangent plane at p, there is only one associated curvature k_t. There are two priviledged directions of the surface, called the principal directions (t_1 and t_2), which correspond to the two extremal values of the curvature: k_1 and k_2. There are many more parameters to determine the characterization of surfaces, but we have considered the latter two (k_1 and k_2) being enough to describe what at last will be called ridge lines or crest lines.

4 Coding Scheme and Objective Function

Our proposal is based on solving the IR problem by searching in the matching space (See Section 2). So, a coding scheme specifying the matching between model and scene primitives (points in our case) has to be defined. First, a preprocessing step (a 3D crest lines edge detector [10]) is applied to extract the most relevant feature points describing the surfaces. Then the point matching between both images is represented as a permutation π of size $N_{max} = max(N_1, N_2)$, with N_1 and N_2 being the number of 3D points in the scene and model shapes.

Therefore, we will be able to infer the parameters $(t_x, t_y, t_z, \alpha_x, \alpha_y, \alpha_z, s)$ of the implicit registration transformation f related to the point matching π by means of simple numerical optimization methods such as least squares estimation (see Section 2). Once we know the expresion of f, we can estimate the registration error measured by the *Mean Square Error*, tipically given in IR by:

$$MSE = \frac{\sum_{i=1}^{N_{min}} \|f(x_i) - y_i\|^2}{N_{min}}$$

where f is the estimated registration function; $N_{min} = min(N_1, N_2)$; $x_i, i = 1, 2, ..., N_{min}$, are the N_{min} scene points considered (the f function is applied to each of them); and $y_i, i = 1, 2, ..., N_{min}$, are the N_{min} model points matching the scene ones.

As said, the main novelty of our method is that the features of the image isosurfaces (the curvature information seen in Section 3) are used to guide both the matching and the transformation estimation. So, we define a function $m_{error}(\cdot)$ evaluating the goodness of the matching stored in π by using (one of) the ridge measures shown in Section 3. In this contribution, we have chosen the following:

$$m_{error}(\pi) = \Delta k_1 + \Delta k_2 \quad \text{where} \quad \Delta k_j = \sum_{i=1}^{N_{min}} (k_j^i - k_j^{\pi_i})^2, \; j = \{1, 2\}$$

Δk_1 and Δk_2 measure the error associated to the matching of scene and model points with different values for the first and second principal curvatures, respectively (see Section 3).

This way, the objective function (noted $F(\cdot)$) will include information regarding both previous criteria as follows:

$$\min \; F(\pi) = w_1 \cdot \sum_{i=1}^{N_1} \sum_{j=1}^{N_2} M_{ij} \|X_i - t - sR(\alpha)Y_j\|^2 \; + \; w_2 \cdot m_{error}(M) \quad (1)$$

where the first term stands for the registration error (M is the binary matrix storing the matching encoded in π, and (t,α,s) are the similarity transform parameters to be estimated (rotation, traslation and scaling respectively), the second one for the matching error, and w_1, w_2 are weighting coefficients defining the relative importance of each.

With such a function we will have a more suitable similarity measurement to make a better search process in the space of solutions. Instead of considering a function based on a single registration error criterion, the use of the previous two terms working together to solve the IR problem, is an important part of our novel proposal.

5 A Scatter Search Algorithm for IR

SS fundamentals were originally proposed by Fred Glover and have been later developed in some texts like [9]. The main idea of this technique is based on a *systematic* combination between solutions from a *Reference Set*, instead of a randomized one like that usually done in genetic algorithms. In the next subsections, we will present a brief description of our implementation proposal for each SS component following Glover's usual template structure [6].

Improvement Method. It involves applying local search strategies. In our work, we have chosen the *"best-first"* local search with the *2–opt* neighborhood operator. Moreover, our intention was to promote diversification strategies to achieve high quality solutions. Therefore, the improvement method was carried out using a selective application of the local optimizer that is only applied when the new solution improves any of its parents.

Besides, two improvements have been considered on the local search procedure in order to speed it up. On the one hand, a primary strategy is applied in the neighborhood generation by only making those 2–opt moves being promising taking as a base the curvature information. On the other hand, each of the neighbor solutions generated is not completely re-evaluated but its objective value is computed from that of the current solution by only altering the coefficients of the linear equations related to the matchings modified by the applied move in the least square estimation.

Diversification Generation Method. The aim of this method is to generate P_{size} diverse trial solutions composing the *initial set of solutions* noted by P. Firstly, at the begining of the algorithm the process starts by randomly generating $\frac{P_{size}}{2}$ distinct solutions, optimizing them with the *Improvement Method*, and including the optimized solutions in P. The second phase generates the remaining $\frac{P_{size}}{2}$ solutions in the same way that the former but forcing to have a certain distance with each of them. The distance metric used in our case computes the number of different matching assignements for two given permutations, noted by $d(\pi_a, \pi_b)$. We have considered $0.5 \cdot \pi_{size}$ as a threshold value for such distance measurement.

The Reference set is composed of some solutions selected from the initial solution set P. It is partitioned in two subsets *Quality Reference set* and *Diversity Reference set*, respectively noted Ref^1 and Ref^2.

We have considered that Ref^1 will be comprised by the Ref^1_{size} best solutions from P according to the objective value, while Ref^2 will include the remaining Ref^2_{size} solutions from P with the greatest diversity value D:

$$D(\pi_a, Ref^1) = \frac{min\{d(\pi_a, \pi_i) \ : \ 1 \leq i \leq Ref^1_{size}\}}{F(\pi_a)}$$

where π_a is a solution from P not included in Ref^1 and $F(\cdot)$ is the objective function.

Subset Generation Method. This method groups the solutions in the Reference set in several subsets S_i^n and gives them to the *Solution Combination Method* to generate new solutions. In our implementation, such subsets are composed of pairs of solutions.

As described in other approaches, there are several ways to build the subsets with solutions from the Reference set as combinations between $Ref^1 - Ref^2$, $Ref^1 - Ref^1$ and $Ref^2 - Ref^2$. In our case, we consider all of them.

Solution Combination Method. This method takes each solution subset S_i^n built by the *Subset Generation Method* and obtains new solutions from it by applying a combination operator. As our coding scheme is based on a permutation, we make use of the classical *PMX* recombination operator (which showed several interesting properties in [7]) to combine each pair of solutions from each subset.

Reference Set Update Method. In our approach, the *Solution Combination Method* first generates all the new solutions from the combinations of each subset S_i^n, and then the Reference set is updated with these new solutions. Such updating process is called a *static updating mechanism* [9].

The method applies the updating process using both quality and diversity criteria. Firstly, the list of new solutions is increasingly sorted by their objective values where the first solution is the best one generated by the combination method in the current iteration. If such solution has a lower objective value than the worst solution in Ref^1, the former solution from the list will replace the latter in Ref^1, and so on checking each solution of the list till either list or the last condition is false or the list gets empty.

Secondly, when a given solution of those remaining in the list is not better than its respective in the Ref^1 set, the diversity updating will start by recomputing the diversity value for each solution in Ref^2 and for the remaining solutions in the list with regard to the updated Ref^1 set, in the way described in the *Reference Set Building Method*. Then, the solution in the list with the highest diversity is compared to the solution in Ref^2 with the lowest diversity and replaces it in case the former introduces more diversity. The process goes on with the remaining solutions in the list till every solution in the list is checked.

Finally, in case no solution in the Reference set is updated, a restart process is applied. The process involves maintaining the half part of the best solutions from Ref^1 (Quality Reference subset) into the new P set, and completing it with new improved random trial solutions with a $0.7 \cdot \pi_{size}$ distance value to the former ones, and so a new run can be performed.

6 A Basic Memetic Algorithm for IR

The most simple form of a memetic algorithm [11] is the structure of a classical genetic algorithm with an improvement phase based on a local search strategy applied after offspring generation to improve the search intensification. The components of the BMA used in this work are described as follows:

- *Initial population generation*: The L chromosomes in the population are randomly generated.
- *Selection*: *Tournament* selection of size 3 has been considered.
- *Crossover*: The PMX crossover is considered (as done in the SS *Solution Combination Method*).
- *Mutation*: To carry out a mutation upon a given offspring, we apply a *2-opt* exchange movement according to a certain probability value.
- *Local improvement*: The same employed by SS in its *Improvement Method*.
- *Replacement*: A classical generational scheme with elitism is considered.

7 Experiments

7.1 Image Registration Problems Considered

The experiments developed correspond to six registration problems for two different 3D images that have suffered the same three global similarity transformations which must be estimated by the SS, the BMA and the ICP algorithms. After preprocessing both images, a superellipsoid and a brain model surfaces, 222 and 1052 points are obtained, respectively. We will refer to each of them as the "Piece of cheese" and "Brain" images, and both original and preprocessed images are presented in Figure 2. The three transformations considered are stored in Table 1. In such table (and from now on), all the 3D rotations have been expressed in terms of rotation angle ($RAngle°$) and rotation axis ($RAxis_x, RAxis_y, RAxis_z$) to achieve a better understanding of the geometric transformation involved.

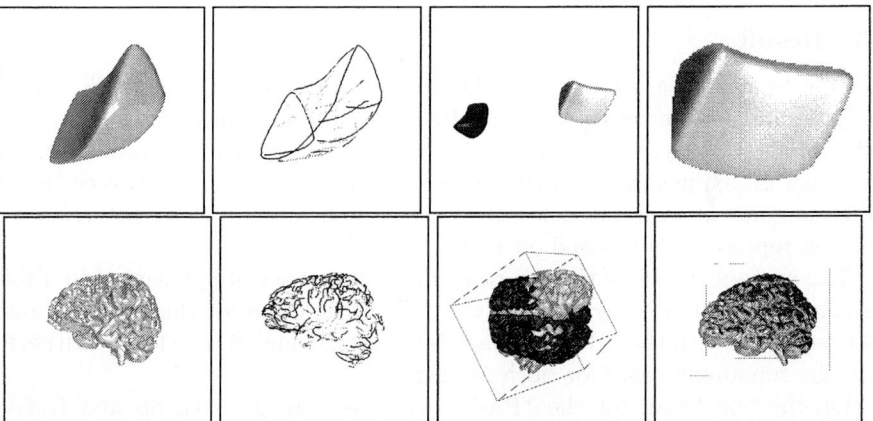

Fig. 2. From left to right, and top to bottom: original images, their respective crest lines points, the scene and model shapes for the first and second transformations in both images, and the best registration estimation obtained by SS and BMA.

Table 1. Transformations applied to every 3D image.

	Tr. 1	Tr. 2	Tr. 3
$RAngle°$	122.699997	95	202.5
$RAxis_x$	0.727393	0	-0.536895
$RAxis_y$	0.363696	1	0.59655
$RAxis_z$	-0.581914	0	0.59655
Δ_x	7.568	-1.5	24
Δ_y	-15.97	19.969999	10.6
Δ_z	-23.879999	2.8	5.2
S	0.7	1	2

7.2 Parameter Settings

SS and BMA are run ten different times for the same fixed time of 50 seconds for the "Piece of cheese" image, and 900 seconds for the "Brain" image. However, ICP is run just once because of its deterministic nature. All the runs have been performed on a 900 MHz. AMD K7 processor. As regards the BMA parameter values, the crossover and mutation probabilities are $P_c = 0.6$ and $P_m = 0.1$, while the population size is $L = 50$ individuals in all cases. The number of initial solutions in P for SS is 30, and the sizes of the Ref^1 and Ref^2 sets are 5 and 1 for the "Brain" image, and 3 and 1 for the "Piece of cheese" image, respectively. As common parameters for both algorithms, the weights w_1 and w_2 are initiated to 0.1 and 0.9, respectively; the PMX crossover sites length do not exceed a 20 % of the solution (permutation) size; while the number of iterations in the local search method are 200 for "Piece of cheese" and 500 for "Brain". All the previous parameter values have been derived from a preliminary experimentation developed with both methods.

7.3 Results

In order to achieve a better comprehension, we present both the *MSE* value and the *percentage of perfect matchings* of every solution as metrics to compare the different algorithms considered. The latter percentage corresponds to the number of correct matchings coded in the finally obtained permutation. Notice that this value can not be computed for ICP since such method does not maintain a solution representation based on matching.

The average values of the ten runs for both metrics are presented in Table 2. As can be seen, ICP only achieves the best MSE value for the second transformation (TR2) with the "Brain" image but both SS and BMA clearly outperform it in the remaining cases for both images.

On the one hand, for the "Piece of cheese", image both SS and BMA algorithms achieve the best possible solution with a null registration error and a perfect matching in the first and the second transformations. However SS obtains a lower MSE and a perfect matching percentage value in the remaining one. Moveover, SS converges to its best solution faster than BMA, with an average of 15 and 37 seconds, respectively.

Table 2. MSE and percentage of perfect matchings corresponding to the three transformations in Table 1 applied to both the "Piece of cheese" and the "Brain" images.

"Piece of cheese" image								
MSE					perfect matchings (%)			
		TR1	TR2	TR3			TR1	TR2	TR3
	ICP	13.76	24.56	97.99		ICP	-	-	-
Best	BMA	0	0	0	Best	BMA	100	100	86
	SS	0	0	0		SS	100	100	100
Mean	BMA	0	0	0.028	Mean	BMA	100	100	98.6
	SS	0	0	**0**		SS	100	100	**100**
SDev	BMA	0	0	0.085	SDev	BMA	0	0	4.2
	SS	0	0	0		SS	0	0	0.0

"Brain" image								
MSE					perfect matchings (%)			
		TR1	TR2	TR3			TR1	TR2	TR3
	ICP	324.16	0	931.14		ICP	-	-	-
Best	BMA	0.618	0.477	6.084	Best	BMA	16.3	3.9	4.1
	SS	0.007	0.010	0.021		SS	81.7	12.9	17.5
Mean	BMA	4.7124	40.589	145.325	Mean	BMA	21.8	21.3	21.84
	SS	**0.039**	**31.096**	**117.135**		SS	**86.3**	**79.1**	**80.1**
SDev	BMA	6.281	114.005	390.056	SDev	BMA	2.3	6.2	7.1
	SS	0.029	93.050	350.448		SS	2.4	22.2	21.2

On the other hand, for the "Brain" image, the SS algorithm significantly outperforms BMA in the three transformations according to the mean and minimum MSE and to the percentage of perfect matching values. As for the "Piece of cheese" image, the convergence of SS remains faster.

The third column of Figure 2 shows different views of the first (top) and second (bottom) transformations (see Table 1) for each image, representing the model and scene to be registered. Finally, the last column shows the respective best registration estimation carried out by SS (top) and BMA (bottom).

8 Concluding Remarks and Future Works

In this contribution, a new feature-based 3D IR technique has been proposed based on SS, which got a good performance with respect to two other algorithms (a BMA and ICP, classical in the topic) in the six registration problems considered.

Our SS-based IR process is still in a full development state, and there are many new possible designs for each of the SS components to achieve more accurate solutions than those obtained in this first study. One of such new extensions can be that making a more agressive solution combination by applying a *dynamic updating* strategy within the SS *Reference set updating method*. Moreover, since the algorithm is fundamented on a linear combination of solutions, other relevant extension could be to consider *Path-Relinking* to combine solutions.

References

1. P. J. Besl and N. D. McKay : A method for registration of 3-D shapes, IEEE Transactions on Pattern Analysis and Machine Intelligence, 14: 239–256, 1992.
2. L. G. Brown : A survey of image registration techniques, ACM Computing Surveys, 24(4):325–376, 1992.
3. O. Cordón, S. Damas, and J. Santamaría : A CHC evolutionary algorithm for 3D image registration, In: Bilgic, T., Baets, B.D., and Bogazici, O., Eds., Lecture Notes in Artificial Intelligence 2715, Heidelberg, Springer, pp. 404-411, 2003.
4. O. Cordón, S. Damas, and E. Bardinet : 2D image registration with iterated local search, In: J.M. Benítez, O. Cordón, F. Hoffmann, R. Roy, Eds., Advances in Soft Computing. Engineering Design and Manufacturing, Springer, pp. 233-242, 2003.
5. J. Feldmar and N. Ayache : Rigid, affine and locally affine registration of free-form surfaces, International Journal of Computer Vision, 18(2):99–119, 1996.
6. F. Glover : A template for scatter search and path relinking, Selected Papers from the Third European Conference on Artificial Evolution, P.3-54, October, 1997.
7. C. Cotta and J.M. Troya : Genetic forma recombination in permutation flowshop problems, Evolutionary Computation, 6(1):25-44, 1998.
8. K. P. Han, K. W. Song, E. Y. Chung, S. J. Cho, and Y. H. Ha : Stereo matching using genetic algorithm with adaptive chromosomes, Pattern Recognition, 32:1729–1740, 2001.
9. M. Laguna and R. Martí : Scatter Search: Methodology and Implementations in C, Kluwer Academic Publishers, Boston, 2003.
10. O. Monga, S. Benayoun, and O. D. Faugeras : Using partial derivatives of 3D images to extract typical surface features, Proc. IEEE Computer Vision and Pattern Recognition (CVPR 92), Urbana Champaign, Illinois (USA), pp. 354–359, 1992.
11. P. Moscato : On evolution, search, optimization, genetic algorithms and martial Arts: towards memetic algorithms, Technical Report, Caltech Concurrent Computation Program, C3P Report 826, 1989.
12. S. M. Yamany, M. N. Ahmed and A. A. Farag : A new genetic-based technique for matching 3D curves and surfaces, Pattern Recognition, 32:1817–1820, 1999.

A Hybrid GRASP – Evolutionary Algorithm Approach to Golomb Ruler Search

Carlos Cotta and Antonio J. Fernández

Dept. Lenguajes y Ciencias de la Computación, ETSI Informática,
University of Málaga, Campus de Teatinos, 29071 - Málaga, Spain
{ccottap,afdez}@lcc.uma.es

Abstract. We consider the problem of finding small Golomb rulers, a hard combinatorial optimization task. This problem is here tackled by means of a hybrid evolutionary algorithm (EA). This EA incorporates ideas from greedy randomized adaptive search procedures (GRASP) in order to perform the genotype-to-phenotype mapping. As it will be shown, this hybrid approach can provide high quality results, better than those of reactive GRASP and other EAs.

1 Introduction

The concept of Golomb rulers was first introduced by W.C. Babcock in 1953 [1], and further described by S.W. Golomb [2]. Golomb Rulers are a class of undirected graphs that, unlike usual rulers, measure more discrete lengths than the number of marks they carry. The particularity of Golomb Rulers is that on any given ruler, all differences between pairs of marks are unique. This feature makes Golomb Rulers really interesting in many practical applications (e.g., [3, 4] explain the connection of Golomb Rulers to real world problems in diverse fields such as radio communications, X-ray crystallography, coding theory, radio astronomy, and pulse phase modulation communications).

Traditionally, researchers are usually interested in discovering rulers with minimum length and Golomb rulers are not an exception. An *Optimal Golomb Ruler* (OGR) is defined as the shortest Golomb ruler for a number of marks. There may be multiple OGRs for a specific number of marks.

The search for OGRs is an extremely difficult task as it is a combinatorial problem whose bounds grow geometrically with respect to the solution size [5]. This has been a major limitation as each new ruler to be discovered is by necessity larger than its predecessor. Fortunately, the search space is bounded and, therefore, solvable [6]. To date, the highest Golomb ruler whose shortest length is known is the ruler with 23 marks [7, 8]. Best solutions for OGRs with a number of marks between 20 and 23 were obtained by massive parallelism projects, and it took several months to find optimum for each of those instances [9, 4]. In July 2000, distributed.net started the web search for the 24 and 25 OGR's, although no news exists about the success in finding these optimums.

To our knowledge, there have been three attempts to apply evolutionary algorithms (EAs) to the search for OGRs (see section 2.2). In this paper, we present a hybrid evolutionary approach designed to speed-up the process of searching good solutions. This approach is based on using ideas taken from the GRASP metaheuristic [10]. To be precise, we propose the use of a GRASP-like mechanism to perform the genotype-to-phenotype mapping.

2 Background

The OGR problem can be classified as a fixed-size subset selection problem, such as e.g., the p-median problem [11]. It exhibits some very distinctive features though. A brief overview of the problem, and how it has been tackled in the literature is provided below.

2.1 Golomb Rulers

A *n-mark Golomb ruler* is an ordered set of n distinct non-negative integers, called *marks*, $a_1 < ... < a_n$, such that all the differences $a_i - a_j$ $(i > j)$ are distinct. Clearly we may assume $a_1 = 0$. By convention, a_n is the *length of the Golomb ruler*. A Golomb ruler with n marks is an optimal Golomb ruler if, and only if,

- there exists no other n-mark Golomb rulers having smaller length, and
- the ruler is canonically "smaller" with respect to the the equivalent rulers. This means that the first differing entry is less than the corresponding entry in the other ruler.

Fig. 1 shows an OGR with 4-marks. Observe that all distances between any two marks are different.

Typically, Golomb Rulers are represented by the values of the marks on the ruler, i.e., in a n-mark Golomb ruler, $a_i = x$ $(1 \leqslant i \leqslant n)$ means that x is the mark value in position i. The sequence $(0, 1, 4, 6)$ would then represent the ruler in Fig. 1. However, this representation turns out to be inappropriate for EAs (for example, it is problematic with respect to developing good crossover operators [12]). An alternative representation consists of representing the Golomb ruler via the lengths of its segments, where the length of a segment of a ruler is defined as the distance between two consecutive marks. Therefore, a Golomb Ruler can

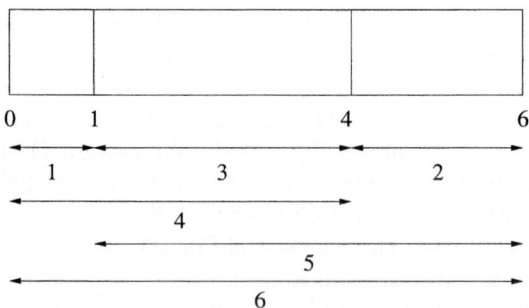

Fig. 1. A Golomb Ruler with 4 marks.

be represented with $n-1$ marks specifying the lengths of the $n-1$ segments that compose it. In the previous example, the sequence $(1,3,2)$ would encode the ruler depicted in Fig. 1.

2.2 Evolutionary Approaches to the OGR

Golomb rulers have been solved by using very different techniques. We will restrict here just to the evolutionary approaches considered so far. The interested reader on other techniques is referred to [7, 8].

To our knowledge, there have been three attempts to apply Evolutionary Computation (EC) techniques to the search for OGRs. In 1995, Soliday, Homaifar and Lebby [12] used a genetic algorithm on different instances of the Golomb Ruler problem. In their representation, each chromosome is composed by a permutation of $n-1$ integers that represents the sequence of the $n-1$ lengths of its segments. In order to assure the uniqueness of each segment length in all the individuals of the population, certain precautions were taken: initially, an array with numbers 1 to m (i.e. the maximum segment length) was loaded; then a repetitive sequence of random swaps between two positions i, j ($i \neq j$ and $i, j > 1$) in the array was executed; finally the first $n-1$ are selected and position 1 (initially containing the value 1) was randomly swapped with some of those selected positions. Soliday et al. also prevented mirror image representations by aligning the ruler. Two evaluation criteria were followed: the overall length of the ruler, and the number of repeated measurements. The mutation operator consisted of two types: a permutation in the segment order, or a change in the segment lengths. As with the population generation, special precautions were taken to assure that segment of length 1 is retained in the ruler as it was proved that all good Golomb rulers should have a segment of length one [2]. A special crossover operator was designed to guarantee that descendants are valid permutations and that length 1 is also retained.

Later, Feeney studied the effect of hybridizing genetic algorithms with local improvement techniques to solve Golomb rulers [3]. Namely, Feeney examined three methods of searching for Golomb Rulers, using genetic algorithms on its own, with local search and Baldwinian learning, and with local search and Lamarckian learning (see e.g. [13–15] for more information on Lamarckian and Baldwinian learning). It is known that, combined with EAs, local search techniques often reduces drastically the number of generations to find a near-optimum solution (see e.g., [16]). However, this can be also a weakness since it can result in premature convergence to suboptimal solutions in certain problems. Moreover, distinct learning techniques may behave differently in solving the same problem; therefore, these techniques tend to depend greatly on the problem itself. The representation used consisted of an array of integers corresponding to the marks of the ruler. The crossover operator was similar to that used in Soliday et al.'s approach although a sort procedure was added at the end. Mutation process was applied on each segment of the ruler with a mutation probability, and consisted basically in the addition to the segment mark selected for mutation of a random amount in the range $[-x, x]$ where x is the maximum difference between any pair of marks in any ruler of the initial population.

Table 1. Results obtained by Soliday *et al.*'s and Feeney's approaches. The columns denoted by Len, Pob, Gen and Err, respectively indicate the length of the best solution calculated, the initial population size, the number of generations required to produce the reported length, and the relative error with respect to the shortest known length (shown in column opt).

Instances	opt.	Soliday *et al.*				Feeney			
		Len	Pob	Gen	Err	Len	Pob	Gen	Err
OGR-5	11	11	512	10	0%	11	100	6	0%
OGR-6	17	17	512	22	0%	17	100	6	0%
OGR-7	25	25	512	22	0%	25	100	23	0%
OGR-8	34	35	1024	84	2.94%	34	100	18	0%
OGR-9	44	44	1024	433	0%	47	100	166	6.81%
OGR-10	55	62	1024	458	12.73%	62	100	229	12.72%
OGR-11	72	79	1024	152	9.72%	80	100	166	11.11%
OGR-12	85	103	1024	59	21.18%	101	100	138	18.82%
OGR-13	106	124	1024	664	16.98%	122	100	128	15.09%
OGR-14	127	168	2048	1506	32.28%	146	100	135	14.96%
OGR-15	151	206	2048	858	36.42%	281	100	79	18.86%
OGR-16	177	238	2048	708	36.46%	213	100	48	20.33%

Table 1 shows the results produced by Soliday *et al.*'s and Feeney's approaches. The best known OGR for every instance size have been taken from [7, 8]. With respect to the different approaches studied by Feeney, we have selected the best result obtained in [3], that corresponds to the execution of a genetic algorithm (with high mutation and no crossover) without local search. The maximum number of generations allowed was 250; the program was executed three times and the most typical result[1] found is shown. These results indicate that Soliday *et al.*'s approach is not very good compared to further EA approaches to solve the Golomb problem. Observe that, for rulers with 10 to 16 marks, the relative error is far from the known OGRs as it is between 9.72% and 36.46%. On its turn, Feeney's approach behaves better and maintains, for the same rulers, this error between 6.81% and 20.33%, that means a significant improvement.

The hybrid approach of Feeney was found to be successful in generating near optimum rulers and in generating optimal Golomb rulers of a short length. Observe also that the error remains in the short range [14.96%, 20.33%] for rulers with marks from 12 to 16. This clearly indicates a stabilization of the error. However, as it is reported in [3], performance was really poor, as it was expected, mainly due to the local search.

Recently, Pereira *et al.* [17] have presented a new EA approach to find OGRs. This new approach uses the concept of random keys [18] to codify the information contained in each chromosome. As in the Soliday *et al.*'s approach, any candidate solution for a n-mark OGR is represented with the length of each of its $n-1$ segments. In fact, a chromosome is composed by a permutation

---

[1] The most typical result is the ruler whose length is closest to the average of the three, unless two had the same length in which case it was their length.

of λ distinct values (where λ is the maximum segment length), and encoding of the permutation is done with random keys (RK). The basic idea consists of generating n random numbers (i.e., the keys) sampled from the interval $[0, 1]$ and ordered by its position in the sequence $1, \ldots, n$; then all positions of the keys are sorted, in decreasing order, according to the value that they contain. This guarantees to obtain always a permutation of n unique numbers between 1 and n. The codification uses a more advanced principle based on the concept of NetKeys (an extension of RK to problems dealing with tree network design) although the basic idea is that described above. Two evaluation criteria, similar to those described in [12], were followed: ruler length and whether the solution contains repeated measurements. They also presented an alternative algorithm that adds a heuristic, favoring the insertion of small segments, to the RK approach already proposed. We will return later to this approach since it has been included in our experimental comparison.

3 A GRASP-Based Hybrid Approach

As anticipated in Sect. 1, the EA approach proposed is based on incorporating ideas from GRASP. It is thus necessary discussing firstly the deployment of this latter metaheuristic on the OGR problem.

3.1 Basic GRASP for the OGR Problem

Greedy randomized adaptive search procedures can be viewed as repetitive sampling techniques [19]. Each iteration of the algorithm produces a tentative solution for the problem at hand by means of a greedy randomized construction algorithm. This latter algorithm assumes that solutions are represented by a list of attributes, and builds incrementally solutions by specifying values for these attributes. More precisely, the values for each attribute are ranked according to some local quality measure, and selected using a quality-biased mechanism. The pseudocode of this process would be as follows:

1. $sol \leftarrow \emptyset$
2. **while** $\neg$completed(sol) **do**
   (a) $RCL \leftarrow$ build a ranked candidate list.
   (b) $s \leftarrow$ select attribute value from RCL.
   (c) $sol \leftarrow sol \cup \{s\}$
3. **return** sol

One of the key steps in this pseudocode is the selection of an attribute from RCL. This can be typically done by using a qualitative criterion (i.e., a candidate is selected among the best k elements in RCL, where k is a parameter), or a quantitative criterion (i.e., a candidate is selected among the elements whose quality is between q_1 and $q_1 + \alpha \cdot (q_{|RCL|} - q_1)$, where q_i is the quality of the i-th element of RCL and α is a parameter). Notice that having $k = 1$ or $\alpha = 0$ would thus result in a plain greedy heuristic. GRASP is based on iterating this construction procedure (possibly applying some local improvement technique to the so-obtained solutions), keeping the best solution generated along the run.

In the OGR problem, the attributes of solutions are obviously the position of the marks. The construction procedure would then iteratively place each of the $n-1$ marks (the first mark is assumed to be $a_1 = 0$). The $(i+1)$-th mark can be obtained as $a_{i+1} = a_i + l_i$, where $l_i \geq 1$ is the i-th segment length. We thus have a potential list of candidates based on tentative values for $l_i \in \{1, 2, \cdots\}$. Actually, this potential list of candidates can be as long as desired, although a bound $\lambda \in O(n)$ is typically chosen. Of course, many candidates from this potential list are infeasible since they would lead to repeated distances between marks. A potential value l_i would then be feasible if, and only if, for all j, k, r such that $1 \leq j \leq i$ and $1 \leq k < r \leq i$, it holds that $(a_i + l_i - a_j) \neq (a_r - a_k)$. After filtering infeasible segment lengths (only values $l_i \leq \max_{1 \leq k < r \leq i}(a_r - a_k)$ have to be checked) we come up with the elements of the actual RCL. A quality measure is now required. In this problem, the natural measure is the length of the ruler. Since at each step the value of a_i is known, it turns out that the ranked list consists of the sequence of increasing feasible values for l_i. A qualitative selection criterion can then be defined by picking a random candidate among the smallest k feasible values for l_i.

3.2 Reactive GRASP vs. Hybrid EA

One of the potential problems of the basic GRASP procedure described before relies on the selection of the parameter for selecting an attribute value from the RCL. As shown in [20], using a single fixed value for this parameter may hinder finding high-quality solutions. Several options are possible to solve this problem. In particular, a learning-based strategy termed *reactive* GRASP has been proposed [21]. In this case, the value of the parameter is chosen in each iteration from a set of discrete values $\Pi = \{\pi_1, \cdots, \pi_m\}$. The selection of the precise value of the parameter at each iteration can be done on the basis of the goodness γ_i of the best solution ever generated by using each parameter π_i. Any of the selection mechanisms typically used in EAs can be utilized for this purpose. For example, in [21], a roulette-wheel procedure is proposed. Since we are dealing here with a minimization problem, such a proportional approach would not be possible unless goodness values were appropriately transformed. We have opted for a simpler approach: using a non-proportionate approach. To be precise, we have considered binary tournament for selecting parameter values.

Using a reactive approach allows the algorithm focusing on the more appropriate subset of parameter values. However, it can still face difficulties if optimal (or near-optimal) solutions comprise an attribute value whose rank in the RCL is high: a low value of the selection parameter would preclude picking this attribute value; a high enough value of the selection parameter could select it, but many other low-quality attributes as well. A finer-grain mechanism would be required here, an approach that allowed for using different values of the parameter not just in each application of the construction phase, but in each internal step of the construction algorithm. This is where EAs come into play.

EAs can be used to evolve the sequence of $n-1$ selection parameters used within an application of the construction algorithm. In principle, this implies that each individual would be a sequence $\langle r_1, \cdots, r_{n-1}\rangle$, where r_i would be the parameter used in the i-th iteration of the construction algorithm. Two practical consideration must be taken into account though. The first one refers to the genotype-to-phenotype mapping: by making randomized choices of attribute values this mapping would be stochastic. Since this would result in an increased level of complexity of the algorithm, a deterministic choice is made. To be precise, the value r_i indicates that the r_i-th best attribute value should be selected in the i-th step. The second consideration refers to the last step of the construction algorithm. In this last step it does not make sense to pick any other attribute value than the smallest one. For this reason, $r_{n-1} = 1$, and individuals need only contain the sequence $\langle r_1, \cdots, r_{n-2}\rangle$. Notice that this representation of solutions is orthogonal [22], i.e., any sequence represents a feasible solution, and hence, standard operators for crossover and mutation can be used to manipulate them.

4 Experimental Results

The experiments have been performed using four different algorithms: plain GRASP, reactive GRASP, a permutational EA following [17], and the hybrid EA-GRASP approach described in previous section. The plain GRASP algorithm used a qualitative selection mechanism using $k = n$ as parameter. In the case of reactive GRASP, five different equally-spaced values between 2 and n were considered. As to the EAs, an elitist generational model (popsize = 100, $p_X = .9$, $p_M = 1/n$) with binary tournament selection has been utilized. For the hybrid EA, each gene can take values $r_i \in \{1, \cdots, n\}$, uniform crossover is used, and mutation is done by randomly increasing or decreasing a gene by 1. The permutational EA uses the interpretation mechanism described in [17]. Random keys are here directly substituted by permutations, being PMX used for crossover, and the swap operator for mutation. In all cases, the algorithms have been run 30 times for 10^6 evaluations. No fine tuning of these parameters has been attempted.

The results of plain GRASP and reactive GRASP are shown in Table 2. As it can be seen, reactive GRASP quickly outperforms plain GRASP as the instance size increases. Notice also that the results of this reactive GRASP are better than those of the basic EA approaches reported in Sect. 2.2.

Focusing on the EAs, the results are shown in Table 3. Notice firstly that the permutational EA provides comparable results to those of reactive GRASP. The hybrid EA provides roughly the same performance that the permutational EA for small instance sizes, but becomes clearly superior when the number of marks increases. A non-parametrical statistical test – Wilcoxon ranksum – indicates that the differences are significant for 10, 11, 14, 15, and 16 marks.

5 Conclusions

We have presented a hybrid EA that incorporates a GRASP-like procedure for decoding the chromosome into a feasible solutions. The advantages of this approach are twofold: first of all, problem-knowledge is exploited by means of the

Table 2. Results (averaged for 30 runs) of plain GRASP and reactive GRASP.

	Plain GRASP			
	ruler length			evaluations
instance	best	median	mean $\pm\sigma$	mean $\pm\sigma$
OGR-5	11	11	11.0 $\pm$ 0.0	44.0 $\pm$ 45.0
OGR-6	17	17	17.0 $\pm$ 0.0	128.7 $\pm$ 106.9
OGR-7	25	25	25.0 $\pm$ 0.0	1634.0 $\pm$ 1243.2
OGR-8	34	34	34.0 $\pm$ 0.0	202710.6 $\pm$ 230112.6
OGR-9	44	44	44.8 $\pm$ 0.9	377499.8 $\pm$ 204172.4
OGR-10	60	62	61.7 $\pm$ 0.8	546206.5 $\pm$ 226282.5
OGR-11	78	81	80.8 $\pm$ 1.6	443928.7 $\pm$ 204992.1
OGR-12	103	105	104.8 $\pm$ 1.3	478968.6 $\pm$ 304395.1
OGR-13	127	129	129.9 $\pm$ 2.2	641836.0 $\pm$ 180381.4
OGR-14	148	163	161.9 $\pm$ 5.1	645870.3 $\pm$ 226777.6
OGR-15	191	200	199.1 $\pm$ 4.3	380212.7 $\pm$ 313521.6
OGR-16	226	242	242.1 $\pm$ 6.1	463089.9 $\pm$ 237976.0
	Reactive GRASP			
	ruler length			evaluations
instance	best	median	mean $\pm\sigma$	mean $\pm\sigma$
OGR-5	11	11	11.0 $\pm$ 0.0	10.3 $\pm$ 9.7
OGR-6	17	17	17.0 $\pm$ 0.0	99.8 $\pm$ 65.7
OGR-7	25	25	25.0 $\pm$ 0.0	213.2 $\pm$ 135.2
OGR-8	34	34	34.0 $\pm$ 0.0	114.1 $\pm$ 113.0
OGR-9	44	44	44.5 $\pm$ 0.5	346344.0 $\pm$ 307876.9
OGR-10	59	59	59.6 $\pm$ 0.7	433369.0 $\pm$ 259147.5
OGR-11	74	74	74.1 $\pm$ 0.3	436378.1 $\pm$ 270748.4
OGR-12	95	96	96.1 $\pm$ 0.7	523898.1 $\pm$ 221195.5
OGR-13	117	119	119.1 $\pm$ 1.3	517139.2 $\pm$ 288309.9
OGR-14	141	147	146.9 $\pm$ 2.9	336471.1 $\pm$ 296678.9
OGR-15	161	179	176.7 $\pm$ 5.8	371481.4 $\pm$ 296244.4
OGR-16	209	212	211.6 $\pm$ 0.9	185518.7 $\pm$ 312827.9

pseudo-greedy mapping from genotype to phenotype; secondly, the representation turns out to be orthogonal, and hence standard string-oriented operators for recombination and mutation can be used. Of course, this does not preclude using those *ad hoc* operators that might be defined. In this sense, reinforcement learning techniques are prime candidates for defining these informed operators.

The hybrid EA has been applied to the Golomb ruler problem, with encouraging results: reactive GRASP and plain EA approaches could be beaten. A permutational EA based on the proposal of [17] was also outperformed. In this sense, it must be noted that results similar to those of the hybrid EA have been reported for this latter permutational EA when executed in long runs using larger population sizes. In a forthcoming work [23], Tavares *et al.* also propose the utilization of *insertion* and *correction* procedures for improving the performance of the algorithm. We believe that these ideas can be fruitfully combined with the hybrid model presented in this work. Another interesting line for future developments lies in the combination of EAs and constraint-satisfaction techniques (e.g., [24]). Work is in progress in this area.

Table 3. Results (averaged for 30 runs) of the permutational EA and the hybrid EA-GRASP.

	Permutational EA			
	ruler length			evaluations
instance	best	median	mean ±σ	mean ±σ
OGR-5	11	11	11.0 ± 0.0	217.8 ± 192.0
OGR-6	17	17	17.0 ± 0.0	514.8 ± 348.1
OGR-7	25	25	25.0 ± 0.0	1821.6 ± 1809.9
OGR-8	34	34	34.1 ± 0.3	157340.7 ± 141192.3
OGR-9	44	44	44.4 ± 0.5	342441.0 ± 254397.7
OGR-10	55	60	59.2 ± 2.3	348509.7 ± 285652.0
OGR-11	74	75	75.7 ± 1.9	468586.8 ± 257449.5
OGR-12	93	95	94.6 ± 1.5	464557.5 ± 257854.7
OGR-13	113	115	115.1 ± 1.0	296010.0 ± 267214.4
OGR-14	143	148	148.0 ± 3.1	548529.3 ± 328350.1
OGR-15	174	177	177.4 ± 2.7	537718.5 ± 259515.4
OGR-16	207	214	213.1 ± 4.1	283229.1 ± 259644.9
	Hybrid GRASP-EA			
	ruler length			evaluations
instance	best	median	mean ±σ	mean ±σ
OGR-5	11	11	11.0 ± 0.0	9.9 ± 29.7
OGR-6	17	17	17.0 ± 0.0	39.6 ± 65.7
OGR-7	25	25	25.0 ± 0.0	514.8 ± 444.5
OGR-8	34	34	34.0 ± 0.0	2465.1 ± 682.2
OGR-9	44	44	44.2 ± 0.4	202761.9 ± 213130.8
OGR-10	55	55	55.4 ± 1.2	245361.6 ± 206552.0
OGR-11	74	74	74.0 ± 0.0	13394.7 ± 10110.6
OGR-12	94	95	94.9 ± 0.3	123542.1 ± 93508.0
OGR-13	111	114	114.2 ± 1.5	341708.4 ± 232391.5
OGR-14	135	139	138.6 ± 2.2	461062.8 ± 271222.9
OGR-15	162	166	166.3 ± 2.2	523531.8 ± 273372.0
OGR-16	189	197	196.5 ± 3.4	429877.8 ± 260082.7

Acknowledgements

The authors wish to thank Jorge Tavares for kindly providing copies of [17] and [23]. This work is partially supported by Spanish MCyT and FEDER under contract TIC2002-04498-C05-02.

References

1. Babcock, W.: Intermodulation interference in radio systems. Bell Systems Technical Journal (1953) 63–73
2. Bloom, G., Golomb, S.: Aplications of numbered undirected graphs. Proceedings of the IEEE **65** (1977) 562–570
3. Feeney, B.: Determining optimum and near-optimum golomb rulers using genetic algorithms. Master thesis, Computer Science, University College Cork (2003)
4. Rankin, W.: Optimal golomb rulers: An exhaustive parallel search implementation. Master thesis, Duke University Electrical Engineering Dept., Durham, NC (1993)

5. Shearer, J.: Some new optimum golomb rulers. IEEE Transactions on Information Theory **36** (1990) 183–184
6. Klove, T.: Bounds and construction for difference triangle sets. IEEE Transactions on Information Theory **35** (1989) 879–886
7. Shearer, J.B.: Golomb ruler table. Mathematics Department, IBM Research, http://www.research.ibm.com/people/s/shearer/grtab.html (2001)
8. Schneider, W.: Golomb rulers. MATHEWS: The Archive of Recreational Mathematics, http://www.wschnei.de/number-theory/golomb-rulers.html (2002)
9. Garry, M., Vanderschel, D., et al.: In search of the optimal 20, 21 & 22 mark golomb rulers. GVANT project, http://members.aol.com/golomb20/index.html (1999)
10. Feo, T., Resende, M.: Greedy randomized adaptive search procedures. Journal of Global Optimization **6** (1995) 109–133
11. Mirchandani, P., Francis, R.: Discrete Location Theory. Wiley-Interscience (1990)
12. Soliday, S., Homaifar, A., Lebby, G.: Genetic algorithm approach to the search for golomb rulers. In Eshelman, L., ed.: 6th International Conference on Genetic Algorithms (ICGA'95), Pittsburgh, PA, USA, Morgan Kaufmann (1995) 528–535
13. Houck, C., Joines, J., Kay, M., Wilson, J.: Empirical investigation of the benefits of partial lamarckianism. Evolutionary Computation **5** (1997) 31–60
14. Julstrom, B.: Comparing darwinian, baldwinian, and lamarckian search in a genetic algorithm for the 4-cycle problem. In Brave, S., Wu., A., eds.: Late Breaking Papers at the 1999 Genetic and Evolutionary Computation Conference, Orlando, FL (1999) 134–138
15. Giraud-Carrier, C.: Unifying learning with evolution through baldwinian evolution and lamarckism: A case study. In Zimmermann, H.J., Tselentis, G., van Someren, M., Dounias, G., eds.: Advances in Computational Intelligence and Learning: Methods and Applications. Kluwer Academic Publishers (2002) 159–168
16. Moscato, P.: Memetic algorithms: A short introduction. In Corne, D., Dorigo, M., Glover, F., eds.: New Ideas in Optimization. McGraw-Hill, Maidenhead, Berkshire, England, UK (1999) 219–234
17. Pereira, F., Tavares, J., Costa, E.: Golomb rulers: The advantage of evolution. In Moura-Pires, F., Abreu, S., eds.: Progress in Artificial Intelligence, 11th Portuguese Conference on Artificial Intelligence. Number 2902 in Lecture Notes in Computer Science, Berlin Heidelberg, Springer-Verlag (2003) 29–42
18. Bean, J.: Genetic algorithms and random keys for sequencing and optimization. ORSA Journal on Computing **6** (1994) 154–160
19. Resende, M., Ribeiro, C.: Greedy randomized adaptive search procedures. In Glover, F., Kochenberger, G., eds.: Handbook of Metaheuristics. Kluwer Academic Publishers, Boston MA (2003) 219–249
20. Prais, M., Ribeiro, C.: Parameter variation in GRASP procedures. Investigación Operativa **9** (2000) 1–20
21. Prais, M., Ribeiro, C.: Reactive GRASP: an application to a matrix decomposition problem in TDMA traffic assignment. INFORMS Journal on Computing **12** (2000) 164–176
22. Radcliffe, N.: Equivalence class analysis of genetic algorithms. Complex Systems **5** (1991) 183–205
23. Tavares, J., Pereira, F., Costa, E.: Understanding the role of insertion and correction in the evolution of golomb rulers. In: Congress on Evolutionary Computation Conference (CEC2004), Portland, Oregon, IEEE (2004)
24. Galinier, P., Jaumard, B., Morales, R., Pesant, G.: A constraint-based approach to the golomb ruler problem. In: Third International Workshop on Integration of AI and OR Techniques, Kent, UK (2001) 321–324

Design of an Efficient Search Algorithm for P2P Networks Using Concepts from Natural Immune Systems[*]

Niloy Ganguly[1], Geoff Canright[2], and Andreas Deutsch[1]

[1] Center for High Performance Computing, Dresden University of Technology, Dresden, Germany
{niloy,deutsch}@zhr.tu-dresden.de
[2] Telenor Research and Development, 1331 Fornebu, Norway
geoffrey.canright@telenor.com

Abstract. In this paper we report a novel and efficient algorithm for searching p2p networks. The algorithm, termed *ImmuneSearch*, draws its basic inspiration from natural immune systems. It is implemented independently by each individual peer participating in the network and is totally decentralized in nature. *ImmuneSearch* avoids query message flooding; instead it uses an immune systems inspired concept of affinity-governed proliferation and mutation for message movement. In addition, a protocol is formulated to change the neighborhoods of the peers based upon their proximity with the queried item. This results in topology evolution of the network whereby similar contents cluster together. The topology evolution coupled with proliferation and mutation help the p2p network to develop 'memory', as a result of which the search efficiency of the network improves as more and more individual peers perform search. Moreover, the algorithm is extremely robust and its performance is stable in face of the transient nature of the constituent peers.

1 Introduction

Due to their flexibility, reliability and adaptivity, p2p solutions can overcome a lot of disadvantages of traditional client-server systems, and can fit to the dynamically changing Internet environment [1]. This explains the high popularity of file sharing systems like Gnutella, Napster, and Freenet [1]. However, the development of an efficient search algorithm for p2p networks poses a fundamental challenge to researchers. The big share of Internet users still uses dial-up modems, which, besides being slow and unreliable, also leave the community (p2p network) at very short intervals. Therefore, to efficiently manage this totally decentralized system, there is urgent need for developing robust decentralized algorithms, i.e. algorithms which are capable of adjusting to the highly changeable structure of p2p networks.

---

[*] This work was partially supported by the Future & Emerging Technologies unit of the European Commission through Project BISON (IST-2001-38923).

The algorithm for search in *p2p* network proposed by us in this paper is termed *ImmuneSearch*. It has been inspired by the simple and well known concept of the humoral immune system where B cells undergo mutation and opportunistic proliferation to generate antibodies which track the antigens (foreign objects). From an information-processing perspective, the immune system is a highly parallel intelligent system. Its general features provide an excellent model of adaptive processes operating at a local level and of useful behavior emerging at the global level. Due to these desirable features of the immune system, there is a growing number of intelligent methodologies inspired by the immune system for solving real-world problems. Examples are: searching for mines [2], anomaly detection in time series data [3], pattern recognition [4], and virus detection [5]. However, to the best of our knowledge, immune system concepts have not been used for designing search algorithms in p2p networks.

ImmuneSearch uses affinity-governed proliferation and mutation to spread query message packets (antibodies) across the network. It also evolves the topology of the p2p network in terms of adjusting the neighborhood of the participating peers (information in peers – antigens). This gives rise to a loosely structured network where the overlay topology [1] roughly corresponds to the content in the network. Consequently, the algorithm ensures better quality of service (in terms of the number of search items found within a specified number of steps), and greater efficiency (in terms of the network congestion arising from the query packets) compared to the conventional schemes of random walk and message flooding [6]. The algorithm ensures robustness, that is, stability of performance in face of the transient nature of the network. It also guarantees autonomy to the users, who are not required to store any replicated files on their own machine.

The next section describes the *ImmuneSearch(IS)* algorithm in detail. For modeling pusposes, the overlay network [1] responsible for maintaining connections between the peers is represented as a 2-dimensional regular grid topology. *Section 3* details the different simulations performed based upon the algorithm *ImmuneSearch*.

2 Simulation Model

This section is divided into two parts. In the first part (Section 2.1) we describe the framework chosen to model the p2p environment. In the second part (Section 2.2) we describe the *ImmuneSearch* algorithm.

2.1 Environment Definition

The factors which are important for simulating p2p environments are the overlay topology, the profile management of each individual peer, the nature of distribution of these profiles and the affinity measure based upon which the search algorithm is developed. Each of these factors is discussed one by one.

Topology: The overlay topology responsible for maintaining the neighborhood connections between the peers in the p2p network is considered to be a toroidal grid where each node in the grid is conceived to be hosting a member (peer) of the p2p network. Due to the grid structure, each node has a fixed set of eight neighbors. A peer[1] residing in a particular node has correspondingly eight neighbors. Each peer carries two profiles – the *informational profile* and the *search profile*. The concept of *information* and *search* profile is explained next.

Profile: The *informational profile* (P_I) of the peer is formed from the information which it shares with the other peers in the p2p network. The *search profile* (P_S) of a peer is built from the informational interest of the user; formally it is represented in the same way as is P_I. In general, the search profile may differ from the information stored on the peer. For instance, a peer may contain some information about scientific researches in the field of distributed networks, but, in addition, the user may also be interested in football. For simplicity we assume that there are 1024 coarse-grained profiles, and let each of these profiles be represented by a unique ($d = $) 10-bit binary token. The query message packet (M) is also a 10-bit binary token. From now on we interchangeably use the term profile and token. Similarity between a profile P and a query message packet (M) is measured by the number of bits that are identical. That is, $sim(P, M) = d - HD(P, M)$, where HD is the *Hamming distance* between P and M. Zipf's distribution[7], is chosen to distribute each of the 1024 unique alternatives in the network. The ranking of tokens in terms of frequency is the same for both information and search profiles.

We now present the search algorithm *ImmuneSearch*.

2.2 ImmuneSearch

The *ImmuneSearch* is a distributed algorithm and will be executed individually and independently by each peer. The search algorithm consists of two parts, the dynamics of packet movement through the network and the topology evolution initiated as a result of search.

Packet Movement: The search in our p2p network is initiated from the user peer. The user (U in *Fig. 1*) emanates message packets (M) to its neighbors – the packets are thereby forwarded to the surroundings. The message packets (M) are formed from the search profile P_S of U. The method of spreading message packets forms the basis of the algorithm.

In the system, the packets undergo a random walk on the grid, but when they come across a matching profile (information profile of any arbitrary peer), that is, the similarity between a message packet and informational profile is above a threshold, the message packet undergoes proliferation (as around peer

---

[1] Although, in standard literature, 'peer' and 'node' are synonymous terms, the terms have been differentiated in the paper for ease of understanding. Node here means a position in the grid and essentially indicates a neighborhood configuration. A peer entering the network is assigned a node by the overlay management protocol. During topology evolution (discussed next) peers occupy new nodes and acquire new sets of neighbors.

A of *Fig. 1*), so as to find more peers with similar information profile around the neighborhood. Some of the proliferated packets are also mutated. (Cf. the message packets distinguished by different gray levels around A in *Fig. 1*). Due to mutation the chance of message packets meeting similar items increases, which in turn helps in packet proliferation.

In order to realize the above described processes (random walk, proliferation and mutation) of message packets, each peer, executing the algorithm locally, should react when a message packet (M) enters the node. The algorithm named *Reaction_p2p* is executed by a peer A, with information profile P_I, when it encounters a packet (M).

Algorithm 1 Reaction_p2p(A)
Input : Message packet(M)
If $(sim(P_I, M) \geq$ Threshold(Pro/Mut)) /*Threshold(Pro/Mut) – Similarity
    threshold required to launch Proliferation/Mutation */
    {Proliferate the packet M in the neighboring peers
    Mutate some of the proliferated packets M to M'}
else   *{Send the packet M to a randomly chosen neighbor peer}*

It is clear from the algorithm, that the effect of proliferation and mutation is to initiate an intensified search around the neighbors of the peers which are already found to be similar to the queried profile. This implicitly points to the importance of topology evolution of the network, which should ensure that peers which have similar profiles come close to each other. This clustering would naturally increase the effectivity of the search, because packets after proliferation will immediately begin to find peers with similar information profiles, thus enhancing the efficiency of search.

Topology Evolution: In the topology evolution scheme, the individual peers change their neighborhood configuration during search so as to place them 'closer' to U. *Fig. 1* illustrates the exact mechanism of this movement. In the figure, peer A moves (changes its neighborhood configuration) from node 7 to node 13 to place itself 'closer' to U. Correspondingly, other peers adjust their positions. We now explain the factors based upon which a peer decides to change position as well as the rules guiding the degree of change.

A peer (say A) decides to change its neighborhood configuration and places itself 'closer' to the user, when similarity between the profile of peer (P) and the message (M) sent by user peer (say U) is above a threshold level. The amount of movement of A towards the user peer (U) is determined by several factors. The distance moved is proportional to (a) the similarity between them $(P$ and $M)$ either in terms of (i) P_I or (ii) P_S; and (b) proportional to the distance between node U and node A. (c) The movement is also controlled by a further important process which is inspired by natural immune systems – *aging*. The movement of a peer gets restricted as it ages. The age of a peer is determined in terms of the number of times it undergoes movement as a result of encountering similar message packets. That is, the longer it stays in the environment (p2p network), the more it is assumed that the peer has found its correct node position, and hence the less it responds to any call for change in

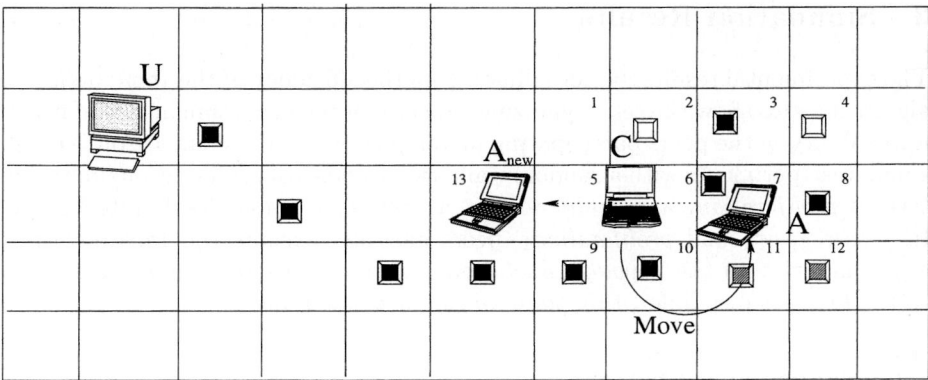

Fig. 1. Search Mechanism (packets passing and topology evolution). The figure shows topology evolution of a particular peer A, which moves to new position A_{new} after evolution. To do so, it swaps its position with intermediate nodes (for example C). Other peers undergo identical evolution mechanism when query packets reach them.

neighbors towards any user peer U. If the search profile (P_S) of peer A matches M, but peer (A) has performed the search operation more times than U, then there is no movement of peer A towards user peer U. The aging concept lends stability to the system; thus a peer entering the p2p network, after undergoing initial changes in neighborhood, finds its correct position.

Algorithm 2 Topology_Evolution(A)
Input : Message packet(M)
If ([sim(P_I,M) or sim(P_S,M)] $\geq$ d) /* d - Similarity threshold required to perform
                                 topology evolution */
    { $x_1 = sim(P_I,M)$ /* P_I - information profile of A */
    $x_2 = age(A);$
    $x_3 = dist(A, U)$ /*distance between A and U*/
    $x_4 = sim(P_S,M)$ /* P_S - search profile of A */
    $x_5 = search\_performed(A) - search\_performed(U)$ /*search_performed(X) -
                               No of times X has previously performed search*/
    if ($x_1 >$ Threshold)
        mov(A) α $\frac{x_1 \cdot x_3}{x_2}$ /*mov(A) - Amount of movement of A towards U*/
    else   if ($x_4 >$ Threshold and $x_5 < 0$)
        mov(A) α $\frac{x_4 \cdot x_3}{x_2}$ }

We are now in a position to present the main algorithm *ImmuneSearch* which is a combination of *Algorithms 1 & 2*. Each peer applies the *ImmuneSearch* algorithm whenever it encounters a message packet.

Algorithm 3 *ImmuneSearch(A)*
Input : Message packets (M)
Output : Search Result
if (sim(P_I,M) $\geq$ d - 1) /* Similarity threshold for a successful search */
        Output ("Successful Search")
Topology_Evolution(A)
Reaction_p2p(A)

3 Simulation Results

The experimental results, besides illustrating the efficiency of the *ImmuneSearch* algorithm, also show the self-organizing capacity of the algorithm in face of heavy unreliability of the peers participating in a p2p network. For comparison, we also simulate experiments with a random walk, two schemes of proliferation/mutation termed *proliferation*$_1$ and *proliferation*$_2$, as well as a simple flooding technique. In *proliferation*$_1$ and *proliferation*$_2$, peers basically execute the *ImmuneSearch* algorithm without the *Topology_Evolution* step. The threshold conditions applied to the two schemes differ; this point will be discussed later.

3.1 Experimental Setup

To understand the effect of proliferation and mutation rates, experiments with different rates and different threshold values (Threshold(Pro/Mut) – Algorithm 1) have been performed. From these, we report two cases which represent two main trends observed by us. In both cases, the proliferation and mutation rate is the same; however, the value of Threshold(Pro/Mut) differs. For the first case, Threshold(Pro/Mut) is $(d-1)$; while in the second case, it is $(d-2)$ (d is the length (= 10) of the token). *ImmuneSearch* and *proliferation*$_1$ represent the first case, while *proliferation*$_2$ represents the second case. The number of packets proliferated (NR) in the neighborhood is given by the following equation – $NR = 8 \cdot S$, where $S = \frac{sim(P_I, M)}{d}$; while the probability of each of those NR packets undergoing one bit mutation (MP) is 0.05.

Each search is initiated by a peer residing at a randomly chosen node and the number of search items (n_s) found within 50 time steps from the commencement of the search is calculated. A generation is defined as a sequence of 100 searches. The search output (n_s) is averaged over 100 different searches (a generation), whereby we obtain N_s.

In the graphs (*Fig. 2 & 4*) we plot this average value N_s against generation number to illustrate the efficiency of different models. We perform two types of experiments within the above mentioned experimental setup. In the first experiment, no peers leave the system, while the second experiment represents a more transient situation where peers leave/join the network at random.

3.2 Expt. I: Search in Stable Conditions

This experiment is carried out under the assumption that no peer leaves the system. The system is represented by a 100 × 100 toroidal grid, that is, it consists of 10^4 peers. We have initiated experiments with random walk, two types of proliferation/mutation schemes (*proliferation*$_1$ and *proliferation*$_2$), limited flooding, and *ImmuneSearch*. The graph of *Fig. 2* displays the performance of the five different models. The x-axis of the graph shows the generation number while the y-axis represents the average number of search items (N_s) found in the last 100 searches. The performance comparison of the above mentioned five methods obeys fairness criteria with respect to 'power' which are discussed next.

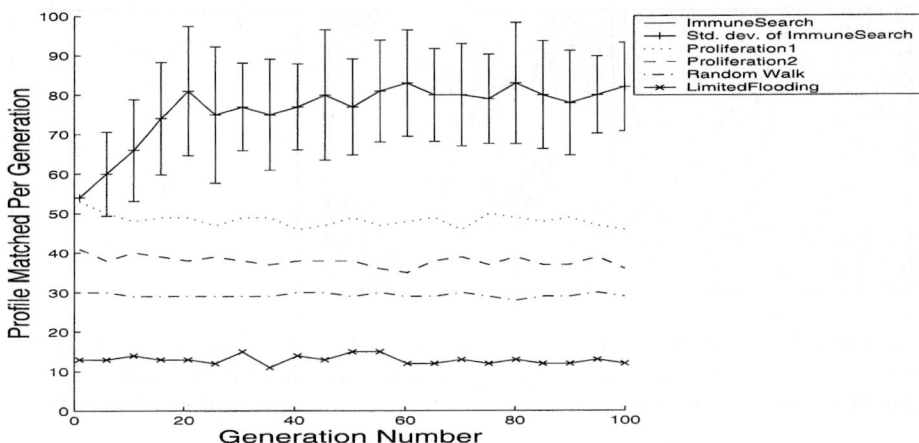

Fig. 2. Efficiency of different techniques of search namely *ImmuneSearch*, *proliferation$_1$*, *proliferation$_2$*, random walk and limited flooding. (Search results are averaged over 20 simulation runs). Standard deviation of the results is also shown for *ImmuneSearch* algorithm.

To provide fairness in 'power', two different approaches are taken. The first approach defines fairness among *ImmuneSearch*, *proliferation$_2$*, random walk, and limited flooding, while the second approach defines fairness between *ImmuneSearch* and *proliferation$_1$*. The initial conditions (number of message packets) for *ImmuneSearch*, *proliferation$_2$*, and random walk, are chosen in a way such that the total number of packets used over 50 time steps of each individual search is roughly the same. In the case of flooding, we have allowed the process to run for x number of steps where x (< 50) steps uses the same number of packets as the aforesaid three cases used in 50 time steps. The fairness in 'power' between *Proliferation$_1$* and *ImmuneSearch* is maintained by employing the same threshold level for proliferation, and the same proliferation/mutation rate.

Search Efficiency: In *Fig. 2*, it is seen that the number of search items (N_s) found is progressively higher in limited flooding, random walk, *proliferation$_2$*, *proliferation$_1$*, and *ImmuneSearch*, respectively. The *proliferation$_1$*, *proliferation$_2$*, random walk, and limited flooding maintain a steady average search output of around 50, 40, 30, and 15 hits respectively. The standard deviation of the output is roughly around 10% of mean in each case. In the *ImmuneSearch* algorithm, it is observed that after it starts at an initial output of around 55 items per search, it steadily increases to 80 within the 25th generation, and then maintains a steady output of about 80 per search.

The difference in performance among the first four schemes which don't undergo any topology evolution can be directly attributed to the different frequencies, with which multiple message packets visit the same peer. The probability is particularly high in limited flooding where each message packet at every instance floods packets to all its neighbors. Therefore, at every instance, a multiple number of packets visits the same peer. In random walk, the probability of

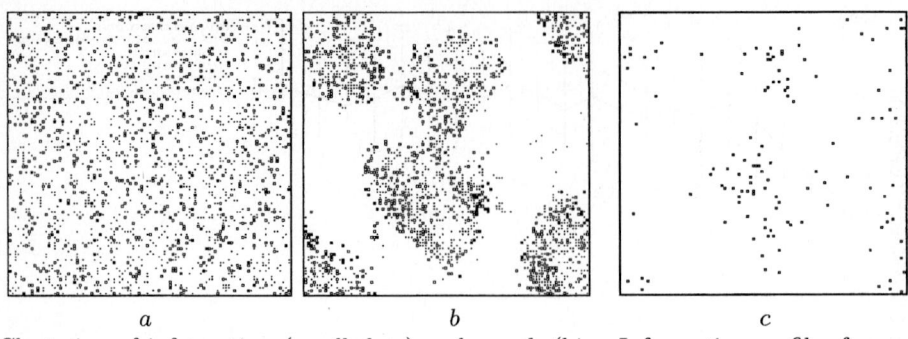

| a | b | c |

Clustering of information (small dots) and search (big dots) profile of peers possessing most frequent tokens at generation no. 0, 24 respectively.   Information profile of peers hosting 11th most frequent tokens at generation 100.

Fig. 3. Snapshots showing clustering of similat peers in the p2p network.

multiple packets visiting the same peer is high at the beginning of the search when they are clustered around the neighborhood of the user peer. The proliferation/mutation scheme in this respect has an advantage, in that initially it starts with a lower number of packets; only when they are sufficiently far apart, they do proliferate. Thus the probability of multiple packets visiting the same region is low. Proliferation/mutation schemes can also control the number of packets produced according to requirement. Since proliferation is dependent upon affinity between the message packets and the information profile, typically a lower number of packets is produced when the searched item is sparse in the system. This stops unnecessary wastage and in turn improves the effectivity of message packets. However, the experiments show that merely more proliferation does not necessarily imply a high rate of success, but that regulation of the proliferation/mutation scheme is also very important. It is seen that although $proliferation_2$ produces more message packets than $proliferation_1$, the search success rate is higher in $proliferation_1$ than $proliferation_2$.

In *ImmuneSearch*, the first 25 generations can be termed as 'learning' phase. During this time, similar to natural immune systems, the p2p network *develops memory* by repositioning the peers. The repositioning results in clustering of peers with similar profiles which is discussed next.

Clustering Impact: The series of snapshots in *Fig. 3* demonstrates the clustering effect in the p2p network as a result of *ImmuneSearch*. Each figure represents the configuration on the 100 × 100 overlay grid taken to host the 10,000 peers. In *Fig. 3a. & b.*, each peer displays its two profiles P_I and P_S. (The big dots represent the search profile of a peer (P_S) while the small dots are the informational profile (P_I)). In *Fig. 3c*, we show only the informational profile represented as dots.

The second snapshot (*Fig. 3b*) exhibits the clustering of the most frequently occurring profile at generation number 24 (the generation around which 'learning' is more or less complete) from the initial scattered setting (*Fig. 3a*). The snapshot of generation 24 shows that peers with search profile P_S intermingle with the peers with information profile P_I. That is, execution of the algorithm results in the peers with search profile (P_S) positioning themselves in 'favorable' positions whereby, when these peers initiate a search, the message packets emanated by them immediately begin to find peers with similar profiles. The clustering of the peers, as seen in *Fig. 3b*, is roughly divided into four major clusters; and it is notable that the clusters are porous. The porous and separated clusters are a result of ongoing competition among the differently frequent tokens and as a result of it also less frequent tokens obtain space to form clusters. Subsequently, their search output is also enhanced. (As an example, *Fig. 3c* shows clusters of peers hosting the 11th most frequent token).

3.3 Expt II: Search in Transient Conditions

The robustness of the algorithm is demonstrated by the following experiment. In this experiment, 0.5%, 1%, 5%, or 50% of the population, respectively, is replenished after every generation. This mimics the transient nature of p2p networks where peers regularly join and leave the system. *Fig. 4* shows the performance of the *ImmuneSearch*, under various degrees of replacement.

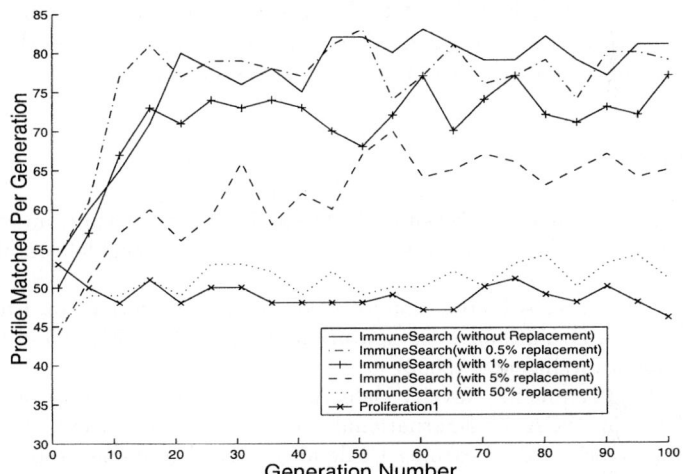

Fig. 4. Performance efficiency of ImmuneSearch when 0%, 0.5%, 1%, 5%, and 50% of peers are respectively replaced after each generation. The performance efficiency of *proliferation*$_1$ is also plotted as a base case. (Results are avg. of 20 simulation runs).

The results of *Fig. 4* illustrate two important aspects. (i) First of all, even in face of dynamic change, the *ImmuneSearch* algorithm 'learns', in that, after some initial generations, the efficiency increases. The rate of increase in search efficiency during the initial generations is generally dependent on the amount of replacement the p2p network undergoes after each generation. We find that the performance of *proliferation*$_1$ is roughly the same when there is 50% replacement.

But replacement of 50% of all peers in only 100 searches is likely far higher than any realistic turnover rate. (ii) However, the more important point to be noted is that at 0.5% replacement, we observe that the performance is in fact at par and sometimes slightly better than *ImmuneSearch* without replacement! The result establishes one important advantage of the algorithm – that is, a little transience is helpful, rather than detrimental, to the performance of the algorithm. This happens because the problem of developing a search algorithm is in fact a multi-objective optimization problem, and due to the enormous complexity, we are obtaining a 'good', however not optimal solution. So a little change in peers is probably enabling the system to move quickly towards a better solution.

4 Conclusion

This paper has presented a search algorithm which derives its inspiration from natural immune systems. The beauty of the algorithm lies in its simplicity. However, this simple decentralized algorithm generates emergent properties like a *complex adaptive system*, whose underlying guiding rules are generally also very simple. We find that as a result of the algorithm, the p2p network 'learns' and subsequently develops memory, whereby the search efficiency improves dramatically after some initial learning/training phase. The basic strengths displayed by the *ImmuneSearch* algorithm need to be further explored and developed, by applying it in more realistic circumstances in the near future.

References

1. Canright, G., Deutsch, A., Jelasity, M., Ducatelle, F.: Structures and functions of dynamic networks. Bison Deliverable, www.cs.unibo.it/bison/deliverables/D01.pdf (2003)
2. Singh, S., Thayer, S.: A Foundation for Kilorobotic Exploration. In: Proceedings of the Congress on Evolutionary Computation at the 2002 IEEE World Congress on Computational Intelligence. (2002)
3. Dasgupta, D., Forrest, S.: Novelty Detection in Time Series Data using Ideas from Immunology. In: ISCA 5th International Conference on Intelligent Systems. (1996)
4. Hunt, J.E., Cooke, D.E.: Learning Using an Artificial Immune System. Journal of Network and Computer Applications **19** (1996) 189–212
5. Kephart, J.O.: A Biologically Inspired Immune System for Computers. In: Proceeding of Artifical Life. (1994)
6. Lv, Q., Cao, P., Cohen, E., Shenker, S.: Search and Replication in Unstructured Peer-to-Peer Networks. In: Proceedings of the 16th ACM International Conference on Supercomputing. (2002)
7. Zipf, G.K. In: Psycho-Biology of Languages. Houghton-Mifflin (1935)

A Novel Ant Algorithm for Solving the Minimum Broadcast Time Problem

Yehudit Hasson and Moshe Sipper

Department of Computer Science, Ben-Gurion University, Israel
{hassonj,sipper}@cs.bgu.ac.il
www.moshesipper.com

Abstract. The problem of Minimum Broadcast Time (MBT) seeks to find the minimal number of times steps required to broadcast a message through a communication network. We describe a novel ant algorithm for solving this NP-Complete problem and compare it to three other known algorithms, one of which is genetic. Through experimentation on randomly generated graphs we show that our algorithm finds the best solutions.

1 Introduction

Communication in networks – in its many guises and forms – is one of the prime areas of research and application today. The performance of a network is influenced by many parameters, one of the most important being the time required to send a message between two communication sites: the message delay. In this paper, we describe a technique to reduce the delay when sending an identical message from one computer (or set of computers) to all other computers in the network – a process known as *broadcasting*. Broadcasting can be used to send control messages throughout a network, or for cable television.

A communication network can be modeled as a connected, undirected graph, wherein the nodes represent computers and the edges represent the communication lines between them. A node communicates with another by transmitting a message, or making a *call*. Theoretically, there is no limitation on the amount of information that can be exchanged during a given call. A *round* is a series of calls carried out simultaneously, each round assumed to require one unit of time. The efficiency of a broadcast scheme is measured by the number of time units it takes to complete the broadcast.

The problem of Minimum Broadcast Time (MBT) – our focus in this paper – is defined as follows: Given a connected, undirected graph G = {V,E} and a subset of nodes, $V_0 \subseteq V$, which initially contain a given message; and given that at each time step every node can transmit the message to *one* other node that has not already received the message; then, find a transmission plan that minimizes the number of steps needed to execute the *broadcast* operation, namely, transmit the message to all nodes in the graph.

Formally, let $V_0 \subseteq V$ be a distinguished vertex (or set of vertices) that holds the message at step 0. A broadcast from V_0 is a sequence $V_0, E_1, V_1, E_2, \ldots, E_k, V_k$ such that for $1 \leq i \leq k$ the following constraints hold:

1. $V_i \subseteq V$, $E_i \subseteq E$, and $V_k = V$.
2. Every edge in E_i has exactly one end point in V_{i-1}.
3. No two edges in E_i have an endpoint in common.
4. $V_i = V_{i-1} \cup \{v : (u, v) \in E_i\}$.

The MBT problem is to find the minimal k needed to complete the broadcast.

In this paper we describe an ant algorithm for solving MBT. The next section delineates previous work on solving MBT, followed by Section 3, which describes ant algorithms. Section 4 presents our novel algorithm, and our results are detailed in Section 5. Finally, we present concluding remarks and future work in Section 6.

2 Previous Work

Since the MBT problem is NP-Complete [1], available solutions are heuristic in nature. These are reviewed in this section.

Scheuermann and Wu [2] represented the broadcast operation as finding at each step an optimal matching in a bipartite graph.

$G = \{V, E\}$ is called a *bipartite* graph if $V = X \cup Y$, $X \cap Y = 0$, and each edge $e \in E$ has one endpoint in X and one in Y. A *matching* in a bipartite graph is a subset $E_s \subseteq E$ such that no two edges in E_s have an endpoint in common. A *maximal matching* in such a graph is the largest set $E_s \subseteq E$.

Scheuermann and Wu developed an algorithm based on dynamic programming that builds a state tree, wherein each node represents different choices of maximal matching. The algorithm searches for the shortest path in the tree by applying backtracking with pruning techniques. Being exponential in the network size, this algorithm becomes inefficient for large networks (over a few dozen nodes).

Scheuermann and Wu [2] also developed a few heuristics based on greedy techniques. Each node in the graph is assigned a *d*-value, which may either be the node degree, the length of the shortest path to the farthest node from it, or the maximum between these two values. The *d*-value can be calculated for different variations of the graph:

- The original graph G.
- The subgraph $G - S$, where S denotes the subgraph formed by the nodes that have the message.
- The subgraph $(G - S) \oplus E_r$, where E_r denotes the subgraph of G formed by the edges with both ends in R (i.e., both ends are nodes without a message), and $\oplus$ is the xor operator.

At each time step, the algorithm searches for an optimal matching between the group of nodes that have the message and the group of those that do not.

Scheuermann and Wu presented two types of search mechanisms:
1. LWMM (Least Weight Maximum Matching), which searches for a maximum matching with minimum weight (the weight of an edge is the d-value of the target node).
2. AM (Approximate Matching), which attempts to find a matching between the target node with the highest d-value and the source node with the lowest vertex degree.

Hoelting, Schoenfeld, and Wainwright [3] developed a genetic algorithm-based (GA) heuristic to the problem. The algorithm begins with a random population of chromosomes, each one being a permutation of the graph nodes.

In order to calculate an individual's fitness, the chromosome is reversed and divided into two lists: the s-list, containing nodes with the message, and the r-list, containing nodes without the message. The algorithm traverses the lists from left to right, trying to match a node in the s-list with a node in the r-list (if more than one match exists, only the first one found is taken into account). The node that receives the message in the current step is added to the end of the s-list in the same order as in the original chromosome. The fitness is the number of steps needed to complete the broadcast.

The crossover operation takes two chromosomes and compares them according to a global precedence vector (GPV), which contains the nodes in the graph sorted according to their vertex degree in ascending order. The idea behind this operation is to force lower-degree vertices toward the front of the chromosome (left) and nodes with a higher degree toward the end of the chromosome (right). To decode the chromosome (in order to evaluate the individual) it is reversed and the message is transmitted to nodes with high degree first. The mutation operation switches between two alleles in the chromosome. The GA used in Section 5 is based on that of Hoelting, Schoenfeld, and Wainwright [3].

3 Ant Algorithms

Swarm Intelligence algorithms [4], which have received increased attention in recent years, are inspired by swarms in nature, e.g., of bees, ants, wasps, and birds. Such swarms give rise to intelligent behavior through the continual operation and interaction of thousands of autonomous, relatively simple members. No central controller is involved in the process.

When the swarm members do not communicate directly but rather do so indirectly – by using the environment as a "blackboard" – this is called stigmergy. Ants, for example, interact by depositing a chemical substance known as a pheromone along their trails. This substance can be sensed by fellow nest members, which tend to follow higher concentrations of pheromone, in turn increasing said concentration yet further. This is a form of indirect communication through the environment. Another example is nest building by wasps, which was simulated beautifully by Theraulaz and Bonabeau [5].

The Ant Colony System (ACS) algorithm was developed by Dorigo, Maniezzo, and Colorni [6], who applied it to the traveling salesman problem (TSP). Since then, much research has been carried out on so-called ant algorithms.

Das et al. [7] applied an ant colony approach to the Minimum Power Broadcast problem in wireless networks, a problem that shares certain similarities with MBT. In this problem we assume a fixed N-node network with a specified source node, which must broadcast a message to all other nodes in the network. In a wireless network (as opposed to a wired one), a node can transmit a message to *any* other node in the network, and thus multiple nodes can be reached by a single transmission. The power required to transmit a message between two nodes depends on the Euclidean distance between them and a channel loss coefficient.

An ant under Das et al.'s scheme maintains a strategy for building a broadcast tree. The ant decides according to its strategy to which node the message should be sent. There are two types of ants (strategies):

1. Greedy "vision," preferring to send the message to the closest node.
2. Wide vision, choosing the next node according to roulette-wheel selection.

The algorithm executes several ants of both types in parallel. For each ant a broadcast tree is built, whereupon two functions are applied to improve its cost, the cost of a tree being the number of steps needed to execute the broadcast. The first function – multiple transmission removal (MTR) – removes multiple transmissions from a node, because the highest-powered transmission will also cover nodes which are reached by lower-power transmissions from that node. The second function – edge trimming (ET) – removes a transmission edge if no new node is reached by it.

The algorithm stores the best tree built so far and updates the pheromone on the tree edges after each ant's traversal and after choosing the best tree. In the end, the algorithm returns the tree with the best cost.

4 Solving MBT Using Ants

Our algorithm employs nine types of ants, each of which dynamically builds a broadcast tree. An ant decides to which node to send the message in the broadcast tree, based on the node's local environment – i.e., its neighbors.

An ant maintains the following information:

– s-list: nodes with message.
– t-list: nodes without message.
– mutation: an ant has a small probability of being "olfaction-less," i.e., its decisions are not influenced by the trail left by other ants.

Tree-building by an ant is an iterative process, which starts with the s-list containing only the source node, and ends when the s-list contains all nodes in the graph. In each step, the ant builds an edge-list, with all the edges connecting nodes in the s-list (source nodes) with nodes in the t-list (target nodes). The ant chooses the next edge from the edge-list according to three parameters: 1) source value, 2) target value, and 3) trail. The chosen edge is added to the tree and any other edge in the edge-list that connects the corresponding source or target is removed from the list. The process of choosing edges from the edge-list continues until the edge-list is empty. Then all nodes that have reached this step are added to the s-list and removed from the t-list – and the step counter is increased by one. The number of steps needed to build the tree is the tree's cost.

The value of an edge is evaluated according to its source and target nodes. In order to do so, each node i maintains information about its neighbors:

- nm-list$_i$: neighbors of node i with message.
- nwm-list$_i$: neighbors of node i without message.
- nwms-list$_i$: neighbors of node i without message that cannot receive message at this step (because they have no edge to a node currently holding message).

The source is assigned a higher value (S), the smaller the number of neighbors that can receive the message from it (nwm-list). Moreover, the value of the target (T) can be calculated by three different methods (depending on the ant type):

1. Number of neighbors that have a message and can send it to the target node at this step (nm-list). The target value is higher, the smaller the size of the nm-list.
2. Number of neighbors without a message (nwm-list).
3. Number of neighbors without a message that cannot receive the message at this step (nwms-list).

For methods 2 and 3, the target value is higher the larger the list size. An ant can choose an edge whose sum of source and target values is maximal, or it can choose first the source that has maximum value and then the target connected to that source with the highest target value – and vice versa. We thus have 9 types of ants, one ant for each version (Table 1): as can be seen, our use of nine types of ants arises from the nine heuristics attained by the various ways of combining source and target costs into an edge score. The use of nine ant types increases diversity, thus boosting the search process.

Table 1. The ants differ in the way they choose the next edge from edge-list. S and T are the respective source and target values for edge (i, j). The ant can choose an edge with max S+T, or first choose the source with max S and then the edge with max T connected to that source – and vice versa. In case more than one edge has the same value, selection is random. The precise formulas for calculating S and T are specified in Figure 1.

Ant 1 – S + T_1	Ant 2 – S + T_2	Ant 3 – S + T_3
Ant 4 – S $\rightarrow$ T_1	Ant 5 – S $\rightarrow$ T_2	Ant 6 – S $\rightarrow$ T_3
Ant 7 – T_1 $\rightarrow$ S	Ant 8 – T_2 $\rightarrow$ S	Ant 9 – T_3 $\rightarrow$ S

The algorithm stores the best tree built so far and updates the trail on the tree edges after running all ants for one cycle, according to the number of ants that choose the edge and the step at which they chose it. In the end, the algorithm returns the tree with the best cost. Figures 3 and 4 describe the pseudocode of our algorithm (the nomenclature is given in Figure 2).

$$S = \tau_{ij}^p * \left(\frac{|V|}{|nm-list_i|+1}\right)^s \qquad T_2 = \tau_{ij}^p * \left(\frac{|nwm-list_j|*100+1}{|V|}\right)^t$$
$$T_1 = \tau_{ij}^p * \left(\frac{|V|}{|nm-list_j|+1}\right)^t \qquad T_3 = \tau_{ij}^p * \left(\frac{|nwms-list_j|*100+1}{|V|}\right)^t$$

Fig. 1. Computing S and T values for edge (i,j). τ_{ij} is the pheromone amount on this edge; p is set to 0 when ant's mutation is false, otherwise it is set to 1; s and t were both set empirically to 1.

$T_k(t)$ – tree built by ant k at iteration t	$Y_k(t)$ – cost of said tree
$T\text{-}LIST^{best}(t)$ – list of best trees at iteration t	$Y^{best}(t)$ – cost of best tree at t
T^{best} – best tree found so far	Y^{best} – cost of best tree
$P_s(e)$ – e's node which is in s-list	$P_t(e)$ – e's node which is in t-list
$E_{st}(step)$ – list at broadcast $step$ containing all edges with source node in s-list and target node in t-list	
$E(step)$ – list containing all edges chosen at $step$	

Fig. 2. Nomenclature for pseudocodes in Figures 3 and 4.

1. $t \leftarrow 0$ // iteration index
2. $\tau_e \leftarrow \tau_0$, $\forall e \in E$ // pheromone amount on edge e
3. while $(t < t_{max})$
    $Y^{best}(t) \leftarrow \infty$
    for k = 1 to NUMANTS // run ant k
        $type = k$ mod ANT-TYPES // ant's type, where ANT-TYPES=9
        $T_k(t) \leftarrow buildTreeByAnt(type)$ // pseudocode given in Figure 4
        if $Y_k(t) = Y^{best}(t)$ then T-LIST$^{best}(t) \leftarrow$ T-LIST$^{best}(t) \cup T_k(t)$
        if $Y_k(t) < Y^{best}(t)$ then
            T-LIST$^{best}(t) \leftarrow \{\ T_k(t)\ \}$
            $Y^{best}(t) \leftarrow Y_k(t)$
    endfor
    for i = 1 to num elements in T-LIST$^{best}(t)$
        foreach $e \in$ T-LIST$_i^{best}(t)$ do   // edge in tree i of T-LIST$^{best}(t)$
            sumSteps $\leftarrow$ sumSteps + 1/step   // step when edge reached
            numVisitors $\leftarrow$ numVisitors + 1   // num ants visiting edge
        endforeach
    endfor
    if $(t = 0)$ OR $(Y^{best}(t) < Y^{best})$
        $T^{best} \leftarrow$ T-LIST$_0^{best}(t)$
        $Y^{best} \leftarrow Y^{best}(t)$
    endif
    foreach $e \in E$ do   // update pheromone on edge
        $\tau_e(t+1) \leftarrow \tau_e(t)^\rho + \left(\frac{numVisitors}{NUMANTS+1}\right)^\alpha + \left(\frac{sumSteps}{NUMANTS+1}\right)^\beta$
        numVisitors $\leftarrow$ 0
        sumSteps $\leftarrow$ 0
    endforeach
    $t \leftarrow t + 1$
4. endwhile
5. return T^{best} and Y^{best}

Fig. 3. ANT-MBT-algorithm: main. The following values were set empirically: $\alpha = 20$, $\beta = 20$, $\rho = 0.1$, and $\tau_0 = 1$.

```
1. initialize ant:
     has-mutation ← true with probability MUTATION-RATIO
     T ← { }
     foreach node i∈V do
         nm-list_i←{}           // neighbors of node i with message
         nwm-list_i←{ Neighbors{i} }   // neighbors of i without message
         nwms-list_i←{ Neighbors{i} }  // neighbors of i in nwm-list that
                                      // can't receive message at this step
     endforeach
2. execute in step 0:
     step ← 0       // broadcast step
     s-list ← { sourceNode }      // nodes with message
     t-list ← { V - sourceNode }  // nodes without message
     nwms-list_{sourceNode} ← { }
     foreach neighbor i of sourceNode
         move sourceNode from nwm-list_i to nm-list_i
         remove sourceNode from nwms-list_i
     endforeach
3. while t-list is not empty
     step ← step + 1
     build $E_{st}(step)$
     foreach e ∈ $E_{st}(step)$
         foreach neighbor i of $P_t(e)$
             remove $P_t(e)$ from nwms-list_i
         endforeach
     endforeach
     have-msg-list ← { i | i ∈ s-list and nwm-list_i != { } }
     while have-msg-list is not empty
         //choose the next edge in the broadcast tree according to
         //ant's type and has-mutation value
         foreach e ∈ $E_{st}(step)$
             compute S ant T values    // see Figure 1
         endforeach
         chosenEdge ← choose the next edge   // see Table 1
         E(step) ← E(step) ∪ chosenEdge
         remove $P_s(chosenEdge)$ from have-msg-list
         remove every e ∈ $E_{st}(step)$ with one endpoint
                equal to either $P_s(chosenEdge)$ or $P_t(chosenEdge)$
         nwms-list_{$P_t(chosenEdge)$} ← { }
         foreach neighbor i of $P_t(chosenEdge)$
             move $P_t(chosenEdge)$ from nwm-list_i to nm-list_i
             if nwm-list_i is empty and i ∈ have-msg-list
                 remove i from have-msg-list
         endforeach
     endwhile
     T ← T ∪ E(step)
     update s-list and t-list
4. endwhile
5. return T
```

Fig. 4. ANT-MBT-algorithm: buildTreeByAnt(*type*). This function returns the broadcast tree built by the ant. MUTATION-RATIO was set empirically to 0.05.

5 Results

Given a connected undirected graph G = {V,E}, with $V_0 = \{u\}$ and $|V| = n$, we can conclude a number of things about the broadcast:

1. A broadcast from a vertex u defines a spanning tree rooted at u.
2. In each step the set of nodes that have received the message increases by at least one. Therefore, the time needed to execute a broadcast in G is a value in the set $\{\lceil \log_2\{n\} \rceil, \ldots, n-1\}$.

We tested the algorithms on graphs containing 15 to 250 nodes with low edge connectivity probabilities, running 10 randomly generated networks for each variation. Note that a low connectivity probability entails a harder problem, since in highly connected graphs the broadcast is easily achieved.

Both GA and Ant are population algorithms, each member in the population representing a candidate solution. We compared both algorithms using the same parameter values (population size, number of cycles, mutation rate), and under the same assumptions:

1. If an optimal solution (treeCost = $\log |V|$) is found, execution of the algorithm is stopped and the solution is returned.
2. The best solution in a cycle moves on to the next generation.
3. The algorithm is said to have converged to a solution if 85% of the population have held the same solution for the past 10 generations, and there is no better solution.

Table 2 shows our results. As can be seen our algorithm emerges as the winner. Though some results may seem only slightly better than the other algorithms, one should bear in mind that *every decrease of even a single broadcast step is significant and hard to attain*.

Table 2. A comparison of algorithm performance rates. For GA and ANT, population size = $2|V|$ (where $|V|$ is the network size), number of generations/cycles = 50, and mutation rate = 0.05. We ran the variants of LWMM and AM that were reported in [2] to produce the best results: 1) LWMM: d-value is the vertex degree, calculated in the subgraph $G - S$; 2) AM: d-value is the vertex degree, calculated in the subgraph $(G-S) \oplus E_r$. Results for AM and LWMM are per one run (algorithms are deterministic), and for ANT and GA averaged over 10 runs.

Network size	Edge Probability	AM	LWMM	GA	ANT
15	0.1	6.9	6.9	**6.3**	**6.3**
30	0.1	6.5	6.4	6.3	**5.9**
60	0.05	8.4	8.3	7.8	**7.7**
60	0.075	7.4	7.5	7.1	**6.6**
60	0.1	7.0	7.0	6.7	**6.4**
120	0.05	8.0	7.9	8.0	**7.3**
120	0.075	8.0	7.3	7.4	**7.0**
120	0.1	8.0	**7.0**	**7.0**	**7.0**
250	0.05	9.0	8.2	9.0	**8.0**
250	0.075	9.0	**8.0**	8.2	**8.0**
250	0.1	9.0	**8.0**	**8.0**	**8.0**

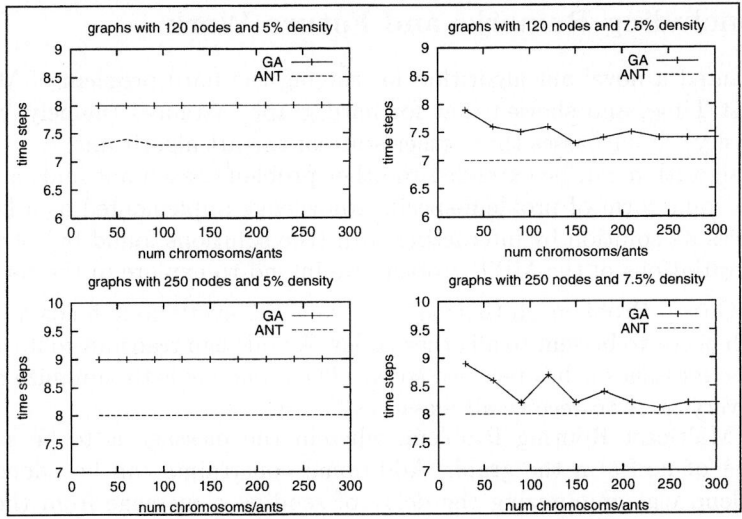

Fig. 5. Effect of population size on performance (shown for the hard problem range, i.e., low density – for higher densities the problem becomes easier).

Figure 5 shows the effects of population size on performance of the GA and ANT algorithms. For the GA, increasing the number of the chromosomes improves performance, while for ANT the effect of increasing the ant population is less significant – the ANT algorithm finds better solutions even with a small number of ants.

Given G={V, E}, the time complexity of the four algorithms discussed herein is a function of several parameters: $|V|$ – number of nodes, $|E|$ – number of edges, $|N|$ – maximal degree of a node, $|K|$ – number of broadcast steps needed to reach a solution, $|C|$ – number of cycles/generations, and $|CH|/|ANTS|$ – number of chromosomes/ants. The time complexities are:

- AM: $O(|K||V|^2)$. This algorithm has proved to be the fastest of the four.
- LWMM: $O(|K||V|^3|E|)$.[1]
- GA: $O(|C||CH||K||V|^2)$.
- ANT: $O(|C||ANTS||K||V||E|)$.

As an example, if $|V|=60$, $|N|=5$, and $|CH|/|ANTS|=2|V|$, then AM and LWMM take about a second to complete, the GA takes 0.2 seconds per generation, and ANT takes a second per cycle.

---

[1] This algorithm finds a least weight maximum matching in a bipartite graph according to the Ford-Fulkerson algorithm [8], i.e., it finds a least weight augmenting path and defines the symmetric difference of the path with the old matching to be the new matching. In the implementation we find an augmenting path with minimal last edge because the weights of the intermediate edges cancel each other out [2].

6 Concluding Remarks and Future Work

We presented a novel ant algorithm for solving the hard problem of Minimum Broadcast Time, and showed that for hard graph instances (namely, with low edge density), it surpasses three other state-of-the-art algorithms.

Our algorithm can be extended to other problems: each ant finds a solution based on some form of problem-specific knowledge implemented as a heuristic; it improves its solution by interacting with (the solutions found by) other ants.

Two variations of the MBT problem we intend to explore in the future are:

- The Gossip Problem. In this variation of MBT every node holds a message, which needs to be sent to all other nodes. A node can transmit to its neighbor all the messages it has received so far. The objective is to minimize the time for every node to receive all messages [9, 10].
- The Multicast Routing Problem, wherein the message is to be sent to a subset of nodes in the graph. Additional constraints can be added to the problem, e.g., minimizing the delay of sending a message from the source to a target, and minimizing the cost of sending the message to all target nodes [11].

References

1. Garey, M.R., Johnson, D.S.: Computers and Interactability: A Guide to the Theory of NP-Completeness. W. H. Freeman and Company, San Francisco, CA (1979)
2. Scheuermann, P., Wu, G.: Heuristic algorithms for broadcasting in point-to-point computer networks. IEEE Transactions on Computers **C-33** (1984)
3. Hoelting, C.J., Schoenefeld, D.A., Wainwright, R.L.: A genetic algorithm for the minimum broadcast time problem using a global precedence vector. In: Proceedings of the 1996 ACM Symposium on Applied Computing, Philadelphia, PA, ACM Press (1996) 258–262
4. Bonabeau, E., Dorigo, M., Theraulaz, G.: Swarm Intelligence: From Natural to Artificial Systems. SFI Studies in the Sciences of Complexity. Oxford university Press (1999)
5. Theraulaz, G., Bonabeau, E.: Coordination in distributed building. Science **269** (1995) 686–688
6. Dorigo, M., Maniezzo, V., Colorni, A.: The ant system: Optimization by a colony of cooperating agents. IEEE Transactions on Systems, Man, and Cybernetics—Part B **26** (1996) 1–13
7. Das, A.K., II, R.J.M., El-Sharkawi, M.A., Arabshahi, P., Gray, A.: The minimum power broadcast problem in wireless networks: An ant colony approach. In: Proceedings of IEEE CAS Workshop on Wireless Communications and Networking, Pasadena, CA (2002)
8. Ford, L.R., Fulkerson, D.R.: Flows in Networks. Princeton University Press, New Jersey (1962)
9. Baker, B., Shostak, R.: Gossips and telephones. Discrete Mathematics **2** (1972) 191–193
10. Hedetniemi, S.M., Hedetniemi, S.T., Liestman, A.L.: A survey of gossiping and broadcasting in communication networks. Networks **18** (1988) 320–349
11. Hakimi, S.L.: Steiner's problem in graphs and its implications. Networks **1** (1971) 113–133

Designing Multiple-Use Primer Set
for Multiplex PCR by Using Compact GAs

Yu-Cheng Huang[1], Han-Yu Chuang[1], Huai-Kuang Tsai[1],
Chun-Fan Chang[2,*], and Cheng-Yan Kao[1,*]

[1] Dept. of Computer Science and Information Engineering,
National Taiwan University, Taiwan
{r91021,r90002,d7526010,cykao}@csie.ntu.edu.tw
[2] Chinese Culture University, Taiwan
chunfan@ms17.hinet.net

Abstract. Reducing the number of needed primers in multiplex polymerase chain reaction experiments is useful, or even essential, in large scale genomic research. In this paper, we transform this multiple-use primer design problem into a set-covering problem, and propose a modified compact genetic algorithm (MCGA) approach to disclose optimal solutions. Our experimental results demonstrate that MCGA effectively reduces the primer numbers of multiplex PCR experiments among whole-genome data sets of four test species within a feasible computation time, especially when applied on complex genomes. Moreover, the performance of MCGA further exhibits better global stability of optimal solutions than conventional heuristic methods that may fall into local optimal traps.

1 Introduction

Molecular analyses and extended diagnostic applications are often restricted by limited availability of biological materials. The Polymerase Chain Reaction (PCR) [1], which uses primers to amplify specific DNA segments, is thus with crucial essence to current genomic researches, such as constructing full-genome spotted microarrays [2] on the preparation of DNA spotting material. Multiplex PCR [3], while using multiple primers to concurrently amplify multiple target DNA segments in single reaction [4], is considered as a time and reagent saving technique for simultaneous amplification of different targets, respectively. In current multiplex PCR, the primer length is often designed between 17 and 25 nucleotides (nt) and the number of primers is exactly twice of target number (with forward and reverse primer pair). The primer length ranging 17~25 nt is due to that the specificity by all random permutations of 17 nt (4^{17} approximately equals to 1.7×10^{10}) has already exceeded the size of human genome (3×10^9 bps) and therefore would cause least random priming in human genome. Many primer selection programs have been commercialized [5, 6], such as Primer 3 [7], and focused on designing unique left and right primers for each gene

---

* Correspondance authors.

targets. Obviously, a substantial percentage of PCR experimental expense inevitably drained into the synthesis cost of needed unique primers in large scale research projects.

To greatly reduce the indicated synthesis cost of needed primers, a demand-driven multiple-use primer design is useful in concurrent amplification of several interested targets from a single sample. Welsh and McClelland [8] proposed the Arbitrarily Primed PCR (AP-PCR) method by using short (8 to 12 nt) arbitrary primers in order to match several targets and to produce more fragments while without prior sequence information. Nevertheless, the multiple-use primer design problem is a difficult and NP-complete [9] combinational optimization problem, which can not be solved by applying commercial primer selection programs mentioned above. Heuristic approaches were hence developed to find the minimal multiple-use primer set, such as linear time heuristic (LTH), densest subgraph heuristic (DSH) [9], and other greedy methods [10]. Albeit, these heuristic algorithms produce sub-optima solutions for multiple-use PCR primer design problem in which the probability of getting local optimal results tends to arise with the growing number of amplification targets in large scale projects.

This paper transforms the multiple-use primer design problem into a constrained set-covering problem and proposes a modified compact genetic algorithm (MCGA) in order to get global and optimal quality results and as well to save the number of required primers within a reasonable amount of time. The MCGA can save tasks from falling into local optima status and give tasks a quick estimate on computational difficulty [14]. Being considered as global search mechanisms, the genetic algorithms (GAs) are one of the main categories of evolutionary algorithms and have very well become increasingly popular for solving complex optimization problems, such as function optimization [11], traveling salesman problem [12], and set-covering problem [13]. The GAs are adaptable concepts for problem-solving and are especially well suited for solving difficult optimization problems based on the ideas borrowed from genetics and natural selection. The GAs have been applied to solve problems of large search spaces, where conventional optimization methods are less effective.

In this paper, our MCGA of primer design algorithm was applied on four test datasets with three different ranges of melting temperature (Tm). In order to match multiple positions in the DNA genome by one primer, the proposed method designs primers with a short length (8-12 nt). Our experimental results show that MCGA overcomes the trade-off between quality and time of feasible solution during minimizing needed primers. Specifically, the solution quality of MCGA is more stable and efficient when compared with most frequently used heuristic methods. Thus, this paper concludes that MCGA is a feasible solution for exploring complex genomes in minimizing multiple-use primers.

The rest sections of this paper are organized as of the followings. Section 2 describes the multiple-use primer design problems, and transforms it into the set-covering problem with more constraints. Section 3 introduces the evolutionary nature of the proposed MCGA approach. Section 4 demonstrates and discusses the experimental results on four datasets with three Tm ranges. Lastly, concluding comments are drawn in Section 5.

2 Multiple-Use PCR Primer Design Problems

2.1 Problem Definition

In a PCR experiment, two primers (forward and reverse primer) are required to amplify the target sequence (as shown in Fig. 1). A primer is an oligo-nucleotide with a constant length that is much shorter than the target sequence. This paper uses the following notations. Assuming there are n DNA sequences, a primer Pi is denoted by (j, p, f/r) to represent that primer Pi hybridizes to sequence j in which the start position is p, where f and r represent forward and reverse primer, respectively. |Pi| denotes the length of primer Pi.

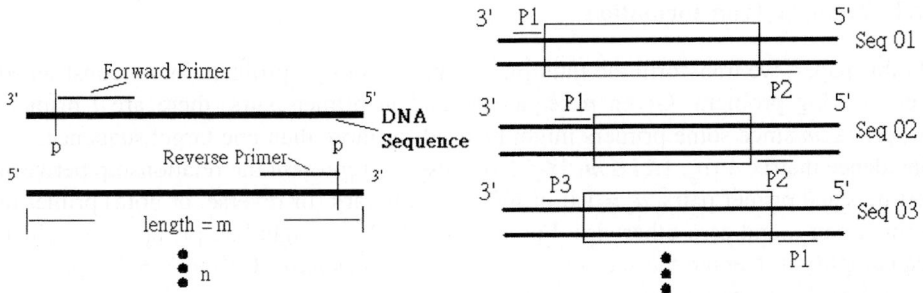

Fig. 1. The PCR primer design.

Fig. 2. The multiplex PCR with multiple-use primers. P1, P2, and P3 are three different primers. The rectangular boxes are the amplified DNA regions.

Figure 2 shows an example of the multiplex PCR problem with three target sequences simultaneously amplified by multiple-use primers. Specifically, primer P1 can be used as the forward primer for Seq01 and Seq02 and the reverse primer for Seq03 simultaneously, while P2 is used as the reverse primer for Seq01 and Seq02. Primers P1 and P2 are re-used for the PCR experiment and thus reduce the total primer number of the PCR experiment. Briefly, the defined multiple-use primer problem can be as follows. Given n DNA sequences, the multiple-use primer problem is to find a primer set with minimal number of primers that can amplify these n sequences simultaneously. Each primer in the set might be forward or reverse, and they satisfy certain desired constraints (described in the next paragraph). For each target sequence, the corresponding forward and reverse primers are contained in the set. Most importantly, primers can be used for amplifying different target sequences. In this paper, certain criteria and biological constraints are considered.

Primer Length: The length of a primer is 12 nt so that each primer can match multiple positions in the genome.

Primer Composition: Primers that contain a skewed AT/GC ratio can fail to give high specificity, or yield primers that are not well performed in other ways.

Melting Temperature (Tm): Tm is the key to deciding whether a primer candidate is appropriate or not. To enhance the discriminative ability of the oligo-nucleotides, the conditions of hybridization and washing need to be optimal. Therefore, it is crucial that all oligo-nucleotides should perform well under similar hybridization conditions. In this recent study, the Tm is set to 40 degrees centigrade and different ranges are used to accommodate more primer candidates.

GC Content: The GC content is 40-60% as in the common cases.

Length of Amplified Regions: The amplified regions are between 300-1200 base pairs long.

2.2 Problem Transformation

In this paper, we transform the multiple-use primer design problem into a constrained set-covering problem. Given n sequences and m primer pairs, there are l primers where $l \leq 2m$ since some primers might be used for more than one target sequence. An incidence matrix A (a_{ij}, $1 \leq i \leq m$, $1 \leq j \leq l$) is used to represent the relationship between primers and primer pairs. $a_{ij} = 1$ if primer j is a forward (or reverse, or both) primer in primer pair i, and zero otherwise. For sequence k, there might be t primer pairs which can amplify it. Denote the set of these t primer pairs as $pair_k$. Define $X_j = 1$ if primer j is in the solution and $X_j = 0$ otherwise.

In the transformed set-covering problems, we intend to find a subset of primers with minimal number of primers which can amplify all target sequences. A sequence k is covered if at least one of $pair_k$ is included in the solution set. Formally, the problem can be stated as a set-covering problem in the following way:

$$\text{Minimize} \sum_{j=1}^{l} X_j \quad (1)$$

subject to

$$\forall k, 1 \leq k \leq n, \exists i \in pair_k \text{ s.t.} \sum_{j}^{l} a_{ij} X_j = \sum_{j=1}^{l} a_{ij}. \quad (2)$$

Constraint (2) guarantees that each sequence k is covered by at least one primer pair, which is different from the traditional set-covering problem. It is well known that set-covering problem has been proven to be NP-complete [15] and is a model for several important applications [16, 17]. Description of set-covering problem could be found in [18, 19].

3 Modified Compact Genetic Algorithm (MCGA)

A genetic algorithm, combining the spirits of compact genetic algorithm (CGA) [14] and a local search based on edge replacement, is proposed to minimize the multiple-use primer number of PCR. The main mechanism of CGA is to represent the population as a probability distribution over the set of solutions, applying the principle of survival of the fittest [20] to produce successively better approximations to a solution. The local search, inspired by the study [9], is considered as an efficient heuristic. Based on the CGA with local search modification, our proposed MCGA approach substantiates both global and local strategies by probability-based mutations.

Figure 3 shows the main steps of MCGA. First, a probability vector V is generated where each entry is equal to 0.5. Then two individuals are generated according to V. A uniform crossover is applied on these two individuals to generate two new intermediates. The local search (Section 3.2) is applied on two intermediates to produce two children. The competition mechanism (Section 3.3) then updates V according to these two children. The above process is repeated until the probability V converges. In the following subsections, the chromosome representation, the local search, and the competition mechanism are described in detail.

3.1 Chromosome Representation

Assume there are l primers. A chromosome is represented as $(u_1, ..., u_l)$, where, $u_j = 1$ implies that primer j should be selected and $u_j = 0$ otherwise ($1 \leq j \leq l$). A probability vector $V=(v_1, ..., v_l)$, is used to represent the population. v_j represents the possibility of selecting the primer j. In the beginning, all v_j is set to 0.5 for random sampling. All chromosomes are generated according to the probability vector V. That is, the probability of setting u_j to 1 is v_j.

3.2 The Local Search

After applying a uniform crossover, two intermediates are generated. A new local search is applied to improve them. The local search mechanism works as follows. Since an intermediate is not always feasible, we first select proper primer pairs into the primer set to make sure that all targets are fully covered. Then for each primer pair, we replace it with other primer pair for the same target sequence to check if the number of primers decreases or not. If the number of primers is less than the previous one, the primer pair is replaced. After all pairs are checked, all primer pairs in the primer set without any shared common primer for other sets are removed. The above process is repeated until there is no more reduction in primer number.

3.3 The Competition Mechanism

After the local search, two children are produced. The one with higher fitness is *winner*, while the other one is *loser*. The competition mechanism applies the following steps to update probability vector V. For a primer i, there are three cases to update v_i: 1) If *winner* selects primer i but *loser* does not, then $v_i = v_i + 1/n$; 2) If *loser* selects primer i but *winner* does not, then $v_i = v_i - 1/n$; 3) If both *winner* and *loser* selects primer i, then v_i stays the same, where n is the population size. The above updating steps are repeated for l times, where l is the number of primers.

4 Experimental Result

In the experiments, we first solved general set-covering problems and then applied our MCGA to the real-world multiple-use primer design problems. In the test of solving general set-covering problems, we used the test sets from Beasley's OR library [21] and compared our approach with present literature [13], including a direct genetic algorithm labeled BeCh [22], a Lagrangean-based heuristic labeled CFT [18], an indirect genetic algorithm labeled IGA [13], a linear time heuristic labeled LTH and a densest subgraph heuristic labeled DSH [9]. Moreover, we applied our CGA to primer design problems in genome-level PCR for four different species, *Schistosoma mansoni* (SMA), *Medicago truncatula* (MTR), *Hordeum vulgare* (HV), and *Ciona intestinalis* (CIN). The proposed MCGA method was tested on three Tm ranges, including 39-41, 38-42, and 37-43 degrees in centigrade, which are much narrower when compared with previous studies. Furthermore, the proposed MCGA approach was compared with the currently fast heuristic LTH and best heuristic DSH of multiple-use primer design to manifest MCGA's optimal performance and stability.

4.1 The Result of Set-Covering Problem by MCGA

The computational experiment was carried out on a 450 MHz Pentium II PC with 128 MB RAM. From the data of Beasley's OR library [21], 60 test sets were used, ranging in size from 200 rows × 1000 columns to 1000 rows × 10000 columns and in density (average proportion of rows covered by a column) from 2% to 20%. The deviation (Dev.) represents the ratio of variance between the problem's optimal solution and the best results out of 10 runs for each data instance. The corresponding deviation and time consumed in finding optimal solutions for these testing problems using different methods are summarized in Table I, where we can see the trade-off between solution quality and time consumption when using commonly available methods. Most excitingly, the MCGA seems to overcome the above drawbacks effectively. The MCGA offered better solution quality of no deviation in the experiments than most other methods did with exceptions of CFT and DSH. Moreover, MCGA spent fewer seconds to find the optimal solution than CFT and DSH did. Based on these comparisons, we are confident to claim that the proposed MCGA approach can find a better solution in a shorter amount of time than common used methods.

4.2 The Improvement in Reducing Needed Primers of LTH Within Acceptable Calculation Time

The multiple-use primer design problem is a set-covering problem with more constraints in the real world. We used the MCGA to design genome-level PCR primers for four datasets of different species, including *Schistosoma mansoni* (SMA), *Medicago truncatula* (MTR), *Hordeum vulgare* (HV), and *Ciona intestinalis* (CIN), downloaded from NCBI UniGene database. The GC content and the length of a primer were set to 40-60% and 12, respectively. We focused on amplifying segments of length between 300-1200 bps. In our implementation, the program automatically translates the genome files in the FASTA database format into appropriate input for the Primer 3 [7].

The proposed method was tested on three Tm ranges of 39-41, 38-42, and 37-43 degrees in centigrade, which are much narrower when compared with previous studies. Obviously, a larger range of melting temperatures produces more primer candidates and gets more reduced primers even when the reduced rate does not improve. However, the range of melting temperature from 39 to 41 is the most desirable condition for real-world experiments since all the primer candidates can work at the most similar temperature in a multiplex PCR experiment.

The proposed approach was compared with the currently fast heuristic LTH and best heuristic DSH of multiple-use primer design to manifest its optimal performance and stability. The experiments were performed on a Pentium 2.6 GHz PC with 1 GB memory running on Linux operation system.

4.2.1 Reducing Needed Primers Within Feasible Calculation Time

Table II shows the simulation results on primer pair design in the test datasets with three Tm ranges by MCGA, DSH and LTH. Each experiment is repeated 30 times, and the results are summarized in Table II. From Table II, we can see that the rate and number of reduced primers grows as the number of primer pair candidates grows. This indicates that the importance of multiple-use primers is more explicit when we plan to explore more complex organisms.

As shown in Table II, MCGA reduces more primers than LTH in all the tested dataset, even small ones. Moreover, the number of reduced primers of MCGA is much greater than that of LTH when applied to larger genomes. Take *Ciona intestinalis* (CIN) with Tm range of 37-43 as an example. MCGA reduces 3239.5 primers more than LTH does. If a 12mer primer cost $7 at least, we could save about $22673 in this experiment. Figure 4 further demonstrates that MCGA can reduce more primers in average than the LTH at all conditions. The y-axis represents the difference in reduced primers between MCGA and LTH; the x-axis contains the four datasets. Each curve represents different Tm ranges. MCGA gets a significant reduction when the data set grow. While MCGA spends a little more time than LTH, it saves a noticeable experimental cost. Because the calculation time of MCGA is acceptable, such a trade-off is worthwhile when the size of simultaneously amplified genes becomes larger.

In addition, Table II also reveals that MCGA finds optimal solutions much faster than DSH in all the test datasets, even in large ones. In such a short calculation time, the number of reduced primers of MCGA is quite close to and even better than that of DSH when they are applied to larger genomes. Take *Ciona intestinalis* (CIN) with Tm range of 37-43 as an example. MCGA spends fewer 455334.85 secs (which is close to 5.27 days) than DSH while the average solution quality of MCGA is better than DSH. MCGA saves more time than DSH when the data set grows. The result shows that MCGA is a more applicable way to deal with larger data set such as the human genome data and get reliable solutions within an acceptable amount of time.

4.2.2 Stable Solution Quality

Figure 5 displays the comparison of reduced primer numbers among LTH, DSH, and MCGA applied on *Ciona intestinalis* (CIN) under Tm range of 37-43 degrees in centigrade for 30 repeated experiments. According to [9], LTH will make a random selection with probability of 1/2 when there is no improvement of the primer's reduction. Therefore, the LTH will get the sub-optima solution depending on its initial state. From figure 5, we can see that MCGA exhibits a stable performance in all the 30 repetitions, whereas the other two with highly variable solutions. Although the maximal reduced primer number of DSH is 17707, which is a little larger than the one of CGA (17254), the average reduced primer number and reduction rate of DSH is much less than those of MCGA. More specifically, the standard deviations of primer numbers reduced by LTH and DSH in the 30 repetitions are 417.16 and 1163.67, respectively. Meanwhile, MCGA is only 26.2. The experimental results indicate that our MCGA approach derives much more reliable solutions than the other two methods do.

Furthermore, Table II shows that the standard deviation of reduced primer number in parentheses seems to be increasing as the data set increases. There are some exceptions such as HV of LTH and MTR of DSH because of the instable solution quality may cause the result. Based on the observation of the standard deviation of solution quality, MCGA has the best solution stability and solution quality in large datasets

5 Conclusion and Future Work

In this paper, we formulated the multiple-use PCR primer design problem for multiplex PCR experiments, and proposed the MCGA approach to solve it with good solution quality and feasible calculation time. We demonstrated MCGA's superiority towards previous heuristic method in reducing the primers needed for PCR experiments of four species. In the experiments, MCGA shows its ability in achieving good and stable reduction of needed primers even in large datasets. The reasons why MCGA performs better may be uniquely due to its generation from the local optima that was often not considered in most heuristic cases.

As in the case of multiple-use PCR primer design, GAs incorporating powerful heuristic methods as the local search mechanisms may offer an adequate way for detecting pathogens causing similar syndrome in the same time. For instance, the multiple-use primers may be designed to simultaneously detect respective *SARS* virus, *Flu* virus, and even the common cold virus in a clinical task-oriented set of target sequences.

In the future, we proceed to combine better heuristic method and genetic algorithms to design multiple-use PCR primers with optimal solution quality and feasible computation time. Our recent work on establishing a better heuristic method may focus on more biological characteristics in order to directly preselect the qualified candidates for subsequent optimization. For the optimal solution quality, we pursue to develop more efficient selection and adaptation rules in GAs. Furthermore, our goal is to develop a user-friendly tool for biologists to design multiple-use PCR primers and develop applications on detecting task-oriented pathogen sets.

Designing Multiple-Use Primer Set for Multiplex PCR by Using Compact GAs

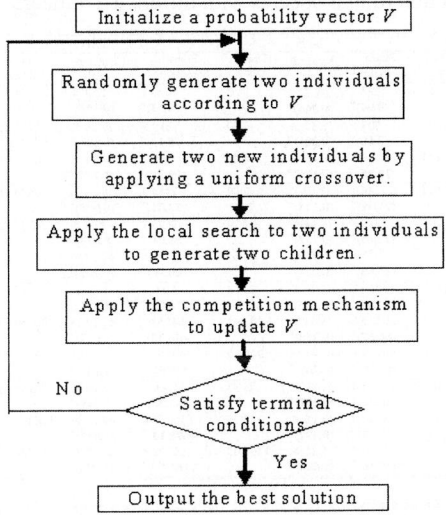

Fig. 3. Overview of the proposed genetic algorithm.

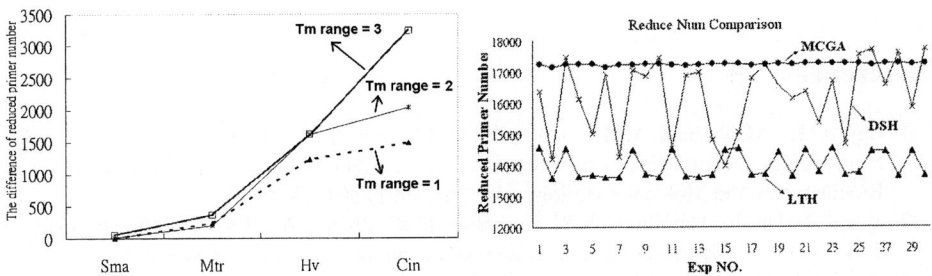

Fig. 4. The difference in the number of reduced primers between MCGA and LTH. The size increasing order of the 4 datasets are from SMA to CIN.

Fig 5. Comparison of reduced primer numbers between LTH, DSH and MCGA at Ciona intestinalis (CIN) in 30 repeated experiments.

Table 1. Summarized results averaged for data sets of same size and density.

Problem	BeCh Dev.	BeCh Time	CFT Dev.	CFT Time	IGA Dev.	IGA Time	LTH Dev.	LTH Time	DSH Dev.	DSH Time	MCGA Dev.	MCGA Time
4	0.00	163.00	0	6.50	0.00	93.30	0.00	3.11	0	28.10	0	44.59
5	0.09	540.20	0	3.20	0.00	61.20	0.00	1.11	0	13.10	0	28.98
6	0.00	57.20	0	9.40	0.00	7.60	0.00	2.25	0	36.33	0	3.52
A	0.00	149.40	0	106.60	0.00	81.00	5.56	27.36	0	466.44	0	38.37
B	0.00	155.40	0	7.40	0.00	30.40	5.53	2.34	0	33.77	0	15.07
C	0.00	199.20	0	66.00	0.00	82.80	3.56	12.00	0	279.38	0	37.13
D	0.00	230.40	0	17.20	0.32	69.00	4.47	5.49	0	76.67	0	30.27
E	0.00	8724.20	0	118.20	0.00	56.00	6.31	28.55	0	499.73	0	25.87
F	0.00	2764.80	0	109.00	0.00	142.80	10.01	10.49	0	452.84	0	67.47
G	0.13	12851.40	0	504.80	0.13	342.80	4.72	62.34	0	2299.68	0	152.04
Overall	0.02%	2583.52	0%	94.83	0.05%	96.69	4.02%	15.50	0%	418.60	0%	44.33

Table 2. Primer reduction in four species with different Tm range. (Primer length = 12).

Species[a]	Input Properties			LTH			DSH			MCGA		
	Tm	Amplified Genes[b]	Primer Pair Candidates[c]	Primer Reduction[d]	Reduced[e] Rate	Time (Sec.)	Primer Reduction	Reduced[e] Rate	Time (Sec.)	Primer Reduction	Reduced[e] Rate	Time (Sec.)
SMA[a]	39-41	706	83,915	193.5 (0.94)*	13.7% (0.066)*	0.53	196.2 (2.13)*	13.9% (0.151)*	637.74	196.1 (1.70)*	13.89% (0.120)*	55.50
	38-42	785	403,092	308.5 (3.16)*	19.65% (0.201)*	0.80	319.9 (5.11)*	20.38% (0.325)*	1875.26	319.9 (3.01)*	20.38% (0.192)*	135.50
	37-43	817	1,015,285	340.7 (19.28)*	20.85% (0.176)*	8.03	407.2 (19.23)*	24.92% (1.180)*	30151.11	398.1 (3.26)*	24.36% (0.200)*	1824.70
MTR[a]	39-41	3937	313,744	2534.7 (11.31)*	32.19% (0.144)*	2.00	2854.3 (73.64)*	36.25% (0.935)*	6676.01	2771.9 (5.32)*	35.2% (0.068)*	359.19
	38-42	4305	1,471,105	3229.7 (22.16)*	37.51% (0.257)*	7.14	3495.9 (58.01)*	40.6% (0.674)*	28743.73	3428.9 (7.38)*	39.83% (0.086)*	1373.17
	37-43	4466	3,711,383	3448.6 (25.62)*	38.61% (0.287)*	18.52	3771.4 (100.18)*	42.22% (1.122)*	74549.02	3815.6 (10.81)*	42.72% (0.121)*	3121.42
HV[a]	39-41	10796	3,370,774	11712.8 (61.85)*	54.25% (0.286)*	38.18	13360.4 (374.23)*	61.88% (1.733)*	45317.04	12942.5 (13.09)*	59.94% (0.061)*	1711.25
	38-42	10982	15,171,875	12855.1 (56.62)*	58.53% (0.258)*	153.41	14742.2 (435.23)*	67.12% (1.982)*	108060.02	14470.5 (15.79)*	65.88% (0.072)*	3922.50
	37-43	11180	36,571,728	14155.1 (59.79)*	63.31% (0.267)*	1069.92	16055.37 (477.83)*	71.8% (2.137)*	227001.40	15778.5 (16.10)*	70.57% (0.072)*	7294.19
CIN[a]	39-41	11690	4,202,249	11973.4 (48.36)*	51.21% (0.207)*	45.38	13360.3 (432.36)*	57.14% (1.849)*	75286.80	13459.0 (17.06)*	57.57% (0.073)*	2213.37
	38-42	12260	19,965,597	13034.0 (120.57)*	53.16% (0.492)*	177.30	15881.4 (698.13)*	64.77% (2.847)*	186067.80	15071.6 (24.56)*	61.47% (0.100)*	5103.37
	37-43	12669	48,507,108	13990.0 (417.16)*	55.21% (1.646)*	1765.03	16212.4 (1163.67)*	63.98% (4.593)*	467867.35	17229.5 (26.20)*	68.0% (0.103)*	12532.50

Note:
a. The data set of four respective species: Schistosoma mansoni, SMA; Medicago truncatula, MTR; Hordeum vulgare, HV; and Ciona intestinalis, CIN.
b. the gene can be amplified with appropriate primer pair.
c. the number of primer pair candidates which were generated by Primer3.
d. the mean value of primer's reduced number in 30 repetitions.
e. the mean value of primer's reduced rate in 30 repetitions.
*. the standard deviation of 30 repetitions.

References

1. Bej, A. K., Mahbubani, M. H., and Atlas, R. M.: Amplification of nucleic acids by polymerase chain reaction (PCR) and other methods and their applications. Critical Reviews in Biochemistry and Molecular Biology, vol. 26. (1991) 301-334.
2. Wang, J., Hu, L., Hamilton, S.R., Coombes, K.R., Zhang, W.: RNA amplification strategies for cDNA microarray experiments. BioTechniques, Vol. 34. (2003) 394-400.
3. Wenijn, S., Siyang, S., Minnan, L., and Guangming L.: Multiplex polymerase chain reaction/membrane hybridization assay for detection of genetically modified organisms. J. Bio-technology, Vol. 105(3). (2003) 227-233.
4. Chamberlain, J.S., Gibbs, R.A., Ranier, J.E., Nguyen, P.N., and Caskey, C.T.: Deletion screening of the duchenne muscular dystrophy locus via multiplex DNA amplification. Nucleic Acids Research, Vol. 16. (1988) 11141-11156.
5. Mitsuhashi, M., Cooper, A., Ogura, M., Shinagawa, T., Yano, K., and Hosokawa, T.: Oligonucleotide probe design – a new approach. Nature, Vol. 367. (1994) 759-761.
6. Lowe, T., Sharefkin, J., Yan, S.Q., and Dieffenbach, C.W.: A computer program for selection of oligonucleotide primers for polymerase chain reactions. Nucleic Acids Research, Vol. 18. (1990) 1757-1761.
7. Rozen, S. and Skaletsky, H.J.:
http://www-genome.wi.mit.edu/genome_software/other/primer3.html.
8. Welsh, J., McClelland, M.: Fingerprinting genomes using PCR with arbitrary primers. Nucleic Acids Research, Vol. 18. (1990) 7213-7218.
9. Rohan J., F., and Steven S. S.: Microarray synthesis through multiple-use PCR primer design. Bioinformatics, Vol.18. (2002) S128-S135.

10. William, R.P., Gabriel, R., Dallas E.W., Tongtong, Z.: On the primer selection problem in polymerase chain reaction experiments. Discrete Applied Mathematics, Vol. 71. Issue 1-3 (1996) 231-246.
11. Srinivas, N., Deb, K.: Multi-Objective function optimization using non-dominated sorting genetic algorithms. Evolutionary Computation, Vol. 2. (1995) 221-248.
12. Jayalakshmi, G.A., Sathiamoorthy, S., Rajaram, R.: A HYBRID GENETIC ALGORITHM – A NEW APPROACH TO SOLVE TRAVELING SALESMAN PROBLEM. International Journal of Computational Engineering Science, Vol. 2. (2001) p339-355.
13. Aickelin, U.: An indirect genetic algorithm for set covering problems. Journal of Operational Research Society, Vol. 50(10). (2002) 1118-1126.
14. Harik, G.R., Lobo, F.G., Goldberg, D.E.: The compact genetic algorithm. IEEE Transactions on Evolutionary Computation, Vol. 3, (1999) 287-297.
15. Garey, M., Johnson, D.: Computers and Intractability: A guide to the theory of NP-completeness. W. H. Freeman, San Francisco, (1979).
16. Gonzalez, B., Hector, Latombe, Jean, C.: A randomized art-gallery algorithm for sensor placement. Proc. of the 17th annual symposium on Computational Geometry, (2002).
17. Karp, R.M.: Mapping the genome: some combinatorial problems arising in molecular biology. Proceedings of the 25th annual ACM symposium on Theory of Computing, (1993).
18. Caprara, A., Fischetti, M., Toth, P.: A heuristic method for the set covering problem. Operations Research, Vol. 47, (1999) 730-743.
19. Caprara, A., Fischetti, M., Toth, P.: Algorithms for the set covering problem. working paper, DEIS. University of Bologna, Italy. (1999)
20. Srinivas, M., Patnaik, L.M.: Genetic algorithms: A survey. Computer Journal, Vol. 27, (1994) 17-26.
21. Beasley, J.: OR-library: distributing test problems by electronic mail. Journal of the Operational Research Society, Vol. 41, (1990) 1069-1072.
22. Beasley, J., Chu, P.: A genetic algorithm for the set covering problem. European Journal of Operational Research, Vol. 94, (1996) 392-404.

Robust Inferential Sensors Based on Ensemble of Predictors Generated by Genetic Programming

Elsa Jordaan[1], Arthur Kordon[2], Leo Chiang[2], and Guido Smits[1]

[1] Dow Benelux B.V., Terneuzen, The Netherlands
{EMJordaan,GFSmits}@dow.com
[2] Dow Chemical, Freeport(TX), USA
{AKKordon,HChiang}@dow.com

Abstract. Inferential sensors are mathematical models used to predict the quality variables of industrial processes. One factor limiting the widespread use of soft sensors in the process industry is their inability to cope with non-constant noise in the data and process variability. A novel approach for inferential sensors design with increased robustness is proposed in the paper. It is based on three techniques. The first technique increases robustness by using explicit non-linear functions derived by Genetic Programming. The second technique applies multi-objective model selection on a Pareto-front to guarantee the right balance between accuracy and complexity. The third technique uses ensembles of predictors for more consistent estimates and possible self-assessment capabilities. The increased robustness of the proposed sensor is demonstrated on a number of industrial applications.

1 Introduction

Inferential or soft sensors are mathematical models used to predict the outcome of processes. These sensors are often needed because online measurements of the outcome of the processes can not be made with ease or are very costly. There are thousands of industrial applications of soft sensors from several vendors like Pavilion Technology, Aspen Technology, Gensym Corporation, etc. However, one factor limiting the widespread use of soft sensors in the process industry is the inability of these sensors to cope with non-constant noise in the data and processes variability. The existing soft sensors are mostly based on back propagation neural networks and have limited capabilities for improved robustness toward process changes. As a result, there is a necessity of frequent re-training which increased maintenance cost and gradually decreased performance and credibility [10].

There are a number of steps that can be taken to improve the robustness of soft sensors. One way is to use explicit nonlinear functions that are derived by Genetic Programming (GP) [8]. A major advantage of this approach is that there is a potential physical interpretation of the model. Other advantages are ability to examine the extrapolation behavior of the model and to impose external constraints on the modeling process. Furthermore, process engineers are more open to take the risk of implementing such type of models. The applicability of symbolic-regression-based soft sensors has already been demonstrated in several industrial applications of continuous processes [1],

[2], [3], and recently - in a batch process [11]. However, in this first approach there is one open issue that influences the robustness toward process changes, namely the control of the model complexity. It is well-known from Statistical Learning Theory, that to construct a model with the best generalization ability one needs to find the optimal complexity for the available data. Here the complexity can be quantified using the Vapnik-Chervonenkis (VC) dimension [5]. Unfortunately, direct application of these theoretical results to GP-based model faces difficulties. In a second approach the idea of balancing the modeling performance and complexity is used to increase the robustness. This approach uses the Pareto-front to find the best trade-off between the model's performance and its complexity [9]. The third approach that could improve robustness toward process changes is to use an ensemble of predictors. The key idea is to use combined predictors and their statistics as a confidence indicator of soft sensor's performance. Most of the literature in this area is based on the use of Neural Networks as individual predictors [4].

In this the paper we will demonstrate how ensembles of GP-based predictors are used to improve the robustness of the soft sensors. In the following section the issues of the soft sensor design of an ensemble of GP-based predictors with optimal performance-complexity properties are discussed. The proposed approach is illustrated in the third section with successful industrial applications in continuous and batch processes. In the final section, concluding remarks about the results presented in this paper are given.

2 Ensemble of GP-Generated Predictors in Soft Sensors

The section describes the nature of GP-based models and focuses on the novel model procedure for selecting the models on the Pareto-front of the performance-complexity plane. Thus, the ensemble is based on predictors with the best generalization capabilities and potential for robust performance in industrial conditions.

2.1 Genetic Programming

One modeling approach that is increasingly being used in the industry is Genetic Programming (GP). GP is of special interest to soft sensor development due to its capability for symbolic regression [8]. GP-generated symbolic regression is a result of simulation of the natural evolution of numerous potential mathematical expressions. The final results is a list of "the best and the brightest" analytical forms according to the selecting objective function. Of special importance to industry are the following unique features of GP [1]:

- no *a priori* modeling assumptions
- derivative-free optimization
- few design parameters
- natural selection of the most important process inputs
- parsimonious analytical functions as a final result.

The last feature has a double benefit. On one side, a simple soft sensor often has a potential for better generalization capability, increased robustness, and needs less frequent re-training. On the other side, process engineers and developers prefer to use non-black box empirical models and are much more open to take the risk to implement soft sensors based on functional relationships. An additional advantage is the low implementation cost of such type of soft sensors. It can be applied directly into the existing Distributed Control Systems (DCS) avoiding additional specialized software packages, typical for neural net-based soft sensors.

At the same time there are still significant challenges in implementing industrial soft sensors generated by GP: function generation with noisy industrial data, dealing with time delays, sensitivity analysis of large data sets, to name a few. Of special importance is the main drawback of GP - the slow speed of model development due to the inherent high computational requirements of this method. For real industrial applications the calculation time is in the order of several hours, even with the current high-end PCs.

2.2 Ensembles of GP Generated Predictors

Ensembles consist of several models that are used to predict future measurements. For a given input the final prediction is the average of the predictions of all the models in the ensemble. There are a number of advantages to use ensembles of predictors instead of a single model, which all relate to the robustness requirements.

Firstly, since the prediction is a combination of a number of predictions, one obtains a more consistent estimate of the output. The soft sensor is more robust as the predicted outcome does not depend on the accuracy of one single model anymore, but on the outcome of several models.

Secondly, the spread or variance of the different predictions can be used to derive a measure of confidence, called the model disagreement indicator. The idea is that in areas of high data density the models in the ensemble will have the same behavior because there were enough information available during training to force all models through the mean of the data in that region. However, in areas of low data density the various models will have more freedom and therefore exhibit different behavior. A small difference in behavior gives the operators more certainty about the soft sensor's prediction.

A third advantage is that the model disagreement indicator can be used for problem detection. Here the idea is that whenever something has changed in the process the models in the ensemble will show a high variance in their predictions where under normal circumstances the variance was much lower. This way drifting processes, faulty equipment or novelty can be detected easily.

Another advantage of an ensembles is that it enables redundancy. Since soft sensors are mainly used in processing conditions it often occurs that one or more of the instruments measuring the input variables can fail. If the ensemble consists of models that depend on different input variables, there will be at least one model available than can predict in the absence of a certain input variable. This prediction may not be the most accurate one, but at least there is a prediction instead of nothing. The soft sensor can be made robust toward the failure of equipment measuring the input variables.

There are several methods to design an ensemble of predictors [4], [12], [13],[16], [17], [18]. The key issue is that one should be careful not to use models in the ensemble that are too similar in performance, because then a false sense of trust can be created as the standard deviation will be very small. On the other hand, the models should not be too different in performance, because then the predictive power of the soft sensor will be lost. Ideally, the selected models are diverse enough to capture uncertainties, but similar enough to predict well.

Designing such a robust ensemble can be very difficult, even for an experienced soft sensor developer. Utilizing the Pareto-front, robust ensembles can be constructed with much more ease and objectivity.

2.3 Pareto-Front Method for Ensemble Model Selection

Several thousand empirical models are generated in a typical GP run with at least 20 simulated evolutionary processes of 200 generations. Most of the generated models have similar performance and proper model selection is non-trivial. The direct approach is to use the R^2-statistic as model selection criterion and to select the "best" model based on the fitness measure at the end of the run. However, the fitness measure does not take complexity or smoothness of the function into account. Furthermore, it is possible that for a slight decrease in the measure a far less complex function may be obtained that may have higher robustness. For this the experience of the analyst is needed. Therefore it is necessary to extract a manageable number of models to inspect.

In order to find the right trade-off between complexity and accuracy, the Pareto-front is constructed. The Pareto-front is a concept commonly used in multi-objective optimization [6]. In multi-objective optimization, apart from the solution space, which is constructed by the constraints in terms of the input variables, there is also an objective space. The objective space is a mapping of the solution space onto the objectives. In classical multi-objective optimization, the problem is cast into a single objective optimization problem by defining an *a priori* weighted sum. The solution to the single objective optimization problem is one point in the objective space. The Pareto-front represents a surface in the objective space of all possible weighted combinations of the different objectives that optimally satisfy the constraints.

Since the model selection task is in principle a multi-objective problem (i.e. accuracy vs. complexity), the fundamentals of the Pareto-front can be applied. Using the Pareto-front for GP-generated models has many advantages [7]. Firstly, the structural risk minimization principle [5] can be easily applied to GP-generated models. Fig. 1 shows how the structural risk minimization is used in finding the optimal model through balancing the complexity and accuracy. Currently in GP the measure that is used for the complexity is the number of nodes needed to define the model.

A second advantage is that the Pareto-front effectively displays the trade-off between the measures, which enables the analyst to make an unbiased decision. The Pareto-front models are models for which no improvement on one objective can be obtained without deteriorating another objective. The optimal model will therefore lie somewhere on the Pareto-front. Its position will depend on the problem at hand. Typically, the most interesting models would lie in the lower left corner of the Pareto-front.

The third advantage is that the number of models that needs to be inspected individually is decreased tremendously as only a small fraction of the generated models in GP will end up on the Pareto-front. This is clearly seen in Fig. 1. Although in total there are 88 models depicted in the figure, only 18 of them lie on the Pareto-front. Furthermore, as none of the models with a ratio of nodes higher than 0.3 significantly improve on the R^2, these may by omitted too.

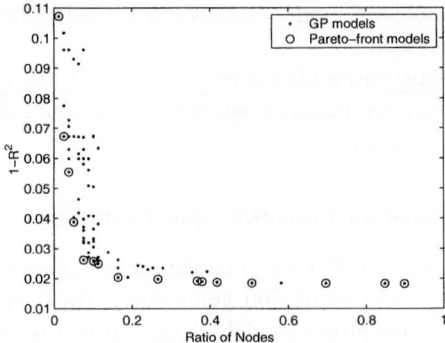

Fig. 1. Pareto-front based on the performance of the training data.

Finally, additional considerations such as diversity in input variables used for ensemble construction can be taken into account. For example, if a Pareto-optimal model uses an undesirable transformation or input variable, one could look for an alternative model among the models close to the Pareto-front. It is also possible to perform model selection in an interactive way such that the analyst can request a model's functional form, error statistics, and response surface by clicking on the particular model depicted in the figure.

3 Applications

The described methodology for designing robust soft sensors based on an ensemble of GP-type predictors will be illustrated with two industrial applications of a different nature. The symbolic regression-type models used in these applications have been derived on a GP toolbox in MATLAB that was developed internally in The Dow Chemical Company. For both these applications several GP-runs were made with different parameter setting. The parameters that were varied are the number of generations, population size, parsimony pressure and fitness measure.

3.1 Ensemble of GP-Based Predictors for a Continuous Process

For better control of a distillation column, it is desirable to obtain an accurate and fast prediction of a process quality variable (in this case - propylene concentration). Current analytical technique allows measurement of propylene every 10 minutes, which is not sufficient for control purposes. The problem has been resolved by an soft sensor, developed by the described approach that can provide minute prediction of propylene.

The soft sensor was developed by training data contained 1300 data points with 23 process variables as candidate inputs to the symbolic regression models. The training data set was selected to cover the normal range of operation. One of the specific requirements of the design was to test the self-assessment capability of the soft sensor toward expected process changes. That is why the selected testing data set included 1250 data points with some process variables slightly outside the training range. Additional requirements were to have model predictions even in case of input measurement faults and to detect drifts in the output analytical instrument.

Using the approach described in the previous section, an ensemble of GP-models was constructed. The following three nonlinear models have been selected for the ensemble:

$$f_1 = 5.44e^{-4} + 1.18e^{-12}\frac{x_{21}^3 x_8^2}{x_4} \tag{1}$$

$$f_2 = -0.216 + 6.96e^{-7}\frac{x_6^3 x_8^2}{x_4^2} \tag{2}$$

$$f_3 = 0.0193 + 8.90e^{-6}\frac{x_6^2 x_{21}^2 x_8^4}{x_4^3 x_{18}^2} \tag{3}$$

As illustrated in the top graph of Fig. 2, the ensemble model performs well for the testing data ($R^2 = 0.985$; $RMSEP = 0.0791$). This performance is well above the requirement for implementing the soft sensor on-line. The model disagreement indicator is the standard deviation of the three models and a critical limit was defined to quantify the effect. The critical limit is equal to the average plus three times the standard deviation of the model disagreement indicator in the training data. A large model disagreement indicator means that individual models do not agree with each other and that the process conditions have deviated from the training set conditions. For this testing data, model disagreement indicators are below the critical limit for most of the data points. This suggests that the testing data and training data are similar and that the prediction is reliable.

The self-assessment capability of the ensemble is illustrated in the lower plot in Fig. 2, where the key inputs (inputs of the selected models) are increased by 15% in the testing data. The model disagreement indicator is now above the critical limit, which

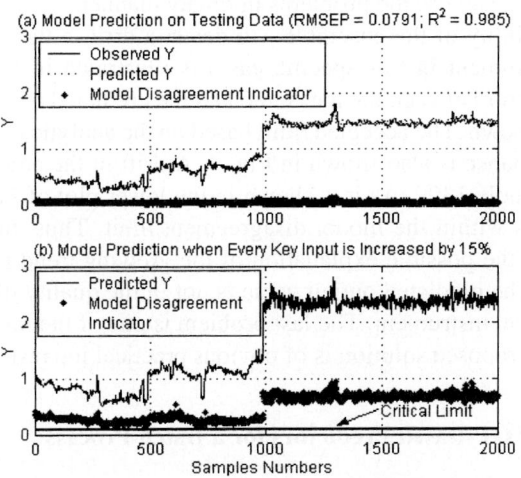

Fig. 2. Performance of the ensemble on the test data with normal and disturbed process conditions.

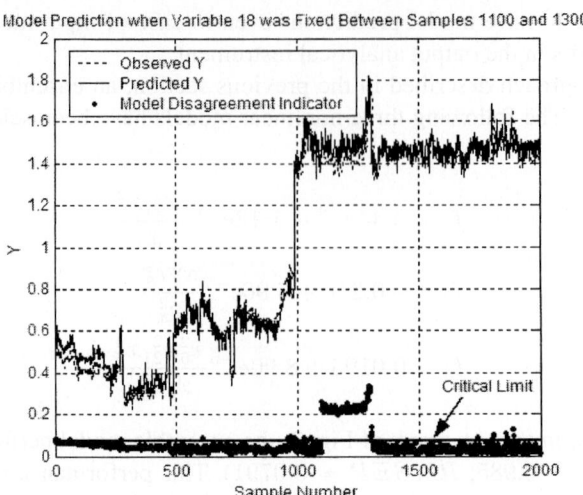

Fig. 3. Performance of the ensemble in the presence of measurement fault.

means that the simulated testing data are now outside the training range. The simulated abnormal process condition has been captured reliably by the model disagreement indicator. This self-assessment capability allows the definition of supervisory protective logic around the soft sensor that can guard process operators from model estimation outside the accepted range, defined by the critical limit.

To test the ensemble robustness in the presence of bad measurements, variable 18 was fixed between samples 1100 to 1300 in Fig. 3. Because x_{18} was used f_3, but not in f_1 and f_2, the median of the three models (which is the predicted Y in Fig. 3) was able to give a robust estimate of the true measurement. Note that the model disagreement indicator specifies abnormal process conditions during this period. This information allows operators to diagnose the problems in timely manner.

The third capability of the ensemble - to detect a drift in the output measurement (an analytical instrument in this specific case) is illustrated in Fig. 4. On the upper plot of Fig. 4 the error between the measured and the predicted output value (propylene concentration) is shown. The accepted limit based on the analytical instrument accuracy and model performance is also shown in Fig. 4. A drift in the analytical instrument is simulated after sample 1300. As it is shown in the lower plot of Fig. 4, the ensemble-based prediction is within the model disagreement limit. Thus, the model prediction is trustworthy and the possible explanation of the growing trend in the error between the measured and the predicted output value is not in the quality of the model but in a drift in the analytical instrument. The last problem is one of the most difficult for early detection and the proposed solution is of obvious practical interest.

3.2 Ensemble of GP-Based Predictors for a Batch Process

Biomass monitoring is fundamental to tracking cell growth and performance in bacterial fermentation processes [14]. Usually the biomass concentrations are determined off-

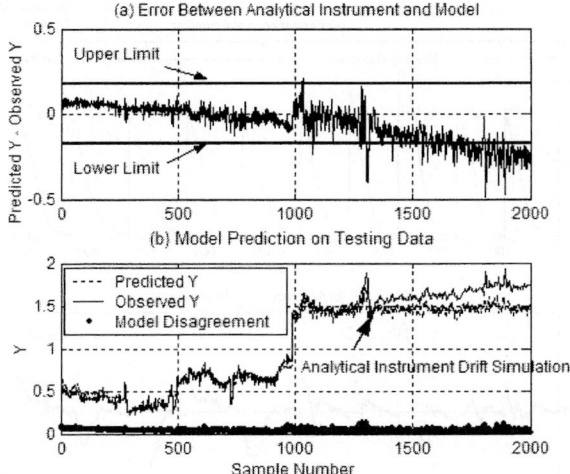

Fig. 4. Analytical instrument drift detection by the ensemble.

line by lab analysis every 2-4 hours. This low measurement frequency, however, can lead to poor control and on-line estimates are needed. Several neural networks-based soft sensors have been implemented since the early 90s [15]. Unfortunately, due to the batch-to-batch variations, it is difficult for a single neural network-based soft sensor to guarantee robust predictions in the whole spectrum of potential operating conditions. As an alternative, the proposed ensemble of GP-generated predictors was developed and tested in real industrial process.

Data from 8 batches has been used for model development (training data) and the test data included 3 batches. Seven process parameters like pressure, agitation, oxygen uptake rate (OUR), carbon dioxide evolution rate (CER), etc. have been used as inputs to the model. The output was the measured optical density (OD) which is proportional to the biomass.

For the biomass soft sensor it was important that all the models have similar performance on both the training and test data. An ensemble of 5 models was constructed using the Pareto-front approach (a detailed description of the design is given in [11]). The accuracy requirements for the ensemble were to predict OD within 15% of the observed OD-level at the end of the growth phase. The performance of the ensemble on the training data used by GP can be seen in Fig. 5. For the training data one sees that for three batches (B_3, B_4 and B_8), the ensemble predicts outside the required accuracy. For batch B_3 it was known that the run was not consistent with the rest of the batches. However, this batch was added in order to increase the range of operating conditions captured in the training set. We see that the performance of the ensemble at the end of the run for all the batches of the test data is within the required error bound.

4 Conclusions

In this paper we have shown a novel approach to improve the robustness of soft sensors. This approach involves the use of GP-generated models in an ensemble of predictors.

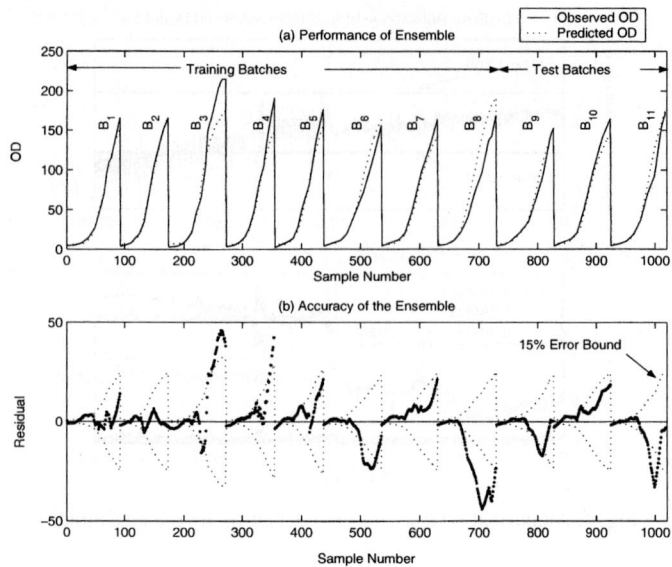

Fig. 5. Performance of the ensemble on the training and test data.

We have described a mechanism which is based on the Pareto-front to effectively construct ensemble. This mechanism enables us to compare the models produced by the various GP runs qualitatively through a performance-complexity trade-off. Furthermore, the number of interesting models to inspect manually is decreased to a manageable number.

The approach was successfully implemented on both continuous and batch processes. For the case of the continuous process, we have also shown how the model disagreement indicator can be effectively used to detect measurement faults and instrument drifting.

Finally, a number of open issues for further research still exist. For one, the way that the complexity of the GP models is defined is not optimal. The measure may be misleading for it doesn't consider the complexity of operators used. Another open issue is the optimal number of models to be used in the ensemble. Furthermore, it is not complete clear what kind of threshold to be used for constructing the ensemble. Also, the hypothesis that there is link between the model disagreement indicator and model error when it extrapolates is not proven yet.

References

1. Kordon, A., Smits, G.: Soft Sensor Development Using Genetic Programming. Proceedings of GECCO'2001, San Francisco (2001) 1346-1351
2. Kalos A., Kordon, A., Smits, G., Werkmeister, S.: Hybrid Model Development Methodology for Industrial Soft Sensors. Proceedings of the ACC'2003, Denver CO (2003) 5417-5422
3. Kordon, A.K, Smits, G.F., Jordaan, E., Rightor, E.: Robust Soft Sensors Based on Integration of Genetic Programming, Analytical Neural Networks, and Support Vector Machines: Proceedings of WCCI'2002, Honolulu (2002) 896-901

4. Sharkey, A. (ed.): Combining Neural Nets. Ensemble and Modular Multi-Net Systems. Springer, London UK (1999)
5. Vapnik, V.: Statistical Learning Theory. Wiley, New York (1998)
6. Deb K.: Multi-Objective Optimization Using Evolutionary Algorithms. Wiley, Chichester UK (2001)
7. Bleuer, S., Brack, M., Thiele, L., Zitzler, E.: Multi-Objective Genetic Programming. Reducing Bloat bt Using SPEA-2. In Proceedings of CEC 2001, (2001) 536-543
8. Koza, J.: Genetic Programming. On the Programming of Computers by Means of Natural Selection. MIT Press, Cambridge MA (1992)
9. Smits, G. and Kotanchek, M.: Pareto-Front Exploitation in Symbolic Regression. In: Riolo, R. and Worzel, B. (eds): Genetic Programming Theory and Practice. Kluwer, Boston (in press) (2004)
10. Lennox, B., Montague, G., Frith, A., Gent, C. Bevan, V.: Industrial Applications of Neural Networks - An Investigation. Journal of Process Control, 11 (2001) 497-507
11. Kordon A., Jordaan, E., Chew, L., Smits, G., Bruck, T., Haney, K., Jenings, A.: Biomass Inferential Sensor Based on Ensemble of Models Generated by Genetic Programming. Accepted for GECCO'2004, (2004)
12. Liu, Y., Yao, X., Higuchi, T.: Evolutionary Ensembles with Negative Correlation Learning. IEEE Transactions on Evolutionary Computation, 4(4) November (2000) 380-387
13. Imamura K., Soule, T., Hechendorn, R., Foster, J.: Behavior Diversity and a Probabilistically Optimal GP Ensemble. Genetic Programming and Evolvable Machines, 4 (2003) 235-253
14. Hodge D., Simon, L., Karim, M.: Data Driven Approaches to Modeling and Analysis of Bioprocesses. Some Industrial Examples. Proceedings of the ACC'2003, Denver (2003) 2062-2076
15. Cheruy A.: Software Sensors in Bioprocess Engineering. Journal of Biotechnology, 52 (1997) 193-199
16. Soule, T.: Heterogenesity and Specialization in Evolving Teams. In: Goldberg, D., Cantu-Paz, E., Parmee, I., Beyer, H.-G. (eds): Proceedings of GECCO'2000, Las Vegas (2000)
17. Brameier, M. and Banszaf, w.: Evolving Teams of Predictors with Linear Genetic Programming. Genetic Programming and Evolvable Machines, 2 (2001) 381-407
18. Iba, H.: Bagging, Boosting, and Bloating in Genetic Programming. Proceedings of GECCO'1999, (1999)

Searching Transcriptional Modules Using Evolutionary Algorithms

Je-Gun Joung[1], Sok June Oh[3], and Byoung-Tak Zhang[1,2]

[1] Biointelligence Laboratory, Graduate Program in Bioinformatics
Seoul National University, Seoul 151-742, Korea
Phone: +82-2-880-5890, Fax: +82-2-883-9120
{jgjoung,btzhang}@bi.snu.ac.kr
[2] School of Computer Science and Engineering,
Seoul National University, Seoul 151-742, Korea
[3] Department of Pharmacology, College of Medicine,
Inje University, Busan 614-735, Korea
juno@bi.snu.ac.kr

Abstract. The mechanism of gene regulation has been studied intensely for decades. It is important to identify synergistic transcriptional motifs. Its search space is so large that an efficient computational method is required. In this paper, we present the method that can search automatically both transcriptional motif list and gene expression profiles for synergistic motif combinations. It uses evolutionary algorithms to find an optimal solution for the problems which have the huge search space. Our approach includes the additional evolutionary operator performing local search to improve searching ability. Our method was applied to four *Saccharomyces cerevisiae* gene expression datasets. The result shows that genes containing synergistic motif combination from our optimization technique are highly correlated than those from k-means clustering. In cell cycle as well as other expression datasets, our results generally coincide with the previous experimental results.

1 Introduction

One of the great challenges in the post-genome era is to understand gene regulation on a genomic scale. The availability of complete genome sequences and large-scale gene expression data of many species has opened up new possibilities of understanding gene regulatory mechanisms. From this point of view, functional combination of transcription factor binding sites (TFBS) is an essential part to understanding gene regulations and a variety of computational techniques will play a key role in generating hypotheses for further study of regulatory mechanisms.

Transcriptional regulation in eukaryotes depends on the activities of hundreds of sequence specific DNA binding proteins known as transcription factors (TFs). In other words, complex expression patterns are mediated by a combination of transcription factors which bind to *cis*-regulatory regions. Each TF recognizes a specific site in the promoter region that is a unique family of short sequence elements, usually from 5 to 15 base pairs in length. Although the number of transcriptional factors are limited, the combinatorial transcriptional control makes it possible to regulate genes in response to a variety of signals from the environment.

There have been several works which identify regulatory elements by using microarray data [1][2][3]. These approaches take the following procedure. First, gene expression data is clustered to look for the co-expressed gene group. Then a motif finding algorithm scans shared patterns over the sequences. It is based on the underlying hypothesis that co-expression of genes implies common regulatory mechanism. Pilpel *et al.* [4] attempted to identify synergistic motif combinations that control gene expression patterns in *Saccharomyces cerevisiae*. Their result was obtained through exhaustive computing of expression coherence for genes containing each motif pair. Currently, one of more systemic approaches is generating of probabilistic frameworks integrated by the models of Segal *et al.* [5]. Further, there are several approaches that apply machine learning techniques such as self-organizing maps (SOM), associative clustering (AC) to this problem [6][7]. If we define this problem as an optimization problem, EAs is one of the most appropriate methods for solving it.

In this paper, our goal is to search motif combinations that importantly participate in several regulatory processes of conditions, including the cell cycle. We introduce a technique searching potential transcriptional motif combinations that affect a regulation in several experimental conditions. Our method corresponds to a searching technique through optimum search algorithms based on the mechanism of natural selection in a population and incorporating local search [8]. Here, each individual in the population represents a set of possible motif indexes in the upstream region of a gene. The fitness measure is based on the clustering for gene expression profiles containing common motifs.

For transcriptional motifs, we used the dataset of known and putative transcription regulatory motifs identified by applying motif finding algorithm in each gene of the *Saccharomyces cerevisiae* [4]. We evaluated on four expression profile datasets including cell cycle and protein interactions extracted from MIPS protein complex database [9]. Our results were compared with k-means clustering of measuring coherent motifs in four expression datasets. Also, we examined whether the algorithm recovers previous known synergistic motifs from four expression datasets.

2 Methods

The main point in search problem for motif combination is to find several motif sets correlated in different expression patterns over total expression space. Our approach is designed to perform both searching motif combinations and clustering gene expression profiles.

Let G be a gene set for the analysis. G consists of $\{g^1, g^2 \ldots, g^N\}$ with total number of genes, N. g^i given by i-th gene has the set of motif indexes, g^i_M

and the expression profile, $v(g^i)$. Here g_M^i consists of $\{m_1^i, m_2^i, \ldots, m_z^i\}$ that is a subset of total motif index set. z is the size of motif indexes for each gene and has variable size. For each gene, the set of motif indexes has different combination and there is the set of common motif indexes for several genes which is M. Let g_M be genes with this set of motif indexes. The algorithm finds best K motif combinations that make diverse gene clusters over expression profiles.

2.1 Individual Representation

Given the number of clusters K, each individual is represented as the set of strings, $S = \{s_1, s_2, \ldots, s_K\}$. Here i-th string s_i is represented as $[l, m_1, m_2, \ldots, m_{q_{max}}]$. Each m is the index of motif picked from total motif indexes. l is the size of actual motifs so that only motif combination is considered from m_1 to m_l and the rest are not used to measure fitness. At initial generation, each m is randomly selected from motif list. This representation provides motif combination with variable size. The size l is converged by evolutionary procedure. For K cluster, there are $l_1, l_2, \ldots, l_K$ and let L be a set of them. The motif combination used to measure fitness is $M = \{m_1, m_2, \ldots, m_l\}$. Given the number of clusters K, the aim of learning is to find a set of optimal motif combinations, $\mathcal{M}^* = \{M_1, \ldots, M_K\}^{best}$.

2.2 Algorithm Overview

The individual represents a set of motif combinations and it is a possible solution of motif combinations. These solutions are fitted as the generation goes. At the last generation, the best motif combinations are selected and it is verified with other resource such as protein complexes. Figure 1 presents the summary of algorithm for searching synergistic motif combination.

An initial population is randomly created by the population size Pop. Each individual I_i in the population is then evaluated using the fitness function for motif combinations $\mathcal{M}_i$. Then, selection is performed by randomly choosing a pair of individuals from the mating pool. Our selection strategy is roulette wheel selection (RWS) that is based on probabilistic selection [10]. After selection, crossover operation is performed with probability p_c. Two offsprings are produced through the exchange of genetic information between the two parent strings. In this paper, crossover operator creates two new individuals through swapping all strings with the randomly-chosen crossover point. It can be defined as $[s_1^a, s_2^a, \ldots, s_K^a] \times [s_1^b, s_2^b, \ldots, s_K^b]$. Mutation operators were performed by choosing a mutation point with a low probability. They flipped the bit at that point for the actual motif size. Then hill-climbing search is performed for motif indexes. The above steps are repeated until a termination condition is reached. Otherwise, it stops if the number of generations reaches maximum generation.

2.3 Fitness Function

The fitness of each individual is defined by

$$Fitness = \alpha EC + S. \tag{1}$$

Procedure TranscriptionalModuleSearching(*K*, *Pop*)
K: number of clusters
Pop: size of population
begin
   Initialize population: $I_1, \ldots, I_{Pop}$.
   for motif combinations $\mathcal{M}_i$ of each individual I_i **do**
      fitness evaluation
   end
   $t := 0$
   while (not termination condition) **do**
      for $i := 1$ **to** #*recombinations* **do**
         Select two parents I^a, I^b randomly
         Crossover motif combination sets S^a, S^b
         Add offsprings $I^{a'}$, $I^{b'}$ to next population
      end
      for $i := 1$ **to** #*mutation* **do**
         Select an offspring I^c randomly
         Mutate size of actual motif L^c
         Local search for motif combinations $\mathcal{M}^c$
      end
      $t := t+1$
end

Fig. 1. Summary of the algorithm.

EC (expression coherence) represents how well the related genes are clustered in expression space and *S* (separation) explains how several groups are separated each other. In other words, the fitness induces clustering of genes in expression space. Here α is a parameter to control trade-off of two terms. If α is highly weighted, it emphasizes condensation of each gene group, otherwise it is emphasis on the separation among groups.

When M_k is the *k*-th motif combination in a certain individual of the algorithm and g_{M_k} defines the genes containing M_k, *EC* is defined as

$$EC = \frac{1}{K} \sum_{k=1}^{K} C(g_{M_k}), \qquad (2)$$

where $C(g_{M_k})$ is a mean of correlation coefficients as follows:

$$C(g_{M_k}) = \frac{1}{P} \sum_{i=1}^{J_k} \sum_{j=i+1}^{J_k} r(v(g_{M_k}^i), v(g_{M_k}^j)). \qquad (3)$$

Where r is the similarity between gene pair over expression profiles. It is measured by the Pearson correlation coefficient. $v(g_{M_k}^i)$ indicates the expression profile of *i*-th gene containing M_k. P is the total number of possible gene pairs, $(J_k^2 - J_k)/2$. J_k is the total number of genes in *k*-th group.

EC is the similarity measure among gene expression profiles in the gene group containing the motif combination. On the other hand, S is the dissimilarity measure among K groups that contain each expression profiles. S is defined as follows:

$$S = \frac{1}{P} \sum_{i=1}^{K} \sum_{j=i+1}^{K} d(\hat{v}(g_{M_i}), \hat{v}(g_{M_j})). \quad (4)$$

Where $\hat{v}(g_{M_i})$ is a mean of expression profiles of genes containing motif combination M_i and the distance d is $1 - r$.

3 Experimental Setup

Our method was applied to the following datasets. Motif dataset contains yeast motif information extracted by Pilpel [4]. This motif dataset consists of 37 known motifs and 329 putative motifs that are upstream DNA promoter motifs obtained using the AlignACE program. We generated dataset by checking an occurrence of motifs for each gene.

To verify our method, we used the result of microarray analysis of 800 ORFs involved during the yeast cell cycle [11]. This dataset was used to examine a characteristic of our method in synergistic effect of motifs. As another test for synergistic effect, algorithm was additionally applied to sporulation, heat-shock and diauxic shift expression data for over 6000 ORFs [12].

The parameter setting of algorithm is as follows. The size of individuals is 100 and the maximum generation is 200. Crossover probability p_c is 0.9 and mutation probability p_m is 0.01. In reproduction, we use elitist selection. Elitism ensures that at least one copy of the best individual in the population is always passed onto the next generation. For local search, hill-climbing was performed during 30 iteration. The maximum size of motif combination in representation, l_{max} set 5. In the fitness function, α is set to 0.8 and it is heuristic value from the repeated runs. The size of cluster K sets 5.

4 Results

First, we examined the learning effect of the algorithm from expression profiles of 800 ORFs associated with cell cycle and 37 known motifs. Figure 2 shows the result of comparison between our method and k-means clustering for expression coherence distribution. The curve represents the distribution of pair-wise correlations. The distribution for our result is strongly shifted to the right. This figure explains that the gene pair obtained by our algorithm is highly correlated in expression.

We tested correlations between genes containing motif combination from our method. k-means clustering algorithm was used as a baseline algorithm for comparison. Figure 3 shows the comparison between our method and k-means clustering for the protein interaction ratio. Our test is based on investigation of the

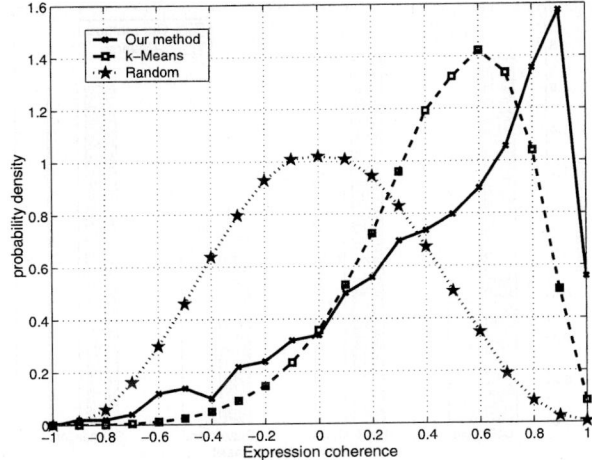

Fig. 2. The comparison between our method and k-means clustering for expression coherence distribution (k=30).

relationship between expression profiles and protein-protein interactions [13][14]. Their results showed many interactions between proteins encoded by genes in the same cluster over expression or subunit.

We define the protein interaction score as the correlation measurement of genes in the same group. The list for yeast protein interactions was extracted from MIPS protein complex database. The interaction list was extracted from 971 complex entries and the size is 92068. Protein interaction score is calculated as the difference between $PID(M)$ and $PID(R)$ as follows.

$$PI\ score = log(PID(M)/PID(R)) \qquad (5)$$

PID is protein interaction density (PID) which is the ratio of the number of observed protein interaction pairs to the total number of possible pair-wise combinations of protein pairs. According to analysis of correlation between transcriptome and interactome, clusters with a significantly higher PID tend to be tighter in expression profiles [13].

$PID(M)$ is protein interaction density in the genes containing motif combination M. $PID(R)$ is protein interaction density in random set. At k-means clustering, the number of cluster k set 30. After k-means clustering algorithm was performed, the gene set containing motif combination correlated with cluster showed lower protein interaction ratio than set from our method.

Finally we present synergistic motif combination for motif dataset in four different expression profile datasets. Figure 4 shows the result of the putative synergistic motif combinations searched by our algorithm. Motif combinations given from our method are significantly related with particular biological condition.

The result from the cell cycle data presents well known MCB and SCB motif combination as well as several combination. SBF (SCB-binding factor) and MBF

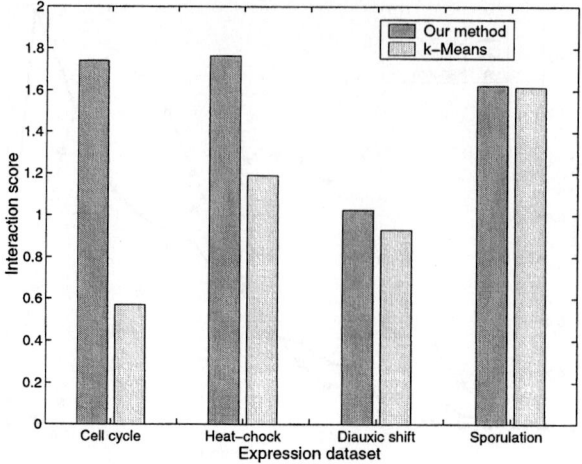

Fig. 3. The comparison between our method and k-means clustering for protein interaction score (k=30). This score indicates the measure of the correlation in specific gene group.

(MCB-binding factor) regulate genes necessary for the transition through G1/S [15]. These two are sequence-specific transcription factors and the two regulatory elements (MCB and SCB) are well known synergistic motifs. These motifs lead to combinatorial control and synergistic effects.

In the sporulation, m155 is MSE which is bound in specific transcriptional factor Ndt80 [16]. Ndt80 is strongly induced during the middle stages of the sporulation pathway. It is important to perform sporulation procedure. Moreover, MSE is related to about 150 genes through meiosis. In the heat-shock dataset, several motifs (RAP1, m301, m303, 306 and 308) are RPE (ribosomal protein element) which is negatively correlated to this condition.

5 Conclusions

We have proposed an effective method to search for the motif combination of genes that are co-regulated in the set of experiments. Our approach is based on the evolutionary algorithm known to be highly effective for several combinatorial optimization problems. It is designed to perform both searching motif combinations and clustering gene expression profiles. Through clustering, our method prevents the generation of similar motif combinations.

Our results show that the method can find several significant motif combinations from highly coherent gene expressions. Genes with motif combination found by our approach were highly correlated than those which are obtained by previous approach. Consequently, the comparison for coherence supports that the searching result has high confidence for finding synergistic motif combinations. Our approach can be used to study the regulatory mechanism at the genome level.

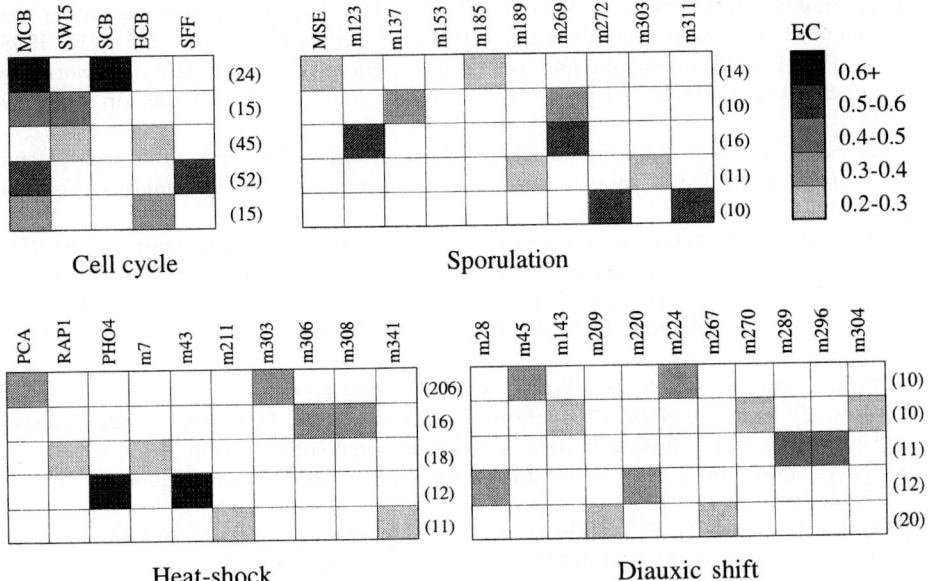

Fig. 4. The putative synergistic motif combinations in several conditions. In each grid, a gray square indicates that particular motif is present in gene set. In top of the grid, motifs are listed and the value on the right side shows the number of genes in each cluster.

As the future works, we consider that the method is improved in several parts. Our searching strategy will be tested by the diverse local searches such as simulated annealing. Also, we consider a co-evolutionary searching technique in an aspect of efficient optimization. The co-evolutionary searching technique can make search both sides. The algorithm will try to find motif combinations in one side as well as clustering gene expressions in the other side.

Acknowledgments

This research was supported in part by NRL, the Korean Ministry of Science and Technology (Korean Systems Biology Research Grant, M10309000002-03B5000-00110).

References

1. S. Sinha, M. Tompa, A statistical method for finding transcription factor binding sites, *Proc. Int Conf. Intell. Syst. Mol. Biol.*, Vol. 8, pp. 344–354, 2000.
2. S. Tavazoie, J. D. Hughes, M. J. Campbell, R. J. Cho, and G. M. Church, Systematic determination of genetic network architecture, *Nature Genetics*, Vol. 22, pp. 281–285, 1999.

3. A. Brazma, I. Jonassen, J. Vilo and E. Ukkonen, Predicting gene regulatory elements *in silico* on a genomic scale, *Genome Research*, 8(11), pp. 1202–1215, 1998.
4. Y. Pilpel, P. Sudarsanam and G. Church, Identifying regulatory networks by combinatorial analysis of promoter elements, *Nat. Genet.*, Vol. 29, pp. 153–159, 2001.
5. E. Segal, R. Yelensky and D. Koller, Genome-wide discovery of transcriptional modules from DNA sequence and gene expression, *Bioinformatics*, Vol. 19, pp. i273–i282, 2003.
6. J. Kasturi, R. Acharya, Clustering of diverse genomic data using information fusion, *2004 ACM symposium on Applied computing*, pp. 116–120, 2004.
7. J. Sinkkonen, J. Nikkila, L. Lahti and S. Kaski, *Associative Clustering by Maximizing a Bayes Factor*, Technical Report A68, Helsinki University of Technology, 2003.
8. P. Moscato, *On Evolution, Search, Optimization, Genetic Algorithm and Martial Arts: Towards Memetic Algorithms*, Technical Report C3P Report 826, Caltech Concurrent Computation Program, California Institute of Technology, 1998.
9. H. W. Mewes, et al., MIPS: a database for genomes and protein sequences, *Nucleic Acids Res.*, 30(1), pp. 31–34, 2002.
10. B. L. Miller and D. E. Goldberg, *Genetic Algorithms, Selection Schemes and the Varying Effect of Noise*, IlliGAL report, No. 95009, 1995.
11. P. T. Spellman, G. Sherlock, M. Q. Zhang, V. R. Iyer, K. Anders, M. B. Eisen, P. O. Brown, D. Botstein and B. Futcher, Comprehensive identification of cell cycle-regulated genes of the yeast *Saccharomyces cerevisiae* by microarray hybridization, *Molecular Biology of the Cell*, Vol. 9, pp. 3273–3297, 1998.
12. M. B. Eisen, P. T. Spellman, P. O. Brown and D. Botstein, Cluster analysis and display of genome-wide expression patterns, *Proc. Natl. Acad. Sci.*, USA, Vol. 95, pp. 14863–14868, 1998.
13. H. Ge, Z. Liu, G. Church and M. Vidal, Correlation between transcriptome and interactome mapping data from *Saccharomyces cerivisia*, *Nature Genet.*, Vol. 29, pp. 482–486, 2001.
14. R. Jansen, D. Greenbaum and M. Gerstein, Relating whole-genome expression data with protein-protein interactions, *Genome Res.*, Vol. 12, pp. 37–46, 2002.
15. I. Simon, J. Barnett, N. Hannett, C. T. Harbison, N. J. Rinaldi, T. L. Volkert, J. J. Wyrick, J. Zeitlinger, D. K. Gifford, R. S. Jaakkola and R. A. Young, Serial regulation of transcriptional regulators in the yeast cell cycle, *Cell*, Vol. 106, pp. 697–708, 2001.
16. S. L. Jason, S. David, T. Roger, W. Cynthia and J. N. M. Glover, Structure of the sporulation-specific transcription factor Ndt80 bound to DNA, *EMBO*, 21(21), pp. 5721–5732, 2002.

Evolution of Voronoi-Based Fuzzy Controllers

Carlos Kavka[1] and Marc Schoenauer[2]

[1] LIDIC, Departamento de Informática, Universidad Nacional de San Luis
D5700HHW, San Luis, Argentina
ckavka@unsl.edu.ar

[2] Équipe TAO, INRIA Futurs – LRI, Université de Paris Sud
91405, Orsay Cedex, France
Marc.Schoenauer@inria.fr

Abstract. A fuzzy controller is usually designed by formulating the knowledge of a human expert into a set of linguistic variables and fuzzy rules. One of the most successful methods to automate the fuzzy controllers development process are evolutionary algorithms. In this work, we propose a so-called "approximative" representation for fuzzy systems, where the antecedent of the rules are determined by a multivariate membership function defined in terms of Voronoi regions. Such representation guarantees the ϵ-completeness property and provides a synergistic relation between the rules. An evolutionary algorithm based on this representation can evolve all the components of the fuzzy system, and due to the properties of the representation, the algorithm (1) can benefit from the use of geometric genetic operators, (2) does not need genetic repair algorithms, (3) guarantees the completeness property and (4) can implement previous knowledge in a simple way by using adaptive a priori rules. The proposed representation is evaluated on an obstacle avoidance problem with a simulated mobile robot.

1 Introduction

One of the most successful areas of application of fuzzy logic is control, where fuzzy controllers have proved to be very effective in the context of controlling complex ill defined processes [7]. A fuzzy controller is usually designed by formulating the knowledge of a human expert into a set of linguistic variables and fuzzy rules [4]. However, there is still no systematic way to perform this process. A large number of methods to automate this process and to evaluate and fine tune the obtained fuzzy controllers have been proposed in the literature, with methods based on reinforcement learning, neural networks and evolutionary algorithms being the most successful ones (see [8, 11] and references therein).

Defining a fuzzy rule amounts to select the membership functions for the input variables, and the corresponding values for the outputs of the rule. An important issue is to ensure that the whole search space is covered by the set of fuzzy rules. A way to overcome this problem is to use the so-called grid representation, i.e. to define fuzzy sets from intervals of the values of the input variables. However, this requires a large number of parameters (the interval values), especially as the dimension of the input space increases.

On the other hand, partitions of an n-dimensional space can be easily evolved using Voronoi diagrams [12], and a complete set of fuzzy rules can hence be defined by attaching a linear function to each subset of a such Voronoi partition: this is the basic idea of the *Fuzzy Voronoi* representation for fuzzy systems that is proposed in this work.

The paper is organized as follows: section 2 introduces the FV representation for fuzzy systems and its evolution, and discusses some interesting properties like the ϵ-completeness, and the way a priori rules can be added by the user while their application domain is evolved by the evolution. Section 3 validates the proposed approach with some experimental results on a simple problem of Evolutionary Robotics. Finally, section 4 draws some quick conclusions.

2 The Fuzzy Voronoi Representation

This section introduces the basic concepts of computational geometry used to construct the FV representation, and describes how these concepts are used to represent Takagi-Sugeno fuzzy systems, before discussing the main properties of this representation.

2.1 Domain Partition

The domain partition strategy is based on Voronoi diagrams. A Voronoi diagram induces a subdivision of the space based on a set of points called *sites*. Formally [2], a Voronoi diagram of a set of p points $\mathcal{P} = \{P_1, \ldots, P_p\}$ is the subdivision of the plane into p cells, one for each site in $\mathcal{P}$, with the property that a point M lies in the cell corresponding to a site P_i if and only if the distance between M and P_i is smaller than the distance between P and all other P_j ($j \neq i$). Formally, the Voronoi cell defined by the site P_i is defined as: $\mathcal{V}(P_i) = \{Q \mid dist(Q, P_i) \leq dist(Q, P_j) \; \forall \; i \neq j\}$, where $dist(x, y)$ is the Euclidean distance between the points x and y. A related concept is the so called Delaunay

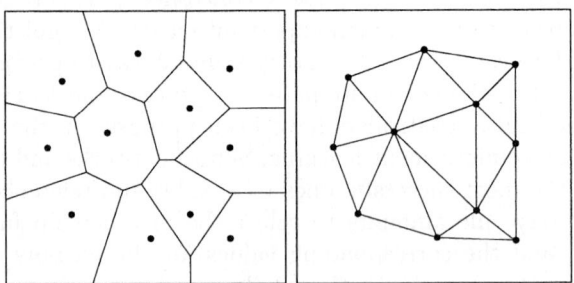

Fig. 1. An example of a Voronoi diagram (left) and the corresponding Delaunay triangulation (right) for a set of points in $\mathbb{R}^2$.

triangulation $\mathcal{T}$, defined as the maximal planar subdivision (i.e. a subdivision such that no edge connecting two vertices can be added to S without destroying its planarity) whose vertex set is $\mathcal{P}$ and such that the circumcircle of any triangle in T does not contain any point of $\mathcal{P}$ in its interior. Figure 1 illustrates an example of a Voronoi diagram and its corresponding Delaunay triangulation in $\mathbb{R}^2$. Note that these definitions can be straightforwardly extended to $\mathbb{R}^n$, with $n \geq 2$ – all details can be found in [2].

2.2 The FV Representation for Takagi–Sugeno Fuzzy Systems

A general Takagi-Sugeno fuzzy system has l input variables $x_1, x_2, \ldots, x_l$ and m output variables $v_1, v_2, \ldots, v_m$ [1]. Rule R_k of such a fuzzy system has the following form:

$$
\begin{aligned}
\text{if } x \text{ is } S_k \text{ then } v_1^k &= a_{10}^k + a_{11}^k x_1 + \ldots + a_{1l}^k x_l \\
&\text{and } \ldots \text{ and} \\
v_m^k &= a_{m0}^k + a_{m1}^k x_1 + \ldots + a_{ml}^k x_l
\end{aligned}
\quad (1)
$$

where S_k is a fuzzy set, $x = (x_1, x_2, \ldots, x_l)$ the input vector, and a_{j0}^k and a_{ji}^k ($1 \leq i \leq l, 1 \leq j \leq m$) are the real valued parameters defining the outputs as a linear combination of the inputs.

The membership value of the input vector x to the fuzzy set S_k can be defined in different ways. For instance, all input variables can be fuzzified independently: assume x_i is fuzzified by $p_i \geq 1$ fuzzy sets A_{ij} ($1 \leq i \leq l, 1 \leq j \leq p_i$) with membership functions μ_{ik_i} ($k_i = 1, 2, \ldots, p_i$). Then the left-hand side of Equation (1) becomes *if x_1 is A_1^k and $\ldots$ and x_l is A_l^k* , where each A_i^k is one of the A_{ij}, the antecedent fuzzy sets (or linguistic labels) associated to the input variable x_i.

The FV representation on the other hand considers joint fuzzy sets defined from a Voronoi diagram $\mathcal{P} = \{P_1, \ldots, P_p\}$. There are as many rules as Voronoi sites, and fuzzy set S_k is defined as by its multivariate membership function μ_k that takes its maximum value 1 at site P_k, and decreases linearly to reach value 0 at the centers of all neighbor Voronoi sites. An example of such a joint fuzzy set is shown in figure 2-a for $n = 2$. Formally, the membership value of the input vector x to the joint fuzzy set S_k is defined by:

$$
\mu_{S_k}(x) = \begin{cases} l_C(x) & x \in \mathcal{V}(P_k) \\ 0 & \text{elsewhere.} \end{cases}
\quad (2)
$$

where $C = P_k$ is the Voronoi site defining S_k and the Voronoi cell $\mathcal{V}(P_k)$, and $l_C(x)$ is the barycentric coordinate of x in the simplex $T_C(x)$ of the Delaunay triangulation of $\mathcal{P}$ that has C as a vertex and to which x belongs. Figure 2-b shows an example of the Voronoi diagram and the associated Delaunay triangulation. On Figure 2-c, the barycentric coordinate $l_C(x)$ corresponds to the (normalized) gray area (volume if $n > 2$) of the sub-simplex formed by x and vertices of simplex $T_C(x)$ but C.

Note that a very large triangle containing all points in the domain is defined in such a way that there are no open Voronoi regions in the input domain.

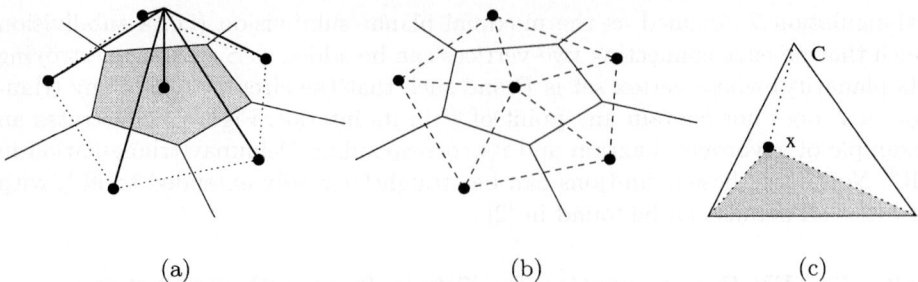

Fig. 2. An example of a (a) joint fuzzy set for a single Voronoi region for $n = 2$, where the membership value is represented in the z-axis, and a (b) Voronoi diagram (solid line) and its corresponding Delaunay triangulation (dotted line) for $n = 2$. The graphic (c) shows an example of the membership computation for $n = 2$. The outer triangle corresponds to the simplex defined by the Delaunay triangulation to which x belongs. The membership value corresponds to the area of the shadowed triangle. Note that the value of the area is 1 when x is equal to C and it goes down linearly to 0 on the side of the triangle opposite to C.

Representation: the FV representation is hence defined by a (variable length) Voronoi diagram $\mathcal{P} = \{P_1, \ldots, P_p\}$ (each P_i is defined by n coordinates), and for each $k \in [1, \ldots, p]$, the set of coefficients $a_{ij}^k, i \in [1, \ldots, l], j \in [1, \ldots, m]$ defining the value of the outputs.

2.3 Evaluation of a FV Takagi–Sugeno Fuzzy System

In order to evaluate the output of such a FV Takagi-Sugeno fuzzy system at point x, the Delaunay triangulation of the set $\mathcal{P}$ has to be computed. Then, the membership functions corresponding to all Voronoi cells that intersect the simplex $T(x)$ to which x belongs have to be computed. Finally, the value of the output variable v_j is computed by summing up the values v_j^k of each activated rule, weighted by their corresponding membership:

$$v_j = \sum_{S_k / T(x) \wedge S_k \neq \emptyset} \mu_{S_k}(x) v_j^k(x). \tag{3}$$

2.4 Evolution of FV Systems

There are two possible approaches for optimizing a FV system: either freeze the number of rules (Voronoi sites), and use any parametric optimization algorithm – but the power of this representation would somehow fade away if the number of sites has to be fixed in advance – or use the flexibility of Evolutionary Algorithms to evolve variable-length genotypes, letting evolution adjust the granularity of the fuzzy rules, i.e. the number and location of the Voronoi sites.

The evolutionary algorithm is described in details in [12, 6]. The crossover operator is based on geometrical exchange of Voronoi sites between both parents with respect to a random hyperplane. The mutation operator can either modify the parameters of a particular rule by some standard Gaussian mutation, or add or delete a Voronoi site, i.e. a rule (see next subsection 2.5). Practical details on the algorithms, including all parameters, will be given in section 3. But before experimentally validating the FV representation, next subsection will discuss some of its properties.

2.5 Properties

First of all, the FV representation belongs to the class of approximative representations [1], where each fuzzy rule defines its own fuzzy sets. It also provides continuous output, as most fuzzy systems. However, it also has a number of useful properties, that we shall now discuss in turn.

ϵ-completeness property: All FV-based fuzzy systems defined with the FV representation fulfills the ϵ-completeness property at any required level, which establishes that any input must belong to at least one fuzzy set with a membership value not smaller than a threshold value ϵ:

$$\forall x \in U \; \exists A \in \{A_1, \ldots, A_n\} \; \mu_A(x) \geqslant \epsilon. \tag{4}$$

For the FV representation, it is clear from the definition of the membership function of equation (2) that this property will hold with $\epsilon = \frac{1}{2}$, as $l_C(x)$ will be above 0.5 if x lies in the Voronoi cell defined by C. This property guarantees an adequate representation for every input point, since there is always a rule that is applied with at least a known value of membership.

No need for genetic repair algorithms: Since it is not possible to define wrong or non complete fuzzy systems, the fuzzy systems produced by applying mutation or crossover operators are always valid control systems.

Adaptive fuzzy rules: The influence on the output of a particular fuzzy rule in the FV representation does not only depend on the rule itself, it also depends on all neighbor rules. The area of application $\mathcal{A}_k$ of a fuzzy rule R_k is defined as the union of all Delaunay regions which contain the point P_k, center of the rule R_k. Formally:

$$\mathcal{A}(R_k) = \bigcup_{P_k \in D_j} D_j \quad D_j \in D = \{D_1, \ldots, D_\gamma\}. \tag{5}$$

where P_k is the center of the rule R_k and $D = \{D_1, \ldots, D_\gamma\}$ is the Delaunay partition of the set $\mathcal{P} = \{P_1, \ldots, P_p\}$. Figure 3 shows an example of the application area of some rules in a regular partition, and illustrates the interdependency of application areas of neighboring rules when some rules are removed or added.

The evolutionary algorithm evolves individuals that represent complete fuzzy systems defined by a set of fuzzy rules that are synergistically related, and not fuzzy systems defined with a set of independent fuzzy rules. The variation operators hence modify the application areas of all fuzzy rules, while still maintaining the required ϵ-completeness level.

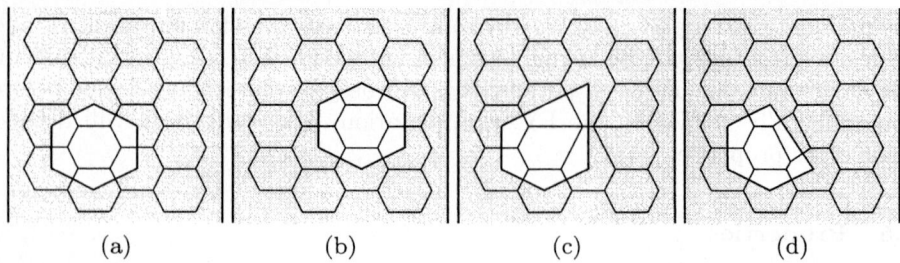

Fig. 3. Diagram (a) shows the application area of a fuzzy rule. Diagram (b) shows the application area of one of its neighbor rule. Diagram (c) shows the application area of the rule of diagram (a) when the rule of diagram (b) is removed, and diagram (d) the application area of the rule of diagram (a) when a rule is added between both rules.

Adaptive a priori rules: In most fuzzy systems, the user can incorporate a priori knowledge by manually defining fuzzy sets and the corresponding fuzzy rules. This process implies that some restriction on the output values and the partition of the input space is introduced in the evolutionary process, but the expected benefit is that the evolutionary process, biased toward hopefully good parts of its search space, will converge faster to better solutions. Similarly, the FV representation allows the definition of a priori rules, i.e. fixed Voronoi sites that will not be modified by evolution. But one big advantages of the FV representation is that the expert does not need to specify the application area of such rules: thanks to the synergistic effect described above, the evolutionary process, by adding rules more or less close to the a priori rules will also tune its domain of application – as will be clear on the experimental results in next section.

3 Experiments

3.1 Obstacle Avoidance with a Khepera Robot

Control problems are among the most successful applications of fuzzy systems: we have chosen a simple control problem in Evolutionary Robotics (ER) to validate the FV representation. For its simplicity, because it has been the hardware basis for many experiments in ER [10], and because there exists many good simulation platforms (we have used [9]), the Khepera robot was chosen: it has 8 infrared sensors to measure proximity to objects and levels of ambient light; two independent motors are used to control the speed and direction of the robot.

The obstacle avoidance is one of the simplest problems in ER. Following [10], the fitness of a controller is defined by testing the controller on the (simulated) robot in some given arena during a number r of *epochs*, the robot being positioned randomly in the arena at start of each epoch. During each epoch, fitness accumulates at each time step proportionally to the robot speed, but is decreased if the robot gets too close to a wall. An epoch stops if the robot hits a wall, or after a predefined number of times steps s. The total fitness is the sum of the fitness obtained during all r epochs. More formally, the fitness (to be maximized) is defined by

$$\text{fitness}(I) = \frac{1}{r} \sum_{i=1}^{r} \sum_{t=1}^{s} d(t) * (1 - a(t)) \tag{6}$$

where t is the time step, $d(t)$ is the normalized forward speed of the robot (sum of the speed of both motors), and $a(t)$ is the normalized maximum activation of the infrared sensors (i.e. a(t)=1 means that the robot is against a wall).

3.2 Experimental Results

In the results reported here, to keep things simple, but not trivial, the controllers have four inputs and two outputs: the inputs are, respectively, the average of the two left sensors, the two front sensors, the two right sensors and the two back sensors; the outputs are the speeds of the two motors. The precise parameters of the evolutionary algorithm are given in table 1.

Table 1. Parameters of the evolutionary algorithm.

Parameter	value
Dimension of the input space	4
Dimension of the output space	2
Population size	50
Number of generations	300
Selection - replacement	Roulette - Generational
Number of epochs per evaluation	40
Number of time steps per epoch	200
Minimum and maximum size of individuals	10 - 30
Crossover rate (Voronoi)	0.8
Mutation rates (Gaussian - addition - deletion)	0.3 - 0.15 - 0.15

The performance of the individuals is evaluated on the scenery shown in Figure 4-a, by performing $r = 40$ evaluations from valid random positions of at most $s = 200$ steps each one. The performance of a representative controller found after evolution is shown in the same Figure 4-a, where the little boxes represent the robot displayed every 30 time steps, for a total of 5000 time steps. It can be appreciated that the robot can successfully navigate through the arena, avoiding obstacles, and moving slowly in narrow regions (boxes are more dense).

Generalization abilities: Figure 4-b shows the performance of the same controller, evaluated in the same conditions but in a different arena from the one it had evolved in during evolution. It can be seen that the controller has successfully learned the navigation rules, since it can move and avoid obstacles in an unknown environment. The performance is comparable with the results provided e.g. in [10] and [5], where neuro controllers are trained in a similar arenas.

A priori rules: Figure 5 shows the usual plot of best fitness (averaged over 5 runs) vs number of generations, together with error bars, when the evolution

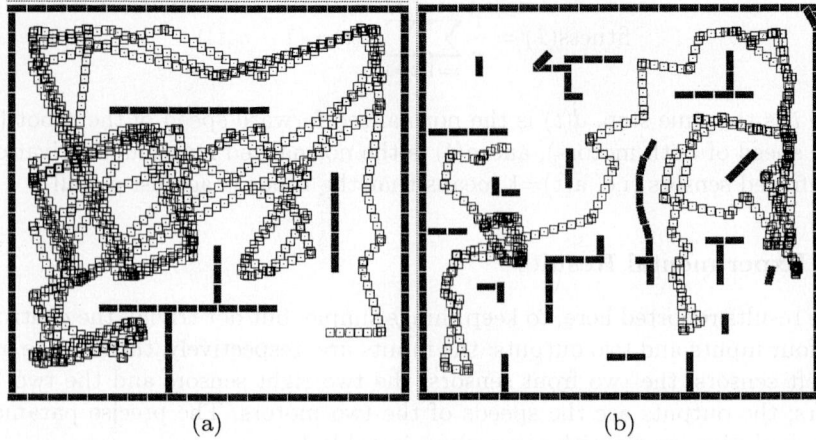

Fig. 4. The graph (a) shows the performance of the best fuzzy controller obtained through evolution in the scenery used for evaluation and the graph (b) shows the performance of the same controller on an unknown environment.

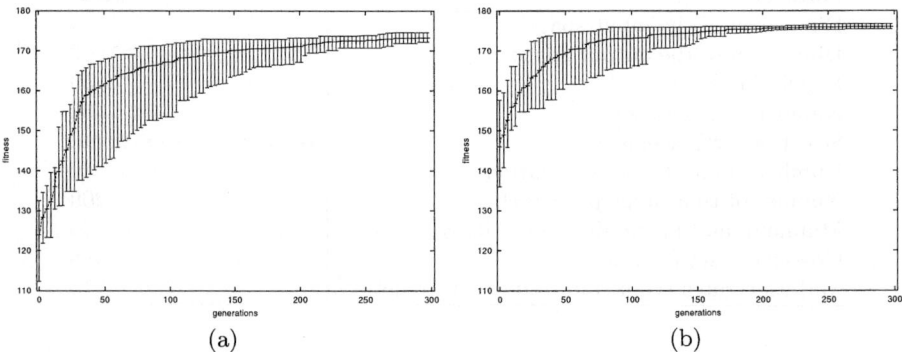

Fig. 5. Fitness vs number of generations, averaged over 5 runs. (a) without a priori rules, and (b) with a priori rules.

Table 2. A priori rules used during evolution.

point				output v_0					output v_1				
left	center	right	back	a_1	a_2	a_3	a_4	a_5	a_1	a_2	a_3	a_4	a_5
0	0	0	0	1.0	0.0	0.0	0.0	0.0	1.0	0.0	0.0	0.0	0.0
1.0	0	1.0	1.0	1.0	0.0	0.0	0.0	0.0	1.0	0.0	0.0	0.0	0.0

is performed without (a) and with (b) the a priori rules shown in table 2. The first rule establishes that the robot should go straight ahead (both motors at full speed) when there are no obstacles around (normalized value 0 for all sensors), and the second rule establishes the same behavior when there are no obstacles in front, but obstacles in all other directions (normalized value 1). Though the final

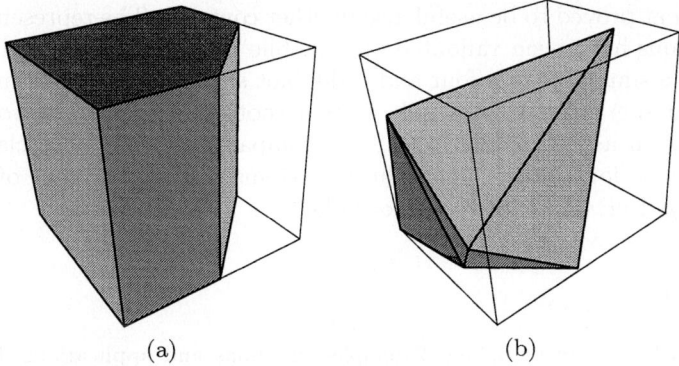

Fig. 6. The (a) original area of application of the first a priori rule and the (b) modified area of application of the same rule at the end of the evolution.

performances reached by the best controllers in the case where a priori rules are used are only slightly better than those in the case without a priori rules, the results in the latter case are obtained more quickly, and, more importantly, are much more robust (smaller error bars). The use of a priori rules makes certainly sense when the simulation is highly costly so the number of runs and the number of generations per run have to be kept small.

The areas of application of the first rule (projected in their first three coordinates) are plotted on Figure 6: (a) shows the initial application area, before evolution started, while (b) is the application of the very same rule after evolution. The algorithm did indeed adjust this domain of application – the user only had to specify the expected behavior at a single point in the input space. Table 3 shows two rules obtained through evolution. The first rule is applied when the only possibility is to move to the left and the second rule when the best option is to move to the right. The normalized outputs produced by the first rule in the center point are 0.01 and 1.0, producing a fast turn to the left. The outputs of the second rule are 0.75 and 0.3, producing a slower turn to the right.

Table 3. An example of rules obtained after evolution.

point				output v_0					output v_1				
left	center	right	back	a_1	a_2	a_3	a_4	a_5	a_1	a_2	a_3	a_4	a_5
0.61	0.98	0.97	0.92	-0.51	-0.04	0.01	0.17	-0.66	0.9	-0.14	0.66	0.48	-0.82
0.82	0.54	0.11	0.67	0.65	-0.46	-0.11	3.31	-0.12	-0.14	-0.31	-0.11	3.54	-0.46

4 Conclusions

A representation for fuzzy controllers based on Voronoi diagrams has been proposed, that can represent fuzzy systems with synergistic rules, fulfilling the ϵ-completeness property and providing a simple way to introduce a priori knowledge. The geometric interpretation of the rules allows the use of geometric genetic operators that proved to be useful also in other contexts. The representation and the algorithms have been validated on a mobile robot obstacle avoidance problem run on a simulator in a four and eight (not shown) dimensions input space, and also on the inverted cart pole system (not shown). Future work include experiments on a real mobile robot, and comparisons with more classical grid representations for Takagi-Sugeno fuzzy systems, and the impact of using the so-called *Symbolic Controllers* approach [3].

References

1. R. Babuška. Fuzzy modeling: Principles, methods and applications. In C. Bonivento, C. Fantuzzi, and R. Rovatti, editors, *Fuzzy Logic Control: Advances in Methodology*, pages 187–220. World Scientific, Singapore, 1998.
2. M. de Berg, M. van Kreveld, M. OVermars, and O. Schwarzkopf. *Computational Geometry, Algorithms and Applications*. Springer Verlag, 1998.
3. N. Godzik, M. Schoenauer, and M. Sebag. Evolving symbolic controllers. In G. Raidl et al., editor, *Applications of Evolutionary Computing*, LNCS 2611, 2003.
4. F. Hoffmann. Evolutionary algorithms for fuzzy control system design. *Proceedings of the IEEE, Special Issue on Industrial Innovations using Soft Computing*, 2001.
5. M. Hülse, B. Lara, F. Pasemann, and U. Steinmetz. Evolving neuro-modules and their interfaces to control autonomous robots. *Lecture Notes in Computer Science*, 2130, 2001.
6. C. Kavka and M. Schoenauer. Voronoi diagrams based function identification. In *Proceedings of the Genetic and Evolutionary Computation Conference*, 2003.
7. C. Lee. Fuzzy logic in control systems: Fuzzy logic controller - part i. *IEEE Transactions on Systems, Man and Cybernetics*, 20(2):404–418, March/April 1990.
8. P. McQuesten. *Cultural Enhancement of Neuroevolution*. PhD thesis, The University of Texas at Austin, August 2002.
9. O. Michel. Kephera simulator package version 2.0.
10. S. Nolfi and D. Floreano. *Evolutionary Robotics, The Biology, Intelligence, and Technology of Self-Organizing Machines*. Bradford Books, 2000.
11. A. Saffiotti. The uses of fuzzy logic in autonomous robot navigation. *Soft Computing*, 1(4):180–197, 1997.
12. M. Schoenauer, F. Jouve, and L. Kallel. Identification of mechanical inclusions. In D. Dasgupta and Z. Michalewicz, editors, *Evolutionary Algorithms in Engineering Applications*. Springer Verlag, 1997.

Analyzing Sensor States and Internal States in the Tartarus Problem with Tree State Machines

DaeEun Kim

Cognitive Robotics
Max Planck Institute for Human Cognitive and Brain Sciences
Munich, 80799, Germany
daeeun@cbs.mpg.de

Abstract. The Tartarus problem is a box pushing task in a grid world environment. It is one of difficult problems for purely reactive agents to solve, and thus a memory-based control architecture is required. This paper presents a novel control structure, called tree state machine, which has an evolving tree structure for sensorimotor mapping and also encodes internal states. As a result, the evolutionary computation on tree state machines can quantify internal states and sensor states needed for the problem. Tree state machines with a dynamic feature of sensor states are demonstrated and compared with finite state machines and GP-automata. It is shown that both sensor states and memory states are important factors to influence the behavior performance of an agent.

1 Introduction

Several grid world problems have been tackled with evolutionary computation based on memory architecture. Finite state machines and recurrent neural networks were used in the artificial ant problems [7]. Koza [10] applied genetic programming with a command sequence function to the artificial ant problem. Wilson designed the Woods problems to study memory-based approaches [14]. Finite state machines were applied to solve the Woods problem [9]. Tartarus problem is also one of agent problems to need internal memory. It has been shown that agents using memory in the Tartarus problem have an advantage over agents that do not use memory [13,2,12]. Especially the Tartarus problem requires handling many environmental configurations, several sensors and internal states. There have been evolutionary approaches to solve the Tartarus problem. Teller used indexed memory in tree structures with genetic programming [13]. Recurrent neural networks have been evolved to solve the problem [4,12]. New structures with memory encoding, called GP-automata and ISAc (If-Skip-Action) lists, were introduced [1,2]. The researches so far have focused on what kind of memory architecture can be organized to solve the problem. The complexity level of the Tartarus problem, however, has not been studied in detail. As an alternative, internal states can be counted as a measure of complexity of an agent problem [3,9]. In fact, there exist many factors to be considered for the complexity of an agent task; sensors and their numbers, effectors, an

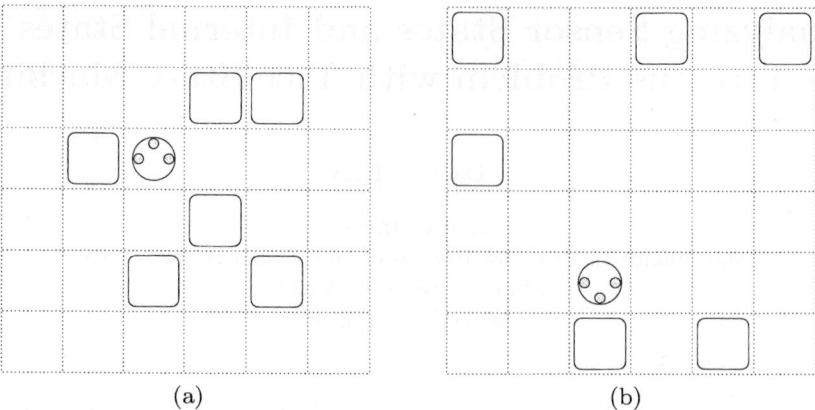

Fig. 1. Examples of the Tartarus environment (a) initial configuration (b) final configuration with score 8.

agent morphology, the controller type, environmental states, and the interaction level between agents and environments. Here we will focus on internal memory and perception states that an agent can use, by assuming that other factors are invariant for the task. Internal states can be used to link subtasks to form a complex task, and the number of internal states may greatly depend on perceptual configurations. Thus, for the complexity of the Tartarus problem, two criteria will be estimated, the number of internal states and the number of sensory configurations[1] in an evolved control structure. For this purpose, we suggest a new memory architecture, called tree state machine, which can represent a set of internal states as well as sensory configurations based on a dynamic tree structure.

The Tartarus problem was originally designed by Teller [13]. It has a 6×6 board environment and six boxes randomly distributed in the inner 4×4 grid. A single agent has eight sensors for its eight nearest neighbors, each of which can detect a box, wall, or empty space. The agent has three motor actions; move forward, turn left or turn right. The agent can move forward only if there is an empty space in front of the agent itself or there is a box in front with an empty square beyond it. Attempting to push two boxes, or a box against a wall, results in no movements. The agent can have four possible directions and the direction can be changed by two operations, turn left or turn right. In the initial configuration six boxes are randomly placed in the inner grid and an agent is put in an empty random position in the inner grid, facing in a random direction. The agent's goal is to push all six boxes to the walls. After a given exploration time passes, the agent gets a score by checking the number of boxes against walls. Score two is given for boxes in corners and score one for boxes in non-corner edge positions. The maximum score that the agent can achieve is thus 10. Eighty time steps are allowed for an agent and the time limit will lead the agent to find an efficient strategy for high score. Fig. 1 shows examples of the Tartarus environment.

---

[1] They will be defined as sensor states in this paper.

The Tartarus problem is different from other grid problems in several respects. An agent has several sensors with integer values to distinguish wall, box, and empty space. Its environment is small in size, but random configurations are allowed. More precisely, an agent has eight sensors to look around the environment and there are more than 300,000 Tartarus boards ($\approx_{16} C_6 \cdot_{10} C_1 \cdot 4 = \frac{16!}{6! \cdot 10!} \cdot \frac{10!}{1! \cdot 9!} \cdot 4$). The agent position and box positions are randomly selected in the initial configuration of the Tartarus environment.

2 Tree State Machines

The Finite State Machine (FSM) approach is powerful in obtaining state transition functions and can easily count the number of memory elements. FSM, however, has a difficulty in representing multi-thresholds for each sensor or handling many sensor configurations, since the encoding size is greatly increasing in proportion to the partitions of sensor space. It also needs a complete encoding for each internal state and scales badly with growing machine complexity. Thus, a tree structure to process sensor readings and the technique of encoding memory states are combined together in this paper, which will be called a tree state machine.

A Tree State Machine (TSM) is defined as a machine $M = (Q, T, \Sigma, \Delta, q_0)$ where q_0 is an initial state, Q is a finite set of states, T is a set of trees assigned to a state, Σ is a set of sensor states and Δ is the set of motor output values. A tree T_i is assigned for a state q_i, and it is defined as

$$T_i(M) = \{(S_k, q_k^*, D_k) | S_k \in \Sigma^i, q_k^* \in Q, D_k \in \Delta\}$$

where Σ^i is a set of sensor states for a given state q_i, and a sensor state in tree state machines is defined with n decision boundaries as $S_k = (r_{k1}, \sigma_{k1}, \theta_{k1}) \wedge (r_{k2}, \sigma_{k2}, \theta_{k2}) \wedge ... (r_{kn}, \sigma_{kn}, \theta_{kn})$, where $(r_{kj}, \sigma_{kj}, \theta_{kj})$ is a decision classifier[2] for the sensor $\sigma_{kj} \in \Sigma$. The symbol r_{kj} is a relation operator which will be an element of the set $\{<, \geq\}$ in a decision tree, $\sigma_{kj} \in \Sigma$ is the j-th sensor, and θ_{kj} is a threshold for the j-th sensor. As a result, TSM provides axis-parallel decision boundaries. We can omit insignificant sensors in the sensor state equation by evolving decision trees for sensor states. For the k-th sensor state, $(q_k^*, D_k) = (q_k^*, (d_{k1}, d_{k2}, d_{k3}, ..., d_{km}))$ will be the form of a terminal value in evolved decision trees. D_k is a motor output string for m motors, and q_k^* is the next memory state after the activation of motor output for a given sensor state.

Strictly speaking, a *sensor state* is defined to be a set of sensor values that have the same motor outputs and the same internal state to be activated next. It is defined within a fixed internal state[3] and a sensor state for a given internal state q_i is written as

---

[2] All the internal nodes traversed from the root node are linked together by logic AND operation over sensors and their thresholds. The structure is similar to a decision tree often used to classify data. Instead of defining classification class at leaf nodes in decision trees, motor actions and the next state transition are specified at leaf nodes.

[3] The internal state will also be called *memory state* to be disambiguated from sensor state.

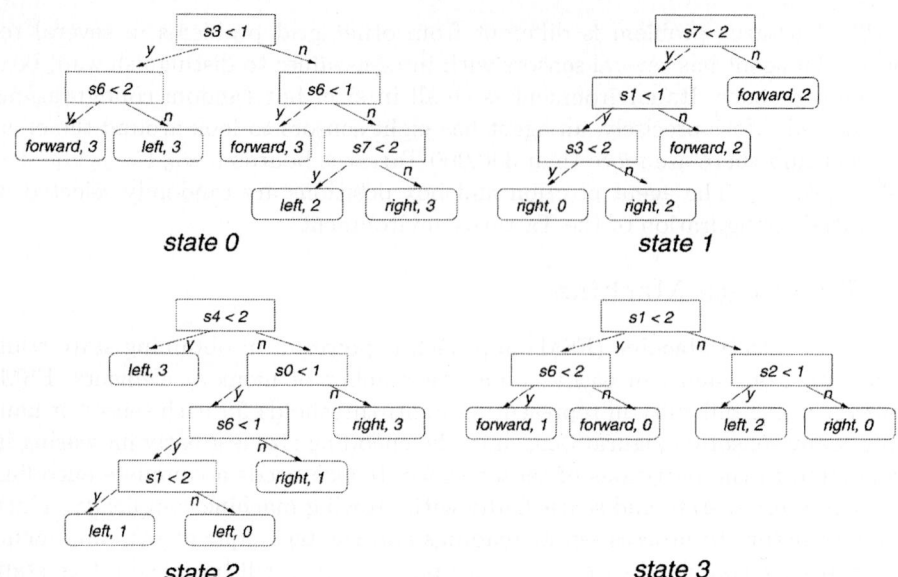

Fig. 2. A tree state machine with 4 memory states and maximum 5 sensor states (terminal nodes); each terminal node defines one sensor state to specify a motor action and the next memory state transition.

$$\epsilon(s^i) = \{s^* | \lambda(q_i, s^i) = \lambda(q_i, s^*) \wedge \delta(q_i, s^i) = \delta(q_i, s^*)\}$$

where S is a set of sensor values with $s^i \in S$, λ is a mapping from $Q \times S$ to Δ, and δ is a memory state transition function from $Q \times S$ to Q. A sensor state is then an equivalence class over observed sensor values, such that all the sensor values in the sensor state have the same motor actions and the same next memory state in the transition functions. The equivalence classes of sensor state form a partition of the set Σ^i of sensor values. The function ϵ maps from a sensor value s^i to one of perceptual states, which is represented as $\sigma_k, k = 0, 1, 2, \ldots$. Then the sensor space Σ^i for a memory state q_i is the set $\{\sigma_k\}$ of all sensor states. Within the same sensor state, all the sensor values induce the same future actions for the next time step.

Fig. 2 shows an example of tree state machine with 4 internal states where the maximum number of leaf nodes is limited to five. The internal nodes define a selected sensor variable and its threshold. Terminal nodes have the values for a motor action and the next state transition.

3 Methods

The chromosome of a tree state machine is defined as a set of trees and each internal state has its own decision tree. A tree state machine thus has trees as many as the number of internal states. The crossover operator on tree state machines is defined as swapping a subset of trees of two parents; some part of the whole chromosome is exchanged among two parents. There are seven mutation operators available for one chromosome. The first operator deletes a subtree and creates a new random subtree. The subtree to be replaced will be randomly selected in a state tree. The state tree is also randomly chosen. The second operator first picks up a random internal node and then changes the sensor variable or its threshold. This keeps the parent tree and modifies only one node. The third operator randomly chooses a leaf node and then changes the motor action or the state transition. The fourth operator selects a branch of a subtree and reduces it into a leaf node with a random motor action and state transition. It will have the effect of removing redundant subtrees. The fifth operator randomly chooses two state trees within one chromosome and then swaps two state trees. The sixth operator randomly chooses two state trees, picks up a subtree inside each state tree and then swaps two subtrees. The seventh operator also chooses two state trees, and then one state tree is replaced by the other state tree. The last three operators are applied to two internal states of one chromosome, and the first four mutation operators are taken on one internal state.

The Tartarus problem intrinsically has a large number of possible configurations and it is not efficient to evaluate a controller over all of these while evolving. The *N-K sampling method* (also called a random subset selection [5, 8]) is applied to this kind of random environment. First, N initial configurations to represent the entire possible configuration of environments are randomly selected. Every generation K samples among N configurations are evaluated for each genome controller and as the evolutionary process continues, it intermittently but regularly evaluates all of N configurations for the best chromosome and records its fitness. This strategy can greatly reduce computation time and effectively accumulate the result of evolving controllers in random environments. Ultimately it will find the best controller to survive in the N environments. The number of random boards, K, is fixed for one experiment. K boards are randomly selected among N configurations each generation and all the individuals in the same population are evaluated with the same K boards. In our experiments, N boards are randomly chosen every 50 generations, evaluated for the best chromosome and then the best fitness results are saved.

4 Experiments

We test finite state machines, GP-automata and tree state machines to analyze internal states needed for the Tartarus problem. In the Tartarus environment, an agent has eight sensors each of which needs three different values to detect wall, box or empty space. First, an FSM is constructed with integer encoding over three sensors at front, left and right among the 8 neighbor sensors to detect the environment. Each internal (memory) state defines a motor action and the next memory state for each of $27(=3^3)$ sensor states and thus the chromosome length is reduced to a reasonable size $3^3 \cdot 2n = 54n$ for a n-state machine (an agent with 8 sensors will have a chromosome size $3^8 \cdot 2n = 13,122n$ for a n-state machine and the size is not feasible for evolutionary computation). It is written as a type

start: 0 → 0			
	if even	if odd	deciders
0	1 → 3	0 → 1	(ITE x1 2 (max x8 x8))
1	2 → 0	0 → 3	(ITE x1 0 (max x6 x7))
2	2 → 1	0 → 3	(- (ITE x5 (ITE x1 0 x6) (Odd x7)))
3	2 → 1	2 → 2	(<> (max x6 x7) (>= x6 (ITE x7 (Odd x8) 0)))

Fig. 3. An example of GP automata with four states ($\alpha \to \beta$ indicates motor action α and the next state β).

of Mealy machine model [6]. Second, GP-automata suggested by Ashlock [1] is reproduced. In GP-automata, sensor readings are handled with tree structures using genetic programming as shown in Fig. 3, where eight sensors are allowed to see the surrounding environment. Each internal state has its own tree and state transitions, but each memory state defines two branches, depending on an even or odd value of an evolved decider function. GP-automata thus allows only two sensor states; two sensor states are determined by odd or even values of deciders. The decider function consists of if-then-else ternary operator, arithmetic operators $(+, -)$, relative operators $(=, \geq, \leq, >, <)$, negation $(-)$, complement function, max/min function, odd/even function, constant and sensor variables. Third, a tree state machine is built with a dynamic tree structure for each internal state, as described in the previous section. It allows as many sensor states as the number of leaf nodes in a tree.

Exploration time was fixed at 80 time steps for every experiment. In the N-K sample selection, we used 50 samples for one genome evaluation every generation ($K=50$, $N=10,000$). Each experiment was run with 5,000 generations 25 times and tournament selection with a group size of four was applied with an elitism strategy. It employed a crossover rate of 0.6. Genetic algorithm for FSM used a mutation rate of 0.01, and genetic programming for GP-automata and TSM used a mutation rate of 0.5.

For each control structure, various numbers of internal states were tested to see the memory effect, and the fitness distributions with 95% confidence intervals were examined by assuming t-distribution. FSM and GP-automata have a fixed number of sensor states, 27 sensor states and 2 sensor states, respectively. Fig. 4(a)-(b) shows the performance of FSM and GP-automata depending on the number of internal states. A 1-memory state machine corresponds to a memoryless reactive control system and its average score is poor, below 1. As the number of memory states increases, the average performance improves remarkably. The results demonstrate that FSMs outperform GP-automata for the same number of internal states within a limited computing time, except for one internal state (this is the comparison of the average performance). Also the performance of GP-automata degrades with a small population. In contrast, the FSM approach is not influenced by the population size when the same computing cost is given. This may be due to the fact that genetic programming tends to develop new good offspring through crossover of individuals in a large sized population rather than with the mutation operator [11]. The FSM approach used only three sensors

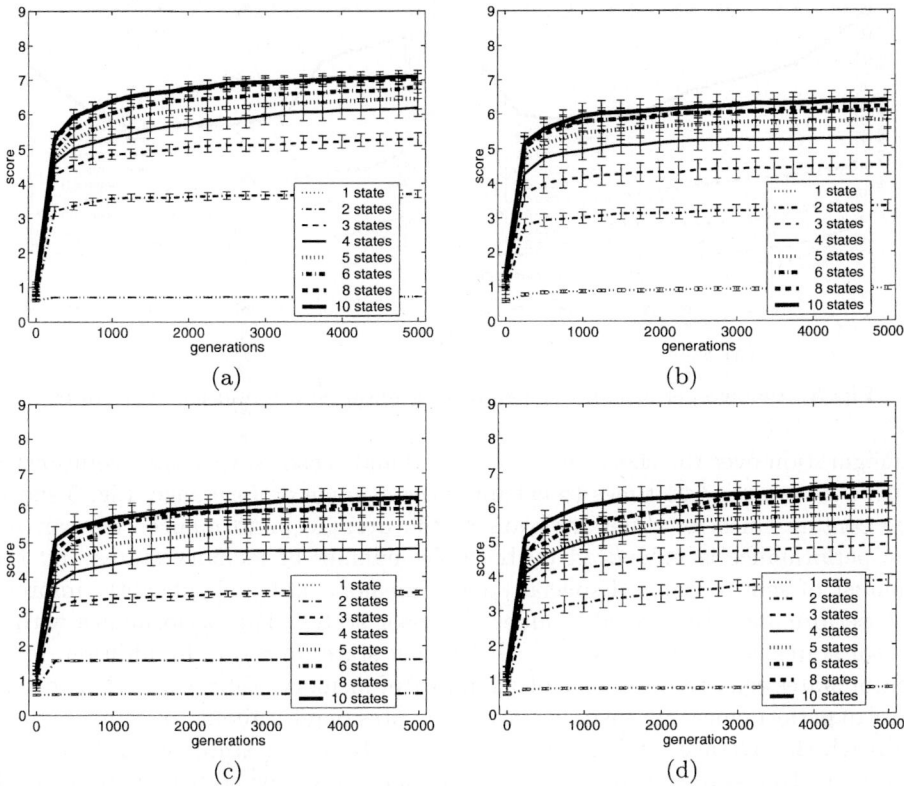

Fig. 4. Performance depending on various sizes of memory states (a) FSM (b) GP-automata (c) TSM with 2 sensor states (d) TSM with 10 sensor states.

among the eight possible sensors. The above results imply that the three sensors are sufficient to generate desirable behaviors for the Tartarus problem.

In tree state machines, we can control the number of sensor states for each internal state. The maximum number of sensor states can be selected in advance. Fig. 4(c)-(d) show the performance of tree state machines for two different maximum numbers of sensor states, 2 sensor states and 10 sensor states, respectively. For 2-4 memory states, TSM with 10 sensor states is significantly better in performance than TSM with 2 sensor states. Moreover, TSM with 10 sensor states shows better average performance than GP-automata, though it is not statistically significant. However, tree state machines have worse performance than FSM. Finite state machines have pre-defined sensor configurations and each gene only defines motor action and the next transition. Evolving tree state machines can have a random perturbation of search for desirable sensor configurations, which often declines the convergence speed to a desirable tree structure. It needs more search time of finding which sensor is effective and what is the desirable sensor threshold for the selected sensor.

We evolved tree state machines with various sizes of memory states (1, 2, 3, 4, 5, 6, 8, 10, 12) and various sizes of sensor states (2, 5, 10, 15, 20). For each

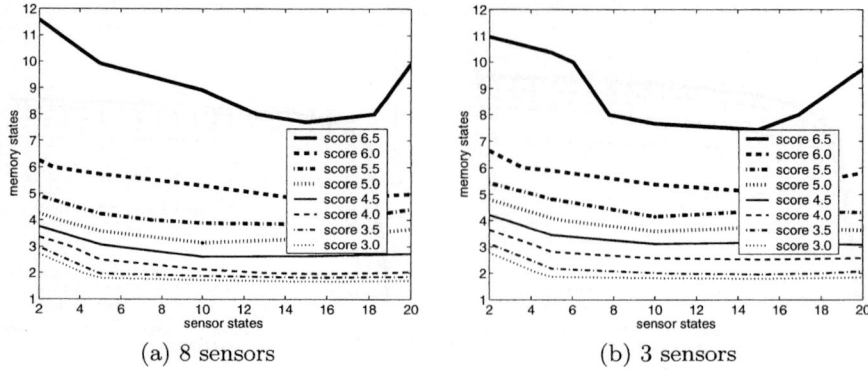

Fig. 5. Average performance depending on sensor states and memory states.

configuration over the size of memory states and sensor states, the evolutionary runs were repeated 25 times to calculate the average performance. Fig. 5 shows the contour lines for different levels of the average performance. We can see the performance is influenced by both the number of memory states and the number of sensor states. Especially more memory states significantly improve the performance for a fixed number of sensor states. The performance with 2 sensor states is worse than that with 5 sensor states or more. In addition, more sensor states tend to need a smaller number of memory states to reach a certain level of performance. For instance, 5 sensor states require about 10 memory states to reach the average performance of 6.5, and 15 sensor states need 8 memory states. In tree state machines, a large number of sensor states (more than 15 sensor states) can decrease the convergence speed to a high score, since the tree structure becomes more complex and it needs more computing time to evolve the parameters. It explains why the contour curve is increasing when the number of sensor states, more than 15 states, increases. Normally more sensor states with a fixed number of memory states produce better performance if a plentiful computing time is provided for evolving parameters. When a sufficient number of memory states are available (larger than 11 states), the number of sensor states seems to be no more a significant factor to improve the performance. In Fig. 5, it is observed that 8 sensors need a smaller number of memory states or sensor states to achieve some level of performance below score 6.0 than 3 sensors (front, left and right sensors).

The FSM, shown in Fig. 4(a), reaches the peak performance with around 8 memory states. For more than 8 states, there is no significant change. One can say that the Tartarus problem requires at least 8 internal states to obtain satisfactory performance (above score 6.5). In contrast, GP-Automata requires 10 memory states to obtain the performance. Here it is noteworthy that they differ in the number of sensor states. The experiments with tree state machines prove that the number of sensor states is correlated with the number of memory states needed for the problem.

We have handled the issue of how many sensor states will be useful to build desirable controllers. In the experiments, TSM with 2 sensor states is worse than GP-automata especially for 2-6 memory states – see Fig. 4(b)-(c). The decider function of TSM is a simple binary function dividing the sensor space by a threshold, while GP-automata use a complex decider function for each state. There may be an issue of how complex functions or what kind of decider functions will be helpful when the number of sensor states is fixed. Linear regression trees or neural networks, instead of a binary decision tree used in this paper, can be explored to build sensor states for the future study.

We have used the average score over 10,000 boards by 25 trial evolutionary runs with 5000 generations. The best score evaluated over 10,000 random boards was 7.99 for TSM with 8 sensors (10 sensor states and 10 memory states), 7.86 for TSM with 3 sensors (15 sensor states and 12 memory states), 7.82 for FSM with 3 sensors and 7.80 for GP-automata with 8 sensors (10 memory states). TSM has more fluctuation on the evolutionary fitness than FSM and its average score is lower. For reference on the Tartarus problem, recurrent neural networks have the best score 4.74 over 500 boards [4] and ISAc lists have the score 7.987 over 5000 boards. They used a small computing time and different evolutionary parameters, and so the performance may not reflect the accurate estimation on the methods.

5 Conclusion

A dynamic structure to represent sensory features is a tree structure which can increase or decrease its size depending on the problem. In this paper, we applied a new memory architecture, called tree state machine, to the Tartarus problem. It has an advantage of encoding memory states as well as various sizes of sensor configurations with a tree structure. The tree state machine can expand sensor states up to its maximum limit, which can be defined by the user. The complexity of the Tartarus problem was measured by the structure of evolved controllers with the best performance, where internal states and sensor states were quantified to estimate the complexity. It was shown that the sensor states as well as internal states influence the performance, which have not been considered together so far. Tree state machine experiments prove that internal states are deeply correlated to sensor states for desirable performance.

The Tartarus environment has no noise in sensor readings. It will be an interesting issue to study the effect of noise on the sensor states and internal states. We will investigate how neural networks or clustering methods organize sensor states in noisy environments. It can be a good comparison with tree state machines. The Tartarus problem is a grid world problem to simplify the real world environment. The importance of sensor states and memory states may be observed in robotic tasks which include more fine-grained sensor values and more motor actions. We leave the application of tree state machines to robotic tasks for future work.

The TSM has worse performance than the FSM approach when the same computing time is given. Our algorithm with tree state machines needs an improvement to accelerate the convergence speed for a large size of sensor states.

In TSM, motor actions and state transitions are combined into one terminal node. We can build two separate trees for them and explore their effect on the performance. In this paper, we focused on counting the number of sensor states and internal states, but the study of the quality of sensory features for the performance has not been covered here. This study could reveal more clearly the relation between sensory features and internal memory.

Acknowledgments

The author would like to thank anonymous reviewers for fruitful comments and suggestions.

References

1. D. Ashlock. GP-automata for dividing the dollar. In *Genetic Programming 97*, pages 18–26. MIT Press, 1997.
2. D. Ashlock. ISAc lists, a different representation for program induction. In *Genetic Programming 98*, pages 3–10. Morgan Kauffman, 1998.
3. B. Bakker and M. de Jong. The epsilon state count. In *From Animals to Animats 6*, pages 51–60. MIT Press, 2000.
4. K. Balakrishnan and V. Honavar. On sensor evolution in robotics. In *Proceedings of the first Conf. on Genetic Programming*, pages 455–460. MIT Press, 1996.
5. C. Gathercole. *An Investigation of Supervised Learning in Genetic Programming*. Ph. D. dissertation, University of Edinburgh, 1998.
6. J.E. Hopcroft and J. D. Ullman. *Introduction to automata theory, languages, and computation*. Addison Wesley, Reading, MA, 1979.
7. D. Jefferson and R. Collins. Evolution as a theme in artificial life. In C. Langton, editor, *Artificial Life II*. Addison Wesley, 1991.
8. D. Kim and J. Hallam. Mobile robot control based on Boolean logic with internal memory. In *Lecture Notes in Computer Science vol. 2159*, pages 529–538, 2001.
9. D. Kim and J. Hallam. An evolutionary approach to quantify internal states needed for the Woods problem. In *From Animals to Animats 7*, pages 312–322. MIT Press, 2002.
10. J.R. Koza. *Genetic Programming*. MIT Press, Cambridge, MA, 1992.
11. S. Nolfi and D. Floreano. *Evolutionary Robotics : The Biology, Intelligence, and Technology of Self-Organizing Machines*. MIT Press, Cambridge, MA, 2000.
12. A. Silva, A. Neves, and E. Costa. Genetically programming networks to evolve memory mechanism. In *Genetic and Evolutionary Computation Conference*, 1999.
13. A. Teller. The evolution of mental models. In *Advances in Genetic Programming*. MIT Press, 1994.
14. S.W. Wilson. ZCS: A zeroth level classifier system. *Evolutionary Computation*, 2(1):1–18, 1994.

Evolving Genetic Regulatory Networks for Hardware Fault Tolerance

Arne Koopman[1] and Daniel Roggen[2]

[1] Adaptive Intelligence Laboratory, Intelligent Systems Group,
Institute for Information and Computing Sciences, Utrecht University, The Netherlands
[2] Autonomous Systems Laboratory
Institute of Systems Engineering, EPFL, Lausanne, Switzerland
acmkoopm@cs.uu.nl

Abstract. We present a new approach that is able to produce an increased fault tolerance in bio-inspired electronic circuits. To this end, we designed hardware-friendly genetic regulatory networks based on a bio-inspired hardware architecture called POEtic tissue. To assess its preliminary functionality, the parameters of the genetic regulatory networks were evolved using genetic algorithms to achieve elementary behaviours, including patch growth and oscillations at various frequencies. The tolerance to faults was explored by inflicting several types of damage, and results show that the system exhibits capabilities to recover from them.

1 Introduction

Nothing lives forever. However, when we look at nature we see that when parts of an organism fail to operate, other parts may adapt to recover its functionality. This is not at all the case for electronics, as failing sub-circuits usually lead to overall disrupted operation. This paper discusses a new approach based on a bio-inspired technique to gain fault tolerance in electronic circuits. More specifically, it presents a hardware-friendly genetic regulatory network (GRN), able to grow structures based on artificial proteins and genomes.

The system is targeted for a new bio-inspired hardware chip called POEtic tissue, able to implement the three distinguished ways of biological adaptation: evolution, growth and learning [6]. Each chip can be used to implement a particular combination of these adaptation methods. In the work presented here, multi-cellular tissues are created from a collection of identical cells, which differentiate to attain specific functions based upon genetic information and inter-cellular signalling mediated by artificial proteins. The artificial proteins determine which genes are expressed, and in this fashion, the static genetic information is able to generate dynamic patterns, as proteins continuously arise, diffuse, and decay. These dynamic properties may improve fault tolerance of electronic based circuitry, as damage may be counteracted by protein production. We induce faults during the evolution of the genetic regulatory networks, to see how resilient this method is to damage.

2 Genetic Regulatory Network Cells

The multi-cellular system consists of totipotent cells, each of them having the capability to replace another due to an identical 'blue print'. Each cell has an identical genome combined with a unique protein mixture, the proteome, which determines its cell type. Implementation is done by means of POEtic "molecules": small FPGA hardware elements that can be configured to perform elementary arithmetic operations. The resulting tissue aims at creating bio-inspired evolvable hardware, which is not restricted to amplifiers or similar typical electronic blocks, but extends to higher level applications like neurons or oscillators. As a whole, it can be considered as a PO model, a combination of evolution (phylogeny) with growth (ontogeny). On top of this an epigeny layer can be added, for example in the form of neurons, although this is not addressed in this paper [5].

Each cell contains a genetic regulatory network (GRN). In a GRN, artificial genomes are divided into genes that can be unlocked when cell environmental requirements are met. This locking and unlocking of genes is inspired by the transcription of biological genetic material, and is initiated by the binding of proteins onto specific gene related regions, called cis regions. Connected proteins can either initiate or cease protein production, called expression or inhibition respectively. This relation is encoded in the gene: it encodes which protein type can bind and which protein type is produced. The complete system is situated in a simulated environment in which proteins can exist in various concentrations within the cell. These protein concentrations have to be beyond a genetically encoded threshold for the gene to be 'unlocked'. Since the proteins in the system act upon the genome, the genome is paired with the proteins within the cell. Multicellular GRNs contain multiple copies of identical genomes and allow proteins to be diffused between neighbouring cells (4 immediate neighbours). Different diffusion rates of the related proteins that flow from cell to cell give rise to variations in viscosity. Moreover, protein types in a system may vary in their half-life (decay rate), which limits the temporal effect of produced proteins. In this sense the system may exhibit temporal behaviour due to production and decay of proteins, while diffusion may be used to generate spatial patterns.

3 Implementation

Most simulations utilising GRNs have almost no restrictions laid upon them, in contrast to designing hardware friendly versions [2]. Minimal size constraints and computational tractability are key-points of the minimalist GRN system presented here [3]. All parameters have been encoded in 7 bit values and are manipulated by fixed point arithmetic. The GRN mechanism is divided into three separate pathways: protein decay, diffusion and production.

Digital hardware systems don't allow real valued chemical diffusion; therefore proteins diffuse according to integer protein gradients among neighbouring cells. Diffused proteins to neighbouring cells are added to their proteomes. Cells located at the borders are connected to the other side of the tissue, making it boundless for the diffusion mechanism. Produced proteins arise from the regulatory pathway which uses a specific genome encoding. In this work we will discuss two hardware friendly encodings from which one was selected for implementation in hardware.

3.1 Minimal Level Encoding

Four main regions make up the gene. Genes are activated when a particular protein, encoded in the *cis* region, is available in the proteome of the cell. Upon activation the gene produces a protein type encoded in the second field, *prod* (see fig. 1b). Not only the mere absence or presence of the proteins is of importance: another field includes the minimal protein concentration, *min*, for the gene to become active. This relation can be flipped by a bit, *i*, which determines whether the gene is an excitatory or inhibitory gene. The former starts producing proteins (P_{prod}), dependant on how far the level is exceeded, the later slowly diminishes production as the protein concentration of type *cis* (P_{cis}) reaches the encoded level (Eq. 1). Note that due to hardware friendliness, this relation is linear. In total each gene of this encoding consists of 12 bits, 2 for the *cis* and *prod* field each, 1 bit indicating its behaviour and 7 remaining bits encoding the minimal level.

$$P_{prod} = \begin{cases} \max(min - P_{cis}, 0) & i = 0 \\ \max(P_{cis} - min, 0) & i = 1 \end{cases} \quad (1)$$

3.2 MinMax Level Encoding

While the former encoding is still quite biological plausible, this encoding adds another level which is unseen in nature. This extra level, *max*, encodes the concentration at which the behaviour of the gene switches back (see fig. 2c bottom). In the excitatory case, the exceeding of this maximum level leads to no proteins generation. In the inhibitory case, proteins gradually arise when biased to this maximum level (Eq. 2). The addition of this extra 7 bits level makes it a 19 bits gene.

$$P_{prod} = \begin{cases} \max(min - P_{cis}, 0) & i = 0 \ \& \ P_{cis} < min \\ \max(P_{cis} - max,) & i = 0 \ \& \ P_{cis} > max \\ \max(P_{cis} - min, 0) & i = 1 \ \& \ P_{cis} < max \end{cases} \quad (2)$$

3.3 Hardware GRN Cells

The simulated GRN model is used to derive experimental results and is translated in POEtic hardware molecules, for use in future intrinsic EHW experiments. The current serial implementation of the min level GRN cell is about 200 molecules (elementary functional units). Estimates of the final POEtic chip also lead to approximately 200 molecules, meaning that one cell could be implemented in one chip.

Larger cell grids can be created by combining several chips together, an inherent property of POEtic tissue. The exact size depends on the amount of genes in the cell, as they are included in a separate memory module of the system. The hardware implementation operates on one gene at a time. As genes reside in memory cells, memory extensions easily lead to additional genes. The current design is targeted for 4 proteins, extending this requires a redesign of the implementation. Given the fact that our minimal level encoding seemed to perform quite well in simulation, its low space requirement made it a logical candidate for hardware implementation.

Inside the cell a table contains the protein decay rates for all available types. In the decay pathway, each entry in the protein table is cycled through and scaled by this value. In the regulation pathway, the cis-region produces an address for a selectable memory cell; this outputs the current concentration, which is compared by a switchable comparator that receives the min level and an inhibition bit as an input. Its output, the biased value, is added to the temporary protein table, which points to the entry directed by the production region in the gene. Since this pathway expresses only one gene at a time, all genes are cycled through before proceeding to the next pathway. The diffusion pathway involves the communication between neighbouring cells forms the most intricate and space consuming pathway. Each current protein concentration has to be scaled by diffusion rates stored within a table and transmitted to neighbouring cells. At the same time it has to process received concentrations to the current concentrations.

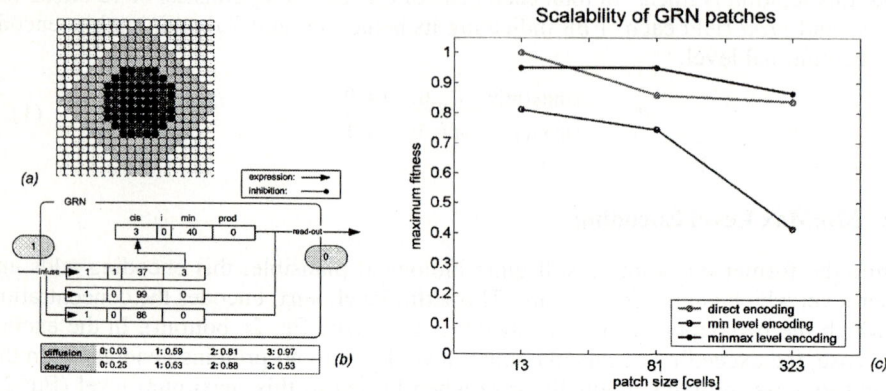

Fig. 1. (a) A grown patch on simulated tissue. (b) The evolved GRN that generates the patch. (c) Maximum obtained fitness for different encodings: direct, min- and minmax level GRN, after 200 generations and averaged over 5 runs [3].

4 Applications

Genetic regulatory networks have been mostly used for creating systems that can grow and develop structures in space [1]. Since the proteome in a single cell behaves dynamically due to infused proteins from neighbouring cells and external injections, it is also possible to generate spatial-temporal patterns [4]. Furthermore, this dynamic nature could also make the tissue somehow fault tolerant. As functionality is not directly encoded in the genome, but comes from the interaction of produced proteins, complete structures and functionality could be more stable when parts of the tissue fail to operate properly as they may be compensated by internal dynamics.

Before looking at fault tolerance, we address the basic capabilities of the GRN tissue. First of all, its ability to grow basic structures in fault-free conditions is compared to a direct encoding. As fault tolerance in our case is related to the ability to utilise the dynamic behaviour, the next series of experiments focuses on oscillation capabilities. Successfully evolved behaviour suggests that the system can produce dynamics to compensate for induced damage.

In the experiments, specific proteins are infused in the GRN tissue in the first clock cycle after which the tissue operates without external influences. The growth period is defined as the number of cycles the GRN system is run. During the growth period, normally 40 cycles, the tissue is evaluated by the fitness function, and results in an averaged fitness value at the end of the growth period. This value is used by a genetic algorithm operating with truncation selection (25%), 1 point-crossover (50%) and a uniform mutation rate of (1%). Genome lengths vary upon the task and are measured in amount of genes, each either 12 or 19 bits long, dependent on the used encoding scheme. Protein specific parameters are also encoded within the genome. For each four protein types, two specific parameters defining protein diffusion and decay are encoded each on 7 bits.

4.1 Patch Growth

The objective of this task is to grow patches of specific target sizes (ranging from 13 to 323 cells), which is initiated by a single protein infusion in the centre of the tissue (fig. 1a). Next to the GRN encodings a direct encoding was used to compare the scalability of the encodings, in which case each bit directly encodes the state of the cell. Maximum fitness is obtained when exclusively the cells within the target area contain the required target protein type 0 (Eq. 3&4). Figure 1 shows that direct encodings compete quite fairly to the developmental encodings on a 13 cell patch (radius is quarter of tissue size), but loses some performance when this patch is scaled relatively to 81 cells with a larger tissue size of 20 by 20 cells. A patch of 323 cells (radius of half the tissue size), shows that the minimal level encoding starts to degrade, this in contrast to the minmax level encoding (see fig. 1 c).

$$f_t = \frac{COUNT_{IN}}{patchsize} \cdot \frac{COUNT_{OUT}}{tissuesize - patchsize} \qquad (3)$$

$$fitness = \frac{1}{growthperiod} \sum_{t=0}^{growthperiod} f_t \qquad (4)$$

When we look at the evolved GRNs, we see that the stable equilibrium state is obtained due to the decay and diffusion parameters; proteins are precisely triggered to vanish due to decay at the edge of the patch (see fig. 1 a). Differently sized patches can be the result of different decay and diffusion rates. The better performance of the minmax level encoding in the relative larger patch may be explained by the fact that this encoding can trigger also on a maximal level, so the 'edge' of the regulating protein does not have to be as sharp as with the minimal encoding. At the same time, this seems to force the min level encoding to grow at a slower pace.

4.2 Oscillation

Initial experiments showed that the genetic regulatory system automatically produces temporal behaviours (which resulted in spatial checkerboard patterns as well as oscillating cells). While these auto-oscillations contain high frequencies, it is interesting to see whether evolution can fine-tune oscillation to a specified oscillation frequency. Fitness is obtained for minimising the difference, *diff*, between a protein concentration, P_0, and a target sine of a given period (Eq. 5&6).

First we infuse a maximum quantity, *max*, of proteins at time step 0 in the centre cell; we look solely at one cell to determine its fitness. Although in practice it is shown that neighbouring cells mimic the oscillating behaviour of the centre cell, leading to growing circles that emerge from the injection spot (see fig. 2a).

$$diff = \left| \frac{max}{2} + \frac{max}{2} * \sin(\frac{t}{period}) - P^t{}_0 \right| \qquad (5)$$

$$\text{fitness} = 1 - \frac{1}{\text{growthperiod}} \sum_{t=0}^{\text{growthperiod}} \frac{\text{diff}}{\text{MaxConcentration}} \qquad (6)$$

We want to assess the ability of the tissue to produce oscillatory behaviour at different frequencies. To this end we swept the target oscillation period between 4 and 20 cycles (see fig. 2b). Environmental conditions were slightly altered by adding one gene in the genome, leading to 5 genes. Both encodings successfully evolved the desired oscillation frequency when we look at the maximum fitness of 5 equal runs (see fig. 2b). This freedom to oscillate at different frequencies can be attributed to the evolvable decay rates, which can fine-tune the decay for it to reach a critical level near the beginning of the oscillation period. In the evolved individuals 3 out of the 4 proteins have been exploited by evolution

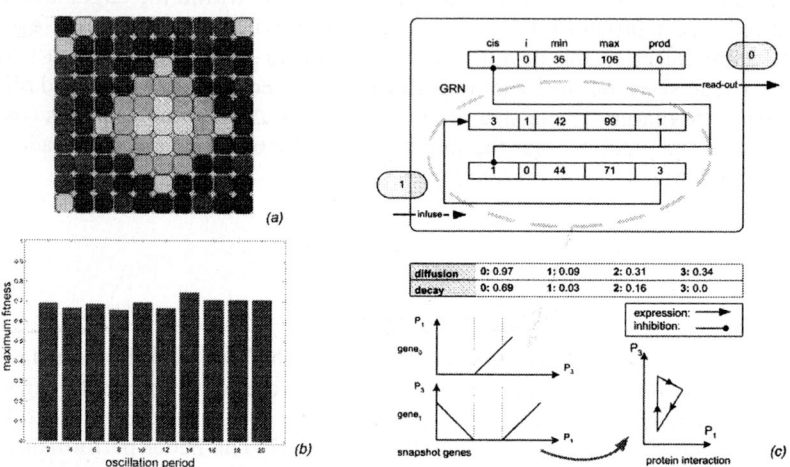

Fig. 2. (a) Growing rings emerge from an oscillating cell. (b) Various target frequencies are equally evolvable. The shown results are maximum obtained fitness values derived form the minmax encoding after 5 averaged runs of 200 generations. (c) 2 genes in the GRN interact with each to produce oscillations [3].

The evolved GRN has 2 main operating genes that produce the oscillatory behaviour (see fig. 2c). The first gene, *gene 0*, (seen bottom in fig. 2c) produces protein 3 in the presence of protein 1. The lack of protein 3, due to decay, activates the second gene, *gene 1*, (seen middle in fig. 2c), and starts to produce protein 1. This in effect leads to intertwined genes, in which each stimulates the other. The remaining genes in the network are evolved as read-out genes, and map protein type 1 to the target type 0.

5 Fault Tolerance

We can inspect the fault tolerance of a system in various ways. To our knowledge GRNs have never been used in fault tolerance tasks. We chose to damage aspects directly related to the gene regulation process. First of all, we flushed the protein concentration, similar to a memory, of random cells and at random time steps during the growth period. A second type of failure was induced by stopping the gene regulation process of random cells, but allowing proteins to be infused into the cell and thus indirectly determine the proteome of the cell. Finally, we looked at how the system performs when cells are killed; no input and output of any kind was allowed, and no regulation occurs in the cell, making it a dead cell in the tissue.

We applied all of these types of fault injuries to both developmental encodings and rerun the experiments 5 times, each lasting 200 generations. Environmental conditions are similar to the previous task: a growth period of 40 cycles, 5 genes in each genome, 4 protein types available in the system and the tissue consists of 10 by 10 cells.

5.1 Flush Cells

During the whole growth period of the individual, each cell has a certain probability to have its proteome flushed. Such error is random in both time and space, and can be conceived as a memory reliability error. Although both encodings seem to handle minor injuries, we see that the performance of the min level encoding drops sharply when the flush damage rate is increased (see fig. 3). The performance stabilises above a 10 percent damage rate, but it has to be noted that the corresponding behaviour is quite erratic. Performance degrades more gradually for the minmax level encoding, which still performs reasonably well at the 20 percent damage rate. In contrast to the fault-free evolution, we observe that proteins are evolved to be more dynamic (higher diffusivity and decay). More dynamic proteins in combination with a production interaction can counteract the loss of proteins more easily.

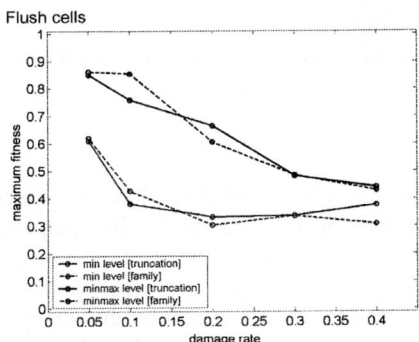

Fig. 3. Maximum fitness values averaged over 5 runs, when flushing the proteins during the growth period at various damage rates.

5.2 Freeze GRN Regulation

At the first time step of the growth period, random cells have a probability to lose their ability to generate proteins in their subsequent life time. Note that these damage probabilities are incomparable to the former ones. Damage is only induced during the first cycle and kept spatially constant, which may be easier for the GRN to handle.

When applied to both encodings we see that the min level encoding performs worse with low damage rate (see fig. 5 left). A possible explanation is that min level encoding only has one boundary region, and thus protein level have to be sharp decaying at the edge of the patch. This suggests that for low damage rate the production of proteins has to be "tamed", to limit the growing patch. As fitness is measured during the whole growth period, this slower growing patch leads to less fitness. This is supported by the evolved diffusion and decay constants; which are less dynamic in fault free conditions than in the fault induced case (see fig. 1b & 4). Resulting, we see that the minmax level encoding performs slightly better than the min level encoding. Moreover we also performed the identical injuries on patches grown by a GRN evolved in fault free conditions (dashed lines are single runs). We see that performance decreases considerably, suggesting that the fine-tuning of protein properties trough evolution is beneficial. We also verified the same behaviour on a patch 6 times bigger, in which a similar response is shown, but starts to degrade at 10 percent lower damage rate.

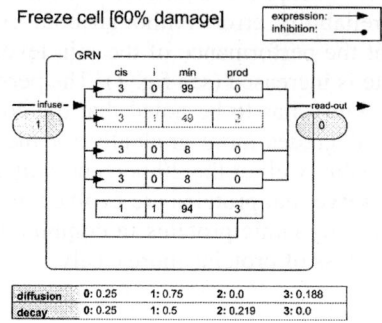

Fig. 4. An evolved GRN that grows a patch in freeze regulation conditions at a 60 damage rate.

5.3 Kill Cells

While the former experiments only disabled the decoding mechanism at the beginning of the growth period, we now disabled random cells completely. We see a linear decrease of performance when we increase the damage rate (see fig. 5 right). This is comparable with a non adaptive technique in which damage directly causes cell malfunction. Also in a system using a direct genetic encoding, performance would degrade also linearly. As in the freeze regulation we induced the same type of damage on a GRN evolved in fault free conditions. Like previously, we see that evolutionary pressure on the GRN and its diffusion and decay constants is beneficial for system performance, which is indicated in the right side of Figure 5 (dashed lines are GRN evolved in fault free conditions).

6 Discussion

In this paper we described results derived from a hardware-friendly multi-cellular genetic regulatory network which has been implemented on a new bio-inspired electronic circuit called POEtic tissue. Simulations were conducted to derive experimental results before committing to the hardware implementation. As fault tolerance is one of the main topics in current bio-inspired electronic architectures, we explored the capacity of the GRN to withstand faults and recover from them. Thanks to gene reuse, GRN may scale better than direct encodings when the phenotype size increases. We compared a direct encoding to the two developmental encodings: min- and minmax level encoding. Minmax level encoding performs better compared to the direct encoding. The comparatively slower growth of the patch when using the min level encoding, leads to a lower fitness. If damage has to be counteracted by internal dynamics, evolution has to be able to tame the dynamics of the GRN. Oscillation is an obvious task to measure temporal capabilities of a GRN. Both GRN mechanisms handle various target oscillation periods well, thanks to the evolvable decay and production constants.

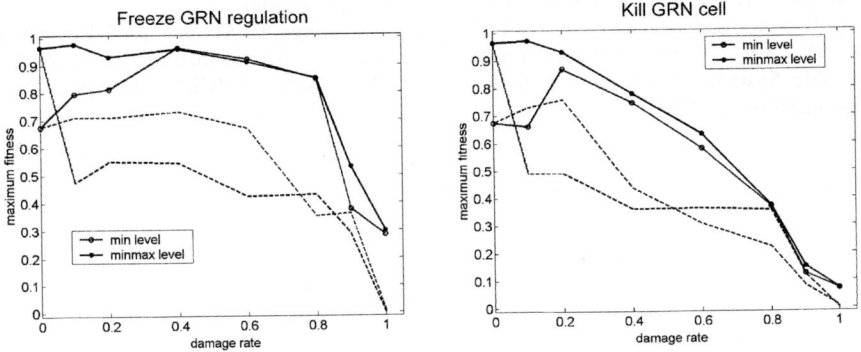

Fig. 5. Maximum fitness (5 runs, 200 generations) when freezing the regulation (left) or killing the cells (right). The evolved GRN handles quite some damage during regulation freezing. Damaging a normal fault free evolved patch leads to a drop in performance (dashed).

The two GRN mechanisms behave differently to faults. Both can sustain slight damage when faults consist of flushing the proteome. However, the minmax level outperforms the min level encoding and obtains a high fitness even at a considerable damage rate. The difference between both encodings also becomes apparent when freezing the regulation process. The min level encoding needs a limited growth speed in order to grow the specified patch. An increased damage rate allows a quicker growth and thus leads to a higher average fitness. Patches stay quite stable until damage reaches 80 percent and stability of the phenotype collapses. However, the GRN systems are more tolerant to faults than direct genetic encodings and show a less than linear decrease of the fitness with an increase in damage rates. When killing cells, the performance degrades in a linear fashion. This is normal as the tissue is considered irreversibly damaged. However if evolution occurs with faults, it manages to adapt to such condition to minimize the performance degradation, in comparison to evolution without faults. Although these results seem promising, they come at a high cost. The current hardware implementation uses about 200 molecules, which corresponds to a full POEtic chip. Developing a more compact implementation is the first step to create more realistic experiments. The ease at which these GRNs could be evolved may indicate a fruitful application in future work on more complex tasks like robotic control in extreme conditions.

References

1. Eggenberger, P. & Dravid, R.: An evolutionary approach to pattern formation mechanisms on Lepidopteran wings. In the Proceedings of CEC1999, pp. 470-473 (1999).
2. Gordon, T.: Exploring models of development for evolutionary circuit design. In CEC2003, the Congress on Evolutionary Computation, pp. 2050-2057 (2003).
3. Koopman, A.C.M.: Hardware-Friendly Genetic Regulatory Networks in POEtic tissue. M.Sc. thesis. Institute for Information and Computing Sciences, Utrecht University (2004).
4. Quick, T. et al.: Evolving embodied genetic regulatory network-driven control systems. In Proceedings of the Seventh European Conference on Artificial Life, ECAL'03 (2003).
5. Roggen, D., Floreano, D. & Mattiussi, C.: A Morphogenetic Evolutionary System: Phylogeny of the POEtic Circuit. In Proceedings of the Fifth International Conference ICES 2003, Evolvable Systems: From biology to Hardware. 153-164 (2003).
6. Tyrell, A.M., Sanchez, E. Floreano, D. Tempesti, G. Mange, D. Moreno, J-M. Rosenberg, J. & Villa, A.E.P.: POEtic Tissue: An integrated architecture for bio-inspired hardware. In Evolvable Systems: From biology to Hardware. Proceedings of ICES 2003, pp. 129-140, Springer-Verlag (2003).

Evolving Dynamics in an Artificial Regulatory Network Model

P. Dwight Kuo[1], André Leier[2], and Wolfgang Banzhaf[1]

[1] Department of Computer Science, Memorial University of Newfoundland,
St. John's NL A1B 3X5, Canada
[2] Department of Computer Science, University of Dortmund,
D–44221 Dortmund, Germany

Abstract. In this paper artificial regulatory networks (ARN) are evolved to match the dynamics of test functions. The ARNs are based on a genome representation generated by a duplication / divergence process. By creating a mapping between the protein concentrations created by gene excitation and inhibition to an output function, the network can be evolved to match output functions such as sinusoids, exponentials and sigmoids. This shows that the dynamics of an ARN may be evolved and thus may be suitable as a method for generating arbitrary time-series for function optimization.

1 Introduction

It has been recognized that understanding the differences between species (and thus the key to evolution) lies in the DNA information controlling gene expression since only a tiny fraction of DNA is translated into proteins [1]. Regulation appears to be a very reasonable answer for a functional role for unexpressed DNA. According to Neidthardt [2] and Thomas [3], 88% of the genome of *E. Coli* is expressed with 11% suspected to contain regulatory information.

Since many evolutionary effects can be traced back to their regulatory causes, regulatory networks mediate between development and evolution and thus serve to help shape organism morphology and behavior [4]. Studying models of regulatory networks can help us to understand some of these mechanisms by providing lessons for both natural and artificial systems under evolution.

It has been previously shown that our regulatory network model is able to reproduce dynamic phenomena found in natural genetic regulatory networks [5]. One example is the ability to capture shifts in the onset and offset of gene expression (heterochrony) based on single bit-flip mutations. As such, this model can relate changes in time and intensity to tiny pattern changes on bit strings. This could possibly provide the algorithmic "missing link" between genotypes subject to constant evolutionary changes and the remarkably stable phenotypes found in the real world. In addition, this model has previously been shown to generate scale-free and small world topologies [6] and network motifs [7].

Recently, there has been significant interest in modelling regulatory networks in the evolutionary computation literature [5, 8–14]. Features of regulatory networks have been previously used in the context of optimization by [8, 10, 14].

However, these models have been explicitly designed for artificial ontogeny. Here we propose the use of a regulatory network framework as a general method for evolving arbitrary time series. Obtaining arbitrary functions through evolutionary means for the purpose of model optimization has been previously performed for flying [15], locomotion [16] and the inference of differential equations [17].

In addition, previous models of ARNs primarily use boolean representations of network dynamics [8, 9, 12, 13]. Here we show that an ARN model using differential equations (approximated as difference equations) can also display complex behaviors which may be selected by evolution.

Other ideas relating to genetic transcription have also previously been used in function optimization such as genetic-code transformations [18], gene expression [19, 20], gene signaling [21] and diploidity [22].

2 Artificial Regulatory Network Model

The ARN consists of a bit string representing a genome with direction (i.e. 5' → 3' in DNA) and mobile "proteins" which interact with the genome through their constituent bit patterns. In this model, proteins are able to interact with the genome most notably at "regulatory" sites located upstream from genes. Attachment to these sites produces either inhibition or activation of the corresponding protein. Therefore, these interactions may be interpreted as a regulatory network with proteins acting as transcription factors.

The genome itself is created through a series of whole length duplication / divergence events. Creation of a genome in such a manner has been shown to generate network topologies which have similarities to biological networks such as having scale-free and small world topology as well as network motifs [6, 7]. First, a random 32-bit string is generated. This string is then used in a series of length duplications similar to those found in nature [23] followed by mutations in order to generate a genome of length L_G. A "promotor" bit sequence of 8-bits was then arbitrarily selected to be "01010101". By randomly choosing "0"s and "1"s to generate a genome, any one-byte pattern can be expected to appear with probability $2^{-8} = 0.39\%$. Since the promotor pattern itself is repetitive, overlapping promotors or periodic extensions of the pattern are not allowed, i.e. a bit sequence of "0101010101" (10-bits) is detected as a single promotor site starting at the first bit. However regions associated with one gene may overlap with another should a promotor pattern also exist within a portion of the coding region of a gene.

The promotor signals the beginning of a gene on the bit string analogous to an open reading frame (ORF) on DNA – a long sequence of DNA that contains no "stop" codon and therefore encodes all or part of a protein. Each gene is set to a fixed length of $l_{gene} = 5$ 32-bit integers which results in an expressed bit pattern of 160 bits. Genes can thus be created on the genome by complete duplications of previously created genes, mutation, and / or combinations of the ending and starting sequences of the genome during duplication.

Immediately upstream from the promotor sites exist two additional 32-bit segments which represent the enhancer and inhibitor sites. As previously mentioned, attachment of proteins (transcription factors) to these sites results in changes to protein production for the corresponding genes (regulation). In this model, we assume only one regulatory site for the increase of expression and one site for the decrease of expression of proteins. This is a radical simplification since natural genomes may have 5-10 regulatory sites that may even be occupied by complexes of proteins [4].

Processes such as transcription, diffusion, spatial variations and elements such as introns, RNA-like mobile elements and translation procedures resulting in a different alphabet for proteins are neglected in this model. This last mechanism is replaced as follows: Each protein is a 32-bit sequence constructed by a many-to-one mapping of its corresponding gene which contains five 32-bit integers. The protein sequence is created by performing the majority rule on each bit position of these five integers so as to arrive at a 32-bit protein. Ties (not possible with an odd number for l_g) for a given bit position are resolved by chance.

Proteins may then be examined to see how they may "match" with the genome, specifically at the regulatory sites. This comparison is implemented by using the XOR operation which returns a "1" if bits on both patterns are complementary. In this scheme, the degree of match between the genome and the protein bit patterns is specified by the number of bits set to "1" during an XOR operation. In general it can be expected that a Gaussian distribution results from measuring the match between proteins and bit sequences in a randomly generated genome [4]. By making the simplifying assumption that the occupation of both of a gene's regulatory sites modulates the expression of its corresponding protein, we may deduce a gene-protein interaction network comprising the different genes and proteins which can be parameterized by strength of match. The bit-string for one gene is shown in Figure 1.

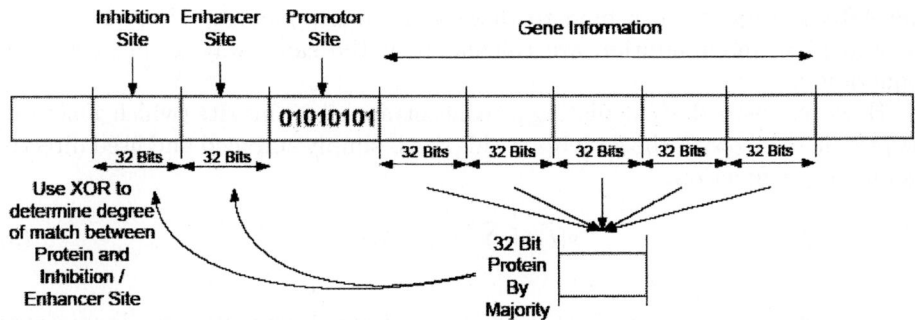

Fig. 1. Bit string for one gene in the ARN model.

The rate at which protein i is produced is given by:

$$\frac{dc_i}{dt} = \frac{\delta \left(e_i - h_i\right) c_i}{\sum_j c_j} \quad (1)$$

$$e_i, h_i = \frac{1}{N} \sum_j^N c_j \exp\left(\beta(u_j - u_{max})\right) \quad (2)$$

where e_i and h_i represent the excitation and inhibition of the production of protein i, u_j represents the number of matching bits between protein j and activation or inhibition site i, u_{max} represents the maximum match (in this case, 32), β and δ are positive scaling factors, and c_i is the concentration of protein i at time t. Note that the concentrations of the various proteins are required to sum to 1. This ensures that there is a competition between binding sites for proteins.

It can be noted that the ARN model presented bears some resemblance to a recurrent neural network (RNN). In the ARN, genes and the match strength between inhibition / activation sites and proteins are analogous to the neurons and connection strengths in an RNN framework.

3 Optimization

By simulating the ARN model presented in the previous section, we obtain a dynamical view of the protein concentrations in the system. However, such a system has no assigned semantics – the protein concentrations have no meaning outside the system. In addition, since the protein concentrations are limited to sum to 1 (i.e. $\sum c_i = 1$), generation of some functions is excluded. In order to use such a system for the purpose of optimization, a mapping is required. An additional 64-bit sequence is randomly selected along the genome as a binding site for the desired output function. The first 32-bits specify the inhibition site while the second 32-bits specify the activation site. The proteins generated by the ARN are free to also bind to these additional regulatory sites. The levels of activation and inhibition are calculated in the same way as in Section 2, Equation 2.

However, instead of calculating a "concentration" of this site (which generates no protein of its own), the activity at this site is simply summed and used directly as an output function:

$$s(t) = \sum_i (e_i - h_i) \quad (3)$$

Subsequent normalization of $s(t)$ to between -1 and 1 generates the dynamics of the specific genome. Thus, the additional binding sites added to the genome may be thought of as a method with which to extract dynamics from the changes in concentrations of the proteins in the ARN model. Further sites may be added to the genome for the extraction of additional signals.

In order to evolve solutions $s(t)$, a simple (50+100)-Evolutionary Strategy (ES) is used [24]. Genomes were generated by 10 duplication events per genome subject to 1% mutation (without selection) leading to individual genomes of length $L_G = 32768$. It has been shown that a mutation rate of 1% during the duplication / divergence process is sufficient to "rewire" parts of the topology of the network without making it completely random [6].

The number of genes in each genome is given by the number of promotor patterns present as was previously defined in Section 2. Each generation, 100 new individuals are created from the current population using a 1% single-point (bit-flip) mutation (i.e. on average, 328 mutations per genome). The fitness of these solutions was calculated and the best 50 of 150 (parents + children) proceed to the next generation. ES was stopped when the best solution found was not improved upon for 250 generations.

The objective is to minimize the fitness function calculated as the mean square error (MSE) between the desired function and the evolved function. The following cases were examined and are shown in Figure 2.

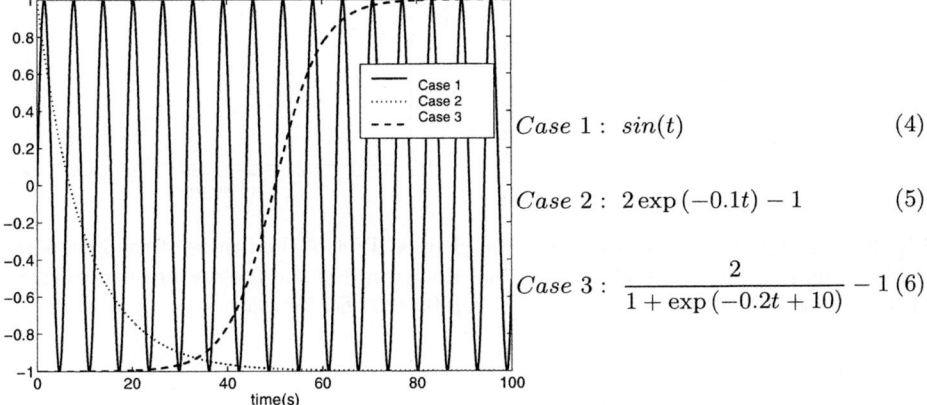

$$\text{Case 1}: \sin(t) \qquad (4)$$

$$\text{Case 2}: 2\exp(-0.1t) - 1 \qquad (5)$$

$$\text{Case 3}: \frac{2}{1 + \exp(-0.2t + 10)} - 1 \quad (6)$$

Fig. 2. Plot of the three fitness cases.

All solutions were generated with a time step, $dt = 0.1s$. The initial protein concentrations (the initial conditions for the differential equation) are set to be $\frac{1}{\#of genes}$ to remain within the simplex. In addition, the first 100 time steps (10s) are ignored. This is done in order to exclude the startup dynamics of the model. Thus, for calculation of the fitness function, the normalized output generated by the ARN model from time $t = 10...110s$ is compared with the fitness case $f(t)$ from time $t = 0...100s$.

4 Results

Tables 1, 2 and 3 summarize the results of 10 evolutionary runs each for the three fitness cases. Figures 3, 5 and 7 show the actual function generated by the best individual of each run for the three fitness cases. Figures 4, 6 and 8 show the progress of the best evolutionary run for each fitness case.

It is clearly shown that the ARN model accurately generates dynamics approximating the sinusoid (Figure 3), the exponential (Figure 5) and the sigmoid (Figure 7) functions with good accuracy for all runs. In all fitness cases and evolutionary runs, the MSE calculated was less than 0.00588654. Additional support for the success of these simulations can be seen in the final population fitness averages shown in Tables 1, 2 and 3. The average population fitness values (MSE) are relatively small with low standard deviation. This indicates that the population is such that all or virtually all individuals when simulated generate functions that closely approximate the respective objective functions.

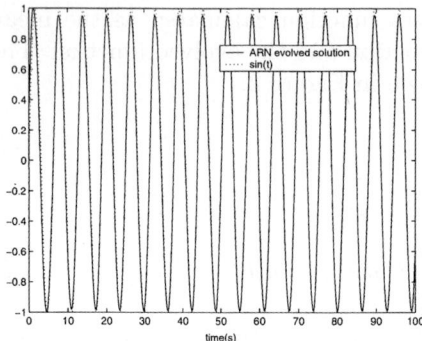
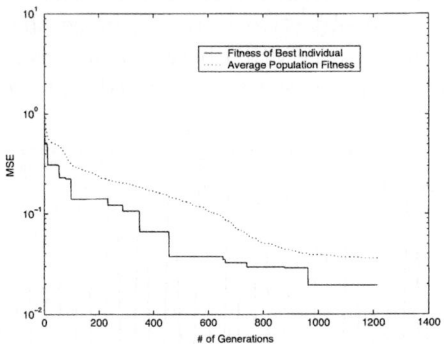

Fig. 3. Plot of best solution (run #8) compared to ideal solution for Case #1. The MSE is 0.000151746.

Fig. 4. Plot of the fitness of the best solution (run #8) and the average fitness using (50+100)-ES for Case #1.

Table 1. Results of 10 runs of (50+100)-ES on Case 1. Standard deviation in brackets.

Run #	Best MSE	#Generations	#Genes	Avg. MSE(Pop.)	Avg. #Genes (Pop.)
1	0.001445217	731	47	0.00287(0.000765)	45.31(5.72)
2	0.001165628	381	74	0.00316(0.000780)	76.92(3.42)
3	0.000614281	1214	105	0.00114(0.000147)	117.59(4.57)
4	0.000747053	835	234	0.00291(0.000817)	244.00(13.2)
5	0.001861556	428	63	0.00326(0.000684)	75.08(9.34)
6	0.000640149	1077	101	0.00186(0.000347)	102.49(4.08)
7	0.001561523	315	26	0.00440(0.000847)	32.78(5.55)
8	0.000151746	1040	124	0.00058(0.000131)	135.63(6.32)
9	0.000519559	933	71	0.00134(0.000341)	92.88(53.2)
10	0.000846462	858	55	0.00270(0.000449)	48.57(3.22)

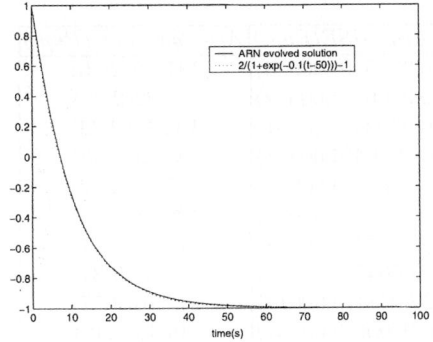

Fig. 5. Plot of best solution (run #3) compared to ideal solution for Case #2. The MSE is 0.00363873.

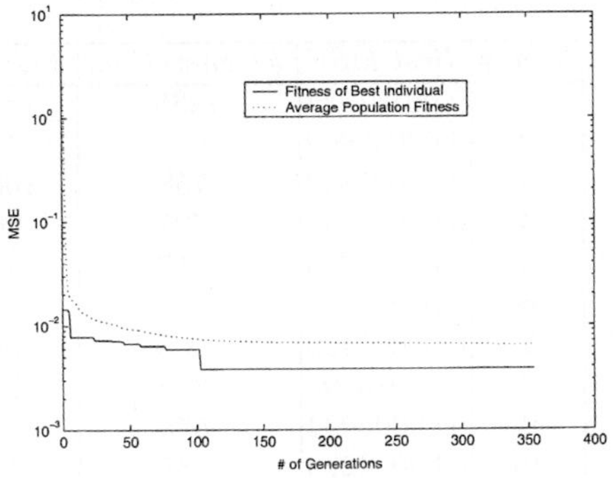

Fig. 6. Plot of the fitness of the best solution (run #3) and the average fitness using (50+100)-ES for Case #2.

Table 2. Results of 10 runs of (50+100)-ES on Case 2. Standard deviation in brackets.

Run #	Best MSE	#Generations	#Genes	Avg. MSE(Pop.)	Avg. #Genes (Pop.)
1	0.00411971	708	133	0.00447(0.000134)	142.83(5.88)
2	0.00478168	642	166	0.00554(0.000250)	185.95(13.5)
3	0.00363873	354	27	0.00641(0.000553)	52.22(7.00)
4	0.00441011	359	20	0.00660(0.000610)	31.95(7.38)
5	0.00381064	747	97	0.00505(0.000303)	106.81(5.71)
6	0.00402240	877	63	0.00464(0.000180)	58.83(4.17)
7	0.00426413	501	128	0.00574(0.000354)	116.14(8.75)
8	0.00537858	287	176	0.00661(0.000458)	164.40(11.1)
9	0.00511630	466	58	0.00688(0.000563)	54.26(3.73)
10	0.00588654	519	45	0.00643(0.000171)	45.65(3.10)

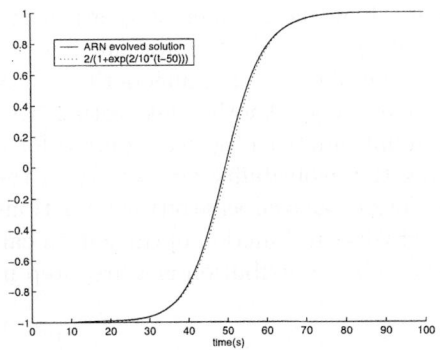
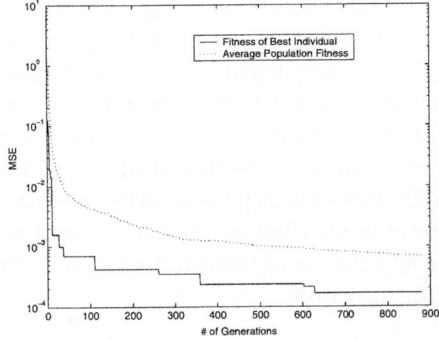

Fig. 7. Plot of best solution (run#4) compared to ideal solution for Case #3. The MSE is 0.0000173162.

Fig. 8. Plot of the fitness of the best solution (run#4) and the average fitness using (50+100)-ES for Case #3.

Table 3. Results of 10 runs of (50+100)-ES on Case 3. Standard deviation in brackets.

Run #	Best MSE	#Generations	#Genes	Avg. MSE(Pop.)	Avg. #Genes (Pop.)
1	0.00101533	1235	154	0.00150(0.00013)	147.59(20.6)
2	0.00035992	557	36	0.00068(0.00012)	39.22(2.40)
3	0.00001843	758	100	0.00004(0.00001)	102.45(2.93)
4	0.00001732	721	96	0.00004(0.00001)	96.55(2.80)
5	0.00011328	617	97	0.00025(0.00006)	102.78(4.02)
6	0.00002073	825	104	0.00013(0.00005)	109.78(5.03)
7	0.00005429	465	108	0.00044(0.00018)	112.37(11.4)
8	0.00016598	879	177	0.00047(0.00022)	186.02(9.87)
9	0.00005034	575	195	0.00031(0.00012)	212.16(9.57)
10	0.00002219	987	39	0.00006(0.00001)	39.49(2.42)

5 Conclusions

It has been demonstrated that the dynamics of a differential equation based ARN model initially created through a duplication / divergence process can be evolved towards simple functions. This might suggest that such an approach may also be appropriate for generating arbitrary functions suitable for use in applications such as model optimization.

Due to the way in which the genes are detected on the genome, there are plentiful opportunities for individuals in the population to acquire neutral mutations. It has been previously shown that neutral mutation can be extremely beneficial in the context of evolution [25]. Since there may exist extensive non-coding regions of the genome, neutral mutations are free to be collected in such regions with new genes appearing suddenly when a new promotor pattern has been created through mutation. As well, each of the networks generated for each fitness case contains a different topology (number of genes). Therefore, due to the quality of solutions, it may be inferred that there are many different networks which can give good approximations to each of the fitness cases.

Unfortunately, it is difficult to determine how the number of genes in the genome affects the evolvability or richness of dynamics in the system. It is an open question within this framework how the number of genes affects the ability of the system to generate functions of a given type. Another interesting area of further inquiry is to determine the minimum number of genes required for a given function. Further studies investigating the evolvability and ability of the ARN model to represent other classes of functions as well as arbitrary functions are necessary before the use of regulatory networks in function optimization can be systematically and fully realized. However, this contribution is a first step in that direction.

Acknowledgements

The authors would like to thank William Langdon and the reviewers for helpful comments.

References

1. Hood, L., Galas, D.: The digital code of DNA. Nature **421(6921)** (2003) 444–448
2. Neidhardt, F.C.: Escherichia Coli and Salmonella Typhimurium. ASM Press, Washington, DC (1996)
3. Thomas, G.H.: Completing the E.Coli proteome: a database of gene products characterised since completion of the genome sequence. Bioinformatics **15(10)** (1999) 860–861
4. Banzhaf, W.: On the dynamics of an artificial regulatory network. In Banzhaf, W., Christaller, T., Dittrich, P., Kim, J.T., Ziegler, J., eds.: Advances in Artificial Life – Proceedings of the 7th European Conference on Artificial Life (ECAL). Volume 2801 of Lecture Notes in Artificial Intelligence., Springer-Verlag (2003) 217–227
5. Banzhaf, W.: Artificial regulatory networks and genetic programming. In Riolo, R.L., Worzel, B., eds.: Genetic Programming Theory and Practice. Kluwer (2003) 43–62
6. Kuo, P.D., Banzhaf, W.: Scale-free and small world network topologies in an artificial regulatory network model. Ninth International Conference on the Simulation and Synthesis of Living Systems (ALIFE) **(in press)** (2004)
7. Banzhaf, W., Kuo, P.D.: Network motifs in artificial and natural transcriptional regulatory networks. Journal of Biological Physics and Chemistry **(in submission)** (2004)
8. Watson, J., Wiles, J., Hanan, J.: Towards more relevant evolutionary models: Integrating an artificial genome with a developmental phenotype. In: Proceedings of the Australian Conference on Artificial Life (ACAL). (2003) 288–298
9. Hallinan, J., Wiles, J.: Evolving genetic regulatory networks using an artificial genome. In Chen, Y.P.P., ed.: Second Asia-Pacific Bioinformatics Conference (APBC2004). Volume 29 of CRPIT., Dunedin, New Zealand, ACS (2004) 291–296
10. Bongard, J.: Evolving modular genetic regulatory networks. In: Proceedings of the IEEE 2002 Congress on Evolutionary Computation, IEEE Press (2002) 1872–1877
11. Hotz, P.E.: Genome-physics as a new concept to reduce the number of genetic parameters in artificial evolution. In: Proceedings of the IEEE 2003 Congress on Evolutionary Computation, IEEE Press (2003) 191–198
12. Willadsen, K., Wiles, J.: Dynamics of gene expression in an artificial genome. In: Proceedings of the IEEE 2003 Congress on Evolutionary Computation, IEEE Press (2003) 199–206
13. Reil, T.: Dynamics of gene expression in an artificial genome: Implications for biological and artificial ontogeny. In Floreano, D., Nicoud, J.D., Mondada, F., eds.: Advances in Artificial Life – Proceedings of the 5th European Conference on Artificial Life (ECAL). Volume 1674 of Lecture Notes in Computer Science., Springer-Verlag (1999) 457–466
14. Bongard, J.C., Pfeifer, R.: Evolving complete agents using artificial ontogeny. In Hara, F., Pfeifer, R., eds.: Morpho-functional Machines: The New Species (Designing Embodied Intelligence). Springer-Verlag (2003) 237–258
15. Augustsson, P., Wolff, K., Nordin, P.: Creation of a learning, flying robot by means of evolution. In Langdon, W.B., Cantú-Paz, E., Mathias, K., Roy, R., Davis, D., Poli, R., Balakrishnan, K., Honavar, V., Rudolph, G., Wegener, J., Bull, L., Potter, M.A., Schultz, A.C., Miller, J.F., Burke, E., Jonoska, N., eds.: GECCO 2002: Proceedings of the Genetic and Evolutionary Computation Conference, Morgan Kaufmann Publishers (2002) 1279–1285

16. Dittrich, P., Burgel, A., Banzhaf, W.: Learning to move a robot with random morphology. In Husbands, P., Meyer, J.A., eds.: Proceedings of the First European Workshop on Evolutionary Robotics. Volume 1468 of Lecture Notes in Computer Science., Springer-Verlag (1998) 165–178
17. Cao, H., Kang, L., Chen, Y., Yu, J.: Evolutionary modeling of systems of ordinary differential equations with genetic programming. Genetic Programming and Evolvable Machines **1(4)** (2000) 309–337
18. Kargupta, H., Ghosh, S.: Toward machine learning through genetic code-like transformations. Genetic Programming and Evolvable Machines **3(3)** (2002) 231–258
19. Kargupta, H.: The gene expression messy genetic algorithm. In: Proceedings of the IEEE 1996 Congress on Evolutionary Computation, IEEE Press (1996) 814–819
20. Eggenberger, P.: Evolving morphologies of simulated 3d organisms based on differential gene expression. In Harvey, I., Husbands, P., eds.: Proceedings of the 4th European Conference on Artificial Life (ECAL), MIT Press (1997) 205–213
21. Goldberg, D.E., Korb, B., Deb, K.: Messy genetic algorithms: Motivation, analysis and first results. Complex Systems **3(5)** (1989) 493–530
22. Yoshida, Y., Adachi, N.: A diploid genetic algorithm for preserving population diversity – pseudo-meiosis GA. In Davidor, Y., Schwefel, H.P., Männer, R., eds.: The Third Conference on Parallel Problem Solving from Nature(PPSN). Volume 866 of Lecture Notes in Computer Science., Springer-Verlag (1994) 36–45
23. Wolfe, K., Shields, D.: Molecular evidence for an ancient duplication of the entire yeast genome. Nature **387(6634)** (1997) 708–713
24. Beyer, H.G., Schwefel, H.P.: Evolution strategies: A comprehensive introduction. Natural Computing **1(1)** (2002) 3–52
25. Yu, T., Miller, J.: Neutrality and the evolvability of boolean function landscapes. In: Proceedings of the 4th European Conference on Genetic Programming (EuroGP). Volume 2038 of Lecture Notes in Computer Science., Springer-Verlag (2001) 204–217

The Application of Bayesian Optimization and Classifier Systems in Nurse Scheduling

Jingpeng Li and Uwe Aickelin

School of Computer Science and Information Technology
The University of Nottingham
Nottingham, NG8 1BB, UK
{jpl,uxa}@cs.nott.ac.uk

Abstract. Two ideas taken from Bayesian optimization and classifier systems are presented for personnel scheduling based on choosing a suitable scheduling rule from a set for each person's assignment. Unlike our previous work of using genetic algorithms whose learning is implicit, the learning in both approaches is explicit, i.e. we are able to identify building blocks directly. To achieve this target, the Bayesian optimization algorithm builds a Bayesian network of the joint probability distribution of the rules used to construct solutions, while the adapted classifier system assigns each rule a strength value that is constantly updated according to its usefulness in the current situation. Computational results from 52 real data instances of nurse scheduling demonstrate the success of both approaches. It is also suggested that the learning mechanism in the proposed approaches might be suitable for other scheduling problems.

1 Introduction

Scheduling problems are generally NP-hard combinatorial problems, and a lot of research has been done to solve these heuristically ([2], [3], [8], [10]). However, research into the development of a general scheduling algorithm is still in its infancy.

Genetic Algorithms (GAs) ([6], [7]) mimicking the natural evolutionary process of the survival of the fittest, have attracted much attention in solving difficult scheduling problems in recent years. Some obstacles exist when using GAs: there is no canonical mechanism to deal with constraints, which are commonly met in most real-world scheduling problems, and small improvements of a solution are difficult. To overcome both difficulties, indirect approaches have been presented ([3], [9], [10]) for nurse scheduling and driver scheduling. In these indirect GAs, the solution space is mapped and then a separate decoding routine builds solutions to the original problem.

In our previous indirect GAs, learning was implicit and restricted to the efficient adjustment of weights for a set of rules that are used to construct schedules. The major limitation of those approaches is that they learn in a non-human way. Like most existing construction algorithms, once the best weight combination is found, the rules used in the construction process are fixed at each iteration. However, normally a long sequence of moves is needed to construct a schedule. Using fixed rules at each move is unreasonable and not coherent with human learning processes.

When a human scheduler works, he normally builds a schedule systematically following a set of rules. After much practice, the scheduler gradually masters the knowledge of which solution parts go well with others. He can identify good parts and is aware of the solution quality even if the scheduling process is not completed yet, thus having the ability to finish a schedule by using flexible, rather than fixed, rules. In this paper, we will present two more human-like scheduling approaches, by using a cutting-edge Bayesian Optimization Algorithm (BOA) and an Adapted Classifier System (ACS) individually, to implement explicit learning from past solutions.

In our test problem (nurse scheduling) problem, the number of the nurse is fixed (about 30), and the target is to create a weekly schedule by assigning each nurse one out of up to 411 shift patterns in the most efficient way. Both of the proposed approaches achieve this by using one suitable rule, from a rule set that contains a number of available rules, for each nurse's assignment. Thus, a potential solution is represented as a sequence of rules corresponding to the first nurse to the last nurse.

The long-term aim of our research is to model the learning of a human scheduler. Humans can provide high quality solutions, but this is tedious and time consuming. Typically, they construct schedules based on rules learnt during scheduling. Due to human limitations, these rules are typically simple. Hence, our rules will be relatively simple, too. Nevertheless, human generated schedules are of high quality due to the ability of the scheduler to switch between the rules, based on the state of the current solution. We envisage the proposed BOA and the ACS to perform this task.

2 The Nurse Scheduling Problem

Nurse scheduling has been widely studied recently ([4], [5]). The schedules generated have to satisfy working contracts and meet the demand for a given number of nurses of different grades on each shift. The problem is complicated by the fact that higher qualified nurses can substitute less qualified nurses but not vice versa. Thus scheduling the different grades independently is not possible. Due to this characteristic, finding and maintaining feasible solutions for most local search algorithms is difficult.

2.1 Integer Linear Programming

The nurse scheduling problem can be formulated as an Integer Program as follows:

Indices:
    $i = 1...n$ nurse index;
    $j = 1...m$ shift pattern index;
    $k = 1...14$ day and night index (1...7 are days and 8...14 are nights);
    $s = 1...p$ grade index.

Decision variables:
    $x_{ij} = 1$ if nurse i works shift pattern j otherwise $x_{ij} = 0$.

Parameters:
  m = Number of shift patterns;
  n = Number of nurses;
  p = Number of grades;
  a_{jk} = 1 if shift pattern j covers day/night k otherwise a_{jk} = 0;
  q_{is} = 1 if nurse i is of grade s or higher otherwise q_{is} = 0;
  p_{ij} = Preference cost of nurse i working shift pattern j;
  R_{ks} = Demand of nurses with grade s on day/night k;
  N_i, D_i, B_i = Shifts per week of nurse i if night / day / both shifts are worked;
  $F(i)$ = Set of feasible shift patterns for nurse i, where $F(i)$ is defined as

$$F(i) = \begin{cases} \sum_{k=1}^{7} a_{jk} = D_i, & \forall j \in \text{day shifts} \\ \sum_{k=8}^{14} a_{jk} = N_i, & \forall j \in \text{night shifts} \\ \sum_{k=1}^{14} a_{jk} = B_i, & \forall j \in \text{combined shifts} \end{cases}, \forall i.$$

Target function is to minimize total preference cost of all nurses, denoted as

$$\sum_{i=1}^{n} \sum_{j \in F(i)}^{m} p_{ij} x_{ij} \to \min! \cdot \qquad (1)$$

Subject to:

1. Every nurse works exactly one feasible shift pattern:

$$\sum_{j \in F(i)} x_{ij} = 1, \forall i \ ; \qquad (2)$$

2. The demand for nurses is fulfilled for every grade on every day and night:

$$\sum_{j \in F(i)} \sum_{i=1}^{n} q_{is} a_{jk} x_{ij} \geq R_{ks}, \forall k, s \ \cdot \qquad (3)$$

Constraint set (2) ensures that every nurse works exactly one shift pattern from his/her feasible set, and constraint set (3) ensures that the demand for nurses is covered for every grade on every day and night. Note that the definition of q_{is} is such that higher graded nurses can substitute those at lower grades if necessary.

Typical problem dimensions are n = 30 nurses of p = 3 grades and m = 411 shift patterns for each nurse. Thus, the integer programming has some 12000 binary variables and about 100 constraints. This is a moderately sized problem. However, some problem cases remain unsolved after overnight computation using professional software [4].

2.2 A Graphic Representation for Nurse Scheduling

Figure 1 shows a graphical representation of the solution structure of the problem: a hierarchical and acyclic directed graph. The node $N_{ij} (i \in \{1,2,...,n\}; j \in \{1,2,...,r\})$ in the graph denotes that nurse i is assigned by using rule j, where n is the number of nurses to be scheduled and r is the number of rules to be used in the building process. The directed edge (arrow) from node N_{ij} to node $N_{i+1,j'}$ denotes a causal relationship of "N_{ij} following $N_{i+1,j'}$", i.e. a rule sub-string for nurse i where the previous rule is j and the current rule is j'. In this graph, a possible solution (a complete rule string) is represented as a directed path from nurse 1 to nurse n connecting n nodes.

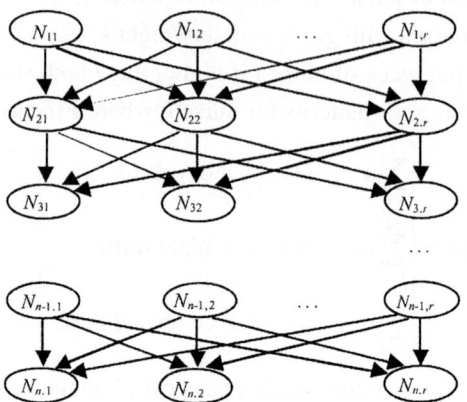

Fig. 1. A directed graph for nurse scheduling.

3 A Building Heuristic for Nurse Scheduling

Similar to the human's working pattern, a building heuristic is designed to build a schedule step by step by using a set of rules. As far as the domain knowledge of nurse scheduling is concerned, the following four rules are currently applied.

The first rule, called '*Random*' rule, is used to select a nurse's shift pattern at random. Its purpose is to introduce randomness into the search thus enlarging the search space, and most importantly to ensure that the proposed algorithm has the ability to escape from local optimum. This rule mirrors much of a scheduler's creativeness to come up with different solutions if required.

The second rule is the '*k-Cheapest*' rule. Disregarding the feasibility of the schedule, it randomly selects a shift pattern from a k-length list containing patterns with k-cheapest cost p_{ij}, in an effort to reduce the cost of a schedule as much as possible.

The third rule '*Cover*' is designed to consider only the feasibility of the schedule. It schedules one nurse at a time to cover those days and nights with the highest number of uncovered shifts. For each shift in a nurse's feasible set, we calculate the total number of uncovered shifts that would be covered if the nurse worked that shift pattern. In order to ensure that high-grade nurses are not 'wasted' covering unnecessarily for lower-grade nurses, for nurses of grade s, only the shifts requiring grade s nurses are counted as long as there is a single uncovered shift for this grade. If all these are covered, shifts of the next lower grade are considered and once these are filled those of the next lower grade. Hence, the '*Cover*' rule can be summarised as finding those shift patterns with the largest amount of undercover of the highest feasible grade.

The fourth rule '*Contribution*' is biased towards solution quality but includes some aspects of feasibility by computing an overall score for each feasible pattern for the nurse currently being scheduled. It is designed to take into account the nurses' preferences. It also takes into account some covering constraints in which it gives preference to patterns that cover shifts that have not yet been allocated sufficient nurses to meet their total requirements. This is achieved by going through the entire set of feasible shift patterns for a nurse and assigning each one a score. The one with the highest (i.e. best) score is chosen. In formulation, the score of a shift pattern S_{ij} is denoted as

$$S_{ij} = w_p(100 - P_{ij}) + \sum_{s=1}^{3} w_s q_{is} (\sum_{k=1}^{14} a_{jk} d_{ks}), \quad (4)$$

where w_p is the weight of the nurse's p_{ij} value for the shift pattern, w_s is the weight of covering an uncovered shift of grade s, and $d_{ks} = 1$ if there are still nurses needed on day k of grade s otherwise $d_{ks} = 0$.

Independent of the rules used, the fitness of completed solutions has to be calculated. Unfortunately, feasibility cannot be guaranteed. This is a problem-specific issue and cannot be changed. Therefore, we need a penalty function approach. Since the chosen encoding automatically satisfies constraint set (2), we can use the following formula to calculate the fitness of solutions:

$$\sum_{i=1}^{n}\sum_{j=1}^{m} p_{ij} x_{ij} + w_{demand} \sum_{k=1}^{14}\sum_{s=1}^{p} \max\left[R_{ks} - \sum_{i=1}^{n}\sum_{j=1}^{m} q_{is} a_{jk} x_{ij}; 0 \right] \rightarrow \min!, \quad (5)$$

where w_{demand} is the penalty weight. Note that the penalty is proportional to the number of uncovered shifts.

4 A Bayesian Optimization Algorithm

Bayesian networks [11] are often used to model multinomial data with both discrete and continuous variables by encoding the relationship between the variables contained in the modelled data. Thus, they represent the structure of a problem. Moreover, Bayesian networks can be used to generate new instances of the variables with similar properties as those given. Each node in the network corresponds to one variable, and each variable corresponds to one position in the strings representing the solutions. The relationship between two variables is represented by a directed edge between the two corresponding nodes (as seen in Figure 1).

Any complete probabilistic model of a domain must represent the joint distribution, i.e. the probability of every possible event as defined by the values of all the variables. The number of such events is exponential. To achieve compactness, Bayesian networks factor the joint distribution into local conditional distributions for each variable.

Mathematically, an acyclic Bayesian network encodes a full joint probability distribution by the product

$$P(x_1,...,x_n) = \prod_{i=1}^{n} P(x_i \mid pa(X_i)); \qquad (6)$$

where x_i denotes some values of the variable X_i, $pa(X_i)$ denotes a set of values for parents of X_i in the network (the set of nodes from which there exists an individual edge to X_i), and $P(x_i \mid pa(X_i))$ denotes the conditional probability of X_i conditioned on variables $pa(X_i)$. This distribution can be used to generate new instances using the marginal and conditional probabilities.

4.1 Learning Based on the Bayesian Network

The graph shown in Figure 1 can be regarded as a Bayesian network, which denotes the solution structure of the problem. In this network, learning the best rule sequence amounts to counting the frequency of using each rule. Hence, we use the symbol '#' meaning 'the number of' in the following equations. It calculates the conditional probabilities of each possible value for each node given all possible values of its parents. For example, for node $N_{i+1,j'}$ with a parent N_{ij}, its conditional probability is

$$P(N_{i+1,j'} \mid N_{ij}) = \frac{P(N_{i+1,j'}, N_{ij})}{P(N_{ij})} = \frac{\#(N_{i+1,j'} = true, N_{ij} = true)}{\#(N_{i+1,j'} = true, N_{ij} = true) + \#(N_{i+1,j'} = false, N_{ij} = true)}. \qquad (7)$$

Note that nodes N_{1j} have no parents. In this circumstance, their probabilities are

$$P(N_{1j}) = \frac{\#(N_{1j} = true)}{\#(N_{1j} = true) + \#(N_{1j} = false)} = \frac{\#(N_{1j} = true)}{T}. \qquad (8)$$

These probability values can be used to generate new rule strings, or new solutions. Since the first rule in a solution has no parents, it will be chosen from nodes N_{1j} according to their probabilities. The next rule will be chosen from nodes N_{ij} according to their probabilities conditioned on the previous nodes. This building process is repeated until the last node has been chosen from nodes N_{nj}, where n is number of the nurses. A link from nurse 1 to nurse n is thus created, representing a new possible solution. Since all the probability values are normalized, the roulette-wheel method is a good strategy for rule selection.

4.2 A BOA Approach for Nurse Scheduling

The BOA is applied to learn good partial solutions and then to complete them by building a Bayesian network of the joint distribution of solutions [12]. The nodes, or variables, in the Bayesian network correspond to the individual rules from which a schedule will be built step by step. In the proposed BOA, the first population of rule strings is generated at random. From the current population, a set of better rule strings is selected. Any selection method biased towards better fitness can be used, and in this paper, the traditional roulette-wheel selection is applied. The conditional probabilities of each node in the Bayesian network are computed. New rule strings are generated by using these conditional probability values, and are added into the old population, replacing some of the old rule strings. In detail:

1. Set $t = 0$, and generate an initial population $P(0)$ at random;
2. Use roulette-wheel to select a set of promising rule strings $S(t)$ from $P(t)$;
3. Compute the conditional probabilities of each node according to this set of promising solutions;
4. For each nurse's assignment, use the roulette-wheel method to select one rule according to the conditional probabilities of all available nodes, thus obtaining a new rule string. A set of new rule strings $O(t)$ will be generated in this way;
5. Create a new population $P(t+1)$ by replacing some rule strings from $P(t)$ with $O(t)$, and set $t = t+1$;
6. If the termination conditions are not met, go to step 2.

5 An Adapted Classifier System

The classifier system is an induction self-learning system in which a set of condition-action rules, called classifiers, compete to control the system and gain credit based on the system's receipt of reinforcement from the environment. It was first introduced by Holland in 1975 and has been extensively studied by others in recent years. In original classifier systems [7], the learning procedures consist of two parts: *credit assignment* and *rule discovery*. The former is critical, which is achieved by using a "bucket brigade" algorithm to rate the rules the system already has. The latter is applied very seldom, which is achieved by using GAs to replace rules of low strength and provide new rules when environmental situations are ill handled.

The design of our ACS is based on the idea of learning from the environment by providing the system with some measure of its performance. In particular, we study reinforcement learning for entities (i.e. for each nurse/rule combination shown in Figure 1). Each entity is given a learning task and when all tasks are completed, a solution is built. This solution will then receive a positive or negative reward according to its quality. The reward is shared among all entities involved. Thus, the process is similar to a game such as chess, where many moves are made before feedback is received.

In this approach, each building unit has its strength showing its usefulness in the current situation, and this strength is constantly assessed and updated. To implement learning based on previous solutions, an ACS for nurse scheduling is designed, which consists of the following four steps:

1. Initialise the strengths of all nodes in Figure 1 by assigning each node a same constant value, and create an initial solution by randomly picking a rule from the rule set for each nurse's assignment;

2. Considering the strengths of all nodes in the graph, we use the roulette-wheel method to select one node for each nurse, i.e. selection is biased towards higher strength. New solutions are generated in this way;
3. If a new solution is better than the previous one, a positive reward is received by this solution and evenly assigned to every associated node, otherwise a negative reward is received and evenly assigned to associated nodes;
4. Keep the best solution found so far. If ending conditions (maximum number of iterations) are not met, go to step 2.

To help understanding how the reward is assigned and shared, we will give a simple example of scheduling three nurses using four rules. The initial strength of each node is set to 10, and the reward of an improved solution is set to 3. The initial solution is generated by using rule 1 for nurse 1, rule 4 for nurse 2 and rule 3 for nurse 3. The next solution is generated by using rule 4 for nurse 1, rule 2 for nurse 2 and rule 3 for nurse 3. Thus, the strength matrix after each generation is updated as follows:

$$\begin{pmatrix} 10 & 10 & 10 & 10 \\ 10 & 10 & 10 & 10 \\ 10 & 10 & 10 & 10 \end{pmatrix} \Rightarrow \begin{pmatrix} 11 & 10 & 10 & 10 \\ 10 & 10 & 10 & 11 \\ 10 & 10 & 11 & 10 \end{pmatrix} \Rightarrow \begin{pmatrix} 11 & 10 & 10 & 11 \\ 10 & 11 & 10 & 11 \\ 10 & 10 & 12 & 10 \end{pmatrix}$$

It is worth mentioning here, that our proposed two approaches in the way of building schedules may have similarity with ant colony optimisation. However, their search mechanisms are very different. In our BOA, the search is based on the conditional probabilities of all available moves, rather than on the local and global trail updating in the ants' method. In our ACS, the searching method is still under development. It is currently based on the improvement of a single path, rather than the evolution of a group of paths in ant algorithms.

6 Computational Results

In this section, we present the results of extensive computer experiments on 52 real data instances and compare them to results of the same data instances found previously by other algorithms. Figure 2 summarises results of 20 runs with different random seeds for the BOA and the ACS respectively. Figure 3 gives an overall comparison between various algorithms. The runtime of both algorithms is approx 10-20 seconds per run and data instance on a Pentium 4 PC.

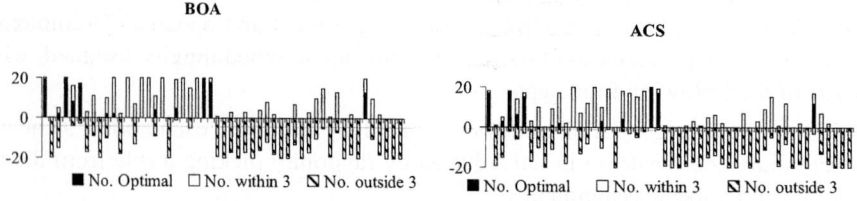

Fig. 2. Results of the BOA and the ACS.

In Figure 2, the *x*-axis represents the number of data sets, and the bars above the *y*-axis represent solution quality. The black bars show the number of optimal, the white near-optimal (within three units) solutions. The bars below the y-axis represent the number of times the algorithm failed to find a feasible solution or the solution was feasible but non-optimal (more than three units from optimum). The value of three units was chosen in consultation with the hospital involved. Hence, the shorter the bar below the y-axis and the longer above, the better the algorithm's performance.

Figure 2 shows that for the BOA 38 out of 52 data sets are solved to or near to optimality. Additionally, feasible solutions are always found for all data sets. Broadly speaking, the results for the ACS are similar, but a little weaker. This is unsurprising as in its present form the ACS is simple and its search is based on a single solution.

Figure 3 gives the optimal or best-known solutions found by an IP software package, and compares performance of different GAs ([1], [3]) with the BOA and the ACS presented here. The results are encouraging, with a fraction of the development time and simpler algorithms, the complex genetic algorithms are outperformed in terms of feasibility, best and average results. Only the hill-climbing GA, which includes an additional local search, has a better 'best case' performance. We believe that once this feature is added into our approach, by using the ACS as the hill-climber for the BOA, we will see the best possible results. Our plan is to implement a post-processor that is similar to a human scheduler who 'improves' a finished schedule.

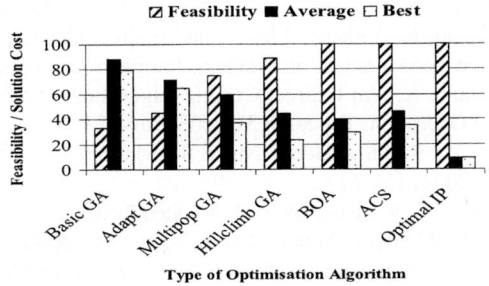

Fig. 3. Summary results of various algorithms.

Another direction for further research is to see if there are good constructing sequence for a fixed nurses' scheduling order. If so, the good patterns could be recognized and then extracted as new domain knowledge. Then using the extracted knowledge, we can assign specific rules to the corresponding nurses beforehand, and only need to schedule the remaining nurses, hence reducing the solution space.

7 Conclusions

This paper presents two scheduling algorithms based on the Bayesian optimization and classifier systems. The approach is novel because it is the first time that ideas from classifier systems are applied to personnel scheduling. Two effective methods are proposed to implement explicit learning from past solutions. Unlike most existing approaches, the new approach has the ability to build schedules using flexible, rather than fixed rules. Experimental results from real-world nurse scheduling problems demonstrate the strength of the proposed approaches.

Although we have presented this work in terms of nurse scheduling, it is suggested that the main ideas of the approaches could be applied to many other scheduling problems where the schedules will be built systematically according to specific rules. It is also hoped that this research will give some preliminary answers about how to include human-like learning into scheduling algorithms and may therefore be of interest to practitioners and researchers in areas of scheduling and evolutionary computation. In future, we aim to extract the 'explicit' part of the learning process further, e.g. by keeping learnt rule sequences from one data instances to the next.

Acknowledgements

The work was funded by the UK's, Engineering and Physical Sciences Research Council (EPSRC), under grand GR/R92899/01.

References

1. Aickelin, U., Dowsland, K.: Exploiting Problem Structure in a Genetic Algorithm Approach to a Nurse Rostering Problem. Journal of Scheduling 3(2000) 139-153
2. Aickelin, U., Dowsland, K.: Enhanced Direct and Indirect Genetic Algorithm Approaches for a Mall Layout and Tenant Selection Problem. Journal of Heuristics 8(2002) 503-514
3. Aickelin, U., Dowsland, K.: An Indirect Genetic Algorithm for a Nurse Scheduling Problem. Computers and Operations Research 31(2003) 761-778
4. Aickelin, U., White P.: Building Better Nurse Scheduling Algorithms. Annals of Operations Research 128 (2004) 159-177
5. Burke, E.K., Cowling, P.I., Causmaecker, P., Vanden Berghe, G.: A Memetic Approach to the Nurse Rostering Problem. In: Applied Intelligence, Vol. 15. Kluwer (2001) 199-214
6. Goldberg, D.E.: Genetic Algorithms in Search, Optimization and Machine Leaning. Addison-Wesley (1989)
7. Holland, J.H.: Adaptation in Natural and Artificial Systems. University of Michigan Press (1975), Republished by MIT Press (1992)
8. Li, J., Kwan, R.S.K.: A Fuzzy Simulated Evolution Algorithm for the Driver Scheduling Problem. In: Proceedings of Congress on Evolutionary Computation. (2001a) 1115-1122
9. Li, J., Kwan, R.S.K.: A Fuzzy Theory Based Evolutionary Approach for Driver Scheduling. In: Spector, L. et al. (eds.): Proceedings of Genetic and Evolutionary Computation Conference (GECCO). Morgan Kaufmann Publishers (2001b) 1152-1158
10. Li, J., Kwan, R.S.K.: A Fuzzy Genetic Algorithm for Driver Scheduling. European Journal of Operational Research 147 (2003) 334-344
11. Pearl, J.: Probabilistic Reasoning in Intelligent Systems: Networks of Plausible Inference. Morgan Kaufmann Publishers (1988)
12. Pelikan, M., Goldberg, D.: Research on the Bayesian Optimization Algorithms. IlliGAL Report No 200010, University of Illinois (2000)

An Evolutionary Approach to Modeling Radial Brightness Distributions in Elliptical Galaxies

Jin Li[1], Xin Yao[1], Colin Frayn[1], Habib G. Khosroshahi[2], and Somak Raychaudhury[2]

[1] The Centre of Excellence for Research
in Computational Intelligence and Applications (CERCIA), School of Computer Science,
The University of Birmingham, Edgbaston, Birmingham B15 2TT, UK
{J.Li,X.Yao,C.M.Frayn}@cercia.ac.uk
http://www.cercia.ac.uk/index.html
[2] Astrophysics and Space Research Group, School of Physics and Astronomy
The University of Birmingham, Edgbaston, Birmingham, B15 2TT, UK
{habib,somak}@star.sr.bham.ac.uk

Abstract. A reasonably good description of the luminosity profiles of galaxies is needed as it serves as a guide towards understanding the process of galaxy formation and evolution. To obtain a radial brightness profile model of a galaxy, the way varies both in terms of the exact mathematical form of the function used and in terms of the algorithm used for parameters fitting for the function given. Traditionally, one builds such a model by means of fitting parameters for a functional form assumed beforehand. As a result, such a model depends crucially on the assumed functional form. In this paper we propose an approach that enables one to build profile models from data directly without assuming a functional form in advance by using evolutionary computation. This evolutionary approach consists of two major steps that serve two goals. The first step applies the technique of genetic programming with the aim of finding a promising functional form, whereas the second step takes advantage of the power of evolutionary programming with the aim of fitting parameters for functional forms found at the first step. The proposed evolutionary approach has been applied to modeling 18 elliptical galaxies profiles and its preliminary results are reported in this paper.

1 Introduction

The basic building block of the universe is the galaxy. Nevertheless, even though the physics of the formation and evolution of individual stars is well understood, how galaxies form and evolve in various environments is not very well understood. In optical images, galaxies have a wide range of shapes and sizes. The appearance of a galaxy is expected to be related to its formation evolutionary history, and thus the morphological classification of galaxies is considered to be an important exercise in astrophysics [21].

Most regular galaxies can be divided into two types, namely, ellipticals and spirals. Elliptical galaxies appear smooth and structureless and have elliptical isophotes. In contrast, spiral galaxies comprise of a central brightness condensation resembling an elliptical, called the bulge, and a thin disk, which contains obvious spiral features. To develop a deeper understanding of the evolution of galaxies, it is important to quantify the morphological features as a first stage in an attempt to link them to the physics of their formation.

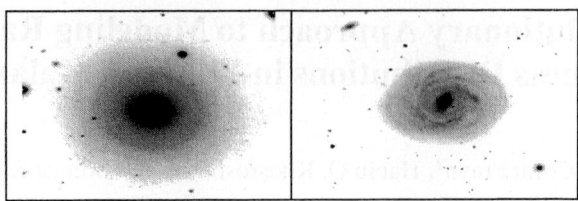

Fig. 1. Monochromatic (negative) images of a typical elliptical (left) and spiral (right) galaxy.

For this purpose it is necessary to express the structural features of a galaxy in terms of a small set of parameters. One way of doing this is to obtain a radial brightness profile of the galaxy, i.e., how the galaxy surface brightness varies as a function of radial distance from its center. Substantial work has been done towards finding better analytic fitting functions for radial brightness profiles (this will hereafter be simply referred to as the "profile") of galaxies. These include work by Hubble [7], de Vaucouleurs [3], King [11], Sersic [19] and Kormendy [13]. The most commonly used fitting functions for elliptical galaxy profiles are the Hubble's law given by

$$I(r) = I_0/(r/a + 1)^2 \qquad (1)$$

and the de Vaucouleurs $r^{1/4}$ law given by

$$I(r) = I_e \exp\{-3.33[(r/r_e)^{1/4} - 1]\}. \qquad (2)$$

Each function has two parameters, a brightness scale I_0 or I_e and a size scale a or r_e. I_0 is the surface brightness at $r = 0$, i.e. the central surface brightness. The scale length a is the distance at which the surface brightness falls to a quarter of its central value. In constrast, r_e, known as the effective radius, contains half of the total light of the galaxy, and I_e is the brightness at r_e. Both laws give a reasonably good description of the luminosity profiles of elliptical galaxies and the bulges of some types of spiral galaxies. However, they do not describe well these profiles beyond certain bounds of r or the bulges of spiral galaxies with pronounced spiral features. For the latter, a popular model is an exponential form

$$I(r) = 5.36 I_e \exp[-1.68(r/r_e)]. \qquad (3)$$

Neither (2) nor (3) have been formally linked to a physical model of galaxy formation, and remain mere empirical fits to observed profiles. Hubble's model (1) is not a very good fit to a wide range of observed ellipticals, but is related to possible density profiles of self-gravitating isothermal spheres of gas. It would be desirable to have a single model that would describe all elliptical galaxies with a variation of parameters, in particular if this model could be linked with the physics of collapsing gas clouds and the formation of self-gravitating ellipsoidal systems.

On the other hand, spiral galaxies are dominated by a disk which seems to be reasonably described by a simple exponential brightness profile [6]

$$I(r) = I_0 \exp(-r/h) \qquad (4)$$

where I_0 is the central surface brightness and h represents the scale-length of the disk.

There has been a lot of effort in the literature to find appropriate mathematical functions to describe a wide range of profiles of various components of spiral and elliptical galaxies, and to find plausible values for parameters that would fit observed profiles. Both tasks are non-trivial. The usual approach is to postulate a mathematical model comprising of common mathematical functions, then to apply fitting algorithms to find suitable parameters for these functions. The parameter fitting algorithm usually adopted is the non-linear reduced χ^2 minimization given by

$$\chi^2 = \frac{1}{\upsilon}\sum_i \frac{[I_{model}(i) - I_{obs}(i)]^2}{\delta^2}, \qquad (5)$$

where $I_{obs}(i)$ is the individual observed profile value, $I_{model}(i)$ is the value calculated from the fitting function, υ is the number of degrees of freedom, and δ is the standard deviation of the data. One disadvantage of non-linear minimization algorithms is their sensitivity to the initial values provided. Unreasonable initial values could cause the fitting program to trap in a local minimum. (see [1], [2] and [24]).

As more and more galaxy images have become available, the popular models seem to be suitable for an increasingly smaller fraction of observed galaxies. With the imminent prospect of photometry of millions of galaxies becoming publicly available through the Virtual Observatory project (www.ivoa.net), it is crucial to find reasonably good generic mathematical models that would describe a much larger number of galaxies with variation in model parameters.

In our approach presented here, the technique of genetic programming (GP) [14] plays the role as the first step to find alternative promising functional forms. The second step in our approach aims at fitting parameters in the function thus derived. To achieve the second goal, we take the evolutionary programming (EP) technique [4], [5] rather than non-linear reduced χ^2 minimization algorithms. The main reason for this is that EP has successfully worked for many numerical and combinatorial optimization problems in recent years [22], [23]. With its population of solutions, EP makes it easier to escape local minima and is more likely to find global minima.

The structure of the paper is as follows. Section 2 describes the sample of 18 radial brightness profiles of elliptical galaxies that we use in this study. Section 3 presents details of the evolutionary approach that involve genetic programming and evolutionary programming. In Section 4, we present our experiments on the application of our evolutionary approach to modeling 18 profiles and also report preliminary results. We draw conclusions and discuss our further work in Section 5.

2 The Distribution of Light in Elliptical Galaxies

The data chosen for this study is a set of 18 elliptical galaxies in the Coma cluster observed in near-infrared band (central wavelength 2.2 μm; for further description of the observations see [9]). Elliptical galaxies are chosen for this study because of their smooth brightness distribution compared to the more complicated morphologies of spiral galaxies. They are also chosen from the same cluster of galaxies to enable us to eliminate the signature of different environments on the surface brightness of the sample galaxies. Elliptical galaxies historically have been characterized by the de Vaucouleurs ($r^{1/4}$) profile, which is an empirical fit, not yet shown to emerge from theoretical or semi-analytic scenarios of galaxy formation. Careful observations reveal a far greater variety of profiles, leading, among others, Khosroshahi et al [9], [10] to advocate the use of generalized models that allow for shallower or steeper profiles to elliptical galaxies and bulges of disk galaxies.

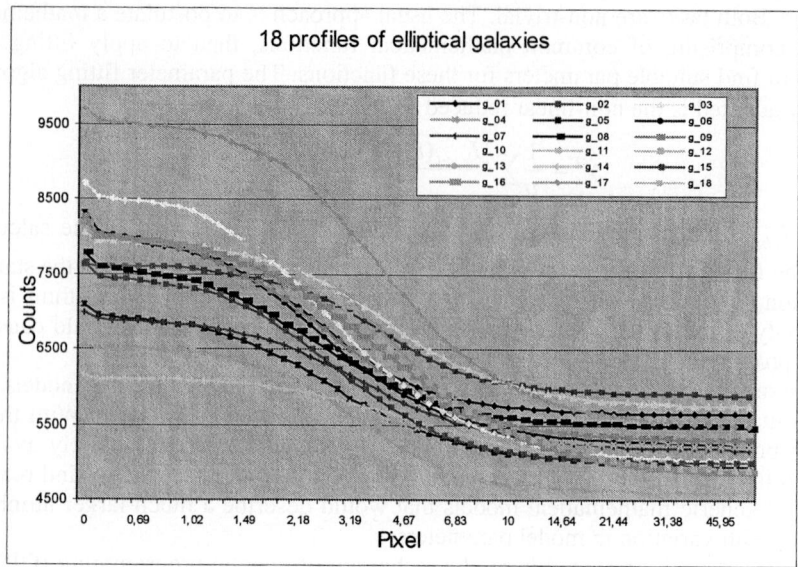

Fig. 2. The brightness intensity distribution of 18 elliptical galaxies.

In this exercise, one dimensional radial profiles have been extracted from fitting elliptical contours of the same brightness (isophotes) to the images of the galaxies, and computing the average brightness as a function of radius along the major axis of the ellipse at various values of the radial distance r. Each profile has 50 data points (see Fig. 2). The sky background is highly variable at near-infrared wavelengths. Therefore the local background is highly variable.

3 The Evolutionary Approach

Our evolutionary approach consists of two major steps with its distinct target. First we aim to seek promising a functional form using genetic programming. We then apply a simple generalization process on the function generated. The form is generalized in the way of replacing a few numeric values by a few parameter variables.

The second step is aimed at fitting parameters in the functional form thus found, using evolutionary programming techniques. The details of both algorithms used in our approach are described below.

3.1 Genetic Programming

Genetic programming (GP) is a class of evolutionary computation inspired by Darwin's evolution theory. It operates iteratively evolving a population of individuals. On each iteration, all individuals are evaluated in terms of the fitness function. A new population is then generated by probabilistically selecting the most fit individuals from the current population. Some members in the new population are carried forward from the last generation population intact via reproduction operation. The rest are generated by applying genetic operators: crossover or mutation. Such a process continues until sufficiently fit individuals are found.

GP has been applied to a variety of fields [17]. One important application is symbolic regression (or function identification). Problems of symbolic regression require finding a function, in symbolic form, which fits a given limited sampling of data points. One individual in GP is an executable tree structure/parse tree, which can be interpreted as a mathematical expression. GP is capable of generating mathematical formulas which approximate many or even whole data points among a set of data sample given. In addition, because GP algorithm is a stochastic process, it is able to generate a variety of function forms when modeling even on the same data. These facts make GP a strong candidate for finding alternative promising forms.

For simplicity, the detail of GP algorithms is not presented here. For readers interested, please refer to the book [16]. In the case of GP here, we take a function set, $F = \{+, -, *, /, \exp, \log, \sin, \cos\}$ and a terminal set, $T = \{r, \Re\}$ where r is the variable radius and $\Re$ is a random float-point value between −10.0 and 10.0. Theoretically, all profile models (function 1-4) introduced in Section 1 could be potentially generated by GP. Examples of individual expressions are illustrated in Fig, 3.

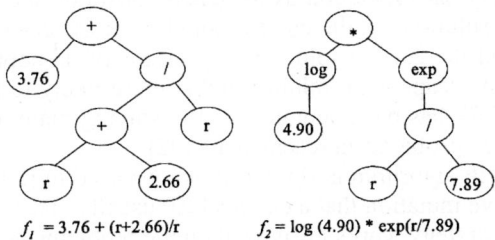

$f_1 = 3.76 + (r+2.66)/r$ $f_2 = \log(4.90) * \exp(r/7.89)$

Fig. 3. Examples of mathematical formula forms created by GP.

The fitness function is an important component in GP. Here it determines how well an individual expression fits an observational profile. The overall fitness function used here for GP consists of two items. We take *hits* as the first part of the fitness function. The 'hits measure' here counts the number of fitness data points for which the numeric value returned by the model expression lies within a small tolerance (the 'hits criterion') of the observed intensity value. For example, the hits criterion taken in this paper is 0.005 for GP. Selecting an appropriate value for the hit criterion seems a bit tricky here. In general, a higher hit criterion could fail to guide GP to find a good shape of function which better fit profiles. In contrast, a lower hit criterion does allow GP to find a good form which could possibly over-fit a particular profile, but lack generality to match other profiles. This is also known as the over-fitting problem in machine learning. The aim of using GP is to find functional forms that potentially have capability to describe as many profiles as possible. Therefore, in our approach, taking a higher hit criterion for GP is preferable as long as the maximum number of hits (i.e. 50 in this study) is achievable in terms of the results on 18 galaxies profiles.

In addition, we add a second item into the fitness function to penalize any complex expression because a simple functional form is almost always preferable. The complexity of an expression is measured by the length of the expression, i.e. the number of nodes within the expression. The extent to which an expression should be penalized is changeable by a weight w. In summary, the fitness function that we use is given by

$$f_{\text{fitness function}} = Hits - w * \text{ the length of the expression.} \qquad (6)$$

It is worth noting that the second item in the fitness function is also essential. Without it, our GP tends to generate rather complicated mathematical functional forms, which are difficult to generalize.

The criteria for terminating a GP run are either the maximum run time allowed or the maximum of generation that we set, whichever reached first.

3.2 Evolutionary Programming

GP is good at finding a function or a symbolic form. However, it lacks mechanism to tune parameters in the form. This is partly because existing genetic operations, such as crossover or mutation, affect only the structure of the trees, not the composition of the nodes. The numeric constants in nodes thus cannot benefit much from them.

Like GP, evolutionary programming is one class of evolutionary computation [5]. Unlike GP, EP merely uses mutation as its genetic operator and has only two major steps: 1) mutate the solutions in the current population; 2) select the next generation from the mutated and the current solutions. By means of its population of solutions, EP makes it easier to escape local minima and is more likely to find global minima. The effectiveness of EP has been demonstrated in solving many numerical and combinatorial optimization problems in recent years [22].

In this study, the EP algorithm is similar to one we used in [23], except that we do not apply self-adaptive mutation that a classical EP usually takes. It is simply because the simple mutation strategy works fairly well on the problems being solved here. We use the Cauchy mutation rather than traditional Gaussian mutation as our previous work has demonstrated that the former performs much better than the latter [23]. The fitness function we take is merely the *hits*, the first item of the fitness function for GP. The termination criterion taken here is that the maximum generation has reached.

4 Experiments and Results

The experiments in this study were carried out as follows. We first ran the GP system on each of 18 galaxy profile datasets. It is common practice to fit in the logarithmic (magnitude) regime when decomposing 1D profiles. We adopt this approach and let GP run to fit the model function forms to data points in the logarithmic regime for each profile. The parameter settings for running GP are listed in the Table 1.

One profile model is created after each GP run. 18 different profile models with different mathematical forms are generated in total. They seem different in their shapes of tree structure. Therefore, finding similarity between those forms generated is needed in order to find a more generic model form.

We simplify a tree-structured function form in the way of cutting each possible sub-tree and replacing it by a single numerical node if the ultimate return value of the sub-tree is a numerical value. After the simplification, the form has to be generalized in the way of replacing a few numerical values by variables (e.g. *a, b,* and *c*) respectively.

Table 1. Parameter settings used in our GP for experiments.

Target	To find a regression mathematical function based on the galaxy profile given
Terminals	R, $\Re$=[–10, 10]
Non-terminals	+, -, *, /, exp, sin, cos, log
Crossover rate	0.9
Mutation rate	0.01
Population size	6,000
Maximum no. of generations	100
Termination criterion	Generation limit or Time limit, whichever reached first
Selection strategy	Tournament selection, Size = 6
Max depth of individual expressions	17
Hit criterion	0.005
Fitness criterion	Hits – 0.01 * the length of the expression
Max depth of initial individual expressions	6
Maximum run time (hours)	6

After the generalization process, there emerge a few forms with parameters that are relatively simple. Among these forms we only select the following two simplest function forms f_{g1} (see 7) and f_{g2} (see 8) for further investigation.

$$f_{g1} = a + b / (c + r) \qquad (7)$$
$$f_{g2} = a' + b'/(b' + c' r^2) \qquad (8)$$

Each of the two forms involves three parameters i.e. a, b, and c for f_{g1}; a', b' and c' for f_{g2}, and one radius r. Now, we use EP to seek proper values for three parameters within the both functions respectively to fit each galaxy profile in the logarithmic regime. The parameter settings for running EP are listed in the Table 2.

Table 2. Parameters used in our EP for experiments.

Target	To find proper parameters
Mutation rate	0.9
Population size	10,000
Maximum no. of generations	150
Termination criterion	Maximum generation reach
Selection strategy	Tournament selection, Size = 6
Fitness criterion	Hits (maximum hit = 50)
Hit criterion	0.005

For brevity, results of fitting parameters found by EP for f_{g1} and for f_{g2} are not listed here. However, Several points are worth indicating here. First of all, EP algorithms almost always achieve the maximum hits: 50 (the number of data points for each profile), with the above EP parameter settings while running based on either function forms for each galaxy profile. This is partly attributed to a large population of solutions. Secondly, unlike non-linear fitting algorithms, EP is not sensitive to the initial values provided at all. Throughout our experiments we keep the same initial values for those parameters (i.e. a, b, and c; a', b' and c'), which do not need to be tuned in order to avoid failure of a run. This is attributed to the mutation in EP. Thirdly, the hit criterion is one of the most important parameter settings in EP because it determines how well the resulting models fit the empirical galaxy profile. The smaller the value of the hit criterion is, the better fit the resulting model could be. This will be further discussed shortly.

To evaluate the accuracy and overall success of a model fit, we use statistical measure, the reduced χ^2, given in (5). In general, the resultant χ^2 above 2 means that the model does not seem to describe the empirical galaxy profile very well. Otherwise, the model is a good description for the brightness distribution of a galaxy. We calculate the reduced χ^2 for each galaxy based on both functions respectively. Both results are shown under the columns with hit criterion = 0.005 in Table 3.

Table 3. The reduced χ^2 for 18 models based on two function f_{g1} and f_{g2} using two hit criteria.

Profiles	χ^2 for f_{g1}		χ^2 for f_{g2}	
	Using hit criteria =0.005	Using hit criteria = 0.002	Using hit criteria =0.005	Using hit criteria = 0.002
1	7.4460	7.8961	11.4012	**1.1141**
2	9.1809	6.2876	12.8405	**1.8633**
3	8.7796	5.0199	6.3452	**0.7113**
4	6.8782	6.8221	2.8035	2.8385
5	4.1948	3.8105	5.7141	**0.8685**
6	3.1867	2.7282	3.2442	**0.7194**
7	9.7797	4.8050	17.9798	**0.9289**
8	6.8756	4.9609	11.0505	**0.1353**
9	5.8373	5.0018	3.4484	1.0390
10	2.8263	2.8807	**1.9078**	**0.3318**
11	34.0802	8.2256	25.2975	7.9733
12	5.8477	5.0861	7.9886	**1.5150**
13	7.6026	7.6528	10.6681	**1.2615**
14	9.1534	**1.8299**	13.8083	**1.2896**
15	5.9548	5.8170	2.1233	**1.2062**
16	4.8048	**1.98719**	3.7705	**0.6759**
17	2.9778	3.0106	**1.3418**	**0.3138**
18	**1.2161**	1.0233	**0.8031**	**0.0796**

According to the value of the reduced χ^2, only one model based on f_{g1} fits the observational profile very well (i.e. galaxy 18; its χ^2 = 1.2161<2), whereas three models based on f_{g2} perform well for galaxy 10, galaxy 17 and galaxy 18 as each χ^2 is less than 2. We may argue that f_{g2} is a better model than f_{g1} in terms of the total number of good model fittings. Apart from this fact, the results do not seem promising at all. The poor performance is partly due to the higher hit criterion we set in EP.

As mentioned earlier, the hit criterion in EP determines how closely a resulting model fits an empirical galaxy profile. A lower hit criterion potentially guides EP to find appropriate values of parameters which can match empirical models better. The poor results here imply that a lower hit criterion is necessary to make models better.

We then carry out a set of experiments using a smaller hit criterion 0.002. Other parameter settings for EP are the same except for the maximum number of generations. We double the maximum number of generation to 300 as the termination criterion for EP. For simplicity, results of parameter values found by EP for f_{g1} (i.e. a, b, and c) and f_{g2} (i.e. a', b' and c') are not shown in this paper. We only list the results of the reduced χ^2 based on both function models to see how good those resultant models are. The results are shown under the column with the hit criterion = 0.002 in Table 3.

With the smaller hit criterion, only three models based on f_{g1} have been found to be fairly good because their χ^2s calculated are all less than 2. In contrast, based on f_{g2}, 16 models among the total 18 are good descriptions for corresponding galaxy profiles except for two models, i.e. the model 4 for galaxy 4 and the model 11 for galaxy 11. The χ^2s of model 4 and model 11 are 2.8385 and 7.7933 respectively.

While comparing the results by using 0.005 as a hit criterion, we note that more good fitting models can be found by using 0.002 for both f_{g1} and f_{g2} in terms of the standard of the reduced χ^2. The number of good models found increases from 1 to 3 for f_{g1} and from 3 to 16 for f_{g2}. In terms of the total number of good fitting galaxies found here, we argue again that f_{g2} is a more promising mathematical form compared with f_{g1} to describe 18 galaxy profiles studied here.

5 Conclusions and Future Work

In the study of galaxy formation and evolution, it is important to find functional forms that best describe the distribution of starlight in galaxy images. Limitations of traditional approaches are: a) an exact mathematical function form must be given before applying any fitting algorithms; b) the commonly used fitting algorithm like non-linear reduced χ^2 tends to be sensitive to initial values provided and more likely culminates in wrong local minima, resulting in unsatisfactory fits.

An evolutionary approach has been proposed in this paper. It attempts to overcome the above weakness of traditional methods. The approach takes two major steps to achieve distinct goals. The first step uses a GP technique to find promising mathematical functional forms based on observed radial profiles of elliptical galaxies. The second step applies evolutionary programming aimed at finding appropriate values for the parameters within the form found. Between the two steps, the process of generalization is required to make the overall approach succeed. The main novelty of the approach lies in the fact that the whole procedure of modelling profiles is a data-driven process without assuming a functional form beforehand. This bottom up process is particularly useful when one faces a large number of galaxy profiles without any prior knowledge of them. It allows one to find a good functional form first and then to fit parameters for the function in order to build reasonably good galaxy profile models.

The approach has been demonstrated on 18 galaxy profiles given. Two major different mathematical function forms are found at its first step. Through a generalization process, three parameters are introduced into each function. Parameter fittings by EP using two different hit criteria have been carried out at its second step. Experimental results demonstrate that a good mathematical form plays a more important part in finding good descriptions of galaxy profiles. On the other hand, a smaller hit criterion is preferable to use in order to guide EP to achieve better models.

In this paper, we have conducted a preliminary study to apply a proposed evolutionary approach to modelling 18 galaxy profiles. Though initial results are promising, the effectiveness of our approach needs further investigation. In particular, we would like to test the effectiveness of the evolutionary approach to a great extent. The number of galaxy profile samples would be increased in our future study. Meanwhile, other types of galaxies should also be considered in our research. As two-dimensional decomposition techniques are becoming more promising for modeling galaxy profiles [10], [24], exploring the possibility of combining the evolutionary approach with two-dimensional decomposition techniques certainly merits further investigation.

References

1. Andredakis, Y.C., Sanders, R.H. (1994). Exponential bulges in late-type spirals: an improved description of the light distribution, Monthly Notices of the Royal Astronomical Society (MNRAS), Vol. 267, No. 2, 283-296.
2. De Jong, R.S. (1996), Near-IR photometry of 86 galaxies. II. *Astronomy & Astrophysics Supplement Series,* 118, 557-573.
3. De Vaucouleurs G. (1948). Recherches sur les Nebuleuses Extragalactiques. *Annales d'Astrophysique*, Vol. 11, 247.
4. Fogel, D.B. (1991). *System Identification Through Simulated Evolution: A Machine Learning Approach to Modeling.* Needham Heights, MA: Ginn.
5. Fogel, L.J., Owens, A. J. and Walsh, M. J. (1966). *Artificial Intelligence Through Simulated Evolution.* New York: Wiley.
6. Freeman, K.C. (1970). On the Disks of Spiral and S0 Galaxies. *The Astrophysical Journal* 160: 811-830
7. Hubble, E.P. (1930). Distribution of luminosity in elliptical nebulae. *The Astrophysical Journal 71*, 231-276.
8. Khosroshahi, H.G., Raychaudhury, S., Ponman, T.J., Miles, T.A., Forbes, D.A. (2004). Scaling relations in early-type galaxies belonging to groups. *Monthly Notices of the Royal Astronomical Society,* 349: 527-534.
9. Khosroshahi, H.G., Wadadekar, Y., Kembhavi, A., Mobasher, B. (2000a). Correlations among global photometric properties of disk galaxies. *The Astrophysical Journal letters* 531: 103-106.
10. Khosroshahi, H.G., Wadadekar, Y., Kembhavi, A. (2000b). Correlations among global photometric properties of disk galaxies. *The Astrophysical Journal* 533: 162-171.
11. King, I. R. (1962). The structure of star clusters. I. An empirical density law, *Astronomical Journal*, Vol. 67, 471.
12. King, I R. (1966). The structure of star clusters. III. Some simple dynamical models. *Astronomical Journal,* Vol. 71, 64.
13. Kormendy, J. (1977). Brightness distributions in compact and normal galaxies. III - Decomposition of observed profiles into spheroid and disk components. *The Astrophysical Journal*, Vol. 217, 406-419.
14. Koza, J.R. (1992). *Genetic Programming: on the programming of computers by means of natural selection.* MIT Press.
15. Koza, J.R. (1994). *Genetic Programming II: Automatic Discovery of Reusable Programs.* MIT Press.
16. Koza, J.R. (1992). *Genetic Programming: on the programming of computers by means of natural selection.* MIT Press.
17. Koza, J.R. (1994). *Genetic Programming II: Automatic Discovery of Reusable Programs.*
18. Schombert, J.M. & Bothun, G. D. (1987). The methodology and reliability of determining bulge-to-disk ratios for spiral galaxies. *Astronomical Journal (ISSN 0004-6256)*, Vol. 93, 60-73.

19. Sersic, J.L. (1968) *Atlas de Galaxies Australes* Cordoba: Observatorio Astronomica
20. Sparke, L.S. & Gallagher III, J. S. (2000). *Galaxies in the Universe: An introduction.* Cambridge University Press.
21. Van den Bergh, S. (1998) *Galaxy Morphology and classification.* Cambridge University Press.
22. Yao, X., (1996) An overview of evolutionary computation, *Chinese J. Adv. Software Res.*, Vol. 3, No. 1, 12–29.
23. Yao, X, Liu, Y. and Lin, G. (1999) Evolutionary Programming Made Faster. In: *IEEE Transaction on Evolutionary Computation* Vol. 3, No. 2. 82-102.
24. Wadadekar, Y., Robbason, B., Kembhavi, A. (1999). Two-dimensional Galaxy Image Decomposition. *Astronomical Journal,* Vol 117, Issue 3, 1219-1228.

Conference Paper Assignment Using a Combined Greedy/Evolutionary Algorithm

Juan Julián Merelo-Guervós and Pedro Castillo-Valdivieso

GeNeura Team, Depto. Arquitectura y Tecnología de Computadores,
Universidad de Granada, Spain
tutti@geneura.ugr.es
http://geneura.ugr.es

Abstract. This paper presents a method that combines a greedy and an evolutionary algorithm to assign papers submitted to a conference to reviewers. The evolutionary algorithm tries to maximize match between the referee expertise and the paper topics, with the constraints that no referee should get more papers than a preset maximum and no paper should get less reviewers than an established minimum, taking into account also incompatibilities and conflicts of interest. A previous version of the method presented on this paper was tested in another conference obtaining not only a good match, but also a high satisfaction of referees with the papers they have been assigned; the current version has been also applied on that conference data, and to the conference where this paper has been submitted; results were obtained in a short time, and yielded a good match between reviewers and papers assigned to them, better than a greedy algorithm. The paper finishes with some conclusions and reflections on how the whole submission and refereeing process should be conducted.

1 Introduction

Assigning paper to reviewers in a conference is an essential part of the organization of those events. From an optimization point of view, the problem consists in assigning paper to reviewers so as to maximize the match between the reviewer's expertise and the paper topic, taking into account several constraints: no paper should receive less than a pre-established number of reviewers, no referee should get more than a previously agreed number of papers, conflicts of interest should be avoided, and, if possible, papers should be distributed as evenly as possible among the reviewers.

In fact, while every field increases its diversification, and its number of practitioners, expertise is concentrated in increasingly narrow fields, and paper assignment to reviewers by journal editors or conference organizing committees is an increasingly difficult problem. Some authors are already calling for changes [1] in the journal/conference reviewing process. Even within a field such as Parallel Problem Solving from Nature, it is almost impossible to find a reviewer that is able to deal with any paper within it; even more so, it is impossible to manually assign paper to reviewers in the best, or, at least, in a good enough way. Any person who has willingly participated in a recent conference will have probably received several papers that have nothing to do with her skills.

In practice, paper assignment is often an obscure process, being usually done randomly and evenly among reviewers; at most, reviewers and papers are divided by tracks, corresponding to broad topics, and paper distributed as above within each track. Needless to say, this process often leads to a low match among the paper topic and the referee expertise, resulting in a low return rate (many papers are left without revision, or the referee indicates that she is not able to review the paper), and low quality of revisions.

Automatically assigning paper to referees while maximizing match between is not a difficult problem, and has actually got two different parts. The *first phase* is to establish the match among reviewers and papers, which can be approached either using information retrieval techniques [2], or by having the reviewers express their preferences, or else by making reviewers and paper authors select a set of keywords that best describe their skills and topic, respectively. Any of them is a valid technique, although in our case we have chosen the last option, due to the facility of its implementation.

The *second phase* in the paper assignment problem is the optimization process itself, assigning paper to referees so as to maximize match, which can be visualized as a bipartite graph, composed by two kinds of nodes, paper and reviewer. A link, or *graph edge* would represent the relation "match is different from zero". Each paper would be linked to the reviewers whose match is different from zero; in the algorithm presented here, those reviewers with at least a keyword in common. An optimal assignment is appropriately called a *matching* [3], that is, given an undirected graph $G = (V, E)$ with n vertexes V and m edges E, a *matching M* is a subset of the edges such that no two edges in M share a vertex. A *max cardinality matching* is a matching that includes as many edges as possible; a *max weight matching* maximizes the sum of all edges weight; a *max weight, max cardinality matching* maximizes both the number of edges and the cardinality. An *assignment* is a *matching* that includes every vertex in the graph.

In the case at hand, vertexes (papers or reviewers) *do* have to share an edge, since each reviewer gets several papers, with a maximum on p papers; and every paper must get at least r reviewers; however, this can also be expressed in terms of the aforementioned definition by representing each paper by r vertexes (which would roughly correspond to *paper slots*) and each reviewer by p (*reviewer-slots*) vertexes. In this case, the conference paper assignment problem consists in finding the max weight matching in this graph, with the restriction that no *paper slot* can be left unfilled (some reviewer slots can be left unfilled, however).

In this paper, as has been already a tradition [4, 5] in the PPSN (Parallel Problem Solving from Nature) series of conferences [6, 7], papers have been assigned to reviewers using a hybrid greedy/evolutionary algorithm, which afforded assignment hours after the submission process was closed, and which has also allowed an assignment that maximizes match between the paper and the referee keywords, which will probably yield high-quality reviews and also a higher satisfaction of referees with papers assigned to them. This is obviously not proved for this conference; however, we will show figures for the previous edition of the conference that prove this claim.

The rest of the paper is organized as follows: next section (section 2) shows the state of the art in the paper assignment problem. Section 3 describes the algorithm used to assign papers to reviewers, and results for the current and previous PPSN conferences. The paper finishes with some discussion, conclusions and future work in section 4.

2 State of the Art

Automatic paper assignment has been approached in the past quite often, in several possible ways; different methods have been used to, first, compute reviewer/paper match, and then, to assign paper to reviewers in an optimal way. One of the earliest paper found in the literature is by Dumais et al. [8], who used referee ranking of paper abstracts to assign whole papers later on; besides, reviewers had to submit an abstract of their own topics of interest, which was compared, using Latent Semantic Indexing [2], with submitted papers. Yarovsky [9] refines the method by requiring no intervention from reviewers: the reviewer profile is obtained from their online published papers, and it is then matched, using also LSI, to the paper content; papers are assigned based on matches. Another paper [10], deals also with the topic, presenting it as an instance of the capacitated transshipment problem, and solving using "classical" optimization techniques. In fact, these papers are more focused on the first phase of assignment, computing reviewer/paper match, than in the second phase, optimal assignment based on those matching scores.

Conference paper assignment can also be formulated as a scheduling problem, where resources are the paper themselves and the "jobs" are the reviewers. This problem has been approached extensively in the past using evolutionary algorithms: for instance, Bierwirth et al. [11] studies permutation and several kind of crossover operators applied to scheduling problems, specially job shop scheduling. It can also be considered a knowledge management problem, since, in general, it deals with assigning a document to the person that can best handle it; a similar problem has been approached using genetic algorithms in [12].

In our version of the conference assignment problem, the first phase is solved by making reviewers and paper authors to select several keywords from the same pre-established list, that tries to cover all subjects in the area of biologically-inspired computation. Paper/reviewer match was only a matter of computing how many keywords in common they had.

In previous instances of this conference, evolutionary algorithms were also used to assign papers to reviewers. It was done for the first time for PPSN 2000 by Pierre Collet [4]. In this first instance reviewers, besides selecting keywords, could chose the papers they preferred to review. However, there were several problems with his implementation: not all referees had selected keywords, and the algorithm did not make sure that there was at least one keyword match among the referee and the paper. Thus, some referees received papers they had not chosen or seen before, and were disappointed. Besides, one of the four referees assigned to each paper was finally chosen by hand, and the result obtained by the genetic algorithm had to be improved by a greedy algorithm.

In the next edition of the conference, a similar method was used [6, 5], but, in this case, keyword selection was enforced for all reviewers. Referees were also allowed to choose which papers they would rather review, but, when applying the evolutionary algorithm, this was considered only a very soft constraint, and many reviewers received papers they had chosen not to review, resulting in a good amount of frustration. However, as is usual in the review forms, reviewers were asked about their confidence in their decision, so there is an *a posteriori* measures of referee confidence in their decision: 1.7 ± 0.7, with 1 meaning *very high* confidence and 2 *somewhat high* confidence. In this case, no correction was done by hand, other than including conflicts of interest in the assignment problem.

3 Results

In this section, we will describe the algorithm used for paper assignment, and how it was applied to the the previous PPSN conference data (2002) and the conference this paper has been submitted to.

During the PPSN2002 conference, the process of paper assignment proceeded as follows:

1. Reviewers are asked to select keywords from a set of around 90 keywords distributed in different categories, such as Technique or Theory of Evolutionary Computation.
2. The authors of every paper were also asked to select keywords from the same set when submitting it.
3. Reviewer keywords were revised according to the papers that had been submitted. If some area was underrepresented, new reviewers were called. This problem is particularly dire for papers that select a single keyword; in that case, the program committee had to include at least r reviewers with that keyword. This was usually a problem for applied papers.
4. When all papers were submitted, it was checked that every paper could have, at least, r reviewers. Tentative assignments were made, so that conflicts of interest could be detected by the organizing committee, and included into the database, so that they were taken into account in subsequent assignments.

The evolutionary algorithm uses a greedy algorithm to assign papers in the following way: each individual in the population is a permutation in the order of paper assignment. Fitness of each permutation is computed by assigning to each paper, in order, the first $r = 4$ referees whose paper slots have not been filled. If a paper receives less than 4 referees, a penalty of 0.5*number of missing referees is applied. In the algorithm that was actually used for that conference, a "good" amount of papers per referee was also considered as a soft constraint; if a referee was assigned more than this "good" amount (which is strictly less than the hard constraint of $p = 6$), a small penalty was also applied. However, during the run it was found that this soft constraint made the fitness landscape rougher, resulting in assignments with a lower overall match, and, besides, with that "good amount" constraint unfulfilled. That is why it was not actually used in the experiments described below.

Distribution of keywords, as well as the number of keywords and referees were different for the two conference editions. Results for each one will be shown separately, one in subsection 3.1 and the other in subsection 3.2.

3.1 Previous Conference: PPSN2002

In this section, we will show the results of the algorithm presented in this paper on last conference data. In this conference, 181 papers were submitted, and there were 159 reviewers admitted in the program committee. As is usual in other PPSN conferences, every paper was assigned to $r = 4$ reviewers while the agreement was that no referee would get more than $p = 4$ reviewers. However, according to keywords selected, not all papers could be assigned to any reviewer. Table 2 shows the range of possible choices for each paper and reviewer in the column labeled PPSN 2002.

The bipartite graph that paper and referees form is shown in figure 1, which allows us to visualize, more or less easily, the shape of the problem. In this graph, that represents papers via white squares and reviewers via red rhombus, a paper is joined to a reviewer if there is at least a keyword in common. Reviewers are arranged according to the number of links; the closer they are to the center, the higher the number of links; as can be seen, there is a wide range of variation. In practice, that means a possible conflict regarding constraints: since not all reviewers can review any paper, and papers are assigned reviewers in order, a paper can be left without referees if it is one of the last and its referees are all *popular* referees with all their slots filled already.

The algorithm for paper assignment was run in several different configurations, without the soft restriction of a *good* amount for papers per referee (which was the one actually used for that conference [5]. Every experiment was repeated 10 times.

The baseline experiment used parameters shown in table 1, and obtained an average fitness of 280.09 ± 0.01. This was a small improvement over the first gen-

Table 1. Evolutionary algorithm parameters used for the paper assignment problem.

Parameter	Value
Population size	400
Stopping criterion	10 generations without change in fitness
Mutation operators	2 & 10 places permutation
Selection	2-Tournament
Replacement	Steady-state, 80% substituted

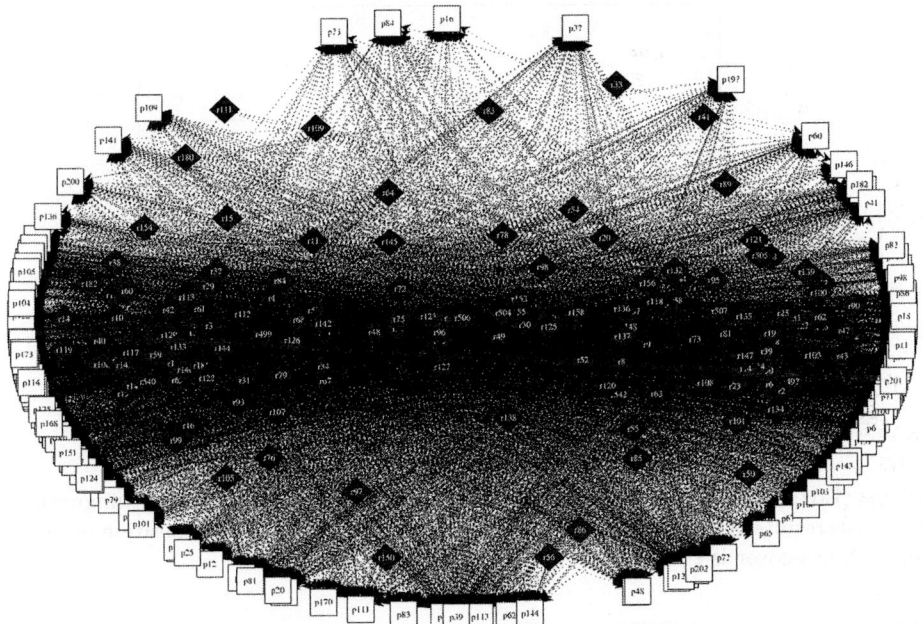

Fig. 1. Representation of the referee/paper bipartite graph using Visone. Referees, represented by blue rhombus, are linked to the papers (represented by white squares) they can possibly review (that is, with at least one keyword in common), and arranged according to the number of links; those closest to the center have the highest number of links, that is, they can potentially review the highest number of papers, those placed more off-center have a smaller range of possible assignments.

eration, whose best individual roamed around 279.9; however, this improvement obviously results in several papers getting better reviewers than if just a random paper order had been used to assign the papers using a greedy algorithm. Best fitness was 280.1, that is, an average match per paper per referee equal to 0.39. Paper distribution among reviewers is quite even. Most reviewers get 6 papers, while 30 out of 135 got less than that. This is usually not desirable; however, a balance must be kept between quality of reviews and evenness in paper distribution.

Several sets of runs were made with other configurations: adding the CX operator [13] (labeled cx), changing tournament size to 5 (labeled t5, and eliminating the 10-permutation operator (labeled nom2). The boxplot of results is shown figure 2 indicates that the best results are obtained when 2 permutation operators (for 2 and 10 papers) plus CX are used, while tournament size does not seem to have much influence on result. In that case, the best match obtained is 283.8, with an average match per review of .392. This result should be compared with the absolute maximum of 320.76 (0.44 per review), achieved when every paper is assigned the 4 best-matching referees, which obviously violates constraints, and results in some reviewers getting as many as 34 papers. The proposed algorithm obtains 88.48% of this absolute maximum.

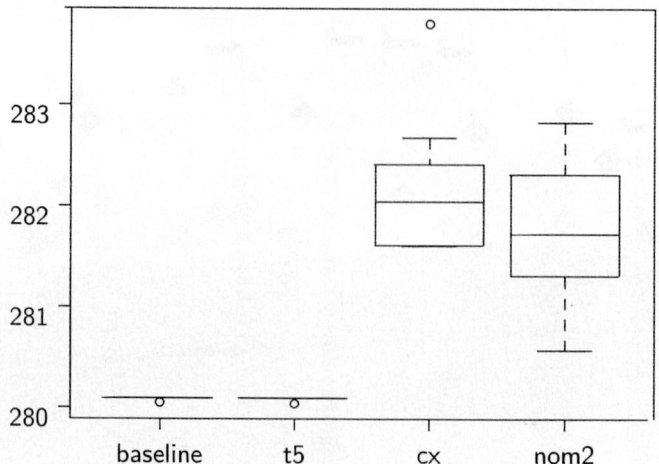

Fig. 2. Boxplot representation of fitness reached for different operator configuration. The best results is reached when tournament size is 2, 2- and 10-permutation are used, and CX crossover is turned on.

3.2 Results for PPSN2004

Situation for PPSN2004 was completely different from the previous conference. For starters, 2/3rds of the papers were submitted in the last 2 days, which meant that it was difficult to have an adequate supply of referee slots. All in all, around 350 papers had to be reviewed.

However, the assignment algorithm was used to create different paper-assignment scenarios, and see which areas needed more reviewers. Several runs were made with combinations of 7 papers per referee/3 reviews per paper, 8/3, 8/4, 6/4, resulting in a compromise scenario of 7/4; however, more reviewers had to be called at that point.

Final overall situation is shown in table 2 (column PPSN 2004). The average and maximum number of non-zero match papers per reviewer is higher than in the previous edition, which means more choice, and probably a higher match, however, since there are many papers, this choice is constrained by the number of slots per reviewer.

356 papers were finally suitable for revision, and the pool of referees was populated by 244 persons. Most papers chose only a few keywords, which obviously limits the amount of reviewers available for them but, on the other hand, makes any choice sharper. The problem is that the choice of keywords does not correspond exactly to paper content; sometimes, *general* keywords are not used, and the authors concentrate only on what makes its paper really apart from the rest (for instance, choice of operators or application area); on the other hand, sometimes just general keywords are chosen, which makes difficult to find the correct reviewers.

The evolutionary algorithm was run as explained above, using the same operators and rates that have been proved to find the best results in the previous

Table 2. Range of possible paper/reviewer assignment: the range of referees that could be assigned to each paper in the PPSN2002 conference went from a minimum of 7 through an average of 51.34 to a maximum of 101.

Data	PPSN 2002	PPSN 2004
Min. number of papers per referee	1	3
Min. number of referees per paper	7	3
Mean number of papers per referee	58.81	114.0
Mean number of referees per paper	51.34	74.31
Max. number of papers per referee	154	317.0
Max. number of referees per paper	101	161.00

conference data. The only difference was that, since individuals are twice as long as before (twice the number of papers), population had to be increased to 1000, and the number of generations without change before stopping was also increased to 20.

Running, as before, an greedy algorithm that did not take constraints into account, assigning to each paper the 4 best-matched referees yielded a 717.63 score, that is, a 0.51 average match per assigned review; slightly higher than the previous conference, due mainly to the higher number of reviewers available.

Final assignment data cannot be provided at this stage, but the best fitness assignments hovered around 596, that is, around 0.41 per paper, and around 81% of the optimal assignment (vs. 88.46% for the same algorithm applied to the previous conference), which is a bit less than for the previous conference, due mainly to the different paper/reviewer ratio in this edition.

4   Conclusion and Discussion

In general, the work presented in this paper achieved its objective: being able to assign papers to referees using keywords so that match is maximized, and constraints are met. In fact, it has been the method actually used in this conference.

Using an automated method as opposed to manual processing allowed to run different scenarios of assignment, and the evolutionary algorithms achieved a match several percentage points better that could have been achieved using only a greedy algorithm. Using keywords as a way of assessing paper match might also pose some problems. Keywords do not have the same weight, they are very different in scope. *Evolutionary computation-general* can be applied to most reviewers and papers, while *Estimation of distribution algorithms* refer to a specific algorithm used by a rather small community; while a match in the former is worth the same as the latter, it is quite clear that it is much more important to choose a referee that is an expert in EDAs than in EC-General. That can be fixed by assigning weights to every keyword, but that might complicate things more than would be necessary. However, any complication in the assignments of matches would probably result also in a complication in the referee choice phase. Another option would be to make paper authors select at least one keyword in each of several areas: one in *Techniques* and another in *Applications*, for instance; however, this could result in reduced usability of the submission form, however. An additional problem is that keywords do not tell the whole story of referee abilities; in some cases, new keywords must be drawn, or else, assignments revised so that papers can be assigned to the person that is most related to them.

From this, another lesson must be drawn: program committee choice should take into account keyword distribution during the last editions of the conference, and should be done according to that; even so, it is much better to choose in advance many more reviewers than would be probably needed. It is not a big problem if some reviewer receives one or a few papers to review (or none), but it can be a big problem if a reviewer gets more papers than she expected; not only for the reviewer herself, but also for the resulting quality of reviews.

As future lines of work, paper information will be used to create a network of papers, so that paper recommendation can be done during the conference. Several alternative greedy algorithms will be tested, as well as a multi-objective optimization algorithm, that will look not only at keyword match, but also at paper distribution, trying to make it as even as possible. Different greedy algorithms will be also tested, and compared with this hybrid algorithm.

Acknowledgements

This paper has been funded by project TIC2003-09481-C04-01, of the Spanish Ministry of Science and Technology. Data and source code is available from the authors.

References

1. Ron Weber. The journal review process: a manifesto for change. *Commun. AIS*, 2(2es):3, 1999.
2. Scott C. Deerwester, Susan T. Dumais, Thomas K. Landauer, George W. Furnas, and Richard A. Harshman. Indexing by latent semantic analysis. *Journal of the American Society of Information Science*, 41(6):391–407, 1990.
3. Zvi Galil. Efficient algorithms for finding maximum matching in graphs. *ACM Comput. Surv.*, 18(1):23–38, 1986.
4. P. Collet, E. Lutton, M. Schoenauer, and J. Louchet. Take it EASEA. In Marc Schoenauer, Kalyanmoy Deb, Guenter Rudolph, Xin Yao, and Hans-Paul Schwefel Evelyne Lutton, Juan Julian Merelo, editors, *PPSN VI*, number 1917 in LNCS, pages 891–901. Springer Verlag, 2001.
5. Juan-Julián Merelo-Guervós, Francisco-Javier García-Castellano, P.A. Castillo, and M.G. Arenas. How Evolutionary Computation and Perl saved my conference. In Luciano Sánchez, editor, *MAEB03, Segundo Congreso Español sobre Metaheurísticas, Algoritmos Evolutivos y Bioinspirados*, pages 93–99, Febrero 2003.
6. J.-J. Merelo Guervós, P. Adamidis, H.-G. Beyer, J.-L. Fernández-Villacañas, and H.-P. Schwefel, editors. *Parallel Problem Solving from Nature - PPSN VII, 7th International Conference, Granada, Spain, September 7-11, 2002. Proceedings*, number 2439 in Lecture Notes in Computer Science, LNCS. Springer-Verlag, September 2002. Available from Amazon and http://www.springeronline.com/sgw/cda/frontpage/0,10735,5-40109-22-2240086-0,00.html.

7. Marc Schoenauer, Kalyanmoy Deb, Günter Rudolph, Xin Yao, Evelyne Lutton, Juan Julián Merelo, and Hans-Paul Schwefel, editors. *Parallel Problem Solving from Nature - PPSN VI*, number 1917 in Lecture Notes in Computer Science. Springer, 2000. Available from http://www.springeronline.com/sgw/cda/frontpage/0,10735,5-146-22-2040755-0,00.html and Amazon.
8. Susan T. Dumais and Jakob Nielsen. Automating the assignment of submitted manuscripts to reviewers. In *Research and Development in Information Retrieval*, pages 233–244, 1992.
9. D. Yarowsky and R. Florian. Taking the load off the conference chairs: towards a digital paper-routing assistant. In *Proceedings of the 1999 Joint SIGDAT Conference on Empirical Methods in NLP and Very-Large Corpora*, 1999.
10. Jerry Cheyung Wei; D. Hartvigsen and R. Czuchlewski. The conference paper-reviewer assignment problem. *Decision Sciences*, 30(3), 1999.
11. Christian Bierwirth, Dirk C. Mattfeld, and Herbert Kopfer. On permutation representations for scheduling problems. In Hans-Michael Voigt, Werner Ebeling, Ingo Rechenberg, and Hans-Paul Schwefel, editors, *Parallel Problem Solving from Nature – PPSN IV*, pages 310–318, Berlin, 1996. Springer.
12. W. H. Ip; Min Huang; K. L. Yung; Dingwei Wang. Genetic algorithmnext term solution for a risk-based partner selection problem in a virtual enterprise. *Computers & Operations Research*, 30(2), February 2003,. Available online 26 November 2001.
13. I. M. Oliver, D.J. Smith, and J. R. C. Holland. A study of permutation crossover operators on the traveling salesman problem. In *Procs. ICGA-87*, pages 224–230, 1987.

A Primer on the Evolution of Equivalence Classes of Bayesian-Network Structures

Jorge Muruzábal[1] and Carlos Cotta[2]

[1] Grupo de Estadística y Ciencias de la Decisión, ESCET,
University Rey Juan Carlos, 28933 - Móstoles, Spain
j.muruzabal@escet.urjc.es
[2] Dept. Lenguajes y Ciencias de la Computación, ETSI Informática,
University of Málaga, Campus de Teatinos, 29071 - Málaga, Spain
ccottap@lcc.uma.es

Abstract. Bayesian networks (BN) constitute a useful tool to model the joint distribution of a set of random variables of interest. To deal with the problem of learning sensible BN models from data, we have previously considered various evolutionary algorithms for searching the space of BN structures directly. In this paper, we explore a simple evolutionary algorithm designed to search the space of BN *equivalence classes*. We discuss a number of issues arising in this evolutionary context and provide a first assessment of the new class of algorithms.

1 Introduction

A Bayesian Network (BN) is a graphical model postulating a joint distribution for a set of discrete random variables. Critical qualitative aspects in this model are given by the underlying graphical structure, a *directed acyclic graph* (DAG) **G**; quantitative aspects are provided by the set of marginal and conditional probabilities attached to this DAG, say $\theta = \theta(\mathbf{G})$. To deal with the problem of learning sensible BN models from data (a problem known to be NP-hard), a number of evolutionary algorithms (EAs) have been considered to search the space of DAG structures or *b-space*, see e.g. [1–3]. Just like other *score-and-search* methods [4], DAG structures **G** are often evolved according to some standard scoring measure based on the data. Promising results have been obtained in general following this evolutionary approach in b-space.

Two DAGs are *(Markov) equivalent* if they encode the same statistical model, that is, the same set of independence and conditional independence statements. If we denote the equivalence class containing **G** as [**G**], each [**G**] corresponds to a different statistical model (our true object of interest). Hence, as DAGs can be meaningfully grouped together in equivalence classes, we can also consider the alternative *e-space*, the space of equivalence classes, as a more direct target [5]. This strategy will be useful, of course, provided that we can traverse the more complex e-space in some computationally efficient manner. It must be noted that e-space is known to be not much smaller than b-space [6], and the computational load in the former may be somewhat heavier. While the issue seems far from settled at this point (see the concluding section), in this paper we follow what we think is an appealing framework for initiating the investigation of evolutionary search in e-space.

It turns out that equivalence classes [**G**] can be compactly represented by certain class of *partially* directed acyclic graphs or PDAGs, see e.g. [7]. PDAGs may include directed as well as *undirected* arcs. Let **Ḡ** denote the *unique* PDAG structure representing some [**G**]. Then **Ḡ** and all **H** ∈ [**G**] share the same connectivity pattern (ignoring directionality), and all directed arcs in **Ḡ** show up in every **H** ∈ [**G**]. A complicating factor is that not all PDAGs represent equivalence classes, only *completed* PDAGs (CPDAGs) do. On this matter, Chickering [7] presents various operators designed to modify a given CPDAG **Ḡ** (representing [**G**]) so that the resulting PDAG **H̄** represents (after being completed) some other [**H**] ≠ [**G**]. Templates are also provided for calculating the corresponding change in score after the modification is done.

The design of efficient learning algorithms in e-space can thus be assisted by using the CPDAG space, and building on Chickering's basic results. We explore below what we believe is the first EA designed to adopt exactly this approach. The key operators look much like *mutations*, so we have adopted an *evolutionary programming* (EP) approach as the natural paradigm to get started [2, 8].

2 Background

This section provides basic ideas and notational details. We first introduce the central BN framework, then continue with the learning paradigm based on equivalence classes.

2.1 Bayesian Networks

A Bayesian Network is a tuple $(\mathbf{G}, \boldsymbol{\theta})$, where **G** is a Directed Acyclic Graph (DAG) and $\boldsymbol{\theta} = \boldsymbol{\theta}(\mathbf{G})$ is a set of probability distributions attached to **G**. The DAG is the set of links or *arcs* among variables or *nodes*. If we denote the whole set of variables as $\mathbf{X} = \{X_1, X_2, ..., X_n\}$, each X_i has a set of *parents*, denoted by $\Pi_i = \{X_j \in \mathbf{X} \mid (X_j \to X_i) \in \mathbf{G}\}$, and the DAG **G** represents the joint distribution $P(\mathbf{X}) = P(\mathbf{X}|\mathbf{G}) = \prod_{i=1}^{n} P(X_i \mid \Pi_i)$, where $\Pi_i = \emptyset$ at least once. A standard parametric model arises when this $P(\mathbf{X})$ is viewed as a family of distributions indexed by $\boldsymbol{\theta} = \boldsymbol{\theta}(\mathbf{G})$. In particular, it is often assumed that variables follow (conditionally) independent Multinomial distributions, that is, $P(X_i = k \mid \Pi_i = j) = \theta_{ijk}$, where $j = 1, ..., q_i$; $k = 1, ..., r_i$; r_i is the number of distinct values that X_i can assume and q_i is the number of different configurations that Π_i can present. Hence, $\boldsymbol{\theta} = \{\theta_{ijk}\}$ collects all parameters in **G** with the constraint that $\sum_k \theta_{ijk} = 1$ for all (i, j).

A crucial issue is how to evaluate DAG structures. Given a standard Multinomial likelihood $P(\mathbf{D}|\mathbf{G}, \boldsymbol{\theta})$, estimates $\hat{\boldsymbol{\theta}} = \hat{\boldsymbol{\theta}}(\mathbf{D})$ are usually based on the sufficient count statistics $\mathbf{N} = \{N_{ijk}\}$ (interpreted as $\boldsymbol{\theta}$). For example, the maximum likelihood (frequentist) approach leads to $\hat{\theta}_{ijk} = N_{ijk}/N_{ij}$, where $N_{ij} = \sum_k N_{ijk}$. The (intra-network) Bayesian approach assumes a *prior* density on parameter space, say $\pi(\boldsymbol{\theta}|\mathbf{G})$, and uses it to compute the *marginal likelihood* $P(\mathbf{D}|\mathbf{G}) = \int P(\mathbf{D}|\mathbf{G}, \boldsymbol{\theta})\pi(\boldsymbol{\theta}|\mathbf{G})d\boldsymbol{\theta}$. This integration will be difficult in general, but it is possible analytically (under certain assumptions) if $\pi(\boldsymbol{\theta}|\mathbf{G}) = \prod_{i,j} \pi(\theta_{ij})$, where θ_{ij} denotes the vector containing the r_i probabilities θ_{ijk}, $\pi(\theta_{ij}) \propto \prod_k \theta_{ijk}^{\alpha_{ijk}-1}$, and $\boldsymbol{\alpha} = \{\alpha_{ijk}\}$ is the *virtual count* or Dirichlet hyperparameter ($\alpha_{ijk} > 0$), see [9]. We adopt this criterion in what follows. Since $\boldsymbol{\alpha}$ must be supplied by the user just like the complete data set $\mathbf{D}$, we write $\Psi(\mathbf{G}|\mathbf{D}, \boldsymbol{\alpha}) = \log P(\mathbf{D}|\mathbf{G})$ as our basic (standard) scoring metric in b-space.

2.2 Learning Equivalence Classes of BN Models

As mentioned earlier, an equivalence class of DAGs contains all structures yielding exactly the same set of independence and conditional independence statements. For example, DAGs $X \to Y \to Z$ and $X \leftarrow Y \to Z$ are equivalent, for they both express that X is conditionally independent of Z given Y. Equivalence classes [**G**] can be compactly represented by the class of completed partially directed acyclic graphs or CPDAGs [5, 7]. If an arc $X \to Y$ shows up in all $\mathbf{H} \in [\mathbf{G}]$, then that arc is *compelled* in [**G**]. If an arc is not compelled, then it is *reversible*, i.e., there exist $\mathbf{H}, \mathbf{K} \in [\mathbf{G}]$ such that $\mathbf{H}$ contains $X \to Y$ and $\mathbf{K}$ contains $Y \to X$. The unique CPDAG $\bar{\mathbf{G}}$ representing [**G**] contains a directed arc for each compelled arc in [**G**] and an undirected arc for each reversible arc in [**G**]. In our previous example, the CPDAG $X - Y - Z$ represents the equivalence class containing $X \to Y \to Z$, $X \leftarrow Y \to Z$ as well as $X \leftarrow Y \leftarrow Z$. However, $X \to Y \leftarrow Z$ belongs to a different equivalence class, namely, that represented by the CPDAG containing the *v-structure* (or "inmorality") $X \to Y \leftarrow Z$. It follows that providing arbitrary directionality to reversible arcs in a CPDAG [**G**] does not necessarily result in a member of [**G**]. On the contrary, very specific algorithms must be used to obtain a correct DAG from a given CPDAG and *vice versa* (see [7] and below).

With regard to some other research [4, 9, 10], Chickering's approach introduces a clear semantics and up to six different operators for performing local variation in existing CPDAGs. These operators can be scored locally, and score-updating formulae are provided for them. Hence, search algorithms can traverse much faster through different equivalence classes [7]. The basic operators are termed InsertU, DeleteU, InsertD, DeleteD, ReverseD and MakeV. The first four either increase or reduce the number of arcs by one, the rest maintain the number of arcs in the current CPDAG. Specifically, the fifth reverses the directionality of a single directed arc, whereas the sixth transforms the substructure $X-Y-Z$ (where X is not linked to Z directly) into the v-structure $X \to Y \leftarrow Z$.

When locally manipulating a given CPDAG $\bar{\mathbf{G}}$ in these ways, the resulting PDAG may not be initially completed. In essence, we could use the basic PDAG-to-DAG routine [7] to find out if any proposed operation is *valid*: if this routine failed to return a proper DAG structure, say $\mathbf{H}$, then the operation can not be carried out. Otherwise the operation would be valid, and we could call the basic DAG-to-CPDAG routine (with input $\mathbf{H}$) to determine the resulting $\bar{\mathbf{H}} \neq \bar{\mathbf{G}}$. In practice, each operator comes with its own *validity test*, a compact set of conditions to check that **H** exists in each case [7]. Note that there may be "cascading" implications in this process; for example, `DeleteD` may make other directed arcs undirected. Or, after applying `MakeV`, many arcs may switch from undirected to directed.

Chickering also provides the corresponding change in score after the modification is done [7]. Here it makes sense to use a basic DAG scoring metric which is *score-equivalent*, that is, constant over each equivalence class. Many familiar measures are score-equivalent – the present $\Psi(\mathbf{G}|\mathbf{D}, \boldsymbol{\alpha}) = \log P(\mathbf{D}|\mathbf{G})$ may or may not be depending on $\boldsymbol{\alpha}$. Let $\alpha_{ij} = \sum_k \alpha_{ijk}$ and $\alpha_i = \sum_j \alpha_{ij}$. Heckerman, Geiger and Chickering [9] show that $\Psi(\mathbf{G}|\mathbf{D}, \boldsymbol{\alpha})$ is score-equivalent if $\alpha_i \equiv \alpha$ for some $\alpha > 0$ (the BDe metric). Parameter α reflects strength of belief in the proposed priors for the θ_{ijk}. We consider below the well-known BDeu(α) metric $\alpha_{ijk} = \alpha/r_i q_i$. Another typical option is the K2 metric $\alpha_{ijk} = 1$, but this is not score-equivalent.

Once an initial CPDAG structure is evaluated, we can update the score via Chickering's results. The key idea behind this local scoring is that a *decomposable* scoring function Ψ – making use of local evaluations only – is typically used (for example, both K2 and BDeu(α) are decomposable). That is, for some function σ (and implicit data), $\Psi(\mathbf{G}) = \sum_{i=1}^{n} \sigma(X_i, \Pi_i)$, where calculation is restricted in each case to a single node X_i and its parents Π_i. To illustrate, the change in score attributed to a particular valid mutation deleting $X \to Y$ in $\bar{\mathbf{G}}$ and leading to some $\bar{\mathbf{H}}$ can be expressed as $\Psi(\bar{\mathbf{H}}) - \Psi(\bar{\mathbf{G}}) = \sigma(Y, \Lambda_1) - \sigma(Y, \Lambda_2)$, where $\Lambda_1 \subset \mathbf{X}$ is the set of nodes connected to Y (with either a directed or undirected arc), and $\Lambda_2 = \Lambda_1 \cup \{X\}$. Similar (or slightly more complex) expressions hold for the remaining operators.

3 Evolutionary Framework

A number of NP results motivate the use of heuristic methods for the problem of learning BNs from data [7]. Score-and-search methods are relatively simple to use and constitute a major alternative to locate sensible models. In particular, a number of evolutionary algorithms have been proposed (see e.g., [1–3] and the references therein). In essence, these evolutionary approaches can be classified within two main categories: *direct* and *indirect*. Direct approaches are those in which the search is conducted over the space of all possible DAGs (b-space). Indirect approaches use an auxiliary space to conduct the search. Selected elements from this auxiliary space are fed to a suitable (decoder) algorithm to obtain the actual BNs they represent. The algorithm considered in this work falls within the first category, although with the twist that the search is conducted over the space of all possible CPDAGs (e-space).

The first issue to be tackled is the choice of evolutionary paradigm to work with. The graph modifications discussed in Sect. 2.2 can be seen as natural counterparts of the familiar mutation operators found in the evolutionary DAG arena, see e.g. [2]. Thus, our basic algorithm is currently of evolutionary programming (EP) nature (e.g., see [8,11]). We begin with a population of P CPDAGs. At each generation, members of the population are selected by means of binary tournament to produce mutated structures (i.e., different CPDAGs), which we locally evaluate and store. Finally, the best P out of the $2P$ available structures are selected for the next generation (the rest are discarded) and a new mutation sweep takes place. We simply let this process continue for T generations in all experiments below. Initial CPDAGs are generated by the DAG-to-CPDAG routine on either randomly or heuristically constructed DAGs (by applying the K2 heuristic using a random permutation of the variables as seed). In the first case, the initialization process is parameterized by $\delta \in [0,1]$, the arc density of the random graph [3]; in the second case, it is controlled by $\pi_{\max}$, the maximum number of parents per variable in the initial population. In either case, each DAG is evaluated by our basic scoring metric $\Psi(\mathbf{G}|\mathbf{D}, \boldsymbol{\alpha}) = \log P(\mathbf{D}|\mathbf{G})$ and the result passed to the associated CPDAG.

There are many interesting research questions in this scenario – we provide some discussion and empirical evidence now and we discuss some further issues later. Two key roles that we do investigate are those played by the fitness BDeu(α) metric and the various mutation operators. More specifically, what is the effect of α in the EP process? Are all six operators needed for best operation? If so, how to decide which operator ω will act on a selected CPDAG $\bar{\mathbf{G}}$?

At the moment, we try to gain some familiarity with this environment by analyzing a simple (default) variant. Specifically, mutation operators ω are selected by (independent) drawings from the uniform probability distribution Ω over the whole set of available operators. Note that some operators ω may not find a suitable entry point in the selected CPDAG and hence may become non-applicable (in which case a different operator should be selected etc.). If, on the other hand, one or more appropriate entry points can be found for the selected ω, then the operator is tentatively applied at a randomly selected point. Since the mutated CPDAG $\bar{\mathbf{H}} = \omega(\bar{\mathbf{G}})$ may not pass the corresponding validity test, we monitor the operators' *validity* ratio $v = v(\omega)$. If the mutated CPDAG is valid, it is incorporated to the offspring population. We also track the *success* ratio of each operator $\varepsilon = \varepsilon(\omega)$ during the replacement stage, i.e., the number of CPDAGs that ω produced and made it to the next population. We believe some knowledge about these basic aspects of performance should be acquired before we can embark into more elaborate designs.

4 Experimental Results

The basic algorithm described above has been deployed on the familiar ALARM network, a 37-variable network for monitoring patients in intensive care [12]. The equivalence class [ALARM] is represented by a CPDAG with 4 undirected and 42 directed arcs. A training set of $N = 10,000$ examples was created once by random probabilistic sampling as customary. The BDeu(α) metric $\Psi(\mathbf{G}|\mathbf{D}, \boldsymbol{\alpha}) = \log P(\mathbf{D}|\mathbf{G})$ is the fitness function (to be maximized). All experiments have been performed using a population size of $P = 100$ individuals and $T = 500$ generations (i.e., 50,000 individuals generated). Five different initialization settings have been considered: on one hand, random initialization using density values

Table 1. Results (averaged for ten runs) of the EA using a different set of operators. Random initialization with parameter δ is denoted by R_δ, and heuristic initialization with parameter $\pi_{\max}$ is denoted as $H_{\pi_{\max}}$. U and D indicate the average number of undirected and directed arcs in the final population.

	Basic Set				Basic Set ∪ {ReverseD}			
	best	mean ± SD	U	D	best	mean ± SD	U	D
$R_{0.05}$	-107006	-107499 ± 516	45.23	19.03	-106519	-106899 ± 357	33.79	23.30
$R_{0.10}$	-106680	-107236 ± 401	39.03	23.49	-106707	-107099 ± 470	35.14	24.85
H_2	-106656	-106933 ± 252	31.31	25.40	-106532	-106681 ± 113	28.07	25.00
	Basic Set ∪ {MakeV}				Basic Set ∪ {ReverseD, MakeV}			
	best	mean ± SD	U	D	best	mean ± SD	U	D
$R_{0.01}$	-107308	-108108 ± 533	6.34	56.73	-106506	-107039 ± 324	7.49	46.60
$R_{0.05}$	-106994	-108191 ± 559	8.02	59.82	-106621	-107045 ± 280	10.69	47.68
$R_{0.10}$	-107186	-108281 ± 820	6.22	59.45	-106703	-107175 ± 351	8.82	51.93
H_1	-106594	-106915 ± 267	9.59	45.58	-106503	-106723 ± 232	7.68	43.65
H_2	-106591	-106867 ± 208	7.57	46.17	-106503	-106602 ± 209	7.96	39.31

$\delta \in \{0.01, 0.05, 0.10\}$; on the other, heuristic initialization using a greedy (K2) heuristic with maximum number of parents per variable $\pi_{\max} \in \{1, 2\}$.

The initial experiments aim to assess the operators as follows. We have considered a *basic* set of operators for traversing the space of CPDAGs, namely InsertD, DeleteD, InsertU, and DeleteU. Subsequently, we have tested the addition of ReverseD and/or MakeV, implying a total of four operator sets. The results are shown in Table 1. In all cases, the BDeu($\alpha = 1$) metric has been used. To put these results in perspective, the fitness of the original network is -106587.

Note firstly the essential role played by MakeV: by inspecting the networks in the final populations, it can be seen that a high number of undirected arcs arise when this operator is not available. The injection of v-structures appears thus crucial for balancing the adequate proportion of directed and undirected arcs. Actually, whenever the population is initialized with low-density networks ($R_{0.01}$ or H_1), the lack of MakeV makes all directed arcs vanish in a few iterations. Besides turning DeleteD and ReverseD inapplicable, the population achieves in this situation a degenerate state of high-density undirected networks. For this reason, we have not included these low-density initial conditions in the experiments omitting MakeV. Note also that results are best when using MakeV together with ReverseD. Indeed, the best network found in this case just differs from the original network in a directed arc of the latter that is substituted by a different undirected arc in the former. The ReverseD operator seems also very important in practice. Here, it seems to help the networks size down appropriately.

Regarding the properties of the operators, consider first the validity ratio $v = v(\omega)$. We note that this ratio is close to 1 for InsertU and DeleteU. For DeleteD and ReverseD, it raises from 0.5 up to 1 in about 100 generations, then stays at that level for the rest of the run. For InsertD, it oscillates between 0.8 and 1. Finally, MakeV exhibits the lowest v ratio (oscillating between 0.5 and 1).

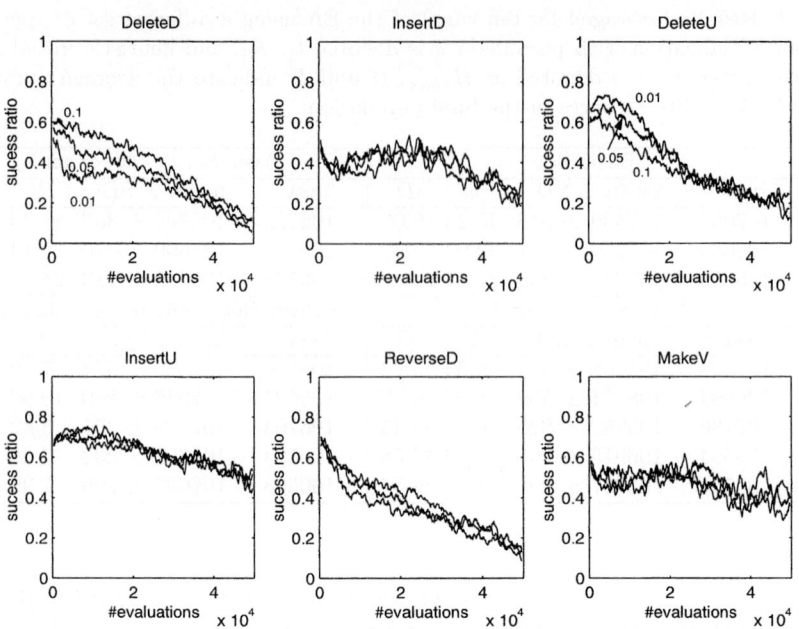

Fig. 1. Mean success ratio (averaged for ten runs) of each operator when using random initialization.

As refers to success ratios, consider the trajectories shown in Fig. 1. There exists naturally a general decreasing trend (improvements are less frequent in the latter stages of the run). Also for this reason, lower success levels (not shown) are obtained when using heuristic initialization (the algorithm performs its run at a higher fitness level). The overall aspect of the trajectories is nevertheless the same in this latter case. The different decreasing rates shed some light on the relative contribution of operators though. In particular, note that the undirected-arc-based, "brick and mortar" operators InsertU and MakeV tend to maintain the highest success ratios. On the other hand, DeleteD, ReverseD and DeleteU are the ultimately least useful. This suggests that the evolved structures manage to consolidate some useful set of both compelled and reversible arcs.

Using the full set of operators, our second set of experiments intends to test the influence of the BDeu parameter α. For this purpose, we compare the difference between the best structure found in each run and the original ALARM CPDAG. The values $\alpha \in \{0.01, 0.1, 1, 10\}$ have been tried, see Table 2. A first inspection indicates that there are some trends that can be appreciated in this range. For the randomly initialized runs, the number of shared (*true*) arcs of either kind tends to decrease for larger values of α. For the heuristically initialized runs, this is only true for the undirected arcs. On this matter, Kayaalp and Cooper [13] show that, for big enough sample size N, arcs are more likely to be incorporated into the network for larger values of α. Actually, the average number of arcs (either directed or undirected) for each value of α is 48.88, 49.84, 53.78, and 60.78 respectively, an uprising pattern. The simple $\alpha = 1.0$ seems

Table 2. Networks generated by the EA for different values of α. S_U and S_D stand for shared arcs (undirected or directed), i.e., arcs present in both the original and the evolved networks). The number of arcs in the evolved network is denoted as n_{arcs}. All results are the average of ten runs.

	$\alpha = 0.01$			$\alpha = 0.1$			$\alpha = 1$			$\alpha = 10$		
	S_U	S_D	n_{arcs}	S_U	S_D	n_{arcs}	S_U	S_D	n_{arcs}	S_U	S_D	n_{arcs}
$R_{0.01}$	3.3	32.9	48.0	3.0	36.1	49.1	2.2	30.9	54.0	1.5	29.5	61.1
$R_{0.05}$	3.1	32.6	49.3	2.8	33.0	51.3	2.2	28.9	56.5	1.3	26.9	67.6
$R_{0.10}$	2.4	29.4	53.5	1.8	30.1	54.9	1.6	28.5	59.1	1.3	25.1	70.8
H_1	3.8	34.6	46.7	3.6	36.8	47.4	3.7	35.0	51.3	1.5	37.8	50.9
H_2	3.8	33.9	46.9	4.0	37.5	46.5	4.0	36.4	48.0	1.1	34.6	53.5

to provide the best overall results. For example, the best network (according to BDeu) found for $\alpha = 0.1$ captures all 4 original undirected arcs, and 39 original directed arcs from the ALARM structure. As to $\alpha = 10$, just 1 undirected and 37 directed arcs are reflected. By contrast, 4 undirected arcs and 41 directed arcs are captured in the best run for $\alpha = 1$. This level of performance is comparable to that achieved by the state-of-the-art algorithms [7, 14].

5 Discussion and Further Developments

We have considered a basic EP algorithm based on equivalence classes (EPQ say) and studied a number of performance issues in a novel evolutionary framework based on equivalence classes represented as CPDAGs. We have observed the adequacy of having all six operators introduced by Chickering [7] cooperating together in order to achieve satisfactory results in the benchmark ALARM problem. We have also illustrated the relatively low sensitivity of the evolved structures with regard to the α scaling of the BDeu fitness metric. Our results are thus encouraging albeit preliminary, for there are some key issues still in dispute in the broader machine learning context. We now briefly discuss some of these issues, and the implications for our current EPQ algorithm.

Castelo and Kočka [14] highlight the relevance of the *inclusion boundary* (IB) principle in graph learning. This principle stresses the need for the traverse set of operators to be able to produce *any* model in some "tight" neighbourhood of the current model. A number of algorithms (backed by some useful convergence results holding under reasonable sampling assumptions) have been proposed and tested with success [14–16]. As it turns out, the desired connectivity is given by the *ENR* (equivalence-no-reversals) neighbourhood of a DAG **G**: the set of all DAGs that can be reached from any DAG **H** ∈ [**G**] by (valid) single directed arc addition or deletion. This neighbourhood might appear to be relatively simpler to implement in b-space [14] than in e-space [15]. Indeed, our traverse set made up by the six operators proposed in [7] does not verify the IB principle since some DAGs in ENR may not be reachable (although many other DAGs not in ENR can be covered). Chickering [15] has subsequently introduced (more complex) `Insert` and `Delete` operators respecting the IB principle (covering ENR). Thus, a first line for future work would address the tradeoff between simplicity and ENR-coverage towards the design of more efficient traverse operators in e-space [16]. On the other hand, we have already begun the evaluation of EPQ with regard to other inclusion-driven EP algorithms in b-space.

Moving beyond this overview of the general learning scenario, we would also like to furnish some prospects for future evolutionary developments based on the present EPQ. First of all, there is a very interesting research line in connection with the Ω distribution used for selecting operators. We would like to tackle the design of strategies for dynamically adapting Ω. In this sense, we envision both adaptive approaches – in which some population-wide rules are used to modify Ω during the run –, and self-adaptive approaches – in which each individual l carries its own Ω_l distribution (whose population is also subject to evolution). Some lessons from the utilization of these mechanisms in the field of *evolution strategies* can be used for this purpose [17].

Recombination operators are also in perspective. We face here a difficult scenario for recombination, for not only acyclicity constraints apply (as in the case of DAGs), but also additional constraints due to the nature of CPDAGs. Of course, we could instantiate $\bar{\mathbf{G}}$ and $\bar{\mathbf{H}}$ (using the PDAG-to-DAG routine) to obtain DAGs $\mathbf{G}$ and $\mathbf{H}$, use standard operators over DAGs as in [3] to produce some DAG $\mathbf{K}$, and finally apply the DAG-to-CPDAG routine to obtain an offspring $\bar{\mathbf{K}}$ derived from $\bar{\mathbf{G}}$ and $\bar{\mathbf{H}}$. However, we could not guarantee that $\bar{\mathbf{K}} \neq \bar{\mathbf{G}}$ and $\bar{\mathbf{K}} \neq \bar{\mathbf{H}}$. To deal with this, we have in mind the decomposition of the recombination process in a sequence of basic operations assimilable to the mutation operators we have used, much in the line of what is done in path-relinking [18]. This and the basic EP approaches can be completed with the incorporation of *phenotypic* measures based on the availability of local scoring measures, e.g. [3].

We have used a variant of BDe or $\log P(\mathbf{D}|\mathbf{G})$ as our basic scoring metric. An alternative is provided by the log posterior $\Psi(\mathbf{G}|\mathbf{D}, \boldsymbol{\alpha}) = \log \pi(\mathbf{G}|\mathbf{D}) = \log \pi(\mathbf{G}) + \log P(\mathbf{D}|\mathbf{G})$, where $\pi(\mathbf{G})$ is some prior on DAG structures [9]. For example, letting $g = \sum_i (r_i - 1)q_i$, the number of free parameters in $\boldsymbol{\theta}$, $\pi(\mathbf{G}) \propto N^{-g/2}$ penalizes complex structures (as in our previous work [3]). These ideas may be useful to counter-balance biases towards denser networks that could appear when working with BDeu [13].

Acknowledgement

We are grateful to D.M. Chickering and R. Castelo for some useful conversations on these ideas, and to Alicia Puerta and Quique López for valuable assistance. The authors are partially supported by the DMR Foundation's Decision Engineering Lab and by grants TIC2001-0175-C03-03 and TIC2002-04498-C05-02 from the Spanish MCyT.

References

1. Larrañaga, P., Poza, M., Yurramendi, Y., Murga, R., Kuijpers, C.H.: Structure learning of bayesian networks by genetic algorithms: A performance analysis of control parameters. IEEE Transactions on Pattern Analysis and Machine Intelligence **10** (1996) 912–926

2. Wong, M., Lam, W., Leung, K.: Using evolutionary programming and minimum description length principle for data mining of bayesian networks. IEEE Transactions on Pattern Analysis and Machine Intelligence **21** (1999) 174–178
3. Cotta, C., Muruzábal, J.: Towards a more efficient evolutionary induction of bayesian networks. In Merelo, J., Adamidis, P., Beyer, H.G., Fernández-Villacañas, J.L., Schwefel, H.P., eds.: Parallel Problem Solving From Nature VII. Volume 2439 of Lecture Notes in Computer Science. Springer-Verlag, Berlin (2002) 730–739
4. Heckerman, D.: A tutorial on learning with bayesian networks. In Jordan, M., ed.: Learning in Graphical Models. Kluwer, Dordrecht (1998) 301–354
5. Andersson, S., Madigan, D., Perlman, M.: A characterization of markov equivalence classes for acyclic digraphs. Annals of Statistics **25** (1997) 505–541
6. Gillespie, S., Perlman, M.: Enumerating Markov equivalence classes of acyclic digraph models. In Goldszmidt, M., Breese, J., Koller, D., eds.: Proceedings of the Seventh Conference on Uncertainty in Artificial Intelligence, Seatle WA, Morgan Kaufmann (2001) 171–177
7. Chickering, D.: Learning equivalence classes of Bayesian-network structures. Journal of Machine Learning Research **2** (2002) 445–498
8. Fogel, L., Owens, A., Walsh, M.: Artificial Intelligence Through Simulated Evolution. Wiley, New York NY (1966)
9. Heckerman, D., Geiger, D., Chickering, D.: Learning bayesian networks: the combination of knowledge and statistical data. Machine Learning **20** (1995) 197–243
10. Acid, S., de Campos. L.M.: Searching for bayesian network structures in the space of restricted acyclic partially directed graphs. Journal of Artificial Intelligence Research **18** (2003) 445–490
11. Eiben, A., Smith, J.: Introduction to Evolutionary Computing. Springer-Verlag, Berlin Heidelberg (2003)
12. Beinlich, I., Suermondt, H., Chavez, R., Cooper, G.: The ALARM monitoring system: A case study with two probabilistic inference techniques for belief networks. In Hunter, J., Cookson, J., Wyatt, J., eds.: Proceedings of the Second European Conference on Artificial Intelligence and Medicine, Berlin, Springer-Verlag (1989) 247–256
13. Kayaalp, M., Cooper, G.: A bayesian network scoring metric that is based on globally uniform parameter priors. In Darwiche, A., Friedman, N., eds.: Proceedings of the Eighteenth Annual Conference on Uncertainty in Artificial Intelligence, San Francisco CA, Morgan Kaufmann (2002) 251–258
14. Castelo, R., Kočka, T.: On inclusion-driven learning of bayesian networks. Journal of Machine Learning Research **4** (2003) 527–574
15. Chickering, D.: Optimal structure identification with greedy search. Journal of Machine Learning Research **3** (2002) 507–554
16. Nielsen, J., Kočka, T., Peña, J.: On local optima in learning bayesian networks. In Rulff, U., Meek, C., eds.: Proceedings of the Nineteenth Conference on Uncertainty in Artificial Intelligence, Acapulco, Mexico, Morgan Kaufmann (2003) 435–442
17. Beyer, H.G.: Toward a theory of evolution strategies: Self adaptation. Evolutionary Computation **3** (1996) 311–347
18. Glover, F., Laguna, M., Martí, R.: Fundamentals of scatter search and path relinking. Control and Cybernetics **39** (2000) 653–684

The Infection Algorithm: An Artificial Epidemic Approach for Dense Stereo Matching

Gustavo Olague[1], Francisco Fernández de Vega[2],
Cynthia B. Pérez[1], and Evelyne Lutton[3]

[1] CICESE, Research Center, Applied Physics Division
Centro de Investigación Científica y de Educación Superior de Ensenada,
B.C., Km. 107 Carretera Tijuana-Ensenada, 22860, Ensenada, B.C., México
olague@cicese.mx
[2] University of Extremadura, Computer Science Department
Centro Universitario de Merida, C/Sta Teresa de Jornet, 38. 06800 Mérida, Spain
[3] INRIA Rocquencourt, Complex Team
Domaine de Voluceau BP 105
78153 Le Chesnay Cedex, France

Abstract. We present a new bio-inspired approach applied to a problem of stereo images matching. This approach is based on an artifical epidemic process, that we call "the infection algorithm." The problem at hand is a basic one in computer vision for 3D scene reconstruction. It has many complex aspects and is known as an extremely difficult one. The aim is to match the contents of two images in order to obtain 3D informations which allow the generation of simulated projections from a viewpoint that is different from the ones of the initial photographs. This process is known as view synthesis. The algorithm we propose exploits the image contents in order to only produce the necessary 3D depth information, while saving computational time. It is based on a set of distributed rules, that propagate like an artificial epidemy over the images. Experiments on a pair of real images are presented, and realistic reprojected images have been generated.

1 Introduction

The problem of matching the contents of a stereoscopic system is a classical (and extremely difficult!) problem in computer vision. Image matching has been shown recently to be NP-complete [14]. Stereo image matching has multiple practical applications, including robot navigation, object recognition, and more recently, realistic scene visualization or image-based rendering. Many approach exist today that attempts to solve this problem. These approaches are now classified in terms of local and global methods. Local methods are typically block matching, gradient based optimization, and feature matching, while global approaches are dynamic programming, intrinsic curves, graph cuts, nonlinear diffusion, belief propagation, and correspondenceless methods, see [2].

The matching of two images can be formulated as a constrained optimization problem. It is however necessary to deal with a huge search space and with

a) Left image.　　　　　　　　　b) Right image.

Fig. 1. A stereo pair taken at the EvoVisión laboratory, notice several classical problems: occlusion, textureless areas, sensor saturation, and optical constraints.

some aspects that are hard to model, such as the occlusion of parts on the scene, regions with a regular pattern, or even regions with similar textures. Classical techniques are limited and fail, due to the complexity and nature of the problem. This is the main reason why artificial life and evolutionary methods are considered now in this framework, see: [11] and [6].

Our work aims to improve the speed and the quality of a stereo matching, while considering simultaneously local and global information. The local information is obtained from the correlation or objective function used to match the contents of both images, and from the constraints which are used to improve the matching process. The objective function and constraints are considered as local because they only depend on a local neighborhood. The global information is encapsulated within the algorithm that we will describe in section 3.

Artificial life obviously does not try to reproduce natural life, but to create systems that generate characteristics, responses or behaviors, similar to the ones observed in natural systems. One of the favorite topics of this domain is the study of emergence of complex behaviors from a set of elementar components acting according to simple rules.

This paper is organized as follows. The next section describes the nature of the matching problem, the objective function and constraints we consider. Section 3 introduces the proposed algorithm, with the main goal of saving on the number of calculations while maintaining the quality of the virtual reprojected image. Finally, a set of images and graphs illustrate the behavior and performances of the infection algorithm.

2 Statement of the Problem

Computational stereo or the correspondence problem refers to the problem of determining three-dimensional structure of a scene from two or more images taken from different viewpoints. The fundamental assumption used by stereo algorithms is that a single three-dimensional physical point projects onto a unique pair of image points for two cameras. On the other hand, if it is possible to locate the image projected points on two observing cameras that correspond to the same physical point in space, then it is possible to calculate its precise 3D position. However, the problem becomes intractable for several reasons so that there exists no closed form solution to this problem. Stereo matching is an ill-posed problem with inherent ambiguities, due to ambiguous matches produced by occlusions, specularities, or lack of texture. Therefore, a variety of constraints and assumptions are commonly exploited to make the problem tractable. Figure 1 shows a classical pair of images illustrating the usual difficulties of computational stereo. The movement between both images is typically a translation plus a small rotation. The wooden house and the calibration grid are clearly visible in both images. However, the wooden puppet only appears in the right image, while the file organizer behind the box with the children face only appears on the left image.

These are examples of visibility constraints : due to obstructions in the workplace, all points of interest that lie within the field of view are not always projected on both cameras. Thus, the visibility of a feature of an object from a particular viewpoint depends if it is occluded by either some part of the object itself (self-occlusion), or by other objects in the environment. This problem is due to the opaqueness of the objects. Additionnally, if the feature lies outside the field-of-view of the sensor it is not visible. Hence, matching is impossible for these previous cases. Moreover, matching large homogeneous (textureless) areas is also an ill-posed problem, since there is no way to decide which point corresponds to which other point over the entire area (no characteristic feature, ambiguity). This is clearly the case for the *EvoVisión* house as well as for the calibration grid of the test stereo pair.

2.1 Correlation as an Objective Function

A correlation measure can be used as a similarity criterion between image windows of fixed size. The input is a stereo pair of images, I_l (left) and I_r (right). The process of correlation can be thought as a search process in which the correlation gives the measure used to identify the corresponding pixels on both images. This process attempts to maximize the similarity criterion within a search region. Let p_l and p_r be pixels in the left and right image, $2W+1$ the width (in pixels) of the correlation window, $R(p_l)$ the search region in the right image associated with p_l, and $\phi(I_l, I_r)$ a function of both image windows. The ϕ function is defined as the Zero-mean Normalized Cross-Correlation (ZNCC) in order to match the contents of both images. This function is used to match points in two images, as it is invariant to local linear radio-metric changes.

$$\phi(I_l, I_r) = \frac{\sum_{i,j}[(I_l(x+i,y+j)-\overline{I_l(x,y)})(I_r(x'+i,y'+j)-\overline{I_r(x',y')})]}{\sqrt{\sum_{i,j}(I_l(x+i,y+j)-\overline{I_l(x,y)})^2 \sum_{i,j}(I_r(x'+i,y'+j)-\overline{I_r(x',y')})^2]}} \quad (1)$$

2.2 Constraints on Dense Stereo Matching

Stereo matching is a very difficult search process. In order to minimize false matches, some matching constraints must be set. The constraints we have considered in our algorithm are the following.

- Epipolar geometry. Given a feature point p_l in the left image, the corresponding feature point p_r must lie on the corresponding epipolar line. This constraint reduces the search space from two-dimensions to one-dimension. Unlike all other constraints, the epipolar constraint would never fail and could be applied reliably once the epipolar geometry is known (stereo calibrated system).
- Ordering. If $p_l \leftrightarrow p_r$ and $p'_l \leftrightarrow p'_r$ and if p_l is on the left of p_r then p'_l should also lie on the left of p'_r and reversely. That is the ordering of features is preserved.
- Orientation. We use as a constraint not only the grey value of a pixel but also the orientation of the epipolar line on which the pixel lies.

3 Artificial Epidemics for Dense Stereo Matching

The motivation to use what we called the infection algorithm has two main origins. First, when we observe a scene, we do not observe everything in front of us. Instead of it, we focus our attention to some parts which keeps our interest on the scene. Hence, we believe that many of the attention process are handled by guessing, while we are developing our activities (which also may be the source of optical illusions). The process of information guess from characteristic points can be implemented via a matching propagation. This point also has some intuitive connections with disease spread in a population.

Invasion of disease into a population is a natural phenomenon. This phenomenon can be noticed in any species populations, and has been a concern for human beings for centuries. The problem has been deeply studied during the last fifty years, with the aim of obtaining ideas about how a given disease will spread into a population, and also to decide how to vaccinate the people in order to stop the propagation of the disease. Although there have been several approaches to the study of disease propagation, researchers agree that the first attempt to formulate a mathematical model is due to Lowell Reed and Wade Hapton in the 1920s [1], and the model was called SIR (Susceptible/Infective/Recovered) model. In this model a population is divided into three classes according to their status in relation to the disease of interest: *susceptible*, meaning they are free of the disease but can catch it, *infective*, meaning they have the disease and can pass it to others, and *recovered*, meaning they have recovered from the disease and cannot longer pass it on. Some probability values per unit of time are employed to calculate transitions from a given state to another one. Contact patterns between individuals from the population are also required for modeling the phenomenon.

The model has been later revised and several researchers have studied exact solutions for this timely called *epidemic models* [5]. Given the features of epidemic models, some authors have employed them to study different behaviors in computer networks and parallel machines. For instance, in [9] an epidemic based protocol is applied for implementing computer models on Parallel Machines. Ganesh [4] presents an epidemic based protocol for decentralized collection of information in a distributed network. Very recently, a new kind of models aimed at describing interaction through social, technological and biological networks has been presented, and also employed for the study of the spread of disease. These models have been called *small-world networks*, and try to study how information traverses a network featuring some properties [17]. The concept of small-world network is being recently applied to study the effect of epidemic algorithms [10]. But epidemic algorithms can also be seen from another point of view. Given that the model employs transition rules from the different states that each individual from the population may have during the epidemic process, other authors have studied and modeled the disease spread in population by means of cellular automata [8], which is another very well-known algorithm inspired by nature.

Cellular automata (CA) are fundamental computational models of spatial phenomena, in which space is represented by a discrete lattice of cells. Each cell concurrently interacts with its neighborhood which, in traditional CA, is limited to the cells nearest neighbors. Cellular automata are considered as one of the best representatives of parallel algorithms inspired by nature [15].

The new algorithm we present in this paper is called the *infection algorithm*. It possesses some properties borrowed from epidemic models: information is transmitted between individuals from the population based on some transition rules. Nevertheless, as we will see later, the number of different states that each individual from the population may feature is larger than in an epidemic model. On the other hand, the pattern of contacts among individuals is restricted to the close neighbors, instead of establishing complex networks of contacts. The algorithm is also inspired by cellular automata, because transition rules are employed to determine the next state of each individual from the population. But these transition rules not only uses the states of the individual and its neighbors, but also employ some external information, correlation and constraints, which are computed from the problem we are addressing. With this in mind, the infection algorithm is described in the following section.

4 The Infection Algorithm

The infection algorithm is based on the concept of natural virus for searching the correspondences between real stereo images. The purpose is to find all existing corresponding points in stereo images while saving the maximum number of calculations and maintaining the quality of the reconstructed data.

The search process is based on transition rules, similarly to cellular automata. Cellular automata are models of dynamic systems based on simple rules that

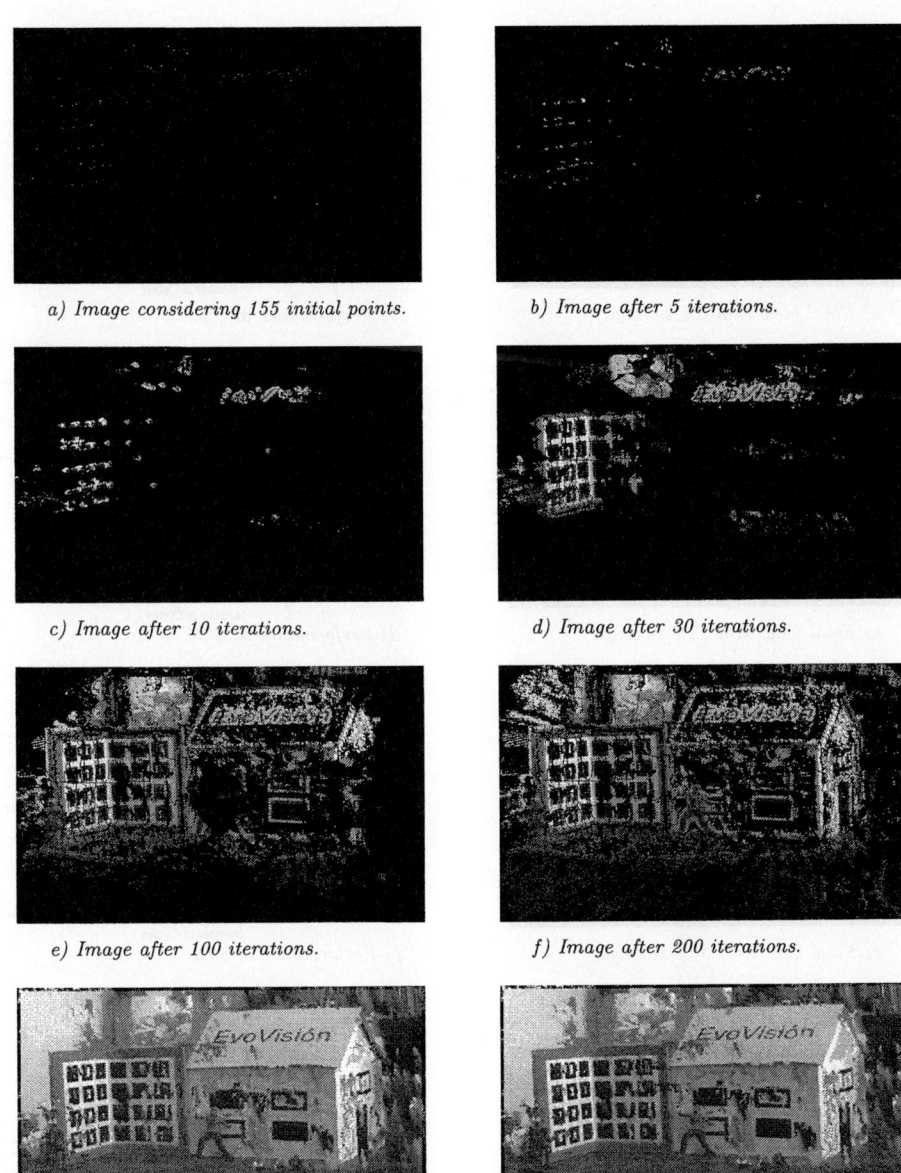

a) Image considering 155 initial points.

b) Image after 5 iterations.

c) Image after 10 iterations.

d) Image after 30 iterations.

e) Image after 100 iterations.

f) Image after 200 iterations.

g) Final view of our algorithm.

h) Final image with an exhaustive search.

Fig. 2. These 8 images show the evolution of our algorithm within a synthetic view. The new image represents a new viewpoint between the two original images. The last two images show the final step of our algorithm. We apply a median filter to achieve the new synthetic image g), as well as to obtain image h), which is product of an exhaustive search. We compared images g) and h): the quality is slightly better on g), while saving 47% of calculations.

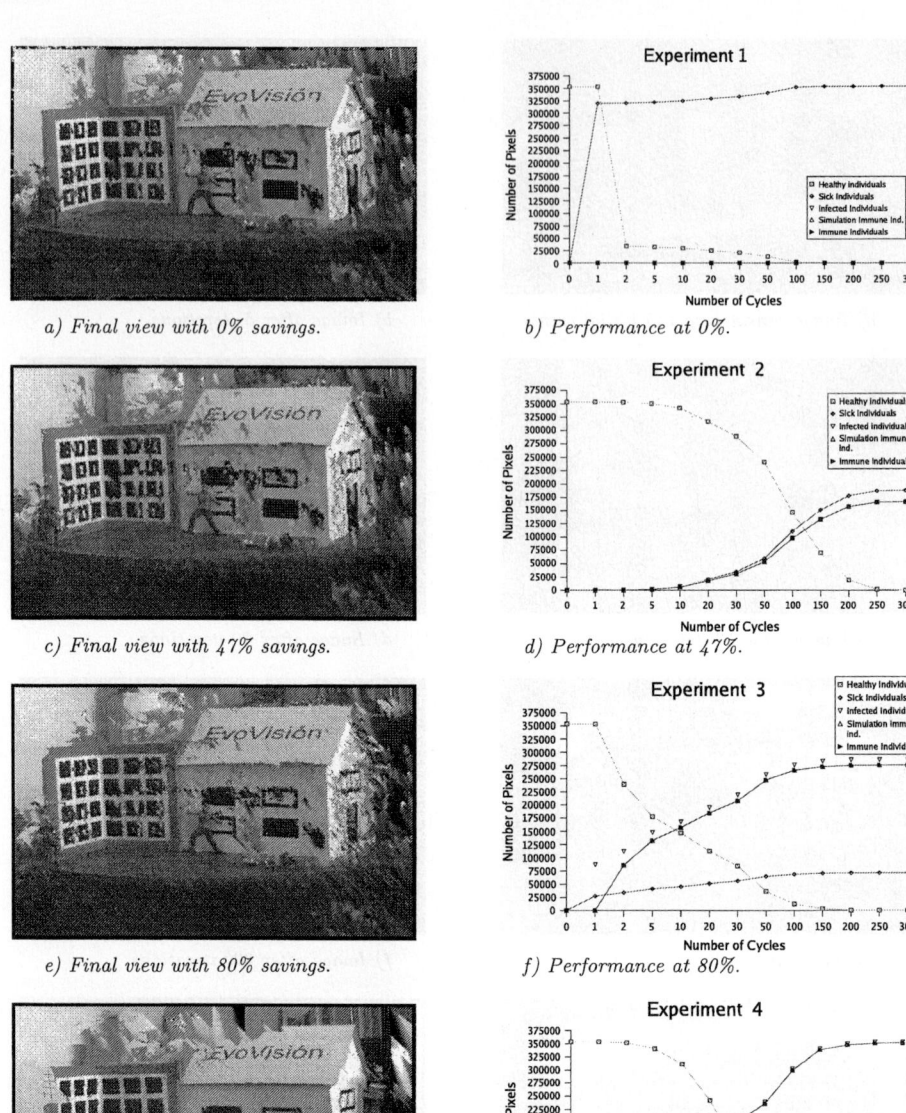

a) Final view with 0% savings.   b) Performance at 0%.

c) Final view with 47% savings.   d) Performance at 47%.

e) Final view with 80% savings.   f) Performance at 80%.

g) Final view using mainly the seeds.   h) Performance at 99%.

Fig. 3. These 4 images show the final results of our algorithm after modifying the rules in order to obtain different levels of savings on the number of computations. The quality of the virtual image is deteriorated, when the level of automatically allocated pixels is increased. However, the quality of the final image is relatively good due to the quality of the nucleus of infection.

interact to produce a global and complex behavior. Our automaton can be seen as a distributed sequence of discrete time steps governed by a fixed set of rules. The rule entries depends on the state of the pixel's neighborhood. The neighborhood structure considered here is a 25 neighbors lattice including the central cell: it is positioned inside a 7x7 window centered on the pixel of interest, with 9 close neighbors and 16 external ones.

The initialisation of the process is based on a set of seed – or nucleus of infection – distributed over the whole image, that attack their neighboring cells. The infection nucleus are generated on the left image with the O&H and K&R corner detectors [13]. The infection evolves over the image according to a set of rules that changes the state of a pixel depending on the state of its neighborhood. Four states are defined as follows.

1. **Healthy individuals** (Not-Explored). Nothing has been decided yet for the pixel.
2. **Sick individuals** (Explored). The pixel has been computed using constraints of dense stereo matching.
3. **Infected individuals** (Proposed). The value of the pixel is guessed on the basis of its neighborhood state. Some controversial information from various neighbors prevent to fix its status at the moment,
4. **Immune individuals** (Automatically allocated). All the information from the neighborhood are coherent and the guessed value has been confirmed.

Healthy individuals are the cells which have not been affected by the virus at time t (initial state). The Sick individuals are the cells which have been affected by the virus, and represent pixels which have been calculated or explored in order to find the correspondence on the right image. The proposed or infected individuals represent cells or pixels which we don't know yet if we need to calculate it, or automatically allocate it a correspondence or matching. Finally, the immune individuals are the most important state because they represent the automatic allocation of the corresponding pixels in the right image without the need of calculating the matching. The assignment is made only through the consideration of the set of local rules, which produces then a global behavior.

The algorithm works in the following way using the above information. First, we need to calculate the projection matrix and the fundamental matrix. We consider a calibrated system using a calibration grid from which we calculate a set of correspondences with a high-accurate corner detector, see Olague et al. [12]. The obained information is used to calibrate rigorously the stereo system. It is important to mention that because the correspondence problem is focused on a calibrated system using real stereo images we work now for simplicity with a scene that is rigid. The camera is moving but not the scene. It is also important to mention that within the cells we create data structures composed of the following information: cell state, corresponding coordinates, and angle of the epipolar line. The whole virtual image is initialized to healthy state (Not-Explored). The lattice is examined cell by cell in a number of cycles.

The aim is to find the maximum number of existing correspondences according to the employed rules. These rules are defined and coded in a file according to the nature of the problem. They determine the desired global behaviour, even if their application only involves local informations (state of the neighborhood). At each step, the algorithm scans the set of rule in order to make a decision based on local informations.

This structure is flexible: rules and neighborhood system directly tune the global behaviour of the system. For example it allows to obtain various infection percentages (that is directly related to the saving of computational cost) and various quality levels of stereo matching results.

Each central cell is analyzed in order to precisely define its state, as well as the state of its neighborhood. The algorithm searches the set of rules in order to apply the rules that match the current local state (state of central cell, number of external neighbors in each state, and precise state of the close neighbors). An action is then activated that produces a path and sequence around the initial nucleus. When the algorithm needs to execute a rule to evaluate a pixel, it calculates the corresponding epipolar line using the fundamental matrix information. The correlation window is defined and centered with respect to the epipolar line when the search process is started. The correlation is the main measurement that is used to identify which pixel on the right image corresponds to the studied pixel of the left image (of course, improvements may be drawn from employing both directions).

In the case of automatic allocation of the central cell, angle of the epipolar line, and orientation constraints of the explored neighbors are checked to be coherent with the corresponding values of the central cell. The algorithm then saves the coordinates of the corresponding pixel, otherwise the algorithm calculates the pixel. On the other hand, if the central cell is in the state "proposed", the central cell is only marked as "infected." Finally, when the search is finished, the algorithm saves a synthetic image, which is the projection of the scene between the two original images. This algorithm approaches then the problem of dense stereo matching. It is summarized as follows.

1. All pixels in the images are initiated to the state "not-explored".
2. Then, pixels of maximum interest are extracted. They are in the state "explored" (nucleus of infection).
3. Transition rules are applied to any pixel in the images except if their state is "automatically allocated" or "explored."
4. While there still exists pixels that are not "automatically allocated" or "explored," go to step 3.

5 Experiments and Conclusions

Experiments are presented in figures 2 and 3. Figure 2 shows a virtual image which represents the match data reprojected on a new viewpoint. Figure 3 shows a set of experiments where the local rules were changed in order to modify the behaviour of the algorithm. The latter case represents a high percentage of automatically allocated pixels producing a good quality image.

We have derived a new bio-inspired algorithm, that we have for the moment applied to dense stereo matching. It has been proved efficient for the aim of computational saving without losing the quality of the virtual image. In the future we intend to extend this model in order to identify occluded regions and vantage viewpoints for stereovision. However it seems that the infection algorithm may be useful in other image applications, where local informations needs to be propagated in a coherent way, such as: monocular vision or "shape fom ..." problems, among others.

Acknowledgments

This research was funded by Ministerio de Ciencia y Tecnología, SPAIN, research project number TIC2002-04498-C05-01, and by CONACyT and INRIA through the LAFMI project 634-212.

References

1. H. Abbey. An Examination of the Reed Frost Theory of Epidemics. Human Biology, 24:201-233, 1952.
2. Myron Z. Brown, Darius Burschka, and Gregory D. Hager. Advances in Computational Stereo. IEEE Trans. on Pattern Analysis and Machine Intelligence. Vol. 25, No. 8, August 2003, pp. 993-1008.
3. Gabriel Fielding and Moshe Kam. Weighted Matchings for Dense Stereo Correspondence. Pattern Recognition, Vol. 33 (2000) 1511-1524.
4. Ayaldi J. Ganesh, Anne-Marie Kermarrec, and Laurent Massoulié. Scamp: Peer-to-peer lightweight membership service for large-scale group communication. In Jon Crowcroft and Marcus Hofman, editors. Third International COST264 Workshop (NGC 2001), LNCS 2233, pp. 44-55, London, UK, November 2001.
5. W.O. Kermark and A.G. McKendrick. A Contribution to the Mathematical Theory of Epidemics. Proceedings of the Royal Society of London. Series A, 115, 772:700-721, 1927.
6. Jean Louchet, Using an Individual Evolution Strategy for Stereovision, Genetic Programming and Evolvable Machines Journal, Kluwer, Vol.2 No 2 (2001) 101-109.
7. Qiuming Luo, Jingli Zhou, Shengsheng Yu, and Degui Xiao. Stereo Matching and Occlusion Detection with Integrity and Illusion Sensitivity. Pattern Recognition Letters. Vol. 24 (2003) 1143-1149.
8. W. Maniatty, B. Szymanski, and T. Caraco. Parallel Computing with Generalized Cellular Automata. Nova Science Publishers, Inc. 2001.
9. W. Maniatty, B.K. Szymanski, and T. Caraco. Epidemics Modeling and Simulation on a Parallel Machine. In IASTED, editor, Proceedings of the International Conference on Applied Modeling and Simulation, pp. 69-70. Vancouver, Canada, 1993.
10. C. Moore and M.E.J. Newman. Epidemics and Percolation in Small-World Networks. Phys. Rev. E, 61:5678-5682, 2000.
11. Gustavo Olague. Automated Photogrammetric Network Design using Genetic Algorithms. Photogrammetric Engineering & Remote Sensing. Vol.68, No.5, pp.423-431, May 2002. Paper awarded the "2003 First Honorable Mention for the Talbert Abrams Award", by ASPRS.

12. Gustavo Olague, Benjamín Hernández, and Enrique Dunn. Accurate L-Corner Measurement using USEF Functions and Evolutionary Algorithms. Applications of Evolutionary Computing. EvoWorkshops 2003, LNCS 2611, pp. 410-421.
13. Gustavo Olague and Benjamín Hernández. A New Accurate and Flexible Model Based Multi-corner Detector for Measurement and Recognition. Pattern Recognition Letters, to appear.
14. Daniel Keysers and Walter Unger. Elastic Image Matching is NP-complete. Pattern Recognition Letters. Vol. 24, Issue 1-3, pp. 445-453, January 2003.
15. M. Sipper. Evolution of Parallel Cellular Machines. Springer-Verlag, 1997.
16. Jian Sun, Nan-Ning Zheng, and Heung-Yeung Shum. Stereo Matching using Belif Propagation. IEEE Transactions on Pattern Analysis and Machine Intelligence. Vol. 25, No. 7, July 2003, pp. 787-800.
17. D.J. Watts. Small Worlds. Princeton University Press, 1999.
18. C. Lawrence Zitnick and Takeo Kanade. A Cooperative Algorithm for Stereo Matching and Occlusion Detection. IEEE Trans. on Pattern Analysis and Machine Intelligence. Vol. 22, No. 7, July 2000, pp. 675-684.

Optimising Cancer Chemotherapy Using Particle Swarm Optimisation and Genetic Algorithms

Andrei Petrovski*, Bhavani Sudha, and John McCall

School of Computing,
The Robert Gordon University,
St. Andrew Street,
Aberdeen, AB25 1HG, UK
{ap,bs,jm}@comp.rgu.ac.uk

Abstract. Cancer chemotherapy is a complex treatment mode that requires balancing the benefits of treating tumours using anti-cancer drugs with the adverse toxic side-effects caused by these drugs. Some methods of computational optimisation, Genetic Algorithms in particular, have proven to be useful in helping to strike the right balance. The purpose of this paper is to study how an alternative optimisation method - Particle Swarm Optimisation - can be used to facilitate finding optimal chemotherapeutic treatments, and to compare its performance with that of Genetic Algorithms.

1 Introduction

Many decision-making activities involve searching through a large space of possible solutions. In the chemotherapy problem we have studied, the size of the solution space increases exponentially with the number of decision variables, the values of which need to satisfy certain feasibility criteria.

The requirements imposed on decision variables often make the structure of a solution space quite intricate - regions of feasible solutions are scattered irregularly throughout the solution space, and only one of these regions contains the optimal solution. To find the optimal solution in such situations becomes a difficult task for conventional optimisation methods (gradient-based or simple heuristics). Similarly, the methods of mathematical programming cannot easily deal with multiplicity of feasible regions in the solution space.

It has been found [6], [7], [8], [10] that Genetic Algorithms show a good and robust performance on a class of non-linear, multi-constrained chemotherapy design problems. However, the field of evolutionary computation is growing, and alternative techniques of computational optimisation are being developed. One of such technique is the Particle Swarm Optimisation (PSO), introduced by Kennedy and Eberhart [3].

The appeal of PSO is that it is also a population-based optimisation technique based on the 'social-psychological tendency of individual particles' within the swarm to 'emulate the success of other individuals' [3]. The search behaviour of a particle is influenced by the experience of its neighbours and represents a 'kind of symbiotic cooperative algorithm', aimed at efficient search through unpredictable solution spaces that have complex structures.

---

* Corresponding author.

This property of PSO may make it particularly suitable to the optimisation problem of cancer chemotherapy, which exhibits such properties as multimodality and disjoint nature of feasible regions in the solution space. The purpose of this paper is to study the capabilities of PSO and to compare it with those of genetic algorithms.

In Section 2 we are going to explain the salient features of the chemotherapy optimisation problem. Section 3 describes the methodology of solving this optimization problem using two approaches – Genetic Algorithms and PSO. In Section 4 the details of experiments based on the identified approaches are given. Finally, Section 5 illustrates the experimental results and draws some conclusions, whereas in Section 6 we discuss the significance and our interpretation of the results obtained.

2 Problem Background

Amongst the modalities of cancer treatment, chemotherapy is often considered as inherently the most complex [14]. As a consequence of this, it is extremely difficult to find effective chemotherapy treatments without a systematic approach. In order to realise such an approach, we need to take into account the medical aspects of cancer treatment.

2.1 Medical Aspects of Chemotherapy

Drugs used in cancer chemotherapy all have narrow therapeutic indices. This means that the dose levels at which these drugs significantly affect a tumor are close to those levels at which unacceptable toxic side-effects occur. Therefore, more effective treatments result from balancing the beneficial and adverse effects of a combination of different drugs, administered at various dosages over a treatment period [7].

The beneficial effects of cancer chemotherapy correspond to treatment objectives which oncologists want to achieve by means of administering anti-cancer drugs. A cancer chemotherapy treatment may be either curative or palliative. Curative treatments attempt to eradicate the tumour; palliative treatments, on the other hand, are applied only when a tumour is deemed to be incurable with the objective to maintain a reasonable quality of life for as long as possible.

The adverse effects of cancer chemotherapy stem from the systemic nature of this treatment: drugs are delivered via the bloodstream and therefore affect all body tissues. Since most anti-cancer drugs are highly toxic, they inevitably cause damage to sensitive tissues elsewhere in the body. In order to limit this damage, toxicity constraints need to be placed on the amount of drug applied at any time interval, on the cumulative drug dosage over the treatment period, and on the damage caused to various sensitive tissues [14]. In addition to toxicity constraints, the tumour size (i.e. the number of cancerous cells) must be maintained below a lethal level during the whole treatment period for obvious reasons.

The goal of cancer chemotherapy therefore is to achieve the beneficial effects of treatment objectives without violating any of the abovementioned constraints

2.2 Problem Formulation

In order to solve the optimisation problem of cancer chemotherapy, we need to find a set of treatment schedules, which satisfies toxicity and tumour size constraints yielding at the same time acceptable values of treatment objectives. This set will allow the oncologist to make a decision on which treatment schedule to use, given his/her preferences or certain priorities. In the remainder of this section we will define the decision vectors and the search space for the cancer chemotherapy optimisation problem, specify the constraints, and particularise the optimisation objectives.

Anti-cancer drugs are usually delivered according to a discrete dosage program in which there are n doses given at times $t_1, t_2, \ldots t_n$ [5]. In the case of multi-drug chemotherapy, each dose is a cocktail of d drugs characterised by the concentration levels $C_{ij}, i \in \overline{1,n}, j \in \overline{1,d}$ of anti-cancer drugs in the bloodplasma. Optimisation of chemotherapeutic treatment is achieved by modification of these variables. Therefore, the solution space Ω of the chemotherapy optimisation problem is the set of control vectors $\mathbf{c} = (C_{ij})$ representing the drug concentration profiles.

However, not all of these profiles will be feasible as chemotherapy treatment must be constrained in a number of ways. Although the constraint sets of chemotherapeutic treatment vary from drug to drug as well as with cancer type, they have the following general form.

1. Maximum instantaneous dose C_{max} for each drug acting as a single agent:
$$g_1(\mathbf{c}) = \{C_{max\,j} - C_{ij} \geq 0 : \forall i \in \overline{1,n}, \forall j \in \overline{1,d}\} \tag{1}$$

2. Maximum cumulative C_{cum} dose for drug acting as a single agent:
$$g_2(\mathbf{c}) = \left\{C_{cum\,j} - \sum_{i=1}^{n} C_{ij} \geq 0 : \forall j \in \overline{1,d}\right\} \tag{2}$$

3. Maximum permissible size N_{max} of the tumour:
$$g_3(\mathbf{c}) = \{N_{max} - N(t_i) \geq 0 : \forall i \in \overline{1,n}\} \tag{3}$$

4. Restriction on the toxic side-effects of multi-drug chemotherapy:
$$g_4(\mathbf{c}) = \left\{C_{s\text{-eff}\,k} - \sum_{j=1}^{d} \eta_{kj} C_{ij} \geq 0 : \forall i \in \overline{1,n}, \forall k \in \overline{1,m}\right\} \tag{4}$$

The factors η_{kj} in the last constraint represent the risk of damaging the kth organ or tissue (such as heart, bone marrow, lung etc.) by administering the jth drug. Estimates of these factors for the drugs most commonly used in treatment of breast cancer, as well as the values of maximum instantaneous and cumulative doses, can be found in [1, 2].

Regarding the objectives of cancer chemotherapy, we focus our study on the primary objective of cancer treatment – tumour eradication. We define eradication to mean a reduction of the tumour from an initial size of around 10^9 cells (minimum detectable tumour size) to below 10^3 cells.

In order to simulate the response of a tumour to chemotherapy, a number of mathematical models can be used [5]. The most popular is the Gompertz growth model with a linear cell-loss effect [14]:

$$\frac{dN}{dt} = N(t) \cdot \left[\lambda \ln\left(\frac{\Theta}{N(t)}\right) - \sum_{j=1}^{d} \kappa_j \sum_{i=1}^{n} C_{ij} \{H(t-t_i) - H(t-t_{i+1})\} \right] \quad (5)$$

where $N(t)$ represents the number of tumour cells at time t; λ, Θ are the parameters of tumour growth, $H(t)$ is the Heaviside step function; κ_j are the quantities representing the efficacy of anti-cancer drugs, and C_{ij} denote the concentration levels of these drugs. One advantage of the Gompertz model from the computational optimisation point of view is that the equation (5) yields an analytical solution after the substitution $u(t) = \ln(\Theta/N(t))$ [5]. Since $u(t)$ increases when $N(t)$ decreases, the primary optimisation objective of tumour eradication can be formulated as follows [8]:

$$\underset{\mathbf{c}}{\text{minimise}} \quad F(\mathbf{c}) = \sum_{i=1}^{n} N(t_i) \quad (6)$$

subject to the state equation (5) and the constraints (1)-(4).

3 Methodology

In this section we are going to explain how the optimisation problem of cancer chemotherapy can be solved by two computational optimisation techniques – GA and PSO.

3.1 Genetic Algorithms

The search process aims at finding chemotherapy schedules that satisfy treatment constraints and optimize the optimisation objective (6).

The search for such treatment schedules may be accomplished using the GA approach. Multi-drug chemotherapy schedules, represented by decision vectors $\mathbf{c} = (C_{ij}), i \in \overline{1,n}, j \in \overline{1,d}$, are encoded as binary strings. The representation space $\mathbf{I}$ (a discretized version of Ω) can then be expressed as a Cartesian product

$$\mathbf{I} = A_1^1 \times A_1^2 \times ... \times A_1^d \times A_2^1 \times A_2^2 \times ... \times A_2^d \times ... \times A_n^1 \times A_n^2 \times ... \times A_n^d \quad (7)$$

of allele sets A_i^j. Each allele set uses a 4-bit representation scheme

$$A_i^j = \{a_1 a_2 a_3 a_4 : a_k \in \{0,1\} \forall k \in \overline{1,4}\} \quad (8)$$

so that each concentration level C_{ij} takes an integer value in the range of 0 to 15 concentration units [6], [7]. In general, with n treatment intervals and up to 2^p concentration levels for d drugs, there are up to 2^{npd} individual elements. Henceforth we assume that $n=10$ and that the number of available drugs in restricted to ten [8]. The values $n=10$ and $d=10$ result in the individual (search) space of power $|\mathbf{I}| = 2^{400}$ individuals, referred to as chromosomes.

Thus, a chromosome $x \in \mathbf{I}$ can be expressed as

$$x = \{a_1 a_2 a_3 \ldots a_{4nd} : a_k \in \{0,1\} \; \forall k \in \overline{1, 4nd}\} \tag{9}$$

and the mapping function $m : \mathbf{I} \to \mathbf{C}$ between the individual $\mathbf{I}$ and the decision vector $\mathbf{C}$ spaces can be defined as

$$C_{ij} = \Delta C_j \sum_{k=1}^{4} 2^{4-k} a_{4d(i-1)+4(j-1)+k}, \; \forall i \in \overline{1, n}, j \in \overline{1, d} \tag{10}$$

where ΔC_j represents the concentration unit for drug j. This function symbolizes the decoding algorithm to derive the decision vector $\mathbf{c} = m(x)$ from a chromosome x. Applying the evaluation function F to $\mathbf{c}$ yields the value of the optimisation objective.

3.2 Particle Swarm Optimisation

The PSO algorithm is initialised with a population of random candidate solutions, conceptualised as particles. These particles are flown through the hyperspace Ω of solutions to the chemotherapy optimisation problem described in the previous section. The position of each particle $\overline{c}_i^{k+1}$ at iteration $k+1$ corresponds to a treatment regimen of anti-cancer drugs and is determined by the following formula:

$$\overline{c}_i^{k+1} = \overline{c}_i^k + \overline{v}_i^k \tag{11}$$

where is $\overline{v}_i^k$ a randomised velocity vector assigned to each particle in a swarm. The velocity vector drives the optimisation process and reflects the 'socially exchanged' information.

There exist different algorithms that regulate how this 'social' information is exchanged [3]. In the first algorithms – *individual best* – each particle compares its current position in the solution space Ω to its own best position found so far; no information from other particles is used. In the second algorithm – *local best* – particles are influenced by the best position within their neighbourhood, as well as their own past experience. In the third algorithm – *global best* – the 'social' knowledge used to drive the movements of particles includes the position of the best particle from the entire swarm.

Therefore, each particle in the swarm is attracted towards the locations representing best chemotherapeutic treatments found by the particle itself, its neighbours, and/or the entire population. This is achieved by defining the velocity vector in (11) for each particle as:

$$\overline{v}_i^k = w \cdot \overline{v}_i^{k-1} + b_1 \cdot r_1 \cdot \left(\overline{c}_i^* - \overline{c}_i^{k-1}\right) + b_2 \cdot r_2 \cdot \left(\overline{c}_i^{**} - \overline{c}_i^{k-1}\right) \tag{12}$$

where:
- w is the inertia coefficient;
- b_1 and b_2 are empirical coefficients used to improve PSO performance;
- r_1 and r_2 are random numbers is the range $[0,1]$;

- $\bar{c}_i^*$ and $\bar{c}_i^{**}$ are the best locations in Ω found by the particle i and the entire population respectively;
- $\bar{v}_i^{k-1}$ is the value of particle i velocity at previous iteration of the algorithm; the values $\bar{v}_i^0$ are initialised at random.

The PSO algorithm works by finding a new position for each particle using (11) and (12), evaluating them and updating the personal and global best values.

4 Experiments

In our study we compared three algorithms - Genetic Algorithms, global best PSO, and local best PSO. The comparison has been done on the problem of multi-drug cancer chemotherapy optimisation addressed in [6], [7], [8]. The optimisation objective is to minimise the overall tumour burden $F(\mathbf{c})$ defined by (6) with the aim to eradicate the tumour.

In our attempt to solve this problem, the following settings of algorithms' properties and parameters have been chosen.

4.1 Genetic Algorithms

The initial GA population of 50 individuals is chosen at random in accordance with the representation scheme (8)-(9). The selection procedure is based in the roulette-wheel selection, augmented by a linear fitness normalization technique [8] and an elitist strategy that reserves two best chromosomes in the population. Recombination is implemented as a 2-point crossover followed by a uniform mutation applied with the probabilities $p_c = 0.5$ and $p_m = 0.2$ respectively. (These setting are the same as in our previous studies [6], [7], [8].)

4.2 Particle Swarm Optimisation

Similar to the GA population, initial positions of 50 PSO particles are generated at random. Each particle in the swarm is assigned a random velocity value from the range $[0,2]$, i.e. $\bar{v}_i^0 \in [0,2]$, $i \in [1,50]$; this value changes at each iteration of the algorithm according to (12) with the following settings of parameters as recommended in [11]:

➢ ω is assigned a randomly generated value from the range $[0.5, 1]$;
➢ $b_1 = b_2 = 4$;
➢ r_1, r_2 are randomly generated from the range $[0,1]$;
➢ the velocity bound values $|v_{max}|$ are set to 1 to help keep the swarm under control [9].

For the local best PSO algorithm, the neighbourhood size was chosen to be 20% of the population, i.e. each neighbourhood contains 10 particles and is formed on the basis of the numerical indexes assigned to these particles.

The programs implementing both GA and PSO algorithms are written in Java; these programs run until a predefined termination criterion is satisfied. The termination criterion was chosen to be 25,000 fitness function evaluations, because it has been empirically found that this number of evaluations guarantees finding a feasible solution for all trial runs of at least one algorithm, which happened to be the global best PSO.

Because of the randomised nature of algorithms under investigation, the programs implementing GA, local and global best PSO were run 30 times each. In order to sharpen the comparison of performance, the same set of 30 random starting populations was used for each of the algorithms tested. This ensures that differences in performance between algorithms cannot be ascribed to a relatively poor set of random starts. In addition, repeated runs allowed us to gather empirical data, statistical analysis of which can lead to reliable results. These results are presented in the next section.

5 Results

During each trial run of the programs implementing GA, local and global PSO, the following outcomes were recorded:

- the number of algorithms' iterations (referred to as generations) required to find at least one feasible (i.e. satisfying all the constraints (1)-(4)) solution;
- the maximum value of the fitness function found at each iteration of the algorithms;
- the best solution found at the end of a trial run.

Figure 1 presents the comparative results based on the first measure - the mean number of generations required to find a feasible solution. The data are represented in the format adopted in [4].

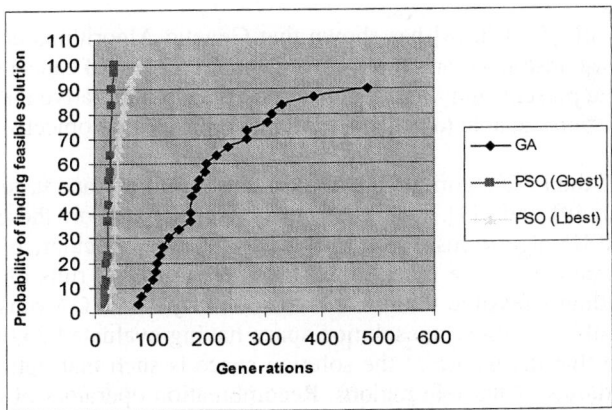

Fig. 1. Number of generations needed to find a feasible solution.

From the above graph it is clear that the PSO algorithms find the feasible region in the solution space of chemotherapeutic treatments faster than Genetic Algorithms. This conclusion is confirmed by the statistical analysis based on interquartile ranges of experimental samples and on t-test comparison of means, summarised in Table 1.

Table 1. T-test comparison of the algorithms' speeds.

Pair	Difference in Means	Std. Error Mean	t-test	p-value
GA vs. global PSO	170.9259	18.87354	9.056	.000
GA vs. local PSO	152.7778	19.00002	8.041	.000
Global vs. local PSO	-17.200	2.6920	-6.389	.000

As can be seen from the last column of Table 1, all p-values are $\ll 0.05$; this indicates that the difference in algorithms' performance originates from their respective effectiveness rather than from random noise.

The second outcome of our comparison is that in addition to finding a feasible solution faster, the PSO algorithms yield the overall best solution (found at the end of each trial run) of the same quality as that of Genetic Algorithms as can be seen from Table 2.

Table 2. T-test comparison of best solutions found by each algorithm.

Pair	Difference in Means	Std. Error Mean	t-test	p-value
GA vs. global PSO	-1.4063	.76898	-1.829	.078
GA vs. local PSO	-1.4040	.76872	-1.826	.078
Global vs. local PSO	.0023	.00446	.523	.605

This is an important observation implying that the PSO algorithms do not achieve efficiency at the expense of effectiveness.

6 Discussions

Our previous work [6], [7], [8] has shown that Genetic Algorithms can be useful in solving the multi-constrained and multi-dimensional problem of cancer chemotherapy optimisation. The present study has demonstrated that an alternative method - Particle Swarm Optimisation - is able to achieve the same optimisation objective in a new and faster way.

The ability of the PSO algorithms to explore the solution space faster than GA has been reported in [9] and [11]. Our experimental results support these findings and show that the PSO algorithms, the global best PSO in particular, optimise cancer chemotherapy treatments in a more robust manner – all trial runs of the PSO programs led to finding a feasible solution. On the contrary, some GA runs did not result in finding a feasible region in the solution space having evaluated 25,000 treatments. We hypothesize that the nature of the solution space is such that optimal treatments lie on the boundaries of feasible regions. Recombination operators of Genetic Algorithms may cause these boundaries to be crossed, leading to infeasible solutions. The PSO algorithms, on the other hand, tend to keep particles within feasible regions by pulling them toward remembered locations in the solution space that proved their trustworthiness. In this respect, a PSO algorithm can rely on its memory – the advantage that Genetic Algorithms do not have. Presumably, historical information on the best solutions found by each particle and the population on the whole is a valuable asset in the context of cancer chemotherapy optimisation, where multiple constraints and a very large solution space lead to a disjoint and sparse nature of the feasible region.

Although there is only a soft real-time constraint on finding a good treatment schedule, the cost of evaluating a chemotherapeutic treatment is likely to increase with the introduction of new anti-cancer drugs and imposing patient-specific constraints. Therefore, finding a solution to the problem of cancer chemotherapy optimisation faster without compromising its quality is an important and useful goal for oncologists. The results of this study show that PSO algorithms can be a viable, and even better, alternative to Genetic Algorithms in achieving this goal.

References

1. Cassidy, J., McLeod, H.: Is it possible to design a logical development plan for an anti-cancer drug. Pharmaceutical Medicine, (1995), **9**, 95-103.
2. Dearnaley, D., et al.: Handbook of adult cancer chemotherapy schedules. The Medicine Group (Education) Ltd., Oxfordshire, (1995).
3. Eberhart, R.: Computational Intelligence PC Tools, Academic Press Professionals (APP), (1996) 185-196.
4. Hoos, H., Stutzle, T.: Local Search Algorithms for SAT: An Empirical Evaluation. J. Automated Reasoning, special Issue "SAT 2000", 1999.
5. Martin, R., Teo, K.: Optimal Control of Drug Administration in Cancer Chemotherapy. World Scientific, Singapore New Jersey London Hong Kong (1994).
6. McCall, J., Petrovski, A.: A Decision Support System for Cancer Chemotherapy Using Genetic Algorithms. Proceedings of the International Conference on Computational Intelligence for Modelling, Control and Automation, Vol. 1. IOS Press (1999) 65-70.
7. Petrovski, A., McCall, J. A. W. Multi-objective optimisation of cancer chemotherapy using evolutionary algorithms. Proceedings of the First International Conference on Evolutionary Multi-Criterion Optimisation, Zurich, Switzerland (2001).
8. Petrovski, A.: An Application of Genetic Algorithms to Chemotherapy Treatment. PhD thesis, The Robert Gordon University, Aberdeen, U.K., (1999).
9. Robinson, J., Sinton, S., Rahmat-Samii, Y.: Particle Swarm, Genetic Algorithm, and their Hybrids: Optimisation of a Profiled Corrugated Horn Antenna. IEEE International Symposium on Antennas & Propagation. San Antonio, Texas, (2002).
10. Kay Chen Tan, Khor, E. F., Cai, J., Heng, C. M., Lee, T. H.: Automating the drug scheduling of cancer chemotherapy via evolutionary computation. Artificial Intelligence in Medicine 25(2): 169-185 (2002).
11. Trelea, I.: The particle swarm optimization: convergence analysis and parameter selection. Information Processing Letters (2003), **85**, 317-25.
12. Ujjin, S., Bentley, P.: Particle Swarm Optimization Recommender System. In Proceedings of the IEEE Swarm Intelligence Symposium, Indianapolis, 2003.
13. Venter, G., Haftka, R., Sobieszczanski-Sobieski, J.: Robust Design Using Particle Swarm and Genetic Algorithm Optimisation. 5th World Congress of Structural and Multidisciplinary Optimization, Lido di Jesolo, Italy , May 19-23, 2003 .
14. Wheldon, T.: Mathematical models in cancer research. Adam Hilger, Bristol Philadelphia (1988).

An Evolutionary Algorithm for Column Generation in Integer Programming: An Effective Approach for 2D Bin Packing*

Jakob Puchinger and Günther R. Raidl

Institute of Computer Graphics and Algorithms
Vienna University of Technology, Vienna, Austria
{puchinger,raidl}@ads.tuwien.ac.at

Abstract. We consider the 3-stage two-dimensional bin packing problem, which occurs in real-world problems such as glass cutting. For it, we present a new integer linear programming formulation and a branch and price algorithm. Column generation is performed by applying either a greedy heuristic or an Evolutionary Algorithm (EA). Computational experiments show the benefits of the EA-based approach. The higher computational effort of the EA pays off in terms of better final solutions; furthermore more instances can be solved to provable optimality.

1 Introduction

The Two-Dimensional Bin Packing (2BP) problem occurs in different variants in important real-world applications such as glass, paper, and steel cutting. A recent survey on 2D packing problems is given in Lodi et al. [5]. Among the algorithms for exactly solving the general 2BP problem are the branch and bound algorithm of Martello and Vigo [7] and the hybrid Branch and Price / Constraint Programming algorithm presented by Pisinger and Sigurd [8].

In many cases there is a special requirement on the cutting patterns: only orthogonal *guillotine* cuts are allowed, i.e., pieces may only be cut horizontally or vertically from one border to the one opposite. Furthermore, the number of stages of such cuts, i.e., the height of the cutting tree of each bin, is often limited in real-world applications. The case of two-stage cutting was first considered by Gilmore and Gomory [3]. More recently two-stage 2BP was considered in Lodi et al. [4] and Belov and Scheithauer [1]. Three-stage cutting problems were treated in Vanderbeck [10] and Puchinger et al. [9], where particular real-world problems with specific additional properties were considered.

In Sec. 2 we present an Integer Linear Programming (ILP) model for classical 3-stage 2BP, based on the model of [4]. In Sec. 3 a column generation formulation and a Branch and Price (B&P) framework, based on [8], are proposed. We describe a greedy heuristic in Sec. 4 and an evolutionary algorithm in Sec. 5 for solving the pricing problem within the B&P approach, i.e., for generating new columns. In Sec. 6 experimental results are given and analyzed.

---

* This work is supported by the Austrian Science Fund (FWF) under grant P16263-N04.

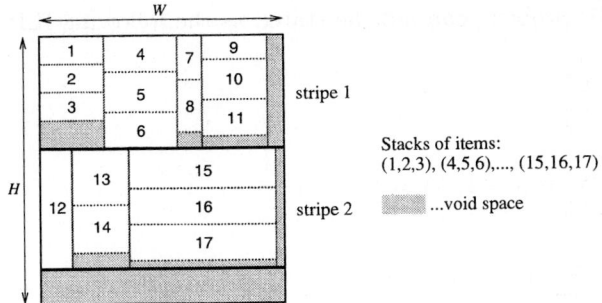

Fig. 1. A three-stage cutting pattern for one bin in normal form.

2 Three-Stage Two-Dimensional Bin Packing

The 2BP problem consists of a set of n rectangular items, each having a height h_i and a width w_i, $i = 1, ..., n$. The objective is to pack them into a minimum number of rectangular bins, each having height H and width W. Items may not overlap and we do not consider rotation.

A feasible layout for *3-stage* 2BP consists of a set of *bins*, each bin consists of a set of *stripes*, each stripe consists of a set of *stacks*, and each stack consists of *items* having equal width. Every such pattern can be reduced into its so-called *normal form* by moving each item to its uppermost and leftmost position, so that void space appears only at the bottom of stacks, to the right of the last stack in each stripe and below the last stripe, see Fig. 1. In the sequel we consider only patterns in normal form.

In [4] a polynomial-sized ILP model for 2-stage 2BP has been proposed. We extend this model in order to get a polynomial-sized ILP formulation for 3-stage 2BP.

The items are sorted so that $h_1 \geq h_2 \geq ... \geq h_n$. The order of the items within each stack is not relevant, so they can always be ordered according to their indices. A solution may contain at most n stacks. We label each stack with the index of the highest item it contains, i.e., the smallest item index. Similarly, a solution has at most n stripes, and a stripe's label is the label of its highest stack. Finally at most n bins are needed and we label each of them with the smallest index of the stripes it contains. The model uses the following 0/1-variables:

- $\alpha_{j,i}$, $j = 1, ..., n$, $i = j, ..., n$: rectangle i is contained in stack j;
- $\beta_{k,j}$, $k = 1, ..., n$, $j = 1, ..., n$: stack j is contained in stripe k;
- $\gamma_{l,k}$, $l = 1, ..., n$, $k = l, ..., n$: stripe k is contained in bin l;
- $\delta_{l,i,j}$, $l = 1, ..., n-1$, $i = l+1, ..., n$, and $j = l, ..., i-1$: item i contributes to the total height of all stripes in bin l; i.e., item i appears in stack j, stack j appears in stripe j, and stripe j appears in bin l.

The 3-stage 2BP problem can now be stated as the following ILP:

$$\text{minimize} \quad \sum_{l=1}^{n} \gamma_{l,l} \tag{1}$$

$$\text{subject to} \quad \sum_{j=1}^{i} \alpha_{j,i} = 1, \quad \forall i = 1, \ldots, n \tag{2}$$

$$\sum_{i=j+1}^{n} \alpha_{j,i} \leq (n-j)\alpha_{j,j}, \quad \forall j = 1, \ldots, n-1 \tag{3}$$

$$\alpha_{j,i} = 0, \quad \forall j = 1, \ldots, n-1 \; \forall i > j \mid w_i \neq w_j \wedge h_i + h_j > H \tag{4}$$

$$\sum_{k=1}^{n} \beta_{k,j} = \alpha_{j,j} \quad \forall j = 1, \ldots, n \tag{5}$$

$$\sum_{i=j}^{n} h_i \alpha_{j,i} < \sum_{i=k}^{n} h_i \alpha_{k,i} + (H+1)(1 - \beta_{k,j}),$$
$$\forall k = 2, \ldots, n, \quad \forall j = 1, \ldots, k-1 \tag{6}$$

$$\sum_{i=j}^{n} h_i \alpha_{j,i} \leq \sum_{i=k}^{n} h_i \alpha_{k,i} + H(1 - \beta_{k,j}),$$
$$\forall k = 1, \ldots, n-1, \quad \forall j = k+1, \ldots, n \tag{7}$$

$$\sum_{j=1}^{n} w_j \beta_{k,j} \leq W \beta_{k,k}, \quad \forall k = 1, \ldots, n \tag{8}$$

$$\sum_{l=1}^{k} \gamma_{l,k} = \beta_{k,k}, \quad \forall k = 1, \ldots, n \tag{9}$$

$$\sum_{i=l}^{n} h_i \left(\gamma_{l,i} + \sum_{j=l}^{i-1} \delta_{l,i,j} \right) \leq H \gamma_{l,l}, \quad \forall l = 1, \ldots, n-1 \tag{10}$$

$$\alpha_{j,i} + \gamma_{l,j} - 1 \leq \delta_{l,i,j} \leq (\alpha_{j,i} + \gamma_{l,j})/2,$$
$$\forall l = 1, \ldots, n-1, \; \forall i = l+1, \ldots, n, \; \forall j = l, \ldots, i-1 \tag{11}$$

$$\sum_{k=l+1}^{n} \gamma_{l,k} \leq (n-l)\gamma_{l,l}, \quad \forall l = 1, \ldots, n-1 \tag{12}$$

The objective function (1) minimizes the number of used bins. Equations (2) state that each item has to be packed once. In (3) it is ensured that items are only assigned to a *used* stack j, i.e., the stack contains item j. The fact that the items packed into the same stack must have identical width is guaranteed by (4). In an implementation, it is not necessary to use all of the $\alpha_{j,i}$, $j \neq i$, but only those for which $w_i = w_j$ and $h_i + h_j \leq H$. However, we keep them in our model for the sake of clarity. Each used stack is packed exactly once according to (5). Constraints (6) and (7) ensure for each stripe k and each contained stack j that the stack's height does not exceed the stripe's height (= stack k's height). Constraints (8) guarantee that width W is not exceeded and no stacks are packed into unused stripes ($\beta_{k,k} = 0$). Equations (9) ensure each used stripe being packed into a bin. In (10) it is guaranteed that height H is not exceeded and no stripes are packed into unused bins ($\gamma_{l,l} = 0$). Constraints (11) force variables $\delta_{l,i,j}$ to be set to one iff rectangle i appears in stack j, stripe j is used, and stripe j appears in bin l. In (12) it is ensured that no stripes are packed into an unused bin.

3   Column Generation Formulation

A general introduction to integer linear programming, B&P, and column generation can be found in Wolsey [11]. Our column generation formulation for 3-stage 2BP is based on the set covering model from [8] and the ILP from the last section.

Let $\mathcal{P}$ be the set of all feasible 3-stage packings of a single bin. The 0/1-variable x_p indicates whether packing $p \in \mathcal{P}$ appears in the solution. For every rectangle $i = 1, \ldots, n$ and every packing $p \in \mathcal{P}$, let $A_i^p = 1$ iff packing p contains rectangle i; otherwise $A_i^p = 0$. The 3-stage 2BP problem can now be formulated as:

$$\text{minimize} \quad \sum_{p \in \mathcal{P}} x_p \tag{13}$$

$$\text{subject to} \quad \sum_{p \in \mathcal{P}} x_p A_i^p \geq 1 \quad \forall i = 1, \ldots, n, \tag{14}$$

$$x_p \in \{0, 1\} \quad \forall p \in \mathcal{P}. \tag{15}$$

In general, $\mathcal{P}$ is too huge for explicitly considering all variables $x_p, p \in P$. Fortunately, we can use delayed column generation to solve the Linear Programming (LP) relaxation of the problem without explicitly considering the majority of the variables [11]. We start with a small set of initial patterns $\mathcal{P}' \subset \mathcal{P}$ taken from an initial feasible solution, and solve the LP relaxation of the problem restricted to $\mathcal{P}'$. Based on the obtained solution, we search for a new variable/pattern whose inclusion in the restricted problem might improve the result. The extended LP is resolved and the whole process repeated until no further improvements are possible.

In addition, every M-th iteration the restricted problem is solved to integrality by using branch and cut, possibly providing a new incumbent solution ($M = 100$ turned out to be a reasonable choice).

The *reduced costs* of a packing $p \in \mathcal{P}$ are

$$c_p^\pi = 1 - \sum_{i=1}^{n} A_i^p \pi_i, \tag{16}$$

where π_i are the dual variables of the restricted LP-relaxed problem. Only variables with negative reduced costs can improve the current solution of the master problem leading us to the challenge of finding such a variable/pattern.

The Pricing Problem. consists of finding a packing p with the smallest reduced costs c_p^π. It is a 3-Stage 2D Knapsack Packing (2DKP) problem with respect to the profits π_i. It can be modeled as follows:

$$\text{maximize} \quad \sum_{i=1}^{n} \pi_i \sum_{j=1}^{i} \alpha_{j,i} \tag{17}$$

$$\text{subject to} \quad \sum_{j=1}^{i} \alpha_{j,i} \leq 1, \quad \forall i = 1, \ldots, n \tag{18}$$

$$\sum_{i=1}^{n} h_i \sum_{j=1}^{i} \delta_{i,j} \leq H \tag{19}$$

$$\alpha_{j,i} + \beta_{j,j} - 1 \leq \delta_{i,j} \leq \frac{\alpha_{j,i} + \beta_{j,j}}{2}$$
$$\forall i = 1, \ldots, n, \ \forall j = 1, \ldots, i \tag{20}$$

and the constraints:

(3), (4), (5), (6), (7), and (8).

Variables $\alpha_{j,i}$ and $\beta_{k,j}$ have the same meaning as in the ILP of Sec. 2. The 0/1-variables $\delta_{i,j}$ are set to one iff item i contributes to the total height of all used stripes, i.e., iff item i appears in stack j, and stack j appears in stripe j.

Branching. If no further variables with negative reduced costs can be determined, and the difference between the solution value of the LP-relaxed restricted problem and the value of the so-far best integer solution is greater than or equal to one, branching becomes necessary. We use a branching rule similar to the one described in [8]. The solution space is divided into two parts, where two different items i_1 and i_2 have not to be or have to be in the same bin. We always choose the two highest possible items from a pattern/variable with an LP solution value closest to 0.5.

The first branch corresponds to adding the constraint

$$\sum_{p \in \mathcal{P}} x_p A_{i_1}^p A_{i_2}^p = 0, \tag{21}$$

the second branch corresponds to adding the two constraints

$$\sum_{p \in \mathcal{P}} x_p A_{i_1}^p (1 - A_{i_2}^p) = 0 \quad \text{and} \quad \sum_{p \in \mathcal{P}} x_p (1 - A_{i_1}^p) A_{i_2}^p = 0. \tag{22}$$

In the actual implementation we do not explicitly add the constraints (21) and (22), but the variables violating them are fixed to zero.

The following constraints have to be added to the pricing problem in order to guarantee that patterns violating the branching constraints cannot be generated. In the first branch

$$\sum_{j=1}^{i_1} \alpha_{j,i_1} + \sum_{j=1}^{i_2} \alpha_{j,i_2} \leq 1, \tag{23}$$

and in the second branch

$$\sum_{j=1}^{i_1} \alpha_{j,i_1} = \sum_{j=1}^{i_2} \alpha_{j,i_2}. \qquad (24)$$

In the sequel, we call i_1 and i_2 *conflicting* if constraint (23) is active and say that i_1 *induces* i_2 and vice-versa if equation (24) is active.

Initial Feasible Solution. In order to initialize the column generation algorithm, a feasible solution is needed. The packing patterns of its bins are used as initial $\mathcal{P}'$. This solution is generated by the order-based Finite First Fit heuristic from [9] without considering the additional application-specific constraints described there. The heuristic is called $20n$ times for different item orders, and the best obtained solution is used. The first five item orders are determined by sorting the items according to decreasing height, width, area, $2h_i + w_i$, and $h_i + 2w_i$; all further orders are random permutations.

4 Solving the Pricing Problem

The pricing problem is solved by a greedy First Fit heuristic respecting the Branching Constraints (FFBC); see Fig. 2.

Similarly to the initialization heuristic, FFBC considers the items in a given order. One item after the other is packed into the first stack it fits. If the item does not fit into any existing stack, a new stack is created in the first stripe it fits. If no such stripe exists and there is enough space left in the bin, a new stack is created and packed into a new stripe. Otherwise, the algorithm proceeds with the next item. If the addition of an item to a stack would increase the corresponding stripe's height, we check if enough vertical space is left in the bin and actually add the item with a probability of 0.5.

The constraints resulting from branching are handled as follows. If an item is considered for packing, we first check whether there are any conflicts with already packed items in the bin (checkNoConflicts in Fig. 2); if there are, the item is skipped. Otherwise we recursively check if other items are induced, and if any of those stay in conflict with any other induced or already packed item (recursiveCheck in Fig. 2). If such a conflict occurs, none of these items can be packed. Otherwise, we immediately try to also pack all the induced items. If this is impossible we skip the whole chain of items.

FFBC is iteratively applied to up to 100 different item orders until a solution with negative reduced costs is found. The first five orders are determined by sorting the items according to decreasing π_i, $\frac{\pi_i}{h_i \cdot w_i}$, $\frac{\pi_i}{h_i + w_i}$, $\frac{\pi_i}{h_i}$, and $\frac{\pi_i}{w_i}$; all further orders are random permutations.

If the heuristic does not find a packing pattern with negative reduced costs, the general purpose ILP-solver CPLEX is finally called on the pricing problem in order to perform an exact search, eventually proving that no such patterns exist anymore.

```
Algorithm FFBC(items, bin)            Function pack(b, i)
forall items i with π_i > 0             forall stripes s in b
  if checkNoConflicts(i)                  forall stacks a in s
    induced = recursiveCheck(i)             if w_i == a.w
    if induced == ∅                           if h_i + a.h ≤ s.h
      pack(bin, i)                              pack i into a
    else                                        return true
      tmp = bin                             else if a.h + h_i − s.h ≤ b.uh ∧ R < ½
      packed = pack(tmp, i)                     pack i into a
      if packed                                 return true
        forall items j in induced       forall stripes r in b
          packed = pack(tmp,j)            if w_i ≤ s.uw ∧ h_i ≤ s.h
          if not packed                     create stack containing i, pack it into s
            break                           return true
      if packed                         else if w_i ≤ s.uw ∧ h_i − s.h ≤ b.uh ∧ R < ½
        bin = tmp                         create stack containing i, pack it into s
                                          return true
Abbreviations:                          if h_i ≤ b.uh
*.h: height of *                          create stack containing i
*.w: width of *                           pack it into new stripe, pack it into b
*.uh: unused height of *                  return true
*.uw: unused width of *                 return false
R: random value ∈ [0, 1)
```

Fig. 2. First fit heuristic respecting the branching constraints.

5 An Evolutionary Algorithm for the Pricing Problem

Since the 2DKP problem is strongly NP-hard, calling the ILP-solver may be very time-consuming. A more sophisticated metaheuristic, performed when FFBC did not find a variable with negative reduced costs and before solving the problem in an exact way, could lead to a faster overall column generation since significantly fewer calls of the ILP-solver may be needed. We decided to apply an Evolutionary Algorithm (EA) operating directly on stripes, stacks, and items.

Structure of the EA. We use a standard steady-state algorithm with binary tournament selection and duplicate elimination. In each iteration, one new candidate solution is created by always applying recombination, and applying mutation with a certain probability. The new solution replaces the worst solution in the population if it is not identical to an already existing solution.

Representation and Initialization. The chosen representation is direct: Each chromosome represents a bin as a set of stripes, each stripe as a set of stacks, and each stack as a set of item references. Using such a hierarchy of sets makes it easy to ignore the order of items, stacks, and stripes and to avoid symmetries.

Initial solutions are created via the FFBC heuristic using randomly generated item orders. These orders are created in a biased way by assigning each item i a random value $r_i \in [0, 1)$ and sorting the items according to decreasing $r_i \pi_i$.

Recombination. This operator first assigns a random value $r_s \in [0,1)$ to each stripe s in the two parent solutions. All these stripes are then sorted according to decreasing $r_s p_s$, with p_s being the sum of the π_i of the items contained in stripe s. The stripes are then considered in this order and packed into the offspring's bin when they fit into it (i.e., their height is smaller than the remaining unused height of the bin). Identical stripes of both parents appear twice in the ordered list, but they are considered at their first appearance only.

When all stripes have been processed, repairing is usually necessary in order to guarantee feasibility. First, the bin is traversed in order to check if items appear twice, the first of these items is deleted. Then, the branching constraints are considered: Items conflicting with others are removed. Afterwards, we try to pack induced items; if this is not possible the corresponding original items are also removed from the bin. Finally, FFBC is applied to the remaining items, possibly improving the solution.

Mutation. The mutation operator removes a randomly chosen item i from the bin. If the branching constraints induce other items for i, they are also deleted. Finally, FFBC is applied to the remaining items for local improvement.

6 Experimental Results

We performed experiments on the benchmark instances from Berkey and Wang [2] (classes 1 to 6) and Martello and Vigo [7] (classes 7 to 10).

We compare CPLEX 8.1 directly applied to the ILP model (1) to (12) and the two variants of the B&P approach with and without the EA for solving the pricing problem. The B&P algorithm was implemented using the opensource framework COIN/Bcp (version 2004/04) [6], the LPs were solved using COIN/Clp. The computational experiments were performed on a Pentium 4 PC with 2.8 GHz. The EA's population size was 100, the mutation was performed with probability 0.75, and the EA terminated when either 1 000 iterations were performed without an improvement of the best solution or after a total of 100 000 iterations. Each of the experiments had a time limit of 1 000 seconds, which was occasionally exceeded because CPLEX is given the same time limit of 1 000 seconds.

Table 1 shows results obtained for the 10 problem classes; in each class there are 50 instances divided into 5 subclasses with $n = 20, \ldots, 100$ items. For each of the considered algorithms (CPLEX, B&P, B&P with EA), average objective values $\bar{z}$ of finally best integer solutions, numbers of instances solved to provable optimality Opt (out of 10), and average times $\bar{t}$ in seconds are given. The last rows show totals and averages over all instances.

When CPLEX is directly applied to the ILP model, 335 out of 500 instances could be solved to provable optimality. This is not bad, but substantially less than B&P's 402 instances and in particular the 409 completely solved instances of the EA-enhanced B&P. The differences in the objective values of the finally best integer solutions found by the three algorithms for instances that could not be

Table 1. Experimental results of the presented algorithms.

Class	n	CPLEX $\bar{z}$	CPLEX Opt	CPLEX $\bar{t}$ [s]	B&P $\bar{z}$	B&P Opt	B&P $\bar{t}$ [s]	B&P with EA $\bar{z}$	B&P with EA Opt	B&P with EA $\bar{t}$ [s]
1	20	7.2	10.0	0.0	7.2	10.0	0.3	7.2	10.0	6.3
	40	13.6	6.0	404.8	13.6	8.0	206.1	13.6	8.0	204.0
	60	20.2	3.0	748.9	20.2	8.0	256.9	20.1	8.0	221.6
	80	27.8	0.0	1000.6	27.6	9.0	182.1	27.6	9.0	183.9
	100	32.7	0.0	1001.3	32.3	4.0	845.6	32.0	6.0	590.4
2	20	1.0	10.0	0.0	1.0	10.0	0.1	1.0	10.0	0.1
	40	2.0	9.0	100.2	2.0	9.0	113.0	2.0	9.0	118.3
	60	2.8	7.0	300.8	2.8	7.0	317.9	2.8	7.0	411.2
	80	3.4	7.0	302.4	3.4	7.0	377.9	3.4	7.0	410.1
	100	4.1	8.0	206.7	4.1	8.0	344.0	4.1	8.0	220.8
3	20	5.4	10.0	0.0	5.4	10.0	0.2	5.4	10.0	0.3
	40	9.7	8.0	307.2	9.8	9.0	124.3	9.7	10.0	7.0
	60	14.2	5.0	704.3	14.2	7.0	386.9	14.1	9.0	184.4
	80	20.3	0.0	1000.4	19.5	7.0	423.9	19.3	8.0	280.2
	100	23.9	0.0	1000.8	23.2	2.0	950.1	22.9	3.0	946.9
4	20	1.0	10.0	0.0	1.0	10.0	0.1	1.0	10.0	0.1
	40	2.0	9.0	100.1	2.0	9.0	100.7	2.0	9.0	166.6
	60	2.6	7.0	353.7	2.7	6.0	413.3	2.7	6.0	736.5
	80	3.3	7.0	300.9	3.3	7.0	402.3	3.3	7.0	303.3
	100	4.0	7.0	302.0	4.0	7.0	378.2	4.0	7.0	306.9
5	20	6.6	10.0	0.0	6.6	10.0	0.2	6.6	10.0	0.8
	40	12.3	10.0	24.2	12.3	10.0	23.0	12.3	10.0	3.1
	60	18.3	10.0	10.3	18.3	10.0	19.0	18.3	10.0	89.0
	80	25.0	5.0	530.1	24.8	9.0	199.4	24.8	9.0	213.7
	100	29.4	1.0	901.5	28.9	5.0	621.6	28.9	7.0	536.3
6	20	1.0	10.0	0.0	1.0	10.0	0.1	1.0	10.0	0.1
	40	1.9	10.0	14.2	1.9	6.0	401.7	1.9	6.0	405.7
	60	2.3	8.0	200.2	2.3	8.0	202.2	2.3	8.0	201.3
	80	3.0	10.0	0.4	3.0	10.0	3.1	3.0	10.0	3.1
	100	3.6	6.0	400.8	3.6	6.0	405.5	3.6	6.0	405.6
7	20	5.7	10.0	0.0	5.7	10.0	0.3	5.7	10.0	0.7
	40	11.5	6.0	566.3	11.5	10.0	4.9	11.5	10.0	39.7
	60	16.2	0.0	1000.2	16.2	9.0	128.5	16.1	10.0	24.7
	80	23.5	0.0	1000.4	23.2	10.0	60.2	23.3	9.0	157.3
	100	28.0	0.0	1000.7	27.1	10.0	292.1	27.1	10.0	269.6
8	20	6.1	10.0	0.0	6.1	10.0	0.8	6.1	10.0	0.9
	40	11.4	10.0	0.6	11.5	9.0	133.7	11.4	10.0	120.1
	60	16.4	10.0	8.6	16.5	9.0	116.0	16.5	9.0	118.6
	80	22.6	8.0	288.6	22.7	9.0	177.8	22.9	7.0	346.5
	100	28.2	8.0	410.0	28.3	7.0	506.4	28.4	6.0	508.9
9	20	14.3	10.0	0.0	14.3	10.0	0.1	14.3	10.0	0.2
	40	27.8	10.0	0.0	27.8	10.0	0.4	27.8	10.0	0.6
	60	43.7	10.0	0.1	43.7	10.0	1.4	43.7	10.0	1.5
	80	57.7	10.0	0.2	57.7	10.0	3.6	57.7	10.0	3.8
	100	69.5	8.0	200.3	69.5	10.0	7.9	69.5	10.0	8.5
10	20	4.5	10.0	0.0	4.5	10.0	0.7	4.5	10.0	0.5
	40	7.7	9.0	185.8	7.7	9.0	166.1	7.8	8.0	217.4
	60	10.7	3.0	822.1	10.7	2.0	857.2	10.5	3.0	825.1
	80	14.0	0.0	1000.4	13.9	0.0	1048.8	13.6	0.0	1114.5
	100	16.9	0.0	1000.7	16.9	0.0	1048.5	16.6	0.0	1151.4
Total		741.0	335.0	17702.0	737.5	402.0	12254.9	735.9	409.0	12068.2
Average		14.82	6.70	354.04	14.75	8.04	245.10	14.72	8.18	241.36

solved to optimality are in general relatively small. Nevertheless, B&P's solution values are in several cases significantly better than those of CPLEX, and the EA-enhanced B&P performs best on average. The two variants of B&P with and without the EA exhibit approximately the same total running times. Applying CPLEX directly was significantly slower in most cases. Thus, the application of the EA within the B&P framework is worth the additional effort.

7 Conclusions and Future Work

For 3-stage 2BP, we presented a compact ILP model having only $O(n^3)$ variables. In practice, however, the proposed column generation approach having a number of potential variables that grows exponentially with n turns out to be more efficient. Using the described EA as an additional strategy for solving the pricing problem pays off in terms of a higher capability of solving instances to provable optimality, but also slightly better average solution values. The combination of B&P and an EA in this form is also highly promising for other combinatorial optimization problems. Research on more sophisticated interaction and a parallel execution of these algorithms will be done next.

References

1. G. Belov and G. Scheithauer. A branch-and-cut-and-price algorithm for one-dimensional stock cutting and two-dimensional two-stage cutting. Technical Report MATH-NM-03-2003, Dresden University of Technology, Germany, 2003.
2. J.O. Berkey and P.Y. Wang. Two-dimensional finite bin packing algorithms. *Journal of the Operational Research Society*, 38:423–429, 1987.
3. P.C. Gilmore and R.E. Gomory. Multistage cutting-stock problems of two and more dimensions. *Operations Research*, 13:90–120, 1965.
4. A. Lodi, S. Martello, and D. Vigo. Models and bounds for two-dimensional level packing problems. *Journal of Combinatorial Optimization*. To appear.
5. A. Lodi, S. Martello, and D. Vigo. Recent advances on two-dimensional bin packing problems. *Discrete Applied Mathematics*, 123:373–390, 2002.
6. R. Lougee-Heimer. The Common Optimization INterface for Operations Research: Promoting open-source software in the operations research community. *IBM Journal of Research and Development*, 47(1):57–66, 2003.
7. S. Martello and D. Vigo. Exact solutions of the two-dimensional finite bin packing problem. *Management Science*, 44:388–399, 1998.
8. D. Pisinger and M. Sigurd. Using decomposition techniques and constraint programming for solving the two-dimensional bin packing problem. Technical Report 03/01, University of Copenhagen, Denmark, 2003.
9. J. Puchinger, G.R. Raidl, and G. Koller. Solving a real-world glass cutting problem. In J. Gottlieb and G. R. Raidl, editors, *Evolutionary Computation in Combinatorial Optimization – EvoCOP 2004*, volume 3004 of *LNCS*, pages 162–173. Springer, 2004.
10. F. Vanderbeck. A nested decomposition approach to a 3-stage 2-dimensional cutting stock problem. *Management Science*, 47(2):864–879, 1998.
11. L.A. Wolsey. *Integer Programming*. Wiley-Interscience, 1998.

An Improved Evaluation Function for the Bandwidth Minimization Problem*

Eduardo Rodriguez-Tello[1], Jin-Kao Hao[1], and Jose Torres-Jimenez[2]

[1] LERIA, Université d'Angers,
2 Boulevard Lavoisier, 49045 Angers, France
{ertello,hao}@info.univ-angers.fr
[2] ITESM Campus Cuernavaca, Computer Science Department,
Av. Paseo de la Reforma 182-A. 62589 Temixco Morelos, Mexico
jtj@itesm.mx

Abstract. This paper introduces a new evaluation function, called δ, for the Bandwidth Minimization Problem for Graphs (BMPG). Compared with the classical β evaluation function used, our δ function is much more discriminating and leads to smoother landscapes. The main characteristics of δ are analyzed and its practical usefulness is assessed within a Simulated Annealing algorithm. Experiments show that thanks to the use of the δ function, we are able to improve on some previous best results of a set of well-known benchmarks.

Keywords: Bandwidth Evaluation Function, Bandwidth Minimization Problem, Heuristics, Simulated Annealing.

1 Introduction

The Matrix Bandwidth Minimization Problem (MBMP) seems to be originated in the 1950's when structural engineers first analyzed steel frameworks by computer manipulation of their structural matrices [1]. In order that operations like inversion and finding determinants take the least time as possible, many efforts were made to discover an equivalent matrix in which all the nonzero entries would lay within a narrow band near the main diagonal (hence the term "bandwidth") [2]. On the other hand the Bandwidth Minimization Problem for Graphs (BMPG) was proposed independently by Harper [3] and Harary [4]. The MBMP is equivalent to the BMPG, given that a graph can be transformed into an incidence matrix. The BMPG has a large number of applications including for instance circuit design and information retrieval in hypertext.

The BMPG can be defined formally as follows. Let $G = (V, E)$ be a finite undirected graph, where $V = \{1, 2, .., n\}$ defines the set of vertices and $E \subseteq V \times V = \{\{i, j\} \mid i, j \in V\}$ is the set of edges. Let $\tau = \{\tau_1, \tau_2, ..., \tau_n\}$ be a permutation of V. The bandwidth β of G for τ is defined by:

$$\beta_\tau(G) = Max\{|\tau_i - \tau_j| : (i, j) \in E\} \qquad (1)$$

---

* This work was partially supported by the CONACyT Mexico.

Then the BMPG consists in finding a permutation τ for which $\beta_\tau(G)$ is minimum.

Since there are $n!$ possible permutations for a graph with n vertices, the BMPG is a highly combinatorial problem. Papadimitriou has shown that finding the bandwidth of a graph is NP-Complete [5]. Later, it was demonstrated that the BMPG is NP-Complete even for trees with a maximum degree of three [6].

Several algorithms for the BMPG have been reported. They can be divided into two classes: exact and heuristic algorithms. Exact algorithms guarantee always to discover the optimal bandwidth. Two examples are proposed in [7]. Both methods solve problems up to 100 vertices, for some classes of matrices. On the other hand, heuristic algorithms try to find good solutions as fast as possible, but they do not guarantee the optimality of the solution found. Some examples are: the Cuthill–McKee algorithm [8] and the Gibbs Poole and Stockmeyer algorithm (GPS) [9]. More recently, metaheuristics have been applied to the BMPG: Simulated Annealing (SA) [10], Tabu Search [11] and Genetic Algorithms [12].

The most common practice in all these algorithms is to evaluate the quality of a configuration as the change in the objective function $\beta_\tau(G)$. This provides little or no information during the search process because $\beta_\tau(G)$ only takes into consideration the maximum absolute difference between labels of adjacent vertices in the graph (see Equation 1).

Three exceptions are reported in the literature. In [10], the authors take into account the five maximum absolute differences to evaluate a configuration. In [13], an evaluation function, called γ, is presented. It takes into consideration all the edges of the graph, unfortunately due to its nature it can only be used in graphs with less than 150 vertices. In [11], the value of a move between two vertices u and v is defined as the number of vertices adjacent to v or u whose bandwidth increases due to the move.

Following these ideas, and given that one of the most important elements in heuristic search is how the quality of a configuration is evaluated, a new evaluation function (namely δ) is proposed in this paper. This new evaluation function is able to capture even the smallest improvement that orients the searching of better solutions and permits to find configurations in which all the absolute differences are minimized.

The rest of this paper is organized as follows: Section 2 concentrates on an analysis of the β evaluation function, the cardinality of its equivalence classes and some possible drawbacks of it. In Section 3 a new evaluation function called δ is proposed. It takes into account all the edges of the graph. Section 4 makes a comparison between β and δ. Section 5 shows the implementation details of the SA algorithm used to study the performance obtained when it uses either δ or β. Section 6 explains the computational results obtained with the SA algorithm for both evaluation functions and a comparison with the best heuristics reported in the literature. Finally, in Section 7 some conclusions are presented.

2 The β Evaluation Function

Given that an undirected graph G could potentially have n reflexive edges and $\frac{n(n-1)}{2}$ non-reflexive edges, then the total number of possible edges is given by: $n + (\frac{n(n-1)}{2}) = \frac{n(n+1)}{2}$, and given that a particular edge can be present or absent (please note that we are counting even the graph with no edges), the number of possible graphs is: $2^{\frac{n(n+1)}{2}}$.

β is the most used evaluation function in the BMP algorithms [9, 14, 8, 12]. Next, some features of β are analyzed.

β can only take n different values $(0 \leq \beta \leq n-1)$, $\beta = 0$ implies that the graph G has either no edges or only reflexive edges. Consequently the search space of $n!$ possible configurations (permutations of $\{1, 2, ..., n\}$) can be partitioned into n different equivalence classes[1] under β. Additionally, let ω_i be the cardinality of the equivalence class under $\beta = i$. Then, it is easy to show that $\omega_0 = 2^n$, and $\omega_1 = 2^n \left(2^{(n-1)} - 1\right)$ then:

$$\omega_i = (2^{(n-i)} - 1) \prod_{j=1}^{i-1} 2^{(n-j)} \qquad (2)$$

Now, in order to verify that all the possible graphs are taken into account, the summation of all cardinalities of the equivalence classes is given in Equation 3, as can be verified the summation equals the total number of graphs.

$$\omega_0 + \sum_{i=1}^{n-1} \omega_i = 2^n + \sum_{i=1}^{n-1}(2^{(n-i)} - 1)\prod_{j=1}^{i-1} 2^{(n-j)} = 2^{\frac{n(n+1)}{2}} \qquad (3)$$

It is very important to remark that the β evaluation function does not take into account all the absolute differences between labels of adjacent vertices, but the maximum absolute difference. In this sense there is no way to make distinctions between elements that belong to the same β equivalence class. For example, the two permutations for the graph showed in Fig. 1 belong to the same β equivalence class ($\beta = 3$), which can be a potential drawback when searching a solution, since the permutation in Fig. 1(b) is better than the one in Fig. 1(a) (it is better because it has only one absolute difference with value two).

The β evaluation function is very gross with very few equivalence classes, in consequence, each equivalence class has high cardinality.

3 The δ Evaluation Function

Given the negative features of β it has been developed a new evaluation function, called δ, which takes into account all the edges of the graph. The proposed

---
[1] Let S be a set with an equivalence relation R. An equivalence class of S under R is a subset $T \subset S$ such that: If $x \in T$ and $y \in S$, then $x \, R \, y$ if and only if $y \in T$. And if $S \neq \emptyset$, then $T \neq \emptyset$.

An Improved Evaluation Function for the Bandwidth Minimization Problem

Fig. 1. (a) Permutation τ with $\beta=3$. (b) Permutation τ' with $\beta=3$.

evaluation function for a permutation τ is defined by Equation 4 where d_x refers to the number of absolute differences with value x between adjacent vertices, and β_τ the bandwidth for the permutation τ.

$$\delta(\tau) = \beta_\tau + \sum_{x=0}^{\beta_\tau}\left(\frac{d_x}{\prod_{y=x}^{\beta_\tau}(n+(\beta_\tau-y)+1)}\right) \qquad (4)$$

To illustrate the computation of this new evaluation function, let us consider the graph in Fig. 1(a). For this particular graph: $d_0 = 2$, $d_1 = 1$, $d_2 = 2$, $d_3 = 2$, $d_4 = 0$; additionally it is easy to observe that $\beta = 3$ and $n = 5$.

Then, by making the substitution of these values in the Formula 4 and simplifying we obtain: $\delta(\tau) = 3 + \frac{2}{3024} + \frac{1}{336} + \frac{2}{42} + \frac{2}{6} = 3.3846$.

In contrast if δ is computed for the permutation τ' showed in Fig. 1(b) a different and smaller value is obtained $\delta(\tau') = 3.3638$.

Next the analysis of the equivalence classes of δ is presented. Two permutations belong to the same equivalence class if they have the same set of counters d_x, for instance the set of counters for the permutation in Fig. 2(a) is: $\{d_0 = 2, d_1 = 1, d_2 = 2\}$ and for the permutation in Fig. 2(b) is: $\{d_0 = 2, d_1 = 1, d_2 = 2\}$. In this sense both permutations, in Fig. 2, belong to the same equivalence class. Now, given that d_x takes values between 0 and $n - x$, the cardinality of possible values for d_x is $(n - x + 1)$, and the total number of equivalence classes is described by the equation:

$$\prod_{x=0}^{n-1}(n-x+1) = (n+1)!$$

The number of graphs that belong to the same equivalence class is:

$$\binom{1}{d_{n-1}}\binom{2}{d_{n-2}}\cdots\binom{n-1}{d_1}\binom{n}{d_0} = \prod_{x=1}^{n}\binom{x}{d_{n-x}} \qquad (5)$$

To demonstrate that the summation of the cardinalities of all equivalency classes equals the number of possible graphs, it is necessary to use the Formula 5 instantiated with all possible values for the d_{n-x} counters and compute the sum. This can be expressed as:

Fig. 2. Two permutations of a graph which belong to the same equivalence class.

$$\prod_{x=1}^{n}\left(\sum_{d_{n-x}}^{x}\binom{x}{d_{n-x}}\right) = \prod_{x=1}^{n} 2^x = 2^{\sum_{x=1}^{n} x} = 2^{\frac{n(n+1)}{2}} \quad (6)$$

Then given that the Equation 6 gives the same value as the total number of graphs, we conclude that all the $(n+1)!$ equivalence classes capture all the possible graphs.

4 Comparing β and δ

In this section the differences between the evaluation functions β and δ are contrasted. First we compare the total number of equivalence classes (ω_β and ω_δ) for each evaluation function and then the average values of the cardinalities for these equivalence classes. This is presented in the Table 1 for some graphs with different number of vertices n. The second and third columns show the number of equivalence classes for β and δ respectively, while the fourth and fifth columns show the average of their cardinalities.

It is important to emphasize that ω_β has a linear increment while ω_δ has an exponential one. Thanks to the data presented in Table 1 it is possible to conclude that δ is finer than β since it has the ability to create more equivalence classes with a lower cardinality. This is an important characteristic which allows to capture even the smallest improvement that orients the searching process of solutions and permits to find configurations where all the absolute differences between labels of adjacent vertices are minimized; and not only the maximum one as it happens with β.

Table 1. Comparison between the total number of equivalence classes and the average of their cardinalities.

n	ω_β	ω_δ	$2^{\frac{n(n+1)}{2}}/\omega_\beta$	$2^{\frac{n(n+1)}{2}}/\omega_\delta$
5	5	$7.20E+2$	$6.55E+3$	$4.55E+1$
10	10	$3.99E+7$	$3.60E+15$	$9.03E+8$
70	70	$8.50E+101$	$1.64E+746$	$1.35E+646$
150	150	$8.63E+264$	$9.73E+3406$	$1.70E+3144$
300	300	$9.21E+616$	$1.06E+13589$	$3.47E+12974$

5 A Simulated Annealing Approach to Solve the BMPG

To evaluate the practical usefulness of the δ evaluation function, a Simulated Annealing (SA) algorithm was developed. Next some details of the implementation proposed are presented:

Internal Representation. Let τ be a potential solution of the problem, that is a permutation of V. Then τ is represented as an array of integers of length n, in which the i-th element denotes the label assigned to the vertex i of the graph. The solution space is obviously the set of all the permutations of order n, where n is the number of vertices in the graph.

Evaluation Function. The choice of the evaluation function is an important aspect of any search procedure. Firstly, in order to efficiently test each potential solution, the evaluation function must be as simple as possible. Secondly, it must be sensitive enough to locate promising search regions on the space of solutions. Finally, the evaluation function must be consistent: a solution that is better than others must return a better value. All these characteristics are present in the new δ evaluation function whose formal definition is presented in Formula 4.

Neighborhood Function. The neighborhood of a solution $N(\tau)$ in our implementation contains all the permutations τ' obtained by swapping two adjacent vertices of the current permutation τ.

Initial Solution. The initial solution is the starting configuration used for the algorithm to begin searching better configurations using the neighborhood function. In this implementation the initial permutation is generated randomly.

Cooling Schedule. In a SA algorithm the way in which the temperature is decreased is known as the cooling schedule, in our implementation the proportional cooling schedule is used ($T_n = T_{n-1} * 0.92$). The initial temperature was fixed at $1.0E$-03 and the final temperature (T_f) at $1.0E$-09.

Termination Condition. The algorithm stops either if the current temperature reaches T_f, or the number of accepted configurations at each temperature falls below the limit of 25. The maximum number of accepted configurations at each temperature ($maxConfigurations$), depends directly on the number of edges ($|E|$) of the graph, because more moves are required for denser graphs ($maxConfigurations = 15 * |E|$).

All the parameters of the SA algorithm were chosen experimentally, and taking into account some related work reported in [15, 13, 10].

6 Computational Experiments

In this section, we present the experiments accomplished to evaluate the performance of δ over a set of 125 benchmark instances. For these experiments the above SA algorithm is used. The code, programmed in C, was compiled with *gcc* using the optimization flag -$O2$ and ran into a Pentium 4@2.8 GHz. with 1 GB of RAM. Due to the incomplete and non-deterministic nature of the method 20 independent runs were executed for each of the selected benchmark instances. All the results reported here are data averaged over the 20 corresponding runs.

6.1 Benchmark Instances and Comparison Criteria

Two sets of problem instances were used. The first set has 12 structured instances, randomly generated according to the model proposed by [10]. It consists of six different classes of graphs of increasing sizes including: grids, paths, cycles, binary trees, ternary trees and quaternary trees.

The second set of instances is the same test data used by Martí et al. [11] and Piñana et al. [16]. It has 113 problem instances from the Harwell-Boeing Sparse Matrix Collection[2], divided into two subsets. The first is composed of 33 instances with 30 to 199 vertices. The second consists of 80 large instances whose sizes vary from 200 to 1000.

The criteria used for evaluating the performance of δ are the same as those used in the literature: the average bandwidth over each instance set and the average CPU time in seconds.

6.2 Comparison Between β and δ

The purpose of the first experiment is to compare the new δ evaluation function and the classical β evaluation function. To do this, we use δ and β within the SA algorithm presented in Section 5 (call these SA algorithms SA-δ and SA-β) and test them on the first set of 12 random instances. Both SA-δ and SA-β were run 20 times on each instance and the results are presented in Table 2. In this table columns 1 to 3 show the name of the graph, the number of vertices and edges. Columns SA-β and SA-δ represent the average bandwidth for the 20 runs of the SA algorithm that uses the metric β and δ respectively. The sixth and seventh columns show the best bandwidth obtained for each of the SA variants. Finally the last column presents the improvement obtained when the δ metric was used.

The results presented in Table 2 show clearly that the SA that uses δ consistently has much better results for many classes of graphs than the one that uses β. We can observe an average improvement of 42% (see column Improvement). So we could conclude that δ is a better evaluation function than β.

In order to illustrate the behavior of SA-δ and SA-β in Fig. 3 the bandwidth reduction versus the annealing temperature is shown. In this figure it can be seen that the SA-δ reduces the bandwidth almost continuously while the SA-β gets stuck longer time, and the final bandwidth reached by SA-δ is significantly lower than the bandwidth reached by SA-β.

6.3 Comparison Between SA-δ and the Best Known Results

In this experiment a performance comparison of our SA-δ procedure with the following heuristics was carried out: GPS [9], Dueck and Jeffs' Simulated Annealing

---

[2] http://math.nist.gov/MatrixMarket/data/Harwell-Boeing

Table 2. Results obtained with two SA for the BMPG using δ and β.

Graph	n	Edges	SA-β	SA-δ	Best SA-β	Best SA-δ	Improvement
Path100	100	99	10.0	1.2	10	1	90%
Path150	150	149	15.6	1.4	15	1	93%
Cycle100	100	99	10.6	2.2	10	2	80%
Cycle150	150	149	15.8	2.6	15	2	87%
TreeB63	63	62	8.0	7.0	8	7	13%
TreeB127	127	126	15.6	11.0	15	11	27%
TreeT40	40	39	7.0	7.0	7	7	0%
TreeT121	121	120	17.8	15.0	17	15	12%
TreeQ85	85	84	15.0	14.0	15	14	7%
TreeQ205	205	204	30.6	26.0	30	26	13%
Grid100	100	180	15.8	10.0	15	10	33%
Grid225	225	420	31.2	15.0	30	15	50%
Average					15.6	9.3	42%

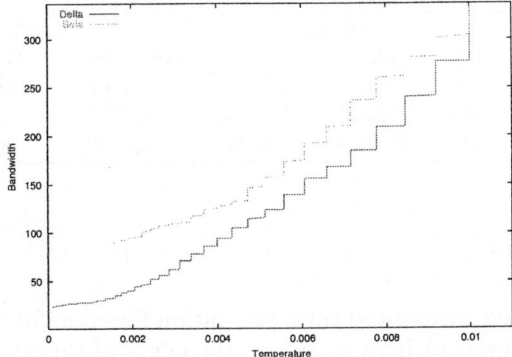

Fig. 3. SA-β and SA-δ behavior comparison on the instance dwt_361.mtx.rnd from the Harwell-Boeing Sparse Matrix Collection.

(SA-DJ) [10], Tabu Search (TS) [11], GRASP with Path Relinking (GRASP-PR) [16] and Genetic Algorithm with Hill Climbing (GA-HC) [12].

Table 3 shows for each algorithm the average bandwidth over each instance set along with the average CPU time in seconds and the average deviation from the best solutions found by applying all the heuristics to the same instance. It is important to remark that the CPU times for the algorithms GPS, TS, GRASP-PR and GA-HC are taken from [12] where a Pentium 4@1.6 GHz. was used for the experiments. Note that SA-DJ has a cooling schedule that is very slow. Our SA-δ uses a set of parameters, presented in Section 5, that speeds up the cooling and allows to reach better configurations.

We can observe from Table 3 that the performance of the classic GPS algorithm, though very fast, gives inferior results in comparison with the other heuristics. In particular, it has an average deviation several orders of magnitude larger than those obtained with SA-δ. For the subset of small instances the average deviation from the best known values for SA-δ is 0.45%, while GRASP-PR (the second best heuristic) obtains a 2.47%. For the large instances it is important to note the remarkable improvement in the average bandwidth obtained with our algorithm (*i.e.*, 94.80 for SA-δ versus 97.05 for GA-HC). In summary, the best solution quality, for the both experiments, is obtained by SA-δ. It was able to match 101 out of the 113 best known solutions, which outperforms the GA-HC (the best heuristic here) that was only able to find 48 of the best solutions.

Table 3. Performance comparison according to problem size.

	33 instances with $n = 30, ..., 199$					
	GPS	SA-DJ	TS	GRASP-PR	GA-HC	SA-δ
Average β	31.42	29.36	23.33	22.52	22.67	22.03
Deviation	35.49%	56.50%	9.63%	2.47%	5.66%	0.45%
CPU sec.	0.003	1434.97	2.36	4.21	2.54	11.18
	80 instances with $n = 200, ..., 1000$					
	GPS	SA-DJ	TS	GRASP-PR	GA-HC	SA-δ
Average β	156.38	164.59	100.78	99.43	97.05	94.80
Deviation	46.96%	222.32%	11.77%	6.59%	6.22%	1.14%
CPU sec.	0.11	1800.00	121.66	323.19	85.22	199.25

7 Conclusions

In this paper, we have introduced the δ evaluation function for the BMPG. It has two important features: a) It considers all the edges of the graph and b) It produces more equivalence classes with lower cardinality. δ orients better the search process with a smoother landscape and permits to find configurations where all the absolute differences between labels of adjacent vertices are minimized.

To validate the practical usefulness of δ, two versions of a basic SA (SA-δ and SA-β) was implemented. They were compared using a set of randomly generated structured graphs and the results showed that for many classes of graphs an average improvement of 42% can be achieved when δ is used.

On the other hand, the goodness of the SA-δ algorithm was also validated using a set of benchmarks from the Harwell-Boeing Sparse Matrix Collection. Our approach was able to match 101 out of the 113 best known solutions, and outperforms thus other state-of-the-art heuristics.

Finally, let us notice that the δ evaluation function proposed in this paper can be used by other metaheuristic algorithms (Genetic Algorithms, Tabu Search, Scatter Search) to boost their performance.

More generally, we think that the research of new evaluation functions for combinatorial problems is a very important topic, because it permits to improve the search power of metaheuristics.

Acknowledgments

The authors would like to thank Rafael Martí who have kindly provided us with his test data and detailed results.

References

1. Livesley, R.: The analysis of large structural systems. Computer Journal **3** (1960) 34–39
2. Chinn, P., Chvatalova, J., Dewdney, A., Gibbs, N.: The bandwidth problem for graphs and matrices - a survey. Journal of Graph Theory **6** (1982) 223–254
3. Harper, L.: Optimal assignment of numbers to vertices. Journal of SIAM **12** (1964) 131–135
4. Harary, F.: Theory of Graphs and its Aplications. Czechoslovak Academy of Science, Prague (1967) M. Fiedler.
5. Papadimitriou, C.: The NP-Completeness of the bandwidth minimization problem. Journal on Computing **16** (1976) 263–270
6. Garey, M., Graham, R., Johnson, D., Knuth, D.: Complexity results for bandwidth minimization. SIAM Journal of Applied Mathematics **34** (1978) 477–495
7. Corso, G.D., Manzini, G.: Finding exact solutions to the bandwidth minimization problem. Computing **62** (1999) 189–203
8. Cutchill, E., McKee, J.: Reducing the bandwidth of sparse symmetric matrices. In: Proceedings of the ACM National Conference, New York (1969) 157–172
9. Gibbs, N., Poole, W., Stockmeyer, P.: An algorithm for reducing the bandwidth and profile of a sparse matrix. SIAM Journal on Numerical Analysis **13** (1976) 235–251
10. Dueck, G., Jeffs, J.: A heuristic bandwidth reduction algorithm. Journal of Combinatorial Mathematics and Computers **18** (1995) 97–108
11. Martí, R., Laguna, M., Glover, F., Campos, V.: Reducing the bandwidth of a sparse matrix with tabu search. European Journal of Operational Research **135** (2001) 211–220
12. Lim, A., Rodrigues, B., Xiao, F.: Integrated genetic algorithm with hill climbing for bandwidth minimization problem. Lecture Notes in Computer Science **2724** (2003) 1594–1595
13. Torres-Jimenez, J., Rodriguez-Tello, E.: A new measure for the bandwidth minimization problem. Lecture Notes in Computer Science **1952** (2000) 477–486
14. Esposito, A., Catallano, M.F., Malucelli, F., Tarricone, L.: A new matrix bandwidth reduction algorithm. Operations Research Letters **23** (1999) 99–107
15. Kirkpatrick, S., Gelatt, C., Vecchi, M.: Optimization by simulated annealing. Science **220** (1983) 671–680
16. Piñana, E., Plana, I., Campos, V., Martí, R.: GRASP and path relinking for the matrix bandwidth minimization. European Journal of Operational Research **153** (2004) 200–210

Coupling of Evolution and Learning to Optimize a Hierarchical Object Recognition Model

Georg Schneider, Heiko Wersing, Bernhard Sendhoff, and Edgar Körner

Honda Research Institute Europe GmbH
Carl-Legien-Strasse 30, D-63073 Offenbach/Main, Germany
{Georg.Schneider,Heiko.Wersing}@honda-ri.de

Abstract. A key problem in designing artificial neural networks for visual object recognition tasks is the proper choice of the network architecture. Evolutionary optimization methods can help to solve this problem. In this work we compare different evolutionary optimization approaches for a biologically inspired neural vision system: Direct coding versus a biologically more plausible indirect coding using unsupervised local learning. A comparison to state-of-the-art recognition approaches shows the competitiveness of our approach.

1 Introduction

Evolutionary algorithms provide a general method for system design optimization and their successful combination with neural networks has been shown in various applications [1]. In the work presented here we optimize neural structures applied to object recognition problems. A critical problem in the application of neural vision systems is the introduction of invariance properties, such as translation, scaling and rotation of the input stimuli. We propose to use hierarchical architectural principles, which are inspired by the human vision system. There is strong biological evidence that hierarchical processing is an important principle in the visual cortex [2]. Barlow [3] proposed that these hierarchical neural representations are structured according to the principle of redundancy reduction. Along this line, unsupervised local learning rules were used to obtain visual features similar to the ones found in early visual brain areas [4].

In order to apply evolutionary algorithms to the design of neural systems their structure and parameters must be represented or encoded. Most approaches [1] use *direct* or *explicit coding*, e.g., via a *connection matrix*, where each entry represents a connection between two neurons. Biologically this scheme is implausible as the amount of information needed to be stored in the genome is far too large. This makes *indirect coding* approaches, where not every neuron with every connection is explicitly encoded in the genome, attractive. By using for example a predefined building process which controls the development of the phenotype, the only information which have to be encoded in the genome are process control parameters [5]. The next step is not only to use a set of fixed rules for the development, but an active learning process for the indirect coding. Interesting approaches which focus on this combination of evolution and learning can be found [6,7]. This scheme of an indirect coding using local learning rules for the building process of a complex neural system is biologically far more realistic [8, 9]. Few researchers use a form of indirect coding in their evolutionary optimizations of neural networks. Kitano [5] suggests a graph generation grammar to indirectly code neural networks and shows that the indirectly coded networks exhibit a magnitude of speed-up in convergence of the evolutionary optimization. Sendhoff and Kreutz [7] have included a developmental phase – a growth process – in the analysis of the dynamic interaction between genetic information and information learned during development. A strongly neurobiologically inspired approach to the combination of evolution and learning for the design of neural networks has been suggested by Rolls and Stringer [6]. Their optimized networks are restricted to three canonic architectures: pattern association memory, auto-association network and competitive neural network. In summary, most contributions which focus on indirectly coded evolutionary optimization schemes did not approach complex tasks, like 3D object recognition.

In our work presented here we combine biologically inspired hierarchical networks with evolution strategies in a novel way to obtain powerful recognition architectures for general 3D object recognition. Our focus is a comparison of direct versus indirect coding of the features in the visual hierarchy with regard to the generalization capabilities of the network. In the case of the indirect coding, we use a coupling of evolution and different local learning processes. The target value of the optimization is the classification performance of the vision network in an 3D object recognition task. Our vision model architecture is introduced in Section 2. The details of the evolutionary optimization are described in Section 3. We state and discuss the results, including a comparison to other state-of-the-art algorithms, in Section 4. In the last section, we conclude our work.

2 The Neural Vision System for Object Recognition

In the following, we define the hierarchical model architecture that we will use for the evolutionary optimization. The model is based on a feedforward architecture with weight-sharing and a succession of feature-sensitive matching and pooling stages (see also [10] for a discussion on the general properties and biological relevance of this architecture). The model comprises three stages arranged in a processing hierarchy (see Figure 1). The input image is presented as a 64×64 pixel image. The S1 layer

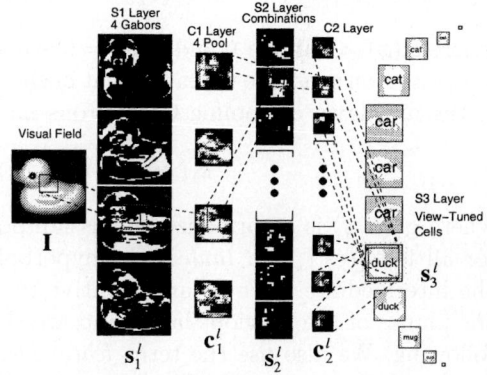

Fig. 1. Sketch of hierarchical network.

consists of 4 Gabor feature planes at 4 orientations with a dimension of 64×64 each. The C1 layer subsamples by pooling down to a resolution of 16×16 for each of the 4 S1 planes. The S2 layer contains combination coding cells with possible local connections to all of the C1 cells. The C2 layer pools the S2 planes down to a resolution of 8 × 8. The final S3 cells are tuned to particular views, which are represented as the activity pattern of the C2 planes for an input image.

The first processing stage consists of a convolution with 4 differently oriented first-order Gabor filters, a Winner-Take-Most (WTM) mechanism between these features and a final threshold function. We adopt the notation, that vector indices run over the set of neurons within a particular feature plane of a particular layer. To compute the response $s_1^l(x,y)$ of a neuron in the first layer S1, responsive to feature type l at position (x, y), first the image vector $\mathbf{I}$ is multiplied with a weight vector $\mathbf{w}_1^l(x,y)$ characterizing the receptive field profile:

$$q_1^l(x,y) = |\mathbf{w}_1^l(x,y) * \mathbf{I}|, \tag{1}$$

where the inner product is denoted by $*$, i.e. for a 10×10 pixel image, $\mathbf{I}$ and $\mathbf{w}_1^l(x,y)$ are 100-dimensional vectors. All neurons in a feature plane l have the same receptive field structure, given by $\mathbf{w}_1^l(x,y)$, but shifted receptive field centers, as in a classical weight-sharing architecture [11]. In a second step, a Winner-Take-Most mechanism is performed with

$$r_1^l(x,y) = \begin{cases} 0 & \text{if } \frac{q_1^l(x,y)}{M} < \gamma_1 \text{ or } M = 0, \\ \frac{q_1^l(x,y) - M\gamma_1}{1-\gamma_1} & \text{otherwise,} \end{cases} \tag{2}$$

where $M = \max_k q_1^k(x,y)$ and $r_1^l(x,y)$ is the response after the WTM mechanism which suppresses sub-maximal responses and provides a model of latency-based competition [10]. The parameter $0 < \gamma_1 < 1$ controls the strength of the competition. The activity is then passed through a simple threshold function with a common threshold θ_1 for all neurons in layer S1:

$$s_1^l(x,y) = \mathrm{H}(r_1^l(x,y) - \theta_1), \tag{3}$$

where $\mathrm{H}(x) = 1$ if $x \geq 0$ and $\mathrm{H}(x) = 0$ otherwise and $s_1^l(x,y)$ is the final activity of the neuron sensitive to feature l at position (x,y) in the S1 layer. The activities of the first layer of pooling C1-neurons are given by

$$c_1^l(x,y) = \tanh\left(\mathbf{g}_1(x,y) * \mathbf{s}_1^l\right), \tag{4}$$

where $\mathbf{g}_1(x,y)$ is a normalized Gaussian pooling kernel with width σ_1, identical for all features l, and *tanh* is the hyperbolic tangent function. The features in the intermediate layer S2 are sensitive to local combinations of the features in the planes of the previous layer, and are thus called *combination neurons* in the following. We also use the term *feature bank* to denote the set of features of a particular layer. We introduce the layer activation vector $\bar{\mathbf{c}}_1 = (\mathbf{c}_1^1, \ldots, \mathbf{c}_1^K)$ and the layer weight vector $\bar{\mathbf{w}}_2^l = (\mathbf{w}_2^{l1}, \ldots, \mathbf{w}_2^{lK})$ with K=4. Here $\mathbf{w}_2^{lk}(x,y)$ is the receptive field vector of the S2 neuron of feature l at position (x,y), describing connections to the plane k of the previous $C1$ neurons. The combined linear summation over previous planes is then given by $q_2^l(x,y) = \bar{\mathbf{w}}_2^l(x,y) * \bar{\mathbf{c}}_1$. The weights of these combination neurons are a main target of our evolutionary optimization. After the same WTM procedure with strength γ_2 as in (2), the activity in the S2 layer is given by $s_2^l(x,y) = H(r_2^l(x,y) - \theta_2)$ after thresholding with a common threshold θ_2. The step from S2 to C2 is identical to (4) and given by $c_2^l(x,y) = \tanh(\mathbf{g}_2(x,y) * \mathbf{s}_2^l)$, with Gaussian spatial pooling kernel $\mathbf{g}_2(x,y)$ with range σ_2. The nonlinearity parameters $\gamma_1, \theta_1, \sigma_1, \gamma_2, \theta_2, \sigma_2$ will be subject to evolutionary optimization.

Classification of an input image with C2 output $\bar{\mathbf{c}}_2$ is done by nearest neighbor match to previously stored template activations $\bar{\mathbf{c}}_2^v$ for each training view v. This can be realized e.g. by view-tuned units (VTU) in an additional S3 layer with a radial basis function characteristics according to $s_3^v = \exp(-||\bar{\mathbf{w}}_3^v - \mathbf{c}_2||^2)$ where $\bar{\mathbf{w}}_3^v = \mathbf{c}_2^v$ is tuned to the training C2 output of pattern v. Classification can then be performed by detecting the maximally activated VTU.

3 Evolutionary Optimization of the Neural Vision System

3.1 Evolution Strategies

We employ a standard evolution strategy (ES) [12] with a semi-global step-size-adaptation with two different step-sizes to optimize the vision system. This turned out to be sufficient: one step-size for the 6 nonlinearity parameters and one for the combination feature weights, described in more detail in the following sections. In the case of the indirect coding, we need just one step-size since the combination features are optimized by the local learning process. We used discrete recombination for the 6 nonlinearity parameters. The strategy parameters were recombined by a generalized intermediate recombination. In our studies, we used the "ES-typical" deterministic (μ, λ) selection.

3.2 First and Second Order Generalization

For the evaluation of the optimized vision systems we introduce the concept of first and second order generalization (Note that the more common terms test and validation error are not suitable, since we are working on different databases and not on two subsets of one database.), which is displayed in Figure 2. The flow of the evolutionary optimization of the hierarchical neural vision system is the following: We code the vision system into the chromosome (directly for the first two and indirectly for the next three settings). Then we apply evolutionary operators like mutation and recombination to the population. Thereafter, we construct the offsprings – different vision systems –

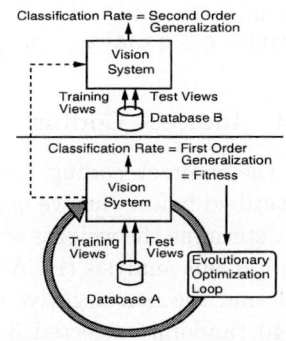

Fig. 2. Concept of first and second order generalization.

and train these using a few views from objects of an image database A. Then we test the systems with the classification of test object views from database A, not contained in the training set. We use the classification rate as the fitness for the following selection of the parents, which constitute the next generation. After a sufficient number of generations we get vision systems which are well structured and successfully classify objects of database A. We call this performance *first order generalization*. With *second order generalization* we denote the ability of the system optimized on database A, to successfully classify objects from a database B, without any changes to features or nonlinearities.

3.3 Direct Coding

In the representation of the vision system we differentiate between system nonlinearities and the combination features. The system nonlinearities are 6 parameters which efficiently characterize the quality of the nonlinear processing steps of the system. These are: 1. the WTM selectivities $\gamma_1, \gamma_2 \in [0,1]$, which control the competition between the different features at the same image location within the same layer, 2. the threshold parameters $\theta_1, \theta_2 \in [0,3]$, which control the number of neurons firing, and 3. the pooling ranges $\sigma_1, \sigma_2 \in [0.0001, 7]$, which control the sizes of the Gaussian pooling kernels used in layer C1 and C2. The parameters $\gamma_1, \gamma_2, \theta_1, \theta_2, \sigma_1, \sigma_2$ are coded as real values into the chromosome. Additionally, to the system nonlinearities the weights $\bar{\mathbf{w}}_2^l = (\mathbf{w}_2^{l1}, \ldots, \mathbf{w}_2^{l4})$, which define the combination feature bank, are directly coded into the chromosome, $l = 1, \ldots, L$, where L is the number of S2 feature planes. For comparison with the different indirect codings we explored two different domains for the weights: a non-negative one with $w_{2i}^{lk} \in [0,1]$ and one with $w_{2i}^{lk} \in [-1,1]$. The coding of the combination feature bank is organized as follows: We define the size of one feature of the combination feature bank $\bar{\mathbf{w}}_2^l \in \mathbb{R}^{36=4 \times 3 \times 3}$. Each of the 4 planes of layer C1 corresponding to four different local orientations in the image is convolved with a 3×3 filter. We define w_{2i}^{lk}, with $k = 1, \ldots, 4$, and $i = 1, \ldots, 36$ as the ith entry of $\mathbf{w}_2^{lk}$. The optimization was carried out with $L = 9, 36, 50$ features. With 50 features $50 \times 36 = 1800$ values have to be optimized. Thus the full optimization (including also the nonlinearities) took place in a 1806-dimensional $(1800 + 6 = 1806)$ search space.

3.4 Indirect Coding

In the indirect coding approach, we still code the nonlinearities directly like described before but we use three different unsupervised local learning processes to determine the weights of the combination feature bank. These are the principal component analysis (PCA), the fast independent component analysis (fastICA) [13] and the non-negative sparse coding scheme (nnSC) [14]. The processes use 1440 randomly selected 3×3 pixel patches of the C1 layer (which contains 4 planes) to learn a filter bank. These patches therefore consist of 36 entries each $(3 \times 3 \times 4 = 36)$. The combination feature bank then consists of the L principal component vectors of the C1 patches for the PCA and of the L independent component vectors in the case of the fastICA. In the case of the nnSC the bank is the basis for a sparse coding of the patches. In contrary to PCA and fastICA it can be an overcomplete set and $L > 36$ is therefore possible. This learning process is also controlled by a sparsity factor which determines the trade-off between sparsity and reconstruction ability of the patch inputs. We code this parameter in addition to the 6 nonlinearities into the chromosome and therefore perform the optimization in a just 7-dimensional search space. The space for the PCA and ICA optimization is 6-dimensional, as we have here no additional parameters which are needed. In the following, we briefly summarize the procedure of our indirect coding scheme from the genotype to the phenotype to the fitness evaluation: For each genotype in the population do:

1. Construction of the phenotype up to the C1 layer.
2. Generation of C1 layer activations using the database A.
3. Collecting 3×3-patches of the activated C1 layer.
4. Use of unsupervised local learning for the generation of the combination feature bank using the patches (and the sparsity parameter, which is explicitly coded in the genotype, for the case of the nnSC).
5. Construction of the complete phenotype – the vision system – with all nonlinearities and the combination feature bank.
6. Training of the vision system with training views of database A (storing C2 activations as a VTU for each training view).
7. Calculation of the classification rate using test views of database A in a nearest-neighbor classification based on C2 feature output. The result is the fitness of the individual.

4 Results and Discussion

For the evolutionary optimization of the combination features and nonlinearity parameters we used the object database COIL20 [15]. This database contains 20 different objects with 72 images of varying angles of rotation in depth, reaching from 0 to 360 degrees in 5 degree steps. After the vision system is generated according to the parameters in the chromosome, it is trained with 3 views (0, 120 and 240 degrees) of each object, by simply storing the highest order C2 feature activation vectors of each training view (see Section 2). In the test phase, the vision system has to classify 24 remaining views, which are equally distributed between 0 and 360 degrees. These test views are matched in a nearest-neighbor fashion to the stored training vectors. We note that other classifiers like linear discriminators could also be applied, see [10], but the nearest-neighbor approach has the advantage of not requiring an additional weight adaptation on the view-tuned units. The target of the optimization is the determination of the nonlinearities and the combination features in a way that the system will have a minimal classification error after training, i.e., that the first order generalization of the hierarchical vision system is maximal. A further test for the system is the second order generalization. For this test, we use a subset of the COIL100

[15][1] database which contains 100 objects, also with 72 images of continually varying rotation angle. We have to note that 17 objects of the COIL20 are also objects of the COIL100 database. We excluded these objects to ensure a proper measure of the second-order generalization. We call this reduced database of 83 objects *COILselect*. In the following tests, we optimized each setting 10 times for 400 generations using a (7,19)-ES, which we identified to be a good setting in preliminary studies, considering the trade-off between evaluation time and performance. We ran 3 different settings with the number of features contained in the combination feature bank set to $L = 9, 36, 50$.[2]

The results are displayed in Table 1. Note that we focus in the following discussion of the results on the average, and not on the best results achieved with a setting. When we compare the performances with respect to the first order generalization (the errors on the COIL20), we find that the direct coding outperforms the indirect one significantly (with respect to the Student-t test). This can be explained by the fact that the number of degrees of freedom is in the direct case much higher than in the indirect case and therefore the vision system could be adapted to perform particularly well on database A. Among the direct codings the one which allows also negative values for the combination features (denoted with "neg. CF") performs better than the one with non negative values (denoted with "non neg. CF") for the same reason. The possibilities of the vision system with negative values are in that sense higher, that not only the existence of features could be combined, but also the absence of features. The neg. CF setting again performs best with $L = 36$ features. Only 9 features seem to be too few to represent the objects properly. With 50 features the performance degrades compared to 36 because of the larger search space dimension.

Table 1. Results of directly and indirectly coded evolutionary optimization. L=number of features, b=best result, m=mean, and s=standard deviation of 10 runs.

direct coding		error COIL20			error COILsel.		
	L	b	m	s	b	m	s
non- neg. CF	9	7.9	8.6	0.5	24.2	27.6	3.0
	36	7.7	8.3	0.5	23.2	26.5	2.2
	50	7.3	8.6	0.8	23.2	24.8	1.5
neg. CF	9	**6.5**	8.1	1.2	22.8	26.3	2.4
	36	7.1	**7.8**	0.5	22.9	24.2	1.8
	50	7.1	8.1	0.7	22.4	24.3	1.7

indirect coding		error COIL20			error COILsel.		
	L	b	m	s	b	m	s
PCA	9	9.4	10.6	1.1	23.4	25.1	1.2
	36	8.1	9.6	1.1	23.6	25.8	3.1
fast ICA	9	8.5	9.4	0.7	24.4	26.7	1.8
	36	8.8	9.7	1.0	22.5	24.7	2.8
nnSC	9	9.0	10.0	0.6	24.1	26.5	1.6
	36	8.5	9.7	1.3	22.4	**24.1**	1.4
	50	8.8	9.5	0.6	**21.7**	24.2	1.4

---

[1] We converted the color images of the COIL100 database to grey value images and scaled them down to 64x64 pixels.
[2] Except for the indirect coding with PCA and fastICA where L must be less or equal to the data vector dimension.

We now focus on the errors on the COILselect database which give us a measure of how good the vision system performs on an arbitray database – the second order generalization. We find that now both main settings (direct and indirect coding) perform almost equally well. The advantage of the indirect coding is not significant. From this result, we can draw the conclusion, that the unsupervised learning processes have enough freedom and are capable of building up a high performing vision system with regard to second order generalization. Among the indirect coding settings the nnSC performs best, although only positive values for the combination features are allowed in this method. Equally to the first order generalization also here 36 features seem to be adequate as a trade off between adaptability and increasing the search space too much.

In order to understand more about the properties of the optimization problem, it is interesting to find out whether similar sets of combination features have been found during different optimization runs. For a comparison of two sets of combination features we have to define a distance measure D_{CF} which is invariant under permutation of single features (as these permutations have no effect on the fitness). D_{CF} is defined as follows: Starting with the first feature of one of the two CF-sets we search for the closest (in Euclidean metric) feature in the second CF-set. We measure the distance d_1 between these two features and exclude both of them from the sets. Then we repeat this procedure with the next feature of the first set and so forth. To have a symmetric measure, we repeat the process with the two sets interchanged. The resulting distance measure D_{CF} is equal to the sum of all calculated distances divided by two: $D_{CF} = \frac{1}{2}\sum_{i=1}^{2L} d_i$, where L denotes the number of combination features in each set. Using the described distance measure we observed, that there exist a large number of significantly different CF-sets that have similar performance.

In the following we shortly discuss the case: direct coding; $L = 9$; negative CFs. In order to be able to interpret the absolute distance values, we take the best vision system and add Gaussian noise to its CFs. We do this ten times and for three different noise levels. After that, we measure D_{CF} and the misclassification rates of the changed system. For Gaussian noise with a standard deviation of $\sigma_{noise} = 0.025$ the mean distance measure is $\bar{D}_{CF} = 1.4$ and the misclassification rate increased on average from 6.5% to 7.7% (i.e. $\Delta \bar{f} = 1.2$). For $\sigma_{noise} = 0.05(0.1)$, we get $\bar{D}_{CF} = 2.6(5.2)$ and $\Delta \bar{f} = 1.6(3.2)$. Then we calculate $\bar{D}_{CF} = 40.1$ for all pairs of two of the best CF-sets out of the 10 optimization runs. Next, we derive $\bar{D}_{CF}$ for 10 randomly generated CF-sets and get $\bar{D}_{CF} = 40.5$. Comparing the similarities of optimized and random features, we conclude, that the optimized CFs have almost no similarity to each other and seem to be widely spread over the whole parameter space.

To assess the performance of the best result of the indirectly coded evolutionary optimization, we have performed a comparison to a previous, manually tuned version of the vision system (mtVS) [14], and to other state-of-the-art systems. Here we use the results of Roobaert & van Hulle [16], who performed an extensive study on the COIL100 database, comparing support vector machines (SVM), and the eigenspace-based system of Nayar et al. [15] (denoted

Columbia in the table). The results are shown in Table 2, where the number of objects and the number of training views is varied (for less than 100 objects the first n objects are taken). We see, that the evolutionary optimization could effectively improve the performance of the manually tuned vision system (mtVS). Compared to other classifiers the optimized vision system (optVS) is highly competitive and shows superior performance especially in the most difficult cases of the task, where only few training views are available and a high number of objects have to be classified. The results of the nearest-neighbor classifier based on the plain image data (NNC) illustrate the baseline similarity of the images in the database.

Table 2. Comparison of misclassification rates on COIL100 database.

Method	30 Objects Training Views			4 Training Views Number of Objects		
	36	8	2	10	30	100
NNC	0	7.5	29.5	13.5	18.2	29.9
Columbia	0	4.4	32.9	7.9	15.4	23.0
SVM	0	4.8	29.0	9.0	15.1	25.4
mtVS	0	7.3	28.3	18.4	15.8	23.9
optVS	0	4.4	22.9	12.4	12.9	20.2

5 Conclusion

The work presented here is the first study of the evolutionary optimization of a biologically inspired vision network, which is capable of performing a complex 3D real world object classification task. We compared the optimization using a direct and an indirect coding of the combination feature bank. We showed that the used biologically inspired hierarchical architecture has a very robust behavior, where a lot of different combination feature banks are equally well suited for classification. Therefore, the directly coded evolutionary optimization found good results with a good convergence behavior despite the huge dimensionality of the search space for the direct coding with $L = 50$ features (1806-dimensional). Considering second order generalization, the results are even better than the ones for only 9 features (330-dimensional). For the more difficult COILselect database, 36 or even 50 filters for the combination feature bank seem more adequate [14] and the drawback of a harder optimization is compensated by the enhanced representational capability of the network.

We found, that the coupling of evolutionary search with unsupervised local learning processes yields good results. Hereby we can realize a biologically more sensible encoding and work in a 6 respectively 7 dimensional search space (compared to over 1800 before). Comparing direct and indirect coding, we find that the direct evolutionary optimization yields significantly better results in the first order generalization. This performance advantage stems from specialization to the database used during evolution as the performance gain cannot be observed for the second order generalization. Here we see even a slight advantage for the indirect coding, which, however, does not have high statistical significance. We also showed that the optimized architecture is highly competitive with other current high-performing recognition methods like support vector machines.

Acknowledgment

This work was supported by the BMBF under grant LOKI 01IB001E.

References

1. X. Yao, "Evolving artificial neural networks," *Proc. IEEE*, vol. 87, no. 9, pp. 1423–1447, 1999.
2. M. Riesenhuber and T. Poggio, "Hierarchical models of object recognition in cortex," *Nature Neuroscience*, vol. 2, no. 11, pp. 1019–1025, 1999.
3. H. B. Barlow, "The twelfth Bartlett memorial lecture: The role of single neurons in the psychology of perception," *Quart. J. Exp. Psychol.*, vol. 37, pp. 121–145, 1985.
4. B. A. Olshausen and D. J. Field, "Sparse coding with an overcomplete basis set: A strategy employed by V1 ?" *Vision Research*, vol. 37, pp. 3311–3325, 1997.
5. H. Kitano, "Designing neural networks using genetic algorithms with graph generation system," *Complex Systems*, vol. 4, pp. 461–476, 1990.
6. E. T. Rolls and S. M. Stringer, "On the design of neural networks in the brain by genetic evolution," *Progress in Neurobiology*, vol. 6, no. 61, pp. 557–579, 2000.
7. B. Sendhoff and M. Kreutz, "A model for the dynamic interaction between evolution and learning," *Neural Processing Letters*, vol. 10, no. 3, pp. 181–193, 1999.
8. S. Quartz and T. Sejnowski, "The neural basis of cognitive development: A constructivist manifesto," *Behavioral and Brain Sciences*, vol. 9, pp. 537–596, 1997.
9. A. G. Rust, R. Adams, S. George, and H. Bolouri, "Towards computational neural systems through developmental evolution," in *LNCS*, S. W. et al., Ed., vol. 2036, 2001, pp. 188–202.
10. H. Wersing and E. Körner, "Learning optimized features for hierarchical models of invariant recognition," *Neural Computation*, vol. 15, no. 7, pp. 1559–1588, 2003.
11. K. Fukushima, "Neocognitron: A self-organizing neural network model for a mechanism of pattern recognition unaffected by shift in position," *Biol. Cyb.*, vol. 39, pp. 139–202, 1980.
12. H.-P. Schwefel and G. Rudolph, "Contemporary evolution strategies," in *Proc. of the Third European Conf. on Artificial Life : Advances in Artificial Life*, ser. LNAI, F. M. et al., Ed., vol. 929. Berlin: Springer Verlag, June 1995, pp. 893–907.
13. A. Hyvärinen and E. Oja, "A fast fixed-point algorithm for independent component analysis," *Neural Computation*, vol. 9, no. 7, pp. 1483–1492, 1997.
14. H. Wersing and E. Körner, "Unsupervised learning of combination features for hierarchical recognition models," in *Int. Conf. Artif. Neur. Netw. ICANN*, J. R. D. et al., Ed. Springer, 2002, pp. 1225–1230.
15. S. K. Nayar, S. A. Nene, and H. Murase, "Real-time 100 object recognition system," in *Proc. of ARPA Image Understanding Workshop*, Palm Springs, 1996.
16. D. Roobaert and M. V. Hulle, "View-based 3d object recognition with support vector machines," in *Proc. IEEE Int. Workshop on Neural Networks for Signal Processing, Madison, USA*. New York, USA: IEEE, 1999, pp. 77–84.

Evolution of Small-World Networks of Automata for Computation

Marco Tomassini, Mario Giacobini, and Christian Darabos

Information Systems Department, University of Lausanne, Switzerland
{marco.tomassini,mario.giacobini,christian.darabos}@hec.unil.ch

Abstract. We study an extension of cellular automata to arbitrary interconnection topologies for the majority problem. By using an evolutionary algorithm, we show that small-world network topologies consistently evolve from regular and random structures without being designed beforehand. These topologies have better performance than regular lattice structures and are easier to evolve, which could explain in part their ubiquity.

1 Introduction

In recent years there has been substantial research activity in the science of networks. Networks, which can be formally described by the tools of graph theory, are a central model for the description of many phenomena of scientific, social and technological interest. Typical examples include the Internet, the World Wide Web, social acquaintances, electric power networks, and many others. This activity has mainly been spurred by the pioneering studies of Watts and Strogatz [14,13], which have been followed by many others. Their key observation was that most real networks have mathematical properties that set them apart from regular lattices and from random graphs, which were the two main topologies that had been studied until then. In particular, they introduced the concept of *small-world networks*, in which most pairs of vertices seem to be connected by a short path through the network.

Another type of networks which also differs from both the regular and the random ones, the *scale-free* graphs, are more typical of real-world networks; they are fully described in [1], which is a very readable and complete account of modern network theory.

The topological structure of a network has a marked influence on the processes that may take place on it. Regular and random networks have been thoroughly studied from this point of view in many disciplines. In computer science, for instance, variously connected networks of processors have been used in parallel and distributed computing [7], while lattices and random networks of simple automata have also received a great deal of attention [4,5]. On the other hand, due to their novelty, there are very few studies of the computational properties of small-world networks. One notable exception is Watts' book [13] in which cellular automata (CAs) computation on small-world networks is examined in detail. Another recent study for CAs on small worlds appears in [10]. However, there is no hint in these works as to how such networks could arise in the first place. In other words, the graphs are generated by a prescribed algorithm. In our opinion, how these networks could form is an interesting yet unanswered question. In contrast, for scale-free networks there exist several models that account for their genesis [1], although all of them make some hypothesis as to how new nodes become linked to existing ones. For example, *preferential attachment* posits that the likelihood of connecting to a node depends on the node's degree: high-degree nodes are more likely to attract other nodes.

To attempt to find how networks might come to be selected, we let an artificial evolutionary process find "good" network structures according to a predefined fitness measure, without prescribing the fine details of the wiring. We take as a prototypical problem the *majority classification* problem which is the same that Watts discusses in [13] as a useful first step. This will also allow us to compare the products of artificial evolution with Watts' results.

In the next section some background material on graphs is briefly discussed. Section 3 describes the CA majority problem and previous results. Section 4 presents our evolutionary search for networks and discusses the results. Section 5 gives our conclusions and ideas for future work.

2   Useful Definitions for Graphs

For ease of reference, here we collect a few definitions and some nomenclature for graphs that is used throught this work. The treatment is necessarily brief: a more detailed account can be found for example in [1, 13].

Let V be a nonempty set called the set of *vertices* or *nodes*, and let E be a symmetric binary relation on V, i.e. a set of unordered pairs of vertices. Then $G = (E, V)$ is called a *undirected graph* and E is the set of *edges* or *links* of G. In *directed graphs* edges have a direction, i.e. they go from one vertex to another and the pairs of vertices are ordered pairs. When vertices (u, v) form an edge they are said to be *adjacent* or *neighbors*.

The *degree* k of a vertex in an undirected graph is the number of edges incident on it (or, equivalently, the number of neighbors). The *average degree* $\langle k \rangle$ is the average of all the vertex degrees in G.

A *path* from vertex u to vertex v in a graph G is a sequence of edges that are traversed when going from u to v with no edge traversed more than once. The *length* of a path is the number of edges in it. The *shortest path* between two vertices u and v is the path with the smallest length joining u to v.

A graph is *connected* if there is a path between any two vertices. A *completely connected* undirected graph G with $|V| = N$ vertices has an edge between any two vertices. The total number of edges is $N(N-1)/2$.

A *random graph* is a graph in which pairs of nodes are connected with a given probability p. Consequentely, the total number of edges in a random graph is a random variable whose expectation value is $p[N(N-1)/2]$. Several useful results on random graphs are described in [1].

Four statistics are particularly useful for small-world and random graphs: the average degree described above, the *clustering coefficient*, the *characteristic path length*, and the *degree distribution*. They are briefly described below and in more detail in [1].

Let us take a particular node j in a graph, and let us assume that it has k edges connecting it to k neighboring nodes. If all k vertices in the neighborhood were completely connected then the number of edges would be equal to $k(k-1)/2$. The clustering coefficient C is defined as the ratio between the E edges that actually exist between the k neighbors and the number of possible edges between these nodes:

$$C = \frac{2E}{k(k-1)}$$

The clustering coefficient of a random graph is simply $\langle k \rangle/N$, where N is the total number of vertices. For a regular lattice, C is given by the following formula: $3(k-2)/(4(k-1))$, where k is the (constant) number of nodes that are connected to a given node. C is thus independent of N for a regular lattice, and approaches $3/4$ as k increases.

The characteristic path length L is defined in [13] as the median of the means of the shortest path lengths connecting each vertex $v \in G$ to all other vertices.

The degree distribution $P(k)$ of a graph G is a function that gives the probability that a randomly selected vertex has k edges incident on it. For a random graph $P(k)$ is a binomial peaked at $\langle k \rangle$. But most real networks do not show this kind of behavior. In particular, in scale-free graphs which are frequent in real-life, $P(k)$ follows a power-law distribution.

According to Watts and Strogatz (see [13, 14], where details of the construction are given), a small-world graph can be constructed starting from a regular ring of nodes in which each node has k neighbors ($k \ll N$) by simply systematically going through successive nodes and "rewiring" a link with a certain probability p. When the edge is deleted, it is replaced with an edge to a randomly chosen node. This procedure will create a number of shortcuts that join distant parts of the lattice. These shortcuts are the hallmark of small worlds and, while L scales logarithmically in the number of nodes for a random graph, in small-world graphs it scales approximately linearly for low rewiring probability and tends to the random graph limit as the probability increases. This is due to the progressive appearance of shortcut edges between distant parts of the graph, which obviously contract the path lengths between many vertices. However, small worlds typically have a higher clustering coefficient than random graphs. Small-world networks have a degree distribution $P(k)$ that is close to binomial for intermediate and large values of the rewiring probability p, while $P(k)$ tends to a delta function for $p \to 0$. Following Watts [13], we will show our results as a function of the parameter ϕ, which is the fraction of edges in a graph that are shortcuts. Shortcuts are defined to be edges that join vertices that would be more than two edges apart if they were not connected directly.

3 The Cellular Automata Majority Problem

CAs are dynamical systems in which space and time are discrete. A standard CA consists of an array of cells, each of which can be in one of a finite number of possible states, updated synchronously in discrete time steps, according to a local, identical rule. Here we will only consider boolean automata for which the cellular state $s \in \{0, 1\}$. The state of a cell at the next time step is determined by the current states of a surrounding neighborhood of cells. The regular cellular array (grid) is d-dimensional, where $d = 1, 2, 3$ is used in practice. For one-dimensional grids, a cell is connected to r local neighbors (cells) on either side where r is referred to as the *radius* (thus, each cell has $2r+1$ neighbors, including itself). The term *configuration* refers to an assignment of ones and zeros to all the cells at a given time step. It can be described by $\mathbf{s}^t = (s_0^t, s_1^t, \ldots, s_{N-1}^t)$, where N is the lattice size. Often CAs have periodic boundary conditions $s_{N+i}^t = s_i^t$.

Here we will consider an extension of the concept of CA in which, while the rule is the same on each node, nodes can be connected in any way, that is, the topological structures are general graphs, provided the graph is connected and self and multiple links are disallowed.

The majority (also called density) task is a prototypical distributed computational task for CAs. For a finite CA of size N it is defined as follows. Let ρ_0 be the fraction of 1s in the initial configuration (IC) $\mathbf{s}^0$. The task is to determine whether ρ_0 is greater than or less than $1/2$. If $\rho_0 > 1/2$ then the CA must relax to a fixed-point configuration of all 1s; otherwise it must relax to a fixed-point configuration of all 0s, after a number of time steps of the order of the grid size N (N is odd to avoid the case $\rho_0 = 0.5$). This computation is trivial for a computer having a central control. Indeed, just scanning the array and adding up the number of, say, 1 bits will provide the answer in $O(N)$ time. However, it is nontrivial for a small radius one-dimensional CA since such a CA can only transfer information at finite speed relying on local information exclusively, while density is a global property of the configuration of states [9].

It has been shown that the density task cannot be solved perfectly by a uniform, two-state CA with finite radius [6], although a slightly modified version of the task can be shown to admit perfect solution by such an automaton [2]. The *performance* P of a given rule on the majority task is defined as the fraction of correct classifications over 10^4 randomly chosen ICs. The ICs are sampled according to a binomial distribution (i.e., each bit is independently drawn with probability $1/2$ of being 0). Clearly, this distribution is strongly peaked around $\rho_0 = 1/2$ and thus it makes a difficult case for the CA to solve.

Nevertheless, the lack of a perfect solution does not prevent one from searching for imperfect solutions of as good a quality as possible. In general, given a desired global behavior for a CA (e.g., the density task capability), it is extremely difficult to infer the local CA rule that will give rise to the emergence of a desired computation due to possible nonlinearities and large-scale collective effects that cannot in general be predicted from the sole local CA updating rule. Since exhaustive evaluation of all possible rules is out of the question except for elementary ($d = 1, r = 1$) automata, one possible solution of the problem consists in using evolutionary algorithms (EAs), as first proposed by Mitchell et al. [8, 9] for uniform CAs and by Sipper for nonuniform ones [11].

Watts [13] studied a general graph version of the density task. Since a CA rule table depends on the number of neighbors, given that a small-world graph has vertices with different degrees, he considered the simpler problem of fixing the rule and evaluating the performance of small-world graphs on the task. The chosen rule was a variation of the *majority* rule (not to be confused with the majority problem). The rule simply says that, at each time step, each node will assume the state of the majority of its neighbors in the graph. If the number of neighbors having state 0 is equal to the number of those at 1, then the next state is assigned at random with equal probability. When used in a 1-d CA this rule has performance $P \simeq 0$ since it gives rise to stripes of 0s and 1s that cannot mix at the borders. Watts, however, has shown that the performance can be good on other network structures, where "long" links somewhat compensate for the lack of information transmission of the regular lattice case, in spite of the fact that the node degrees are still low. Indeed, Watts built many networks with performance values $P > 0.8$, while the best evolved lattices with the same average number of neighbors had P around 0.77 [8, 9] and was difficult to evolve.

In a remarkable paper [12], Sipper and Ruppin had already examined the influence of different connectivity patterns on the density task. They studied the co-evolution of network architectures and CA rules at the same time, resulting in non-uniform, high-performance networks, while we are dealing with uniform CAs here. Since those were pre-small-world years, it is difficult to state what kind of graphs were obtained. However, it was correctly recognized that reducing the average cellular distance, i.e. the characteristic path length, has a positive effect on the performance.

4 Artificial Evolution of Small Worlds

We use a cellular EA (cEA) with the aim of evolving small-world networks for the density task as cEAs have proved effective in finding good solutions and maintaining population diversity [3]. The population is arranged on a 20×20 square grid for a total of 400 individuals. Each individual represents a network topology and is coded as an array of integers denoting vertices, each one of which has a list of the vertices it is connected to. As the graph is undirected the information is redundant (e.g. if X is connected to Y, then both have the other in their own connections list). The automaton rule is the generalized majority rule described above for all cases. During the evolution the networks are constrained to have a maximum degree of 50, and a minimum degree of two. The termination condition is reached after computing 100 generations.

The fitness of a network of automata in the population is calculated by randomly choosing 100 out of the 2^N possible initial configurations (ICs) with uniform density – i.e. any configuration has the same probability of being selected – and then iterating the automaton on each IC for $M = 2N$ time steps, where $N = 149$ is the grid size. The network's fitness is the fraction of ICs for which the rule produced the correct fixed point, given the known IC density. At each generation a different set of ICs is generated for each individual. Selection is done locally using a central individual and its north, east, south and west first neighbors in the grid. Binary tournament selection is used with this pool. The winner is then mutated (see below) and evaluated. It replaces the central individual if it has a better fitness.

Mutation is designed to operate on the network topology and works as follows. Each node of an individual is mutated with probability 0.5. If chosen, a vertex (called target vertex) will have an edge either added or removed to a randomly chosen vertex (called destination vertex) with probability 0.5. This will only happen if all the requirements are met (minimum and maximum degree are respected). If the source vertex has already reached its maximum degree and should be added one edge or its minimum degree and should be removed one edge, the mutation will not happen. If the same case happens with the target, another one is randomly chosen. This version of the algorithm does not use recombination operators.

4.1 Evolution from Regular Lattices

In this first series of experiments we started from regular rings, which is the customary way for constructing small-world graphs [13]. In order not to unduly bias the evolution, the initial population was composed by individuals that are regular rings with node degree $k = 4$, i.e. each vertex is connected to its four nearest neighbors in the ring, instead of rings with $k = 6$, which is the case treated by Watts. Moreover, we slightly modify each of them by adding an edge with a probability of 0.1 applied to each vertex.

Figure 1 (a) shows the population entropy, ϕ (see section 2), fitness, and performance of the best individual (as defined in sections 4 and 3) as a function of the generation number. The curves represent data from a typical run out of 50 independent runs of the EA.

We see that fitness quickly reaches high levels, while performance, which is a harder measure of the generalization capabilities of the evolved networks on the density task, stays lower and then stabilizes at a level greater than 0.8. The population entropy remains high during all runs, meaning that there is little diversity loss during evolution. Note that the entropy refers to the "genotype" and not to fitness. This is unusual and probably due to the spatial structure of the cEA, which only allows slow diffusion of good individuals through the grid [3]. The ϕ curve is particularly interesting as it permits a direct comparison with Watts' hand-constructed graphs [13]. The results fully confirm his measurements, with networks having best performance clustering around ϕ values between 0.6 and 0.8. This is clearly seen in figure 1 (b) where the 50 best networks found are reported as a function of their ϕ, which is to be compared with figure 7.2 in [13]. Therefore, we see that even a simple EA is capable of consistently evolving good performance networks in the small-world range. This is not the case for the standard CAs for the majority task, which are notoriously difficult to evolve. In fact, while we consistently obtain networks having performance around 0.8

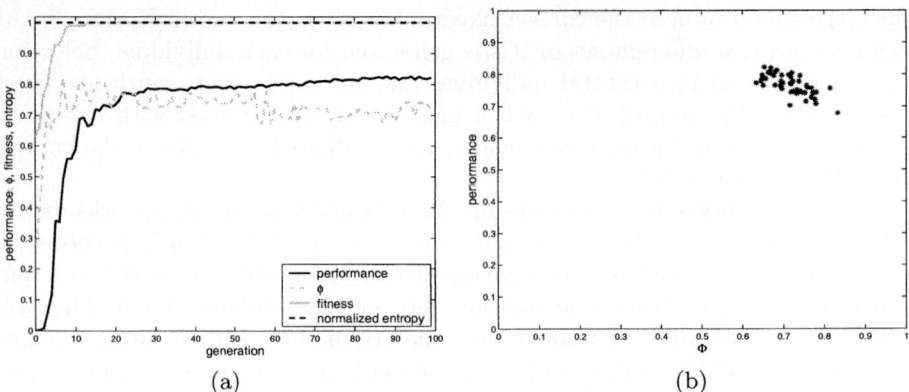

Fig. 1. A typical evolutionary run starting from a perturbed ring population (a). The ϕ - performance values of the 50 best individuals found in the 50 evolutionary runs (b).

in each evolutionary run, Mitchell et al. [8] found that only a small fraction of the runs lead to high-performance CAs. As well, our networks and Watts' reach higher performance: 0.82 against 0.77 for the lattice. Evidently, the original fitness landscape corresponding to the 2^{128} possible ring CAs with radius three is much more difficult to search than the landscape corresponding to all possible graphs with N vertices. To this we may add that the performance of the small-world solutions are better than those of the original lattices as N increases, as was observed by Watts and confirmed by our study (not shown here for lack of space). Work is under way to study the basic statistics of the above landscapes in order to obtain a better understanding of their structures.

4.2 Evolution from Random Graphs

Although the results of artificial evolution from rings are appreciable, giving rise to networks of automata with small-world topology and good performance, the way the initial population is generated might nevertheless contain a bias towards such graphs. In order to really assess the power of this artificial evolution, we designed a second series of experiments in which all the parameters are the same except that the initial population is now formed by arbitrary random graphs. A random graph having N vertices can be constructed by taking all possible pair of vertices and connecting each pair with probability p, or not connecting it with probability $1 - p$. In the experiments $p = 0.03$ and there is no constraint on the minimum node degree, which means that disconnected graphs are also possible. However, we discarded such graphs and ensure that all the networks in the initial population are connected with average degree $\langle k \rangle = Np$ of 4.47.

Figure 2 depicts the same curves starting from random graphs as figure 1 does for the perturbed ring initial population. Here too, 50 independent runs have been performed and a typical one is plotted in the figure. We see again that genotypic diversity is maintained through evolution as the entropy is always high. Likewise, fitness rises quickly and stays near the maximum. Performance has a different behavior initially. While it started low and rapidly and steadily increased in the previous case, here it has an approximate value of 0.4 at the beginning. The difference is due to the fact that, in the perturbed ring case, the initial population is still mainly constituted by regular rings, which we know are uncapable of performing the density task using the majority rule as CA rule. In the random graph case, a fraction of the networks in the initial population does a better job on the task. The same conclusion can be reached by looking at the ϕ curve. While in the perturbed ring case ϕ starts low (ϕ is 0 for a lattice) and then slowly increases toward values around 0.7, in the random graph case the contrary happens: ϕ is rather high at the beginning because truly random graphs predominate during the first part of the evolution, i.e. about 20 generations. After that, graphs are more of the small-world type and converge toward the same ϕ region in both cases. This can be clearly seen in figure 2 (b), where the best 50 individuals of all runs are plotted superimposed on the same number of best networks originating from the ring evolution.

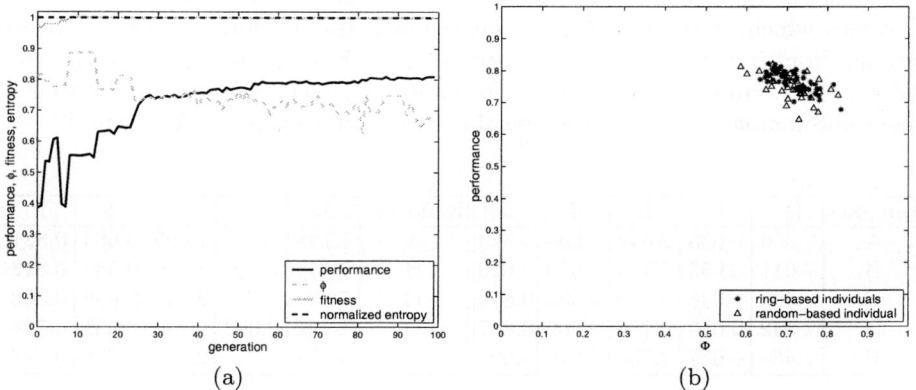

Fig. 2. A typical evolutionary run starting from a random graph population (a). The ϕ - performance values of the 50 best individuals found in the 50 evolutionary runs (b).

It should be noted that in both figures 1 and 2 performance does not stop improving even though fitness has reached its maximum value. This is an indication of the good learning and generalization capabilities of the evolved networks.

The following figure 3 shows the degree distribution of the best networks found by evolution in the ring case (a), and the random graph case (b). Although the number of vertices is too small for a rigorous statistical treatment, it is easily seen that the distribution is close to binomial in both cases, which is what one would have expected.

Finally, figure 4 summarizes the graph-theoretical properties of the five best evolved individuals for the ring case (left), and for the random graph case (right). It is interesting that, although no provision was explicitly made for it, the average

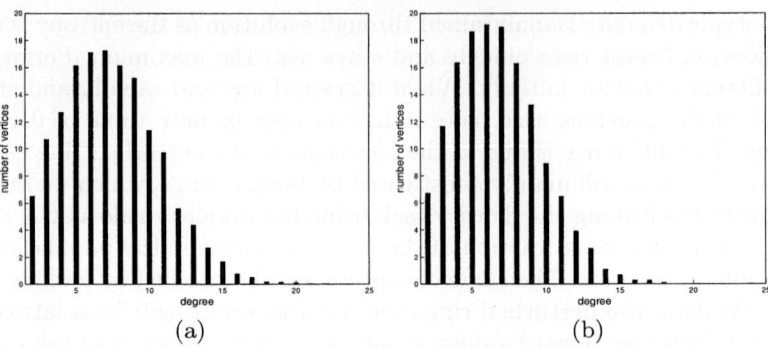

Fig. 3. Degree distribution of best evolved networks. Initial ring population (a); initial random graph population (b).

number of neighbors $\langle k \rangle$ ended up being around seven, very close to six used by construction in Watts [13] (remember that his construction for small-world graphs leaves the initial $\langle k \rangle$ for a ring unchanged). Measured average path lengths L and clustering coefficients C have expected values, given the corresponding ϕ values which, without being in the random graph regime, are nevertheless not far from it for both for initial rings and initial random graphs. In other words, the networks with good performance constructed by Watts as well as those automatically found by artificial evolution have many links rewired.

Ring-net	$\langle k \rangle$	C	L	Φ	P	Rand-net	$\langle k \rangle$	C	L	Φ	P
A	7.906	0.053	2.649	0.654	0.823	A	7.798	-*	2.695	0.664	0.821
B	7.611	0.053	2.703	0.670	0.820	B	7.543	-*	2.736	0.585	0.812
C	7.409	0.048	2.750	0.685	0.813	C	7.355	-*	2.729	0.686	0.800
D	7.342	0.049	2.736	0.669	0.807	D	7.422	0.062	2.736	0.631	0.798
E	7.450	0.057	2.730	0.679	0.807	E	6.778	-*	2.858	0.748	0.797

Fig. 4. The ten best evolved networks. $\langle k \rangle$ is the mean node degree. C is the clustering coefficient. L is the characteristic path length. ϕ is the percentage of shortcuts, and P is the network performance on the density task. Left part: ring-based evolved individuals. Right part: random-based evolved individuals (a -* in random based graphs means that the clustering coefficient is not computable since those graphs are allowed to have vertices with a degree smaller than 2).

5 Conclusions

Starting from the work of Watts on small-world automata for the density task, we have used an evolutionary algorithm to evolve networks that have similar capabilities. Without including any preconceived design issue, the evolutionary algorithm has been consistently able to find high-performance automata networks in the same class of those constructed by Watts. The power of artificial evolution is seen in the fact that, even starting from a population of completely random graphs, the algorithm finds automata in the same class. This result is an indication that small-world network automata in this range have above average distributed computation capabilities, although we only studied one problem of this type. This is also in line with the results of recent research which point to a pervasive presence of small-world and scale-free graphs in many different domains. In future work we will study other typical CA tasks from this point of view. We would also like to investigate the simultaneous co-evolution of network topologies and automata rules.

References

1. R. Albert and A.-L. Barabasi. Statistical mechanics of complex networks. *Reviews of Modern Physics*, 74:47–97, 2002.
2. M. S. Capcarrère, M. Sipper, and M. Tomassini. Two-state, r=1 cellular automaton that classifies density. *Physical Review Letters*, 77(24):4969–4971, December 1996.
3. B. Dorronsoro, E. Alba, M. Giacobini, and M. Tomassini. The influence of grid shape and asynchronicity in cellular evolutionary algorithms. In *Congress on Evolutionary Computation (CEC 2004)*, 2004. (To appear).
4. M. Garzon. *Models of Massive Parallelism: Analysis of Cellular Automata and Neural Networks*. Springer-Verlag, Berlin, 1995.
5. S. A. Kauffman. *The Origins of Order*. Oxford University Press, New York, 1993.
6. M. Land and R. K. Belew. No perfect two-state cellular automata for density classification exists. *Physical Review Letters*, 74(25):5148–5150, June 1995.
7. F. Thomson Leighton. *Introduction to Parallel Algorithms and Architectures: Arrays, Trees, Hypercubes*. Morgan Kaufmann, San Mateo, CA, 1992.
8. M. Mitchell, J. P. Crutchfield, and P. T. Hraber. Evolving cellular automata to perform computations: Mechanisms and impediments. *Physica D*, 75:361–391, 1994.
9. M. Mitchell, P. T. Hraber, and J. P. Crutchfield. Revisiting the edge of chaos: Evolving cellular automata to perform computations. *Complex Systems*, 7:89–130, 1993.
10. R. Serra and M. Villani. Perturbing the regular topology of cellular automata: implications for the dynamics. In S. Bandini, B. Chopard, and M. Tomassini, editors, *Cellular Automata, ACRI 2002*, volume 2493 of *Lecture Notes in Computer Science*, pages 168–177. Springer-Verlag, Heidelberg, 2002.
11. M. Sipper. *Evolution of Parallel Cellular Machines: The Cellular Programming Approach*. Springer-Verlag, Heidelberg, 1997.
12. M. Sipper and E. Ruppin. Co-evolving architectures for cellular machines. *Physica D*, 99:428–441, 1997.
13. D. J. Watts. *Small worlds: The Dynamics of Networks between Order and Randomness*. Princeton University Press, Princeton NJ, 1999.
14. D. J. Watts and S. H. Strogatz. Collective dynamics of 'small-world' networks. *Nature*, 393:440–442, 1998.

Recognizing Speed Limit Sign Numbers by Evolvable Hardware

Jim Torresen[1], Jorgen W. Bakke[1], and Lukas Sekanina[2]

[1] Department of Informatics, University of Oslo
P.O. Box 1080 Blindern, N-0316 Oslo, Norway
{jimtoer,jorgenwa}@ifi.uio.no
[2] Faculty of Information Technology, Brno University of Technology
Bozetechova 2, 612 66 Brno, Czech Republic
sekanina@fit.vutbr.cz

Abstract. An automatic traffic sign detection system would be important in a driver assistance system. In this paper, an approach for detecting numbers on speed limit signs is proposed. Such a system would have to provide a high recognition performance in real-time. Thus, in this paper we propose to apply evolvable hardware for the classification of the numbers extracted from images. The system is based on incremental evolution of digital logic gates. Experiments show that this is a very efficient approach.

1 Introduction

For the last years there has been an increasing focus on enhancing traffic safety by applying intelligent systems in vehicles to assist drivers. One of the reasons for this becoming possible is the recent advance in computer hardware providing affordable technology with a high processing capability. In the work presented in this paper, we consider recognizing speed limit signs. Such a system could assist drivers on signs they did not notice before passing them. It will inform drivers about the present speed limit as well as possibly giving an alert if a car is driven faster than the speed limit. More actively, it could be applied to avoid using today's physical obstacles in the road. This would require that the system could control the vehicle so that it becomes impossible to drive faster than the speed limit. This will mainly be relevant on roads with low speed limits. In the future, autonomous vehicles would have to be controlled by automatic road sign recognition. We have found very little work on speed limit sign classification. There exists a system based on Global Position System (GPS) and digital road maps with speed limits included [4]. However, such a system depends on much external infrastructure. Further, problems like lack of updated speed limits on road maps question the reliability of such a system.

This paper concerns detection of the *numbers* on speed limit signs specifically. This is by classifying numbers extracted from the sign. This will be undertaken in digital logic gates configured by evolution (evolvable hardware – EHW). The complete image recognition system will be presented shortly as well.

The goal of the design is to provide an architecture with a high classification performance at a high speed. This is important since images in such a real-time system are input from a normally *fast moving* vehicle. To obtain sufficient performance and speed at an affordable cost, we plan to migrate computational demanding parts of the software into dedicated hardware. This paper shows the first step in this direction by undertaking the *number classification* part in dedicated (evolved) hardware.

To make the system affordable, expensive hardware is not applicable. A promising technology which also allows for adaptation and upgrades is reconfigurable technology. Thus, we believe Field Programmable Gate Arrays (FPGA) would be an appropriate technology for hardware implementation. Other parts of the system would run as software on a processor. Earlier research has shown that classification can be conducted effectively in evolvable hardware [7]. We are not aware of any other work combining evolvable hardware and road sign classification.

One of the main problems in evolving hardware systems seems to be the difficulties in evolving systems for complex real-world application. The limitation seems to be in the chromosome string length [2, 9]. A long string is normally required for solving a complex problem. However, a larger number of generations is required by the evolutionary algorithm as the string increases. This often makes the search space becoming too large. Thus, work has been undertaken to try to diminish this limitation. One promising approach – incremental evolution of EHW, was first introduced in [5] for a character recognition system. The approach is a divide-and-conquer on the evolution of the EHW system. It consists of a division of the *problem* domain together with incremental evolution of the hardware system. Evolution is first undertaken individually on a set of basic units. The evolved units are the building blocks used in further evolution of a larger and more complex system. The benefits of applying this scheme is both a *simpler* and *smaller* search space compared to conducting evolution in one single run. In this paper, it is applied to evolve a number classification architecture applied on extracted bit arrays from road images. An EHW architecture as well as how incremental evolution is applied are described.

The next section introduces the speed limit signs recognition. This is followed by an outline of the proposed evolvable hardware for classification in Section 3, respectively. Results from the implementation is given in Section 4. Finally, Section 5 concludes the paper.

2 Speed Limit Sign Recognition System

Speed limit signs have features making them feasible for automatic detection. First, there is a limited number of signs to distinguish. The following speed limit signs – see Fig. 1, are used in the experiments: 30, 40, 50, 60, 70 and 80 km/h (other speed limit signs are not included due to lack of images). The outer circle of a sign is in *red* color.

Fig. 1. Speed limit signs.

Fig. 2. An example of an input image.

Second, there are rules (named a road grammar) for how signs can be placed along the road. After a "80" sign you will never find a "30" sign, but rather another "80" sign or a "60" sign. Third, the numbers on the signs are positioned vertically making the matching simpler. In curves only, the signs may be marginally tilted. Forth, each time a *new* speed limit is given, there are speed limit signs at *both* sides of the driving lane. These features make it promising to undertake speed limit sign detection with a very high rate of correct prediction. A typical input image is shown in Fig. 2.

The algorithm is divided into *three* parts: 1) Image filtering to emphasize the red parts of the sign(s), 2) Template matching to locate possible sign(s) in an image and 3) Sign number recognition [3]. These will be presented below.

In the first part, a specialized robust color filter is applied on the image to emphasize the *red circle* surrounding the speed limit numbers. Further, this part of the algorithm effectively limits the number of red pixels in the image to be further processed.

In the second part, possible signs are located in the image by searching for the *red circle* surrounding the numbers. The search is based on matching with a set of circular templates of various size. In addition to locating the sign, the algorithm tries to reject objects that are not signs and signs that are not speed limit signs. That is, to improve recognition at the same time as reducing the computation time.

2.1 Sign Number Recognition

The last part of the algorithm is to detect the speed limit *number* on a sign. This is conducted as follows:

1. Clean the space defined by the best template (remove RED and surrounding colors), but keep the numbers.
2. Find boundaries of numbers (width and height).
3. Work only with the first number (the second is always zero).
4. Create a 7 (rows) x 5 (columns) bit array of the given number (down-scaling): Set each bit of the array to 1 if there is more BLACK than WHITE pixels, else set the bit to 0.
5. Classify the bit array using the evolved classifier circuit (described in the next section).

345678

Fig. 3. Examples of extracted arrays from real images to be classified by EHW.

Some randomly picked examples of bit arrays with different numbers are included in Fig. 3.

Number Classification in EHW. To be able to correctly classify the bit array containing the extracted number, some kind of classification tool is needed. We would like to show that evolved digital logic gates are appropriate. The initial reason for this is the format of the array: it is *small* and contains *binary* values. If applying other approaches like artificial neural network (ANN), a large number of floating point operations would be needed. The EHW architecture, on the other hand, could be implemented in combinational logic where classification is performed in parallel. The next section presents the architecture applied for classification.

3 An Evolvable Architecture for Classification

In this section, the proposed classifier architecture is described. This includes the algorithm for undertaking the incremental evolution. Earlier experiments have shown that the number of generations required for evolution by this architecture can be substantially reduced compared to evolving a system directly in one operation. In experiments for prosthetic hand control [7], better classification results than for artificial neural networks were obtained.

The architecture is illustrated in Fig. 4. It consists of one subsystem for *each* of the six numbers to be classified. In each subsystem, the binary inputs $x_0 \ldots x_{31}$ (3 bits

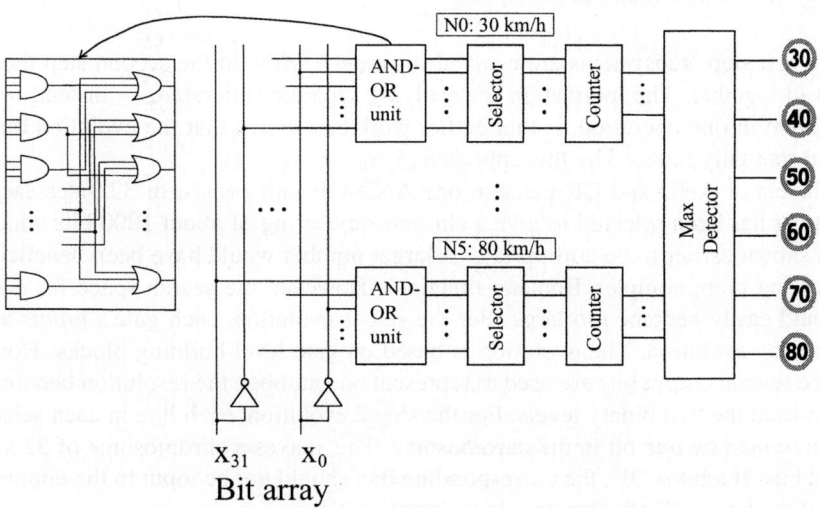

Fig. 4. The digital gate based architecture of the sign number classifier.

from the array are not used) are processed by a number of different units, starting by the AND-OR unit. This is a layer of AND gates followed by a layer of OR gates. Each gate has three inputs. The outputs of the OR gates are routed to the Selector. This unit selects *which* of these outputs that are to be counted by the succeeding counter. That is, for each new input, the Counter is counting the number of *selected* outputs being "1" from the corresponding AND-OR unit. Finally, the Max Detector outputs which counter – corresponding to *one* specific number, is having the largest value. If the Counter having the *largest* value corresponds to the correct number, the input has been correctly classified. E.g. if a bit array with "8" is input, we want as *many* outputs as possible of the lowermost (N5) AND-OR unit in Fig. 4 being "1". For the other five subsystems, we want as *few* outputs as possible outputs being "1". The reason for using more than one output for each number is to provide generalisation.

One of the motivations for introducing the selectors is to be able to adjust the *number* of outputs from each AND-OR unit in a flexible way. Earlier experiments have shown that this effectively increases the performance. A scheme, based on using multi-input AND gates together with counters, has been proposed earlier [10]. However, the architecture used in this paper is distinguished by including OR-gates, together with the selector units involving incremental evolution. The incremental evolution of this system can be described by the following steps:

1. **Step 1 evolution.** Evolve the AND-OR unit for each subsystem *separately* one at a time. Apply *all* vectors in the training set for the evolution of each subsystem. There are no interaction among the subsystems at this step, and the fitness is measured on the output of the AND-OR units.
2. **Step 2 evolution.** Assemble the six AND-OR units into one system as seen in Fig. 4. The AND-OR units are now fixed and the *Selectors* are to be evolved in the assembled system – in one common run. The fitness is measured using the same training set as in step 1 but the evaluation is now on the output of the Max Detector.
3. The system is now ready to be applied.

In the first step, subsystems are evolved separately, while in the second step these are evolved together. The motivation for evolving separate subsystems – instead of a single system in one operation, is that earlier work has shown that the evolution time can be substantially reduced by this approach [5, 6].

The layers of AND and OR gates in one AND-OR unit consist of 32 gates each. This number has been selected to give a chromosome string of about 1000 bits which has been shown earlier to be appropriate. A larger number would have been beneficial for expressing more complex Boolean functions. However, the search space for evolution could easily become too large. For the step 1 evolution, each gate's *inputs* are determined by evolution. The evolution is based on gate level building blocks. However, since several output bits are used to represent one number, the resolution becomes increased from the two binary levels. For the step 2 evolution, each line in each selector is represented by *one* bit in the chromosome. This makes a chromosome of 32 x 6 bits= 192 bits. If a bit is "0", the corresponding line should *not* be input to the counter, whereas if the bit is "1", the line *should* be input.

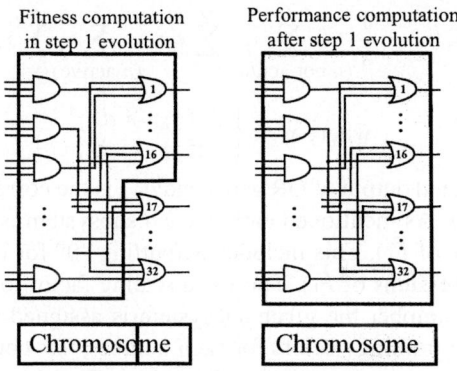

Fig. 5. A "fitness measure" equal to 16.

Fitness Measure

In step 1 evolution, one would normally think about measuring fitness on all the 32 outputs of each AND-OR unit. However, several earlier experiments have shown a great benefit when the fitness is measured on a *limited* number (16 are used here) of the outputs [8]. That is, each AND-OR unit still has 32 outputs but – as seen in Fig. 5, only 16 are included in the computation of the fitness function:

$$\text{Fitness} = \sum_{i=1}^{16} \text{Output OR gate } i \qquad (1)$$

The 16 outputs not used are included in the chromosome and have *random* values. That is, their values do not affect the fitness of the circuit. After evolution, all 32 outputs are applied for computing the performance:

$$\text{Performance} = \sum_{i=1}^{32} \text{Output OR gate } i \qquad (2)$$

Since 16 OR gates are used for fitness computation, the "fitness measure" equals 16. In the figure, gate 1 to 16 are used for the fitness function. However, in principle any 16 gates out of the 32 can be used. Other numbers than 16 were tested in earlier experiments but 16 showed to give the best performance results and was used in the following reported experiments. This approach has shown to be important to improve the generalisation of the circuit [7]. Only the OR gates in the AND-OR unit are "floating" during the evolution since all AND gates may be inputs to the 16 OR gates used by the fitness function. The 16 "floating" OR-gates then provide additional combination of these *trained* AND gates.

Fitness Function

The fitness function is important for the performance when evolving circuits. For the step 1 evolution, the fitness function – applied for each AND-OR unit separately, is as follows for the number n ($n \in \{0, \ldots, 5\}$) unit:

$$F_1(n) = \frac{1}{s} \sum_{(n \text{ not active})} \sum_{i=1}^{O} x_i + \sum_{(n \text{ active})} \sum_{i=1}^{O} x_i \qquad (3)$$

$$\text{where } x_i = \begin{cases} 0 \text{ if } y_{i,j} \neq d_{n,j} \\ 1 \text{ if } y_{i,j} = d_{n,j} \end{cases}$$

where $y_{i,j}$ in the computed output of OR gate i and $d_{n,j}$ is the corresponding target value of the training vector j. As mentioned earlier, each subsystem is trained for *one* number (the last expression of F_1). This includes outputting "0" for input vectors for other numbers (the first expressions of F_1). The s is a scaling factor to implicitly emphasize on the vectors for the number the given subsystem is assigned to detect. Since there is a variable number of training vectors for each number, this constant was set specifically for each subsystem (as seen in the result section). The O is the number of outputs included in the fitness function and is 16 in the following experiments (referred to as "fitness measure" in the previous section).

The fitness function for the step 2 evolution is applied on the complete system and is given as follows:

$$F_2 = \sum_{j=0}^{P-1} x_j \qquad (4)$$

$$\text{where } x_j = \begin{cases} 1 \text{ if } d_{n,j} = 1 \text{ and } n = i \text{ for which } \max_{i=0}^{5}(Counter_i) \\ 0 \text{ else} \end{cases}$$

This fitness function counts the number of training vectors for which the target *output* being "1" *equals* the *id* of the counter having the maximum output (only *one* output bit is "1" for each training vector). P is the total number of vectors in the training set ($P = 100$ in the following experiments).

The Evolutionary Algorithm

The simple Genetic Algorithm (GA) – given by Goldberg [1], was applied for the evolution with a population size of 50. For each new generation an entirely new population of individuals is generated. Elitism is used, thus, the best individuals from each generation are carried over to the next generation. The (single point) crossover rate is 0.8, thus the cloning rate is 0.2. Roulette wheel selection scheme is applied. The mutation rate – the probability of bit inversion for each bit in the binary chromosome string, is 0.01.

Various experiments have been undertaken to find appropriate GA parameters. The ones that seemed to give the best results were selected and fixed for all the experiments. This was necessary due to the large number of experiments that would have been required if GA parameters should be able vary through all the experiments. The initial experiments indicated that the parameter setting was not a major critical issue.

The proposed architecture fits into most FPGAs. The evolution is undertaken off-line using software simulation. However, since no feed-back connections are used and the number of gates between the input and output is limited, the real performance should equal the simulation. Any spikes could be removed using registers in the circuit.

For each experiment presented, four different runs of GA were performed. Thus, *each* of the four resulting circuits from step 1 evolution is taken to step 2 evolution and evolved for four runs.

Effective Processing in EHW

In the last part of Section 2.1, the benefits of the EHW architecture compared to ANN were introduced. In this section more details will be given. The EHW architecture do classification in *parallel* for all the different numbers. Each path consists of *two* layers of gates in the AND-OR unit. The selector could be implemented with a *one* gate layer. The counter could effectively be implemented as a tree of gates. The Max Detector would consist of a comparator structure. Thus, all can be implemented in combinational logic. However, to improve the speed if necessary, registers could be introduced in the architecture together with pipelined processing. Thus, the architecture should be able to process one bit array *each* clock cycle. A neural network would typically have 32 inputs, 32 hidden units and 6 outputs. This would result in at least (32x32 + 32x6 = 1216) multiply-accumulate operations and (32+6) sigmoid function operations. This would normally have to be executed as serial floating point operations on a processor. This seems to be a waste of resources since the input would still be binary values.

4 Results

This section reports the results from the experimental work undertaken. A database of 198 images from traffic situations were used in the experiments. 115 contained a speed limit sign and 83 contained other signs or no sign at all. Many of the images were in various ways "difficult" (different brightness on sign, faded color on sign etc). The results were as follows (before number recognition was undertaken):

- Is there a speed limit sign? A speed limit sign was found in 100 of the 115 images (87%). In those not found, the system stated that a speed limit sign was not present in the image.
- 78 of the 83 images without a speed limit was correctly refused (94%). Thus, only five images were sent to the final sign number recognition.

For *all* the 100 images (P) that the system correctly detected a speed limit sign, the extracted number arrays were applied for evolving the hardware to perform classification. The number of arrays for the different speed limits is given in Table 1. The values for fitness scaling (see equation (3)) are also included. They are computed according to the following equation:

$$s = \frac{P}{P_n} \cdot k = \frac{100}{P_n} \cdot 0.7 = \frac{70}{P_n}$$

P_n is the number of arrays for the given class (column two in the table) and k is a constant determining the ratio between the fitness from P_n training vectors (active) and $(P - P_n)$ training vectors (not active). I.e. for speed limit 40, the *total* fitness for the 11 arrays counts a factor 0.7 less than the *total* of the fitness for the other 89 arrays. The value of k was determined by experiments.

Table 2 summarizes the classification performance. All the experiments are based on a "fitness measure" equal to 16. In the table, "A" shows the performance when only the outputs applied in the fitness function are applied in computing the performance (after step 1 evolution is finished). However, we see that it is better to apply all 32 outputs ("B") since the average performance is about 8% higher. Thus, 16 OR gates

Table 1. The number of extracted arrays classified for each speed limit.

Speed limit	Number of arrays (P_n)	Fitness scaling factor (s)
30	4	18
40	11	7
50	32	2
60	35	2
70	12	7
80	6	12

Table 2. The correct number classification performance in %.

Type of system	Step of evolution	Min	Max	Average
A: Performance of 16 outputs	1	67.6	75.7	71.44
B: Performance of 32 outputs	1	71.8	90.9	79.2
C: Performance of 32 outputs	2	92.9	96.0	94.5

Table 3. Performance of the best classifier architecture evolved.

Speed Limit	30	40	50	60	70	80
Performance (in %)	100	100	84.4	91.4	100	100

with random input connections improve the performance. We see the importance of the step 2 evolution in "C" in which the performance is substantially increased. The average performance is more than 15% higher than for "B". The best classifier provided a performance of 96%.

The performance for each speed limit for the best classifier is shown in Table 3. Only two speed limits have less than 100% correct classification.

In step 1 evolution, each AND-OR unit was evolved for 25,000 generations. Step 2 evolution needed less than 500 generations before the performance stopped increasing. We have not yet studied the performance of the 5 images that were wrongly sent to the number recognizer. However, these could probably be eliminated by a combination of matching on the "0" number and applying road grammar (as explained in Section 2). We have not fully explored all possible parameter settings for the architecture. Thus, there is a potential for further improving the performance. Further, a threshold unit could be introduced to avoid misclassifying numbers by rather indicating no distinct match.

In addition to achieve a high rate of correct classification, we have made much effort at the same time to reduce the processing time. This would be highly needed in a future real-time system. By applying digital logic gates for the number classification, we have almost eliminated the processing time for this operation. To have a robust and reliable system, more images should be analyzed and this is a part of our future work. With the promising results so far, future work also consists of further improving the algorithms and implementing the most computational demanding parts in special hardware. More image data should be applied to better test the generalisation performance. Further, possible inclusion of evolution in other parts of the system is of interest as well. Finally, a prototype to be applied in a vehicle will be implemented.

5 Conclusions

The paper has presented a novel approach to detect extracted numbers from speed limit signs using evolvable hardware. It is focused on reducing computation time at the same time as getting high recognition performance. The results show that performance can be substantially increased by applying incremental evolution. In average, 94.5 % correct classification is achieved in the experiments.

Acknowledgments

The research is funded by the Research Council of Norway through the project *Biological-Inspired Design of Systems for Complex Real-World Applications* (project no 160308/V30). The research is also performed with funding from the Grant Agency of the Czech Republic under No. 102/03/P004 *Evolvable hardware based application design methods*.

References

1. D. Goldberg. *Genetic Algorithms in search, optimization, and machine learning.* Addison-Wesley, 1989.
2. W-P. Lee, J. Hallam, and H.H. Lund. Learning complex robot behaviours by evolutionary computing with task decomposition. In A. Birk and J. Demiris, editors, *Learning Robots: Proc. of 6th European Workshop, EWLR-6 Brighton*, volume 1545 of *Lecture Notes in Artificial Intelligence*, pages 155–172. Springer-Verlag, 1997.
3. L. Sekanina and J. Torresen. Detection of Norwegian speed limit signs. In *Proc. of the 16th European Simulation Multiconference (ESM'2002)*, pages 337–340. SCS Europe, June 2002.
4. R. Thomas. Less is more [intelligent speed adaptation for road vehicles]. *IEE Review*, 49(5):40–43, May 2003.
5. J. Torresen. A divide-and-conquer approach to evolvable hardware. In M. Sipper et al., editors, *Evolvable Systems: From Biology to Hardware. Second International Conference, ICES 98*, volume 1478 of *Lecture Notes in Computer Science*, pages 57–65. Springer-Verlag, 1998.
6. J. Torresen. Scalable evolvable hardware applied to road image recognition. In J. Lohn et al., editor, *Proc. of the 2nd NASA/DoD Workshop on Evolvable Hardware*, pages 245–252. IEEE Computer Society, Silicon Valley, USA, July 2000.
7. J. Torresen. Two-step incremental evolution of a digital logic gate based prosthetic hand controller. In *Evolvable Systems: From Biology to Hardware. Fourth International Conference, (ICES'01)*, volume 2210 of *Lecture Notes in Computer Science*, pages 1–13. Springer-Verlag, 2001.
8. Jim Torresen. A scalable approach to evolvable hardware. *Journal of Genetic Programming and Evolvable Machines*, 3(3):259–282, 2002.
9. X. Yao and T. Higuchi. Promises and challenges of evolvable hardware. In T. Higuchi et al., editors, *Evolvable Systems: From Biology to Hardware. First International Conference, ICES 96*, volume 1259 of *Lecture Notes in Computer Science*, pages 55–78. Springer-Verlag, 1997.
10. M. Yasunaga et al. Genetic algorithm-based design methodology for pattern recognition hardware. In *Evolvable Systems: From Biology to Hardware. Third International Conference, ICES 2000*, volume 1801 of *LNCS*, pages 264–273. Springer-Verlag, 2000.

Dynamic Routing Problems with Fruitful Regions: Models and Evolutionary Computation*

Jano I. van Hemert and J.A. La Poutré

Dutch National Research Institute for Mathematics and Computer Science,
P.O. Box 94079, NL-1090 GB Amsterdam, The Netherlands
{jvhemert,hlp}@cwi.nl

Abstract. We introduce the concept of fruitful regions in a dynamic routing context: regions that have a high potential of generating loads to be transported. The objective is to maximise the number of loads transported, while keeping to capacity and time constraints. Loads arrive while the problem is being solved, which makes it a real-time routing problem. The solver is a self-adaptive evolutionary algorithm that ensures feasible solutions at all times. We investigate under what conditions the exploration of fruitful regions improves the effectiveness of the evolutionary algorithm.

1 Introduction

Vehicle routing forms an interesting line of research, because of its high complexity and intractable nature, as well as because of its importance to the transport industry. It has been studied in many different forms, whereby introducing concepts as uncertainty [1] and pickup-and-delivery scenarios [2]. In practice, dynamic routing problems occur widely [3], in which matters are further complicated as one needs to cope with a lack of knowledge while solving.

We concentrate our study on dynamic vehicle routing problems over an extended time period. This paper reports on the problem of collecting loads and delivering them to a central depot, during which requested pickups appear dynamically, i.e., while vehicles are on-route. We consider having knowledge about the probability where loads appear, especially in the form of regions. This knowledge could have been obtained from, for instance, data of previous routes on customer demands. We address the problem whether this knowledge may improve upon the quality of solutions.

In this paper we shall provide a mathematical model of this dynamic routing problem, for which we will introduce an evolutionary algorithm in order to solve it. Our main contribution is the discovery that exploration of fruitful regions is beneficial to the effectiveness of the solver for various types of problem settings.

2 Relation to and Embedding into Previous Research

Often in practice, a problem may develop over time, that is, some variables in the problem may change or be set at a later stage such that a new evaluation of the

---
* This work is part of DEAL (Distributed Engine for Advanced Logistics) supported as project EETK01141 under the Dutch EET programme.

problem is required. Basically, this inserts uncertainties and lack of information into the problem. The literature distinguishes between two ways of analysing such problems, stochastic routing and dynamic routing [4]. The latter is also referred to as real-time routing or on-line routing [5]. In stochastic routing we are presented with a routing problem that has a number of its variables stochastically determined. This still requires a solution to the static problem, i.e., an a priori solution, but we can use only an expected value of the optimisation function. Examples of stochastic variables are uncertain supplies [6] and stochastic travel times [7]. The dynamic routing problem requires that the solver keeps waiting for events to occur to which it should act accordingly. Such events may be more customer requests, but they can also be changed travel times or other incidents that endanger the success of the current plan. A solver should thus make sure that it creates its solution to the current status in such a way that it may be altered successfully to changes in the future. Our interest lies in the second approach as these become more common in practice, due to an increasing amount of computing and communication resources and due to an increasing amount of flexibility demanded by customers [3, 8].

In the same book [9] where Psaraftis [10] laid out the differences between dynamic and static vehicle routing problems, Powell [11] first reviews the idea of forecasting the uncertainties within dynamic routing. Powell's work is targeted towards solving assignment problems, where the objective is to assign available loads to individual vehicles such that the whole fleet of vehicles is able to maintain a steady flow of work. In [12], a model is presented that deals with long-haul transport, which has led to a hybrid model that assigns jobs to trucks and forecasts jobs in future time periods. Thus, Powell's work is essentially about work flows, and not about dynamic routing.

Our objective is to use the concept of demand forecasting and use this in dynamic routing problems that occur real-time, i.e., the vehicles are on route when the problem changes. This is different to the work of Laporte and Louveaux, which is concerned with creating routes beforehand. It is also different to Powell's work on forecasting, as he uses it in combination with the assignment problem in the application area of dispatching, a fact that is underlined in [13]. In the assignment problem, the routing aspect, i.e., the optimisation problem where one minimises route length or the number of vehicles, is fully ignored in favour of having the fleet spread over the network such that the expected loads are covered.

In this paper, the application lies in transport that occurs in and between areas with a dense distribution of customers, where routing is required to achieve cost effective solutions. The problem is a dynamic in a sense that customer requests are handled dynamically, and where the problem is solved in real-time. Furthermore, the solver possibly makes use of the knowledge about high-potential, i.e., fruitful, regions.

3 Definition of the Problem

A routing problem consists of a set of nodes N, connected by a graph $G = (N, E)$ with edges E that are labelled with the cost to traverse them, a set of loads L and a set of vehicles V. An optimisation function determines the goal of the routing problem, which is further specified by a set of constraints that places restrictions on the aforementioned resources. Here we consider loads that need to be picked up from nodes and then delivered to a central depot.

A load $l \in L$ is a quadruple $\langle s, d, t, \Delta \rangle$, where $s \in N$ is the source node, and $d \in \mathbb{N}$ is the size of the load, which is fixed to one here. $t \in T$ is the entry time, i.e., the time when the load is announced to the solver, with T the time period of the problem. Every load should be delivered to a central depot $n_0 \in N$ within Δ time steps with $l \in L$, i.e., before $t + \Delta$. Here we assume that Δ is equal for each load.

A vehicle $v \in V$ is characterised by a capacity q and a start position $sp \in N$. We assume that all vehicles have the same capacity. Each vehicle has a speed of 1 and starts at the depot ($sp = n_0$). The dynamic status of a vehicle v, i.e., its route, assigned loads and current position, is defined with two functions. Both functions use the assumption that a vehicle always travels directly from node to node, i.e., it is not possible to stop half way and choose another route. This enables us to talk about the position of a vehicle in terms of nodes. We define the current position of a vehicle v as $p \in N$ where p is the node last visited by v. Then, we define the current situation using v and p as,

$$\text{current}(v, p) = \langle \mathbf{r}_{\leq p}, A_{\leq p}, A_p \rangle, \tag{1}$$

where $\mathbf{r}_{\leq p} = (r_0, \ldots, r_j)$ is an ordered list of nodes with $r_i \in N$ for $0 \leq i \leq j$ and $r_0 = sp$, denoting the route of the vehicle through the network up until and including node r_j where $r_j = p$. $A_{\leq p}$ is the set of loads that were assigned and were collected and delivered to the central depot by v so far, and A_p is the set of loads that were assigned and were collected by v so far, but not yet delivered.

$$\text{future}(v, p) = \langle \mathbf{r}_{>p}, A_{>p} \rangle, \tag{2}$$

where $\mathbf{r}_{>p} = (r_{p+1}, \ldots, r_k)$ is an ordered list of nodes with $r_i \in N$, which denotes the route planned for vehicle v from the next location r_{p+1} onwards. $A_{>p}$ is the set of loads that are assigned to be collected by v in the future.

We define some additional functions that are helpful in our futher formulation of the problem. The function arrival-time(v, p) returns the time vehicle v arrives at node $r_p \in N$ as the pth node of its route. The function loads(v, p) returns the set of all loads assigned to vehicle v; loads$(v, p) = A_{\leq p} \cup A_p \cup A_{>p}$.

The constraints of the routing problem are given next.

$$\forall v \in V, \forall p : \text{future}(v, p) = \langle (r_{p+1}, \ldots, r_k), A_{>p} \rangle \wedge p + 1 = k \Rightarrow A_{>p} = \emptyset \tag{3}$$

$$\forall v_1, v_2 \in V, \forall p_1, p_2 : v_1 \neq v_2 \Rightarrow \text{loads}(v_1, p_1) \cap \text{loads}(v_2, p_2) = \emptyset \tag{4}$$

$$\forall v \in V, \forall p : \forall \langle s, d, t, \Delta \rangle \in A_p \cup A_{<p} : \text{arrival-time}(v, p) \geq t \tag{5}$$

$$\forall l = \langle s, d, t, \Delta \rangle \in L : \forall v \in V : \text{current}(v, p) =$$
$$\langle \mathbf{r}_{\leq p}, A_{\leq p}, A_p \rangle \wedge \langle s, d, t, \Delta \rangle \in A_p \wedge \exists p' : r_{p'} = d \wedge p \leq p' \Rightarrow$$
$$\text{arrival-time}(v, p') \leq t + \Delta \tag{6}$$

$$\forall \langle v \rangle \in V : \forall p : \text{current}(v, p) = \langle r_p, A_{\leq p}, A_p \rangle \Rightarrow \sum_{\langle s, d, t, \Delta \rangle \in A_p} d \leq q \tag{7}$$

The constraint (3) restricts vehicles from carrying loads at the end of their route. To enforce that a load is carried by at most one vehicle the constraint (4) is used. The notion of time appears in three places; in the definition of a load, where the *entry time* is set, in constraint (5), where we make sure loads are only carried after their entry time, and in constraint (6), where we make sure loads are delivered at their destination within a fixed time after entering the system. Finally, constraint (7) is introduced to have vehicles carry only as much as their capacity lets them.

Three differences with the classic static routing problem can be identified as in this dynamic model:

1. vehicles may drive routes where they pass through nodes without performing a loading or unloading action,
2. loads may become available while vehicles are already on route, and
3. it is let open that each load must be assigned to a vehicle.

The latter enables us to choose as the objective of the routing problem to carry as many loads as possible, i.e., to maximise the number of loads successfully delivered at the central depot: let p_v be the last position of vehicle v at the end of time period T, then $\max \sum_{v \in V} \text{loads}(v, p_v)$. In the experiments we shall report as a performance measure the success ratio, which is defined as the number of loads successfully delivered at the depot divided by the total number of loads generated during a run of the whole system.

4 Fruitful Regions

In practice, customers are often clustered into regions as opposed to scattered around equally over the total domain [14]. Often, the amount of service requested in total from one region may differ much from another. This is due to all types of reasons, such as the production capacities of customer in a region. Depending on the distribution of the customers and the distribution of service requests, it might be beneficial for a vehicle to visit nodes in the customer graph that have a high probability for a service request in the near future.

The grouping of customers into clusters is achieved either a posteriori, by observing the distribution of service requests in historical data, or a priori, by modelling them explicitly. In both cases we assume that a partition $C = \{C_1, C_2, \ldots, C_c\}$ of clusters exists in the layout of the problem, where each $C_i \subseteq N$. Next, we define the vector $\boldsymbol{f} = (f_1, f_2, \ldots, f_{|N|})$, where f_j is the probability that a load in the simulation originates from customer $j \in N$. The following holds: $\sum_{j \in N} f_j = 1$. We define the potential of a cluster C_i as the sum over the probabilities of its nodes: $\sum_{j \in C_i} f_j$.

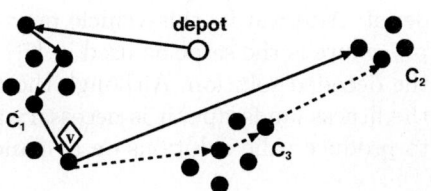

Fig. 1. An example of an anticipating route.

An example of three clusters and one central depot is presented in Figure 1. The vehicle v that left the depot and then visited several nodes in C_1, is now on its route to a node in C_2. If the potential for new loads in C_3 is high enough, it might want to perform an anticipated move, visiting nodes in C_3 along the dotted lines, as this could provide another load without much additional driving.

5 Evolutionary Algorithm

In the context of dynamic optimisation, evolutionary computation has the advantage of being able to cope with changes in the environment during its optimisation [15]. By maintaining a diverse set of candidate solutions, the evolutionary algorithm can adapt to the changes. Evolutionary algorithms can quickly converge to a suboptimal or optimal solution. Together with the current speed of processors, this makes it possible to keep providing solutions to a dynamic routing problem.

Bräysy and Gendreau [16] have reviewed many successful evolutionary algorithms and other meta-heuristic approaches for the classic vehicle routing problem. These were often tested using the well known Solomon benchmark [14]. All these implementations make extensive use of heuristics and other hybrid solutions to increase the efficiency and effectiveness of the final routing algorithm. Our objective is to verify whether or not the concept of fruitful regions can help increase performance. We shall start with a straightforward representation of the problem together with basic operators, then add the possibility to move vehicles to fruitful regions. Precise details of the evolutionary algorithm are given next.

5.1 An Evolutionary Algorithm for Dynamic Routing

Representation. Each individual represents a plan for all the vehicles in the system. It is a list of routes, where each route corresponds to exactly one vehicle. A route consists of potential assignments for that vehicle, which it will perform in that order. Assignments are either pickup assignments or moves to a location. This representation is then decoded into a valid solution, i.e., a solution where none of the constraints are violated. Assignments that violate one or more time constraints are ignored by the decoder. When a vehicle reaches its capacity or when adding more assignments will violate a time constraint, the decoder forces a visit to the depot. Afterwards, this vehicle may be deployed to service customers again. This procedure is the same as used in [7]. The fitness of the individual will be based on the decoded solution. Although the decoding process may have a large impact on the fitness landscape, it is necessary as in a dynamic environment we must be able to produce valid solutions on demand.

Initialisation. At the start, i.e., at $t = 0$, every available load $l \in \{\langle s, d, t, \Delta \rangle \in L | t = 0\}$ is randomly assigned to a vehicle. When fruitful regions are considered, a self-adaptative mechanism is used that lets an individual decide for itself how much it values to explore such regions. This employs an alpha value initialised uniform randomly between 0 and 1, which is further explained in the fitness function. The population size is set to 30.

Fitness Function. The basis for the fitness function is the number of loads that can be transported successfully, i.e., that can be transported without violating the time and capacity constraints. We call these *feasible loads*. The fitness of an individual x is defined as,

$$\text{fitness}_1(x) = \frac{\#\text{ feasible loads}}{\#\text{ total loads available}}.$$

Only available loads are considered, that is, loads that are not yet picked up. The rationale here is that loads are removed from individuals of the evolutionary algorithm once they are picked up. As individuals only concern with future routing these loads play no role and should therefore not be included in the evaluation of an individual. Note that for assessing the overall quality of the evolutionary algorithm, we will use every load in the system over the whole period T.

We add the mechanism that allows the evolutionary algorithm to explore the possibility of employing vehicles to nodes that have not yet requested service. The fitness function, which has to be maximised, is extended with anticipated moves, i.e., moves that have no direct loading action attached. These moves are performed only when the constraints allow this. Thus, some moves may be cancelled during decoding to make sure that the final plan satisfies the constraints placed upon a vehicle because of previous assigned actions, such as, picking up a load. If we would perform such a move, the planning would become infeasible and hence, such a move is called an *infeasible anticipated move*. A candidate solution is penalised for every infeasible anticipated move in order to restrict the number of anticipated moves. The fitness of an candidate solution is decreased by the fraction of infeasible anticipated moves out of all planned anticipated moves. The amount with which this decreases the fitness function depends on an alpha value (α), which is encoded into every candidate solution. Using this self-adaptive mechanism, each candidate solution is able to determine by itself how much it values the effect of inserting anticipated moves.

$$\text{fitness}_2(x) = \text{fitness}_1(x) - \alpha \frac{\#\text{ infeasible anticipated moves}}{\#\text{ total anticipated moves of } x}.$$

To asses the effectiveness of the evolutionary algorithm, with or without anticipated moves, we measure the ratio of the loads successfully delivered to the total number of loads made available for transport, at the end of the run.

Selection. A 2-tournament selection is used to select an individual for mutation. A generational scheme is used, known in evolution strategies as (μ, μ), with elitism of size one.

Variation Operator. Only mutation is considered. Two vehicles, possibly the same one, are chosen uniform randomly. In both vehicles two nodes are selected uniform randomly. If only one vehicle is chosen these nodes are chosen to be distinct. Then, the nodes are swapped. This way, visits, both for loading or as an anticipated move, can be exchanged between vehicles as well as within the route of one vehicle.

Furthermore, the individual's alpha value, which influences the fitness function, is changed according to the common update rule from evolution strategies.

Stop Condition. The algorithm is terminated once the time period T is expired, i.e., at the end of the simulation.

5.2 Dynamism

In practice, dealing with a dynamic problem means that we have limited time to contemplate the solution as vehicles need to be kept going and changes may be on their way. In reality we have the world and the solver running in parallel, and then we need to decide how often the solver's view of the world is updated. Here, we choose a time period based on the number of times the evolutionary algorithm evaluates one of its candidate solutions. These fitness evaluations take up most of the time in an evolutionary algorithm. For each time unit of the simulation the evolutionary algorithm may perform one generation. Thus the evolutionary algorithm will perform *population size* × *time steps* ($= 30|T|$) fitness evaluations in a simulation run.

The whole simulation operates by alternatively running the evolutionary algorithm and the simulated routing problem. The routing simulator calculates when the next event will occur, e.g., a vehicle will pickup or deliver a load, or, a load is announced for pickup. Then, the evolutionary algorithm may run up until this event occurs. This way we simulate an interrupt of the evolutionary algorithm when it needs to adapt to changes in the real world. The best individual from the last generation before the "interrupt" is used to update the assignments of the vehicles in the routing simulation. Then, the routing problem is advanced up until the next event. Afterwards, the individuals of the evolutionary algorithm are updated by removing finished assignments and adding loads recently made available. This process is repeated for time period T. Note that it is possible that multiple events occur at the same time, which will be handled in one go.

6 Experiments

To simulate a dynamic environment with fruitful regions we introduce a particular arrangements of the customers by clusters. First a set of points called the set of cluster centres C is created by randomly selecting points (x, y) in the 2-dimensional space such that these points are uniformly distributed in that space. Then for each cluster centre $(x, y) \in C$ a set of locations $R_{(x,y)}$ is created such that these locations are scattered around the cluster centre by using a Gaussian random distribution with an average distance of τ to choose the diversion from the centre. This way we get clusters with a circular shape. The set of nodes N is defined as $N = \{n | n \in R_{(x,y)} \land (x, y) \in C\}$. The set of locations form the nodes of the graph $G = (N, E)$. This graph is a full graph and its edges E are labelled with the costs to traverse them. For each $(n_1, n_2) \in E$, this cost is equal to the Euclidean distance between n_1 and n_2.

A set of loads is randomly generated, which will represent the work that needs to be routed in the time period T. Every load starts at a node and needs to be carried to a central depot, which is located in the centre of the map. Each node is assigned a number of loads, this number is taken from a Gaussian distribution

Table 1. Parameters of the problem instances, experiment parameters in bold.

parameter	value
maximum width and height of the map	200×200
number of locations	$|N| = 50$
number of clusters	$|C| = 5$
spread of locations in a cluster	$\tau = 10$
number of vehicles	$|V| = 10$
capacity constraint	$q \in \{1, 2, 3, 4, 5, 6\}$
delivery time constraint	$\Delta \in \{20, 40, \ldots, 380\}$
average number of loads per cluster	5
deviation of the number of loads over clusters	5
deviation of loads per node within a cluster	4
average time spread	$\lambda = 10 \ (\sigma = 50)$

with as average the potential of the cluster and a deviation of loads within a cluster parameter set in Table 1. Clusters are assigned a potential in the same way using the average number of loads per cluster.

The entry times of loads is chosen by considering all loads one at a time. The i-th load is generated at time $i \times \lambda + N(0, \sigma)$, where λ is the average time spread σ is the deviation of the average time between entry times (see Table 1). This way we spread the loads over time using a normal distribution.

To show the effect of performing anticipated moves to fruitful regions we fix the capacity q of each vehicle to one and vary the time delivery constraint Δ. By increasing the time available for performing a delivery, we are loosening this constraint, which makes it possible that more loads are transported. We clearly notice three stages, separated by the two vertical lines. Figure 2(a) shows the result for both with and without performing anticipated moves. The first stage, where delivery time is very restricted, and consequently only few loads can be transported. There, anticipated moves will not influence the success ratio. Then, in the next stage, the exploration of fruitful regions shows its potential for increasing the success ratio. Last, when the time restriction is removed further, there is plenty of time to deliver loads, thus the best result is achieved by sticking to routing vehicles for pickup and deliveries only. For the last stage, a vehicle can take a long

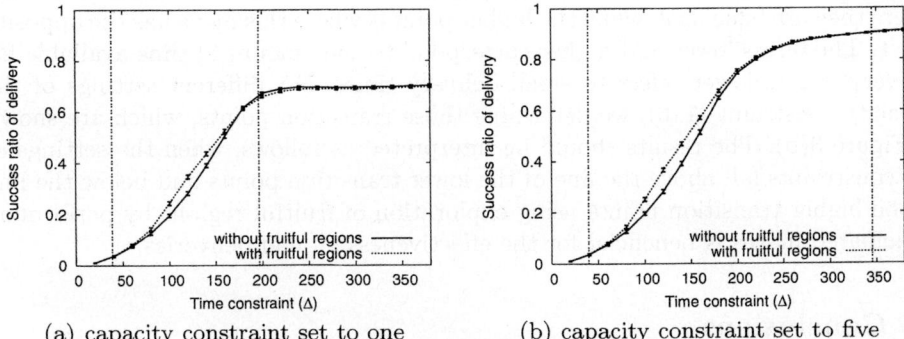

(a) capacity constraint set to one (b) capacity constraint set to five

Fig. 2. Average ratio of successfully delivered loads with increasing delivery time for both with and without using anticipated moves. Results for each setting of the time delivery constraint are averaged over 40 problem instances with 10 independent runs of the evolutionary algorithm and include 95% confidence intervals.

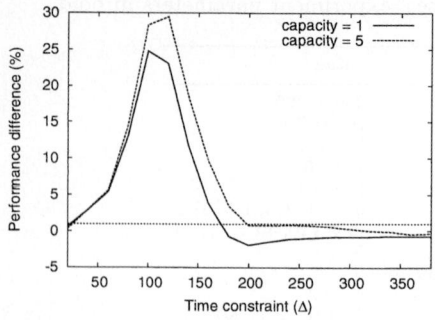 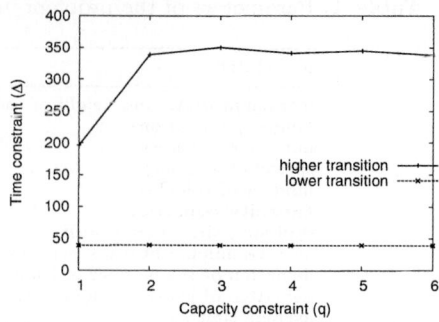

(a) Performance ratios, where the success ratio of with anticipated moves is divided by the success ratio of without anticipated moves

(b) Relating the capacity and time constraints using transition points to determine the boundaries wherein anticipated moves to fruitful regions may improve effectiveness

Fig. 3. Performance ratios and transition points.

time to fetch any load, as it will have more than enough time to return to the depot.

With the capacity constraint set to five we get the result shown in Figure 2(b). Most notably, the phase where the exploration of fruitful regions are beneficial widens. In Figure 3(a), we show by how much anticipated moves improves the effectiveness. The largest benefit is found at a time constraint setting of 100 and 120 for $q = 1$ and $q = 5$ respectively, where the success ratio is improved by 25% and 30%. For tight time constraints no significant difference can be noted and for loose time constraints the success ratio is at most 1.8% and 0.8% lower, for the settings of 1 and 5 respectively. This shows that knowledge of the constraint settings is important, but as long as the tightness of the time constraint is not too restrictive, an exploration of fruitful regions is recommendable.

To take into consideration the effect of both constraints, capacity and time, we show how they relate for the lower and higher transition points. The lower point is where we move from a stage where anticipated moves are not beneficial to a stage where they are beneficial, while the higher point is where this move has the opposite effect. The terms lower and higher correspond to the amount of time available for delivery, where lower refers to small delivery times. For different settings of the capacity constraint (1–6), we determine those transition points, which are shown in Figure 3(b). The results should be interpreted as follows, when the settings of the constraints fall above the line of the lower transition points and below the line of the higher transition points using exploration of fruitful regions by performing anticipated moves is beneficial for the effectiveness of load deliveries.

7 Conclusions

Dynamic constrained optimisation problems play an increasingly more import role in many areas, not only because of faster computers and telecommunication, but because of the increasing demand of customers for flexible and fast service as well.

Vehicle routing is a scientifically interesting problem as its static version is known to be intractable. By moving into the realm of dynamic routing problems, with the given constraint that we should be able to maintain viable solutions, we make this problem even more challenging.

In this paper, we introduced a dynamic routing model that defines a load collection problem, i.e., the pickup and return of loads to one depot. Especially, we introduced a model for taking into account regions with high potentials for the origin of new loads. Furthermore, we have provided an evolutionary algorithm that is able to provide solutions in real-time. Using the evolutionary algorithm, and an extention to let it perform anticipated moves, we have determined the transition points where between the exploration of fruitful regions is of benefit. The potential of using the concept of fruitful regions is evident from the significant increase in the effectiveness for settings within these transition points.

References

1. Bertsimas, D., Simchi-Levi, D.: A new generation of vehicle routing research: Robust algorithms, addressing uncertainty. Operations Research **44** (1996) 286–304
2. Savelsbergh, M., Sol, M.: The general pickup and delivery problem. Transportation Science **29** (1995) 17–29
3. Psaraftis, H.: Dynamic vehicle routing: status and prospects. Annals of Operations Research **61** (1995) 143–164
4. Ghiani, G., Guerriero, F., Laporte, G., Musmanno, R.: Real-time vehicle routing: Solution concepts, algorithms and parallel computing strategies. Technical report, Center of Excellence for High Performance Computing, Univ. of Calabria, Italy (2003)
5. de Paepe, W.: Complexity Results and Competitive Analysis for Vehicle Routing Problems. PhD thesis, Research School for Operations Management and Logistics, Technical University of Eindhoven (2002)
6. Laporte, G., Louveaux, F. In: Formulations and bounds for the stochastic capacitated vehicle routing problem with uncertain supplies. Elsevier Science Publishers B.V. (1990) 443–455
7. Laporte, G., Louveaux, F., Mercure, H.: The vehicle routing problem with stochastic travel times. Transportation Science **26** (1992) 161–170
8. Bianchi, L.: Notes on dynamic vehicle routing — the state of the art. Technical report, IDSIA, Galleria 2, 6928 Manno-Lugano, Switzerland (2000)
9. Golden, B., Assad, A.: Vehicle Routing: methods and studies. Elsevier Science Publishers B.V. (1988)
10. Psaraftis, H.: Dynamic vehicle routing problems. [9] chapter 11 223–248
11. Powell, W.: A comparative review of alternative algorithms for the dynamic vehicle routing problem. [9] chapter 12 249–291
12. Powell, W.: A stochastic formulation of the dynamic assignment problem, with an application to truckload motor carriers. Transportation Science **30** (1996) 195–219
13. Gendreau, M., Potvin, J.Y.: Dynamic vehicle routing and dispatching. In Crainic, T., Laporte, G., eds.: Fleet Management and Logistics. Kluwer, Boston (1998) 115–126
14. Solomon, M.: The vehicle routing and scheduling problems with time window constraints. Operations Research **35** (1987) 254–265
15. Branke, J.: Evolutionary Optimization in Dynamic Environments. Volume 3 of Genetic Algorithms and Evolutionary Computation. Kluwer Academic Publishers (2001)
16. Bräysy, O., Gendreau, M.: Vehicle routing problem with time windows, part II: Metaheuristics. Transportation Science (to appear)

Optimising the Performance of a Formula One Car Using a Genetic Algorithm

Krzysztof Wloch and Peter J. Bentley

Department of Computer Science, University College London, Gower St., London, UK
{k.wloch,p.bentley}@cs.ucl.ac.uk

Abstract. Formula One motor racing is a rich sport that spends millions on research and development of highly optimized cars. Here we describe the use of a genetic algorithm to optimize 66 setup parameters for a simulation of a Formula One car and demonstrate performance improvements (faster lap times) better than all other methods tested.

1 Introduction

Formula One is arguably the première motor racing sport of the world. In the quest to produce ever more competitive racing cars, the teams that design, build and race them spend millions each year on research and development. A modern Formula One car has almost as much in common with a jet fighter as it does with an ordinary road car[1].

Even minor changes in wing height, suspension stiffness, or tyre rubber compound can make the difference between a car winning and coming last in a race. And with sponsors' money dependent on the television coverage a car receives, a losing car may result in its team losing funding and going out of business.

It is therefore very important, both for the sport and for business, to have effective methods of optimising Formula One car settings. Here we describe the use of a genetic algorithm (GA) to optimise such settings, and demonstrate that the resulting performance is better than all other methods tested of producing car setups.

2 Background

Formula One is notoriously secretive, so it is difficult to know if any teams have begun using genetic algorithms for similar purposes as those described here. A recent press release from the Jordon team [1] hints that they may be considering such technologies. It describes how the team has "...signed up *Scientio Inc.*, an artificial intelligence and data mining specialist, to assist the team in various problem-solving projects," and, "The company's technology includes: data mining techniques, fuzzy logic, genetic algorithms and software which learns optimum solutions to problems."

But it seems that published work in the area of car optimization using genetic algorithms is rare. Deb and Saxena [2] describe work on the optimization of car suspen-

---

[1] From www.formula1.com, the official formula one website.

sion design for comfort, by minimizing factors such as bouncing, pitching and rolling. They claim to have evolved a suspension design that is "better than a design used by one automobile industry."

The most common research in this area seems to focus on car design optimization, with numerous examples, including automobile valvetrain optimization [3], structural automobile design [4], and aerodynamic conceptual design of a sports car [5].

The apparent lack of work using GAs to optimize Formula One car settings is surprising, especially given the success demonstrated in this work.

3 System

Although the authors did not have access to real Formula One cars or data, the popularity of the sport means that accurate car and track simulators capable of data logging are widely available. The Formula One evolutionary optimization system combines a genetic algorithm with such a simulator (linked using additional macro and data parsing software), see figure 1.

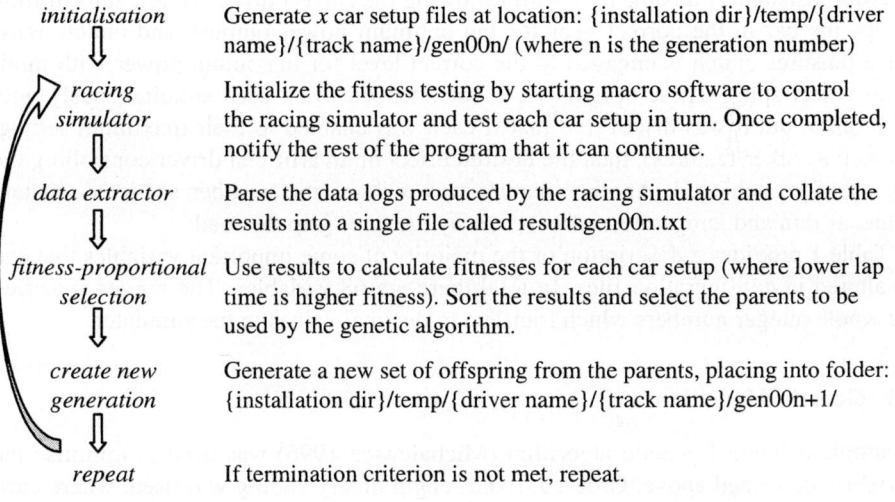

Fig. 1. The Formula One evolutionary optimization system.

3.1 Macro-software

From the outset of the development of this system, it was clear that a method for automation would be essential. Linking the GA optimiser to the racing simulator efficiently was critical, so it was determined that macro software would enable the automation of the testing of the cars. The macro would have to be able to launch the simulation software, and initialize any required options, such as loading the current evolved configurations of the car. It would need to be able to simulate the pressing of combinations of any keys which might be necessary, for example throttle control. The final solution was to use a combination of two different programs, each handling a different section of the automation. *Macro Scheduler*™ was used to load the car simulator; *Hot Keyboard Pro*™ was used to simulate the throttle of the car being pressed and to load the desired configuration into the vehicle simulator.

3.2 Racing Simulator

Several existing racing simulations were considered but the option selected was *Formula One Challenge '99-'02* by *Electronic Arts*™. Released in 2003, it has an advanced real time physics engine, and models specific cars and tracks with remarkable accuracy, in addition to details such as track/tyre temperatures, and weather effects. Other important factors included the feature for F1 Challenge to output track results to disk[2], have 68 input parameters for configuration[3], and artificially driven cars. The latter ability was enabled by altering the configuration of the program to control the steering, braking, and throttle level, see below. The throttle was 'pressed' using a windows macro while the simulator controlled the throttle pressure and the gears.

The software included a driver aids options to help the driving with tasks such as: steering assistance (aids the user with following the correct driving line), auto shifting (keeps the car in the correct gear for the optimum power output), and clutch assistance (ensures clutch is engaged to the correct level for maximum power with minimum wheel spin). These options were not intended to be used simultaneously with each other, but it was discovered that if each was enabled to their maximum setting, (as well as other features), then the desired effect of an artificial driver controlling the car could be achieved. Another feature was to have the weather set to a constant value, as rain and temperature affect the way the tyres grip the road.

Table 1 provides a description of the majority of some important variables that can be altered in configuration files. In total there are 68 variables. The ranges specified are whole integer numbers which translate to decimal values in the simulator.

3.3 Genetic Algorithm

A simple canonical genetic algorithm (Michalewicz 1996) was used to optimise the variables described above. Ordered, fixed-length binary coding was used, where each parameter was encoded into a binary string with maximum length for range of that value, e.g. for the range 0-31, the value 14 is encoded as 01110. Parents were randomly picked from the best 40 percent of the population each generation. Single point crossover was used 100 percent of the time, mutation occurred with a probability of 0.01 (within the permissible range of the parameter). Elitism was used to preserve the best individual in the population each generation.

---

[2] Track results are logged to a location within the installation directory and stored within text files for easy extraction. Each file is named in reference to the time it was created. This feature is enabled by changing the logging settings within the config file in the root of the simulator.

[3] See [6] for an exact list of all the parameters available.

Table 1. Main variables that affect the performance of the car. Other variables include fuel consumption and steering controls.

Setting name	Range	Its function
Suspension		
Anti-Sway	0-25	Has an effect on the under/oversteer of the car, and the contact that the tyres have with the ground. The value relates to the stiffness of the anti-sway bar.
Toe In settings	0-40	Relates to the angle of the wheels in relation to each other. The variable alters how much the wheels point forwards. This has an effect on directional stability.
Camber settings	0-80	Camber is the angle of the wheel relative to the vertical. The variable alters this angle, and affects the tyres' performance while cornering.
Spring rates.	0-40	The spring rates determine how stiff the springs are and how the vehicle responds in cornering and bumpier surfaces. They can affect understeer/oversteer also. Measured in N/mm.
Packer settings.	0-40	Useful in high-speed situations the packers are related to the spring and ride height.
Ride height.	0-40	This can be varied in millimetres and affects the down force of the car on the track.
Bump damping.	Multiple	There are several variables associated with these settings, with ranges from 0-40. They affect how quickly the suspension responds to the road surface.
Engine		
Rev Limit	0-10	Variations to how many revolutions per minute the engine can reach. Affects acceleration in certain rev ranges.
Gear Ratios	Multiple	There are 15 variables associated with changing the gear ratios. They effect the acceleration of the vehicle. They vary in range up to 0-75.
Aerodynamics		
Brake duct size	0-6	Relates to the size of the ducts, and affects cooling.
Radiator size	0-4	Also affects cooling, and the aerodynamics of the car.
Wings	0-49	Varies the height and position of the wings, changing the down force of the vehicle and its grip on the road.
Other		
Tyre pressure	0-105	Can be set individually for each tyre.
Brake pressure and bias	Multiple	Varies how hard the brakes are applied, and the distribution between front and rear break pressure. Several variables associated with this ranging from 0-45.

4 Experiments

The racing simulator permitted many different racing tracks and cars to be simulated. For this work two tracks and one car was chosen. Several factors were considered in deciding to select two racing circuits which are considerably different to each other:

- **Silverstone, Great Britain**
  The Silverstone circuit, located in Northamptonshire, is a generally fast circuit with several slow corners, and a selection of fast sweeping turns. This means that the car should be tuned for higher speeds, with less down force for cornering and aerodynamics designed to provide greater straight line speed.
- **Nürburgring, Germany**
  The Nürburgring circuit was chosen for exactly the opposite reason to Silverstone. It is a very twisty and tough circuit. The track is quite uneven and the car would need to be configured for high down-force to handle tight corners at speed.

The racing car chosen was the *Williams BMW, 2002*, for purely personal reasons of the first author. The car uses a 10 cylinder engine provided by BMW, while Williams provides the chassis and aerodynamic design. The FW25 chassis in this model was a new generation design with notable differences from the previous models. The 900bhp engine was the most powerful of the Formula One cars at the time, capable of 19,050rpm.

Table 2. The five experiments performed using the Formula One evolutionary optimization system.

Test	Track Name	Vehicle	Pop. Size	Generations Completed
1	Great Britain, Silverstone	2002 Williams	10	23
2	Great Britain, Silverstone	2002 Williams	30	20
3	Great Britain, Silverstone	2002 Williams	40	43*
4	Great Britain, Silverstone	2002 Williams	40	40*
5	Germany, Nürburgring	2002 Williams	40	40

4.1 Testing Procedure

In total, five experiments were performed, detailed in Table 2. Population sizes were varied to determine the effect on optimisation. The first four experiments tested the 2002 Williams car on the Silverstone track. The final experiment tested the system on Nürburgring. Because the racing simulator models Formula One cars in real time, fitness evaluation was lengthy and each experiment took several days to complete. Evolution was halted manually when convergence of the GA had occurred.

5 Results

Figure 2 shows graphs of fitness against time for the five experiments.

5.1 Experiment 1

The first test that was performed was with a population size of 10. The initial population, as with all tests, was randomly generated. The aim of this was to initially test the system, see how quickly it converged, and fine-tune GA parameters. The algorithm was halted after 23 generations.

The graph in figure 2 shows the lap time of the fastest car setup for that generation. It was observed that the population appeared to converge after the 14th generation, but when watching the vehicles being fitness tested it became apparent that not all the variables were being optimized.

The fastest time achieved was 1 minute 26.608 seconds. Although elitism is being employed, because of noise, the lap time may appear to increase minutely at the 22nd generation.

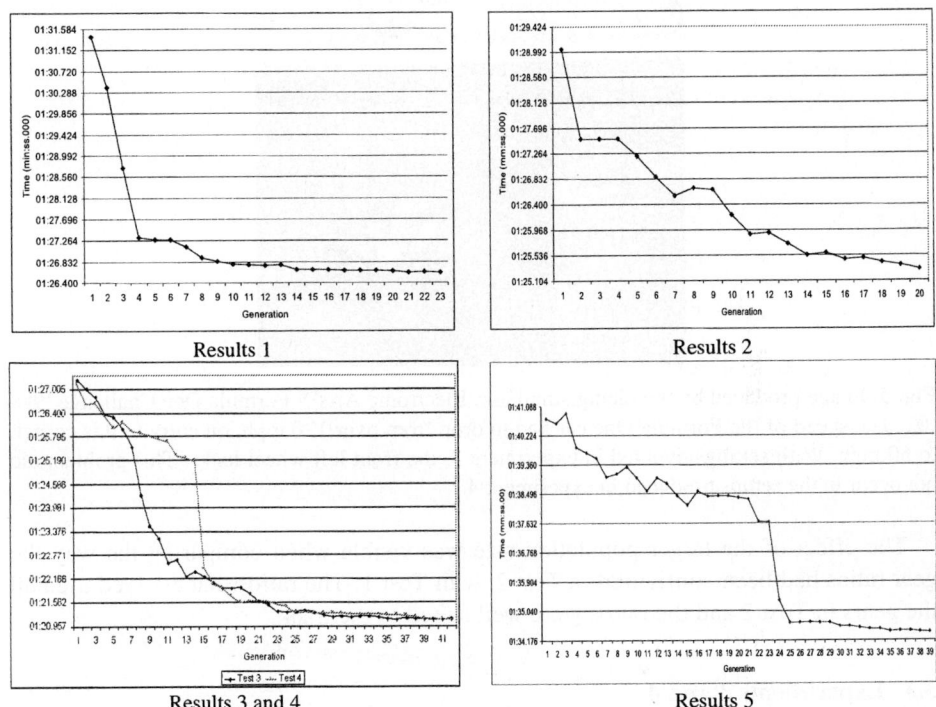

Fig. 2. Results of experiments 1 to 5.

It was decided to run until the 23rd generation to see what affect it would have on the vehicle on track. Although the lap time did not appear to decrease any further, noticeably, when doing so, it became apparent that certain variables did improve over time, and this was taken into account when planning further runs of the algorithm. The decrease in lap time from the initial randomly generated variables to the final optimized 23rd generation car setups was very significant. The lap times improved by up to 5 seconds from some of the better initial configurations. It seems likely that the apparent inability of the algorithm to optimize some of the parameters was because the population size was so limited. For example, only the first 3 gear ratios were properly optimized with the top gears not even being used when testing the car.

5.2 Experiment 2

This test was with a population size of 30. The aim of this was to see what effect slightly increasing the population size would have on the algorithm's ability to optimize the variables. It was run for 20 generations.

The fastest lap time achieved was 1 minute 25.397 seconds after 20 generations, see figure 2, Results 2. The car setups appeared to converge after the 18th generation (note the difference in scale). The increase in population size had a marked effect on the ability of all the variables to converge to their optimum.

Fig. 3. Image produced by the racing simulator, Electronic Arts™ Formula One Challenge '99–'02. The speed of the Formula One car had to drop from over 170 mph, on entry to this corner, to 50 mph. With settings evolved in experiment 3, the front left wheel locks. This problem did not occur in the setups produced in experiment 4.

The effect of the larger population size was visible when comparing the way the gear ratios had been configured in Test 2, with Test 1. The ratios that evolved used all the gears in Test 2 and the ratios were well suited to the track.

5.3 Experiments 3 and 4

Test 3 and 4 were carried out in the same manner, and are included in this section together as the comparison of their results and the setups generated are revealing.

The algorithm was run on test 3 until the lap time no longer appeared to decrease significantly. Test 4 was then run for the same number of generations. The two were then compared, see figure 2, Results 2 and 3. The same optimum is reached after 40 generations on each run of the algorithm. The fastest time was 1 minute 21.050 secs.

Although the same lap time was reached after 40 generations there were significant differences in the way the algorithm produced the results. For example, a common fault with all the car configurations developed after 40 generations on test 3. When turning into one corner on Silverstone, known as 'Club,' there was a tendency for the front left wheel to lock up under braking, see fig. 3.

Other differences between the evolved settings existed in the suspension settings, although there were similarities. For example, the brake bias between front and rear wheels, the weight distribution on the vehicle, the engine rev limit and the aerodynamic parameters all evolved to almost exactly the same settings in both experiments. The exact parameters can be found in [6].

5.4 Experiment 5

The test at Nürburgring was carried out to see how effective the genetic algorithm would be at optimizing the car setup on a very different type of track. The test was carried out in an identical method to tests 3 and 4, running for 40 generations.

The graph shows that the program was capable of effectively optimizing the car setup on a track style which was totally different to Silverstone. The parameters appeared to converge at around the same generation number as in Test 3 and 4: generation 25. Nevertheless, the variables continued to evolve to better settings the longer the simulation was run.

The graph gives an impression that the track times increase and decrease quite considerably as the tests continue, but this is due to how difficult it is to achieve a consistent lap time on a more demanding track. The gear ratios which evolved were perfectly suited to the track, in that for each corner the engine revolutions stayed consistently high allowing for fast acceleration out of the corners, and a high enough final gear ratio so that in the straight part of the track the car could reach a top speed of 193mph. No visible problems developed with the car setup, as with test 3.

6 Discussion

The default settings of the car (provided by the simulation software itself) produce lap times which on all occasions were beaten by everything generated by the tests shown in the results. The initial results from Test 1 did not provide very significant gains over the default setups, but they were certainly visible, and subsequent tests showed huge increases in performance. The setups generated towards the end of Tests 3 and 4 produced gains, consistently, of over 5 seconds in lap times. Running the tests for longer and with larger populations could only have increased those gains.

Tests 3 and 4 also showed that the system is capable of producing various solutions to optimizing the car around the track. This was visible in the way that in test 3 the front left wheel of the car locked up under braking while in test 4 a different solution was created without similar problems. Although test 3 produced a setup which could cope with the lock up, in reality it would not be good for tyre and brake wear.

In comparison with tunings produced by a human, the system was easily able to compete and beat settings that the author was able to produce, and in every case that was tested it had faster lap times on car setups that were obtained from the internet, from sources that had greater experience with F1 Challenge than the author.

The best car setup, produced from Tests 3 and 4 (which was provided by test 4), was compared against 3 car setups. The first was recommended settings provided by the simulator, the second was a configuration produced by the first author, and the third was from an 'internet expert.' For the sake of consistency, all the vehicles were tested in exactly the same manner. The automatic driver drove the vehicles around the track and controlled all the usual functions, such as throttle level, braking and steering. The amount of fuel that the cars were carrying was set to the lowest level to allow them to complete the laps, each car was given the same tyres (soft compound), and the track/outside temperature was fixed on each test. Silverstone was the testing track. Table 3 summarises the results.

Table 3. Comparison of lap times produced by cars with evolved settings with three other sets of parameter settings.

Car setup	Lap time (mm:ss.000)	Difference (ss.000)
Evolved Settings	1:20.349	
Expert Setup	1:21.221	+0.879
Krzysztof's Setup (author)	1:21.439	+1.090
Default System Setup	1:22.769	+2.420

The reduction in fuel weight carried by the cars is the explanation for the difference between the results quoted earlier and in table 3, but as is clearly visible, the reduction in lap time by the evolved settings is considerable, although the stresses on the car are probably far greater and it is visible that the car is driving on the limit.

7 Conclusions

This work drew together several different software technologies to produce a system that fulfilled its goals of optimising the settings of a Formula One car using evolutionary computing, and achieving real improvements in lap times compared with all other methods tested. The choice to use the EA developed simulator proved highly successful when it came to the implementation. The automatic control of the cars around the track provided a highly consistent method of fitness testing, and the data output by the program was used very effectively by the genetic algorithm.

7.1 Future Work

If the program was to be developed further, then the telemetry feature on F1 Challenge should be employed. Although the data is encoded in an unrecognisable format, the belief is that a far more effective algorithm could be created if the exact details of the results from a lap could be incorporated into an evolutionary process. This would involve looking at the effectiveness of individual components of the car and certain parts of the track, and evolving the parameters, in a similar method to before, to take into account this extra information.

A faster testing method, which would reduce the time for fitness testing, and also the overall optimization process, would be very useful. Currently the time for testing makes using large population sizes unattractive.

Finally, it is anticipated that the same methods could be used to optimise real Formula One car setups with equal success, so useful collaborations with willing teams are a real possibility.

References

1. Jordan Grand Prix (2004). Jordan finds a new technical partner. Jordon Press Release, published on F1-Live.com at 15:07, 09/02/04.
2. Deb, K. and Saxena, V. (1997). Car suspension design for comfort using genetic algorithms. In Thomas Bäck (Ed.) Proceedings of the Seventh International Conference on Genetic Algorithms (pp. 553--560).
3. Emre Kazancioglu, Guangquan Wu, Jeonghan Ko, Stanislav Bohac, Zoran Filipi, S. Jack Hu, Dennis Assanis and Kazuhiro Saitou. (2003) Robust Optimization Of An Automobile Valvetrain Using A Multiobjective Genetic Algorithm. Proc. of ASME 2003 Design Engineering Technical Conferences Chicago, Illinois.
4. Leiva, J.P., Wang, L., Recek S. and Watson, B. (2001), Automobile Design Using the GENESIS Structural Optimization Program , Nafems Seminar: Advances in Optimization Tecnologies for Product Design, Chicago, Ilinois, USA, October 22-23, 2001.
5. Bentley, P. J. & Wakefield, J. P. (1997). Generic Evolutionary Design. Chawdhry, P.K., Roy, R., & Pant, R.K. (eds) Soft Computing in Engineering Design and Manufacturing. Springer Verlag London Limited, Part 6, 289-298.
6. Wloch, K. (2004) Optimising Formula One Settings using a Genetic Algorithm. B.Sc. final project report, Department of Computer Science, University College London.
7. Michalewicz, Z. (1996). Genetic Algorithms + Data Structures = Evolution Programs. 3rd edn. Springer-Verlag, Berlin Heidelberg New York .

An Inexpensive Cognitive Approach for Bi-objective Optimization Using Bliss Points and Interaction

Hussein A. Abbass

Artificial Life and Adaptive Robotics Laboratory (ALAR),
School of Information Technology and Electrical Engineering,
University of New South Wales,
Australian Defence Force Academy,
Canberra, ACT 2600, Australia
h.abbass@adfa.edu.au

Abstract. When an optimization problem encompasses multiple objectives, it is usually difficult to define optimality. The decision maker plays an important role when choosing the final single decision. Pareto-based *evolutionary multiobjective optimization* (EMO) methods are very informative for the decision making process since they provide the decision maker with a set of efficient solutions to choose from. Despite that this set may not be the global efficient set, we show in this paper that this set can still be informative within an interactive session with the decision maker. We use a combination of EMO and single objective optimization methods to guide the decision maker in interactive sessions.

1 Introduction

The majority of real life problems have a number of conflicting objectives, where improving one objective comes with the cost of worsening the others. Problems with multiple conflicting objectives are called *multiobjective optimization problems* (MOPs). Methods for solving MOPs have been applied to many domains including, recently, novel applications such as neural networks' design [2], evolutionary ensemble of neural networks [1] and evolutionary robotics [19].

In MOPs, Pareto-optimality replaces the traditional concept of optimal solutions in single objective optimization. If there exists a solution x_1 which is better than or equal to another solution x_2 when compared on all objectives and strictly better than x_2 when measured on at least one objective, the corresponding objective vector $F(x_1)$ is said to dominate the objective vector $F(x_2)$ and $F(x_2)$ is labelled dominated while $F(x_1)$ is labelled non-dominated. A solution x^* is said to be Pareto-optimal if there is no other solution x in the feasible region such that x dominates x^*. Evolutionary methods [10, 20, 21] for solving MOPs are called *evolutionary multiobjective optimization* (EMO) methods. In EMO, the non-dominated set changes during the evolutionary run since the population is merely a sample of the search space. Therefore, we distinguish between the Non-dominated set defined by the evolutionary process, ND_e, and the Pareto optimal set, ND_a.

A distinct group of techniques for solving MOPs is evolutionary algorithms (EAs) [6, 7]. This group is inspired by different theories of evolution and works with a population of solutions at each time step (iteration/generation) in contrast to the majority of traditional approaches which work with a single solution at a time. EMO problems fall into one of three categories: plain aggregating [11, 13, 22]; non-Pareto approaches [16]; and Pareto-based approaches [8, 9, 14, 17, 15, 25]. The majority of EMO methods attempt to generate the set of Pareto optimal solutions independent of the decision maker.

The ultimate goal of any decision making process is to reach a decision. In the existence of multiple conflicting objectives, the Pareto set can be very informative to the decision maker since each solution in this set presents a tradeoff between the different objectives. Visualizing this set can guide the decision maker in choosing the right solution. Here, interactive approaches play a key role in constructing some sort of a dialogue with the decision maker to assist in making a suitable decision. Interactive methods are also known as interactive programming [23].

In this paper, we present an interactive EMO method. The contribution of the method is two folds. One is a mechanism that can assist an EMO method to get as close as possible to the actual Pareto front using human interaction. The second is a mechanism for involving the decision maker to focus on and filter areas of the search space that she is interested in.

2 Motivation

In traditional optimization methods, the problem needs to satisfy certain mathematical properties such as linearity or convexity. Therefore, traditional methods stand shorthanded when these assumptions are violated. Even in traditional derivative free global optimization methods [12, 18], the majority of these methods assume the function to be locally Lipschitz (see [5] for a definition of Lipschitz functions). If these assumptions are violated, these methods become inappropriate. Here, evolutionary computation methods can play an important role in optimizing those problems.

If we focus on traditional methods for interactive programming, two more disadvantages related specifically to interactive programming can be identified.

First, the decision maker either needs to identify the value or utility matrix, which is an extremely difficult and challenging task, or the decision maker needs to propose a new solution. For those methods depending on the existence of value functions, a simple inconsistency in the decision maker choices during the process will simply cause failure of these methods. Even when fuzzy or utility functions are used, it is hard to believe that the decision maker is always working towards some implicit function, especially if the decision maker does not have long experience with the problem domain. Proposing a new bliss point (*i.e.* desired solution) in an inconsistent manner, can cause many problems for the interactive method. For example, if the decision maker cycles between two bliss points, the method will never converge to a solution. Therefore, the cognitive complexity of the interactive method based on the mechanism where the decision maker proposes new solutions is extremely high. This is because these methods assume that the decision maker is maintaining a memory or cognitive map of previous solutions being presented and proposed by the solver. This memory imposes a multiobjective problem in its own right; that is, the trade-off between the amount of information to be presented to the decision maker (*i.e.* letting the interface presents the history during the interactive session instead of exhausting the decision maker memory) and the amount of information and cognitive map the decision maker needs to maintain. If the interface is over-loaded with information, it will become a very difficult task to comprehend these information in any meaningful way. On the other hand, if the interface presents a few amount of information, the decision maker will need to use her own memory for the interactive session to be successful.

The solution to the second disadvantage is to use a memoryless interactive approach as we propose in this paper. The idea is to present the decision maker with the output from the EMO method. The decision maker then proposes an interval of bliss points. The solutions found corresponding to this interval are then incorporated into the existing Pareto front and the decision maker continues with her choice. The process continues till the decision maker is satisfied with the available set of solutions.

It is clear that the decision maker does not need to maintain a memory because visualizing the efficient set captures more information than simply enumerating a number of solutions. Humans can understand patterns easily and can spot trends in a graph much easier than extracting patterns from a bunch of numbers. Therefore, the cognitive capacity needed for selecting an interval from a simple graph depicting the Pareto front is less than that needed to identify an interval from a set of numbers.

Second, many algorithms start with proposing an initial solution to the decision maker. This causes what is known as the Anchoring problem. Here, the decision maker gets biased with the initial point and sometimes focuses only on areas of the search space surrounding the initial point. Buchanan [4] argued that the effect of the Anchoring problem is less when the method used is based on free search. Meanwhile, if the method is based on structured or directed search, the effect of the initial point is critical.

In our proposed method, we start by visualizing the set of efficient solutions as determined by the evolutionary process, which is a free search method. Therefore, the decision maker won't be biased with a single initial point. On the contrary, the decision maker will be in a better position to see the alternatives available in the problem. The decision maker can see the patterns during the visualization instead of a simple enumeration of the set. Human can understand and perceive patterns more efficiently than crunching numbers.

In the current paper, we only deal with bi-objective problems. For space consideration, we will not present results with more than two objectives. However, it is worth mentioning that we use parallel coordinates to visualize higher dimensions.

3 Algorithm

The underlying EMO method is based on a modified version of the *Pareto Differential Evolution Algorithm* (PDE). Interested readers can refer to [3] for a detailed explanation of PDE. It is worth mentioning, however, that the software is written to allow other EMO methods to be encoded with minimal modifications. We have also implemented different mutation and crossover operators for future use and extendibility of the software to other EMO algorithms. The interface is presented in Figure 1.

The neighborhood function used in the original PDE is replaced by a simple niching function as follows: the range of the first objective function in the non-dominated set

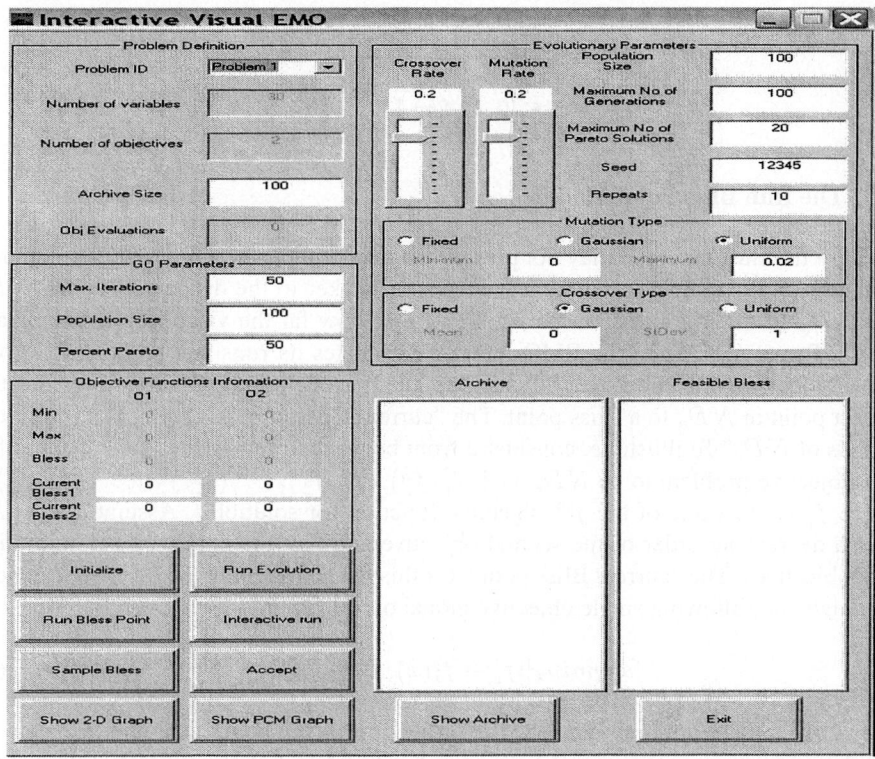

Fig. 1. A screen dump of the user interface.

is calculated and divided into $MaxPareto$ intervals of equal length. A non-dominated solution is chosen at random from each interval. If the interval is empty, the closest solution to the lower bound of the interval or the closest solution to the upper bound of the interval is chosen. The niching function works on the first objective only for a bi-objective problem. This niching function provides better spread than the previously used neighborhood function.

The interactive software is composed of a number of components. The rest of the paper will present each component and an example will be used to facilitate the explanation.

4 Example 1: Convex Pareto Front

In explaining the method, we will use the first benchmark minimization problem ZDT1 used in [24] which is formulated as follows:

$$f_1(x) = x_1$$

$$f_2(x) = g \times (1 - \sqrt{\frac{f_1}{g}})$$

$$g = 1 + 9 \times \frac{\sum_{i=2}^{n} x_i}{n-1}$$

$$x_i \in [0,1], i = 1, \ldots, 30$$

4.1 The Run Bliss Point Module

Because the EMO method may not present the decision maker with ND_a, we adopt a method which can help in pointing the decision maker to the distance between ND_e and ND_a so that the decision maker is aware of how far the visualized solutions are for the Pareto set. When the EMO method completes its runs and reports ND_e, we use a global optimization method, such as another evolutionary method, to find the closest point in ND_a to a Bliss point. The "current Bliss point" is formulated from the bounds of ND_e. To illustrate, consider a front being reported by the EMO method for a bi-objective problem to be $ND_e = \{(f_1^1, f_1^2), (f_1^2, f_2^2), \ldots, (f_1^i, f_2^i), \ldots, (f_1^k, f_2^k)\}$, where f_j^i is the value of the jth objective function for solution i. Assume that ND_e is of a decreasing order of the second objective and that the problem is to minimize both objectives. The "current Bliss point" for this list is therefore (f_1^1, f_2^k). We can now formulate the following single objective global optimization

$$argmin_{\hat{x}} \|f_1^1 - f_1(\hat{x}), f_2^k - f_2(\hat{x})\| \tag{1}$$

where $\|.\|$ is the L_2 norm and $\hat{x}$ is the projection of the solution to this problem in the objective space onto the decision space. In other words, $\hat{x}$ is a vector of the values of the decision variables that satisfy the minimum of this function. We can speed up this global optimization process by initializing the process with solutions from ND_e, where the user can control the percentage of the population in the global optimization algorithm to be initialized from ND_e. The solution to this global optimization problem will result in the "feasible Bliss point". We may note that the current Bliss point is very likely to be infeasible because its projection onto the decision space will fall outside the bounds on the variables. A feasible Bliss point is the closest point to the current Bliss point in the objective space, whom projection onto the decision space is feasible.

In Figure 2(left), we used a bad combination of parameters for PDE to obtain a non-dominated set ND_e that is quiet far from ND_a for the first benchmark minimization problem ZDT1 used in [24]. We used a bad combination of parameters on purpose so that the distance between the evolutionary output and the interaction appears clearly when the figures are printed out. It is clear from the figure that the feasible point corresponding to the Bliss point is far from ND_e which is a clear indication that $ND_e \neq ND_a$ in this run.

4.2 The Interactive Run Module

After running the *Bliss point module*, the user can see an estimate of how far ND_e is from ND_a. This estimate can be calculated as $(d_1, d_2)^t = (f_1^1 - f_1(\hat{x}), f_2^k - f_2(\hat{x}))^t$, where $(d)^t$ stands for the transpose of d. A series of global optimization problems is

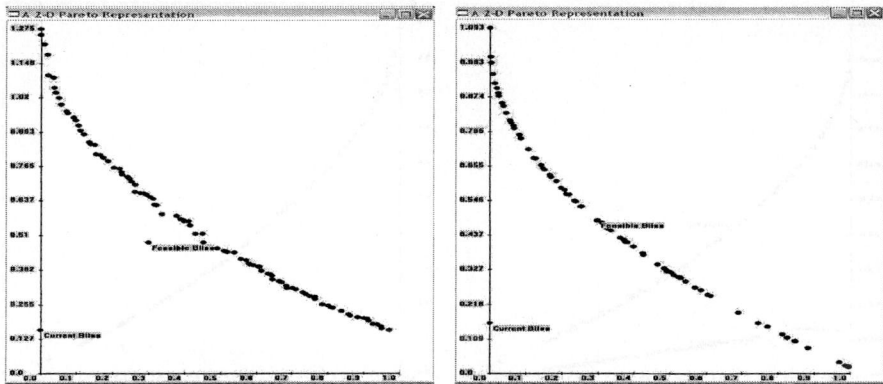

Fig. 2. On left: The Bliss point and the corresponding feasible point are shown in a sample run. On right: The non-dominated set after being pushed towards the actual non-dominated set using the *interactive run module*.

constructed for the solutions in ND_e. Let (f_1^i, f_2^i) be the ith solution in ND_e. Define $\hat{f}_1^i = (f_1^i + U_1(0, Step) * d_1)$ and $\hat{f}_2^i = (f_2^i + U_2(0, Step) * d_2)$.

$$argmin_{\hat{x}} \|\hat{f}_1^i - f_1(\hat{x}), \hat{f}_2^i - f_2(\hat{x})\| \qquad (2)$$

The solution $\hat{x}$ replaces solution x_i in ND_e. In other words, the *interactive run module* shifts each solution in ND_e in the direction between the Bliss point and the Feasible Bliss point in the objective space.

In Figure 2(right), we show the non-dominated set of Figure 2(left) after calling the *interactive run module*. It is clear that the non-dominated set is almost the actual non-dominated set of the problem. This illustrates that this approach is quite efficient in pushing a sub-optimal non-dominated set to the actual non-dominated set. We may note here that the scale of the figure changes automatically because it allows better visualization of the points to the decision maker. This may have a negative effect if the decision maker does not realize the large shifts in the curve, but this problem can be overcome by training the user on the system; otherwise if we leave the scale unchanged, the curve can become very small and hard to see.

4.3 The Sample Bliss Module

The *sample Bliss module* is where the user interaction plays the main role in biasing the search. Here, the user needs to specify two Bliss points B_1 and B_2. The user specifies these bliss points by either typing the required Bliss values in the specified text boxes in the interface or by clicking on the required area in the Graphical interface. Once B_1 and B_2 are specified, the user is allowed to call the *Sample Bliss Module*, where a population of Bliss points is generated within the interval $[B_1, B_2]$. For each of these Bliss points, a global optimization problem is constructed similar to the one presented in the *run bliss point module* and the corresponding feasible Bliss point is calculated and added to a list of feasible Bliss points.

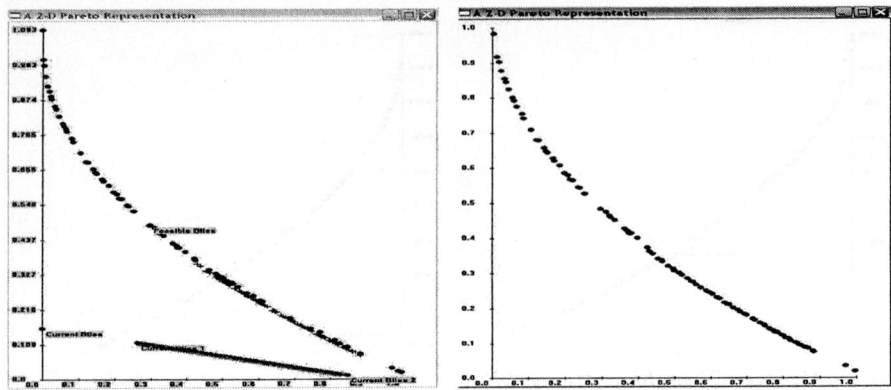

Fig. 3. On left: Filling the gaps in the non-dominated set found by the evolutionary method using the *sample Bliss module*. On right: The new non-dominated front after accepting the solutions resultant from running the *sample Bliss module*.

Another possible use for the *sample Bliss module* is to fill gaps in the non-dominated set found because of genetic drift in the EMO method. We can see in Figure 2(right) a gap in the lower right side of the non-dominated front. In Figure 3(left), we show a sample of Bliss points being generated after the user has chosen two bliss points: *Current Bliss 1* and *Current Bliss 2*. The Bliss points are marked with "x" while the corresponding feasible solutions are marked with "+". The power of the method is clear from this Figure, where the gap in the Pareto set is filled and a better distribution of solutions around the Pareto front is generated.

4.4 The Accept Module

If the user is happy with the feasible Bliss points being generated by the *sample Bliss module*, she can then accepts this list and adds it to the archive. Figure 3(right) depicts the new non-dominated front after the user has accepted the solutions resultant from the *sample Bliss module*.

Overall, the contribution of the method is two folds. One is a mechanism for formulating a series of global optimization problems to improve the quality of efficient solutions obtained by the EMO method. The second is a mechanism for involving the decision maker to guide the evolutionary method as close as possible to the Pareto set; thus overcoming the drawbacks in exiting EMO.

5 Example 2: Discontinuous Pareto-Front

In this section, we will use ZDT3 defined as follows:

$$f_1(x) = x_1$$

$$f_2(x) = g * (1 - \sqrt{\frac{f_1}{g}} - \frac{f_1}{g}\sin(10\pi f_1))$$

$$g = 1 + 9 \times \frac{(\sum_{i=2}^{n} x_i)}{(n-1)}$$

$$x_i \in [0,1], i = 1, \ldots, 30$$

Figures 4,5 demonstrate a different case from the first example. Here, we still used a combination of evolutionary parameters that produce a non-dominated set that is quiet far from the actual one as shown in Figure 4 on the left. After calling the interactive run module, as the solutions are pushed hard toward the Pareto front, the archive lost spread of solutions. The idea here is to demonstrate that when solution spread is lost, we can still overcome this problem through interaction. Once more, the same bliss module is used for 3 rounds of interaction to fill the gaps and the results are presented in Figure 5. This example also demonstrates that the approach is suitable to ensure that a discontinuous Pareto front can be generated easily.

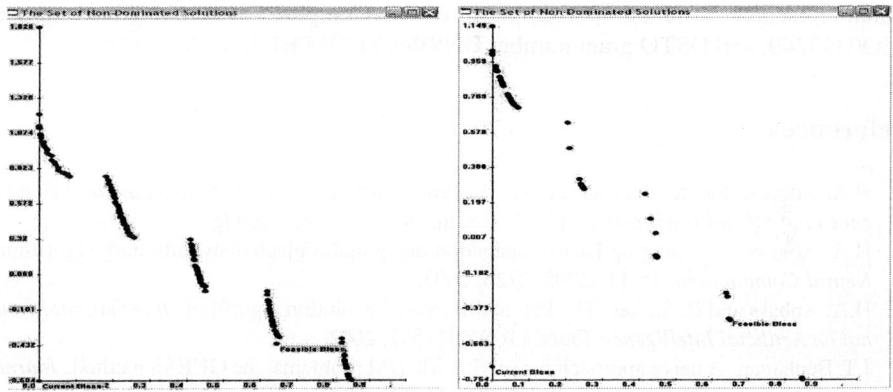

Fig. 4. On left: The initial Pareto front for ZDT3. On right: the Pareto front after running the *interactive run module*.

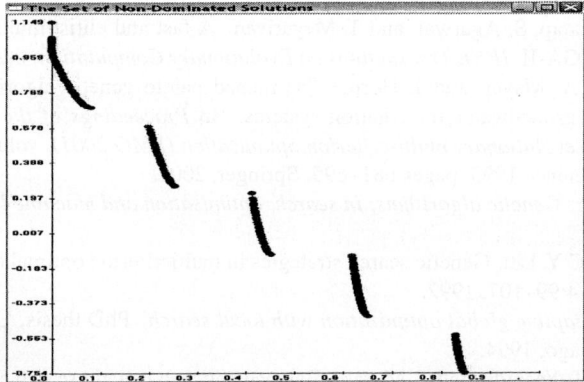

Fig. 5. The final Pareto front after 3 rounds of interaction using the *sample Bliss module*.

6 Conclusions

In this paper, we presented an interactive approach for assisting the decision maker in refining solutions obtained by evolutionary multiobjective methods. The visualization of Pareto solutions reduces the cognitive cost of inspecting the solutions. Although we have presented the approach using the PDE method, other evolutionary methods such as PAES, SPEA2, or NSGA II can be coded very easily into the software. Our main objective here was not to introduce a new method, but to introduce a generic interactive framework that can be potentially useful for any Pareto evolutionary multiobjective method. Currently, we are investigating the use of this approach in real life applications.

Acknowledgment

This work is supported by the University of New South Wales grant PS04411, the Australian Research Council (ARC) Centre on Complex Systems grant number CEO0348249, and DSTO grant number UNSWA ZCOM RE228 RM01821.

References

1. H.A. Abbass. Pareto neuro-ensemble. In *Proceedings of the 16th Australian Joint Conference on Artificial Intelligence (AI'03)*, Berlin, 2003. Springer-Verlag.
2. H.A. Abbass. Speeding up back-propagation using multiobjective evolutionary algorithms. *Neural Computation*, 15(11):2705–2726, 2003.
3. H.A. Abbass and R. Sarker. The Pareto differential evolution algorithm. *International Journal on Artificial Intelligence Tools*, 11(4):531–552, 2002.
4. J.T. Buchanan. A naïve approach for solving MCDM problems: the GUESS method. *Journal of the Operations Research Society*, 48(2):202–206, 1997.
5. F. Clarke. *Optimization and Nonsmooth Analysis*. John Wiley & Sons, New York, 1983.
6. C.A. Coello, D.A. Van Veldhuizen, and G.B. Lamont. *Evolutionary Algorithms for Solving Multi-Objective Problems*. Kluwer Academic publishers, New York, 2002.
7. K. Deb. *Multi-objective optimization using evolutionary algorithms*. John Wiley & Sons,, New York, 2001.
8. K. Deb, A. Pratap, S. Agarwal, and T. Meyarivan. A fast and elitist multiobjective genetic algorithm: NSGA-II. *IEEE Transactions on Evolutionary Computation*, 6(2):182–197, 2002.
9. M. Erickson, A. Mayer, and J. Horn. The niched pareto genetic algorithm 2 applied to the design of groundwater remediation systems. In *Proceedings of the 1st international conference on evolutionary multi-criterion optimization (EMO 2001)*, volume Lecture notes in computer science,1993, pages 681–695. Springer, 2001.
10. D.E. Goldberg. *Genetic algorithms: in search, optimisation and machine learning*. Addison Wesely, 1989.
11. P. Hajela and C.Y. Lin. Genetic search strategies in multicriterion optimal design. *Structural Optimization*, 4:99–107, 1992.
12. W.E. Hart. *Adaptive global optimization with local search*. PhD thesis, University of California, San Diago, 1994.
13. H. Ishibuchi, T. Yoshida, and T. Murata. Balance between genetic search and local search in memetic algorithms for multiobjective permutation flowshop scheduling. *IEEE transactions on evolutionary computation*, 7(2):204–223, 2003.

14. J. Knowles and D. Corne. Approximating the nondominated front using the pareto archived evolution strategy. *Evolutionary Computation*, 8(2):149–172, 2000.
15. F. Menczer, M. Degeratu, and W.N. Street. Efficient and scalable pareto optimization by evolutionary local selection algorithms. *Evolutionary computation*, 8(2):223–247, 2000.
16. J.D. Schaffer. Multiple objective optimization with vector evaluated genetic algorithms. *Genetic Algorithms and their Applications: Proceedings of the First International Conference on Genetic Algorithms*, pages 93–100, 1985.
17. K.C. Tan, T.H. Lee, and E.F. Khor. Evolutionary algorithms for multi-objective optimization: performance assessments and comparisons. In *Proceedings of the 2001 congress on evolutionary computation (CEC 2001)*, pages 979–986. IEEE press, 2001.
18. A. Törn and A. Žilinskas. Global optimization. In G. Goos and J. Hartmanis, editors, *Lecturer Notes in Computer Science*. Springer-Verlag, 1987.
19. J. Teo and H.A. Abbass. Trading-off mind complexity and locomotion in a physically simulated quadruped. In L. Wang, K.C. Tan, T. Furuhashi, J.H. Kim, and X. Yao, editors, *Proceedings of the 4th Asia-Pacific Conference on Simulated Evolution And Learning (SEAL'02)*, volume 2, pages 776–780, 2002.
20. B. Thomas. *Evolutionary algorithms in theory and practice*. Oxford university press, 1996.
21. B. Thomas, F. David, and M. Zbigniew. *Handbook of evolutionary computation*. Institute of physics publishing and Oxford University, 1997.
22. E.L. Ulungu, J. Teghem, P.H. Fortemps, and D. Tuyttens. MOSA method: a tool for solving multiobjective combinatorial optimization problems. *Journal of multicriteria decision analysis*, 8:221–236, 1999.
23. M. Zeleny. Multiple criteria decision making: Eight concepts of optimality. *Human Systems Management*, 17:97–107, 1998.
24. E. Zitzler, K. deb, and L. Thiele. Comparison of multiobjective evolutionary algorithms: empirical results. *Evolutionary Computation*, 8(2):173–195, 2000.
25. E. Zitzler and L. Thiele. Multiobjective evolutionary algorithms: A comparative case study and the strength pareto approach. *IEEE Transactions on Evolutionary Computation*, 3(4):257–271, 1999.

Finding Knees in Multi-objective Optimization

Jürgen Branke[1], Kalyanmoy Deb[2], Henning Dierolf[1], and Matthias Osswald[1]

[1] Institute AIFB, University of Karlsruhe, Germany
branke@aifb.uni-karlsruhe.de
[2] Department of Mechanical Engineering, IIT Kanpur, India
deb@iitk.ac.in

Abstract. Many real-world optimization problems have several, usually conflicting objectives. Evolutionary multi-objective optimization usually solves this predicament by searching for the whole Pareto-optimal front of solutions, and relies on a decision maker to finally select a single solution. However, in particular if the number of objectives is large, the number of Pareto-optimal solutions may be huge, and it may be very difficult to pick one "best" solution out of this large set of alternatives. As we argue in this paper, the most interesting solutions of the Pareto-optimal front are solutions where a small improvement in one objective would lead to a large deterioration in at least one other objective. These solutions are sometimes also called "knees". We then introduce a new modified multi-objective evolutionary algorithm which is able to focus search on these knee regions, resulting in a smaller set of solutions which are likely to be more relevant to the decision maker.

1 Introduction

Many real-world optimization problems involve multiple objectives which need to be considered simultaneously. As these objectives are usually conflicting, it is not possible to find a single solution which is optimal with respect to all objectives. Instead, there exist a number of so called "Pareto-optimal" solutions which are characterized by the fact that an improvement in any one objective can only be obtained at the expense of degradation in at least one other objective. Therefore, in the absence of any additional preference information, none of the Pareto-optimal solutions can be said to be inferior when compared to any other solution, as it is superior in at least one criterion.

In order to come up with a single solution, at some point during the optimization process, a decision maker (DM) has to make a choice regarding the importance of different objectives. Following a classification by Veldhuizen [16], the articulation of preferences may be done either before (a priori), during (progressive), or after (a posteriori) the optimization process.

A priori approaches basically transform the multi-objective optimization problem into a single objective problem by specifying a utility function over all different criteria. However, they are usually not practicable, since they require the user to explicitly and exactly weigh the different objectives before any alternatives are known.

Most Evolutionary Multi-Objective Optimization (EMO) approaches can be classified as a posteriori. They attempt to discover the whole set of Pareto-optimal solutions or, if there are too many, at least a well distributed set of representatives. Then, the decision maker has to look at this potentially huge set of Pareto-optimal alternative solutions and make a choice. Naturally, in particular if the number of objectives is high, this is a difficult task, and a lot of research has been done to support the decision maker during this selection step, see e.g. [14].

Hybrids between a priori and a posteriori approaches are also possible. In this case, the DM specifies his/her preferences as good as possible and provides imprecise goals. These can then be used by the EMO algorithm to bias or guide the search towards the solutions which have been classified as "interesting" by the DM (see e.g. [2, 9, 1]). This results in a smaller set of more (to the DM) interesting solutions, but it requires the DM to provide a priori knowledge.

The idea of this paper to do without a priori knowledge and instead to "guess" what solutions might be most interesting for a decision maker. Let us consider the simple Pareto-optimal front depicted in Figure 1, with two objectives to be minimized. This front has a clearly visible bump in the middle, which is called a "knee". Without any knowledge about the user's preferences, it may be argued that the region around that knee is most likely to be interesting for the DM. First of all, these solutions are characterized by the fact that a small improvement in either objective will cause a large deterioration in the other objective, which makes moving in either direction not very attractive. Also, if we assume linear preference functions, and (due to the lack of any other information) furthermore assume that each preference function is equally likely, the solutions at the knee are most likely to be the optimal choice of the DM. Note that in Figure 1, due to the concavity at the edges, similar reasoning holds for the extreme solutions (edges), which is why these should be considered knees as well.

In this paper, we present two modifications to EMO which allow to focus search on the aforementioned knees, resulting in a potentially smaller set of solutions which, however, are likely to be more relevant to the DM.

The paper is structured as follows: In the following section, we briefly review some related work. Then, Section 3 describes our proposed modifications. The new approaches are evaluated empirically in Section 4. The paper concludes with a summary and some ideas for future work.

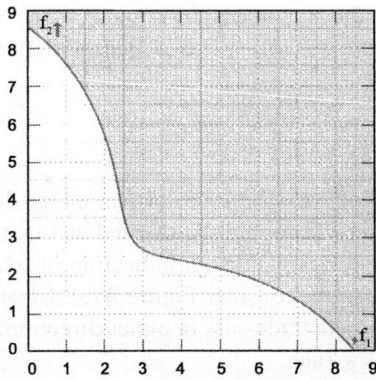

Fig. 1. A simple Pareto-optimal front with a knee.

2 Related Work

Evolutionary multi-objective optimization is a very active research area. For comprehensive books on the topic, the reader is referred to [8, 4].

The problem of selecting a solution from the set of Pareto-optimal solutions has been discussed before. Typical methods for selection are the compromise programming approach [17], the marginal rate of substitution approach [15], or the pseudo-weight vector approach [8].

The importance of knees has been stressed before by different authors, see e.g. [15, 9, 6]. In [14], an algorithm is proposed which determines the relevant knee points based on a given set of non-dominated solutions.

The idea to focus on knees and thereby to better reflect user preferences is also somewhat related to the idea of explicitly integrating user preferences into EMO approaches, see e.g. [3, 1, 5, 12].

3 Focusing on Knees

In this section, we will describe two modifications which allow the EMO-approach to focus on the knee regions, which we have argued are, given no additional knowledge, the most likely to be relevant to the DM.

We base our modifications on NSGA-II [10], one of today's standard EMO approaches. EMO approaches have to achieve two things: they have to quickly converge towards the Pareto-optimal front, and they have to maintain a good spread of solutions on that front. NSGA-II achieves that by relying on two measures when comparing individuals (e.g. for selection and deletion): The first is the non-domination rank, which measures how close an individual is to the non-dominated front. An individual with a lower rank (closer to the front) is always preferred to an individual with a higher rank. If two individuals have the same non-domination rank, as a secondary criterion, a crowding measure is used, which prefers individuals which are in rather deserted areas of the front. More precisely, for each individual the cuboid length is calculated, which is the sum of distances between an individual's two closest neighbors in each dimension. The individuals with greater cuboid length are then preferred.

Our approach modifies the secondary criterion, and replaces the cuboid length by either an angle-based measure or a utility-based measure. These will be described in the following subsections.

3.1 Angle-Based Focus

In the case of only two objectives, the trade-offs in either direction can be estimated by the slopes of the two lines through an individual and its two neighbors. The angle between these slopes can be regarded as an indication of whether the individual is at a knee or not. For an illustration, consider Figure 2 (a). Clearly, the larger the angle α between the lines, the worse the trade-offs in either direction, and the more clearly the solution can be classified as a knee.

More formally, to calculate the angle measure for a particular individual x_i, we calculate the angle between the individual and its two neighbors, i.e. between (x_{i-1}, x_i)

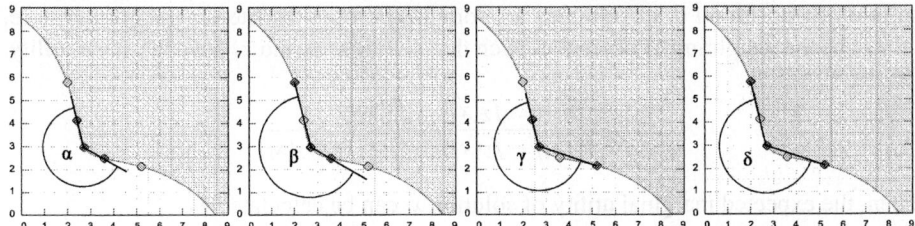

Fig. 2. Calculation of the angle measure. The standard version just calculates α, the intensified version takes 4 neighbors into account and calculates the maximum of $\alpha, \beta, \gamma,$ and δ.

and (x_i, x_{i+1}). These three individuals have to be pairwise linearly independent, thus duplicate individuals (individuals with the same objective function values, which are not prevented in NSGA-II per se) are treated as one and are assigned the same angle-measure. If no neighbor to the left (right) is found, a vertical (horizontal) line is used to calculate the angle. Similar to the standard cuboid-length measure, individuals with a larger angle-measure are preferred.

To intensify the focus on the knee area, we also suggest a variant which uses four neighbors (two in either direction) instead of two. In that case, four angles are computed, using on either side either the closest or the second closest neighbor (cf. angles $\alpha, \beta, \gamma, \delta$ in Figure 2). The largest of these four angles is then assigned to the individual.

Calculating the angle measure in 2D is efficient. For more than two objectives, however, it becomes impractical even to just find the neighbors. Thus, we restrict our examination of the angle-based focus to problems with two objectives only. The utility-based focus presented in this section, however, can be extended to any number of objectives.

3.2 Utility-Based Focus

An alternative measure for a solution's relevance could be the expected marginal utility that solution provides to a decision maker, assuming linear utility functions of the form $U(x, \lambda) = \lambda f_1(x) + (1-\lambda) f_2(x)$, with all $\lambda \in [0, 1]$ being equally likely. For illustration, let us first assume we would know that the DM has a particular preference function $U(x, \lambda')$, with some known λ'. Then, we could calculate, for each individual x_i in the population, the DM's utility $U(x_i, \lambda')$ of that individual. Clearly, given the choice among all individuals in the population, the DM would select the one with the highest utility. Now let us define an individual's marginal utility $U'(x, \lambda')$ as the additional cost the DM would have to accept if that particular individual would not be available and he/she would have to settle for the second best, i.e.

$$U'(x_i, \lambda') = \begin{cases} \min_{j \neq i} U(x_j, \lambda') - U(x_i, \lambda') & : \quad i = \arg\min U(x_j, \lambda') \\ 0 & : \quad \text{otherwise} \end{cases}$$

The utility measure we propose here assumes a distribution of utility functions uniform in the parameter λ in order to calculate the expected marginal utility. For the case of only two objectives, the expected marginal utility can be calculated exactly by integrating over all possible linear utility functions as follows: Let us denote with x_i the solution on position i if all solutions are sorted according to criterion f_1. Furthermore, let $\lambda_{i,j}$ be the weighting of objectives such that solutions x_i and x_j have the same utility, i.e.

$$\lambda_{i,j} = \frac{f_2(x_j) - f_2(x_i)}{f_1(x_i) - f_1(x_j) + f_2(x_j) - f_2(x_i)}$$

Then, the expected marginal utility of solution x_i can be calculated as

$$E(U'(x_i,\lambda)) = \int_{\alpha=\lambda_{i-1,i}}^{\lambda_{i-1,i+1}} \alpha(f_1(x_i) - f_1(x_{i-1})) + (1-\alpha)(f_2(x_i) - f_2(x_{i-1}))d\alpha$$
$$+ \int_{\alpha=\lambda_{i-1,i+1}}^{\lambda_{i,i+1}} \alpha(f_1(x_i) - f_1(x_{i-1})) + (1-\alpha)(f_2(x_i) - f_2(x_{i-1}))d\alpha$$

Unlike the angle measure, the utility measure extends easily to more than two objectives, by defining $U(x,\lambda) = \sum \lambda_i f_i(x)$ with $\sum \lambda_i = 1$. The expected marginal utilities can be approximated simply by sampling, i.e. by calculating the marginal utility for all individuals for a number of randomly chosen utility functions, and taking the average as expected marginal utility. Sampling can be done either randomly or, as we have done in order to reduce variance, in a systematic manner (equi-distant values for λ). We call the number of utility functions used for approximation *precision* of the measure. From our experience, we would recommend a precision of at least the number of individuals in the population.

Naturally, individuals with the largest overall marginal utility are preferred. Note, however, that the assumption of linear utility functions makes it impossible to find knees in concave regions of the non-dominated front.

4 Empirical Evaluation

Let us now demonstrate the effectiveness of our approach on some test problems. The test problems are based on the DTLZ ones [11, 7]. Let n denote the number of decision variables (we use $n = 30$ below), and K be a parameter which allows to control the number of knees in the problem, generating K knees in a problem with two objectives.

Then, the DO2DK test problem is defined as follows:

$$\min f_1(x) = g(x)r(x_1)\left(\sin\left(\pi x_1/2^{s+1}\right) + \left(1 + \frac{2^s - 1}{2^{s+2}}\right)\pi\right) + 1\right)$$
$$\min f_2(x) = g(x)r(x_1)(\cos(\pi x_1/2 + \pi) + 1)$$
$$g(x) = 1 + \frac{9}{n-1}\sum_{i=2}^{n} x_i$$
$$r(x_1) = 5 + 10(x_1 - 0.5)^2 + \frac{1}{K}\cos(2K\pi x_1) \cdot 2^{\frac{s}{2}}$$
$$0 \leq x_i \leq 1 \quad i = 1, 2, \ldots, n$$

The parameter s in that function skews the front.

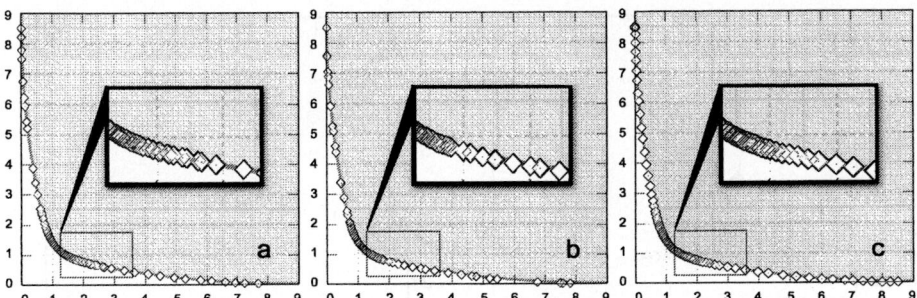

Fig. 3. Comparison of NSGA-II with (a) angle-measure, (b) 4-angle-measure and (c) utility-measure on a simple test problem.

Let us first look at an instance with a very simple front which is convex and has a single knee, using the parameters $K = 1, n = 30$, and $s = 0$. Figure 3 compares the non-dominated front obtained after running NSGA-II with the three proposed methods, the angle-measure, the 4-angle-measure, and the utility-measure for 10 generations with a population size of 200. As can be seen, all three methods clearly focus on the knee. The run based on the utility-measure has the best (most regular) distribution of individuals on the front. As expected, the 4-angle-measure puts a stronger focus on the knee than the standard angle-measure.

Now let us increase the number of knees ($K = 4$) and skew the front ($s = 1.0$). The non-dominated front obtained after 10 generations with a population size of 100 is depicted in Figure 4. As can be seen, both measures allow to discover all knees. The utility-measure shows a wider distribution at the shallow knees, while the angle-based measure emphasizes the stronger knees, and also has a few solutions reaching into the concave regions.

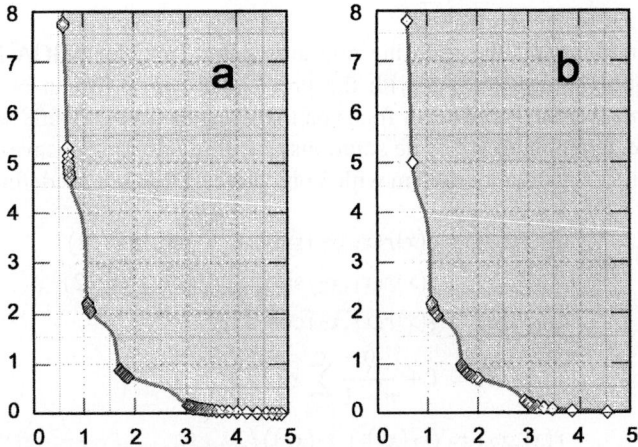

Fig. 4. Comparison of NSGA-II with (a) utility-measure and (b) angle-based measure on a test problem with several knees. Populations size is 100, result after 10 generations, for utility-measure a precision of 100 was used.

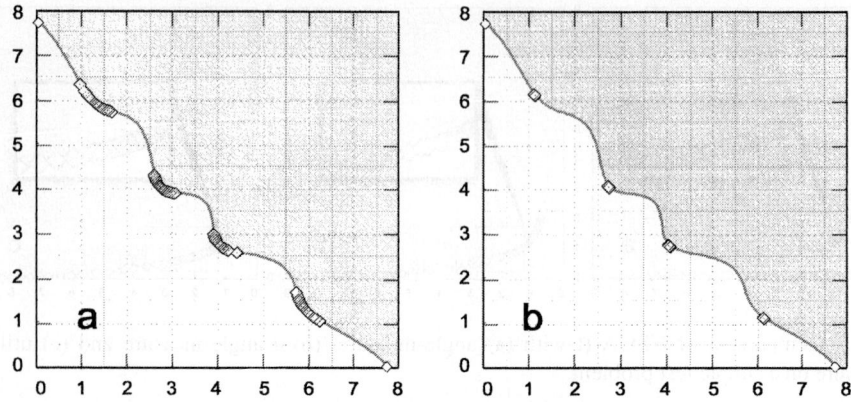

Fig. 5. Comparison of NSGA-II with (a) angle-measure and (b) utility-measure on a test problem with several knees. Populations size is 200, result after 15 generations, for utility-measure a precision of 100 was used.

The DEB2DK problem is similar, but concave at the edges of the Pareto front. It is defined as follows:

$$\min f_1(x) = g(x)r(x_1)\sin(\pi x_1/2)$$
$$\min f_2(x) = g(x)r(x_1)\cos(\pi x_1/2)$$
$$g(x) = 1 + \frac{9}{n-1}\sum_{i=2}^{n} x_i$$
$$r(x_1) = 5 + 10(x_1 - 0.5)^2 + \frac{1}{K}\cos(2K\pi x_1)$$
$$0 \leq x_i \leq 1 \quad i = 1, 2, \ldots, n$$

Figure 5 again compares the resulting non-dominated front for NSGA-II with angle-measure and utility-measure. As with the previous function, it can be seen that the utility-based measure has a stronger focus on the tip of the knees, while with the angle-based measure, again there are some solutions reaching into the concave regions.

Finally, let us consider a problem with 3 objectives. DEB3DK is defined as follows:

$$\min f_1(x) = g(x)r(x_1,x_2)\sin(\pi x_1/2)\sin(\pi x_2/2)$$
$$\min f_2(x) = g(x)r(x_1,x_2)\sin(\pi x_1/2)\cos(\pi x_2/2)$$
$$\min f_3(x) = g(x)r(x_1,x_2)\cos(\pi x_1/2)$$
$$g(x) = 1 + \frac{9}{n-1}\sum_{i=2}^{n} x_i$$
$$r(x_1,x_2) = (r_1(x_1) + r_2(x_2))/2$$
$$r_i(x_i) = 5 + 10(x_i - 0.5)^2 + \frac{2}{K}\cos(2K\pi x_i)$$
$$0 \leq x_i \leq 1 \quad i = 1, 2, \ldots, n$$

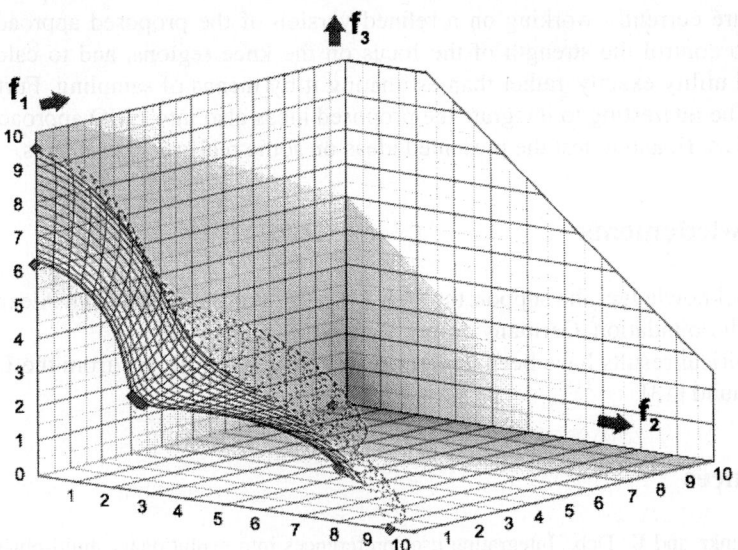

Fig. 6. NSGA-II with utility-measure on a 3-objective problem with knees. Populations size is 150, result after 20 generations, precision is 100.

Note that this test problem can also be extended to more than three objectives as it is based on the DTLZ functions. The number of knees then increases as K^{M-1}, where M is the number of objectives.

Since with three objectives, only the utility-based measure can be used, Figure 6 only shows the resulting non-dominated front for that approach. Again, NSGA-II with utility-measure is able to find all the knee points.

5 Conclusions

Most EMO approaches attempt at finding all Pareto-optimal solutions. But that leaves the decision maker (DM) with the challenge to select the best solution out of the potentially huge set of Pareto-optimal alternatives. In this paper, we have argued that, without further knowledge, the knee points of the Pareto-optimal front are likely to be the most relevant to the DM. Consequently, we have then presented and compared two different ways to focus the search of the EA to these knee regions.

The basic idea was to replace NSGA-II's cuboid length measure, which is used to favor individuals in sparse regions, by an alternative measure, which favors individuals in knee regions. Two such measures have been proposed, one based on the angle to neighboring individuals, another one based on marginal utility.

As has been shown empirically, either method was able to focus search on the knee regions of the Pareto-optimal front, resulting in a smaller number of potentially more interesting solutions. The utility-measure seemed to yield slightly better results and is easily extendable to any number of objectives.

We are currently working on a refined version of the proposed approach, which allows to control the strength of the focus on the knee regions, and to calculate the marginal utility exactly, rather than estimating it by means of sampling. Furthermore, it would be interesting to integrate the proposed ideas also into EMO approaches other than NSGA-II, and to test the presented ideas on some real-world problems.

Acknowledgments

K. Deb acknowledges the support through Bessel Research Award from Alexander von Humboldt Foundation, Germany during the course of this study.
The empirical results have been generated using the KEA library from the University of Dortmund [13].

References

1. J. Branke and K. Deb. Integrating user preferences into evolutionary multi-objective optimization. In Y. Jin, editor, *Knowledge Incorporation in Evolutionary Computation*. Springer, to appear.
2. J. Branke, T. Kaußler, and H. Schmeck. Guidance in evolutionary multi-objective optimization. *Advances in Engineering Software*, 32:499–507, 2001.
3. J. Branke, T. Kaußler, and H. Schmeck. Guidance in evolutionary multi-objective optimization. *Advances in Engineering Software*, 32(6):499–508, 2001.
4. C. A. Coello Coello, D. A. Van Veldhuizen, and G. B. Lamont. *Evolutionary Algorithms for Solving Multi-Objective Problems*. Kluwer, 2002.
5. D. Cvetković and I. C. Parmee. Preferences and their Application in Evolutionary Multiobjective Optimisation. *IEEE Transactions on Evolutionary Computation*, 6(1):42–57, February 2002.
6. I. Das. On characterizing the 'knee' of the pareto curve based on normal-boundary intersection. *Structural Optimization*, 18(2/3):107–115, 1999.
7. K. Deb. Multi-objective genetic algorithms: Problem difficulties and construction of test problems. *Evolutionary Computation Journal*, 7(3):205–230, 1999.
8. K. Deb. *Multi-objective optimization using evolutionary algorithms*. Chichester, UK: Wiley, 2001.
9. K. Deb. Multi-objective evolutionary algorithms: Introducing bias among Pareto-optimal solutions. In A. Ghosh and S. Tsutsui, editors, *Advances in Evolutionary Computing: Theory and Applications*, pages 263–292. London: Springer-Verlag, 2003.
10. K. Deb, S. Agrawal, A. Pratap, and T. Meyarivan. A fast and elitist multi-objective genetic algorithm: NSGA-II. *IEEE Transactions on Evolutionary Computation*, 6(2):182–197, 2002.
11. K. Deb, L. Thiele, M. Laumanns, and E. Zitzler. Scalable multi-objective optimization test problems. In *Proceedings of the Congress on Evolutionary Computation (CEC-2002)*, pages 825–830, 2002.
12. G. W. Greenwood, X. S. Hu, and J. G. D'Ambrosio. Fitness Functions for Multiple Objective Optimization Problems: Combining Preferences with Pareto Rankings. In Richard K. Belew and Michael D. Vose, editors, *Foundations of Genetic Algorithms 4*, pages 437–455, San Mateo, California, 1997. Morgan Kaufmann.
13. Ls11. The Kea-Project (v. 1.0). University of Dortmund, Informatics Department, online: http://ls11-www.cs.uni-dortmund.de, 2003.

14. C. A. Mattson, A. A. Mullur, and A. Messac. Minimal representation of multiobjective design space using a smart pareto filter. In *AIAA/ISSMO Symposium on Multidisciplinary Analysis and Optimization*, 2002.
15. K. Miettinen. *Nonlinear Multiobjective Optimization*. Kluwer, Boston, 1999.
16. D. Van Veldhuizen and G. B. Lamont. Multiobjective evolutionary algorithms: Analyzing the state-of-the-art. *Evolutionary Computation Journal*, 8(2):125–148, 2000.
17. P. L. Yu. A class of solutions for group decision problems. *Management Science*, 19(8):936–946, 1973.

Multi-objective Parallel Tabu Search

Daniel Jaeggi, Chris Asselin-Miller, Geoff Parks, Timoleon Kipouros,
Theo Bell, and John Clarkson

Engineering Design Centre, Cambridge University Engineering Department,
Trumpington Street, Cambridge CB2 1PZ, UK

Abstract. This paper describes the implementation of a parallel Tabu Search algorithm for multi-objective continuous optimisation problems. We compare our new algorithm with a leading multi-objective Genetic Algorithm and find it exhibits comparable performance on standard benchmark problems. In addition, for certain problem types, we expect Tabu Search to outperform other algorithms and present preliminary results from an aerodynamic shape optimisation problem. This is a real-world, highly constrained, computationally demanding design problem which requires efficient optimisation algorithms that can be run on parallel computers: with this approach optimisation algorithms are able to play a part in the design cycle.

1 Introduction

1.1 Background

In recent years, there has been a large amount of interest in meta-heuristic optimisation techniques. These have proved effective in solving complex, real-world optimisation problems with many local minima, problems to which traditional, gradient-based methods are ill suited. Four significant methods to have emerged are Simulated Annealing (SA), Genetic Algorithms (GA), Evolution Strategies (ES) and Tabu Search (TS) [1]. Each of these methods has been successfully applied to single-objective combinatorial and continuous optimisation problems. Other meta-heuristics such as Ant Colony Optimisation, Variable Neighbourhood Search and Greedy Randomised Adaptive Search Procedures have been shown to be effective in single-objective combinatorial optimisation problems [2].

With increases in computing power and the realisation that most real-world design problems involve compromises between conflicting objectives, there has been much recent interest in developing multi-objective optimisation algorithms. The first multi-objective GA was developed in 1985 and research in this field has been very active [3]. Similarly, multi-objective SA algorithms have also been developed [4]. However, very little work has been done on multi-objective TS algorithms. Jones et al. [1] surveyed 115 articles concerned with multi-objective meta-heuristics: they found 70% of the articles used GA or ES as the primary meta-heuristic, 24% SA and 6% TS.

1.2 Motivation

In this work we have developed a multi-objective TS code for continuous optimisation problems and compared its performance with a leading multi-objective GA. Over a variety of test functions, we find that we achieve comparable performance. Our multi-objective TS also lends itself naturally to a parallel implementation.

Our motivation for this development is our interest in aerodynamic shape optimisation problems. Such problems have high computational demands, are highly constrained, and cannot be solved by gradient-based methods due to the lack of gradient information and the large number of local minima. Previous research on a single-objective aerodynamic problem had found TS to be a particularly effective optimisation algorithm for this application domain [5].

2 Existing Multi-objective TS Algorithms

2.1 The Multi-objective Problem and Pareto Equivalence

We consider a problem where multiple objective functions are each to be minimised. The solution to such a problem is a set of solutions representing the optimal set of trade-offs between the objectives. This set is known as the *Pareto optimal* (PO) set: solutions in the set are said to be *Pareto equivalent* (PE) to each other and non-dominated by any other solution. If c_n is the vector of objective function values for design point x_n, x_n is said to be PE to another point x_m if some components of c_n are larger than the corresponding components of c_m while other components of c_n are smaller than the corresponding components of c_m. Similarly, x_n dominates x_m if all components of c_n are less than or equal to the corresponding components of c_m and at least one component is less.

2.2 Solving the Multi-objective Optimisation Problem

There are two fundamentally different approaches to solving this problem. The first reduces the multi-objective problem to a single-objective one by generating a composite objective $g(x)$ from a (usually) linear sum of the multiple objectives $f_i(x)$:

$$g(x) = \sum_{i=1}^{n} W_i f_i(x)$$

This function can be optimised using existing single-objective optimisers. However, the weights W_i (which by convention are non-negative and sum to unity) must be pre-set, and the solution to this problem will be a single vector of control variables rather than the entire PO set. This can have undesirable consequences: setting the weights implicitly introduces the designer's preconceptions about the relative trade-off between objectives. Real-world problems can produce surprising PO sets which may profoundly affect design decisions, and the potential to generate novel designs is a key benefit of optimisation [4].

The second approach to solving the multi-objective problem is to search directly for the entire PO set. This can be achieved in a number of ways and requires modification to existing single-objective algorithms.

The authors know of only two attempts to produce a multi-objective TS algorithm which finds multiple PO solutions in a single run. Hansen's algorithm [6] is an extension of the composite objective approach: his algorithm performs a number of composite objective Tabu searches in parallel. Each search has a different and dynamically updated set of weights, and in this way the search can be driven to explore the entire Pareto front. This algorithm, although a good implementation of TS, suffers the one problem common to all weighted-sum approaches: for problems with concave Pareto fronts, there may be regions of the front that are not defined by a combination of weights and certain combinations of weights represent two points on the front. Thus, this algorithm may not adequately locate the entire PO set.

Baykasoglu *et al.* [7] developed a TS algorithm combining a downhill local search with an *intensification memory* (IM) to store non-dominated points that were not selected in the search. When the search fails to find a downhill move, a point from the IM is selected instead. When the IM is empty and all search paths exhausted, the algorithm stops. This cannot be considered a true TS algorithm: in restricting the search to only downhill moves they reject one of the basic tenets of TS, that "a bad strategic choice can yield more information than a good random choice" [8]. Also, the lack of any diversification strategy renders the algorithm incomplete and merely an elaborate local search algorithm.

3 Basic Algorithm Description

As a starting point for our multi-objective variant, we use the single-objective TS implementation of Connor and Tilley [9]. This uses a Hooke and Jeeves (H&J) local search algorithm (designed for continuous optimisation problems) [10] coupled with short, medium and long term memories to implement search intensification and diversification as prescribed by Glover and Laguna [8].

TS operates in a sequential, iterative manner: the search starts at a given point and the algorithm selects a new point in the search space to be the next current point. The basic search pattern is the H&J search.

Recently visited points are stored in the *short term memory* (STM) and are tabu – the search is not allowed to revisit these points. Optimal or near-optimal points are stored in the *medium term memory* (MTM) and are used for intensification, focusing the search on areas of the search space with good objective function values. The *long term memory* (LTM) records the regions of the search space which have been explored and is used on diversification, directing the search to regions which are under-explored. This is achieved by dividing each variable into a certain number of regions and counting the number of solutions evaluated in those regions. A local iteration counter i_local is used and reset upon a successful addition to the MTM. When i_local reaches user-specified values, the algorithm will diversify or intensify the search, or reduce the search step size and restart the search from the best solution found.

Thus, TS combines an exhaustive, systematic local search with a stochastic element and an intelligent coverage of the entire search space. Our multi-objective TS implementation of [9] is modified in the following areas:

3.1 Search Point Comparison

In a single-objective optimisation problem, points may be compared using the operators ==, > and < acting on the objective function values for those points. Similarly, points in a multi-objective problem can be compared in the same way (thus preserving the logic of the single-objective algorithm) by using the concepts of Pareto equivalence (==) and dominance (> and <).

The concept of a PO set (see 2.1) allows us to define a container we call a ParetoPointSet, which is central to our algorithm. This container stores points which are PE. A candidate for addition to the set is only added if it is non-dominated by any existing solutions in the set. Upon successful addition to the set, any points which consequently become dominated are removed.

3.2 The Hooke and Jeeves Move

At each iteration, a H&J move is made. $2n\_var$ new points are generated by incrementing and decrementing each design variable by a given step around the current point. The objective functions for each new point are evaluated and, as long as the point is neither tabu (*i.e.* not a member of the STM) nor violates any constraints, it is considered as a candidate for the next point in the search.

In the single-objective TS algorithm, these candidates are sorted and the point with the lowest objective is chosen as the next point. A similar logic can be applied to the multi-objective case: however, the possibility of multiple points being PE and optimal must be allowed for. We use a ParetoPointSet container to store our candidate points. If, after all candidates have been considered for addition, one point remains in the container, it is selected as the next point. If there are multiple points, one is selected at random and the others become candidates for intensification (see 3.4). Thus, our strategy accepts both downhill and uphill moves – the next point is simply the "best" point (or one of the PE best points) selected from the candidate solutions.

In addition, we implement a *pattern move* strategy in the same way as Connor and Tilley [9]. Before every second H&J move, the previous move is repeated. This new point is compared to the current point, and, if it dominates it, is accepted as the next point; if not, the standard H&J move is made. In this way, the search may be accelerated along known downhill directions.

3.3 Optimal Point Archiving and the Medium Term Memory

In Connor's single-objective TS [9], the MTM is a bounded, sorted list of near-optimal solutions. As the concept of a single optimal point does not exist in multi-objective optimisation (see 2.1), we replace the MTM in our multi-objective TS variant by a ParetoPointSet of optimal solutions produced by the search. As new points are evaluated, they become candidates for addition to this set. Thus, the MTM represents the PO set for the problem at that stage in the search.

3.4 Intensification and Restart Strategy

The original single-objective TS produced intensification points by using the MTM to generate points in the neighbourhood of good solutions. Although the replacement of the MTM by a PO set of solutions allows us to use a variant of this strategy, a feature of multi-objective optimisation suggests an alternative strategy, similar to that used by Baykasoglu [7].

A multi-objective H&J iteration may produce multiple PO points (see 3.2). As only one point may be selected as the next point, it seems wasteful to discard the other points. Therefore, we incorporate an intensification memory into our algorithm. This memory is a ParetoPointSet, and unselected PO points are considered as candidates for addition to the set. At search intensification, a point is chosen randomly from the IM. As the IM is a ParetoPointSet, points within it that become dominated by the addition of new points are removed, ensuring it only contains points that are, or are almost, globally Pareto optimal. The single-objective TS restart strategy returns the search to the current best point in the MTM. As this has been replaced by a ParetoPointSet (with multiple PO points), we select a point at random from this set. More intelligent restart strategies are possible [4] and these are under investigation.

4 Search Efficiency Improvements and Parallelisation Strategy

4.1 Improving Local Search Efficiency

The H&J local search strategy requires roughly $2n\_var$ solution evaluations (allowing for points that are tabu or violate constraints) at each step, where n_var is the number of design variables. A real-world problem may contain a large number of variables (the shape optimisation of a Boeing 747 wing required 90 variables [11]) and this strategy could become prohibitively expensive. Our solution to this is to incorporate an element of random sampling in the H&J step.

We generate the $2n\_var$ new points, remove those that are tabu, and only evaluate $n\_sample \leq 2n\_var$ points from those that remain, selecting randomly to avoid introducing any directional bias. If one of these points dominates the current point, it is automatically accepted as the next point. If more than one point dominates the current point, a non-dominated point from these is randomly selected. If no points dominate the current point, a further n_sample points are sampled and the comparison is repeated. If all the feasible, non-tabu points have been sampled without finding a point that dominates the current solution, the standard selection procedure is employed.

This procedure may incur some performance penalty: where there are a number of possible downhill moves, an inferior move may be selected. However, where there is only one downhill move, we would, on average, find this move in fewer function evaluations. As the search progresses, we would expect more instances of the latter situation; thus, any performance penalty would be incurred in the earlier stages of the search, and this procedure should be beneficial on balance.

4.2 Parallelisation Strategy

Any optimisation procedure that forms part of a real-world design cycle must be able to complete in a reasonable time-frame. Parallel processing offers a large potential speed-up; any serious optimisation algorithm should be designed with this in mind, and there are three ways in which TS may be parallelised [8]:

1. *Functional Decomposition* – Operations necessary for each iteration of the search are executed in parallel.
2. *Domain Decomposition* – The search domain is decomposed and individually searched.
3. *Multi-threaded Search* – Several searches are executed in parallel and information is shared between the searches.

All three strategies have advantages and disadvantages, but we can reject domain decomposition immediately: this is likely to perform poorly if the search domain cannot be easily equally divided, as is the case with highly constrained problems.

A multi-threaded TS may give certain performance benefits: coupled parallel search algorithms may give a super-linear speed-up in certain conditions [12]. Hansen's multi-objective TS has also used this strategy successfully [6]. However, it is more complex to implement and the optimal level of information sharing between threads still needs to be determined.

A functionally decomposed TS is straightforward to implement and fits well with H&J search, which requires a number of solution evaluations at each iteration. It does not alter the fundamental TS algorithm used (which is tested and known to perform well [5, 9]), and has the potential to give near optimal parallel speed-up (for problems with costly objective function evaluations).

We have used functional decomposition for our parallel multi-objective TS. We perform parallel objective function evaluations at two stages in the search: at the H&J move and the diversification move. We have implemented the algorithm as a master/slave MPI program with n_slave slave processes. The main search algorithm runs on the master program; the slaves perform the objective function evaluations in parallel. At the H&J move, we set $n\_sample = n\_slave$ (see 4.1) and evaluate each solution on a different slave. On diversification, instead of sampling one point from the design space, we sample n_slave points in parallel and select a non-dominated point from these as the next point.

5 Comparison with a Multi-objective GA

Deb et al. [13] developed a multi-objective GA (NSGA-II) and compared it to other leading multi-objective GAs. They found NSGA-II (in real or binary coded versions) outperformed the other algorithms on a set of nine test problems [13].

We have tested our multi-objective TS (MOTS) on the same nine test problems using the same test conditions as Deb et al.: they allowed a maximum of 25000 solution evaluations and the mean and variance of the performance metrics were calculated from the results of 45 test runs (using the same set of randomly selected random number seeds). We have not optimised the TS parameter settings for the problems: we use the same settings for all problems, and, indeed, our experience shows that MOTS is reasonably robust to the parameter settings chosen. The only exception is the initial step-size setting which must be chosen to give adequate search space coverage: a step of 5-10% of the total parameter range of the problem is normally suitable (from experience). The settings used are shown in Table 1.

Table 1. Tabu search parameter settings.

Parameter	Value	Description
i_d	10	Diversify search when $i\_local == i\_d$
i_i	20	Intensify search when $i\_local == i\_i$
i_r	50	Reduce step sizes and restart when $i\_local == i\_r$
n_stm	20	STM size – the last n_stm visited points are tabu
$n\_regions$	2	In the LTM each variable is divided into $n\_regions$ regions
SS	8%	Initial H&J step size as percentage of variable range
$SSRF$	0.5	Factor by which step sizes are reduced on restart
n_sample	6	Number of points randomly sampled at each H&J move – see 4.1

Tables 2 and 3 show the mean and variance of the convergence and diversity metrics (used by Deb et al.) for real-coded NSGA-II and MOTS on the nine test problems. Real-coded (as opposed to binary-coded) NSGA-II was chosen for comparison, because we are interested in real-coded problems and it cannot be known a priori which NSGA-II variant will perform better on a given problem.

The convergence metric Υ measures the mean distance between the generated PO set and an ideal set (which is known). The diversity metric Δ gives a measure of the spread of the solutions: how close to the extreme ends of the ideal PO set the generated PO set is, and how evenly spaced are the solutions along it. An ideal PO set will have $\Upsilon = 0$ and $\Delta = 0$. A PO set A is better than PO set B if $\Upsilon_A < \Upsilon_B$. If $\Upsilon_A = \Upsilon_B$ then A is better than B if $\Delta_A < \Delta_B$.

6 Discussion

The results in Tables 2 and 3 show that our multi-objective TS outperforms NSGA-II on 5 test functions out of 9. Overall, MOTS performs comparably with NSGA-II over this range of test functions. On problem KUR, MOTS gives a slightly better value of Υ than NSGA-II; however, Δ is worse indicating the PO solutions are less well spread. On problem ZDT4, MOTS performs poorly due to a feature of TS. This problem has 21^9 local PO fronts in the search space

Table 2. Mean (first rows) and variance (second rows) of the Convergence Metric Υ for NSGA-II and MOTS on the nine test problems.

	SCH	FON	POL	KUR	ZDT1	ZDT2	ZDT3	ZDT4	ZDT6
MOTS	0.00323	0.00083	0.01582	0.02763	0.04136	0.06642	0.01540	22.6888	0.37582
	0	0	0.00050	0.00473	0.00082	0.00164	0.00101	10.9659	0.17450
NSGA-II	0.00339	0.00193	0.01555	0.02896	0.03348	0.07239	0.11450	0.51305	0.29656
	0	0	0	0.00002	0.00475	0.03169	0.00794	0.11846	0.01314

Table 3. Mean (first rows) and variance (second rows) of the Diversity Metric Δ for NSGA-II and MOTS on the nine test problems.

	SCH	FON	POL	KUR	ZDT1	ZDT2	ZDT3	ZDT4	ZDT6
MOTS	0.37888	1.12977	1.59330	1.11656	0.77136	0.81349	0.82339	1.00441	0.37216
	0.02516	0.03436	0.01200	0.14368	0.07888	0.03603	0.02247	0.00469	0.26475
NSGA-II	0.47790	0.37807	0.45215	0.41148	0.39031	0.43078	0.73854	0.70261	0.66803
	0.00347	0.00064	0.00287	0.00099	0.00188	0.00472	0.01971	0.06465	0.00992

[13]; TS uses a local search and contains less of a stochastic element than a GA. Thus, TS may become trapped in a local PO front and may not adequately cover the search space. We expect this behaviour to improve in a multi-threaded implementation [12].

This behaviour, which is a disadvantage on ZDT4, is desirable on certain types of problems – such as our aerodynamic applications – where the search space is highly constrained and too much random jumping in search space could lead to unnecessary time being spent evaluating infeasible solutions (which can only be determined after a costly flow simulation).

In addition, Computational Fluid Dynamics (CFD) codes (for the problem types we are interested in) work in an iterative manner and their rate of convergence depends on the quality of the initial solution. Thus, the cost of a function evaluation depends on how close the new point is to an existing solution. The search pattern of the H&J algorithm in our implementation guarantees that most objective function evaluations are close (in design space) to the current search point. This reduces the computational cost of each CFD evaluation [14]. Adjoint methods [11, 14] also offer a potential means of reducing the cost of the function evaluations required at each H&J step.

7 CFD Test Case

We are currently testing our MOTS on an aerodynamic shape optimisation problem. Harvey optimised a turbomachinery compressor blade with a single objective function [5]. We have used the same 26 variable parameterisation scheme and CFD code, but we have modified the problem; we have now defined two objectives – minimisation of the blockage and of the RMS spatial variation of blockage. The blockage measures the extent to which viscous forces restrict the effective flow area in a blade passage and is an important 1D performance measure. The spatial variation of the blockage quantifies its homogeneity - effectively a 2D measure of blade performance.

This is a computationally hard and highly constrained problem [5]. Each solution evaluation takes about 3 minutes on a 2.8 GHz Pentium 4 processor and we are using a 9 node cluster on this problem. The TS parameter settings are: $i\_i = 25$, $i\_d = 75$, $i\_r = 95$, $n\_stm = 15$, $n\_regions = 4$, $SS = 10\%$, $SSRF = 0.5$, and $n\_sample = 8$. Figure 1 shows the Pareto front obtained after 1000 iterations and 36071 function evaluations, all evaluated solutions, and the datum point (an actual blade geometry - used as the search's initial point).

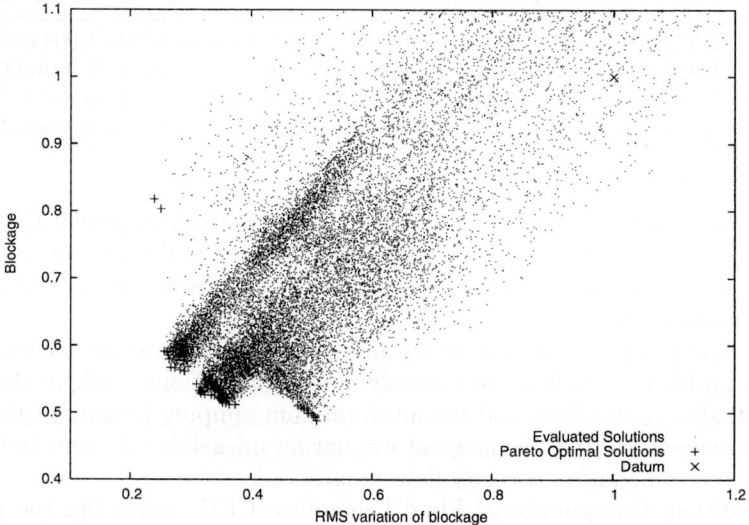

Fig. 1. Pareto front and evaluated solutions for the CFD optimisation problem.

The preliminary results in Fig. 1 show that MOTS can indeed tackle real-world problems. A range of points have been located on a Pareto front and the algorithm appears to be exploring the objective function space thoroughly.

8 Conclusions

In this paper we have successfully developed a true multi-objective, TS-based, parallel optimisation algorithm. Relatively few modifications were required to adapt an existing single-objective TS algorithm for use on multi-objective problems. A number of performance improvements were introduced and various parallelisation strategies were considered. We opted to functionally decompose our problem; however, a multi-threaded scheme may offer performance benefits and this is currently under development.

We have compared the performance of our algorithm with a leading multi-objective GA on a range of bound-constrained test problems. We find that our algorithm performs comparably. We argue that there are other reasons why TS methods should be particularly effective on problems using CFD for objective function evaluation, based on previous work in this group [5] and others [14]. We have presented preliminary results from a two-objective aerodynamic shape optimisation problem currently being run on a 9 node Linux cluster.

Acknowledgements

This research is supported by the UK Engineering and Physical Sciences Research Council (EPSRC) under grant number GR/R64100/01. The authors would also like to thank Prof. Bill Dawes for his support and encouragement.

References

1. Jones, D., Mirrazavi, S., Tamiz, M.: Multi-objective meta-heuristics: An overview of the current state-of-the-art. European Journal of Operational Research **137** (2002) 1–9
2. Blum, C., Roli, A.: Metaheuristics in combinatorial optimization: overview and conceptual comparison. ACM Computing Surveys **35** (2003) 268–308
3. Deb, K.: Multi-Objective Optimization using Evolutionary Algorithms. John Wiley & Sons, Ltd. (2001)
4. Suppapitnarm, A., Seffen, K., Parks, G., Clarkson, J.: A simulated annealing algorithm for multiobjective optimization. Engineering Optimization **33** (2000) 59–85
5. Harvey, S.: The Design Optimisation of Turbomachinery Blade Rows. PhD thesis, Cambridge University Engineering Department (2002)
6. Hansen, M.: Tabu search for multiobjective optimization: MOTS. In: MCDM, Cape Town, South Africa. (1997)
7. Baykasoglu, A., Owen, S., Gindy, N.: A taboo search based approach to find the pareto optimal set in multiple objective optimization. Engineering Optimization **31** (1999) 731–748
8. Glover, F., Laguna, M.: Tabu Search. Kluwer Academic Publishers (1997)
9. Connor, A., Tilley, D.: A tabu search method for the optimisation of fluid power circuits. IMechE Journal of Systems and Control **212** (1998) 373–381
10. Hooke, R., Jeeves, T.: Direct search solution of numerical and statistical problems. Journal of the ACM **8** (1961) 212–229
11. Jameson, A.: A perspective on computational algorithms for aerodynamic analysis and design. Progress in Aerospace Sciences **37** (2001) 197–243
12. Shirts, M., Pande, V.: Mathematical analysis of coupled parallel simulations. Physical Letters Review **86** (2001) 4983–4987
13. Deb, K., Pratap, A., Agarwal, S., Meyarivan, T.: A fast and elitist mulitobjective genetic algorithm: NSGA–II. IEEE Transactions on Evolutionary Computation **6** (2002) 182–197
14. Nemec, M., Zingg, D., Pulliam, T.: Multipoint and multi-objective aerodynamic shape optimization. AIAA Journal **42** (2004) 1057–1065

SPEA2+: Improving the Performance of the Strength Pareto Evolutionary Algorithm 2

Mifa Kim[1], Tomoyuki Hiroyasu[2], Mitsunori Miki[2], and Shinya Watanabe[3]

[1] Graduate School, Department of Knowledge Engineering and Computer Sciences,
Doshisha University, 610-0321 Kyoto, Japan
kim@mikilab.doshisha.ac.jp

[2] Department of Knowledge Engineering and Computer Sciences,
Doshisha University, 610-0321 Kyoto, Japan
{tomo@is,mmiki@mail}.doshisha.ac.jp

[3] Department of Computer Science Faculty of Science & Engineering,
Ritsumeikan University, Shiga, Japan
sin@sys.ci.ritsumei.ac.jp

Abstract. Multi-objective optimization methods are essential to resolve real-world problems as most involve several types of objects. Several multi-objective genetic algorithms have been proposed. Among them, SPEA2 and NSGA-II are the most successful. In the present study, two new mechanisms were added to SPEA2 to improve its searching ability a more effective crossover mechanism and an archive mechanism to maintain diversity of the solutions in the objective and variable spaces. The new SPEA2 with these two mechanisms was named SPEA2+. To clarify the characteristics and effectiveness of the proposed method, SPEA2+ was applied to several test functions. In the comparison of SPEA2+ with SPEA2 and NSGA-II, SPEA2+ showed good results and the effects of the new mechanism were clarified. From these results, it was concluded that SPEA2+ is a good algorithm for multi-objective optimization problems.

1 Introduction

Shaffer's Vector Evaluated Genetic Algorithm (VEGA[1]) spawned several attempts to apply evolutionary computation to multi-objective optimization problems(MOPs), and several algorithms have been proposed. Among them, SPEA2[2] developed by Zitzler and NSGA-II [3] developed by Deb have been reported to perform well and contain methods useful for multi-objective genetic algorithms. However, in these proposed algorithms, the crossover mechanism, which is an operator in genetic algorithms, has not yet been explored. Many multi-objective genetic algorithms have operations to maintain diversity in the objective space, but diversity in the variable space has not yet been considered.

In this paper, a new algorithm, SPEA2+, is presented. SPEA2+ attempts to improve the problem space exploration abilities of SPEA2 by adding a more effective crossover mechanism and an algorithm to maintain diversity in the two object and variable spaces.

In this paper, SPEA2+ is compared to SPEA2 and NSGA-II to discuss the feasibility of the proposed algorithm.

2 SPEA2+

Many algorithms have been proposed in recent years, and SPEA2[2] proposed by Zitzler has been reported to perform well in searching. SPEA2 contains the important operations such as archiving of individuals with good fitness, density estimation, and fitness assignment, and is able to obtain a population with both "precision" and "diversity".

However, there has been insufficient discussion concerning effective crossover, one of the major operators in GA, in SPEA2. Most multi-objective GAs include operations to maintain a wide diversity of individuals in the objective space, but do not consider the population distribution in the design variable space.

In this paper, SPEA2+ is proposed as a different model to SPEA2 that includes more effetive crossover and a method to obtain diverse solutions in the objective and variable spaces. SPEA2+ adds the following operations to SPEA2:
1) Neighborhood crossover, which crosses over individuals close to each other in objective space.
2) Mating selection, which reflects all archived good individuals in the search.
3) Applying archive to allow holding of diverse solutions in the objective space and variable space.
These operations are explained in the following section.

2.1 Neighborhood Crossover

In multi-objective GAs, effective crossover often cannot be performed, as the searching directions of each parent individual are very different from one another. Therefore, we propose neighborhood crossover, which performs crossover with individuals neighboring each other in objective space. In neighborhood crossover, individuals that match in the search direction are crossed over to generate offspring that are similar to the parent. Watanabe reported that the neighborhood crossover mechanism is effective in multi-objective GA[8].

Neighborhood crossover is performed as follows:

Step 1: Sort the population with one of the function values. The function value used in the sort is altered each generation.
Step 2: Neighborhood shuffle is performed for the sorted population.
Step 3: Select ith and $i+1$th items as parents and crossover is performed.

In neighborhood crossover, individuals that are next to each other within the population sorted based on arbitrary function values are defined as neighboring individuals.

To avoid crossing over with the same individuals, the neighborhood shuffling operation is applied after sorting ; neighborhood shuffling counterchanges individuals in the randomized range, which is less than 10% of the population size.

2.2 Mating Selection

The operation to create a population by selecting individuals from the archive is called mating selection. Binary tournament selection is used in SPEA2 as a method for mating selection[4]. Binary tournament selection obtains two individuals from the archive and selects the individual with the higher fitness. By this operation, SPEA2 can obtain a population with individuals with high precision solutions.

However, searching with SPEA2 results in an increase in non-dominated individuals within the archive, and in most cases all individuals become non-dominated individuals in the later stages of the search. Thus, use of binary tournament selection to generate the population sacrifices diversity of non-dominated individuals.

Therefore, in the proposed method, as the mating selection method, all of the archive is copied to the population used in the search. This copy operation maintain the diversity of the population to allow for a more global search.

2.3 Archive Truncation

The archive truncation method[2] is used to reduce the number of non-dominated individuals when there are more non-dominated individuals than the size of the archive. Two individuals closest to each other in Euclid distance in the objective space within the non-dominated solution are chosen. The distances between second-closest individuals and the chosen individuals are evaluated, and the individual that is closer to its second-closest individual is reduced. By this operation, the archive will hold a more diverse solution in the objective space.

Most multi-objective GAs consider diversity in objective space but not in the variable space. In MOPs, in the final stages of the search, it is necessary to select a good solution from the non-dominated individuals, where the variable values forming the solutions become important. Therefore, if comparable objective function values can be achieved using different design variables, having the diversity of design variables in the non-dominated solution within the variable space is effective.

In the present study, a method with two archives holding diverse solutions in the objective and variable spaces was used. In the operation, non-dominated solutions in each generation are copied to both archives, and in each archive, archive truncation is performed based on both the objective and variable space Euclid distance. The archive will thus hold a diverse range of solutions in both spaces.

2.4 SPEA2+ Algorithm

The algorithm flow of SPEA2+ is as follows:
Input N (archive size)
T (maximum number of generations)
Step 1: Initial population P_0 is generated. A_0^O and A_0^V are the empty archives. Generation is $t = 0$.

Step 2: Fitness values of all individuals in P_t, A_t^O, A_t^V are calculated with fitness assignment method[2].
Step 3: All non-dominated individuals in P_t, A_t^O, and A_t^V are copied to A_{t+1}^O A_{t+1}^V. If the number of individuals of A_{t+1}^O and A_{t+1}^V have exceeded N, archive truncation in objective space is applied to the individuals in A_{t+1}^O, and archive truncation in variable space is A_{t+1}^V to reduce the number of individuals. If the number of individuals of A_{t+1}^O or A_{t+1}^V is less than N, individuals with good fitness from P_t A_t^O A_t^V are used to fill A_{t+1}^O A_{t+1}^V.
Step 4: Terminate the search if $t \geq T$ or other termination conditions are met.
Step 5: P_{t+1} is generated by copying A_{t+1}^O. The neighborhood crossover and mutation operations are performed. Return to step 2 with $t = t + 1$.

3   Numerical Experimentation

To clarify the effects of neighborhood crossover and copy operations, the results of SPEA2_NC and SPEA2_copy, which are SPEA2 with the operations built in, were examined. In addition, the searching effectiveness of SPEA2+ will be discussed. For diversity of the variable space, the results of the variable space archive are compared with SPEA2. To visualize the variable space distribution, 3-variable KUR was used as the test problem. By comparison with NSGA-II[3], which has also been reported to perform well alongside SPEA2, the effectiveness of the proposed method SPEA2+ is discussed.

3.1   Target Problem

Several different test functions with different characteristics were used. All of the functions used were minimization problem with 2 objectives. In this experiment, ZDT4[6] reported by Zitzler and Deb, KUR[5] reported by Kursawe, and F_{dis}[7] reported by Deb were used. The formulae of each problem are presented in Table 3.1. However, as stated above, to see the diversity of the variable space distribution, 3-variable F_{dis} was used.

Table 3.1. Test problem

Problem	n	Variable bounds	Objective functions
ZDT4	10	$x_1 \in [0,1]$	min $f_1 = x_1$
		$x_i \in [-5,5]$	min $f_2 = g(x)[1 - \left(\frac{f_1}{g}\right)^{0.5}]$
			$g = 1 + 10(N-1) + \sum_{i=2}^{N}(x_i^2 - 10\cos(4\pi x_i))$
F_{dis}	100	$x_i \in [0,1]$	min $f_1 = x_1$
			min $f_2 = g(x)[1 + 10\frac{\sum_{i=2}^{N} x_i}{N-1}]$
			$g = 1 - \left(\frac{f_1}{g}\right)^{0.25} - \frac{f_1}{g}\sin(10\pi f_1)$
KUR	100	$x_i \in [-5,5]$	min $f_1 = \sum_{i=1}^{N-1}(-10\exp(-0.2\sqrt{x_i^2 + x_{i+1}^2}))$
			min $f_2 = \sum_{i=1}^{N}(|x_i|^{0.8} + 5\sin(x_i)^3)$

3.2 Comparison Method

In this experiment, the precision of the obtained population was evaluated from the ratio of non-dominated individuals as described below. The width of the population was compared with the maximum, minimum, and mean values for each axes of the target function. In this experiment, 30 runs were performed for all target problems. In each run, the ratio of non-dominated individuals, maximum, minimum, and mean values were obtained, and used as the result. The ratio of non-dominated individuals is explained below.

Ratio of Non-dominated Individuals

Ratio of Non-dominated Individuals (RNI) is a method for evaluation by comparing the dominance of two populations obtained by two different algorithms. In RNI, the populations obtained from the two algorithms, S_1 and S_2 are combined to make a union set S_U. Obtain the set of non-dominated individuals S_P from S_U. The number of individuals contained in S_P from each algorithm is used to obtain the ratio, and the value is used as the result of evaluation. When the value is closer to the maximum value of 100%, the algorithm can be said to have obtained a better population.

3.3 GA Parameters

In this experiment, the population number was set as 100 in all problems. The number of generations for ZDT4 was set to 500. For KUR and F_{dis}, the number of generations was set to 250. The bit-coding method is used for representation of individuals, and the number of bits per variable was set to 20, as used in other studies[2],[3]. For mutation, bit-flipping was used, and one-point crossover was used for crossover. The crossover rate was 1.0, and mutation rate was 1/bit-length.

3.4 Performance Comparison Results

ZDT4

The results for ZDT4 as target problem are shown in Fig.1. The distribution graph shown in Fig.1(a) is the result of collecting all solutions for 30 runs, and the pie chart shows the RNI value compared with SPEA2. Graph (b) shows the means for maximum, minimum, and mean values for each objective function axes.

ZDT4 is a multimodal problem in $f_2(x)$, and the main problem is how to escape from a local optimal value to the Pareto-optimal solution. Fig.1(a) indicates that SPEA2 falls to the local optimal value several times in the 30 runs, and the proposed methods of SPEA2 with neighborhood crossover and copy operations reached closer to the Pareto-optimal solution, although they still fell in the local optimal solution. From Fig.1(b), it can be seen that the mean value for SPEA2+ is the smallest, indicating that on average it is performing a good search.

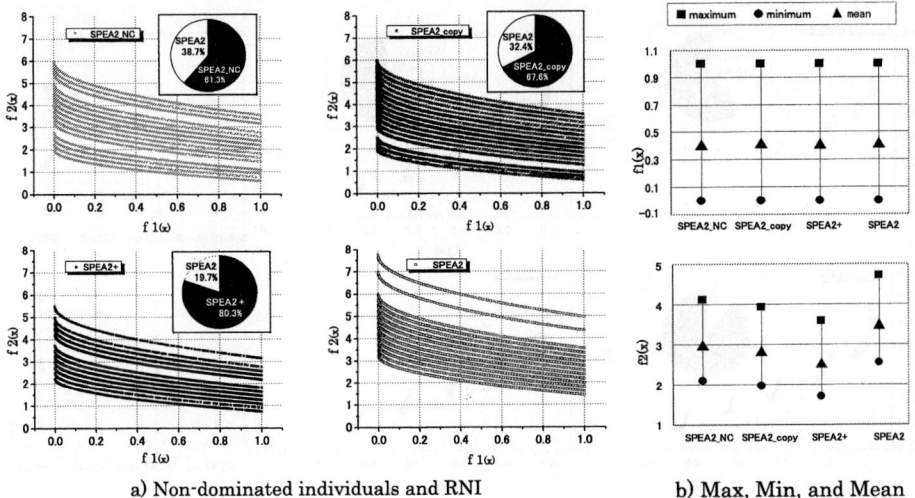

Fig. 1. Result ZDT4.

F_dis

Fig.2 shows the results using F_{dis} as the target function. The method of presenting the diagram is the same as described for Fig.1.

This is an example of a problem where the Pareto-optimal solution is non-continuous. The number of design variables was 100, and thus the problem is more difficult than ZDT4. As shown in Fig.2(b), the differences in maximum, minimum, and mean values for each target function value axes were not markedly different between the algorithms. However, the SPEA2+ distribution chart in Fig.2(a) shows that the search precision deviated less between each run, and RNI showed that SPEA2+ was better than SPEA2.

KUR

The results obtained with KUR as the target problem are shown in Fig.3. The method of display is the same as described for Fig.1.

This problem has interdependency between neighboring variables on $f_1(x)$ and has multimodal characteristics on $f_2(x)$. From Fig.3(a), it can be seen that SPEA2_NC and SPEA2+ with neighborhood crossover achieved a more diverse population. In addition, SPEA2_copy, which included the copy operation in mating selection, obtained better solutions more often than SPEA2, which used tournament selection.

3.5 Comparison with NSGA-II

Comparison of proposed SPEA2+ and NSGA-II was performed for each target function. RNI, maximum, minimal, and mean values are shown in Fig.4.

Fig.4 indicates that both algorithms show comparable results in target problem F_{dis}, and the difference in search ability between SPEA2+ and NSGA-II

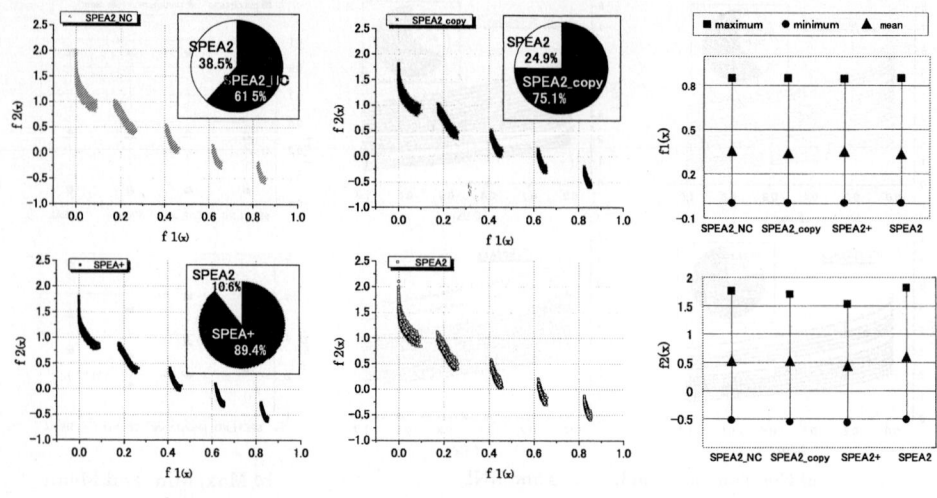

a) Non-dominated individuals and RNI   b) Max, Min, and Mean

Fig. 2. Result F_{dis}.

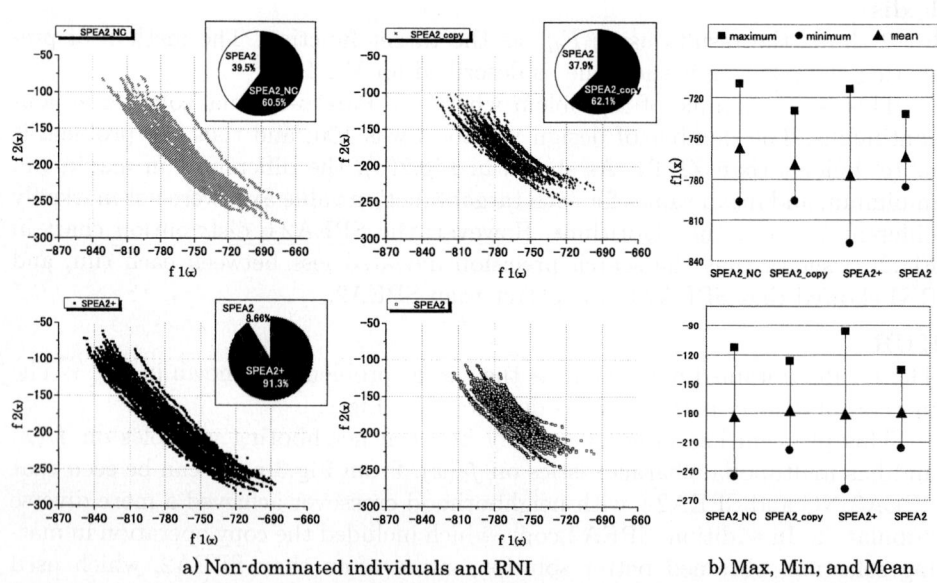

a) Non-dominated individuals and RNI   b) Max, Min, and Mean

Fig. 3. Result KUR.

was smaller than that in comparison with SPEA2. This was probably because congestion is considered in binary tournament selection in NSGA-II mating selection. In tournament selection in NSGA-II, when the fitness values of two individuals being compared are equal, the individual with lower congestion is selected. Therefore, it can generate a more uniformly distributed population than SPEA2+. This focus on population diversity is common with SPEA2+,

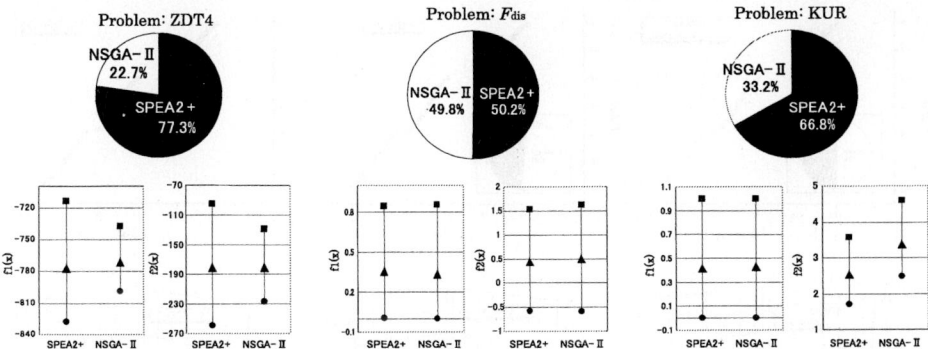

Fig. 4. Comparison of SPEA2+ with NSGA-II.

and in SPEA2+ diversity is maintained by copying all individuals. SPEA2+, which utilizes neighborhood crossover, obtained a wider solution than NSGA-II in the KUR problem, demonstrating the effectiveness of neighborhood crossover in the search.

3.6 Comparison by Design Variable Space

The results of the algorithms applied to the three-variable KUR problem are shown in Fig.5. The distribution charts on the top plot the objective archive on the objective space, and the charts on the bottom plot the variable archive on the variable space. The pie-charts show the RNI values in comparison with SPEA2.

This problem is a three-variable problem, and is relatively simple. In each method, the precision of the solution in the target function field resulted in a similar value. On the other hand, the chart on the bottom of Fig.5 shows that SPEA2_twoArchive (which introduced two archives to SPEA2) and SPEA2+ obtained a wider variety of individuals in the variable space. This was caused by having two archives to maintain diversity in both objective space and variable space.

3.7 Discussion of Results

In this experiment, three test problems were used for comparison. To clarify the effects of neighborhood crossover and the copy operation proposed in this paper, the results of SPEA2_NC and SPEA2_copy, which are SPEA2 with the respective additions, are shown, and the results of SPEA2+ were compared with SPEA2 and NSGA-II.

The results of the experiments verified the improvement of searching precision after adding copy operation to mating selection. This was considered due to the avoidance of local optimal solutions by generating populations with a wide variety of individuals. On the other hand, when neighborhood crossover was

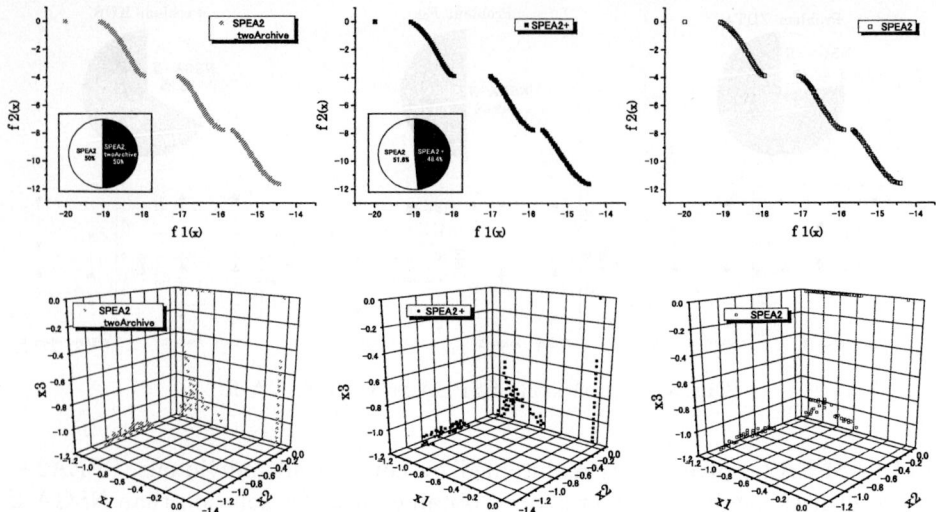

Fig. 5. Distributions of individuals in objective space and variable space.

performed, the results showed improved diversity of individuals along with precision. This was considered due to the generation of offspring close to the parents by neighborhood crossover, which maintains a wider range of individuals.

In comparing the diversity of the solutions in the variable space, after introducing two archives, it was possible to obtain a wider variety of individuals in the variable space without affecting the searching ability. This was due to the use of only the objective archive at mating selection for the population. Therefore, individuals in the variable archive do not affect usual searches.

4 Conclusions

In this paper, SPEA2+, which is an improved SPEA2 algorithm, was presented. SPEA2+ is based on SPEA2 with neighborhood crossover to perform better crossover, as well as a copy operation for mating and two archives for maintenance of a wider variety of variable space and objective space.

The experiments yielded the following points:
· By performing neighborhood crossover, population diversity can be obtained.
· By performing copy operation, solutions with better precision can be obtained.
· By using two archives, it is possible to obtain a wider variety of individuals in the variable space without affecting the search ability.

SPEA2+, which included the above operations, mostly showed better results than SPEA2 or NSGA-II. These observations suggest that SPEA2+ is an effective algorithm.

References

1. J.D. Schaffer: Multiple objective optimization with vector evaluated genetic algorithms, Proceedings of 1st International Conference on Genetic Algorithms and Their Applications,93-100,1985
2. E. Zitzler and M. Laumanns and L. Thiele, "SPEA2: Improving the Performance of the Strength Pareto Evolutionary Algorithm", Technical Report 103, Computer Engineering and Communication Networks Lab (TIK), Swiss Federal Institute of Technology (ETH) Zurich (2001)
3. Kalyanmoy Deb, Samir Agrawal, Amrit Pratab, and T. Meyarivan, "A Fast Elitist Non-Dominated Sorting Genetic Algorithm for Multi-Objective Optimization: NSGA-II", KanGAL report 200001, Indian Institute of Technology, Kanpur, India (2000)
4. D.E. Goldberg, and K. Deb. A comparison of selection schemes used in genetic algorithms.In Foundations of Genetic Algorithms 1(FOMA-1),pp69-93.(1991)
5. F. Lirsawe, "A Variant of Evolution Strategies for Vector Optimization, *PPSN I*", volume 496 of Lecture Notes in Computer Science, (1991)
6. E.Zitzler, and K. Deb, and L. Thiele,"Comparison of Multiobjective Evolutionary Algorithms: Empirical Results", EC, Vol. 8, No. 2, pp. 173–195, (2000)
7. K. Deb and T. Meyarivan,"Constrained Test Problems for Multi-Objective Evolutionary Optimization",KanGAL report 200005, Indian Institute of Technology, Kanpur, India,2000
8. Shinya Watanabe, Tomoyuki Hiroyasu and Mitsunori Miki, "Neighborhood Cultivation Genetic Algorithm for Multi-Objective Optimization Problems",Proceedings of the 4th Asia-Pacific Conference on Simulated Evolution And Learning (SEAL-2002), pp.198-202, 2002

An Extension of Generalized Differential Evolution for Multi-objective Optimization with Constraints

Saku Kukkonen and Jouni Lampinen

Department of Information Technology
Lappeenranta University of Technology
P.O. Box 20
FIN-53851 Lappeenranta, Finland
Saku.Kukkonen@lut.fi

Abstract. In this paper an extension of Generalized Differential Evolution for constrained multi-objective (Pareto-)optimization is proposed. The proposed extension adds a mechanism for maintaining extent and distribution of the obtained non-dominated solutions approximating a Pareto front. The proposed extension is tested with a set of five benchmark multi-objective test problems and results are numerically compared to known global Pareto fronts and to results obtained with the elitist Non-Dominated Sorting Genetic Algorithm and Generalized Differential Evolution. Results show that the extension improves extent and distribution of solutions of Generalized Differential Evolution.

Keywords: multi-objective optimization, Pareto-optimization, constraint handling, evolutionary algorithms, differential evolution

1 Introduction

Many situations in engineering and economics deal with optimization. One may want to optimize, *e.g.*, manufacturing processes, shape of products, and number of different products to be manufactured. Typical goals are minimizing costs, maximizing profits, and improving performance. Several natural aspects limit feasible solutions, *e.g.*, resources may cause limitations and/or the number of products cannot be a negative number.

Optimization is an intensively studied problem field in mathematics. However, functions to be optimized in traditional mathematics are relatively simple (continuous, convex, unimodal, differentiable, *etc.*), yet functions to be optimized in practice are often far more complicated (discontinuous, non-convex, multi-modal, non-differentiable, *etc.*). In such cases various stochastic optimization methods have shown their effectiveness.

Most optimization research deals with single-objective optimization problems. The basic nature of many optimization problems is, however, multi-objective and these problems are usually first converted to single-objective problems.

Single-objective problems are commonly considered easier to solve but conversion from a multi-objective problem to a single-objective problem requires some *a priori* knowledge which is not necessarily available or which is hard to determine, *e.g.*, the relative importance of each individual sub-objective. For this reason interest exists in solving multi-objective problems in multi-objective form.

Several extensions of Differential Evolution (DE) for multi-objective optimization have already been proposed [1–5]. Most of these methods use a non-dominated sorting for reproduction in each generation and some distance metric to prevent crowding.

This paper continues with the following parts: In Section 2 the concept of multi-objective optimization with constraints is handled briefly. Section 3 describes Differential Evolution algorithm and Section 4 describes proposed extension for constrained multi-objective optimization. Section 5 describes experiments and finally conclusions are given in Section 6.

2 Multi-objective Optimization with Constraints

Many practical problems have multiple objectives. For example, designing a wing of an aircraft may have objectives such as maximizing strength, minimizing weight, minimizing manufacturing costs, maximizing lifting force, minimizing drag, *etc*. Multiple objectives are almost always more or less conflicting.

Several aspects cause constraints to problems. In the previous example of the wing, the thickness of the metal parts used must be a positive number, shape limitations exist, some parts are available only in some predefined standard sizes, *etc.* Constraints can be divided into box or boundary constraints and constraint functions. Boundary constraints are used when the value of some optimized variable is limited to some range and constraint functions are representing more complicated constraints which are expressed as functions.

Multi-objective problems are often converted to single-objective problems by predefining weighting factors for different objectives, expressing the relative importance of each objective. However, this is impossible in many cases because a decision-maker does not necessarily know beforehand how different objectives should be weighted. Thus, a more convenient way is to keep multiple objectives of multi-objective problems and try to solve them in this form even though this may be harder to do in practice. Optimizing several objectives simultaneously without articulating the relative importance of each objective *a priori*, is often called Pareto-optimization [6]. An obtained solution is Pareto-optimal if none of the objectives can be improved without impairing at least one other objective [7, p. 11–12]. If the obtained solution can be improved in such way that at least one objective improves and other objectives do not decline, then the new solution dominates the original solution. A set of Pareto-optimal solutions form a Pareto front. An approximation of the Pareto front is called a set of non-dominated solutions because the solutions in this set are not dominating each other in the space of objective functions. From the set of non-dominated solutions the decision-maker may select one which has suitable values for different objectives.

This can be viewed as *a posteriori* articulation of the decision-makers preferences concerning the relative importance of each objective.

A mathematically constrained multi-objective optimization problem can be presented in the form [7, p. 37]

$$\begin{array}{l}\text{minimize } \{f_1(\boldsymbol{x}), f_2(\boldsymbol{x}), \ldots, f_K(\boldsymbol{x})\} \\ \text{subject to } \boldsymbol{x} \in S = \{\boldsymbol{x} \in \mathbf{R}^D | \boldsymbol{g}(\boldsymbol{x}) = (g_1(\boldsymbol{x}), g_2(\boldsymbol{x}), \ldots, g_M(\boldsymbol{x}))^T \leq \mathbf{0}\}\end{array} \quad (1)$$

Thus, there are K functions to be optimized and M constraint functions.

The major part of earlier mathematical research has concentrated on optimization problems where the functions are linear, differentiable, convex, or otherwise mathematically well behaving. However, in practical problems objective functions are often nonlinear, non-differentiable, discontinuous, multi-modal, *etc.* and no presumptions can be made about their behavior. Variables may also be integers or discrete instead of being continuous. Most traditional optimization methods cannot handle such complexity or do not perform well in these cases in which the assumptions they are based on do not hold. For such problems stochastic optimization methods such as Simulated Annealing (SA) and Evolution Algorithms (EAs) have been demonstrated to be effective because they do not rely on any assumptions concerning the objective and constraint functions.

3 Differential Evolution

The Differential Evolution (DE) algorithm [8, 9] [10, pp. 79–108] belongs to the family of Evolution Algorithms and was introduced by Storn and Price in 1995 [11]. Design principles in DE were simplicity, efficiency, and use of floating-point encoding instead of binary numbers.

Like in a typical EA, the idea in DE is to have some random initial population which is then improved using selection, mutation, and crossover operations. Several ways exist to determine a stopping criterion for EAs but usually a predefined upper limit G_{max} for the number of generations to be computed provides an appropriate stopping condition.

A trial vector $\boldsymbol{u}_{i,G}$ created by mutation and crossover operations is compared to an old objective vector $\boldsymbol{x}_{i,G}$. Here i is an index of the vector in the population and G is a generation index. If the trial vector has equal or lower objective value, then it replaces the old vector. This selection operation can be presented as follows [10, p. 82]:

$$\boldsymbol{x}_{i,G+1} = \begin{cases} \boldsymbol{u}_{i,G} & \text{if } f(\boldsymbol{u}_{i,G}) \leq f(\boldsymbol{x}_{i,G}) \\ \boldsymbol{x}_{i,G} & \text{otherwise} \end{cases} \quad (2)$$

The average objective value of the population will never increase, because the trial vector replaces the old vector only if it has equal or lower objective value.

4 An Extension of Generalized Differential Evolution

Generalized Differential Evolution (GDE) [12–17] extends the selection operation of the basic DE algorithm for constrained multi-objective optimization. GDE has been demonstrated to have good convergence properties but distribution of solutions and extent of the obtained non-dominated front need to be improved. GDE does not contain any mechanism for maintaining these. As an attempt to improve GDE from this point of view, a modified selection operation for GDE is proposed in this paper. The proposed selection operation for M constraint and K objective functions is presented formally in (3).

$$x_{i,G+1} = \begin{cases} u_{i,G} \text{ if } \begin{cases} \begin{cases} \exists j \in \{1,\ldots,M\} : g_j(u_{i,G}) > 0 \\ \wedge \\ \forall j \in \{1,\ldots,M\} : g'_j(u_{i,G}) \leq g'_j(x_{i,G}) \end{cases} \\ \vee \\ \begin{cases} \forall j \in \{1,\ldots,M\} : g_j(u_{i,G}) \leq 0 \\ \wedge \\ \exists j \in \{1,\ldots,M\} : g_j(x_{i,G}) > 0 \end{cases} \\ \vee \\ \begin{cases} \forall j \in \{1,\ldots,M\} : g_j(u_{i,G}) \leq 0 \wedge g_j(x_{i,G}) \leq 0 \\ \wedge \\ \begin{cases} \forall k \in \{1,\ldots,K\} : f_k(u_{i,G}) \leq f_k(x_{i,G}) \\ \vee \\ \begin{cases} \neg [\forall k \in \{1,\ldots,K\} : f_k(u_{i,G}) \geq f_k(x_{i,G}) \wedge \\ \exists k \in \{1,\ldots,K\} : f_k(u_{i,G}) > f_k(x_{i,G})] \\ \wedge \\ d_{u_{i,G}} \geq d_{x_{i,G}} \end{cases} \end{cases} \end{cases} \end{cases} \\ x_{i,G} \text{ otherwise} \end{cases} \quad , \quad (3)$$

where $g'_j(x_{i,G}) = \max(g_j(x_{i,G}), 0)$ and $g'_j(u_{i,G}) = \max(g_j(u_{i,G}), 0)$ are representing the constraint violations, and d_i is a distance measure for measuring the distance from a particular solution i to its neighbor solutions.

The selection rule given in (3) selects the trial vector $u_{i,G}$ to replace the old vector $x_{i,G}$ in the following cases:

1. Both the trial vector and the old vector violate at least one constraint but the trial vector does not violate any of the constraints more than the old vector does.
2. The old vector violates at least one constraint whereas the trial vector is feasible.
3. Both vectors are feasible and
    - the trial vector dominates the old vector or has equal value for all objectives, or
    - the old vector does not dominate the trial vector and the old vector resides in a more crowded region of the objective space.

Otherwise the old vector $x_{i,G}$ is preserved.

The basic idea in the selection rule is that the trial vector is required to dominate the compared old population member in constraint violation space or in objective function space, or at least provide an equally good solution as the old population member. If both vectors are feasible and they do not dominate each other, then the one residing in a less crowded region of the objective space is chosen to the population of the next generation. The principle of constraint handling is effectively rather similar to the method described in [18] even though the formulation is different. The main difference is in the case of two infeasible solutions. In this case the selection rule given in (3) compares solutions based on dominance of the constraint violations whereas the selection method described in [18] compares solutions based on a sum of the constraint violations which needs evaluation of all constraint functions and normalization of their values.

The whole selection rule given in (3) is effectively almost same as a constrained tournament method in [19, pp. 301–308]. In the selection rule given in (3) the trial vector is preferred over the old vector also in the cases when the trial vector is equally good as the old vector, *i.e.*, constraint violations are equal or objective function values are equal.

The selection rule given in (3) can be implemented in such a way that the number of function evaluations is reduced because not always all the constraints and objectives need to be evaluated, *e.g.*, inspecting constraint violations (even one constraint) is often enough to determine which vector to select for the next generation [13, 14]. However, in the case of feasible solutions all the objectives need to be evaluated which was not always necessary in earlier GDE. This will increase the total number of function evaluations as well as execution time. Also calculation of the distance measure, d_i, will increase execution time. In principle, any measure of distance from a solution to its neighbor solutions can be applied. A crowding distance [19, pp. 248–249] was applied here as the distance measure, d_i, because it does not need any extra parameters.

After the selected number of generations the final population presents a solution for the optimization problem. The non-dominated solutions can be separated from the final population if desired. There is no sorting of non-dominated solutions during the optimization process.

Later on in this paper the proposed method with the selection rule given in (3) is called *Generalized Differential Evolution 2 (GDE2)*. The selection rule given in (3) handles any number M of constraints and any number K of objectives. When $M = 0$ and $K = 1$, the selection rule is identical to the selection rule of the basic DE algorithm.

Usually large values (such as 0.9) are suggested as initial settings for the crossover rate *CR* and mutation factor F in the case of single-objective problems. In the case of multiple objectives, it was observed that using a large crossover rate often leads to faster convergence along one objective compared to another [15–17]. This causes the solution to converge to a single point of the Pareto front, which is not desired. Based on this observation, our initial recommendations for the control parameter values used for multi-objective optimization problems are $CR \in [0.05, 0.5]$ and $F \in [0.05, 1+)$ for initial settings. In line with these observations, use of small values for *CR* was also reported by other researchers in [2, 3]. However, the current recommendations are based on limited experimentation, and the problem of selecting the control parameter values is remaining mostly open.

5 Experiments

GDE and GDE2 were implemented in C and tested with a set of five bi-objective benchmark problems described in [20] and [21, pp. 57–59]. These problems are known as ZDT1, ZDT2, ZDT3, ZDT4, and ZDT6 [19, pp. 356–360]. They are designed to test the ability of a multi-objective optimization method to handle convexity (ZDT1), non-convexity (ZDT2), discontinuity (ZDT3), multi-modality (ZDT4), and non-uniformity (ZDT6) of the Pareto front.

5.1 Experimental Results and Discussions

In all the test problems the size of the population was 100, the number of generations was 250, and the control parameter values for GDE and GDE2 were $CR = 0.05$ and $F = 0.1$. In preliminary tests control parameter values 0.05, 0.1, 0.2, 0.3, and 0.4 were tested and suitable crossover rate and mutation factor were thereby approximately determined. It was noticed that suitable values for the crossover rate and mutation factor should be drawn from a rather narrow range for some problems, e.g., problem ZDT4, while the underlying reason for this remains open.

The results of a single run of GDE and GDE2 for solving the multi-objective benchmark problems are shown in Fig. 1, where known global Pareto fronts and the results obtained with the Strength Pareto Evolutionary Algorithm (SPEA) [22] and the elitist Non-Dominated Sorting Genetic Algorithm (NSGA-II) [23] are also shown for comparison and visual assessment.

Tests for NSGA-II, GDE, and GDE2 were repeated 100 times with different random number generator seeds and the results were compared with different metrics. NSGA-II was selected for comparison because of its good performance in previous comparison tests [23] and since it is well known within the multi-objective optimization community.

Closeness to the Pareto front was measured with an error ratio (ER) and a generational distance (GD) [19, pp. 324–327]. Diversity of the obtained solution was measured using spacing (S), spread (Δ), and maximum spread (D) metrics [19, pp. 328–331]. Smaller values for the error ratio, generational distance, spacing, and spread are preferable. The optimal value for the maximum spread is 1.

Average numbers of needed function evaluations for GDE and average execution times for the methods are reported in Table 1. For NSGA-II and GDE2 2×25100 function evaluations were needed on each run. All the tests were run on a Sun Sparc Ultra2. Table 2 contains the performance measurements solving the benchmark problems. Solutions contained the non-dominated members of the final population.

The results show that GDE2 improved extent and diversity of solutions over GDE without impairing the convergence property of GDE and increasing execution time only by little. NSGA-II was slightly better than GDE2 in most of the problems according to the metrics but NSGA-II needed more execution

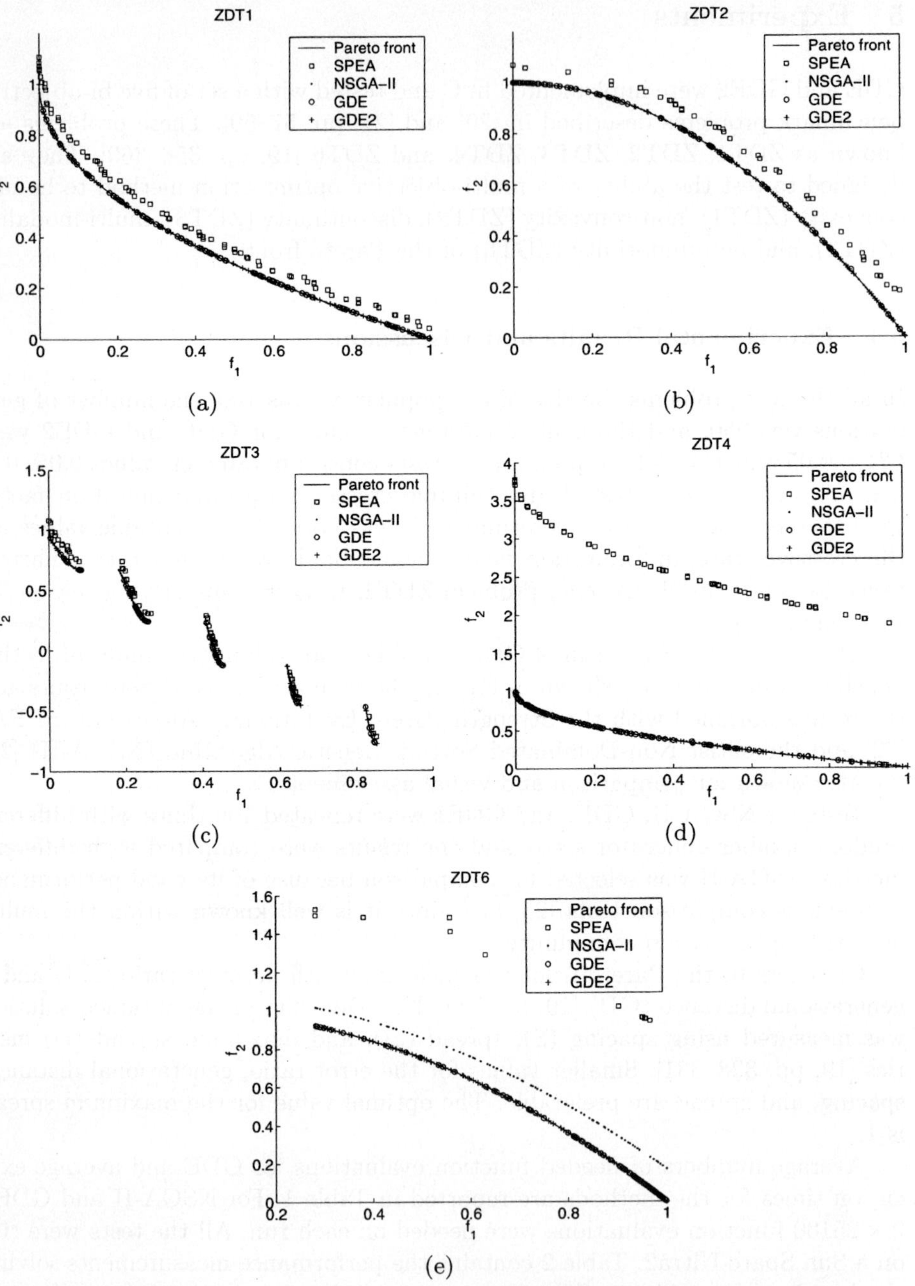

Fig. 1. Global Pareto front and solutions obtained with SPEA, NSGA-II, GDE, and GDE2 for a) ZDT1 b) ZDT2 c) ZDT3 d) ZDT4 e) ZDT6.

Table 1. Average execution times of NSGA-II, GDE, and GDE2 solving multi-objective benchmark test problems. Average number of needed function evaluations (f_1 and f_2) of GDE are also shown. Standard deviations are in parenthesis.

	NSGA-II	GDE			GDE2
	Execution time	Execution time	f_1	f_2	Execution time
ZDT1	4.0040(0.3661) s	1.0166(0.0071) s	25100(0.0)	24079.2(29.3)	1.0875(0.0091) s
ZDT2	4.0315(0.2389) s	1.0230(0.0163) s	25100(0.0)	24080.2(27.9)	1.0820(0.0067) s
ZDT3	3.9735(0.3963) s	1.0477(0.0085) s	25100(0.0)	24078.3(32.8)	1.1169(0.0081) s
ZDT4	3.9341(0.4769) s	0.5537(0.0085) s	25100(0.0)	23280.5(37.1)	0.6329(0.0151) s
ZDT6	4.0762(2.6311) s	0.5782(0.0097) s	25100(0.0)	22885.3(68.0)	0.6554(0.0106) s

Table 2. Means of the solution cardinality ($\aleph$), error ratio (ER), generational distance (GD), spacing (S), spread (Δ), and maximum spread (D) of NSGA-II, GDE, and GDE2 for the multi-objective benchmark test problems. Standard deviations are in parenthesis.

ZDT1	$\aleph$	ER	GD	S	Δ	D
NSGA-II	91.7(2.7)	**0.000**(0.000)	**0.000**(0.000)	**0.008**(0.001)	**0.418**(0.036)	**1.000**(0.000)
GDE	**98.9**(1.3)	**0.000**(0.000)	**0.000**(0.000)	0.012(0.003)	0.764(0.045)	0.949(0.028)
GDE2	83.6(4.7)	**0.000**(0.000)	**0.000**(0.000)	0.011(0.001)	0.518(0.048)	**1.000**(0.000)

ZDT2	$\aleph$	ER	GD	S	Δ	D
NSGA-II	74.7(37.1)	**0.000**(0.000)	**0.000**(0.000)	**0.008**(0.001)	0.535(0.236)	0.800(0.402)
GDE	78.1(9.8)	**0.000**(0.001)	**0.000**(0.000)	0.018(0.005)	0.864(0.067)	0.978(0.024)
GDE2	**87.9**(4.4)	0.020(0.141)	**0.000**(0.000)	0.010(0.001)	**0.470**(0.052)	**1.000**(0.001)

ZDT3	$\aleph$	ER	GD	S	Δ	D
NSGA-II	**92.9**(2.3)	**0.000**(0.000)	**0.000**(0.000)	**0.006**(0.001)	**0.573**(0.036)	0.971(0.083)
GDE	69.1(4.8)	0.003(0.007)	**0.000**(0.000)	0.018(0.008)	1.044(0.068)	0.968(0.020)
GDE2	40.3(3.8)	0.007(0.014)	**0.000**(0.000)	0.020(0.005)	0.712(0.063)	**1.000**(0.001)

ZDT4	$\aleph$	ER	GD	S	Δ	D
NSGA-II	**95.5**(16.8)	**0.031**(0.113)	**0.001**(0.001)	**0.007**(0.001)	**0.389**(0.113)	0.971(0.172)
GDE	66.7(25.4)	0.235(0.357)	0.003(0.007)	0.026(0.015)	0.775(0.123)	0.968(0.052)
GDE2	55.2(21.1)	0.318(0.384)	0.004(0.006)	0.019(0.010)	0.532(0.067)	**1.006**(0.025)

ZDT6	$\aleph$	ER	GD	S	Δ	D
NSGA-II	89.5(2.9)	1.000(0.000)	0.008(0.001)	**0.008**(0.001)	0.513(0.031)	0.965(0.006)
GDE	**99.8**(2.1)	0.010(0.100)	0.002(0.021)	0.017(0.005)	1.018(0.079)	0.988(0.050)
GDE2	97.2(2.3)	**0.000**(0.000)	**0.000**(0.000)	**0.008**(0.001)	**0.388**(0.046)	**1.000**(0.001)

time than GDE and GDE2, probably because of additional operations, *e.g.*, the non-dominated sorting. GDE2 outperforms NSGA-II in the problem ZDT6.

6 Conclusions and Future Research

In this paper an extension of Generalized Differential Evolution algorithm is proposed. The extension, GDE2, adds to GDE a mechanism for improving extent and diversity of the obtained Pareto front approximation without impairing convergence speed of GDE and increasing execution time only little. GDE2 is demonstrated to be effective, and does not introduce any extra control parameters to be preset by the user.

GDE and GDE2 were tested with a set of five benchmark multi-objective test problems. The numerical results show that GDE2 is able to provide a solution for all the test problems and performs comparably to NSGA-II and GDE providing a relatively good approximation of the Pareto front. However, the proposed method was found rather sensitive to control parameter values.

The effect of parameters on the optimization process, extensive comparison of GDE2 with latest multi-objective evolutionary algorithms and test problems, and applying GDE2 for practical multi-objective problems remains among the topics to be studied.

Acknowledgements

Authors wish to thank K. Deb and E. Zitzler for providing source codes of NSGA-II and results of SPEA respectively, and reviewers for useful commends.

References

1. Chang, C.S., Xu, D.Y., Quek, H.B.: Pareto-optimal set based multiobjective tuning of fuzzy automatic train operation for mass transit system. IEE Proceedings on Electric Power Applications **146** (1999) 577–583
2. Abbass, H.A., Sarker, R.: The Pareto Differential Evolution algorithm. International Journal on Artificial Intelligence Tools **11** (2002) 531–552
3. Madavan, N.K.: Multiobjective optimization using a Pareto Differential Evolution approach. In: Proceedings of the 2002 Congress on Evolutionary Computation, CEC'02, Honolulu, Hawaii (2002) 1145–1150
4. Babu, B.V., Jehan, M.M.L.: Differential Evolution for multi-objective optimization. In: Proceedings of the 2003 Congress on Evolutionary Computation, CEC'03, Canberra, Australia (2003) 2696–2703
5. Feng Xue, Arthur C. Sanderson, R.J.G.: Multi-objective differential evolution and its application to enterprise planning. In: Proceedings of IEEE International Conference on Robotics and Automation, Taiwan (2003) 3535–3541
6. Pareto, V.: Cours D'Economie Politique. Libraire Droz, Geneve (1964 (the first edition in 1896))
7. Miettinen, K.: Nonlinear Multiobjective Optimization. Kluwer Academic Publishers, Boston (1998)
8. Storn, R., Price, K.V.: Differential Evolution - a simple and efficient heuristic for global optimization over continuous spaces. Journal of Global Optimization **11** (1997) 341–359
9. Lampinen, J., Storn, R.: Differential Evolution. In: New Optimization Techniques in Engineering. Springer (2004) 123–166
10. Corne, D., Dorigo, M., Glover, F.: New Ideas in Optimization. McGraw-Hill, London (1999)
11. Storn, R., Price, K.V.: Differential Evolution - a simple and efficient adaptive scheme for global optimization over continuous spaces. Technical report, ICSI (1995) [Online] Available: ftp.icsi.berkeley.edu/pub/techreports/1995/tr-95-012.ps.gz, 3.5.2004.

12. Lampinen, J.: A constraint handling approach for the Differential Evolution algorithm. In: Proceedings of the 2002 Congress on Evolutionary Computation, CEC'02, Honolulu, Hawaii (2002) 1468–1473
13. Lampinen, J.: DE's selection rule for multiobjective optimization. Technical report, Lappeenranta University of Technology, Department of Information Technology (2001) [Online] Available: http://www.it.lut.fi/kurssit/03-04/010778000/MODE.pdf, 3.5.2004.
14. Lampinen, J.: Multi-constrained nonlinear optimization by the Differential Evolution algorithm. Technical report, Lappeenranta University of Technology, Department of Information Technology (2001) [Online] Available: http://www.it.lut.fi/kurssit/03-04/010778000/DECONSTR.PDF, 3.5.2004.
15. Kukkonen, S., Lampinen, J.: A Differential Evolution algorithm for constrained multi-objective optimization: Initial assessment. In: Proceedings of the IASTED International Conference on Artificial Intelligence and Applications, Innsbruck, Austria (2004) 96–102
16. Kukkonen, S., Lampinen, J.: Mechanical component design for multiple objectives using Generalized Differential Evolution. In: Proceedings of the 6th International Conference on Adaptive Computing in Design and Manufacture (ACDM2004), Bristol, United Kingdom (2004) 261–272
17. Kukkonen, S., Lampinen, J.: Comparison of Generalized Differential Evolution algorithm to other multi-objective evolutionary algorithms. In: Proceedings of the 4th European Congress on Computational Methods in Applied Sciences and Engineering, Jyväskylä, Finland (2004) Accepted for publication.
18. Deb, K.: An efficient constraint handling method for genetic algorithms. Computer Methods in Applied Mechanics and Engineering **186** (2000) 311–338
19. Deb, K.: Multi-Objective Optimization using Evolutionary algorithms. John Wiley & Sons, Chichester, England (2001)
20. Zitzler, E., Deb, K., Thiele, L.: Comparison of multiobjective evolutionary algorithms: Empirical results. Evolutionary Computation **8** (2000) 173–195 Also available: ftp.tik.ee.ethz.ch/pub/people/zitzler/ZDT2000.ps, 15.1.2004.
21. Zitzler, E.: Evolutionary Algorithms for Multiobjective Optimization: Methods and Applications. PhD thesis, Swiss Federal Institute of Technology (ETH) Zurich, TIK-Schriftenreihe Nr. 30, Diss ETH No. 13398, Shaker Verlag, Germany (1999)
22. Zitzler, E., Thiele, L.: Multiobjective evolutionary algorithms: A comparative case study and the Strength Pareto approach. IEEE Transactions on Evolutionary Computation **4** (1999) 257–271
23. Deb, K., Pratap, A., Agarwal, S., Meyarivan, T.: A fast and elitist multiobjective genetic algorithm: NSGA-II. IEEE Transactions on Evolutionary Computation **6** (2002) 182–197

Adaptive Weighted Particle Swarm Optimisation for Multi-objective Optimal Design of Alloy Steels

Mahdi Mahfouf, Min-You Chen, and Derek Arthur Linkens

Institute for Microstructure and Mechanical Properties Engineering,
The University of Sheffield (IMMPETUS)
Department of Automatic Control and Systems Engineering,
The University of Sheffield, Mappin Street, Sheffield S1 3JD, UK
{M.Mahfouf,minyou.chen,d.linkens}@shef.ac.uk

Abstract. In this paper, a modified Particle Swarm Optimisation (PSO) algorithm is presented to improve the performance of multi-objective optimisation. The PSO algorithm search capabilities are enhanced via the inclusion of the adaptive inertia weight and acceleration factor. In addition, a weighted aggregation function has been introduced within the algorithm to guide the selection of the personal and global bests, together with a non-dominated sorting algorithm to select the particles from one iteration to another. The proposed algorithm has been successfully applied to a series of well-known benchmark functions as well as to the multi-objective optimal design of alloy steels, which aims at determining the optimal heat treatment regimes and the required weight percentages for the chemical composites in order to obtain the pre-defined mechanical properties of the material. The results have shown that the algorithm can locate the constrained optimal design with a very good accuracy.

1 Introduction

Multi-objective optimisation is becoming more and more the focus of active research for many real-world problems most of which are indeed 'multi-objective' in nature. In many scientific and engineering environments, it is not uncommon to face design challenges when there are several criteria or design objectives which need to be met concomitantly. If these objectives happen to conflict with each other, then the problem becomes equivalent to finding the best possible design(s) that satisfy the competing objectives under predefined trade-off scenarios. In the steel industry in particular, optimal metal design represents a challenging multi-objective optimisation problem, which consists of finding the optimal processing parameters and the corresponding chemical compositions to obtain certain pre-defined mechanical properties. Particle Swarm Optimisation (PSO) is a relatively new technique for finding optimal regions of complex search spaces through the interaction of individuals in a population of particles. J. Kennedy and C. Eberhart originally introduced the technique in 1995 [1]. Unlike evolutionary algorithms, which are based on the principle of survival of the fittest, PSO is motivated by the simulation of the social behaviour of flocks. As Kennedy stated [2], the algorithm is based on a metaphor of social interaction, searches a space by adjusting the trajectories of individual vectors, called "particles" as they are conceptualised as moving points in the multidimensional space. The individual particles evaluate their positions, at each iteration, relative to a goal (fitness). They are drawn stochastically towards the positions of their own previous best performance and the best previous performance of their companions. The PSO algorithm has been shown to be a successful optimiser over a wide range of functions [3]-[6], and attracted wide attention from several scientific and engineering communities. This paper represents an enhancement of the original PSO algorithm by introducing adaptive weighting and a weighted aggregation function for performance evaluation. The modified algorithm has been successfully tested on a set of difficult functions and subsequently applied to multi-objective optimal design of alloy steels.

The remaining parts of the paper are organised as follows: Section 2 presents the adaptive weighted non-dominated sorting PSO algorithm. Section 3 will show the results of simulations using the proposed algorithm to solve the multi-objective optimisation test problems ZDT1~ZDT4. This section will also conduct a comparative study between the proposed algorithm and other commonly recognised effective multi-objective optimisation algorithms. The analysis and results relating to the optimal design of alloy steels will be given in Section 4. Finally, concluding remarks will be given in Section 5.

2 The Modified Particle Swarm Optimisation Algorithm

The particle swarm algorithm imitates human social behaviour. Individuals interact with one another while learning from their own experience(s), and gradually, the population members move into better regions of the problem space. The algorithm is incredibly simple – it can be described in one straightforward formula – but is able to circumvent many of the obstacles that optimisation problems usually present, including those associated with Genetic Algorithms (GA).

The PSO algorithm defines each particle as a potential solution to a problem in a dimensional space, with the particle I, represented by the following vector:

$$x_i = (x_{i1}, x_{i2}, \ldots, x_{id}), \qquad i=1, 2, \ldots N$$

Where d is the search dimension and N is the number of particles in the population.

The original formula, which was developed by Kennedy and Eberhart, was later improved by Shi and Eberhart by introducing an inertia weight w [6]. During each iteration, the particle's position is modified according to the following equations:

$$v_i(t) = w\, v_i(t-1) + c_1 r_1 (p_i - x_i(t-1)) + c_2 r_2 (p_g - x_i(t-1)) \qquad (1)$$

$$x_i(t) = v_i(t) + x_i(t-1) \qquad (2)$$

where v_i is the velocity, w is the inertia weight, c_1 and c_2 are positive constants, and r_1 and r_2 are random numbers obtained from a uniform random distribution function in the interval [0, 1]. The parameter p_i represents the best previous position of the ith particle and p_g denotes the best particle among all the particles in the population.

The inertia weight w plays the role of balancing the global and local searches and its value may vary during the optimisation process. A large inertia weight encourages a global search while a small value pursues a local search. In [6], Shi and Eberhart suggested to change the inertia weight linearly from 1 to 0.4 to restrict the global search ability of the PSO algorithm at the end of a run. They also proposed a 'fuzzy adaptation' of the inertia weight [7] due to the fact that a linearly-decreasing weight would not be adequate to improve the performance of the PSO due to its non-linear nature.

To improve the performance of the PSO for multi-objective optimisation problems, we hereby propose an Adaptive Weighted PSO (AWPSO) algorithm, in which the velocity in Equation (1) is modified as follows:

$$v_i(t+1) = w\, v_i(t) + \alpha\, [r_1(p_i - x_i(t)) + r_2(p_g - x_i(t))] \tag{3}$$

The second term in Equation (3) can be viewed as an acceleration term, which depends on the distances between the current position x_i, the the personal best p_i, and the global best p_g. The acceleration factor α is defined as follows:

$$\alpha = \alpha_0 + t/N_t \qquad t=1, 2, \ldots, N_t \tag{4}$$

where N_t denotes the number of iterations, t represents the current generation, and the suggested range for α_0 is [0.5, 1].

As can be seen from Equation (4), the acceleration term will increase as the number of iterations increases, which will enhance the global search ability at the end of run and help the algorithm to jump out of the local optimum, especially in the case of multi-modal problems.

Furthermore, instead of using a linearly-decreasing inertia weight, we use a random number, which was proved by Zhang et al. [8] to improve the performance of the PSO in some benchmark functions. Hence, in this study, we change the inertia weight at every generation via the following formula:

$$w = w_0 + r(1 - w_0) \,; \tag{5}$$

where $w_0 \in [0, 1]$ is a positive constant, and r is a random number uniformly distributed in [0, 1]. The suggested range for w_0 is [0, 0.5], which makes the weight w randomly varying between w_0 and 1.

In order to evaluate the performance of individual particles, an appropriate evaluation function (or fitness function) should be defined. Instead of using a 'dominance-based evaluation', we simply use a *weighted aggregation* approach to construct the evaluation function F for multi-objective optimisation:

$$F = \sum_{i=1}^{m} w_i f_i \,; \qquad \sum_{i=1}^{m} w_i = 1 \tag{6}$$

where m is the number of objectives, $i=1, 2, \ldots, m$.

To approximate the Pareto front instead of a certain Pareto solution, the weights w_i for each objective are changed systematically and normalised as follows:

$$w_i = \lambda_i \Big/ \sum_{i=1}^{m} \lambda_i \,; \qquad \lambda_i = U(0,1) \tag{7}$$

The function $U(0,1)$ generates a uniformly distributed random number within the interval [0,1]. In this way, we can obtain a uniformly distributed random weight combination, which is generated at every iteration. The idea here is to use dynamic weights instead of fixed weights to obtain the Pareto solutions. This dynamically *weighted aggregation* approach was introduced for the selection of the best p_i and p_g. We will show that this approach works very well with both multi-modal test problems and our industry-related problem.

Finally, in order to strengthen the convergence properties of the multi-objective optimisation, the 'non-dominated sorting' technique, which was proposed and improved by Deb [9]-[10] and then introduced into the PSO based algorithm by Li [11], has been also used in our AWPSO algorithm. In the light of above considerations, the proposed algorithm can be summarised as follows:

1. Initialisation.
   Set population number N and iteration number N_t. Initialise the position x_i and velocity v_i of the particles with random numbers within the pre-defined decision variable range. V_{max} is set to the upper bound of the decision variables. Set personal best position $p_i = x_i$, iteration counter $t=0$.

2. Evaluation.
   $t=t+1$. Evaluate each particle in the current population using equation (6). If $F_i(t) < F_i(t-1)$, then $p_i = x_i$. Find $F_{min} = \min\{F_i\}$, and corresponding position X_{min}. Select global best $p_g = X_{min}$.

3. New particles generation.
   Calculate the new velocity NV_i and new position NX_i based on the current x_i (i=1, 2, ..., N), using equations (3) and (2), and the objective function values for all the new particles. Combine all x_i and NX_i ($2N$ particles) together and store them in a temporary list *tempList*.

4. Non-dominated Sorting.
   Identify non-dominated solutions in *tempList* and store them in a matrix *PFront* (Pareto front). Set front number $k=1$.
   a) Remove the non-dominated particles from *tempList*.
   b) $k=k+1$. Identify non-dominated solutions in the remaining *tempList* and store them in a matrix *Frontk* (front k).
   c) Repeat b) and c) until all $2N$ particles are ranked into different fronts.

5. Select particles for next iteration.
   If *PFront* size $>N$, then randomly select N particles from *PFront* and store them as *NextX*. Otherwise, store *PFront* as *NextX* then randomly select particles in next front (*Frontk*) and add them to *NextX* until *NextX* size=N.

6. Calculate objective functions values for all particles in NextX and set the NextX as the current positions x for the next iteration.

7. If all $v_i < 0.1 V_{max}$, execute the following steps, otherwise go to 8).
   a) Randomly select 20% particles in current population and randomly change their positions by 10% of the V_{max}. Store them in *Xtemp*.
   b) Evaluate the *Xtemp* and find the particles which dominate any particles in the current Pareto front. Use these dominating particles to replace the corresponding particles in the current x.
   c) Repeat a) and b) K times (K=1~10), make sure the number of x dose not exceed N.

8. If $t < N_t$, go to 2).

9. Store the non-dominated solutions from the final population and calculate the performance metric values (see equations (8) and (9) in the next section).

3 The Multi-objective Optimisation Problems

In order to demonstrate the effectiveness of the proposed AWPSO algorithm, we used a set of commonly recognised test problems (ZDT1~ZDT4 functions) [12]. The function ZDT1 has a convex Pareto front while ZDT2 has a concave Pareto front. Discreteness in the Pareto front for ZDT3 causes difficulties in finding a diverse set of solutions. ZDT4 is a multi-modal problem, the multiple local Pareto fronts cause difficulties for many algorithms to converge to the true Pareto-optimal front. For all test functions, the proposed AWPSO algorithm performed very well and converged to the Pareto-optimal with a high accuracy while maintaining a good diversity among the Pareto solutions.

For ZDT1~ZDT3, we set w_0=0.15, α_0 = 0.5, the population size N=100, the number of iterations N_t=100. The Pareto solutions found by AWPSO after a single run are shown in Fig1.(a) to (c) respectively. For the ZDT4 function, the parameters setting are w_0=0.15, α_0 = 0.5, N=100, N_t=300. Figure 1 (d) shows the Pareto solutions found by the AWPSO algorithm. It can be seen that the algorithm possesses very good convergence properties while maintaining a good diversity among the Pareto solutions. To compare the performance of the AWPSO to other recently developed algorithms, such as NSGA II, SPEA and NSPSO, two performance metrics, namely the Generational Distance (GD) and the Spread Δ, which were described in [12], were used. GD measures the closeness of the obtained Pareto solution set Q from a known set of the Pareto-optimal set P^*, which is defined as follows:

$$GD = \frac{(\sum_{i=1}^{|Q|} d_i^m)^{1/m}}{|Q|} ; \qquad (8)$$

For a two-objective problem (m=2), d_i is the Euclidean distance between the solution $i \in Q$ and the nearest member of P^*. A set of $|P^*|$ =500 uniformly distributed Pareto-optimal solutions is used to calculate the closeness metric GD.

The Spread Δ measures the diversity of the solutions along the Pareto front in the final population and is defined as follows:

$$\Delta = \frac{\sum_{m=1}^{M} d_m^e + \sum_{i=1}^{|Q|} |d_i - \bar{d}|}{\sum_{m=1}^{M} d_m^e + |Q| \bar{d}} \qquad (9)$$

where d_i is distance between the neighbouring solutions in the Pareto solution set Q. $\bar{d}$ is the mean value of all d_i. d_m^e is the distance between the extreme solutions of P^* and Q along the mth objective. It is worth noting that for an ideal distribution of the solutions (uniform distribution), Δ=0.

In order to establish repeatability, the AWPSO algorithm was run 10 times independently. The average performance metric values and the corresponding variance σ^2 are summarised in Tables 1 and 2 respectively. In these Tables, the compared results for SPEA, NSGA-II and NSPSO were obtained from [12] and [11] respectively. It can be seen that the proposed algorithm performed very well as far as convergence and diversity are concerned. From Table 1 we can see that AWPSO has achieved a better convergence. Table 2 shows that NSGA II has achieved better Δ values overall. However, from the Pareto fronts as shown in Fig. 1, AWPSO still has a good coverage of P^*.

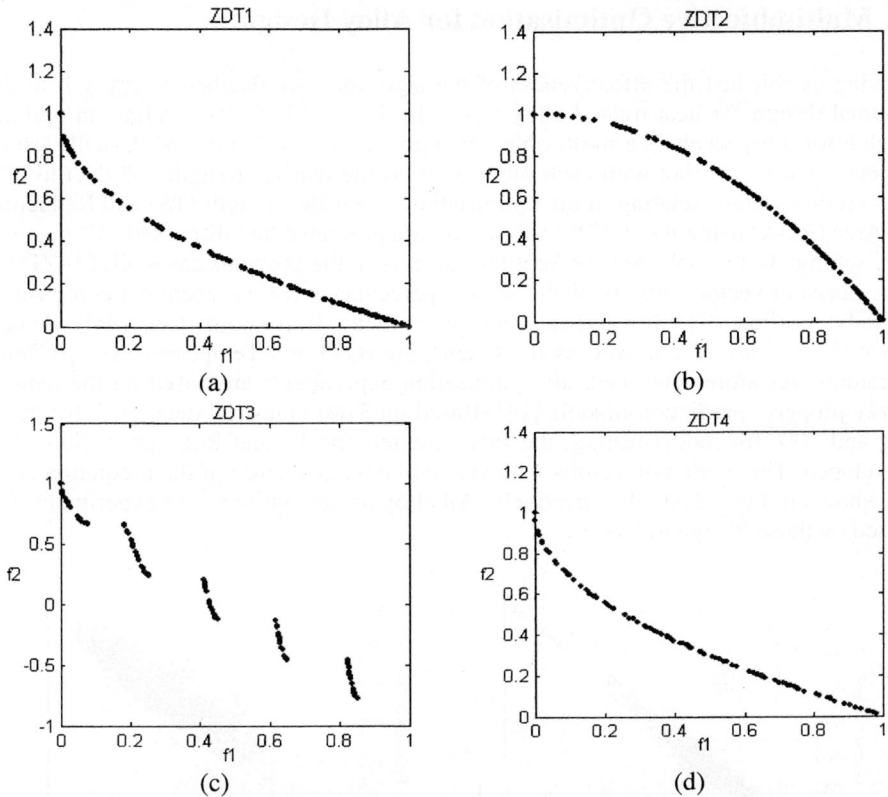

Fig. 1. Pareto solutions of AWPSO on ZDT1~ZDT4.

Table 1. Mean and variance values of the convergence measure GD.

Algorithm	ZDT1		ZDT2		ZDT3		ZDT4	
	GD	σ^2	GD	σ^2	GD	σ^2	GD	σ^2
SPEA	1.25e-3	0	3.04e-3	2.00e-5	4.42e-2	1.90e-5	9.514	11.321
NSGA II	8.94e-4	0	8.24e-4	0	4.34e-2	4.20e-5	2.92e-2	4.67e-2
NSPSO	7.53e-4	4.18e-5	8.05e-4	3.05e-5	3.4e-3	2.54e-4	7.82e-4	6.91e-5
AWPSO	1.01e-4	2.61e-9	1.210e-4	1.4e-9	5.206e-4	2.85e-9	5.34e-4	3.92e-8

Table 2. Mean and variance values of the diversity measure Δ.

Algorithm	ZDT1		ZDT2		ZDT3		ZDT4	
	Δ	σ_Δ^2	Δ	σ_Δ^2	Δ	σ_Δ^2	Δ	σ_Δ^2
SPEA	0.730	9.07e-3	0.678	4.48e-3	0.666	6.66e-4	0.732	1.13e-2
NSGA II	0.463	4.16e-2	0.435	2.46e-2	0.576	5.08e-3	0.655	1.98e-1
NSPSO	0.767	3.00e-2	0.758	2.77e-2	0.869	5.81e-2	0.768	3.57e-2
AWPSO	0.759	1.71e-3	0.758	4.92e-3	0.891	1.10e-2	0.680	3.00e-3

4 Multi-objective Optimisation for Alloy Design

Having established the effectiveness of the algorithm, we decided to apply it to the optimal design for heat-treated alloy steels. In the steel industry, finding an optimal design for alloy steels is a multi-objective optimisation problem [13]. Usually, some objectives may conflict with each other, such as the tensile strength and ductility. In this section, details relating to the optimisation of tensile strength (TS) and Reduction of Area (ROA) using the AWPSO algorithm are presented and discussed. All parameters settings in the AWPSO are kept the same as in the previous cases ZDT1~ZDT3. The decision vector consists of the weight percentages for the chemical composites, namely: Carbon (C), Silica (Si), Manganese (Mn), Chromium (Cr), Molybdenum (Mo), Vanadium (V), as well as the Quenching (QT) and Tempering (Temp) Temperatures. As aforementioned, all optimisation experiments are based on the neural-fuzzy property prediction models [14]. Based on 3760 industrial data, 50% for training and 50% for model testing, the fuzzy models for TS and ROA prediction were developed. The prediction results with standard deviation (SD) of the prediction error are shown in Figs. 2 and 3 respectively. All alloy design optimisation experiments are based on these fuzzy models.

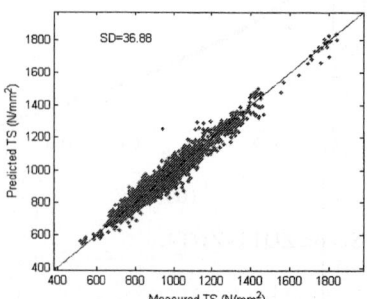

Fig. 2. Fuzzy model prediction for TS. **Fig. 3.** Fuzzy model prediction for ROA.

4.1 The Two-Objective Optimisation Problem

In order to achieve the pre-defined tensile strength (TS) and the corresponding 95% confidence error band EB_t for model predictions, such variables were selected as the objectives. It is worth noting that the error band, which depends upon the model accuracy and training data density, provides an accurate guide with respect to the model prediction error. The smaller the error band, the more reliable the corresponding model prediction. Hence, the objectives are defined as follows:

$$\text{Minimise } J_1 = \begin{cases} |TS - TS_t| & \text{if } |TS - TS_t| < 0.1TS_T \\ 1000|TS - TS_t| & \text{otherwise} \end{cases} \quad (10)$$

$$\text{Minimise } J_2 = EB_T$$

The first objective function J_1 indicates that the ideal solutions should be close to the target TS value TS_t and the acceptable variation is 10% of TS_t. The penalty will be given to the solutions that are greater than the 10% variation range of the target. Fig. 4 illustrates the TS values against the error band corresponding to the obtained Pareto solutions with the target value TS_t=868 (N/mm^2). It indicates that based on the Pareto solutions, the obtained TS values are close to the target. Table 3 shows the average values of the Pareto solutions in all five independent runs. It can be seen that the produced solutions are very consistent and always converged to a specific area that minimised the above objective functions.

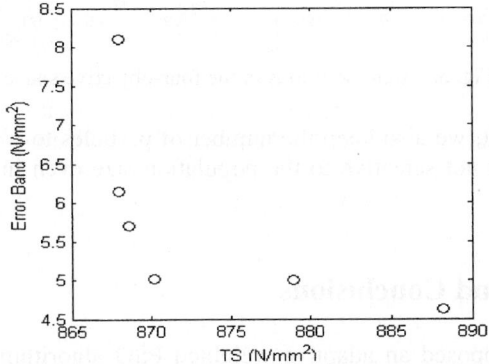

Fig. 4. Obtained Pareto solutions in the objective space.

Table 3. Mean values of the Pareto solutions across five runs.

	C	Si	Mn	Cr	Mo	Ni	V	QT	Temp	TS	EB
Run1	0.388	0.251	0.761	1.219	0.304	0.642	0.009	867	650	870	5.06
Run2	0.379	0.252	0.780	1.027	0.271	0.688	0.009	856	626	872	8.69
Run3	0.391	0.256	0.765	1.247	0.279	0.689	0.003	859	642	873	4.81
Run4	0.387	0.250	0.741	1.194	0.308	0.709	0.013	859	653	873	8.01
Run5	0.392	0.256	0.718	0.938	0.261	0.882	0.006	858	619	874	5.76

4.2 The Four-Objective Optimisation Problem

This experiment aims at finding the optimal chemical compositions and heat-treatment process parameters to obtain the required TS and ROA, the latter reflecting the ductility of steels. Again, the model prediction error bands EB_t and EB_r for TS and ROA respectively are included in the objective functions. The target values for TS and ROA are set to 868 (N/mm^2) and 60%, respectively. Among the four objectives, J_1 and J_2 are defined similarly to the previous section, while J_3 and J_4 relating to ROA and the corresponding error band are defined as follows:

$$\text{Minimise: } J_3=|ROA-60|, \qquad J_4=EB_r \qquad (11)$$

Figure 5 shows the Pareto-solutions produced by the AWPSO algorithm in the objective space. Again, it is seen that the algorithm converged to the region close to the pre-defined TS and ROA target values and also provided different solutions which meet the mechanical property requirements of the alloy steels.

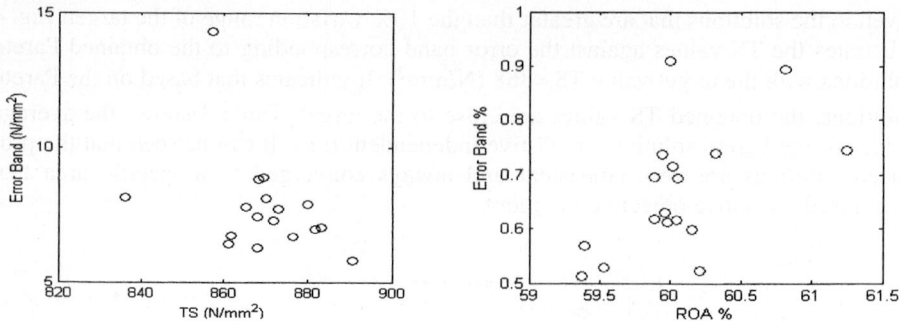

Fig. 5. Pareto-solutions in the four-objective space.

In this experiment, we also keep the number of particles to $N=100$. This indicates that the algorithm is not sensitive to the population size even in a high-dimensional objective space.

5 Discussions and Conclusions

In this paper we proposed an adaptive weighted PSO algorithm (AWPSO) and applied it to a series of benchmark functions and to the optimal design of heat-treated alloy steels based on data-driven neural-fuzzy predictive models. The main aim of the research was to determine the optimal heat treatment regime and the required weight percentages for the chemical composites to obtain the desired mechanical properties of steels. Using the adaptive weights w_0 and α in the AWPSO we overcame the problem commonly found in the standard PSO algorithm which related to its limitation for effective local search in the early stages of the run coupled with its limitation for effective global search during the late stages of the run. The introduction of the *adaptive weighted aggregation* evaluation function improved the diversity of the Pareto solutions while keeping the algorithm simple. Compared to other recently developed algorithms, such as NSGA II, SPEA and NSPSO, the proposed algorithm can achieve better convergence while keeping a good diversity (we used the well-known functions ZDT1~ZDT4 for benchmark testing). The proposed algorithm has also been successfully applied to multi-objective optimal design of alloy steels. The results have shown that the algorithm can locate the constrained optimal design with very good accuracy, and other simulation experiments (not reported here) have also established the superiority of the algorithm when compared to the SPEA2 algorithm. The simulation results also indicate that the algorithm produced very consistent solutions and can be effectively applied to other industrial optimisation problems.

Acknowledgement

The authors would like to thank the UK Engineering and Physical Sciences Research Council (EPSRC) for their financial support via the IMMPETUS Phase II Programme Award, under Grant GR/R70514/01.

References

1. J. Kennedy and R. Eberhart, Particle Swarm Optimization, Neural Networks, Perth; Australia, p. 1942-1948, 1995
2. J. Kennedy, The Particle Swarm: Social adaptation of knowledge, Proc. 1997 Int. Conf. Evolutionary Computation, Indianapolis, IN, 1997, P. 303-308.
3. J. Kennedy, Stereotyping: Improving Particle Swarm Performance with Cluster Analysis, Evolutionary Computation, La Jolla, CA, p. 1507-1512, 2000.
4. P.J. Angeline, Evolutionary Optimization Versus Particle Swarm Optimization: Philosophy and Performance Differences, LNCS, p. 601-610, 1998
5. R. Eberhart and Y. Shi, Comparison between Genetic Algorithms and Particle Swarm Optimisation, Lecture Notes in Computer Science, p. 611-618, 1998
6. Y. Shi and R. Eberhart, Empirical Study of Particle Swarm Optimization, Evolutionary Computation, Washington DC, p.1945-1950, 1999
7. Y. Shi and R. Eberhart, Fuzzy Adaptive Particle Swarm Optimization, Congress on Evolutionary Computation, Seoul, Korea, p. 101-106, 2001.
8. L.H. Zhang and S. Hu, A New Approach to Improve Particle Swarm Optimization, Lecture Notes in Computer Science, vol. 2723, p. 134-139, 2003.
9. K. Deb, S. Agrawal, A. Pratap and T. Meyarivan, A Fast Elitist Non-Dominated Sorting Genetic Algorithm for Multi-Objective Optimization: NSGA-II, Proceedings of Parallel Problem Solving from Nature-PPSN VI, Springer, p.849-858, 2000.
10. K. Deb and T. Goel, Controlled Elitist Non-Dominated Sorting Genetic Algorithms for Better Convergence, Lecture Notes in Computer Science, vol. 1993, p. 67-81, 2001.
11. X. Li, A Non-dominated Sorting Particle Swarm Optimizer for Muli-objective Optimization, Lecture Notes in Computer Science, vol. 2723, p. 37-48, 2003.
12. K. Deb, Multi-objective optimization using evolutionary algorithms, New York; Chichester: Wiley, 2001.
13. M. Mahfouf, M. Jamei, and D.A. Linkens, Optimal Design of Metals using Fuzzy Specified Multi-Objective Functions, IFAC Fuzzy-GA 2004.
14. M-Y Chen and D.A. Linkens, A Systematic Neuro-fuzzy Modeling Framework with Application to Material Property Prediction, IEEE Transactions on Systems, Man and Cybernetics, Part B, 31(5), p. 781-790, 2001.

Multi-objective Optimisation by Co-operative Co-evolution

Kuntinee Maneeratana[1], Kittipong Boonlong[1], and Nachol Chaiyaratana[2]

[1] Department of Mechanical Engineering, Chulalongkorn University
Phaya Thai Road, Pathum Wan, Bangkok 10330, Thailand
kuntinee.m@chula.ac.th, kittipong_toy@yahoo.com
[2] Research and Development Center for Intelligent Systems,
King Mongkut's Institute of Technology North Bangkok
1518 Piboolsongkram Road, Bangsue, Bangkok 10800, Thailand
nchl@kmitnb.ac.th

Abstract. This paper presents the integration between a co-operative co-evolutionary genetic algorithm (CCGA) and four evolutionary multi-objective optimisation algorithms (EMOAs): a multi-objective genetic algorithm (MOGA), a niched Pareto genetic algorithm (NPGA), a non-dominated sorting genetic algorithm (NSGA) and a controlled elitist non-dominated sorting genetic algorithm (CNSGA). The resulting algorithms can be referred to as co-operative co-evolutionary multi-objective optimisation algorithms or CCMOAs. The CCMOAs are benchmarked against the EMOAs in seven test problems. The first six problems cover different characteristics of multi-objective optimisation problems, namely convex Pareto front, non-convex Pareto front, discrete Pareto front, multi-modality, deceptive Pareto front and non-uniformity of solution distribution. In contrast, the last problem is a two-objective real-world problem, which is generally referred to as the continuum topology design. The results indicate that the CCMOAs are superior to the EMOAs in terms of the solution set coverage, the average distance from the non-dominated solutions to the true Pareto front, the distribution of the non-dominated solutions and the extent of the front described by the non-dominated solutions.

1 Introduction

Genetic algorithms (GAs) have a unique niche in the area of multi-objective optimisation. Due to the parallel search nature of the algorithms, the approximation of multiple Pareto optimal solutions can be effectively executed. Various genetic algorithms are currently available for use in multi-objective optimisation [1–8]. Similar to the case of single-objective optimisation, as the search space or problem size increases, the performance of the algorithms always degrade. As a result, the non-dominated solutions identified by the algorithms may deviate from the true Pareto front. In addition, the coverage of the Pareto front by the solutions generated may also be affected. A number of strategies have been used to solve the problem. Examples of the strategies that have been successfully embedded into the algorithms include elitism [6–8], diversity control [9] and co-evolution [10, 11]. Although the strategies mentioned can be used with almost all genetic algorithms designed for multi-objective optimisation, these strategies have rarely been used with more than one algorithm and hence the effect of the same strategy on different genetic algorithms cannot be determined directly. In particular, the strategy interested for a detailed study in this paper is the co-operative co-evolutionary strategy.

A co-evolutionary search involves the use of multiple species as the representation of a solution to the optimisation problem. Each species can either compete or co-operate during the search evolution. One particular algorithm that stands out as one of the algorithms that truly exploit the concept of co-evolution is a co-operative co-evolutionary genetic algorithm or CCGA [12, 13]. In brief, a species member in the CCGA represents a part of the decision variable set where all species will co-operatively produce a complete solution to the problem. Each species member will then independently evolve using a standard genetic algorithm. By partitioning the problem in this manner, the search space that each sub-population has to cover would significantly reduce. Although the CCGA is originally developed for use in single-objective optimisation, the co-operative co-evolutionary effect has also been successfully embedded into a multi-objective genetic algorithm [10]. Keerativuttitumrong et al. [10] have proven that the multi-objective co-operative co-evolutionary genetic algorithm or MOCCGA outperforms the original multi-objective genetic algorithm or MOGA [2, 5] in six test problems introduced by Zitzler et al. [14]. As suggested by Keerativuttitumrong et al. [10], the effects of co-operative co-evolution in other genetic algorithms that are designed for use in multi-objective optimisation will be investigated in this paper. The candidate algorithms for the study include a niched Pareto genetic algorithm or NPGA [3], a non-dominated sorting genetic algorithm or NSGA [4] and a controlled elitist non-dominated sorting genetic algorithm or CNSGA [7]. In addition, the modification on the MOCCGA for a further performance enhancement will also be covered in this paper. All modified algorithms will be benchmarked against the original algorithms by means of a performance comparison. The benchmark problems used include six test problems proposed by Zitzler et al. [14] and an engineering problem called a topology design [15].

The organisation of this paper is as follows. In section 2, the genetic algorithm integration and additional genetic operators used for the performance enhancement will be discussed. The test problems and the performance evaluation criteria will be described in sections 3 and 4, respectively. In section 5, the benchmarking results and discussions are given. Finally, the conclusions are drawn in section 6.

2 GA Integration and Additional Genetic Operators

The CCGA will be integrated with each one of the four genetic algorithms for multi-objective optimisation. In order to enhance the combined algorithms, two additional genetic operators are utilised: a crowding distance selection [7, 8] and an elitist strategy. The algorithm integration and the elitist strategy are described as follows.

2.1 Genetic Algorithm Integration

Similar to the original CCGA, the population of its multi-objective counterpart also contains a number of species or sub-populations where each species represents a decision variable or a part of solution. The objective vector of a species member or an individual is obtained after combining it with the remaining species extracted from a non-dominated solution, which is randomly picked from a preserved non-dominated solution set. It is noted that the preserved non-dominated solution set is initially created by combining different species together randomly and choosing only the non-dominated solutions. If the complete solution obtained after combining the individual of interest with other species is neither dominated by any solutions in the preserved set nor a duplicate of a solution in the preserved set, then this complete solution will be added to the preserved set. At the same time, if the newly created solution dominates any existing solutions in the preserved set, the dominated solutions will be expunged from the set. In order to maintain the diversity within the preserved non-dominated solution set, the crowding distance selection [7, 8] is used to regulate the size of the preserved set. After the objective values have been assigned to every individual in all sub-populations, the evolution of every species is then commenced by one of the four genetic algorithms for multi-objective optimisation. The resulting co-operative co-evolutionary multi-objective optimisation algorithms (CCMOAs) can be uniquely referred to as a co-operative co-evolutionary multi-objective genetic algorithm (CCMOGA), a co-operative co-evolutionary niched Pareto genetic algorithm (CCNPGA), a co-operative co-evolutionary non-dominated sorting genetic algorithm (CCNSGA) and a co-operative co-evolutionary controlled elitist non-dominated sorting genetic algorithm (CCCNSGA). The name given to the resulting algorithm obtained after combining the MOGA with the CCGA in this paper differs from that used by Keerativuttitumrong et al. [10] since the integration protocol is quite different.

2.2 Elitist Strategy

Elitism has been proven to be an important part in the success of multi-objective optimisation using a genetic algorithm [7, 8]. Since the use of an elitist strategy has not been mentioned in the original publications of MOGA, NPGA and NSGA, such a strategy will be used in conjunction with the MOGA, CCMOGA, NPGA, CCNPGA, NSGA and CCNSGA. Similar to the case of single-objective genetic algorithm, the implemented elitist strategy involves passing a number of individuals (of the same species) from one generation to the next without either crossover or mutation. However, the elite individuals in this case will be the non-duplicated non-dominated individuals. The prevention of using duplicated individuals as elite individuals would promote genetic diversity [16, 17]. Note that if the number of non-duplicated non-dominated individuals acquired exceeds a preset limit, the crowding distance selection will be used to select the individuals for the elite individual set.

3 Test Problems

In order to assess the performance of the four combined algorithms, they will be benchmarked using six optimisation test cases developed by Zitzler et al. [14] and an engineering problem called a topology design [15]. The optimisation problems T_1–T_6 proposed by Zitzler et al. [14] are minimisation problems with m decision variables and two objectives. T_1 is a 30-dimensional problem with a convex Pareto front, which is continuous and uniformly distributed. T_2 is also a 30-dimensional problem but has a non-convex Pareto front. T_3 is a 30-dimensional problem with five discrete Pareto fronts. T_4 is a 10-dimensional problem with 21^9 local Pareto fronts and therefore is used to test the algorithm's ability to deal with multi-modality. T_5 is an 11-dimensional problem with deceptive Pareto fronts. T_6 is a 10-dimensional problem with the non-uniform search space.

In contrast, a 2D heat transfer problem is used as a real life case study for topology design optimisation [15]. Given a wall with linear distributed temperature profile, a limited space is available for attaching a solid protruding configuration that facilitates heat loss from the wall as shown in Fig. 1 (left). The optimisation aims to obtain lightweight configuration with high dissipated heat from the wall and body into the surroundings. The boundary between the protruding body and the environment is assumed to be convective with very good air circulation that the ambient air temperature in close proximity to the wall and the protruding body remains unchanged. Domains of the available space are dividing into uniform grids with 10 rows and 10 columns. The problem is thus encoded using a 100-bit binary representation in the on-off style. The block insertion on a grid is represented by '1' whilst '0' signifies a void in the corresponding location. A complete solution can be divided into 5 parts, each containing 20 bits that represents 2 rows in the grid. The heat dissipation performance of each configuration is numerically evaluated by the finite volume simulation and, thus, the true Pareto front of the problem can only be generated by an exhaustive search. Hence, for this problem solutions obtained from an algorithm will only be compared with solutions generated by a different algorithm.

4 Performance Evaluation Criteria

Zitzler et al. [14] suggest that in order to assess the optimality of non-dominated solutions identified by a multi-objective optimisation algorithm, these solutions should be compared with either the solutions obtained from a different algorithm or the true Pareto optimal solutions. Four corresponding measurement criteria are considered: the solution set coverage (C), the average distance between the non-dominated solutions to the Pareto optimal solutions (M_1), the distribution of the non-dominated solutions (M_2) and the normalised absolute difference between the extent of the front described by the non-dominated solutions and that obtained from the Pareto optimal solutions (M_3'). The solution set coverage is evaluated in the decision variable space while the remaining three criteria are calculated from the objective vectors of the solutions obtained. It is noted that the first three indices are taken directly from Zitzler et al. [14] while the final index is adapted from the M_3 index discussed in Zitzler et al. [14]. The M_3' index is introduced in this paper since the extent of the true Pareto front for each problem has a specific value and hence only the difference between the M_3 index calculated from the non-dominated solution set and that obtained from the true Pareto optimal solutions that yields a meaningful measurement [9].

5 Optimisation Results and Discussions

In this section, the results from using the evolutionary multi-objective optimisation algorithms (EMOAs) with the elitist strategy described in section 2.2 and the co-operative co-evolutionary multi-objective optimisation algorithms (CCMOAs) to solve T_1–T_6 problems and the topology design problem will be presented. The parameter setting for the algorithms that is used in all problems is displayed in Table 1. It is noted that after all repeated runs have completed, the final non-dominated solutions are then retrieved from either the individuals in the last generation from each run of a EMOA or the solutions in the preserved non-dominated solution set from every CCMOA run. The performance indicators introduced in section 4, i.e. M_1, M_2 and M_3', of each run are calculated and then averaged to obtain the final indices.

The M_1, M_2 and M_3' indices of the EMOAs and CCMOAs on the test problems T_1–T_6 are summarised in Table 2. In addition, the non-dominated solutions of the topology design problem in the objective space and the non-dominated solutions and the true Pareto optimal solutions of the test problems T_1–T_6 are displayed in Figs. 1–4 while the box plots of the C indices [14] from all seven problems are illustrated in Fig. 5. It is noted that the results displayed in Figs. 1 (right), 2, 3 and 4 (right) cover only the solutions from the MOGA and CCMOGA searches while Fig. 4 (left) illustrates only the solutions produced by the MOGA, CCMOGA and CCCNSGA. This is because most of the results from two different algorithms in the same category are very close to one another. Hence, the display of all search results would render the graphical representation useless and the displayed results are only used to present the overall effect of co-evolution.

From Table 2, in terms of the average distance from the identified non-dominated solutions to the true Pareto front as described by the M_1 criterion, a major improvement in the search performance of all algorithms can be observed in the test problems T_1, T_2, T_3, T_4 and T_6. In the test problem T_5, although the introduction of the co-operative co-evolutionary effect seems to produce only a minor improvement, this improvement is enough to push the solutions from the best deceptive Pareto front to the true Pareto front in the case of CCMOGA. This observation is confirmed by Fig. 4 (left). Nonetheless, even with the use of the co-operative co-evolution, the CCNPGA, CCNSGA and CCCNSGA are still unable to locate the true Pareto optimal solutions of the test problem T_5.

Moving onto the consideration of the distribution of the identified non-dominated solutions. The M_2 indices in Table 2 indicate that the use of the

Table 1. Parameter setting for the algorithms that is used in all problems. The fitness sharing, selection and elitist strategy listed here is not used in the implementation of CNSGA and CCCNSGA.

Parameter	EMOA	CCMOA
Chromosome representation	Binary chromosome	
Chromosome length of a complete solution	900 (T_1, T_2, T_3); 300 (T_4, T_6); 80 (T_5); 100 (Topology design problem)	
Fitness sharing	Triangular sharing function with the sharing radius estimated in the objective space [2]	
Selection method	Stochastic universal sampling or tournament selection (NPGA and CCNPGA only)	
Crossover method	Uniform crossover with probability = 1.0	
Mutation method	Bit-flip mutation with probability = 0.025	
Population/Sub-population size	200	200
Maximum size of preserved non-dominated solution set	-	50
Maximum number of elitist individuals	50	50
Number of generations	600	Number required for an equivalent number of objective evaluations
Number of repeated runs	30	30

Table 2. Summary of the EMOA and CCMOA performances on the test problems T_1–T_6. The neighbourhood parameters (σ) for the calculation of M_2 indices from normalised objective vectors are set to 0.04082. These parameters are set with the extent of the true Pareto front in the objective space as the guideline.

T	Index	MOGA	CCMOGA	NPGA	CCNPGA	NSGA	CCNSGA	CNSGA	CCCNSGA
T_1	M_1	0.1469	0.0000	0.1047	0.0002	0.1267	0.0001	0.0426	0.0002
	M_2	48.061	47.980	48.245	47.980	48.245	48.000	48.041	48.000
	M_3'	0.1629	0.0117	0.1542	0.0032	0.1937	0.0042	0.0805	0.0044
T_2	M_1	0.2033	0.0001	0.3237	0.0002	0.3156	0.0002	0.0608	0.0003
	M_2	43.244	48.000	25.255	47.959	27.571	47.959	47.980	47.960
	M_3'	0.0682	0.0015	0.0503	0.0006	0.0776	0.0006	0.0181	0.0003
T_3	M_1	0.0721	0.0000	0.0638	0.0001	0.0806	0.0001	0.0239	0.0001
	M_2	46.980	47.776	47.592	47.878	47.510	47.878	47.592	47.755
	M_3'	0.1194	0.0038	0.1093	0.0033	0.1084	0.0033	0.0468	0.0017
T_4	M_1	2.9706	0.0001	5.7623	0.0000	4.1912	0.0000	2.1231	0.0000
	M_2	47.082	48.041	11.309	48.000	27.537	48.041	48.674	48.041
	M_3'	1.8915	0.0047	2.5086	0.0016	4.5755	0.0021	0.7483	0.0012
T_5	M_1	0.0481	0.0456	0.0709	0.0712	0.0788	0.0661	0.0864	0.0847
	M_2	41.041	46.776	39.347	46.898	40.347	46.857	46.837	46.939
	M_3'	0.5754	0.2000	0.5876	0.3000	0.5267	0.3000	0.5000	0.4500
T_6	M_1	1.1317	0.0000	2.6990	0.0000	2.4099	0.0000	0.4288	0.0000
	M_2	17.134	48.000	5.0000	48.000	6.1670	48.000	37.010	47.959
	M_3'	0.1112	0.0000	0.3359	0.0000	0.2240	0.0000	0.0866	0.0000

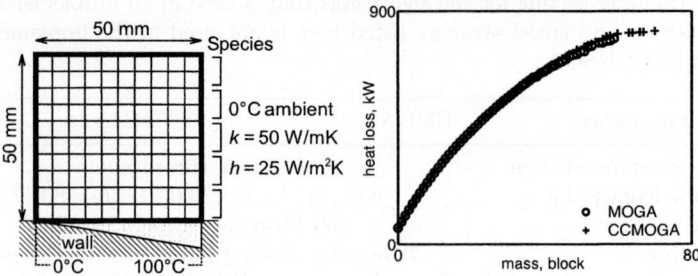

Fig. 1. Topology design problem (left) and the corresponding optimisation results (right).

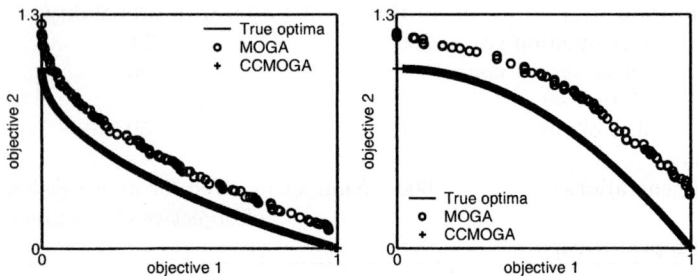

Fig. 2. Optimisation results of the T_1 (left) and T_2 (right) problems.

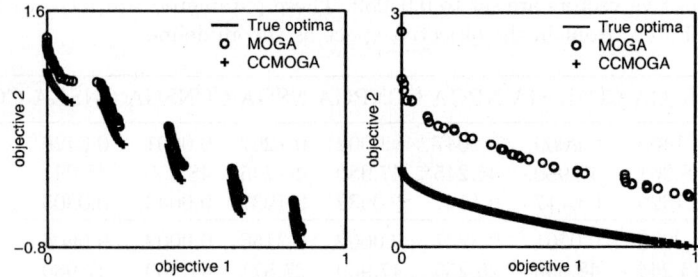

Fig. 3. Optimisation results of the T_3 (left) and T_4 (right) problems.

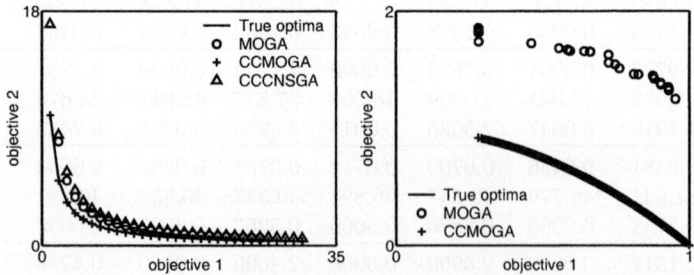

Fig. 4. Optimisation results of the T_5 (left) and T_6 (right) problems.

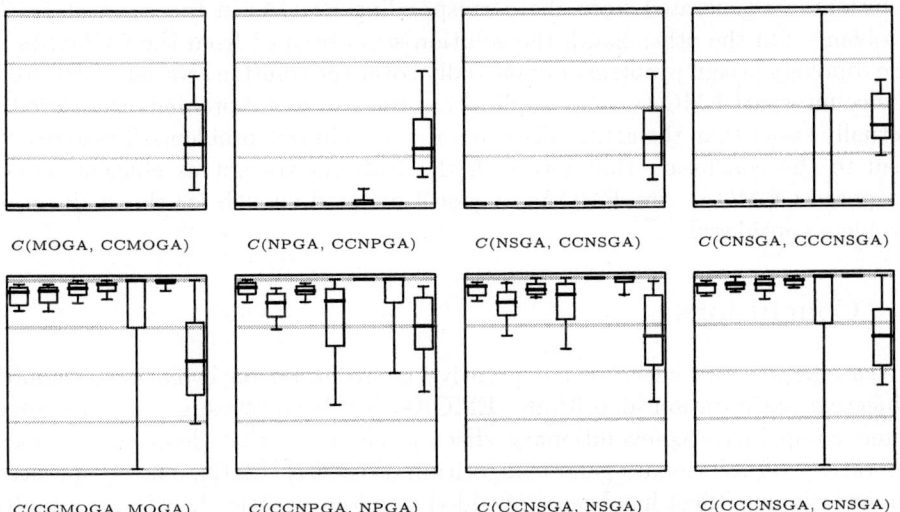

Fig. 5. Box plots of function $C(X, Y)$ which is covered by X) indices for each pair of EMOA and CCMOA. Each rectangle contains seven box plots representing the distribution of the C values; the leftmost box plot relates to T_1 while the rightmost to the topology design problem. The scale is 0 (no coverage) at the bottom and 1 (total coverage) at the top per rectangle.

co-operative co-evolution does not improve the solution distribution in the test problems T_1, and T_3. In contrast, a major improvement in the search results produced the CCNPGA and CCNSGA can be noticed in the test problems T_2, T_4, T_5 and T_6. In addition, some improvements can also be observed from the CCMOGA and CCCNSGA searches in the case of test problem T_6. In overall, the co-operative co-evolutionary effect helps creating a uniform distribution of solutions across the front.

In terms of the normalised absolute difference between the extent of the front described by the non-dominated solutions and that obtained from the true Pareto optimal solutions via the M_3' index, the co-operative co-evolutionary effect improves the performance of all algorithms. However, the search improvement in test problem T_5 is rendered less obvious numerically since the extent of the best deceptive Pareto front is very close to that of the true Pareto front. In other words, the M_3' index calculated from the solutions at the best deceptive Pareto front would only be slightly higher than that obtained from the solutions at the true Pareto front. For the test problem T_5, an additional use of graphical representation of solutions as shown in Fig. 4 (left) is required for the correct interpretation of the M_3' indices.

Finally, the solution set coverage using the C index is analysed. In contrast to the M_1, M_2 and M_3' indices, the C index can only be used to indicate whether the solution set obtained from one algorithm is dominated or equal to the solution set generated by another algorithm or not. The box plots illustrated in Fig. 5 clearly show that the solution sets obtained from the CCMOAs cover the solution sets generated from the corresponding EMOAs in the cases of T_1–T_6 problems. On the other hand, the solution sets obtained from the CCMOAs in the topology design problem only partially cover the solution sets generated from the counterpart EMOAs. This implies that the real-world problem considered is actually easier than the artificially generated benchmark problems. These results lead to the conclusion that although the EMOAs are not as efficient as the proposed CCMOAs, the EMOAs may still be good enough for the engineering problem considered.

6 Conclusions

In this paper, the effect of co-operative co-evolution on evolutionary multi-objective optimisation algorithms (EMOAs) has been investigated. The interested co-operative co-evolutionary effect is based on that described in a co-operative co-evolutionary genetic algorithm or CCGA [12, 13]. The co-operative co-evolutionary effect has been embedded into four genetic algorithms: a multi-objective genetic algorithm or MOGA [2, 5], a niched Pareto genetic algorithm or NPGA [3], a non-dominated sorting genetic algorithm or NSGA [4] and a controlled elitist non-dominated sorting genetic algorithm or CNSGA [7]. Subsequently, the co-operative co-evolutionary multi-objective optimisation algorithms (CCMOAs) have been benchmarked against the EMOAs in seven test problems. The first six problems cover different characteristics of multi-objective optimisation problems, namely convex Pareto front, non-convex Pareto front, discrete Pareto front, multi-modality, deceptive Pareto front and non-uniformity of solution distribution [14]. In contrast, the last problem is a two-objective real-world problem, which is generally referred to as a topology design [15]. The simulation results indicate that in general the CCMOAs are superior to the EMOAs. This conclusion is based upon the solution set coverage, the average distance from the non-dominated solutions and the true Pareto front, the distribution of the non-dominated solutions and the extent of the front described by the non-dominated solutions [14].

Acknowledgements

The support from the Thailand Research Fund (TRF) for Prof. P. Dechaumphai is acknowledged.

References

1. Hajela, P. and Lin, C. Y.: Genetic search strategies in multicriterion optimal design. Structural Optimization **4** (1992) 99–107
2. Fonseca, C. M. and Fleming, P. J.: Genetic algorithms for multiobjective optimization: Formulation, discussion and generalization. In: Proceedings of the Fifth International Conference on Genetic Algorithms, Urbana-Champaign, IL (1993) 416–423

3. Horn, J. and Nafpliotis, N.: Multiobjective optimization using the niched Pareto genetic algorithm. IlliGAL Report No. 93005, Illinois Genetic Algorithms Laboratory, University of Illinois at Urbana-Champaign, Urbana-Champaign, IL (1993)
4. Srinivas, N. and Deb, K.: Multi-objective function optimization using non-dominated sorting genetic algorithms. Evolutionary Computation **2**(3) (1994) 221–248
5. Fonseca, C. M. and Fleming, P. J.: Multiobjective optimization and multiple constraint handling with evolutionary algorithms–Part 1: A unified formulation. IEEE Transactions on Systems, Man, and Cybernetics–Part A: Systems and Humans **28**(1) (1998) 26–37
6. Zitzler, E. and Thiele, L.: Multiobjective evolutionary algorithms: A comparative case study and the strength Pareto approach. IEEE Transactions on Evolutionary Computation **3**(4) (1999) 257–271
7. Deb, K. and Goel, T.: Controlled elitist non-dominated sorting genetic algorithms for better convergence. In: Proceedings of the First International Conference on Evolutionary Multi-Criterion Optimization–Lecture Notes in Computer Science **1993**, Zurich, Switzerland (2001) 67–81
8. Deb, K., Pratap, A., Agarwal, S., and Meyarivan, T.: A fast and elitist multiobjective genetic algorithm: NSGA-II. IEEE Transactions on Evolutionary Computation **6**(2) (2002) 182–197
9. Sangkawelert, N. and Chaiyaratana, N.: Diversity control in a multi-objective genetic algorithm. In: Proceedings of the 2003 Congress on Evolutionary Computation, Canberra, Australia (2003) 2704–2711
10. Keerativuttitumrong, N., Chaiyaratana, N., and Varavithya, V.: Multi-objective co-operative co-evolutionary genetic algorithm. In: Proceedings of the Seventh International Conference on Parallel Problem Solving from Nature (PPSN VII)–Lecture Notes in Computer Science **2439**, Granada, Spain (2002) 288–297
11. Lohn, J. D., Kraus, W. F., and Haith, G. L.: Comparing coevolutionary genetic algorithm for multiobjective optimization. In: Proceedings of the 2002 Congress on Evolutionary Computation, Honolulu, HI (2002) 1157–1162
12. Potter, M. A. and De Jong, K. A.: A cooperative coevolutionary approach to function optimization. In: Proceedings of the Third International Conference on Parallel Problem Solving from Nature (PPSN III)–Lecture Notes in Computer Science **866**, Jerusalem, Israel (1994) 249–257
13. Potter, M. A. and De Jong, K. A.: Cooperative coevolution: An architecture for evolving coadapted subcomponents. Evolutionary Computation **8**(1) (2000) 1–29
14. Zitzler, E., Deb, K., and Thiele, L.: Comparison of multiobjective evolutionary algorithms: Empirical results. Evolutionary Computation **8**(2) (2000) 173–195
15. Boonlong, K. and Maneeratana, K.: A preliminary study on the multi-objective topology design by genetic algorithm and finite volume method. In: Proceedings of the 17th Conference of the Mechanical Engineering Network of Thailand, Prachinburi, Thailand (2003) CS024
16. Shimodaira, H.: DCGA: A diversity control oriented genetic algorithm. In: Proceedings of the Second International Conference on Genetic Algorithms in Engineering Systems: Innovations and Applications, Glasgow, UK (1997) 444–449
17. Shimodaira, H.: A diversity-control-oriented genetic algorithm (DCGA): Performance in function optimization. In: Proceedings of the 2001 Congress on Evolutionary Computation, Seoul, Korea (2001) 44–51

Sequential Process Optimisation Using Genetic Algorithms

Victor Oduguwa, Ashutosh Tiwari, and Rajkumar Roy

Enterprise Integration, School of Industrial and Manufacturing Science,
Cranfield University, Cranfield, Bedford, MK43 0AL, UK
voduguwa@hotmail.com,
{a.tiwari,r.roy}@cranfield.ac.uk

Abstract. Locating good design solutions within a sequential process environment is necessary to improve the quality and overall productivity of the processes. Multi-objective, multi-stage sequential process design is a complex problem involving large number of design variables and sequential relationship between any two stages. The aim of this paper is to propose a novel framework to handle real-life sequential process optimisation problems using a Genetic Algorithm (GA) based technique. The research validates the proposed GA based framework using a real-life case study of optimising the multi-pass rolling system design. The framework identifies a number of near optimal designs of the rolling system.

1 Introduction

Process optimisation involves the generation of optimal design solutions for individual units of the process including both design information such as the geometrical size of a unit and the operating conditions for the unit which are used to meet the desired reqirements of the overall process. Process optimisation problems are complex and can be charateritised as having multiple stages. Individual units of the process systems are connected to form multiple stages of the overall process problem. The nature of this association could be sequential or non-sequential. Sequential nature of the process offers the separate subsystems a dependency link where the output relationship of a subsystyem becomes the input relationship of the subsequent subsystem in an orderly manner. Non-sequential on the other hand is non-ordered association. This paper aims to propose a novel optimisation framework for handling sequential process optimisation problems.

Traditional methods of solving the sequential process optimisation problems are based on trial and error. This relies on manually adopting existing designs to produce the required design where a large set of design variables are changed, one variable at a time. Since the human can only deal with up to 5-10 variables at any single time [1], the optimisation task becomes slow and often results to sub optimum solutions.

A review of the literature reveals that there is very little work based on optimisation approaches reported for dealing with sequential process optimisation problems.

However, there are some related works reported in metal forming in general. Several authors have adopted the finite element (FE) based method since it provides detailed information about the domain being studied. Kobayashi [2] applied a FE based backward tracing technique to design a pre-form in a shell housing. This was also applied to plane-strain rolling problems [3] and disk forging. This technique has been shown to discover the desired final shape in various forming problems. However, backward tracing technique, when used alone, cannot uniquely determine the optimal solutions due to the presence of diverse and multiple loading solution paths. It tends to be more efficient when the loading path is known, however this can lead to difficulties in those problems where the search space is unknown especially when multiple diverse loading paths are present.

Several authors have also used derivative based approaches to solve sequential process optimisation problems. Joun and Hwang [4] developed a FE based process optimisation technique and applied it to a die profile design extrusion problem. In spite of reported successes, the derivative based approaches require an initial guess, which can influence the search. They also tend to get stuck in sub-optimal solutions and an algorithm that is efficient in solving one optimisation problem may not be efficient in solving a different optimisation problem [5].

In order to address these limitations, a number of authors [6] are now adopting genetic algorithms (GAs) with embedded FE solver to automate the search for good quality solutions. GAs are adaptive methods used to solve search and optimisation problems, based on genetic processes of biological organisms [7]. Roy *et al.* [8] implemented an adaptive Micro Genetic Algorithm for shape optimisation of process variables in multi-pass wire drawing processes. Hwang and Chung [9] proposed a modified micro genetic algorithm for the optimisation of die shape in extrusion. These GA based techniques provide an algorithmic framework to deal with the parameter optimisation in sequential process optimisation problems. The techniques can deliver multiple good solutions, which speed up the design process. However, the GA based approach using the FE solver as embedded optimiser incurs severe computational cost in real-life problems. This problem intensifies since GA techniques require large number of solutions for convergence. This inhibits the use of algorithmic approaches to real-life sequential process optimisation. Therefore, this paper applies the proposed framework for the multi-objective design optimisation of a four pass oval-round rolling pass using mathematical process model developed from rolling theory.

2 Proposed Optimisation Framework

This section proposes a novel optimisation framework for handling real-life sequential optimisation problems. The solution strategy adopted by the optimisation framework is based on the GA. The dependency link between stages is modelled based on informing the subsequent stage (i) of the move made by the ($i-1$)th stage such that the solution alternatives considered for the ith stage take into account the move made by the previous stage.

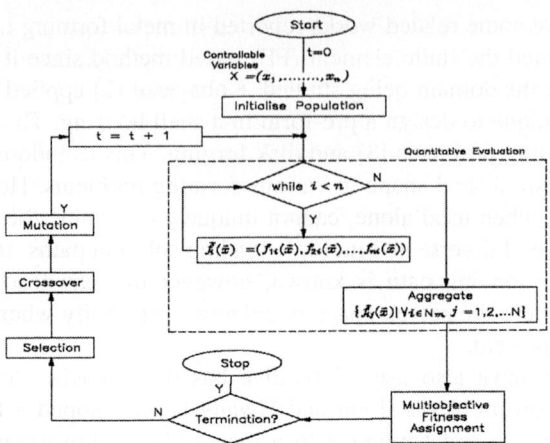

Fig. 1. NSGA-II for Sequential Optimisation Problems.

The GA based approach was selected because they have been used extensively as search and optimisation tools in various problem domains and the primary reasons for their success are applicability, ease of use and global perspectives. NSGA II was selected as the most popular multi-objective GA algorithm for the optimisation [5]. The following section presents the optimisation framework for real-life sequential optimisation problems. Figure 1 shows a flow chart of the solution technique. The solution algorithm consists of three main parts: the NSGA-II algorithm, the multi-stage model and the multi-objective fitness assignment. A brief description of the model and the coding scheme adopted is given below.

The model is used in two steps to evaluate individual members of the population. The first step is a local evaluation of a sub-set of strings in the chromosomes. This represents the objective function values for each stage of the sequential process optimisation problem while the second part is a global evaluation. This aggregates the objective function values of all the stages using a suitable aggregation operator. The objective function value of the global evaluation represents the fitness of the chromosome. The dependency relationship is modelled by incorporating design variables (stock variables) from a previous pass $k=j-1$ into the objective function of pass j. This relationship is peculiar to those sequential processes, where the output stock of one stage serves as input stock into the deforming tool of the other stage (e.g. metal forming). This is expressed for a given stage j by Equation 1, and the global evaluation is given by Equation 2 to illustrate this evaluation concept.

$$\vec{f}_j(\vec{x}) = \{f_{ij}(x_{1j}, x_{2j},....x_{mj}, x_{1k}, x_{2k},....x_{rk}) \mid (j=1,2,...n), k=j-1, r<m\} \quad (1)$$

$$\vec{F}_i^k(\vec{x}) = \sum_{j=1}^{n} \vec{f}_{ij}^k(\vec{x}) \mid i=1,2,...p \quad (2)$$

where i is the ith objective, p is the number of objectives, m is the number of design variables at stage j, k is the design variable from stage $j-1$, r is the number of design variables from stage $j-1$ that is considered at stage j, and n is the number of passes.

2.1 Genetic String Representation Printing Area

Figure 2 illustrates the string structure adopted for the sequential process optimisation problem. This coding procedure expresses all the design variables in binary code and combines them into a set of genetic strings that simulate the initial version of the design solution before conducting the evolutionary search. A genetic string is made up of sub-strings representing the number of stages, where the number of stages is assumed fixed. Since there is only one finishing stage, the genetic string has n-1 string segments for roughing and one segment for the finishing pass. Each of the sub-strings consists of product and process variables. Only controllable variables are represented in the genetic string and random values are chosen for these variables within the allowable range for each of the passes.

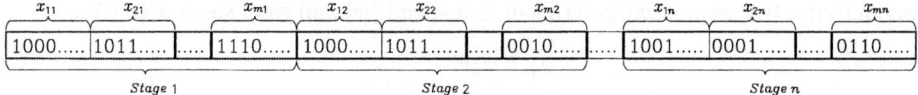

Fig. 2. String Structure of a Chromosome.

3 Case Study: Multi-pass Rolling System Optimisation

The multi-pass rolling system is a high-speed continuous metal forming process where the metal from the reheating furnace (referred to as stock) is continuously deformed into the desired product geometry by passing through a series of rotating cylindrical rolls. The multi-pass rolling system design (RSD) optimisation attempts to locate optimal design solutions for individual passes of the rolling process including both design information such as the geometrical size of a roll and the operating conditions for the mills.

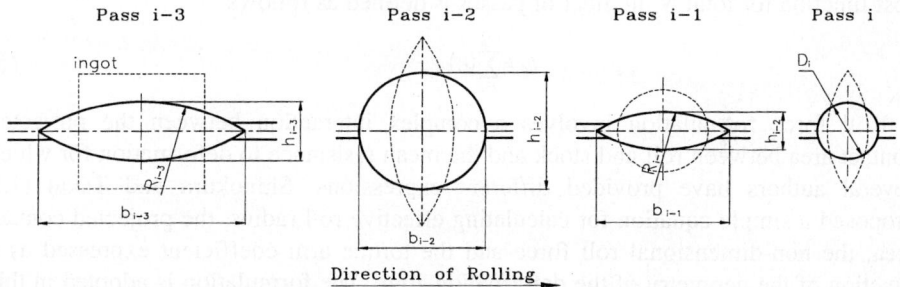

Fig. 3. Round-Oval-Round Breaking-Down Sequence.

3.1 Development of Multi-pass Rolling Model

A process model is required to evaluate the quality of each solution over the design space in order to conduct optimisation. Therefore, this section presents the development of a multi-pass rolling model. Figure 3 shows the process geometry addressed in this section. The overall breakdown sequence consists of a number of cascaded passes. The ith pass is denoted by P_i. Each pass is physically separated from its neighbours, and the output from the P_{i-1} is provided to the P_i as input. The breakdown sequence shows the oval stock turned through 90° with its major axis in-line with the vertical axis of the round pass. This is repeated for all the subsequent passes. The model development is detailed as follows. A detailed description of the model is available in [10].

Determination of Objective Function

Throughput
Throughput (T_p) is an important roll design objective that expresses the effect of mill productivity. It is expressed in terms of exit speed (w) and final stock area (A_2):

$$T_p = A_2 w \qquad (3)$$

Calculation of Pass Dimensions
The pass variables for each oval pass are: b_j and h_j; and round pass diameter, D. This assumes that the oval section is composed of two equal arcs of circle, its area is approximately [11]:

$$A = \frac{2h_j b_j}{2.85} \qquad (4)$$

The suffix 'j' = (1,2) is for inlet and outlet variables respectively.

Calculation of Roll Force
One of the most important objectives in the scheduling is to provide an optimum rolling load (P_T) required for deformation at each stand. Excessive loading in various passes can affect the productivity of the rolling process. The total deformation load cost function for total N_p number of passes is defined as follows:

$$P_T = \sum_{i=1}^{N_p} (P_i) \qquad (5)$$

Roll force formulation involves a complex interaction between the projected contact area between roll and stock and the mean resistance to deformation for which several authors have provided different expressions. Shinokura and Takai [12] proposed a simple equation for calculating effective roll radius, the projected contact area, the non-dimensional roll force and the torque arm coefficient expressed as a function of the geometry of the deformation zone. The formulation is adopted in this study since it is suitable for oval-to-oval passes. The equation is:

$$P_i = Q_s A_p (2k) \qquad (6)$$

where Q_s is a multiplier, A_p is the projected contact area and $2k$ is the mean flow strength in the pass.

Constraints for Validity Checks

The industrial application imposes the introduction of some constraints related to the quality of the product, technical function and organisational considerations. These factors can be classified into mechanical design constraints and variable constraints. The variable constraints are the upper and lower limits of the variables.

Roll Load

The total roll force is limited to the mechanical design limits of the rolling mills imposed by the roll manufactures. Excessive roll load can cause roll breakage that can be detrimental to production efficiency. This constraint can be formulated as follows:

$$g_1(\mathbf{x}) \equiv P_i \leq P_{max} \tag{7}$$

Related Process Functions

λ_T and λ_k are the total elongation and elongation at stage k, therefore:

$$g_2(\mathbf{x}) \equiv \sum_{k=1}^{n} \lambda_k - \lambda_T \geq 0 \tag{8}$$

The following constraint is required to ensure the breakdown sequence is achieved with reduction taking place from pass to pass. For every pass i;

$$\text{Inter-pass reduction} \quad g_3(\mathbf{x}) \equiv \lambda_i > 1 \tag{9}$$

Rod Size

The overall rod size is a measure of product quality. This is allowed to vary within a given tolerance limit K. This is treated as a soft constraint to allow the possibility to explore designs within the specified boundaries. This is specified as:

$$g_4(\mathbf{x}) \equiv K_{min} \leq \sqrt{(D_{Np} - D)^2} \leq K_{max} \tag{10}$$

The breakdown sequence shows the oval stock turned through 90° with its major axis in the vertical diagonal of the square pass. The square stock is provided as flat into the oval pass and the oval stock is turned through 90° with its major axis in-line with the vertical axis of the round pass. Constraints on inter-pass sections can be shown as:

$$h_3(\mathbf{x}) \equiv b_i^j = h_{i-1}^{j+1}; i = 1, 2 \ldots n; j = 1, 2 \tag{11}$$

$$h_4(\mathbf{x}) \equiv h_i^j = b_{i-1}^{j+1}; i = 1, 2 \ldots n; j = 1, 2 \tag{12}$$

3.2 Multi-pass Rolling System Optimisation

This section presents an application of the novel framework (Section 2) for optimal shape design of a pass schedule in long product hot rolling of sections. The aim is to determine the geometry of each pass that would ensure the reduction of an ingot from a given section to a prescribed final section with respect to some cost objectives, while satisfying some constraints. The problem is solved using the proposed framework and the results are compared with work reported in the literature. GA computes the objective function for each string of the solution space so that the individual with the better fitness value is determined. Equation 13 gives a formal definition of the multi-objective RSD optimisation problem. It aims to minimise deformation load and maximise rolling throughput, subject to given constraints for a four pass oval to round design. The deformation load is a cost objective while throughput is a function of mill productivity. Excessive deformation load results in excessive roll wear and hence overall production cost. Both objectives are assumed conflicting in nature since metal compression by the cylindrical rolls encourages metal flow in the direction of rolling, increasing the metal deformation load, also increasing the metal flow.

Equation 13:

Minimise Total Deformation Load (5) $\quad f_1(\mathbf{x}) \equiv P_T(x)$

Maximise Throughput (3) $\quad f_2(\mathbf{x}) \equiv T_p(x)$

Subject to:

Roll Load (7) $\quad g_1(\mathbf{x}) \equiv P_i \leq P_{max}$

Total elongation (8) $\quad g_2(\mathbf{x}) \equiv \sum_{k=1}^{n} \lambda_k - \lambda_T \geq 0$

Inter-pass reduction (9) $\quad g_3(\mathbf{x}) \equiv \lambda_i > 1$

Rod size (10) $\quad g_4(\mathbf{x}) \equiv K_{min} \leq \sqrt{(D_{Np} - D)^2} \leq K_{max}$

Inter-pass sections (11) $\quad h_3(\mathbf{x}) \equiv b_i^j = h_{i-1}^{j+1}; i = 1,2...n; j = 1,2$

Inter-pass sections (12) $\quad h_4(\mathbf{x}) \equiv h_i^j = b_{i-1}^{j+1}; i = 1,2...n; j = 1,2$

Experimental Details

The NSGA-II based algorithm solves a multi-pass roll design problem to minimise deformation load while maximising the mill throughput. Experiments were carried out using the proposed framework for the two objectives to illustrate how the algorithm deals with the multi-objective multi-pass search space problem. The following additional parameters were set for the experiment. P_{max} = 750KN per stand, final rod diameter (D) = 20.1±0.25 mm, where k_{min} is set as 19.85 mm and k_{max} is set as 20.35 mm, and the tolerance range was estimated based on design experience.

Results were obtained using the process model developed in Section 3.1. The performances of the solution algorithm for different values of crossover and mutation probabilities were first investigated. Ten independent GA runs were performed in each case using a different random initial population. The crowded tournament selector operator was used to select new offspring. Tests were carried out with the following parameters: population of size 500 for 2000 generation with a 3-point crossover probability of 0.8 and a mutation probability of 0.03, and tournament selection with size 3. The 3-point crossover was chosen to ensure more effective transfer of genetic material during reproduction since the total chromosome length is

225. These results form the typical set obtained from 10 runs with different random number seeds. Six out of ten runs obtained similar results. A random search of 10000 points is also conducted in order to get an indication of the search space. This will be used to identify the likely presence of a Pareto front in the design problem. Details of results are discussed as follows.

Discussion of Results

The results obtained from the NSGA-II algorithm are compared to empirical results published in the literature [11]. Results shown in Figure 4 were obtained for the NSGA-II parameters outlined above. Comparison of the random search space and the results achieved from the algorithm confirms that the solution algorithm has been able to converge to the Pareto front. Since the search space is not known in absolute terms, the results reported in Figure 4 have converged to the near optimal Pareto front locating a reasonable spread of multiple optimal solutions. The presence of a Pareto front also confirms the conflicting relationship between deformation load and throughput. The empirical design point obtained from the literature was superimposed in the search space and compared with the near optimal solutions. Since this point does not lie on the identified near optimal Pareto front, it is clear that the solutions obtained are superior to the empirical based solution.

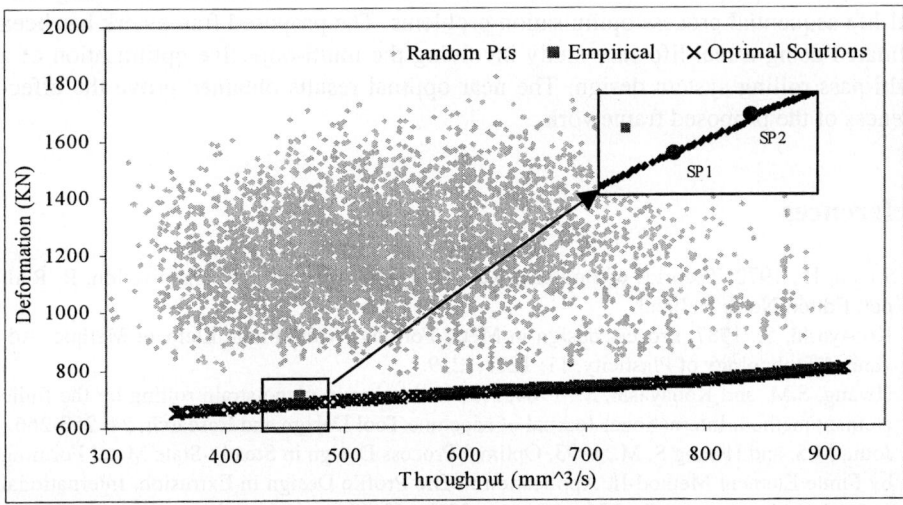

Fig. 4. Pareto Front for Four Pass Rolling Process.

SP1 (see insert in Figure 4) demonstrates a classic example of how this algorithmic-based approach can locate better solutions compared to the single point methods. Since the deformation load is lower and the throughput is higher than the empirical solution, the NSGA-II based solution is better than the empirical based solution for both objectives. This implies that the proposed approach is capable of identifying solutions with higher outputs at lower deformation loads than the empirical based solution. Two solution points SP1 and SP2 are selected (see insert in Figure 4) and compared with the empirical solution in terms of throughput, deformation load, elongation coefficient and the deformed sections. Results obtained from the proposed approach not only identify good solutions, but also provide insight into the complex behaviour of the design problem.

The optimisation framework is limited to process optimisation problems with sequential relationships between consecutive stages. Also, the case study only considers a four pass rolling design, in practice there can be many more passes required for rod rolling (usually up to 25 passes). The scalability of the framework is not tested in this research. It is also observed that aggregation of the contributions from different passes may even out fluctuations caused by many of the underlying unknown factors, this can lead to deception problem for the GA. In future it would be useful to study the nature of behaviour between the different stages during the GA search. Such information could be valuable in understanding the convergence behaviour of the search space, which could result in improved GA based optimisation algorithms.

4 Conclusion

This paper has proposed a novel GA-based optimisation framework for dealing with real-life sequential process optimisation problems. The proposed framework has been validated using a real-life case study involving the multi-objective optimisation of a multi-pass rolling system design. The near optimal results obtained prove the effectiveness of the proposed framework.

References

1. Simon, H., 1972, Theories of Bounded Rationality, in Decision and Organization, R. Radner, Editor, North Holland.
2. Kobayashi, S., 1987, Process design in Metal Formng by the Finite Element Method. Advanced Technology of Plasticity, 11: 1213-1219.
3. Hwang, S.M. and Kobayashi, S., 1984, Preform design in plane-strain rolling by the finite element method. International Journal of Machine Tool Design and Research, 24: 253-266.
4. Joun, M.S. and Hwang S. M., 1993, Optimal Process Design in Steady-State Metal Forming by Finite Element Method-II. Application to Die Profile Design in Extrusion. International Journal of Machine and Tool Manufacture, 33(1): 63-70.
5. Deb, K., 2001, Multi-objective Optimization Using Evolutionary Algorithms. John Wiley and Sons Ltd.
6. Chakraborti, N. and Kumar, A., 2003, The Optimal Scheduling of a Reversing Strip Mill: Studies Using Multi-population Genetic Algorithms and Differential Evolution. Journal of Material Processing Technology. Submitted for publication.
7. Goldberg, D.E., 1989, Genetic Algorithm in Search, Optimization and Machine Learning. Addison Wesley, Massachusetts.

8. Roy, S., Ghosh, S., and Shivpuri, R., 1996, Optimal Design of Process Variables in Multi-Pass Wire Drawing by Genetic Algorithms. Journal of Manufacturing Science and Engineering, 118-124.
9. Hwang, S.M. and Chung, J.S., 1997, Application of genetic algorithm to optimal design of the die shape in Extrusion. Journal of Materials Processing Technology, 72: 69-77.
10. Oduguwa, V., 2003, Rolling System Design Optimisation using Soft Computing Techniques, EngD Thesis, Cranfield University, UK.
11. Wusatowski, Z., 1969, Fundamentals of rolling, Pergamon.
12. Shinokura, T. and Takai, K., 1982, A new method for calculating spread in rod rolling. Journal of Application in Metalworking, 2: 147-160.

On Test Functions for Evolutionary Multi-objective Optimization

Tatsuya Okabe, Yaochu Jin, Markus Olhofer, and Bernhard Sendhoff

Honda Research Institute Europe GmbH
Carl-Legien-Strasse 30, 63073 Offenbach/Main, Germany

Abstract. In order to evaluate the relative performance of optimization algorithms benchmark problems are frequently used. In the case of multi-objective optimization (MOO), we will show in this paper that most known benchmark problems belong to a constrained class of functions with piecewise linear Pareto fronts in the parameter space. We present a straightforward way to define benchmark problems with an arbitrary Pareto front both in the fitness and parameter spaces. Furthermore, we introduce a difficulty measure based on the mapping of probability density functions from parameter to fitness space. Finally, we evaluate two MOO algorithms for new benchmark problems.

1 Introduction

In the recent literature, several multi-objective evolutionary optimization algorithms have been proposed [1, 3]. In order to compare their performance and in order for practitioners to decide which algorithm to employ, benchmark problems (test functions) are extensively used. Therefore, the properties of test functions and their difficulty and representativeness are of utmost importance. Although some work on summarizing the properties of test functions for multi-objective optimization can be found in the literature [1], we will see in the next section that a majority of all test functions share the same property: their Pareto front in parameter space is piecewise linear. This restriction of benchmarks to a limited class of functions is dangerous since we cannot expect that most real-world problems will also have piecewise linear Pareto fronts in parameter space. It is the target of this paper to present an "easy to follow" recipe to construct test functions for multi-objective optimization problems with arbitrary, user-specified Pareto curves in the parameter space *and* fitness space. Furthermore, in Section 4, we will present a measure for the difficulty of benchmark problems based on the mapping between parameter space and fitness space[1]. In Section 5, examples of generated test functions will be given. We will compare two multi-objective evolutionary algorithms for these new test problems in Section 6 and summarize this paper in the last section.

---

[1] Note that the fitness space is the space spanned by the number of objectives in MOO. It should not be confused with the fitness landscape, which in single objective optimization is sometimes also referred to as fitness space.

2 Properties of Test Functions

Coello et al. [1] have summarized test functions for MOO according to their properties in the fitness space (FS) and in the parameter space (PS). However the geometry of the Pareto front in parameter space and in particular the mapping between the PS and the FS has not received much attention. We investigated the geometry of the Pareto front in the PS of the test functions found in [1, 3]. The results are shown in Table 1 for the two-dimensional case. It is noticed that the Pareto fronts of most test functions consists of piecewise linear curves and/or single points in the PS.

Table 1. Geometry of Pareto fronts in the parameter space. The properties of test functions with "*" are obtained empirically.

Geometry	Test Functions	Geometry	Test Functions
1 Point	Binh(3), Osyczka	4 Lines	Schaffer(2),ZDT3
31 Points	ZDT5	5 Lines	Osyczka(2)
1 Line	Binh(1),Binh(2),Fonseca, Fonseca(2),Laumanns,Lis, Murata,Rendon(2),Schaffer, Belegundu,Kita,Srinivas, ZDT1,ZDT2,ZDT4,ZDT6	1 Point and 3 Lines	Kursawe*
		1 Point and 4 Lines	Poloni*,Viennet(3)*
		1 Curve	Binh(4),Obayashi
		3 Curves	Tanaka
		1 Surface	Viennet*,Tamaki
2 Lines	Jimenez	1 Surface and 1 Line	Viennet(4)*
3 Lines	Rendon,Viennet(2)*	6 Parts of Surface	Quaglizrella

In [2,3], Deb has proposed the following method to construct "tunable" test functions for MOO:

$$\min (f_1(\boldsymbol{x}), f_2(\boldsymbol{x})) = (f_1(x_1, x_2, ..., x_m), g(x_{m+1}, x_{m+2}, ..., x_n) \cdot h(f_1, g)). \quad (1)$$

Here, $f_i, i = 1, 2$ and $x_j, j = 1, \ldots, n$ are the i-th objective function, and the j-th component of the parameter vector with dimension n. Functions g and h are defined by the user. In Equation (1), function h determines the shape of the Pareto front in the fitness space, function g controls the difficulty for an algorithm to converge to the Pareto front, and function f_1 influences the diversity of the Pareto optimal solutions. By applying deceptive or multi-modal test functions from single objective optimization (SOO) to g, one can realize the same difficulty, i.e. deceptiveness or multi-modality, in MOO. Therefore, it is possible to determine the shape of the Pareto front in FS and to tune the difficulty with respect to "standard" measures of difficulty from single objective optimization. However, we can decompose the optimization problem resulting from such test functions in the following way: (1) minimize the g function; (2) generate proper f_1 values to get widely spread and well-distributed solutions. Since all values of f_1 locate on the boundary of the feasible region and might be Pareto optimal solutions, it is sufficient to generate well-distributed f_1 values to get well-distributed Pareto-optimal solutions. The mapping between the parameter and the fitness spaces, and the shape of the Pareto front in parameter space have not been taken into account in the framework outlined above. This might be the reason for the similarity of the class of test functions created using the framework.

Although many papers in the literature concentrate on bi-objective optimization and/or optimization without constraints, most of real-world problems have more than two objectives and a lot of constraints. Three different approaches for generating test functions with more than two objectives in [4, 6] and the one for constrained test functions in [5] are proposed. These are frontier work for more practical test functions.

3 A New Method to Build Test Functions

This section proposes a method to construct different types of test functions with arbitrary, customized Pareto fronts in fitness *and* in parameter space. The basic idea is to start from a starting space between a parameter space and a fitness space[2], which we denote by $\mathcal{S}^2$, and to construct the parameter space and the fitness by applying appropriate functions to $\mathcal{S}^2$. Using the inverse of the generation operation, i.e. deformation, rotation and shift, for the parameter space, we arrive at the mapping from PS to FS. The basic procedure is outlined in Figure 1 and will be described in detail in the next sections.

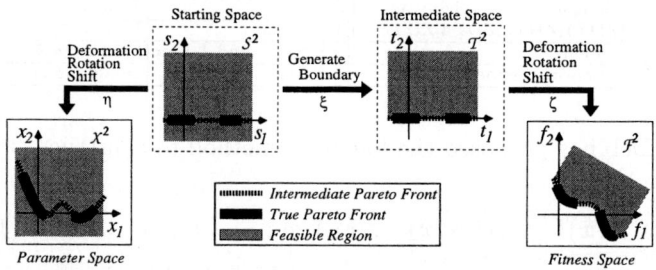

Fig. 1. Basic idea to generate test functions with arbitrary Pareto fronts in the PS and the FS. The space $\mathcal{S}^2$ is the starting space. The final result is given by the Pareto fronts in the PS $\mathcal{X}^2$ and the FS $\mathcal{F}^2$ and the mapping from PS to FS.

3.1 Determine Intermediate Pareto Front in the PS

The space $\mathcal{S}^2(s_1, s_2)$ with the Pareto front $s_2 = 0$ is used as the starting point. The mapping between $\mathcal{S}^2$ and the parameter space $\mathcal{X}^2(x_1, x_2)$ is given by

$$x_1 = \eta_1(s_1, s_2), \quad x_2 = \eta_2(s_1, s_2). \tag{2}$$

The following equations correspond to the intermediate Pareto front in PS

$$x_1 = \eta_1(s_1, s_2 = 0), \quad x_2 = \eta_2(s_1, s_2 = 0). \tag{3}$$

Since a true Pareto front will be determined later, we added the term *intermediate*. If the defining space for η_1^{-1} is denoted as $\mathcal{X}^2_{\eta_1^{-1}}$, the functional relation for the Pareto front in the parameter space is given by

---
[2] Note that we will restrict the discussion in the following to two dimensions, however, the identical approach can be used to construct test functions in higher dimensions (both of a parameter space and a fitness space).

$$x_2 = \eta_2(\eta_1^{-1}(x_1, s_2 = 0), s_2 = 0), \quad x_1 \in \mathcal{X}_{\eta_1^{-1}}^2 \tag{4}$$

Therefore, functions η_1 and η_2 define the Pareto front in parameter space. Additionally, some constraints are introduced if $\mathcal{X}_{\eta_1^{-1}}^2 \neq I\!R^2$, e.g. if $\eta_1 = s_1^2$, the constraint is given by $x_1 \geq 0$. However, besides defining the (intermediate) Pareto front in parameter space, η_1 also has a more hidden property. It relates the probability density (PD) in $\mathcal{S}^2$ space to the probability density in $\mathcal{X}^2$ space. This is an important aspect because the search process in multi-objective evolutionary optimization can be understood by mapping the search distribution in parameter space to the one in fitness space [8]. Two examples of the mapping of a uniform distribution on $s_2 = 0$ in $\mathcal{S}^2$ space to the Pareto front in parameter space are shown in Figure 2 with $\eta_2 = \sin(s_1)$. Here, the points are generated with $s_1 = 0.1i - 4.0$ $(i = 0, 1, \cdots, 80)$. We refer to this property of η_1 as *deformation*.

In order to analyze the effect of the functions η_1 and η_2 on the whole $\mathcal{X}^2$ space (not just the Pareto front), we decompose them into functions that depend on s_1 or s_2 only[3].

$$x_1 = \eta_1(s_1, s_2) \equiv g_1(s_1) + g_2(s_2), \quad x_2 = \eta_2(s_1, s_2) \equiv g_3(s_1) + g_4(s_2). \tag{5}$$

To simplify our discussion, $g_2(s_2) = 0$ will be used for the rest of this paper. If we assume $g_4(s_2) = 0, \forall s_2 = 0$, then our comments above on the role of η_1 equally apply to $g_3(s_1)$. Thus, $g_3(s_1)$ determines the relationship of the probability density on the Pareto front from the $\mathcal{S}^2$ space to the $\mathcal{X}^2$. The role of $g_4(s_2)$ is similar, however, it controls the mapping of the probability density function *approaching* the Pareto front. Again in Figure 3 two examples are shown. Here, the points are generated with $s_1 = 0.1i - 4.0$ $(i = 0, 1, \cdots, 80)$, $s_2 = 0.25j - 1.0$ $(j = 0, 1, \cdots, 8)$. Needless to say that the function $g_4(s_2)$ is very important as a measure for the difficulty of the optimization problem. In the extreme case, the Pareto front might be an "island" surrounded by areas of extremely low probability (under the assumption of a uniform distribution in $\mathcal{S}^2$ space).

In order to extend the possible degree of variation, the Pareto front in $\mathcal{X}^2$ space can additionally be *rotated* using a standard rotation matrix.

So far we have discussed the mapping from the starting space $\mathcal{S}^2$ to $\mathcal{X}^2$ space, because this is the direction for constructing the Pareto front. Of course the mapping direction during search is the opposite. The projected probability distributions for the mapping from $\mathcal{X}^2$ space to $\mathcal{S}^2$ space assuming uniform distribution of (x_1, x_2) in $[-\pi, \pi]^2$ is shown in Figure 4(a) for the example of

$$\eta_1(s_1, s_2) = s_1^3, \quad \eta_2(s_1, s_2) = \sin(s_1^3) + s_2, \tag{6}$$

and in Figure 4(b) for the example of

$$\eta_1(s_1, s_2) = s_1, \quad \eta_2(s_1, s_2) = \sin(s_1) + s_2^3. \tag{7}$$

In Figure 4(b), we can observe the "island effect" which we mentioned above.

---

[3] To simplify our discussion, we assume that η_1 and η_2 can be decomposed. However, this assumption is not necessary for generating test functions in practice.

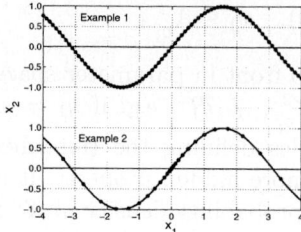
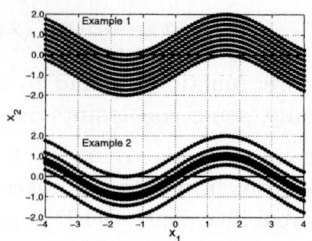

Fig. 2. The effect of η_1 function. Probability density of solutions along the Pareto front for $\eta_1(s_1, s_2 = 0) = s_1$ (top) and $\eta_1(s_1, s_2 = 0) = s_1^3$ (bottom). Data points (dots) are uniformly generated in $\mathcal{S}^2$ space.

Fig. 3. The effect of g_4 function. Probability density for $g_4(s_2) = s_2$ (top) and $g_4(s_2) = s_2^3$ (bottom). Here, $\eta_1(s_1, s_2) = s_1$ and $g_3(s_1) = \sin(s_1)$ are assumed. Data points (dots) are uniformly generated in the $\mathcal{S}^2$ space.

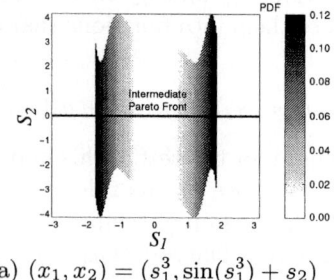
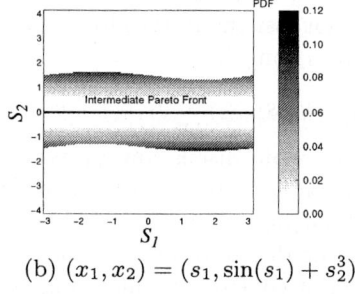

(a) $(x_1, x_2) = (s_1^3, \sin(s_1^3) + s_2)$ (b) $(x_1, x_2) = (s_1, \sin(s_1) + s_2^3)$

Fig. 4. Projected distribution in the $\mathcal{S}^2$ space. The distribution in the PS (the $\mathcal{X}^2$ space), is assumed to be uniform in $(x_1, x_2) \in [-\pi, \pi]^2$.

3.2 Generate Boundary

The first step from the intermediate space $\mathcal{S}^2$ toward the fitness space is the generation of a boundary, since the Pareto front in fitness space usually consists of parts of a boundary.

There are two approaches to generating boundaries. First, the boundary can explicitly be defined by introducing appropriate constraints. Second, it can implicitly be defined by using functions that generate a boundary. We will concentrate on the second approach and define a second intermediate space $\mathcal{T}^2 = (t_1, t_2)$. The following functions will be used as "boundary generators":

(1) $t_1 = \xi_1(s_1) = s_1$ (2) $t_1 = \xi_1(s_1) = s_1$ (3) $t_1 = \xi_1(s_1) = s_1$
    $t_2 = \xi_2(s_2) = s_2^2$ $t_2 = \xi_2(s_2) = |s_2|$ $t_2 = \xi_2(s_2) = \sqrt{|s_2|}$.

Now, the distribution in the $\mathcal{T}^2$ space can be calculated theoretically [8]. The distribution in the $\mathcal{S}^2$ space is assumed to be uniform in $[-1, 1]^2$. The results are shown in Figure 5. As explained in [8], the sphere function results in the highest value of the probability density function (PDF) near the intermediate Pareto front. Theoretically, the PDF of case (1) at $t_2 = 0$ is infinity. For the absolute function, case (2), the distribution remains uniform. The square root function, case (3), generates difficult problems to reach the intermediate Pareto front.

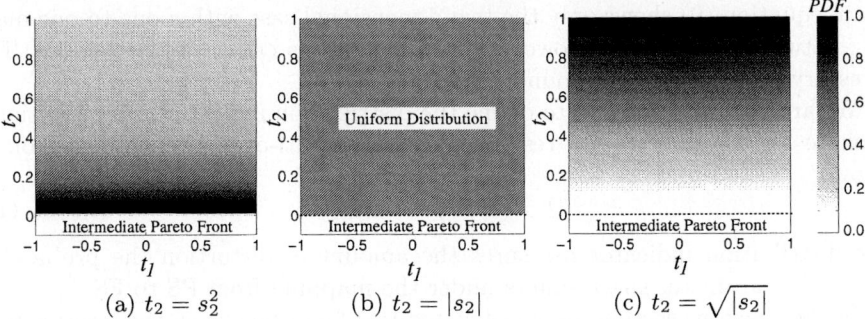

Fig. 5. Projected Distribution in the $\mathcal{T}^2$ space. The distribution in the $\mathcal{S}^2$ space is assumed to be uniform in $[-1, 1]^2$.

3.3 Determine Intermediate and True Pareto Front in FS

To generate the shape of the intermediate Pareto front in the FS, the same procedure as in Section 3.1 can be used. In the $\mathcal{T}^2$ space, the boundary of $t_1 = 0$ is the candidate for the Pareto front in the FS. The relationship between the space $\mathcal{T}^2$ and the fitness space can be written as:

$$f_1 = \zeta_1(t_1, t_2), \quad f_2 = \zeta_2(t_1, t_2). \tag{8}$$

It is worth noticing that the mapping direction from $\mathcal{T}^2$ to $\mathcal{F}^2$ is the same as for the optimization, i.e. from the PS to the FS. Thus, the discussion of the properties of ζ_1 and ζ_2 carry directly over to the discussion of the PS to FS mapping for the optimization.

After generating the intermediate Pareto front, the true Pareto front in the FS will be determined. According to the definition of Pareto optimality [1], only parts of the generated boundary will be the Pareto front. Here, we can also generate a disconnected Pareto front by selecting proper functions of ζ_1 and ζ_2. To know which parts are the Pareto front in the PS, the boundary information can be mapped back to the PS using the functions and their inverses outlined in the previous sections.

4 Distribution Indicator

In this section, we will discuss the difficulty of test functions from the viewpoint of the transformation of a given probability density under the mapping from the parameter space to the fitness space. For this purpose, the *Distribution Indicator* will be proposed.

Assume the distribution before projection to be $\phi(x_1, x_2)$ in the parameter space $\mathcal{X}^2$. Using the following equation, the projected distribution, $\psi(f_1, f_2)$, in the fitness space $\mathcal{F}^2$ can be calculated with the Jacobian matrix J as follows [8]:

$$\psi(f_1, f_2) = \frac{1}{|J|} \phi(x_1, x_2), \quad |J| = \frac{\partial f_1}{\partial x_1} \frac{\partial f_2}{\partial x_2} - \frac{\partial f_1}{\partial x_2} \frac{\partial f_2}{\partial x_1}. \tag{9}$$

Again equation (9) shows only the two-dimensional case with a one-to-one mapping between both spaces, however, both conditions can easily be relaxed. The necessary extension can be found in [8].

We are now in a position to define the distribution indicator as an additional measure for the difficulty of test problems for multi-objective optimization as follows:

$$\mathcal{D} = (\det J)^{-1} = |J|^{-1}. \tag{10}$$

The distribution indicator measures the amount of distortion the probability density in parameter space suffers under the mapping from PS to FS.

In the previous section, we constructed test functions using the intermediate spaces $\mathcal{S}^2$ and $\mathcal{T}^2$ and the additional rotation operation. The rotation results in no distortion and will therefore be neglected in the following. The remaining distribution indicators can simply be multiplied to yield the overall indicator:

$$\mathcal{D} \equiv \mathcal{D}_{x \to f} = \mathcal{D}_{x \to s} \times \mathcal{D}_{s \to t} \times \mathcal{D}_{t \to f} \tag{11}$$

The *Distribution Indicators* $\mathcal{D}_{x \to s}$ for the functions that we used in the previous sections are given as follows

(1) $(x_1, x_2) = (s_1, \sin(s_1) + s_2) \quad \to \quad \mathcal{D}_{x \to s} = 1$
(2) $(x_1, x_2) = (s_1^3, \sin(s_1^3) + s_2) \quad \to \quad \mathcal{D}_{x \to s} = 3s_1^2$
(3) $(x_1, x_2) = (s_1, \sin(s_1) + s_2^3) \quad \to \quad \mathcal{D}_{x \to s} = 3s_2^2$

Case 1 results in no changes in the probability density. For the second case, the distribution is uniform in the direction of s_2 but not in s_1. Since the *Distribution Indicator* becomes low near $s_1 = 0$, the probability density in this area becomes sparse whereas it is high for $s_1 \gg 0$ and $s_1 \ll 0$. Case 3 is similar to case 2, however, the role of s_1 and s_2 is exchanged. These results which show good agreement with Figure 4 demonstrate that difficult MOO problems can be generated with a smaller *Distribution Indicator* close to the Pareto front.

The *Distribution Indicators* $\mathcal{D}_{s \to t}$ are given by

(1) $(t_1, t_2) = (s_1, s_2^2) \quad \to \quad \mathcal{D}_{s \to t} = (2\sqrt{t_2})^{-1}$
(2) $(t_1, t_2) = (s_1, |s_2|) \quad \to \quad \mathcal{D}_{s \to t} = 1$
(3) $(t_1, t_2) = (s_1, \sqrt{|s_2|}) \quad \to \quad \mathcal{D}_{s \to t} = 2t_2$

For case 1 the PDF becomes infinite on the intermediate Pareto front. Additionally, the area near the intermediate Pareto front has higher values of the PDF. This situation is the same as for SCH1 test function in [9]. Case 2 results in a uniform distribution due to $\mathcal{D} = 1$. In case 3, the distribution depends on $2t_2$. Thus, the area far from the intermediate Pareto front has high value. The minimum PDF is on the intermediate Pareto front.

The *Distribution Indicators* $\mathcal{D}_{t \to f}$ can be calculated in the same way with $\mathcal{D}_{x \to s}$ due to the same generation operation.

5 Illustrative Examples

With the framework presented in this paper, a variety of test functions can be generated. Due to the space limit, only two examples are shown here.

Test Function OKA1

Suppose that the desired Pareto front in the PS is defined by $x_2 = 3\cos(x_1) + 3$ with 15-degree rotation clockwise and the one in the FS by $f_2 = \sqrt{2\pi} - \sqrt{f_1}$. To control the hardness of the test function, the distribution in the f_1 direction is assumed to be uniform (see Example 1 in Figure 2) and the one in the f_2 direction is assumed to become more sparse towards the Pareto front, see Figure 4 (b). For this purpose, we can use the following mapping functions:

$$\eta_1(s_1, s_2) = \cos(\pi/12)s_1 + \sin(\pi/12)\left(3\cos(s_1) + 3 + s_2^3\right),$$
$$\eta_2(s_1, s_2) = -\sin(\pi/12)s_1 + \cos(\pi/12)\left(3\cos(s_1) + 3 + s_2^3\right)$$
$$\xi_1(s_1) = s_1, \quad \xi_2(s_2) = |s_2|, \quad \zeta_1(t_1, t_2) = t_1, \quad \zeta_2(t_1, t_2) = \sqrt{2\pi} - \sqrt{|t_1|} + 2t_2. \quad (12)$$

Here, η_1 and η_2 define the Pareto front in the PS. To generate the boundary, the simple mapping functions $\xi_1 = s_1$ and $\xi_2 = |s_2|$ is used. Finally, mappings ζ_1 and ζ_2 determine the Pareto front in the the FS. In this way, the following MOO test function is created:

$$f_1 = x_1', \quad f_2 = \sqrt{2\pi} - \sqrt{|x_1'|} + 2\left|x_2' - 3\cos(x_1') - 3\right|^{\frac{1}{3}},$$
$$x_1' = \cos(\pi/12)x_1 - \sin(\pi/12)x_2, \quad x_2' = \sin(\pi/12)x_1 + \cos(\pi/12)x_2,$$
$$x_1 \in [6\sin(\pi/12), 6\sin(\pi/12) + 2\pi\cos(\pi/12)], \quad x_2 \in [-2\pi\sin(\pi/12), 6\cos(\pi/12)]$$
Pareto Front in the PS $\quad x_2' = 3\cos(x_1') + 3 \quad (x_1' \in [0, 2\pi])$
Pareto Front in the FS $\quad f_2 = \sqrt{2\pi} - \sqrt{f_1} \quad (f_1 \in [0, 2\pi])$
Distribution Indicator $\quad \mathcal{D}_{x \to f} = \dfrac{3}{2}\left|x_2' - 3\cos(x_1') - 3\right|^{\frac{2}{3}}. \quad (13)$

Test Function OKA2

Similarly, we can construct the following three-dimensional test function:

$$f_1 = x_1, \quad f_2 = 1 - \frac{1}{4\pi^2}(x_1 + \pi)^2 + |x_2 - 5\cos(x_1)|^{\frac{1}{3}} + |x_3 - 5\sin(x_1)|^{\frac{1}{3}}$$
$$x_1 \in [-\pi, \pi], \quad x_2, x_3 \in [-5, 5]$$
Pareto Front in the PS $\quad (x_1, x_2, x_3) = (\xi, 5\cos(\xi), 5\sin(\xi)) \quad (x_1 \in [-\pi, \pi])$
Pareto Front in the FS $\quad f_2 = 1 - \dfrac{1}{4\pi^2}(f_1 + \pi)^2 \quad (f_1 \in [-\pi, \pi])$
Distribution Indicator $\quad \mathcal{D}_{x \to f} = 9\left|x_2 - 5\cos(x_1)\right|^{\frac{2}{3}}\left|x_3 - 5\sin(x_1)\right|^{\frac{2}{3}}. \quad (14)$

To show the Pareto front, 10000 data points are generated randomly in the PS and projected into the FS, see Figure 6 and 7. In the FS, all data points are plotted to show the entire fitness landscape. In the PS, only non-dominated points are shown. The true Pareto front is denoted by the solid curves. It can be seen from Figure 6 and 7 that the designed test functions address our concerns discussed in Section 1 and 2.

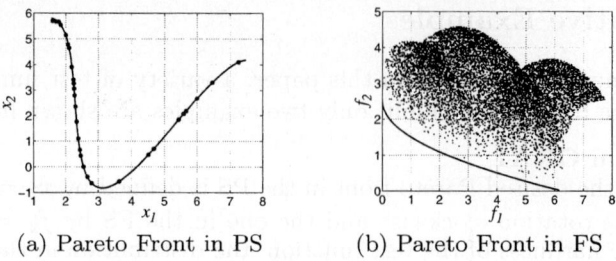

(a) Pareto Front in PS (b) Pareto Front in FS

Fig. 6. Pareto front (OKA1) in the parameter space (PS) and in the fitness space (FS).

6 Performance Comparison

In this section, the performance of NSGA-II (GA version) [6] and Hybrid Representation (HR) [9] will be compared on the two given test functions OKA1 and OKA2. Each algorithm was executed 30 times to reduce the randomness. The parameters used are summarized in Table 2 and the results are shown in Figure 8 (a)-(b) for NSGA-II, and (d)-(e) for HR, respectively. It can be seen that the performance of both optimizers on OKA1 and OKA2 is not sufficient.

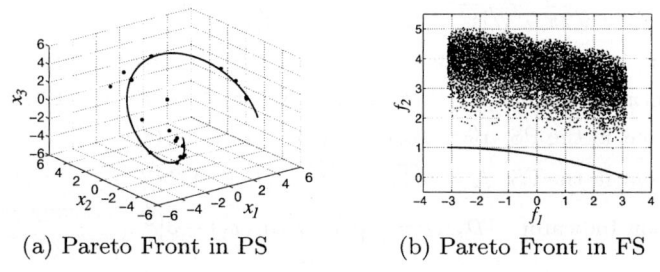

(a) Pareto Front in PS (b) Pareto Front in FS

Fig. 7. Pareto front (OKA2) in the parameter space (PS) and in the fitness space (FS).

The main reason is that for both test functions, the closer the population gets to the Pareto front, the more sparse the probability density becomes. To illustrate this, we show the parent (denoted by dots) and offspring (denoted by circles) individuals at the final generation in Figure 8 (c) of NSGA-II and (f) of HR. Clearly, both optimizers cannot generate promising offspring even if parents have converged to the Pareto front (denoted by the curve). Using the new test functions, we show that although both optimizers can solve existing test functions of a low dimension perfectly, neither of them is able to solve the test functions proposed in this work satisfactorily even if the dimensionality is very low.

7 Summary

Most test functions have piecewise linear Pareto fronts in parameter space. In order to circumvent this undesirable restriction, we proposed in this paper a

Table 2. Parameters used in the experiments.

	NSGA-II	HR
Population size	100	100
Maximum iterations	500	500
Coding	Gray coding	Gray coding
Crossover	One-point crossover	One-point crossover
Crossover rate	0.90	0.90
Mutation (GA)	Bit flip	Bit flip
Mutation rate (GA)	0.025	0.025
Number of bits per one design parameter	20	20
Initial step size (ES)	N/A	$\sigma_i = [0.0, 0.1]$
Lower bound	N/A	$\sigma_i \geq 0.004 \times |x_i|$
Minimum number of individuals	N/A	5%
Mutation rate (Switching)	N/A	0.01
Selection	Crowded Tournament	Crowded Tournament

method to construct benchmark problems for multi-objective optimization problems with arbitrary, customized Pareto fronts in fitness *and* parameter space. As a "by-product" of this method we suggested an additional measure for the difficulty of test problems which is based on the mapping of probability density functions from parameter to fitness space. We termed this measure *distribution indicator*. If the value of this indicator is small, the corresponding region is difficult to search for the optimizer. Finally, we gave examples of test functions with a higher order Pareto curve in parameter space and compared the performance of two evolutionary algorithms.

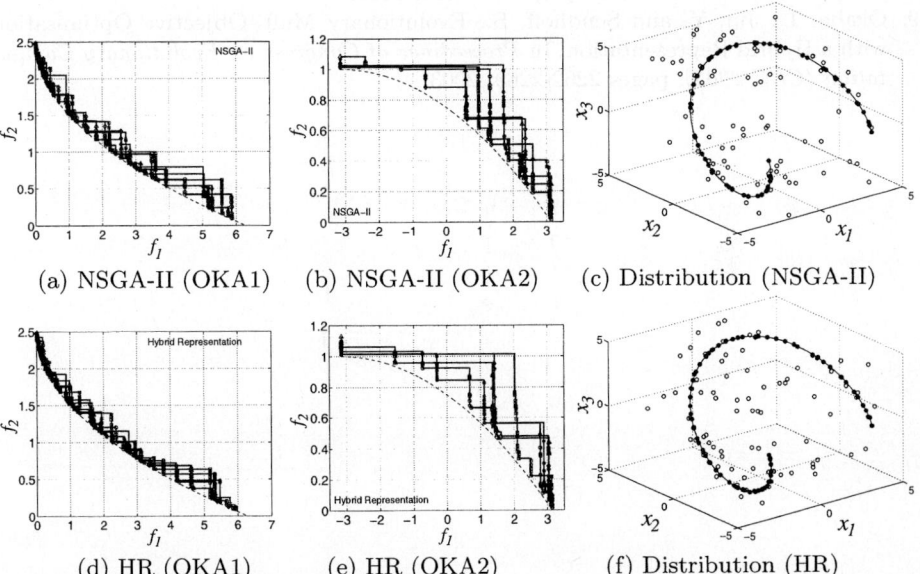

Fig. 8. Solutions obtained by NSGA-II (a)-(b) and HR (d)-(e) on OKA1 and OKA2. Only 5 results are shown to avoid complicated figures. Parents and offspring at the final generation of NSGA-II (c) and HR (f) on OKA2.

Acknowledgment

The authors would like to thank E. Körner and A. Richter for their kind support.

References

1. Coello, C. A. C., Van Veldhuizen, D. A. and Lamont, G. B., *Evolutionary Algorithms for Solving Multi-Objective Problems*, Kluwer Academic Publishers, 2001.
2. Deb, K., Multi-Objective Genetic Algorithms: Problem Difficulties and Construction of Test Problems, *Evolutionary Computation*, 7(3), pages 205–230, 1999.
3. Deb, K., *Multi-Objective Optimization using Evolutionary Algorithms*, John Wiley & Sons, LTD., 2001.
4. Deb, K., Thiele, L., Laumanns, M. and Zitzler, E., Scalable Test Problems for Evolutionary Multi-Objective Optimization, KanGAL Report 2001001, 2001.
5. Deb, K., Pratap, A. and Meyarivan, T., Constrained Test Problems for Multi-Objective Evolutionary Optimization, In *Evolutionary Multi-Criterion Optimization (EMO-2001)*, pages 284–298, 2001.
6. Deb, K., Pratap, A., Agarwal, S. and Meyarivan, T., A Fast and Elitist Multi-Objective Genetic Algorithms: NSGA-II, *IEEE Transactions on Evolutionary Computation*, 6(2), pages 182–197, 2002.
7. Deb, K., Thiele, L., Laumanns, M. and Zitzler, E., Scalable Multi-Objective Optimization Test Problems, In *Proceedings of Congress on Evolutionary Computation (CEC-2002)*, pages 825–830, 2002.
8. Okabe, T., Jin, Y. and Sendhoff, B., On the Dynamics of Evolutionary Multi-Objective Optimisation, *Proceedings of Genetic and Evolutionary Computation Conference (GECCO-2002)*, pages 247–255, 2002.
9. Okabe, T., Jin, Y. and Sendhoff, B., Evolutionary Multi-Objective Optimisation with a Hybrid Representation, In *Proceedings of Congress on Evolutionary Computation (CEC-2003)*, pages 2262-2269, 2003.

Multi-objective Optimization of a Composite Material Spring Design Using an Evolutionary Algorithm

Frédéric Ratle[1], Benoît Lecarpentier[1], Richard Labib[2], and François Trochu[1]

[1] Centre de Recherche Appliquée Sur les Polymères, Département de Génie Mécanique,
École Polytechnique de Montréal, C.P. 6079, Succ. Centre-ville, Montréal,
Québec, Canada H3C 3A7
{Frederic.Ratle,Benoit.Lecarpentier,Trochu}@polymtl.ca

[2] Département de Mathématiques et de Génie Industriel, École Polytechnique de Montréal,
C.P. 6079, Succ. Centre-ville, Montréal, Québec, Canada H3C 3A7
Richard.Labib@polymtl.ca

Abstract. A multi-objective evolutionary algorithm is applied to optimize the design of a helical spring made out of a composite material. The criteria considered are the minimization of the mass along with the maximization of the stiffness of the spring. Considering the computation time required for finite element analyses, the optimization is performed using approximate relations between design parameters. Dual kriging interpolation allows improving the accuracy of the classical model of spring stiffness by estimating the error between the model and the results of finite element analyses. This error is taken into account by adding a correction function to the stiffness function. The NSGA-II algorithm is applied and shows satisfactory results, while using the correction function induces a displacement of the Pareto front.

1 Introduction

The problem addressed here consists of optimizing mechanical properties, e.g. stiffness and mass, of springs made out of composite materials given a set of design parameters, which constitutes the design space of the problem. Rather than considering an aggregation of the objectives, a multi-objective evolutionary algorithm, which can deal with two or more contradictory objectives, is used in this investigation. For instance, in the case of spring design, maximizing stiffness for a given geometry results in increasing the mass, whereas the latter has to be minimized. The maximum admissible load is also a contradictory objective with respect to the mass: a lighter spring admits a lower load before failure, while it is interesting in applications to maximize this load. However, only mass and stiffness will be considered in this paper.

1.1 Helical Springs and Composite Materials

With the development of new composite manufacturing technology based on resin injection through fibrous reinforcements, it is nowadays possible to replace the classical metal wire helical springs by a lightweight composite version particularly well adapted for torsional loads and efficient at storing elastic deformation energy. This change of material brings about the possibility of substantially reducing spring mass while the other desired mechanical properties, such as stiffness and maximum deflection, could remain reasonably unchanged compared to metallic springs.

At the design stage, optimal geometric and material-related parameters are required to get the best compromise among many possible spring configurations. Parameters can be divided into two categories, geometric and material-related. Unlike metal springs, it is possible to adapt the structure of a composite spring to the specific requirements of an application. In our case, the material-related variable is the braid angle, assuming that each ply has the same fiber orientation. All the design parameters (D, d_{int}, e, p, N, θ) are described in Fig. 1.

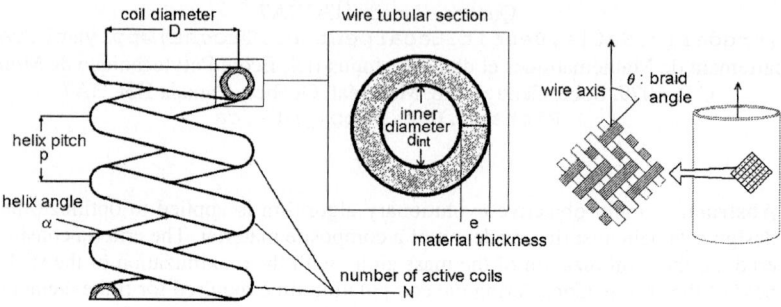

Fig. 1. Geometric and material-related design parameters.

These design variables lie within the boundary values specified in Table 1. Note that the composite material is a laminate made of fiberglass and epoxy resin.

Table 1. Design space of the problem.

Parameter	Description	Minimum value	Maximum value	Units
D	coil diameter	60	200	mm
d_{int}	inner diameter	8	16	mm
e	thickness	2	6	mm
p	helix pitch	50	70	mm
N	number of active coils	2	7	-
θ	braid angle	30	55	degrees

It is convenient for the sake of brevity to introduce the following notations: the helix angle α (1), the wire outer diameter d_{ext} (2), the spring index C (3), and the thickness ratio ξ (4), given by the following relations:

$$\alpha = \arctan\left(\frac{p}{2D}\right), \tag{1}$$

$$d_{ext} = d_{int} + 2e, \tag{2}$$

$$C = \frac{D}{d_{ext}}, \tag{3}$$

$$\xi = \frac{e}{d_{ext}}. \tag{4}$$

1.2 Classical Formula for Helical Spring Design

The following formula is used in classical spring theory to evaluate the stiffness k of a helical tubular spring with an empty core:

$$k = \frac{G_{12}(d_{ext}^4 - d_{int}^4)}{8ND^3} . \tag{5}$$

where G_{12} is the in-plane material shear modulus. However, this formula results from an approximation, i.e., only the torsion component of the applied load matters. In fact, this component is usually dominant over the flexural one, but in the case of small spring indices ($C \leq 5$) or important helix angles ($\alpha \geq 15°$) a gap exists with the theoretical formula. Since flexural stress can reach half the value of the torsional stress, it cannot be neglected. Furthermore, this formula has been established for isotropic materials and cannot be straightforwardly applied to orthotropic materials such as braided composites. To solve this problem, a correction function was devised for the output values of the classical stiffness formula. The approach proposed in this investigation is described in section 3.

1.3 Previous Work in Spring Design Optimization

Very few studies have been conducted on the optimization of spring design. Yokota et al. [1] have worked with a single-objective genetic algorithm to solve the constrained nonlinear integer programming problem of minimizing the weight of a helical metallic spring. Also, Gobbi and Mastinu [2] have applied multi-objective programming, a branch of Operations Research, to optimize simultaneously the mass and the stiffness of a spring. To improve the classical stiffness formula, they have introduced an analytical formula based on the moment of inertia of thin-walled tubular composite materials.

The present work aims at applying multi-objective evolutionary algorithms to this type of problem. However, the problem settings in [1, 2] being different from that of this paper (particularly the thin-walled material assumption), comparison is difficult. Nevertheless, the results obtained with the correction function are compared to a direct application of NSGA-II on the classical formulae of stiffness and mass.

2 Multi-objective Evolutionary Optimization

Evolutionary algorithms have emerged in the recent years as one of the most efficient approaches to solve multi-objective optimization problems. Their intrinsically parallel nature allows finding the best trade-off solutions among a pool of potential designs.

When dealing with multiple objectives, finding a set of optimal solutions rather than a single optimum is in many ways more convenient. On one hand, from a computational point of view, it is much more straightforward to optimize a single-objective function. On the other hand, this presupposes that the designer is able to aggregate the objectives in a single function expressing the relative importance of each criterion. This *a priori* knowledge is usually hard to translate into quantitative information, and the choice of the weighting coefficients is somewhat arbitrary.

During the last decade, *Pareto-based* algorithms have been studied extensively [3, 4, 5]. These algorithms allow the decision-maker to choose among many optimal solutions and do not require quantitative *a priori* information. As a result, the decision concerning the optimal design can be made *a posteriori*.

2.1 Pareto Dominance

The main difference between single- and multi-objective evolutionary algorithms is the way of performing the selection of individuals. The original concept of fitness is no longer significant in multi-objective optimization. It is rather the concept *Pareto-dominance* that is relevant to rank the individuals in a given generation. If x and y are two individuals, x is said to be *Pareto-dominant* over y if x is not worse than y with respect to all objectives and is strictly better than y for at least one objective. This way of comparing individuals enables the algorithm to pick the best solutions of compromise by considering all criteria at once.

2.2 The NSGA-II Algorithm

The original non-dominated sorting genetic algorithm (NSGA) is presented by Srinivas and Deb [3], while NSGA-II, the faster version of the algorithm, is described by Deb et al. [4]. The algorithm is based on the concept of domination rank. Individuals of a certain generation are selected (originally with the deterministic tournament method [3]) on the basis of their domination rank in the population. When two individuals are compared, the one with the smallest domination rank wins. Selection is based on this rank, while crossover and mutation remain unchanged.

If the domination ranks of two individuals are equal, the crowding distance will guide the selection process. This distance is a measure of the local sparseness and aims to promote diversity in the population. The individual with the largest crowding distance will be favored. Thus, individuals lying in a region with a high density of potential solutions will be penalized to prevent premature convergence.

The most valuable advantages of NSGA-II over NSGA are the introduction of elitism, the less computationally expensive sorting of individuals with respect to their domination rank, and the concept of crowding distance, which does not require a user-specified niche radius parameter, as would require a classical fitness sharing method. Some practical applications of NSGA-II have been studied in [6, 7, 8] and have demonstrated the efficiency of this approach.

3 Correction Function

As stated in section 1, the problem of composite springs has been addressed with approximate relations rather than numerical analyses because of the computational cost involved. However, stiffness calculation is inaccurate for composite springs. A first approach that could be considered consists, as described by Jin [9], of updating the fitness function during the evolution process. Yet, by looking at the differences between the classical model and the results of finite element analysis, it is clear that some regions of the search space are very well approximated, while some other regions show a non negligible error. Adaptive fitness function approximation would then result in evaluating a great amount of points which are already well approximated by the classical formula, while uncertain regions could remain unexplored.

An interesting alternative to the latter approach is to build a function representing the approximation error as a function of the design parameters using dual kriging. This error is the difference between the output of the analytical formula and numerical results. The principles underlying kriging can be found in Cressie [10] or Trochu [11].

The first step of the correction approach consists of performing a uniform experimental design in the search space. Different spring configurations are evaluated by the analytical formula and the finite element analysis. The points evaluated then constitute the training set to build the kriging model, which output is the approximation error. The objective function can then be expressed as a combination of the analytical formula and the correction function. The main drawback of this approach is the time required to build a substantial training set, the search space being multi-dimensional and the numerical simulation computationally expensive. Consequently, two steps are undertaken to reduce both dimensionality and the number of function evaluations.

Firstly, a sensitivity analysis shows that parameters responsible for the gap with finite element calculations are the spring index C, the helix angle α, the thickness ratio ξ, the number of active coils N and the material used, namely here the braid angle θ. The experimental design is thus established with these five parameters only. The stiffness can hence be expressed as

$$k = k_o[1 + L(C, \alpha, \xi, N, \theta)], \quad (6)$$

where k_0 is the stiffness obtained from (5). Function L has the following form:

$$L(\mathbf{x}) = a(\mathbf{x}) + W(\mathbf{x}), \quad (7)$$

where $\mathbf{x}$ is the input vector, $a(\mathbf{x})$ is the drift, a known function representing the global trend of the phenomenon, and $W(\mathbf{x})$, a random function representing the local deviation from the drift. In the present case, the following functions have been used:

$$a(\mathbf{x}) = a_0 + a_1 \mathbf{x}, \quad (8)$$

$$\text{cov}(W(\mathbf{x}^i), W(\mathbf{x}^j)) = \mathbf{K}(c(\mathbf{x}^i, \mathbf{x}^j)), \quad (9)$$

where $\mathbf{K}$ is the correlation matrix, and c the correlation function between any two of the N training samples. In this study, function c is assumed to be linear:

$$c(\mathbf{x}^i, \mathbf{x}^j) = \sum_{k=1}^{n} b_j |x_k^i - x_k^j|. \quad (10)$$

where the b_j are the correlation parameters, and n the dimension of the design space.

Secondly, an approach based on the query learning paradigm [12, 13] is used to reduce the number of function calls required to build the correction function. From the initial experimental design, different independent datasets are picked using the bootstrap method, i.e., sampling with replacement from the original data, and used to construct a kriging estimator. The point which splits most evenly the predictors is added to the original training set. This procedure is repeated for a fixed number of iterations and the improvement is measured by a cross-validation estimation of the error on the current data. The general idea of this approach takes root in the "Query by Bagging" algorithm presented by Abe and Mamitsuka [13].

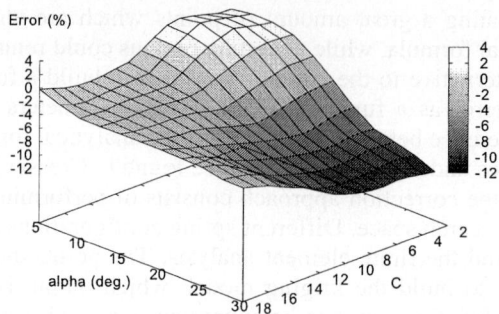

Fig. 2. Correction function.

The aim of this method is to decrease more rapidly the generalization error than by a passive learning approach, where training data is selected at random. Knowing that the amount of information provided by a randomly selected point decreases as points are added to the training set, such an approach will hopefully provide pertinent information to the learner and allow using a smaller dataset for the construction of the correction function. For the sake of clarity, the correction function is plotted in Fig. 2. Only the influence of C and α is showed here (ξ, N and θ are kept constant).

From the previous figure, it can be seen that the springs presenting a large index C are well approximated by the analytical formula, especially for small helix angles. As C decreases, a gap appears. For small angles, there is a positive error, which means that stiffness is underestimated by the classical theory. This is due to the flexural component of the stress. A higher load has to be applied to attain the same deflection. The stiffness of the spring thus appears higher. At high angles, the error is negative. This means that the stiffness is overestimated. At such angles, the resulting stiffness of the spring is reduced since the compression load contributes to increase D, the spring diameter.

Therefore, the optimization problem can finally be stated as follows:

$$\text{Max} \quad k = \frac{G_{12}(d_{ext}^4 - d_{int}^4)}{8ND^3}[1 + L(C, \alpha, \xi, N, \theta)], \quad (11)$$

$$\text{Min} \quad mass = \frac{\rho \pi ND(d_{ext}^2 - d_{int}^2)}{4\cos\alpha}, \quad (12)$$

$$\text{s.t.} \quad p - d_{ext} > 0. \quad (13)$$

The above constraint ensures that coils do not touch each other. It is handled by assigning a penalty to unfeasible individuals. The parameter ρ is the density of the material. Of course, mass calculation does not require a correction function. It is computed directly from the geometric and material-related parameters of the spring.

4 Experimental Results

4.1 Experimental Conditions

The NSGA-II is built on the basis of the Evolving Objects library, with a real representation. Variation relies solely on Gaussian mutation. The mutation is continuous for all the design parameters except the number of active coils N and the braid angle θ, for which the Gaussian law is approximated by a binomial law, the latter variables being discrete. For all the experiments, the population size is 200, the stopping criterion is the maximum number of generations, which is set to 200, and the mutation rate is $1/n$, where n is the space dimension. The deterministic tournament size is set to 2. These parameters have been statically determined using a sensitivity analysis. All experiments are performed with a Pentium IV processor running at 2.8GHz under Windows XP.

4.2 Results and Discussion

Table 2 shows the average CPU time for the NSGA-II algorithm with and without the correction function. As an indication, NSGA, the former version of the algorithm, has been tested on the same problem. Twenty runs of each algorithm were conducted.

Table 2. CPU time.

Algorithm	Average CPU time (sec.)
NSGA-II with correction function	20.218
NSGA-II	13.130
NSGA with correction function	179.197
NSGA	152.566

As we can see, NSGA-II is much faster than its former version. It is known [4] that NSGA is of complexity $O(mN^3)$ while NSGA-II is $O(mN^2)$, m being the number of objectives, and N the population size. Looking at Table 2, NSGA-II seems to be more than 10 times faster than NSGA for this particular problem. The ratio is different when the correction function is considered because of the time required by the kriging calculations.

The Pareto front obtained with the NSGA-II algorithm and the correction function is compared in Fig. 3 with the one derived with the classical stiffness formula only.

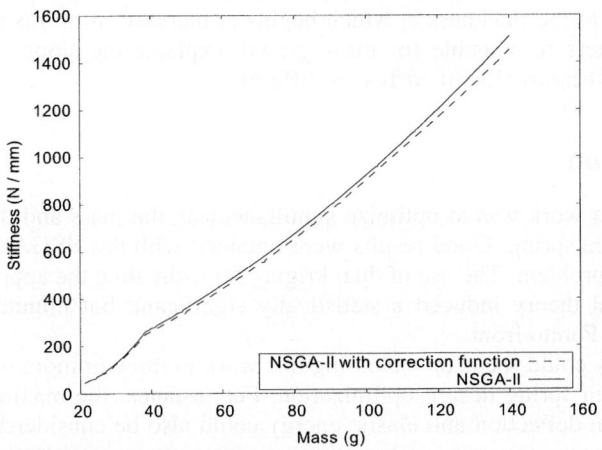

Fig. 3. Pareto fronts for NSGA-II with and without the correction function.

According to Fig. 3, the classical spring model overestimates the stiffness for a given mass. Indeed, as mass and stiffness increase, a minute displacement of the Pareto front is noticeable. This displacement reaches a maximum of approximately 4% of the stiffness value. To ensure that this value is statistically significant, the maximal displacement of the front was measured for all the runs of the algorithm and showed an average of 3.93% and a standard deviation of 0.05%. Such a difference in the value of stiffness is physically significant and justifies using the correction function.

Another important point is the presence of an inflection point, which is zoomed in Fig. 4.

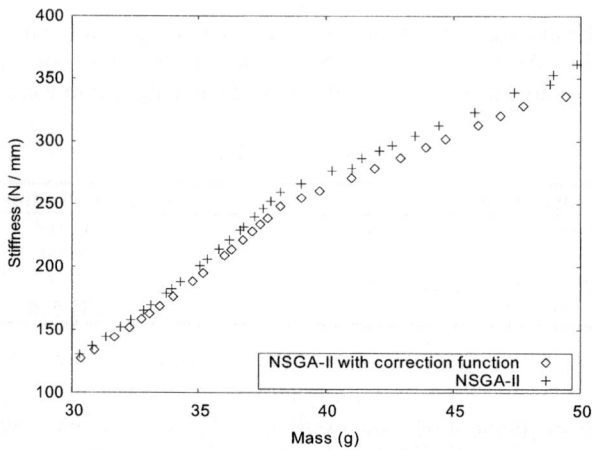

Fig. 4. Zoom on the Pareto front in the neighborhood of the inflection point.

This bilinear behaviour has been noted in every run of the algorithm and is due to the boundary limits of the different parameters. As the springs are getting larger, d_{int} increases and reaches its maximum value around $m = 40$. Afterwards, mass grows proportionally to the thickness e, which begins to increase from this point. This shift in the parameters responsible for mass growth explains the slope change, because their effect on the variation of stiffnss is different.

5 Conclusion

The aim of this work was to optimize simultaneously the mass and the stiffness of a composite-made spring. Good results were obtained with the NSGA-II algorithm for this particular problem. The use of dual kriging for estimating the approximation error of the classical theory induced a statistically significant, but minute change in the position of the Pareto front.

Future study could focus on extending this work to three or more objectives which are important in spring design optimization. For instance, the maximum admissible load, maximum deflection and elastic energy could also be considered in the optimization process.

It would also be interesting to compare the results with the direct use of numerical simulations in order to evaluate the accuracy of the fitness model. However, this would require problem-level approximations. For instance, Parmee [14] reports the use of mesh refinement techniques during the evolution process, or coevolution with meshes of different precisions.

Acknowledgements

Authors wish to thank NSERC, FQRNT, the Auto21 Network of Centres of Excellence as well as Composites Atlantic Ltd. for their financial support.

References

1. Yokota, T., Taguchi, T., Gen, M.: A solution method for optimal weight design problem of helical spring using genetic algorithms. In: Computers Ind. Engng., Vol. 33, Nos 1-2 (1997) 71-76
2. Gobbi, M., Mastinu, G.: On the optimal design of composite material tubular helical springs. In: Meccanica, Vol. 36. Kluwer Academic Publishers (2002) 525-553
3. Srinivas, D., Deb, K.: Multiobjective optimization using nondominated sorting in genetic algorithms. In: Journal of Evolutionary Computation, Vol. 2, No. 3 (1995) 221-248
4. Deb, K., Agrawal, S., Pratap, A., and Meyarivan, T.: A fast elitist non-dominated sorting genetic algorithm for multi-objective optimization: NSGA-II. In: M. Schoenauer et al. (eds): Parallel Problem Solving from Nature, Vol. 6 (2000) 849-858
5. Zitzler, E., Deb, K., Thiele, L.: Comparison of multiobjective evolutionary algorithms: empirical results. In: Evolutionary Computation, Vol. 8, No. 2 (2000) 173-195
6. Hamda, H., Roudenko, O., Schoenauer, M.: Application of a multi-objective evolutionary algorithm to topological optimum design. In: I. Parmee (ed): Fifth International Conference on Adaptive Computing in Design and Manufacture (2002)
7. Lahanas, M., Baltas, D. and Zamboglou, N.: A hybrid evolutionary multiobjective algorithm for anatomy based dose optimization algorithm in HDR brachytherapy. In: Physics in Medecine and Biology, Vol. 48 (2003) 399-415
8. Wu, J.-L., Agogino, A.M.: Automating keyphrase extraction with multi-objective genetic algorithms. In: Proceedings of the 37th Hawaii International Conference on Systems Sciences (2004)
9. Jin, Y.: Fitness approximation in evolutionary computation: a survey. In: Soft Computing Journal, Vol. 4 (2003), In press
10. Cressie, N.: Statistics for Spatial Data. Wiley (1993)
11. Trochu, F.: A contouring program based on dual kriging interpolation. In: Engineering with Computers, Vol. 9 (1993) 160-177
12. Cohn, D.A., Ghahramani, Z., Jordan, M.I.: Active learning with statistical models. In: Journal of Artificial Intelligence Research, Vol. 4 (1996) 129-145
13. Abe, N., Mamitsuka, H.: Query learning strategies using boosting and bagging. In: Proceedings of The Fifteenth International Conference on Machine Learning (1998) 1-9
14. Parmee, I.: Evolutionary and Adaptive Computing in Engineering Design. Springer-Verlag, 2001

Dominance Based Crossover Operator for Evolutionary Multi-objective Algorithms

Olga Rudenko and Marc Schoenauer

TAO Team, INRIA Futurs
LRI, bat. 490, Université Paris-Sud
91405 Orsay Cedex, France
Olga.Roudenko@lri.fr, Marc.Schoenauer@inria.fr

Abstract. In spite of the recent quick growth of the Evolutionary Multi-objective Optimization (EMO) research field, there has been few trials to adapt the general variation operators to the particular context of the quest for the Pareto-optimal set. The only exceptions are some mating restrictions that take in account the distance between the potential mates – but contradictory conclusions have been reported. This paper introduces a particular mating restriction for Evolutionary Multi-objective Algorithms, based on the Pareto dominance relation: the partner of a non-dominated individual will be preferably chosen among the individuals of the population that it dominates. Coupled with the BLX crossover operator, two different ways of generating offspring are proposed. This recombination scheme is validated within the well-known NSGA-II framework on three bi-objective benchmark problems and one real-world bi-objective constrained optimization problem. An acceleration of the progress of the population toward the Pareto set is observed on all problems.

Introduction

The idea of *restricted mating* is not new in Evolutionary Computation: Goldberg [7] already suggested to forbid, or at least restrict, the crossover between too different individuals (i.e. that are too far apart for some distance on the genotypic space) – which makes sense for single-objective problems as soon as the population has started to accumulate on different fitness peaks, as recombining individuals from different peaks would often lead to lethal individuals. This idea has been transposed in the framework of Evolutionary Multi-objective Algorithms (EMAs) by Hajela and Lin [8], and by Fonseca and Fleming [6]. Nevertheless, Zitzler and Thiele [17] did not observe any improvement when mating similar individuals. On the other hand, Horn et al. [9] present an argument supporting mating of dissimilar individuals: in the multi-objective framework, because the population diversity is enforced, the information provided by very different solutions can be combined in such way that a new type of (good) compromises can hopefully be obtained. Nevertheless, Schaffer reported the absence of the improvement when mating dissimilar individuals. To sum up, no clear conclusion can be drawn from existing experiments on the usefulness of restricted mating based on the (dis)similarity between mates.

On a real-world design problem, using a very specific representation, Wildman et Parks [13] have investigated different pairing strategies based on maximizing or minimizing different similarity measures. In particular, the similarity in the sense of the dominance rank has been considered, and enforcing the mating of the individuals from the elite archive with the individuals from the population, in an archive-based EMA, has been observed to be beneficial.

However, in all studies enumerated above, the efficiency of the proposed mating restrictions has been measured by the quality of the final non-dominated solutions, without addressing the issue of computational time. In this paper, we propose a restricted mating strategy whose main effect is to accelerate the progress of the population of an EMA toward the Pareto set. The main idea is fairly simple, and consists in using the Pareto dominance relation when choosing a mate for the best (non-dominated) individuals. Note that a more detailed presentation (in French) can be found in [10].

The paper is organized as follows. Next section briefly introduces evolutionary multi-objective optimization, and describes in more detail the NSGA-II algorithm, one of the best performing EMA to-date, that will be used in all experiments. Two slightly different implementations of the dominance-based crossover operator are then proposed in Section 2, based on BLX-α crossover, used throughout this study. Section 3 presents some experimental results witnessing the acceleration of the progress toward the Pareto set when using the proposed mating restrictions. Finally, Section 4 gives some guidelines for a more rigorous and complete validation of the proposed strategy, as well as for its possible refinements.

1 Evolutionary Multi-objective Optimization

Multi-objective optimization aims at simultaneously optimizing several contradictory objectives. For such kind of problems, there does not exist a single optimal solution, and compromises have to be made.

An element of the search space x is said to *Pareto-dominate* another element y if x is not worse than y with respect to all objectives, and is strictly better than y with respect to at least one objective. The set of all elements of the search space that are not Pareto-dominated by any other element is called the *Pareto set* of the multi-objective problem at hand: it represents the best possible compromises with respect to the contradictory objectives.

Solving a multi-objective problem amounts to choose one solution among those non-dominated solutions, and some decision arguments have to be given. Unlike classical optimization methods, that generally find one of the Pareto optimal solutions by making the initial optimization problem single-objective, EMAs are to-date the only algorithms that directly search for the whole Pareto set, allowing decision makers to choose one of the Pareto solutions with more complete information.

1.1 Pareto-Based Evolutionary Algorithms

In order to find a good approximation of the Pareto set (a uniform and well spread sampling of the non-dominated solutions, close to the actual Pareto set of the problem at hand), EMAs have to enforce some progress toward the Pareto set while, at the same time, preserving diversity between the non-dominated solutions.

Numerous evolutionary methods have been designed in the past years for the particular task of searching for the Pareto set (the interested reader will find a good summary in [2]). The best performing among them (NSGA-II [3], SPEA2 [16], PESA [1]) are directly based on the Pareto dominance relation, that actually ensures progressing toward the non-dominated set.

Among the diversity preserving techniques, some were transposed to EMAs from single-objective EAs (such as sharing, for instance), while others, like the crowding distance described in next subsection, are specific to the multi-objective framework.

Another recognized important feature of EMAs is elitism [15], directly related to the notion of the Pareto dominance in EMAs: the non-dominated individuals can be preserved either by maintaining an archive (SPEA2 and PESA) or by using a deterministic replacement procedure (NSGA-II).

1.2 NSGA-II

The NSGA-II algorithm has been proposed by Deb et al. in 2001 [3]. The progress toward the Pareto set is here favored by using a selection based on the *Pareto ranking*, that divides the population into a hierarchy of non-dominated subsets, as illustrated by figure 1(a). All non-dominated individuals of the population are first labeled as being of rank 1; they are then temporarily removed from the population, and the process is repeated: the non-dominated individuals of the remainder of the population are given rank 2, and so on, until the whole population is ranked.

NSGA-II diversity preserving technique is based on the *crowding distance* – one of the possible estimations of the density of the solutions belonging to the same non-dominated subset. The crowding distance of each individual i is computed as follows: the non-dominated subset to which the individual i belongs is ordered following each of the objectives; for each objective m, the distance $d_i^{(m)} = f_m(i+1) - f_m(i-1)$ between the surrounding neighbors of individual i according to objective m is computed (Fig. 1(b)); the sum over all objectives of these distances is the crowding distance of individual i.

The following comparison operator $\succ$ is then used during the Darwinian stages (selection and replacement) of NSGA-II:

$x \succ y$ **iff** $\quad$ rank$(x) <$ rank(y)
$\qquad\qquad$ **or** $\quad$ rank$(x) =$ rank(y)
$\qquad\qquad$ **and** $\quad$ crowding_dist$(x) >$ crowding_dist(y)

NSGA-II selection is based on tournament: it chooses an individual for reproduction by uniformly drawing T individuals (generally, $T = 2$) from the

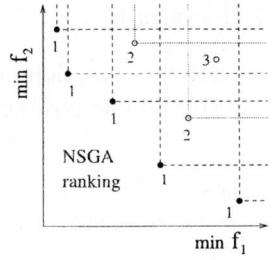 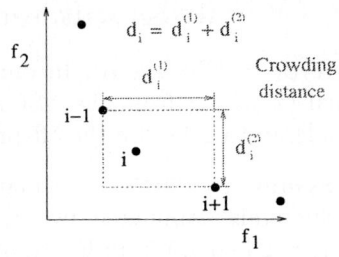

(a) Ensuring progress toward the Pareto set (b) Preserving diversity technique

Fig. 1. NSGA-II comparison criteria.

population and returning the best of them with respect to the comparison operator $\succ$. NSGA-II replacement is deterministic: it consists in merging parents and offspring together, and choosing the N best individuals in that global population, again using comparison operator $\succ$. The algorithm NSGA-II is said to be elitist because the best (less crowded non-dominated) individuals are preserved from one generation to another.

2 Dominance-Based Crossover

The basic mechanism of the proposed mating restriction consists in allowing the mating of each of the best individuals only with an individual it dominates (if any), where *best individuals* means non-dominated individuals when applying NSGA-II, or members of the archive when using SPEA2 ou PESA.

The rationale behind using the dominance relation to form the couples for the crossover is the following. If x dominates y, then x is better than y for all objectives. Hence, the direction $y \to x$ is likely to improve all criteria simultaneously. Furthermore, a natural continuation of the same idea is to bias the distribution of the offspring toward the dominant parent, as better individuals are more likely to be found close to it. However, it is clear that success of this idea depends on the behavior of the objective functions in the region of the decision space where the mated individuals sit.

The resulting crossover, called Dominance-Based Crossover (DBX) will proceed as follows: a first mate is chosen using the usual selection procedure of the EMA at hand (e.g. tournament based on the $\succ$ operator for NSGA-II). If the chosen individual is non-dominated and dominates some other individuals in the population, its mate is chosen among those. Otherwise, the mate is chosen using the usual selection procedure. In any case, crossover then proceeds with the chosen operator.

In this study, the well-known BLX-α crossover ($0 < \alpha < 1$), proposed by Eshelman and Schaffer [5] for real representations, has been used. Formally, given two parents $(x_i)_{i \in [1,n]}$ and $(y_i)_{i \in [1,n]}$, this operator produces an offspring by a random linear recombination of the parents as follows:

$$((x_i)_{i\in[1,n]}, (y_i)_{i\in[1,n]}) \longrightarrow (\phi_i x_i + (1-\phi_i)y_i)_{i\in[1,n]}, \qquad (1)$$

where $\phi_i = U[\alpha, 1+\alpha]$. In our particular case, given a non-dominated individual $(x_i)_{i\in[1,n]}$ from the NSGA-II population, two possible strategies will be considered to generate the offspring:

1. **Symmetric DBX:** The mate $(y_i)_{i\in[1,n]}$ is chosen from the list of the individuals dominated by $(x_i)_{i\in[1,n]}$, if any, by tournament otherwise, and $\phi_i = U[-0.5, 1.5]$ in Equation (1).
2. **Biased DBX:** Similarly, the mate $(y_i)_{i\in[1,n]}$ is chosen from the list of the individuals dominated by $(x_i)_{i\in[1,n]}$, if any, but now $\phi_i = U[0.5, 1.5]$ in Equation (1), i.e. the offspring will be closer to the first parent $(x_i)_{i\in[1,n]}$.

3 Experimental Results

3.1 Experimental Conditions

This section presents some experimental results, on three standard benchmark problems [15] and on an industrial problem [12]. All experiments are run with population size 100 and tournament size 2. The two DBX crossovers are compared to the standard BLX-0.5, the crossover rate is set to 0.9. The uniform mutation operator is applied with rate 0.05. The algorithms run for at most 150 (resp. 250) generations for ZDT-benchmarks (resp. the industrial problem).

3.2 Bi-objective ZDT Benchmarks

For each of ZDT1–ZDT3 test problems 31 NSGAII runs have been performed for biased DBX, symmetric DBX and standard BLX-0.5 operators starting with the same 31 initial populations. The non-dominated individuals over all 31 runs have been calculated at each 10th generation approximately until the moment when the whole population is non-dominated, that means that DBX crossover is not applied any longer. These snapshots corresponding to biased DBX and standard BLX-0.5 are shown in the figures 2, 3 and 4 for ZDT1, ZDT2 and ZDT3 respectively. On all three test problems, a small but steady acceleration of the progress toward the Pareto front is observed when using DBX crossover. On those problems, very similar results have been obtained with the symmetric and biased DBX operators (the snapshots corresponding to the symmetric DBX are not shown for the space reasons).

3.3 Constrained Bi-objective Optimization

This industrial problem consists in optimizing the structural geometry, described by 13 continuous parameters, of the front crash member of the car in order to minimize its mass while maximizing the internal energy absorbed during a crash (two competitive objectives) under 8 constraints arising from the acoustic and static mechanical domains [12].

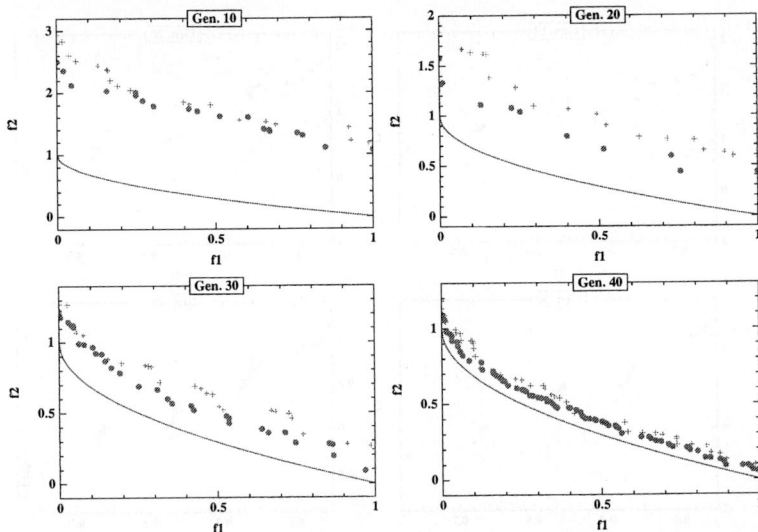

Fig. 2. ZDT1: the black bullets (for the biased DBX) and the gray crosses (for the standard BLX-0.5) represent the non-dominated individuals over 31 runs at generations 10, 20, 30 and 40.

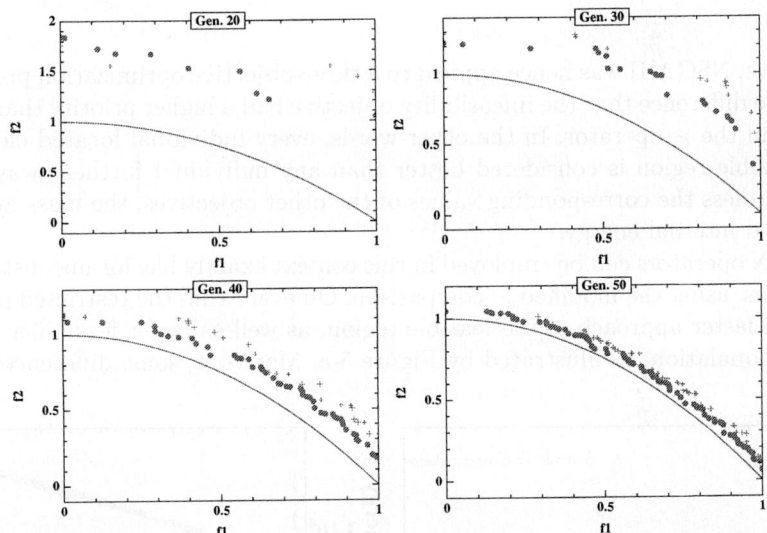

Fig. 3. ZDT2: the black bullets (for the biased DBX) and the gray crosses (for the standard BLX-0.5) represent the non-dominated individuals over 31 runs at generations 20, 30, 40 and 50.

The constraints have been handled using the so-called *infeasibility objective approach* [14]: the aggregated sum of the scaled constraint violations (that can be viewed as a measure of distance separating each individual from the feasible region) was considered as an additional optimization criterion – the infeasibility

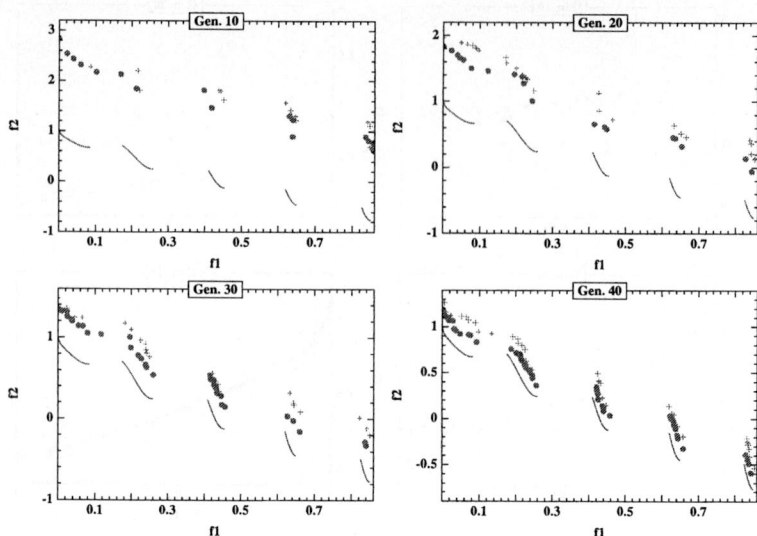

Fig. 4. ZDT3: the black bullets (for the biased DBX) and the gray crosses (for the standard BLX-0.5) represent the non-dominated individuals over 31 runs at generations 10, 20, 30 and 40.

objective. NSGA-II was hence applied to a three-objective optimization problem, with the difference that the infeasibility objective had a higher priority than both others in the $\succ$ operator. In the other words, every individual located closer to the feasible region is considered better than any individual further away from it, regardless the corresponding values of the other objectives, the mass and the absorbed internal energy.

DBX operators can be employed in this context exactly like for unconstrained problems, using the modified $\succ$ comparison. On every run, the restricted mating allowed faster approach of the feasible region, as well as faster feasibility of the whole population, as illustrated by Figure 5-a. Moreover, some differences with

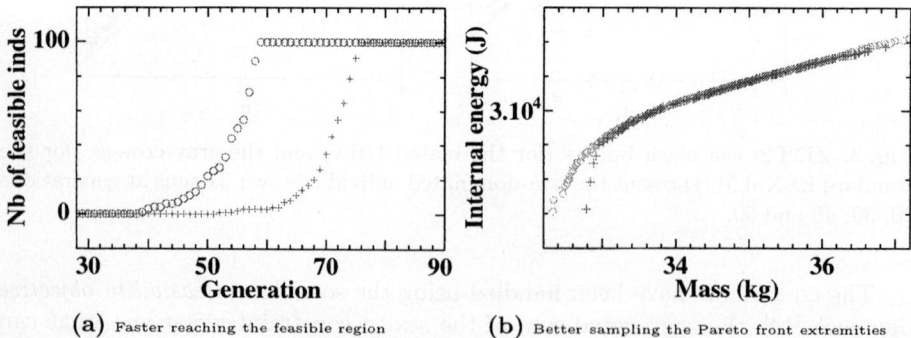

(a) Faster reaching the feasible region (b) Better sampling the Pareto front extremities

Fig. 5. Effect of the dominance-based mating restriction in the presence of constraints: biased DBX (rings) VS standard BLX-0.5 (crosses).

the results on the test problems ZDT have been steadily observed. First, biased DBX was more efficient than symmetric DBX. Then, and more importantly, the use of mating restriction not only accelerated the search, it also provided solutions of better quality at the extremities of the Pareto front, as it can be seen on figure 5-b.

4 Discussion and Future Work

For all four problems considered in this study, the DBX operators (that only allow the mating of dominant individuals with individuals they dominate) have been shown to accelerate the progress of the populations toward the Pareto set. Moreover, for the optimization of the car front crash member, it also allowed finding solutions of better quality at the extremities of the Pareto set that could not be reached when using the usual recombination strategy.

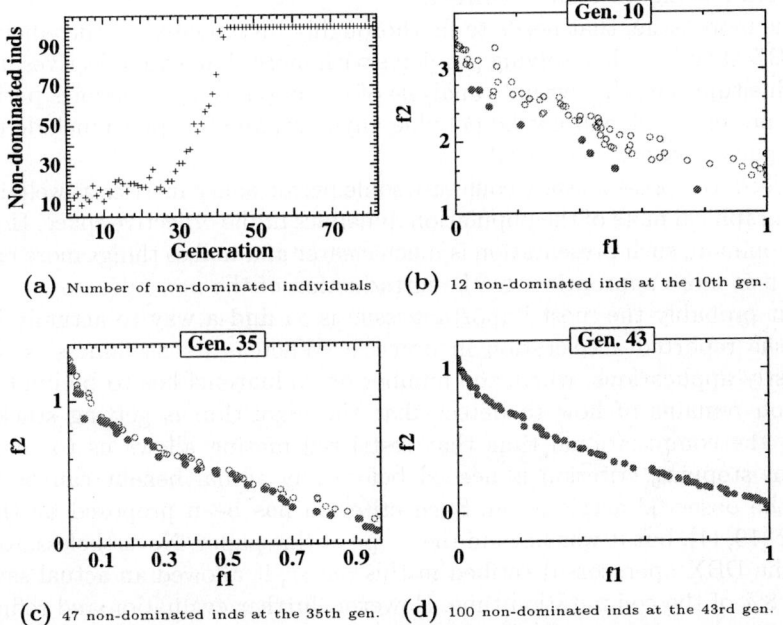

(a) Number of non-dominated individuals (b) 12 non-dominated inds at the 10th gen.

(c) 47 non-dominated inds at the 35th gen. (d) 100 non-dominated inds at the 43rd gen.

Fig. 6. Evolution of the number of non-dominated individuals during a run of NSGA-II.

The observed acceleration is relatively small, but is systematic. When observing NSGA-II dynamics (the typical NSGA-II evolution process is illustrated by Figure 6), we realize that in fact only a small number of DBX crossovers are actually applied. First, note that restricted mating is applied at most as many times as there are non-dominated individuals in the population. There are few non-dominated individuals at the beginning of evolution (Fig. 6-a,b), but each of them dominates a lot of other individuals (Fig. 6-b). As the population gets closer to the Pareto set, the number of non-dominated individuals rapidly increases (Fig. 6-a,c), but each of them dominates only a few individuals if any (Fig. 6-c). Finally, when the whole population is non-dominated (Fig. 6-d), DBX crossover cannot be applied because no individual actually dominates anyone in the population! The actual rate of application of the DBX operator is maximal about the moment when the half of the population gets the rank 1 (Fig. 6-c).

One possible improvement would be to increase the rate of application of DBX operators at the beginning of evolution by mating each non-dominated individual with not only one but several individuals it dominates.

Note that dynamic behavior of the populations described here above and, in particular, the disappearance of the dominated individuals is due to the the replacement procedure in NSGA-II, and might not be so prominent with other EMAs. It is hence worth investigating the use of DBX restricted mating with other EMAs paradigms, such as SPEA2 or PESA, for instance.

Furthermore, there exist other crossover operators used in EAs (such as SBX [2], for example) that could be applied together with dominance based restricted mating, instead of BLX-α.

One more issue, that needs to be thoroughly investigated, is the efficiency of the DBX strategy when solving problems with more than two objectives. Indeed, in such situations, the "visual" analysis of the populations dynamics performed in the present work will not be possible anymore, and our plans include the use of so-called *running metrics* [4].

Indeed, the present study could use some performance metrics as well, instead of the graphical plots of the population dynamics in the objective space. However, in our opinion, such presentation is much clearer and makes things more explicit, hence it is more appropriate to the introduction of the new operator.

But probably the most important issue is to find a way to actually benefit from the reported acceleration in practice. Whereas its usefulness is obvious for costly applications, where the number of evaluations has to be limited, the question remains of how to detect that the algorithm is getting stuck, thus saving the computational time that restricted mating allows us to spare. An efficient stopping criterion is needed before any actual benefit can be gained from the observed acceleration. Such criterion has been proposed by the first author [10, 11], but it was beyond the scope of this paper. Nevertheless, together with the DBX operators described in this paper, it allowed an actual saving of about 8% of the computation time. However, further evaluation and refinement of that stopping criterion are still needed before definite strong conclusions can be drawn.

References

1. D. W. Corne, J. D. Knowles, and M.L. Oates. The Pareto Envelope-based Selection Algorithm for Multiobjective Optimization. In M. Schoenauer and al., editors, *Proc. PPSN 2000*, pages 839–848. LNCS 1917, Springer Verlag, 2000.
2. K. Deb. *Multi-Objective Optimization using Evolutionary Algorithms*. John Wiley, 2001.

3. K. Deb, S. Agrawal, A. Pratap, and T. Meyarivan. A Fast Elitist Non-dominated Sorting Genetic Algorithm for Multi-objective Optimization: NSGA-II. In M. Schoenauer and al., editors, *Proc. PPSN 2000*, pages 849–858. LNCS 1917, Springer Verlag, 2000.
4. K. Deb and S. Jain. Running performance metrics for evolutionary multi-objective optimization. Technical Report 2002004, Indian Institute of Technology, Kanpur, May 2002.
5. L. Eshelman and J. D. Schaffer. Real-coded genetic algorithms and interval-schemata. In L. D. Whitley, editor, *Foundations of Genetic Algorithms 2*, pages 187–202, Morgan Kaufmann, 1993.
6. Carlos M. Fonseca and Peter J. Fleming. Genetic algorithms for multiobjective optimization: Formulation, discussion and generalization. In *ICGA'93*, pages 416–423. Morgan Kaufmann, 1993.
7. D. E. Goldberg. *Genetic algorithms in search, optimization and machine learning.* Addison Wesley, 1989.
8. P. Hajela and C. Y. Lin. Genetic search strategies in multicriterion optimal design. *Structural Optimization*, 4:99–107, 1992.
9. J. Horn, S. N. Nafpliotis, and D. E. Goldberg. A niched pareto genetic algorithm for multiobjective optimization. In Z. Michalewicz et al., editors, *Proc. of ICEC'94*, pages 82–87. IEEE Press, 1994.
10. O. Rudenko. *Application des algorithmes évolutionnaires aux problèmes d'optimisation multi-objectif avec contraintes.* PhD thesis, +cole Polytechnique, 2004.
11. O. Rudenko and M. Schoenauer. A steady performance stopping criterion for pareto-based evolutionary algorithms. In *Proc. 6th Intl Conf. on Multi Objective Programming and Goal Programming*, 2004.
12. O. Rudenko, M. Schoenauer, T. Bosio, and R. Fontana. A multiobjective evolutionary algorithm for car front end design. In P. Collet et al., editors, *Artificial Evolution'2001*, pages 205–216, LNCS 2310, Springer Verlag, 2001.
13. A. Wildman and G. Parks. A comparative study of selective breeding strategies in a multiobjective genetic algorithm. In C. M. Fonseca et al., editors, *Proc. EMO'03*, pages 418–432. LNCS 2632, Springer Verlag, 2003.
14. J. Wright and H. Loosemore. An infeasibility objective for use in constrained pareto optimization. In E. Zitzler et al., editors, *Proc. EMO'01*, pages 256–268, LNCS 1993, Springer-Verlag, 2001.
15. E. Zitzler, K. Deb, and L. Thiele. Comparison of multiobjective evolutionary algorithms: Empirical results. *Evolutionary Computation*, 8(2):125–148, 2000.
16. E. Zitzler, M. Laumanns, and L. Thiele. SPEA2: Improving the strength pareto evolutionary algorithm. Technical Report 103, Computer Engineering and Networks Laboratory, ETH, Zurich, Switzerland, 2001.
17. E. Zitzler and L. Thiele. Multiobjective optimization using evolutionary algorithms – a comparative case study. In A.-E. Eiben, T. Bäck, M. Schoenauer, and H.-P. Schwefel, editors, *Proc. PPSN'98*, pages 292–301. LNCS 1498, Springer Verlag, 1998.

Evolutionary Bi-objective Controlled Elevator Group Regulates Passenger Service Level and Minimises Energy Consumption

Tapio Tyni and Jari Ylinen

KONE Corporation, Global R&D, Myllykatu 3
05801 Hyvinkää, Finland
{tapio.tyni,jari.ylinen}@kone.com
http://www.kone.com

Abstract. This paper introduces an elevator group control system based on bi-objective optimisation. The two conflicting objectives are passenger waiting times and energy consumption. Due to the response time requirements the powerful but computationally demanding Pareto-dominance based Evolutionary Multiobjective Optimisers cannot be used in this real-world-real-time control application. Instead, an evolutionary variant of the modest Weighted Aggregation method has been applied without prejudice. The presented approach solves the weight-scaling problem of the Weighted Aggregation method in dynamically changing environment. In addition, the method does not solve, but copes with the disability of the WA-method to reach the concave Pareto-front regions in the fitness space. A dedicated controller acts as a Decision Maker guiding the optimiser to produce solutions that fulfil the specified passenger waiting times over a longer period of time with minimum consumption of energy. Simulation results show that the control principle is able to regulate the service level of an elevator group and at the same time decrease the consumption of energy and system wearing.

1 Introduction

The elevator routing or landing call allocation problem may be considered as a version of the Travelling Salesman Problem (TSP). In the elevator car routing context the TSP problem can be converted to Multiple Travelling Salesmen Problem (MTSP), where salesmen (elevator cars) visit the cities (car calls and landing calls) so that each city (call) is visited only once and the cost function $\sum C(\mathbf{S}_i, \mathbf{C}_i \cup \mathbf{L}_i)$ is minimised. The partial cost C is gathered along the route when a set of car and landing calls $\mathbf{C}_i \cup \mathbf{L}_i$ is visited by the elevator i, starting the roundtrip from the elevator's initial state $\mathbf{S}_i$.

The size of the problem space is $N_s = E^n$, where E is number of elevators and n is the number of active landing calls. The problem is too large to be solved systematically, except only in the smallest elevator groups, so other methods have to be applied to solve the landing call allocation problem. In [1] we have presented a landing call allocation method based on Genetic Algorithms (GA). In [8] the approach was studied with double deck elevators. The optimisation in [1] and [8] was based on a single-objective: the call time or waiting time of passengers. Here we extend the algorithm to multi-objective optimisation (MO) capability and utilise two conflicting objectives – the landing call waiting time and energy consumption of elevators along their routes. Due to the asymmetric properties of the elevator hoisting function, by selecting the elevator car routes carefully, it is possible to conserve energy and still serve passengers well.

The landing call allocation decisions are needed in real time, the elevator route optimisation problem has to be solved twice a second. Due to the processing time restrictions the paper presents an approach based on the straightforward and computationally efficient Weighted Aggregation (WA) method. The WA-optimisation returns the original MO-problem to a single optimisation one, which have run times in $O(GN)$, where G is the number of generations and N is the population size, whereas the run times of the nondominated sorting methods, like NSGA-II, are in $O(MGN^2)$, where M is the number of objective function [2]. Despite their benefits dealing with non-convex Pareto-fronts the nondominated Evolutionary Multiobjective Optimisation methods (EMO) cannot be used in this real time application because of the unacceptable processing times they would yield.

The WA-method presented in this paper is able to perform the bi-objective optimisation task with contradicting objectives in real time within the given 500-milliseconds time frame. The drawback of the WA-method is that it has problems in two areas: (i) the definition of the weight values depends of the optimisation problem and (ii) it cannot obtain solutions lying on the non-convex regions in the Pareto-optimal front [3].

To overcome the problem (i) we present a general method which normalises the objective functions in the beginning of the evolutionary search letting the Decision Maker (DM) all the time simply express his preferences with weight values in range [0..1]. To deal with problem (ii) a control loop is established to assure that the time averaged solutions meet the requirements given by the system operator. In the control loop a PI-controller acts as a DM adjusting the weights of the WA-optimiser according to the deviations from the target passenger's waiting time defined by a system operator, who is usually the Building Manager in our case.

The ultimate goal behind the approach we present here is to regulate the service level of the elevator system in terms of passenger waiting times or call time. During the design phase of the building the elevators are sized to give appropriate service during intensive traffic peaks [4,6,7]. During other traffic periods, when traditionally optimising only the passenger waiting time, the system provides inadequate good service at the expense of energy consumption and the system wearing. The bearing idea is to specify the average waiting time the system should maintain in all traffic situations - the elevator car routes should satisfy the specified average passenger waiting time with the least consumption of energy.

2 Objective Functions

The traditional objective function to control the elevator group operation has been the landing call on time [4], which describes to some extent the passenger waiting times as well as the service level of an elevator system. Besides the average call time we use the energy consumption of the elevator routes as the second optimisation objective.

The components of an elevator hoisting mechanics are dimensioned so that the system is in balance when the counterweight resides at the same height h as the half-loaded car

$$m_{cw} + \tfrac{1}{2} m_{ropes}(h) = m_{car} + \tfrac{1}{2} m_{L\max} + \tfrac{1}{2} m_{ropes}(h) , \qquad (1)$$

where m_{Lmax} is the maximum rated load. When the car and counterweight are located at different heights in the shaft the ropes get imbalance. In the mid and high-rise elevators with shaft lengths up to several hundreds meters the imbalance due to ropes has to be compensated with another set of ropes connecting the car and counterweight through the pit. In that case (1) reduces to

$$m_{cw} = m_{car} + \tfrac{1}{2} m_{L\max} . \qquad (2)$$

In the low-rise elevators, the rope masses are much smaller compared to the car and counterweight masses and (2) can be applied with sufficient accuracy as well.

When an elevator car runs from a floor at height h_1 to some other floor at height h_2 the potential energy in the system changes

$$\Delta E = mg(h_2 - h_1) = mg\Delta h . \qquad (3)$$

In (3) the mass m is the static mass balance of the system

$$m = m_{car} + m_L - m_{cw} = m_L - \tfrac{1}{2} m_{L\max} . \qquad (4)$$

Consider an empty car moving downwards. The counterweight is heavier than the car and the hoisting motor has to apply energy to the system in order to increase the system's potential energy. In the opposite case, when the empty car moves upward, the heavier counterweight pulls the car and the motor has to brake, i.e. it operates as a generator. Depending of the motor drive electronics the released potential energy is either wasted into a braking resistor or, as in the more advanced systems, it can be restored back to the power supply network. When the car is full loaded the directions reverse – moving the car upward consumes energy and moving downward restores the potential energy. In fact, the passengers transported into the building conserve energy, which in turn is released when passengers leave the building. All the potential energy bounded to the passengers cannot be restored because of the mechanical and electrical losses in the transportation system.

Figure 1 shows measured example drive upwards (2-15 seconds) and then downwards (30–43 seconds) with a full loaded car. The nominal speed of the hoisting system is 3.5m/s, acceleration 1.2m/s² and maximum load 1600kg equals 21 persons. This 13-floor hoisting system is used in the examples through this paper. Figure 2 shows the energy surfaces of the elevator trips up and down with different loads and travelling distances.

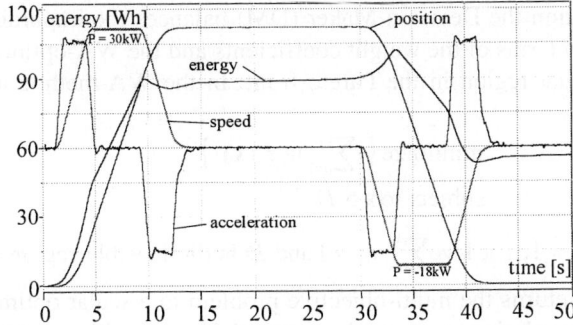

Fig. 1. Measured car acceleration, speed, position and energy consumption of a flight up and then a returning flight down to the initial floor, with full load of 21 persons.

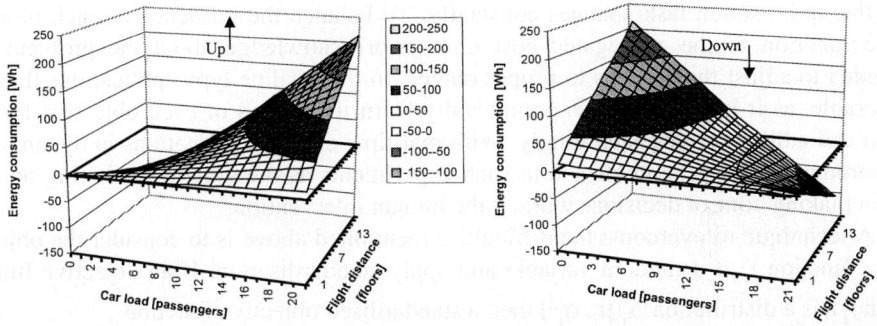

Fig. 2. Energy consumption of the example elevator as a function of car load and flight distance. Up (*left*) and down (*right*) directions, car accommodates 21 passengers.

3 The Control Principle

The literature on the evolutionary multi-objective optimisation deals much with problems of analysis and design type, e.g. optimising some mechanical structure. The focus can be seen e.g. in [5]. These problems are off-line in nature, the computational expense of the algorithm is important but not the most crucial aspect when considering the algorithm.

Instead, in real time control type optimisation problems, the time frame available to achieve the solution is limited and crucial. For example, in case of our elevator group control application, the routing decisions have to be made twice a second. With the popular Pareto-dominated EMOs the processing times obey $O(MGN^2)$, where M is the number of objective functions, G is the number of generations and N is the population size [2]. As the Weighted Aggregation (WA) method is essentially a single optimisation method the processing times are in $O(GN)$. Using Pareto-dominated sorting algorithms would yield $O(MN)$ longer processing times as compared to the WA-algorithms, which would be unacceptable in this real time application.

In this application the Decision Maker (DM) balances the importance of each objective function in terms of the weight coefficients and the WA-optimiser then returns a solution from that region in the Pareto-front. In the WA-method a problem to be solved is

$$\text{minimize}\left\{ \sum_{i=1}^{n} w_i f_i(\mathbf{x}) \right\},$$
$$\text{subject to } \mathbf{x} \in D \tag{5}$$

where $w_i \geq 0 \ \forall \ i = 1, \ldots, k \wedge \sum_{i=1}^{k} w_i = 1$ and D is the feasible region of the solutions [3]. The method returns the multi-objective problem to a scalar optimisation one and all the developed evolutionary methods on that field are readily available.

To obtain the nondominated set of decision vectors $\mathbf{x}$ the optimisation problem is normally run with different linear combinations of weights w_i. Problem arises when the ranges of each objective function differ significantly or are not known beforehand or the optimisation task changes constantly. To balance the influence of each objective function to the aggregated cost C, a priori knowledge about the problem is needed to adjust the weights to proper ranges. In the off-line type applications this is tolerable, as it is possible to experimentally learn the ranges of each objective function and adjust weights accordingly. With real-time control applications in dynamical environments there is no chance to such experiments as the system is running on its own making control decisions without the human intervention.

A technique to overcome the difficulties mentioned above is to consider the objective function f_i as a random variable and apply standardisation. If an objective function f_i has a distribution $\Delta_i(\mu_i, \sigma_i^2)$ then a standardised objective function

$$\phi_i = \frac{f_i - \mu_i}{\sigma_i} \tag{6}$$

has distribution $\Delta_i(0,1)$. The underlying mean μ and variance σ^2 of the objective functions are not (normally) known a priori. Instead, they have to be estimated with their counterparts, sample mean m and sample variance s^2

$$m_i = \frac{1}{N} \sum_{j=1}^{N} f_{i,j}$$
$$s_i^2 = \frac{1}{N-1} \sum_{j=1}^{N} (f_{i,j} - m_i)^2, \tag{7}$$

where N is the sample size. The standardisation gets now to form

$$\hat{\phi}_i = \frac{f_i - m_i}{s_i} \tag{8}$$

and the optimisation problem is now

$$\text{minimize}\left\{ \sum_{i=1}^{n} w_i \hat{\phi}_i(\mathbf{x}) \right\},$$
$$\text{subject to } \mathbf{x} \in D \tag{9}$$

where again $w_i \geq 0 \ \forall \ i = 1, \ldots, k \wedge \sum_{i=1}^{k} w_i = 1$.

With the evolutionary algorithms, the sampling is a built in feature of the algorithm. The initial, (uniformly) randomly generated first generation of decision vectors **x** take N random samples from the objective function space for each f_i: $R^n \rightarrow R$. The sampling and normalisation approach with the evolutionary algorithms with population size N is straightforward as illustrated in the Table 1.

Table 1. Steps of the Evolutionary Standardised Objective Weighted Aggregation Method.

Step	Action
1	Create the initial population of the N decision vectors randomly, compute the sample mean m_i and variance s_i^2 in equation (7)
2	Compute the standardised objective functions $\hat{\phi}_i$ in (8)
3	Compute the aggregated cost C in (9)
4	Apply the genetic operators (selection, crossover and mutation) specific to your (single objective) evolutionary optimiser to create the next generation of population
5	If not converged go to the step 2.

The severe limitation of typical WA method is its disability to deal with the non-convex regions of the Pareto-front [3]. The non-convexity is present also in the elevator car routing problem. Figure 3 shows an elevator group of 7 elevators, an optimisation problem instance and the corresponding fitness space. The example implies that the Pareto-front in this application may possess none, one, two, or even more local concave regions not reachable by WA-method.

The control principle of the elevator group is to find such routes for the elevator cars that satisfy the given target passenger waiting time with minimum consumption of energy, i.e.

$$\text{Minimise } \{ f_1(\mathbf{x}), f_2(\mathbf{x}) \} \quad \text{Subject to } \mathbf{x} \in D, \tag{10a}$$

$$\mathbf{x}^* = \{ \mathbf{x} \in P^* \mid (f_1(\mathbf{x}) - f_1^*)^2 = \min \}. \tag{10b}$$

In the Decision-Maker's utility function (10b) f_1^* is the specified target for the average call time the system should maintain in the prevailing traffic conditions and $\mathbf{x}^*$ is the decision vector or allocation decisions from the set of nondominated solutions P^* forming the Pareto-front. In order to obtain the P^* with the WA-method the optimisation should be run with a number of linear combinations of weights w_i and then apply (10b). To reduce the computational burden and further, to compensate for the difficulties of the WA-method with the concave Pareto-regions, we take an approach where the optimisation is executed only once per control cycle.

To reach the correct regions of the Pareto-front the weights w_i are adjusted continuously during the course of the operation so that the time average of term $(f_1(\mathbf{x})-f_1^*)^2$ in (10b) is minimised. During each control cycle a dedicated controller acts as a Decision Maker comparing the differences between the predicted average call time

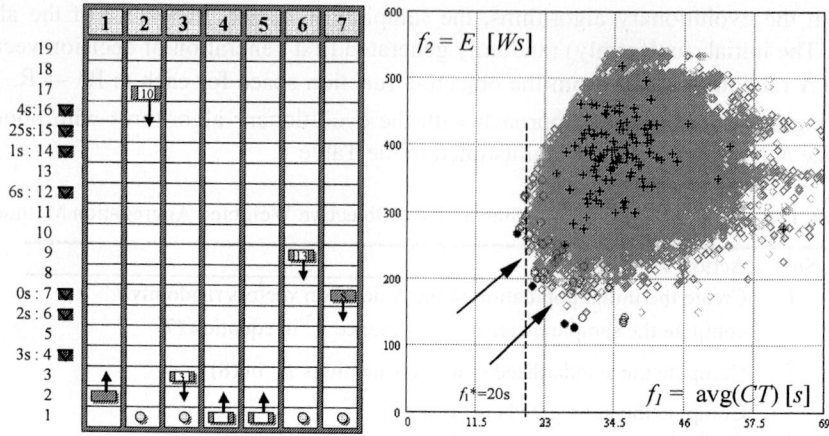

Fig. 3. A traffic situation (*left*) and corresponding fitness space (*right*). Objective f_1 is the average Call Time and f_2 is the Energy consumption of the route alternatives. The optimisation was run for 11 times with weights $w_1 = \{0, 0.1,..., 1.0\}$ and $w_2 = \{1-w_1\}$. 4 distinct solutions was found by ESOWA shown with dots. Also shown best fitness from each generation (*circles*), random initial values for the search (*crosses*) and 64000 randomly generated routes (*diamonds*). Two arrows pointing locally convex regions in the Pareto-front.

$f_1(\mathbf{x}^*)$, produced by the elevator system model in evolutionary optimiser, to the target value f_1^*. The DM thus guides the optimiser by adjusting the objective function weights according to the PI-control rule (Proportional and time-Integral terms) in order to satisfy (10b) over the course of time. Block diagram of the approach is shown in Figure 4.

4 Results

As it is not possible to obtain comprehensive data in controlled manner from elevator system running in a real building, building simulators with simulated passenger traffic and elevators are standard development tools in the elevator industry [4,6]. The selected building for the performance tests is a high-rise building with an elevator group of 7 elevators and 19 floors as illustrated in the Figure 3. The specifications of the hoisting system were given in the beginning of the paper. The nominal transportation capacity of the system is 200 passengers in five minutes, which equals 13.1% of the building population and is classified as good [7]. Three independent simulation series were run with pure outgoing traffic. The results shown here are averages of the three series. The pure outgoing traffic was selected because in that traffic type the optimiser has most freedom to arrange the routes, as there is no constraining car calls, thus revealing most clearly the capabilities of the control principle. Within one simulation series the traffic intensity was increased from 2% of the building population to 20%, in 2% steps. Each intensity step was run for 30 minutes.

Evolutionary Elevator Group Regulates Passenger Service Level   829

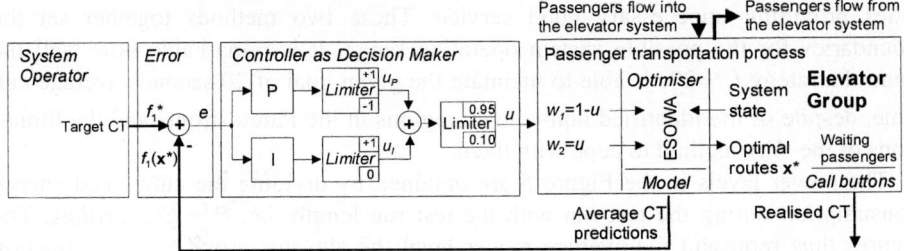

Fig. 4. Overall system structure. A PI-controller acts as a Decision Maker guiding the Optimiser to provide specified service level in terms of Average Call Time. The predicted Average Call Time $f_1(\mathbf{x}^*)$ is obtained from the Optimiser's system model as "side product" of the optimisation.

Figures 5 and 6 collect the main results from the three simulation series with three different control strategies. The horizontal axis is traffic intensity in percentages of the building population. The three different routing strategies are pure call time optimisation with $f_1^*=0$s, pure energy optimisation with $f_1^*=\infty$s, and adequate service level with $f_1^*=20$s.

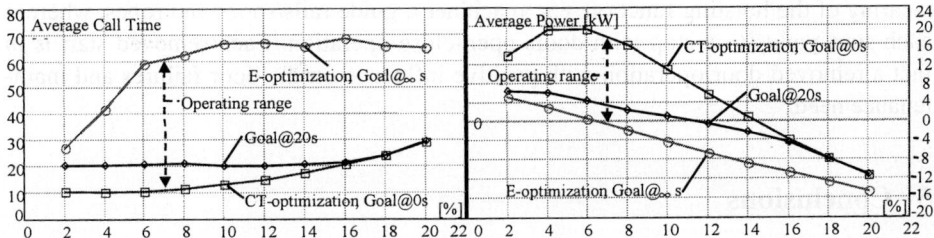

Fig. 5. Average call time (*left*) and the average power level (*right*) of the hoisting system to provide that service level. Outgoing traffic, intensity % of the building population.

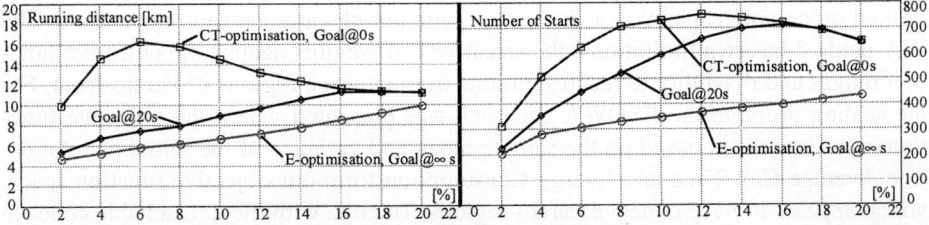

Fig. 6. Running distance of the elevator group (*left*) and number of starts (*right*) during the 30-minutes simulation run. Outgoing traffic, intensity % of the building population.

When looking at the call times in the Figure 5 the results produced by the pure energy optimisation would be useless in practice. The standard approach, the pure call time optimisation, pushes the figures down to 10 seconds during the low traffic intensities providing unnecessary good service. These two methods together set the boundaries for the possible system operating range. It is remarkable how well the control strategy f_1^*=20s is able to maintain the given goal of 20 seconds average call time, despite of the identified non-convex regions in the Pareto-fronts and the limitations of the WA-method to cope with them.

The power levels in the Figure 5 are obtained by dividing the cumulated energy consumption during the test run with the test run length, i.e. $P = Energy/time$. The figures thus represent the average power level the elevator group hoisting function has applied during the 30 minutes run to provide the specified service level. The decrease in energy consumption and the required power level is outstanding in the low and medium traffic intensities. The largest reduction is at the intensity 6% where the hoisting system power drops by 14 kilowatts – from 19 kilowatts to 5 kilowatts. Obviously the shorter waiting times the ordinary call time optimisation provides to passengers are expensive in terms of energy consumption.

Figure 6 shows the side effects of the different control methods. With the control strategy f_1^*=20s there is a drastic reduction in the total running distance of the elevators when compared to the ordinary CT-optimisation. Also the number of starts is reduced significantly. Both the running distance and the number of starts have impact on system wearing and maintenance needs. Running distance affects directly to the wearing of the hoisting function, e.g. machinery, guide rails/shoes and ropes, whereas each start yields to a stop with doors open-close operation. Each removed start is in fact a removed door operation with positive influence on the door failures and maintenance need.

5 Conclusions

In the field of EMO the main interest and research is in the algorithms based on Pareto-domination. These algorithms are powerful but have run times of $O(MGN^2)$. On the other hand the modest WA-method has run times in $O(GN)$, meeting more easily the needs for response times in real time commercial control applications with limited processing capacity – as is the case with our elevator car routing problem. The WA-method has two limitations: the sensitivity of weights against the objective function ranges and disability to reach solutions from concave regions of Pareto-front. For the scaling problem the ESOWA approach was presented where the objective functions are normalised based on the sample mean and variance of the initial population. The Average Call Time and Energy Consumption form our objective function space, which appears to have concave Pareto-regions. To cope with the unreachable concave regions, the PI-controller based DM balances the biased solutions, found from the closest convex regions by the WA-method, over longer period of time. The simulation results show that the presented approach is successful in this application. As a result the service level of the elevator group is regulated while the energy consumption is minimised. This is a novel approach and control concept in the elevator industry. An important additional result of the approach is the reduction in the number of starts and running distance that the elevators perform, which reduces wearing of the system, failure rate and service need. Although the results obtained with the pure outgoing traffic show the potential of the approach, with real traffic there will more constraints for the route optimisation. In the future, the capabilities of the method will be studied with daily traffic patterns from typical office and residential buildings. Also the performance of the presented method will be compared to the dominance based ranking EMOs, like NSGA-II.

References

1. Tyni, T. and Ylinen, J.: Genetic Algorithms in Elevator Car Routing Problem. In: Spector, L., et. al. (eds.): Proceedings of the Genetic and Evolutionary Computation Conference, GECCO-2001. Morgan Kaufmann Publishers, San Francisco (2001)
2. Jensen, M., T.: Reducing the Run-Time Complexity of Multiobjective EAs: The NSGA-II and Other Algorithms. IEEE Transactions on Evolutionary Computation, Vol.7, NO.5 (2003) 503–515
3. Coello Coello, C., A., Van Veldhuizen, D., A., Lamont, G., B.: Evolutionary Algorithms for Solving Multi-Objective Problems. Kluwer Academic/Plenum Publishers, New York (2002)
4. Barney, G.: Elevator Traffic Handbook, Theory and Practice. Spon Press, London and New York (2003)
5. Bugeda, G., Desideri, J., A., Periaux, J., Schoenauer M., Winter, G. (eds.): Evolutionary Methods for Design, Optimisation and Control with Applications to Industrial and Societal Problems. In: Proceedings of Eurogen 2003, CIMNE Barcelona (2003)
6. Siikonen, M-L.: Planning and Control Models for Elevators in High Rise Buildings. Doctorate thesis, Helsinki University of Technology (1997)
7. KONE Corporation: Recommendations for traffic handling capacity for different building types. In: Traffic planning software "KONE Trafcal" (2003)
8. Sorsa, J., Siikonen, M-L., Ehtamo, H.: Optimal Control of Double Deck Elevator Group using Genetic Algorithm. International Transactions on Operational Research, Vol.10, No.2 (2003) 103-114

Indicator-Based Selection in Multiobjective Search

Eckart Zitzler and Simon Künzli*

Swiss Federal Institute of Technology Zurich
Computer Engineering and Networks Laboratory (TIK)
Gloriastrasse 35, CH–8092 Zürich, Switzerland
{zitzler,kuenzli}@tik.ee.ethz.ch

Abstract. This paper discusses how preference information of the decision maker can in general be integrated into multiobjective search. The main idea is to first define the optimization goal in terms of a binary performance measure (indicator) and then to directly use this measure in the selection process. To this end, we propose a general indicator-based evolutionary algorithm (IBEA) that can be combined with arbitrary indicators. In contrast to existing algorithms, IBEA can be adapted to the preferences of the user and moreover does not require any additional diversity preservation mechanism such as fitness sharing to be used. It is shown on several continuous and discrete benchmark problems that IBEA can substantially improve on the results generated by two popular algorithms, namely NSGA-II and SPEA2, with respect to different performance measures.

1 Motivation

In a multiobjective scenario, the goal of the optimization process is often to find a good approximation of the set of Pareto-optimal solutions. The difficulty, though, is that there is no general definition of what a good approximation of the Pareto set is. Each particular definition represents specific preference information that depends on the user. For instance, one could formalize the goal as maximizing the hypervolume of the objective space dominated by the resulting approximation (cf. [11, 18]). In certain scenarios this definition may be appropriate, in others it can be inappropriate because the goal of the optimization process may vary for each decision maker and problem.

In the light of this discussion, one may reconsider the criteria that guided the design of multiobjective evolutionary algorithms (MOEAs) in the last decade. We make two observations here:

1. The basis of most MOEAs is the assumption that there are two conflicting goals: (i) to minimize the distance to the Pareto-optimal set, and (ii) to maximize the diversity within the approximation of the Pareto-optimal set [3]. However, recent studies [10, 18] have shown that this assumption

---

* Simon Künzli has been supported by the Swiss Innovation Promotion Agency (KTI/CTI) through the project KTI 5500.2.

is problematic; to our best knowledge, there exists no formal definition of two separate objectives, one for convergence and one for diversity, that is compliant with the Pareto dominance relation. Furthermore, there are also practical problems related to this issue as discussed in [1].

2. In most popular MOEAs, the above assumption is implemented in terms of a Pareto-based ranking of the individuals that is refined by additional density information in objective space. The algorithms, though, differ in various aspects, and therefore each of them realizes a slightly different optimization goal, which is usually not explicitly defined. That means current approaches have not been designed for flexibility with respect to the preference information used; instead, they directly implement one particular type of preference information.

As to the first aspect, the alternative is to use Pareto-compliant formalizations of the decision maker's preferences (cf. [9, 10, 18]). This, in turn, leads to a question that is directly related to the second aspect: How to design MOEAs with respect to arbitrary preference information?

The issue of integrating preference information into multiobjective search has been addressed by different researchers, see [2] for an overview. For instance, Fonseca and Fleming [8] proposed an extended dominance relation that integrates predefined priorities and goals; however, the two observations stated above also apply to the algorithm introduced by them, similarly to many other algorithms used in this context: a diversity preservation mechanism is implemented that implicitly encodes unspecified preference information. In contrast, Knowles [11] presented a multiobjective hill climber that can be combined with arbitrary unary performance measures and does not require niching methods. This approach, though, is – depending on the performance measure used – computationally expensive, and it is not clear how to extend it to population-based multiobjective optimizers that implement both mating and environmental selection.

In this paper, we extend the idea of flexible integration of preference information by Fonseca and Fleming [8] and Knowles [11] and propose a general indicator-based evolutionary algorithm, IBEA for short. The main idea is to formalize preferences in terms of *continuous* generalizations of the dominance relation, which leads to a simple algorithmic concept. Thereby, IBEA not only allows adaptation to arbitrary preference information and optimization scenarios, but also does not need any diversity preservation techniques, in contrast to [8]. In comparison to [11], IBEA is more general, since the population size can be arbitrary, and faster, because it only compares pairs of individuals and not entire approximation sets. As will be shown, the proposed approach can significantly improve the quality of the generated Pareto set approximation with respect to the considered optimization goal – in comparison to prominent Pareto-based MOEAs.

2 Preliminaries

In the following, we consider a general optimization problem that is defined by a decision space X, an objective space Z, and n objective functions $f_1, f_2, \ldots, f_n$

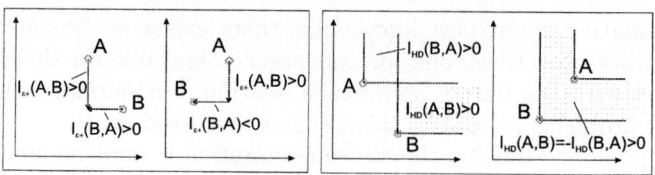

Fig. 1. Illustration of the two binary quality indicators used in this paper where A and B contain one decision vector each (left: $I_{\epsilon+}$-indicator; right: I_{HD}-indicator).

that assign to each decision vector $x \in X$ a corresponding objective vector $z = (f_1(x), f_2(x), \ldots, f_n(x)) \in Z$. Without loss of generality, it is assumed that all objective functions are to be minimized and that $Z \subseteq \mathbb{R}^n$. Furthermore, the outcome of an MOEA is defined as a set of incomparable decision vectors, i.e., no decision vector dominates[1] any other decision vector in the set. Such a set will also be denoted as Pareto set approximation, and the entirety of all Pareto set approximations is represented by the symbol Ω, where $\Omega \subseteq 2^Z$. The set of all Pareto-optimal solutions is called the Pareto set S with $S \in \Omega$.

We assume that the preferences of the decision maker are given in terms of a binary quality indicator $I : \Omega \times \Omega \to \mathbb{R}$. A quality indicator in general is a function that maps k Pareto set approximations to a real number; most common are unary quality indicators where $k = 1$ (cf. [18]). Binary quality indicators can be used to compare the quality of two Pareto set approximations relatively to each other. For instance, the binary additive ϵ-indicator $I_{\epsilon+}$ [18] gives the minimum distance by which a Pareto set approximation needs to or can be translated in each dimension in objective space such that another approximation is weakly dominated[2]. Formally, it is defined as follows (cf. Fig. 1 for an illustration):

$$I_{\epsilon+}(A, B) = \min_\epsilon \left\{ \forall x^2 \in B \; \exists x^1 \in A \; : \; f_i(x^1) - \epsilon \leq f_i(x^2) \text{ for } i \in \{1, \ldots, n\} \right\}$$

The reason why we consider binary quality indicators here is that they represent a natural extension of the Pareto dominance relation, and therefore can directly be used for fitness calculation similarly to the common Pareto-based fitness assignment schemes. One requirement, though, is that the considered indicator I is compliant with Pareto dominance as defined as follows.

Definition 1. *A binary quality indicator I is denoted as* dominance preserving *if (i) $x^1 \succ x^2 \Rightarrow I(\{x^1\}, \{x^2\}) < I(\{x^2\}, \{x^1\})$ and (ii) $x^1 \succ x^2 \Rightarrow I(\{x^3\}, \{x^1\}) \geq I(\{x^3\}, \{x^2\})$ for all $x^1, x^2, x^3 \in X$.*

We will see later how these properties ensure that the proposed fitness assignment scheme is also Pareto dominance compliant. Note that the $I_{\epsilon+}$-indicator

---

[1] A decision vector x^1 is said to dominate another decision vector x^2, written as $x^1 \succ x^2$, if $f_i(x^1) \leq f_i(x^2)$ for all $i \in \{1, \ldots, n\}$ and $f_j(x^1) < f_j(x^2)$ for at least one $j \in \{1, \ldots, n\}$.
[2] A ecision vector x^1 weakly dominates another one x^2, written as $x^1 \succeq x^2$, if x^1 dominates x^2 or the corresponding objective vectors are equal.

is dominance preserving; for instance, the indicator values become negative as soon as x^1 dominates x^2 (cf. [18]).

Now, given an arbitrary optimization problem and a corresponding binary quality indicator I, we can define the goal of the optimization process as minimizing $I(A, S)$ for $A \in \Omega$ where S is the Pareto set. If I is dominance preserving, then $I(A, S)$ is minimum for $A = S$; in the case of the additive ϵ-indicator, $I_{\epsilon+}(S, S) = 0$. Note that we do not require here that S is known, it just serves the formalization of the optimization goal.

3 Indicator-Based Selection

Taking the scenario described in Section 2, the question is how I can be integrated in an MOEA to minimize $I(A, S)$, where A is the generated Pareto set approximation. This section deals with this issue.

3.1 Fitness Assignment

The population P represents a sample of the decision space, and fitness assignment tries to rank the population members according to their usefulness regarding the optimization goal. Among the different ways how the exploit the information given by P and I, one possibility is to simply sum up the indicator values for each population member with respect to the rest of population, i.e.: $F'(x^1) = \sum_{x^2 \in P \setminus \{x^1\}} I(\{x^2\}, \{x^1\})$ This fitness value F', which is to be maximized, is a measure for the "loss in quality" if x^1 is removed from the population. For $I_{\epsilon+}$, e.g., $F'(x^1)$ divided by the population size N equals the average ϵ needed to cover x^1 by other population members. However, we will use a slightly different scheme in the following that amplifies the influence of dominating population members over dominated ones:

$$F(x^1) = \sum_{x^2 \in P \setminus \{x^1\}} -e^{-I(\{x^2\},\{x^1\})/\kappa}$$

We use one property of dominance preserving indicators here, namely that $I(\{x^1\}, \{x^2\}) < I(\{x^2\}, \{x^1\})$ if $x^1 \succ x^2$. Thereby, the influence of small indicator values contributes much more to the overall fitness than large values. The parameter κ is a scaling factor depending on I and the underlying problem; κ needs to be greater than 0. The following theorem shows that this fitness scheme is compliant with the Pareto dominance relation.

Theorem 1. *Let I be a binary quality indicator. If I is dominance preserving, then it holds that $x^1 \succ x^2 \Rightarrow F(x^1) > F(x^2)$.*

Proof. From Def. 1 and property (i) it follows that the indicator value $I(\{x^1\}, \{x^2\}) < I(\{x^2\}, \{x^1\})$. Due to property (ii) of Def. 1, we know that $I(\{x^3\}, \{x^1\}) \geq I(\{x^3\}, \{x^2\}), \forall x^3 \notin \{x^1, x^2\}$. Since $-e^{-x/\kappa} > -e^{-y/\kappa}$, if $x < y$ and $\kappa > 0$, it follows that $F(x^1) > F(x^2)$. □

3.2 Example Indicators

We have now seen how the additive ϵ-indicator can be used to assign fitness values to the population members. However, many other dominance preserving indicators can be defined that could be used instead. For instance, the following I_{HD}-indicator is based on the hypervolume concept [17]:

$$I_{HD}(A, B) = \begin{cases} I_H(B) - I_H(A) & \text{if } \forall \bm{x}^2 \in B \; \exists \bm{x}^1 \in A \; : \; \bm{x}^1 \succ \bm{x}^2 \\ I_H(A + B) - I_H(A) & \text{else} \end{cases}$$

Here, $I_H(A)$ gives the hypervolume of the objective space dominated by A, and accordingly $I_{HD}(A, B)$ measures the volume of the space that is dominated by B but not by A with respect to a predefined reference point $\bm{Z}$. While the calculation of the $I_{HD}(A, B)$-values is computationally expensive for approximations containing several decision vectors, it is of order $\mathcal{O}(n)$ if two decision vectors are compared. The I_{HD}-indicator will be used in addition to the $I_{\epsilon+}$-indicator later in this paper. A graphical interpretation for I_{HD} can be found on the right hand side of Fig. 1.

Other examples for binary quality indicators that could be used here are described in Hansen and Jaszkiewicz's study [9].

3.3 Basic Algorithm

Based on the above fitness assignment scheme, we propose a general indicator-based evolutionary algorithm (IBEA) that performs binary tournaments for mating selection and implements environmental selection by iteratively removing the worst individual from the population and updating the fitness values of the remaining individuals. Its running-time complexity is $\mathcal{O}(\alpha^2)$ with regard to the population size α. Details of the algorithm are given below; note that it represents only the basic version of IBEA (denoted B-IBEA in the following), an extended version will be specified later.

Algorithm 1 (Basic IBEA)

Input: α (population size)
             N (maximum number of generations)
             κ (fitness scaling factor)
Output: A (Pareto set approximation)

Step 1: *Initialization:* Generate an initial population P of size α; set the generation counter m to 0.

Step 2: *Fitness assignment:* Calculate fitness values of individuals in P, i.e., for all $\bm{x}^1 \in P$ set $F(\bm{x}^1) = \sum_{\bm{x}^2 \in P \setminus \{\bm{x}^1\}} -e^{-I(\{\bm{x}^2\},\{\bm{x}^1\})/\kappa}$.

Step 3: *Environmental selection:* Iterate the following three steps until the size of population P does not exceed α:
  1. Choose an individual $\bm{x}^* \in P$ with the smallest fitness value, i.e., $F(\bm{x}^*) \leq F(\bm{x})$ for all $\bm{x} \in P$.
  2. Remove $\bm{x}^*$ from the population.
  3. Update the fitness values of the remaining individuals, i.e.,
$F(\bm{x}) = F(\bm{x}) + e^{-I(\{\bm{x}^*\},\{\bm{x}\})/\kappa}$ for all $\bm{x} \in P$.

Step 4: *Termination:* If $m \geq N$ or another stopping criterion is satisfied then set A to the set of decision vectors represented by the nondominated individuals in P. Stop.

Step 5: *Mating selection:* Perform binary tournament selection with replacement on P in order to fill the temporary mating pool P'.

Step 6: *Variation:* Apply recombination and mutation operators to the mating pool P' and add the resulting offspring to P. Increment the generation counter ($m = m + 1$) and go to Step 2.

3.4 Simulation Results

The proposed algorithm was tested on several well-known benchmark problems: the 2-dimensional knapsack problem instance from [17] with 100 items, a network processor application comprising problem instances with two (EXPO2), three (EXPO3), and four (EXPO4) objectives (cf. [14]), and four continuous test functions, namely ZDT6 [15] and KUR [12] with two objectives as well as DTLZ2 and DTLZ6 [6] with three objectives each[3]. For all problems, the population size α was set to 100 and the maximum number of generations N to 200. Overall, 30 runs with different initial populations were carried out per algorithm and per benchmark problem.

To assess the performance values, we have compared the solutions found by the two new algorithms B-IBEA$_{\epsilon+}$ and B-IBEA$_{HD}$ with NSGA-II [5] and SPEA2 [16]. The performance comparison was carried out using the quality indicators $I_{\epsilon+}$ and I_{HD}, i.e., we have computed 30 indicator values $I(A, R)$ for different seeds for all the tested algorithms. In this formula, A stands for the output that the evolutionary algorithm produced; the reference set R was determined by merging all solutions found by all the different algorithms into one set and keeping the non-dominated solutions. R was used instead of the Pareto set S, because S is usually unknown.

For the results obtained using B-IBEA$_{\epsilon+}$, B-IBEA$_{HD}$, NSGA-II and SPEA2, we can observe in the comparison that B-IBEA$_{\epsilon+}$ and B-IBEA$_{HD}$ perform significantly better than the other algorithms regarding both performance indicators and for appropriately chosen parameter κ. Although for the variation parameter settings described above, the choice for the parameter κ does not influence the performance of the algorithm much, we found other parameter settings that indicate that the optimal choice of κ can vary and is dependent on the problem and the indicator used. This is, e.g., the case for ZDT6 if both mutation and recombination probability are set to 1. In Figure 2a (top), the influence of different values κ for the performance of B-IBEA$_{\epsilon+}$ on the problem ZDT6 is given. The performance of B-IBEA$_{HD}$ not only depends on the choice of κ but also on the choice of the reference point. In Figure 2a (bottom), we can see that for a particular choice of both κ and the reference point, the performance of B-IBEA$_{HD}$ for problem ZDT6 is better than SPEA2 and NSGA-II, but for other choices for κ and the reference point the performance is substantially worse. We do not give all the results for the basic versions of IBEA in a table due to space limitations.

---

[3] For the continuous problems, the individuals are coded as real vectors, where the SBX-20 operator is used for recombination and a polynomial distribution for mutation [4]. The recombination and mutation probabilities were set to 1.0 and to 0.01, resp., according to [7]. For the knapsack problem, an individual is represented by a bit string, recombination is performed as one-point crossover with probability 0.8 according to [17], and point mutations are performed with bit-flip probability 0.04, as suggested in [13]. For the design-space exploration problems EXPO, the representation of individuals and the operators are described in [14]. The recombination probability was set to 0.5 and the probability for mutation was set to 0.8. (These are the same parameter settings as proposed in [14]).

The question that arises inspecting the results obtained so far is how we can improve the algorithms such that (i) the same κ value can be used for different problems and indicators, and (ii) B-IBEA$_{HD}$ becomes less sensitive to the choice of the reference point for I_{HD}.

4 Improving Robustness

4.1 Adaptive IBEA

The values for the indicators $I(A, B)$ can be widely spread for different problems. This makes it difficult to determine an appropriate value for κ. We can ease this task by adaptively scaling the indicator values such that they lie in the interval $[-1, 1]$ for all points in the population. Thereby, we can use the same value κ for all the problems.

To tackle the problem of determining a good reference point for the I_{HD} indicator, we propose to use adaptive scaling not only for the indicator values, but also for the objective values. After scaling, the objective values lie in the interval $[0, 1]$. Like this, we can choose the worst values for each objective found in the population as reference point to calculate I_{HD}, i.e. the reference point would be set to 1 for all objectives. If we use this strategy, the only problem remaining is that the corner points found in a population do not add to the hypervolume. To overcome this problem, for the reference point we used a value of 2 for all objectives in the experiments with IBEA$_{HD}$.

Algorithm 2 (Adaptive IBEA)

...

Step 2: **Fitness assignment:** First scale objective and indicator values, and then use scaled values to assign fitness values:
1. Determine for each objective f_i its lower bound $\underline{b_i} = min_{\boldsymbol{x} \in P} f_i(\boldsymbol{x})$ and its upper bound $\overline{b_i} = max_{\boldsymbol{x} \in P} f_i(\boldsymbol{x})$.
2. Scale each objective to the interval $[0, 1]$, i.e., $f'_i(\boldsymbol{x}) = (f_i(\boldsymbol{x}) - \underline{b_i})/(\overline{b_i} - \underline{b_i})$.
3. Calculate indicator values $I(\boldsymbol{x}^1, \boldsymbol{x}^2)$ using the scaled objective values f'_i instead of the original f_i, and determine the maximum absolute indicator value $c = max_{\boldsymbol{x}^1, \boldsymbol{x}^2 \in P} |I(\boldsymbol{x}^1, \boldsymbol{x}^2)|$.
4. For all $\boldsymbol{x}^1 \in P$ set $F(\boldsymbol{x}^1) = \sum_{\boldsymbol{x}^2 \in P \setminus \{\boldsymbol{x}^1\}} -e^{-I(\{\boldsymbol{x}^2\},\{\boldsymbol{x}^1\})/(c \cdot \kappa)}$.

Step 3: **Environmental selection:** ...
1. ...
2. ...
3. Update the fitness values of the remaining individuals, i.e., $F(\boldsymbol{x}) = F(\boldsymbol{x}) + e^{-I(\{\boldsymbol{x}^*\},\{\boldsymbol{x}\})/(c \cdot \kappa)}$ for all $\boldsymbol{x} \in P$.

...

The algorithms IBEA$_{\epsilon+}$ and IBEA$_{HD}$ denote the adaptive versions of the basic algorithms. For these versions, the choice of κ only marginally depends on the problem and the indicator under consideration. The changes in the initial algorithm are shown in Algorithm 2. For the experiments discussed in Section 4.2, we have used $\kappa = 0.05$ for all the problems and algorithms. Preliminary tests have shown that this value for κ produced good results on the problems considered. Furthermore, the value for κ was chosen such that in the implementation no numerical problems occur, because smaller values led to fitness values larger than the maximum allowed double value in the PISA-specification ($= 10^{99}$).

Table 1. Comparison of different MOEAs for the $I_{\epsilon+}$-indicator using the Wilcoxon rank test. The "P value" columns give the adjusted P value of the corresponding pairwise test that accounts for multiple testing; it equals the lowest significance level for which the null-hypothesis (the medians are drawn from the same distribution) would still be rejected. The "T" columns give the outcome of the test for a significance level of 5%: either the algorithm corresponding to the specific row is significantly better (↑) resp. worse (↓) than the algorithm associated with the corresponding column or there is no significant difference between the results (⇌).

		SPEA2 P value	T	NSGA-II P value	T	SPEA2$_{adap}$ P value	T	IBEA$_{\epsilon, adap}$ P value	T
ZDT6	NSGA-II	$5.6073 \cdot 10^{-4}$	↑						
	SPEA2$_{adap}$	$> 5\%$	⇌	$8.1975 \cdot 10^{-6}$	↓				
	IBEA$_{\epsilon, adap}$	$8.1014 \cdot 10^{-9}$	↑	$2.0023 \cdot 10^{-5}$	↑	$1.9568 \cdot 10^{-9}$	↑		
	IBEA$_{HD, adap}$	0.0095	↑	$> 5\%$	⇌	$5.4620 \cdot 10^{-5}$	↑	$1.3853 \cdot 10^{-5}$	↓
DTLZ2	NSGA-II	$3.0199 \cdot 10^{-10}$	↓						
	SPEA2$_{adap}$	$> 5\%$	⇌	$3.0199 \cdot 10^{-10}$	↑				
	IBEA$_{\epsilon, adap}$	$3.0199 \cdot 10^{-10}$	↑	$3.0199 \cdot 10^{-10}$	↑	$3.0199 \cdot 10^{-10}$	↑		
	IBEA$_{HD, adap}$	$3.0199 \cdot 10^{-10}$	↑	$3.0199 \cdot 10^{-10}$	↑	$3.0199 \cdot 10^{-10}$	↑	$5.5329 \cdot 10^{-7}$	↓
DTLZ6	NSGA-II	$8.1014 \cdot 10^{-9}$	↓						
	SPEA2$_{adap}$	$> 5\%$	⇌	$6.1210 \cdot 10^{-9}$	↑				
	IBEA$_{\epsilon, adap}$	$3.0199 \cdot 10^{-10}$	↑	$3.0199 \cdot 10^{-10}$	↑	$3.0199 \cdot 10^{-10}$	↑		
	IBEA$_{HD, adap}$	$3.0199 \cdot 10^{-10}$	↑	$3.0199 \cdot 10^{-10}$	↑	$3.0199 \cdot 10^{-10}$	↑	$3.5923 \cdot 10^{-4}$	↓
KUR	NSGA-II	$> 5\%$	⇌						
	SPEA2$_{adap}$	$> 5\%$	⇌	$> 5\%$	⇌				
	IBEA$_{\epsilon, adap}$	$3.0199 \cdot 10^{-10}$	↓	$3.0199 \cdot 10^{-10}$	↓	$6.6955 \cdot 10^{-10}$	↓		
	IBEA$_{HD, adap}$	$3.0199 \cdot 10^{-10}$	↓	$3.0199 \cdot 10^{-10}$	↓	$4.9752 \cdot 10^{-10}$	↓	$> 5\%$	⇌
Knap.	NSGA-II	$> 5\%$	⇌						
	SPEA2$_{adap}$	$> 5\%$	⇌	$> 5\%$	⇌				
	IBEA$_{\epsilon, adap}$	$> 5\%$	⇌	$> 5\%$	⇌	$> 5\%$	⇌		
	IBEA$_{HD, adap}$	$> 5\%$	⇌	$> 5\%$	⇌	$> 5\%$	⇌	$> 5\%$	⇌
EXPO2	NSGA-II	$> 5\%$	⇌						
	SPEA2$_{adap}$	$> 5\%$	⇌	0.0189	↑				
	IBEA$_{\epsilon, adap}$	$1.0837 \cdot 10^{-8}$	↑	$2.6753 \cdot 10^{-9}$	↑	$6.4048 \cdot 10^{-8}$	↑		
	IBEA$_{HD, adap}$	$1.9638 \cdot 10^{-7}$	↑	$1.2260 \cdot 10^{-8}$	↑	$6.6261 \cdot 10^{-7}$	↑	$> 5\%$	⇌
EXPO3	NSGA-II	$> 5\%$	⇌						
	SPEA2$_{adap}$	$> 5\%$	⇌	$> 5\%$	⇌				
	IBEA$_{\epsilon, adap}$	$4.3165 \cdot 10^{-8}$	↑	$5.0801 \cdot 10^{-8}$	↑	$3.1159 \cdot 10^{-7}$	↑		
	IBEA$_{HD, adap}$	$2.4189 \cdot 10^{-7}$	↑	$1.5732 \cdot 10^{-7}$	↑	$1.1653 \cdot 10^{-6}$	↑	$> 5\%$	⇌
EXPO4	NSGA-II	$> 5\%$	⇌	-					
	SPEA2$_{adap}$	$> 5\%$	⇌	$9.4209 \cdot 10^{-4}$	↓				
	IBEA$_{\epsilon, adap}$	$1.8546 \cdot 10^{-10}$	↑	$6.9754 \cdot 10^{-10}$	↑	$1.8390 \cdot 10^{-10}$	↑		
	IBEA$_{HD, adap}$	$1.9883 \cdot 10^{-10}$	↑	$1.0221 \cdot 10^{-9}$	↑	$1.9716 \cdot 10^{-10}$	↑	$> 5\%$	⇌

4.2 Simulation Results

In Fig. 2 (b), the comparison results for the problems DTLZ6 and EXPO2 are shown. For both problems, the proposed algorithms IBEA$_{\epsilon+}$ and IBEA$_{HD}$ perform significantly better than SPEA2 and NSGA-II with respect to the performance indicators $I_{\epsilon+}$ and I_{HD}. Note that these IBEA versions all work with the same value for κ.

In addition to SPEA2, NSGA-II and the proposed IBEA$_{\epsilon+}$ and IBEA$_{HD}$, we have implemented an adaptive version of SPEA2 to see the impact of adaptive objective-value scaling as such. The performance of the adaptive version of SPEA2 is comparable to the original algorithm on the test problems, and the Wilcoxon rank test returns false for all the problems investigated, i. e. the

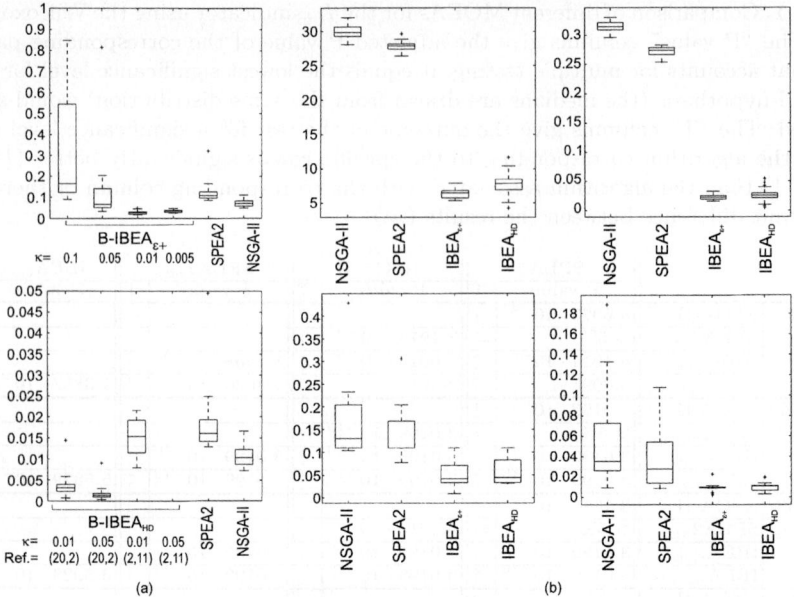

Fig. 2. (a) (top) The indicator values $I_{\epsilon+}$ for SPEA2, NSGA-II and B-IBEA$_{\epsilon+}$ for different values of κ. For all the different algorithms one outlier was removed from the result sample for improved readability. (bottom) The indicator values I_{HD} for SPEA2, NSGA-II and B-IBEA$_{HD}$ for different values of κ and the reference point. In the 4th column, no values are given because they are about 10 times greater than the values given. (b) Performance comparison for adaptive IBEA$_\epsilon$, IBEA$_{HD}$, SPEA2 and NSGA-II solving problems DTLZ6 (top) and EXPO2 (bottom). On the left, values for $I_{\epsilon+}$, on the right for I_{HD} are given.

distributions of $I(A, R)$ for SPEA2 and the adaptive version of SPEA2 are not significantly different.

An overview of the results for $I_{\epsilon+}$ is given in Table 1. We do not give a table with results for I_{HD} due to space limitations. Overall, we can see that for the continuous problems DTLZ2, DTLZ6 and ZDT6, the proposed algorithms IBEA$_{\epsilon+}$ and IBEA$_{HD}$ perform significantly better than SPEA2 or NSGA-II; only for KUR, the latter provide better performance than the two IBEA instances. For the discrete knapsack problem, the significance tests return false, i.e. the indicator value distributions generated by the different search algorithms are statistically not different from each other. In contrast, the indicator-based algorithms show significantly better performance for the design-space exploration problem EXPO in two, three and four dimensions.

5 Conclusions

Every MOEA implementation inevitably makes assumptions about the decision maker's preferences which are usually hard coded in the algorithm. These preferences, though, may vary for each user and application. Therefore, we have

- argued that ideally MOEAs would be designed and evaluated with regard to the specific preferences of the user, formalized in terms of a performance measure, and
- proposed a general indicator-based evolutionary algorithm (IBEA) that, contrarily to existing population-based MOEAs, allows to adapt the search according to arbitrary performance measures. For two different performance measures, this approach has be shown to generate significantly better results on six of eight benchmark problems in comparison to SPEA2 and NSGA-II, while no statistically significant performance difference could be observed on one of the test function.

IBEA as well as the other MOEAs and the benchmark problems considered in the paper can be downloaded as precompiled, ready-to-use components from the PISA Website http://www.tik.ee.ethz.ch/pisa/.

References

1. P. A. N. Bosman and D. Thierens. The balance between proximity and diversity in multiobjective evolutionary algorithms. *IEEE Transactions on Evolutionary Computation*, 7(2):174–188, 2003.
2. C. A. Coello Coello, D. A. Van Veldhuizen, and G. B. Lamont. *Evolutionary Algorithms for Solving Multi-Objective Problems*. Kluwer, New York, 2002.
3. K. Deb. *Multi-objective optimization using evolutionary algorithms*. Wiley, Chichester, UK, 2001.
4. K. Deb and R. B. Agrawal. Simulated binary crossover for continuous search space. *Complex Systems*, 9:115–148, 1995.
5. K. Deb, S. Agrawal, A. Pratap, and T. Meyarivan. A fast elitist non-dominated sorting genetic algorithm for multi-objective optimization: NSGA-II. In M. Schoenauer et al., editors, *PPSN VI*, LNCS Vol. 1917, pages 849–858. Springer, 2000.
6. K. Deb, L. Thiele, M. Laumanns, and E. Zitzler. Scalable multi-objective optimization test problems. In *CEC 2002*, pages 825–830. IEEE Press, 2002.
7. K. Deb, L. Thiele, M. Laumanns, and E. Zitzler. Scalable test problems for evolutionary multi-objective optimization. In A. Abraham et al., editors, *Evolutionary Computation Based Multi-Criteria Optimization: Theoretical Advances and Applications*. Springer, 2004. To appear.
8. C. M. Fonseca and P. J. Fleming. Multiobjective optimization and multiple constraint handling with evolutionary algorithms – part ii: Application example. *IEEE Transactions on Systems, Man, and Cybernetics*, 28(1):38–47, 1998.
9. M. P. Hansen and A. Jaszkiewicz. Evaluating the quality of approximations of the non-dominated set. Technical report, Institute of Mathematical Modeling, Technical University of Denmark, 1998. IMM Technical Report IMM-REP-1998-7.
10. J. Knowles and D. Corne. On metrics for comparing non-dominated sets. In *CEC 2002*, pages 711–716, Piscataway, NJ, 2002. IEEE Press.
11. J. D. Knowles. *Local-Search and Hybrid Evolutionary Algorithms for Pareto Optimization*. PhD thesis, University of Reading, 2002.
12. F. Kursawe. A variant of evolution strategies for vector optimization. In H.-P. Schwefel and R. Männer, eds., *PPSN I*, pages 193–197. Springer, 1991.

13. M. Laumanns, E. Zitzler, and L. Thiele. On the effects of archiving, elitism, and density based selection in evolutionary multi-objective optimization. In *Proceedings of the First International Conference on Evolutionary Multi-Criterion Optimization*, pages 181–196. Springer, 2001.
14. L. Thiele, S. Chakraborty, M. Gries, and S. Künzli. Design space exploration of network processor architectures. In M. Franklin et. al., eds, *Network Processor Design Issues and Practices, Vol. 1*, chapter 4, Morgan Kaufmann, Oct. 2002.
15. E. Zitzler, K. Deb, and L. Thiele. Comparison of multiobjective evolutionary algorithms: Empirical results. *Evolutionary Computation*, 8(2):173–195, 2000.
16. E. Zitzler, M. Laumanns, and L. Thiele. SPEA2: Improving the Strength Pareto Evolutionary Algorithm for Multiobjective Optimization. In K. Giannakoglou et al., editors, *EUROGEN 2001*, pages 95–100. International Center for Numerical Methods in Engineering (CIMNE), 2002.
17. E. Zitzler and L. Thiele. Multiobjective Evolutionary Algorithms: A Comparative Case Study and the Strength Pareto Approach. *IEEE Transactions on Evolutionary Computation*, 3(4):257–271, 1999.
18. E. Zitzler, L. Thiele, M. Laumanns, C. M. Fonseca, and V. Grunert da Fonseca. Performance assessment of multiobjective optimizers: An analysis and review. *IEEE Transactions on Evolutionary Computation*, 7(2):117–132, 2003.

Intransitivity in Coevolution

Edwin D. de Jong

Universiteit Utrecht
Decision Support Systems Group
The Netherlands
http://www.cs.uu.nl/~dejong
dejong@cs.uu.nl

Abstract. We review and investigate the current status of intransitivity as a potential obstacle in coevolution. Pareto-Coevolution avoids intransitivity by translating any standard superiority relation into a transitive Pareto-dominance relation. Even for transitive problems though, cycling is possible. Recently however, algorithms that provide monotonic progress for Pareto-Coevolution have become available. The use of such algorithms avoids cycling, whether caused by intransitivity or not. We investigate this in experiments with two intransitive test problems, and find that the IPCA and LAPCA archive methods establish monotonic progress on both test problems, thereby substantially outperforming the same method without an archive.

Coevolution offers algorithms for problems where the performance of individuals can be evaluated using tests [1–7]. Since evaluation in coevolution is based on evolving individuals, coevolution setups can suffer from inaccurate evaluation, leading to problems such as over-specialization, Red Queen dynamics, and disengagement [8, 9].

A problem feature that has received particular interest in the past is that of *intransitivity* [9]. A relation R is *transitive* if $aRb \wedge bRc$ implies aRc; if this cannot be guaranteed, the relation is intransitive. An example of a problem where the relation used to compare individuals is intransitive, is *Rock, Paper, Scissors*; while *scissors* beats *paper* and *paper* beats *rock*, *scissors* is beaten by *rock*. The existence of such intransitive relations in a coevolution problem can lead to *cycling*, i.e. the recurrence of previously visited states of the population.

Intransitivity has been viewed as an inherent feature of coevolution that can render algorithms unreliable. Indeed, the resulting problem of *cycling* has been thought of as an obstacle that could prevent coevolution from becoming a reliable problem solving technique, as attested to by the following quote: "We believe that the cycling problem, like the local minima problem in gradient-descent methods..., is an intrinsic problem of coevolution that cannot be eliminated completely" [10].

Recently, it has been shown that coevolution can in principle approximate *ideal evaluation* [11], i.e. equivalence to evaluation on the space of all tests. This result is based on the solution concept offered by Pareto-Coevolution [12, 13], consisting of all candidate solutions whose performance cannot be improved on any test without decreasing the individual's outcome on some other test.

Another approach to achieve reliability in coevolution is to use an *archive* to maintain promising candidate solutions and informative tests. If an archive can avoid regress, then generating all possible individuals with non-zero probability guarantees that the algorithm can only make progress and will occasionally do so, thus enabling the coevolutionary goal of open-ended, sustained progress.

Rosin's *covering competitive algorithm* [14], alternates between finding a first-player strategy that beats all second-player strategies in the archive and *vice versa*. This guarantees that regress can be avoided, but the strict criterion of defeating all previous opposition is likely to result in stalling as soon as mutually exclusive tests exist, i.e. tests that cannot all be solved by a single learner but can be solved individually by different learners. Ficici and Pollack's Nash Memory [15] guarantees progress for the solution concept of the Nash Equilibrium. It is limited to symmetric games, but extension to the case of asymmetric games is noted to be straightforward. The Incremental Pareto-Coevolution Archive (IPCA) [16] guarantees progress for Pareto-Coevolution, and is applicable to both symmetric and asymmetric problems. All of the above archive methods can only guarantee progress however if the archive size is unlimited. A layered variant of IPCA was found empirically to produce reliable progress on test problems using a bounded archive [17].

Our aim here is to investigate the role of intransitivity in coevolution in the light of the above developments. It is known that the use of Pareto-coevolution transforms intransitive superiority relations into transitive relations; we provide a concise proof demonstrating this. While this transitive relation provides an appropriate basis for reliable coevolution, cycling is also possible for transitive relations, as shown in a simple example. We discuss the potential of coevolution methods to avoid cycling, and investigate the performance of two recent algorithms on test problems featuring intransitivity.

The structure of this paper is as follows. Section 1 discusses intransitivity and recent results in achieving reliable progress in coevolution. Section 2 presents experimental results, and Section 3 concludes.

1 Intransitivity

1.1 Intransitivity Can Lead to Cycling

A familiar example of intransitivity is provided by the game of *Rock, Paper, Scissors*, where *scissors* beats *paper*, *paper* beats *rock*, and *rock* beats *scissors*. Suppose we administer this problem to the minimal setup that may be called coevolution, namely a hillclimbing individual that learns by self-play. The expected transcript of this experiment if the population is initialized with *Rock* (R), and a newly generated individual replaces the current individual if and only if the former beats the latter is R, P, S, R. As this example demonstrates, the application of a hillclimber to an intransitive problem can lead to cycling.

1.2 Pareto-Coevolution

In Pareto-Coevolution [12,13], the individuals that are used as tests in evaluating other individuals are used as *objectives*, in the sense of Evolutionary Multi-Objective Optimization. Table 1 shows an example of interactions between three different individuals, A, B, and C. The outcomes in the matrix may be viewed for example as the score of the row player against the column player in a two-player game G with the row player as first player, so that for example $G(a,a) = 0, G(a,b) = 1)$. The outcomes can be used to define a relation R that specifies which games result in a win for the first player: aRb, bRa, cRa, cRb. In standard coevolution, this relation is used directly to assess the quality of the different individuals by interpreting it as a 'greater than' relation. Fitness can then for instance be based on the number of wins an individual achieves. However, as the example shows, this direct use of the relation can yield conflicting information (e.g. aRb and bRa), resulting from the fact that first player strategies are compared against second player strategies.

Table 1. Example outcomes for three individuals, a, b, and c. Each table entry lists the outcome of a row player against a column player.

	a	b	c
a	0	1	0
b	1	0	0
c	1	1	0

When Pareto-Coevolution is used, a distinction is made between *learners* (candidate solutions) and *tests* (individuals used to evaluate the quality of learners). If our aim is to find an optimal first player strategy, then individuals functioning as first (row) players are learners, and the second (column) players are tests. This shift in perspective is illustrated by renaming the column players as a', b', and c' respectively to signal their different role when used as a test.

Pareto-Coevolution now evaluates a learner by viewing its outcomes against tests as *objectives*. Two learners are compared using the Pareto dominance relation, defined as follows: an individuals x with objective values x_i dominates another individual y with objective values y_i if and only if:

$$\forall i : x_i \geq y_i \quad \wedge \quad \exists i : x_i > y_i$$

Thus, in the example, c dominates a, as c's score is at least as high as a's score for all tests, and higher for at least one test (a'). Likewise, c also dominates b, while a and b do not dominate any other learners. The dominance relation is a new relation that can be used to evaluate and compare learners. By viewing a learner's outcomes against tests as objectives and comparing learners based on Pareto-dominance, we have obtained a second relation R' that can be derived from R. In this new relation conflicting information, such as $aR'b \wedge bR'a$, cannot occur.

1.3 Pareto-Coevolution Transforms Intransitive Relations into Transitive Ones

The previous section illustrated how Pareto-Coevolution takes a given relation R between individuals and uses it to define a new relation R' specifying dominance relations between learners, and using test outcomes as objectives. It has been observed that using test outcomes as objectives results in an evaluation function that is transitive in each objective, and that the relation induced on learners by Pareto-Coevolution cannot be intransitive for any fixed set of tests [18, 11]. Bucci and Pollack [19] observe that Pareto-Coevolution induces a preorder relation on learners which can be embedded into $\mathbb{R}^n$, and is therefore transitive.

In summary, Pareto-Coevolution transforms a given, possibly intransitive superiority relation between individuals into a transitive dominance relation. This can be seen with the following brief proof:

Let R be a relation over a set of individuals I. For any $a, b \in I$, aRb may be interpreted as stating that a obtains a positive outcome against b. Without loss of generality, we assume that the first players x in interactions xRy are the learners whose outcome are to be maximized, and the second players y are tests. Then Pareto-Coevolution transforms the initial relation R into a new relation R', defined as the Pareto-dominance over learners that uses the tests as objectives:

$$a_1 R' a_2 \iff \forall x \in I \quad a_1 Rx \geq a_2 Rx \quad \land \quad \exists x \in I \quad a_1 Rx > a_2 Rx \tag{1}$$

$$R' \text{ is transitive if } \forall a, b, c \in I \quad aR'b \land bR'c \implies aR'c \tag{2}$$

Assume $aR'b \land bR'c$. Then

$$\forall x \in I \quad aRx \geq bRx \quad \land \tag{3}$$
$$\exists x \in I \quad aRx > bRx \tag{4}$$
$$\forall x \in I \quad bRx \geq cRx \quad \land \tag{5}$$
$$\exists x \in I \quad bRx > cRx \tag{6}$$

From (3) and (5): $\forall x \in I \quad aRx \geq cRx \tag{7}$

From (4) and (5): $\exists x \in I \quad aRx > cRx \tag{8}$

By combining (7) and (8): $\forall x \in I \quad aRx \geq cRx \quad \land \quad \exists x \in I \quad aRx > cRx$

Therefore $aR'c$. ∎

1.4 Transitive Games Can Lead to Cycling

Even in a transitive game, cycling is possible. This can be shown by a small example, see the payoff matrix for learners (a1, a2) in Table 2; the payoff for tests (b1, b2) is the inverse. Table 2 shows the sequence of learner and test populations when two size one populations are initialized with learner $a1$ as the learner population and test $b1$ as the test population. Both populations are hillclimbers that maximize their score against the other population. Given $a1$ as a learner, the best strategy for the test population is $b2$. Given $b2$, the best strategy for the learner population is $a2$, and so on. After four replacement steps, the populations are back to their initial state, and cycling has thus occurred.

Table 2. Example demonstrating cycling in a transitive problem. Left: payoff matrix. Right: After four transitions, both population are in their initial state again.

	b1	b2
a1	1	0
a2	0	1

L	a1	a1	a2	a2	a1
T	b1	b2	b2	b1	b1

1.5 Monotonic Progress Avoids Cycling

Recently, an archive method for coevolution has been presented that guarantees monotonic progress for Pareto-Coevolution. The archive, called the Incremental Pareto-Coevolution Archive (IPCA) [16] maintains a learner archive and a test archive. The archive accepts learners and tests from a *generator*, which can be any coevolutionary algorithm. The generator can use the reliability of the archive by using individuals from the archive as a basis for generating new learners and test, and does not need to be reliable itself.

IPCA provides conditions determining which learners and tests produced by the generator are accepted into the archive. The learner archive accepts individuals that are non-dominated and different from existing individuals in the learner archive, and discards any individuals dominated by newly introduced individuals. The test archive accepts tests required to detect the uniqueness or value of learners, and grows incrementally. For a detailed description, please consult [16].

IPCA guarantees monotonic progress, i.e. the archive avoids regress. This criterion is defined as follows. The learner archives obtained over time form a series of approximations of the solution concept of the non-dominated front of learners relative to the set of all possible tests. Let these approximations be denoted as $L^1, L^2, \ldots L^t$, and let the test archives obtained over time be written as $T^1, T^2, \ldots T^t$. Then progress is monotonic if for any $t' > t$:

1. $\forall TS \subseteq T^t: \quad [\exists L \in L^t : solves(L, TS) \implies \exists L' \in L^{t'} : solves(L', TS)]$
2. $\exists TS \subseteq T^{t'}: \quad [\nexists L \in L^t : solves(L, TS) \wedge \exists L' \in L^{t'} : solves(L', TS)]$

From these definitions, it follows that any archive guaranteeing monotonic progress avoids cycling. This can be seen as follows. Since each test set in the sequence must contain a subset of tests that is not solved by a single learner in any previous learner set yet is solved by some learner in the current learner set, the learner set must therefore be different from any previous learner set. Therefore, cycling in the sense of a recurring population state is ruled out. In fact, the definition of monotonic progress is much stricter than the avoidance of cycling; it guarantees that actual improvements must be made between subsequent versions of the archive.

2 Experimental Results

As discussed in the previous section, cycling (whether due to intransitivity or not) can be avoided. This suggests that intransitivity should present no problem to coevolutionary algorithms with a progress guarantee. To test this conclusion, we apply the IPCA algorithm to two intransitive problems.

The first problem is the Intransitive Numbers Game introduced in [9]. We employ the version of the problem defined in [15], and use a value of 0.05 for the ϵ parameter. The problem is discretized with a granularity of 0.05. Mutation randomly adds a constant from [-.065,.035], and when used is applied to randomly selected dimensions twice. This mutation bias makes it more likely that mutation results in regress than progress, and is meant to model the situation in problems of practical interest where this is generally the case.

The generator that supplies candidate learners and tests to IPCA produces offspring using crossover (50%) and mutation (50%). With probability 0.1, it uses an archive member as a parent. For IPCA, archive members are chosen for this purpose based on recency, where $x = \frac{index+1}{archivesize}$ is used as the relative probability of an archive member in a Boltzmann distribution with temperature 1, i.e. $P_{rel} = e^x$. The generator maintains a learner and test populations, both of size 10. The objectives for learners are their outcomes against tests and the distinctions between tests. The learner objectives are based on the union of the current population and new generation of tests. The objectives for the tests are analogous, namely their outcomes against and distinctions between individuals in the current population and new generation of learners, resulting in a symmetric setup.

For each objective achieved by an individual, a score is assigned that equals one over the number of other individuals that achieve the objective, as in *competitive fitness sharing* [14]. The weighted sum of an individual's scores on the n outcome objectives (weight 0.75 for learners and 0.25 for tests) and on the n^2 distinction objectives, where n is the size of the population plus the new generation, are added to yield a single total score for the individual.

The highest scoring individuals of the new generation are lined up with the lowest scoring individuals of the current population. Then k is determined as the highest number for which the summed scores of the first k generation members is still at least as high as that of the first k population members. The lowest scoring k population members are discarded and replaced by the k highest scoring individuals from the new generation.

As a control experiment, we also measure the performance of the generator by itself, without the use of the IPCA archive. In addition to these two methods, the LAPCA method is used. This is a layered variant of IPCA design to achieve reasonable (but not guaranteed) reliability while maintaining limited archive sizes. LAPCA is described in detail elsewhere [17]. Briefly, the learner archive in LAPCA maintains a number n of layers of learners, analogous to the NSGA algorithm for EMOO [20], while the test archive maintains tests that *separate* these layers from one another; for each distinction [7] between learners in the same or subsequent layers, tests are kept that maintain the distinction.

The performance criterion is the lowest value among all dimensions of an individual; if this value increases, progress is made on all dimensions. Performance is plotted as a function of the number of actual generations, and averaged over 50 runs.

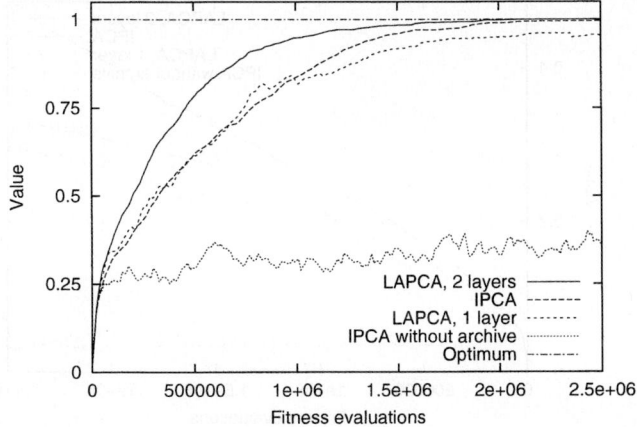

Fig. 1. Performance on the Intransitive Numbers game. IPCA and LAPCA converge to the optimum of 1, and LAPCA with two layers is most efficient in doing so. The archive methods perform substantially better than the method that does not use an archive.

Figure 1 shows the performance of the different methods on the two-dimensional version of the Intransitive Numbers Game with mutation bias. The results validate the expectation that monotonic progress can be made.

The second test problem is the LINT game, introduced by Richard Watson [21]. LINT stands for Locally INTransitive game, and can be defined as follows.

$$G(a,b) = \begin{cases} a < b & \text{if } |a - b| < d \\ a > b & \text{otherwise} \end{cases} \quad (9)$$

Figure 2 shows the results of the methods on the LINT problem. Again, all archive methods achieve sustained progress, and the two-layered LAPCA is most efficient in doing so.

3 Conclusions

Intransitivity has long been seen as a substantial obstacle to progress in coevolution, as it can lead to cycling. Recent developments in coevolution clarify how reliable progress can be guaranteed. Informed by these developments, we review and investigate the remaining significance of intransitivity and cycling for coevolution research.

Pareto-Coevolution transforms intransitive problems into transitive problems, as known and as shown with a concise proof. Apart from intransitivity, the loss of informative tests can also lead to cycling. Several recent coevolution archives provide a guarantee of permitting progress only. Since cycling is thereby avoided, it is expected that intransitivity no longer presents an insurmountable obstacle to coevolution methods. This expectation is confirmed in experiments with two intransitive problems, where the IPCA and LAPCA archive methods

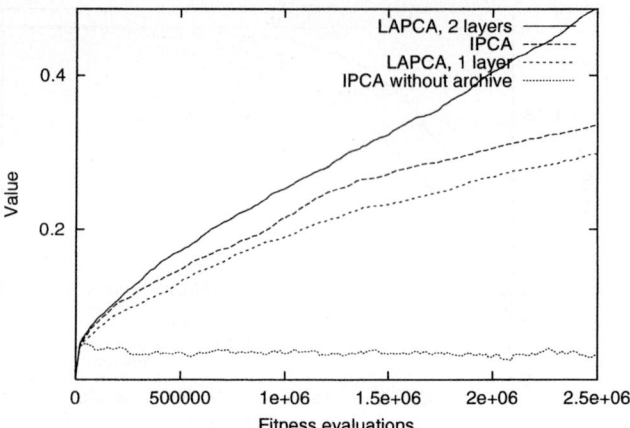

Fig. 2. Performance of the same methods on the LINT game. Again, all archive methods achieve sustained progress.

achieved sustained progress and the same method without an archive fails to do so. A main further question regarding reliable algorithms for coevolution is how methods can be made more efficient while retaining reliability.

References

1. Barricelli, N.A.: Numerical testing of evolution theories. Part I: Theoretical introduction and basic tests. Acta Biotheoretica **16** (1962) 69–98
2. Axelrod, R.: The evolution of strategies in the iterated prisoner's dilemma. In Davis, L., ed.: Genetic Algorithms and Simulated Annealing. Research Notes in Artificial Intelligence, London, Pitman Publishing (1987) 32–41
3. Hillis, D.W.: Co-evolving parasites improve simulated evolution in an optimization procedure. Physica D **42** (1990) 228–234
4. Paredis, J.: Coevolutionary computation. Artificial Life **2** (1996)
5. Pagie, L., Hogeweg, P.: Evolutionary consequences of coevolving targets. Evolutionary Computation **5** (1998) 401–418
6. Juillé, H.: Methods for Statistical Inference: Extending the Evolutionary Computation Paradigm. PhD thesis, Brandeis University (1999)
7. Ficici, S.G., Pollack, J.B.: Pareto optimality in coevolutionary learning. In Kelemen, J., ed.: Sixth European Conference on Artificial Life, Berlin, Springer (2001)
8. Cliff, D., Miller, G.F.: Tracking the Red Queen: Measurements of adaptive progress in co-evolutionary simulations. In Morán, F., Moreno, A., Merelo, J.J., Chacón, P., eds.: Proceedings of the Third European Conference on Artificial Life: Advances in Artificial Life. Volume 929 of LNAI., Berlin, Springer (1995) 200–218
9. Watson, R.A., Pollack, J.B.: Coevolutionary dynamics in a minimal substrate. In Spector, L., Goodman, E., Wu, A., Langdon, W., Voigt, H.M., Gen, M., Sen, S., Dorigo, M., Pezeshk, S., Garzon, M., Burke, E., eds.: Proceedings of the Genetic and Evolutionary Computation Conference, GECCO-01, San Francisco, CA, Morgan Kaufmann (2001) 702–709
10. Nolfi, S., Floreano, D.: Co-evolving predator and prey robots: Do 'arms races' arise in artificial evolution? Artificial Life **4** (1998)

11. De Jong, E.D., Pollack, J.B.: Ideal evaluation from coevolution. Evolutionary Computation **12** (2004) 159–192
12. Ficici, S.G., Pollack, J.B.: A game-theoretic approach to the simple coevolutionary algorithm. In Schoenauer et al., M., ed.: Parallel Problem Solving from Nature, PPSN-VI. Volume 1917 of LNCS., Berlin, Springer (2000)
13. Watson, R.A., Pollack, J.B.: Symbiotic combination as an alternative to sexual recombination in genetic algorithms. In Schoenauer et al., M., ed.: Parallel Problem Solving from Nature, PPSN-VI. Volume 1917 of LNCS., Berlin, Springer (2000)
14. Rosin, C.D.: Coevolutionary Search among Adversaries. PhD thesis, University of California, San Diego, CA (1997)
15. Ficici, S.G., Pollack, J.B.: A game-theoretic memory mechanism for coevolution. In Cantú-Paz et al., E., ed.: Genetic and Evolutionary Computation – GECCO-2003. Volume 2723 of LNCS., Chicago, Springer-Verlag (2003) 286–297
16. De Jong, E.D.: The Incremental Pareto-Coevolution Archive. In: Proceedings of the Genetic and Evolutionary Computation Conference, GECCO-04. (2004)
17. De Jong, E.D.: Towards a bounded Pareto-Coevolution archive. In: Proceedings of the Congress on Evolutionary Computation, CEC-04. (2004)
18. De Jong, E.D., Pollack, J.B.: Principled Evaluation in Coevolution. Technical Report CS-02-225; May 31 2002, Brandeis University (2002)
19. Bucci, A., Pollack, J.B.: Focusing versus intransitivity. Geometrical aspects of coevolution. In Cantú-Paz et al., E., ed.: Proceedings of the Genetic and Evolutionary Computation Conference, GECCO-03, Berlin, Springer (2003)
20. Srinivas, N., Deb, K.: Multiobjective Optimization Using Nondominated Sorting in Genetic Algorithms. Evolutionary Computation **2** (1994) 221–248
21. Watson, R.A. Personal communication (2003)

Group Transport of an Object to a Target That Only Some Group Members May Sense

Roderich Groß and Marco Dorigo

IRIDIA - Université Libre de Bruxelles - Brussels, Belgium
{rgross,mdorigo}@ulb.ac.be

Abstract. This paper addresses the cooperative transport of a heavy object, called *prey*, towards a sporadically changing target location by a group of robots. The study is focused on the situation in which some robots are given the opportunity to localize the target, while the others (called the *blind* ones) are not. We propose the use of relatively simple robots capable of self-assembling into structures which pull or push the prey. To enable a blind robot to contribute to the group's performance, it can locally perceive traction forces, and whether it is moving or not. The robot group is controlled in a distributed manner, using a modular control architecture. A collection of simple hand-coded and artificially evolved control modules is presented and discussed. For group sizes ranging from 2 to 16 and different proportions of blind robots within the group, it is shown that controlled by an evolved solution, blind robots make an essential contribution to the group's performance.
The study is carried out using a physics-based simulation of a real robotic system that is currently under construction.

1 Introduction

The transport of heavy objects by groups of robots can be motivated by low cost of manufacture, high robustness, high failure tolerance, or high flexibility – all desirable properties for a robotic system to have. Instead of using one robot powerful enough to transport the object (called *prey* hereafter) on its own, the task is accomplished in cooperation by a group of less powerful robots.

This paper addresses the situation in which the target location may be localized by some robots, while the others (the *blind* ones) cannot perceive it. In reality, such a constraint may exist due to various reasons. For a robot the target could be not visible because it is shadowed by the prey, or because of environmental conditions such as fog, steam or smoke. Or, it may happen that the robot's sensory system responsible for the perception of the target fails.

We propose the use of a group of relatively simple, autonomous robots (hereafter called *s-bots*) capable of self-assembling into structures which pull or push the prey. Thus, this paper addresses the self-organization of s-bots into assembled structures and the transport of heavy prey by groups of assembled s-bots. The robot group is controlled in a distributed manner. To enable a blind s-bot to contribute to the transport performance, it can locally perceive traction forces, and whether it is moving or not.

The paper is organized as follows. Section 2 provides a brief overview of some works related to this study. In Section 3, the simulation model is introduced. Section 4 details the different control policies that are used. Finally, in Sections 5 and 6 the results are discussed and conclusions are drawn.

2 Related Work

The field of distributed robotics has received growing attention by researchers within the last 15 years. Multi-robot systems have been studied in various topic areas and in different application domains [Parker, 2000]. Several works considered the cooperative transport of objects by a group of mobile robots. Some of these have been inspired by studies of social insect behavior.

Deneubourg et al. [1990] proposed the use of self-organized approaches for the collection and transport of objects by robots in unpredictable environments. Each robot unit could be simple and inefficient in itself, but a group of robots could exhibit complex and efficient behaviors. Cooperation could be achieved without any direct communication among robots [Grassé, 1959, Deneubourg and Goss, 1989]. Indirect communication is prevalent in the robotic system realized by Aiyama et al. [1999] in which two autonomous legged robots are carrying a common load in a pre-defined direction. In their system, the robots were communicating via the object to be moved. In order to synchronize its own actions with its teammate, each robot is provided with a sensor to measure the force exerted by the common load on the robot itself.

The use of force sensors for the coordinated motion of a group of pre-assembled robots has been studied by Dorigo et al. [2004]. In their system, the group was also able to move objects, if not too heavy, in an arbitrary direction.

Kube and Zhang [1993] studied a distributed approach to let a group of simple robots find and push a box towards a light. The box was too heavy to be moved by a single robot. Inspired by the observation that the behavior of ants during transport (e.g., changes in their spatial arrangement) can be associated with the detection of the stagnation of movement, Kube and Zhang [1995] extended their system with a stagnation recovery mechanism.

3 Simulator

3.1 Environment and Task

The simulated environment that we use in our experiments consists of a flat plane, a prey, and eight beacons which are uniformly arranged in a circle at a distance of 500 cm from a position called the *center*. The prey emits green light. It is modeled as a cylinder with a radius (in cm) in the range [5.8, 10], and a mass (in grams) in the range [$200N, 300N$], where N denotes the number of s-bots used. For each simulation, radius and mass are chosen randomly according to uniform distributions.

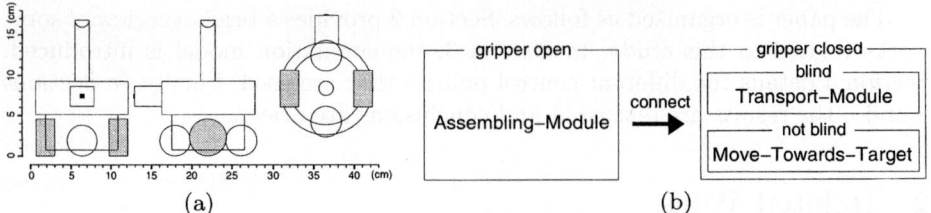

Fig. 1. The s-bot: (a) front, side and top view of the s-bot model and (b) the control scheme. For details see Section 3.2 and Section 4.

A simulation lasts 35 simulated seconds. At any point in time, there is only one beacon emitting white light indicating the target location. The beacon is selected randomly according to a uniform distribution once prior and twice during simulation (after 15 and 25 seconds). Initially, the prey is put in the center, and N s-bots are placed at random positions and with random orientations no more than 50 cm from the prey. In principle, all s-bots are able to sense the light-emitting beacon from any position in the environment. However, the controllers of the blind s-bots are not provided with the corresponding sensory information.

The s-bot controllers are supposed to let the s-bots localize and approach the prey, self-assemble into structures, each of them physically linked to the prey, and pull or push the prey towards the light-emitting beacon.

3.2 S-Bot Model

The s-bot model is illustrated in Figure 1 (a). It is an approximation of a real s-bot, currently under construction within the SWARM-BOTS project [Mondada et al., 2004, Dorigo et al., 2004, see also www.swarm-bots.org]. In the following, the actuators and sensors are detailed. Both the actuators and the sensors are affected by noise.

Actuators. The s-bot is equipped with two motorized wheels, a rotational base, a gripper element and an LED ring. Each motorized wheel can be controlled by setting the desired angular speed (in rad/s) in the range $[-8, 8]$. The s-bot's upper part (the turret) can rotate with respect to the lower part (the chassis) by means of a motorized axis. Therefore, the s-bot can align its turret with respect to its chassis to any angular offset in $[-\pi, \pi]$. The gripper element is modeled as a box heading forward with a small contact plate in the front. If the element is in *gripping* mode, a rigid connection will be established as soon as the contact plate touches the turret of another s-bot or the prey. The LED ring can emit green light. It can either be switched on or off. In this study, each s-bot uses its LED ring to signal whether an object is gripped or not.

Sensors. The simulated s-bot is equipped with a gripper status sensor, two proximity sensors, a rotational base sensor, a traction sensor, and an omnidirectional camera. These sensors have their counterparts on the real s-bot.

The gripper status sensor is able to detect whether the gripper is connected to another object or not. The proximity sensors measure the proximity of objects in the front left and front right directions. The rotational base sensor is able to perceive the angular offset between the turret and the chassis. The traction sensor provides an estimate of the magnitude and orientation of the horizontal component of the traction force that acts on the hinge joint between the turret and the chassis of the s-bot. This force is affected by the s-bot's actions and by the force exerted by all the objects that are physically linked to the s-bot.

The camera sensor is able to estimate the horizontal angle to the light-emitting beacon with respect to the s-bot's forward motion. The camera sensor can detect the presence and the coarse orientation of green objects in the front of the s-bot up to a distance of 60 cm, and 20 cm, respectively. In addition, the s-bot is able to detect whether it is moving or not. For the real s-bot, this ability can be implemented using the camera system, for example by comparing the position of light landmarks in its vicinity over time.

4 Control Policies

In a previous study on cooperative transport by a group of non-blind s-bots, we addressed the entire task utilizing a single neural network controller synthesized by artificial evolution [Groß and Dorigo, 2004]. We observed that the evolutionary process required a large number of generations to provide controllers that performed quite well, and the attained performance level differed essentially between the replications of the experiment.

On the contrary, in this paper we have decomposed the problem of control at the level of an s-bot into sub problems (see Figure 1 (b)): an s-bot can be in one of two main states as indicated by the status of its LED ring: if the s-bot has gripped the (green) prey or another s-bot, the LED ring emits a green light, otherwise it is switched off. Initially all s-bot are not connected and the rotational bases are locked. In this initial status, the *Assembling-Module* procedure is in charge of controlling the s-bot so that it locates a green object, approaches it and eventually establishes a physical connection with it. The s-bot is not allowed to grip objects other than green. Therefore, a green s-bot is, either directly or indirectly, always connected to the prey. Once a connection has been established, the gripper remains closed and the rotational base is unlocked. Unless the s-bot is *blind*, a simple but effective behavior for the robot is to align the chassis towards the target location and to set the speed of the wheels to the maximum value (*Move-Towards-Target* procedure). If the s-bot is *blind*, it locally perceives traction forces, and whether it is moving or not, and it determines the desired orientation of the chassis and a nonnegative speed for the wheels (*Transport-Module* procedure). In the following, several strategies implementing the *Assembling-Module* and *Transport-Module* procedures are detailed.

4.1 Hand-Coded Solutions, Lower and Upper Bounds

For the *Assembling-Module* procedure a parameterized, hand-coded controller has been developed: as long as no green object is perceived in its forward direction, the s-bot turns applying the speed vector $(s_1, -s_1)$ to the wheels. Once an object is perceived, and if it is more than 20 cm away, the s-bot approaches it at maximum speed. As soon as the object is close, the s-bot estimates whether it is more to the left or to the right, in order to approach it while turning in the appropriate direction (applying the speed vector (s_2, s_3), or (s_3, s_2), respectively to the wheels). Based on a training set of 200 trials with 2, 4, 6 or 8 s-bots, 1000 combinations of s_1, s_2 and s_3 have been evaluated, and the one exhibiting the fastest average assembly time has been selected for the analysis.

For the *Transport-Module* procedure we implemented the following two simple policies to control the s-bots that are *blind*: the first one, in which the s-bots do not move their wheels nor their rotational bases; and the second one, in which the s-bots pull the objects gripped with maximum force.

As a lower bound to the performance of *Transport-Module* procedures for which blind s-bots contribute to the group's performance, we consider the case in which the blind s-bots are removed from the simulation. As an upper bound we consider the case in which the blind s-bots are replaced by non-blind ones.

4.2 Evolved Solutions

As an alternative to the hand-coded solutions, implementations of both modules have been obtained by artificial evolution. The evolutionary algorithm used is a self-adaptive $(\mu + \lambda)$ evolution strategy [Schwefel, 1975, Beyer, 2001]. The number of parents is $\mu = 20$ and the number of offspring is $\lambda = 80$.

An individual is composed of real-valued object parameters, and real-valued strategy parameters specifying the mutation strength used for each component of the object parameter vector. The object parameters encode the weights of two neural networks: a simple perceptron for the *Assembling-Module* procedure, and a simple recurrent neural network [Elman, 1990] with 4 hidden nodes for the *Transport-Module* procedure. In the latter case, having memory might be beneficial, since the s-bot can remember past sensory patterns (e.g., the readings from the traction sensor) that are not affected by its current motor actions.

The initial population is generated randomly. With a probability of 0.8 an offspring is created by mutation, otherwise two parent individuals are selected and recombined. In the latter case, the mutation operator is applied to the created offspring. The recombination operator acts on both, object and strategy parameters, and combines two genotypes a) by swapping the parameter sets belonging to the first or second neural network, b) by intermediate recombination, or c) by dominant recombination [Beyer, 2001], each with the same probability.

In the following, the fitness function is described.

Fitness. An individual represents a common controller which is cloned and uploaded to each s-bot in the group. Its fitness is evaluated by performing five tests of 35 simulated seconds each; the group size $N \in [2, 3, 4, 5]$ and the number of blind s-bots in the group $N_B \in [1, 2, \ldots, \lceil N/2 \rceil]$ are chosen randomly according to uniform distributions. The fitness score is computed as the average of the quality values observed in the five trials.

The quality Q exhibited in a trial is defined as $Q = cA + (1-c)B$, where $c = \frac{1}{5}$, A measures the overall assembling performance, and B measures the transport performance of the blind s-bots. Q can be computed based solely on information the s-bots perceive locally during simulation. A is the average of the assembling performance of all s-bots for all control steps, while B is the average of the transport performance of all blind s-bots for a subset of all control steps: only control steps happening in the 6 seconds preceding a target change or the end of the simulation are taken into account, as during the other control steps the s-bots are busy assembling or adapting to the current target location[1].

The assembling performance rewards s-bots for approaching and gripping green objects: $A^t(j) = 1$, if s-bot j grips a green object at time t, and otherwise

$$A^t(j) = \begin{cases} \frac{1}{2} + \frac{1}{4}(1 - h^t(j)) & \text{if s-bot } j \text{ senses a green object } (\leq 20\,\text{cm}); \\ \frac{1}{4} & \text{if s-bot } j \text{ senses a green object } (> 20\,\text{cm}); \\ 0 & \text{otherwise;} \end{cases} \quad (1)$$

where $h^t(j) = \min(1, \alpha^t(j)/\frac{\pi}{6})$, and $\alpha^t(j)$ denotes the angular deviation (in rad) of s-bot j's heading with respect to the green object perceived at time t.

The transport performance is defined as $B^t(j) = 0$ if s-bot j is not gripped to any object at time t. Otherwise $B^t(j) = B_1^t(j) + B_2^t(j)$, where $B_1^t(j) = \frac{1}{2}\max(0, o^t(j))$ rewards the s-bot for having its chassis oriented towards the target[2], while $B_2^t(j) = \frac{1}{4} + \frac{1}{4}s^t(j)o^t(j)$ additionally takes into account the setting $s^t(j) \in [0,1]$ for the nonnegative speed of the left and right wheels.

5 Results

Ten independent evolutionary runs have been performed for 300 generations each. A single run lasts almost one week on a cluster of 10 computers, each one equipped with an AMD Athlon XP™ 2400+ processor.

Figure 2 shows the development of fitness values for the ten runs performed. The fitness values are very noisy. It is hard for a human observer to assess the attained quality level of the whole transport system by using the given fitness function. Therefore, we introduce another quality measure, the *gained distance*, defined as the difference between the initial and final distances of the prey from the light-emitting beacon. Since the target location changes twice, we take as performance measure the sum of the corresponding three gained distances. Using this new measure, we post-evaluated the $\mu = 20$ best individuals of the final generation of each evolutionary run on a sample of 200 different trials. For each evolution, we consider the individual exhibiting the highest average performance to be the best. We observed that the best individuals of all evolutionary runs exhibit a similar average performance (on average 151 with standard deviation 7.6). In the following, we focus on the performance of the best evolved individual.

Figure 3 (a) shows the performance by means of the gained distance observed for 4, 8, 12 and 16 s-bots, all of which are not blind. Hand-coded and evolved

---
[1] An s-bot may take up to 2 seconds to realign its rotational base.
[2] $o^t(j) \in [-1, 1]$; the value 1 (-1) refers to alignment with the target (opposite to it).

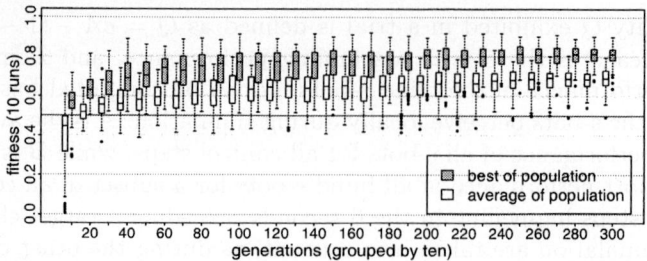

Fig. 2. Box-and-whisker plot providing information about the fitness development in ten evolutionary runs. Each box comprises observations ranging from the first to the third quartile. The median is indicated by a bar. The whiskers extend to the farthest data points that are within 1.5 times the interquartile range. Outliers are indicated as circles. The bold line at fitness level 0.5 marks an upper bound to the average performance of robotic systems in which blind s-bots do not contribute to transport: once an s-bot is connected, having its chassis oriented in a random direction and pulling with maximum speed, the expected reward the s-bot receives is 0.5 (see Section 4.2).

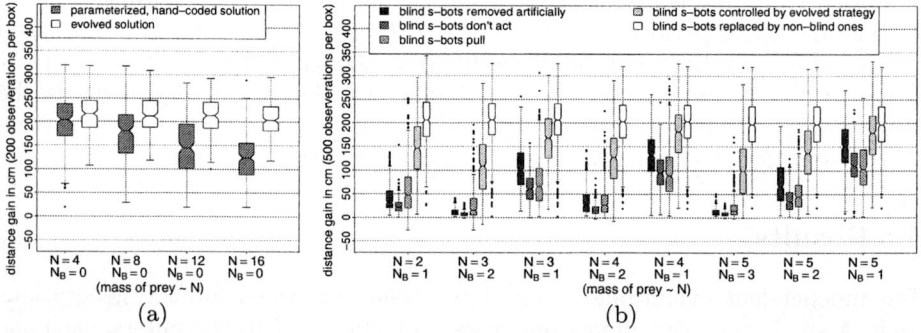

Fig. 3. Performance of solutions for (a) the *Assembling-Module* procedure for groups of 4 to 16 non-blind s-bots, and (b) the *Transport-Module* procedure for N s-bots of which N_B are blind; to assemble, the hand-coded *Assembling-Module* procedure is used.

implementations of the *Assembling-Module* procedure are compared; since no blind s-bots are present, the *Transport-Module* procedure is not required. It can be seen that the evolved solution scales better with group size. The bigger the group, the higher the density of s-bots. Thus, the better performance of the evolved controller might be due to an efficient use of the front left and front right proximity sensors. An s-bot controlled by the hand-coded solution avoids only obstacles shadowing green objects in its forward direction.

Figure 3 (b) shows the performance of several transport strategies for those combinations of group size and number of blind s-bots that occur during evolution. In every case, the parameterized, hand-coded solution with the most successful parameter set is used as *Assembling-Module* procedure.

The first, and the last, box in each group represent the lower, and upper, bounds (respectively) for the performance of *Transport-Module* procedures in which blind s-bots contribute to the group's performance. Blind s-bots are either artificially removed from the simulation (first box) or replaced by non-blind ones (last box). Thus, the first, and the last, box display to what extent $N - N_\mathrm{B}$, or N, non-blind s-bots have transported the prey by pulling with the maximum speed towards the target. By looking at the figure, we observe that in the scenarios in which the percentage of blind s-bots is more than 50% (groups 2 and 6 from left to right) $N - N_\mathrm{B}$ s-bots are nearly incapable of moving the prey.

The second and third boxes in each group (from left to right) correspond to the hand-coded solutions for the *Transport-Module* procedure. During transport, the blind s-bots either don't act (second box) or pull with maximum force (third box). In general, if the non-blind s-bots are not powerful enough to overcome the prey's resistance to motion, blind s-bots pulling in random directions can contribute to the group's performance (on average). However, the higher the number of blind s-bots, the less likely it is that all their pulling forces are properly directed. On the other hand, if the non-blind robots are capable of transporting the prey, the blind s-bots, because of their lack of knowledge about the target location, may end up being an additional weight to be carried, determining a decrease in performance.

The fourth box refers to observations in which the *Transport-Module* procedure of the best evolved solution has been used. The performance of this controller clearly outperforms the hand-coded solutions. With this controller blind s-bots make an essential contribution to the group's performance.

So far we have shown that we can control blind s-bots so that they contribute to the transport. However, to what extent there is an advantage by using blind s-bots seems to depend on the values of the parameters N and N_B. Let $\mathrm{P}(x, y, z)$ be the performance of a group of x s-bots of which y are blind and whose task is to transport a prey of mass $z \cdot m$ (in grams), where m is chosen uniformly random in $[200, 300]$. Given the group size N and the number of blind s-bots N_B, we can define the relative system performance as

$$\mathrm{RSP}(N, N_\mathrm{B}) = \frac{\mathrm{P}(N, N_\mathrm{B}, N)}{\mathrm{P}(N, 0, N)}. \qquad (2)$$

In other words, $\mathrm{RSP}(N, N_\mathrm{B})$ is the ratio between the performance of N s-bots of which N_B are blind and the performance of N non-blind s-bots. In addition, we define the contribution factor of blind s-bots as

$$\mathrm{CF}(N, N_\mathrm{B}) = \frac{\mathrm{P}(N, N_\mathrm{B}, N) - \mathrm{P}(N - N_\mathrm{B}, 0, N)}{\mathrm{P}(N, 0, N) - \mathrm{P}(N - N_\mathrm{B}, 0, N)}. \qquad (3)$$

$\mathrm{CF}(N, N_\mathrm{B})$ is the ratio between the contribution of N_B blind s-bots and the contribution that N_B non-blind s-bots would provide if put in the same situation.

Using the mean distance gain over 200 trials as performance measure, Table 1 lists the relative system performance and the contribution factor of blind s-bots for the case in which both, the *Transport-Module* procedure and the *Assembling-Module* procedure are specified by the genotype of the best evolved individual. It can be seen that blind s-bots contribute to the system's performance unless all s-bots are blind (last column). In all cases in which no more than half of

Table 1. Relative system performance RSP(N, N_B) and contribution factor of blind s-bots CF(N, N_B) (both expressed as percentages) for the best evolved solution, and for different group sizes (N) and different numbers of blind s-bots (N_B).

N_B:		0	1	2	3	$\frac{1}{4}N$	$\frac{2}{4}N$	$\frac{3}{4}N$	N
$N = 4$	RSP	100.00	80.54	64.53	40.57	80.54	64.53	40.57	0.19
	CF	100.00	50.20	57.88	39.14	50.20	57.88	39.14	0.19
$N = 8$	RSP	100.00	93.86	85.01	72.56	85.01	58.91	24.87	-0.43
	CF	100.00	60.41	55.66	53.97	55.66	50.93	22.73	-0.43
$N = 12$	RSP	100.00	94.70	89.01	84.48	84.48	56.95	22.09	-0.70
	CF	100.00	50.54	46.15	50.45	50.45	48.37	19.14	-0.70
$N = 16$	RSP	100.00	96.90	95.34	91.39	82.88	56.96	20.80	0.10
	CF	100.00	51.70	54.29	58.06	40.42	47.41	16.85	0.10

the s-bots are blind, the contribution of the blind s-bots is 40 to 60% of the contribution non-blind s-bots would provide (in average).

6 Conclusions

In this paper a robotic system composed of relatively simple robots capable of self-assembling is proposed for the cooperative transport of a heavy prey. In principle, the advantage of our robotic system with respect to robotic systems used in previous studies in cooperative transport is twofold. First, due to the ability to establish physical links among s-bots, the system is applicable to scenarios in which the number of robots necessary to push/pull the prey is higher than the number of robots which can directly manipulate it. Second, even if some of the robots are blind (i.e., they cannot localize the target), they can contribute to the overall system performance.

We assessed the performances of simple hand-coded and evolved solutions and we put them in relation to lower and upper bounds. Unless no robot is able to localize the target, having blind robots controlled by an evolved individual is superior in performance to the alternative of removing them from the experiment. On the contrary, in most of the trials, controlling the blind s-bots by the hand-coded solutions is inferior in performance to the alternative of removing them from the experiment. If no more than half of the robots are blind, the contribution of the blind robots, if controlled by the best evolved controller, is 40 to 60% of the contribution non-blind robots would provide (in average) if put in the same situation.

For the best evolved solution the performance scales well with group size, making it possible to transport heavier prey by larger swarms of robots.

Acknowledgments

This work was supported by the Belgian FNRS, of which Marco Dorigo is a Research Director, via the grant "Virtual Swarm-bots" (contract no. 9.4515.03);

by the Scientific Research Directorate of the French Community of Belgium via an "Action de Recherche Concertée" (the "ANTS" project); and by the Future and Emerging Technologies programme (IST-FET) of the European Commission, via the "SWARM-BOTS" project (grant IST-2000-31010). The information provided is the sole responsibility of the authors and does not reflect the Community's opinion. The Community is not responsible for any use that might be made of data appearing in this publication. The authors also wish to thank Tom Lenaerts and all the members of the "SWARM-BOTS" project.

References

Y. Aiyama, M. Hara, T. Yabuki, J. Ota, and T. Arai. Cooperative transportation by two four-legged robots with implicit communication. *Robotics and Autonomous Systems*, 29:13–19, 1999.

H.-G. Beyer. *The Theory of Evolution Strategies*. Springer, Berlin, Germany, 2001.

J.-L. Deneubourg and S. Goss. Collective patterns and decision-making. *Ethology, Ecology and Evolution*, 1:295–311, 1989.

J.-L. Deneubourg, S. Goss, G. Sandini, F. Ferrari, and P. Dario. Self-organizing collection and transport of objects in unpredictable environments. In *Proc. of Japan – U.S.A Symp. on Flexible Automation*, pages 1093–1098. ISCIE, Kyoto, Japan, 1990.

M. Dorigo, V. Trianni, E. Şahin, R. Groß, T.H. Labella, G. Baldassarre, S. Nolfi, J.-L. Deneubourg, F. Mondada, D. Floreano, and L.M. Gambardella. Evolving self-organizing behaviors for a swarm-bot. *Autonomous Robots*, 17(2–3):223–245, 2004.

J. L. Elman. Finding structure in time. *Cognitive Science*, 14:179–211, 1990.

P.-P. Grassé. La reconstruction du nid et les coordinations inter-individuelles chez *Bellicositermes natalensis et Cubitermes sp*. La théorie de la stigmergie : essai d'interprétation du comportement des termites constructeurs. *Insectes Sociaux*, 6: 41–81, 1959.

R. Groß and M. Dorigo. Cooperative transport of objects of different shapes and sizes. In *Ant Colony Optimization and Swarm Intelligence – Proceedings of ANTS 2004 – Fourth International Workshop*, volume 3172 of *Lecture Notes in Computer Science*, pages 107–118. Springer Verlag, Berlin, Germany, 2004.

C. R. Kube and H. Zhang. Collective robotics: from social insects to robots. *Adaptive Behaviour*, 2(2):189–218, 1993.

C. R. Kube and H. Zhang. Stagnation recovery behaviours for collective robotics. In *1994 IEEE/RSJ/GI Int. Conf. on Intelligent Robotics and Systems*, pages 1883–1890. IEEE Computer Society Press, Los Alamitos, CA, 1995.

F. Mondada, G. C. Pettinaro, A. Guignard, I. V. Kwee, D. Floreano, J.-L. Deneubourg, S. Nolfi, L. M. Gambardella, and M. Dorigo. SWARM-BOT: A new distributed robotic concept. *Autonomous Robots*, 17(2–3):193–221, 2004.

L. E. Parker. Current state of the art in distributed autonomous mobile robotics. In *Distributed Autonomous Robotic System 4*, pages 3–12. Springer, Tokyo, Japan, 2000.

H.-P. Schwefel. *Evolutionsstrategie und numerische Optimierung*. PhD thesis, Technische Universität Berlin, Germany, 1975.

Hawks, Doves and Lifetime Reproductive Success

Philip Hingston[1] and Luigi Barone[2]

[1] Edith Cowan University, WA 6020, Australia
p.hingston@ecu.edu.au
[2] The Univeristy of Western Australia, WA 6009, Australia
luigi@csse.uwa.edu.au

Abstract. Evolutionary game theory is an adaptation of classical game theory used to analyse and explain observed natural phenomena where organisms choose between alternative behavioural strategies. Recent analyses and simulations of evolutionary games have shown that implementation choices such as population size and selection method can have unexpected effects on the course of evolution. In this paper, we propose a new evolutionary interpretation of such games that uses a more biologically faithful selection scheme, in which selection and population size emerge from the interactions of the players and their environment. Using the well-known Hawks and Doves game as an example, we show that the resulting models are also tractable, easily simulated, and flexible.

1 Introduction

Evolutionary game theory [7] is an adaptation of classical game theory used to analyse and explain observed natural phenomena where organisms choose between alternative behavioural strategies. In recent years, simulation studies based on co-evolutionary algorithms have been applied to such scenarios.

One feature of these simulations is an explicit fitness value for each genotype, which is used in the fitness proportionate selection mechanism of the co-evolutionary algorithm. In nature, there is no such explicit fitness value. Individual organisms are born, interact with each other and with their environment, reproduce and die, and their *lifetime reproductive success* emerges out of this complex system - it depends upon how long the organism lives, how frequently it reproduces, and the reproductive success of its offspring. These in turn depend on the behaviour of the organism, as well as on factors outside its control, such as the environment in which it lives, the number of other organisms in the population and their behaviours. The same phenotype could thus have different reproductive success at different times, depending on such factors as well as on chance events. A simple fixed fitness value is a simplification that is intended to capture a kind of expectation of lifetime reproductive success for a random individual with a particular genotype.

Standard analytical methods also posit an explicit fitness value, and a selection mechanism based on this fitness value, similar to that used in these simulations (giving rise to the so-called *replicator dynamics*). At first it might seem that using an explicit fitness value is a reasonable simplification that facilitates analysis. If that were the case, though, one would expect that simulation models would generally be in agreement with analytical results. Experience has shown that this is not so. Simulations are sensitive to implementation choices that need to be made [2,3,4,5].

This suggests that a different approach, more faithful to biological reality, is needed. In this paper, we present a simulation study and some initial analysis using a new "Artificial Life" model that does not rely on an explicit reproductive fitness value, and we show that the model is easily simulated, flexible, tractable, and is capable of demonstrating phenomena similar to those predicted by evolutionary game theory, such as evolutionarily stable strategies.

2 The Hawks and Doves Game

The Hawks and Doves game is the classic game-theoretic example used to illustrate the concept of evolutionarily stable strategies [7,8]. Imagine a scenario in which pairs of agents from a population of agents compete for a shared resource. The agents might be animals and the resource might be food or access to nesting sites. Or the agents might be corporations and the resource might be potential customers. In each contest between a pair of agents, two strategies are available: the aggressive *hawk* strategy and the pacifist *dove* strategy. If both agents choose to play hawk, they will fight, with the winner taking the resource and the loser suffering an injury. If a hawk plays a dove, the dove will run away, avoiding injury, but the hawk takes the resource. If two doves meet, they will each try to bluff the other, until one gives up and lets the other take the resource, but both agents suffer a penalty for wasted effort.

In an evolutionary biology setting, these outcomes are normally interpreted as changes to an artificial construct called "reproductive fitness":

- when two hawks meet, a winner is randomly selected. The winner's fitness increases by 50 units of reproductive fitness and the loser loses 100 units. Thus, on average, each hawk will lose 25 units.
- when a hawk meets a dove, the hawk gets 50 units and the dove gets nothing.
- when two doves meet, a winner is randomly selected. The winner gets 50 units, but both the winner and the loser lose 10 units. Thus, on average, each dove will gain 15 units.

The resulting reproductive fitness values are used to perform fitness proportionate selection on the population. What will happen to a population of agents under this regime? Will the evolving population favour the hawk or the dove strategy, or is an equilibrium position with a mixture of hawk and dove behaviours possible?

To investigate this question, in [7], Maynard Smith et al. consider the proportion, p, of times hawk is the strategy used. By computing the expected changes in hawk and dove reproductive fitness from each contest, they show how to derive an equilibrium proportion $p = \frac{7}{12}$. Further analysis shows this equilibrium proportion is also an *evolutionarily stable strategy (ESS)*, meaning that any small deviation from this proportion will cause evolutionary pressure back toward the equilibrium.

The analysis of the scenario above is only really valid under unrealistic assumptions such as an infinite supply of the shared resource, an infinite population, and equal probabilities of contests between all pairs of agents (*perfect mixing*). The effects of randomness and discreteness, imperfect mixing and a limited resource in a real, finite population mean that the analysis is only an approximation. Indeed, various simulation studies have shown that implementation choices such as population size, degree of mixing and selection method can have unexpected effects on the simulated course of evolution, including limit cycles instead of equilibria, or mean p values that are statistically significantly different from the ESS [2,3,4,5]. There has been some debate about whether these difficulties should lead us to question the value of simulation studies, or the concept of ESS's, or to be more careful in implementing and analyzing these simulation models. In this paper, we propose a different response, namely, moving away from models based on explicit reproductive fitness values and towards more biologically faithful models based on emergent lifetime reproductive success.

3 Artificial Life Model

We propose an alternative interpretation for evolutionary games such as Hawks and Doves, in which each agent has its own health or energy level (we deliberately avoid the term "fitness", as we mean something different from reproductive fitness). This energy idea has similarities to other "Artificial Life" style models such as Holland's Echo [6], Menczer and Belew's Latent Energy Environments [9], Ray's Tierra [11], or Barone's peacock's tails and predator/prey models [1]. It is also similar in spirit to Sharov's life-system paradigm in the field of population ecology [12].

In our interpretation, individual agents wander about in their environment, using up energy in doing so, meeting other agents and competing for the shared resource. Whenever a contest takes place, the energy levels of the protagonists go up or down according to the rules laid out above. If an agent's energy level goes too low, she dies. If an agent's energy level gets high enough, she reproduces, sharing her energy with her offspring (although we have used the female pronoun, reproduction is asexual).

An important difference from the normal interpretation is that the population size, while finite, is not fixed. The number of birds varies as individual birds die or reproduce. The shared resource (we might as well call it "food") is replenished at a constant rate, and any unused food expires after a certain amount of time, so the "ecosystem" supports a limited population size, which depends on how much energy the birds expend. For example, in a population with a high proportion of hawks, much energy is wasted in fighting, so the population will be smaller than one with a high proportion of doves would be.

Recall the three requirements for an evolutionary process:
1. Variation of phenotypes
2. Differential survival and reproduction depending on phenotype
3. Inheritance of phenotypic traits

The usual interpretation of an evolutionary game operationalises both differential survival and differential reproduction, using fitness proportionate selection, as outlined in Section 2. In our interpretation, these differential rates emerge from the interactions of all the agents in a complex system. Energy level alone, for example, does not determine survival and reproduction rates. These also depend on the availability of food, whether the bird plays hawk or dove, and whether she encounters a hawk or a dove when competing for food. Changes in energy levels cannot be interpreted as predictable changes in survival or reproduction rates. For example, losing a competition for food will have a greater effect on the survival chances of a bird that already has a low energy level, the loss will be felt more if food is scarce. Again, the effect may be greater for a hawk than for a dove. Factors like the scarcity of food and the proportion of hawks to doves will also vary over the lifetime of an individual bird.

Thus, the proposed model eliminates two of the main problematic aspects of existing models – fixed (or infinite) population size, and an artificial selection method based on a simplified notion of reproductive fitness.

To investigate this model, we developed an agent-based simulation. To keep it simple, in this first version there is no notion of spatial location. These are the parameters we used for our simulations:

- Initial population: 100 hawks and 100 doves
- Energy value of food items: $v = 50$ units
- Energy loss for injury: $i = 100$ units
- Energy loss for bluffing: $b = 10$ units
- Death threshold: $d = 20$ units
- Reproduction threshold: $r = 140$ units
- Initial energy level for each hawk or dove: sampled uniformly from (d, r)
- Base energy requirement per time period: $base = 2$ units
- Time periods before a food item expires: 5
- Food supply: 100 new food items per time period

Of these, v, i, and b are fixed by the rules of the game, the initial population sizes are not important (the population grows or shrinks as needed) and the rest are just reasonable guesses. The parameters d, $base$, and r have been chosen by experimentation to ensure that the food supply is sufficient to support the resulting ecosystem. The last two parameters can be used to manipulate the carrying capacity of the ecosystem, which we experiment with later.

The simulation maintains a population of agents, each of which is genetically programmed as either a hawk or a dove. In each time period, the following procedure is executed:

```
Remove expired food
Add new food
For each agent
    If the agent has not yet competed in this time period
        If food is available
            If another agent wants the food
                Compete for the food and update Energy
            Else
```

```
        Take the food and update Energy
Subtract base from Energy
If Energy < d
   Remove the agent from the population
Else if Energy > r
   Create an offspring with Energy/2 initial energy
   and reduce this agent's Energy to Energy/2
```

To complete the description, we need to explain what "food is available" and "another agent wants the food" mean. In this version of the simulation, "food is available" simply means that there is some uneaten food when this agent's turn comes around (the order of treatment of the agents in the "For each agent" loop is determined randomly for each time period). Likewise, in this version "another agent wants the food" simply means that there are some other agents that have not yet tried for food in this time period. The agent to compete against is selected randomly from these agents. Thus each agent takes part in at most one competition for food in each time period.

4 Simulation Results

We carried out 10 simulation runs with the parameters listed above. Figure 1 shows a plot of population size and proportion of hawks over time in a typical simulation run over 1000 time periods. After an initial settling down period, the proportion of hawks remains fairly constant in the range 0.65 to 0.7, while the population size varies between about 375 and 500.

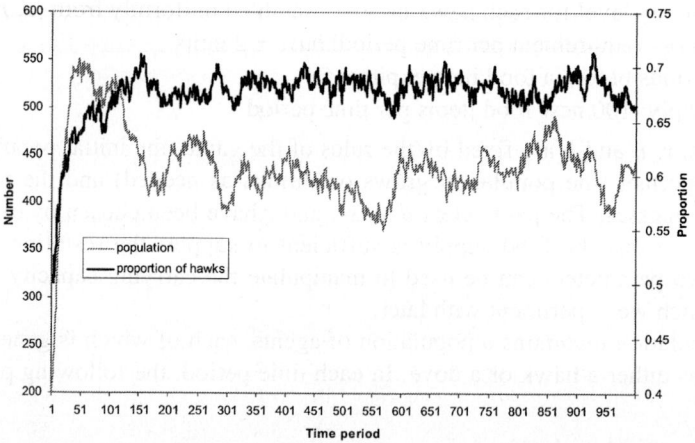

Fig. 1. Plot of the proportion of hawks and population size: a typical simulation run.

The mean values over the 10 runs for the mean proportion of hawks and the mean population size were 67.74% (stdev. 0.07%) and 438.6 (stdev. 1.35) respectively. These results are not sensitive to the initial numbers of hawks and doves. The tendency for proportion of hawks in the population to fluctuate around 68% reminds us of the ESS seen in the traditional interpretation of the game. It is worth emphasizing, however, that, as the selection mechanism is so different from fitness proportionate selection, there is no reason to expect that the equilibrium proportion should be in any way related to the 7/12 proportion of the ESS.

To investigate the effect of varying the food supply, we repeated the simulations using the same parameter values, but a food supply rate of 50 new food items per time period, and again with 200 new food items per time period. Table 1 shows the mean values of proportion of hawks and population size over 10 runs for each food supply rate. As can be seen from the table, the proportion of hawks remains constant, and the population size varies in direct proportion to the food supply rate.

Table 1. Mean values for proportion of hawks and population size for different food supply rates.

Rate	Proportion of hawks	Population size
50	0.676	221.4
100	0.677	438.7
200	0.676	883.6

5 Analysis

In this section, we derive some results to explain the observed behaviour of the simulations. We saw that the population size fluctuates a good deal, but the proportion of hawks fluctuates much less, staying around 68%. Therefore, we will try to determine conditions that are consistent with a roughly equilibrium *proportion* of hawks.

If an equilibrium were to occur, then it must be that the proportionate rate of increase (or decrease) of hawks in the population equals the proportionate rate of increase of doves. These rates are determined by how many hawks (or doves) die in a given time period, and how many reproduce. Specifically, if we define d_h as the probability that a hawk will die in a given period, and r_h as the probability that a hawk will reproduce in a given period, then the expected rate of increase of hawks is $1 + r_h - d_h$. Making the equivalent definition for doves, we can express the condition for equilibrium as:

$$1 + r_h - d_h = 1 + r_d - d_d. \tag{1}$$

Consider, then, what may happen to a hawk in a given time period. Firstly, the hawk may find no food to compete for (if there are more agents than food). Let us use f to denote the probability that an agent will find food. Secondly, if the hawk finds food, there will probably be another agent that also wants the food. The only exception is if all the other agents have already competed in this time period, so at most one agent can find herself in this situation. Let us use c to denote the probability of having to compete (c will be very close to 1). The other agent might be a hawk or a dove. Let us use p for the probability that the opponent is a hawk (p is just the proportion of hawks in the population). If the opponent is another hawk, then our hawk has a 50-50 chance of winning the food, whilst if it is a dove, our hawk will definitely win the

Table 2. Probabilities of changes in energy levels for a hawk in one time period.

Change in energy level	Probability
$-base$	$1-f$
$v-base$	$f \cdot (1-c) + f \cdot c \cdot p \cdot \frac{1}{2} + f \cdot c \cdot (1-p)$
$-i-base$	$f \cdot c \cdot p \cdot \frac{1}{2}$

food. Taking all these possibilities into account, we can complete the following table of probabilities for possible changes in the hawk's energy level in one time period:

Using Table 2, we can calculate the probability that our hawk will die in the given period, as well as the probability that she will reproduce. Let us start with the probability of death. At the start of the period, the hawk's energy level is between d and r. If the hawk is to die, its energy level must go down during the period. Assuming that the energy value of a food item is greater than the base energy requirement (otherwise all the agents will quickly starve), a drop in energy level corresponds to either row 1 or row 3 of Table 2. If the hawk's energy level is less than $d+base$ then either row 1 or row 3 lead to death. If the hawk's energy level is more than $d+base$ but less than $d+base+i$, only row 3 is fatal. In all other cases, the hawk cannot die in the given time period. The probability of death, then, depends on the energy level of the hawk at the start of the period, E, so we denote it $d_h(E)$. Table 3 lists the three cases:

Table 3. Probability of death for hawks with various energy levels.

Range for E	$d_h(E)$
$E < d+base$	$(1-f) + f \cdot c \cdot p \cdot \frac{1}{2}$
$d+base \leq E < d+base+i$	$f \cdot c \cdot p \cdot \frac{1}{2}$
$d+base+i \leq E$	0

The probability distribution of energy levels for hawks determines the probability of the precondition for each case. In order to push the analysis further, we will assume that it is reasonable to approximate this distribution with empirical data from the simulations. We define $k_1 = p(E < d+base)$ and $k_2 = p(d+base \leq E < d+base+i)$.

Hence we can write the probability of death for a hawk as:

$$d_h = k_1 \cdot ((1-f) + f \cdot c \cdot p \cdot \tfrac{1}{2}) + k_2 \cdot f \cdot c \cdot p \cdot \tfrac{1}{2}. \qquad (2)$$

We can use the same method to derive the probability that a hawk will reproduce in a given time period. This time there are two cases:

We define $k_3 = p(E > r - v + base)$, and we can write:

$$r_h = k_3 \cdot (f \cdot (1-c) + f \cdot c \cdot p \cdot \tfrac{1}{2} + f \cdot c \cdot (1-p)). \qquad (3)$$

Table 4. Probability of reproduction for hawks with various energy levels.

Range for E	$r_h(E)$
$E > r - v + base$	$f \cdot (1-c) + f \cdot c \cdot p \cdot \frac{1}{2} + f \cdot c \cdot (1-p)$
$E \leq r - v + base$	0

We carry out the same calculations to find the probabilities of death and reproduction for doves, d_d and r_d respectively. Considering what can happen to a dove in a given time period, we derive Table 5. From this, we derive Table 6 and Table 7.

Table 5. Probabilities of changes in energy levels for a dove in one time period.

Change in energy level	Probability
$-base$	$(1-f) + f \cdot c \cdot p$
$v - base$	$f \cdot (1-c)$
$v - b - base$	$f \cdot c \cdot (1-p) \cdot \frac{1}{2}$
$-b - base$	$f \cdot c \cdot (1-p) \cdot \frac{1}{2}$

Table 6. Probability of death for doves with various energy level ranges, and probability of being in these ranges.

Range for E	p(E in range)	$d_d(E)$
$E < d + base$	k_4	$(1-f) + f \cdot c \cdot p + f \cdot c \cdot (1-p) \cdot \frac{1}{2}$
$d + base \leq E < d + base + b$	k_5	$f \cdot c \cdot (1-p) \cdot \frac{1}{2}$
$d + base + b \leq E$	0	0

Table 7. Probability of reproduction for doves with various energy level ranges, and probability of being in these ranges.

Range for E	p(E in range)	$r_d(E)$
$E > r - v + b + base$	k_6	$f \cdot (1-c) + f \cdot c \cdot (1-p) \cdot \frac{1}{2}$
$r - v + base < E \leq r - v + b + base$	k_7	$f \cdot (1-c)$
$E \leq r - v + base$	0	0

Now we can write formulae for d_d and r_d:

$$d_d = k_4 \cdot (1 - f + f \cdot c \cdot p + f \cdot c \cdot (1-p) \cdot \tfrac{1}{2}) + k_5 \cdot f \cdot c \cdot (1-p) \cdot \tfrac{1}{2}. \qquad (4)$$

$$r_d = k_6 \cdot (f \cdot (1-c) + f \cdot c \cdot (1-p) \cdot \tfrac{1}{2}) + k_7 \cdot f \cdot (1-c). \qquad (5)$$

Substituting these expressions into equation (1) and solving for p, we get:

$$p = \frac{2}{c \cdot f} \cdot \frac{(k_4 - k_1) + f \cdot (k_3 + k_1 - k_6 - k_7 - k_4 + c \cdot (k_6/2 + k_7 + k_4/2 + k_5/2))}{k_3 + k_1 + k_2 - k_6 - k_4 + k_5}. \quad (6)$$

Approximate mean values for $k_1, k_2, \ldots, k_7$ from simulations are 0.008, 0.717. 0.385, 0.009, 0.054 and 0.173 respectively. f varies between about 0.4 and 0.5, with a mean of about 0.46, and c is approximately equal to 1. Substituting these values into equation (6) yields a value of $p \approx 0.678$, which agrees very well with the simulations. Notice that, as k_4 and k_1 are small and approximately equal, the right hand side of equation (12) can be approximated as in equation (7):

$$p \approx \frac{2}{c} \cdot \frac{k_3 - k_6 - k_7 + c \cdot (k_6/2 + k_7 + k_4/2 + k_5/2)}{k_3 + k_2 - k_6 + k_5}, \quad (7)$$

which is independent of f, in agreement with the simulations results. But the two sides of equation (1), the rates of population change for hawks and doves, do depend on f. If the population is low, there is more food available, i.e. f is higher, so rates of population increase go up. Conversely, a high population will cause a relative shortage of food, i.e. a lower f, so rates of population increase go down. Thus, the population size is maintained within a range that the available food supply can support, for a given proportion of hawks. We see, then, that the main observed features of the simulations are in accordance with equation (1).

6 Conclusion

We have presented a new interpretation of evolutionary games, using the well-known Hawks and Doves game as our example, in which game payoffs are interpreted as short term changes to energy levels of players, resulting in emergent changes to lifetime reproductive success. This has numerous advantages over the traditional interpretation. It avoids the contrivance of positing an explicit, fixed fitness function. It avoids the need to arbitrarily fix the population size. Previous simulation studies have shown that such arbitrary choices can unexpectedly affect the outcome of the simulation. We also claim that this is a more faithful way of modeling reality, can readily accommodate additional model features, and is easily simulated.

We have shown that we can combine simulation and analysis of such models to obtain useful insights into the behaviour of the systems they describe. We believe that with further effort, better analysis methods can be developed, offering a potentially superior alternative to the traditional approach.

References

1. Barone, L.: Computer Modeling of Evolution, Honours Thesis, Department of Computer Science, The University of Western Australia (1994)

2. Fogel, D.B., Fogel, G.B., Andrews, P.C.: On the instability of evolutionary stable strategies, BioSystems 44 (1997), 135-152
3. Fogel, G.B., Andrews, P.C., Fogel, D.B.: On the instability of evolutionary stable strategies in small populations, Ecological Modelling 109(1998), 283-294
4. Ficici, S.G., Melnik, O., Pollack, J.B.: A Game-Theoretic Investigation of Selection Methods Used in Evolutionary Algorithms, Proceedings of the 2000 Congress on Evolutionary Computation, IEEE Press (2000), 880-887
5. Ficici, S. G., Pollack, J.B.: Effects of Finite Populations on Evolutionary Stable Strategies, Proceedings of the Genetic and Evolutionary Computation Conference, Morgan Kaufmann (2000), 927-934.
6. Hraber, P., Jones, T. Forrest, S.: The Ecology of Echo, ALife 3(3), pp 165-190, (1997).
7. Maynard Smith, J.: Evolution and the Theory of Games, Cambridge U.P. (1982)
8. Maynard Smith, J., Price G.R.: The Logic of Animal Conflict, Nature 246 (1973), 15-18
9. Menczer, F., Belew, R.K.: Latent Energy Environments, In: Belew, R., Mitchell, M. (eds.): Adaptive Individuals in Evolving Populations: Models and Algorithms, Addison Wesley (1996), 191-208
10. Oliphant, M.: Evolving Cooperation in the Non-Iterated Prisoner's Dilemma: The Importance of Spatial Organization, In: Brooks, R., Maes, P. (eds.): Proceedings of the Fourth Artificial Life Workshop, MIT Press (1994)
11. Ray, T.S.: An approach to the synthesis of life. In C.G. Langton, C. Taylor, J.D. Farmer, and S. Rasmussen, editors, Artificial Life II, Vol. X, 371-408. Addison-Wesley (1992).
12. Sharov, A.A.: Life-system approach: a system paradigm in population ecology. Oikos, vol. 63 (1992), 485-494.

Evolutionary Multi-agent Systems

Pieter J. 't Hoen[1] and Edwin D. de Jong[2]

[1] Center for Mathematics and Computer Science (CWI)
P.O. Box 94079, Amsterdam, The Netherlands
hoen@cwi.nl
[2] Utrecht University, Decision Support Systems Group
P.O. Box 80.089, Utrecht, The Netherlands
dejong@cs.uu.nl

Abstract. In Multi-Agent learning, agents must learn to select actions that maximize their utility given the action choices of the other agents. Cooperative Coevolution offers a way to evolve multiple elements that together form a whole, by using a separate population for each element. We apply this setup to the problem of multi-agent learning, arriving at an evolutionary multi-agent system (EA-MAS). We study a problem that requires agents to select their actions in parallel, and investigate the problem solving capacity of the EA-MAS for a wide range of settings.
Secondly, we investigate the transfer of the COllective INtelligence (COIN) framework to the EA-MAS. COIN is a proved engineering approach for learning of cooperative tasks in MASs, and consists of re-engineering the utilities of the agents so as to contribute to the global utility. It is found that, as in the Reinforcement Learning case, the use of the Wonderful Life Utility specified by COIN also leads to improved results for the EA-MAS.

1 Introduction

In Multi-Agent learning, agents must learn to select actions that maximize their utility given the action choices of the other agents [14, 3, 6, 13]. Cooperative Coevolution [9] offers a way to evolve multiple elements that together form a whole, by using a separate population for each element. We propose that this setup can be applied to the problem of Multi-Agent learning, arriving at an evolutionary multi-agent system (EA-MAS).

In the experiments presented in [9], the different populations evolve sequentially. Each population thereby evolves in a temporarily static context as only one population is evolved at a time. This solves part of the credit assignment problem posed when multiple populations adapt simultaneously. However, the possibility of simultaneous adaptation is mentioned by the authors, and viewed as a possible alternative to sequential adaptation. In the multi-agent decision-making problem studied here, it is part of the problem formulation that agents must simultaneously select their actions. We therefore employ a multiple population setup in which all populations evolve simultaneously. We investigate the problem solving capacity of the EA-MAS for a wide range of settings. It is found that the EA-MAS model is able to converge to high fitness for suitable conditions.

Experimental results are presented for the full Dispersion Games [2, 11]. In this cooperative game, n agents each have to decide which of the n tasks they are to undertake. Agents acting and learning in parallel while using local feedback with no central control must evolve towards an optimal distribution over the available tasks. Such problems are typical for a growing class of large-scale distributed applications such as load balancing, niche selection, division of roles within robotics, or application in logistics.

The COllective INtelligence (COIN) framework has originally been applied in the context of multi-agent Reinforcement Learning (RL). Here, we investigate its application to the EA-MAS setup. COIN is a proved engineering approach for learning of cooperative tasks in MASs [16, 12, 10]. In typical problem settings, as in the full Dispersion Games, individual agents in a MAS contribute to some part of the collective through their individual actions. The joint actions of all agents derive some reward from the outside world. To enable local learning, this reward has to be suitably divided among the individual agents where each agent aims to increase its received reward. However, unless special care is taken as to how reward is assigned, there is a risk that agents in the collective work at cross-purposes. For example, agents can reach sub-optimal solutions by competing for scarce resources or by inefficient task distribution among the agents as they each only consider their own goals (e.g. a Tragedy of the Commons [4] or policy oscillations [8]). In general, the performance of a MAS is difficult to predict. In the COIN framework, the utilities of the agents are re-engineered to contribute to the global utility. We show how the improved results for MAS RL in COIN can be translated to similar results for the EA-MAS.

The rest of this document is structured as follows. Section 2 introduces our generalized EA-MAS. Section 3 discusses our experimental settings. Section 4 shows the analysis of the full Dispersion Games for the EA-MAS. Section 5 presents the COIN framework and Section 6 presents the novel use of COIN in an EA setting. Section 7 discusses and concludes.

2 EA-MAS Setup

An EA-MAS is represented by several parameters. For a full Dispersion Game with n agents and hence n tasks, we represent each agent i ($1 \leq i \leq n$) in the MAS by one separate population pop_i. This population consists of chromosomes representing preference for tasks by the agent.

Each chromosome consists of a number of genes equal to the number of tasks from which the agent has to choose. For each chromosome, the gene g_j ($1 \leq j \leq n$) encodes the preference of the chromosome for task j. The behavior dictated by this chromosome, i.e. the task actually chosen, is stochastic. For this we use the Boltzmann probability. The chance of choice of task j at timestep k is equal to:

$$\frac{e^{\frac{g_j(k)}{\tau}}}{\sum_{l=1}^{n} e^{\frac{g_l(k)}{\tau}}} \qquad (1)$$

where τ is the temperature that determines the exploration/exploitation of each chromosome in choosing its actions. We set τ at the reasonable value of 0.5.

For each population representing one agent, like in [9], the chromosome with the highest fitness determines the behavior of the agent. The expected utility for a chromosome c_i in population i is given by the probability that its selected action will be executed. This probability however depends on the action choices of the other populations in the MAS. The fitness function is designed to yield an accurate approximation of this ideal utility.

The fitness of a chromosome c_i for population pop_i is determined in several steps. First, the highest fitness[1] chromosomes c_l, where $l \neq i \wedge 1 \leq l \leq n$, are taken from each other population pop_l. Chromosome c_i now represents agent i and the rest of the MAS is represented by the other selected chromosomes. The choice of task execution by each of the agents, represented by their respective chromosomes, is determined. The task chosen by agent j (i.e. chromosome c_j representing the agent) is randomly assigned to one (possibly exactly one) of the contenders for this task. The sought for fitness of chromosome c_i is 1 if the task is assigned to the agent represented by chromosome c_i, and 0 otherwise. A more accurate approximation of the utility can be obtained by averaging over a series of such fitness calculations, which we call samples (the number of samples in the experiments is detailed in Section 3).

We have defined the fitness measure for one individual chromosome above. The fitness of the MAS as a whole is calculated by first calculating the fitness of each chromosome for each of the populations of the EA-MAS. Like in [9], the highest valued chromosome for each population then determines the choice of action for the respective agent. For each of these chromosomes, the most likely task choice is selected. The fitness of the MAS, scaled from 0 to 1, is then defined as the proportion of tasks that has at least one agent as executor. A fitness of 1 is only reached if, and only if, all agents choose a distinct task.

The fitness of the MAS is improved, hopefully, through learning. In each epoch, for each population pop_i, C new children/offspring (chromosomes) are generated. For each offspring, a randomly chosen chromosome c_i from pop_i is chosen as a parent. The child c'_i replaces its parent if and only if the fitness of this newcomer is higher. Alternative replacement rules, as for example discussed in [9], are of course possible.

Each new offspring c'_i is generated as a copy of its parent but with a mutation of $\epsilon \in [-\alpha, \alpha]$ of gene g_j to $g_j + \epsilon$ for a random index j. We have used a value of $\alpha = 0.5$. We hence modify the preference of a chromosome for one of the tasks by mutating the gene indicating the preference for this task. In our presented results, we have used a uniform chance of mutation per gene of $\frac{1}{n}$ for the offspring as this produced better results for all studied settings. No cross-over is used. Like in [9], each population is a distinct species in the sense that there is no exchange of genetic material between the populations.

All chromosomes in the initial populations are formed with the value 0 for each of their genes. They hence have an equiprobable preference for all tasks

---

[1] Ties are broken at random.

available to the MAS. The MAS initially hence shows uniform random behavior. To save computation, the initial fitness of all the chromosomes is set at 0.5 as this is a reasonable initial approximation of their utility that will be improved as the EA-MAS evolves.

Furthermore, the fitness of a chromosome in the EA-MAS is only actually calculated when this chromosome is considered as a parent for a child. The fitness of the chromosomes used in calculation of the MAS is hence only an approximation. Investigation of the converged populations however reveals that all chromosomes have converged to a 99% preference for one task. This seems to indicate that our reduced use of computation cost did not skew the results. This is in line with [9] where populations in the experiments converged once a population had found a niche to exploit.

The process of generating new children and updating the individual populations is executed in parallel for all the populations and newcomers. All new offspring hence calculate their fitness relative to the original MAS of the previous epoch. The new children therefore may introduce new conflicts as the other agents, i.e. populations, also evolve in parallel.

In [9], the evolution of the separate populations in one epoch is executed sequentially; once population p_i has been updated, population p_{i+1} can evolve relative to the updated behavior of populations p_0 to p_i. For a MAS using RL for the full Dispersion Games [11] we found that such a sequential implementation considerably simplified learning the studied problems. Here, the sequentializing of the learning made it possible to arrive at optimal solutions as each agent was easily able to improve its behavior relative to the fixed other agents of the MAS. Experiments for the EA-MAS (not shown) indicate that similar results hold when learning in the Dispersion Games is sequentialized.

3 Experimental Settings

Our experiments, for the EA-MAS with and without COIN, investigate several settings. Most importantly, we vary the size of the populations representing the agents and the number of children produced per such population in one epoch. Similar to traditional single population EA's, we aim to quantify the possible added power of computation offered by larger populations. We use the variable S to indicate the size of one population and C for the number of children. As settings we investigate for $S = C$ the values 1, 5, and 10.

Also, we investigate the impact of a greedy choice in action selection[2] in determining the fitness of a chromosome. In determining the fitness of a chromosome c, we can choose whether or not to choose the most likely action by the chromosomes representing the other agents the MAS. As a hypothesis, we expect for a EA-MAS to more easily achieve good solutions for a greedy setting as agents clearly indicate their preferred actions to facilitate learning.

---

[2] A greedy choice of action selection for our chromosomes is the choice of action with the highest probability as determined by Equation 1.

Furthermore, as sketched in Section 2, the fitness of one chromosome is defined as 1 if a task is assigned to the agent represented by the chromosome and 0 otherwise. We experiment with using the fitness averaged over 1, 10 and 100 such calculations, which we call samples, to hopefully better approximate the utility of a chromosome.

Lastly, to investigate the scaling properties of the EA-MAS, we investigated the full Dispersion Games for 10, 30 and 60 agents. The results shown are averaged over 30, 30, and 10 runs respectively. We can then also conclude whether settings appropriate for few agents carry over to larger systems.

4 Results EA-MAS

In Figure 1, we give the results for the EA-MAS for the full Dispersion Game with 10 agents. The performance of the system improves as either the number of samples or the size of the populations is increased. The $S = C = 1$ population has difficulty in achieving full utility. The $S = C = 5$ population performs optimally and clearly benefits from a larger sample size. The difference between 10 and a 100 samples in determining the fitness of an individual chromosome is however marginal. The added benefit of more samples becomes even smaller for $S = C = 10$, supporting the hypothesis that larger population sizes in a EA-MAS are a dominating factor.

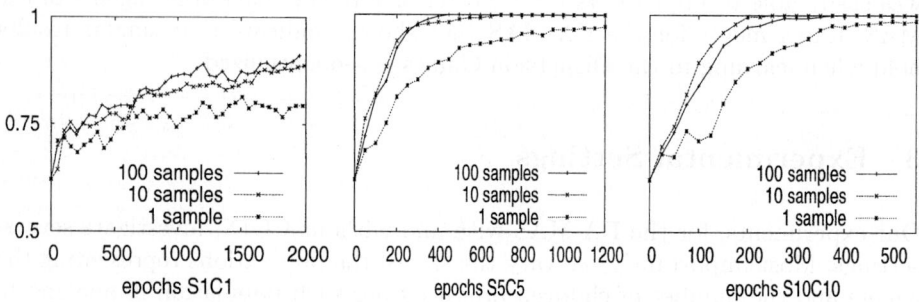

Fig. 1. Fitness 10 agents for the EA-MAS.

In Figure 2, we show results for the EA-MAS again for 10 agents, but with non-greedy choice of action in determining the fitness of an individual chromosome; i.e. the chromosomes representing the other agents do not take their greedy action, but take an action according to the Boltzmann distribution of Equation 1. The increased stochasticity of the MAS makes it more difficult for agents to achieve good results. We further present only results for a greedy choice of action due to the representative better results, as also for COIN in Section 6, for this setting.

In Figure 3 we show the performance of the EA-MAS for similar settings as in Figure 1, but now for 30 agents. In Figure 4, we extend the full Dispersion

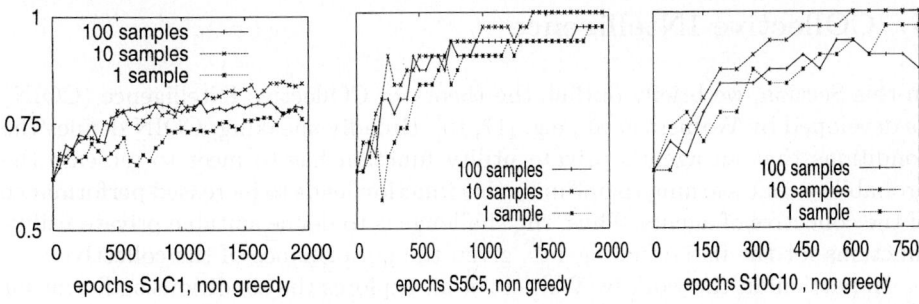

Fig. 2. Fitness 10 agents for the EA-MAS, non greedy.

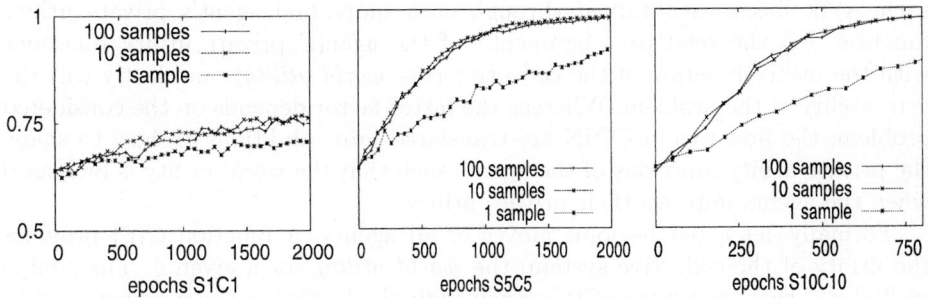

Fig. 3. Fitness 30 agents for the EA-MAS.

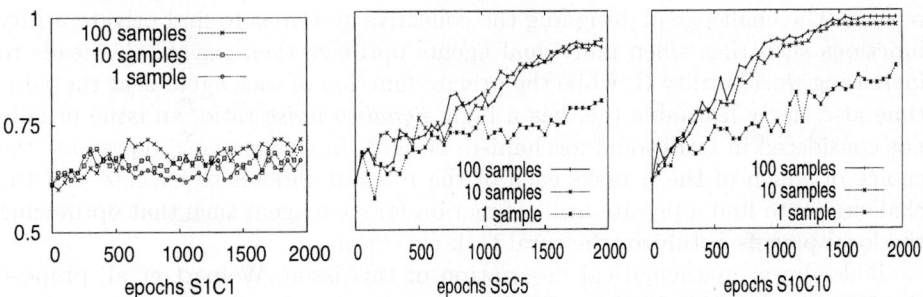

Fig. 4. Fitness 60 agents for the EA-MAS.

Game to 60 agents. In scaling the system, it becomes essential to use the larger population size of $S = C = 10$ to quickly achieve good results and a larger sample size is more beneficial.

As related work, the coevolving string covers of [9] pose a similar problem to the full Dispersion Game. In this work, binary strings are used to cover a target problem. Each population must find a niche of patterns in the target set. This work uses 2 to 8 populations seeded with 50 chromosomes each. Of interest is to study how the choice of parameters S and C would affect the results of [9] or whether the good results of [9] are sustained as the number of populations is increased significantly.

5 COllective INtelligence

In this Section, we briefly outline the theory of COllective INtelligence (COIN) as developed by Wolpert et al., e.g. [17, 15]. Broadly speaking, COIN defines the conditions that an agent's private utility function has to meet to increase the probability that learning to optimize this function leads to increased performance of the collective of agents. Thus, the challenge is to define suitable private utility functions for the individual agents, given the performance of the collective.

In particular, the work by Wolpert et al. explores the conditions sufficient for effective emergent behavior for a collective of independent agents each employing their private utility. These conditions relate to (i) the learnability of the problem each agent faces, as obtained through each individual agent's private utility function, (ii) the relative "alignment" of the agents' private utility functions with the utility function of the collective (the *world utility*), and lastly (iii) the learnability of the problem. Whereas the latter factor depends on the considered problem, the first two in COIN are translated into conditions on how to shape the private utility functions of the agents such that the world utility is increased when the agents improve their private utility.

Formally, let ζ be the joint moves of all agents. A function $G(\zeta)$ provides the utility of the collective system, the *world utility*, for a given ζ. The goal is to find a ζ that maximizes $G(\zeta)$. Each individual agent η has a private utility function g_η that relates the reward obtained by the collective to the reward that the individual agent collects. Each agent will act such as to improve its own reward. The challenge of designing the collective system is to find private utility functions such that when individual agents optimize their payoff, this leads to increasing world utility G, while the private function of each agent is at the same time also easily learnable (i.e. has a high *signal-to-noise* ratio, an issue usually not considered in traditional mechanism design). In this paper, ζ represents the choice of which of the n tasks each of the n agent chooses to execute and the challenge is to find a private utility function for each agent such that optimizing the local payoffs optimizes the total task execution.

Following a mathematical description of this issue, Wolpert et al. propose the **Wonderful Life Utility** (WLU) as a private utility function that is both *learnable* and *aligned* with G, and that can also be easily calculated.

$$WLU_\eta(\zeta) = G(\zeta) - G(CL_{S_\eta^{eff}}(\zeta)) \qquad (2)$$

The function $CL_{S_\eta^{eff}}(\zeta)$ as classically applied[3] "clamps" or suspends the choice of task by agent η and returns the utility of the system without the effect of agent η on the remaining agents $\hat{\eta}$ with which it possibly interacts. For our problem domain, the clamped effect set are those agents $\hat{\eta}$ that are influenced in their utility by the choice of task of agent η. Hence $WLU_\eta(\zeta)$ for agent η is equal to the value of all the tasks executed by all the agents minus the value of the tasks executed by the other agents $\hat{\eta}$ if agent η had not been in the system.

---

[3] Ongoing work investigates more general clamping functions.

If agent η picks a task τ, which is not chosen by the other agents, the first term of Equation 2 increases appropriately while the second term remains unchanged. Agent η hence receives a reward of $V(\tau)$, where V assigns a value to a task τ. As defined in Section 2, this reward is equal to 1. If the task chosen and executed by η is however also chosen by any of the other agents, then the first term $G(\zeta)$ of Equation 2 is unchanged (at least one of the agents executes this task). The second term however increases with the value of $V(\tau)$ as agent η "no longer" competes for completion of the task. Agent η then receives a penalty $-V(\tau)$ for competing for a task targeted by one of the other agents $\hat{\eta}$. The WLU hence has a built in incentive for agents to find an unfulfilled task and hence for each agent to strive for a high global utility in its search for maximizing its own rewards.

6 COIN for EA-MAS

In Figures 5, 6, and 7 we show the results for a EA-MAS using the WLU of the COIN framework as fitness measure for individual chromosomes. The EA-MAS enhanced with COIN shows improved convergence results across the board compared to the settings of Section 4.

In Figure 5, we show the performance for COIN in a system with 10 agents. Compared to Figure 1 for the "standard" EA-MAS, the convergence time of the system is remarkably improved. The added benefit of increased sampling is reduced as the system quickly steers to good solutions.

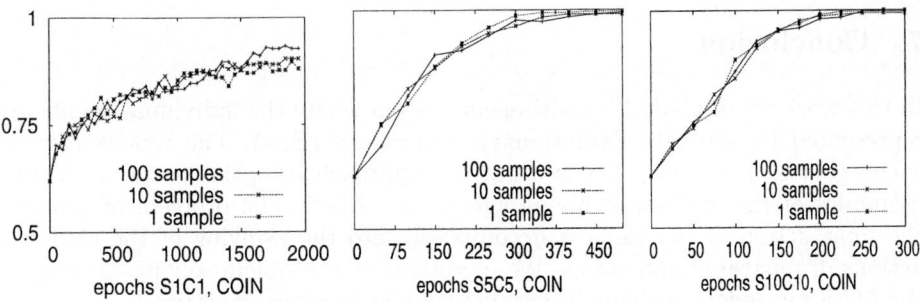

Fig. 5. Fitness 10 agents for the EA-MAS, COIN.

In Figure 6, we show the performance for COIN in a system with 30 agents. Compared to Figure 3, the convergence time of the system is once again improved. The added benefit of increased sampling is once more reduced as the system quickly steers to good solutions. The added value of COIN can even replace the need for sampling as can be seen for populations $S10C10$. This can lead to substantial reduction in computation times.

Lastly, in Figure 7, we show the performance for COIN in a system with 60 agents. Compared to Figure 4, the convergence for few samples is improved while other settings show a slight increase in convergence rates. Of interest for future work is to investigate whether the incentives for a high MAS utility of [7] or [5] can produce similar benefits as a COIN approach.

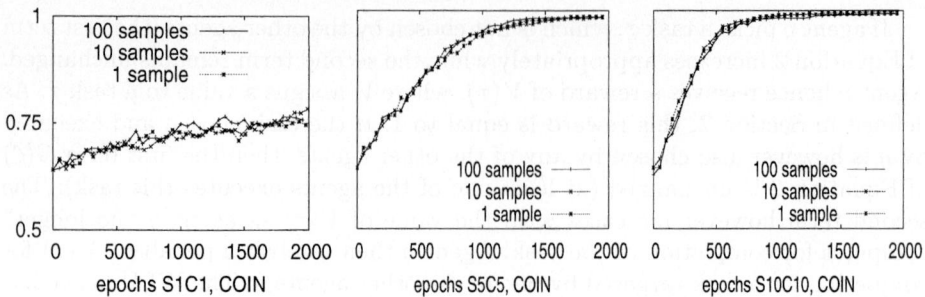

Fig. 6. Fitness 30 agents for the EA-MAS, COIN.

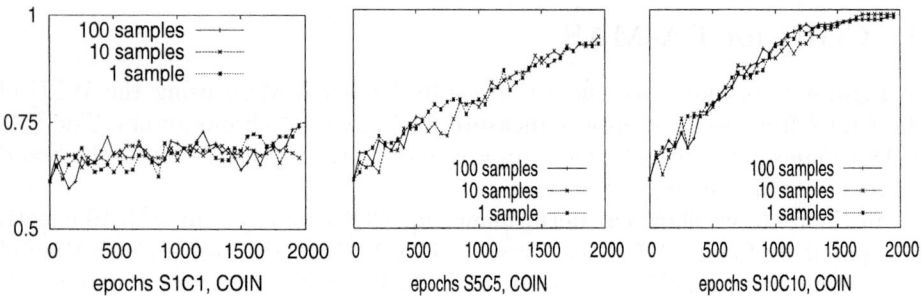

Fig. 7. Fitness 60 agents for the EA-MAS, COIN.

7 Conclusion

In this work we presented a multi-agent system where the individual agents are represented by separate Evolutionary Algorithms (EAs). The representing of each agent as a separate EA is a natural approach to optimize the individual dynamics of the learning/evolving agents in a MAS. The problem of evolving the joint action of the MAS is decomposed into the evolving of the choice of actions of separate populations. We investigate the problem solving capacity of the MAS for agents evolving in parallel for a wide range of settings.

Secondly, we show how the COllective INtelligence (COIN) framework traditionally applied to Reinforcement Learning can be successfully applied to the EA approach. COIN is a proved engineering approach for learning of cooperative tasks in MASs. The utilities of the agents are re-engineered to contribute to the global utility. We show how the improved results for MAS RL in COIN can be translated to similar results in EA.

The setup is a form of coevolution. A recent finding in coevolution is that the accuracy of evaluation can be optimized by taking the informativeness of co-evolving individuals into account [1]. An interesting issue for further research therefore is whether the performance of the system can be improved by taking a population's informativeness in evaluating other populations into consideration.

References

1. E. D. De Jong and J. B. Pollack. Ideal evaluation from coevolution. *Evolutionary Computation*, 12(2), 2004.
2. T. Grenager, R. Powers, and Y. Shoham. Dispersion games: general definitions and some specific learning results. In *AAAI 2002*, 2002.
3. C. Guestrin, D. Koller, C. Gearhart, and N. Kanodia. Generalizing plans to new environments in relational MDPs. In *International Joint Conference on Artificial Intelligence (IJCAI-03)*, 2003.
4. G. Hardin. The tragedy of the commons. *Science*, 162:1243–1248, 1968.
5. M. Kisiel-Dorohinicki and K. Socha. Crowding Factor in Evolutionary Multi-Agent System For Multiobjective Optimization. In H. R. Arabnia, editor, *Proceedings of IC-AI'01 – International Conference on Artificial Inteligence*, volume 1. CSREA Press, June 2001.
6. J. Kok and N. Vlassis. Sparse cooperative Q-learning. In *International Conference of Machine Learning*, 2004.
7. H. S. Miu, K. S. Leung, and Y. Leung. An evolutionary multi-agent system for object recognition in satellite images. In *Evolutionary Computation, CEC '03, The 2003 Congress on*, pages 520– 527, 2003.
8. A. Nowé and K. Verbeeck. Distributed Reinforcement Learning, loadbased routing a case study. In *Notes of the Neural, Symbolic and Reinforcement Methods for sequence Learning Workshop at IJCAI*, 1999.
9. M. A. Potter and K. A. De Jong. Cooperative coevolution: An architecture for evolving coadapted subcomponents. *Evolutionary Computation*, 8(1):1–29, 2000.
10. P. 't Hoen and S. Bohte. COllective INtelligence with sequences of actions. In *14th European Conference on Machine Learning*, Lecture Notes in Artificial Intelligence, LNAI 2837. Springer, 2003.
11. P. 't Hoen and S. Bohte. COllective INtelligence with task assignment. In *Proceedings of CDOCS03, fortcoming. Also available as TR*, Lecture Notes in Artificial Intelligence. Springer, 2003.
12. K. Tumer and D. Wolpert. COllective INtelligence and Braess' paradox. In *Proceedings of the Sixteenth National Conference on Artificial Intelligence*, pages 104–109, Austin, Aug. 2000.
13. N. Urquhart, P. Ross, B. Paechter, and K. Chisholm. Solving a real world routing problem using multiple evolutionary agents. In *Parallel Problem Solving From Nature (PPSN) VII, Springer Verlag, LNCS 2439*, pages 871–882, 2002.
14. G. Weiss, editor. *Multiagent Systems: A Modern Approach to Distributed Artificial Intelligence*. The MIT Press, Cambridge, MA, 1999.
15. D. Wolpert and K. Tumer. Optimal payoff functions for members of collectives. *Advances in Complex Systems*, 4(2/3):265–279, 2001.
16. D. H. Wolpert, K. Tumer, and J. Frank. Using collective intelligence to route internet traffic. In *Advances in Neural Information Processing Systems-11*, pages 952–958, Denver, 1998.
17. D. H. Wolpert, K. R. Wheeler, and K. Tumer. General principles of learning-based multi-agent systems. In O. Etzioni, J. P. Müller, and J. M. Bradshaw, editors, *Proceedings of the Third Annual Conference on Autonomous Agents (AGENTS-99)*, pages 77–83, New York, May 1–5 1999. ACM Press.

Credit Assignment Among Neurons in Co-evolving Populations

Vineet R. Khare[1], Xin Yao[1], and Bernhard Sendhoff[2]

[1] Natural Computation Group, School of Computer Science,
The University of Birmingham, Birmingham B15 2TT, UK
{V.R.Khare,X.Yao}@cs.bham.ac.uk
http://www.cs.bham.ac.uk/research/NC/
[2] Honda Research Institute Europe GmbH, Carl-Legien-Straße 30,
63073 Offenbach/Main, Germany
Bernhard_Sendhoff@de.hrdeu.com
http://www.honda-ri.de

Abstract. Different credit assignment strategies are investigated in a two level co-evolutionary model which involves a population of Gaussian neurons and a population of radial basis function networks consisting of neurons from the neuron population. Each individual in neuron population can contribute to one or more networks in network population, so there is a two-fold difficulty in evaluating the effectiveness (or fitness) of a neuron. Firstly, since each neuron only represents a partial solution to the problem, it needs to be assigned some credit for the complete problem solving activity. Secondly, these credits need to be accumulated from different networks the neuron participates in. This model, along with various credit assignment strategies, is tested on a classification (Heart disease diagnosis problem from UCI machine learning repository) and a regression problem (Mackey-Glass time series prediction problem).

1 Introduction

Co-evolution is one of the ways, used in literature [1–4], to implement the *divide-and-conquer* strategy for tackling complex computational problems. These implementations differ from each other on the basis of interactions between individuals, species and populations. Co-evolution occurs either at intra or inter-population level. The idea is to co-evolve complete solutions (systems) and sub-solutions (modules) simultaneously. These can be divided into two categories – single and two-level co-evolutionary methods. In single-level co-evolutionary methods the sub-components/modules are evolved in separate genetically isolated sub-populations. Fitness evaluation for these modules is carried out either by combining representative individuals from these sub-populations and then passing back the fitness of the system, thus created, to the representative individual [1, 2] or by sharing the fitness of current best module with other modules with similar input-output function [3]. While in two-level co-evolutionary methods [4] modules are evolved in a separate population along with systems in another. These modules are evaluated on the basis of their contribution to various systems in the second population.

In this work, we present one such two-level co-evolutionary model which co-evolves RBF Networks and Gaussian neurons in separate populations. This is similar to the Symbiotic Adaptive Neuro-Evolution or SANE [4]. Main differences between SANE and this model are the use of RBF Networks instead of Multi-Layer Perceptrons (MLPs) and the credit assignment strategies used for the fitness evaluation of neurons (which are Radial Basis Gaussian Functions (RBGFs) in this case). Also, in each generation, RBF networks can be trained using iRprop [5] (an improved version of Rprop [6]). SANE co-evolves a population of neurons and a population of two-layer feed forward networks. For the fitness of an individual in neuron population it uses the sum of fitnesses of a few good MLPs in the MLP population, in which that individual participates. We argue that this credit assignment strategy among neurons would work only if the problem is decomposable into modules that are mostly independent but otherwise, as is mostly the case, the fitness of a neuron should depend on the other neurons present in the MLP to model the interdependencies between the modules. This inspires the use of Gaussian Kernel Functions along with RBF networks instead of MLPs, where we can get a nice localized property. In other words, the influence of a RBGF on some distance from its center can be neglected. Thus, we should expect them to be relatively independent of each other, i.e., the effectiveness of one RBGF in a network should not be influenced by the presence of others. It does not hold for MLPs, where the effect of all hidden neurons should be taken into account at each point of the input space. Locality in RBF Networks has been exploited [7, 8] to solve the aforementioned credit assignment problem.

The rest of the paper is organized as follows. In Sect. 2 we describe the co-evolutionary model. Section 3 discusses various credit assignment strategies used, followed by the description of experiments and results in Sect. 4. Finally we conclude in Sect. 5 with discussion on results obtained.

2   Co-evolutionary Model

The co-evolutionary model consists of a network population (*netPop*) and a neuron population (*neuPop*). This is similar to SANE except for the use of RBGFs in *neuPop* and RBF networks in *netPop*. Figure 1 gives a pseudo code for the model. RBF networks in *netPop* consist of pointers to RBGFs. Each network is represented by an array of integers that stores the indices of RBGFs from *neuPop*. Each RBGF has the following real valued parameters associated with it

$$\mu_j, \sigma_j, w_k,$$
$$j \in \{0, \ldots, d-1\}, k \in \{0, \ldots, n-1\},$$

where d and n are the dimensionalities of input and output spaces respectively. In *neuPop* each RBGF is initialized with its center (μ) randomly chosen from one

```
Initialize neuPop and netPop
repeat
        clear fitness in neuPop and netPop
        for all networks in netPop do
                if LEARNING do
                        initialize all weights randomly
                        train the network partially on training data
                        evaluate the network on validation data
                        if LAMARCKIAN LEARNING do
                                accumulate the changes in neuron parameters in neuPop
                else evaluate the network on validation data
        sort netPop according to fitness
        if LAMARCKIAN LEARNING do
                write back the average changes in neuron parameters in neuPop
        evaluate neurons in neuPop using one credit assignment strategy (Sect. 3)
        sort neuPop according to fitness
        for all networks in netPop do
                reassign pointers to new positions of neurons
        apply variational operators to neuPop and netPop
until fixed number of generations
```

Fig. 1. Pseudo Code.

of the input data points. Widths (σ) and weights (w) are initialized randomly. Individuals in *netPop* point to random individuals in the *neuPop* initially.

For each individual i in *netPop* one RBF network *net*, consisting of the RBGFs from *neuPop* corresponding to the array entries of the individual i, is constructed. The fitness of this individual depends on how well the RBF Network performs on the validation data set

$$fitness^i = \frac{1}{MSE^{net}_{validation\_data} + \epsilon}, \qquad (1)$$

which is the inverse of mean-squared error achieved by RBF network *net* on the validation data set and ϵ is a small constant to prevent very high values of fitness if the mean-squared error approaches zero. Before evaluating the network on validation data it can be trained partially on a training data set to help evolution find good solutions in fewer generations. It can be viewed as lifetime learning of an individual in the evolutionary process. Now we can choose to copy the modified (trained) values of various neuron parameters back to the RBGF population (Lamarckian evolution) or we can choose not to copy them back and just use the trained individual to evaluate fitness (Baldwinian evolution). Since one neuron can take part in many networks, we need to make averaged genotypic changes, in the *neuPop*, corresponding to training in each network in *neuPop*. After training all the networks in the network population average modifications are made on neurons in *neuPop*, which is similar to the *Averaged Lamarckian Evolution Heuristic* proposed in [9]. Different fitness assignment strategies for fitness of neurons in *neuPop* are discussed in Sect. 3.

The breeding strategy used is similar to the one in SANE, though different crossover and mutation operators are used for the real coded parameters. After sorting the neuron population, each neuron from the top 25% of the population is crossed (crossover operator produces an equally distributed random number in between the two parent chromosomes) with another neuron chosen randomly from the top 25% neurons to produce an offspring. One random parent and the offspring replace two worst performing neurons in the *neuPop*. Thus in each generation 25% of population is replaced by new offspring. This aggressive strategy is balanced by a strong mutation strategy. For mutation, neuron centers and widths, for each neuron in the population, are perturbed with normally distributed noises with zero mean and one standard deviation. Weights are evolved only in absence of learning. Evolutionary algorithm used for the network level is identical to the neuron level. Since networks consist of pointers one point crossover is used. Each array value corresponding to the bottom 75% networks is then mutated to a random value with probability 0.01.

3 Fitness Assignment in Neuron Population

Fitness of a neuron in *neuPop* depends on the fitness of networks in *netPop*. It should depend on the number of networks it participates in, effectiveness of those networks and its contribution to those networks. The following three fitness assignment strategies try to take these factors into consideration.

3.1 Using a Few Good Networks

Each neuron gets the summed fitness of the top 25% networks, from *netPop*, in which the neuron participates. Though the fitness assignment strategy is exactly the same as SANE, yet improvement in performance is expected because of local characteristics of RBGFs. We will compare the performance of SANE and our model with this and other credit assignment strategies in Sect. 4.

3.2 Credit Sharing Along Orthogonal Dimensions

Here a credit apportionment strategy (proposed in [8]) is used to split the credit for the overall performance of the RBF network, first, into orthogonal niches and then the credit available for each individual niche is apportioned among individual RBGFs depending on how much they contribute to that niche. In an RBF Network for a set of (say) m basis functions ϕ_is, singular value decomposition (SVD) of transformed training data matrix $\mathbf{A}$, whose elements are $a_{ki} = \phi_i(\mathbf{x}_k)$, gives $\mathbf{A} = \mathbf{U}\mathbf{\Sigma}\mathbf{V}^\mathbf{T}$, where $\mathbf{U}$ has orthogonal columns $\mathbf{u}_1, \ldots \mathbf{u}_m$, $\mathbf{\Sigma}$ is a diagonal matrix with positive or zero elements (the *singular values*), and $\mathbf{V}$ an orthogonal matrix with entries v_{ij}. Credit available to each basis function ϕ_i is given by (for details refer to [8])

$$credit(\phi_i) = \sum_{j'=0}^{m-1} v_{ij'} f_{j'}/\sigma_{j'} \sum_{j=0}^{m-1} \sigma_j v_{ij} f_j, \qquad (2)$$

where $f_j(= \mathbf{u}_j \cdot f)$ is the inner product in the finite Euclidean basis $\{\delta_k\}, k = 1, \ldots, p$, where $\delta_k(\mathbf{x})$ is 1 at $\mathbf{x} = \mathbf{x}_k$ and 0 elsewhere and p is the number of training points. Credit available from a particular network is then multiplied with the network's fitness and summed over all networks in which the neuron participates to obtain neuron fitness.

3.3 Weights-Based Credit Assignment

Since the output of a RBF Network (net_j) is a weighted sum of activations of each RBGF (ϕ_i), these weights (w_{ij}s) can be used to evaluate the relative contribution of a RBGF to network j as

$$contribution(\phi_i) = |w_{ij}|^\beta / E(|w_{i'j}|^\beta), \qquad (3)$$

where $E(\cdot)$ denotes the mean value over all RBGFs (ϕ_is) in net_j. As discussed in [7], while evolving a single network we should have $\beta \in (1, 2)$ to encourage the desired behaviour of competition and cooperation among RBGFs with similar and different functionalities, respectively. Also, $\beta = 2.0$ produces too much of competition and $\beta = 1.0$ is insufficient to prevent competition among RBGFs with dissimilar activations, while $\beta = 1.5$ yields the desired behavior. In our experiments, we have used the three values of β (1, 1.5 and 2) although we do not expect to observe the aforementioned phenomenon as the neurons obtain their fitness from a group of networks rather than a single network.

4 Experimentation and Results

In the following, the co-evolutionary model (Sect. 2) along with different fitness assignment strategies (Sect. 3) are tested on a classification problem (Sect. 4.1) and a regression problem (Sect. 4.2). Different parameters used for experimentation are listed in table 1.

4.1 Heart Disease Diagnosis Problem

Heart disease diagnosis dataset, taken from UCI benchmark database [10], is used as the classification problem. This dataset has 270 instances with 13 continuously valued attributes; based on these attributes, any given pattern has to be classified into 2 classes, which are either presence or absence of the disease. The whole dataset is divided into - Training Set ($\frac{3}{4}$th of full dataset) and Testing Set (remaining $\frac{1}{4}$th). If learning is used then Training Set is further split into Training (half of full dataset) and Validation Set ($\frac{1}{4}$th of full dataset). Figure 2 shows the best and average fitnesses of individuals in the two populations for a simulation run with Baldwinian learning and a credit assignment strategy using weights (Sect. 3.3, $\beta = 1.5$).

Plot (a) in fig. 2 also shows the number of neurons that are in use at a given generation. From this plot we can observe that, with generations, the networks in

Table 1. Parameters used for experiments.

Parameter	Heart Disease		Mackey-Glass	
	no-learning	learning	no-learning	learning
Size of training data set	202	135	-	500
Size of validation data set	-	67	-	-
Size of test data set	68	68	-	500
Neuron population size	360	360	360	360
Network population size	20	20	20	20
Neurons per network	18	18	18	18
Top Neurons	90	90	90	90
Top Networks	6	6	6	6
Number of best networks for neuron fitness	5	5	5	5
Mutation Rate	10%	10%	10%	10%
Num. of generations - no learning	1000	-	-	-
- Baldwinian learning	-	100	-	200
- Lamarckian learning	-	50	-	100

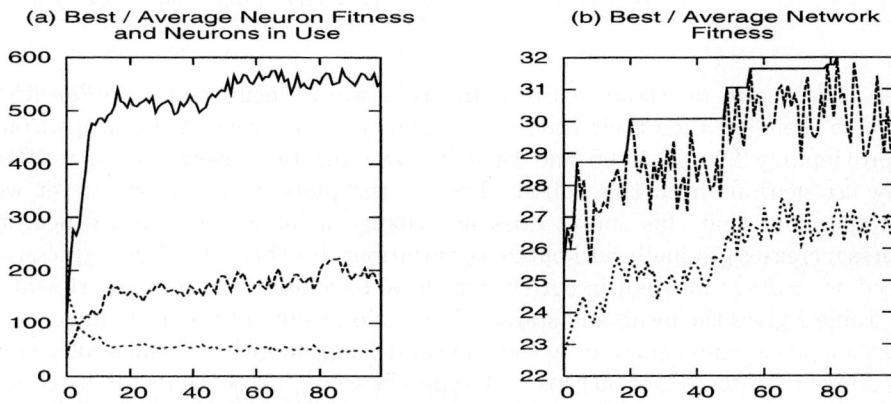

Fig. 2. Fitness variations in *neuPop* and *netPop* with number of generations. Plotted for a simulation run with Baldwinian learning. In plot (a) solid line (—), dashed line (- - -) and dotted line (···) show the maximum neuron fitness, average neuron fitness of the neurons in use and the neurons in use with the number of generations, respectively. In plot (b) they show the fitness of best network over all generations, fitness of best network in current generation and average fitness of all networks in *netPop* with the number of generations, respectively.

netPop are specialized to certain neurons in *neuPop*. After 100 generations these networks use 54 neurons from *neuPop*, with maximum neuron fitness being 553.5. Similar plots with Lamarckian learning show that this number is approximately the same ($\sim$ 53 after 50 generations and 55 after 100 generations) with maximum neuron fitness being 480.4 after 50 and 470.1 after 100 generations along with a much sharper rise in fitness early on. This lower fitness of best neuron is the result of averaging in Lamarckian evolution. Also, we observe the co-evolutionary effect where networks in *netPop* first search for good neurons in *neuPop* and

Table 2. Heart Disease diagnosis results (percentage correct classifications averaged over 30 runs).

Credit Assignment Strategy		No learning		Learning					
				Baldwinian			Lamarckian		
		Training	Testing	Training	Validation	Testing	Training	Validation	Testing
SANE	Mean	73.89	80.19						
	Std Dev	2.83	3.09						
Using good networks	Mean	84.24	80.07	90.62	91.59	82.99	89.68	89.95	82.45
	Std Dev	3.46	4.41	2.09	2.30	3.06	2.13	2.71	2.78
Credit sharing along orthogonal dimensions	Mean	73.68	75.22	89.95	91.69	82.55	88.58	88.47	83.87
	Std Dev	3.22	4.79	2.41	2.44	3.18	1.27	1.80	2.51
Using weights $\beta = 1.0$	Mean	82.52	78.89	89.98	91.14	83.48	89.80	90.50	82.84
	Std Dev	6.85	5.71	2.27	2.25	2.67	2.63	2.20	1.94
Using weights $\beta = 1.5$	Mean	83.93	79.58	89.93	91.84	82.99	89.23	90.4	82.75
	Std Dev	3.95	3.55	2.15	2.10	3.15	2.07	2.21	3.30
Using weights $\beta = 2.0$	Mean	85.10	80.97	90.49	91.69	82.21	89.16	90.05	82.89
	Std Dev	2.07	3.88	2.18	2.02	1.98	1.96	2.58	2.40

then concentrate on those neurons. In other words, neurons in *neuPop* first increase their use then their fitness. The number of neurons in use drops from approximately 220 to 30-60 and then it stays constant. Networks in *netPop* only use neurons from this subset. Though the plots do not show it, yet we can speculate that this subset does not change a lot as the average neuron fitness increases gradually without large variations. It is because of the aggressive breeding strategy inherent in SANE, which we have used for these experiments.

Table 2 gives the mean and standard deviation values of the percentage classification accuracies achieved by the co-evolutionary model with different credit assignment strategies, for 30 runs with different seeds. These values are listed for experiments without learning, Baldwinian learning and Lamarckian learning. In addition results obtained with SANE are also listed. Few observations can be made from these results - (1) Though SANE performs as good as others on test set, it is unable to fit the training data that well. On average, same credit assignment strategy with RBF networks produce 170 correct classifications out of 202 as against 149 correct classifications by SANE. (2) Learning does improve the performance significantly. (3) Lamarckian learning does not improve the performance over Baldwinian learning, though it produces similar results in half the number of generations (table 1). (4) As expected (Sect. 3.3) different values of β do not produce significantly different results. (5) These results are comparable with the existing results available in the literature (83.9% [11] and 84.9% [12]).

4.2 Mackey-Glass Time Series Prediction Problem

The Mackey-Glass time series is generated by the following differential equation using fourth order Runge-Kutta method with initial condition $x(0) = 1.2$ and time step of 1.

$$\dot{x}(t) = \beta x(t) + \frac{\alpha x(t-\tau)}{1+x^{10}(t-\tau)}, \quad (4)$$

where $\alpha = 0.2$, $\beta = -0.1$, $\tau = 17$ as used in [7,8,13-15]. Each network receives four past data points $x(t)$, $x(t-6)$, $x(t-12)$ and $x(t-18)$ as inputs and predicts 6 time steps ahead ($x(t+6)$). For predicting further steps ahead iterative predictions of $x(t+6)$, $x(t+12)$, ..., $x(t+84)$ are used during testing, e.g. the network uses its own prediction for time step $t+6$ and the input points $x(t)$, $x(t-6)$ and $x(t-12)$ to predict $x(t+12)$. For training $x(t+6)$ values are used as targets. This setup is same as that used in [13,16]. 500 points starting from 118 are used for training and following 500 points are used for testing. No validation set is used for comparison purposes. For fitness evaluation of networks in (1) training set is used instead of validation set.

Table 3. Mackey-Glass time series prediction results (normalized RMS Error on test set, averaged over 30 runs) with Baldwinian learning.

Credit Assignment Strategy		Generalization Performance	
		$\Delta t = 6$	$\Delta t = 84$
Using good networks	Mean	0.0296	0.0995
	Std Dev	0.0019	0.0156
Credit sharing along	Mean	0.0299	0.1021
orthogonal dimensions	Std Dev	0.0020	0.0093
Using weights $\beta = 1.0$	Mean	0.0303	0.1032
	Std Dev	0.0015	0.0085
Using weights $\beta = 1.5$	Mean	0.0301	0.1013
	Std Dev	0.0019	0.0119
Using weights $\beta = 2.0$	Mean	0.0298	0.1043
	Std Dev	0.0019	0.0140
Other Results			
Ensemble of 20 RBF	mean	0.0358	0.1106
networks	Std Dev	0.0038	0.0206
EPNet [13]	mean	0.02	0.06

Table 3 gives the mean and standard deviation values, of the normalized root-mean-squared (RMS) errors achieved on test set by the co-evolutionary model with different credit assignment strategies, for 30 runs with different seeds. Here normalized RMS errors are obtained by dividing the absolute RMS error values by the standard deviation of $x(t)$ [13,14,16]. Results are listed only for experiments with Baldwinian learning as no-learning does not produce good generalization performance (normalized RMS error ~ 1.2 in 2000 generations) and Lamarckian learning results are again very similar to Baldwinian learning. Observations 2, 3 and 4 from Sect. 4.1 are again verified from these results. These results are comparable to those obtained by an ensemble of RBF networks with similar computational overhead (20 networks with 18 neurons each), though there are better results available in the literature [13] (see table 3). Each network in the ensemble is trained using iRprop with centers initialized using K-means-Clustering [17, pages 187–188], widths initialized randomly between 0 and 1 and weights and bias values initialized by means of linear regression. After training, best network was tested on testing data.

5 Conclusion

A two-level co-evolutionary model which co-evolves RBF Networks and Gaussian neurons in separate populations was presented in this work along with different credit assignment strategies for evaluating the fitness of neurons in neuron population. These strategies were evaluated, on the basis of their performance, in conjunction with the co-evolutionary model on two test problems. In between these two populations a co-evolutionary effect was observed, where networks in network population first search for good neurons in neuron population and then consolidate on these neurons.

It was argued that the use of RBF networks instead of MLPs was beneficial in such a co-evolutionary model because of local characteristics of Gaussian neurons. Which was also verified by a comparison of the model with SANE on heart disease diagnosis problem. Other than the use of RBF networks, this model only differed with SANE in real-coded parameters and variational operators and had same fitness assignment strategy and breeding strategy.

The introduction of learning produced a significant improvement in performance of the system on both heart disease diagnosis problem and Mackey-Glass time series prediction problem. The number of generations for experiments with or without learning were chosen to allow similar running times. Further, Lamarckian learning was able to produce similar results in half the number of generations.

The results obtained on the two test problems were comparable to the results available in literature, although different credit assignment strategies used did not produce significantly different results, specially in the presence of learning, for the two test problems used. Also, more experiments with other benchmarks are needed to make firm conclusions about the applicability of the introduced approach.

References

1. Potter, M.A., Jong, K.A.D.: Cooperative Coevolution: An Architecture for Evolving Coadapted Subcomponents. Evolutionary Computation **8** (2000) 1–29
2. Yong, C.H., Miikkulainen, R.: Cooperative Coevolution of Multi-Agent Systems. Technical Report AI01-287, Department of computer Sciences, The University of Texas at Austin, Austin, TX 78712 USA (2001)
3. Smalz, R., Conrad, M.: Combining Evolution With Credit Apportionment: A New Learning Algorithm for Neural Nets. Neural Networks **7** (1994) 341–351
4. Moriarty, D.E., Miikkulainen, R.: Forming Neural Networks Through Efficient and Adaptive Coevolution. Evolutionary Computation **5** (1997) 373–399

5. Igel, C., Hüsken, M.: Empirical Evaluation of the Improved Rprop Learning Algorithm. Neurocomputing **50** (2003) 105–123
6. Riedmiller, M., Braun, H.: A Direct Adaptive Method for Faster Backpropagation Learning: The RPROP algorithm. In: Proceedings of the IEEE International Conference on Neural Networks, San Francisco, CA (1993) 586–591
7. Whitehead, B.A., Choate, T.D.: Cooperative-Competitive Genetic Evolution of Radial Basis Function Centers and Widths for Time Series Prediction. IEEE Transactions on Neural Networks **7** (1996) 869–880
8. Whitehead, B.A.: Genetic Evolution of Radial Basis Function Coverage Using Orthogonal Niches. IEEE Transactions on Neural Networks **7** (1996) 1525–1528
9. Hüsken, M., Gayko, J.E., Sendhoff, B.: Optimization for Problem Classes - Neural Networks that Learn to Learn. In X.Yao, ed.: IEEE Symposium on Combinations of Evolutionary Computation and Neural Networks, IEEE Press (2000) 98-109.
10. Blake, C., Merz, C.: UCI Repository of machine learning databases (1998) http://www.ics.uci.edu/~mlearn/MLRepository.html.
11. Khare, V., X.Yao: Artificial Speciation and Automatic Modularisation. In Wang, L., Tan, K.C., Furuhashi, T., Kim, J.H., Yao, X., eds.: Proceedings of the 4th Asia-Pacific Conference on Simulated Evolution And Learning (SEAL'02). 1, Singapore (2002) 56–60
12. Yao, X., Liu, Y.: Making Use of Population Information in Evolutionary Artificial Neural Networks. IEEE Transactions on Systems, Man and Cybernetics, Part B: Cybernetics **28** (1998) 417–425
13. Yao, X., Liu, Y.: A New Evolutionary System for Evolving Artificial Neural Networks. IEEE Transactions on Neural Networks **8** (1997) 694–713
14. Farmer, J.D., Sidorowich, J.J.: Predicting chaotic time series. Physical Review Letters **59** (1987) 845–848
15. Mackey, M.C., Glass, L.: Oscillation and chaos in physiological control systems. Science **197** (1977) 287–289
16. Martinetz, T.M., Berkovich, S.G., Schulten, K.J.: 'Neural-Gas' Network for Vector Quantization and its Application to Time-Series Prediction. IEEE Transactions on Neural Networks **4** (1993) 558–569
17. Bishop, C.M.: Neural Networks for Pattern Recogntion. Oxford University Press (1995)

A Visual Demonstration of Convergence Properties of Cooperative Coevolution

Liviu Panait, R. Paul Wiegand*, and Sean Luke

George Mason University, Fairfax, VA 22030
{lpanait,sean}@cs.gmu.edu, paul@tesseract.org

Abstract. We introduce a model for cooperative coevolutionary algorithms (CCEAs) using partial mixing, which allows us to compute the expected long-run convergence of such algorithms when individuals' fitness is based on the maximum payoff of some N evaluations with partners chosen at random from the other population. Using this model, we devise novel visualization mechanisms to attempt to qualitatively explain a difficult-to-conceptualize pathology in CCEAs: the tendency for them to converge to suboptimal Nash equilibria. We further demonstrate visually how increasing the size of N, or biasing the fitness to include an ideal-collaboration factor, both improve the likelihood of optimal convergence, and under which initial population configurations they are not much help.

1 Introduction

Cooperative coevolutionary algorithms (CCEAs) are coevolutionary algorithms where individuals from different populations are evaluated based on how well they perform together as a team. Commonly all individuals in a team receive the same resulting fitness (payoff). Applications of this method include optimization of inventory control systems [1], learning constructive neural networks [2], rule learning [3], and multi-agent learning [4]. The presumed advantage of CCEAs is decomposition of the search space: each of the N populations learns a different aspect (projection) of the problem, instead of one single population having to learn the joint problem at one time. Unfortunately, though each CCEA population is searching its projection of the problem at a time, that projection is constantly changing. The result is that it is easy for the algorithm to get tricked by misleading information provided by poor samples of the projected space. This leads to algorithms that tend to prefer individuals in one population that will do well with *many* individuals in the other population(s) (*relative overgeneralization*), whether or not these combinations are globally optimal [5].

We have recently examined approaches to overcome relative overgeneralization. In [4,6] we showed that this can be countered through judicious *biasing* of how individuals are evaluated. Specifically, the fitness of an individual is a

---

* R. Paul Wiegand currently holds a postdoctoral position with the American Society for Engineering Education and conducts research at the Naval Research Laboratory.

weighted sum of how well it performed when teamed with individuals from the other population(s), plus how well it performed with its *ideal collaborator* (or some approximation thereof). This biasing is quite effective at eliminating relative overgeneralization, at least in the simple problems we presented and analyzed formally.

Conceptualizing the phenomenon of overgeneralization, and the effects of ideal-collaboration, is quite difficult. A goal of this paper is to provide an intuitive understanding of the issues involved. The paper begins by extending the existing theoretical framework for analyzing cooperative coevolution by replacing the *complete mixing* model for fitness assessment with one using expected maximum payoff with multiple partners. This model can be used to determine the basins of attraction for the coevolutionary search. Then we will introduce a technique for visualizing these basins of attraction in a coevolutionary search space for small numbers of dimensions. As each "dimension" is a separate genome in the search space, obviously only trivial search spaces can be visualized in this way, but it will be more than sufficient for our goal. Last, we will use this new technique to show expected outcomes with and without biasing.

2 Evolutionary Game Theory

Our approach to coevolution follows Potter's [7] model of cooperative coevolution: each population contains individuals that represent a particular component of the problem, so that one member from each population is needed in order to assemble a complete solution. Evaluation of an individual from a particular population is performed by assembling the individual with collaborating partners from other populations. To combat noise in the evaluation process due to choice of partners, multiple evaluations may be performed. Aside from evaluation, the populations are evolved independently.

An appealing abstract mathematical model for this system comes from the biology literature: evolutionary game theory [8,9]. EGT provides a formalism based on traditional game theory and dynamical systems techniques to analyze the limiting behaviors of interacting populations under long-term evolution. For specifics about applying EGT to the analysis of multi-population cooperative coevolutionary algorithms, see [5].

In this paper, we consider only two-population models. Expressing the quality of complete solutions through a pair of *payoff matrices*, one for each population. For this paper, we assume a symmetric model where each payoff matrix is the transpose of the other. When individuals from the first population interact with individuals from the second, a payoff matrix A is used, while individuals from the second population receive payoffs defined by A^T. We will also use an *infinite population* model. A population can be thought of not as a set of individuals, but rather as a finite-length vector x of proportions, where each element in the vector is the proportion of a given *genotype* in the population. As the proportions in a valid vector must sum to one, all legal vectors make up what is commonly known as the *unit simplex*, denoted Δ^n, n here is the number of distinct genotypes possible, $\mathbf{x} \in \Delta^n : x_i \in [0,1], \sum_{i=1}^{n} x_i = 1$. The joint, two-population space of a CCEA is the product simplex $\Delta^n \times \Delta^m$.

Previous approaches to modeling CCEAs via EGT [4–6, 10] assume that an individual's fitness is assessed as the *average* of payoffs received when in combination with *every* member of the cooperating population; this is also known as *complete mixing*. Instead we will use a more realistic fitness assessment: the maximum payoff obtained when the individual is combined N times with individuals, chosen with replacement, from the other population. Maximum has been shown to produce superior results to average in recent studies [11].

Theorem 1. *Let the payoff for individual i when teamed with individual j be a_{ij}, and $(p_j)_{j \in 1..n}$ be the probability distribution for the individuals in the population of partners for i. If the a_{ij} values are sorted in increasing order $(a_{i1} \leq a_{i2} \leq .. \leq a_{in})$, the expected maximum payoff of i over N pairwise combinations with random partners $j_1...j_N$ from the other population is*

$$\sum_{j=1}^{n} a_{ij} \left(\left(\sum_{k=1}^{j} p_k \right)^N - \left(\sum_{k=1}^{j-1} p_k \right)^N \right)$$

Proof. The expected maximum payoff is a linear combination of the actual payoff a_{ij} times the probability that it is the maximum of pairwise combinations with N random partners. As the a_{ij} values are sorted, it follows that $\left(\sum_{k=1}^{j} p_k \right)^N$ represents the probability of choosing all N partners from the $1....j$ set. Therefore, the probability that a_{ij} is the maximum of N combinations is equal to the probability of extracting all partners from the $1...j$ set, minus the probability of choosing all such partners except j (that is, $\left(\sum_{k=1}^{j-1} p_k \right)^N$). Hence, the expected maximum is $\sum_{j=1}^{n} a_{ij} \left(\left(\sum_{k=1}^{j} p_k \right)^N - \left(\sum_{k=1}^{j-1} p_k \right)^N \right)$. ■

Interestingly, the extreme setting $N = 1$ results in same fitness per individual as in the complete mixing model. As we will see later on, our extension shows improvements as the number of partners is increased in the two populations.

3 Related Work

Traditionally, EC applications of evolutionary game theory have focussed almost entirely on modeling coevolutionary algorithms that use proportionate selection and employ complete mixing. There are several exceptions, however. Ficici [12] considers several alternative selection methods, including truncation selection, (μ, λ)-ES selection, linear ranking selection, and Boltzman selection; however, this work concerns single population, competitive models of coevolution. Wiegand [5] presents two partial mixing models for cooperative coevolution, one for a complete mixing but weighted with a scheme that prefers more fit individuals (from previous generations) over less fit ones; and one that models fitness assessment as the average result of partnering with a finite number of collaborators.

Table 1. Examples of coordination games: (a) a simple 2x2 coordination game; (b) the Climb game; (c) the Penalty game.

20	0
10	15

(a)

21	0	10
0	17	16
10	10	15

(b)

20	10	0
10	15	10
0	10	20

(c)

Finally, Ming [13] analyzes CEA behaviors on two-bit landscapes using various partnering strategies, indicating that even in such a simple setting such choices can have profound effects on runtime behavior.

Visualization of basins of attraction is a common approach for understanding behaviors in many kinds of dynamical systems [14]; however, they are often restricted to two dimensions and they are not commonly employed by the evolutionary computation community. Elsewhere, visualizing dynamical system properties have proved helpful in understanding aspects of other kinds of evolutionary systems. Visualizing reverse iterates of dynamical trajectories in genetic algorithms has revealed interesting properties of locations of fixed points outside the population space one normally considers [15]. In coevolutionary systems, the aforementioned paper by Ficici [12] attempts to illustrate chaotic and periodic behaviors using cobweb plots. Recent work in the analysis of cooperative coevolutionary algorithms has demonstrated the usefulness of plotting measures of relative sizes of basins of attraction using rain-gauge methods [4,10]. Additionally, trajectory plots in the simplex and Cartesian-product simplex spaces of evolutionary and coevolutionary systems have revealed the at-times-counterintuitive dynamics of these systems [5,10,8]. Finally, visualization of transitional state information in finite populations using Markov models of evolution [16] and coevolution [17] have helped illustrate the differences between the long-term dynamical systems predictions and the true algorithm behaviors.

4 Visualizing Basins of Attraction

We employ the EGT model with expected maximum fitness as described in the previous section, using fitness proportionate selection and no variational operators. We iterate the model until the proportion for one of the genotypes in each population exceeds a threshold of 0.99995, or until 50000 generations. Given the initial configuration, EGT models the coevolutionary search as a deterministic process. That is, for each initial point in the search space, we can compute to which equilibrium point it converges. As [5] shows, the populations are expected to converge to Nash equilibrium points in the payoff matrix (elements that are maximal on their row and column).

4.1 2x2 Coordination Games

Imagine the payoff matrix (a) in Table 1, where each population contains two kinds of genotypes: "1"s and "2"s. The higher payoffs are achieved by either

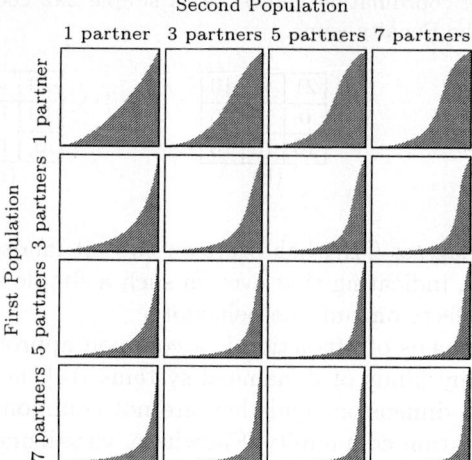

Fig. 1. Basins of attraction for the simple 2x2 coordination game, when using different numbers of partners for each of the two populations. The proportion of 1s in the first population decreases from 1.0 (top) to 0.0 (bottom) in each squared image. Similarly, the proportion of 1s in the second population decreases from 1.0 (left) to 0.0 (right) in each squared image. The basin of attraction for the (1,1) point is colored white, and the one for (2,2) is colored gray.

pairs (1,1) and (2,2). Both of these are Nash equilibria points. A payoff of 10 is received by the pair (2,1); this increases the difficulty of the search process.

As there are only two genotypes, the state of the coevolutionary search as modeled by EGT can be described at each instant by only two proportions – p_1 and p_2 (proportions of 2s in the first and in the second population). For visualization, we consider the cartesian product of the two spaces of initial configurations (ICs) for the two populations, which is a two dimensional square from (0.0,0.0) to (1.0,1.0). p_1 increases from top to bottom, and p_2 increases from left to right. The width and height of the square are divided into 100 segments, and the center of each segment is taken as the proportion of 2s in the initial configuration.

To visualize the basins of attraction, we mark with different colors the sets of initial configurations from which the EGT model converges to the specific equilibrium point. As we have only two Nash equilibria in our example, we use white for the (1,1) equilibrium and gray for (2,2).

Figure 1 show the basins of attraction when using different numbers of partners for each of the populations. As expected, if both populations start with very high proportions of 1s, the system converges to the (1,1) equilibrium. Similarly, if both populations start with very high proportions of 2s, the system converges to the (2,2) equilibrium. The visualization shows that using more partners for both populations leads to an increase in the size of the basin of attraction of the optimal Nash equilibrium point (1,1). This result is in accordance with empirical findings reported in [11].

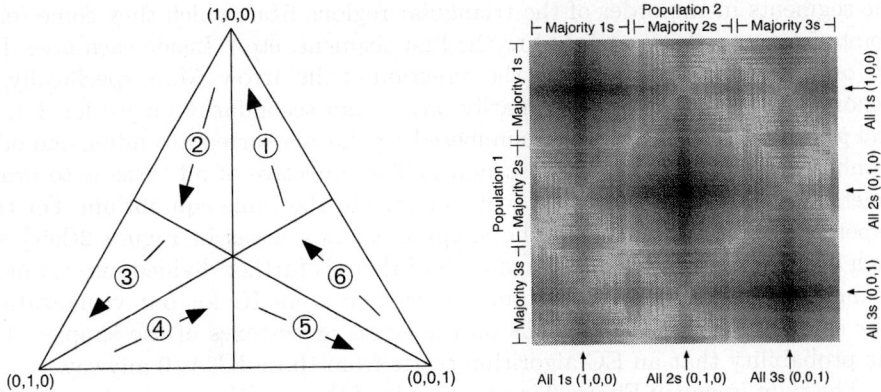

Fig. 2. (left): Our projection divides the simplex Δ^3 into six equal-area triangles; arrows shows the direction for sorting points in each area. (right): Visualization of the cartesian product of two simplexes; see details in the text.

Additionally, gains in performance decrease with more partners. As more partners lead to longer runtimes, there may be a maximal justifiable number of partners. We plan to investigate this issue in the future.

Also, the visualization of the basins of attraction reveals an interesting artifact: the basin of attraction for the suboptimal peak tends to *grow* in the upper area of each image as we increase the number of collaborators for the second population. Thus, when the first population starts with a majority of 1s and the second population with a majority of 2s, the final results are *worse* if we provide the second population with more collaborators. One explanation: an increase in the number of partners for the second population significantly increases the expected fitness of the 2s, but does not dramatically affect the fitness of the 1s.

4.2 3x3 Coordination Games

Visualizing basins of attraction in 2x2 coordination games is relatively straightforward. In this section, we describe how the visualization can be extended to the more complicated case of 3x3 coordination games.

For a given population, possible proportions (points from the Δ^3 space) are projected onto the vertical or (for the second population) horizontal axis by first dividing the Δ^3 space into subregions, where all points in a given subregion have the same ordering of genotype proportion (1s more common than 2s, which are more common than 3s, for example). These subregions define the primary sorting for projecting points onto the axis. In this way we hope to see patterns emerging based on similarity in overall proportion.

Our projection of Δ^3 onto one dimension starts by dividing it into six equal-area triangles, as in Figure 2 (left). ICs in areas 1-2 have a majority of 1s in the population, and similarly areas 3-4 and 5-6 have majorities of 2s and 3s. The single axis is divided into six equal segments and points are assigned to the segments in the order of the triangular regions from which they come (e.g., points from area 1 are assigned to the first segment, etc.). Inside each area, ICs are ordered lexicographically in the direction of the arrow. More specifically, in regions 1-2, sorting is done primarily on p_1, and secondarily on p_2; for 3-4, p_2 and p_3; for 5-6, p_3 and p_1. Even-numbered regions are sorted ascending and odd-numbered regions are sorted descending. The objective of all these is to group together regions that we expect will converge to the same equilibrium. For this paper, we sample 216 ICs in the simplex: the six areas in Figure 2(left) are each divided into six triangles, and each of them is further divided into six more triangles. The center of each resulting triangle is an IC for our visualization. Our sampling does not cover ICs on the edges or vertexes of the simplex, but the probability that an EC algorithm starts from those ICs is 0 anyway.

The right image in Figure 2 is an example of the resulting projection of $(\Delta^3)^2$ onto 2-D. The sorting described above creates 2-D regions reflecting majority-1, majority-2, and majority-3 areas. Borders between those regions are the mixture of the two areas respectively. Dark lines in the figure show locations that are all 1s, 2s, and 3s in one or the other population (the vertices of the simplex).

In [4], we introduced a biased cooperative coevolution approach, and studied its application to two multi-agent coordination problems: Climb and Penalty. Both domains represent problems that associate penalties with miscoordinated actions, while providing suboptimal collaborations that avoid penalties. In this paper, we visualize basins of attraction for equilibria points in these two problems. The payoff matrices for Climb and Penalty are presented in Figure 1. Climb has two Nash equilibria, the optimum (1,1) and the suboptimum (2,2), and is strongly deceptive. Penalty has three Nash equilibria: both 1s, both 2s, and both 3s; both 2s is suboptimal, but is more forgiving if one or the other population deviates from the Nash equilibrium.

Figure 3(a) shows the basins of attraction[1] for the Climb coordination game when using different numbers of partners in each population. The images show that the "deceptiveness" of the problem domain decreases as the number of partners is increased. When using a single partner, it appears that the coevolutionary search will find the optima if at least one of the populations starts with a large number of 1s. However, as the number of partners is increased we observe that the basin of attraction for the suboptimal equilibria reduces to areas where at least one of the initial populations has a very large proportion of 2s or 3s: the more partners are used, the larger the proportion required to still converge to the sub-optimum.

One interesting feature we note: if either population is dominated by 2s (as opposed to 3s), the system is less likely to converge to the optimum even if the other population is mostly 1s and 3s. This is due to the large, attractive basin of attraction for 2 is very large.

---

[1] Some of the images, especially the one with 1 partner for each population, contain some gray dots. Those are visualization artifacts due to the threshold of 0.99995 we used for convergence.

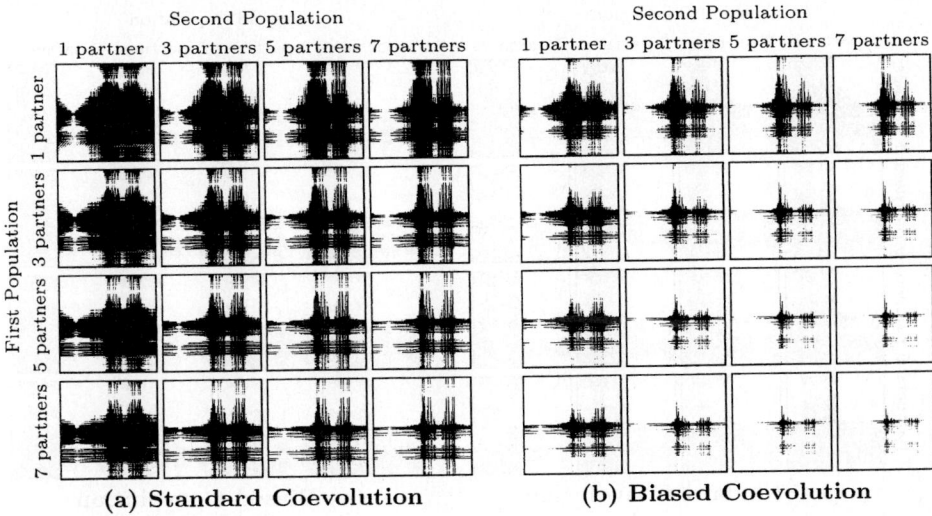

Fig. 3. Basins of attraction in Climb problem when using (a) standard and (b) biased coevolution, and 1, 3, 5 and 7 partners per population. White and black mark the basins of attraction for the (1,1) and (2,2) equilibria.

Figure 4(a) presents the basins of attraction for the Penalty game. We observe that the two global optima cover most of the space even when a single partner is used; the suboptimal equilibria covers mainly areas where at least one of the population started with a high percentage of 2s, and the other population has the 1s and 3s equally distributed – this increases the percentage of miscoordinations. As the number of partners is increased, the basin of attraction for the (2,2) point reduces to only areas where *both* populations start with almost only 2s. The visualization of the basins of attraction suggests that Penalty is a much easier coordination game than Climb.

We note a thin diagonal line in the 1-partner, 1-partner graph in Figure 4(a). Interestingly, this is due to the fact that if the proportion of 1s in one population is *equal* to the proportion of 3s in the other population, such combinations are heavily penalized and the system converges to the suboptimal (2,2) equilibrium.

Biased Coevolution. As discussed in [4–6], much of the convergence to suboptimal solutions is due to relative overgeneralization, and one approach to dealing with this is to bias the fitness by basing it partly on the payoff of collaboration with the ideal partner for that individual (or an approximation thereof). Here, we compute the fitness of an individual as the average of the maximum payoff of N collaborations (as before), and the payoff of the individual with its ideal partner. We assume the ideal partner is known for each individual. Figures 3(b) and 4(b) present the basins of attraction for the equilibrium points for the biased coevolutionary search. The images suggest that biasing further reduces the basins of attraction for suboptimal equilibria, and when biasing, increasing the

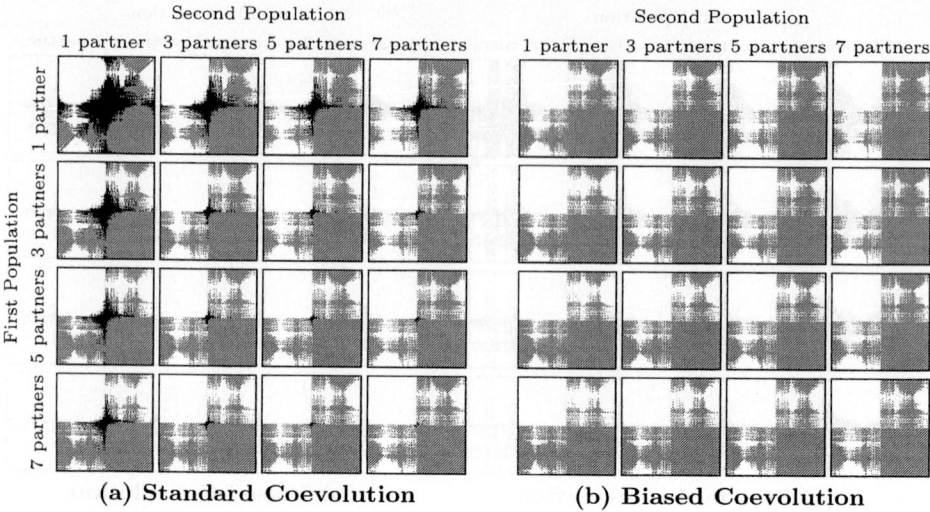

Fig. 4. Basins of attraction in Penalty problem when using (a) standard and (b) biased coevolution, and 1, 3, 5 and 7 partners per population. White, black and gray mark basins of attraction for the (1,1), (2,2) and (3,3) equilibria.

number of partners helps even further. In fact in the Penalty domain, the basins of attraction for the two globally optimal equilibria cover the entire space, even with a single partner.

5 Conclusions and Future Work

In this paper we provided an evolutionary game theoretic formalism for computing the expected convergence when an individual is teamed with partners N times with replacement, and the maximum payoff is used as the individual's fitness. We then used this formalism to provide a visualization of convergence properties when teamed with multiple partners. The goal of the visualization was to demonstrate qualitatively how increases in number of partners affects the likely convergence to the globally optimal Nash equilibria, and how including collaboration with the ideal partner as part of the fitness function, as was done in [5, 4, 6], further reduces convergence to suboptima. This visualization was done straightforwardly for 2-genotype populations, and through a novel linearization of 3-D space, for 3-genotype populations.

Future research will investigate formal models for other complex collaboration schemes, and the visualization of basins of attraction for even more complicated problem domains. We believe that both the model and the visualization techniques improve our intuition of how CCEAs work, and how they can be better applied to optimization tasks.

References

1. Eriksson, R., Olsson, B.: Cooperative coevolution in inventory control optimisation. In Smith, G., Steele, N., Albrecht, R., eds.: Proceedings of the Third International Conference on Artificial Neural Networks and Genetic Algorithms, University of East Anglia, Norwich, UK, Springer (1997)
2. Potter, M., De Jong, K.: Cooperative coevolution: An architecture for evolving coadapted subcomponents. Evolutionary Computation 8 (2000) 1–29
3. Potter, M.A., De Jong, K.A., Grefenstette, J.J.: A coevolutionary approach to learning sequential decision rules. In: Proceedings from the Sixth International Conference on Genetic Algorithms, Morgan Kaufmann (1995) 366–372
4. Panait, L., Wiegand, R.P., Luke, S.: Improving coevolutionary search for optimal multiagent behaviors. In: Proceedings of the Eighteenth International Joint Conference on Artificial Intelligence (IJCAI), Acapulco, Mexico, Morgan Kaufmann (2003) 653–658
5. Wiegand, R.P.: An Analysis of Cooperative Coevolutionary Algorithms. PhD thesis, George Mason University, Fairfax, Virginia (2004)
6. Panait, L., Wiegand, R.P., Luke, S.: A sensitivity analysis of a cooperative coevolutionary algorithm biased for optimization. In Poli, R., et al, eds.: Proceedings of the Genetic and Evolutionary Computation Conference (GECCO) 2004, Berlin, Germany, Springer (2004) (to appear)
7. Potter, M.: The Design and Analysis of a Computational Model of Cooperative CoEvolution. PhD thesis, George Mason University, Fairfax, Virginia (1997)
8. Maynard-Smith, J.: Evolution and the Theory of Games. Cambridge University Press (1982)
9. Hofbauer, J., Sigmund, K.: Evolutionary Games and Population Dynamics. Cambridge University Press (1998)
10. Wiegand, R.P., Liles, W., De Jong, K.: Modeling variation in cooperative coevolution using evolutionary game theory. In Poli, R., et al, eds.: Foundations of Genetic Algorithms (FOGA) VII, Morgan Kaufmann (2002) 231–248
11. Wiegand, R.P., Liles, W., De Jong, K.: An empirical analysis of collaboration methods in cooperative coevolutionary algorithms. In Spector, L., et al, eds.: Proceedings of the Genetic and Evolutionary Computation Conference (GECCO) 2001, Morgan Kaufmann (2001) 1235–1242
12. Ficici, S., Pollack, J.: Game–theoretic investigation of selection methods used in evolutionary algorithms. In Whitley, D., ed.: Proceedings of CEC 2000, IEEE Press (2000) 880–887
13. Chang, M., Ohkura, K., Ueda, K., Sugiyama, M.: Modeling coevolutionary genetic algorithms on two-bit landscapes: Partnering strategies. In Greenwood, G., et al, eds.: Proceedings of CEC 2004, IEEE Press (2004) (to appear)
14. Alligood, K., Sauer, T., Yorke, J.: Chaos: An Introduction to Dynamical Systems. Springer–Verlag (1996)
15. Juliany, J., Vose, M.: The genetic algorithm fractal. Evolutionary Computation 2 (1994) 165–180
16. Spears, W.M., De Jong, K.: Analyzing gas using markov models with semantically ordered and lumped states. In Belew, R., Vose, M., eds.: Foundations of Genetic Algorithms (FOGA) IV, Morgan Kaufmann (1996)
17. Liekens, A., Eikelder, H., Hilbers, P.: Predicting genetic drift in 2×2 games. In Poli, R., et al, eds.: Proceedings of the Genetic and Evolutionary Computation Conference (GECCO) 2004, Berlin, Germany, Springer (2004) (to appear)

Cooperative Coevolution of Image Feature Construction and Object Detection

Mark E. Roberts and Ela Claridge

School of Computer Science, University of Birmingham, B15 2TT, UK
{M.E.Roberts,E.Claridge}@cs.bham.ac.uk

Abstract. Most previous approaches using genetic programming to solve object detection tasks have evolved classifiers which are basically arithmetic expressions using pre-extracted local pixel statistics as terminals. The pixel statistics chosen are often highly general, meaning that the classifier cannot exploit useful aspects of the domain, or are too domain specific and overfit. This work presents a system whereby a feature construction stage is simultaneously coevolved along side the GP object detectors. Effectively, the system learns both stages of the visual process simultaneously. This work shows initial results of using this technique on both artificial and natual images and shows how it can quickly adapt to form general solutions to difficult scale and rotation invariant problems.

1 Introduction

Ever since its inception, people have quite rightly seen the potential of using genetic programming (GP) to aid in the production of algorithms to process and understand images. The size and complexity of the data involved makes the design of imaging algorithms a very hard task, normally requiring the skill of very experienced researchers and, because of the complexity, the easiest route is often to create highly domain specific methods, sacrificing generalisation ability. Obviously, the ideal situation would be one in which expertise in image processing is not necessary in order to create such algorithms and non-experts could create well performing systems just by providing examples of the desired behaviour. This paper outlines a method by which this can be acheived using cooperative coevolution to learn the parts of a vision system that would normally use domain specific knowledge or generic "one size fits all" methods.

1.1 Previous Work

GP has provided many new ways in which to create or enhance imaging algorithms. One way which has seen widespread use is the approach of using GP to evolve object detection algorithms in the form of arithmetic or simple programmatic expressions which use sets of pre-extracted local image statistics as terminals. The end result of this is a classifier which is applied at each pixel and determines its classification based on statistics of the region around it.

Many people have used variations on this technique, with the variations normally due to the use of different sets of statistics as terminals, as shown in Table 1. It can be seen from this table that there is massive variation in the choice of statistics. The sets that are chosen are either highly domain specific, or are at the other end of the spectrum and are extremely general and not suited to harnessing aspects of the domain that might lead to a good classification. It is important to remember here that having extraneous terminals harms the performance of the evolution [1], and that the popular belief that "GP will only use the terminals it needs" is misguided. So, it is therefore very important to extract features conservatively – in effect we need to optimise the set of features chosen.

Table 1. Pixel statistics used in previous work.

Author	Statistic set	Total statistics
Tackett [2]	Means and standard deviations of small and large rectangular windows plus the global mean and standard deviation.	7
Daida [3]	Pixel value, 3x3 area mean, 5x5 area mean, 5x5 Laplacian response, 5x5 Laplacian response of a 3x3 mean.	5
Howard [4]	Rotationally invariant statistics of 4 concentric rings. For each ring the statistics measured mean and standard deviation, number of edges and a measure of edge distribution.	16
Howard [5]	3x3, 5x5, 7x7 and 9x9 means, 5x5, 7x7, 9x9 perimeter means and variances, and the differences between a 3x3 area mean and 5x5, 7x7 and 9x9 perimeter means.	13
Winkeler [6]	Means and variances of 26 zones. Zone 1 was the entire 20x20 area, zones 2-5 were the four 10x10 quadrants, 6-10 were 5 20x4 horizontal strips, and 11-26 were 16 5x5 pixel squares.	52
Ross [7]	Features related to cross and plane polarized microscopy output. Angle of max. gradient, angle of max. position, max. colour during rotation, min. intensity, and min. colour.	9
Zhang [8]	Means and variances of 4 large and 4 small squares, plus the means and variances of 2 long and 2 short line profiles, passing horizontally and vertically through the origin.	20
Zhang [9]	Used 3 different terminals sets using means and variances of each zone. Set 1 used two different sized squares, set 2 had four concentric squares, and set 3 had 3 concentric circles.	4, 8, 6

Most work in this area has focused on the evolution of the detection algorithms and have not studied the choice of pixel statistics (except [9] which compared the performance of 3 different statistic sets). In this work, we propose that instead of using these fixed statistic sets, we can use of cooperative coevolution [10] to allow the pixel statistic sets to adapt to the problem domain. We show how the pixel statistic sets which produce the inputs to the detectors, can be simultaneously coevolved alongside the detectors themselves, allowing the system to optimise both the feature construction and object detection stages.

This work has links with many areas, an important one being the that of *feature transformation*, which is in turn normally broken down into feature subset selection (FSS), feature extraction (FE), and feature construction (FC) [11]. Pixel statistic sets can be viewed as performing feature construction[1], creating new, highler level, features from the raw pixel data. The detection algorithms can also be seen as performing both feature extraction and feature subset selection.

There has been some previous work evolving feature transformations of various sorts, or using evolutionary processes to act on the result of a feature transformation. A common approach is to use a GA to perform a feature subset selection (of pre-determined features) which are then used in the induction of a classifier - usually a decision tree [12, 13]. Other work [14, 15] uses coevolution as a first step to construct features, and then passes these to a decision tree or bayesian classfier. The work by Guarda [16] is closest in concept to this work, in that it evolves feature constructors (in the form of convolution kernels) which are then used as terminals by a GP based classifier. However, the features are first evaluated independently, before being passed to the GP system, rather than being simultaneously co-evolved, as is suggested here.

2 Test Problems

Two sets of greyscale images were used to evaluate the proposed method. The first is an artificial dataset where each image contains between 10 and 20 objects. Each object has a random radius (between 8 and 16 pixels) and a random orientation. An object can be either a circle or a triangle. The task for this dataset is to identify the triangles. Gaussian noise with a standard deviation of 30 grey levels, is then added to the entire image. Each image is 300x300 pixels.

The second dataset contains natural images of two different types of pasta photographed against a textured background. Pasta was chosen as it offers a variety of complex shapes to test the system. Also, the two types are obviously the same colour which makes the task more challenging. There are between 1 and 20 objects in each image, all at random orientations. The task is to detect only the spiral shapes. Each image is 320x240 pixels.

Each dataset contains 100 images, of which 20 are used for training, and 80 for testing. Each picture has the pixel coordinates of the centre of the targets marked. These coordinates were generated automatically in the case of the first dataset, and marked up by the author in the case of the second dataset. An example of each of these datasets can be seen in Figure 1.

3 System Architecture

The system used for these experiments coevolves normal tree based object detection algorithms, alongside the pixel statistics that they use as terminals. In order

---

[1] Although strictly not in accordance with the definition given by Motoda[11], where feature construction adds new features to the original set. That would in this case imply that the raw pixel data were available as features, which they are not.

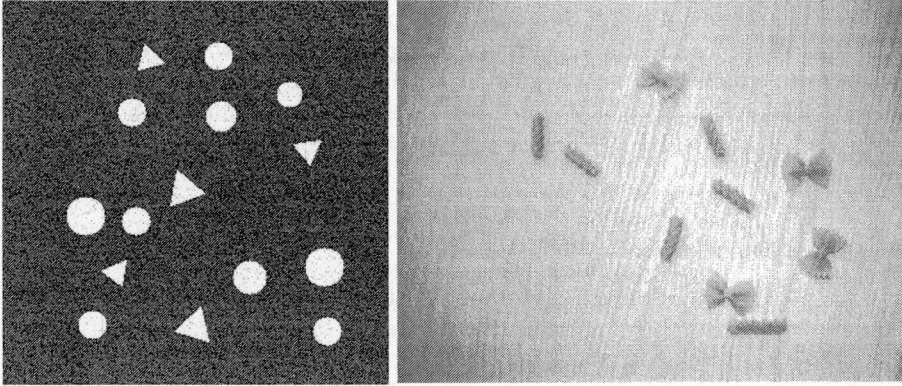

Fig. 1. An example from each dataset.

to evolve these, the system has two main components. The first is a population of object detection algorithms (ODAs), in which each individual is a "normal" GP tree. The terminals used in the ODAs are the results of the calculation of various pixel statistics. These statistics are supplied by a number of pixel statistic populations (PSPs) in which each individual is a single pixel statistic zone (PSZ). One PSZ is selected from each PSP to form the entire pixel statistic set (PSS) which the ODA is evaluated with. This basic architecture and the interaction between the population is inspired by the work of Ahluwalia [17, 18] on "Coevolutionary ADFs".

3.1 Pixel Statistics

Each individual in the PSP is a single pixel statistic zone (PSZ), which is applied as a moving window over the image, and is represented using 7 values which describe its shape and behaviour. The origin of the PSZ is at the pixel that the classifier is currently looking at. Its parameters are as follows -

- The zone's shape. Currently only rectangles are used, but other shapes such as lines and "square-rings" (rectangles with a smaller rectangle cut out of the middle) are supported by the system, but not shown in this work.
- The distance from the origin in pixels, and the angle in radians. These polar coordinates define the zone's centre.
- The orientation of the shape.
- Two fields representing size, which give the dimensions of the zone. In rectangular zones the two sizes represent width and height. Only the first is used in the case of line zones.
- The statistic that the zone returns. Currently only mean and standard deviation are used.

The system uses a set of populations to represent the pixel statistics. One zone from each population will eventually be used to form a complete pixel statistic set (PSS), used for terminal calculations.

Mutation of a PSZ involves a small random change to one of these components. The shape and statistic fields are changed less often, with only 30 percent of selections resulting in a change to one of these fields. Crossover simply interpolates the position and size of two zones, and creates one child. Each population is evolved independently of all other populations i.e. there is no cross-breeding between populations.

3.2 ODA Population

This is a population of object detection algorithms which are normal tree based representations of programs using the operators add, subtract, multiply, divide, power, min, max, and a conditional operator (IFLT) which compares two branches and returns one of two other branches depending on the result of the comparison. The terminals used in these trees $(F_1, F_2, \ldots, F_n)$ refer to the outputs of each PSZ in the PSS currently being evaluated. Crossover and mutation are applied to these trees in the normal fashion.

3.3 Evaluation

The ODAs and PSZs can only be evaluated in the context of each other, which means we cannot evaluate any of the populations independently. To calculate fitness values the system first creates a pixel statistic set (PSS) i.e. one zone from each PSP, which is paired with an ODA. This pairing is then evaluated on the training images. However, just using one of these collaborations is not usually enough to assess fitness, as one of the components may drag down the fitness of the others. In order to form a good estimate of the fitness of each of the components, we must evaluate each individual several times using different collaborators. Choosing collaborators and the subsequent credit assignment problem is not a well understood task, analysed in detail by Wiegand et. al. [19].

The basic evolutionary process is as follows.

```
begin
  foreach individual in the ODA population
    repeat subset_size times
      randomly select an individual from each PSP to create a PSS
      foreach training image
        extract each of the pixel statistic features
        apply ODA to image and calculate fitness (See section 3.4)
      end foreach
      record fitness with ODA and each PSZ
    end repeat
  end foreach
  calculate final fitnesses for each ODA
  calculate final fitnesses for each zone in each PSP
  breed each population independently
repeat until termination criteria met
```

The parameter *subset_size* is the collaboration pool size, i.e. the number of pairings to try for each ODA, and should be as high as possible within the bounds of evaluation time. At the end of each generation we use the "optimistic" credit assignment method [19], whereby each ODA and PSZ are assigned the best fitness value of any evaluation it has been involved in.

3.4 Fitness Calculation

In order to assess how well a combined ODA and PSS perform, we need to first extract the features (i.e. the result of calculating the PSZs) described by the PSS at every pixel in the image. This creates a number of "feature images", one per feature. This may at first seem like an enormous amount of computation, especially for large zones, but it is in fact a constant time operation due to the use of an "integral image" representation [20], which precalculates a version of the image from which mean and standard deviations of any size of rectangle can be calculated using only 5 and 11 arithmetic operations respectively. The ODA (a normal GP tree) is then applied at each pixel in the image, with the terminal set being filled from the corresponding point in each feature image. The resulting output image is then thresholded half way through its range. In the binary image that results from this, white patches represent "objects" and black patches represent background[2]. Each object is reduced down to a single point, its centre of gravity. The resulting set of points are the "guesses" of the algorithm, and are used in the subsequent fitness calculation.

The aim of the fitness function is to minimise the distances between each guess $g \in G$ and a target $t \in T$ and to minimise the number of false guesses i.e. we only want one guess per target, and it should be as close to the target as possible. The fitness is calculated on a per-target basis and then summed. For each target we look at the set of all the guesses around it, G_t, i.e. all the guesses which are closer to t than to any other target. We calculate the fitness of the target as the sum of all of the guess distances. The distances are weighted with a logarithmic function to help them centre on the target more quickly. This figure is then multiplied by the square of the number of guesses G_t to create a sort of fitness sharing, where the target's fitness gets worse in relation to how many guesses there are around it.

$$f = \frac{1}{|T|} \sum_{t \in T} targetTerm(t) \qquad (1)$$

$$targetTerm(t) = \begin{cases} \sum_{g \in G_t} ln\left(\alpha \times dist_{g,t}\right)(|G_t|)^2 & if |G_t| > 0 \\ ln\left(\alpha \times dist_{pen}\right)(count_{pen})^2 & otherwise \end{cases} \qquad (2)$$

Another issue linked to this trade-off is that of what to do if there are no guesses around any target. The target term must return a penalty, but the magnitude

---
[2] We apply an additional condition that objects must be less than 20 percent of the size of the image.

of this penalty must be set depending on the desired balance between over and under-guessing i.e *"Not guessing at all would be as bad as guessing $count_{pen}$ times at a distance of $dist_{pen}$"*. In this work the values of $count_{pen}$ and $dist_{pen}$ are 4 and 70 respectively. The scaling parameter α is set to 5.

4 Results

The fitness function used for training is good at its task of rewarding good solutions and punishing bad ones, but in order to guide the evolution properly it needs to be highly non-linear. However, these non-linearities mean that we cannot easily use it as a measure of actual classification performance. For this purpose we use the *figure of merit* measure used by Howard et. al. [5] as it conveniently sums up the detector's performance on an image.

$$FOM = \frac{TP}{|T| + FP} = \frac{TP}{TP + FN + FP} \qquad (3)$$

This measure is between 0 and 1, with 1 being perfect performance. To qualify as a true positive (TP) a guess must be within 4 pixels of the actual target coordinates. All other guesses are false positives (FP). The number of false negatives (FN) is the number of targets that have no true positives, i.e. they are missed.

4.1 Dataset 1 Results

The best detector (in terms of training performance) for this dataset had an average FOM on the training set of 1.0 (a perfect result). On unseen test data, the detector had an average FOM of 0.96 (standard deviation 0.07). The 31 node solution was generated after 16 generations, and used 4 standard deviation zones and no mean zones. Example output from this detector is shown in Figure 3.

4.2 Dataset 2 Results

The best detector for the pasta dataset had an average FOM on the training set of 1.0 (a perfect result). On the test data, the detector had an average FOM of 0.98 (sd. 0.06). The 25 node solution was generated after 28 generations, and used only two zones, both calculating standard deviation. The solution can be seen in Figure 2 and example output is shown in Figure 3. The runtime of the solution on a 320x240 image is about 0.55 seconds on a 2.0Ghz Athlon CPU.

5 Conclusions

The performance of the coevolved detectors is very impressive. On both datasets the system was able to create detectors which perfectly classified all of the training images, and generalised almost perfectly to a comparitively large unseen test set. Obviously, these images were far more controlled than a real world data set might be, but this is not really important here. What is far more important is

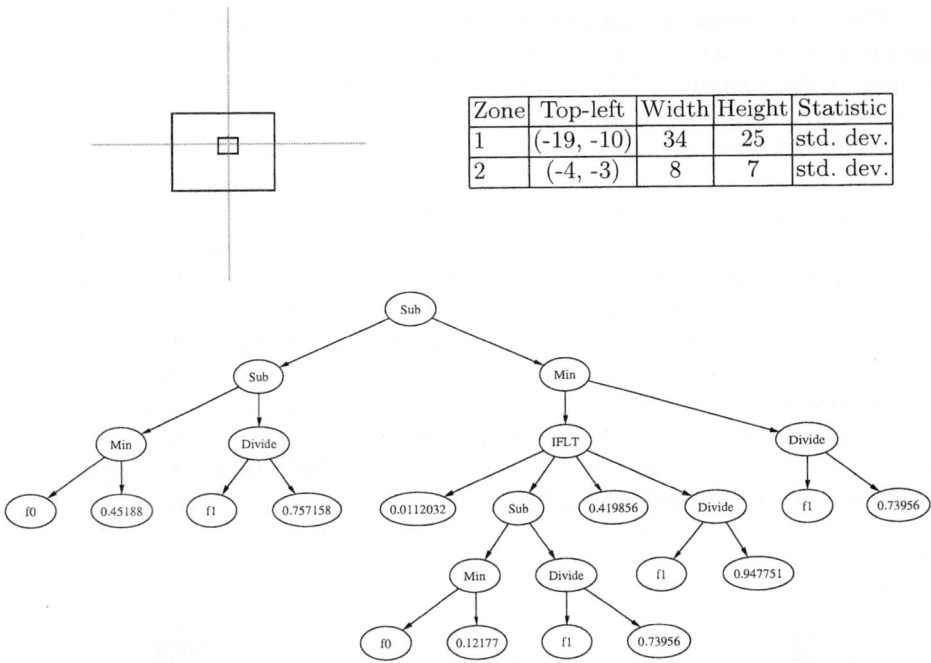

Fig. 2. Shows the solution generated for the pasta detector. Top - Shows the PSS evolved, with the table showing the details of each PSZ, relative to the local origin. Bottom - shows the ODA generated.

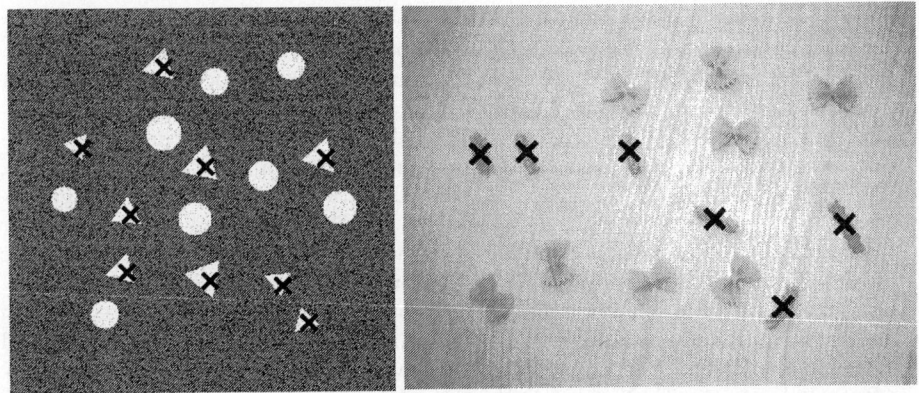

Fig. 3. Example output on each dataset, the crosses mark the detector's guesses.

the fact that the system learned to extract important features from the image, and how to use them, without any domain knowledge.

The solutions produced for the two datasets used only 2 and 4 features respectively. In terms of computation this is far more efficient than the large generic zone sets used in previous work (see Table 1). By adapting the zones to the data, and the detectors to the zones, the system produces a more optimal pairing.

There are several obvious extensions to this work, which are currently in progress. The first of these is to make the number of zones change during the course of the evolution. This is relatively easy to do, and again methods from [17, 18], provide an initial framework for achieving this.

Training time is always an issue with GP systems, and this work is no exception. Every generation, each tree is evaluated once for every pixel of every training image, and this is repeated several times depending on collaboration pool size. For example, in the pasta dataset training, this equates to 6.1×10^9 tree evaluations per generation. Early experiments suggest that techniques such as dynamic subset selection [21] and Tarpeian bloat control [22] can reduce this training time dramatically, while still maintaining accuracy.

In conclusion, this work has shown that by coevolving both feature extraction and object detection together, we can achieve very efficient solutions to vision problems, without supplying *any domain knowledge*. Allowing the algorithm to adapt its own zones gives it the freedom to choose what it thinks are appropriate features, rather than using ones that a human designer thinks might be useful.

References

1. Koza, J.R.: Genetic Programming: On the Programming of Computers by Means of Natural Selection. MIT Press (1992)
2. Tackett, W.A.: Genetic programming for feature discovery and image discrimination. In: Proceedings of the 5th International Conference on Genetic Algorithms, ICGA-93, Morgan Kaufmann (1994) 303–309
3. Daida, J.M., Bersano-Begey, T.F., Ross, S.J., Vesecky, J.F.: Computer-assisted design of image classification algorithms: Dynamic and static fitness evaluations in a scaffolded genetic programming environment. In Koza, J.R., Goldberg, D.E., Fogel, D.B., Riolo, R.L., eds.: Genetic Programming 1996: Proceedings of the First Annual Conference, Stanford University, CA, USA, MIT Press (1996) 279–284
4. Howard, D., Roberts, S.C.: Evolving object detectors for infrared imagery: a comparison of texture analysis against simple statistics. In Miettinen, K., Mäkelä, M.M., Neittaanmäki, P., Periaux, J., eds.: Evolutionary Algorithms in Engineering and Computer Science, Chichester, UK, John Wiley & Sons (1999) 79–86
5. Howard, D., Roberts, S.C., Brankin, R.: Target detection in imagery by genetic programming. Advances in Engineering Software **30** (1999) 303–311
6. Winkeler, J.F., Manjunath, B.S.: Genetic programming for object detection. In Koza, J.R., et. al., eds.: Genetic Programming 1997: Proceedings of the Second Annual Conference, San Francisco, CA, USA, Morgan Kaufmann (1997) 330–335
7. Ross, B.J., Fueten, F., Yashkir, D.Y.: Edge detection of petrographic images using genetic programming. In Proceedings of Genetic and Evolutionary Computation GECCO 2000, San Francisco, USA, Morgan Kaufmann (2000) 658–665
8. Zhang, M.: A Domain Independent Approach to 2d Object Detection Based on Neural Networks and Genetic Paradigms. PhD thesis, Department of Computer Science, RMIT University, Melbourne, Victoria, Australia (2000)
9. Zhang, M., Bhowan, U.: Program size and pixel statistics in genetic programming for object detection. In Raidl, G.R., Cagnoni, S., et. al., eds.: Applications of Evolutionary Computing, EvoWorkshops2004. Volume 3005 of LNCS., Coimbra, Portugal, Springer Verlag (2004) 377–386

10. Potter, M.A., De Jong, K.A.: A cooperative coevolutionary approach to function optimization. In: Proceedings of the Third Conference on Parallel Problem Solving from Nature, Springer (1994) 249–257 Lecture Notes in Computer Science.
11. Motoda, H., Liu, H.: Feature selection, extraction and construction. In: Towards the Foundation of Data Mining Workshop, Sixth Pacific-Asia Conference on Knowledge Discovery and Data Mining (PAKDD'02), Taipei, Taiwan (2002) 67–72
12. Bala, J., Jong, K.D., Huang, J., Vafaie, H., Wechsler, H.: Using learning to facilitate the evolution of features for recognizing visual convepts. Evolutionary Computation **4** (1997)
13. Bala, J., Jong, K.D., Huang, J., Vafaie, H., Wechsler, H.: Visual routine for eye detection using hybrid genetic architectures. In Bolle, R., Dickmanns, E., eds.: Proceedings of the International Conference on Pattern Recognition Volume 3, Vienna, Austria, IEEE (1996) 606–610
14. Krawiec, K., Bhanu, B.: Coevolution and linear genetic programming for visual learning. In Cantú-Paz, E., Foster, J.A., et. al., eds.: Genetic and Evolutionary Computation – GECCO-2003. Volume 2723 of LNCS., Berlin, Springer-Verlag (2003) 332–343
15. Lin, Y., Bhanu, B.: Learning features for object recognition. In Proceedings of Genetic and Evolutionary Computation - GECCO 2003, Chicago, US, Springer (2003) 2227–2239
16. Guardo, A., Gal, C.L., Lux, A.: Evolving visual features and detectors. In da Fontoura, et. al., eds.: International Symposium on Computer Graphics, Image Processing, and Vision (SIGGRAPI 98), Rio De Janeiro, Brazil, IEEE (1998) 246–253
17. Ahluwalia, M., Bull, L.: Coevolving functions in genetic programming. Journal of Systems Architecture **47** (2001) 573–585
18. Ahluwalia, M., Bell, L., Fogarty, T.C.: Co-evolving functions in genetic programming: A comparison in ADF selection strategies. In Koza, J.R., Deb, K., Dorigo, M., Fogel, D.B., Garzon, M., Iba, H., Riolo, R.L., eds.: Genetic Programming 1997: Proceedings of the Second Annual Conference, San Francisco, CA, USA, Morgan Kaufmann (1997) 3–8
19. Wiegand, R.P., Liles, W.C., Jong, K.A.D.: An empirical analysis of collaboration methods in cooperative coevolutionary algorithms. In Raidl, G.R., Cagnoni, S., et. al., eds.: Proceedings of the Genetic and Evolutionary Computation Conference (GECCO). Volume 2611 of LNCS., Berlin, Morgan Kaufmann (2001) 1235–1245
20. Viola, P., Jones, M.J.: Robust real-time face detection. International Journal of Computer Vision **57** (2004) 137–154
21. Gathercole, C., Ross, P.: Dynamic training subset selection for supervised learning in genetic programming. In Davidor, Y., Schwefel, H.P., Männer, R., eds.: Parallel Problem Solving from Nature III. Volume 866 of LNCS., Berlin, Germany, Springer-Verlag (1994) 312–321
22. Poli, R.: A simple but theoretically-motivated method to control bloat in genetic programming. In Ryan, C., et. al, eds.: Proceedings of EuroGP'2003, Essex, UK, Springer-Verlag (2003) 200–210

Spatial Embedding and Loss of Gradient in Cooperative Coevolutionary Algorithms

R. Paul Wiegand* and Jayshree Sarma

Department of Computer Science, George Mason University, Fairfax, VA 22030, USA
paul@tesseract.org, jsarma@cs.gmu.edu

Abstract. Coevolutionary algorithms offer great promise as adaptive problem solvers but suffer from several known pathologies. Historically, spatially embedded coevolutionary algorithms seem to have succeeded where other coevolutionary approaches fail; however, explanations for this have been largely unexplored. We examine this idea more closely by looking at spatial models in the context of a particular coevolutionary pathology: loss of gradient. We believe that loss of gradient in cooperative coevolution is caused by asymmetries in the problem or initial conditions between populations, driving one population to convergence before another. Spatial models seem to lock populations together in terms of evolutionary change, helping establish a type of dynamic balance to thwart loss of gradient. We construct a tunably asymmetric function optimization problem domain and conduct an empirical study to justify this assertion. We find that spatial restrictions for collaboration *and* selection can help keep population changes balanced when presented with severe asymmetries in the problem.

1 Introduction

Coevolutionary algorithms (CEAs) are increasingly popular extensions of traditional evolutionary algorithms (EAs). The most fundamental differences between CEAs and EAs stem from the adaptive nature of fitness evaluation in coevolutionary systems: individuals are assigned fitness values based on direct interactions with other individuals. Examples of such systems include competitive approaches where an individual in one population receives fitness based on the result of a competition with one or more individuals, as well as cooperative approaches where an individual represents a component of a larger, more structured problem, and receives fitness based on how well it performs in conjunction with individuals from other populations.

There is a lot of intuitive appeal to coevolutionary algorithms. In the case of competitive systems, there is the hope of establishing an *arms race*, where steady progress is made by mutual and reciprocal adaptations between competing groups of individuals [1]. Cooperative systems have the same sort of hope, though perhaps the term "parallel adaptive changes" might be more appropriate to its collaborative nature. In spite of their appeal, coevolutionary algorithms are often challenged by seemingly simple problems. Constructing algorithms that facilitate arms-race type behaviors is far from easy.

---

* R. Paul Wiegand currently holds a postdoctoral position with the American Society for Engineering Education and conducts research at the Naval Research Laboratory.

One difficulty common to both competitive and cooperative coevolutionary algorithms is the *loss of gradient* problem, in which one population comes to severely dominate the others, creating an impossible situation where the other populations have insufficient information from which to learn. Suppose a grand master of chess repeatedly plays a child, who is merely learning: if the child gets no more information than the result of the game, he is unlikely to learn much from the process.

Of particular interest to us are cooperative coevolutionary algorithms (CCEAs). These algorithms have appeal when applied to problems with large domain spaces having certain structural properties among interacting components. The intuition behind this advantage is that the algorithm adaptively searches only projections of the space at any given time, thus presenting a narrower search domain in a particular generation. However, loss of gradient can also occur in CCEAs when the diversity of a subset of the populations suddenly decreases, leaving the others searching only a static projection and not the full problem [2].

The key to solving the loss of gradient problem would seem to be found in helping the algorithm maintain some kind of balance between the populations in terms of evolutionary change. Here biology suggests a potential solution: establish some locality constraints in terms of selection and collaborator interactions [3] Indeed there is precedent for such fine-grained spatially embedded population models in both traditional EAs [4], as well as coevolutionary systems [5]. Moreover, recent empirical research has suggested that spatial models may indeed give CEAs some kind of advantage, though the reason for this advantage has remained unexplored. We believe that such spatial CEA successes are due to their ability to thwart the loss of gradient problem by constraining the speeds at which populations themselves can propagate changes, as well as the speeds at which populations can provide interaction information to the other populations. This paper explores the relationship between spatial models and the causes of loss of gradient in cooperative coevolutionary algorithms. We make no claims regarding the general utility of spatial CCEAs for solving static function optimization problems, rather we seek only to expose some of the reasons why spatial embedding may benefit coevolution when solving problems that have certain properties.

The next section provides background of the cooperative coevolutionary framework we consider, the loss of gradient pathology, and spatial embedding in EAs. The third section describes our spatial CCEA, including the effects of constraining the locality of certain operators. Our experimental design and results are described in detail in the fourth section. The paper terminates with a section discussing our conclusions, as well as indicating areas of future work highlighted by our research.

2 Background

There are a variety of models of cooperative coevolution, beginning with the early work of Husbands and Mill [6], to more recent models by Potter [7], as well as Moriarty and Miikkulainen [8]. This paper focusses on the Potter model of cooperative coevolution. Here each population contains individuals that represent a particular component of the problem, so that one member from each population is needed in order to assemble a complete solution. Evaluation of an individual from a particular population is performed by assembling the individual with collaborating partners from other populations. Often multiple collaborators are used to gain a better quality estimate of an individual's contribution to the interaction. An individual's fitness could be the mean of such evaluations, or the max, among other approaches. Aside from evaluation, the populations are evolved independently.

An example may help clarify things. Suppose we are optimizing a two argument function, $f(x, y)$. One might assign individuals in the first population to represent the x argument and the second to represent y. Each population is evolved separately, except that when evaluating an individual in some population (e.g., x), collaborating representatives must be chosen from the other population (y) in order to obtain an objective function value with a complete solution, $f(x, y)$. A simple example collaboration method is to choose a representing member by using the most fit individual from the other other population as determined by the previous round of evaluations. Another approach is to pick partners at random from the other population. Once a complete solution is formed, it can be evaluated and the resulting score can be assigned to the individual as the mean of several of these interactions.

Though the behavior of cooperative and competitive CEAs can certainly differ, they also share some pathologies. One such pathology is that of loss of gradient. In a multi-population model, loss of gradient occurs when one population converges to strategies that provide the other populations no hope for meaningful search due to the unavailability of informational distinctions between individuals. In a competitive system, this suggests that one population has severely dominated the other, such that no information is learned from a contest between individuals from those populations. In a cooperative system, this suggests that one or more populations has converged, and the projection offered by these converged populations during collaboration is misleading or degenerate in some way for the populations that are still attempting to progress.

The term *loss of gradient* stems primarily from three works relating to the analysis of competitive coevolutionary algorithms. Juillé and Pollack [9], as well as Ficici and Pollack [10], primarily focus on methods for measuring and maintaining coevolutionary progress while discussing the need for successful competitive algorithms to maintain a gradient of search. Watson and Pollack [11] specifically introduce the term, using a simple problem structure to help illustrate and identify it as one of several pathologies of competitive coevolutionary systems. While more recent work suggests that loss of gradient may not be as big a problem for competitive algorithms as problems related to overspecialized focussing [12], it seems evident that it remains a significant challenge. Multi-population coevolution works by making parallel adaptive changes in interacting populations, but a balance between these changing populations must exist in order maintain co-adaptive search gradients. When that balance is lost, the search can fail by forcing changes in the populations to become disengaged, resulting in polarization of the populations in terms of subjective fitness assessment [11].

Though loss of gradient is perhaps more easily understood in the context of competitive coevolution, the same problem challenges cooperative models. It can happen, for instance, when rapid asymmetric changes in one population lead it to converge to near homogeneity, forcing the other disengaged populations to be driven into arbitrary equilibria [2]. Such inequality can be created by many factors including initialization effects, asymmetries in algorithmic choices or asymmetries in the problem itself.

Biologists and social scientists have studied spatially embedded evolution and coevolution for some time, typically taking game-theoretic approaches to understanding the dynamics in single population systems playing games such as iterated prisoner's dilemma [13].Researchers in the field of evolutionary computation have also studied spatial models in some detail [4, 14], but analysis of coevolutionary spatial models has primarily been relegated to discussions of general CEA performance measures [1]. Nevertheless, applications of such systems have proved effective [15–17], sometimes demonstrating clear advantages over non-spatial CEAs [5]. Unfortunately, the underlying cause of this advantage has not been addressed.

3 A Spatial CCEA

The basic idea behind spatially embedded evolutionary algorithms is quite simple. In the most obvious case, the individuals in the population are distributed on a 2-D (often toroidal) grid. Each individual occupies a specific location on that grid, and locality is defined by the vertical and horizontal topological connections. The algorithm works the same as a traditional evolutionary algorithm, with the exception of selection. New individuals for each position are selected locally using a pre-defined neighborhood. Virtually any traditional selection operator can be applied in this method, though its purview is limited to the individuals in the local neighborhood of the position under consideration. Updates to the current population may be synchronous or asynchronous.

For example, consider a synchronous spatial variant of a traditional generational evolutionary algorithm. Let's suppose the algorithm uses binary representation with bit-flip mutation, fitness proportionate selection, and a 2×2, von Neumann neighborhood (a diamond shaped subset of the grid covering five points). Individuals are distributed on the grid positions, initialized uniformly at random, then evaluated against the objective function. We then produce a new child for each grid position by selecting from the individuals in the surrounding neighborhood, proportionally according to their fitness values. The offspring produced for that position is subjected to mutation and placed into the next generation's grid at the same position. A new position is then considered in the same way, and the process is repeated until all positions have been considered. At this point the generation is complete and a new generation begins.

The most distinctive parameter of spatial models of this sort is the neighborhood definition. It turns out that for several geometric shapes, a general size measure (called the *radius* of the neighborhood) is useful for understanding diffusive properties of the selection method. The larger the radius, the faster information is propagated throughout the population, the smaller the radius, the slower [4].

In the case of a simple, spatial CCEA, things are very similar. We now consider separate grids for each population, and "align" the 2-D grids in a stacked fashion, forming a 3-D lattice. Now a given population grid position has an adjacent position above or below the current position in another population grid. In addition to selection, collaboration now makes use of the neighborhood mechanism. Representative partners are selected from a neighborhood in the adjacent population(s), providing another type of locality restriction altogether—one that controls the amount of information about interactions a population receives. In this case the larger the radius of the collaboration neighborhood, the more information about potential partners is available, the smaller the radius, the less information.

Controlling these two relative sizes appears to be very important to the success of coevolution in many cases. By restricting the rate of diffusion due to selection, the rates of change of EAs associated with each population can be reduced. By restricting the amount of available interaction information, the EAs can be given time to adapt to radical phenotypic shifts in the collaborating population before being exposed to degenerate partners. If rapid, asymmetric losses of diversity are our major concern then local selection slows the rate at which populations reach homogeneity and local collaboration allows topologically distant partners the chance to make changes before being exposed to the new individuals. The intuition is that the overall effect acts as a kind of cap to population advancement, "locking" the populations together in terms of their relative evolutionary changes.

4 Experimental Results

4.1 The ASYMMTWOQUAD Problem

Recall that asymmetries in a problem can exacerbate the loss of gradient pathology for the CCEA. To help show this, we define a class of problems that allows one to construct instances that vary in terms of degree of problem asymmetry. The problem class defined below consists of two quadratic peaks, one a global maxima and the other a local sub-maxima. Each of these two peaks can be varied independently to adjust asymmetric conditions in the landscape between the two arguments.

Definition 1. *Given constant values k_1 and k_2 defining the relative heights of two peaks; parameters s_{x1}, s_{x2}, s_{y1}, and $s_y 2$ defining peak widths; and points $(\bar{x}_1, \bar{y}_1)$ and $(\bar{x}_2, \bar{y}_2)$ defining the locations of the peaks, the function* ASYMMTWOQUAD $: \mathbb{R} \times \mathbb{R} \to \mathbb{R}$ *(ATQ) is defined by*

$$quad_1(x,y) = k_1 - \left[s_{x1} \cdot (\bar{x}_1 - x)^2 + s_{y1} \cdot (\bar{y}_1 - y)^2 \right]$$

$$quad_2(x,y) = k_2 - \left[s_{x2} \cdot (\bar{x}_2 - x)^2 + s_{y2} \cdot (\bar{y}_2 - y)^2 \right]$$

$$\text{ASYMMTWOQUAD}(x,y) = \max(quad_1, quad_2)$$

For our purposes, the parameters controlling the width of the peaks are most salient. The larger the s_{x1} value is, the narrower the first peak becomes along the x-axis. We can create a situation that endangers the CCEA of suboptimal convergence by tightening the global peak's width relative to the suboptimal peak [2], and we can make this situation increasingly asymmetric by tightening more along one axis than another. Here, the s_{x2} and s_{y2} parameters were both set to 1, and the s_{x1} parameter was held fixed at 8. The s_{y1} parameter, however, was varied using the values $\{8, 16, 32, 64, 128, 256, 512\}$. The two optima are located at $(8, 1)$ and $(1, 8)$, and their objective values (k_1 and k_2) are 180 and 140, respectively. Domain values for x and y were restricted to $[1, 8]$. This problem class is simple enough to intuit salient properties, while allowing a researcher to generate a range of problems from very simple to quite difficult. Though the domain itself is relatively limited in scope, it serves us well here since our goal is to understand the effects spatial representations have on loss of gradient, not to demonstrate any specific advantage of spatial CCEAs over EAs in general.

4.2 Basic Experimental Setup

In all cases, the basic underlying algorithms were generational EAs with fitness proportionate selection. There were two populations, each containing individuals representing one of the two arguments to the ASYMMTWOQUAD function. The genotype of each individual was encoded as a binary string, each argument ranging in $[1, 8]$. The string length and population sizes were fixed for these experiments. There were 100 individuals in each population, each of which were $l = 128$ bits long, thus $n = 256$ bits. Collaboration was handled as follows. Five representatives from the alternate population were selected at random from either the entire population, or from the locally restricted areas defined by the spatial approaches. Each representative was evaluated with the current individual, and the average score was assigned for fitness purposes.

Though other population sizes, string lengths, and collaboration sizes are not shown, some were tested and the results were consistent with those reported here. It is our intent that the population size is linear with respect to the string length and that the number of collaborators is bounded above by the square root of the population size (with a constant factor of 1/2). Such a rule leads to reasonably sized populations for the ASYMMTWOQUAD problem class and provides useful information for future analysts. Bit-flip mutation is used at a rate of $1/l$. There is evidence that crossover may exacerbate the effects of loss of gradient in CCEAs [2], and since our intent is to try to understand the effects of spatial embedding on loss of gradient at the most basic level we choose not to complicate the discussion in this article by including crossover in our discussion. This notwithstanding, though not shown, we also ran our experiments with parameterized uniform crossover operator of varying rates and the results are consistent with the findings stated here. Where possible, we keep things intentionally as simple as possible here to allow for future analysis.

4.3 Balancing Evolutionary Change

As we've already mentioned, the ASYMMTWOQUAD problem described above becomes increasingly more asymmetric as the s_{x1} parameter is increased. The effect of this is to make the global peak narrower in one dimension. This creates a situation in which one population has a clear advantage if for no other reason than the fact that the ratio of domain coverage of the global peak is larger in one dimension than another. The resulting effect on simple CCEAs is a decrease in performance due to loss of gradient.

Our hypothesis is that the locality constraints of selection and collaboration in the spatially embedded model will help keep the system in balance in terms of evolutionary change, thus improving performance. We first consider two algorithms, a more traditional non-spatial CCEA described above and a spatially embedded analog of this algorithm. In the spatial model, individuals in each population are spread out on a 2-D toroidal 10×10 grid. The neighborhood sizes for selection and collaboration are performed in a 2×2 diamond of radius 1 from a given position (covering 5 grid points).

To test these two algorithms we ran 14 experimental groups, 7 with a traditional non-spatial CCEA, and 7 with a spatial CCEA. These 7 groups correspond the ASYMMTWOQUAD problem parameter values $s_{x1} \in \{8, 16, 32, 64, 128, 256, 512\}$. The results are shown in two graphs in Figure 1. In both graphs, the x-axis indicates results from the different experimental groups specified by the s_{x1} parameter. Each point of the top graph illustrates the mean best-ever fitness value of 50 trials and the vertical

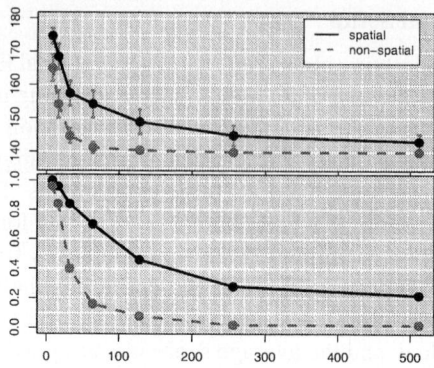

Fig. 1. Spatial and non-spatial CCEA results on the ASYMMTWOQUAD problem as s_{x1} (x-axis) varied. Points in the top graph represent mean and confidence intervals of best-ever (y-axis) values in 50 trials. Points in the bottom graph represent the ratio of trials (y-axis) that are likely to globally converge.

wings surrounding that point illustrate the 95% confidence intervals of that group. Each point in the bottom graph represents the ratio of the 50 trials where the best-ever value exceeded 140, and thus indicates the ratio of populations that plausibly may eventually converge to the global peak.

The best-ever values of the groups were tested using pair-wise t-tests with Bonferoni adjustment. The result indicates that for all values of s_{x1} the spatial model significantly outperforms the non-spatial model (with confidence of 95%). These results were consistent for population size of 49, $l = 64$ using 3 collaborators. They were also consistent with results applying parameterized uniform crossover with a crossover rate of 100% and swap rates of 0.5 and 0.2 (not shown).

The lower panel of the figure gives us some clue as to why the spatial groups resulted in higher performance. As the problem becomes increasingly asymmetric, the ratio of suboptimally converging populations drops much faster for the non-spatial CCEA than for the spatial CCEA.

Although it is not shown here for space reasons, it is also the case that the standard deviations in fitness values are significantly higher for the spatial model than for the non-spatial model in every case, indicating higher levels of diversity. Examining the inter-population diversity, the relative differences in standard deviations between populations of the same model, helps reveal something about the differing rates of change in the two populations. Here, the inter-population diversity within the first ten generations (the early stages of population convergence) reveals that the standard deviations of the two populations in the non-spatial CCEA differ significantly. This is only true for the $s_{x1} = 256$ case for the spatial model. This suggests that the spatial model may very well have an advantage with respect to differing rates of evolutionary change.

4.4 Collaboration *and* Selection

There are at least three ways this spatial model might improve upon the non-spatial model: local restrictions to selection, local restrictions to collaboration, and a combined impact of both of these.

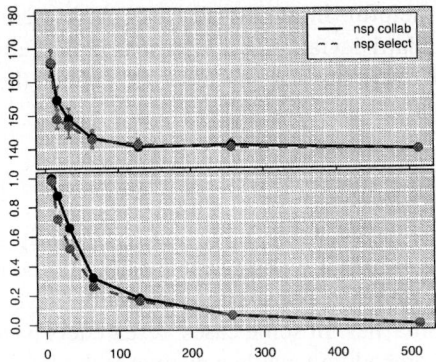

Fig. 2. Results for two CCEAs are presented: non-spatial selection with spatial collaboration and non-spatial collaboration with spatial selection. The results are reported for the ASYMMTWOQUAD problem as s_{x1} (x-axis) varied. Points in the top graph represent mean and confidence intervals of best-ever (y-axis) values in 50 trials. Points in the bottom graph represent the ratio of trials (y-axis) that are likely to globally converge.

First, an argument could be made that restricting selection to local neighborhoods cannot be responsible for the behavioral improvement. After all, the effects of locality on selection are mainly speed effects. One would expect to see a slowing of the pathology, but certainly not its absence. While this is true, it is also the case that spatial representations help maintain diversity, and this has been known to help resolve difficulties in certain kinds of acyclic problems [18].

The second difference between the spatial model and the non-spatial one is the locality restriction imposed upon collaboration. One may again be tempted to dismiss this component as the explanation for improvement since a smaller pool of potential collaborators seems to invite even more challenges to the CCEA. However, restricting collaborators to a local neighborhood restricts the flow of interaction information between the two populations, allowing one population to have more time with a given set of interactions before they are washed away by selection.

The most satisfying answer is that the improvement results from a combination of these two mechanisms. Slowing selection down and maintaining enough diversity to give one population time to catch up to the other, while restricting the information flow between the populations in such a way as to protect distant population members from unhelpful representatives from the collaborating population. We ran the same experiments as before for two more sets of groups, save that this time the spatial restrictions were used for only one of the two mechanisms. In the first set, selection is performed across the entire population but collaboration occurs in the 2×2 diamond neighborhood ("nsp select"), while in the second set the situation was entirely reversed ("nsp collab"). Figure 2 shows these results.

As can be seen from these graphs, the advantage the spatial model has over the non-spatial does indeed require *both* collaboration *and* selection to be restricted. Removing either produces results that are statistically indistinguishable from those of a completely non-spatial CCEA from the perspective of best-of-run performance results. Looking once again at the relative differences in standard deviations between populations in the first ten generations is helpful. In almost all cases there were significant differences between population standard deviation scores, just as in the fully non-spatial case. This again suggests that both restrictions are necessary to explain the spatial CCEA's ability to thwart loss of gradient.

5 Conclusions and Future Work

Coevolution offers much promise, but achieving consistently successful performance from coevolutionary algorithms is a complicated and important research issue. Historically, many of the reported successes with coevolution have employed fine-grained, spatially embedded approaches. In some cases, researchers have reported success on a problem using a spatial embedding, while a distinct lack of success when a non-spatial CEA is applied to the very same problem [5]. This paper begins to answer why. The study of the general performance quality of spatial CCEAs is not germane here.

Recent analytical work has suggested that not only does the loss of gradient pathology affect cooperative coevolutionary algorithms, but it might be caused, or at least exacerbated by an imbalance in evolutionary change between co-adapting populations [2]. Our hypothesis here is that a spatial embedding is one way to help restore this balance by locking together the rates of relative changes between populations. We explore this hypothesis using a simple, tunably asymmetric landscape and use a cooperative coevolutionary algorithm to optimize this function.

We examined the CCEA with and without spatial restrictions for collaboration and selection together, as well as independently. The results showed that as the problem becomes increasingly asymmetric, the degradation in performance is far less in the fully spatial model than any other combination of spatially-restricted algorithms. Moreover, the ratio of trials that optimally converge was typically much higher for the spatial algorithm than for the non-spatial CCEA. Further, there seems to be some evidence that inter-population diversity measures are more disparate in the more non-spatial case. All of this leads us to conclude that spatially embedded cooperative coevolutionary algorithms use locality restrictions as a means of helping maintain balanced evolutionary change between populations, and that *both* the collaboration process *and* the selection process need to be so restricted. This effect appears to be largely due to the spatial model's ability to maintain larger levels of diversity in the population, but *also* because it keeps these levels somewhat balanced between populations.

The exact nature of these diversity differences has yet to be fully explored, and is a topic for further research. Additionally, a much more careful examination of the effects that locality restrictions have on competitive models, where loss of gradient is perhaps more intuitively understood, should be undertaken. Finally, as we develop a greater understanding for the causes of pathologies such as loss of gradient, we should begin exploring augmentations to traditional CEA approaches that help counteract these challenges. Spatial models are not the only solution to loss of gradient, but they are one more tool in a practitioner's toolbox to help them with such difficulties.

References

1. Cliff, D., Miller, G.F.: Tracking the red queen: Measurements of adaptive progress in co-evolutionary sumulations. In: Proceedings of the Third European Conference on Artificial Life, Springer–Verlag (1995) 200–218
2. Wiegand, R.P.: An Analysis of Cooperative Coevolutionary Algorithms. PhD thesis, George Mason University, Fairfax, Virginia (2004)
3. Nuismer, S.L., Thompson, J.N., Gomulkiewicz, R.: Coevolution between hosts and parasites with partially overlapping geographic ranges. Journal of Evolutionary Biology **16** (2003) 1337–1345
4. Sarma, J.: An Analysis of Decentralized and Spatially Distributed Genetic Algorithms. PhD thesis, George Mason University, Fairfax, Virginia (1998)
5. Pagie, L.: Information Integration in Evolutionary Processes. PhD thesis, Universiteit Utrecht, Netherlands (1999)
6. Husbands, P., Mill, F.: Simulated coevolution as the mechanism for emergent planning and scheduling. In Belew, R., Booker, L., eds.: Proceedings of the Fourch International Conference on Genetic Algorithms, Morgan Kaufmann (1991) 264–270
7. Potter, M.: The Design and Analysis of a Computational Model of Cooperative CoEvolution. PhD thesis, George Mason University, Fairfax, Virginia (1997)
8. Moriarty, D., Miikkulainen, R.: Forming neural networks through efficient and adaptive coevolution. Evolutionary Computation **5** (1997) 373–399
9. Juillé, H., Pollack, J.: Coevolving the "ideal" trainer: Application to the discovery of cellular automata rules. In: Proceedings of the Third Annual Genetic Programming Conference, Madison, Wisconsin (1998)
10. Ficici, S., Pollack, J.: Challenges in coevolutionary learning: Arms–race dynamics, open–endedness, and mediocre stable states. In et al, A., ed.: Proceedings of the Sixth International Conference on Artificial Life, Cambridge, MA, MIT Press (1998) 238–247
11. Watson, R., Pollack, J.: Coevolutionary dynamics in a minimal substrate. In Spector, L., *et al*, eds.: Proceedings of the Genetic and Evolutionary Computation Conference (GECCO) 2001, Morgan Kaufmann (2001) 702–709
12. Bucci, A., Pollack, J.B.: Focusing versus intransitivity geometrical aspects of co-evolution. [19] 250–261
13. Nowak, M., May, R.: Evolutionary games and spatial chaos. Nature **359** (1992) 826–29
14. Giacobini, M., Alba, E., Tomassini, M.: Selection intensity in asynchronous cellular evolutionary algorithms. [19] 955–966
15. Hillis, D.: Co-evolving parasites improve simulated evolution as an optimization procedure. Artificial Life II, SFI Studies in the Sciences of Complexity **10** (1991) 313–324
16. Husbands, P.: Distributed coevolutionary genetic algorithms for multi–criteria and multi-constraint optimisation. In: Evolutionary Computing, AISB Workshop for Selected Papers, Springer–Verlag (1994) 150–165
17. Ronge, A., Nordahl, M.G.: Genetic programs and co-evolution developing robust general purpose controllers using local mating in two dimensional populations. In Voigt, H.M., Ebeling, W., Rechenberg, I., Schwefel, H.P., eds.: Parallel Problem Solving from Nature IV, Proceedings of the International Conference on Evolutionary Computation. Volume 1141 of LNCS., Berlin, Germany, Springer Verlag (1996) 81–90
18. Cartlidge, J., Bullock, S.: Caring versus sharing: How to maintain engagement and diversity in coevolutionary populations. In: Proceedings from Seventh International Conference on Evolutionary Computation and Artificial Life. (2003)
19. Cantú-Paz, E., *et al*, eds.: Proceedings of the Genetic and Evolutionary Computation Conference (GECCO) 2003. In Cantú-Paz, E., *et al*, eds.: Proceedings of the Genetic and Evolutionary Computation Conference (GECCO) 2003, Berlin, Germany, Springer (2003)

A High Performance Multi-objective Evolutionary Algorithm Based on the Principles of Thermodynamics

Xiufen Zou[1], Minzhong Liu[2], Lishan Kang[2], and Jun He[3]

[1] College of Mathematics and Statistics, Wuhan University, Wuhan 430072, China
    zouxiufen@yahoo.com
[2] State Key Laboratory of Software Engineering, Wuhan University, Wuhan 430072, China
    kang_whu@yahoo.com
[3] School of Computer Science, The University of Birmingham, Birmingham B15 2TT, UK
    J.He@cs.bham.ac.uk

Abstract. In this paper, we propose a high performance multi-objective evolutionary algorithm (HPMOEA) based on the principles of the minimal free energy in thermodynamics. The main innovations of HPMOEA are: (1) providing of a new fitness assignment strategy by combining Pareto dominance relation and Gibbs entropy, (2) the provision of a new criterion for selection of new individuals to maintain the diversity of the population. We use convergence and diversity to measure the performance of the proposed HPMOEA, and compare it with the other four well-known multi-objective evolutionary algorithms (MOEAs): NSGA II, SPEA, PAES, TDGA for a number of test problems. Simulation results show that the HPMOEA is able to find much better spread of solutions and has better convergence near the true Pareto-optimal front on most problems.

1 Introduction

Most real-world problems are multi-objective optimization problems (MOPs), and the effectiveness of evolutionary algorithms(EAs) in solving these problems has been widely recognized in the last ten years[1]. After David Schaffer's first study on evolutionary multi-objective optimization (EMO) in the mid of 1980s [2], a number of Pareto-based techniques and elitist algorithms have been proposed in the last decade [3][4], such as Pareto-based ranking procedure (FFGA) [5], niched Pareto genetic algorithm (NPGA) [6], Pareto-archived evolution strategy (PAES) [7], nondominated sorting genetic algorithm (NSGA, NSGA II) [8][9], the strength Pareto evolutionary algorithm (SPEA, SPEA2) [10][11] and thermo-dynamical genetic algorithm (TDGA) [12].

Although these techniques performed well in different comparative studies, there is still much room for improvement as recent studies have shown [9][13][14].

In order to increase the convergence rate and get more uniform Pareto optimal solutions, in this paper, we propose a high performance multi-objective evolutionary algorithm (HPMOEA) based on the principles of the minimal free energy in statistical physics, for solving multi-objective optimization problems (MOPs). Two new ideas are introduced in HPMOEA. One is a fitness assignment strategy that combines Pareto dominance relation and Gibbs entropy. The other is density distance and the Metropolis criterion for selection of new individuals in each generation.

The paper is structured as follows: section 2 provides detailed descriptions of the proposed algorithm. In section 3, numerical experiments are conducted, and two measurements proposed by Deb [9] are used to compare HPMOEA with other four well-known multi-objective evolutionary algorithms (MOEAS): NSGAII, SPEA, PAES, TDGA for a number of test problems. Finally, some conclusions and future work are addressed in section 4.

2 Description of the HPMOEA for Multi-objective Optimization

Without loss of generality, we consider the following multi-objective minimization problem with n decision variables(parameters), M objectives and k constrained conditions:

$$\text{minimize } y = F(\vec{x}) = (f_1(\vec{x}), f_2(\vec{x}), \cdots, f_M(\vec{x})) \qquad (1)$$

$$\text{subject to } g_i(\vec{x}) \leq 0, \ i = 1, 2, \cdots, k;$$

2.1 The New Fitness Assignment Strategy

In statistical physics, the Gibbs distribution models a system in thermo-dynamical equilibrium at a given temperature. Further, it is also known that this distribution minimizes the free energy F defined by

$$F = <E> - TS, \qquad (2)$$

Where $<E>$ is the mean energy of the system, S is the entropy and T is the temperature. The minimization of F means minimization of $<E>$ and maximization of TS. It is called "the principle of the minimal free energy".

Such a statistical framework has been introduced into many fields. Since the minimization of the objective function (convergence towards the Pareto-optimal set) and the maximization of diversity in obtained solutions are two key goals in the multi-objective optimization, the working principle of a MOEA and the principle of finding the minimum free energy state in a thermodynamic system is analogous. In order to plunge a multi-objective optimization problem into such a statistical framework, we combine the rank value $R(i)$ calculated by Pareto-dominance relation with Gibbs entropy $S(i)$ to assign a new fitness $F(i)$ for each individual i in the population, that is:

$$F(i) = R(i) - TS(i), \qquad (3)$$

where $R(i)$ is the rank value of individual i, which is equal to the number of solution n_i that dominates solution i [5]. In this way, $R(i) = 0$ corresponds to a non-dominated individual while a high $R(i)$ value means that i is dominated by many individuals.

$$S(i) = -p_T(i) \log p_T(i) \qquad (4)$$

where $p_T(i) = \frac{1}{Z}\exp(-\frac{R(i)}{T})$ is the analogue of the Gibbs distribution, $Z = \sum_{i=1}^{N}\exp(-\frac{R(i)}{T})$ is called the partition function, and N is the population size.

2.2 Density Estimation Technique

From the expression (3), we easily observe that it is difficult to distinguish the different individuals when their Rank values are equal. Therefore, we use a density estimation technique (which proposed by Deb et al[9]) to compute an individual's crowding distance. The crowding distance $d(i)$ for individual i is calculated according to the following steps:

(1) Sort the solution set I according to each objective function in ascending order of magnitude.

(2) Note that $d_m(i)$ is the crowding distance of individual i referring to the m th objective function, then $d_m(1) = d_m(l) = \infty$ (the boundary solutions are assigned an infinite distance value), $d_m(i) = \frac{f_m^{i+1} - f_m^{i-1}}{f_m^{max} - f_m^{min}}$, $i = 2,3,\cdots,l-1$, where f_m^i is the m th objective function, value of the ith individual in the set I, f_m^{max} and f_m^{min} are the maximum and minimum values of the m th objective function.

(3) Calculate the sum corresponding to all objective functions. $d(i) = \sum_{m=1}^{M} d_m(i)$ where M is the number of objective functions.

A solution with a smaller value of this distance measure is, in some sense, more crowded by other solutions. So we use the crowding distance to correct the expression of fitness value (3):

$$fitness(i) = R(i) - TS_i - d(i). \qquad (5)$$

In HPMOEA, the fitness values are sorting in increasing order. The individual in population with the smallest fitness value is called "the best individual", and the individual with the largest fitness value is called "the worst individual".

2.3 The New Selection Criterion

In every generation, new individuals are generated by genetic operator, but it is worthwhile discussing that what kind of way can be used to accept the new individuals, and form new population at next generation. Since the HPMOEA is based on the thermodynamical principle, we attempt to employ the Metropolis criterion of simulated annealing algorithm (SA)[15] and the crowding distance to guide the select process, that is,

(1) If $R(X_{new}) < R(X_{worse})$, then $X_{worst} := X_{new}$
(2) If $R(X_{new}) = R(X_{worse})$ and $d(X_{new}) > d(X_{worse})$, then $X_{worst} := X_{new}$
(3) else if $\exp(\dfrac{R_{worst}-R_{new}}{T}) > \text{random}(0,1)$, then $X_{worst} := X_{new}$

Where R_{worst} and R_{new} are respectively the Rank values of the worst individuals and the new individuals.

The structure of HPMOEA is described as follows:

```
Procedure HPMOEA
Step1: t=0, generate randomly an initial population
   P(t)={X₁ X₂… X_N}, N is the population size;
Step2: Calculate the rank values {R₁(t),…, R_N(t)} of all
   individuals in P(t);
Step3: Save the individuals whose rank values are equal
   to zero;
Step4: Calculate the fitness of all individuals according
   to equation (5),and sort them in increasing order;
Step5: Repeatedly execute step6 to step11 until the ter-
   mination conditions are satisfied;
Step6: t=t+1;
Step7:Randomly select m₁ individuals to do multi-parent
   crossover and m₂ individuals to mutate, and to generate
   n new individuals;
Step8:Compare the new individuals with the worst indi-
   viduals, and accept new individuals according to the
   new selection criterion in section 2.3;
Step9: Calculate the rank values {R₁(t),…, R_N(t)} of all
   individuals in new population P(t);
Step10: Save the individuals whose the rank values are
   equal to zero;
Step11: Calculate the fitness of all individuals accord-
   ing to equation (5), sort them in increasing order, and
   record the worst individuals;
Step12: Output the all results.
```

Remark1. In step 7, multi-parents crossover originated from Guo T. et al [16].

Remark2: Although HPMOEA is based on the same principle of TDGA [12], it is quite different to TDGA in following aspects:

(1) In HPMOEA, entropy of each individual is directly calculated by Gibbs entropy (5) in statistical physics, which is simpler than that of TDGA.

(2) When we evaluate new individuals from crossover and mutation at every generation, we introduce the Metropolis criterion of simulated annealing to accept the new individuals., that is, accept the worse solution in some probability.
(3) The computational complexity of HPMOEA is $O(MN^2)$, which is less than that in TDGA ($O(MN^3)$)[3].

3 The Numerical Experiments

To verify the efficiency and effectiveness of the HPMOEA, we have conducted many numerical experiments and compare its performance with several other MOEAs: NSGA II, SPEA, PAES. Here, we choose nine difficult test problems with no constraints, four problems with constraints and one high-dimensional problem.
(a) Unconstrained Test Problems from Deb [3][9]
SCH1, FON, POL, KUR, ZDT1, ZDT2, ZDT3, ZDT4, ZDT6
(b) Constrained Test Problems
CONSTR[3], TNK[3], SRN[3], BNH[3], KYMN

Where KYMN originated from Kita et al[12]:
(c) A high-dimensional problem VNT[17]

3.1 Performance Measures

Many performance metrics have been suggested [3][10][18]. Here, we use the two performance metrics defined in [9]. The first metric γ measures the extent of convergence to a known set of Pareto-optimal solutions:

$$\gamma = \frac{d_1 + d_2 + \cdots + d_k}{k}, \qquad (6)$$

where d_i is the minimum Euclidean distance of solution i from H chosen solutions on the true Pareto-optimal front ($H = 500$ uniform solutions are chosen in [9]), and k is the number of all solutions obtained with an algorithm). The second metric Δ measures the extent of spread achieved among the obtained solutions:

$$\Delta = \frac{d_f + d_l + \sum_{i=1}^{k-1}|d_i - \overline{d}|}{d_f + d_l + (k-1)\overline{d}}, \qquad (7)$$

here, the parameters d_f and d_l are the Euclidean distances between the extreme solutions and the boundary solutions of the obtained nondominated set. $d_i (i = 1, 2, \cdots, k-1)$ is the Euclidean distance between consecutive solutions in the obtained nondominated set of solutions, and $\overline{d}$ is the average of these distances, assuming that there are k solutions on the best nondominated front.

3.2 Results and Discussion

In order to compare with NSGA II, SPEA, PAES, the setting of parameters is basically the same as that in [9]. The algorithm has been coded in C language and implemented on a Pentium PC 500MHz in double precision arithmetic.

For each problem, 20 runs with different random seeds have been carried out.

Table 1. Parameter settings.

Population Size : $N=100$
Crossover: Multi-parent crossover, the crossover probability is 0.1(different from [9])
Mutate: uniform mutate, the mutate probability is $1/n$ (where n is the number of decision variables)
The maximum generation: $g=250$ (25000 function evaluations)
Temperature : $T=10000$.

Table 2 shows the mean and variance of the convergence metric obtained by four algorithms: HPMOEA, NSGA-II (real-coded), SPEA, and PAES. HPMOEA is able to converge better in all problems except in POL, where NSGA-II found better convergence. In all cases with HPMOEA, the variance in 20 runs is also smaller (In the table, the zero variance means that the variance is less than 10^{-6}), it shows the HPMOEA is more steady in convergence.

Table 2. The mean $\bar{\gamma}$ (first row) and variance σ_γ^2 (second row) of the convergence metric.

Algorithm	SCH1	FON	POL	KUR	ZDT1	ZDT2	ZDT3	ZDT4	ZDT6
HPMOEA	0.000408	0.002245	0.030703	0.022262	0.000150	0.000119	0.000493	0.000290	0.000520
	0	0	0.000043	0	0	0	0	0.000001	0
NSGA-|| (Real-coded)	0.003891	0.001931	0.015553	0.028964	0.033482	0.072391	0.114500	0.513053	0.296564
	0	0	0.000001	0.000018	0.004750	0.031689	0.007940	0.118460	0.013135
SPEA	0.003403	0.125692	0.037812	0.045617	0.001799	0.001339	0.047517	7.340299	0.221138
	0	0.000038	0.000088	0.00005	0.000001	0	0.000047	6.572516	0.000449
PAES	0.001313	0.151263	0.030864	0.057323	0.082085	0.126276	0.023872	0.854816	0.085469
	0.000003	0.000905	0.000431	0.011989	0.008679	0.036877	0.000001	0.527238	0.006664

Table 3 shows the mean and variance of the diversity metric obtained by all four algorithms. HPMOEA performs better than NSGA-II (real-coded), SPEA and PAES in all test problems except in KUR, where NSGA-II found better diversity.

The above results show the good behavior of our algorithm in all test problems with uniformly distributed solutions being obtained on all the Pareto-optimal fronts. In experiments, we find that the second term(Gibbs distribution) of expression (5) gives a gradient to make the algorithm converge quickly, however, it needs to be proved from theory.

Table 3. The mean $\overline{\Delta}$ (first row) and variance σ_Δ^2 (second row) of the diversity metric.

Algorithm	SCH1	FON	POL	KUR	ZDT1	ZDT2	ZDT3	ZDT4	ZDT6
HPMOEA	0.202006	0.351841	0.272671	0.580337	0.321018	0.322464	0.558973	0.487381	0.313715
	0.000416	0.000345	0.001789	0.000297	0.001055	0.000589	0.003799	0.007740	0.000534
NSGAII (Real-coded)	0.477899	0.378065	0.452150	0.411477	0.390307	0.430776	0.738540	0.702612	0.668025
	0.003471	0.000639	0.002868	0.000992	0.001876	0.004721	0.019706	0.064648	0.009923
SPEA	1.021110	0.792352	0.972783	0.852990	0.784525	0.755148	0.672938	0.798463	0.849389
	0.004372	0.005546	0.008475	0.002619	0.004440	0.004521	0.003587	0.014616	0.002713
PAES	1.063288	1.162528	1.020007	1.079838	1.229794	1.165942	0.789920	0.870458	1.153052
	0.002868	0.008945	0	0.013772	0.004839	0.007682	0.001653	0.101399	0.003916

In all experiments, the different parameter settings do not have obvious effects on results, but only the problem ZDT4, which has 21^9 different local Pareto-optimal fronts in the search space, is sensitive to the number of new individuals that generated by multi-parent crossover, if the number of new individuals is set to 1~5 in every generation, the HPMOEA is very quickly converge to the global Pareto front, or it is easy to be trapped in local Pareto front.

About the constrained problems, we use the proposed constraint-handling approach in NSGA-II[9]. The parameters setting is the same as Table-I, Fig.1(a)~(d) shows the obtained nondominated solutions after 500 generations using HPMOEA. The figure shows that HPMOEA is able to uniformly maintain solutions in all Pareto-optimal regions.

Moreover, we compare the nondominated solutions obtained with HPMOEA and TDGA on KYMN when they are run for a same maximum of 100*100 function evaluations, respectively depicted in Fig.2 (a) and Fig.2(b) (it is a copy of Fig.3 (f) from Kita et al. [12]). From the figure, HPMOEA finds a better converged set of non-dominated solutions and a better distribution in solutions.

Fig.3 (f1 against f2, f1 against f3, f2 against f3, f1 against f2 against f3) is the obtained nondominated solutions with HPMOEA on high-dimensional problem VNT after 250 generations. From the figure, we observe that HPMOEA can easily converge to the Pareto-optimal front. So we can conclude that HPMOEA is very fast and effective for solving high-dimensional problems

4 Conclusions and Future Work

In this paper, we have presented HPMOEA, a high performance evolutionary algorithm for multiobjective optimization problems that employs a new fitness assignment strategy and a new accepting criterion based on the principle of the minimal free energy. By using the two metrics, we make extensive experimental comparisons of HPMOEA with NSGA II, SPEA, PESA, TDGA, four other recently proposed algorithms, on many difficult test problems. The proposed HPMOEA has shown better

(a) CONSTR (b) TNK

(c) SRN (d) BNH

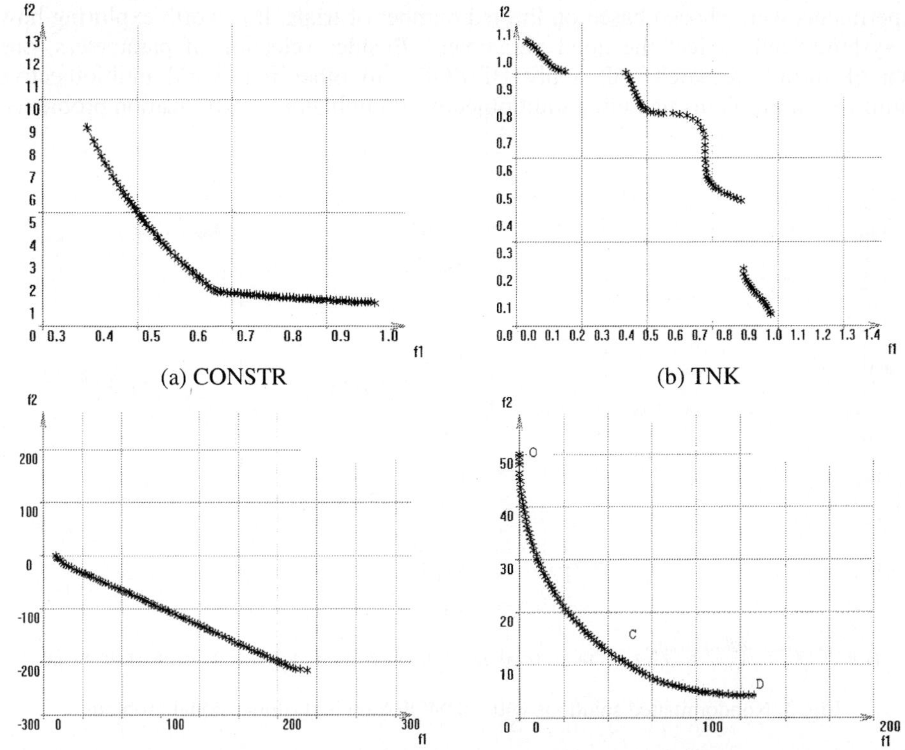

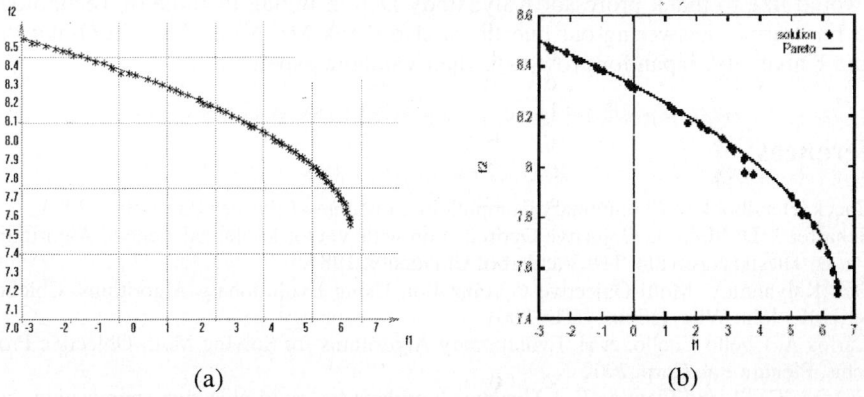

Fig. 1. Nondominated solutions with HPMOEA on CONSTR, TNK, SRN, BNH.

(a) (b)

Fig. 2. Nondominated solutions with HPMOEA and TDGA on KYMN.

performance according to the diversity and convergence. The experiments have shown that HPMOEA converged faster, therefore, in the future, more theoretical work can be done to estimate its convergence rate. The experiments have also shown the parameters can affect HPMOEA's performance. The parameters for HPMOEA in the experiments were chosen based on limited number of trials. It is worth exploring how to systematically select the good parameters. Besides selection of parameters, one area of further research will apply HPMOEA to other real-world multiobjective optimization problems including multiobjective combinatorial optimization problems.

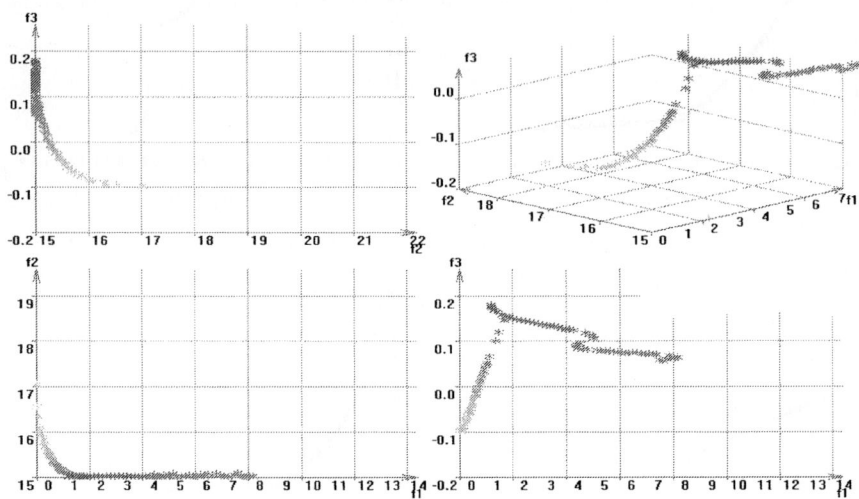

Fig. 3. Nondominated solutions with HPMOEA on high-dimensional problem.

Acknowledgements

We would like to thank professor Kalyanmoy Deb in Indian Institute of Technology, India for warmly answering our questions, also thank Mr. Naoki Mori in Osaka Prefecture University, Japan for provide us their valuable papers.

References

1. Baeck. Handbook of Evolutionary Computation, Institute of Physics Publishing, 2003.
2. Schaffer J. D. Multiple Objective Optimization with Vector Evaluated Genetic Algorithms. Ph. D. Thesis, Nashville, TN: Vanderbilt University, 1984.
3. Deb Kalyanmoy. Multi-Objective Optimization Using Evolutionary Algorithms. Chichester,U.K.: John Wiley&Sons, LTD, 2001.
4. Carlos A. Coello Coello, et al. Evolutionary Algorithms for Solving Multi-Objective Problems, Plenum Pub Corp, 2002.
5. Fonseca C. M. and Fleming P. J. Genetic algorithms for multi-objective optimization: Formulation, discussion and generalization. In: S. Forrest (Ed.), *Proceedings of the Fifth International Conference on Genetic Algorithms,* 1993, pp. 416–423. San Mateo, California.
6. Horn, J., Nafploitis N. and Goldberg D. A Niched Pareto Genetic Algorithm for Multi-objective Optimization, In Proceedings of the first IEEE Conference on Evolutionary Computation, Michalewicz Z. Ed. Piscataway , NJ:IEEE Press, 1994, pp.82-87.

7. Knowles J. and Corne D. The Pareto archived evolution strategy: A new baseline algorithm for multiobjective optimization," in *Proceedings of the 1999 Congress on Evolutionary Computation*. Piscataway, NJ:IEEE Press, 1999, pp. 98–105.
8. Srinivas N. and Deb K. Multiobjective function optimization using nondominated sorting genetic algorithms, *Evolutionary Computation.*, 1995, vol. 2, no.3, pp. 221–248.
9. Deb K., Pratap A. Agarwal S. and Meyarivan T. A Fast and Elitist Multi-objective Genetic Algorithm :NSGA II *IEEE Transaction on Evolutionary Computation*, 2002, Vol6, No 2, pp.182-197.
10. Zitzler E. Evolutionary algorithms for multiobjective optimization:Methods and Applications, Doctoral dissertation ETH 13398, Swiss Federal Institute of Technology (ETH), Zurich, Switzerland, 1999.
11. Zitzler E., Laumanns M. andThiele L. SPEA2: Improving the Strength Pareto Evolutionary Algorithm. TIK-Report 103, ETH Zentrum, Gloriastrasse 35, CH-8092 Zurich, Switxerland. 2001.
12. Kita H., Yabumoto Y., Mori N. and Nishikawa Y. Multi-objective Optimization by means of Thermodynamical Genetic Algorithm, In Proceedings of Parallel Problem Solving from Nature IV(PPSN-IV), 1996, pp.504-512 .
13. Zitzler E., Deb K., and Thiele L. Comparison of Multi-objective Evolutionary Algorithms: Empirical Results. *Evolutionary Computation Journal* **8**(2), 2000, pp.125-148.
14. Zitzler E, Thiele L, Laumanns M et al. Performance Assessment of Multiobjective Optimizers: An Analysis and Review. IEEE Transactions on Evolutionary Computation, vol. 7, no. 2, 2003, pp.117-132.
15. Aarts E.H.H., Korst J.H.M. Simulated annealing and Boltzmann machines, John Wiley and Sons, 1989.
16. Guo T. and Kang L S. A new evolutionary algorithm for function optimization. *Wuhan university Journal of Nature Science*. Vol **4**, 1999, pp. 409-414.
17. Veldhuizen D.V., Lamont G B. Multi-objective Evolutionary Algorithm test suites. In: Proc the 1999 ACM Symposium on Applied Computing, San Antonio, Texas, 1999, pp.351-357.
18. Veldhuizen D.V. Multi-objective Evolutionary Algorithms: Classifications , Analysis and New Innovations, Ph.D. Thesis , Dayton , OH: Air Force Institute of Technology, 1999.

Robustness in the Long Run: Auto-teaching *vs* Anticipation in Evolutionary Robotics

Nicolas Godzik, Marc Schoenauer, and Michèle Sebag

TAO team, INRIA Futurs and LRI, UMR CNRS 8623 bat. 490, Université Paris-Sud
91405 Orsay Cedex, France
{Nicolas.Godzik,Marc.Schoenauer,Michele.Sebag}@lri.fr

Abstract. In Evolutionary Robotics, auto-teaching networks, neural networks that modify their own weights during the life-time of the robot, have been shown to be powerful architectures to develop adaptive controllers. Unfortunately, when run for a longer period of time than that used during evolution, the long-term behavior of such networks can become unpredictable. This paper gives an example of such dangerous behavior, and proposes an alternative solution based on anticipation: as in auto-teaching networks, a secondary network is evolved, but its outputs try to predict the next state of the robot sensors. The weights of the action network are adjusted using some back-propagation procedure based on the errors made by the anticipatory network. First results – in simulated environments – show a tremendous increase in robustness of the long-term behavior of the controller.

1 Introduction

One key challenge of Evolutionary Robotics (ER) [7] is robustness, defined as the ability of the controller to efficiently deal with changing environments and previously unseen situations – in other words, to adapt itself to some real world. One prominent approach aimed at robust controllers in ER is based on the so-called auto-teaching networks[9]. In this approach, the controller is made of two parts, simultaneously optimized by evolutionary algorithms. The first part, referred to as Agent Model, is fixed offline. The second part, the Agent, actually controls the robot; in the same time, the Agent is modified on-line to get closer to the agent model (section 2). This way, evolution constructs a dynamic decision system, the trajectory of which is defined from an attraction center (the model) and a starting point (the agent at time 0). At this point, two time scales must be distinguished. During the training period, the agent is adjusted to the model, the fitness associated to the pair (agent, model) is computed and will serve to find optimal couples of (agent, model). During the robot life-time, referred to as generalization period, the agent is still adjusted to the model in each time step.

However, for feasibility reasons, the training period only represents a fraction of the robot lifetime. Therefore, the long term dynamics of the controller is not examined during the training period. This would make it possible for (opportunistic) evolutionary computation to select controllers with *any* dynamics in the long run, compatible with a good behavior in the short run...

This paper first focuses on the long-term behavior of auto-teaching networks, making every effort to reproduce as closely as possible the experimental setting described in [9]. Though results could not be exactly reproduced, interesting phenomena appear. Intensive experiments show that, not infrequently, auto-teaching networks with good fitness (good behavior during the training period) are found to diverge (repeatedly hitting the walls) as time goes by.

This paper proposes another source of adaptation, more stable in the long term than a fixed model, inspired from the cognitive sensori-motor framework [10]. The adaptation of the controller architecture is centered on an anticipation module; the anticipation module predicts the next state of the environment (the sensor values) depending on its current state *and the agent action*. When the actual state of the environment becomes available, the anticipation module provides an error signal that can be used either to modify the controller weights or as an additional input. The important issue is that the world model can here be evaluated with respect to the world itself, available for free (at next time step) during both the training and the generalization period. In opposition, the agent model in the auto-teaching architecture could not be confronted to the "true actions" during the generalization period. Implementations of this architecture, termed *AAA*, for *Action, Anticipation, Adaptation*, demonstrate an outstanding robustness in the long run of the simulated experiments, comparatively to the reference results.

The paper is organized the following way. Section 2 briefly describes the auto-teaching architecture, the goal and experimental setting [9], and presents and discusses the results obtained along the same settings when observing the behavior of auto-teaching networks in the long run. In section 3, the *AAA* architecture is presented, focusing on the anticipation module and its interaction with the decision module. Section 4 reports on the experimental validation comparatively to the reference results. The paper ends with a discussion of these first results, and points out the numerous avenues for research opened by this study.

2 Long Term Behavior of Auto-teaching Networks

2.1 Settings

With our apologies for the brevity of this reminder (due to space limitation), this section will recall settings and results obtained in [9] (see also [7]). The architecture of auto-teaching networks involves two modules with identical inputs and topologies, feed-forward neural nets without any hidden layer. During the lifetime of the robot, the first module is fixed, while the second module uses the first module as a predictor and adapts its weights using back-propagation.

During evolution, the training period is made of 10 epochs. At the beginning of each epoch, both the target and the Khepera robot are set to random positions; the robot explores the arena (60 × 20 cm) during at most 500 times steps, until either it hits the 2cm radius target, increasing its fitness by $500 - t_{hit}$, or it hits a wall, getting no fitness for that epoch (Note that the target is not "visible").

The main result obtained in [9] was that auto-teaching networks did exhibit an adaptive behavior when the color of the walls changed from black to white.

Building on those results, our plan was to examine how the auto-teaching networks adapt to rapidly changing environments. To this aim, the color of the walls was changed every generation, alternating dark and white walls.

As in [9], we used an ES-like Evolutionary Algorithm in which 20 parents generate 100 offspring. The weights were real-coded genotypes, and their values were limited to $[-10, 10]$. The mutation rate was 10%. However, in order to approach the performances, some slight modifications were necessary: we used a (20+100)-ES rather than a (20,100)-ES; We used Gaussian mutation with fixed standard deviation .5 instead of uniform mutation with amplitude 1; And we used some crossover at rate 40%.

2.2 Training Period

A first remark is that we failed to fully reproduce the results in [9], due to the very high variability of the fitness with respect to the starting positions of the robot and the target. This variability was clearly visible when post-processing the best individuals from the last generation: out of 10 epochs, it never came even close to the same fitness than it had been given during its last evaluation. The only way to get over that variability and to come close to that was to run 10 times 10 epochs and to take the best results out of those 10 evaluations.

Nevertheless, the on-line results (best and average of 11 runs) resemble those of [9] with higher variance, as can be seen on Figure 4-left, and show a rapid increase toward a somehow stationary value of 2500. However, when we started to investigate the behavior of the controllers over a large number of epochs, we discovered drastic changes after the 10 epochs of "normal" lifetime – most robots starting to repeatedly hit the walls (Figure 4-right).

2.3 Generalization Period

Figure 1-right and Figure 2 show typical results in our setting for that experiment. For each epoch (x coordinate), a bar shows whether the robot found the target (positive bar, the smaller the better) or hit the wall (negative bar). To make the figure more readable, no bar is displayed when the robot neither found the target nor hit the wall. The "most decent" individual (Fig. 1-left) only starts hitting the walls after 300 epochs – though it does not find the target very often after the initial 10 epochs. Figure 2 is a disastrous individual, that starts crashing exactly after 10 epochs. More precisely, the best individuals (gathered after a re-evaluation on 10 times 10 epochs of all individuals in the final population) hit the walls on average for 400 epochs out of 1000, the one displayed on Figure 1-left being the best one with only 142 crashes.

The interpretation offered for these results is that once again, evolution found a mouse hole to reach the goal: because what happens after the training period does not influence selection, anything can indeed happen then. The underlying

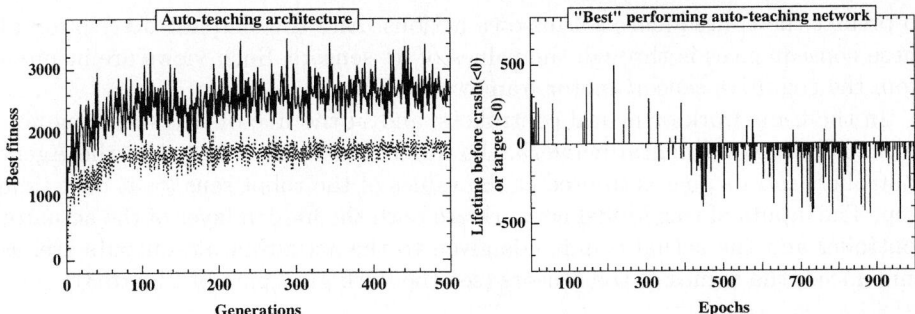

Fig. 1. Experiments with auto-teaching architecture: Left - On-line results (peak and average from 11 independent runs). Right - Life-times for the "Less Disastrous" results on long-term adaptation: negative values indicates that the epoch ended with a crash.

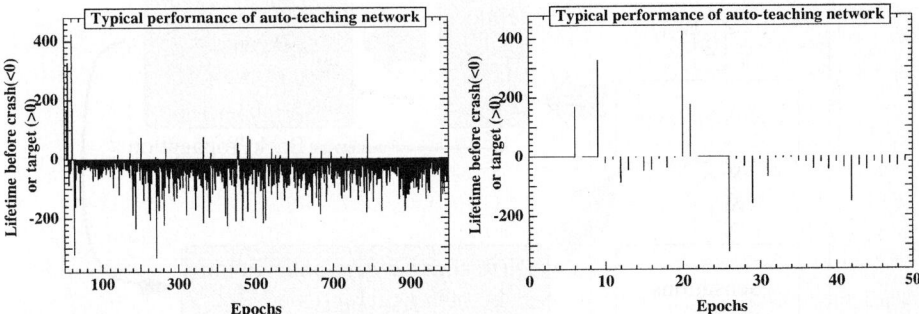

Fig. 2. More typical behaviors on long-term runs: Left - for 1000 epochs. Right - Zoom on the first 50 epochs.

dynamical system modifies the weights according to some evolved model that only has to be accurate during 10 epochs.

A totally unrealistic solution would be to increase the training period by an order of magnitude during evolution. The anticipatory architecture presented in the next section is an attempt to address the above limitations.

3 Action, Anticipation, Adaptation

The *AAA* architecture for neural controllers achieves three tasks: action (controlling the robot effectors); anticipation (based on the robot sensors, and the action output); adaptation (based on the difference between the sensor values anticipated in the previous time step, and the current sensor values).

As mentioned in the introduction, the basic underlying idea of the *AAA* architecture is that the adaptation mechanism must apply only when needed, and must be based on "true errors" rather than errors coming from an arbitrary model purposely evolved. In other words, rather than build a declarative model of the world, the idea is to give the robot a procedural model that will allow him to predict the consequence sof his own actions. And the simplest description of these consequences is through the values of its sensors. Such views are inspired from the cognitive sensori-motor framework [10].

In the framework or neural controllers, and in the line of auto-teaching networks [9], a second neural network, the Model network, is added to the Agent controller, and its goal is to predict the values of the robot sensors at next time step. The inputs of this Model network are both the hidden layer of the actuator controller and the actual commands given to the actuators. Its outputs are, as announced, the values of the sensors (see the dark gray part of Figure 3).

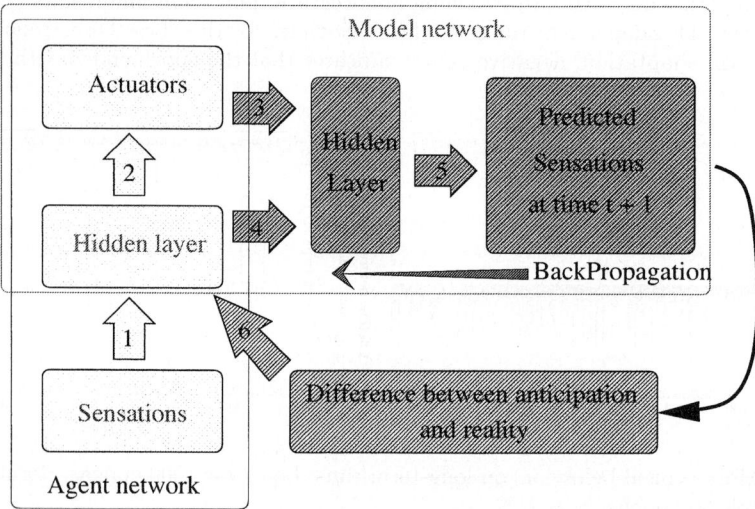

Fig. 3. The complete Anticipatory Neural Architecture. Rounded boxes are neurons, large arrows are connection weights. The classical Agent network gives actuator commands from the sensations. The Model network predicts values for the sensors from the intermediate layer of the actuator network and the actual actuator commands. Back-propagation is applied using the prediction error to all weights backward: 5, then 3 and 4, then 2, then 1. The prediction errors are also added as inputs to the Agent network.

Those predictions are then compared with the actual values sent by the sensors at next time step, and the results of these comparisons are used for a back-propagation algorithm that adjusts the weights of both the Model and the Agent networks, as described on Figure 3. Another possible use of those errors, not used in the experiments described in this paper, is to add them as direct inputs to the actuator network (light gray part of Figure 3). The first author's PhD will consider such alternate architecture.

Note that similar architectures had been proposed in [4], in the framework of robot arm controllers, as an alternative to directly building the inverse problem.

4 Long Term Robustness of *AAA* Architecture

4.1 The Neural Network

In the experimental framework considered in this paper, the Khepera has 4 inputs (pairs of infra-red sensors), 2 outputs (two independent motors). Hence the anticipatory part of the network must also have 4 outputs. Both hidden layers of the actuator network and of the anticipatory network have 5 neurons. Considering that all neurons also have a bias as input, the resulting network hence has 5×5 (arrows 1 and 6 + bias on Figure 3) + 6×2 (arrow 2 + bias) weights on the actuator network, plus 8×5 (arrows 3 and 4 + bias) + 6×4 (arrow 5) weights for the anticipatory network – 101 weights altogether. All those weights are submitted to back-propagation when some error occurs on the sensor predictions.

4.2 Long-Term Robustness

The same simulated experiment than that of [9] was run with the *AAA* Architecture. The learning curves along evolution are given on Figure 4-left, averaged on 11 independent runs: they are not very different from the same plots for the auto-teaching network (Figure 4-left). But the results about long-term adaptation are by no way comparable. Whereas the auto-teaching networks show unpredictable behaviors after the initial 10 epochs the anticipatory controllers stay rather stable when put in the same never-ending adaptation environment (e.g. the color of the walls change every 10 epochs, while adaptation though back-propagation is still going on). A typical summary of the behavior of the best individual of an evolution of the anticipative architecture can be seen on Figure 4-right: apart from a few crashes due to starting positions very close to the wall, almost no crash occurs in that scenario.

More precisely, out of 11 independent runs, 8 never crash in 1000 epochs (plots not shown!) while the 3 others had a behavior similar to that displayed on Figure 4-right: they never crash when the walls are white, and start hitting the dark walls after 700-800 epochs of continuous learning.

All those results clearly demonstrate that the anticipatory architecture does not suffer from the auto-teaching networks' defects, and exhibit very stable behaviors even after thousands of epochs (the 8 crash-free best individuals were run up to 50000 epochs with no crash at all).

4.3 Adaptation in *AAA* Networks

An important issue, however, is that of the adaptivity of the anticipatory architecture. Indeed, more sophisticated architectures than the simple auto-teaching network described in section 2.1 (like for instance a 3 layers network with one fully recurrent hidden layer) can be evolved to be robust in both the white and black environment – the robots will simply stay further away from the walls in

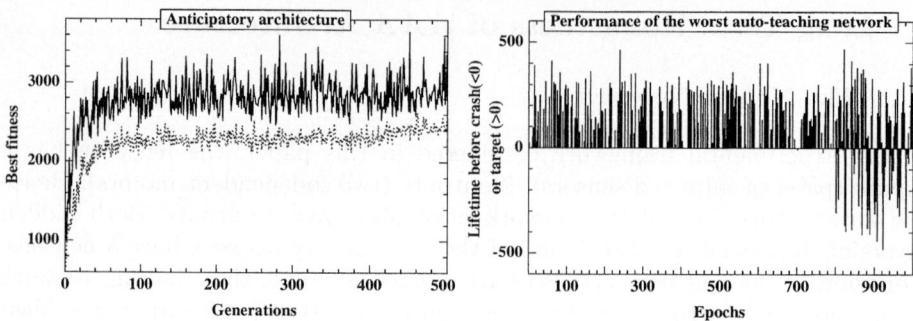

Fig. 4. Experiments with the anticipating architecture: Left - On-line results (average best and average from 11 independent runs). Right - **Worst** result on long-term adaptation (the wall color changes every 10 epochs).

the white environment. But such architectures do not have any adaptive mechanism, and the experiments presented now will demonstrate that the anticipatory architecture does behave adaptively.

The initial a posteriori experiments described in previous section (let the robot live for 1000 epochs, alternating dark and white walls every 10 epochs) did not give any evidence of adaptivity: all anticipatory controllers behave similarly, crashing very rarely against the walls, and behaving almost the same in both dark and white environments: due to the large number of weights, their values change rather slowly.

It was hence decided to let the weights adjust during 100 epochs in the same environment, and some interesting phenomena started to appear. First, after 100 epochs, some individuals began to have trajectories like the ones plotted on Figure 6: whereas the initial weights allow a cautious behavior in case of dark walls (the robot stays farther from the walls, see the thick line on the top plot), this is no longer the case after 100 epochs of weight modification, as witnessed by the bottom plot of Figure 6, where the red cross indicates that the robot hit the wall (dark walls) while it still avoids the walls when they are white. Indeed, after 100 epochs of adaptation to the white walls, the immediate epochs in the dark environment always resulted in a crash. Note that the reverse is not true, and individuals that have spent their first 100 epochs in the white environment never hit any wall, black or white afterward.

But more importantly, after some time in the dark environment, the behavior of the robot comes back to collision-free trajectories. Figure 5 shows two situations in which this happens. When, after the initial 100 epochs in the white environment, the walls remain black forever (left), the number of crashes gradually decreases, and no crash takes place during the last 100 epochs. More surprisingly, when the wall change color every 100 epochs, the rate of crashes also decreases (Figure 5-right), and in fact, it decreases even more rapidly than in the previous scenario – something that requires further investigations.

Note that control experiments with the auto-teaching networks still exhibited an enormous amount of crashes, whatever the scenario.

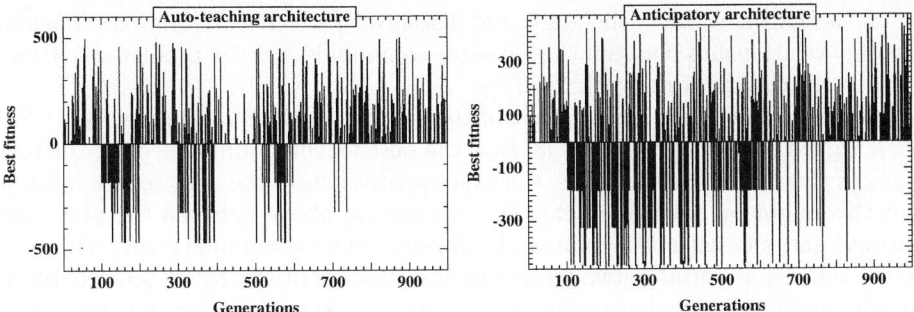

Fig. 5. Adaptation by the Anticipating architecture: 100 epochs are run with white walls; the robot is then put in the dark environment for 900 epochs (left) or is put alternatively in dark and white environments by periods of 100 epochs (right).

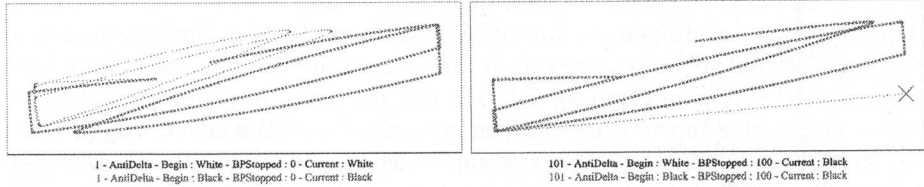

Fig. 6. Trajectories of the best individual of an evolution of an anticipative architecture, where the thick lines correspond to dark walls and the thin line to white walls. The stating points are the same for all trajectories. Left: Initial behavior during the first epoch, before any adaptation could take place. Right: behavior after 100 epochs of adaptation in the white environment.

5 Discussion and Further Work

The idea of using anticipation to better adapt to changing environments is not new, and has been proposed in many different areas. Anticipatory Classifiers Systems [11] are based on anticipation, but in a discrete framework that hardly scales up.

Trying to predict some other entity's action also amounts to anticipation, but does not really try to anticipate on the consequences of one's own actions (e.g. a program playing "psychological" games [1], or multi-agent systems [13]). Trying to directly predict its own sensor values has also been tried to help building Cognitive Maps in Robotics [2]: the prediction error is then used as a measure of interest for an event.

But the architecture the most similar to AAA has been proposed in the Evolutionary Robotic domain by Nolfi, Elman and Parisi [6] in a simpler framework, for artificial organisms foraging food. First of all, no long term experiment was described in that work. Moreover, their architecture did not use the prediction errors as supplementary inputs - but it did use the last output commands ... Furthermore, the sensors and the actuators were closely related: the sensory inputs were the direction and distance of the nearest food, while the commands for the actuators were ... the angle and distance to advance: in our experiments, the only relationship between the actuator commands and the predicted outputs is through the Agent network itself.

Another interesting issue is that of the outputs of the Model network. It has been argued by Nolfi and Parisi [8] that the best teaching inputs are not the correct answers for the network (i.e. the exact predictions of the next sensor values). But this might be because of that link mentioned above between the predicted outputs and the actuator commands. Indeed, some preliminary investigations inside the AAA neural networks during the lifetime of the robot seem to show that its predictions are here rather accurate most of the time: for instance, when the robot is far from any obstacle, the predicted values are indeed very close to 0 (and hence not modification of the weight does take place). But here again deeper investigations are required.

Looking at the behavior of adaptive systems from a long-term perspective asks new questions beyond the traditional debate between Nolfi's model of interaction between learning and evolution [5] and Harvey's claim that the success of learning + evolution only comes from the relearning of weights that have been perturbed by some mutation [3]. Indeed, the successful re-adaptation observed after a long period in the white environment (Section 4.3) seems to suggest that the learning is not limited to correcting some weight modifications. However, more work is needed to understand how such re-adaptation has been made possible by evolution. In particular, a detailed monitoring of how the weights adapt on-line should bring arguments to this debate.

Another important issue is that of the scaling up of the AAA architecture with the number of sensors (e.g. if the robot is equipped with some vision system). A possible answer might come from the *information bottleneck* theory [12]: this model tries to compress the sensor information as much as possible, while still maintaining feasible a reconstruction of the world that is sufficient for the task at hand. In that perspective, the hidden layer of the Agent network (Figure 3) could then be viewed as the set of *perceptions* of the robot, and the Model network could then try to predict this minimal compressed information rather than the numerous sensor values.

Finally, running the AAA architecture in real-world environment will be the ultimate validation of the approach. However, the experiment used in this paper is not likely to be easily portable to real-word, because of the huge variance of the results. Using the amount of area swept by the robot seems a better idea, and preliminary results (in simulation) suggest that the phenomena also happen with such more stable fitness.

6 Conclusion

After having pointed out a major weakness of auto-teaching networks, the unpredictability of their long-term behavior, we have proposed the AAA architecture to remedy this problem: the evolved oracle of auto-teaching networks without any grasp on reality, is replaced by a Model network that will learn to predict the values of the sensors of the robot. The modification of the weights of the

Agent network (the motor control) is then based on the errors made for those predictions. The first results in terms of long-term robustness are outstanding compared to those of the auto-teaching networks. Moreover, at least some of those networks do exhibit a very interesting adaptive behavior: after having evolved during 100 epochs in a white environment, they can gradually re-adapt to dark walls.

However, a lot of work remains to be done to assess the efficiency and usefulness of the AAA architecture, starting with a better understanding of how and why such anticipatory networks can re-adapt their weights on-line without any direct incentive or reward for collision avoidance. Forthcoming experiment will involve other variants of the AAA architecture (e.g. adding the error on the prediction as inputs to the controller), more meaningful scenarios (e.g. tracking regularly moving objects) and more importantly precise monitoring of the weight adaptation in different situations for some evolved controllers. We nevertheless hope that anticipatory networks can somehow help bridging the gap between fully reactive controllers and sensori-motor systems.

References

1. Meyer C., Akoulchina I., and Ganascia J.-G. Learning Strategies in Games by Anticipation. In *Proc. IJCAI'97*. Morgan Kaufmann, 1997.
2. Y. Endo and R.C. Arkin. Anticipatory Robot Navigation by Simultaneously Localizing and Building a Cognitive Map. In *ICOS'03 - Intl. Conf. on Intelligent Robots and Systems*. IEEE/RSJ, 2003.
3. I. Harvey. Is there another new factor in evolution? *Evolutionary Computation*, 4(3):311–327, 1997. Special Issue: 100 Years of the Baldwin Effect.
4. M. Jordan and D. Rumelhart. Forward models: Supervised learning with a distal teacher. *Cognitive Science*, 16, 1992.
5. S. Nolfi. How learning and evolution interact: The case of a learning task which differs from the evolutionary task. *Adaptive Behavior*, 7(2):231–236, 2000.
6. S. Nolfi, J.L. Elman, and D. Parisi. Learning and evolution in neural networks. *Adaptive Behavior*, 3(1):5–28, 1994.
7. S. Nolfi and D. Floreano. How co-evolution can enhance the adaptive power of artificial evolution: implications for evolutionary robotics. In P. Husbands and J.A. Meyer, editors, *Proceedings of EvoRobot98*, pages 22–38. Springer Verlag, 1998.
8. S. Nolfi and D. Parisi. Desired answers do not correspond to good teaching input in ecological neural networks. *Neural Processing Letters*, 2(1):1–4, 1994.
9. S. Nolfi and D. Parisi. Learning to adapt to changing environments in evolving neural networks. *Adaptive Behavior*, 5(1):75–98, 1997.
10. J. Kevin O'Regan and Alva Noë. A sensorimotor account of vision and visual consciousness. *Behavioral and Brain Sciences*, 24(5), 2001.
11. W. Stolzmann. An introduction to anticipatory classifier systems. In P.L. Lanzi et al., editors, *LCS'99*, pages 175–194. LNAI 1813, Springer Verlag, 2000.
12. N. Tishby, F. C. Pereira, and W. Bialek. The information bottleneck method. In *Proc. 37-th Allerton Conf. on Communication, Control and Computing*, pages 368–377, 1999.
13. M. Veloso, P. Stone, and M. Bowling. Anticipation as a key for collaboration in a team of agents: A case study in robotic soccer. In *SPIE Sensor Fusion and Decentralized Control in Robotic Systems II*, volume 3839, 1999.

A Self-adaptive Neural Learning Classifier System with Constructivism for Mobile Robot Control

Jacob Hurst and Larry Bull

Faculty of Computing, Engineering & Mathematical Sciences,
University of the West of England, Bristol BS16 1QY, U.K.
Larry.Bull@uwe.ac.uk

Abstract. For artificial entities to achieve true autonomy and display complex life-like behaviour they will need to exploit appropriate adaptable learning algorithms. In this sense adaptability implies flexibility guided by the environment at any given time and an open-ended ability to learn appropriate behaviours. This paper examines the use of constructivism-inspired mechanisms within a neural learning classifier system architecture which exploits parameter self-adaptation as an approach to realise such behaviour. The system uses a rule structure in which each is represented by an artificial neural network. It is shown that appropriate internal rule complexity emerges during learning at a rate controlled by the learner and that the structure indicates underlying features of the task. Results are presented from using a mobile robot platform.

1 Introduction

The Neural Constructivist [e.g., 1] explanation for the emergence of complex reasoning within brains postulates that the dynamic interaction between neural growth mechanisms and the environment drives the learning process. This is in contrast to related evolutionary selectionist ideas which emphasise regressive mechanisms whereby initial neural over-connectivity is pruned based on a measure of utility [e.g., 2]. The scenario for constructivist learning is that, rather than start with a large neural network development begins with a small network. Learning then adds appropriate structure, particularly through growing/pruning dendritic connectivity, until some satisfactory level of utility is reached. Suitable specialized neural structures are not specified *a priori*. The representation of the problem space is flexible and tailored by the learner's interaction with it. We are interested in the feasibility of a constructive approach to realize flexible learning within both simulated and real entities, in an architecture which combines neural networks, reinforcement learning and evolutionary computing. Such machine learning techniques have often been used to control autonomous entities. However, in almost all cases the entities acquire knowledge within a predefined representation scheme. Conversely, biological systems, through individually experienced sensory input and motor actions, constantly acquire new information and organize it into operational knowledge which then shapes future behaviour. Approaches which generate knowledge representations to bring new meaning to the functionality of the system are fundamental to the realization of truly autonomous entities. The aim of this research is to move toward artificial entities which exhibit such life-like qualities, based around the Learning Classifier System (LCS) [3] framework and neural constructivism.

The production of embodied intelligence requires the consideration of a number of issues including, but not limited to: the learning architecture, which must be flexible and responsive to environmental change, with automatic shifts in computational effort; and the knowledge representation, needed to provide generalization abilities over the input/output space thereby reducing the size of internal models and which must allow the inclusion of dimensions such as temporal context. In this paper we examine the suitability of a self-adaptive learning system which considers these key issues within a coherent whole - the Neural Learning Classifier System [4].

Since their inception Learning Classifier Systems have been compared to neural networks, both conceptually [e.g., 5] and functionally [e.g., 6]. LCS traditionally use a binary rule representation, augmented with 'wildcard' symbols to allow for generalizations. This can become limiting in more complex domains (e.g., see [7] for early discussions). We exploit a neural network-based scheme where each rule's condition and action are represented by a neural network. The weights/variables of each neural rule being concatenated together and evolved under the actions of the genetic algorithm (GA)[8]. The approach is closely related to the use of evolutionary computing techniques in general to produce neural networks (see [9] for an overview). In contrast to most of that work, an LCS-based approach is coevolutionary, the aim being to develop a number of (small) cooperative neural networks to solve the given task, as opposed to the evolution of one (large) network. That is, a decompositional approach to the evolution of neural networks is proposed. Moriarty and Miikulainen's SANE [10] is most similar to the work described here, however SANE coevolves individual neurons to form a large network rather than small networks of neurons as rules.

The paper is arranged as follows: the next section describes the self-adaptive Neural Learning Classifier System containing constructivism-inspired processes and its consideration of continuous time and space. The mobile robot platform is then presented followed by experimentation within a non-stationary problem domain.

2 A Neural Learning Classifier with Constructivism

The Neural LCS (NCS) used in this work is based on TCS [11], which is in turn based on ZCS [12] a simple LCS which has been shown to have the potential to perform optimally through its use of fitness sharing [13]. It periodically receives an input from its environment, determines an appropriate response based on this input and performs the indicated action, usually altering the state of the environment. Desired behaviour is rewarded by providing a scalar reinforcement. Internally the system cycles through a sequence of performance, reinforcement and discovery on each system cycle.

The NCS used here consists of a population of P radial basis function networks (RBFs) [14]. Each rule encodes a series of centres (one per hidden layer node), their spreads (where each hidden layer node has one spread per input node) and the weights of connections from the hidden layer nodes to the output layer nodes (full connection assumed). The centres are seeded uniformly randomly in the range [0.0,1.0], the widths are seeded uniformly randomly in the range [0.0,0.04], and the weights are seeded uniformly randomly in the range [-0.5,0.5]. Also associated with each rule is a fitness scalar f initialised to a predetermined value f_0 and a mutation rate μ initialised uniformly randomly in the range [0.0, 0.1] which is self-adapted as described below.

The basic concept of neural constructivism can be used within NCS to allow for the emergence of appropriate rule complexity to a given task [4]. Here each rule can have from one up to a maximal fixed number of nodes in its hidden layer, fully connected to the input and output layers. At each reproduction event, after mutation, with some probability (ψ), a constructivism event can occur in the given offspring. With some probability (ϖ) this causes connections to a new node to be added with random parameters, otherwise the last connected node is disconnected. The two probabilities are initialised uniformly randomly in the allowed range [0.0, 1.0] and self-adapted in the same way as the mutation rate (see below). Hence the number of hidden nodes exploited by a given rule evolves over time, at a rate determined by the rule and guided by its interactions with the environment.

On receipt of a sensory input all the rules in the rule-base process the input and those that match the input form a match set [M]. There are three output nodes for each RBF rule here. If any one of these has an output of greater than 0, the rule is said to match the input. The action for an individual classifier is decided by which of the output nodes has the highest level of activation. In this way the NCS has three actions available; move continuously left, right or forward. An action is selected from the rules contained in [M]. Action selection is a simple roulette wheel process based on proportional fitness. All rules that match the current input and advocate the chosen action are placed in an action set [A]. The rules that match the current input but do not form part of [A], are subject to a tax (τ) on their fitness.

The NCS exploits actions of continuous duration. While the system is carrying out the ordained action, the input from the environment is continually sampled. To decide if the NCS should continue with an action or drop it, the current input is passed through the RBF rules in the current [A]. In the case where none of the current members of [A] match the input, the procedure is straight forward: the current members of the action set are moved to the previous action set where they receive an internal reward. A new action is then selected. When all the classifiers in [A] match the current input, the effect is to continue with the current action. The situation where a proportion of the classifiers match the current input and a proportion do not is more complex. A decision has to be made either to continue with the current action, or stop and consider a different action. The action set can therefore be divided into two sets: those rules advocating to continue with the action, the "continue set" [C]; and those advocating stopping the current action, the "drop set" [D]. Simple roulette wheel selection is then carried out over the entire action set based on fitness as before. If the rule selected is from the drop set, all members of [C] are removed from [A] and the contents of the action set are moved to the previous action set, where they receive internal reinforcement. If however the rule is selected from [C], all rules contained in [D] are removed from the current action set and taxed by τ. The system continues with the action until a drop decision is taken or an external event occurs. A further test must be made to see if the action proposed by rules in [C] has changed. That is, under the neural representation rules can change which output node has the highest activation with only a slight change in input. Therefore, the action with the highest total fitness in [C] is chosen and the remaining rules are then treated in the same way as the drop set.

For the experiments examined here, the external events that break an action-continue cycle are when the robot hits the wall, hits the light switch (and receives external reward) or if the action has continued longer then a maximum predefined limit (i.e., the robot is most likely to be moving in a circle).

External and internal reward received by the system is not discounted by a fixed factor (as in most LCS, e.g., ZCS) but by a variable factor depending upon the time taken by the system to reach the current state. In the case of the external reward the total time taken from the start state to the goal state is used to discount the reward. With the internal reward the time taken is the time to move from one state to the next. In this way the reinforcement learning process moves away from generalizing over *Markov* decision state spaces to generalizing over *Semi-Markov Decision Processes* (see [15]). More formally:

$$S_{[A]} \xleftarrow{\beta} e^{-\phi t^t} r_{imm} + e^{-\eta t^i} S_{[A]'}$$

where $S_{[A]}$ is the fitness of the current action set, $S_{[A]'}$ is the fitness of the succeeding actionset, r_{imm} is the immediate external reward, $\xleftarrow{\beta}$ is the Widrow Hoff delta rule with learning rate β, t^t is the total time to achieve the task, t^i is the duration of the action, and ϕ and η are their respective discount factors. The overall effect of this algorithm is for the LCS to learn appropriate discretizations in the continuous input space, as it solves the given reinforcement learning task, exploiting its population of rules developed under the GA (other approaches have been presented, e.g., [16]).

NCS employs two discovery mechanisms, a genetic algorithm that operates over the whole rule-set and a covering operator. For this work, the GA is invoked when the goal state is reached only as this has been found to aid on-line performance. When called, the GA uses traditional roulette wheel selection to obtain two parent rules based on their fitness. Two offspring are produced per GA invocation. These offspring are copies of the parental rules that have been mutated at a per gene rate which is determined by themselves. That is, each rule has its own mutation rate μ which is passed to its offspring. Each offspring then applies its mutation rate to itself using the following update $\mu' = \mu * e^{N(0,1)}$ (as in Evolutionary Strategies, see [17] for an overview), before mutating the rest of the rule at the resulting rate. Upon satisfaction of the probability, genes are altered using a step size taken from a Gaussian distribution $N(0,1)$. The parents then donate half of their fitness to their offspring who replace existing members of the population. The deleted rules are chosen using roulette wheel selection based on the reciprocal of fitness. It can be noted that by not using recombination, the potentially troublesome competing conventions problem [18] (similarly fit solutions represented by different encodings) is avoided, as is the need for a modified operator to handle variable length individuals (as experienced under the constructivism process). The GA is invoked twice per trial end here.

If on some time-step, [M] is empty a covering operator is invoked. A random rule is created which matches the environmental input. The new rule is given a fitness equal to the population average and inserted into the population over writing a rule selected for deletion as before.

3 Robotic Environment

The task examined in this paper is a relatively simple robot learning experiment but it is non-stationary since the robot must learn phototaxis and then the same phototaxis with sensor disruption; the task allows for demonstration of the preferable algorithmic characteristics noted in the introduction. A large amount of effort has been taken to automate the setup so experiments can be run without needing human monitoring or direct involvement (after [11]). Motivation for this particular experiment also comes from the only other significant body of work using LCS for the control of real robots, that by Dorigo et al. (see [19] for an overview). They used a hierarchical architecture to learn various phototaxis and obstacle avoidance behaviours. However, their work used step-by-step reinforcement – "behavioural shaping" – rather than the standard delayed reward scenario used here [20]. This work is also related to that undertaken in evolutionary robotics, particularly using neural rule representations (e.g., see [21]).

The robotic platform used in the experiments described is the University of the West of England's "LinuxBot". This is a three-wheeled robot, the rear two wheels of which are powered. It is controlled via a radio LAN system and acts as a probe with motor commands being sent by the LCS algorithm running on a base station. Sensory information takes the form of three real-valued numbers from three light sensors placed on the top of the robot (Figure 1(a)). All sensor values are scaled between 0 and 5. The robot also has three IR proximity sensors placed on the front of the robot which are not used here. Turning actions are obtained by slowing one of the wheels to half its usual speed.

(a)   (b)

Fig. 1. The LinuxBot platform and the experimental setup.

Figure 1(b) shows the experimental setup where the robot runs on a metallic powered floor, allowing experiments to be run for extended time periods. The lights are surrounded with metal bumpers and only one is on at any given time. When the light is on and the bumper surrounding it is hit, this light is then switched off and the light at the opposite end of the arena is switched on. This switching is monitored by a computer base station, which sends a message to the LCS informing it that the robot has reached its goal state. The robot then automatically reverses and rotates by 180 degrees. The curvature of the light bumpers and the different angles by which the robot can hit the bumpers ensures that the robot does not always have the same initial orientation for the next trial. Figure 2(b) illustrates the experimental area (obstacle seen is not incorporated here). The arena is a rectangle 2.2 m x 1.7 m and the optimal time to reach the goal state from a start state is ~12 seconds. As well as possessing light and IR sensors, the robot also has two "bump sensors". When these are hit the robot automatically stops whatever action it is doing and reverses 10 cm and sends a signal to the controlling algorithm.

4 Results

Results presented are the average of five runs, without smoothing (common in LCS simulations [e.g., 12]) to clearly indicate the robot's online performance. The parameters are: $P = 1500, f_0 = 10.0, r_{imm} = 1000$ $\beta = 0.85, \phi = 0.5, \eta = 0.05$. The robot is given 350 trials to learn the phototaxis task, after which the robot's light sensor inputs are swapped. That is, the input to the left sensor is presented to the node which was originally taking input from the right sensor and *vice-versa*, and the robot is then given another 350 trials to re-adapt.

Figure 2(a) shows the performance of the NCS. It can be seen that the time taken to reach the goal drops to around 20 seconds after about 110 trials but there is continued variation – some trials are near optimal whereas others can take over five times as long. This can be attributed to several reasons: the action selection policy is not particularly greedy but allows constant online adaptation; the GA is constantly introducing new rules, again to maintain the learning ability of the system; and, the goal state has only been visited a few hundred times and so unexplored aspects of the environ-

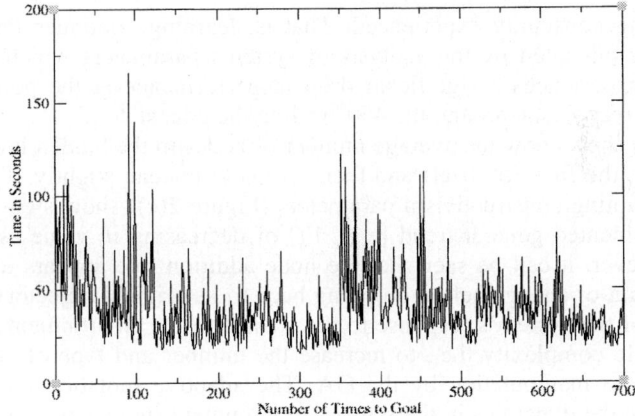

Fig. 2a. Performance of NCS on the dynamic phototaxis task.

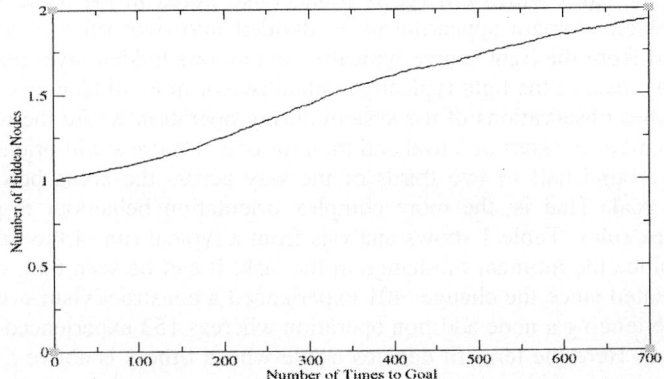

Fig. 2b. Average number of hidden layer nodes.

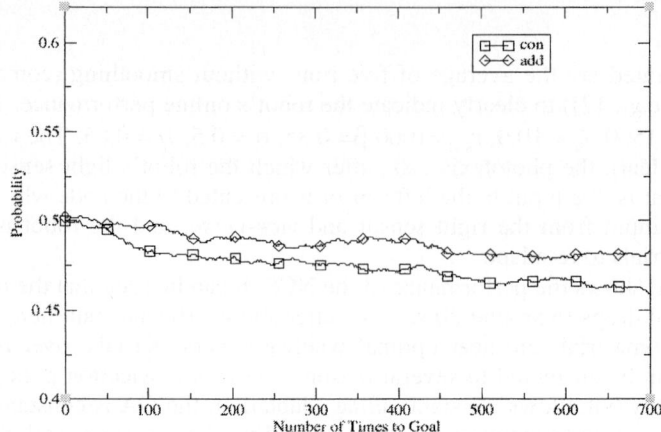

Fig. 2c. Movement of the neural constructivism parameters.

ment are being constantly experienced. That is, learning continues throughout this period, as demonstrated by the analysis of systems parameters which follows. The system then experiences a significant drop in performance at the point of change, from which it recovers at around the 450th visit to the goal state.

Figure 2(b) shows how the average number of nodes in the hidden layer rapidly increases during the first 350 trials and then begins to plateau slightly. The movement of the self-adapting constructivism parameters (Figure 2(c)) show signs of following the well documented general trend [e.g., 17] of decreasing in value as the run progresses. However, it can be seen that the node addition rate appears to rise slightly around the point of change before dropping back to its original trajectory downwards. That is, part of the system's response to the change in the environment appears to be to increase rule complexity, i.e., to increase the number and type of generalizations (basins) open to manipulation by the GA. The adaptive mutation rate shows little change despite the dynamics in the sensory environment (not shown). This is perhaps due to the restricted seeding founded necessary to achieve learning in the time used.

Figure 3 shows some match set analysis of this task. Spatial heterogeneity in the structure of the rules which emerge is found (also noted in [4] using simulations), with the problem domain appearing to be divided into two: rules which match the arena furthest from the light source typically contain one hidden layer node and those which match closer to the light typically contain two or more hidden layer nodes. This finding matches observations of the system during operation where the usual strategy is to go forward at the start of a trial and then for one or more slight orientation moves to be made around half to two thirds of the way across the arena before the robot reaches the goal. That is, the more complex orientation behaviour is produced by more complex rules. Table 1 shows analysis from a typical run of the rules produced by the GA since the moment of change in the task. It can be seen that, of the 618 fit offspring created since the change, 401 experienced a constructivism event, with 248 of them experiencing a node addition operation whereas 153 experienced a node deletion operation. Here the term fit denotes a rule whose fitness is above f_0. That is, the additive response to a change suggested by the slight rise in the self-adapting rate of node addition under a constructivism event is clearly evident.

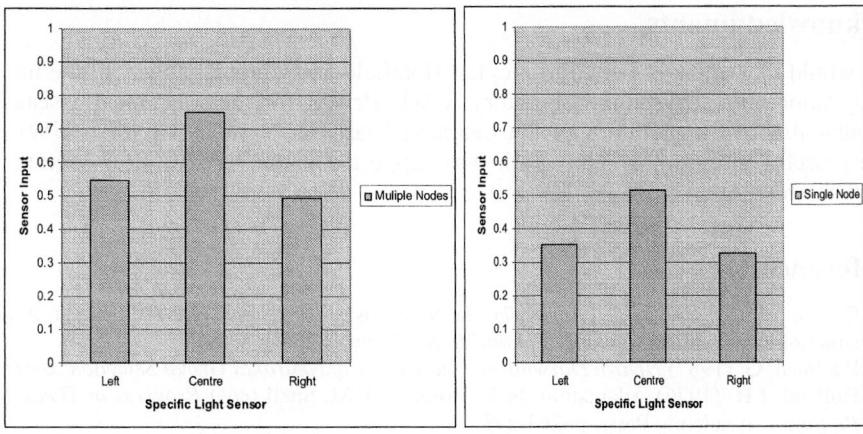

Fig. 3. Analysis of RBF rule structure in phototaxis task.

5 Conclusions

The Neural Learning Classifier System approach to artificial learning entities would appear to, potentially at least, encompass many of the key aspects raised in the introduction. This paper has explored the use of self-adaptive constructivism within the architecture as an approach to aid the realization of complex/appropriate autonomous behaviour, exploiting NCS's basis in evolutionary computing. In particular, it has been shown that the NCS is able to learn appropriate structure whilst interacting with a mobile robotics task.

The results presented here indicate reasonable performance for NCS in simple robotic tasks and adds to the previous work demonstrating that learning classifier systems have the ability to work in continuous space and time within robotic environments [11].

We are currently extending this work with the robot to incorporate gradient descent methods for determining the parameters of the RBF rules to increase the rate of learning (after [22]). Further, since NCS uses neural networks to generalize at the level of state-action pairs it can be used with continuous value actions without alteration (see [4]) and this is also under consideration. Other methods for constructivism are also being explored, along with other neural representations, and an accuracy-based fitness scheme (see [23]).

Table 1. Analysis of rule creation.

		Number of Addition Events	Number of Deletion Events
Number of construction events producing fit children	401	248	153
Number of construction events producing unfit children	84	69	15
Number of replication events with no construction producing fit children.	217		
Number of Replication events with no construction producing unfit children	79		

Acknowledgments

We would like to thank Ian Gillespie, Ian Horsfield and Chris Blythway of the Intelligent Autonomous Systems Laboratory, UWE Bristol for their technical assistance. Thanks also to the members of the Learning Classifier Systems Group at UWE for many useful discussions. This work was supported under EPSRC ROPA grant no. GR/R80469.

References

1. Quartz, S.R & Sejnowski, T.J. (1997) The Neural Basis of Cognitive Development: A Constructionist Manifesto. *Behavioural and Brain Sciences* 20(4): 537-596.
2. Edelman, G. (1987) *Neural Darwinism: The Theory of Neuronal Group Selection*. Basic.
3. Holland, J.H. (1976) Adaptation. In R. Rosen & F.M. Snell (eds) *Progress in Theoretical Biology* 4. Academic Press, pp263-293.
4. Bull, L. (2002) On using Constructivism in Neural Learning Classifier Systems. In J. Merelo, P. Adamidis, H-G. Beyer, J-L. Fernandez-Villacanas & H-P. Schwefel (eds) *Parallel Problem Solving from Nature - PPSN VII*. Springer Verlag, pp558-567
5. Farmer, D. (1989) A Rosetta Stone for Connectionism. *Physica D* 42:153-187.
6. Davis, L. (1989) Mapping Neural Networks into Classifier Systems. In J.D. Schaffer (ed.) *Proceedings of the Third International Conference on Genetic Algorithms,* Morgan Kaufmann, pp375-378.
7. Schuurmans, D. & Schaeffer, J. (1989) Representational Difficulties with Classifier Systems. In J.D. Schaffer (ed.) *Proceedings of the Third International Conference on Genetic Algorithms,* Morgan Kaufmann, pp328-333.
8. Holland, J.H. (1975) *Adaptation in Natural and Artificial Systems*. Univ. Michigan Press.
9. Yao, X. (1999) Evolving Artificial Neural Networks. *Proceedings of the IEEE* 87(9): 1423-1447.
10. Moriarty, D.E. & Miikulainen, R. (1997) Forming Neural Networks Through Efficient and Adaptive Coevolution. *Evolutionary Computation* 5(2): 373-399.
11. Hurst, J., Bull, L. & Melhuish, C. (2002) TCS Learning Classifier System Controller on a Real Robot. In J. Merelo, P. Adamidis, H-G. Beyer, J-L. Fernandez-Villacanas & H-P. Schwefel (eds) *Parallel Problem Solving from Nature - PPSN VII*. Springer Verlag, pp588-600.
12. Wilson, S.W. (1994) ZCS: A Zeroth-level Classifier System. *Evolutionary Computation* 2(1):1-18.
13. Bull, L. & Hurst, J. (2002) ZCS Redux. *Evolutionary Computation* 10(2): 185-205
14. Poggio, T. & Girosi, F. (1990) Networks for approximation and learning *Proceedings of the IEEE*, 78:1481-1497.
15. Parr, R. (1998) *Hierarchical Control and Learning for Markov Decision Processes*. PhD Thesis, University of California, Berkeley.
16. Santamaria, J.C., Sutton, R. & Ram, A. (1998) Experiments in Reinforcement Learning in Problems with Continuous State and Action Spaces. *Adaptive Behaviour* 6(2): 163-217.
17. Baeck, T. (1995) *Evolutionary Computation: Theory and Practice*. Oxford.
18. Montana, D.J. & Davis, L. (1989) Training Feedforward Neural Networks using Genetic Algorithms. In S. Sridharan (ed) *Proceedings of the Eleventh International Joint Conference on Artificial Intelligence*. Morgan Kauffman, pp762-767.
19. Dorigo, M. & Colombetti, M. (1997) *Robot Shaping*. MIT Press.
20. Sutton, R.S. & Barto, R. (1998) *Reinforcement Learning*. MIT Press.
21. Nolfi, S. & Floreano, D. (2000) *Evolutionary Robotics: Biology, Intelligence, and Technology of Self-Organizing Machines*. MIT Press.

22. O'Hara, T. & Bull, L. (2003) Backpropagation in Accuracy-based Neural Learning Classifier Systems. *UWE Learning Classifier Systems Group Technical Report - UWELCSG03-007*. Available from http://www.cems.uwe.ac.uk/lcsg
23. Bull, L. & O'Hara, T. (2002) Accuracy-based Neuro and Neuro-Fuzzy Classifier Systems. In W.B.Langdon, E.Cantu-Paz, K.Mathias, R. Roy, D.Davis, R. Poli, K.Balakrishnan, V. Honavar, G. Rudolph, J. Wegener, L. Bull, M. A. Potter, A.C. Schultz, J. F. Miller, E. Burke & N.Jonoska (eds) *Proceedings of the Genetic and Evolutionary Computation Conference – GECCO-02*. Morgan Kaufmann, pp905-911.

An Approach to Evolutionary Robotics Using a Genetic Algorithm with a Variable Mutation Rate Strategy

Yoshiaki Katada[1], Kazuhiro Ohkura[2], and Kanji Ueda[3]

[1] Graduate School of Science and Technology, Kobe University, Kobe, Japan
[2] Faculty of Engineering, Kobe University, Kobe, Japan
Phone/Fax: +81-78-803-6135
{katada,ohkura}@rci.scitec.kobe-u.ac.jp
[3] RACE (Research into Artifacts, Center for Engineering),
The University of Tokyo, Meguro, Japan
Phone: +81-3-5453-5887 Fax:+81-3-3467-0648
ueda@race.u-tokyo.ac.jp

Abstract. Neutral networks, which occur in fitness landscapes containing neighboring points of equal fitness, have attracted much research interest in recent years. In recent papers [20, 21], we have shown that, in the case of simple test functions, the mutation rate of a genetic algorithm is an important factor for improving the speed at which a population moves along a neutral network. Our results also suggested that the benefits of the variable mutation rate strategy used by the operon-GA [5] increase as the ruggedness of the landscapes increases. In this work, we conducted a series of computer simulations with an evolutionary robotics problem in order to investigate whether our previous results are applicable to this problem domain. Two types of GA were used. One was the standard GA, where the mutation rate is constant, and the other was the operon-GA, whose effective mutation rate at each locus changes independently according to the history of the genetic search. The evolutionary dynamics we observed were consistent with those observed in our previous experiments, confirming that the variable mutation rate strategy is also beneficial to this problem.

1 Introduction

Selective neutrality has been found in many real-world applications of artificial evolution, such as the evolution of neural network controllers in robotics [1, 2] and on-chip electronic circuit evolution [3, 4]. This characteristic is caused by highly redundant mappings from genotype to phenotype or from phenotype to fitness. With these kinds of problems, redundancy is inevitable. Even for problems where redundancy is largely absent, it may be useful to introduce it. A number of researchers have been trying to improve the performance of artificial evolution on more traditional problems by incorporating redundancy in genotype to phenotype mappings[5–8]. Neutrality is also found in natural systems, and has

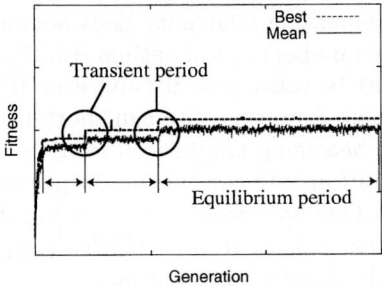

Fig. 1. Typical evolutionary dynamics on a fitness landscape featuring neutral networks, which can be classified into transient periods and equilibrium periods.

been of particular interest to evolutionary theorists [9] and molecular biologists [10, 11].

Landscapes which include neutrality have been conceptualized as containing *neutral networks* [6, 12, 13]. This concept is central to the majority of research in this field. Harvey [12] first introduced the concept of neutral networks into the GA community. His definition is as follows: "A neutral network of a fitness landscape is defined as a set of connected points of equivalent fitness, each representing a separate genotype: here connected means that there exists a path of single (neutral) mutations which can traverse the network between any two points on it without affecting fitness."

Evolutionary dynamics on neutral networks can be classified into transient periods and equilibrium periods (Fig. 1) [14, 15]. During an equilibrium period, the population is clustered in genotype space around the *dominant phenotype*, analogously to *quasi-species* [16], and moves around until it finds a portal to a neutral network of higher fitness. The discovery of a portal leads to a transient period, which is expected to be very short in comparison to an equilibrium period. It has been shown that there is a clear transition in evolutionary dynamics for populations on neutral networks over the mutation rate range. At a very low mutation rate, the population is maintained in a cluster on the neutral network. As the mutation rate increases, the population gradually loses the current network. That is, some individuals fall to lower neutral networks. At a certain critical mutation rate, the whole population will lose the current neutral network. This mutation rate is called the *phenotypic error threshold*[1] [14, 17, 18].

Generally, the error threshold sets the upper limit for a mutation rate that will enable efficient search. This implies that if we adopt a constant mutation rate strategy, we should set a relatively low mutation rate so as to avoid any error threshold effects during the process. From a practical point of view, however, it would be efficient to shorten the equilibrium period which dominates the whole computation (Fig. 1). Additionally, in landscapes which include ruggedness, individuals can easily get trapped on local optima if there is a low mutation rate and high selection pressure. It has been demonstrated in a tunably neutral NK

---

[1] These concepts originate from molecular evolution [10, 11].

landscape [17, 19] that increasing neutrality does not affect the ruggedness, although it does reduce the number of local optima [13, 17, 19]. This means that the effects of ruggedness must be taken into account even if landscapes include neutral networks. Using a high mutation rate can shorten equilibrium periods and help a population avoid becoming trapped on local optima. However, as noted above, using a high mutation rate can be counterproductive because of the effects of error thresholds. One approach to overcoming these problems would be to adopt *variable mutation rate strategies*, which change the effective mutation rate adaptively during the process of evolution.

Recently, we have investigated the effect of mutation rate and selection pressure on the speed of population movement on very simple neutral networks with different levels of neutrality [20]. We also examined the performance of GAs using terraced NK landscapes with different levels of ruggedness and different selection pressures. [21]. Our results can be summarized as follows:

- For a fixed population size, the speed of a population plotted as a function of the mutation rate yields a concave curve with an optimal mutation rate and an error threshold.
- Increasing the selection pressure will improve the speed at which a population moves on a neutral network.
- The variable mutation rate strategy used by the operon-GA [5] is not only beneficial with simple test functions but also with complex test functions. The benefits increase as the ruggedness of the landscapes increases.

We are interested in whether these observations are consistent with more complex problems. This is because we want to solve complex real-world problems. This paper investigates how well our previous results apply to the evolution of artificial neural networks for robot control by comparing a standard GA [22] and the operon-GA on an evolutionary robotics task using a simulated robot. The paper is organized as follows. The next section describes the neural networks adopted in a robot control problem. Section 3 defines the robot control problem where the evolved neural networks are evaluated. Section 4 gives the results of our computer simulations. Section 5 discusses the relationship between the correlation of the landscape and the overall GA performance. Conclusions are given in the last section.

2 The Neural Controller – Spike Response Model

The agent's behavior is controlled by a *spike response model* network [23], which is a form of *Pulsed Neural Network* (PNN). A neuron emits a spike when the total amount of excitation due to incoming excitatory and inhibitory spikes exceeds its firing threshold, θ. After firing, the membrane potential of the neuron is set to a low negative voltage, it then gradually returns to its resting potential; during this refractory period, a neuron cannot emit a new spike. The function η_i, accounting for neuronal refractoriness, is given by:

$$\eta_i(r) = -\exp(-\frac{r}{\tau_m})H(r) \qquad (1)$$

Here $r = t - t_i^{(f)}$ is the difference between the time t and the time of firing $t^{(f)}$ of neuron i, τ_m is a membrane time constant and $H(r)$ is the Heaviside step function which vanishes for $r < 0$ and gives a value of 1 for $r > 0$.

The function ε_{ij} describes the response to postsynaptic spikes: (2).

$$\varepsilon_{ij}(r) = [\exp(-\frac{r - \Delta^{ax}}{\tau_m})(1 - \exp(-\frac{r - \Delta^{ax}}{\tau_s}))]H(r - \Delta^{ax}) \quad (2)$$

where τ_s is a synaptic time constant, Δ^{ax} is the axonal transmission delay.

The membrane potential of a neuron i at time t is given by:

$$u_i(t) = \sum_{t_i^{(f)} \in F_i} \eta_i(t - t_i^{(f)}) + \sum_{j \in \Gamma_i} \sum_{t_j^{(f)} \in F_j} \omega_{ij} \varepsilon_{ij}(t - t_j^{(f)}) \quad (3)$$

where F_i is the set of firing times in a neuron i. The neuron i may receive the input from presynaptic neurons $j \in \Gamma_i$. The weight ω_{ij} is the strength of the connection from the jth neuron, and scales the amplitude of the response given in eq.(2).

3 The Task and the Fitness Function

The control task used in this paper was motion pattern discrimination [24], and is based on a task originally implemented by Beer [25]. The agent must discriminate between two types of vertically falling object based on the object's period of horizontal oscillation; it must catch (i.e., move close to) falling objects that have a long period whilst avoiding those with a short period (see Fig. 2). An array of proximity sensors allow the agent to perceive the falling objects. If an object intersects a proximity sensor, the sensor outputs a value inversely proportional to the distance between the object and the agent. The agent can move horizontally along the bottom of the arena. In our experiment, the agent of diameter 30 had 7 proximity sensors of maximum range 220 uniformly distributed over a visual angle of 45 degrees. The horizontal velocity of the agent was proportional to the sum of the opposing horizontal forces produced by a pair of effectors. It has

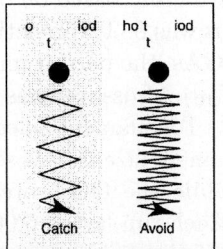
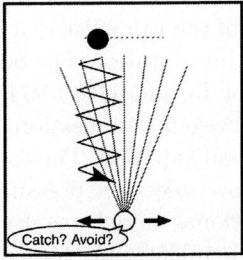

Fig. 2. Experimental setup for the discrimination of the motion patterns. Two kinds of period used in the discrimination experiments (left) and the agent in the arena with its array of the proximity sensors (right).

maximum velocity of 8. Each falling object was circular, with diameter 30, and dropped from the top of the arena with a vertical velocity of 4, a horizontal amplitude of 30 and an initial horizontal offset of ±50. An object's horizontal velocity was ±10 (12 steps in a period) for a long period and ±30 (4 steps in a period) for a short period.

The performance measure to be maximized was as follows:

$$Fitness = 1000 \sum_{i=1}^{NumTrials} \frac{P_i}{NumTrials} \qquad (4)$$

where $P_i = 1 - d_i$ for a long period and $P_i = d_i$ for a short period, $d_i = 1$ when $hd_i > 60$ and $d_i = hd_i/60$ when $hd_i \leq 60$, hd_i is the final horizontal distance between the center of the agent and the object, and $NumTrials$ is the number of trials for an individual (8 trials for each period).

4 Computer Simulations

4.1 Simulation Conditions

For this experiment, an agent's controller was a PNN with 7 sensory neurons, 2 fully interconnected motor neurons and N_h fully interconnected hidden neurons, where $N_h \in \{1, 10\}$. The network's connection weights and the firing threshold for each neuron were genetically encoded and evolved. The total number of parameters was either 33 ($N_h = 1$) or 240 ($N_h = 10$). The parameters were mapped linearly onto the following ranges: connection weights, $\omega \in [-1.0, 1.0]$, and thresholds, $\theta \in [0.0, 3.9]$. The parameters of the neurons and synapses (see section 2) were set as follows: $\tau_m = 4$, $\tau_s = 10$, $\Delta^{ax} = 2$ for all neurons and all synapses in the network following the recommendations given in [26]. Computer simulations were conducted using populations of size 50. Each individual was encoded as a binary string with 10 bits for each parameter. Therefore, the total length of the genotype was either $L_1 = 330$ ($N_h = 1$) or $L_{10} = 2400$ ($N_h = 10$). The standard GA (SGA) and the operon-GA (OGA) were employed to evolve the PNN parameters. The OGA uses standard bit mutation and five additional genetic operators: *connection*, *division*, *duplication*, *deletion* and *inversion*. The probabilities for genetic operations were set at 0.3 for *connection* and *division*, 0.2 for *duplication* and 0.05 for *deletion* and *inversion*, based on our previous results in [21]. The length of the value list in a locus was 6. The genetic operation for the SGA was standard bit mutation. For both GAs, the per-bit mutation rate, q, was set at $1/L$ (0.003 for L_1 and 0.000416 for L_{10}). Crossover was not used for either GA, following Nimwegen's suggestion [14]. Tournament selection was adopted. *Elitism*[2] was optionally applied. The tournament size, s, was set at $\{2, 6\}$ because the SGA prefers low selection pressure while the OGA prefers high selection pressure. A generational model was used. Each run lasted 6,000 generations. We conducted 10 independent runs for each of the sixteen conditions. All results were averaged over 10 runs.

---

[2] The fittest individual of each generation was passed un-mutated to the next generation (if several individuals had the highest fitness, one was randomly chosen.)

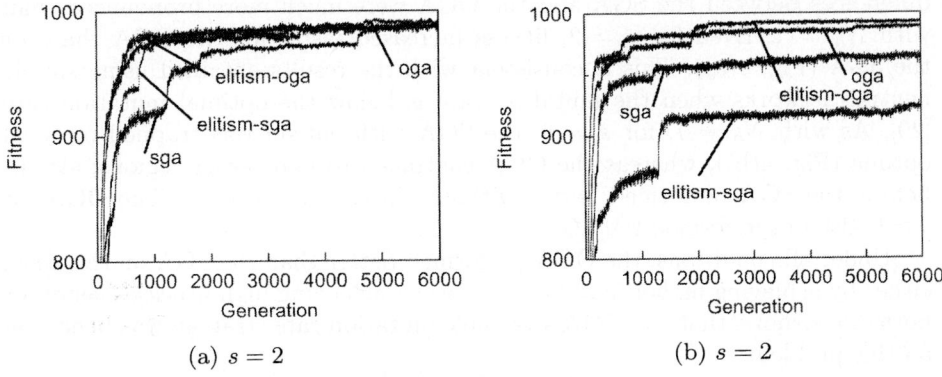

Fig. 3. The maximum fitness at each generation for $N_h = 1$.

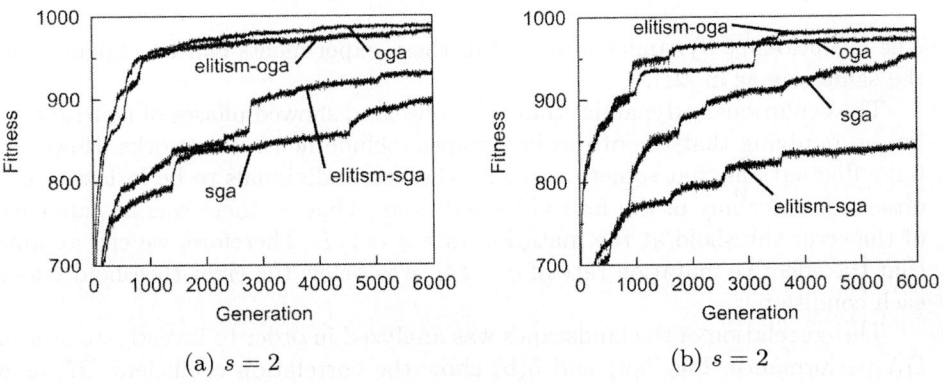

Fig. 4. The maximum fitness at each generation for $N_h = 10$.

4.2 Simulation Results

Fig. 3 shows the maximum fitness at each generation for the SGA and OGA, with and without elitism, for controllers with $N_h = 1$. Fig. 3(a) and 3(b) show the results for the four GA conditions for $s = 2$ and 6 respectively. For $s = 2$, fitness increased faster with the OGA than with the SGA in the early generations. In the final generation, there was no significant difference between the SGA and the OGA. For $s = 6$, the SGA was trapped on local optima, whereas the OGA continued to find better regions of the search space. In addition, the SGA performed better without elitism than with it. These results are consistent with the results obtained using terraced NK landscapes [21]. With respect to final generation fitnesses, there was no significant difference between the SGA with $s = 2$ and the OGA for $s = 6$. However, a closer examination reveals that during the process of evolution the OGA with $s = 6$ performed better than the SGA with $s = 2$ and elitism.

Fig. 4 shows the maximum fitness at each generation for the SGA and OGA, with and without elitism, for $s = 2$ and 6 with $N_h = 10$. With $N_h = 10$, differences between the SGA and the OGA were much more pronounced than with $N_h = 1$. Even for $s = 2$, fitness increased faster for the OGA than for the SGA (Fig. 4(a)). This is consistent with the results obtained using simple neutral networks when the mutation rate is below the optimal mutation rate [20]. As with $N_h = 1$, for $s = 6$, the SGA with elitism was trapped on local optima (Fig. 4(b)), whereas the OGA continued to find better regions; also as before, the SGA performed better without elitism than with it. The OGA for $s = 6$ also outperformed the SGA for $s = 2$.

Under all conditions, the OGA performed better than the SGA on this task, either by achieving higher final fitnesses, or by achieving high fitnesses faster, or both. This shows that the OGA's variable mutation rate strategy was beneficial on this problem.

5 Discussion

The evolutionary dynamics observed in these experiments can be explained in the same way as in [21].

The evolutionary dynamics that were observed showed phases of neutral evolution, implying that the fitness landscapes include neutral networks. However, large fluctuations that sometimes cause the best individuals to be lost were not observed under any of the four GA conditions. That is, there was no influence of the error threshold at the mutation rate $q = 1/L$. Therefore, we can assume that the effective mutation rate of $q = 1/L$ was below the error threshold under each condition.

The correlation of the landscapes was analyzed in order to investigate overall GA performance. Fig. 5(a) and 5(b) show the correlation coefficient [27] as a function of the Hamming distance between parents and offspring for the SGA with and without elitism, with $N_h = 1$ and 10 respectively. They suggest high fitness correlation in both landscapes, with the $N_h = 10$ landscape being more highly correlated that the $N_h = 1$ landscape.

As predicted, with $s = 6$, the SGA with and without elitism was trapped on local optima when $N_h = 1$, due to the low mutation rate and high selection pressure. With $s = 6$ and $N_h = 10$, the SGA with elitism was also trapped on local optima. However, the SGA without elitism for $s = 6$ and $N_h = 10$ was not obviously trapped. Based on the analysis of ruggedness shown in Fig. 5(b), it seems likely that fitnesses would continue improving if the runs were extended beyond their final generation. Further computer simulations were therefore conducted in order to observe the SGA runs over an additional 4,000 generations. Fig. 6 shows the maximum fitness for 10,000 generations of the SGA with $N_h = 10$. The SGA without elitism continued to find better regions of the search space. This indicates that the SGA without elitism can escape from local optima with this level of ruggedness.

When compared on the same landscapes, the OGA continued to find much better regions of search space than the SGA. The continued improvement observed with the OGA was due to the online adaptation of mutation rates during

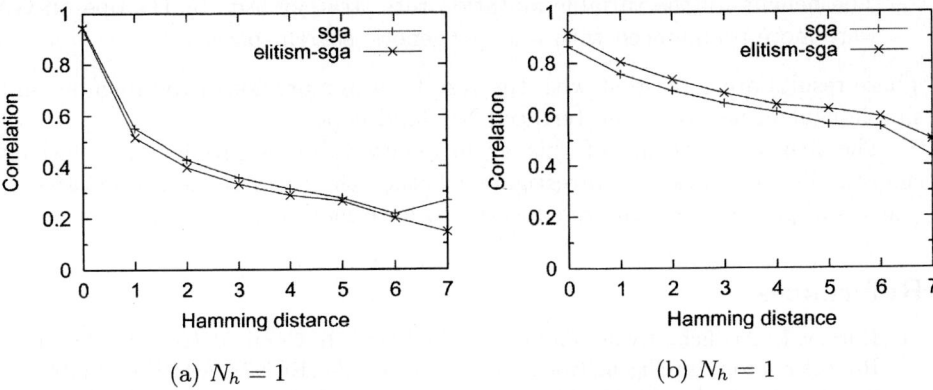

Fig. 5. The correlation coefficient as a function of the Hamming distance between parents and offspring for the SGA.

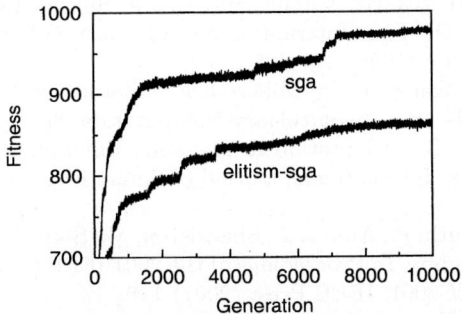

Fig. 6. The maximum fitness over 10,000 generations for the SGA for $s = 6$ and $N_h = 10$.

the process of evolution. In addition to this, with the OGA, the effective mutation rate will have been below the error threshold even with low selection pressure (i.e. when $s = 2$). This is why the variable mutation rate strategy of the OGA was a better approach on this problem with both high and low selection pressure.

6 Conclusions

In this work, we applied the standard GA and the operon-GA to evolution of artificial neural networks for robot control, and investigated their performance using different selection pressures. Our results can be summarized as follows:

– This evolutionary robotics problem does show phases of neutral evolution.
– The standard GA with low selection pressure and the operon-GA were able to continually find better regions of the search space.
– The standard GA can easily get trapped on local optima under conditions of high selection pressure and a low mutation rate.

- The benefits of the variable mutation rate strategy used by the operon-GA were more pronounced with a larger genetic search space.

These results are consistent with the results of our previous experiments using simple neutral networks and terraced NK landscapes.

The fitness landscape of this evolutionary robotics problem is relatively smooth. Future work will investigate whether these results are applicable to real-world problems which are expected to have more rugged landscapes.

References

1. Harvey, I.: Artificial Evolution for Real Problems. In Gomi, T. (ed.): Evolutionary Robotics: From Intelligent Robots to Artificial Life (ER'97), AAI Books (1997)
2. Smith, T., Husbands, P., O'Shea, M.: Neutral Networks in an Evolutionary Robotics Search Space. In Proceedings of the 2001 IEEE Congress on Evolutionary Computation (2001) 136–145
3. Thompson, A.: An Evolved Circuit, Intrinsic in Silicon, Entwined with Physics. In Proceedings of the First International Conference on Evolvable Systems: From Biology to Hardware (1996) 390–405
4. Vassilev, V. K., Fogarty, T. C., Miller, J. F.: Information Characteristics and the Structure of Landscapes. Evolutionary Computation, 8(1) (2000) 31–60
5. Ohkura, K., Ueda, K.: Adaptation in Dynamic Environment by Using GA with Neutral Mutations. International Journal of Smart Engineering System Design, 2 (1999) 17–31
6. Ebner, M., Langguth, P., Albert, J., Shackleton, M., Shipman, R.: On Neutral Networks and Evolvability, In Proceedings of the 2001 IEEE Congress on Evolutionary Computation: CEC2001, IEEE Press (2001) 1–8
7. Knowles, J. D., Watson, R. A.: On the Utility of Redundant Encodings in Mutation-based Evolutionary Search. In Merelo, J.J., Admidis, P., Beyer, H.-G., Fernandes-Villacanas, J.-L., Schwefel, H.-P. (eds.): Proceedings of Parallel Problem Solving from Nature - PPSN VII, Seventh International Conference, LNCS 2439 (2002) 88–98
8. Rothlauf, F., Goldberg, D.: Redundant Representations in Evolutionary Computation. Evolutionary Computation, 11(4) (2003) 381–415
9. Kimura, M.: The Neutral Theory of Molecular Evolution, Cambridge University Press, New York (1983)
10. Huynen, M., Stadler, P., Fontana, W.: Smoothness within Ruggedness: The Role of Neutrality in Adaptation. In Proceedings of the National Academy of Science USA, 93 (1996) 397–401
11. Reidys, C., Stadler, P., Schuster, P.: Generic Properties of Combinatory Maps - Neutral Networks of RNA Secondary Structures. Bulletin of Mathematical Biology, 59 (1997) 339–397
12. Harvey, I., Thompson, A.: Through the Labyrinth Evolution Finds a Way: A Silicon Ridge. In Proceedings of the First International Conference on Evolvable Systems: From Biology to Hardware (1996) 406–422
13. Smith, T. Husbands, P. Layzell, P. O'Shea, M.: Fitness Landscapes and Evolvability. Evolutionary Computation, 10(1) (2002) 1–34
14. Nimwegen, E., Crutchfield, J., Mitchell, M.: Statistical Dynamics of the Royal Road Genetic Algorithm. Theoretical Computer Science, Vol. 229, No. 1 (1999) 41–102

15. Barnett, L.: Netcrawling - Optimal Evolutionary Search with Neutral Networks. In Proceedings of the 2001 IEEE Congress on Evolutionary Computation (2001) 30–37
16. Eigen, M., McCaskill, J., Schuster, P.: The Molecular Quasi-species. Advances in Chemical Physics, 75 (1989) 149–263
17. Barnett, L.: Tangled Webs: Evolutionary Dynamics on Fitness Landscapes with Neutrality. MSc. dissertation, School of Cognitive and Computing Sciences, Sussex University, UK (1997)
18. Nimwegen, E., Ctrutchfield, J.: Optimizing Epochal Evolutionary Search: Population-size Dependent Theory. SFI Working Paper 9810-090, Santa Fe Institute (1998)
19. Newman, M. Engelhardt, R.: Effect of Neutral Selection on the Evolution of Molecular Species. In Proceedings of the Royal Society of London B, Morgan Kaufmann, 256 (1998) 1333–1338
20. Katada, Y., Ohkura, K., Ueda, K.: Tuning Genetic Algorithms for Problems Including Neutral Networks -The Simplest Case: The Balance Beam Function-. In Proceedings of the 7th Joint Conference on Information Sciences (2003) 1657–1660
21. Katada, Y., Ohkura, K., Ueda, K.: Tuning Genetic Algorithms for Problems Including Neutral Networks -A More Complex Case: The Terraced NK Problem-. In Proceedings of the 7th Joint Conference on Information Sciences (2003) 1661–1664
22. Goldberg, D.: Genetic Algorithms in Search, Optimization and Machine Learning. Addison-Wesley (1989)
23. Maass, W., Bishop, C.M.: Pulsed Neural Networks, MIT press (1998)
24. Katada, Y., Ohkura, K., Ueda, K.: Artificial Evolution of Pulsed Neural Networks on the Motion Pattern Classification System. In Proceedings of 2003 IEEE International Symposium on Computational Intelligence in Robotics and Automation(CIRA) (2003) 318–323
25. Beer, R.: Toward the Evolution of Dynamical Neural Networks for Minimally Cognitive Behavior. In Maes, P., Mataric, M., Meyer, J., Pollack, J., Wilson, S. (eds.): Proceedings of From Animals to Animats 4, MIT press (1996) 421–429
26. Floreano, D., Mattiussi, C.: Evolution of Spiking Neural Controllers. In Gomi, T. (ed.): Evolutionary Robotics: From Intelligent Robots to Artificial Life (ER'01), AAI Books, Springer-Verlag (2001) 38–61
27. Manderick, B., Weger, M., Spiessens, P.: The Genetic Algorithm and the Structure of the Fitness Landscape. In Belew, R., Booker, B. (eds): Proceedings of the Fourth International Conference on Genetic Algorithms, Morgan Kaufmann (1991) 143–150

Translating the Dances of Honeybees into Resource Location

DaeEun Kim

Cognitive Robotics
Max Planck Institute for Human Cognitive and Brain Sciences,
Munich, 80799, Germany
`daeeun@cbs.mpg.de`

Abstract. Dance communication of honeybees has been well known since von Frisch's work. Many researchers have believed that the waggle dance of forager bees shows the direction and distance of resources. In this paper, we suggest a possibility that dance followers employ a temporal path integration mechanism to translate the dance. We apply a neural network model consisting of sinusoidal arrays for a representation of the resource vector. The followers keeping in contact with the forager accumulate the activation of head direction relative to a gravity compass and calculate the resource vector in a circular array of neurons. This provides an idea of how bees can translate the sickle dance as well as the waggle dance into the resource location. The neural model is tested with simulated robots to communicate the resource location.

1 Introduction

Honeybees have a unique communication style called dance language. The dance communication is revealed in detail since Karl von Frisch's work [13] and the dance of honeybees is a body language to communicating the resource direction and distance. A forager bee seeks flowers for her nectar and returns to the hive. Then she arouses the other colleague bees for the location of flowers. She uses her waggle dance by walking in a straight line and wagging her abdomen from side to side. Then she moves in a semicircle to the starting point. She repeats waggle dance in a straight line and then draws another semicircle, but this time in the opposite direction. As a result, the waggle dance looks like a figure-eight looping dance.

The experiments by Frisch [13] showed that the angle of this waggle dance to the gravity direction is almost the same as the angle of the food source to the sunlight. When the distance of resource location is closer to the hive, forager bees dance rapidly. The waggle dance thus has two kinds of information for the food, direction and distance to the nectar resource. Frisch [13] assumed that the dance tells other bees the location of the food and chemical odours have the information of what kind of flowers can be detected. There have been arguments about the efficiency and mechanism about this waggle dance. Some researchers claimed that the dance mechanism is attentional and it has a limited information of the resource [14, 11]. The distance to the resource seems involved with several factors of the dance, duration of the waggle run, duration of the return run, duration of the sound, and the number of waggles [6]. Recently it is reported that the duration of the return phase can be an index of food-source profitability while the duration of the waggle phase portion holds constant for equidistant sources [10].

In fact several sensory cues exist simultaneously for the resource location [1]. Sounds produced by wings, vibration of the substrate, odour and tactile cues via the antenna have been considered as sensory modalities for the resource. The forager bee uses sound by wings as well as dance to arouse her followers [15]. Olfactory cues and wingbeat sound together in addition to waggle dance transmits the information about the position of the food source [6]. Also the recruitment can be influenced by the nature of the surface on which a forager bee dances [11]. It implies that the vibration generated by a forager bee can be another resource information transmitted to other bees. The jet air flow generated by the vibrating wings may also guide dance followers [5]. Presumably dance followers record a directional cue provided by the dance, the sound of wings, the vibration of the hive surface or the odours, and they monitor the duration of sensory cues for distance estimation.

We focus on the figure-eight looping movement of bees without auditory or any other sensory cue. It is noteworthy that the followers of a dance bee keep their antennae in contact with a dancing bee or listen to the wingbeat sound of dancer in a close distance [8]. We suggest an integration of direction readings during the dance can be another cue information for resource location. It is assumed that the dance followers accumulate activation for each of directional neuron cells relative to a reference direction, for instance, a gravity compass (in the hive) or a light compass (outdoors), while the dance bee repeats her dances. In this paper, we show a possible neural network mechanism to translate a given dance into the direction and distance of food source, and a simulation result of bee-like robot behavior will be provided.

O'Keefe [7] supposed that a phasor encoding with sinusoidal waves for path integration might be used by biological animals, since it can easily encode direction and magnitude of a given vector. Some researchers reported that a spatial representation of the phase signal is more effective than a temporal representation of the phase signal [12]. The continuous time-dependent signal can be distributed over a sinusoidal array of N units where unit i encodes the amplitude of the sinusoidal wave for phase $\frac{2\pi i}{N}$. The sinusoidal array has been successfully applied to homing navigation [16]. The model in this paper resembles this sinusoidal array.

The main contribution of this paper is to show a possible neural mechanism to translate the dances of honeybees. The neural network calculates the direction of a resource from accumulated observations of the head directions by following the dance bee. This mechanism can translate the information of resource vector by either a sickle dance or a waggle dance while only the accumulated observations do not provide a direct extraction of resource direction for a sickle dance.

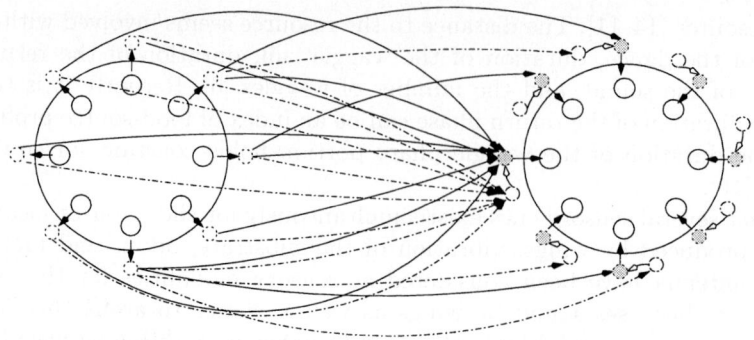

Fig. 1. Mapping for resource vector $N = 8$.

2 Estimation of a Resource Vector

To calculate a resource vector, there are two circular arrays of neurons as shown in Fig. 1. One array is for the accumulation of sensory activation on each direction with a reference direction of gravity or sunlight[1] and the other array is for the activation of resource vector on each directional component (two arrays may have different sizes). Each cell in a circular array of neurons will be activated in parallel. Previously we showed a result of two circular arrays of neurons developed for path integration [3], which used two neurons for integration in Cartesian coordinates between two circular arrays. In this paper, the neuron structure is extended to implement the direct interconnection between two arrays of neurons. Wittmann and Schwegler [16] showed a similar structure of circular neurons, and they assumed all-to-all connections in a circular array of neurons, which includes a short-term memory to store the integrated vector.

Assume there are N units in the circular array. Then the k-th unit codes for travel in a preferred direction $\theta_k = \frac{2\pi k}{N}$ with respect to light compass or gravity compass, for $k = 1, .., N$. The integrated position (x, y) in Cartesian coordinates can be calculated as follows:

$$x = \sum_{k=1}^{N} a_k \cos(\theta_k), \qquad y = \sum_{k=1}^{N} a_k \sin(\theta_k)$$

where N is the number of cells, and a_k is the accumulated activation of the k-th cell, which indicates how long one has moved in the unit's preferred direction. It will be estimated by $a_k(t+1) = a_k(t) + \delta$ where δ is a time step for each command cycle.

Then the temporal path integration (x, y) value is transformed into a given coordinate. There is a second circular array of neurons to represent a direction of resource vector. The direction of resource vector can be estimated by calculating the magnitude of the orthogonal vector to a given directional axis. The path integration (x, y) is changed into (x_j, y_j) by a coordinate transformation which is equivalent to rotating the point (x, y) clockwise with an angle $\theta_j = \frac{2\pi j}{N}$.

---
[1] Dwarf bees (*A. Florea*) use the light compass instead of the gravity compass [13].

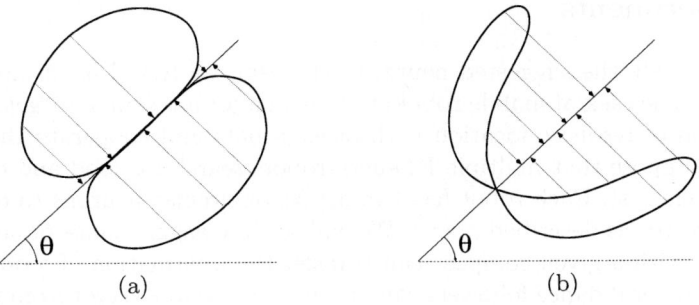

Fig. 2. Direction of resource vector (a) waggle dance (b) sickle dance.

$$x_j = \cos(\theta_j) \sum_{k=1}^{N} a_k \cos(\theta_k) + \sin(\theta_j) \sum_{k=1}^{N} a_k \sin(\theta_k)$$

$$y_j = -\sin(\theta_j) \sum_{k=1}^{N} a_k \cos(\theta_k) + \cos(\theta_j) \sum_{k=1}^{N} a_k \sin(\theta_k)$$

We can simplify the equation as follows:

$$x_j = \sum_{k=1}^{N} \cos(\theta_k - \theta_j) a_k = \sum_{k=1}^{N} w^x_{kj} a_k, \quad y_j = \sum_{k=1}^{N} \sin(\theta_k - \theta_j) a_k = \sum_{k=1}^{N} w^y_{kj} a_k$$

where $w^x_{kj} = \cos(\theta_k - \theta_j) = \cos(\frac{2\pi(k-j)}{N})$ and $w^y_{kj} = \sin(\theta_k - \theta_j) = \sin(\frac{2\pi(k-j)}{N})$. To keep x-component positive, we set $w^x_{kj} = 0$ for $|\theta_k - \theta_j| > \pi/2$.

Fig. 2 shows an example of resource vector direction for two kinds of honeybee dances. It is assumed that followers trace almost the same path as the dance bee walks. If the path integration result has a zero-value in the y-axis in a new coordinate system, the coordinate direction will be a resource vector direction. When y_j is close to zero in the circular array neuron, the j-th direction is the resource vector direction translated from the dance of honeybees. Also the magnitude of x_j represents the distance of the resource vector. Thus, a vector of the integration is projected on each of cell directions in the second array. The resource direction will be estimated by finding the cell in which the component orthogonal to the projected vector is close to zero. We build a gating network with an inhibition term between x_j and y_j, $c_j = \exp(-y_j^2/\sigma^2) x_j$, which is a neuron activation in the second array. We assume local lateral inhibition among resource vector cells with c_k for $k = 1, ..., N$. A winner-take-all method will choose the cell with the maximum activation in the second circular array of neurons. The cell direction corresponds to the preferred direction for resource and its activation itself indicates the distance to resource. Each unit in the neural array has a linear activation and the transcendental function is set into the interconnection weight between the first and the second array.

3 Experiments

To demonstrate the suggested neural mechanism, we tested it on mobile robot platforms. The task of mobile robots is to search for a resource target, share the information of resource location with other robots and cooperate the foraging task. We suppose that multiple Khepera robots search for food and deliver the food to their nest. Each robot has two arrays of circular neurons to encode the resource vector as described above. We will see if a waggle dance or sickle dance movement with a given compass can transfer the information of food source to other robots, or if dance followers can obtain the resource vector from the dance.

We use a kinematic simulation of Khepera robot. The robot has two wheel motors on the left and right, and 10 % noisy level is added on each sensor and each motor action of the simulated Khepera robot. It is assumed that 100 photo sensors are mounted on the top of the robot and a circular array of 100 neurons will be used for the accumulation of the sensor activation. The reference compass will be the ambient light, instead of the gravity. Only one cell with the strongest excitation level will be active at a time, although it is possible to use the integration over a population coding of directional neural cells. The other circular array of 100 neurons will represent the direction of resource location. Thus, the angular resolution will be 3.6 degrees. In simulation, the transmission delay from sensor readings to motor actions is fixed for every command cycle. To follow a forager robot, a robot uses four infrared sensors in front (at angles -45, -12, 12, 45 degrees from the head direction). The readings of infrared sensors will determine motor actions, forward movement, or left/right directional movement; if two sensors at the angles -12 and 12 degrees are strongly perceptive, the robot moves straightforward, if the infrared sensors on the left side are more responsive, then the robot moves left, and otherwise, it moves right. This behavior imitates the behavior of dance-following bees keeping their antennae in contact with the forager bee.

A robot initially explores for food in an arena. Once the food is found, the robot memorizes the resource vector from the nest place to the food location, and it returns to the nest – see Fig. 3. The forager uses a homing navigation based on path integration to return to the nest [3], where the resource vector can be seen as equivalent to the homing vector except with the vector direction reversed. To recruit other robots, the forager robot performs a waggle or sickle dance based on the resource vector as shown in Fig. 4. The robots in the nest simply follow the forager robot, keeping in contact with the forager using infrared sensors. With the neural network representation described in the previous section, the followers collect the information of resource location. Then they can directly go to the food source without any exploration of the whole arena.

Fig. 5(a) shows an example of the accumulated sensor activation during the waggle dance given in Fig. 4(a). The directional component close to the resource direction is dominant but several neighbor angular positions also have protruding activations. After applying the temporal integration, the vector result in Fig. 5(b) shows a pronounced directional cue for the food source. The magnitude of the vector in polar coordinates represents the distance of the food source;

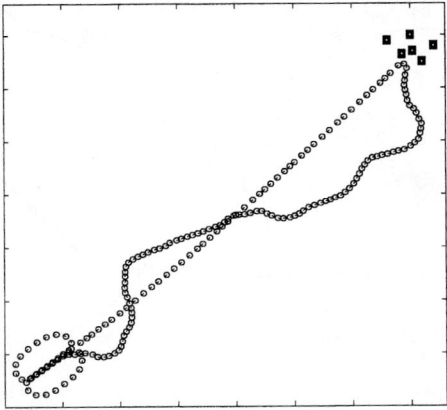

Fig. 3. Exploration of a forager robot and its waggle dance (square: food, circle: robot).

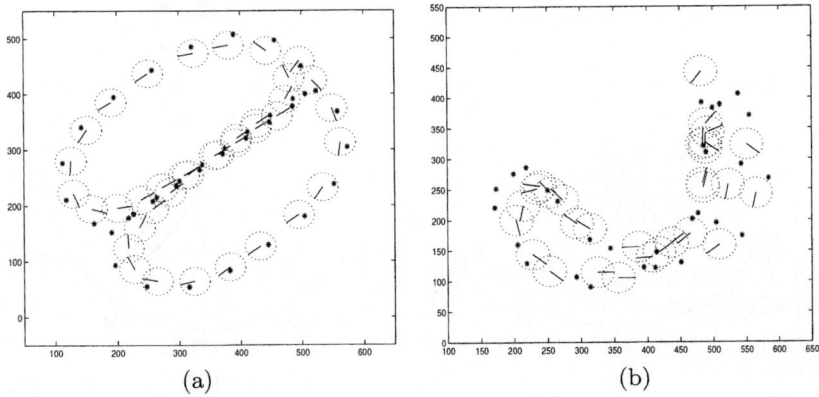

Fig. 4. Robot movements of a dance follower (*: forager, solid: head direction of the follower, dotted: the follower robot) (a) waggle dance (b) sickle dance.

the higher magnitude, the more distant resource. As mentioned above, neuron activations depending on the moving direction relative to the light compass are accumulated in a circular array and so more duration of the waggle phase will more dominantly feature the direction and increase the vector magnitude. The current approach produces two dominant peaks, one for the waggle phase and the other for the return phase as shown in Fig. 5(b). These two peaks can be disambiguated by observing the moving direction at the onset of the dance cycle; both the waggle dance and the sickle dance always take an outward direction in a circular movement. In addition, other sensory cues can be applied to choose the correct direction as the wingbeat sound or the vibration of the hive surface is observed in the dances of honeybees[2].

---

[2] It is unknown so far why several redundant sensory cues exist simultaneously during the dance and also which sensory cue is more influential.

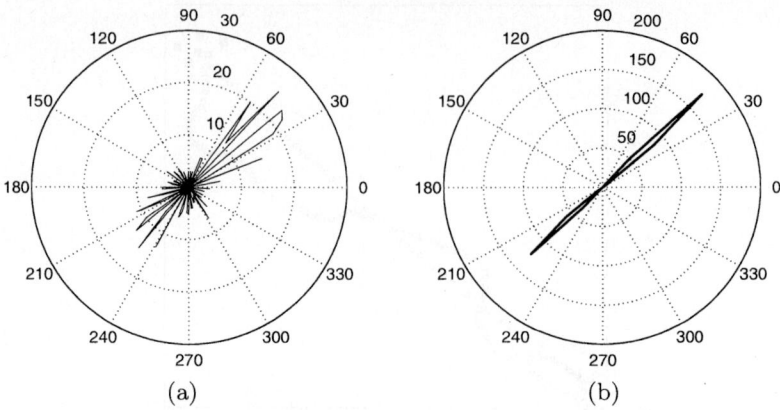

Fig. 5. Result of waggle dance (a) accumulated activation in the first circular array (b) direction and magnitude of the resource vector.

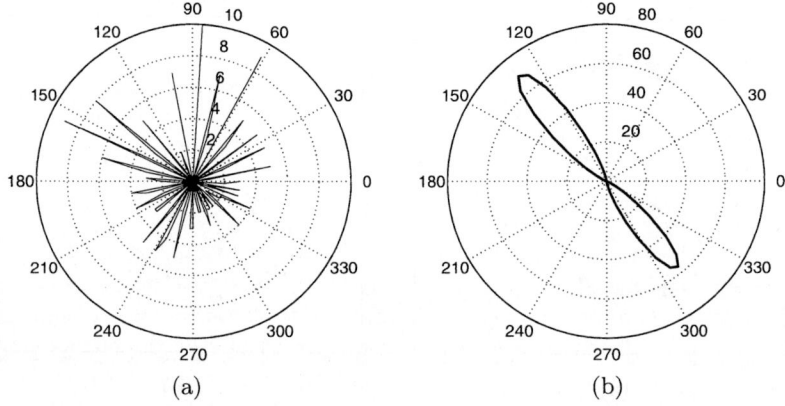

Fig. 6. Result of sickle dance (a) accumulated activation in the first circular array (b) direction and magnitude of the resource vector.

An Italian bee *A. Mellifera ligustica* has a sickle dance in addition to a waggle dance. The bee does not wag her abdomen in the sickle dance, but the dance also provides other bees with the resource vector information [13], which has been neglected among biologists so far. A sickle dance shown in Fig. 4(b) can also record the vector for the food source. In fact *A. Mellifera ligustica* takes this sickle dance when the food source is close to the hive. With large distances of the resource, the bee changes the dance into a waggle dance. For followers of a sickle dance, only the accumulation of head-direction activations in the first array is insufficient to extract the direction of the food source – see Fig. 6(a). However, the path integration can successfully point the food direction and estimate the distance as in Fig. 6(b). Generally the waggle dance shows a sharper curve for the directional cue of the second array than the sickle dance (Fig. 5(b) and 6(b)). It means that the waggle dance can transmit more precise information than the sickle dance.

Many honeybees such as *A. Florea*, *A. Dorsata*, *A. Indica*, *A. Melifera carnica* and *A. Mellifera ligustica* perform a round dance instead of a waggle dance when the resource is very close to their hive. The dance has no definite directional movement and instead repeats moving in a circle anticlockwise and then clockwise. They use a waggle dance to represent more exact direction and distance when the resource is far distant. For the round dance, the neural network with temporal path integration will produce little directional cue as spiky as for the waggle dance (but the turning point even in the round dance can be an indicator of the direction), since the sensor activation is uniformly distributed over most of the directions. The magnitude of the resource vector will be relatively small, because a cycle of the round dance is played in a short time. It is noticeable that more rapid dance indicates shorter distance for honeybees [13].

The dance also expresses the quality or information of the food source by the vigorness and the movement of bees. The food quality is obtained by separating the duration of the waggle phase and the return phase in a dance cycle [10]. The suggested neural structure can encode the duration of the waggle phase and the return phase, which can be a source of information for distance estimation and resource profitability, respectively.

Desert ants (*Cataglyphis fortis*) can measure their travel distance with proprioceptive feedback of motor actions and path integration [9]. The accumulation of the sensory activation for each head direction, which is used in this paper, is more relevant to dance translation rather than that of the proprioceptive signals, since the translation needs to record the duration of each directional movement. This may partly support the fact that the duration of the waggle run is strongly involved with the distance information [10, 13]. The neural network mechanism in this paper is similar to that for homing navigation [3, 16], except that the homing nest is replaced by the food source, and the proprioceptive signals by the sensor activations. It appears that homing navigation and dance communication use similar neural representations to encode the corresponding vector, even though the vector information has a different meaning.

4 Discussion

During the waggle dance the forager bee emits the wingbeat sound as well as wags her abdomen [4]. So the duration of the sound in the waggle run may be an important cue for the distance of the food. In other words, the magnitude of the resource vector can be estimated by how long the sound or odour cue lasts. Also the corresponding direction may be emphasized by the sound together with the integration of movements[3]. Normally other sensory cues in addition to the waggle dance are provided, even though they are redundant. They will probably help bees receive more precise information of resource.

We argued that the integration mechanism is required to translate the sickle dance. To our knowledge, it is not reported yet whether there exists any sensory

---

[3] Without integration, only sound during the waggle run can transmit the resource information, but it is not evident yet whether the integration is required for bees.

cue during the sickle dance. At least two directional components (C-shaped) in a sickle dance should be combined into one averaged vector, while only one direction is prominently observed in the waggle dance. The analysis of the sickle dance may support our hypothesis of integration mechanism for dance translation.

For the integration mechanism, the body of dance followers should be closely aligned with that of the dance bee. Indeed dance followers maneuver themselves behind the dancer during the waggle dance and they are positioned within an approximately 30° arc behind the dancer [2]. The bees staying motionless cannot succeed in extracting the resource information. A mean of 7.8 consecutive waggle runs are required for dance followers to interpret the dance successfully. The translation of the resource direction during the waggle dance would require the calculation of relative body orientations of follower bees along the axis of the waggle dance. The sound field with interaural intensity difference, the jet air flow from the vibration or the contact patterns of antenna may transform the information of spatial orientations for bees which are not exactly aligned with the dancing bee. For future work, the calculation of body orientation angles can be combined with the integration mechanism.

5 Conclusion

The neural network mechanism to translate waggle dance or sickle dance has not been well studied so far, and this paper presents a possible neural mechanism of how the bees following a forager bee recognize the information of resource location. Through a component analysis over accumulated sensor activations, it can translate even a sickle dance where it is not possible to extract the resource direction directly from the sensor activations alone. The neural network representation can easily translate a given dance movement into the resource vector, that is, direction and distance of the resource together. The neural network can also sketch the food quality by reckoning the duration of the return phase in a dance cycle. To support the idea of the temporal integration with circular array neurons, multi-robot simulation was provided.

The suggested neural network or temporal integration hypothesis may not be appropriate to explain the whole mechanism of dance communication when we consider the fact that several sensory modalities are involved together in the dance. The resource vector, however, can be estimated by the current neural mechanism, even without any other sensory cue. To approve our integration hypothesis, the neurophysiological evidence of honeybees should be pursued.

The mobile robots can use better communication tool or method instead of the above dancing communication. Only simple robots without wireless communication can exploit the method. Possibly we can apply our neural network mechanism to the decision of orientation of a mobile robot towards a stimulus when a set of sensor activations for the stimulus are available. The neural network structure would robustly work even if a few neurons malfunction.

Acknowledgments

The author would like to thank anonymous reviewers for useful comments and suggestions.

References

1. F. C. Dyer. The biology of the dance language. *Annual Review of Entomology*, 47:917–949, 2002.
2. T. M. Judd. The waggle dance of the honey bee: which bees following a dancer successfully acquire the information? *Journal of Insect Behavior*, 8:343–354, 1995.
3. D. Kim and J. Hallam. Neural network approach to path integration for homing navigation. In *From Animals to Animats 6*, pages 228–235. MIT Press, 2000.
4. W. H. Kirchner and W. F. Towne. The sensory basis of the honeybee's dance language. *Scientific American*, pages 52–59, 1994.
5. A. Michelsen. Signals and flexibility in the dance communication of honeybees. *Journal of Comparative Physiology A*, 189(3):165–174, 2003.
6. A. Michelsen, B. B. Andersen, J. Storm, W. H. Kirchner, and M. Lindauer. How honeybees perceive communication dances, studied by means of a mechanical model. *Behavioral Ecology and Sociobiology*, 30:143–150, 1992.
7. J. O'Keefe. An allocentric spatial model for the hippocampal cognitive map. *Hippocampus*, 1:230–235, 1991.
8. K. Rohrseitz and J. Tautz. Honey bee dance communication: waggle run direction coded in antennal contacts? *J. of Comparative Physiology A*, 184:463–470, 1999.
9. B. Ronacher, K. Gallizzi, S. Wohlgemuth, and R. Wehner. Lateral optic flow does not influence distance estimation in the desert ant *Cataglyphis fortis*. *Journal of Experimental Biology*, 203:1113–1121, 2000.
10. T. D. Seeley, A. S. Mikheyev, and G. J. Pagano. Dancing bees tune both duration and rate of waggle-run production in relation to nectar-source profitability. *Journal of Comparative Physiology A*, 186:813–819, 2000.
11. J. Tautz. Honeybee waggle dance: recruitment success depends on the dance floor. *Journal Of experimental Biology*, 199:1375–1381, 1996.
12. D. Touretzky, A. Redish, and H. Wan. Neural representation of space using sinusoidal arrays. *Neural Computation*, 6(5):869–884, 1993.
13. K. von Frisch. *The Dance Language and Orientation of Bees*. Harvard University Press, Cambridge, 1967.
14. A. M. Wenner. Recruitment search behavior and flight ranges of honeybees. *Am. Zool.*, 31:768–782, 1991.
15. A.M. Wenner. Sound production during the waggle dance of the honeybee. *Animal Behaviour*, 10:78–95, 1962.
16. T. Wittmann and H. Schwegler. Path integration - a network model. *Biological Cybernetics*, 73:569–575, 1995.

Natural Policy Gradient Reinforcement Learning for a CPG Control of a Biped Robot

Yutaka Nakamura[1,2], Takeshi Mori[2], and Shin Ishii[2,1]

[1] CREST, JST
[2] Nara Institute of Science and Technology, 8916-5 Takayama-cho, Ikoma, Nara 630-0192, Japan
{yutak-na,tak-mori,ishii}@is.naist.jp
http://hawaii.naist.jp/index.html

Abstract. Motivated by the perspective that animals' rhythmic movements such as locomotion are controlled by neural circuits called central pattern generators (CPGs), motor control mechanisms by CPG have been studied. As an autonomous learning framework for a CPG controller, we previously proposed a reinforcement learning (RL) method called the CPG-actor-critic method. In this article, we propose a natural policy gradient learning algorithm for the CPG-actor-critic method, and applied our RL to an automatic control problem by a biped robot simulator. Computer simulations show that our RL makes the biped robot walk stably on various terrain.

1 Introduction

Rhythmic movements are fundamental to animals' movements. For example, locomotion and swimming are crucial abilities for many animals to survive. These rhythmic movements are characterized by their rapid adaptability to variously changing environments, and the mechanism realizing such adaptability has been extensively studied both in biological science and in engineering [1]. Neurobiological studies have revealed that rhythmic motor patterns are produced by neural oscillators called central pattern generators (CPGs) [1]. It has also been suggested that sensory feedback signals play an important role in stabilizing rhythmic movements by coordinating the physical system with the CPGs. Taga et al. devised a model of a human lower body (a biped robot) and a CPG controller and applied them to simulating human-like biped walking [2]. For this biped walking, however, it was necessary to tune the weights of mutual connections among CPG neurons that compose the CPG controller and those of sensory feedback connections from the biped robot. Although the determination of such CPG parameters was necessary, depending on target physical systems (robots) and environments, it was very difficult due to the lack of design principle.

In our previous study [3], we proposed a reinforcement learning (RL) method for a CPG controller, which is called the CPG-actor-critic method. The learning scheme used in this method was based on the SARSA algorithm [4], which is a kind of value-based RL methods. In value-based RL methods, the value of each state (and action) is evaluated, and then, the policy is updated so as to increase the value. Although value-based RL methods have been successfully applied to various Markov decision processes (MDPs) with finite state and action spaces, they have a disadvantage especially when the state and action spaces are large. Namely, as the state and action spaces grows, the value learning becomes quite difficult, which is often referred as "the curse of dimensionality". Because the degree of freedom of a biped robot is fairly large, the state and action spaces become large and hence the learning of value and control policy is difficult. This is one of the major reasons why the CPG-actor-critic model employing the SARSA learning was not very stable when applied to an automatic acquisition task of a biped locomotion.

On the other hand, policy gradient methods have recently been attracting attention because of the robustness of their learning. In these methods, the gradient of the performance indicator, the average reward per step for example, with respect to the policy parameter is calculated, and the policy parameter is updated according to the gradient (policy gradient). Recently it has been shown that an unbiased estimator of the policy gradient can be calculated by using an approximation of the action-value function, which is a parametric linear combination of basis functions determined automatically from the policy's parameterization, and it is proved to converge under certain conditions [5][6]. Furthermore, Kakade et al. derived the natural policy gradient by using this approximate action-value function [7][8].

In many cases, the space spanned by these basis function is smaller than that of the state and action, because the number of parameters necessary for the control policy is usually smaller than that of variables necessary to represent the state and action spaces. In addition, the value function can be represented as a parametric linear function, although the true value function is often nonlinear. The value learning in policy gradient methods thus becomes relatively easy.

In this article, we propose a new learning scheme based on a natural policy gradient method, which is applied to our CPG-actor-critic method. We applied this method to a biped robot simulator adopted from [2]. Computer simulations show that our RL makes the biped robot walk stably on various terrain.

2   CPG-Actor-Critic Model

The motion of a physical system like a biped robot is expressed as

$$\dot{\mathbf{x}} = F(\mathbf{x}, \boldsymbol{\tau}), \tag{1}$$

where $\mathbf{x}$ and $\dot{\mathbf{x}}$ denote the state and velocity, respectively, of the physical system. $\boldsymbol{\tau}$ denotes the control signal (torque) produced by the controller. $F(\mathbf{x}, \boldsymbol{\tau})$ represents the vector field of the system dynamics.

In this article, we assume that a physical system is controlled by a CPG controller as depicted in figure 1. The CPG controller is implemented as a neural oscillator network, and outputs a control signal according to the neurons' state in the oscillator network. The CPG controller receives sensory feedback signals from the physical system, typically the state observations.

A neural oscillator network is an instance of recurrent neural networks (RNNs), and the dynamics of the i-th neuron is given by

$$c_i \dot{\nu}_i = -\nu_i + I_i \qquad y_i = G_i(\nu_i), \tag{2}$$

where ν_i, y_i, I_i and c_i denote the state, output, input and time constant, respectively. Output y_i is calculated from the state ν_i by the transfer function G_i. An identical function, a threshold function, or a sigmoidal function is used as the output function G_i (see section 4.1, for details). Input I_i is given by

$$I_i = \sum_j W_{ij}^{cpg} y_j + I_i^{ext} + B_i, \tag{3}$$

where the first term is the feedback input from the other neurons, the second term is the external input that depends on the sensory feedback signal from the physical system, and the third term is a bias. W_{ij}^{cpg} represents the weight of the mutual connection from the j-th neuron to the i-th neuron. The external input I_i^{ext} is given by

$$I_i^{ext} = \sum_k W_{ik}^{feed} X_k, \tag{4}$$

that is, a sum of the sensory feedback signal $\mathbf{X}$ weighted by connection weight $\mathbf{W}_i^{feed}$. The sensory feedback signal $\mathbf{X}$ is a vector depending on the physical system's state.

A control signal to the physical system is given by a weighted sum of the outputs of CPG neurons:

$$\tau_n = \sum_i T_{ni} y_i, \tag{5}$$

where τ_n is the n-th control signal and $\mathbf{T}_n$ denotes the weight vector for the output of the CPG neurons.

Actor-critic methods are popular reinforcement learning (RL) schemes [4][9]. In a typical implementation, the actor is a controller that provides control signals to the physical system; it observes the physical system's state and outputs a control signal according to this state. The critic evaluates the current state of the physical system to indicate the utility of a control signal, which is the actor's output.

In a naive application of such an actor-critic method, the CPG controller, an instance of RNNs, is regarded as an actor. However, such an approach needs heavy computation to train the RNN by using instantaneous training signals in an on-line RL algorithm. Another difficulty also arises, because the policy, which is a mapping from a state to a control signal, comes to incorporate internal states, i.e., the neurons' state in the CPG controller. In order to avoid the training of the RNN, we formerly proposed an RL method called the CPG-actor-critic method [3]. In this method, the CPG controller is divided into two parts, the basic CPG and the actor, as depicted in figure 1(b). We treat the physical system

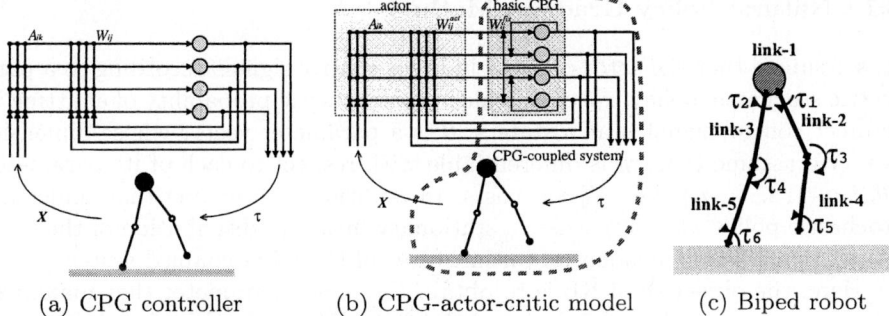

Fig. 1. Control scheme and biped robot simulator.

and the basic CPG as a single dynamical system, which is called the CPG-coupled system. The actor controls the CPG-coupled system, as a feed-forward neural network, i.e., the actor has no mutual connections. Corresponding to this separation, the input to the CPG neuron, I_i, is divided into two parts:

$$I_i = I_i^{fix} + u_i \qquad (6)$$

$$I_i^{fix} = \sum_j W_{ij}^{fix} y_j + B_i \qquad (7)$$

$$u_i = \sum_j W_{ij}^{act} y_j + \sum_k W_{ik}^{feed} X_k, \qquad (8)$$

where W_{ij}^{fix} is the connection weight in the basic CPG, and W_{ij}^{fix} and B_i are fixed. The basic CPG receives an output of the actor, $\mathbf{u}$, which is called an indirect control signal. The actor observes a state of the CPG-coupled system and outputs a control signal to the CPG-coupled system according to equation (8). The control torques are applied to the physical system according to equation (5), where the connection weight $\mathbf{T}$ is fixed. Accordingly, this learning scheme has potential to construct a non-linear controller by tuning the parameter of a linear controller, i.e., W_{ij}^{act} and W_{ik}^{feed} within the actor.

3 Learning Algorithm

In this section, we describe a learning scheme for the CPG-actor-critic model based on the natural policy gradient method. For the sake of simplicity, we assume that equations (1) and (2) are discretized in time by an appropriate method.

At a discrete time step t, the actor observes both a feedback sensory signal $\mathbf{X}(t)$ and an output of the CPG neuron $\mathbf{y}(t)$, and outputs an indirect control signal $\mathbf{u}(t)$ calculated by equation (8). The CPG-coupled system receives an output of the actor $\mathbf{u}(t)$ and changes its state $\mathbf{s}(t) = \{\mathbf{x}(t), \boldsymbol{\nu}(t)\}$ to $\mathbf{s}(t+1)$ according to the dynamics of the basic CPG and the physical system. The state transition probability from $\mathbf{s}(t)$ to $\mathbf{s}(t+1)$ is denoted by $p(\mathbf{s}(t+1)|\mathbf{s}(t), \mathbf{u}(t))$. We also assume that the learning system receives an immediate reward $r(\mathbf{s}(t), \mathbf{u}(t))$ based on the physical system's state and the control signal.

3.1 Natural Policy Gradient Method

It is assumed that the actor outputs indirect control signals according to a parametric stochastic policy, $\pi_\theta(\mathbf{u}|\mathbf{s})$, which represents the probability of emitting an indirect control signal $\mathbf{u}$ at a state $\mathbf{s}$. $\boldsymbol{\theta}$ is a parameter vector whose dimension is n. We assume that π_θ is differentiable with respect to each of its parameters $\{\theta_i | i = 1, 2, \ldots, n\}$, i.e., $\frac{\partial}{\partial \theta_i} \pi_\theta$ exists. In addition, we assume that under any stochastic policy π_θ, there exists a stationary invariant distribution of the state, $D_\theta(\mathbf{s})$, which is independent of initial states of the CPG-coupled system.

Here, the objective of RL is to obtain the policy parameter that maximizes the expected reward accumulation defined by $\rho(\boldsymbol{\theta}) \equiv E_\theta \left[\sum_t \gamma^{t-1} r(\mathbf{s}(t), \mathbf{u}(t)) \right]$ where $\gamma \in (0, 1]$ is a discount factor. The partial differential of $\rho(\boldsymbol{\theta})$ with respect to the policy parameter θ_i is calculated by

$$\frac{\partial \rho(\boldsymbol{\theta})}{\partial \theta_i} = \int_{\mathbf{s},\mathbf{u}} d\mathbf{s} d\mathbf{u} D_\theta(\mathbf{s}, \mathbf{u}) \psi_i(\mathbf{s}, \mathbf{u}) Q_\theta(\mathbf{s}, \mathbf{u}), \tag{9}$$

where $\psi_i(\mathbf{s}, \mathbf{u}) \equiv \frac{\partial}{\partial \theta_i} \ln \pi_\theta(\mathbf{u}|\mathbf{s})$ and $Q_\theta(\mathbf{s}, \mathbf{u})$ denotes the action-value function (Q-function) [5][6].

To estimate the policy gradient (9), we employ a linear approximator of the Q-function: $f_\theta^w(\mathbf{s}, \mathbf{u}) = \sum_i \psi_i(\mathbf{s}, \mathbf{u}) w_i$, where $\mathbf{w}$ is the parameter vector. If we achieve $\tilde{\mathbf{w}} = \arg\min_{\mathbf{w}} (Q_\theta(\mathbf{s}, \mathbf{u}) - f_\theta^w(\mathbf{s}, \mathbf{u}))^2$, using $f_\theta^w(\mathbf{s}, \mathbf{u})$ instead of the true Q-function $Q_\theta(\mathbf{s}, \mathbf{u})$ does not introduce any bias to the calculation of the policy gradient (9) [6], and the parameter $\tilde{\mathbf{w}}$ provides the natural policy gradient [7][8].

Our training of the CPG-actor-critic model is based on the actor-critic model described above. The actor outputs control signals according to the parametric stochastic policy π_θ, and the critic approximates the Q-function. We assume that the critic is represented by a parametric linear mixture of basis functions $\{\phi_j | j = 1, \ldots, m\}$, which include $\{\psi_i | i = 1, \ldots, n\}$: $Q_\theta^w = \sum_{j=1}^{m} w_j \phi_j(\mathbf{s}, \mathbf{u})$, where $\mathbf{w} = \{w_j\}$ is the parameter vector of the critic. $\phi_i = \psi_i$ for $i = 1, \ldots, n$ are determined automatically from the actor parameterization, and the other bases ϕ_i for $i = n+1, \ldots, m$ are arbitrary functions of state $\mathbf{s}$. The basis functions in the latter category are used for representing the state value function, and they have a role in reducing the variance of the policy gradient (9) without introducing any bias [6][8]. The actor parameter is updated as $\theta_i := \theta_i + \eta_a \tilde{w}_i$, where $\tilde{w}_i$ is the parameter that minimizes the approximation error of the Q-function and η_a is the learning rate of the actor.

In order to find the optimal solution $\tilde{\mathbf{w}}$, we employ a learning algorithm for the Q-function based on a least square method, which is called the least square Q (LSQ) [8][10][11]. Note that the Q-function is required to satisfy probabilistically the Bellman's self-consistent equation for a fixed policy: $Q_\theta^w(\mathbf{s}, \mathbf{u}) \approx r(\mathbf{s}, \mathbf{u}) + \gamma Q_\theta^w(\mathbf{s}', \mathbf{u}')$, where $\mathbf{s}'$ and $\mathbf{u}'$ denote the state and action at the next discrete time step, respectively. The least-square estimator of the parameter $\mathbf{w}$ is required to minimize: $E_\theta[\{r(\mathbf{s}, \mathbf{u}) + (\gamma \bar{\phi}(\mathbf{s}', \mathbf{u}'|\mathbf{s}, \mathbf{u}) - \phi(\mathbf{s}, \mathbf{u}))' \mathbf{w}\}^2]$, where $\bar{\phi}(\mathbf{s}', \mathbf{u}'|\mathbf{s}, \mathbf{u})$ denotes the expectation of the basis value after observing the transition from $\mathbf{s}$ and $\mathbf{u}$.

Given a set of samples, $\{\mathbf{s}(t), \mathbf{u}(t) | t = 0, 1, \ldots, T\}$, we assume the stationary distribution is calculated by weighted mean of the empirical distribution: $D_{\boldsymbol{\theta}}(\mathbf{s}, \mathbf{u}) = \alpha(T) \sum_{t=0}^{T} (\prod_{\tau=t+1}^{T} \beta(\tau)) \delta(\mathbf{s}(t), \mathbf{u}(t))$, where $\delta(\cdot)$ denotes the Dirac's delta function, $\beta \in (0, 1]$ is a discount factor, and $\alpha(T)$ is a normalization term. This weighted mean is introduced in order to decrease the effects of the old policy.

The state transition probability is also approximated as an empirical one. $\int_{\mathbf{u}} d\mathbf{u} \phi_i(\mathbf{s}, \mathbf{u}) \pi_{\boldsymbol{\theta}}(\mathbf{u}|\mathbf{s}) = 0$ for $i = 1 \leq i \leq n$, and the other basis functions ϕ_i for $i > n$ are designed not to depend on $\mathbf{u}$. $\bar{\phi}_i(\mathbf{s}', \mathbf{u}'|\mathbf{s}(t), \mathbf{u}(t)) = [0, \ldots, 0, \phi_{n+1}(\mathbf{s}(t+1)), \ldots, \phi_m(\mathbf{s}(t+1))]'$. Then, the least-square solution $\mathbf{w}$ is obtained by using weighted sufficient statistics:

$$\mathbf{w} = \langle\langle \varphi \varphi' \rangle\rangle(t)^{-1} \langle\langle \varphi r(\mathbf{s}, \mathbf{u}) \rangle\rangle(t), \tag{10}$$

where $\varphi(t) = \gamma \bar{\phi}(\mathbf{s}', \mathbf{u}'|\mathbf{s}(t), \mathbf{u}(t)) - \phi(\mathbf{s}(t), \mathbf{u}(t))$ and $\langle\langle \cdot \rangle\rangle$ represents the weighted mean. The normalization term $\alpha(T)$ is calculated iteratively; $\alpha(t) = \alpha(t-1)/(\beta(t) + \alpha(t-1))$, thus the weighted mean $\langle\langle f \rangle\rangle(t)$ is iteratively calculated by $\langle\langle f \rangle\rangle(t) = (1 - \alpha(t)) \langle\langle f \rangle\rangle(t-1) + \alpha(t) f(t)$. The solution of equation (10) is a biased estimator when the system's transition is probabilistic, but an unbiased estimator if the system is deterministic [10].

We summarize the learning procedure in table 1. The i-th learning episode consists of time steps: $\{t_i, t_i + 1 \ldots, t_{i+1} - 1\}$. According to this method, both the actor and the critic are trained in an on-line fashion simultaneously. Since the actor and the critic depend on each other, they are fixed for a certain number of control steps, which is defined as N, in order to stabilize the concurrent learning process.

Table 1. Learning procedure.

//$t_{\text{last-update}}$: Last update time
//N : Fixed interval
//i : Episode's index
Initialize the actor parameter $\boldsymbol{\theta}$
Set $t_0 = 0$ and $i = 0$
for $i = 0$ to ∞ {
Set $\mathbf{s}(t_i)$ to a initial state (for details, see Experiments).
  for $t = t_i$ to $t_i + t_{max}$ {
  Output $\mathbf{u}(t) \sim \pi_{\boldsymbol{\theta}}(\mathbf{u}|\mathbf{s}(t))$
  Change the state to $\mathbf{s}(t+1)$ and observe $r(\mathbf{s}(t), \mathbf{u}(t))$
  Update $\langle\langle \varphi \varphi' \rangle\rangle(t)$ and $\langle\langle \varphi r(\mathbf{s}, \mathbf{u}) \rangle\rangle(t)$
  If $\mathbf{s}(t+1)$ is a terminal state { break }
  }
Set $t_{i+1} = t + 1$
If $t - t_{\text{last-update}} > N$ {
Update $\mathbf{w}$ and $\boldsymbol{\theta}$
Set $t_{\text{last-update}} = t$
} }

---

4 Experiments

We applied our RL based on the CPG-actor-critic model to a control task of a biped robot simulator [2]. The purpose of this simulation is to obtain the parameter of the CPG controller autonomously, which allows the biped robot to walk stably.

4.1 Biped Robot and Basic CPG

The biped robot is composed of five connected links, as depicted in figure 1(c). The motion of these links is restricted within a sagittal plane. Link-1 is a point mass representing the upper body. Each leg consists of a thigh (link-2 and 3) and a shank (link-4 and 5) and has three joints, i.e., hip, knee and ankle. The lengths of the thigh and shank are 0.5 m and 0.6 m, respectively. The robot is controlled by the torques τ_1-τ_6, each of which is applied to a single joint. When a shank is off the ground, no torque is generated at the ankle joint. The active force from the ground is modeled by a spring and damper model. A state of the biped robot is represented by a 12-dimensional vector $\mathbf{x}$, where x_1 and x_2 denote the horizontal and vertical coordinates of link-1, $x_i (i = 3, \ldots, 6)$ denotes the angle of link-$(i-1)$ from the vertical axis, and $x_i (i = 7, \ldots, 12)$ denotes the velocity of x_{i-6}.

The basic CPG is a kind of RNNs, which is composed of 12 primary neurons $i = 1, \ldots, 12$ and 12 supplementary neurons $i = 13, \ldots, 24$; each supplementary neuron is connected exclusively to its corresponding primary neuron. The output functions of a primary neuron and a supplementary neuron are $G_i(\nu_i) = \max(0, y_i)$ and the identical function, respectively. The fixed connection weights in the basic CPG, $\mathbf{W}^{fix}$, are adopted from [2]. With these weights, the CPG neurons autonomously emit oscillatory signals if there is no sensory feedback signal. A group of four neurons $(2i - 1, 2i, 2i + 11, 2i + 12, i = 1, \ldots, 6)$ acts as a single neural oscillator, which controls the corresponding joint.

Torque τ is calculated from the output of the CPG neurons: $\tau_i = -T_i^F y_{2i-1} + T_i^E y_{2i}$ for $i = 1, \ldots, 4$ and $\tau_i = (-T_i^F y_{2i-1} + T_i^E y_{2i}) \Xi_{i-1}$ for $i = 5, 6$ where Ξ_{i-1} represents an indicator function of shank-i ($i = 4, 5$); $\Xi_{i-1} = 1$ (or $= 0$) when the link-i touches (or is off) the ground. τ_1 and τ_2 control hip joints, τ_3 and τ_4 control knee joints, and τ_5 and τ_6 control ankle joints. T_i^F and T_i^E represent the weights of the flexor and extensor, respectively, and their values are adopted from [2]. A sensory feedback signal from the biped robot is given by $\mathbf{X} = \{x_3, x_4, x_5\Xi_4, x_6\Xi_5, \Xi_4, \Xi_5, x_{11}\Xi_4, x_{12}\Xi_5\}$; this is also adopted from [2].

4.2 Experimental Condition

The learning system observes a state of the CPG-coupled system and outputs an indirect control signal every 0.01 second. We assume that the discrete time step t is incremented after 0.01 second elapses in the physical world.

We assume that input signals to the $(2i-1)$-th and $2i$-th CPG neurons are anti-symmetric: $u_{2i-1} = -u_{2i}$. Then, the stochastic policy $\pi_{\boldsymbol{\theta}}(\mathbf{u}|\mathbf{s})$ is defined by the normal distribution $\mathcal{N}(\boldsymbol{\mu}; \bar{\boldsymbol{\mu}}, \sigma)$, in which σ is the standard deviation of the policy and $\boldsymbol{\mu}$ is a six-dimensional vector whose i-th element is $\mu_i \equiv u_{2i-1}$. In order for contra-lateral links to produce anti-symmetric motions, we assume that connection patterns have specific forms referred to [2], i.e., the mean $\bar{\boldsymbol{\mu}}$ is given by

$$\begin{aligned}
\bar{\mu}_1 &= \theta_1 X_1 - \theta_2 X_2 + \theta_3 X_3 + \theta_4 X_6 + \theta_9(y_1 - y_2) \\
\bar{\mu}_2 &= \theta_1 X_2 - \theta_2 X_1 + \theta_3 X_4 + \theta_4 X_5 + \theta_9(y_3 - y_4) \\
\bar{\mu}_3 &= \theta_5 X_4 + \theta_{10}(y_1 - y_2) \\
\bar{\mu}_4 &= \theta_5 X_3 + \theta_{10}(y_3 - y_4) \\
\bar{\mu}_5 &= -\theta_6 X_3 - \theta_7 X_4 - \theta_8 X_7 + \theta_{11}(y_1 - y_2) \\
\bar{\mu}_6 &= -\theta_6 X_4 - \theta_7 X_3 - \theta_8 X_8 + \theta_{11}(y_3 - y_4).
\end{aligned} \quad (11)$$

Accordingly the parameter of the actor, i.e., the stochastic policy $\mathcal{N}(\mu; \bar{\mu}, \sigma)$, is $\boldsymbol{\theta} \equiv \{\theta_1, \ldots, \theta_{11}\}$, and this parameter vector is determined by our RL scheme.

We assume that an immediate reward $r(\boldsymbol{\nu}(t), \mathbf{x}(t), \mathbf{u}(t))$ depends only on the robot state at the next time step $\mathbf{x}(t+1)$:

$$\tilde{r}(\mathbf{x}) = k_h r_h(\mathbf{x}) + k_s r_s(\mathbf{x}) + k_{h2} r_{h2}(\mathbf{x}) + k_{\dot{h}} r_{\dot{h}}(\mathbf{x}), \quad (12)$$

where $r_h(\mathbf{x}) = h_1 - \min(h_4, h_5) - H$, $r_s(\mathbf{x}) = x_7$ if $|x_7| < 1$ or $x_7/|x_7|$ otherwise, $r_{h2}(\mathbf{x}) = -r_h^2$ if $r_h < 0$ or 0 otherwise, and $r_{\dot{h}}(\mathbf{x}) = \exp(x_8 - \dot{H}) - 1$ if $x_8 < \dot{H}$ or 0 otherwise. $h_i(i = 1, 4, 5)$ represents the height of link-i, and x_7 and x_8 are the horizontal and vertical speeds of link-1, respectively. $r_h(\mathbf{x})$ encourages the robot not to fall down, and $r_s(\mathbf{x})$ encourages the robot to proceed to the forward direction. We employ r_{h2} and $r_{\dot{h}}$ in order to incur a large penalty when the robot falls down. k_h, k_s, k_{h2} and $k_{\dot{h}}$ are weight values for r_h, r_s, r_{h2} and $r_{\dot{h}}$, respectively. H and $\dot{H}$ are the thresholds for the leg's height and the vertical speed of link-1, respectively. These parameters are fixed at $k_h = 1.0$, $k_s = 0.1$, $k_{h2} = 1.0$, $k_{\dot{h}} = 1.0$, $H = 0.9$ and $\dot{H} = -0.8$.

At the beginning of an episode, the robot was initialized in such a way that it did not move and its two legs were slightly opened. If the robot tumbled before the maximum time period elapsed, the episode was terminated at that point. The RL proceeded by repeating such a learning episode.

As additional basis functions for the critic, we used a constant basis (bias term), the height of link-1: $x_2(t) - 0.9$, the horizontal speed of link-1: $x_7(t)$, and the vertical speed of link-1: $x_8(t)$.

Acquisition of the Biped Locomotion. In the first experiment, we examined whether our method was able to obtain the CPG controller such that the biped robot could walk stably. For the sake of experimental simplicity, mutual connection weights in the neural oscillator network are fixed, i.e., $\theta_i = 0$ for $i = 9, 10, 11$ ($W_{ij}^{act} \equiv 0$ in equation (8)). Before learning, each weight parameter θ_i for $i = 1, \ldots, 8$ was set to a small random value, which did not allow the robot to walk as can be seen in Figure 2(a). The maximum time period in one episode was set to 5 seconds and the interval N was set to 1,000.

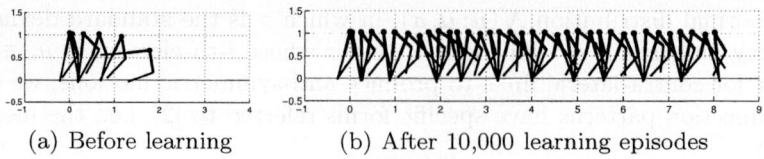

(a) Before learning   (b) After 10,000 learning episodes

Fig. 2. Gait patterns.

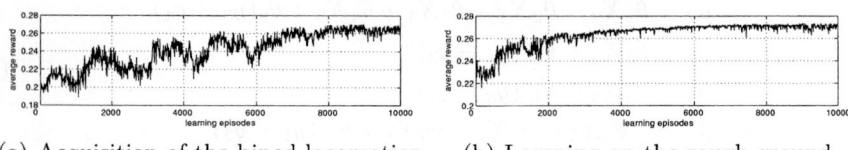

(a) Acquisition of the biped locomotion   (b) Learning on the rough ground

Fig. 3. Learning curve.

Figure 3(a) shows the learning curve. The horizontal axis denotes the number of learning episodes, and the vertical axes denote the average reward. After about 7,000 episodes, the robot was less likely to fall down before 5 seconds elapsed, and the average reward per step got large. Figures 2(a) and 2(b) show stroboscopic gait patterns of the biped robot before learning and after 10,000 learning episodes, respectively.

Learning on the Rough Ground. In the second experiment, we examined whether the CPG controller was able to acquire the policy that produces stable walking on various ground conditions, after starting from near the CPG controller whose connection weight was the hand-tuned value in [2]. Note that the hand-tuned CPG controller could not produce stable walking on such variety of ground conditions. θ_i for $i = 1, \ldots, 8$ were initialized at hand-tuned values in [2] plus small random values, and θ_i for $i = 9, \ldots, 11$ were set to small random values. During each RL episode, the ground surface was set to be piece-wise linear, in which the gradient of each linear piece was set randomly within a specific range. The maximum time period in one episode was set to 10 seconds and the interval N was set to 1,000. Before learning, i.e., with a CPG close to the hand-tuned one, the robot usually fell down before 10 seconds elapsed.

Figure 3(b) shows the learning curve. The horizontal axis denotes the number of learning episodes, and the vertical axes denote the average reward. After about 2,000 learning episodes, the robot acquired a good control that allowed it not to fall down and to walk stably.

5 Concluding Remarks

In this article, we proposed a natural policy gradient learning for the CPG-actor-critic model. According to our RL method, the critic approximated the projection of the Q-function onto a lower dimensional space than the state-action space, and the critic's parameter was estimated by LSQ. The actor's parameter was updated according to the natural policy gradient. We applied our method to an automatic acquisition problem of biped locomotion by using a robot simulator. Using this method, a CPG controller was obtained such to allow the biped robot to walk stably even on various ground conditions. In these simulations, the connection patterns within the actor were restricted. It is not beneficial to train the CPG controller from scratch, because a control scheme using a CPG controller works well by utilizing inherent oscillatory patterns of the CPG.

In our method, there are some factors that possibly introduce a bias to the estimator $\tilde{w}$. In particular, the configuration of an initial state of each RL episode and the maximum time length t_{max} should be determined more carefully, because they may cause the difference between the empirical distribution and the assumed stationary distribution. This problem will be considered in our future study.

References

1. Grillner, S., Wallen, P., Brodin, L., Lansner, A.: Neuronal network generating locomotor behavior in lamprey: circuitry, transmitters, membrane properties and simulations. Annual Review of Neuroscience **14** (1991) 169–199
2. Taga, G., Yamaguchi, Y., Shimizu, H.: Self-organized control of bipedal locomotion by neural oscillators in unpredictable environment. Biological Cybernetics **65** (1991) 147–159
3. Sato, M., Nakamura, Y., Ishii, S.: Reinforcement learning for biped locomotion. In: International Conference on Artificial Neural Networks (ICANN 2002). (2002) 777–782
4. Sutton, R.S., Barto, A.G.: Reinforcement Learning: An Introduction. MIT Press (1998)
5. Konda, V.R., Tsitsiklis, J.N.: Actor-critic algorithms. SIAM Journal on Control and Optimization **42** (2003) 1143–1146
6. Sutton, R.S., McAllester, D., Singh, S., Manour, Y.: Policy gradient method for reinforcement learning with function approximation. In: Proceedings of the 1998 IEEE International Conference on Robotics & Automation. (2000)
7. Kakade, S.: A natural policy gradient. In Advances in Neural Information Processing Systems **14** (2001) 1531–1538
8. Peters, J., Vijayakumar, S., Schaal, S.: Reinforcement learning for humanoid robotics. In: Third IEEE International Conference on Humanoid Robotics 2003, Germany. (2003)
9. Sato, M., Ishii, S.: Reinforcement learning based on on-line em algorithm. Advances in Neural Information Processing Systems **11** (1999) 1052–1058
10. Bradtke, S.J., Barto, A.G.: Linear least-squares algorithms for temporal difference learning. Machine Learning **22** (1996) 33–57
11. Lagoudakis, M.G., Parr, R., Littman, M.L.: Least-squares methods in reinforcement learning for control. In: SETN. (2002) 249–260

Evaluation of Adaptive Nature Inspired Task Allocation Against Alternate Decentralised Multiagent Strategies

Richard Price and Peter Tiňo

School Of Computer Science
University Of Birmingham
Birmingham B15 2TT, UK
{ug73rxp,pxt}@cs.bham.ac.uk

Abstract. Adaptive multiagent algorithms based upon the behaviour of social insects are powerful *decentralised* systems capable of solving complex problems. The intelligence of such a system lies not within a single agent but is a product of a network of simple interactions. Under the context of a mail collection environment different techniques are implemented and evaluated. The paper creates a number of strategies to tackle task allocation problems of this type based upon the principles of self-organisation and greedy search. The paper also investigates factors that may affect their performance.

1 Introduction

Social insects have been colonising the planet for millions of years, part of their ability to survive in numerous climates is due to their ability to react to changing demands with little or no centralised control. Social insects are therefore powerful decentralised problem solving systems. Theories of self-organisation, originally developed in the context of physics and chemistry, can be extended to social insects. Algorithms based upon these principles have been shown to be effective on many complex problems including the travelling salesman problem, combinatorial optimisation and graph partitioning. The success of these algorithms and indeed social insects is (at least partly) due to their ability to adapt to dynamic environments.

The aim of this paper is to investigate how adaptive nature inspired techniques can be applied to a multiagent task allocation problem. The issue with all adaptive algorithms that are designed to deal with dynamically varying problems is that there is no standard way of evaluating their performance [1].

This paper explores nature inspired task allocation in a multiagent environment and compares its performance against other more established strategies.

The problem considered here is a variation of the mail retrieval proposal by Bonabeau et al. in [1]. Batches of mail produced by cities need to be assigned to processing centres all of which are spread across an area. Once produced, a batch of mail waits for collection at its origin and that city cannot produce another batch until it has been collected. Cities can produce different types of batches, each of which need to be processed differently by centres. Each centre has a collecting agent solely responsible for the selection and collection of batches of mail. Centres will eventually develop a queue of batches each of which must be processed in turn. It takes a set amount of time to process a batch of mail but it takes significantly longer to reconfigure the centre if the type of mail needing to be processed is different from the batch previously processed. Therefore the number of these changeovers should be minimised as best as possible.

However, a centre cannot exclusively deal with a single type of mail as a deadlock situation may occur with all the cities having a single type of mail waiting for collection. In addition each centre has a limited size queue of batches that have been collected and are awaiting processing. Therefore each centre needs to specialise as best as possible whilst being able to react to fluctuating demands. It is clear that the performance of each centre is directly dependent upon the decisions of the collecting agent.

The approach taken in this paper investigates a number of new areas. Firstly the project investigates decentralised task allocation rather than the centrally controlled approaches taken in [2, 3]. Secondly the paper compares a number of decentralised algorithms upon the mail retrieval problem to analyse how their performances compare and contrast. Finally the environment is more generalised than previous work in [1, 3, 4] allowing further investigation into the behaviours of the different algorithms.

2   Decentralised Approaches to Task Allocation

Developed by Bonabeau et al. in [5] the fixed response threshold algorithm can explain several aspects of the behaviour of social insects. In this model, individuals are more likely to engage in a task when the level of stimulus associated with that task exceeds their threshold. As a task's stimulus can only increase if the task is not performed at all or with not enough efficiency, removing individuals that normally conduct a specific task will result in the associated stimulus increasing. This will cause other individuals not normally associated with this task being stimulated to conduct it. This behaviour directly relates to the observations of the notable biologist Wilson in [6].

Every individual a is assumed to posses a set of response thresholds $\Theta_a = \{\theta_{a,0}, ..., \theta_{a,N}\}$. Each threshold $\theta_{a,t}$ correspond to a *type of task* $t = 0, 1, 2, ..., N$, that individual is able to perform. The initial values of the thresholds are randomly initialised to ensure that their roles are not predetermined.

A response threshold algorithm combines the associated threshold with the corresponding stimulus intensity of a task to calculate the probability that an individual will engage in that task. A threshold response function ensures that when the stimulus exceeds an individual's corresponding threshold that individual is likely to engage in that task. Correspondingly if the stimulus is less than an individual's threshold then it should be unlikely that the individual engages in that task. Finally if the stimulus is equal to the individual's threshold then there should be a 50% chance of that individual engaging in that task. Formally [1],

$$T_{\theta_{a,t}}(S_j) = \frac{(S_j)^n}{(S_j)^n + (\theta_{a,t})^n}, \qquad (1)$$

where $T_{\theta_{a,t}}(S_j)$ is the probability that the individual a will perform task j of type t. The probability is directly related to the magnitude of the stimulus S_j and the individual's response threshold $\theta_{a,t}$ to that type of task. In this paper, the stimulus S_j is the time waited of batch of mail j whilst $\theta_{a,t}$ is the threshold of agent a corresponding to type of mail t. In addition, the steepness of the threshold response function can be altered through the parameter $n > 2$.

However, fixing an agent's threshold limits the agent's ability to adapt to its environment and this model cannot account for several aspects of social insect behaviour. A fixed threshold model assumes that an individual's role is predetermined, in addition to excluding ageing and learning from the task allocation process. Therefore a fixed threshold model is only a valid model of social insect behaviour over a sufficiently short period of time where thresholds are considered relatively stable.

Theraulaz et al. [7] extended the fixed threshold model by allowing variable thresholds. This model allows thresholds to vary through time in a self-reinforcing way according to what action an agent takes. In our paper, each time an agent a collects a batch of mail of type t, its threshold for collecting that type of batch again is lowered by a small amount $\epsilon > 0$

$$\theta_{a,t}^{new} = \theta_{a,t}^{old} - \epsilon. \qquad (2)$$

In addition, that agent's thresholds for all other types of batches q are increased by a small amount $\phi > 0$,

$$\theta_{a,q}^{new} = \theta_{a,q}^{old} + \phi, \quad q \neq t. \qquad (3)$$

In [1], Bonabeau et al. refers to ϵ and ϕ as learning and forgetting coefficients, respectively. A response threshold function such as (1) is still used to select tasks. In addition each threshold $\theta_{a,t}$ is restricted to a positive interval $[\theta_{min}, \theta_{max}]$[1].

The variable response threshold algorithm does not assume that roles are predetermined and allows the age of an individual to affect response thresholds. In addition a number of experiments and observations imply the existence of a reinforcement process within social insects [8].

The variable response threshold algorithm has been used in several nature inspired systems. Bonabeau et al. in [1] showed that the use of variable thresholds caused individuals to become highly responsive to stimulus associated with specific tasks whilst others only became weakly responsive. By removing these responsive individuals from the experiment individuals with previously high thresholds become more responsive to the associated available tasks. This behaviour is analogous to the observations by Wilson in [6] in contrast to the fixed threshold model in which thresholds cannot respond to perturbations in

---

[1] if $\theta_{a,t}^{new} < \theta_{min}$, then $\theta_{a,t}^{new} = \theta_{min}$, and if $\theta_{a,t}^{new} > \theta_{max}$, then $\theta_{a,t}^{new} = \theta_{max}$

the environment. This paper implements both the fixed and variable response threshold algorithms to further analyse their behaviour.

Other work also investigates the behaviour of the response threshold algorithm. In [4], Cicirello et al. showed that by using a variable response threshold algorithm and a dynamic queueing policy based upon wasp behaviour is capable of producing an efficient and robust system that can adapt to dynamically changing factory environments. Campos et al. [3] explain the similarities between the variable response threshold algorithm and a more established market-based approach. Overall related work shows that the variable response threshold algorithm can be used to create a self-organised system that is flexible, efficient and robust.

A core aim of this paper is to compare the performance of the variable response threshold algorithm against viable alternatives, such the variable response probability algorithm introduced below. Each agent a has an internal value $P_{a,t}$ for each type of mail t. $P_{a,t}$ represents the probability of collecting mail of type t by agent a. Each time an agent a collects a batch of mail of type t, its probability for collecting that type of mail again is increased, while probabilities for collecting all other types of mail are decreased:

$$Q_{a,t} = P_{a,t}^{old} \cdot (1 + \alpha), \tag{4}$$

$$Q_{a,q} = P_{a,q}^{old} \cdot (1 - \alpha), \quad q \neq t, \tag{5}$$

$$P_{a,j}^{new} = \frac{Q_{a,j}}{\sum_r Q_{a,r}}, \tag{6}$$

where $0 < \alpha < 1$.

Note that updates in the variable response probability algorithm are multiplicative in nature, whereas the threshold updates in the variable response threshold algorithm by Theraulaz et al. [7] are additive.

As mentioned earlier the environment created for this paper is different in many respects than alternate approaches. Each agent, regardless of strategy, is supplied with the same information about mail awaiting collection (such as type and time waited). No agent, in any strategy, has access to information about other agent's actions or states. Therefore each strategy is completely decentralised. Many task allocation techniques implement centralised control and/or communication between agents to optimise the overall performance [2, 3]. This paper offers a fresh outlook at decentralised task allocation algorithms within both stationary and dynamically changing environments.

3 Experiments

The experiments in this section analyse the performance of the all the strategies upon increasingly complex environments. However, all the experiments have a few common features. Each simulation is run for a period of 10,000 ticks and each experiment uses 100 simulations for each strategy to ensure comprehensive testing.

Both fixed and variable response threshold algorithms used the following parameter settings: $\theta_{min} = 0$, $\theta_{max} = 100$, $n = 2$. In addition, the variable response threshold algorithm used $\epsilon = 5$ and $\phi = 5$. Parameter α in the variable response probability algorithm was set to 0.2. These parameter settings where chosen as they tended to lead to good performance levels when tested upon the multiple versions of the environment (with varying degrees of complexity) used in this paper.

The work presented here also implemented two base case strategies designed to be the minimum level of acceptable performance for the other strategies. By far the simplest of the algorithms, *'first in - first out'* (FIFO), collects mail in the same order it is produced. Slightly more sophisticated than FIFO is the *greedy algorithm* that always attempts to collect the same type of mail it is currently processing. The type of mail currently being processed has the highest priority, otherwise mail is collected according to the time it has waited. One would expect that the greedy algorithm performs to a higher standard than FIFO by processing more mail and incurring fewer changeovers.

Performance can be evaluated by how much mail each strategy is able to process whilst minimising the number of changeovers. The tables in this section show for each experiment the average amount of mail processed and the average number of changeovers of each strategy over 100 runs. In addition the standard deviations of these figures are shown in brackets below the averages.

We tested for significance in differences between alternate strategies across multiple runs of the same experiment using t-test. Throughout this section the symbol $*$ signifies that a strategy is statistically significantly worse (with probability 0.95) in comparison to the variable response threshold algorithm. Analogously, symbol $+$ signifies that a strategy is statistically significantly worse in comparison to the variable response probability algorithm (with probability 0.95).

3.1 Experiment 1

The initial comparison used an environment of six cities (producing mail), two centres (collecting/processing the mail) and two types of mail. The results of the experiment are shown in Table 1.

As expected, the FIFO strategy was outperformed by every other strategy. In addition, the greedy algorithm was only able to slightly increase throughput and decrease changeovers. The fixed response threshold algorithm outperformed both of these algorithms but was unable to compete with the variable response threshold (VRT) and variable response probability (VRP) algorithms. The VRT algorithm was able to significantly increase throughput and decrease changeovers by almost 50% in comparison to the fixed response threshold algorithm. The VRP algorithm decreased changeovers dramatically, well below all other algorithms, while additionally closely matching the throughput of the VRT algorithm.

Table 1. Average performances of strategies in Experiment 1. FRT, VRT and VRP stand for the fixed response threshold, variable response threshold and variable response probability algorithms, respectively.

Strategy	Mail Processed	Changeovers
FIFO	318.73*,+ (10.676)	162.21*,+ (3.817)
Greedy	321.23*,+ (13.348)	159.75*,+ (5.695)
FRT	332.94*,+ (20.840)	151.37*,+ (11.755)
VRT	401.40 (22.609)	88.27+ (10.419)
VRP	400.78 (33.108)	18.93 (7.137)

3.2 Experiment 2

Further experiments with increasingly complex environments showed similar results – variable response threshold algorithm processes the most mail whilst the VRP algorithm maintains significantly lower changeovers. A typical example (using 30 cities, 10 centres and 2 types of mail) is presented in Table 2.

Table 2. Average performances of strategies in Experiment 2 (30 cities, 10 centres, 2 types of mail).

Strategy	Mail Processed	Changeovers
FIFO	1587.20*,+ (27.167)	805.80*,+ (9.945)
Greedy	1632.51*,+ (44.587)	756.49*,+ (29.533)
FRT	1485.05*,+ (82.864)	508.32*,+ (58.587)
VRT	2318.61 (35.622)	222.67+ (29.330)
VRP	2207.87* (143.795)	65.90 (14.721)

3.3 Experiment 3

The previous experiments only investigated stationary environments where the probabilities of different types of mail appearing remained constant. It was reasoned that because of the relatively high value of parameter α in the variable response probability model ($\alpha = 0.2$) and the multiplicative nature of updates in this model, the response probabilities of agents quickly specialise to a type of mail to process (the probability of picking an alternate type of mail rapidly decreases to negligible values). This makes the model rather inflexible in dynamically changing environments. The next experiment setup an environment where initially one type of mail was twice as likely to appear as the alternate, however after 5000 ticks these probabilities are reversed: There were 9 cities, 3 centres and 2 types of mail. The results are presented in Table 3.

Table 3. Average performances of strategies VRT and VRP in Experiment 3 (dynamically changing environment, 9 cities, 3 centres, 2 types of mail).

Strategy	Mail Processed	Changeovers
VRT	633.68	121.03$^+$
	(29.083)	(17.555)
VRP	507.80*	32.30
	(51.358)	(7.243)

In this experiment, the variable response threshold algorithm consistently devoted two centres to the dominant mail type in the first half of the simulations. At the point where the mail type probabilities switched, the algorithm reliably caused the behaviour of one of the collecting agents to specialise to the alternate and now dominant type of mail. However the VRP algorithm was unable to adapt as suitably to the dynamic probabilities within the environment. Using this strategy, the collecting agents behaviour did not alter despite the new environmental conditions resulting in a significantly lower overall throughput, although the changeovers incurred remained minimal.

4 Discussion

The main findings of this paper are that the adaptive algorithms, namely the variable response threshold (VRT) and variable response probability (VRP) algorithm, where able to significantly outperform the simpler approaches. The performance of these algorithms remained stable over increasingly complex environments. The difference in performance between the fixed and variable response threshold algorithms highlight how a dual reinforcement process enables collecting agents to adapt well to most environments.

Particularly of interest was how the VRP algorithm was able to incur a very small amount of changeovers compared to every other strategy. The changeovers occurred very early in the simulation before the collecting agents could fully specialise to one type of mail. Once the collecting agents had adapted to the environment, changeovers occurred with little or no frequency. Further experiments (not included in this paper) also show that in complex *stationary* environments the VRP algorithm is able to process more mail than the VRT algorithm.

By the nature of the VRP model, parameter α determines the speed of specialisation. Higher values of α lead to faster specialisation, but also to greater inflexibility of the model to adapt to changes in the environment. In dynamic environments, the VRT algorithm consistently outperformed the VRP algorithm. Further observations showed that the more dynamic the environment, the larger the performance gap between the VRT and VRP algorithms becomes.

This paper offers a fresh outlook at decentralised task allocation algorithms within both static and dynamic environments. The transfer of social insect inspired algorithms from static to dynamic environments has rarely been tested [3].

The work presented here also analysed the VRT algorithm in more detail and was shown to have many diverse features. The results highlight that the algorithm is capable of creating a self-organised system through stigmergy alone. This self-organised system also adapts well to most environments. In addition, natural phenomena particularly in comparison to the work of Wilson in [6] are reproducible. The behaviour of the algorithm can be altered through the parameters. Particularly of interest was how the VRT algorithm may reinforce a hypothesis suggested by Anderson in [9]: *"There must be a critical window of correlation of activity among individuals in order for self-organisation to occur. That is above some upper threshold and below some lower threshold, self-organisation breaks down, and the emergent properties no longer exist."*

5 Conclusion

We compared the variable response threshold (VRT) algorithm of Theraulaz et al. [7] for decentralised task allocation with four alternate strategies, namely FIFO, greedy algorithm, fixed response threshold algorithm (FRT) and variable response probability (VRP) algorithm. Each of these strategies where analysed and compared upon increasingly complex environments. It appears that the VRP algorithm can be most suitable in stationary environments where the probabilities of the types of mail appearing remained constant. However if the probabilities of mail types appearing are dynamic within the environment the VRP algorithm is less flexible than the VRT algorithm.

Overall the area of self-organisation is intriguing and new developments are being discovered at a rapid pace. Perhaps in the future such systems will become more widely accepted, as their behaviour is better understood. Until such a time the area will be dominated by theoretical problems and relatively few real-world applications. Even though social insect colonies and other biological systems have utilised self-organisation in the real world with great success for millions of years.

References

1. Bonabeau E., Sobkowski A., Theraulaz G., Deneubourg J.L.: Adaptive Task Allocation Inspired by a Model of Division of Labour in Social Insects. In: Bio-Computation and Emergent Computing. World Scientific (1997) 36-45.

2. Waldspurger, C.A., Hog T., Huberman B.A., Kephart J.O.: Spawn: A Distributed Computational Economy. IEEE Trans. Softw. Engineer **18** (1992) 103-117.
3. Campos M., Bonabeau E., Theraulaz G., Deneubourg J.L.: Dynamic Scheduling and Division of Labour in Social Insects. Adaptive Behaviour **8(2)** (2001) 83-92.
4. Cicirello V.A., Smith S.F.: Wasp Nests for Self-Configurable Factories. In Agents 2001. Proceedings of the Fifth International Conference on Autonomous Agents. ACM Press (2001) 473-480.
5. Bonabeau E., Theraulaz G., Deneubourg J.L.: Quantitative Study of the Fixed Threshold Model for the Regulation of Division of Labour Insect Societies Proc. Roy. Soc. London **B 263** (1996) 1565-1569.
6. Wilson E.O.: The Relation Between Caste Ratios and Division of Labour in the Ant Genus Pheidole (Hymenoptera: Formicidae). Behav. Ecol. Sociobiol. **16** (1984) 89-98.
7. Theraulaz G., Goss S., Gervet J., Deneubourg J.L.: Task Differentiation in Polistes Wasp Colonies: A Model for Self-Organizing Groups of Robots. In Proceedings First International Conference on Simulation of Adaptive Behaviour: From Animals to Animats. (1991) 346-355.
8. Withers G.S., Fahrbach S.E., Robinson G.E.: Selective neuroanatomical plasticity and division of labour in the honeybee. Nature **364** (1993) 238-240.
9. Anderson C.: Self-Organization in Relation to Several Similar Concepts: Are the Boundaries to Self-Organization Indistinct? Biol. Bull, **202** (2002) 247-255.

A Neuroevolutionary Approach to Emergent Task Decomposition

Jekanthan Thangavelautham and Gabriele M.T. D'Eleuterio

Institute for Aerospace Studies, University of Toronto
Toronto, Ontario, Canada, M3H 5T6
thangav@ecf.utoronto.ca, gabriele.deleuterio@utoronto.ca

Abstract. A scalable architecture to facilitate emergent (self-organized) task decomposition using neural networks and evolutionary algorithms is presented. Various control system architectures are compared for a collective robotics (3 × 3 tiling pattern formation) task where emergent behaviours and effective task -decomposition techniques are necessary to solve the task. We show that bigger, more modular network architectures that exploit emergent task decomposition strategies can evolve faster and outperform comparably smaller non emergent neural networks for this task. Much like biological nervous systems, larger Emergent Task Decomposition Networks appear to evolve faster than comparable smaller networks. Unlike reinforcement learning techniques, only a global fitness function is specified, requiring limited supervision, and self-organized task decomposition is achieved through competition and specialization. The results are derived from computer simulations.

1 Introduction

Some of the fundamental goals of machine learning is to develop learning algorithms that require limited supervision but can facilitate the discovery of novel solutions and better handle environmental uncertainties. We have been inspired by social insects such as ants, bees and termites that form *synergistic* (one whose capabilities exceed the sum of its parts) multiagent systems without any centralized supervision. These insects societies consist of simple individuals and as a collective can solve complex tasks. For example, termites have evolved the ability to survive the harsh Australian outback by building towering nests with internal heating and cooling shafts [3].

Evolutionary algorithms (EAs) are specially suited for non-Markovian collective robotics tasks, since only a global fitness function needs to be specified to obtain a desired collective behaviour. Unfortunately, the application of evolutionary algorithms for increasingly complex robotics control tasks has been very challenging due to the *bootstrap problem* [12]. The bootstrap problem occurs when it becomes increasingly difficult for the EAs (particularly for a monolithic control system topology) to pick out incrementally better solutions for crossover and mutation resulting in premature stagnation of the evolutionary run.

A common solution to the bootstrap problem is to decompose a complex task into a set of simpler tasks through supervised task decomposition. This often requires a priori information of the task and supervisor intervention in determining suitable task decomposition strategies. Yet in nature, biological systems can accomplish such feet with no such external intervention.

In this paper we introduce a modular Emergent Task Decomposition Network (ETDN) architecture that requires limited supervision and can decompose a complex task into a set of simpler tasks through competition and self organization. The ETDN architecture is trained using evolutionary algorithms, with only a prespecified global fitness function. The network is composed of *decision neurons* (mediates competition) and several *expert networks* (that compete for dominance).

Limited supervision provides numerous advantages including the ability to discover novel solutions that would otherwise be overlooked by a human supervisor. This strategy is particularly advantageous for decentralized collective robotics where little is known of the interaction of local behaviours resulting in a desired global behaviour. We empirically compare the training performance (using evolutionary algorithms) of various control systems for the tiling pattern formation task (similar to a segment of the termite nest building task [3]). It was found earlier that a memorisation approach (such as a monolithic look-up table-based control system) is unable to solve more complex versions of the task because of the bootstrap problem [14].

2 Related Work

Dorigo and Colombetti [4] introduced the idea of *incremental learning (shaping)* in classifier systems, where a robot learns a simplified version of the task and the task complexity is progressively increased by modifying the learning function. Stone and Veloso [13] developed a task decomposition scheme known as *layered learning*, where the learning function for a complex task (playing soccer) is partitioned into a set of simpler learning functions (corresponding to sub-tasks) and learned sequentially. These traditional task decomposition techniques require the supervisor to have domain knowledge of the task and are very difficult to implement in the collective robotics domain since the necessary local and global (collective) behaviours need to be known.

Jordan and Jacob [8] developed an automated task decomposition technique using a modular neural network architecture for the 'what' and 'where' vision task. The architecture consists of a decision network (mediates competition) and several expert modules (explicitly specialized for predefined subtasks). The expert networks and the decision networks are trained separately according to a set of handcrafted reinforcement learning algorithms. Darwen and Yao [2], Liu, Yao and Higuchi [10] developed a hybrid automated approach to task decomposition. Localized training is done using backpropagation or negative correlation learning and in turn EAs are used to modify training algorithm parameters. Rather than using a gating neuron, a prespecified gating algorithm such as voting is used. Diversity amongst the expert modules is protected through fitness sharing based speciation techniques.

Algorithms such as ESP (Enforced Subpopulations) and SANE (Symbiotic Adaptive Neuro-Evolution) evolve individual neurons, within a fixed neural network topology [6]. ESP uses separate subpopulations to select neurons for each placeholder within the neural network control systems [15, 6, 7]. Unfortunately, this approach is susceptible to premature convergence in some cases, due to a 'greedy' approach to neuron selection [6].

In evolutionary robotics, Nolfi [11] introduced *emergent modular architectures*, where decision neurons arbitrate individual motor control neurons for the garbage collection task [12]. This architecture evolved faster and produced better solutions than other comparable networks including multilayered feed forward and recurrent architectures.

There are some key difference between our ETDN architecture and Nolfi's emergent modular architecture. In his experiments, selection was amongst two motor neurons rather than whole networks. In addition there is 1:1 mapping between his decision neurons and control neurons, where each decision neuron votes for a motor neuron. This implementation is applicable for simpler problems, where individual neuron responses are sufficient for a solution. Using our ETDN architecture (Binary Relative Lookup variant), arbitration could be extended to among $2n$ expert networks.

3 Method

Some of the control system architectures presented in this paper consist of artificial neural networks trained using evolutionary algorithms (neuroevolution). We use a fixed network topology, with a 1:1 genotype-to-phenotype mapping, with a integer encoding scheme and where weights, biases/thresholds are evolved using a global fitness function. Some of the advantages of neuroevolution, over reinforcement learning is that the search space need not be smooth nor differentiable and solutions tend to be more robust against local minima. In addition, unlike traditional machine learning algorithms, EAs could be used to select suitable activation functions during training (as shown with our modular neuron architecture).

3.1 Emergent Task-Decomposition Architecture

We propose an Emergent Task-Decomposition Network (ETDN) architecture that consist of a set of decision neurons that mediate competition and a set of expert network modules that compete for dominance (see Fig. 1b). We exploit network modularity, evolutionary competition, specialization and *functional neutrality* to facilitate emergent (self organized) task decomposition

Unlike traditional machine learning methods where handcrafted learning functions are used to train the decision and expert networks separately, our architecture requires only a global fitness function. The intent is for the architecture to evolve the ability to decompose a complex task into a set of simpler

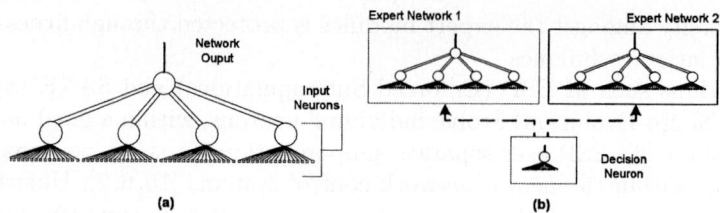

Fig. 1. (a) An example of the non-emergent network used in our experiments. (b) ETDN architecture consisting of a decision neuron that arbitrates between 2 expert networks.

tasks with limited supervision. The decision neuron is connected to all the sensory input and is used to select an expert network based on the output state. In turn, the output from the selected expert network triggers a set of predefined actions.

In nature, it is well known that the brain has adopted a modular architecture. Ballard [1] goes further and suggests that a limitation in the number of neurons in the brain (due to limited volume) have forced the brain to evolve a modular architecture. Geschwind and Galaburda[5] suggest competition between different networks of neurons in the brain drives certain networks to become specialized for a particular function.

3.2 Extending Emergent Task Decomposition

Our proposed ETDN architecture unlike previous work in the field of evolutionary robotics, could be generalized for n_E expert networks. Here we discuss two proposed extensions to the ETDN architecture, namely the Binary Relative Lookup (BRL) architecture and Binary Decision Tree (BDT) architecture.

The Binary Relative Lookup (BRL) architecture consists of a set of n_d non-interconnected decision neurons that arbitrate between 2^{n_d} expert networks. Starting from left to right, each additional decision neuron determines the specific grouping of expert networks relative to the selected group. Since the decision neurons are not interconnected (see Fig. 2), this architecture is well suited for parallel implementation.

The Binary Decision Tree (BDT) architecture could be represented as a binary tree where the tree nodes consist of decision neurons and the leaves consist of expert networks. For this architecture, n_d decision neurons arbitrate between

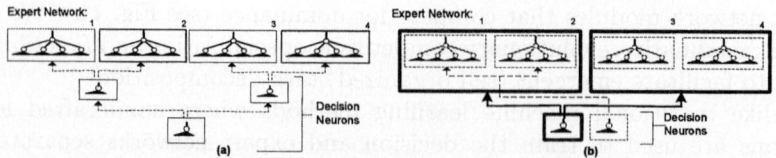

Fig. 2. (left) BDT Architecture with 4 expert networks and 3 decision neurons. (right) BRL Architecture with 4 expert networks and 2 decision neurons.

$n_d + 1$ expert networks. The tree is traversed by starting from the root and computing decisions neurons along each selected branch node until an expert network is selected. For both architectures the computational cost of the decision neurons, $C_d \propto \log n_E$.

3.3 Modular Neurons

We have also developed a modular threshold activation neuron, where the EAs are used to train the weights, threshold parameters and choice of activation function for each neuron. The inputs and outputs from the modular threshold neurons consist of states rather than arbitrary values. The modular neuron could assume one of four different activation functions listed shown below:

$$\phi_1: s_{out} = \begin{cases} s_1, & \text{if } p(x) \le t_1 \\ s_2, & \text{if } p(x) > t_1 \end{cases} \quad \phi_3: s_{out} = \begin{cases} s_1, & \text{if } t_2 < p(x) < t_1 \\ s_2, & \text{otherwise} \end{cases}$$

$$\phi_2: s_{out} = \begin{cases} s_1, & \text{if } p(x) \ge t_2 \\ s_2, & \text{if } p(x) < t_2 \end{cases} \quad \phi_4: s_{out} = \begin{cases} s_1, & \text{if } p(x) > (1 - p(x)) \\ \text{rand}(s_1, s_2), & \text{if } p(x) = (1 - p(x)) \\ s_2, & \text{if } p(x) < (1 - p(x)) \end{cases} \quad (1)$$

Each neuron outputs one of two states $s = (s_1, s_2)$, where t_n is a threshold, $p(x) = (\sum_i w_i x_i)/(\sum_i x_i)$, w_i is a neuron weight and x_i is an element of the active input state vector.

Our intention was to develop a compact modular neuron architecture for implementation on hardware, where a single neuron could be used to simulate AND, OR, NOT and XOR functions. The assumption is that a compact yet sufficiently complex (functional) neuron will speed up evolutionary training since this will reduce the need for more hidden layers and thus result in smaller networks.

4 Example Task: Tiling Pattern Formation Task

The tiling pattern formation task [14] involves redistributing objects (blocks) piled up in a 2-D world into a desired tiling structure (see Fig. 7). The robots need to come to a consensus and form one 'perfect' tiling pattern. This task is similar to a segment of the termite nest construction task that involves redistributing pheromone filled pellets on the nest floor [3]. Once the pheromone pellets are uniformly distributed, the termite use the pellets as markers for constructing pillars to support the nest roof.

More important, the tiling pattern formation task could be decomposed into a number of potential subtasks consisting of emergent behaviours. These may include foraging for objects (blocks), redistributing block piles, arranging blocks in the desired tiling structure locally, merging local lattice structures, reaching a collective consensus and finding/correcting mistakes in the lattice structure. Inspired by nature, we are interested in evolving homogenous decentralized controllers (similar to a nest of termites) for the task [9]. Decentralized control offers

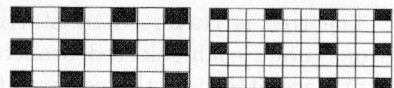

Fig. 3. The 2×2 tiling pattern (left) and 3×3 tiling pattern (right).

some inherent advantages including the ability to scaleup to a larger problem size. Task complexity is dependent on the intended tile spacing, since more sensor data would be required to construct a 'wider' tiling pattern.

Shannon's entropy function has been shown to be a suitable fitness function for the tiling formation task [14]. The test area spans $M \times M$ squares and is divided into J $l \times l$ cells, A_j, where the fitness value, $f_{i,x,y}$, for one set of initial condition i, after T discrete time steps, with cells shifted x squares in the x-direction and y squares in the y-direction is given as follows:

$$f_{i,x,y} = s \cdot \frac{\sum_{j=1}^{J} p_j \ln p_j}{\ln J} \qquad (2)$$

where, $s = 100$ and is a constant scaling factor, I is an index over a set of initial conditions and $p_j = (n(A_j))/(\sum_{j=1}^{J} n(A_j))$, where $n(A_j)$ is the number of blocks in cell A_j. To encourage the desired tiling pattern, the fitness function is applied by shifting the cells a maximum of $l - 1$ squares and the total fitness, $f_i = (\sum_{y=0}^{l-1}(\sum_{x=0}^{l-1} f_{i,x,y}))/l^2$. When the blocks are uniformly distributed over J cells, according to the desired tiling pattern, we have $f_i = 100$ (a successful epoch).

4.1 The Robot

The robots are modelled as modified Khepera robots equipped with a gripper turret. We have developed a fast 2-D grid world simulator for our evolutionary experiments and we have verified this simulator using Webots (Fig. 7). For the 2×2 tiling pattern formation task, each robot could detect blocks and other robots in the 5 squares as shown (Fig. 4). For the 3×3 tiling pattern formation task, the robots could detect object in 7 surrounding squares as shown. The output state from the robot controller activates one of two predefined basis behaviours, namely **Move** and **Manipulate Object**.

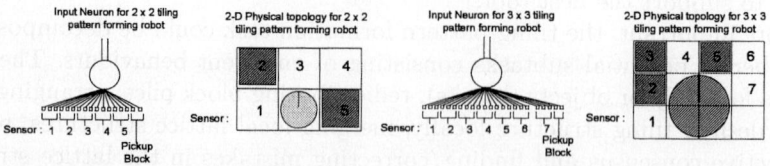

Fig. 4. Input layer neuron and physical topology for the 2×2 (left) and 3×3 (right) tiling pattern forming robots.

5 Experimentation

The evolutionary performance of various control systems architectures are compared for the tiling pattern formation task (see Fig. 5). Through experimentation, we found the best nonmodular network for the tiling pattern formation task as shown in Fig. 1(a). We use this network as our expert network module for the ETDN architectures. In our simulations the EA population size is $P = 100$, number of generations $G = 200$, crossover probability $p_c = 0.7$, mutation probability $p_m = 0.025$ and tournament size of $0.06 p_c$ (for tournament selection). The fitness is evaluated after $T = 3000$ timesteps for a 11×11 world (2×2 task) or 16×16 world (3×3 task) with 11 robots and 36 blocks.

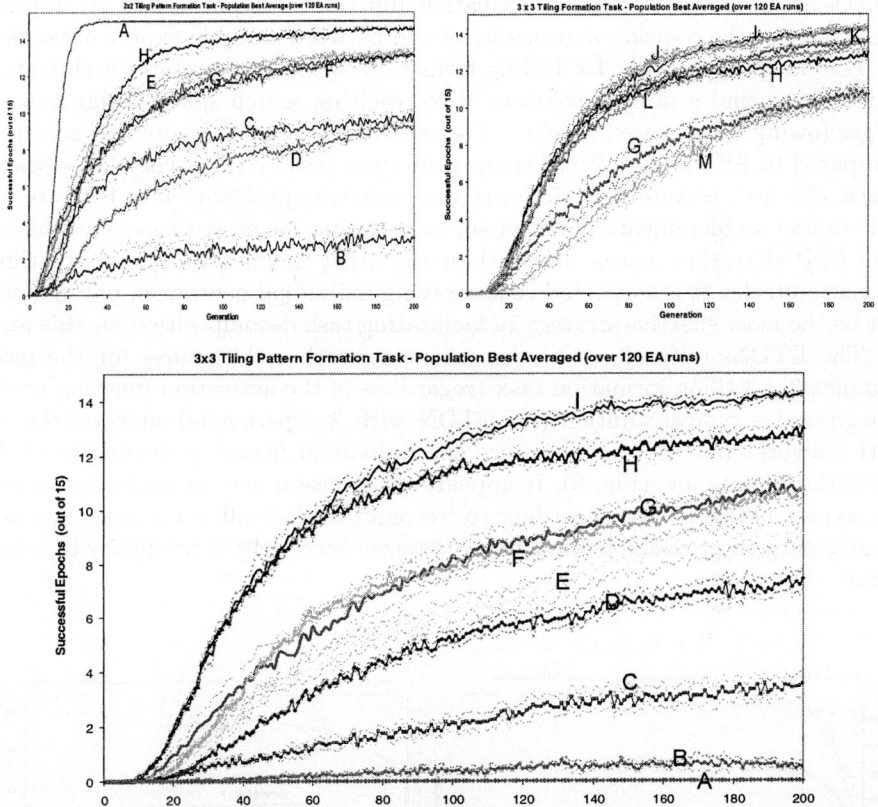

Fig. 5. Evolutionary performance comparison, 2×2 (left), 3×3 (right, bottom) tiling pattern formation task, averaged over 120 EA runs. **(A)** Look-up Table, **(B)** ESP (using Non-Emergent Net), **(C)** Non-Emergent Net(Sigmoid), **(D)** ETDN (Exp. Net 2, Sigmoid), **(E)** Non-Emergent Net. (Threshold), **(F)** ETDN (2 Exp. Nets, Threshold), **(G)** Non-Emergent Net. (Modular), **(H)** ETDN (2 Exp. Nets, Modular), **(I)** BRL (16 Exp. Nets, Modular), **(J)** BRL (32 Exp. Nets, Modular), **(K)** BRL (8 Exp. Nets, Modular), **(L)** BRL (4 Exp. Nets, Modular), **(M)** BDT (4 Exp. Nets, Modular).

6 Results and Discussion

For the 2×2 tiling pattern formation task, the lookup table approach evolves desired solutions faster than the network architectures. This suggests that ETDNs may not be the most efficient strategy for smaller search spaces. Our conventional ETDN architecture consisting of a single threshold activation function evolves slower than the nonemergent architectures.

The ETDN architectures include an additional 'overhead', since the evolutionary performance is dependent on the evolution of the expert networks and decision neurons resulting in slower performance for simpler tasks. However the Emergent Task Decomposition Network architecture that combines our modular neuron architecture outperforms all other network architectures. The performance of the modular neurons appears to offset the 'overhead' of the bigger ETDN architecture. A 'richer' activation function is hypothesized to improve the ability of the decision neurons to switch between suitable expert networks.

For the more difficult 3×3 tiling formation task, a lookup table architecture is unable to find a desired solution. The resulting search space is significantly larger (owing to increased number of sensors required), 2^{4374} potential solutions compared to 2^{486} for the 2×2 tiling formation task. With a very large search space, this architecture falls victim to the bootstrap problem, since EAs are unable to find an incrementally better solution during the early phase of evolution. The ESP algorithm learns slower than the other architectures for both tiling formation tasks. It is suspected that evolving individual neurons in parallel may not be the most effective strategy in facilitating task decomposition for this task.

The ETDNs outperform non-emergent network architectures for the more complex 3×3 tiling formation task (regardless of the activation function used). Analysis of a typical solution (for ETDN with 2 expert nets) suggests the expert networks have specialized since the individual fitness performance of the networks is quite low (Fig. 6). It appears the decision neuron arbitrates among the expert networks not according to 'recognizable' distill behaviours but as a set of emergent proximal behaviours (organized according to proximity in sensor space) [11].

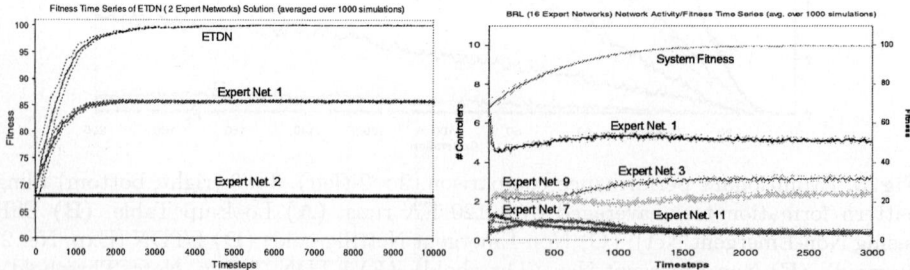

Fig. 6. (Left) Fitness of individual expert networks and the entire control system (ETDN, 2 expert nets.) averaged over 1000 simulations. (right) Expert Network activity and overall system fitness for a BRL (with 16 expert networks).

Table 1. Success rate of population best (generation 200) scaled up to a 100 × 100 world (76 robots, 1156 blocks).

Architecture	% Successful Epochs	% Batch Variance
Non-Emergent (Sigmoid)	0.0	-
Non-Emergent (Modular)	27.0	0.2
ETDN (2 Expert Nets., Modular)	44.5	2.2
BRL (16 Expert Nets., Modular)	70.2	0.4

Although conventional network architecture can perform limited task decomposition, (evident from solutions to the 3×3 tiling formation task), this process is more prone to *spatial crosstalk* [8] resulting in slower evolutionary performance. For the ETDNs, it appears, the task is distributed over several expert networks resulting in fewer hidden neurons being used as feature detectors within each network, thus reducing the overall effect of spatial crosstalk. The decision neurons within the BRL architecture act more 'independently' when selecting an expert network than the BDT network. We suspect this characteristic, in addition to the fewer number of decision neurons for the BRL network improves the ability to select suitable expert networks. This is evident from Fig. 5, where the BDT with 4 expert networks evolves slower than a comparable BRL network.

Much like biological nervous systems, the larger BRL architecture outperformed (or performed as fast as) the smaller ones (evident after about 80 generations). It is hypothesized that by increasing the number of expert networks, competition among candidate expert networks is further increased thus improving the chance of finding a desired solution. However, as the number of expert networks is increased (beyond 16), the relative improvement in performance is minimal, for this particular task.

The larger BRL network solutions generally evolve the ability to limit the number of expert networks used (see Fig. 6 for a typical solution). The other expert networks remain dormant throughout the simulations. The ability to limit the number of expert networks used for task decomposition is particularly advantageous, since 'over segmenting' the task into subtasks would result in over-fitting. Minor differences in fitness performance and 'success rates' for the 19 × 19 training world is 'magnified', once we scaleup to a larger problem size (100 × 100 world). This is where our ETDN and in particular BRL architectures is more advantageous over conventional network architectures (see Table 1).

Fig. 7. Simulation snapshots taken after 0, 100, 400 and 410 timesteps using a evolved solution for the 2 × 2 tiling formation task on a 11 × 11 world (11 robots, 36 blocks). The robots reach a consensus and form a 'perfect' tiling pattern after 410 timesteps.

7 Conclusion and Future Work

A scalable mechanism for emergent task decomposition using artificial neural networks and evolutionary algorithms is presented in this paper. Unlike reinforcement learning techniques, only a global fitness function is specified (unsupervised) and the network is able to decompose a complex task into simpler tasks through self-organization. Emergent Task Decomposition Networks (ETDN) evolve faster than non-emergent architectures and produce more desired solutions for complex tasks. It is interesting that much like biological nervous systems, larger BRL architectures tend to evolve faster than comparable smaller architectures. We are currently planning to compare the performance of our ETDN architecture with other supervised task decomposition methods for potential multirobot control tasks such as robotic soccer, mining and surface exploration.

References

1. Ballard, D.H., Cortical Connections and parallel processing. The Behavioural and Brain Sciences, Vol. 9, (1986) 279–284
2. Darwen, P., Yao X., Speciation as automatic categorical modularization. IEEE Transactions on Evolutionary Computation, 1(2), (1997) 101-108
3. Deneubourg J-L. Application de l'ordre par fluctuations 'a la description de certaines 'etapes de la construction du nid chez les termites. Insectes Sociaux, (1977) 117-130
4. Dorigo M., Colombetti M., Robot Shaping: Developing autonomous agents through learning. Artificial Intelligence, No. 71, (1994) 321-370
5. Gecshwind, N., Galaburda A.M., Cereberal Lateralization : Biological Mechanisms, Associations, and Pathology, MIT Press (1987)
6. Gomez, F., Miikkulainen R., Solving Non-Markovian Control Tasks with Neuroevolution In Proc. of the Int. Joint Conf.on Artificial Intelligence (1999)
7. Gomez, F., Miikkulainen, R., Active Guidance for a Finless Rocket using Neuroevolution. In the Proc. of Genetic and Evolutionary Comp. Conf.,(2003)
8. Jacobs R., Jordan M., Barto A., Task decomposition through competition in a modular connectionist architecture. Cognitive Science, No. 15, (1991) 219-250
9. Kube, R., Zhang, H.: Collective Robotics Intelligence : From Social Insects to robots. In Proc. Of Simulation of Adaptive Behavior (1992) 460–468
10. Liu, Y., Yao X., Higuchi T., Evolutionary Ensembles with Negative Correlation Learning. IEEE Transactions on Evolutionary Computation 4(4), (2000) 380-387
11. Nolfi, S., Using Emergent modularity to develop control systems for mobile robots., Adaptive Behaviour 5, No. 3, ISAB, (1997) 343-363
12. Nolfi, S., Floreano D.: Evolutionary Robotics : The Biology, Intelligence, and Technology of Self-Organizing Machines, MIT Press (2000) 13-15
13. Stone, P., Veloso M., Layered Learning, Proc. of 11th European Conf. on Machine Learning (2000) 369-381
14. Thangavelautham, J., Barfoot, T., D'Eleuterio, G.M.T., Coevolving Communication and Cooperation for Lattice formation Tasks In Adv. in ALife: Proc. Of 7th European Conf. on ALife (2003) 857-864
15. Whiteson, S. et. al.,Evolving Keep-away Soccer Players through Task Decomposition. In the Proc. of Genetic and Evolutionary Comp. Conf., (2003)

Evolving the "Feeling" of Time Through Sensory-Motor Coordination: A Robot Based Model

Elio Tuci, Vito Trianni, and Marco Dorigo

IRIDIA
Univeristé Libre de Bruxelles - Bruxelles - Belgium
{etuci,vtrianni,mdorigo}@ulb.ac.be

Abstract. In this paper, we aim to design decision-making mechanisms for an autonomous robot equipped with simple sensors, which integrates over time its perceptual experience in order to initiate a simple signalling response. Contrary to other similar studies, in this work the decision-making is uniquely controlled by the time-dependent structures of the agent's controller, which in turn are tightly linked to the mechanisms for sensory-motor coordination. The results of this work show that a single dynamic neural network, shaped by evolution, makes an autonomous agent capable of "feeling" time through the flow of sensations determined by its actions.

1 Introduction

Animals that forage in patchy environments, and do not have any *a priori* knowledge concerning the quality of the patch, must decide when it is time to leave a patch to move to another one of potentially better quality. Optimal foraging theory models assume that the experience that the animals have of the patch during time has an incremental or a decremental effect on the animal tendency to remain in the patch. These models show that some animals behave as if they made their decision on information gained while foraging [1]. Artificial autonomous agents might face similar problems: they may be required to change their behaviour because of information gained through a repeated interaction with their environment. In this paper, we aim to design decision-making mechanisms for an autonomous robot equipped with simple sensors, which integrates over time its perceptual experience in order to initiate alternative actions. In other words, the behaviour of the agent should change as a consequence of its repeated interaction with particular environmental circumstances.

We are interested in exploiting an evolutionary biologically-inspired approach, based on the use of dynamical neural networks and genetic algorithms [2]. Generally speaking, the appeal of an evolutionary approach to robotics is twofold. Firstly, and most basically, it offers the possibility of automating a complex design task [3]. Secondly, since artificial evolution needs neither to understand, nor to decompose a problem in order to find a solution, it offers the possibility of exploring regions of the design space that conventional design approaches are often constrained to ignore [4]. In our work, artificial evolution should tightly couple the agent's decision-making mechanisms to the nature of the environment and to the sensory-motor capabilities of the agent.

The experiment, described in details in section 2, requires an autonomous agent to possess both navigational skills and decision-making mechanisms. That is, the agent should prove capable of navigating within a boundless arena in order to approach a light bulb positioned at a certain distance from its starting position. Moreover, it should prove capable of discriminating between two types of environment: one in which the light can be actually reached; the other one in which the light is surrounded by a "barrier" which prevents the agent from proceeding further toward its target. Due to the nature of the experimental setup, the agent can decide in which type of environment it is situated only if it proves capable of (a) moving coordinately in order to bring forth the perceptual experience required to discriminate between the two environments; (b) integrating over time its perceptual experience in order to initiate a signalling behaviour if situated in an environment in which the light cannot be reached.

The contribution of this paper consists in showing that a single dynamic neural network, shaped by evolution, make an autonomous agent capable of "feeling" time through the flow of sensations determined by its actions. In other words, the controller allows an agent to make coordinated movements which bring forth the perceptual experience necessary to discriminate between two different types of environment and thus to initiate a simple signalling behaviour. Low level "leaky-integrator" neurons, which constitute the elementary units of the robot's controller, provide the agent with the required time-dependent structures. This is not the first experiment in which time-dependent structures are evolved to control the behaviour of agents required to make decision based on their experience (see, for example, [5–7]). However, in [7] and in [5] the task was simpler than the one described in here, because the controller was only in charge of making the decision, while the nature of the perceptual experience of the robot was determined by the experimenter. The work illustrated in [6] and the one described in this paper differ in term of the nature of the cue/s exploited by the agent to make the discrimination: in [6] the cues the agent exploits are environmental structures (regularities) which the agent's controller has to extract; in our task, the cue the agent has to exploit concerns the persistence of a perceptual state, which is common to both types of environment.

2 Methods

Description of the task. At the start of each trial, a robot is positioned within a boundless arena, at about 100 cm west of the light, with a randomly determined orientation chosen between north-east and south-east (see Figure 1 left). The light is always turned on during the trial. The robot perceives the light through its ambient light sensors. The colour of the arena floor is white except for a circular band, centred around the lamp, within which the floor is in shades of grey. The circular band covers an area between 40 cm and 60

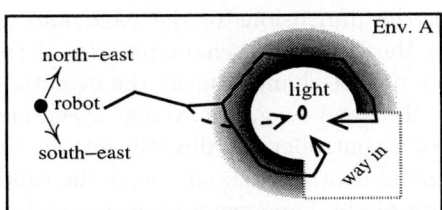
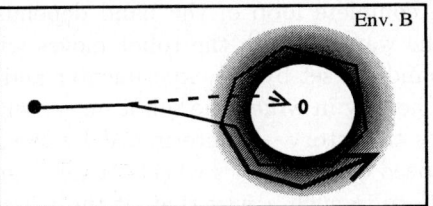

Fig. 1. Depiction of the task. The small black circles represent the robot at starting position. The small empty circles represent the light bulb. The arena floor is white everywhere except within a circular band surrounding the light. The *way in* zone corresponds to the sector of the band, indicated by dotted lines, in which the floor is white. In both pictures, the continuous arrows are examples of good navigational strategies; the dashed arrows are examples of forbidden trajectories. In *Env. B*, the continuous arrow gets thicker to indicate that the robot emits a sound after having made a loop around the light.

cm from the light; the floor is black at exactly 40 cm from the light; the grey level decreases linearly with the distance from the light. The robot perceives the colour of the floor through its floor sensor, positioned on its belly. The robot can freely move within the band, but it is not allowed to cross the black edge. The latter can be imagined as an obstacle, a trough, that prevents the robot to further approach the light (see dashed arrows in Figure 1). The area in shades of grey is meant to work as a warning signal which "tells" the robot how close it is to the danger—i.e., the black edge.

There are two types of environment. In one type, referred to as *Env. A*, the band presents a discontinuity (see Figure 1, left). This discontinuity, referred to as the *way in* zone, is a sector of the band in which the floor is white. In the other type, referred to as *Env. B*, the band completely surrounds the light (see Figure 1, right). The *way in* zone represents the path along which the robot is allowed to safely reach the light. A successful robot should prove to be capable of performing phototaxis as well as looking for the *way in* zone to avoid to cross the black edge of the band. Such a robot should always reach the light in *Env. A*, whereas, in *Env. B*, besides avoiding to cross the black edge, the robot should signal the absence of the *way in* zone by emitting a tone. How can the robot distinguish between *Env. A* and *Env. B*? The cue the agent should use is a temporal one: that is, the *Env. B* can be "recognised" by the persistence of the perception of the band for the amount of time that, given the trajectory and speed of the robot, corresponds to the time required to make a loop around the light. If the perception of the band persists long enough, this means that there is no *way in* zone, and a tone has to be emitted.

The difficulty of this experiment resides in synthesising a controller which, by solely integrating over time the perception of the colour of the floor under the robot's belly, brings forth something similar to the "feeling" of being travelling within the band for the time required to complete a loop, so to "recognise" that there is no *way in* zone. The amount of time required for the robot to perform a complete loop of the band depends on the dimensions of the band and on the way in which the robot moves within the band. The characteristics of the band are set by the experimenter and they do not change during the evolution. The way in which the robot moves within the band—e.g., its average speed and its trajectory—is determined by the robot's controller, by directly setting the speed of the robot's wheels. Thus, a successful controller should make the robot move in such a way that, if the perception of the band persists over a certain amount of time, the following conclusions can be drawn: (i) the band does not present any discontinuity; (ii) the sound signalling must be activated. Continuous time recurrent neural networks (CTRNNs), shaped by evolution, seem to be a suitable tool to obtain this kind of mix between mechanisms for sensory-motor coordination and time-dependent structures required to perform this task [5].

The simulation model. The robot and its world are simulated using a modified version of the "minimal simulation" technique described by Jakobi in [8]. Jakobi's technique uses high levels of noise to guarantee that the simulated controller will transfer to a physically realised robot with no loss of performance. Our simulation models a Khepera robot, a 55 mm diameter cylindrical robot. This simulated robot is provided with two ambient light sensors, placed at 45 degrees (A_1) and -45 degrees (A_2) with respect to its heading, and a floor sensor positioned facing downward on the underside of the robot (F). The light sensors have an angle of acceptance of 120 degrees. Light levels change as a function of the robot's distance from the lamp. The light sensor values are extrapolated from a look-up table which corresponds to the one provided with the Evorobot simulator (see [9]). The floor sensor can be conceived of as a proximity infra-red sensor capable of detecting the level of grey of the floor. It produces an output which is proportional to the level of grey, scaled between 0—when the robot is positioned over white floor—and 1—when it is over black floor.

The controller and the evolutionary algorithm. Fully connected, eight neuron CTRNNs are used. All neurons are governed by the following state equation:

$$\frac{dy_i}{dt} = \frac{1}{\tau_i}\left(-y_i + \sum_{j=1}^{8} \omega_{ji}\sigma(y_j + \beta_j) + gI_i\right) \qquad \sigma(y_j + \beta_j) = \frac{1}{1+e^{-x}} \qquad (1)$$

where, using terms derived from an analogy with real neurons, y_i represents the cell potential, τ_i the decay constant, β_j the bias term, $\sigma(y_j + \beta_j)$ the firing rate, ω_{ji} the strength of the synaptic connection from neuron j^{th} to neuron i^{th}, I_i the intensity of the sensory perturbation on sensory neuron i. Three neurons receive input (I_i) from the robot sensors: e.g., neuron N_1 takes input from A_1, N_2 from A_2, and N_3 from F. These input neurons receive a real value in the range [0,1], which is a simple linear scaling of the reading taken from its associated sensor. The other neurons do not receive any input from the robot's sensors. The cell potential (y_i) of the 6th neuron, mapped into [0,1] by a sigmoid function (σ) and then set to 1 if bigger than 0.5 or 0 otherwise, can be used by the robot to control the sound signalling system The cell potential (y_i) of the 7th and the 8th neuron, mapped into [0,1] by a sigmoid function (σ) and then linearly scaled into [-10,10], set the robot motors output. The strength of synaptic connections ω_{ji}, the decay constant τ_i, the bias term β_j, and the gain factor g are genetically encoded parameters. Cell potentials are set to 0 any time the network is initialised or reset, and circuits are integrated using the forward Euler method with an integration step-size of 0.2.

A simple generational genetic algorithm (GA) is employed to set the parameters of the networks. The population contains 100 genotypes. Generations following the first one are produced by a combination of selection with elitism, recombination and mutation. For each new generation, the three highest scoring individuals ("the elite") from the previous generation are retained unchanged. The remainder of the new population is generated by fitness-proportional selection from the 70 best individuals of the old population. Each genotype is a vector comprising 81 real values (64 connections, 8 decay constants, 8 bias terms, and a gain factor). Initially, a random population of vectors is generated by initialising each component of each genotype to values chosen uniformly random from the range [0,1]. New genotypes, except "the elite", are produced by applying recombination with a probability of 0.3 and mutation. Mutation entails that a random Gaussian offset is applied to each real-valued vector component encoded in the genotype, with a probability of 0.15. The mean of the Gaussian is 0, and its standard deviation is 0.1. During evolution, all vector component values are constrained to remain within the range [0,1]. Genotype parameters are linearly mapped to produce CTRNN parameters with the following ranges: biases $\beta_j \in$ [-2,2], weights $\omega_{ji} \in$ [-6,6] and gain factor $g \in$ [1,12]. Decay constants are firstly linearly mapped onto the range $[-0.7, 1.7]$ and then exponentially mapped into $\tau_i \in [10^{-0.7}, 10^{1.7}]$. The lower bound of τ_i corresponds to a value slightly smaller than the integration step-size used to update the controller; the upper bound corresponds to a value slightly bigger than the average time required by a robot to reach and to perform a complete loop of the band in shades of grey.

The evaluation function. During the evolution, each genotype is coded into a robot controller, and is evaluated 40 times—20 times in *Env. A* and 20 in *Env. B*. At the beginning of each trial, the neural network is reset—i.e., the activation value of each neuron is set to zero. Each trial differs from the others in the initialisation of the random number generator, which influences the robot starting position and orientation, the position and amplitude of the *way in* zone, and the noise added to motors and sensors. For each of the 20 trials in *Env. A*, the position of the *way in* zone is varied to facilitate the evolution of robust navigational strategies. Its amplitude varies within the interval $[\frac{\pi}{6}, \frac{\pi}{2}]$. Within a trial, the robot life-span is 80 s (400 simulation cycles). A trial is terminated earlier if either the robot crosses the black edge of the band (see dashed arrows in Figure 1) or because it reaches an Euclidean distance from the light higher than 120 cm. In each trial t, the robot is rewarded by an evaluation function f_t which corresponds to the sum of the following four components:

$$R_{\text{motion}} = \frac{d_f - d_n}{d_f} \qquad R_{\text{error}} = -\frac{p_b}{t_b}$$

$$R_{\text{near}} = \begin{cases} p_c/t_c & \text{Env. A} \\ 0 & \text{Env. B} \end{cases} \qquad R_{\text{signal}} = \begin{cases} 0 & \text{Env. A} \\ p_a/t_a & \text{Env. B} \end{cases}$$

R_{motion} rewards movements toward the light bulb: d_f and d_n represent respectively the furthest and the nearest Euclidean distance between the robot and the light bulb. In particular, d_f is updated whenever the robot increases its maximum distance from the light bulb. At the beginning of the trial, d_n is fixed as equal to d_f, and it is subsequently updated every time step when (i) the robot gets closer to the light bulb; (ii) d_f is updated. In this latter case, d_n is set equal to the new d_f. In *Env. A*, d_n is set to 0 if the robot is less than 7.5 cm away from the light bulb. In *Env. B*, d_n is set to 0 if the robot makes a complete loop around the light bulb while remaining within the circular band. R_{error} is negative to penalise the robot for (i) signalling in *Env. A*, and (ii) signalling in *Env. B* before having made a loop around the light: p_b is the number of simulation cycles during which the robot has erroneously emitted a tone, and t_b is the number of simulation cycles during which the robot was not required to signal. R_{near} rewards movements for remaining close to the light bulb: p_c is the number of simulation cycles during which the robot was no further than 7.5 cm away from the light bulb in *Env. A*, and t_c is the robot life-span. In *Env. B* the robot cannot get closer than 40 cm to the light, therefore, this component is equal to 0. R_{signal} rewards signalling in *Env. B*: p_a is the number of simulation cycles during which the robot has emitted a tone after having made a loop around the light, and t_a is the number of simulation cycles during which the robot was required to emit a tone. In *Env. A*, this component is always set to zero. Recall that the robot is also penalised for crossing the black edge of the band and for reaching a distance from the light higher than 120 cm. In these cases, the trial is ended and the robot's fitness is computed by considering the current state of the system.

3 Results

Twenty evolutionary simulations, each using a different random initialisation, were run for 6000 generations. We examined the best individual of the final generation from each of these runs in order to establish whether they evolved the required behaviour. During re-evaluation, each of the twenty best evolved controllers was subjected to a set of 100 trials in *Env. A* and a set of 100 trials in *Env. B*. At the beginning of each re-evaluation trial, the controllers are reset. Each trial has a different initialisation (see section 2 for details). During re-evaluation, the robot life-span is 120 s (600 simulation cycles).

Firstly, we analyse the navigational abilities of the best evolved robot in an *Env. A*. Recall that, in these circumstances, a successful robot should reach the light bulb going through the *way in* zone, without signalling. Figure 2 shows the percentage of time each of these robots spent in an area located in the proximity of the light bulb during the 100 re-evaluation trials in *Env. A*, as computed by the fitness component R_{near}. These results prove that almost all the best evolved robots employ successful navigational strategies which allow them to find the *way in* zone, and to spend between 40% and 80% of their life-time close to the target. In both types of environment, the run n. 1 and n. 8 are slightly less successful than the others. We observed that their failure was caused by a tendency to cross the black edge of the band. A qualitative analysis of the robots' behaviour shows that, when the best evolved robots are situated in an *Env. B*, their navigational strategies allow them (i) to approach the light as much as possible without crossing the black edge of the band, and (ii) to make a loop around the light, between 40 cm and 60 cm from the light, following a trajectory nearly circular. The agents are not evolved just to navigate properly toward the light, but also for accurately discriminating between the two types of environment. Recall that the agents are required to make their choice by emitting a tone only if they "feel" they have been situated in an *Env. B*. We observed that none of the best evolved robots emits a tone if situated in *Env. A*. Table 1 shows data concerning the signalling behaviour of the best evolved robots in *Env. B*. In particular, the column (*Succ.*) shows the percentage of successful trials at the discrimination task, for each of these robots, during the 100 re-evaluation trials. We can notice that eleven out of twenty robots never missed to emit a tone if situated in *Env. B* (i.e., run n. 2, 3, 6, 7, 10, 13, 14, 16, 17, 18, 20). The robot run n. 4 shows a 96% success rate. The other eight robots did not emit any tone during each of the 100 re-evaluation trials in *Env. B* (i.e., run n. 1, 5, 8, 9, 11, 12, 15, 19).

The quality of the signalling behaviour can be established with reference to the amount of error of type I (*Err. I*) and error of type II (*Err. II*) made by the successful robots. The *Err. I* refers to those cases in which the robot emits a tone **before** having made a loop around the light. The *Err. II* refers to those cases in which the robot emits a tone **after** having completed the loop. *Err. I* can be considered as a false positive error—i.e., signalling that there is no *way in* zone when there may be one. *Err. II* can be considered as a false negative error—i.e., not accurately signalling that there is no *way in* zone. Both types of error are calculated with respect to the angular displacement of the robot

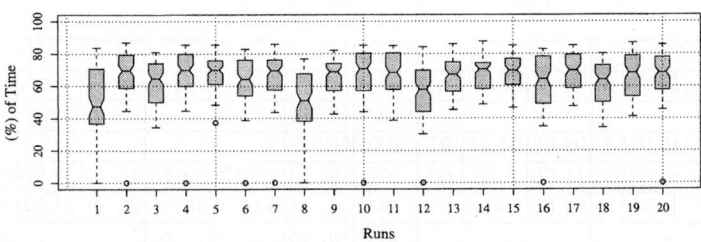

Fig. 2. Box-and-whisker plot visualising the fitness component R_{near} of the best evolved strategies for each run, computed over 100 trials in *Env. A*. The box comprises observations ranging from the first to the third quartile. The median is indicated by a horizontal bar. The whiskers extend to the most extreme data point which is no more than 1.5 times the interquartile range. Outliers are indicated as circles.

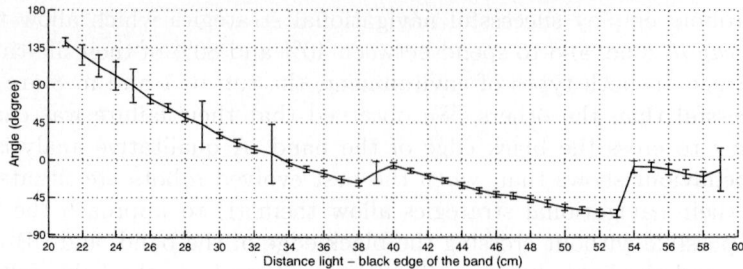

Fig. 3. The graph shows the average and standard deviation of Err I—i.e., negative angles—and Err II—positive angles—for each environmental condition defined by the distance between the black edge of the band and the light. The values are averaged over 100 re-evaluation trials.

around the light from the starting position—the position at the time when the robot enters into the circular band—to the signalling position—the position at the time when the robot starts signalling. If the robot makes no errors, this angle is 2π. The bigger is the angle, the less reliable is the signalling mechanism. However, we should notice that, due to the nature of the task, it is very difficult to make no errors—i.e, emitting a tone precisely at the time in which an entire loop around the light is made. For our purpose, we consider successful an agent that, in order to signal the absence of the *way in* zone, manages to reduce the amount of errors of both types. As shown in column "*Err. I—Avg.*" and in column "*Err. II—Avg.*" of table 1, the robots evolved in runs n. 17, 18 and 20 manage to keep their average error of both types smaller than an angle of 10 degrees. The robots evolved in runs n. 3 and n. 7 are also quite accurate, with both types of error smaller than 16 degrees. All the other "signalling" robots are less accurate, with average errors bigger than 20 degrees.

Table 1. Quality of the performance of the twenty best evolved robots in *Env. B* during the 100 re-evaluation trials. The table shows the average angle (degrees), the standard deviation, and the number of times the error was made for both *Err. I* and *Err. II*. The success rate (%) at the discrimination task is indicated by *Succ.*

run	Err. I			Err. II			Succ.	run	Err. I			Err. II			Succ.
---	Avg.	Std	n.	Avg.	Std	n.	(%)	---	Avg.	Std	n.	Avg.	Std	n.	(%)
n. 1	-			-			0	n. 11	-			-			0
n. 2	18.55	5.05	3	99.96	24.45	97	100	n. 12	-			-			0
n. 3	8.50	5.67	36	11.70	8.68	64	100	n. 13	7.88	8.53	14	34.84	23.29	86	100
n. 4	0	0	0	64.65	13.88	96	96	n. 14	4.05	4.40	11	25.30	21.62	89	100
n. 5	-			-			0	n. 15	-			-			0
n. 6	5.14	3.26	13	30.66	20.92	87	100	n. 16	6.41	4.94	37	22.69	38.80	63	100
n. 7	2.86	4.13	9	15.14	9.02	91	100	n. 17	6.67	3.36	96	1.88	1.44	4	100
n. 8	-			-			0	n. 18	7.65	5.01	70	5.89	4.42	30	100
n. 9	-			-			0	n. 19	-			-			0
n. 10	0	0	0	44.63	15.48	100	100	n. 20	6.11	3.92	59	9.02	6.88	41	100

The mechanisms that the successful robots employ to solve the discrimination task are tuned to those environmental conditions experienced during evolution. As expected, they do not properly work if the environment changes. For example, we observed that both the reduction and the increment of the distance between the black edge of the band and the light disrupt the robots' performance: the smaller is the distance, the bigger is the *Err. II*—i.e., signalling after having made a loop around the light; the higher is the distance, the bigger is *Err. I*—i.e., signalling before having made a loop around the light. However, as far as it concerns the robot evolved in run n. 17, we observed that in particular circumstances it is capable of adjusting its behaviour to the altered environmental conditions. As shown in Figure 3, when the black edge of the band is 34 cm away from the light, the performance of the robot is comparable to the one recorded in those conditions experienced during evolution. Moreover, when this distance is 54 cm, the *Err I* gets smaller. How do we explain the robustness of this behaviour? An explanation could be that the robot is taking into account (i.e., it integrates over time) both the perception of the floor and the intensity of the light. Obviously, in the altered environmental conditions, the perception of the floor is not disrupted. That is, the robot can still freely move within the band in order to bring forth the perception of the colour of the floor that it was used to experience during evolution. However, for a given perception of the floor, the corresponding light intensity is altered by the fact that the black edge of the band is not at the same distance from the light, as during evolution. It is reasonable to conclude that, for an agent that integrates both the perception of the floor and the intensity of the light, the relationship between these two sensory inputs might have a bearing on the emission of the tone. For example, for a given level of grey, the higher/lower is the intensity of the light the shorter/longer is the time it takes to the robot to emit a tone. This mechanism improves the robustness and the adaptiveness of the agent's controller in particular environments that differ from the one experienced during evolution. Interestingly, the evolution of this mechanism has not been favoured by any selective pressures explicitly introduced to encourage the emergence of robust controllers. Serendipitously the artificial neural networks turned out to be capable of tracking significant variations in environmental conditions—i.e., the relationship between the intensity of the light and levels of grey of the floor.

4 Conclusions

In this paper, we have shown that a single dynamic neural network can be synthetised by evolution to allow an autonomous agent to make coordinated movements that bring forth the perceptual experience necessary to discriminate between two types of environments. The results illustrated here are of particular interest because, contrary to other previous similar studies, in this work the decision-making is uniquely controlled by the time-dependent structures of the agent controller, which in turn, are tightly linked to the mechanisms for sensory-motor coordination. Unexpectedly, one of the evolved controllers proved robust to variation in the environmental conditions without being explicitly evolved for this. Based on this preliminary but encouraging results, in future works, we will consider more challenging experimental setups. In particular, the integration of the agent perception over time will not be solely finalised to a simple signalling response, but it will trigger effective alternative actions as it is the case for animal species making decisions about the quality of foraging sites.

Acknowledgement

This work was supported by the "SWARM-BOTS" project, funded by the Future and Emerging Technologies programme (IST-FET) of the European Commission, under grant IST-2000-31010. The authors thank Christos Ampatzis, Paul Graham, Roderich Gross, Thomas Halva Labella, Shervin Nouyan, Peter Todd, and Andreas Wilke for useful comments. Marco Dorigo acknowledges support from the Belgian FNRS, of which he is a Senior Research Associate, through the grant "Virtual Swarm-bots", contract no. 9.4515.03, and from the "ANTS" project, an "Action de Recherche Concertée" funded by the Scientific Research Directorate of the French Community of Belgium. The information provided is the sole responsibility of the authors and does not reflect the Community's opinion. The Community is not responsible for any use that might be made of data appearing in this publication.

References

1. Nonacs, P.: State dependent behavior and the marginal value theorem. Behavioral Ecology **12** (2003) 71–83
2. Beer, R.D.: A dynamical systems perspective on agent-environment interaction. Artificial Intelligence **72** (1995) 173–215
3. Nolfi, S., Floreano, D.: Evolutionary Robotics: The Biology, Intelligence, and Technology of Self-Organizing Machines. MIT Press, Cambridge, MA (2000)
4. Harvey, I., Husbands, P., Cliff, D.: Issues in evolutionary robotics. In Meyer, J.A., Roitblat, H., Wilson, S., eds.: Proc. of the 2nd Int. Conf. on Simulation of Adaptive Behavior, MIT Press, Cambridge, MA (1992) 364–373
5. Beer, R.D., Gallagher, J.C.: Evolving dynamic neural networks for adaptive behavior. Adaptive Behavior **1** (1992) 91–122
6. Nolfi, S.: Evolving robots able to self-localize in the environment: The importance of viewing cognition as the result of processes occurring at different time scales. Connection Science **14** (2002) 231–244
7. Tuci, E., Harvey, I., Todd, P.M.: Using a net to catch a mate: Evolving CTRNNs for the dowry problem. In Hallam, B., Floreano, D., Hallam, J., Hayes, G., Meyer, J.A., eds.: Proceedings of SAB'02, MIT press, Cambridge, MA (2002)
8. Jakobi, N.: Evolutionary robotics and the radical envelope of noise hypothesis. Adaptive Behavior **6** (1997) 325–368
9. Nolfi, S.: EvoRob 1.1 User Manual. Institute of Psychology, National Research Council (CNR). (2000) Available at http://gral.ip.rm.cnr.it/evorobot/simulator.html.

An Artificial Immune System for Fuzzy-Rule Induction in Data Mining

Roberto T. Alves[1], Myriam R. Delgado[1], Heitor S. Lopes[1], and Alex A. Freitas[2]

[1] CPGEI, CEFET-PR, Av. Sete de Setembro, 3165, CEP: 80230-901 Curitiba, Brasil
roberto_alves@msn.com, myriam@dainf.cefetpr.br,
hslopes@cpgei.cefetpr.br
[2] Computing Laboratory, University of Kent, Canterbury, CT2 7NF, UK
A.A.Freitas@kent.ac.uk

Abstract. This work proposes a classification-rule discovery algorithm integrating artificial immune systems and fuzzy systems. The algorithm consists of two parts: a sequential covering procedure and a rule evolution procedure. Each antibody (candidate solution) corresponds to a classification rule. The classification of new examples (antigens) considers not only the fitness of a fuzzy rule based on the entire training set, but also the affinity between the rule and the new example. This affinity must be greater than a threshold in order for the fuzzy rule to be activated, and it is proposed an adaptive procedure for computing this threshold for each rule. This paper reports results for the proposed algorithm in several data sets. Results are analyzed with respect to both predictive accuracy and rule set simplicity, and are compared with C4.5rules, a very popular data mining algorithm.

1 Introduction

Data mining consists of extracting knowledge from real-world data sets. We stress that the goal of data mining is to discover knowledge that is not only accurate, but also comprehensible [1],[2], i.e. knowledge that can be easily interpreted by the user. Hence, the user can validate discovered knowledge and combine it with her/his background knowledge in order to make an intelligent decision, rather than blindly trusting the results of a "black box".

This work focuses on the classification task of data mining, where the goal is to discover a classification model (a rule set, in this work) that predicts the class of an example (a record) based on the values of predictor attributes for that example.

More precisely, this work proposes a new algorithm for inducing a set of fuzzy classification rules based on an artificial immune system (AIS), a relatively new computational intelligence paradigm [3]. The proposed algorithm discovers a set of rules of the form "IF (fuzzy conditions) THEN (class)", whose interpretation is: if an example's attribute values satisfy the fuzzy conditions then the example belongs to the class predicted by the rule. The fuzzy representation of the rule conditions not only gives the system more flexibility to cope with uncertainties typically found in real-world applications, but also improves the comprehensibility of the rules [4],[5].

The remainder of this paper is organized as follows. Section 2 presents a brief overview of AIS, fuzzy systems, and related work. Section 3 describes in detail the proposed algorithm. Section 4 reports computational results. Finally, section 5 presents the conclusions and future research directions.

2 Artificial Immune Systems, Fuzzy Systems and Related Work

AIS consist of methods that are inspired by the biological immune system and designed to solve real-world problems [6]. This work focuses on one kind of AIS inspired by the clonal selection principle of the biological immune system. In essence, when an immune system detector (a lymphocyte) has a high affinity (a high degree of matching) with an antigen (invader microorganism), this recognition stimulates the proliferation and differentiation of cells that produce antibodies. This process, called clonal expansion (because new cells are produced by cloning and mutating existing cells), produces a large population of antibodies targeted for that antigen. This clonal expansion leads to the destruction or neutralization of the antigen and to the retention of some cells in the immunological "memory", so that the immune system can act more quickly the next time the same antigen is found in the body.

This process is a form of natural selection. The better a clone recognizes an antigen, the more it tends to proliferate. This process is also adaptive, because the clones undergo mutation. Since the reproduction rate is very high, the frequency of mutation is also very high. This mechanism is called somatic mutation or hypermutation. Jointly with the selective process, somatic mutation improves the clones' ability in recognizing the antigen (since the best mutations lead to a higher proliferation of the corresponding clones), producing clones with greater affinity for that particular antigen.

Fuzzy systems use symbols – called linguistic terms – that have a well-defined semantics and are represented by membership functions of fuzzy sets. This allows the numerical processing of those symbols or concepts. Fuzzy systems are very effective in expressing the natural ambiguity and subjectivity of human reasoning [4],[5].

Membership functions determine to which degree a given object belongs to a fuzzy set. In a fuzzy system this degree of membership varies from 0 to 1. Membership functions can take different forms, varying from the simplest ones (triangular functions) to more complex functions (parameterized by the user).

According to [7], in a classification problem with n attributes, fuzzy rules can be written as: R_j : If x_1 is A_1^j and .... and x_n is A_n^j then Class C_j, $j = 1,..,N$, where $\mathbf{x}=(x_1,...,x_n)$ is an n-dimensional pattern vector, A_i^j ($i=1,...,n$) is the i-th attribute's linguistic value (e.g. small or large), C is the class predicted by the rule, and N is the number of fuzzy if-then rules. Hence, the antecedent ("IF part") of each fuzzy rule is specified by a combination of linguistic values.

We now briefly review related work. Probably the first AIS specifically designed for the classification task is AIRS [8]. In addition, it has been suggested that an AIS based on the clonal selection principle, called CLONALG, can be used for classification in the context of pattern recognition [6], although originally proposed for other tasks. However, unlike the AIS algorithm proposed in this paper, neither AIRS nor CLONALG discovers comprehensible IF-THEN rules. Hence, neither of those two algorithms addresses the data mining goal of discovering comprehensible, interpretable knowledge (see Introduction). Also, they do not discover fuzzy knowledge, unlike the algorithm proposed in this paper. An AIS for discovering IF-THEN rules is proposed in [9]. Unlike the algorithm proposed in this paper, that work is based on extending the negative selection algorithm with a genetic algorithm. We have avoided the use of the negative selection algorithm because this kind of AIS method has some conceptual problems in the context of the classification task, as discussed in [10]. Also, again that work does not discover fuzzy rules. A fuzzy AIS is proposed in [11]. However, that work addresses the task of clustering, which is very different from the task of classification addressed in this paper. To the best of our knowledge, the algorithm proposed in this paper is the first AIS for discovering fuzzy classification rules based on the clonal selection principle.

3 Description of the IFRAIS Algorithm

The proposed algorithm, called IFRAIS (Induction of Fuzzy Rules with an Artificial Immune System), discovers fuzzy classification rules. In essence, IFRAIS evolves a population of antibodies, where each antibody represents the antecedent (the "IF part") of a fuzzy classification rule. Each antigen represents an example (record, or case). The rule antecedent is formed by a conjunction of conditions (attribute-value pairs, e.g. "*Salary = low*"). Each attribute can be either continuous (real-valued, e.g. *Salary*) or categorical (nominal, e.g. *Gender*), as usual in data mining. Categorical attributes are inherently crisp, but continuous attributes are fuzzified by using a set of three linguistic terms (*low, medium, high*). In this work these linguistic terms are represented by triangular membership functions, for the sake of simplicity.

More precisely, an antibody is encoded by a string with n genes, where n is the number of attributes. Each gene i, $i=1,\ldots,n$, consists of two elements: (a) a value V_i specifying the value (or linguistic term) of the i-th attribute in the i-th rule condition; and (b) a boolean flag B_i indicating whether or not the i-th condition occurs in the classification rule decoded from the antibody. Hence, although all antibodies have the same genotype length, different antibodies represent rules with different number of conditions in their antecedent – subject to the restriction that each decoded rule has at least one condition in its antecedent. This flexibility is essential in data mining, where the optimal number of conditions in each rule is unknown a priori.

The rule consequents (predicted classes) are not evolved by the AIS. Rather, all the antibodies of a given AIS run are associated with the same rule consequent, so that the algorithm is run multiple times to discover rules predicting different classes – as will be explained in more detail in subsection 3.1.

3.1 Discovering Rules from the Training Set

The IFRAIS algorithm (version 1.0) is described in the pseudocodes of Figure 1 – the Sequential Covering (SC) – and Figure 2 – the Rule Evolution (RE).

The SC procedure starts by initializing the *DiscoveredRuleSet* to the empty set, and then it performs a loop over the classes to be predicted [2]. For each class, the algorithm initializes the *TrainSet* with the set of all examples in the training set and iteratively calls the RE procedure, passing as parameters the current *TrainSet* and the class *c* to be predicted by all the candidate rules in the current run of that procedure. The RE procedure returns the best evolved rule, which is then stored in the variable *BestRule*. Next the algorithm adds the *BestRule* to the *DiscoveredRuleSet* and it removes from the current *TrainSet* the examples that have been correctly covered by the best-evolved rule. An example is correctly covered by a rule if and only if the example satisfies the rule antecedent and the example has the same class as predicted by the rule. In order to compute whether or not an example satisfies a rule antecedent we compute the affinity between the rule and the example, as follows.

Input: full training set;
Output: set of discovered rules;

DiscoveredRuleSet = ∅;
FOR EACH class *c*
  TrainSet = {set of all training examples};
  WHILE |*TrainSet*| > *MaxUncovExamp*
    BestRule = RULE-EVOLUTION(*TrainSet*, class *c*);
    DiscoveredRuleSet = *DiscoveredRuleSet* ∪ *BestRule*;
    TrainSet = *TrainSet* − {set of examples correctly covered by *BestRule*};
  END WHILE;
END FOR EACH class;
FOR EACH rule in *DiscoveredRuleSet*
  Recompute the fitness of the rule (antibody) using the full training set of examples;
END FOR;

Fig. 1. Sequential Covering (SC) procedure.

Input: current *TrainSet*;
     the class c predicted by all the rules/antibodies in this run of this procedure;
Output: the best evolved rule;

Create initial population of antibodies at random;
Prune each rule antecedent in a stochastic way;
Compute fitness of each antibody;
FOR *i* = 1 to *Number of Generations*
  Perform tournament selection *T* times, getting *T* winners to be cloned;
  FOR EACH antibody to be cloned
    Produce *C* clones of the antibody, where *C* is proportional to fitness;
    FOR EACH just-produced clone
      Mutate clone with a rate inversely proportional to its fitness;
      Prune each clone in a stochastic way;
      Compute fitness of the clone;
    END FOR EACH clone;
  END FOR EACH antibody;
  Replace the *T* worst-fitness antibodies in the population by the *T* best-fitness clones;
END FOR *i*;
Return the rule whose antecedent consists of the antibody with the best fitness among all antibodies produced in all generations, and whose consequent consists of class *c*;

Fig. 2. Rule Evolution (RE) procedure.

First, for each condition in the rule decoded from an antibody, the algorithm computes the degree to which the original continuous value of the corresponding attribute (in the database) belongs to the fuzzy set associated with the rule condition. These degrees of membership are denoted by $\mu_{A_1}(x_1),...,\mu_{A_n}(x_n)$ where n is the number of conditions in the rule. The next step is to compute the degree to which the example satisfies the rule antecedent as a whole. This is computed by applying the standard aggregation operator *min* to the $\mu_{A_1}(x_1), \ldots, \mu_{A_n}(x_n)$ values. More precisely, the affinity between an antibody *j* and an antigen *k* is given by Equation (1):

$$Afin(k,j) = f\left(\mu_{A_1}(x_1), \cdots, \mu_{A_n}(x_n)\right) = \mu_{A_1}(x_1) \wedge \cdots \wedge \mu_{A_n}(x_n) \qquad (1)$$

An example satisfies a rule (i.e., a rule is activated for that example) if the degree of affinity between the rule and the example is greater than an activation threshold, i.e., if $Afin(k,j) > L_j$, where L_j denotes the activation threshold for the *j*-th rule.

This work proposes an adaptive procedure to automatically choose the best value of affinity threshold L_j for each rule *j*, out of a reasonably large range of values. More precisely, the algorithm considers *m* uniformly distributed values of L_j within the range [0.5, 0.7]. In this work *m* = 20, so that the algorithm considers all values of L_j in {0.50, 0.51, 0.52, …,0.69, 0.70}. For each of these values, the algorithm computes the fitness of the rule in the training set (as will be explained later) and chooses the L_j value that maximizes the fitness of the rule. It should be noted that this mechanism does not require recomputing the degree of matching between each example and the rule, which is the most computationally expensive part of fitness computation. It just requires recomputing the number of examples satisfying and not satisfying each rule, so that its processing time is not too long. In the above range, the lower bound 0.5 is a natural value, since a degree of affinity smaller than 0.5 would mean that the example does not satisfy the rule to a degree greater than the degree to which it satisfies the rule. Intuitively the rule should not be activated in this case. The upper bound of 0.7 and the value of *m* = 20 were empirically determined, and seem to cover a reasonably wide range of useful values for L_j.

The WHILE loop is iteratively performed until the number of uncovered examples is smaller than a user-defined threshold *MaxUncovExamp*, so that this procedure discovers as many rules as necessary to cover the vast majority of the training examples. Finally, in the last step of the SC procedure we recompute the fitness of each rule in the *DiscoveredRuleSet*, by using the full training set.

The RE procedure starts by randomly creating an initial population of antibodies, where each antibody represents the antecedent of a fuzzy classification rule. For each rule, the system prunes the rule and computes the fitness of the antibody. Rule pruning has a twofold motivation: reducing the overfitting of rules to the data and improving the simplicity (comprehensibility) of the rules. The basic idea of this rule pruning procedure is that, the lower the predictive power of a condition, the more likely the condition will be removed from the rule. The predictive power of a condition is estimated by computing its information gain, a very popular heuristic measure of predictive power in data mining [2]. This rule pruning procedure was chosen because it has been shown to be both effective and very computationally efficient in [12]. After rule pruning, the algorithm computes the fitness of each antibody, and then it performs the outer FOR loop over a fixed number of generations.

This outer FOR loop starts by performing *T* tournament selection (with tournament size of 10) procedures, in order to select *T* winner antibodies that will be cloned in the next step. Tournament selection is well-known and often used in evolutionary algorithms [13]. Once *T* antibodies have been selected, the algorithm performs its core step, which is inspired by the clonal selection principle (discussed in Section 2). This step consists of several sub-steps, as follows. First, for each of the *T* antibodies to be cloned the algorithm produces *C* clones. The value of *C* is proportional to the fitness of the antibody. The function used to implement this procedure is shown in Equation (2), where *fit(Ab)* denotes the fitness of a given antibody *Ab* and *MaxNumCl* denotes the maximum number of clones for an antibody. As indicated in the last part of the equation (the "otherwise" condition), the number of clones increases linearly with the antibody fitness when $0 < Fit(Ab) < 0.5$, and any antibody with a fitness greater than or equal to 0.5 will have *MaxNumCl* clones. We set *MaxNumCl* to just 10 to prevent the clone population from being very large, which would not only be inefficient but also possibly lead to overfitting of the rules to the data.

$$NumCl = \begin{cases} 1 & \text{if } fit(Ab) \leq 0 \\ MaxNumCl & \text{if } fit(Ab) \geq 5 \\ round\_to\_integer\left(\dfrac{MaxNumCl \times fit(Ab)}{5}\right) & \text{otherwise} \end{cases} \quad (2)$$

Next, each of the just-produced clones undergoes a process of hypermutation. This process follows [6], where the mutation rate is inversely proportional to the clone's fitness (i.e., the fitness of its "parent" antibody). In words, the lower the fitness (the worse a clone is), the higher its mutation rate. More precisely, the mutation rate for a given clone *cl*, denoted *mut_rate(cl)*, is given by Equation (3):

$$mute\_rate\ (cl) = \alpha + ((\beta - \alpha) \times (1 - fit(cl))) \quad (3)$$

where α and β are the smallest and greatest possible mutation rates, respectively, and *fit(cl)* is the fitness of clone *cl*. The fitness of a clone is a number normalized between 0 and 1, as will be explained later, so that the above equation collapses to α when the clone has the maximum fitness of 1, and it collapses to β when the clone has the minimum fitness of 0. In our experiments we have set α and β to 20% and 50%, respectively – empirically-determined values. These numbers represent the probability that each gene (rule condition) will undergo mutation. Once a clone has undergone hypermutation, its corresponding rule antecedent is pruned by using the previously-explained rule pruning procedure. Finally, the fitness of the clone is recomputed, using the current *TrainSet*.

The next step consists of population updating. More precisely, the *T*-worst fitness antibodies in the current population (not including the clones created by the clonal selection procedure) are replaced by the *T* best-fitness clones out of all clones produced by the clonal selection procedure. This keeps the population size constant at the end of each generation. The parameter *T* was set to 10 in our experiments. The population size was set to 50 and the number of generations was set to 50. These values were empirically determined.

Finally, the RE procedure returns, to the caller SC procedure, the best evolved rule, which will then be added to the set of discovered rules by the caller procedure. The best evolved rule consists of the rule antecedent ("IF part" of the rule) represented by the antibody with the best fitness, across all antibodies produced in all generations, and of the rule consequent ("THEN part" of the rule) containing the class *c*, which was the class associated with all the antibodies created by the RE procedure.

We now turn to the fitness function used by the RE procedure. The fitness of an antibody *Ab*, denoted by *fit(Ab)*, is given by Equation (4):

$$fit(Ab) = \dfrac{TP}{TP + FN} \times \dfrac{TN}{TN + FP} \quad (4)$$

Where the variables TP, FN, TN and FP have the following meaning:
- TP = number of true positives, i.e. number of examples satisfying the rule and having the same class as predicted by the rule;
- FN = number of false negatives, i.e. number of examples that do not satisfy the rule but have the class predicted by the rule;
- TN = number of true negatives, i.e. number of examples that do not satisfy the rule and do not have the class predicted by the rule;
- FP = number of false positives, i.e. number of examples that satisfy the rule but do not have the class predicted by the rule.

This fitness function was proposed by [14] and has also been used by other evolutionary algorithms for discovering classification rules. However, in most projects using this function the discovered rules are crisp, whereas in our project the rules are fuzzy. Hence, in this project the computation of the TP, FN, TN and FP involves, for each example, measuring the degree of affinity (fuzzy matching) between the example and the rule. Note that the same affinity function (Equation (1)) and the same procedure for determining whether or not an example satisfies a rule are used in both the SC and the RE procedures.

3.2 Using the Discovered Rules to Classify Examples in the Test Set

The rules discovered from the training set are used to classify new examples in the test set (unseen during training) as follows. For each test example, the system identifies the rule(s) activated for that example. Recall that a rule j is activated for example k if the affinity between j and k is greater than the affinity threshold for rule j.

When classifying a test example, there are three possible cases. First, if all the rules activated for that example predict the same class, then the example is simply assigned to that class. Second, if there are two or more rules predicting different classes activated for that example, the system uses a conflict resolution strategy consisting of selecting the rule with the greatest value of the product of the affinity between the rule and the example (Equation (1)) by the fitness of the rule (Equation (4)), i.e., it chooses the class C given by Equation (5):

$$C = C_j = \max_j \left(A\!f\!in(k, j) \times fit(j) \right) \quad (5)$$

Third, if there is no rule activated for the example, the example is classified by the "default rule", which simply predicts the most frequent class in the training set [2].

4 Computational Results

The proposed algorithm was evaluated in six public domain data sets: BUPA, CRX, Wisconsin Cancer, Votes, Hepatities, Ljubljana Cancer. These data sets are available from the UCI repository (*http://www.ics.uci.edu/~mlearn/MLRepository.html*). The experiments used a well-known method for estimating predictive accuracy, namely 5-fold cross-validation [2].

Table 1 shows the number of continuous and categorical attributes for each data set (recall that only continuous attributes are fuzzified), as well as the average accuracy rate on the test set computed by the cross-validation procedure. The numbers after the

"±" symbol are the standard deviations. Note that the Votes data set does not have any continuous attribute to be fuzzified. This data set was included in the experiments to evaluate IFRAIS' performance in the "degenerated" case of discovering crisp rules only. The other data sets have 6 or 9 continuous attributes that are fuzzified by IFRAIS. The accuracy rate is shown for IFRAIS and for C4.5Rules, a very popular data mining algorithm for discovering (crisp) classification rules [15]. For each data set, the highest accuracy rate between the two algorithms is shown in bold.

Table 1. Characteristics of data sets and accuracy rate on the test set.

Data Sets	Number of Attributes		IFRAIS	C4.5Rules
	Continous	Categorical		
Crx	6	9	86.29 ± 0.91	**90.22 ± 1.59**
Bupa	6	0	56.22 ± 2.44	**67.40 ± 1.60**
Hepatitis	6	13	**78.66 ± 1.70**	76.32 ± 2.79
Votes	0	16	**95.61 ± 0.86**	94.82 ± 0.82
Wisconsin	9	0	**95.75 ± 0.96**	95.32 ± 1.09
Ljubljana	9	0	**70.18 ± 3.97**	68.80 ± 4.45

In Table 1, IFRAIS obtained higher accuracy than C4.5Rules in four out of the six data sets, but the differences in accuracy rate are not significant – since the accuracy rate intervals (based on the standard deviations) overlap. C4.5Rules obtained a higher accuracy than IFRAIS in only two data sets (Crx and Bupa), and the difference was significant in both cases – since the accuracy rate intervals do not overlap. The reason for this seems to be that the rule sets discovered by IFRAIS in these two data sets were too simple, and so were underfitted to the data.

Table 2. Simplicity of the discovered rule set.

Data Sets	# Rules		# Conditions	
	IFRAIS	C4.5 Rules	IFRAIS	C4.5 Rules
Crx	**7.2 ± 0.20**	15.6 ± 1.12	**19,4 ± 0,24**	63.0 ± 4.03
Bupa	**7.2 ± 0.37**	11.2 ± 1.65	**13.0 ± 1.30**	36.6 ± 6.16
Hepatitis	**4.8 ± 0.20**	5.0 ± 0.44	**10.0 ± 0.70**	10.4 ± 1.53
Votes	**3.4 ± 0.24**	5.6 ± 0.67	**4.0 ± 0.63**	14.4 ± 2.82
Wisconsin	**6.4 ± 0.40**	6.6 ± 0.50	**10.2 ± 1.01**	14.4 ± 1.28
Ljubljana	6.2 ± 3.37	**5.0 ± 0.54**	**11.2 ± 1.06**	15.2 ± 3.08

Table 2 shows the results of both IFRAIS and C4.5Rules with respect to the simplicity of the discovered rule set, measured by the average number of discovered rules and the average total number of conditions in all discovered rules. (Recall that the averages were computed over the five iterations of the cross-validation procedure.) With respect to this rule quality criterion, the results obtained by IFRAIS were much better than the results obtained by C4.5Rules in all data sets. (In the Ljubljana cancer data set, although C4.5Rules discovered a slight smaller number of rules, IFRAIS still discovered a significantly simpler data set, as shown by the total number of conditions.)

5 Conclusions and Future Research

This work proposed a new AIS, called IFRAIS, for discovering fuzzy classification rules. IFRAIS uses a sequential covering procedure that has two important differences with respect to the standard procedure used by conventional rule induction algorithms [2]. First, it stops the covering process when the number of uncovered examples has been reduced to a very low number (smaller than the *MaxUncovExamp* threshold), rather than stopping only when the number of uncovered examples has reached zero, as usual. The motivation for this modification was to avoid overfitting of a rule to just a very small number of examples, where there are not enough examples for a reliable induction of a new rule. In addition, this modification helped to produce simpler rule sets (as shown in Table 2), more easily interpreted by a human user, since it avoids the generation of one or more very specific rules covering very few examples. This modification led to improved results in our preliminary experiments and it was also successfully used in [16].

The second difference was the use of an affinity function and an affinity threshold to decide whether or not an example satisfies a rule. Of course, this modification is not necessary in conventional (crisp) rule induction algorithms, where the matching between an example and a rule is always binary. However, this is fundamental in our case, where the rules have fuzzy antecedents, producing degrees of matching between 0 and 1. We recognize that the value of the affinity threshold can potentially have a significant impact in the performance of the algorithm, and that it is difficult to determine the "optimal" value of this parameter without many experiments. Actually, there is no strong reason to believe that the "optimal" value of this parameter should be the same for all rules. Hence, we developed an adaptive mechanism for choosing the best affinity threshold for each rule – i.e., choosing the affinity threshold that maximizes the fitness of the rule, out of a wide range of possible affinity thresholds. This adaptive mechanism increases the autonomy of the system and relieves the user from the difficult task of adjusting this threshold, whose value has a significant impact in the predictive accuracy of the system.

IFRAIS was compared with C4.5Rules in 6 real-world data sets. IFRAIS obtained classification accuracies slightly better than C4.5Rules in 4 data sets, but classification accuracies significantly worse than C4.5Rules in 2 data sets. However, IFRAIS discovered rule sets were much simpler than the rule sets discovered by C4.5Rules in virtually all the 6 data sets. This is particularly important in the context of data mining, where knowledge comprehensibility is very important [1][2] – since discovered knowledge is supposed to be interpreted by the user, as discussed in the Introduction. In addition, it should be recalled that C4.5Rules is the result of decades of research in decision tree and rule induction algorithms, whereas IFRAIS is still in its first version – and the whole area of AIS is still relatively new.

Some directions for future research, which might improve the predictive accuracy of IFRAIS, are as follows. First, the system could automatically determine the number of linguistic terms for each continuous attribute, rather than just using a fixed number as in the current version. Second, when there are two or more rules predicting different classes activated for a test example, the system could use all the activated rules to compute a predicted class, rather than just choosing the best rule as in the current version. Third, one could develop variations of the rule evolution procedure, which is based on the clonal selection principle, in order to investigate different trade-offs between exploration and exploitation in the search for rules.

References

1. Fayyad, U.M., Piatetsky-Shapiro, G., Smyth, P.: From Data Mining to Knowledge Discovery: an Overview. In: Fayyad, U.M. et al (Eds.) Advances in Knowledge Discovery and Data Mining. AAAI/MIT (1996) 1-34
2. Witten, I. H., Frank, E.: Data Mining: Pratical Machine Learning Tools and Techniques with Java Implementation. Morgan Kaufmann, San Mateo (2000)
3. Dasgupta, D.: Artificial Immune Systems and Their Applications. Springer, Berlin (1999)
4. Zadeh, L.A.: Fuzzy Sets. Inform. Control. 9 (1965) 338-352
5. Pedrycz, W., Gomide, F.: An Introduction to Fuzzy Sets. Analysis and Design. MIT Press, Cambridge (1998)
6. Castro, L.N., Timmis, J.: Artificial Immune Systems: A New Computation Intelligence Approach. Springer-Verlag, Berlin (2002)
7. Ishibuchi, H., Nakashima, T.: Effect of Rule Weights in Fuzzy Rule-based Classification Systems. IEEE T. Fuzzy Syst. 9:4 (2001) 506-515
8. Watkins, A.B., Boggess, L.C.: A Resource Limited Artificial Immune Classifier. Proc. Congress on Evolutionary Computation (2002) 926-931
9. Gonzales, F.A., Dasgupta, D.: An Immunogenetic Technique to Detect Anomalies in Network Traffic. Proceedings of Genetic and Evolutionary Computation. Morgan Kaufmann, San Mateo (2002) 1081-1088
10. Freitas, A.A., Timmis, J.: Revisiting the Foundations of Artificial Immune Systems: a Problem-oriented Perspective. Proc. 2nd International Conference on Artificial Immune Systems. Lecture Notes in Computer Science, Vol. 2787. Springer-Verlag, Berlin (2003) 229-241
11. Nasaroui, O., Gonzales, F., Dasgupta, D.: The Fuzzy Artificial Immune System: motivations, Basic Concepts, and Application to Clustering and Web Profiling. Proceedings of IEEE International Conference on Fuzzy Systems (2002) 711-716
12. Carvalho, D.R., Freitas, A.A.: A genetic Algorithm with Dequential Niching for Discovering Small-disjunct Rules. Proceedings of Genetic and Evolutionary Computation, Morgan Kaufmann, San Mateo (2002) 1035-1042
13. Back, T., Fogel, D.B., and Michalewicz, T. (Eds.): Evolutionary Computation, Vol. 1. IoP Publishing, Oxford, UK (2000)
14. Lopes, H.S., Coutinho, M.S., Lima, W.C.: An Evolutionary Approach to Simulate Cognitive Feedback Learning in Medical Domain. In: Sanchez, E., Shibata, T., Zadeh, L.A. (eds.), Genetic Algorithms and Fuzzy Logic Systems. World Scientific, Singapore (1997) 193-207
15. Quinlan, J.R.: C4.5: Programs For Machine Learning. Morgan Kaufmann, San Mateo, 1993
16. Parpinelli, R.S., Lopes, H.S., Freitas, A.A.: Data Mining With an Ant Colony Optimization Algorithm. IEEE T. Evol. Comput. 6:4 (2002) 321-332

Speeding-Up Pittsburgh Learning Classifier Systems: Modeling Time and Accuracy

Jaume Bacardit[1], David E. Goldberg[2], Martin V. Butz[2], Xavier Llorà[2], and Josep M. Garrell[1]

[1] Intelligent Systems Research Group, Universitat Ramon Llull,
Psg. Bonanova 8, 08022 Barcelona, Catalonia, Spain
{jbacardit,josepmg}@salleURL.edu

[2] Illinois Genetic Algorithms Laboratory (IlliGAL), Department of General Engineering, University of Illinois at Urbana-Champaign,
104 S. Mathews Ave, Urbana, IL 61801
{deg,butz,xllora}@illigal.ge.uiuc.edu

Abstract. Windowing methods are useful techniques to reduce the computational cost of Pittsburgh-style genetic-based machine learning techniques. If used properly, they additionally can be used to improve the classification accuracy of the system. In this paper we develop a theoretical framework for a windowing scheme called *ILAS*, developed previously by the authors. The framework allows us to approximate the degree of windowing we can apply to a given dataset as well as the gain in runtime. The framework sets the first stage for the development of a larger methodology with several types of learning strategies in which we can apply *ILAS*, such as maximizing the learning performance of the system, or achieving the maximum run-time reduction without significant accuracy loss.

1 Introduction

The application of genetic algorithms (GA) [1, 2] to classification problems is usually known as genetic-based machine learning (GBML). One of the traditional ways of addressing it is the Pittsburgh approach, early exemplified by LS-1 [3]. Usually, systems applying this approach have a high computational cost, because each fitness computation means classifying the whole training set.

We can primarily reduce the cost of these fitness computations by either: (a) decreasing complexity of the individuals or (b) decreasing the dimensionality of the domain to be classified (there are other methods such as fitness inheritance or informed competent operators but they may affect the whole *GA* cycle). The former methods are usually referred to as *parsimony* pressure methods [4]. The latter methods are either characterized as feature selection methods, reducing the number of problem attributes, or as incremental learning or windowing methods, reducing the number of training instances per fitness evaluation.

In previous work [5, 6], we empirically tested some training set reduction schemes. These schemes select a training subset to be used for fitness computation. Changing the subsets at every iteration of the *GA* process, the scheme is a kind of windowing method. Our previous results showed that the techniques achieved the run-time reduction objective with no significant accuracy loss. Sometimes, test accuracy actually increased, indicating knowledge generalization pressures that may alleviate over-fitting.

Several open questions remained. From a run-time reduction perspective, we are interested in deriving a model of the maximal learning time reduction we can achieve while avoiding significant accuracy loss. From a learning perspective, we are interested in the learning time reduction that maximizes accuracy in the system, given a constant run time. In order to achieve the latter objective, we need to develop a run-time cost model.

This paper addresses these points. Concentrating our efforts on only one of our windowing schemes, called *ILAS* (incremental learning with alternating strata). We first analyze when a problem gets difficult for *ILAS*. Once we answer this question, we develop a cost model of the system. With the two elements in hand, we finally construct a theory that provides an estimate for optimizing run-time as well as accuracy performance of the system.

The paper is structured as follows. Section 2 presents some related work. Then, we describe the framework of our classifier system in section 3. Section 4 describes the *ILAS* windowing scheme and some previous results that show the motivation of this paper. Section 5 contains the theoretical models of *ILAS* presented in this paper. Finally, section 6 discusses the conclusions and some further work.

2 Related Work

All run-time reduction methods related to training examples share a common idea: using a subset of the training examples for the learning process. From a general machine learning point of view, we can distinguish three main categories:

- **Wrapper methods** [7]. These methods interactively select the most suitable examples for the learning process. The subset of training examples used varies through the iterations until a stopping criteria is met. Such criteria is usually based on the estimation that the current subset of examples is similar enough to the original set.
- **Modified learning algorithms** [8]. These algorithms either are able to learn incrementally from subsets of the training instances, or they include and discard instances based on knowledge-representation specific information.
- **Prototype Selection** [9]. These methods apply a preprocessing stage in which the training set is reduced before the actual learning process. Unlike the two previous categories, prototype selection does not interact with the learner.

The *ILAS* windowing scheme studied in this paper belongs to the second of the categories described above.

3 Framework

In this section we describe the main features of our classifier system. GAssist (*Genetic Algorithms based claSSIfier sySTem*) [10] is a Pittsburgh-style classifier system based on GABIL [7]. Directly from GABIL we have taken the knowledge representation for discrete attributes (rules with conjunctive normal form (CNF) predicates) and the semantically correct crossover operator.

Matching strategy: The matching process follows a "if ... then ... else if ... then..." structure, usually called a *decision list* [11].

Control of the individual's length: Dealing with variable-length individuals raises some important issues. One of the most important one is the control of the size of the evolving individuals [4]. This control is achieved in GAssist using two different operators: (1) *Rule deletion*. This operator deletes the rules of the individuals that do not match any training example. This rule deletion is done after the fitness computation and has two constraints: (a) the process is only activated after a predefined number of iterations (to prevent an irreversible diversity loss) and (b) the number of rules of an individual never goes below a threshold. This threshold is approximately the number of classes of the classification problem. (2) *Minimum description length-based fitness function*. The minimum description length (*MDL*) principle is a metric applied in general to a theory (being a rule set in this paper) which balances the complexity and accuracy of the rule set. In previous work we developed a fitness function based on this principle. A detailed explanation of the fitness function can be found in [12].

4 The *ILAS* Windowing Scheme

In this section we describe the windowing scheme we are using in this paper. We also include some previous results motivating the research presented.

The *ILAS* scheme is basically a standard Pitt-style *GBML* system in which the training set has been stratified (using a methodology similiar to stratified n-fold cross-validation) into s subsets of equal size. Each strata maintains approximately the class distribution of the whole training set. Each GA iteration utilizes a different strata to perform its fitness computation, using a round-robin policy. Figure 1 presents the pseudocode of *ILAS*.

Figure 2 show previous results [6] of the *ILAS* scheme applied to some datasets (Wisconsin breast cancer (bre), ionosphere (int), Pima-indians-diabetes (pim), pen-based recognition of handwritten digits (pen), satimage (sat), thyroid disease (thy)) from the University of California at Irvine (UCI) repository [13]. The first three datasets are small (less than 1000 instances), while the rest of datasets are of medium size (ranging from 6435 to 10992 instances). For the small datasets we tested *ILAS* using 2, 3 and 4 strata and for the medium datasets we used 5, 10 and 20 strata.

The *ILAS* scheme is compared to the standard non-windowed system, labeled *NON*. The table includes results for accuracy and speedup (time of the original system over time of the windowed system, using the same number of

```
Procedure Incremental Learning with Alternating Strata
Input : Examples, NumStrata, NumIterations
Initialize GA
Reorder Examples in NumStrata parts of approximately
equal class distribution
Iteration = 0
StrataSize = size(Examples)/NumStrata
While Iteration < NumIterations
    If Iteration = NumIterations − 1 Then
        TrainingSet = Examples
    Else
        CurrentStrata = Iteration mod NumStrata
        TrainingSet= examples from
            Examples[CurrentStrata · StrataSize] to
            Examples[(CurrentStrata + 1) · StrataSize]
    EndIf
    Run one iteration of the GA with TrainingSet
    Iteration = Iteration + 1
EndWhile
Output : Best individual (set of rules) from GA population
```

Fig. 1. Pseudocode of the incremental learning with alternating strata (ILAS) scheme.

iterations). Note that some speedup values are larger than the expected value of $1/s$. The cause is an implicit generalization pressure introduced by the windowing producing smaller individuals, which are faster to evaluate. This fact is also shown in figure 2 for the Pima dataset.

The datasets shown in figure 2 exhibit different behavior patterns. The runs in the small datasets show that accuracy increases in *bre* and *ion* when using *ILAS* but not in *pim*. Moreover, the maximum accuracy for *bre* is achieved using 3 strata, while in *ion* it is achieved using 4 strata. In the large datasets, a larger number of strata slightly decreases accuracy while strongly improving computational cost. Thus, using *ILAS* can be beneficial in two aspects: an actual accuracy increase may be achieved in small datasets; strong run-time reduction is achieved, while only slightly decreasing accuracy. We are interested in how *ILAS* may be applied to achieve optimal results focusing on learning time and learning accuracy with respect to the number of strata s.

In the next section, we first develop a model of what makes a dataset hard for *ILAS*. Once we achieve this objective and we know which is the maximum

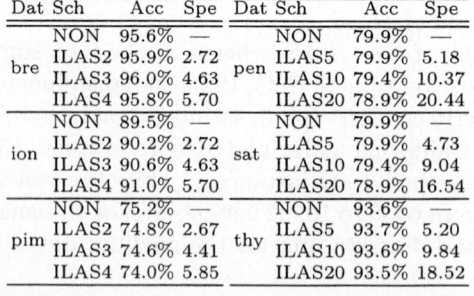 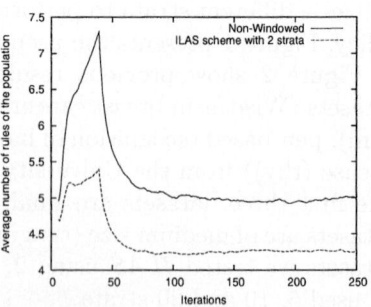

Fig. 2. Previous results of ILAS and plot of individual size reduction. Dat=dataset, Sch = windowing scheme, Acc=Test accuracy, Spe=Speedup.

number of strata we can use for a dataset, we can decide with how many strata
ILAS should be applied to a given problem.

5 Analysis of the *ILAS* Windowing Scheme

This section presents our models for the hardness of a dataset for *ILAS* and a
computational cost model. The models are crucial for estimating the optimal
ILAS settings for a given problem.

5.1 What Makes a Problem Hard to Solve for ILAS?

We start our study focusing on the multiplexer [14] family of problems—a widely
used kind of datasets with a well-known model. Our first step is to perform experiments determining how many iterations are needed to achieve 100% accuracy
(convergence time) using the *ILAS* scheme for a given number of strata. The
results of the experiments for the 6 (MX6) and 11 (MX11) bits multiplexer are
shown in Figure 3. The plots are averaged over 50 independent runs. [1]

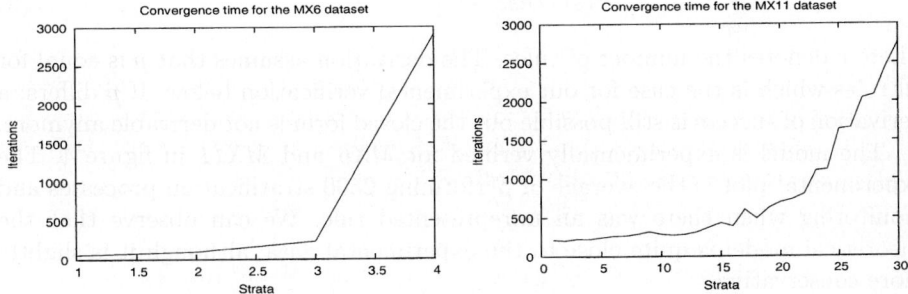

Fig. 3. Convergence time for the MX6 and MX11 datasets.

For both datasets we can see that the convergence time increases with the
number of strata in an exponential way. Before a certain break point, the first
part of the curve can be approximated by a linear increase. This break point is
the maximum number of strata that is worth using in a dataset.

Intuitively we may suspect that after the break point the strata tend to missrepresent the whole training set causing learning disruptions. Since we know
the optimal rule size in the multiplexer dataset, we are able to estimate how
representative a strata may be. In the case of MX6 we have 8 rules, each rule

---

[1] Unless noted otherwise, parameters were set as follows: Crossover probability 0.6;
tournament selection; tournament size 3; population size 300; individual-wise mutation probability 0.6; initial number of rules per individual 20; probability of "1" in
initialization 0.75; Rule Deletion Operator: Iteration of activation: 5; minimum number of rules: number of classes of domain +3; MDL-based fitness function: Iteration
of activation 25; initial theory length ratio: 0.075; weight relax factor: 0.9.

covering 8 instances. In the case of MX11 we have 16 rules, each one covering 128 instances. Only by observing these numbers it is quite easy to see that MX6 has a higher risk of having one of these rules unrepresented in some strata, which translates into having a break point at strata 3 (as seen in figure 3).

In order to predict the break point, we calculate the probability of having a particular rule (which corresponds to a sub-solution) unrepresented in a certain strata. We can approximate this probability supposing uniform sampling with replacement:

$$P(\text{unrepresented rule}/s) = (1-p)^{\frac{D}{s}} \tag{1}$$

where p denotes the probability that a random problem instance represents a particular rule, $\mathcal{D}$ is the number of instances in the dataset and s is the number of strata. The probability essentially estimates the probability that a particular rule is not represented by any problem instance in a strata.

A general probability of success (requiring that no rule is unrepresented) of the whole stratification process can now be derived using the approximation $(1-\frac{r}{s})^s \approx e^{-r}$ twice to simplify:

$$P(success/s) = (1 - P(\text{unrepresented rule}/s))^{rs} \tag{2}$$

$$P(success/s) = e^{-rs \cdot e^{-\frac{pD}{s}}} \tag{3}$$

where r denotes the number of rules. The derivation assumes that p is equal for all rules which is the case for our experimental verification below. If p differs, a derivation of success is still possible but the closed form is not derivable anymore.

The model is experimentally verified for *MX6* and *MX11* in figure 4. The experimental plot is the average of performing 2500 stratification processes and monitoring when there was an unrepresented rule. We can observe that the theoretical model is quite close to the experimental data, although it is slightly more conservative.

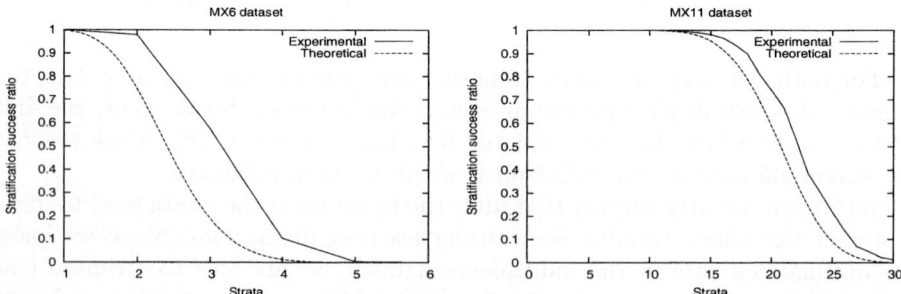

Fig. 4. Probability of stratification success. Verification of model with empirical data.

If we overlap this probabilistic model with the convergence time curve we can see that the exponential area of the convergence time curve starts approximately when the success probability drops below 0.95. We show this observation in figure 5 for the MX6 and MX11 and also for two versions of MX6 that have 2

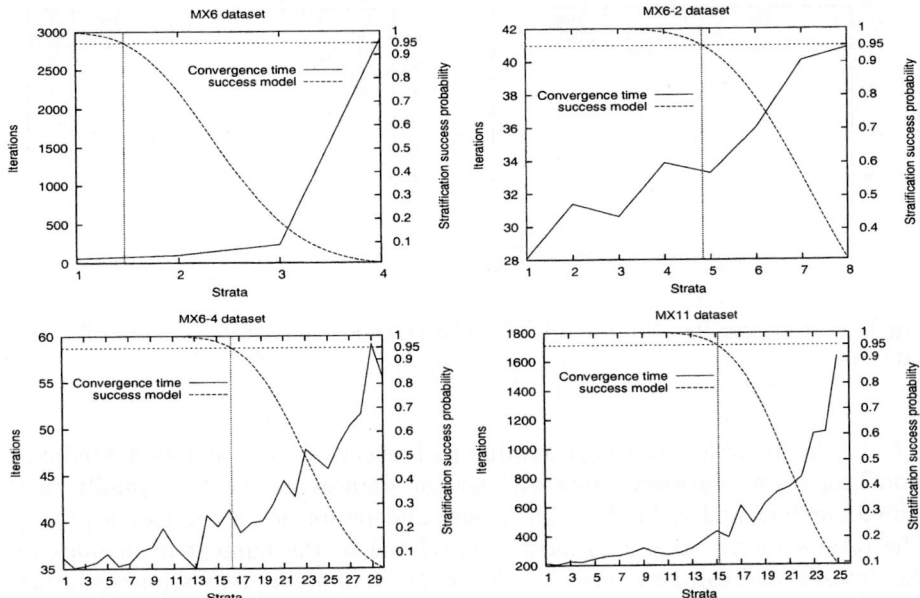

Fig. 5. Comparison of the convergence time and the probability of stratification success. Vertical scale for left hand side of plots corresponds to iterations of convergence time. Scale for right hand side is the probability of stratification success (equation 3). The vertical and horizontal lines mark the 0.95 success point.

(MX6_2) and 4 (MX6_4) additional redundant bits, thus being more robust to the stratification process than MX6. We can approximately predict the break point, achieving one of the objectives of this paper.

5.2 Cost Model of ILAS

The second objective of this paper is the development of a run-time model. Assuming constant run time per iteration, we can model the run-time of the system by

$$T = \alpha \cdot it \tag{4}$$

where T denotes the total time of the learning process, α the time per iteration and it the number of iterations. Figure 6 shows α values for MX6, MX6_2 and MX6_4. Clearly, α is strongly dependent on the number of instances in a dataset. As hypothesized above, time approximately behaves inverse proportional to the number of strata. To have a better insight in α, we compute α' as $\alpha'_s = \alpha_s/\alpha_1$, that is, the value of α for s strata over the value for one strata. Figure 6 also shows α'.

The evolution of α' can be approximated by a formula such as $\alpha' = a/s + b$, where s is the number of strata and b is a constant that needs to be adjusted to the problem at hand (from applying the formula for 1 stratum we know that

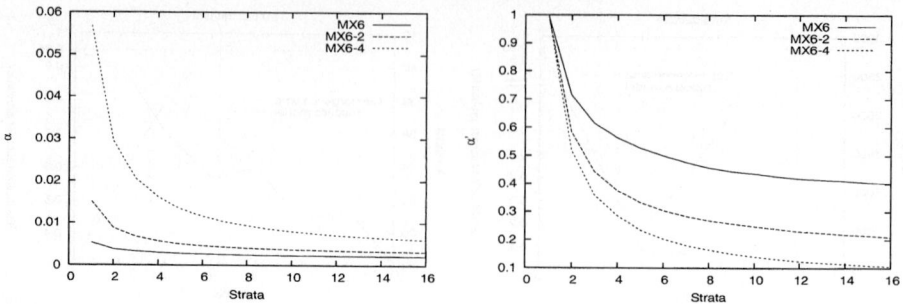

Fig. 6. α (time per iteration) and α' (α relative to a single stratum) values for some datasets.

$a = 1 - b$). In order to assign a value to b effectively developing a predictive model for α', we did some tests with several datasets of the MX6 family (with redundant bits and redundant instances) and performed a regression process. The results showed that b is mostly correlated to the number of instances in the dataset, and can be modeled as $b = c/\mathcal{D} + d$, applying regression again for c and d. These values should, at least, hold across different computers of the same architecture.

The model of α' is verified experimentally with two different datasets: MX11 and an artificial dataset from the *UCI* [13] repository: LED (using 2000 instances with 10% of noise). LED was selected it is more similar to a real problem than the MX datasets due to the added noise. The comparison of the model and the empirical data can be seen in figure 7, which shows that the model is quite accurate.

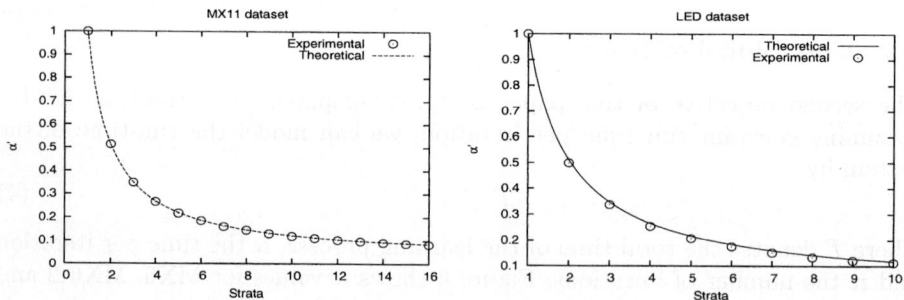

Fig. 7. Verification of the *alpha'* model with MX11 and LED datasets.

With this α' model we can now deduce a formula to approximate the optimal number of iterations to maximize accuracy within a constant running time. The question is how many iterations using s strata (it_s) have the same run time as a base run time using one strata and it_1 iterations. it_s can be estimated by

$$it_s = \frac{it_1 \cdot s}{1 + b(s-1)}, \tag{5}$$

setting $a = 1 - b$. This formula is quite interpretable: b is the overhead of the *GA* cycle. If it were 0, the speedup obtained would be optimal and we could do as many iterations as $it_1 \cdot s$ for s strata. This overhead, however, also depends on the number of strata showing that the stratification does affect not only the evaluation stage of the *GA* cycle but also the resulting model.

6 Summary and Conclusions

This paper focused on a windowing scheme used originally to reduce the run-time of a Pittsburgh approach genetic-based machine learning system. Previous results suggested that the scheme could also improve the accuracy performance of the system. This paper showed how to extract a model to predict when this is possible.

We have developed two theories to model the behavior of the *ILAS* windowing scheme. The first one concerns the maximum number of strata that can be used to separate a dataset before the learning mechanism may be disrupted. The model is based on the number of rules that are needed to classify a dataset correctly and the number of instances that cover each rule. Our model is based on the probability of having all rules represented by at least one instance in each strata. The experimental validation confirmed the derived bound being slightly pessimistic about the outcome.

This model is based on the assumption that all rules represent a uniform number of instances. If the coverage of the rules is not uniform, the probability should decrease. However, given the slightly more conservative behavior of our model versus the empirical ratio of represented rules, we think that we can compensate, to some degree, having unbalanced rules. However, in order to have a fully usable model of *ILAS* we have to answer the pending question of how to model the quasi-linear increase in convergence time before the break point. Future research needs to address this issue in further detail.

The second theory developed in this section concerns the run-time of *ILAS*. Our model can predict the run-time reduction we can achieve in comparison to the system with 1 strata, given the supposition that all individuals (through all iterations) have the same rule size and rule distribution. Given datasets as *Pima*, shown in figure 2, we know that this is not necessarily true. However, the change in rule size is always decreasing when using *ILAS*. Consequently, our model may be considered as an upper bound in the general case.

With these two models we have constructed a framework that permits the use of the *ILAS* scheme in an efficient manner. Based on the expected complexity in the data, practitioners are now able to estimate the number of strata feasible to use in a dataset. They can also predict the relative run time reduction achievable. Future research should focus on putting the framework into practice on real problems, checking which kind of strategies for *ILAS* can be predicted successfully and reliably with these models.

Acknowledgments

The authors acknowledge the support provided by the Spanish Research Agency (CICYT) under grant numbers TIC2002-04160-C02-02 and TIC 2002-04036-C05-03, the support provided by the Department of Universities, Research and Information Society (DURSI) of the Autonomous Government of Catalonia under grants 2002SGR 00155 and 2001FI 00514.

Also, this work was sponsored by the Air Force Office of Scientific Research, Air Force Materiel Command, USAF, under grant F49620-03-1-0129, and by the Technology Research, Education, and Commercialization Center (TRECC), at University of Illinois at Urbana-Champaign, administered by the National Center for Supercomputing Applications (NCSA) and funded by the Office of Naval Research under grant N00014-01-1-0175. The US Government is authorized to reproduce and distribute reprints for Government purposes notwithstanding any copyright notation thereon.

The views and conclusions contained herein are those of the authors and should not be interpreted as necessarily representing the official policies or endorsements, either expressed or implied, of the Air Force Office of Scientific Research, the Technology Research, Education, and Commercialization Center, the Office of Naval Research, or the U.S. Government.

References

1. Holland, J.H.: Adaptation in Natural and Artificial Systems. University of Michigan Press (1975)
2. Goldberg, D.E.: Genetic Algorithms in Search, Optimization and Machine Learning. Addison-Wesley Publishing Company, Inc. (1989)
3. Smith, S.F.: Flexible learning of problem solving heuristics through adaptive search. In: Proceedings of the Eighth International Joint Conference on Artificial Intelligence, Los Altos, CA, Morgan Kaufmann (1983) 421–425
4. Soule, T., Foster, J.A.: Effects of code growth and parsimony pressure on populations in genetic programming. Evolutionary Computation **6** (1998) 293–309
5. Bacardit, J., Garrell, J.M.: Incremental learning for pittsburgh approach classifier systems. In: Proceedings of the "Segundo Congreso Español de Metaheurísticas, Algoritmos Evolutivos y Bioinspirados.". (2003) 303–311
6. Bacardit, J., Garrell, J.M.: Comparison of training set reduction techniques for pittsburgh approach genetic classifier systems. In: Proceedings of the "X Conferencia de la Asociación Española para la Inteligencia Artificial (CAEPIA2003)". (2003)
7. DeJong, K.A., Spears, W.M., Gordon, D.F.: Using genetic algorithms for concept learning. Machine Learning **13** (1993) 161–188
8. Fürnkranz, J.: Integrative windowing. Journal of Artificial Intelligence Research **8** (1998) 129–164
9. Salamó, M., Golobardes, E.: Hybrid deletion policies for case base maintenance. In: Proceedings of FLAIRS-2003. (2003) 150–154
10. Bacardit, J., Garrell, J.M.: Evolving multiple discretizations with adaptive intervals for a pittsburgh rule-based learning classifier system. In: Proceedings of the

Genetic and Evolutionary Computation Conference - GECCO2003, LNCS 2724, Springer (2003) 1818–1831
11. Rivest, R.L.: Learning decision lists. Machine Learning **2** (1987) 229–246
12. Bacardit, J., Garrell, J.M.: Bloat control and generalization pressure using the minimum description length principle for a pittsburgh approach learning classifier system. In: Proceedings of the 6th International Workshop on Learning Classifier Systems, (in press), LNAI, Springer (2003)
13. Blake, C., Keogh, E., Merz, C.: UCI repository of machine learning databases (1998) (www.ics.uci.edu/mlearn/MLRepository.html).
14. Wilson, S.W.: Classifier fitness based on accuracy. Evolutionary Computation **3** (1995) 149–175

A Simple Payoff-Based Learning Classifier System

Larry Bull

Faculty of Computing, Engineering & Mathematical Sciences
University of the West of England
Bristol BS16 1QY, U.K.
larry.bull@uwe.ac.uk

Abstract. It is now ten years since Wilson introduced the 'Zeroth-level' learning classifier system with the aim of simplifying Holland's original system to both aid understanding and improve performance. Despite being comparatively simple, it is still somewhat complex and more recent work has shown the system's sensitivity to its control parameters, particularly with respect to the underlying fitness sharing process. This paper presents a simple payoff-based learning classifier system with which to explore aspects of fitness sharing in such systems, a further aim being to achieve similar performance to accuracy-based learning classifier systems. The system is described and modelled, before being implemented and tested on the multiplexer task.

1 Introduction

Since its introduction Holland's Learning Classifier System (LCS) [1] has inspired much research into 'genetics-based' machine learning [2]. However, the developed system [3,4] was somewhat complex and experience found it difficult to realise the envisaged performance/behaviour [e.g., 5]. As a consequence, Wilson presented the 'Zeroth-level' classifier system, ZCS [6], which "keeps much of Holland's original framework but simplifies it to increase understandability and performance" [ibid.]. It has recently been shown that ZCS can perform optimally through its fitness sharing scheme [7]. Within Genetic Algorithms (GAs) [8], fitness sharing is a well-established approach to multimodal optimization [9]. Under the phenotypic scheme introduced by Holland [4] in the bucket brigade algorithm no problematic distance metric is required (e.g., see [10] for early discussions on such metrics). Although the use of fitness sharing for externally received payoff had been suggested before [e.g., 11], it was not until Wilson introduced the action set-based scheme in ZCS that simple but effective fitness sharing in LCS became possible [7].

Most current research has made a shift away from Holland's original formalism, moving LCS much closer to the field of reinforcement learning [12], after Wilson introduced XCS [13]. XCS uses the accuracy of rules' predictions of expected payoff as their fitness (Holland's original implementation also considered accuracy [14]). In this way a full map of the problem space is created, rather than the traditional search for only high payoff rules, with (potentially) maximally accurate generalizations over the state-action space [15]. That is, XCS uses a GA to evolve generalizations over the space of possible state-action pairs with the aim of easing the use of reinforcement learning in large problems. A primary motivation for accuracy-based fitness is that it explicitly attempts to avoid problematic 'overgeneral' rules which receive a high optimal payoff for some inputs but are sub-optimal for other, lower payoff inputs. Since their average payoff is higher than that for the optimal rules in the latter case, the overgenerals tend to displace them, leaving the LCS sub-optimal. However, the payoffs received by overgeneral rules typically have high variance (they are inaccurate predictors) and so have low fitness in XCS. Holland's LCS was shown to suffer due to such rules emerging [e.g., 15]. It has recently been shown that, when working effectively, fitness sharing in a payoff-based LCS can combat overgenerals [7] but "it would appear that the interaction between the rate of rule updates and the fitness sharing process is critical" [ibid.]. A simplified version of ZCS is presented here to further examine fitness sharing in LCS and the production of solutions with significant generalization by such systems; an equivalent to the "canonical GA" is presented for payoff-based LCS.

2 MCS: A Minimal Learning Classifier System

MCS has no internal memory and the rulebase consists of a number (N) of condition/action rules in which the condition is a string of characters from the usual ternary alphabet $\{0,1,\#\}$ and the action is represented by a binary string. Associated with each rule is a fitness value f, initialized to 1.0 (f_0).

On receipt of an input message, the rulebase is scanned, and any rule whose condition matches the message at each position is tagged as a member of the current match set [M]. An action is then chosen from those proposed by the members of the match set and all rules proposing the selected action form an action set [A]. The grouping of concurrently activated rules by action was used in the purely GA-based LS-1 [16] for action selection, and is used in ZCS and XCS for both action selection and reinforcement updates. A variety of action selection schemes are possible but a version of XCS's explore/exploit scheme will be used here. That is, on one cycle an action is chosen at random and on the following the action with highest total payoff is chosen deterministically.

In this paper the simplest case of immediate reward (payoff P) is considered and hence reinforcement consists of updating the fitness of each member of the current [A] via fitness sharing, using the Widrow-Hoff delta rule with learning rate β:

$$f_j <- f_j + \beta \left((P / |[A]|) - f_j \right) \qquad (1)$$

MCS employs two discovery mechanisms, a panmictic GA and a covering operator. On each time-step there is a probability g of GA invocation. When called, the GA uses roulette wheel selection to determine two parent rules based on their fitness. Offspring are produced via mutation (probability μ, turned into a wildcard at rate p#) and crossover (single point with probability χ), inheriting the parents' fitness values or their average if crossover is invoked. Replacement of existing members of the rulebase is inversely proportional to fitness, i.e., $1/(f_j +1)$, using roulette wheel selection. If no rules match on a given time step, then a covering operator is used which makes a rule that matches the current stimulus (augmented with wildcards at rate p#) and assigns it the default fitness f_0. The GA is not invoked on exploit trials, nor are rule parameters updated (after [17]).

There are a few differences between MCS and ZCS. In particular, in MCS there is no fitness tax on the members of a matchset not forming the current [A] and rules do not donate half of their fitness to their offspring. Also, in MCS cover is not fired if the fitness of a matchset is a defined fraction below the population mean. As will be shown, those mechanisms need not be considered as pre-requisites for the effective use of a payoff-based fitness scheme. The mechanisms of MCS are now modelled, in keeping with its philosophy, in a simple way.

3 A Simple Model

The evolutionary algorithm in MCS, and most LCS, is a steady-state GA. A simple steady-state GA without genetic operators can be expressed in the form:

$$n(k, t+1) = n(k, t) + n(k, t) R(k, t) - n(k, t) D(k, t) \qquad (2)$$

where $n(k, t)$ refers to the number of individuals of type k in the population at time t, $R(k, t)$ refers to their probability of reproductive selection and $D(k, t)$ to their probability of deletion. Roulette-wheel selection is used, i.e., $R(k, t) = f(k, t)/f(K, t)$, where $f(k, t)$ is the fitness of individuals of type k (Equation 1) and $f(K, t)$ is the total population (K) fitness. Replacement is inversely proportional to fitness as described above.

Table 1 shows the payoffs for the single-step task with a single-bit condition and singlebit action considered here (after [17]). The last two entries in Table 1 show the expected payoff for the general rules, i.e., the predicted payoff of a general rule is the average of the payoffs it receives (assuming equal probability). It can be seen that under this scheme for input '1' the general rule #:0 has a higher predicted payoff than the correct rule 1:1; #:0 is an overgeneral rule which would cause sub-optimal performance. The progress of all six rules is examined here, with rulebase size $N = 400$.

Table 1. Reward payoffs for the single-step task considered.

Input	Action	Payoff
1	1	1000
1	0	800
0	1	1000
0	0	3000
#	0	1900
#	1	1000

After [7], with equations of the general form shown in Equation 2 the expected proportions of each rule type in the next generation can be determined; by specifying the initial proportions of each rule in the population ($N/6$), it is possible to generate the trajectory of their proportions over succeeding generations. Note partial individuals are allowed and hence it is in effect an infinite population model. In the following it is assumed that both inputs are presented with equal frequency, that both actions are chosen with equal frequency and that the GA fires once every four cycles (i.e., always explore trials and $g=0.25$). The rules' parameters are updated according to Equation 1 on each cycle with $\beta=0.2$.

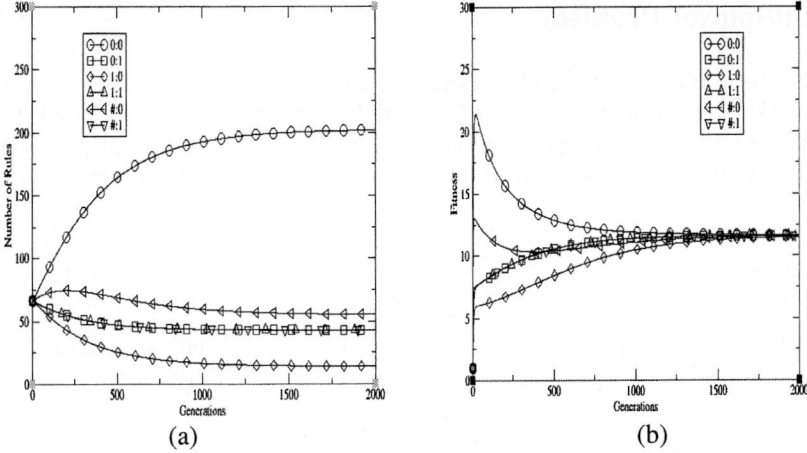

Fig. 1. Behaviour on the task in Table 1, showing numerosities (a) and fitnesses (b).

Figure 1 shows the behaviour of the modelled LCS on the single-step task defined in Table 1. From Figure 1(a) it can be seen that the overgeneral rule #:0 maintains a greater proportion of the population than any rule for the action '1'. Since, as shown in Figure 1(b), under fitness sharing the fitness of all rules goes to the same value (as discussed in [18]), this means that the LCS will provide a sub-optimal response for input '1'. Figure 2 shows the behaviour of the modelled LCS on the same task with $\beta=1.0$. It can be seen that the overgeneral rule #:0 has the lowest numerosity along with the lowest payoff rule (1:0) and that there are an equal number of #:1, 0:1 and 1:1 rules. That is, numerosities reflect rule payoffs more appropriately with the instantaneous update but the more general solution (#:1) does not win out as there is no explicit generalization pressure. Also, given that payoff-based LCS using fitness sharing hold their estimation of utility in *rule numerosity*, the instantaneous fitness update means a rule's fitness can immediately consider the current numerosity, something which is constantly changed by the actions of the GA; it appears that a high learning rate allows the LCS to approximate rule utility more efficiently. This results contrasts with that reported in [7] who showed an instantaneous fitness update failing to solve this task (their Figure 2). However, their model assumed that the fitness of general rules at any time were the average of the corresponding specific rules at that time. The assumption is not made here and hence explains the difference. It can be noted that XCS has also been shown to be sensitive to the learning rate to a degree, although this can be greatly reduced using a rank-based selection scheme [19]. Rank-based selection for LCS was highlighted in [20] after a number of issues were identified, but it is problematic for fitness sharing systems [e.g., 21].

Despite the fact that both XCS and MCS use niche (action set) size to enforce diversity in the rulebase, they do it in different ways, which will usually result in different solutions. XCS uses niche size to equally balance rulebase resources [13]. In contrast, MCS apportions resources based on relative payoff (as highlighted in [7]). Since action '0' receives almost twice as much payoff as action '1' in the task presented in Table 1, MCS converges on a rulebase containing almost twice as many rules for the former action than the latter (Figure 2(a)). The effects, if any, on performance from this difference remain open to further investigation.

4 Multiplexer Problem

MCS has been implemented and investigated using versions of the well-known multiplexer task. These Boolean functions are defined for binary strings of length $l = k + 2^k$ under which the first k bits index into the remaining 2^k bits, returning the value of the indexed bit. A correct classification results in a payoff of 1000, otherwise 0.

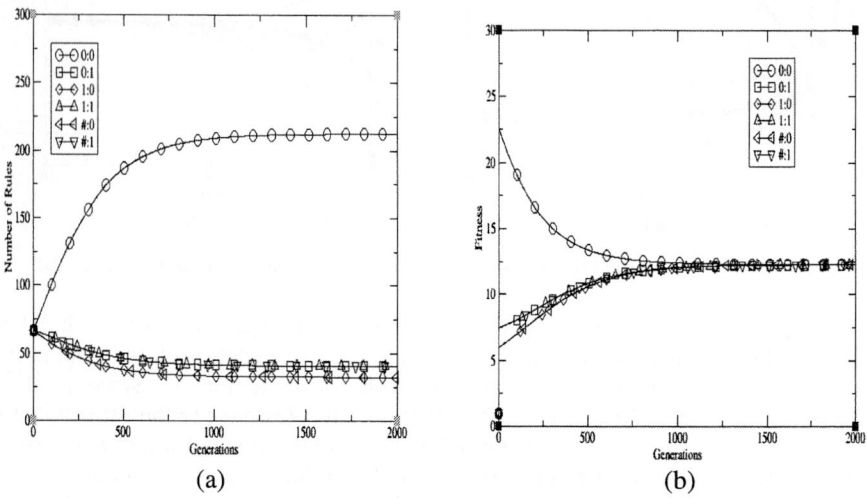

Fig. 2. Behaviour of model LCS on the task in Table 1 with a higher learning rate.

Figure 3(a) shows the performance of MCS, as described in Section 2, on the 6-bit multiplexer problem using the same parameters as in Section 3, with $\beta=0.2$, $p_\#=0.6$, $\chi=0.5$ and $\mu=0.01$. After [13], performance from exploit trials only is recorded (fraction of correct responses are shown), using a 50-point running average, averaged over ten runs. It can be seen that the system is not capable of optimal performance. Figure 3(a) also shows the average specificity, that is, number of non-# bits, of all rules in the solution (as a fraction of condition length). For the 6-bit multiplexer, a maximally general rule contains two address bits and one data bit in its condition, i.e., specificity three (3/6 = 0.5). As can be seen, the specificity is higher. Figure 3(b) shows the performance of the same system on the 6-bit multiplexer with $\beta=1.0$. It can be seen that it achieves optimal performance, as predicted by the model above. Again, its specificity is higher than the optimum. This generalization issue is investigated further in the following section.

5 Default Fitness Allocation

Under the operations of the GA within ZCS, there is a reproduction cost such that parents give half of their fitness to their offspring. No explanation for this mechanism is given in [6] but it has been suggested that it reduces "the initial 'runaway' success of those rules in high payoff niches" [22]. That is, once a rule has reproduced, it and

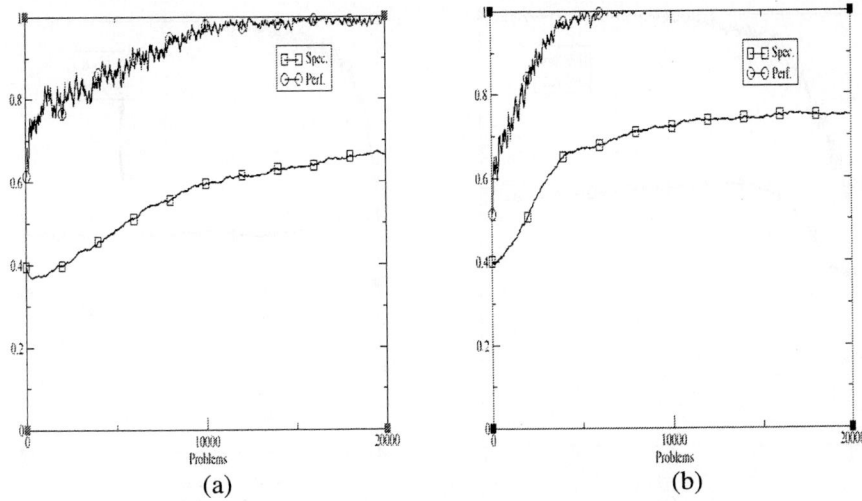

Fig. 3. Performance of MCS on the 6-bit multiplexer task, $\beta=0.2$ (a) and $\beta=1.0$ (b) versions.

its offspring are much less likely to be picked again under the panmictic GA until their niche occurs, at which point they are assigned a new fitness appropriate for the current numerosity. This last point was shown to be significant in Section 3 and is fundamental to the way in which fitness sharing avoids overgeneral rules since it removes any advantage in difference between niche payoff levels [7]; the payoff available to individual rules becomes the same in all niches once numerosities have been adjusted appropriately by the GA. A simpler, tunable mechanism is examined here.

Figure 4(a) shows the effect of assigning the initial default fitness value (f_0) to both the parents and the offspring under the GA of the simple LCS. Further, in Figure 4(b) the GA is fired on every explore trial to increase the rate at which rules are apportioned to niches. Here the GA is constantly working on assigning an appropriate numerosity to each niche, whilst new and existing rules have their fitnesses set according to its latest actions through a maximum learning rate. It can be seen that the default fitness heuristic improves the degree of generalization in the system (compare with Figure 3(b)) and that, combined with the higher GA rate, it now also solves the 6-bit multiplexer with a maximally general solution. All other parameters are as in Figure 3(b).

In Figure 5(a) it can be seen that the system solves the 20-bit multiplexer, with all other parameters as in Figure 4(b) except $N=2000$, producing solutions which are maximally general. Figure 5(b) shows the performance of the same system in the 37-bit multiplexer with all parameters as before, except $N=5000$. It can be seen that optimal performance is obtained around 750,000 exploit trials - equivalent to the performance of XCS using the same parameters (where relevant) as shown in [23]. For this larger multiplexer it can also be seen that the average specificity of the solutions produced by MCS are maximally general (0.17).

This generalization pressure is created by the default fitness allocation heuristic. Consider two breeding rules which are equally correct within their niches but one is more general than the other. Once their fitnesses have been set to the default value

1038   Larry Bull

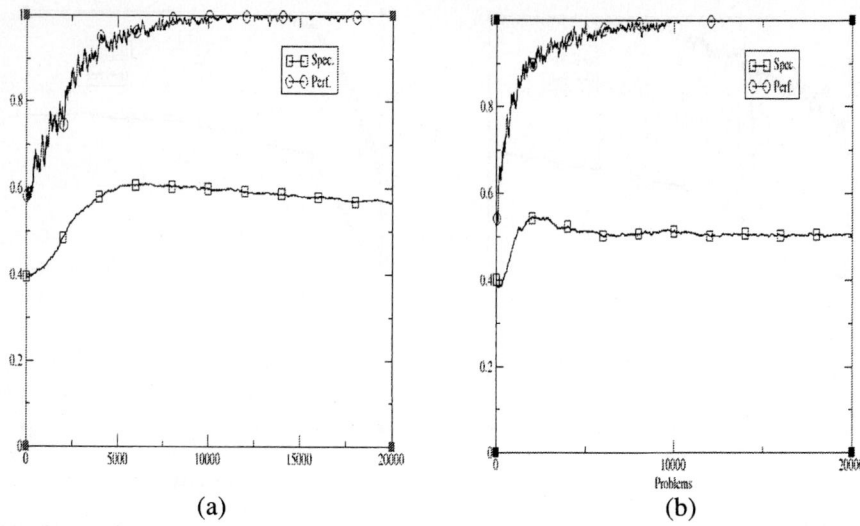

Fig. 4. Performance of MCS on the 6-bit multiplexer task, with $g=0.25$ (a) and $g=1.0$ (b).

they must wait until one of their niches occurs before their fitnesses will be reset. On average, this will occur more quickly for the more general rule meaning it will tend to be selected again for reproduction more quickly than the less general rule; a more general correct rule will increase in numerosity more rapidly than a less general rule. Experiments using the ZCS fitness halving scheme find the system performs more quickly on the 20-bit problem, but does not create maximally general solutions, and does no better than random on the 37-bit multiplexer (Figure 6).

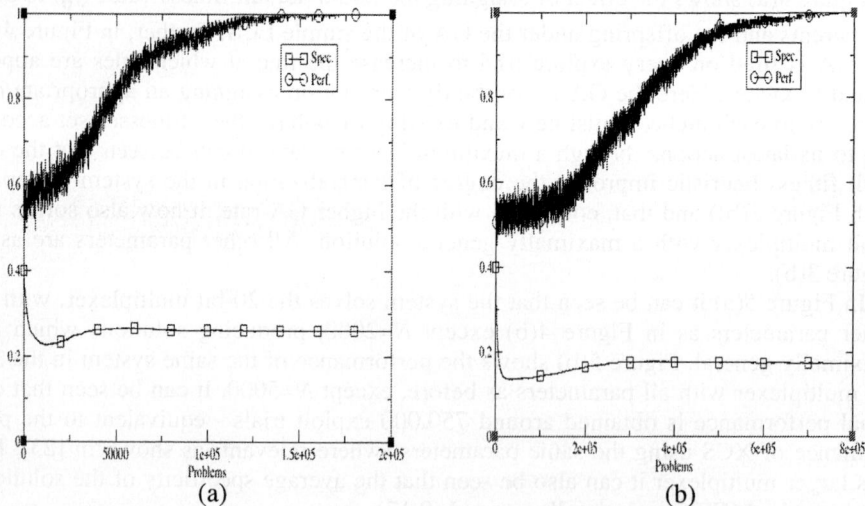

Fig. 5. Performance of MCS on the multiplexer task, 20-bit (a) and 37-bit (b) versions.

6 Conclusions

This paper has investigated a simple payoff-based LCS which draws heavily on Wilson's ZCS, being simple enough to be modelled with difference equations. As in [7], it was shown that the fitness sharing process is sensitive to the learning rate. In this paper it has further been shown that an instantaneous fitness update ($\beta=1.0$) means the fitness sharing can provide an optimal solution. Since such payoff-based LCS store their solutions in rule numerosity together with the fitness value (a fact still often missed [e.g., 19]), this update rate enables the system to rapidly alter fitnesses to consider any changes in numerosity caused by the GA between evaluations. This finding also effectively removes one of the system parameters (β).

Implementation of the system showed that, as predicted by the model, optimal solutions could be obtained, demonstrated using the 6-bit multiplexer problem. However, the degree of generalization was poor, even for such a simple problem, as the basic system contains no explicit generalization pressure. By introducing a simple heuristic which effectively resets the fitness of breeding rules and their offspring to a (low) default value awaiting re-evaluation, and by increasing the rate of GA activity to fire on every system cycle, optimal generalizations were obtained. Further, optimal performance was obtained in larger multiplexer problems. Here the GA is constantly working on assigning an appropriate numerosity to each niche, whilst new and existing rules have their fitnesses set according to its latest actions through a maximum learning rate, as described above. Again, this finding also effectively removes one of the system parameters (g), meaning that the system's behaviour is defined by N, $p_{\#}$, χ, μ, and f_0 for single-step tasks, only two more than the canonical GA.

These results are now being applied to multi-step tasks and systems which create anticipations of the effects of their actions.

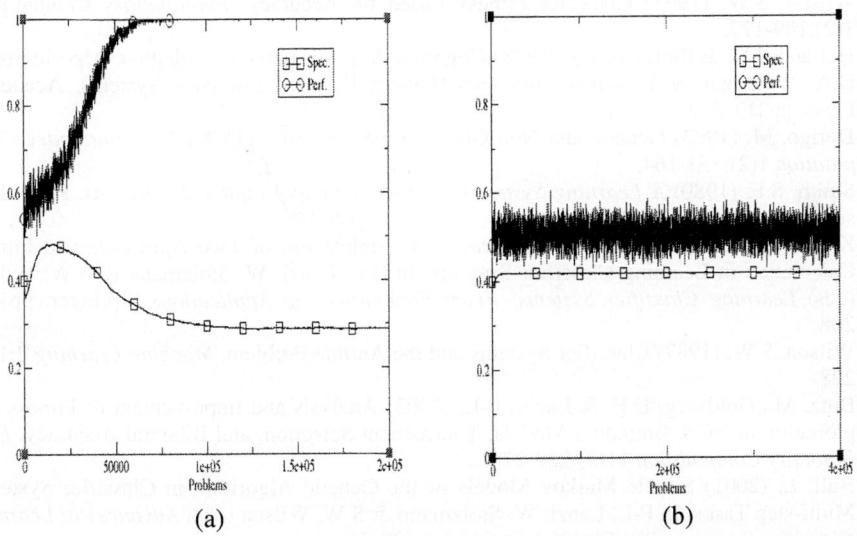

Fig. 6. Performance of MCS using ZCS fitness halving, on 20-bit (a) and 37-bit (b) tasks.

References

1. Holland, J.H. (1976) Adaptation. In R. Rosen & F.M. Snell (eds) *Progress in Theoretical Biology, 4.* Academic Press, pp263-293.
2. Goldberg, D.E. (1989) *Genetic Algorithms in Search, Optimization and Machine Learning.* Addison Wesley.
3. Holland, J.H. (1980) Adaptive Algorithms for Discovering and using General Patterns in Growing Knowledge Trees. *International Journal of Policy Analysis and Information Systems* 4(3): 245-268.
4. Holland, J.H. (1986) Escaping Brittleness. In R.S. Michalski, J.G. Carbonell & T.M. Mitchell (eds) *Machine Learning: An Artificial Intelligence Approach, 2.* Morgan Kauffman, pp48-78.
5. Wilson, S.W. & Goldberg, D.E. (1989) A Critical Review of Classifier Systems. In J.D. Schaffer (ed) *Proceedings of the Third International Conference on Genetic Algorithms.* Morgan Kaufmann, pp244-255.
6. Wilson, S.W. (1994) ZCS: A Zeroth-level Classifier System. *Evolutionary Computation* 2(1):1-18.
7. Bull, L. & Hurst, J. (2002) ZCS Redux. *Evolutionary Computation* 10(2): 185-205.
8. Holland, J.H. (1975) *Adaptation in Natural and Artificial Systems.* University of Michigan Press.
9. Goldberg, D.E. & Richardson, J. (1987) Genetic Algorithms with Sharing for Multimodal Function Optimization. In J.J. Grefenstette (ed) *Proceedings of the Second International Conference on Genetic Algorithms.* Lawrence Erlbaum Assoc., pp41-49.
10. Deb, K. & Goldberg, D.E. (1989) An Investigation of Niche and Species Formation in Genetic Function Optimization. In J.D. Schaffer (ed) *Proceedings of the Third International Conference on Genetic Algorithms.* Morgan Kaufmann, pp42-50.
11. Holland, J.H. (1985) Properties of the Bucket Brigade. In J.J. Grefenstette (ed) *Proceedings of the First International Conference on Genetic Algorithms and their Applications.* Lawrence Erlbaum Associates, pp1-7.
12. Sutton, R.S. & Barto, A.G. (1998) *Reinforcement Learning.* MIT Press.
13. Wilson, S.W. (1995) Classifier Fitness Based on Accuracy. *Evolutionary Computation* 3(2):149-177.
14. Holland, J.H. & Reitman, J.S. (1978) Cognitive Systems based on Adaptive Algorithms. In D.A. Waterman & F. Hayes-Roth (eds) *Pattern Directed Inference Systems.* Academic Press, pp313-329.
15. Dorigo, M. (1993) Genetic and Non-Genetic Operators in ALECSYS. *Evolutionary Computation* 1(2):151-164.
16. Smith, S.F. (1980) *A Learning System Based on Genetic Adaptive Algorithms.* Ph.D. Dissertation, University of Pittsburgh.
17. Kovacs, T. (2000) Strength or Accuracy? A Comparison of Two Approaches to Fitness Calculation in Learning Classifier Systems. In P-L. Lanzi, W. Stolzmann & S.W. Wilson (eds) *Learning Classifier Systems: From Foundations to Applications,* Springer, pp194-208.
18. Wilson, S.W. (1987) Classifier Systems and the Animat Problem. *Machine Learning* 2:199-228.
19. Butz, M., Goldberg, D.E. & Lanzi, P-L. (2003) Analysis and Improvement of Fitness Exploitation in XCS: Bounding Models, Tournament Selection, and Bilateral Accuracy. *Evolutionary Computation* 11(3):239-278.
20. Bull, L. (2001) Simple Markov Models of the Genetic Algorithm in Classifier Systems: Multi-step Tasks. In P-L. Lanzi, W. Stolzmann & S.W. Wilson (eds) *Advances in Learning Classifier Systems - IWLCS 2000,* Springer, pp29-36.
21. Deb, K. (2001) *Evolutionary Multiobjective Optimization Algorithms.* Wiley.

22. Bull, L. & Studley, M. (2002) Consideration of Multiple Objectives in Neural Learning Classifier Systems. In J. Merelo, P. Adamidis, H-G. Beyer, J-L. FernandezVillicanas & H-P. Schwefel (eds) *Parallel Problem Solving from Nature - PPSN VII.* Springer, pp558-567.
23. Butz, M., Kovacs, T., Lanzi, P-L. & Wilson, S.W. (2001) How XCS Evolves Accurate Classifiers. In *Proceedings of the 2001 Genetic and Evolutionary Computation Conference – Gecco 2001.* Morgan Kaufmann, pp927-934.

Lookahead and Latent Learning in a Simple Accuracy-Based Classifier System

Larry Bull

Faculty of Computing, Engineering & Mathematical Sciences
University of the West of England
Bristol BS16 1QY, U.K.
larry.bull@uwe.ac.uk

Abstract. Learning Classifier Systems use evolutionary algorithms to facilitate rulediscovery, where rule fitness is traditionally payoff based and assigned under a sharing scheme. Most current research has shifted to the use of an accuracy-based scheme where fitness is based on a rule's ability to predict the expected payoff from its use. Learning Classifier Systems which build anticipations of the expected states following their actions are also a focus of current research. This paper presents a simple but effective learning classifier system of this last type, using accuracy-based fitness, with the aim of enabling the exploration of their basic principles, i.e., in isolation from the many other mechanisms they usually contain. The system is described and modelled, before being implemented.

1 Introduction

Holland's Learning Classifier System (LCS) [1] represents a form of machine learning which exploits evolutionary computing to produce inductive structures within an artificial entity. Typically, such systems use stimulus-response rules to form chains of reasoning. However, Holland's architecture has been extended to include mechanisms by which higher levels of cognitive capabilities, along the lines of those envisaged in [2, can emerge; the use of predictive modelling within LCS has been considered through alteration to the rule structure [e.g., 3]. Using maze tasks loosely based on those of early animal behaviour experiments, it has been found that LCS can learn effectively when reward is dependent upon the ability to accurately predict the next environment state/sensory input. LCS with such 'lookahead' typically work under latent learning, i.e., they build a full predictive map of the environment without external reinforcement. LCS of this general type have gained renewed interest after Stolzmann presented the heuristics-based ACS [4]. ACS was found to produce overspecific solutions through the workings of its heuristics and was later extended to include a Genetic Algorithm (GA)[5] – ACS2 [6]. Bull [7] presented an extension to Wilson's simple payoff-based LCS – ZCS [8] – which is also able to form anticipations under latent learning. Significantly, this is the only anticipatory system which builds such models through the GA alone; Riolo [3] did not include a GA. Most current work in LCS has shifted to using accuracy as rule fitness, after Wilson presented XCS [9]. In this paper, a simple accuracy-based LCS which can create such anticipations using only the GA is presented and explored.

X. Yao et al. (Eds.): PPSN VIII, LNCS 3242, pp. 1042–1050, 2004.
© Springer-Verlag Berlin Heidelberg 2004

2 YCSL: A Simple Accuracy-Based Anticipatory Classifier System

In this paper, as in ACS [4] (and its related systems [e.g., 10]) and in [7], an explicit representation of the expected next environmental state is used to create a simple accuracy-based anticipatory LCS which uses lookahead under latent learning – YCSL. That is, rules are of the general form:

<condition> : <action> : <anticipation>

Generalizations (#'s) are allowed in the condition and anticipation strings. Where #'s occur at the same loci in both, the corresponding environmental input symbol 'passes through' such that it occurs in the anticipated description for that input. Similarly, defined loci in the condition appear when a # occurs in the corresponding locus of the anticipation.

YCSL is a Learning Classifier System without internal memory, where the rulebase consists of a number (N) of rules with the above form. Associated with each rule is a scalar which indicates the error (ϵ) in the rule's prediction abilities and an estimate of the average size of the niches (action sets - see below) in which that rule participates (σ). The initial random population have these initialized to 10.

On receipt of an input message, the rulebase is scanned, and any rule whose condition matches the message at each position is tagged as a member of the current match set [M]. An action is then chosen from those proposed by the members of the match set at random and all rules proposing the selected action form an action set [A].

Reinforcement consists of updating the error and the niche size estimate of each member of the current [A] using the Widrow-Hoff delta rule with learning rate β:

$$\epsilon_j \leftarrow \epsilon_j + \beta(E - \epsilon_j) \qquad (1)$$
$$\sigma_j \leftarrow \sigma_j + \beta(|[A]| - \sigma_j) \qquad (2)$$

where E is zero if the anticipation of the given rule, created as described above, correctly describes the following state, otherwise 1000. That is, the creation of an internal model of a given environment is cast as a single-step task [7].

YCS employs two discovery mechanisms, a panmictic GA and a covering operator. On each time-step there is a probability g of GA invocation. When called, the GA uses roulette wheel selection to determine two parent rules based on the inverse of their error:

$$\text{fitness}, f_j = 1/(\epsilon_j+1) \qquad (3)$$

Offspring are produced via mutation (probability μ, turned into a wildcard at rate $p_{\#}$) and crossover (single point with probability χ), inheriting the parents' parameter values or their average if crossover is invoked. Replacement of existing members of the rulebase uses roulette wheel selection based on estimated niche size. If no rules match on a given time step, then a covering operator is used which creates a rule with the message as its condition (augmented with wildcards at the rate $p_{\#}$) and a random action and anticipation, which then replaces an existing member of the rulebase in the usual way.

Hence YCSL represents a simple accuracy-based anticipatory LCS which relies solely upon the GA to search the space of possible generalizations; other heuristics need not be considered as pre-requisites for the effective use of an accuracy-based fitness scheme. Here the term effective is taken to mean able to solve problems of low complexity whilst remaining open to close modelling; the canonical GA may be defined in much the same way. The mechanisms of YCSL are now modelled, in keeping with its philosophy, in a simple way.

3 A Simple Model of YCSL

The steady-state GA in YCSL can be expressed without genetic operators by:

$$n(k, t+1) = n(k, t) + n(k, t) R(k, t) - n(k, t) D(k, t) \qquad (4)$$

where $n(k, t)$ refers to the number of individuals of type k in the population at time t, $R(k, t)$ refers to their probability of reproductive selection and $D(k, t)$ to their probability of deletion. Roulette-wheel selection is used, i.e., $R(k, t) = f(k, t)/f(K, t)$, where $f(k, t)$ is the fitness of individuals of type k (Equation 3) and $f(K, t)$ is the total population (K) fitness. Replacement is proportional to estimated action set size, i.e., $D(k, t) = \sigma(k, t)/\sigma(K, t)$.

Table 1. Errors for the maze task.

C:A:Ant	E	C:A:Ant	E	C:A:Ant	E
0:0:0	0	1:0:0	1000	#:0:0	500
0:0:1	1000	1:0:1	0	#:0:1	500
0:0:#	0	1:0:#	0	#:0:#	0
0:1:0	1000	1:1:0	0	#:1:0	500
0:1:1	0	1:1:1	1000	#:1:1	500
0:1:#	1000	1:1:#	1000	#:1:#	1000

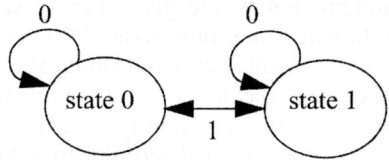

Fig. 1. Simple two-location maze considered.

Table 1 shows the error 'rewards' for each of the rules considered. Those rules which experience two rewards have the average shown (after [11]). Figure 1 shows the maze environment from which the errors are drawn. The maze contains two locations, one providing the LCS with input '0' and the other with input '1'. In both locations an action '0' means no move and action '1' means a move to the other location.

The initial proportions of each rule in the population are equal $(N/18)$. It is assumed that both inputs are presented with equal frequency, that both actions are chosen with equal frequency and that the GA fires once every four cycles (i.e., $g=0.25$). The rules' parameters are updated according to Equations 1 and 2 on each cycle.

Figure 2 shows the behaviour of the modelled YCSL on the simple maze task. Figure 2(a) shows how only the rules which accurately anticipate the next state (i.e.,

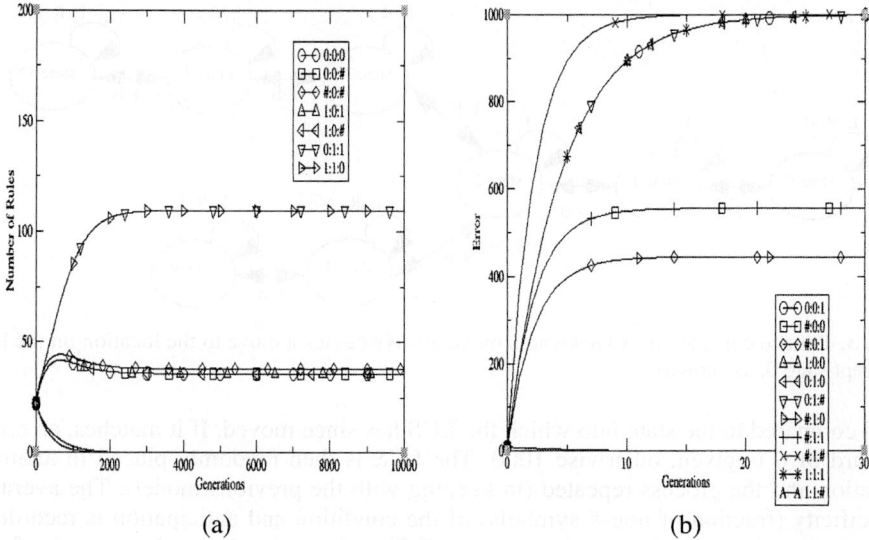

Fig. 2. Behaviour of model YCSL on the maze task, showing numerosities (a) and errors (b).

following their action being taken in the locations they match) exist in the final population. The rulebase is roughly divided between rules with action '0' and those with action '1' but there is no explicit pressure for a maximally general solution. Figure 2(b) shows the corresponding trajectories of the rules' errors with all accurate anticipators having zero error. Therefore the simple accuracy-based fitness scheme of YCSL results in a rulebase which completely maps the maze environment under a latent learning scenario.

4 YCSL in T-Mazes

YCSL has been implemented and investigated using a version of the T-maze presented in [3]. As noted above, motivation for exploring the use of learning without external reinforcement comes from early experiments in animal behaviour. Typically, rats were allowed to run around a T-maze, as shown in Figure 3, where the food cell (state 7) would be empty but a different colour to the rest of the maze. The rats would then be fed in the marked location. Finally, the rats were placed at the start location (state 0) and their ability to take the shortest path (go left at the T-junction in Figure 3) to the food recorded. It was found that rats could do this with around 90% efficiency. Those which were not given the prior experience without food were only 50% efficient, as expected [e.g., 12].

To examine the performance of the simple anticipatory LCS presented here the following scenario is used. The LCS is placed randomly in the maze and a matchset is formed. Sensory input in each location of the maze is the binary encoded number for that state (3 bits) and there are four possible actions - Left, Right, Forwards and Backwards (2 bits). An action is chosen at random from the matchset. All rules which propose the chosen action are updated as described in Section 2 and the GA fires probabilistically. That is, each rule in [A] has the anticipation it created on forming

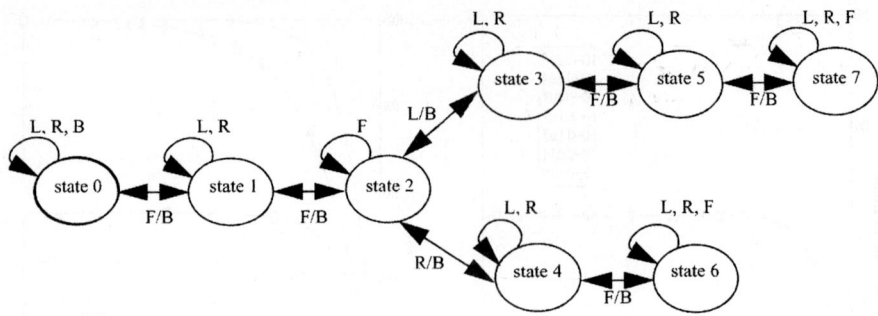

Fig. 3. T-maze considered. A backwards move always causes a move to the location on the left (except state 0, as shown).

[M] compared to the state into which the LCS has since moved. If it matches, an error reward of 0 is given, otherwise 1000. The LCS is then randomly placed in another location and the process repeated (in keeping with the previous model). The average specificity (fraction of non-# symbols) of the condition and anticipation is recorded, as is the number of actions present in each [M], with results shown the average of ten runs.

Figure 4 shows the performance of YCSL on the simple T-maze using the same parameters as in Section 3, with $p_\#=0.33$, $\chi=0.5$ and $\mu=0.01$. Figure 4(a) shows how the fraction of trials upon which the rule with the highest fitness has a correct anticipation quickly rises to 1 (50-point moving average used, after [8]) and the average specificity drops to around 45% indicating the exploitation of generalizations. Figure 4(b) shows how all four actions are present and maintained in each [M] throughout learning. Hence YCSL is able to build a complete and accurate anticipatory map of the simple T-maze (assuming the anticipation of the fittest rules within a given [A] is used in internal processing/planning).

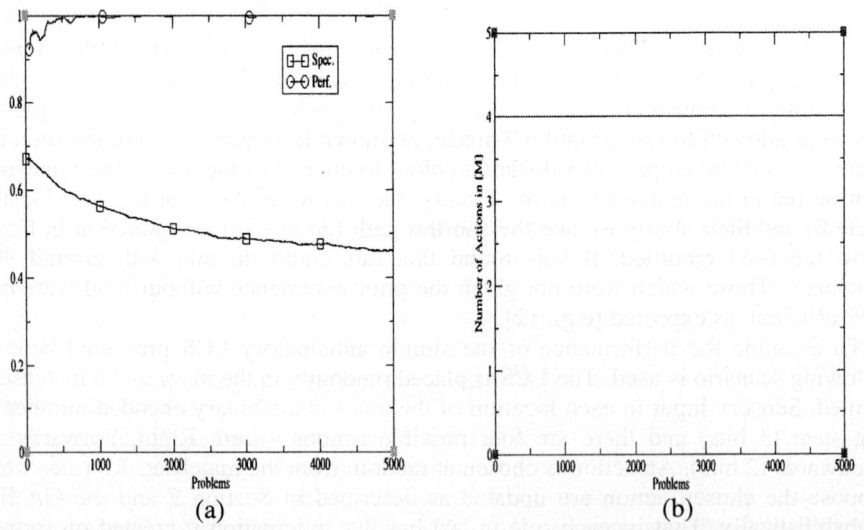

Fig. 4. Showing fittest rule correctness and specificity (a) and number of actions (b) on T-maze.

T	T	T	T	T	T	T
T	F	T	T	T		T
T		T	T	T		T
T						T
T	T	T		T	T	T
T	T	T		T	T	T
T	T	T	T	T	T	T

Fig. 5. The Woods 10 environment.

The maze in Figure 3 is somewhat simple and hence YCSL has also been tested using a more complex version along the lines of other maze tasks typically used in the LCS literature (after [8]) - Woods 10 [7] (Figure 5). The LCS is placed randomly in the maze and a matchset is formed as before. Sensory input in each location of the maze is encoded as a 16-bit binary string with two bits representing each cardinal direction. A blank cell is represented by 00, the food location (F) by 11 and trees (T) by 10 (01 has no meaning). The message is ordered with the cell directly above the LCS represented by the first bit-pair and then proceeds clockwise around it. Again, an action is chosen at random from the matchset where there are now eight possible actions (cardinal moves) and the LCS can move into any one of the surrounding eight cells on each discrete time step, unless occupied by a tree or it is the food location (this avoids creating a sensory ambiguity). All rules which propose the chosen action are updated and all other details are as before. One further mechanism is incorporated for this harder task (after [7]): the first N random rules of the rulebase have their anticipation created using cover (with #'s included as usual) in the first [A] of which they become a member. This goes some way to make " ... good use of the large flow of (non-performance) information supplied by the environment." [13]. Rules created under the cover operator also receive this treatment. In this way the GA explores the generalization space of the anticipations created by the simple heuristic.

Figure 6 shows how the system as used in Figure 4, but with N=5000, $p_{\#}$=0.6, and μ=0.04, is unable to produce a full model of Woods 10. Indeed, the system appears to predict a low number of actions, with increasing specificity, and the rule with the highest fitness in those few [A] rarely anticipates the next state correctly.

The principle mechanism from XCS (and ACS2) that is missing in the simple accuracybased anticipatory LCS described thus far is a triggered niche GA. The general technique was introduced by Booker [14], who based the trigger on a number of factors including the payoff prediction "consistency" of the rules in a given [A], to improve the performance of LCS. XCS uses a simpler time-based mechanism under which each rule maintains a time-stamp of the last system cycle upon which it was part of a GA. The GA is applied within the current [A] when the average number of system cycles since the last GA in the set is over a threshold θ_{GA}. If this condition is met, the GA time-stamp of each rule in [A] is set to the current system time, two parents are chosen according to their fitness using standard roulette-wheel selection, their offspring are potentially crossed and mutated, before being inserted into the (global) rulebase.

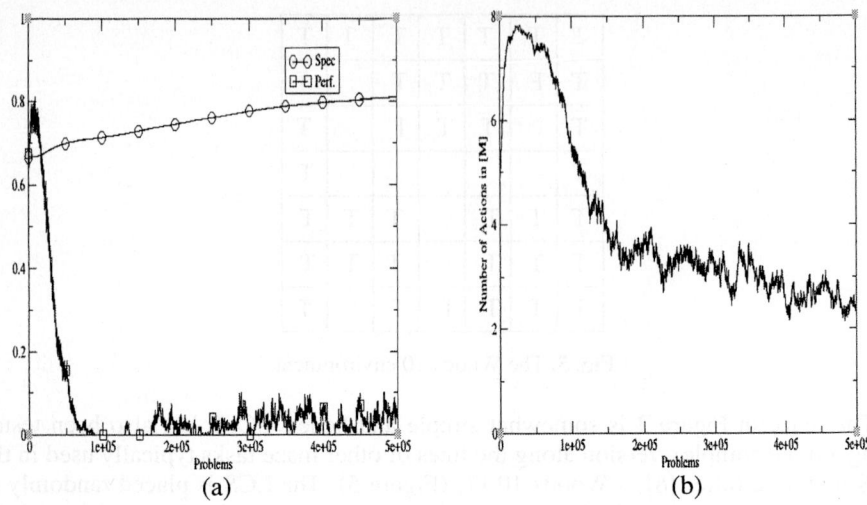

Fig. 6. Showing fittest rule correctness and specificity (a) and no. of actions (b) on 2nd T-maze.

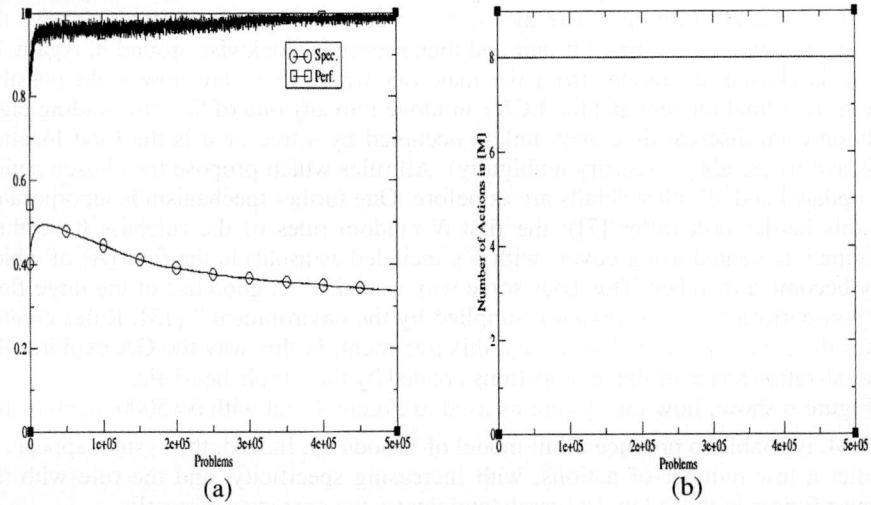

Fig. 7. Showing effects of niche GA on performance (a) and no. of actions (b) on 2nd T-maze.

Figure 7 shows how using the triggered niche GA in YCSL, with $\theta_{GA}= 100$ and all other parameters as before, is able to maintain eight actions and a degree of generalization, but is unable to solve the problem such that the rule with the highest fitness anticipates the next state correctly.

Moving the GA selection and discovery processes to operate within niches – action sets – causes a reduction in the effective population size. In comparison to the panmictic GA, this will almost certainly increase the variance from expected behaviour of the roulette wheel selection operator. A distinguishing feature of XCS is its accuracy function which is a negative power of error. The function is controlled by three variables α, ε_0 and υ, with typical values of 0.1, 10 and 5 respectively, which make it a very harsh, almost step-like, function with a flat top and slight curve at the bottom: $f_j = \alpha\, (\varepsilon_j / \varepsilon_0)^{-\upsilon}$ unless $\varepsilon_j < \varepsilon_0$ where $f_j = 1$. Hence slight differences in error are greatly magnified using this function. In YCSL, as described in Section 2, fitness is simply inversely proportional to error. XCS would seem to indicate that an increase in separation of fitnesses will improve performance in accuracy-based LCS using roulette wheel selection within niches. ACS also uses a power term in its fitness calculation. Figure 8 shows the effects of altering Equation 3 to include a power term υ such that:

$$\text{fitness,}\ f_j = 1/(\varepsilon_j^{\upsilon} + 1) \qquad (5)$$

Figure 8 shows the system with $\upsilon=10$ is able solve the maze task, using all other parameters as in Figure 7, such that the rule with the highest fitness in each [A] correctly anticipates the following sensory state description. $\upsilon=5$ was not as good (not shown).

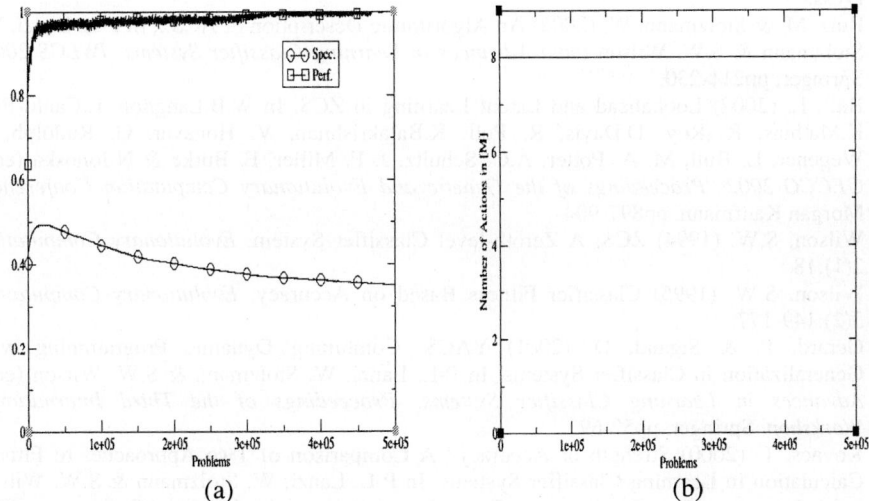

Fig. 8. Showing effects of the altered fitness function on performance (a) and no. of actions (b).

5 Conclusions

Learning Classifier Systems that build a full predictive map of the environment without external reinforcement have recently gained renewed interest. This paper has presented a simple accuracy-based system, termed YCSL, which is capable of this task using only the genetic algorithm. This having been done just once before, through use of payoffbased fitness [7]. Due to its simplicity, an executable model of YCSL has been presented and its finding that optimal performance is possible with such a system was confirmed experimentally. However, it was found that a niche GA was required and the fitness function needed slight alteration for a harder maze task.

Future work will compare the performance and characteristics of YCSL with other anticipatory LCS to improve it and gain a better understanding of such systems in general.

References

1. Holland, J.H. (1976) Adaptation. In R. Rosen & F.M. Snell (eds) *Progress in Theoretical Biology, 4*. Plenum.
2. Holland, J.H., Holyoak, K.J., Nisbett, R.E. & Thagard, P.R. (1986) *Induction: Processes of Inference, Learning and Discovery*. MIT Press.
3. Riolo, R. (1991) Lookahead Planning and Latent Learning in a Classifier System. In J-A. Meyer & S.W. Wilson (eds.) *From Animals to Animats: Proceedings of the First International Conference on Simulation of Adaptive Behaviour*. MIT Press, pp316-326.
4. Stolzmann, W. (1998) Anticipatory Classifier Systems. In J.R. Koza (ed) *Genetic Programming 1998: Proceedings of the Third Annual Conference*. Morgan Kaufmann, pp658-664.
5. Holland, J.H. (1975) *Adaptation in Natural and Artificial Systems*. University of Michigan Press.
6. Butz, M. & Stolzmann, W. (2002) An Algorithmic Description of ACS2. In P-L. Lanzi, W. Stolzmann & S.W. Wilson (eds) *Advances in Learning Classifier Systems: IWLCS 2001*. Springer, pp211-230.
7. Bull, L. (2002) Lookahead and Latent Learning in ZCS. In W.B.Langdon, E.Cantu-Paz, K.Mathias, R. Roy, D.Davis, R. Poli, K.Balakrishnan, V. Honavar, G. Rudolph, J. Wegener, L. Bull, M. A. Potter, A.C. Schultz, J. F. Miller, E. Burke & N.Jonoska (eds) *GECCO-2002: Proceedings of the Genetic and Evolutionary Computation Conference*. Morgan Kaufmann, pp897-904.
8. Wilson, S.W. (1994) ZCS: A Zeroth-level Classifier System. *Evolutionary Computation* 2(1):18.
9. Wilson, S.W. (1995) Classifier Fitness Based on Accuracy. *Evolutionary Computation* 3(2):149-177.
10. Gerard, P. & Sigaud, O. (2001) YACS: Combining Dynamic Programming with Generalization in Classifier Systems. In P-L. Lanzi, W. Stolzmann & S.W. Wilson (eds) *Advances in Learning Classifier Systems: Proceedings of the Third International Workshop*. Springer, pp52-69.
11. Kovacs, T. (2000) Strength or Accuracy? A Comparison of Two Approaches to Fitness Calculation in Learning Classifier Systems. In P-L. Lanzi, W. Stolzmann & S.W. Wilson (eds) *Learning Classifier Systems: From Foundations to Applications*, Springer, pp194-208.
12. Seward, J.P. (1949) An Experimental Analysis of Latent Learning. *Journal of Experimental Psychology* 39: 177-186.
13. Holland, J.H. (1990) Concerning the Emergence of Tag-Mediated Lookahead in Classifier Systems. *Physica D* 42:188-201.
14. Booker, L.B. (1989) Triggered Rule Discovery in Classifier Systems. In J.D. Schaffer (ed) *Proceedings of the Third International Conference on Genetic Algorithms*. Morgan Kaufmann, pp.265-274.

Knowledge Extraction and Problem Structure Identification in XCS

Martin V. Butz[1], Pier Luca Lanzi[2], Xavier Llorà[1], and David E. Goldberg[1]

[1] Illinois Genetic Algorithms Laboratory (IlliGAL)
University of Illinois at Urbana-Champaign
Urbana, IL, 61801
{butz,xllora,deg}@illigal.ge.uiuc.edu
http://www-illigal.ge.uiuc.edu

[2] Artificial Intelligence and Robotics Laboratory
Dipartimento di Elettronica e Informazione
Politecnico di Milano
Milano 20133, Italy
pierluca.lanzi@polimi.it
http://www.elet.polimi.it/index.jsp

Abstract. XCS has been shown to solve hard problems in a machine-learning competitive way. Recent theoretical advancements show that the system can scale-up polynomially in the problem complexity and problem size given the problem is a k-DNF with certain properties. This paper addresses two major issues in XCS: (1) knowledge extraction and (2) structure identification. Knowledge extraction addresses the issue of mining problem knowledge from the final solution developed by XCS. The goal is to identify most important features in the problem and the dependencies among those features. The extracted knowledge may not only be used for further data mining, but may actually be re-fed into the system giving it further competence in solving problems in which dependent features, that is, building blocks, need to be processed effectively. This paper proposes to extract a feature dependency tree out of the developed rule-based problem representation of XCS. The investigations herein focus on Boolean function problems. The extension to nominal and real-valued features is discussed.

1 Introduction

Despite the original proposal of the schema notion by John Holland about three decades ago [1], learning classifier system (LCS) research has hardly addressed the importance of effective schemata processing nor was the effectiveness of the crossover operator addressed extensively. More recent research on genetic algorithms (GAs) suggests that in many problems – namely deceptive problems of bounded difficulty – identification and effective processing of interdependent substructures or schemata, the so called *building blocks* (BBs), is crucial for the success of the applied genetic algorithm [2,3].

The XCS classifier system, proposed by Wilson in 1995 [4], may be the most well-studied LCS to date. It has been shown that the system is able to solve typical data mining problems machine learning competitively [5–7]. Several theoretical advancements have been made recently bounding population size to ensure learning success with high probability [8,9]. Additionally, Wilson's original proposition that XCS may scale polynomially in problem size and problem complexity [10] was confirmed for boundedly difficult $k - DNF$ problems [11]. However, the analysis models learning time as a step-by-step process solely dependent on mutation. Also in XCS, effective BB identification or processing has hardly been addressed. This paper takes a step towards BB identification in XCS using a tree-construction mechanisms that identifies feature importance and interdependencies.

On the other hand, knowledge extraction was recently addressed in the XCS classifier system. Wilson [12] showed that most relevant rules can be extracted from the integer-based XCS system XCSI reducing the rule set by over 95% only marginally degrading performance. Dixon et. al. [13] further analyzed and enhanced the algorithm improving the complexity requirements. Both systems are data-driven in that they use the available training data set to reduce the final problem representation in XCS.

The algorithm proposed herein is not data driven – as the ones mentioned above – but solely considers the classifier population of XCS. Similar approaches for knowledge extraction in populations have already been used successfully for function optimization using genetic algorithms [14]. The algorithm extracts problem knowledge using a heuristic, specificity-based approach. For now, the proposed algorithm is restricted to the binary problem domain. We show that the algorithm does not reduce the accuracy of the final problem knowledge significantly. The resulting tree structure is easily readable and emphasizes the significance and dependency structure of each feature of the problem instances. Additionally, we show that the system clearly identifies the relevant interdependent features even early in a run making the algorithm a valuable candidate for BB identification and processing.

The paper is structured as follows. The next section provides a quick overview over XCS problem representation and learning. Next, we introduce the tree generation algorithm. The algorithm is applied on several typical Boolean function problems revealing its knowledge extraction capabilities as well as its BB identification capabilities. Finally, summary and conclusions are provided.

2 XCS Overview

The XCS classifier system was introduced in [4]. XCS is designed to solve classification problems as well as reinforcement learning problems. The system is learning while interacting online with an unknown problem.

XCS (as all other LCSs) represents the problem solution by a *population* of *classifiers*. At each time step, XCS receives a problem instance. Based on its current knowledge, XCS proposes a solution for the instance. Depending on the problem instance and the solution proposed, XCS receives numerical reward characterizing the goodness of the proposed solution. XCS exploits the incoming reward signal applying an accuracy-based genetic algorithm (GA) to evolve a complete, maximally accurate, and maximally general representation of the optimal problem solution. Accordingly, the learning is biased towards learning a complete representation of the action-value function underlying a particular problem described according to the typical reinforcement learning framework. For a complete introduction to the XCS system, the interested reader is referred to [4, 10, 15]. The remainder of this section gives a short introduction to the mechanisms crucial to ensure understanding of the rest of this paper.

This paper addresses XCS's performance on Boolean functions. A problem instance is coded by a string of l bits and belongs to one of two classes. Knowledge in XCS is represented by a population of rules – very similar to a disjunctive normal form – where each rule specifies one conjunctive term. Essentially, the sought accurate, maximally general problem solution can be represented in disjunctive normal form. Additional to the conjunctive term C (that is, the condition), a rule, or *classifier*, specifies the corresponding binary class A, a prediction of the consequent reward p, the mean absolute deviation of this prediction ϵ, and the fitness F, which estimates the mean relative accuracy of the classifier.

Given a problem instance S, a *match set* $[M]$ is formed consisting of all classifiers in $[P]$ whose conditions match S. The match set $[M]$ essentially represents the knowledge about the current problem instance. $[M]$ is used to decide on the classification on the current problem forming fitness-weighted reward predictions of each possible classification effectively generating a prediction array with entries

$$P(a_i) = \frac{\sum_{cl_k \in [M]|a_i} p_k \times F_k}{\sum_{cl_k \in [M]|a_i} F_k}, \qquad (1)$$

where $[M]|_{a_i}$ refers to the classifiers in $[M]$ that specify action a_i, p_k refers to the reward prediction, and F_k refers to the fitness of the k's classifier in $[M]|_{a_i}$. After the execution of the chosen classification A, and the resulting reward R, an *action set* $[A]$ is formed consisting of all classifiers in $[M]$ that specify the chosen action A. The reinforcement learning component, which updates classifier parameters, is applied in accordance to R. The genetic algorithms reproduces, mutates, and crosses high-fitness rules in $[A]$ and deletes inaccurate and well-supported rules in the population. Thus, the genetic algorithm is designed to evolve maximally accurate, maximally general classifiers.

3 Tree Generation of XCS Knowledge

As mentioned above, XCS is designed to evolve a complete, accurate, and maximally general solution to the provided problem. The solution is represented by a population of classifiers. Previous approaches tried to derive problem knowledge directly out of this rule-based solution representation. However, due to the continuous application of mutation and crossover, despite the generalization pressure in XCS [4, 8], the final population of XCS may still be rather large. In his original work, Wilson [4] proposed a condensation mechanism that reduces

Table 1. Description of the recursive tree generation algorithm.

```
GENERATE_TREE([S], Features):
 1 PA  ← GENERATE_PREDICTION_ARRAY([S])
 2 Class ← arg_max(PA)
 3 Feature ← GET_NEXT_FEATURE_TO_SPLIT([S], Features)
 4 if(Feature is null)
 5    return Leaf(Class)
 6 Features ← Features ∪ Feature
 7 SubTree(0) ← GENERATE_TREE([S.Feature=0], Features)
 8 SubTree(1) ← GENERATE_TREE([S.Feature=1], Features)
 9 SubTree(2) ← GENERATE_TREE([S.Feature=#], Features)
10 return Node(Class, [S], Feature, SubTree(0), SubTree(1), SubTree(2))
```

mutation and crossover rates once accuracy is reached. However, it is often difficult to assess when maximal accuracy is reached (especially in noisy problems). Another approach focuses on extracting rules based on data coverage [12]. The shown results showed promising compression of knowledge and the possibility of generating rules of thumb to express the knowledge. However, the general inter-dependency of the features in the problem remains somewhat obscured. Additionally, the data-dependence of the approaches seems somewhat unsatisfactory.

Our approach focuses on an explicit modeling of the feature dependencies using the current population of classifiers – the same approach used in evolutionary algorithms such as SI3E [14]. The algorithm recursively chooses the most specialized attribute of the available features in the classifier conditions and generates a node specifying the feature. Thus, specificity is used as an indicator of problem- or classification-significance of an attribute. The classifier set is then split into three subsets: the subsets of classifiers that code the chosen attribute as *zero*, *one*, and *don't care*. Next, the algorithm is called recursively for each of those subsets. If there is only one type of classification left in a subset of classifiers, or there is no further node found (because all nodes were split or because all non-split nodes have only don't care symbols), a leaf is created that specifies the class of the subtree choosing the maximum classification in the prediction array of the current subset as the class.

A formal algorithmic description of the recursive algorithm is provided in Table 1. [S] refers to the current subset of classifiers, Features is a set that includes all features which were already used in this subtree. The procedure GENERATE_PREDICTION_ARRAY returns the prediction array as specified in Equation 1 and the procedure GET_NEXT_FEATURE_TO_SPLIT returns the next most specific feature. A node contains information about its class (i.e., the class with the highest prediction array), its support set of classifiers, the feature it splits the support set on, and the three sub-trees which might be nodes and/or leafs.

To avoid the influence of young or unreliable classifiers, we filter the classifier population. Specifically, we generate a filtered classifier set that only contains classifiers that are experienced (they were evaluated more than θ_{exp} times), have a support of at least two ($num \geq 2$ consequently requiring at least one successful selection and reproduction), and have error smaller than 10_0. Additionally, we revert the class of all classifiers that satisfy the above constraints and have a reward prediction below 500. This is possible since there are only two problem classes and a classifier that essentially predicts zero reward predicts the other class (closed-world assumption).

As can be inferred from the algorithm, the complexity is quadratic in the number of features and linear in the population size $O(l^2 N)$. The maximum depth of the tree equals l (when splitting on all attributes), and on each level in the tree the whole population is searched for the current most specific attributes (excluding the attributes already split on). The size of the tree is bounded by $O(lN)$ since each level in the tree needs to maximally store the whole population once (each node in a level stores a part of the whole population). Since Wilson's and Dixon's algorithms depend on the data size, the comparison is difficult. However, note that N itself grows in l as well as in the complexity of the problem [11] and is generally much larger than l and thus dominates the factor l^2. Since also learning time grows in l as well as in problem complexity [16], tree generation is a minor computational effort compared to the learning process.

The resulting tree can also be used as a classifier by itself. However, a slight problem shows up with respect to the don't care branch. Given a problem instance and a node that splits on a particular attribute, should the classification algorithm descent the specified attribute path or the don't care path? Our algorithm makes this decision by counting the support of classifiers in both sub-paths. The branch is chosen in which more classifiers of the corresponding support set match the given problem instance. If a node has less than five (micro-) classifier representatives, the class of this node is chosen as the classification.

The next section will elaborate on the proposed algorithm investigating structure and accuracy of the resulting tree.

4 Structure Extraction

This section investigates how well the generated tree can be used to visualize problem structure as well as how compact the resulting representation is. To do this, we investigate three Boolean function problems: (1) the multiplexer problem [4], (2) a carry problem, and (3) a hierarchical parity-multiplexer problem. The three problems are non-overlapping (accurate, maximally general sub-solutions are non-overlapping), overlapping, unbalanced (accurate, maximally general sub-solutions have a different number of attributes specified), and hierarchically structured, respectively.

4.1 Multiplexer Problem

The multiplexer is a Boolean function problem widely studied in LCS research [4, 17, 5]. The problem is defined for binary strings of length $k + 2^k$. The output is determined by the bit located at the position referred to by the binary value of k *position bits*.

Figure 2(a) shows the resulting tree of the 11-multiplexer problem running the problem for 50,000 problem instances to assure complete convergence. It can be inferred that the tree represents the problem structure perfectly when descending the zero and one branches only. The don't care branches may be regarded as irrelevant but actually convey additional information. Descending down the don't care path on the most left 2=0 node, we can see that XCS also "knows" that if attribute two is ignored but attribute four and six are zero, the output will be zero.

A statistical analysis of 100 runs in the multiplexer problem showed that the conversion to the tree representation does not decrease the accuracy of the classification (all 100 runs showed equal 100% performance). Even when decreasing the population size to $N = 1500$ and the number of learning steps to $30,000$, at which point the accuracy of the knowledge is at a level of about 90%, no significant statistical difference was found between the filtered population and the induced tree – paired t-test and Wilcoxon rank sum test present confidence values greater than 99%. Moreover, results show that the tree removes noisy spurious interactions, providing a stable description of the evolved knowledge in the population.

4.2 Carry Problem

The carry problem is defined by two equally long sub-strings which are added together. If the result has a carry, then the output is one otherwise the output is zero. The different conjunctions that form the solution are (1) overlapping, and (2) do not have the same order. More general conjunctions will match more often and consequently are expected to be expressed by a larger number of classifiers.

The tree generated out of the final population of XCS in the (2,2)-carry problem accurately identified classes of all sub-problems (not shown). In this case, no spurious nodes can be found. Statistical analysis – using the previously introduced t-test and Wilcoxon – confirmed the robustness of the tree generation. Averaged over 100 experiments, there were no statistically significant differences detected between the classification accuracy of the filtered population and the tree with confidence values greater than 99.5%

4.3 Building Block Identification

As the final problem, we construct another Boolean function problem that requires a competent crossover operators to learn efficiently [18]. The problem is structured hierarchically in that the evaluation is pursued in two stages. We combine a parity problem on the lower level with a multiplexer problem on the higher level. The result of the lower level parity function results in a shorter bit string which is then evaluated by the higher level function multiplexer. For example, consider the hierarchical 2-parity, 3-multiplexer problem. The problem is six bits long. On the lower level, blocks of two bits are evaluated by the parity function, that is, if there are an even number of ones, the result will be zero and one otherwise. The result is a string of three bits that is then evaluated by the 3-multiplexer function. The result is the class of the problem instance. For example, the hierarchical 2-parity, 3-multiplexer problem can be written in disjunctive normal form as follows:

$$2\text{-PA},3\text{-MP}(x_1, x_2, x_3, x_4, x_5, x_6) = x_1 x_2 \neg x_3 x_4 \vee x_1 x_2 x_3 \neg x_4 \vee \neg x_1 \neg x_2 \neg x_3 x_4 \vee$$
$$\neg x_1 \neg x_2 x_3 \neg x_4 \vee \neg x_1 x_2 \neg x_5 x_6 \vee \neg x_1 x_2 x_5 \neg x_6 \vee x_1 \neg x_2 \neg x_5 x_6 \vee x_1 \neg x_2 x_5 \neg x_6 \quad (2)$$

Figure 1 show a graphical example of how this problem is extended to a hierarchical 3-parity 6-multiplexer. In [18], we showed that larger instances of this hierarchical problem are very difficult to solve for XCS. Crossover seems to continuously disrupt the found lower-level building blocks so that effective processing of the blocks is impossible. However, we also showed that when applying building-block wise uniform crossover (effectively preventing building block disruption), XCS is able to solve the problem. Thus, for larger hierarchical problems, an operator is necessary to identify and process building blocks.

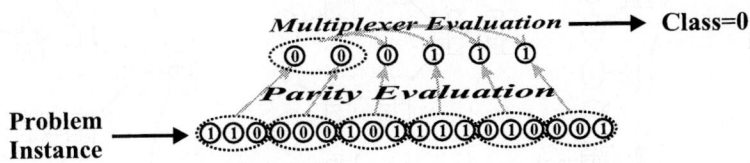

Fig. 1. Combined 3-Parity / 6-Multiplexer Problem.

Figure 2(b) shows the tree generated out of the filtered, converged population in the hierarchical 2-parity, 3-multiplexer problem (that is still solvable with XCS and uniform crossover). Clearly, the tree identifies the dependency of the two parity blocks. Note that the *don't care* branch considers the other two parities and correctly specifies the function outcome in most of those cases. However, since the coverage of the left branches is higher, the hash-branch won't be used for classification. There is also a spurious node (node 3=0 on the left lower side of the tree) that does not influence performance because all branches correctly identify the class as zero.

Finally, we generated a tree in the hierarchical 3-parity, 6-multiplexer problem, which XCS is not able to solve in 500,000 steps even with a population size of 20,000 (performance is at around 65% at that point) when uniform crossover is applied or low mutation rate used. However, XCS with a BB-wise uniform crossover (explicitly preventing the disruption of the parity blocks, exchanging BBs uniformly randomly) is able to solve the problem with the provided resources. The question is if we are able to identify the parity blocks by the means of the tree generation mechanism. Figure 2(c) shows the tree (restricted to depth four and suppressing the hash branches on all levels except for at the root) generated out of the filtered population after 80,000 steps. Whereas XCS's performance at this point is at only 59%, parity blocks (13,14,15) and (7,8,9) are identified by the tree generation mechanism. The tree generation mechanism seems to be able to extract lower-level problem structure that XCS learned albeit XCS is not able to process (that is, propagate and recombine) the lower

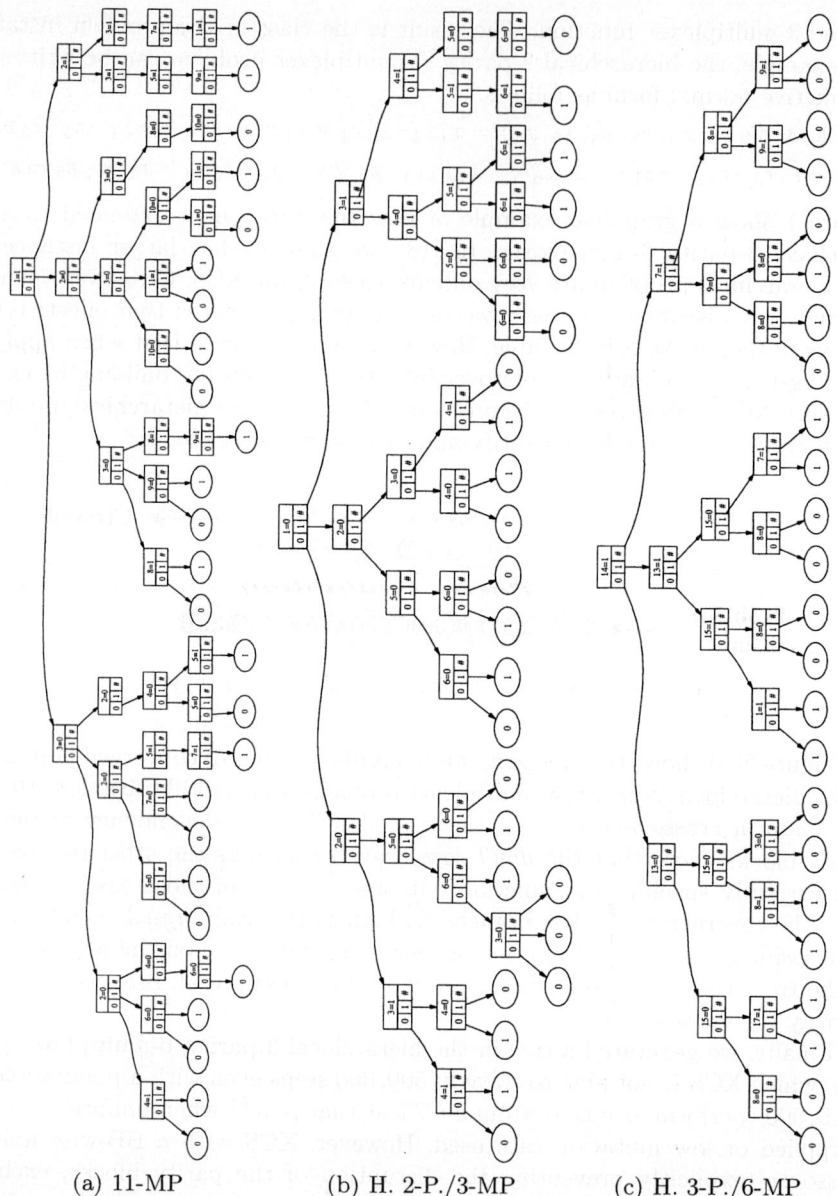

Fig. 2. Each node in a tree specifies the attribute it splits on and the class of the node (attribute=class). The leafs specify the resulting class. **(a)** Tree for the 11-multiplexer problem. **(b)** Tree for the hierarchical 2-parity/3-multiplexer problem. **(c)** Upper part of the tree (plotting up to depth four, suppressing the don't care branches except for at the root) in the hierarchical 3-parity/6-multiplexer problem.

level structure effectively. Thus, we hope to be able to extract the dependencies detected by the tree generation mechanism and propagate building blocks more effectively similar to the competent genetic algorithms such as the extended compact GA [19] or probabilistic model building GAs [20].

5 Conclusions

This paper has addressed two major issues in XCS: (1) knowledge extraction and (2) structure identification. Knowledge extraction addresses the issue of mining problem knowledge from the final solution developed by XCS. The goal was to identify most important features in the problem, as well as the dependencies among those features. Such behavior has two promising applications: (1) obtain a compact representation of the evolved knowledge, and (2) identify the *building blocks* of the problem. One main contribution of our approach is being population-driven instead of data-driven.

We have mainly focused on extracting a compact representation based on the knowledge evolved by XCS. Results show a remarkable ability to obtain compact descriptions out of the final population of classifiers without any significant degradations of the overall accuracy. However, our tree-based approach aims a much broader application: the creation of a first *building block* processing LCS. In order to achieve such purpose our current work is focusing on using the identified *building blocks* in XCS to create a first competent LCS.

Acknowledgments

This work was sponsored by the Air Force Office of Scientific Research, Air Force Materiel Command, USAF (F49620-03-1-0129), and by the Technology Research, Education, and Commercialization Center (TRECC), at University of Illinois at Urbana-Champaign, administered by the National Center for Supercomputing Applications (NCSA) and funded by the Office of Naval Research (N00014-01-1-0175).

References

1. Holland, J.H.: Adaptation in Natural and Artificial Systems. University of Michigan Press, Ann Arbor, MI (1975) second edition 1992.
2. Goldberg, D.E.: The race, the hurdle and the sweet spot: Lessons from genetic algorithms for the automation of innovation and creativity. In Bentley, P., ed.: Evolutionary design by computers. Morgan Kaufmann, San Francisco, CA (1999) 105–118
3. Goldberg, D.E.: The Design of Innovation: Lessons from and for Competent Genetic Algorithms. Kluwer Academic Publishers, Boston, MA (2002)
4. Wilson, S.W.: Classifier fitness based on accuracy. Evolutionary Computation **3** (1995) 149–175

5. Bernadó, E., Llorà, X., Garrell, J.M.: XCS and GALE: A comparative study of two learning classifier systems and six other learning algorithms on classification tasks. In Lanzi, P.L., Stolzmann, W., Wilson, S.W., eds.: Advances in learning classifier systems: Fourth international workshop, IWLCS 2001 (LNAI 2321). Springer-Verlag, Berlin Heidelberg (2002) 115–132
6. Bernadó-Mansilla, E., Garrell-Guiu, J.M.: Accuracy-based learning classifier systems: Models, analysis, and applications to classification tasks. Evolutionary Computation **11** (2003) 209–238
7. Dixon, P.W., Corne, D.W., Oates, M.J.: A preliminary investigation of modified XCS as a generic data mining tool. In Lanzi, P.L., Stolzmann, W., Wilson, S.W., eds.: Advances in learning classifier systems: Fourth international workshop, IWLCS 2001 (LNAI 2321). Springer-Verlag, Berlin Heidelberg (2002) 133–150
8. Butz, M.V., Kovacs, T., Lanzi, P.L., Wilson, S.W.: Toward a theory of generalization and learning in XCS. IEEE Transactions on Evolutionary Computation **8** (2004) 28–46
9. Butz, M.V., Goldberg, D.E., Tharakunnel, K.: Analysis and improvement of fitness exploitation in XCS: Bounding models, tournament selection, and bilateral accuracy. Evolutionary Computation **11** (2003) 239–277
10. Wilson, S.W.: Generalization in the XCS classifier system. Genetic Programming 1998: Proceedings of the Third Annual Conference (1998) 665–674
11. Butz, M.V., Goldberg, D.E., Lanzi, P.L.: PAC Learning in XCS. IlliGAL report 2004011, Illinois Genetic Algorithms Laboratory, University of Illinois at Urbana-Champaign (2004)
12. Wilson, S.W.: Compact rulesets from XCSI. In Lanzi, P.L., Stolzmann, W., Wilson, S.W., eds.: Advances in learning classifier systems: Fourth international workshop, IWLCS 2001 (LNAI 2321). Springer-Verlag, Berlin Heidelberg (2002) 196–208
13. Dixon, P.W., Corne, D.W., Oates, M.J.: A ruleset reduction algorithm for the xcs learning classifier system. In Lanzi, P.L., Stolzmann, W., Wilson, S.W., eds.: Proceedings of the Fifth International Workshop on Learning Classifier Systems, IWLCS 2002. Springer-Verlag, Berlin Heidelberg (in press)
14. Llorà, X., Goldberg, D.E.: Wise breeding ga via machine learning techniques for function optimization. Proceedings of the Fifth Genetic and Evolutionary Computation Conference (GECCO-2003) (2003) 1172–1183
15. Butz, M.V., Wilson, S.W.: An algorithmic description of XCS. Soft Computing **6** (2002) 144–153
16. Butz, M.V., Goldberg, D.E., Lanzi, P.L.: Bounding Learning Time in XCS. IlliGAL report 2004003, Illinois Genetic Algorithms Laboratory, University of Illinois at Urbana-Champaign (2004)
17. De Jong, K.A., Spears, W.M.: Learning concept classification rules using genetic algorithms. IJCAI-91 Proceedings of the Twelfth International Conference on Artificial Intelligence (1991) 651–656
18. Butz, M.V., Goldberg, D.E.: Hierarchical Classification Problems Demand Effective Building Block Identification and Processing in LCSs. IlliGAL report 2004017, Illinois Genetic Algorithms Laboratory, University of Illinois at Urbana-Champaign (2004)
19. Harik, G.: Linkage learning via probabilistic modeling in the ecga. IlliGAL report 99010, Illinois Genetic Algorithms Laboratory, University of Illinois at Urbana-Champaign (1999)
20. Pelikan, M., Goldberg, D.E., Lobo, F.: A survey of optimization by building and using probabilistic models. Computational Optimization and Applications **21** (2002) 5–20

Forecasting Time Series by Means of Evolutionary Algorithms

Cristóbal Luque del Arco-Calderón,
Pedro Isasi Viñuela, and Julio César Hernández Castro

Universidad Carlos III de Madrid, C/Butarque 15, E-28911 Leganés, Spain
{cluque,isasi,jcesar}@inf.uc3m.es
http://www.uc3m.es

Abstract. The time series forecast is a very complex problem, consisting in predicting the behaviour of a data series with only the information of the previous sequence. There is many physical and artificial phenomenon that can be described by time series. The prediction of such phenomenon could be very complex. For instance, in the case of tide forecast, unusually high tides, or sea surges, result from a combination of chaotic climatic elements in conjunction with the more normal, periodic, tidal systems associated with a particular area. Too much variables influence the behaviour of the water level. Our problem is not only to find prediction rules, we also need to discard the noise and select the representative data. Our objective is to generate a set of prediction rules. There are many methods tying to achieve good predictions. In most of the cases this methods look for general rules that are able to predict the whole series. The problem is that usually the time series has local behaviours that don't allow a good level of prediction when using general rules. In this work we present a method for finding local rules able to predict only some zones of the series but achieving better level prediction. This method is based on the evolution of set of rules genetically codified, and following the Michigan approach. For evaluating the proposal, two different domains have been used: an artificial domain widely use in the bibliography (Mackey-Glass series) and a time series corresponding to a natural phenomenon, the water level in Venice Lagoon.

1 Introduction

Time series consists on a data sequence of measures along a time period:

$$y_1, y_2, ..., y_D$$

where the sub-index represents each unit of time. The goal is to predict the values of the series for $i' > D$. In other words, we use the set $\{y_1, \ldots, y_D\}$ to predict $y_{D+\tau}$, where τ is a non negative integer, which receives the name of prediction horizon. In time series related to real phenomenon we have and additional handicap: the measures may have noise. For example, an unusual hard wind will produce unusual measures. A good model needs to detect which elements in the data set can generate knowledge and refuse those that are noise. In this work we developed a model, based on genetic algorithms to search for good rules to detect local behaviours in a time series that allow to improve the prediction level in that area.

This results are applied to predict two examples: The Mackey-Glass series [11][14] as example of artificial series (without noise) and a example of real series extracted from the measures of the water level in the Venice Lagoon.

This problem had been usually approached by means of neural networks. These approaches have mainly used Radial Bases Function Neural Networks [11], with an algorithm that allows to change the net configuration, where neurons are added as needed, during the learning process. In [14], the algorithm combines the growth criterion of the resource-allocating network (RAN) of Platt [11], with a pruning strategy based on the relative contribution of each hidden unit to the overall network output. The resulting network leads toward a minimal topology for the RBFNN. Both papers, [14] and [11], show the results of applying that approach to the Mackey-Glass series. In [15] we can find a time series analysis using nonlinear dynamic systems theory and multilayer neural networks models. This strategy is applied to the time sequence of water level data, recorded from Venice Lagoon during the years 1980-1994. Recent works [5, 13], use a learning method that automatically selects the more appropriated training patterns to the new sample to be predicted. This training method follows a lazy learning strategy, in the sense that it builds approximations centered around the novel sample. Galvan et al. [5] applies his method for the Mackey-Glass, and for the Venice Lagoon time series. Following the Packard's work to predict dynamical systems [10], [8], [9], and using genetic algorithms [4] to generate predictions rules on a time series, we have applied some advanced genetic algorithms' techniques to attain better results. In the experiments explained in this paper, the constants D and τ use the values $D = 24$, and $\tau = 1, 4, 12, 24, 28, 48, 72, 96$. In other words, we use the value of water level along 24 hours to predict the water level 1,4,12... etc. hours later.

2 Genetic Encoding of Rules for Time Series Forecasting

As example of artificial series we selected the Mackey-Glass Series, due to the extensive bibliography about it [11][14]. The chaotic time series known as Mackey-Glass series is defined by the following time-delay ordinary differential equation:

$$\frac{ds(t)}{dt} = -bs(t) + a\frac{s(t-\lambda)}{1 + s(t-\lambda)^{10}}$$

with $a = 0.2$, $b = 0.1$ and $\lambda = 17$.

For our model we want to generate rules that make predictions. For the examples in this paper we use a value $D = 5$. A rule is an assert as "if the series at time unit 1 is smaller than 100 and bigger than 50, at time unit 2 is smaller than 90 and bigger than 40, at time unit 3 is smaller than 5 and bigger than -10,

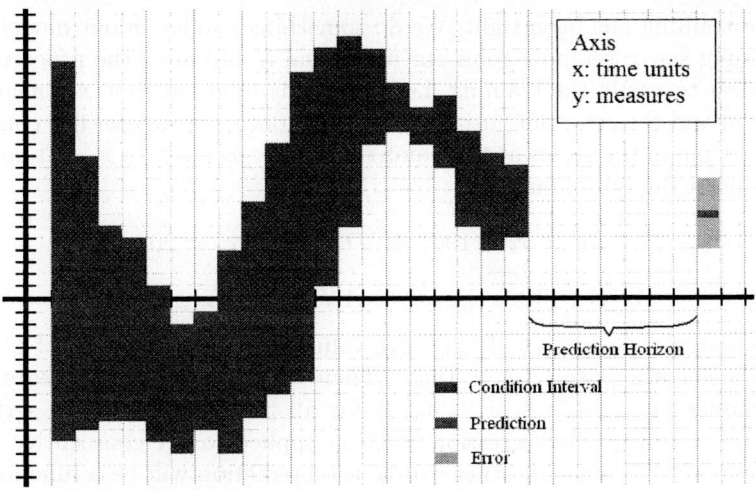

Fig. 1. Graphical representation of a rule.

at time unit 5 is smaller than 100 and bigger than 1, then the measure at time unit 5+τ will be 33 with an error of 5". It could be expressed as

$$IF\ (50 < x_1 < 100)\ AND\ (40 < x_2 < 90)\ AND\ (-10 < x_3 < 5)$$

$$AND\ (1 < x_5 < 100)\ THEN\ prediction = 33 + / - 5$$

We can represent graphically a rule as in figure 1.
We encode this information in an individual as

$$(50, 100, 40, 90, -10, 5, dc, dc, 1, 100, 33, 5)$$

where dc means "don't care". Now we apply the genetic algorithms' paradigm. Two individuals can generate an offspring. This offspring inherits each gene from one parent. A gene is a pair (LL, UL), where LL is the lower limit for a time instant, and UL is the upper limit for the same instant. In other words, the offspring receives a gene from a parent with equal probability for each time instant. The offspring doesn't inherit parent's predictions and errors. We can see an example above:

Parent 1: $(50, 100, 40, 90, -10, 5, dc, dc, 1, 100, 33, 5)$
Parent 2: $(\mathbf{60, 90, 10, 20, 15, 30, 40, 45}, dc, dc, \mathbf{60, 8})$
Offspring: $(50, 100, \mathbf{10, 20}, -10, 5, \mathbf{40, 45}, dc, dc, ?, ?)$

Obviously, the offspring's "prediction" and "error" are not assigned (and appeared as "?" in the above representation). Once generated, an offspring may suffer mutation of some gene. At this point we need to divide the data set in two subsets: a training set and a test set, as we do with neural networks. In Neural Networks we use the training set to train the net, and we use the test set to verify that the training has been right. We do something similar in our model: we use the training set to see how good our individual is and after the process, we use the test set to verify the training. Let C an individual, at first we calculate the prediction and the error of C using the training data: we look for five consecutive values of time in the series at the point i, $(x_i, x_{i+1}, x_{i+2}, x_{i+3}, x_{i+4})$ that fits the conditions of the individual:

$$(50 < x_i < 100) \ AND \ (10 < x_{i+1} < 20)$$

$$AND \ (-10 < x_{i+2} < 5) \ AND \ (40 < x_{i+3} < 45)$$

and we assign $v_i = x_{i+4+\tau}$. If this five values fits the conditions of C, we say $C(i) = true$, otherwise $C(i) = false$. Then we make a multiple regression on the variables $(x_i, x_{i+1}, x_{i+2}, x_{i+3}, x_{i+4})$ for all the points i of the series. The prediction p_i will be the regression function applied to five consecutive values if and only if $C(i) = true$. In other words, the prediction will be a function of the form

$$p_i(x_i, x_{i+1}, x_{i+2}, x_{i+3}, x_{i+4}) = a_0 x_i + a_1 x_{i+1} + a_2 x_{i+2} + a_3 x_{i+3} + a_4 x_{i+4}$$

where a_j are constants, for $j = 1, ..., 4$. Then, for each point i in the time series in which $(x_i, x_{i+1}, x_{i+2}, x_{i+3}, x_{i+4})$ fits the conditions of the individual (i.e. $C(i) = true$), we will have a real value v_i and a prediction p_i. So, the error we use is the maximum absolute error, e, of each prediction to the real value for all the points, i, that fit the conditions of the individual. In other words:

$$e = Max_i\{|p_i - v_i| \ | \ C(i)\}$$

In our model we look for individuals which can predict the maximum number of points with the minimum error possible. The fitness function we used was:

```
IF ((N_C>1) AND (e < VAR_MAX)) THEN
     fitness = (N_C*10) - e
ELSE
     fitness = f_min
```

where C is the individual, and N_C is the number of data points in the training data set satisfying the conditions of C (in other words, $N_C = \sharp\{i|C(i)\}$). VAR_MAX is a constant that makes the fitness function punishes individuals with a variance greater than VAR_MAX. f_min is a minimal value assigned to the individual when the rule is not fitted.

3 Evolution of Simple Rules

We cannot use an standard genetic algorithm, because of the fact that the medium values of the series have more data points than the extreme points or unusual set of data (for example an unusual high tide in the Venice Lagoon) deletes the individuals which makes predictions for that values of data, and the population becomes dominated by individuals which predicts medium values of the series. We decided to use a Michigan's approach [2] using a Steady-State strategy. In the Michigan's approach, the solution to the problem is the total population instead of only one individual. In the Pittsburgh approach [12] [7] [3], the solution to the problem is the best individual of the population, which chromosome encode a set of rules. We decided to use a Michigan's approach because in a complex time series we can find a lot of rules, and for the Pittsburgh approach this produces very big individuals that consume lot of memory and make his fitness evaluation too slow. We apply the Michigan's approach selecting each generation only two parents by three rounds trial to generate only one offspring. Then we replace the nearest individual to the offspring in phenotypic distance. That is, we find the individual whose prediction is nearest to the offspring's prediction, and replace it by the offspring if and only if the offspring fitness is better than the individual's fitness. If this doesn't happen, there isn't any change this generation. That strategy generates a diverse population, in which each individual makes a prediction different to the others individuals, instead of genetic clones of the best individual, produced by the standard genetic algorithm method. Finally, after each execution of the model (75.000 generations), we store in a file, that we called "pool", the individuals which predicts more than 5 points in the training set (and not only one as we do in a standard genetic algorithm model), an execute again the process. After some executions we have a file with a set of individuals. Some individuals predicts the same points of the test set, so the final prediction is the mean of all predictions (we must remember that, possibly, not all the individuals could predict a point of the series).

The last step is to generate the initial population of individuals. We divide the prediction range (i.e., $(-50, 150)$ for the water level) in 40 intervals of 5 centimeters. We create a "void" individual for each interval. For example, for interval $(40, 45)$ we have the "void" individual:

$$(150, -50, 150, -50, 150, -50, 150, -50, 150, -50, ?, ?)$$

Clearly, the upper limit for this "void" individual is -50, and the lower limit is 150, so this individual's rules cannot be complied at any point of the time series. Then we search for all time unit t in the training set the measures $m(t)$ such $m(t) \in (40, 45)$, and adjust the void individual for this interval by this way: we take the 5 measures in the interval of time $[t - 4 - \tau, t - \tau]$, and for all $n \in [1, 5]$ we adjust each hour of the void individual: if the upper limit for the n hour of the individual is lower than the measure of the $t - \tau - 5 + n$ time unit, $m(t - \tau - 5 + n)$, we take the measure as upper limit; if the lower limit for the n hour of the individual is greater than the measure of the $t - \tau - 5 + n$ time unit, $m(t - \tau - 5 + n)$, we take the measure as lower limit. We repeat the process for each hour and for each interval to generate the initial population of 40 individuals.

4 Results

In Table 1 we compare our results with the results obtained in [15] for the high tides prediction in the Venice Lagoon. The experiments have been done with a training data set of 45.000 measures, along 75.000 generations, and the predictions on a data set of 10.000 measures. Individuals use the measures of 24 hours to predict the water level a number of hours equal to the prediction horizon. The individuals in the pool is the number on individuals that we obtained after some executions. "Percentage of prediction" is the percentage of points in the test series which can be predicted by, at least, an individual in the pool. The rest of points cannot be predicted by anyone individual. The error in Table 1, column RMS and in [15] is the root mean square prediction error, where the error is

$$e = \frac{1}{2}(x - \bar{x})^2$$

Table 1. Comparative of predictions for the tides of the Venice Lagoon.

Prediction Horizon	Individuals in the pool	Percentage of prediction	MAE	NRMS	RMS	Error in [15]
1	10412	91,3%	4,22	0,12	3,37	3,30
1	3475	97,2%	5,54	0,15	4,30	3,30
4	3254	99,1%	10,10	0,29	8,26	9,55
12	3227	98,0%	10,35	0,30	8,46	11,38
24	3200	99,3%	10,60	0,31	8,70	11,64
28	3038	98,8%	13,93	0,41	11,62	15,74
48	3076	97,8%	13,19	0,40	11,28	-
72	2870	99,7%	16,99	0,51	14,45	-
96	2613	99,5%	19,08	0,57	16,04	-

The results of the error show an improvement of the prediction level starting from a prediction horizon of 4, and show similar results for a prediction horizon of 1. In all the cases, it has been tried to maximize the percentage of the series that could be predicted by the method. With lower levels of series predicted, even better results, in terms of error, could be reached. It is interesting to remark that, even when the prediction horizon grows up, the number of rules are, more or less, similar,and the percentage of prediction does not decrease. The method seems, therefore, to be stable to the variations of prediction horizon. This property is very interesting, because it points out that the rules are adapted to special and local features of the series. Additionally, it can be seen that as the prediction horizon grows up, less rules are needed to predict even higher percentage of the series. All this without affect, significantly the error committed.

The error in column MAE is the mean of the absolute error. The NRMS error is the normalized RMS error. All errors are measured in centimeters. In Table 1 two experiments with prediction horizon 1 are showed. In the first experiment a value of 12 for the constant VAR_MAX is used. In the second one a value of

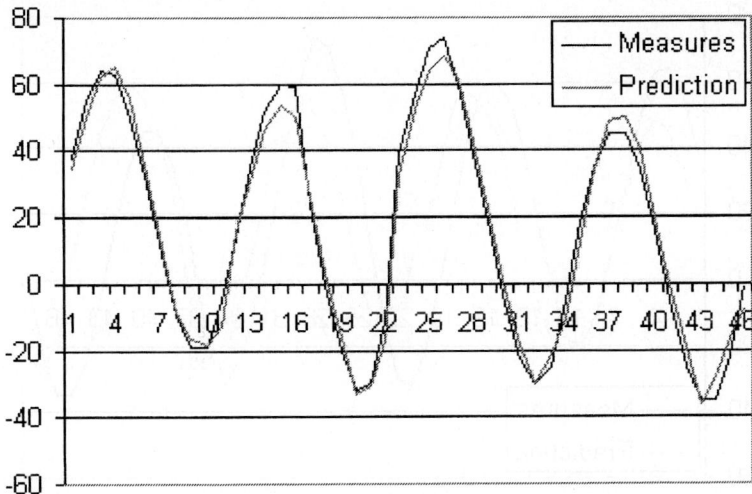

Fig. 2. Prediction of water level with horizon 1.

20 is used. A lower value causes the need of more individuals to increase the percentage of prediction, but decreases the mean error. A greater value for the constant VAR_MAX obtain a greater mean error but we need less individuals for a greater percentage of prediction.

In Table 2 the results of a cross-validation are shown. The total set of data has 50.000 measures of the level water.

Table 2. Cross-validation.

Training Set	Prediction Set	Percentage of prediction	Error (MAE)	Error (RMS)
[0, 30.000]	[30.000, 50.000]	99,1%	5,67	4,33
[10.000, 40.000]	[0, 10.000]∪[40.000, 50.000]	98,9%	5,78	4,45
[20.000, 50.000]	[0, 20.000]	98,7%	5,79	4,45

In graphs 2 and 3 we can see how our model predicts the water level of for a prediction horizon of 1 and 12 hours.

In graph 4 we can see how our model predicts the water level of Venice in a case of abnormally high tides for a prediction horizon 1.

In table 3 we have compared of our algorithm with the results in [11] for the Makey-Glass series with prediction horizon of 85, and the results in [14].

5 Conclusions

Our model uses some very interesting tricks to better face the time series forecasting problem, even though the measures could contains noise. Our model not

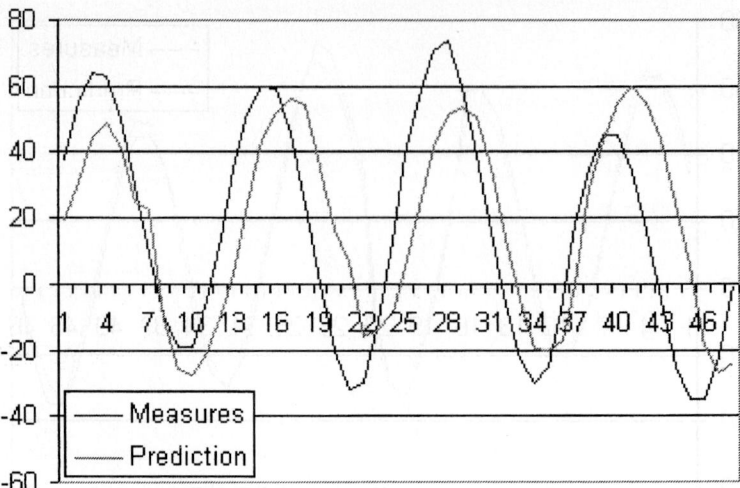

Fig. 3. Prediction of water level with horizon 12.

Table 3. Mackey-Glass series comparative.

Prediction Horizon	Individuals in the pool	Percentage of prediction	Error	Error in [14]	Error in [11]
50	3416	78,9 %	0,025	0,040	-
85	2582	78,2 %	0,046	-	0,050

only gives us predictions, it can also tell as when an abnormal measure is coming. For example, when the percentage of prediction is around a 99% and there isn't any individual to predict for a measure sequence, our model tells us that an abnormal behavior of the series is approaching. Additionally, the model is able to make much better predictions in situations than, being normal, are very unusual. This is due to the fact that the model do not try to generalize all the series, by the opposite it construct small set of rules that better adapt to all situations in a local way.

By increasing the percentage of series predicted, the method performs as any traditional method of generalization, that is, taken into account the whole series to make predictions. In the case that a reduction of the mean of the global error was needed, our approach could be also useful increasing the number of rules allowed. If, by the opposite, it is important to better predict exceptional situations, even though the global error is worse, the system could be adjusted to do so.

Another important feature of this approach, is that the method is able to find the regions of the series, where the behaviour is far from being generalizable. When the series contains regions that have some special particularities, that are different one each other, the method, not only finds this regions, but it constructs particular rules for better predict this special regions.

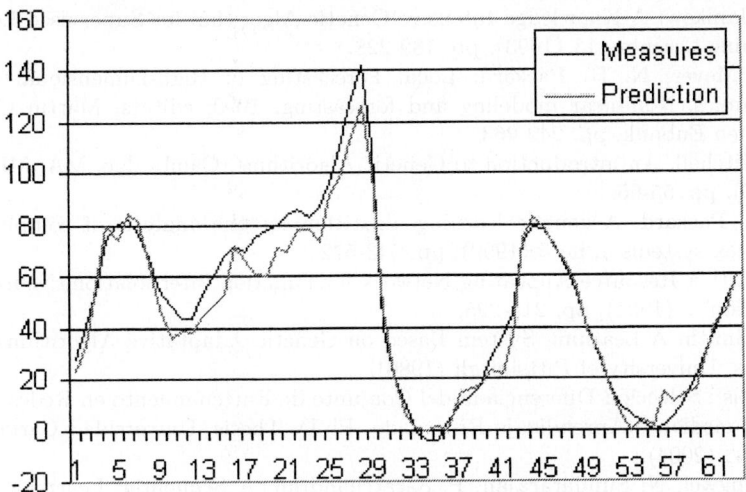

Fig. 4. Prediction of a high tide with horizon 1.

The method is also easily generalizable to others domains different from times series. In particular all domains of inductive learning, where many training examples could be obtained, are susceptible of applying our approach. We are now in the way of modifying the representation schemata of the rules, to makes it more complex and more complete.

Acknowledgements

Investigation supported by the Spanish Ministry of Science and Technology through the TRACER project under contract TIC2002-04498-C05-4

References

1. T. Bäck, H.P. Schwefel.: Evolutionary Algorithms: Some Very Old Strategies for Optimization and Adaptation. In Perret-Gallix (1992), pp. 247-254.
2. L.B. Booker, D.E. Goldberg, J.H. Holland: Classifier Systems and Genetic Algorithms. Artificial Intelligence No 40 (1989), pp. 235-282.
3. K.A. De Jong, W.M. Spears, F.D. Gordon: Usign Genetic Algorithms for Concept Learning. Machine Learning 13 (1993), pp. 198-228.
4. D.B. Fogel: An introduction to simulated evolutionary optimization. IEEE transactions on neural networks, vol 5, n 1, jan 1994.
5. I.M. Galván, P. Isasi, R. Aler, J.M. Valls: A selective learning method to improve the generalization of multilayer feedforward neural networks. International Journal of Neural Systems, Vol 11, No 2 (2001), pp. 167-177.
6. J.H. Holland: Adaptation in Natural and Artificial Systems. University of Michigan Press (1975).

7. C.Z Janikow: A Knowledge Intensive Genetic Algorithm for Supervised Learning. Machine Learning 13 (1993), pp. 189-228.
8. T.P. Meyer, N. H. Packard: Local Forecasting of High-Dimensional Chaotic Dynamics, Nonlinear modeling and forecasting. 1990; editors, Martin Casdagli, Stephen Eubank, pp. 249-263.
9. M. Mitchell: An introduction to Genetic Algorithms, Cambridge, MA: MIT Press (1996), pp. 55-65.
10. N. H. Packard: A genetic learning algorithm for the analysis of complex data. complex systems 4, no 5 (1990), pp. 543-572.
11. J. Platt: A Resource-Allocating Network for Function Interpolation. Neural Computation, 3 (1991), pp. 213-225.
12. S.F. Smith: A Learning System Based on Genetic Adaptative Algorithms. Ph.D. Thesis, University of Pittsburgh (1980).
13. J. Valls : Selección Diferenciada del Conjunto de Entrenamiento en Redes de Neuronas mediante Aprendizaje Retardado. Ph.D. Thesis, Universidad Carlos III de Madrid (2004).
14. L. Yingwei, N. Sundararajan, P. Saratchandran. A Sequential Learning Scheme for Function Aproximation using Minimal Radial Basis Function Neural Networks. Neural Computation, 9 (1997), pp. 461-478.
15. J.M. Zaldívar, E. Gutiérrez, I.M. Galván, F. Strozzi, A. Tomasin: Forecasting high waters an Venice Lagoon using chaotic time series analysis and nonlinear neural network. Journal of Hydroinformatics 02.1 (2000), pp. 61-84.

Detecting and Pruning Introns for Faster Decision Tree Evolution

Jeroen Eggermont, Joost N. Kok, and Walter A. Kosters

Leiden Institute of Advanced Computer Science
Universiteit Leiden
P.O. Box 9512, 2300 RA Leiden
The Netherlands
{jeggermo,joost,kosters}@liacs.nl

Abstract. We show how the understandability and speed of genetic programming classification algorithms can be improved, without affecting the classification accuracy. By analyzing the decision trees evolved we can remove the unessential parts, called *introns*, from the discovered decision trees. Since the resulting trees contain only useful information they are smaller and easier to understand. Moreover, by using these pruned decision trees in a fitness cache we can significantly reduce the number of unnecessary fitness calculations.

1 Introduction

Algorithms for data classification are generally assessed on how well they can classify one or more data sets. However, good classification performance alone is not always enough. Almost equally important can be the understandability of the results and the time it takes to learn to classify a data set. In this paper we focus on ways to improve the speed of our genetic programming (GP) algorithms as well as the understandability of the evolved decision trees.

Evolutionary algorithms generally spend a lot of time on calculating the fitness of the individuals. However, if one looks at the individuals during an evolutionary run, one often finds that some of the genotypes occur more than once. The main reason for this is that generally the diversity in a population decreases over time when a static fitness function is used. We can use these genotypical reoccurrences to speed-up the fitness calculations by storing each evaluated individual and its fitness in a *fitness cache*. If an individual's genotype is already stored in the cache then its fitness can simply be retrieved from the cache instead of the time consuming calculation which would otherwise be needed.

One of the problems of variable length evolutionary algorithms, such as tree-based genetic programming, is that the genotypes of the individuals tend to increase in size until they reach the maximum allowed size. This phenomenon is, in genetic programming, commonly referred to as *bloat* [1] and is caused by GP *introns* [1–3]. The term *introns* was first introduced in the field of genetic programming, and evolutionary computation in general, by Angeline [4] who compared the emergence of extraneous code in variable length GP structures to biological introns. In biology the term introns is used for parts of the DNA, sometimes referred to as junk DNA, which do not have any apparent function as they are not transcribed to RNA. In genetic programming, the term *introns* is used to indicate parts of an evolved solution which do not influence the result produced by, and thus fitness of, the solution (other than increasing its size).

The occurrence of *introns* in evolutionary algorithms has both positive and negative effects. A positive effect is that they might protect against the destructive effects of crossover operators [1]. However, earlier studies [2,3] show that more than 40% of the code in a population can be caused by *introns*.

GP classifiers that use variable length (decision) tree structures are subject to *bloat* and they will thus also contain *introns*. In the case of our decision tree representations we can distinguish between two types of *introns*, *intron subtrees*: subtrees which are never traversed, and *intron nodes*: nodes which do not influence the classification outcome of the decision tree.

The negative effects of *introns* are two-fold. The decision trees found by GP algorithms can contain *introns* which makes them less understandable than semantically equivalent trees without *introns*. The second problem of *introns* is that while they do not influence the classification outcome of a decision tree, their evaluation does take time. More important, *introns* reduce the effectiveness of our fitness cache since it does not recognize semantically equivalent but syntactically different trees.

In this paper we present techniques to detect and prune the *introns* in decision trees. The pruned intron-free decision trees will generally be smaller, and thus easier to understand. By using the pruned intron-free trees for our fitness cache we improve its effectiveness.

The overview of the rest of the paper is as follows. In Section 2 we introduce the representations used by our GP algorithms. Then in Section 3 we show how *introns* can be detected and pruned. In Section 4 we describe the experiments followed by the results. Finally, in Section 5 we present the conclusions.

2   Full Atomic Representations

We use *full atomic* representations. A full atomic representation has atoms in the internal and leaf nodes. Each atom has a predicate of the form (*attribute operator value(s)*), where *operator* is a function returning a Boolean value (e.g., < or =). In the leaf nodes we have *class assignment* atoms of the form (*class := C*), where C is a category selected from the domain of the attribute to be predicted. A small example tree is shown in Figure 1. A full atomic tree classifies an instance I by traversing the tree from root to leaf node. In each non-leaf node an atom is evaluated. If the result is true the right branch is traversed, else the left branch is taken. This process is repeated until a leaf node containing a *class assignment* node is reached, resulting in the classification of the instance.

We next define the precise decision tree representation by specifying what atoms are to be used. In this paper we will use two representations:

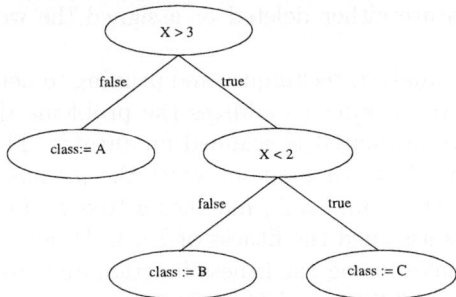

Table 1. Example data set.

X	Y	class
1	a	A
2	b	A
3	a	B
4	b	B
5	a	A
6	b	A

Fig. 1. A full atomic tree.

- *Simple* GP [5], uses atoms based on each possible *attribute-value* combination found in the data set. For non-numerical attributes we use the equality operator (=) and for numerical attributes we use the less-than operator (<). The idea of this approach is to give the GP algorithm the most flexibility and let it decide on the best *attribute-value* combination at a given point in a tree.
- The second representation, *cluster* GP [6], uses unsupervised K-means clustering [7] to partition the domain of numerical valued attributes into a fixed number of clusters. The advantage of the clustering representation is that it leads to smaller search space sizes and better classification performance.

Example. Consider Table 1. In the case of the *simple* representation we get the following atoms:

- Since attribute **X** has six possible values and is numerical valued we get the following atoms: $(\mathbf{X} < 1)$, $(\mathbf{X} < 2)$, $(\mathbf{X} < 3)$, $(\mathbf{X} < 4)$, $(\mathbf{X} < 5)$ and $(\mathbf{X} < 6)$.
- Attribute **Y** is non-numerical resulting in two atoms: $(\mathbf{Y} = a)$ and $(\mathbf{Y} = b)$.
- The two classes result in two terminal nodes: $(class := A)$ and $(class := B)$.

K-means clustering with $k = 3$ results in three clusters for attribute **X**. Thus, in case of the *cluster* GP representation the following atoms are used for attribute **X**: $(\mathbf{X} \in [1,2])$, $(\mathbf{X} \in [3,4])$ and $(\mathbf{X} \in [5,6])$.

3 Intron Detection and Pruning

In [8] Johnson proposes to replace the standard fitness measures by static analysis methods [9]. Through these techniques an individual's behaviour can be evaluated across the entire input space instead of a limited number of test cases. However, for data classification replacing the fitness measure with static analysis techniques does not seem feasible due to the high dimensional nature of the search space. Instead of replacing the fitness function, Keijzer [10] showed how static analysis can be used as a pre-processor for fitness evaluations. By using interval arithmetic to calculate the bounds of symbolic regression trees, functions containing undefined values are either deleted or assigned the worst possible performance value.

We will use a combination of static analysis techniques and pruning to detect and remove *introns* from decision trees in order to address the problems they cause. Each individual T that is to be evaluated is scanned for *introns*. These *introns* are marked and a pruned copy T' of T is made in which the *introns* are removed. If T', which is semantically the same as T, matches a tree T^c found in the *fitness cache* the individual T is assigned the fitness of T^c. If T' does not match any tree in the cache it is evaluated using the fitness function and stored in the cache. In this case T is assigned the fitness of T'.

Since several syntactically different decision trees can have the same *pruned* form this should optimize the effectiveness of the cache. By using the original trees for the evolutionary process (e.g., crossover and mutation) as well as the tree size fitness measure, there is no influence on the classification performance of our algorithms.

3.1 Intron Subtrees

Intron subtrees are subtrees which can and will never be traversed because of the outcome of nodes higher up in the tree. An example of an *intron subtree* is shown in Figure 2(a).

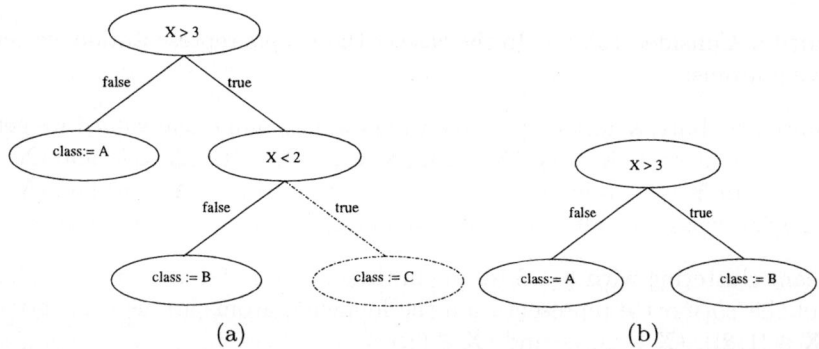

Fig. 2. Two syntactically different trees which are semantically the same. The left tree contains an *intron subtree* indicated by the dotted lines.

In order to detect *intron subtrees* we recursively propagate the possible domains of the attributes through the decision trees in a top-down manner. Given a data set T we can determine for each attribute X_i the domain $D(X_i)$ of possible values. By propagating the domain of each attribute X_i recursively through the trees we can identify situations in which the domain of an attribute becomes empty ($\emptyset$), indicating the presence of a *intron subtree*.

Observe the decision tree T in Figure 3. Let X be a continuous valued attribute in the range $[0, 10]$. Before evaluation of the root node ($X > 3$) the

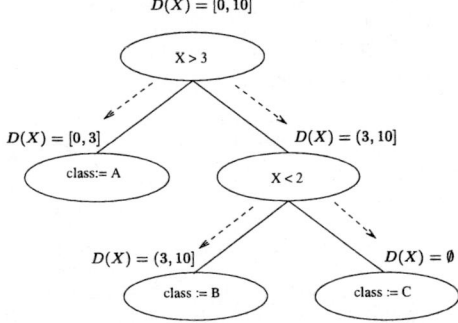

Fig. 3. A full atomic decision tree containing an intron subtree with the domain of attribute X displayed at each point in the tree.

domain of X is $[0, 10]$. Just as the node splits a data set into two parts, the domain of possible values of X is split into two. In the left subtree the domain of X is limited to $[0, 3]$ and in the right subtree the domain of possible values for X is $(3, 10]$. After the evaluation of node $(X < 2)$ the possible domain of X for the left tree is the same as before the atom was evaluated. However, the possible domain of X for the right subtree is reduced to $\emptyset$, and this subtree is therefore marked as an *intron subtree* (see Figure 2 (*a*)).

After *intron subtrees* have been detected and marked the tree can be pruned. During the pruning phase the marked *intron subtrees* are removed and their originating root node ($X < 2$ in our example) is replaced by the remaining *valid* subtree. The resulting pruned tree for the example can be seen in Figure 2(*b*). Note that we assume that all attributes in the data sets are independent. In reality there may be relations between attributes (e.g., attribute X is always larger than attribute Y) in which case some *intron subtrees* are not detected.

3.2 Intron Nodes

Intron nodes are root nodes of subtrees of which each leaf node contains the same *class assignment* atom (e.g., *class := A*). The internal nodes in such a subtree do not influence the classification outcome. While the negative effects of *intron subtrees* are mostly related to size and thus understandability of our decision trees, *intron nodes* have a much more negative influence on the computation times. An example is shown in Figure 4(*a*).

In order to detect *intron nodes* we recursively propagate the set of possible class outcomes through the tree in a bottom-up manner. A leaf node always returns a set containing a single class. In each internal node the sets of possible classes of its children are joined. If the set of possible class outcomes for an internal node contains only a single class the node is marked as an *intron node*. Once all the *intron nodes* have been detected the tree can be pruned. During the pruning phase the tree is traversed in a top-down manner and subtrees with an *intron node* as the root node are replaced by class assignment nodes corresponding to their possible class outcome detected earlier.

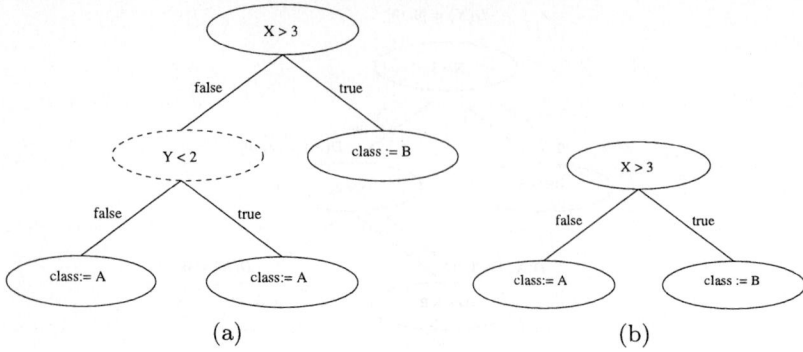

Fig. 4. Two syntactically different trees which are semantically the same. The left tree contains an *intron node* indicated by the dotted lines.

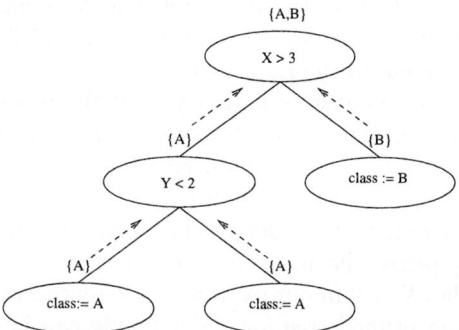

Fig. 5. A full atomic tree with the set of possible target classes for each node.

Consider the tree in Figure 5. The set of possible class outcomes for each leaf node consists of a single class, namely the target class. In the case of node $(Y < 2)$, the sets of possible class outcomes of its subtrees are the same and contain only a single value A. Thus, the set of possible class outcomes for $(Y < 2)$ also contains only a single value and it is therefore marked as an *intron node* (see Figure 4(a)). In the case of node $(X > 3)$ the set of possible class outcomes consists of two classes and this node is therefore not an *intron node*. The resulting tree for the example can be seen in Figure 4(b).

Note that the pruned decision trees in Figures 2(b) and 4(b) are both semantically and syntactically the same although they are derived from syntactically different trees (Figures 2(a) and 4(a)). When *intron node* detection and pruning is used in conjunction with *intron subtree* detection it is important to apply both detection and pruning strategies in the right order. *Intron nodes* should be detected and pruned after *intron subtrees* to assure that all *introns* are found as the pruning of *intron subtrees* can influence the detection of *intron nodes*. Since *intron subtree* detection works top-down and *intron node* detection works bottom-up the two *intron* detection methods can be performed in a single tree traversal.

4 Experiments and Results

In order to determine the effects of *introns* on our GP algorithms we have performed experiments on six data sets from the UCI data set repository [11]. An overview of the data sets as well as the misclassification performance of our GP algorithms and C4.5 (as reported by Freund and Shapire [12]) is given in Table 2. For three data sets (Australian credit, Heart disease and German credit) we applied C4.5 ourselves since no results were reported. Each algorithm is evaluated using n-fold cross-validation and the performance is the average misclassification error over n folds. In n-fold cross-validation the total data set is divided into n parts. Each part is chosen once as the test set while the other $n - 1$ parts form the training set. In all our experiments we use $n = 10$.

Table 2. The data sets used in the experiments.

name	data set records	attributes	classes	misclassification rates simple GP	cluster GP	C4.5
Australian credit (statlog)	690	14	2	22.0	14.8	15.5
German credit (statlog)	1000	23	2	27.1	28.0	27.2
Pima Indians diabetes	768	8	2	26.3	26.3	28.4
Heart disease (statlog)	270	13	2	25.2	21.3	22.2
Ionosphere	351	34	2	12.4	10.5	8.9
Iris	150	4	3	5.6	2.1	5.9

A single GP implementation was used for both representations. It was programmed using the *Evolving Objects* library (EOlib) which is available from http://eodev.sourceforge.net.

In our GP system we use the standard GP mutation and recombination operators for trees. The mutation operator replaces a subtree with a randomly created subtree and the crossover operator exchanges subtrees between two individuals. Both the mutation rate and crossover rate are set to 0.9, optimizing the size of the search space that will be explored. The population was initialized using the ramped half-and-half initialization [1, 13] method to create a combination of full and non-full trees with a maximum tree depth of 6. We used a generational model (comma strategy) with population size of 100, an offspring size of 200 and a maximum of 99 generations, resulting in a maximum of 19.900 individuals. Parents were chosen by using 5-tournament selection. We did not use elitism as the best individual was stored outside the population. Each newly created individual, whether through initialization or recombination, was automatically pruned to a maximum number of 63 nodes. The results are computed over a 100 runs. The cache memory size did not cause any problems.

Whenever the fitness function has to evaluate a decision tree it first checks if the tree is already in the fitness cache. If it is, a *cache hit* occurs and the fitness of the tree is retrieved from the cache. If it is not in the cache the (pruned) decision tree is evaluated by the fitness function and the result is stored in the cache. We will count the number of cache hits to determine the effects of the *intron* detection and pruning strategies on the fitness cache.

Observe the cache hit results for the data sets in Tables 3(a) through (f). When we look at the cache hit percentages of both algorithms it is clear that detecting and pruning *intron subtrees* results in a larger increase in cache hits than detecting and pruning *intron nodes*. As expected the combination of detecting and pruning both *intron subtrees* and *intron nodes* offers the highest number of cache hits. Since the difference between detecting and pruning both types of *introns* on the one hand and detecting and pruning only *intron subtrees* on the other hand is in most cases larger than the difference between no *intron* detection and detecting and pruning *intron nodes* it is clear that first removing the *intron subtrees* allows for a better detection of *intron nodes*. If we look at the average runtimes we see that except for the Ionosphere data, *intron* detection and pruning results in a speed increase of up to 50%. The computation time increase on the Ionosphere data set is probably caused by the relatively large number of attributes combined with a small number of data records.

To determine the effect of intron detection and pruning we have measured the average size of all trees after pruning during an evolutionary run. We also measured the size of trees found to be the best, based on the classification performance on the training set. When we look at the results we see that there is virtually no effect of the representation on the sizes of the evolved decision trees. If we look at the average size of the pruned trees we see that pruning both *intron subtrees* and *nodes* reduces the size of the trees by 30 to 50%. If we look at the average size of the best found trees we see that pruning both the types of *introns* reduces the size by approximately 20%.

5 Conclusions

When we consider the effect of detecting and pruning *introns* on the size of the decision trees, it is clear that the pruned trees will be easier to understand although in some cases they are still quite large. The detection and pruning of *introns* also enables us to identify syntactically different trees which are semantically the same. By comparing and storing pruned decision trees in a fitness cache, rather than the original unpruned decision trees, we can greatly improve the effectiveness of the cache. The increase in cache hits means that less individuals have to be evaluated resulting in reduced computation times.

If we compare the computation times of the algorithms we note that the combination of both *intron* detection and pruning methods has a noticeable effect on the computation times. The decrease in computation time is different from what we would expect when looking at the increase in cache hits and the reduction in tree sizes achieved by the detection and pruning strategies. This difference can be explained by the time spent by our algorithms on detecting and pruning the *introns*, initialization, mutation, recombination and selection as well as choices made during the implementation of the algorithms. Nevertheless, on the smallest data set (Iris) detecting and pruning both *intron subtrees* and *intron nodes* reduces the computation times of the *cluster* GP and *simple* GP algorithms by approximately 50% and 30%, respectively. On the German Credit data set, which contains the most records, the detection and pruning of both

Table 3. The average, minimum and maximum number of cache hits and average runtimes (relative to no *intron* detection and pruning).

(a) Australian Credit

algorithm	intron detection	% cache hits avg	min	max	run-time
simple GP	none	16.9	10.3	31.7	1.0
simple GP	nodes	21.5	12.9	41.0	0.9
simple GP	subtrees	39.0	24.7	53.8	1.0
simple GP	both	46.8	28.9	64.7	0.9
cluster GP	none	18.9	10.9	40.1	1.0
cluster GP	nodes	23.5	13.5	49.1	0.9
cluster GP	subtrees	39.9	25.0	60.9	0.9
cluster GP	both	47.0	29.4	68.4	0.8

(b) German Credit

algorithm	intron detection	# cache hits avg	min	max	run-time
simple GP	none	15.4	9.5	24.7	1.0
simple GP	nodes	19.0	11.8	29.2	0.9
simple GP	subtrees	44.1	25.4	56.9	0.7
simple GP	both	51.1	30.1	65.2	0.6
cluster GP	none	17.3	10.2	28.9	1.0
cluster GP	nodes	20.6	12.5	31.5	0.9
cluster GP	subtrees	30.3	15.5	48.4	0.9
cluster GP	both	35.6	19.7	57.6	0.8

(c) Pima Indians Diabetes

algorithm	intron detection	# cache hits avg	min	max	run-time
simple GP	none	15.2	9.0	24.7	1.0
simple GP	nodes	19.1	11.7	29.4	0.9
simple GP	subtrees	38.6	23.3	57.9	1.1
simple GP	both	45.7	27.6	65.9	1.0
cluster GP	none	16.5	10.6	29.0	1.0
cluster GP	nodes	19.7	13.0	33.2	0.9
cluster GP	subtrees	42.1	23.3	61.0	1.0
cluster GP	both	48.5	27.2	68.8	0.9

(d) Heart Disease

algorithm	intron detection	# cache hits avg	min	max	run-time
simple GP	none	13.7	8.9	22.9	1.0
simple GP	nodes	17.3	11.2	27.8	0.9
simple GP	subtrees	35.3	22.4	49.7	1.0
simple GP	both	42.1	26.4	58.5	0.9
cluster GP	none	13.3	10.0	23.8	1.0
cluster GP	nodes	16.1	12.3	26.7	1.0
cluster GP	subtrees	31.0	18.1	48.4	0.9
cluster GP	both	36.7	22.2	55.8	0.9

(e) Ionosphere

algorithm	intron detection	# cache hits avg	min	max	run-time
simple GP	none	12.4	8.8	21.6	1.0
simple GP	nodes	16.1	11.4	28.7	1.0
simple GP	subtrees	22.7	12.0	45.9	1.5
simple GP	both	28.1	15.2	54.6	1.4
cluster GP	none	14.4	9.2	22.7	1.0
cluster GP	nodes	18.1	11.5	27.8	0.9
cluster GP	subtrees	27.7	14.0	51.0	1.4
cluster GP	both	33.6	17.0	60.0	1.3

(f) Iris

algorithm	intron detection	# cache hits avg	min	max	run-time
simple GP	none	18.4	9.1	30.8	1.0
simple GP	nodes	21.5	10.4	36.3	1.0
simple GP	subtrees	53.0	33.2	65.0	0.7
simple GP	both	58.0	36.1	70.4	0.7
cluster GP	none	29.2	13.2	38.0	1.0
cluster GP	nodes	32.6	14.8	41.9	1.0
cluster GP	subtrees	71.0	57.7	77.5	0.6
cluster GP	both	74.5	61.9	80.0	0.5

types of *introns* reduces the average computation time by over 35% for the *simple* GP and over 20% for the *cluster* GP algorithm.

For future research we are planning to test the *intron* detection and pruning technique on larger data sets. As the number of records in a data set increases the advantage of *intron* removal should become more apparent. We therefore think that the *intron* detection and pruning method will allow GP classifiers to scale better with larger data sets.

References

1. Banzhaf, W., Nordin, P., Keller, R., Francone, F.: Genetic Programming: An Introduction. Morgan Kaufmann (1998)
2. Soule, T., Foster, J.A., Dickinson, J.: Code growth in genetic programming. In et al., J.K., ed.: Genetic Programming 1996: Proceedings of the First Annual Conference, MIT Press (1996) 215–223
3. Soule, T., Foster, J.A.: Code size and depth flows in genetic programming. In et al., J.K., ed.: Genetic Programming 1997: Proceedings of the Second Annual Conference, Morgan Kaufmann (1997) 313–320
4. Angeline, P.: Genetic programming and emergent intelligence. In Kinnear, Jr., K., ed.: Advances in Genetic Programming. MIT Press (1994) 75–98
5. Eggermont, J., Kok, J., Kosters, W.: Genetic programming for data classification: Partitioning the search space. In: Proceedings of the 2004 Symposium on applied computing (ACM SAC'04), ACM (2004) 1001–1005
6. Eggermont, J.: Evolving fuzzy decision trees with genetic programming and clustering. In et al., J.F., ed.: Genetic Programming, Proceedings of the 5th European Conference, EuroGP 2002. Volume 2278 of LNCS., Springer-Verlag (2002) 71–82
7. Witten, I., Frank, E.: Data Mining: Practical Machine Learning Tools and Techniques with Java Implementations. Morgan Kaufmann (2000)
8. Johnson, C.: Deriving genetic programming fitness properties by static analysis. In et al., J.F., ed.: Genetic Programming, Proceedings of the 5th European Conference, EuroGP 2002. Volume 2278 of LNCS., Springer-Verlag (2002) 298–307
9. Nielson, F., Nielson, H., Hankin, C.: Principles of Program Analysis. Springer-Verlag (1999)
10. Keijzer, M.: Improving symbolic regression with interval arithmetic and linear scaling. In et al., C.R., ed.: Genetic Programming, Proceedings of EuroGP'2003. Volume 2610 of LNCS., Springer-Verlag (2003) 71–83
11. Blake, C., Merz, C.: UCI repository of machine learning databases (1998) http://www.ics.uci.edu/~mlearn/MLRepository.html.
12. Freund, Y., Schapire, R.: Experiments with a new boosting algorithm. In: Proceedings of the 13th International Conference on Machine Learning, Morgan Kaufmann (1996) 148–146
13. Koza, J.: Genetic Programming. MIT Press (1992)

Evolutionary Multiobjective Clustering

Julia Handl and Joshua Knowles

Department of Chemistry, UMIST, PO Box 88, Sackville Street,
Manchester M60 1QD, UK
http://dbk.ch.umist.ac.uk/handl/

Abstract. A new approach to data clustering is proposed, in which *two or more* measures of cluster quality are *simultaneously* optimized using a multiobjective evolutionary algorithm (EA). For this purpose, the PESA-II EA is adapted for the clustering problem by the incorporation of specialized mutation and initialization procedures, described herein. Two conceptually orthogonal measures of cluster quality are selected for optimization, enabling, for the first time, a clustering algorithm to explore and improve different compromise solutions during the clustering process. Our results, on a diverse suite of 15 real and synthetic data sets – where the correct classes are known – demonstrate a clear advantage to the multiobjective approach: solutions in the discovered Pareto set are *objectively* better than those obtained when the same EA is applied to optimize just one measure. Moreover, the multiobjective EA exhibits a far more robust level of performance than both the classic k-means and average-link agglomerative clustering algorithms, outperforming them substantially on aggregate.

1 Introduction

The automation of the human ability to recognize patterns in data, and to induce useful hypotheses from them, is the key goal of *data-mining*. A major branch of this project is the development of methods for unsupervised classification of multi-dimensional data, namely the *clustering* of data into homogeneous groups: by now a classic AI problem with algorithms dating back to the 60s [15]. In a broad definition, clustering of data might include the recognition and removal of outliers, the recognition and focusing on key dimensions of the data (i.e. feature selection) and the estimation of the correct number of clusters inherent to the data. In a far more restricted definition, the k-clustering problem (on which we focus here) simply requires us to find a partitioning of a set of data into k disjoint sets such that some objective function operating on this partitioning, and employing a notion of distance in the data space, is optimized. This restricted (but still very broad) problem is NP-complete when stated as a question, and remains NP-complete for many restrictions on the distance functions used and the nature of the objective function, even when $k = 2$ [3].

Both classic and a vast array of new algorithms for k-clustering exist [12]. Common to almost all of them is the fact that they optimize either implicitly or explicitly just one measure on the partitioning of the data. For example, k-means [15] attempts to minimize the summed variance of points within each cluster from their centroid. Although such a method is very effective on certain sets of data, it is also clear that it will fail to find even very obvious cluster structure in other data sets. This is because variance is only a proxy for (i.e. one aspect of) a more fuzzy 'concept' of true cluster structure. Thus, *by focusing on just one aspect of cluster quality, most clustering algorithms can fail catastrophically on certain data-sets*: they are not robust to variations in cluster shape, size, dimensionality and other characteristics.

To combat this problem, practitioners in some fields (where time constraints are secondary) are used to applying several different algorithms to their data, in the hope or expectation that one of them will deliver a good solution. Subsequently, these different partitionings can be tested in the real world: e.g. a biologist with several hypothetical groupings of functionally-related genes can devise experiments that test these alternatives. The idea central to our work is that in such a situation, it may be better to generate alternative solutions using a *single* algorithm, but one that explicitly optimizes *multiple* proxy measures of cluster quality: namely, a Pareto multiobjective EA [7]. This approach may offer greater flexibility and variety in the measures that are used to optimize the clustering, affording higher quality solutions, and, in the process, facilitate greater understanding of the data's structure. In future work we may incorporate feature selection, outlier-removal and determination of k, all within a multiobjective EA framework. However, in this our first paper on multiobjective clustering, we focus on the pivotal question whether this approach can generate objectively high quality solutions.

Readers familiar with clustering research may notice similarities between our proposed approach and other recent methods. Certainly, several EAs for clustering have been proposed ([16, 10, 14, 8]), though none to our knowledge have used a Pareto multiobjective EA. Other recent work has also used the term 'multiobjective' with regard to clustering [13], but the approach was based on using an ensemble of clustering algorithms [18] and then obtaining a consensus clustering from these, similarly to the EA proposed in [10]. Our proposed approach, on the other hand, optimizes different objectives explicitly in one clustering algorithm, enabling different tradeoffs to be explored *during* the clustering process. Its originality derives from this.

The remainder of the paper is organized as follows. Section 2 describes our multiobjective EA, including our selected representation and operators. The objective functions are discussed in Section 3. Section 4 briefly introduces the test suite and points to supporting material where more information on this can be found. Section 5 details our experimental set-up including comparison of our multiobjective EA to two single-objective versions as well as k-means and average-link agglomerative clustering. Section 6 presents results and Section 7 concludes.

2   *VIENNA*: An EA for Clustering

A multiobjective evolutionary algorithm (MOEA) for clustering was developed through extensive preliminary experimentation on a diverse set of clustering problems. This algorithm, employing specialized initialization and mutation operators, is called *VIENNA* (for Voronoi Initialized Evolutionary Nearest-Neighbour Algorithm).

2.1 PESA-II

We based *VIENNA* on the elitist MOEA, PESA-II, described in detail in [5] and [6]. Briefly, PESA-II updates, at each generation, a current set of nondominated solutions stored in an external population (of non-fixed but limited size), and uses this to build an internal population of fixed size to undergo reproduction and variation. PESA-II uses a selection policy designed to give equal reproduction opportunities to all regions of the current nondominated front; thus in the clustering application, it should provide a diverse set of solutions trading off different clustering measures. No critical parameters are associated with this 'niched' selection policy, as it uses an adaptive range equalization and normalization of the objectives. PESA-II may be used to optimize any number of objective functions, allowing us to simultaneously optimize several clustering measures, but in this paper we will use just two (conceptually distant) measures as objectives, described in Section 3.

2.2 Representation Issues

PESA-II can be applied without changes to the clustering problem, given a suitable representation of a partitioning, and related operators. A number of GA clustering representations have been tried and compared in the literature, with seemingly no clear overall winner [4]. In the end, we have chosen to use a straightforward representation in which each gene represents a data item, and its allele value represents the label of the cluster to which it is assigned. This means that for any partition, multiple genotypes code for it, i.e. it is a non-injective encoding – normally thought to be undesirable [17]. This drawback is not serious, however, provided there is not a significant bias or over-representation of certain solutions, and/or we can design operators that work effectively and quickly with this coding. Regarding undesirable bias, the inherent frequency of solutions is free from bias: for every solution that correctly partitions the data into k clusters, there are exactly $k!$ genotypes coding for it. Regarding operators, we have discovered an initialization and mutation operator that work well with this coding, as described next.

2.3 Initialization Based on Random Voronoi Cells

In preliminary work not reported here, we investigated an alternative representation for our EA to use, based on optimizing Voronoi cells. This representation was inspired by [16], where an EA was used to optimize the location of k cluster 'centres', to minimize overall variance when the data points were assigned to the nearest centre. This GA achieves results similar to (but slightly better than) the k-means algorithm. Our idea was to extend this representation by allowing the

EA to use $j > k$ cluster 'centres' (for a partitioning of k clusters) to enable it to cope better with non-hyperspherical, and especially elongated and intertwined, clusters. In our representation, in addition to the location of the j centres, each centre's label is also evolved on the genotype. The kind of clustering solution that this representation affords is depicted in Figure 1.

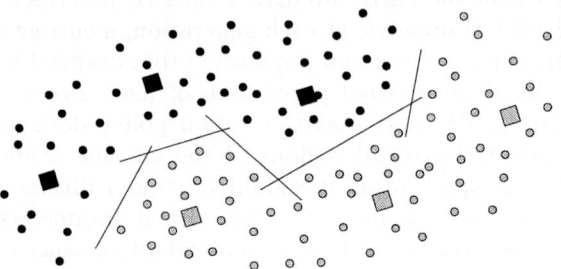

Fig. 1. The kind of complex partitioning boundary enabled by a Voronoi cell genotype coding. Here there are two clusters ($k = 2$) but $j = 6$ centres (squares) have been used to cluster the data. The label of each centre (here visualized by its colour) takes a value in $1..k$. Both the label and location of each centre are coded by the genotype.

Although this representation performs well with PESA-II correctly configured, we have found it slightly inflexible compared with the direct encoding we have opted for, as well as adding an unwelcome parameter j, to be chosen. However, we found that the Voronoi coding is very effective at generating diverse and high-quality clustering solutions that can be used to 'seed' our direct-coded EA. The initialization that we have found effective, and which we use in all our experiments, is to set $j = 2k$, and to place the cluster centres uniformly at random in a rectangular polytope centred on the data, and of side-length twice the range of the data, in each objective. The labels associated with each of the j centres is also assigned uniformly at random, from which it is possible to label all of the data items. We then decode this partitioning into our direct coding, and the Voronoi representation is no longer used. This initialization is used for all members of the initial population in *VIENNA*.

2.4 Directed Mutation Based on Nearest Neighbours

We have explored numerous recombination and mutation operators in preliminary investigations not reported here, including Grouping GA-based methods [9], as well as multi-parent recombinations based on expectation maximization of an ensemble [18]. Overall, we have found it very difficult to design operators that enable a GA to explore broadly enough to escape the very strong local attractors found in some problems when optimizing certain objectives (e.g. variance on non-spherical clusters), without descending into a fruitless random search of what is a very large search space, and whilst also enabling small clustering differences to be explored.

However, in the end, we have found that a single, deceptively simple, directed mutation operator (and no crossover) is sufficient to drive the search. This mutation operator is applied to every gene with probability p_m, which we set to $1/N$ in all experiments, where N is the size of the data set. When a gene undergoes mutation to a different allele value (i.e. cluster), a number g of other genes are simultaneously 'moved' with it into the same target cluster (and the genotype is updated accordingly). The particular data items that undergo this move are the g nearest neighbours to the data item coded for by the initially mutated gene. The integer g itself is chosen, independently at each mutation event, uniformly at random in $0..N/k$.

This operator enables very large changes to result from a single mutation, yet constrains them to be 'reasonable' moves that respect local distance relations. On the other hand, very small changes in the clustering solution are also possible. The operator works in linear time since the nearest neighbours of every data item can be pre-computed once at the beginning of the EA's run.

3 Objective Functions for Clustering

Given a candidate partitioning of the data, numerous 'internal' measures for estimating its quality exist [11]. These measures are based on intuitive notions of the properties of a desirable partitioning – such as the compactness of clusters and their clear separation.

In the EA we present in this paper, we optimize two such internal measures, described next, though we have tried several others in our preliminary testing.

3.1 Overall Deviation

The overall deviation of a clustering solution reflects the overall intra-cluster 'spread' of the data. It is computed as

$$Dev(C) = \sum_{C_k \in C} \sum_{i \in C_k} \delta(i, \mu_k),$$

where C is the set of all clusters, μ_k is the centroid of cluster C_k and $\delta(.,.)$ is the chosen distance function (see Section 4). As an objective, overall deviation should be minimized. Note the relationship to variance (e.g. as used in k-means), which squares the $\delta(.,.)$ in the sum. In preliminary experiments, we found overall deviation to be preferable to variance for use in our EA.

3.2 Connectivity

As a second objective function, we propose a new measure, connectivity, which evaluates the degree to which neighbouring datapoints have been placed in the same cluster. It is computed as

$$Conn(C) = \frac{1}{N} \sum_{i=1}^{N} \left(\frac{\sum_{j=1}^{h} x_{i,nn_i(j)}}{h} \right), \quad \text{where } x_{r,s} = \begin{cases} 1 & \text{if } \exists C_k : r, s \in C_k \\ 0 & \text{otherwise,} \end{cases}$$

$nn_i(j)$ is the jth nearest neighbour of datum i, and h is a parameter determining the number of neighbours that contribute to the connectivity measure. The value of connectivity lies in the interval [0,1], and as an objective, it should be maximized. Connectivity, unlike overall deviation, is relatively indifferent to the shape of clusters, and we have found it robust to the chosen value of h, independently of the data set. It is also fast to compute as the nearest neighbour list can be pre-computed. One drawback of this measure is that trivial attractors, with all, or nearly all, data items placed in the same cluster, exist.

4 Data Sets

Clustering problems vary greatly along a number of important dimensions. For this reason, it is incumbent on the researcher developing new clustering algorithms to test them on a range of problems that exhibit this variety as much as possible. We use eight synthetic and seven real data sets; the former allow us to control several characteristics in isolation, while the latter help to verify that our results are ultimately meaningful in real applications.

For the real data, we first normalize each dimension to have a mean of zero and a standard deviation of one, and use the Cosine similarity as distance function. For the synthetic data, the Euclidean distance is used with no prior normalization.

4.1 Synthetic Data

All eight of our synthetic data sets consist of 500 two-dimensional data items, enabling us to easily visualize the results of a clustering. Pictures and explanations for all these sets are available at [1] but we briefly describe them below. Note: the synthetic data sets are defined in terms of distributions, and the actual data points are sampled from these, independently, in each successive algorithm run.

Three of the data sets (Square1, Square3 and Square5) consist of a square arrangement of four clusters of equal size and spread, each cluster being a Gaussian distribution about a central point. The difference between the sets is the degree of overlap of the four clusters. In Square1, the clusters touch but hardly overlap, whereas for Square5 the overlap is so much that there is little density difference moving from one cluster to the next.

The next three data sets (Sizes1, Sizes3 and Sizes5) are based on Square1, but change the relative cluster sizes (in terms of the number of constituent data items) such that the ratio of the three smaller to the one larger cluster is respectively 2, 6, and 10. Note: the spread of the clusters is unchanged.

The last two of our synthetic data sets (Smile and Long1) contain different, non-spherically shaped clusters, making it more difficult for methods based on minimizing variance. For pictures of these demanding problems, see [1].

4.2 Real Data

For the real data sets we chose seven from the UCI Machine Learning Repository [2] to obtain a good variety in data dimensionality, size of the data set,

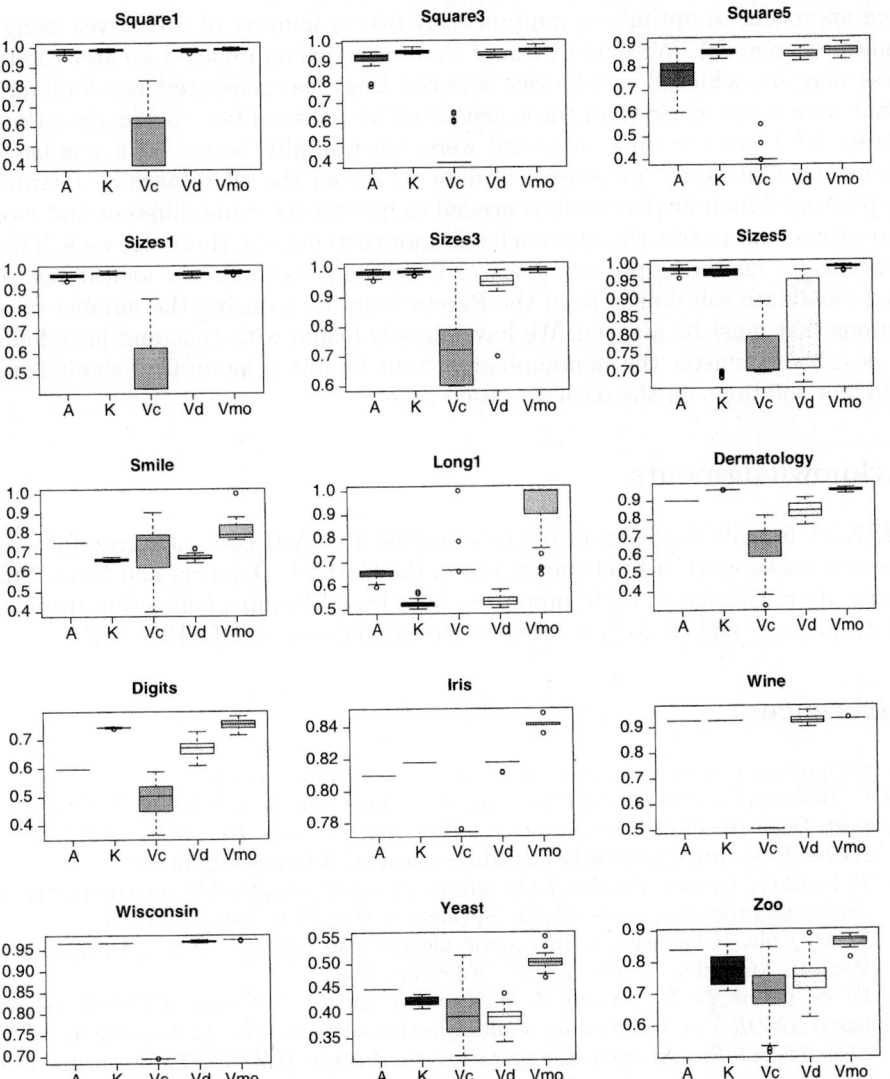

Fig. 2. Boxplots [21] giving the distribution of F measure values achieved for 50 runs of each algorithm on the 15 data sets. Key: A=average-link agglomerative clustering, K = k-means, Vc= VIENNA-conn, Vd= VIENNA-dev, Vmo= VIENNA-moo. Median and IQR values have also been tabulated and can be found at [1].

7 Conclusion

Most clustering algorithms operate by optimizing (either implicitly or explicitly) a single measure of cluster solution quality. Such methods may perform well on certain data-sets but lack robustness with respect to variations in cluster shape, proximity, evenness and so forth. In this paper, we have proposed an alternative approach: to optimize simultaneously over a number of objectives using a multiobjective EA. We demonstrated that with this approach a greater robustness may be achieved – solutions selected from the generated nondominated front were never worse than those generated by either of two classic algorithms, across *all* 15 of our data sets, and were substantially better on a number of them, including three of seven real data sets from the UCI Machine Learning Repository. Much further work is needed to investigate using different and more objectives, and to test the approach still more extensively. However, we will first concentrate on the important issue of developing methods for identifying the best candidate solution(s) from the Pareto front, or reducing the number of solutions that must be assayed. We have already begun with this, and have found it possible to cluster the nondominated front to just a handful of significantly different solutions on the data sets used here.

Acknowledgments

VIENNA is built from David Corne's original PESA-II code. JH gratefully acknowledges support of a scholarship from the Gottlieb-Daimler- and Karl Benz-Foundation, Germany. JK is supported by a David Phillips Fellowship from the Biotechnology and Biological Sciences Research Council (BBSRC), UK.

References

1. Supporting material. http://dbk.ch.umist.ac.uk/handl/vienna/
2. C. Blake and C. Merz. UCI repository of machine learning databases. Technical report, Department of Information and Computer Sciences, University of California, Irvine, 1998. http:://www.ics.uci.edu/~mlearn/MLRepository.html
3. P. Brucker. *Optimization and Operations Research*, chapter On the complexity of clustering problems, pages 45–54. Springer-Verlag, New York, 1977.
4. R. M. Cole. Clustering with genetic algorithms. Master's thesis, University of Western Australia, Nedlands 6907, Australia, 1998.
5. D. W. Corne, N. R. Jerram, J. D. Knowles, and M. J. Oates. PESA-II: region-based selection in evolutionary multiobjective optimization. In *Proceedings of the Genetic and Evolutionary Computation Conference (GECCO'2001)*, pages 283–290. Morgan Kaufmann Publishers, 2001.
6. D. W. Corne, J. D. Knowles, and M. J. Oates. The Pareto envelope-based selection algorithm for multiobjective optimization. In *Proceedings of the Parallel Problem Solving from Nature VI Conference*, pages 839–848. Springer, 2000.
7. K. Deb. *Multi-objective optimization using evolutionary algorithms*. John Wiley & Sons, Chichester, UK, 2001.
8. A. Demiriz, K. Bennett, and M. Embrechts. Semi-supervised clustering using genetic algorithms. Technical report, Rensselaer Polytechnic Institute, Troy, New York, 1999.
9. E. Falkenauer. *Genetic Algorithms and Grouping Problems*. John Wiley & Sons, 1998.
10. W. Gablentz, M. Köppen, and E. Dimitriadou. Robust clustering by evolutionary computation. 5th Online World Conference on Soft Computing in Industrial Applications (WSC5), The Internet (2000), 2000.

11. M. Halkidi, M. Vazirgiannis, and I. Batistakis. Quality scheme assessment in the clustering process. In *Proceedings of the Fourth European Conference on Principles of Data Mining and Knowledge Discovery*, volume 1910 of *LNCS*, pages 265–267. Springer-Verlag, Heidelberg, Germany, 2000.
12. A. K. Jain, M. N. Murty, and P. Flynn. Data clustering: a review. *ACM Computing Surveys*, 31(3):264–323, 1999.
13. M. Law, A. Topchy, and A. K. Jain. Multiobjective data clustering. In *Proceedings of the IEEE Computer Society Conference on Computer Vision and Pattern Recognition*, June 2004. To appear.
14. J. A. Lozano and P. Larrañaga. Applying genetic algorithms to search for the best hierarchical clustering of a dataset. *Pattern Recognition Letters*, 20(911–918), 1999.
15. L. MacQueen. Some methods for classification and analysis of multivariate observations. In *Proceedings of the Fifth Berkeley Symposium on Mathematical Statistics and Probability*, volume 1, pages 281–297. University of California Press, Berkeley, 1967.
16. U. Maulik and S. Bandyopadhyay. Genetic algorithm-based clustering technique. *Pattern Recognition*, 33:1455–1465, 2000.
17. N. J. Radcliffe. Equivalence class analysis of genetic algorithms. *Complex Systems*, 5:183–205, 1991.
18. A. Topchy, A. K. Jain, and W. Punch. A mixture model for clustering ensembles. In *Proceedings SIAM Conf. on Data Mining*, 2004. In press.
19. C. van Rijsbergen. *Information Retrieval, 2nd edition*. Butterworths, London, UK, 1979.
20. E. Vorhees. *The effectiveness and efficiency of agglomerative hierarchical clustering in document retrieval*. PhD thesis, Department of Computer Science, Cornell University, 1985.
21. E. W. Weisstein. Box-and-whisker plot. From MathWorld – A Wolfram Web Resource. http://mathworld.wolfram.com/Box-and-WhiskerPlot.html

Web Page Classification with an Ant Colony Algorithm

Nicholas Holden and Alex A. Freitas

Computing Laboratory, University of Kent
Canterbury, CT2 7NF, UK
{nph4,A.A.Freitas}@kent.ac.uk

Abstract. This paper utilizes Ant-Miner – the first Ant Colony algorithm for discovering classification rules – in the field of web content mining, and shows that it is more effective than C5.0 in two sets of BBC and Yahoo web pages used in our experiments. It also investigates the benefits and dangers of several linguistics-based text preprocessing techniques to reduce the large numbers of attributes associated with web content mining.

1 Introduction

The amount of information available on the web is huge and growing each year. At present Google searches more than 4.2 billion pages. As the web has grown, the ability to mine for specific information has become almost important as the web itself. Data mining consists of a set of techniques used to find useful patterns within a set of data and to express these patterns in a way which can be used for intelligent decision making [1], [2]. In this project the knowledge is represented as classification rules. A rule consists of an antecedent (a set of attribute values) and a consequent (class):

```
IF <attrib = value> AND ... AND <attrib = value> THEN <class>.
```

The class part of the rule (consequent) is the class predicted by the rule for the records where the predictor attributes hold. An example rule might be IF <Salary = high> AND <Mortgate = No> THEN <Good Credit>. This kind of knowledge representation has the advantage of being intuitively comprehensible to the user. This is important, because the general goal of data mining is to discover knowledge that is not only accurate, but also comprehensible to the user [2], [1]. In the classification task, the goal is to discover rules from a set of training data and apply those rules to a set of test data (unseen during training), and hopefully predict the correct class in the test set.

In this project, the goal is to discover a good set of classification rules to classify web pages based on their subject. The main classification algorithm to be used in this paper is Ant-Miner [3], the first Ant Colony Optimisation (ACO) algorithm for discovering classification rules. Investigating the use of Ant-Miner in web mining is an important research direction, as follows. First, an empirical comparison between Ant-Miner and two very popular rule induction algorithms (C4.5 and CN2), across six data sets, has shown that Ant-Miner is not only competitive with respect to predictive accuracy, but also tends to discover much simpler rules [3], [4]. However, that comparison involved only "conventional" data mining – i.e., mining structured data sets.

Web mining is more challenging, because it involves unstructured or semi-structured text found in web pages. In addition, there are a potentially very large number of attributes (words) associated with web pages, and a theoretical analysis of Ant-Miner (under very pessimistic assumptions) shows that its computational time is quite sensitive to the number of attributes [3]. Hence, it is important to understand how scalable Ant-Miner is to data sets with a large number of attributes in practice, in a challenge real-world domain such as web mining. Finally, it is important to investigate the influence of different text preprocessing techniques (which reduce the number of attributes) in the performance of Ant-Miner. This is also addressed in this paper.

2 Web Mining and Linguistic Text Preprocessing

Web mining can be split into three main categories: content mining, usage mining, and structure mining [5]. Content mining involves the automatic analysis of the text stored in the files (i.e. HTML and email), images and any other media available on the web. Usage mining [6] analyses access logs from web servers to discover the patterns that users make when they use the web. Structure mining analyses how web pages link to each other through hyperlinks, for example.

This project focuses on web-content mining. Also, like most web-content mining projects, we mine only text – not images and other media. Web-content mining is a challenging task, as follows. Firstly the amount of attributes (words) is unusually high in comparison to simpler data mining applications. The number of possible classification rules is exponential on the number of words, so that the search space quickly becomes very large. Secondly the English language (all languages in general) is very complicated. There is no program at the moment that can fully understand the meaning of a given web page. We can only hope for a relatively simple interpretation.

There is some hope, however, that html code gives us clues to help us cut down the number of attributes [7]. The authors of web sites leave summaries or descriptions of the web page in <meta> tags: in <meta NAME="keywords"> the content field gives us a list of keywords the author thinks is suitable for the page; and there is also <meta NAME="description"> which gives us hopefully a good overview of the page's content. Going further, it is possible to apply linguistics-based text preprocessing techniques to select the most relevant words from the text.

WordNet is an electronic lexicon that contains several relationships between words [8]. It is an attempt to map the human understanding of words and their relationships into an electronic database. In this project we have used three linguistic resources from WordNet to preprocess the data, as follows.

Firstly, we used the morphological processor of WordNet to perform stemming (i.e., removing the word suffixes). This is useful as instead of having, e.g., the words *borrow*, *borrowing* and *borrowed* we would like to just have the word *borrow* added to our list of attributes. This cuts down the number of attributes and allows us to find patterns more easily. We may not be able to find a pattern with these separate words, but when they are amalgamated together into one attribute, a pattern may emerge.

Secondly, we used WordNet to identify all the nouns in the text. As the amount of words is so high in web mining, it may be useful to only use nouns as attributes, as they are usually the subject of a sentence. Hence we trade off the completeness of the information against the ability to find more useful patterns within a given time.

Thirdly, we use WordNet to capture the idea of a given word in a more generic form and use that instead of the word itself. If different pages have the same idea behind what they contain, then this should allow us to find more trends in the data. For example, if one page contains the words: window, roof, and door, and another web page contains the words chimney, room and brick then we should be able to use WordNet to find the relationship or root of the tree, the word house. As you can see this would reduce the number of attributes from six to just one. Although this is potentially the most rewarding technique discussed, it is also the most risky. If WordNet finds the wrong relationship between the words we may end up with the wrong root word. To perform this kind of word generalization, we use the hypernym/hyponym ("is a") relationship of WordNet, where words are arranged in a tree-like structure.

```
OriginalWordsList = [Words From current web page];
GeneralisedWordsList = [];
RelationshipMaxLength = 2;
WHILE (OriginalWordsList.Size > 2)
   BestRelationShip = NULL;
   CurrentWord = remove first word from OriginalWordsList
   FOR (i = 0; i < OriginalWordsList.Size)
      Get all relationships between all senses of CurrentWord
         and all senses of OriginalWordsList element i, and
         for each relationship compute the number of edges
         in the WordNet taxonomy between CurrentWord and
         OriginalWordsList element i
      Get the relationship with the shortest number of edges,
         out of all relationships identified in previous step
      IF (number of edges in the shortest relationship ≤
         RelationshipMaxLength)
            Save shortest relationship as BestRelationship:
            BestParent = the parent (generalized) word
            BestSecondWord = OriginalWordsList element i
   END FOR
   IF (BestRelationship ≠ NULL)
      Add BestParent to GeneralisedWordList
      Remove BestSecondWord from the OriginalWordsList
   ELSE
      Add CurrentWord to GeneralisedWordsList
END WHILE
```

Alg. 1. Finding the best word-generalisation relationships.

We have developed an algorithm (implemented using the JWNL library) to search for the hypernyms (generalizations) of a pair of words and return the best hypernym. The pseudo-code of the algorithm is shown in Algorithm 1. For each word in the current web page, the algorithm finds the "best hypernym" that is generalizing both that word and another word in the page. The best hypernym is the one associated with the smallest number of edges in the path linking the two generalized words via the hypernym. The best hypernym for each possible pair of words is then added to the "GeneralisedWordList". At the end of the algorithm this list contains the generalized words that will replace their corresponding base words in the representation of the web page.

3 The Ant-Miner Algorithm

In nature ants are seen creating "highways" to and from their food, often using the shortest route. Each ant lays down an amount of pheromone and the other ants are attracted to the strongest scent. As a result, ants tend to converge to the shortest path. This is because a shorter path is faster to transverse, so if an equal amount of ants follow the long path and the short path, the ants that follow the short path will make more trips to the food and back to the colony. If the ants make more trips when following the shorter path, then they will deposit more pheromone over a given distance when compared to the longer path. This is a type of positive feedback and the ants following the longer path will be more likely to change to follow the shorter path, where scent from the pheromone is stronger [9], [10].

The Ant-Miner algorithm takes the ideas from the Ant Colony paradigm and applies them to the field of data mining. Instead of foraging for food the ants in the Ant-Miner algorithm forage for classification rules, and the path they take correspond to a conjunction of attribute-value pairs (terms). A high-level pseudocode of Ant-Miner is shown in Algorithm 2. A detailed description of the algorithm can be found in [3].

Ant-Miner starts by initializing the training set to the set of all training cases (web pages, in this project), and initializing the discovered rule list to an empty list. Then it performs an outer Repeat-Until loop. Each iteration of this loop discovers one classification rule. This first step of this loop is to initialize all trails with the same amount of pheromone, which means that all terms have the same probability of being chosen (by the current ant) to incrementally construct the current classification rule.

```
TrainSet = {all training cases};
DiscoveredRuleList = [];   /* initialized with empty list */
REPEAT
    Initialize all trails with the same amount of pheromone;
    REPEAT
        An ant incrementally constructs a classification rule;
        Prune the just-constructed rule;
        Update the pheromone of all trails;
    UNTIL (stopping criteria)
    Choose best rule out of all rules constructed by all ants;
    Add the best rule to DiscoveredRuleList;
    TrainSet = TrainSet - {cases correctly covered by best rule};
UNTIL (stopping criteria)
```

Alg. 2. High-level pseudocode of Ant-Miner.

The construction of an individual rule is performed by the inner Repeat-Until loop, consisting of three steps. First, an ant starts with an empty rule and incrementally constructs a classification rule by adding one term at a time to the current rule. In this step a $term_{ij}$ – representing a triple <$Attribute_i$ = $Value_j$> – is chosen to be added to the current rule with probability proportional to the product of $\eta_{ij} \times \tau_{ij}(t)$, where η_{ij} is the value of a problem-dependent heuristic function for $term_{ij}$ and $\tau_{ij}(t)$ is the amount of pheromone associated with $term_{ij}$ at iteration (time index) t. More precisely, η_{ij} is essentially the information gain associated with $term_{ij}$ – see e.g. [1] for a discussion on information gain. The higher the value of η_{ij} the more relevant for classification $term_{ij}$ is and so the higher its probability of being chosen. $\tau_{ij}(t)$ corresponds to the amount of pheromone currently available in the position i,j of the trail being followed by the current ant. The better the quality of the rule constructed by an ant, the higher the amount of pheromone added to the trail positions ("terms") visited ("used") by the ant. (Rule quality is measured by *Sensitivity* × *Specificity* [3].) Therefore, as time goes by, the best trail positions to be followed – i.e., the best terms to be added to a rule – will have greater and greater amounts of pheromone, increasing their probability of being chosen to construct a rule.

The second step of the inner loop consists of pruning the just-constructed rule, i.e., removing irrelevant terms – terms that do not improve the predictive accuracy of the rule. In essence, a term is removed from a rule if this operation does not decrease the quality of the rule – as assessed by the same rule-quality measure used to update the pheromones of the trails. The third step of the inner loop consists of updating the pheromone of all trails by increasing the pheromone in the trail followed by the ant, proportionally to the rule's quality. In other words, the higher the quality of the rule, the higher the increase in the pheromone of the terms occurring in the rule antecedent.

The inner loop is performed until some stopping criterion(a) is(are) satisfied, e.g., until a maximum number of candidate rules has been constructed. Once the inner loop is over, the algorithm chooses the highest-quality rule out of all the rules constructed by all the ants in the inner loop, and it adds the chosen rule to the discovered rule list. Next, the algorithm removes from the training set all cases correctly covered by the rule, i.e., all cases that satisfy the rule antecedent and have the same class as predicted by the rule consequent. Hence, the next iteration of the outer loop starts with a smaller training set, consisting only of cases which have not been correctly covered by any rule discovered in previous iterations. The outer loop is performed until some stopping criterion(a) is(are) satisfied, e.g., until the number of uncovered cases is smaller than a user-specified threshold. The output of Ant-Miner is the discovered rule list.

4 Computational Results

4.1 Experimental Setup

A set of 127 web pages in three different classes (Education, Technology and Sport) were harvested from the BBC web site. This site was chosen for analysis because it is arranged in a rigid standard way, and all pages have standard tags which can be used for mining. The standard of writing is also high, making it possible to draw relationships between the content, the information in the Meta fields, and the class (subject) of the page. Some pages published by the BBC are released in more than one class, so a page that appears in, say, the Technology section may also appear in the Education section. In these cases the page in question is removed from the collected set.

We extracted, from each web page, a set of binary attributes (words). Each attribute represents whether or not the corresponding word occurs in a given web page. Since using all words occurring in any web page would produce a huge and impractical number of attributes, we used WordNet to perform the three kinds of linguistics-based text preprocessing discussed in section 2. We also performed controlled experiments to evaluate the effect of each of these preprocessing techniques, as follows.

First, we performed experiments with and without stemming. Second, we performed experiments using only nouns as attributes and using all kinds of words as attributes. In both cases, words that were not recognized by WordNet were presumed to be proper nouns. These proper nouns were left in, as they usually contain important and relevant names. Third, we performed experiments with and without the generalisation of words based on the hypernym relationship of WordNet (using Algorithm 1).

We also performed a basic text preprocessing that is often used in text mining, where stop words, as well as punctuation, were removed. Stop words are words that convey little or no useful information in terms of text mining – e.g. *"the, and, they"*.

To gauge the accuracy of the discovered rules, a conventional five-fold cross-validation procedure was used [1]. Reported results are the average predictive accuracy in the test set over the five iterations of the cross-validation procedure. The following standard Ant-Miner settings [3] (except (d)) were used in all the experiments:

(a) No_of_Ants (number of ants, i.e. maximum number of rules evaluated) = 3000
(b) Min_cases_per_rule (minimum number of cases per rule) = 10
(c) Max_uncovered_cases (maximum number of uncovered cases) = 10
(d) No_rules_converg (number of identical consecutive rules required for indicating convergence) = 20. This parameter was increased from 10 (default value of Ant-Miner) to 20, to try and stop premature convergence to worse rules.

4.2 Results on the Influence of Linguistics-Based Text Preprocessing Techniques

The experiments reported in this section evaluate the influence of different linguistics-based text processing techniques in the performance of Ant-Miner. Tables 1 and 2 report, for each setup, the number of attributes (after text preprocessing) and the average cross-validation accuracy with the standard deviation shown after the "±" symbol. In these figures, WN-generalization denotes WordNet generalization based on the hypernym relation. Title is where the words are harvested from the title field in the documents, Description is where the words are taken from the description field and Union is the union of the two sets of words (Title + Description).

Table 1 shows the accuracies from the different setups when using only nouns (rather than all kinds of words) to create attributes. There are two different ways to analyse this table. First, one can analyse the effect of using nouns from the web page Title only, nouns from the web page Description only, and nouns from both (Union) in the performance of Ant-Miner. There is no clear pattern associated with Title versus Description or Union. However, both when using WordNet generalization and when using Stemming, nouns from Union produced better results than nouns from Description only. Second, it is interesting to analyse the use of WordNet generalization versus the use of stemming as a heuristic to reduce the number of attributes. The use of WordNet was beneficial when the attributes contained only words in the Title. Indeed, WordNet generalization with Title produced the best result (77.34% of accuracy). However, the use of WordNet produced worse results than stemming when the attributes contained words in Description or in Union.

Table 1. Ant-Miner Results in BBC web site – using only nouns.

Test Setup	No. of attrib.	Accuracy
WN-generalisation, Title	41	77.34 ± 2.27
WN-generalisation, Description	125	68.01 ± 2.37
WN-generalisation, Union	188	70.42 ± 5.27
Stemming, Title	46	69.09 ± 5.92
Stemming, Description	159	71.00 ± 1.71
Stemming, Union	293	74.79 ± 2.86

Table 2. Ant-Miner Results in BBC web site – using all words.

Test Setup	No. of Attrib.	Accuracy
WN-generalisation, Title	47	81.00 ± 2.93
WN-generalisation, Description	163	68.69 ± 2.90
WN-generalisation, Union	226	67.81 ± 2.62
Stemming, Title	52	71.28 ± 6.04
Stemming, Description	188	74.29 ± 4.90
Stemming, Union	339	70.97 ± 4.04

Table 2 shows the accuracies from the different setups when using all kinds of words (except, of course, stop words) to create attributes. Again, there are two kinds of analyses to be made. First, one can analyse the effect of using Title only, Description only, and the Union of Title and Description in the performance of Ant-Miner. Unlike the results in Table 1, Table 2 shows that – both when using WordNet generalization and when using stemming – Union produces the worst results. Hence, it seems that when all kinds of words are used, Union leads to a degradation of accuracy because the search space becomes very large, i.e., the large number of attributes (which tends to have many irrelevant attributes) degrades Ant-Miner's performance.

Second, one can analyse the use of WordNet generalization vs. stemming. Similarly to Table 1, Table 2 shows that: (a) the use of WordNet was beneficial when the attributes contained only words in the Title –WordNet generalization with Title produced the best result (81.0% of accuracy); (b) the use of WordNet produced worse results than stemming when the attributes contained words in Description or in Union.

Hence, both Table 1 and Table 2 are evidence that WordNet generalization is a very effective heuristic when the attributes contain words from the Title only, which are the scenarios with the smallest sets of attributes used in our experiments. When the attributes contain words from Description and Union, the larger number of attributes seems to be a serious problem for WordNet generalization, leading to worse results than stemming. Indeed, the title of a web page tends to be a very compact description of its contents in only one sentence, possibly leading to fewer WordNet confusions between different senses of a word.

4.3 Results Comparing Ant-Miner and C5.0

The results with all kinds of words (Table 2) were better than the results with nouns (Table 1) in 4 out of 6 cases. Hence, we decided to focus on the results with all words and do an additional experiment, comparing Ant-Miner with the well-known C5.0 algorithm, implemented in Clementine (an industrial-strength data mining tool). The results of this experiment are reported in Table 3. C5.0 was run with the default settings for its parameters. To make the comparison as fair as possible, both algorithms used exactly the same training and test set partitions in each of the iterations of the cross-validation procedure. Table 3 reports the average cross-validation results with respect to both accuracy and simplicity – number of discovered rules and total number of terms (conditions) in all discovered rules. The reported rule count does not include the default rule for Ant-Miner or C5.0.

Table 3. Comparison between Ant-Miner and C5.0 in BBC news web site, all words.

Test Setup	Algorithm	Accuracy	No. of rules	Total No. of Terms
WordNet generalization, Title, All words	Ant-Miner	**81.00±2.93**	3.0±0.00	9.40±1.91
	C5.0	73.19±4.77	12.00±1.44	24.80±1.71
WordNet generalization, Description, All words	Ant-Miner	**68.69±2.90**	3.0±0.00	12.40±2.58
	C5.0	67.78±1.43	12.40±0.50	27.20±1.46
WordNet generalization, Union, All words	Ant-Miner	67.81±2.62	3.0±0.00	11.60±2.40
	C5.0	**71.83±2.08**	11.60±0.40	23.40±0.87
Stemming, Title, All words	Ant-Miner	71.28±6.04	3.0±0.00	12.13±1.70
	C5.0	**77.08±4.48**	14.00±0.54	26.4±0.74
Stemming, Description, All words	Ant-Miner	**74.29±4.90**	3.0±0.00	11.66±2.56
	C5.0	71.03±4.41	11.00±0.54	22.25±1.79
Stemming, Union, All words	Ant-Miner	70.97±4.04	3.0±0.00	10.06±2.16
	C5.0	**76.39±1.01**	13.80±0.73	27.60±1.63

For each setup in Table 3, the best result is shown in bold. With respect to accuracy, Ant-Miner obtained the best result in three setups, and C5.0 obtained the best result in the other three setups. In 4 out of the 6 setups the difference between the two algorithms is not significant, since the accuracy rate intervals (taking into account the standard deviations) overlap. There were just two setups in which the difference in accuracy was significant (i.e. the accuracy rate intervals do not overlap), namely the first setup (WordNet generalization, Title, All words), where Ant-Miner significantly outperformed C5.0, and the last setup (Stemming, Union, All words), where C5.0 significantly outperformed Ant-Miner.

With respect to the simplicity of the discovered rule set, Ant-Miner discovered a significantly smaller number of rules in all setups. The total number of terms discovered by Ant-Miner was also significantly smaller than the number of terms discovered by C5.0 in all setups. This means that Ant-Miner has performed very well in terms of knowledge comprehensibility in comparison to C5.0. I.e., a user would find it much easier to interpret and possibly use the knowledge discovered by Ant-Miner.

We also did experiments with 429 web pages from the Yahoo web site. Each web page belonged to one of the following three classes: business, tech and entertainment. The results are reported in Table 4.

With respect to accuracy, Ant-Miner obtained the best result in four setups, and C5.0 obtained the best result in the other two setups. However, the differences in accuracy were not significant in any setup, since the accuracy rate intervals overlap. With respect to the simplicity of the discovered rule set, again Ant-Miner discovered a significantly smaller rule set than the rule set discovered by C5.0 in all setups.

Table 4. Comparison between Ant-Miner and C5.0 in Yahoo news web site, all words.

Test Setup	Algorithm	Accuracy	No. of rules	Total No. of Terms
WordNet generalization, Title, All words	Ant-Miner	**88.00±2.16**	**3.6±0.24**	**12.83±2.32**
	C5.0	89.87±1.88	18.6±1.20	42.20±6.80
WordNet generalization, Description, All words	Ant-Miner	**86.50±1.99**	**3.0±0.00**	**14.53±2.93**
	C5.0	86.48±1.25	15.8±1.01	34.60±2.54
WordNet generalization, Union, All words	Ant-Miner	**88.15±1.96**	**3.0±0.00**	**13.53±2.62**
	C5.0	86.46±1.24	16.6±0.74	39.80±2.41
Stemming, Title, All words	Ant-Miner	83.54±2.52	**3.4±0.24**	**12.88±2.48**
	C5.0	**86.70±1.10**	16.8±0.66	30.40±1.80
Stemming, Description, All words	Ant-Miner	**87.91±1.75**	**3.4±0.24**	**11.05±2.19**
	C5.0	83.14±3.63	17.4±1.07	29.00±1.22
Stemming, Union, All words	Ant-Miner	**90.01±2.62**	**3.0±0.00**	**12.00±2.33**
	C5.0	89.29±2.09	11.2±0.19	21.40±0.87

5 Discussion and Future Research

This project was the first attempt to apply Ant-Miner to the challenging problem of web page classification, which is plagued by a large number of attributes and the very complex nature of relationships between words. To the best of our knowledge there are just two other projects on using Ant Colony algorithms in web mining, namely the projects described in [6] and [11]. However, our work is very different from those two projects, since our project addresses the classification task, whereas those projects addressed the clustering task (which is very different from classification [2]).

This paper has the following contributions. First, it showed that: (a) Ant-Miner produces accuracies that are at worst comparable to the more established C5.0 algorithm; and (b) Ant-Miner discovers knowledge in a much more compact form than C5.0, facilitating the interpretation of the knowledge by the user. These results agree entirely with previous results comparing Ant-Miner with C4.5 and CN2 in "conventional" data mining (rather than the more challenging text mining scenario), where Ant-Miner also found much simpler rule sets than those algorithms [3], [4].

Secondly, we also investigated the relative effectiveness of different linguistics-based text preprocessing techniques – used as heuristics to reduce the number of attributes – in the performance of Ant-Miner. This is also, to the best of our knowledge, the first time that an Ant Colony algorithm used WordNet. The results showed that a relatively simple use of WordNet, using the hypernym relationship to generalize words, is often beneficial. However, the errors and misinterpretations it produces when dealing with more complex and longer sentences can sometimes nullify the advantages described. In the scenarios investigated in this paper, WordNet generalisation is most beneficial when the words being generalized occur in a short sentence with a simple meaning, such as in the title field. It is possible that simply stemming the words would be more effective on the more complex sentences, if the number of attributes did not increase so much – overwhelming the Ant Miner algorithm.

Concerning future research, it has been shown that Ant Colony algorithms are good at problems involving continuous learning [12]. It hopefully would be relatively easy to adapt the Ant-Miner algorithm to continuous learning applications as the content available on the web is dynamic by nature. One possibility, for instance, would be to mine data represented in RSS (Really Simple Syndication), which is an XML based web content syndication format. By extending Ant-Miner to continuous learning, the algorithm could be easily used to cope with the dynamic nature of RSS. Another interesting research direction, which could help to achieve a much greater reduction in the number of attributes – while still preserving the most important words from the text – would be to use several other kinds of linguistic relationships available in WordNet.

References

1. I.H. Witten and E. Frank. Data Mining: Practical Machine Learning Tools with Java Implementations, Morgan Kaufmann Publications, 2000.
2. U.M. Fayyad, G. Piatetsky-Shapiro and P. Smyth. From data mining to knowledge discovery: an overview. In: U.M. Fayyad et al (Eds.) Advances in Knowledge Discovery and Data Mining, 1-34. AAAI/MIT, 1996.
3. R.S. Parpinelli, H.S. Lopes and A.A. Freitas. Data Mining with an Ant Colony Optimization Algorithm. IEEE Trans. on Evolutionary Computation, special issue on Ant Colony algorithms, 6(4), pp. 321-332, Aug. 2002.
4. R.S. Parpinelli, H.S. Lopes and A.A. Freitas. An Ant Colony Algorithm for Classification Rule Discovery. In: H.A. Abbass, R.A. Sarker, C.S. Newton. (Eds.) Data Mining: a Heuristic Approach, pp. 191-208. London: Idea Group Publishing, 2002.
5. S. Chakrabarti Mining the web: discovering knowledge from hypertext data. Morgan Kaufmann, 2003.
6. A. Abraham and V. Ramos. Web Usage Mining Using Artificial Ant Colony Clustering and Genetic Programming. Proc. Congress on Evolut. Comp. (CEC-2003). IEEE Press, 2003.
7. M. Cutler, H. Deng, S. S. Maniccam and W. Meng, A New Study Using HTML Structures to Improve Retrieval. Proc. 11th IEEE Int. Conf. on Tools with AI, 406-409. IEEE, 1999.

8. C. Fellbaum (Ed.) WordNet - an electronic lexical database. MIT, 1998.
9. E. Bonabeau, M. Dorigo and G. Theraulaz. Swarm Intelligence: from natural to artificial systems. Oxford, 1999.
10. M. Dorigo and L.M. Gambardella, Ant colonies for the traveling salesman problem. Biosystems 43, 73-81. 1997.
11. K.M. Hoe, W.K. Lai, T.S.Y. Tai. Homogeneous ants for web document similarity modeling and categorization. Ant algorithms, LNCS 2463, 256-261. Springer, 2002.
12. R. Schoonderwoerd, O. Holland, J. Bruten, Ant-like agents for load balancing in telecommunications networks. HP Labs Technical Report, HPL-96-76, May 21, 1996.

Oneiric Processing
Utilising the Anticipatory Classifier System

Julian C. Holley[1], Anthony G. Pipe[2], and Brian Carse[2]

[1] Clares MHE Ltd., Wells, Somerset, England
julian@holley.uklinux.net
[2] University of the West of England, Bristol, England
{anthony.pipe,brian.carse}@uwe.ac.uk

Abstract. The cognitive abilities of the anticipatory classifier system (ACS) have already been successfully shown in earlier work [20]. This report takes inspiration from some philosophical ideas for the purpose of dreaming in animals and humans. This is supported by recent neurological studies that show that rats revisit recent situations in a way that suggests dreaming [25]. An extension is made to the ACS that uses the incomplete information contained in the classifier list as a basis for an abstract world model in which to interact or dream. The abstract thread or dream direction is an emergent property of the selection process, this can be used to recycle around well known states and reduce real world interaction. The system is applied to the classic T-maze experiment and demonstrates that considerably less interactions with the real world are required in order to develop a confident world model.

1 Introduction

There is increasing evidence [8][18][24] that sleep and, in particular, rapid eye movement sleep[1] (REM) [1] where dreaming mostly occurs has important roles in memory and learning amongst both animals and humans. A recent neuro-physiological study has demonstrated that laboratory rats do *dream* or at least replay or rehearse maze experiments while asleep [25]. Psychological studies with animals and humans have shown that REM deprivation (REMD) can impair the learning of complex tasks [17]. Studies, particularly with rats, have demonstrated a distinct correlation between task complexity and onset/longevity of REM sleep [16]. A recent human sleep study has also demonstrated the influence of sleep on insight and reaction time after learning to solve a sequential numerical problem [24]. This paper attempts to relate philosophical concepts of dream sleep with physiological and psychological evidence to improve learning in the machine learning arena [21].

Specifically, a tentative start is made by exploring a modified latent learning architecture, the Anticipatory Classifier System (ACS) [3][19], to simulate simple dreaming.

---

[1] Also known as Paradoxical Sleep, reflecting the paradox of waking brain activity during sleep. For reviews see [10][15].

2 Background

This current research direction has been derived from previous studies controlling unstable dynamic mechanical systems in a failure avoidance framework. Adaptive learning systems, such as the Adaptive Heuristic Critic (AHC) [22] modulating Artificial Neural Networks, (ANNs) were used to control complex systems by avoiding failure [12]. The paradox of learning from failure, experience of the undesirable, led to thoughts into how to best develop off-line or cognitive strategies in such cases. The context of the original problem further shaped development by the batch orientated structure of expensive and dangerous on-line experience and cheap and safe off-line adaption. The natural analogy between the normal wake-sleep cycle and this work set the stage for the investigations into sleep and especially dream sleep adaptation.

3 Dreaming as Model Adaptation

It is well established that humans and higher animals interact with the world through a cognitive abstraction layer. Inputs, such as those in the visual, auditory, and olfactory domains, are combined with memory to form an internal representation and meaning. It is this internal representation that the agent perceives and makes decisions upon. Considering the visual sense, it is difficult for us to accept that the surrounding world does not actually look as we see it, but what we actually *see* is an internal representation of that world updated by external changes.

Combination and internalisation of the environmental stimulus is useful for real time interaction and also essential for more abstract functions such as anticipation, planning and imagination. The ability to predict or estimate the future is clearly a desirable survival attribute and sophisticated planning can be observed in many animals [7]. During sleep the brain is closed off from its usual source of environmental stimulus and during REM sleep (where dreaming mostly occurs) the normal outputs are also inhibited. In such a configuration it is possible that the animal or agent could interact with the internal representation of the world, (conceptualisation of reality) and adapt as though interacting with reality. In the sleep and dream research arena there are many arguments and counter-arguments as to the purpose of such behaviour.

The proposal here is that this delusional interaction has evolved in order to better prepare an agent for the unknown future, a cognitive maintenance program organised to update a predictive model of the future by using some, but not all, of the existing cognitive mechanisms. In short, one purpose of sleep and especially dreaming is to generate and maintain a predictive model of the future. By definition, an agent's anticipatory mechanism is based on a predictive model which, in a constantly changing world, never reaches the state of a true model. Rare or undesirable, and yet critical, scenarios can be generated and safely rehearsed, expanded and extrapolated in preparation for the real future.

4 Improved Convergence Through Model Learning Using the ACS

The long term goal of this work is to improve an agent's cognitive abilities inspired by developing theories from dream research. As an interim step toward this goal the ACS has been employed to reduce learning interactions with the real world by abstractly or cognitively revisiting situations so as to strengthen or weaken state relationships. As the ACS interacts with the environment a generalised model is developed, this knowledge can be exploited to perform some model learning 'Dyna style' [23] and reduce environmental interaction. As with the Dyna architecture the goal is to minimise environmental interaction and utilise information held in the model in order to obtain an accurate model with the least real world interactions. However, the ACS does not hold an explicit world model, but a generalised representation, and this becomes a challenge when employing the model to generate an abstract representation of the real environment. Model learning is applied to the ACS by switching ACS experiences between the real world and the developing model. The model is a snapshot of the classifier list at the time between leaving interactions with the real world and entering the abstract model world. Consider the following example; an ACS system has been interacting with an arbitrary plant and has formed the classifiers shown in Table 1.

Table 1. Example Classifier Set.

Rule	C	A	E	q
1	####	0	####	0.2
2	####	1	####	0.2
3	01##	0	10##	0.9
4	10##	1	01##	0.9

For classifier 3, the list indicates that with a high confidence ($q = 0.9$) if the agent is currently in a state where the first (left most) attributes are '01' and a '0' action is performed, then the first two attributes of the following state will be '10'; the rest of the attributes remain unchanged.

To present the ACS with a model of the real world, an algorithm must extract developing environmental information from the classifier list and present a response in the same format back to the ACS (Fig. 1). The current input state and action are taken as inputs and the next state is presented to the ACS as though the action has taken place in reality. The difference is that the real world response is based in reality whereas the model is an estimate derived from current experience. The algorithm for the model world operation and response is similar to that of the normal ACS selection process. From the snap copy of the classifier list, the model must select the most appropriate next state, given the current state and action. Let us consider that the ACS is running with the

Table 2. Illustration of State Cycling.

Step 1
Input state   = 0100 (matches all classifiers except C4)
C3 Expectation state = 10##
Expected next state = 1000 (last two attributes passed through)
Step 2
Input state   = 1000 (matches all classifiers except C3)
C4 expectation field = 01##
Expected next state = 0100 (last two attributes passed through)
---

previous classifier list. Assume the current state is '0100' and, through the normal selection process, classifier 3 is selected with the action '0'. The classifier expects the next state to become '1000'. At this point before executing the action on the real world, the switch 'S' changes state to allow the ACS to interact with the model world (Fig. 1). The model algorithm takes a copy of the current classifier list and current input state and waits for an action from the ACS. Without distinguishing between the two worlds, the ACS executes action '0' on the model world instead of the real world and the model responds. The model must now reply to the ACS as though the ACS is interacting with the real world. The model replies by performing a selection process (see Table 3) on matching classifiers and uses the winning classifier's expectation field to generate the next state response. After the first cycle the input state therefore becomes uncoupled from reality.

From the previous list only two classifiers match in both the condition and action part, classifier 1 and classifier 3. If (as with the ACS) a high bias is given to classifiers that are more specific, the likelihood that classifier 3 will

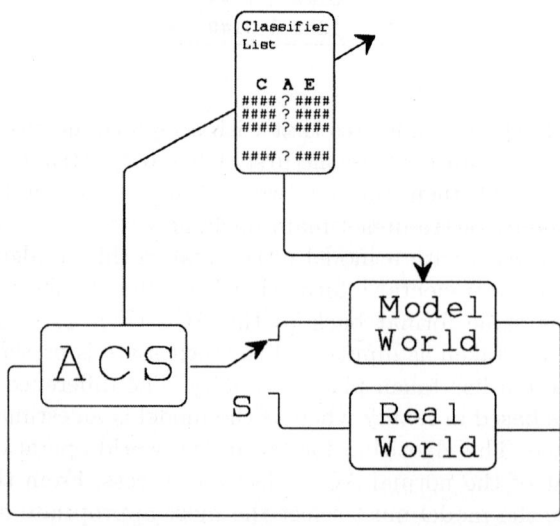

Fig. 1. The 'ACS' switching between the real world and the model of the real world.

win the bid is high (good prediction history, $q = 0.9$ and contains less hash terms). If classifier 3 wins the bid the model algorithm simply responds to the ACS with the next expected state by presenting the current input with a pass through operation using the expectation part of classifier 3 to form '1000'. If classifier 1 wins (even with the small bid), then the current input state will be passed through as the next state (the model presents no change, an *incorrect response*)[2]. When the ACS receives the 'predicted' response from the model, this is taken as the actual response and learning occurs. The input state presented to the ACS is now '1000'. In response to this input the ACS is most likely to choose classifier 4 resulting in issuing action 1 to the model. As with the previous criteria the model now uses classifier 4 to respond, resulting in a return to the first '0100' state as illustrated in Table 2. This can therefore reduce the amount of interactions that are required for the ACS to build up an accurate model in a static environment. When a novel situation is presented to the model and no input-condition and action pair exists, the root classifiers will always win the bid and predict no change. To explore this strategy within the context of *wake* (real world interaction) and *dream* (model world interaction) scenarios, a set of experiments are run whereby interaction between the two are periodically divided. The adapted ACS was applied to a simple maze learning problem, the T-maze adapted from Stolzmann [19] in order to learn a confident world model.

5 Experimental Procedure

The object of the experiment is to record the quantity of total real interactions that are required to reach a confident world model when ACS operation is split between the real and model worlds. Sessions continue to run until a complete sweep of each state with each action predicts the next state correctly and with a classifier that has a high prediction quality ($q > 90\%$). Each of the 10 sessions have a decreasing interaction with the real world and increasing interaction with the developing model. Basic ACS operation and parameterisation are as in Stolzmann's T-maze experiment [19]. Sessions are limited to 5000 cycles, results are averaged over 100 runs[3]. Four experiments are conducted with different selection policies listed in Table 3, for both the ACS and the model selection policy during the model phase of the sessions.

A probabilistic bid is by the roulette wheel selection technique and deterministic selection is a winner takes all technique. Results are illustrated in Fig. 2 and Fig. 3. The X-axis represents each of the 10 sessions with varying percentages of real and model interaction. Session 1 starts with 100% real world interactions (normal ACS) and session 10 ends with just 10% real and 90% model world interactions.

---

[2] The ACS requires environmental causality
[3] Comprehensive experimental detail is publicly available [9]

Table 3. Experimental Exploration Strategies

Experiment	ACS Selection Policy	Model Selection Policy
1	Probabilistic bid	Deterministic
2	Probabilistic bid	Probabilistic bid
3	Deterministic	Deterministic
4	Deterministic	Probabilistic bid

The Y-axis represents the following recordings :-

```
Real     = total real world interaction.
Model    = total model world interaction.
Correct  = independent correct responses.
Restarts = useless responses from the model phase.
```

5.1 Experiment T-Maze 1 and 2

The ACS classifier selection process of probabilistic bidding operates consistently throughout interaction with the real and model worlds. In the first experiment the model selection process is deterministic. In the second experiment the model selection process is probabilistic.

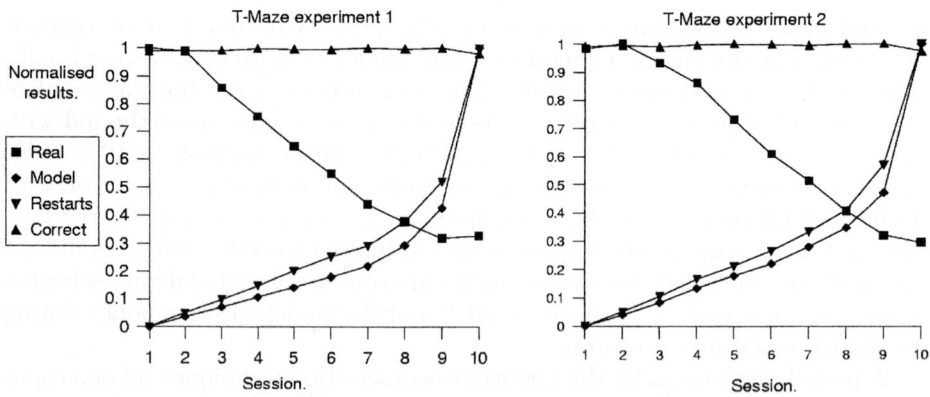

Fig. 2. T-Maze experiments 1 and 2.

5.2 Experiment T-Maze 3 and 4

The ACS classifier selection process of probabilistic bidding operates throughout interaction with the real world, but changes to deterministic during the model phase. In the third experiment the model selection process is also deterministic. In the fourth experiment the model selection process is probabilistic.

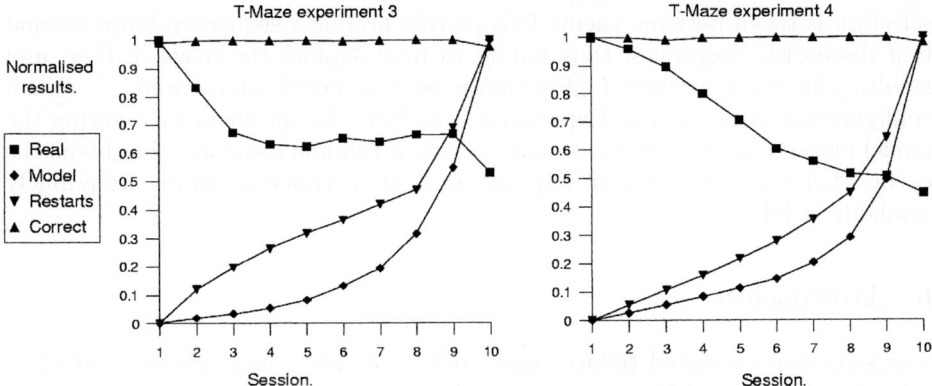

Fig. 3. T-Maze experiments 3 and 4.

5.3 Interpretation of the Results

For each session the ACS interacts between the *real* world (T-Maze) and then with a *model* of that environment. The model responses are generated from the current classifier list at the point of the switch. Switching between the two is distributed throughout the session. For example, in session 10 there are 10 initial interaction steps with the real world followed by 90 steps with the model. Throughout the session, the accumulated real and model interactions are collated until the ACS has developed a confident model of the environment. In all cases, the requirement to interact with the real world decreases in order to generate a confident world model. As interactions with the real world decrease, the ability of the model to generate realistic responses decreases, significantly increasing model cycles and tending towards infinity as real interactions approach zero.

In Experiment 1 and 2 (Fig. 2) the ACS interacts normally, i.e. employing a selection process based on the historical prediction quality of the classifier proportioned by a specificity factor. In Experiment 1 the model selection process replies with a response based on the classifier with the highest bid without introducing an exploratory component implicit in the ACS roulette wheel selection. From the perspective of minimising real world interaction (for reasons outlined in Section 2) this strategy is the most logical and subsequently performs well. This has parallels with Sutton's prioritised sweeping in the Dyna framework [21]. The strategy only allows exploration within the real world session and only allows reiteration by selections of the best generated classifiers in the model session phase. Experiment 2 allows a probabilistic response during the model session, allowing occasional *exploration* by selecting other matching classifiers. Effectively the ACS real world interaction is mirrored in the model world interaction. This is reflected by the slight increase in real world interaction.

Interesting results are shown in Experiments 3 and 4 (Fig. 3). In Experiment 3 both the ACS and the model response choose the best classifiers upon to use, and with which to respond. The only way this configuration can explore is when the selection process is presented with identical bids. In that case, a random selection is taken between them. This pairing produces sequential loops around first discovered sequences, thus failing to fully explore the maze further, and resulting in a consistently high reliance on real world interactions. The final configuration illustrated in Experiment 4 reduces this problem by allowing the model phase to *explore* by occasionally choosing random responses that break the cyclical behaviour observed in Experiment 3. (Experimental details are publicly available at [9]).

6 Discussion

The structure presented reduces real world interaction in a similar method to other Dyna style model learning systems [23]. Other classifier systems have incorporated latent learning [2][13][14] and have also combined Dyna style extensions [5][6][20]. However these systems have developed from a machine learning perspective (with perhaps the exception of Stolzmann et al. [20]). This work is contrasted here in 3 areas, firstly in the model generation scheme. The model generates sequence responses based on current experience represented in the classifier list. Realistic experience, or practice sequences, are an emergent property of the selection requiring no explicit guidance. Secondly, the structure maintains the wake-sleep analogy. The agent learns without differentiating between the real world and the simulated world, the adaptive emphasis falls on the content of the generated model thread. Finally, this work differs in the source of direction and aims. Artificial dreaming has previously been simulated to promote a particular functional stance [4]. It has also been associated with the behaviour of some machine learning systems including the ACS [20]. This work takes the view that dreaming *has* evolved to fulfill some useful function (probably multifaceted)[11]. Those propositions are being explored with existing and new machine learning architectures to develop novel cognitive adaptations.

The function of generating useful threads and how the threads modify existing rules is the subject of continuing work. The selection process could easily be modified further by various methods, such as mutating attributes from classifiers that have a common condition part (in a match or action set) or filling in non-specified attributes from other similar classifiers in uncertain situations. During the dream thread execution, several actions could be taken to generate new rules, assimilate rules or delete rules.

Rules generated during the model interaction present the opportunity for anticipatory behaviour based on real prototypical sequences in situations that have not actually been experienced (dreams). Rules are generated in advance, their generation being guided by real world adaptation (waking). Explicitly, the agent receives no new information during model sessions, but implicit preparation or anticipation could be developed. Research on rodent sleep behaviour recently reported that subjects where more likely to dream about maze running *before* maze runs when sessions were scheduled rather than just after the session, i.e., the rodents appeared to be rehearsing an anticipated event [25].

7 Conclusion

Inspired by developing sleep and dream research, an extension has been applied that allows the ACS agent to replay abstract dreamlike state to state transitions, as though real, on a simple maze problem. The results have shown that this reduces the amount of real world learning interactions that would otherwise be required to develop a confident world model. In the constrained and static mazes so far explored, including the T-maze reported herein, rule creation has been inhibited during the model phase and adaptation occurs through modification of the predictive quality of existing rules. There is considerable scope for further work on static environments including, for example, generalisation and reduction of the rule base during the model phase. However one of the most interesting areas for future work is the prospect of speculative rule creation during the model phase in dynamic environments. This could include rules created from situations that have not actually been experienced yet but could be employed in pending uncertain real situations. With respect to the long term goals of this current research, it is interesting to conclude with a quote from neurological researchers Kenway Louie and Matthew Wilson [25] on results from their research into rodent sleep behaviour. In their recent study they were able to detect temporal reactivation of spatial hippocampal place cells during REM sleep periods that were very similar to activations when awake, in effect they could view rodent dreams during REM sleep:-

> "... This reactivation of previous behavioural representations may be important for the learning of procedural tasks, which is dependent upon REM sleep. Mnemonic information that may have shared characteristics along a particular behavioural axis such as emotion could be juxtaposed and evaluated for common causal links, allowing adaptive behaviour change based on prior experience ...".

References

1. Aserinsky, E. and Klietmen, N. (1953) Regularly Occurring Periods of Eye Mobility, and Concomitant Phenomena, During Sleep. Science 118: 273-274
2. Bull, L. (2001) Lookahead and Latent Learning in ZCS. UWE Learning Classifier Systems Group Technical Report UWELCSG01-004, University of the West of England.
3. Butz, M. V. (2001) Anticipatory Learning Classifier Systems, Genetic Algorithms and Evolutionary Computation, 4. Kluwer Academic Publishers. ISBN 0-792-37630-7
4. Crick, F. and Mitchison, G. (1986) REM Sleep and Neural Nets. Journal of Mind and Behavior 7. 229-250
5. Gerard, P. and Sigaud, O. (2001) YACS: Combining Dynamic Programming with Generalization in Classifier Systems. In Advances in Classifier Systems, Vol. 1996 of LNAI, Springer-Verlag. 52-69
6. Gerard, P., Meyer J. A. and Sigaud, O. (2003) Combining Latent Learning with Dynamic Programming in the Modular Anticipatory Classifier System. European Journal of Operation Research (submitted 2003)

7. Heinrich, B. (2000) Testing Insight in Ravens. In Heyes, C. and Hiber, L. (eds.): The Evolution of Cognition. The MIT Press, Cambridge, MA. ISBN 0-262-09286-1. (2000) 289-305
8. Hobson, J. A., Pace-Schott, E.F., Stickgold, R. and Kahn, D. (1998) To Dream or Not to Dream? Relevant Data from New Neuroimaging and Electrophysiological Studies. Current Opinions in Neurobiology, 8. 239-244
9. Holley, J. (2004) First Investigations of Dream-like Cognitive Processing using the Anticipatory Classifier System. UWE Learning Classifier Systems Group Technical Report UWELCSG04-002, University of the West of England, England.
10. Jouvet, M. (1994) The Paradox of Sleep: The Story of Dreaming. Translated by Laurence Garey (1999). The MIT Press, Cambridge MA. ISBN 0-262-10080-0
11. Kavanau, J. L., (2004) Sleep Researchers need to bring Darwin on Board: Elucidating Functions of Sleep via Adaptedness and Natural Selection (Editorial). Medical Hypotheses Vol. 62. 161-165
12. Miller, T. W., Sutton, R. S. and Werbos, P. J. (1990) Neural Networks for Control, The MIT Press, Cambridge, MA. ISBN 0-262-13261-3
13. Riolo, R. L. (1991) Lookahead Planning and Latent Learning in a Classifier System. Proceedings of the First International Conference on Simulation of Adaptive Behavior. Cambridge, MA: The MIT Press. 316-326
14. Roberts, G. (1993) Dynamic Planning for Classifier Systems. Proceedings of the 5th International Conference on Genetic Algorithms (ICGA93). Morgan Kaufmann. 231-237
15. Rock, A. (2004) The Mind at Night, Basic Books, Cambridge MA. ISBN 0-7382-0755-1
16. Smith, C. and Lapp, L. (1986) Prolonged Increases in both PS and Number of REMs Following a Shuttle Avoidance Task, Physiological Behavior, Vol. 43. 1053-1057
17. Smith, C. (1995) Sleep States and Memory Processes, Behavioral Brain Research, Vol. 69. 137-145
18. Stickgold, R., Hobson, J. A., Fosse, M. and Fosse. M. (2001) Sleep, Learning and Dreams: Off-line Memory Processing, Science, Vol. 294. 1052-1057
19. Stolzmann, W. (1998) Anticipatory Classifier Systems. Genetic Programming 1998: Proceedings of the Third Annual Conference, July 22-25, 1998, University of Wisconsin, Madison, Wisconsin, San Francisco, CA: Morgan Kaufmann. 658-664
20. Stolzmann, W., Butz, M. V., Hoffmann, J. and Goldberg, D. E. (2000) First Cognitive Capabilities in the Anticipatory Classifier System, From Animals to Animats 6, Proceedings from the Sixth International Conference on Adaptive Behavior. 285-296
21. Sutton, R. S. and Barto, A. G. (1998) Reinforcement Learning. The MIT Press, Cambridge, MA. ISBN 0-262-19398-1
22. Sutton, R. S. (1984) Temporal Credit Assignment in Reinforcement in Reinforcement Learning. Ph.D. Dissertation. University of Massachusetts, Amherst.
23. Sutton, R. S. (1991) Dyna, An Integrated Architecture for Learning, Planning and Reacting. SIGART Bulletin, 2: ACM Press. 160-163
24. Wagner, U., Gals, S., Haider, H., Verleger, R. and Born, J. (2004) Sleep Inspires Insight, Nature, Vol. 427. 352-355
25. Wilson, M. A. and Louie, K. (2001) Temporally Structured Replay of Awake Hippocampal Ensemble Activity During Rapid Eye Movement Sleep, Neuron, Vol. 29. 145-156

Self-organizing Neural Grove: Efficient Multiple Classifier System Using Pruned Self-generating Neural Trees

Hirotaka Inoue[1] and Hiroyuki Narihisa[2]

[1] Department of Electrical Engineering and Information Science,
Kure National College of Technology,
2-2-11 Agaminami, Kure-shi, Hiroshima 737-8506, Japan
hiro@kure-nct.ac.jp
[2] Department of Information and Computer Engineering,
Okayama University of Science,
1-1 Ridai-cho, Okayama-shi, Okayama 700-0005, Japan
narihisa@ice.ous.ac.jp

Abstract. Multiple classifier systems (MCS) have become popular during the last decade. Self-generating neural tree (SGNT) is one of the suitable base-classifiers for MCS because of the simple setting and fast learning. However, the computation cost of the MCS increases in proportion to the number of SGNT. In an earlier paper, we proposed a pruning method for the structure of the SGNT in the MCS to reduce the computation cost. In this paper, we propose a novel pruning method for more effective processing and we call this model as self-organizing neural grove (SONG). The pruning method is constructed from an on-line pruning method and an off-line pruning method. Experiments have been conducted to compare the SONG with an unpruned MCS based on SGNT, an MCS based on C4.5, and k-nearest neighbor method. The results show that the SONG can improve its classification accuracy as well as reducing the computation cost.

1 Introduction

Classifiers need to find hidden information in the given large data effectively and classify unknown data as accurately as possible [1]. Recently, to improve the classification accuracy, multiple classifier systems (MCS) such as neural network ensembles, bagging, and boosting have been used for practical data mining applications [2–5]. In general, the base classifiers of the MCS use traditional models such as neural networks (backpropagation network and radial basis function network) [6] and decision trees (CART and C4.5) [7].

Neural networks have great advantages of adaptability, flexibility, and universal nonlinear input-output mapping capability. However, to apply these neural networks, it is necessary to determine the network structure and some parameters by human experts, and it is quite difficult to choose the right network structure suitable for a particular application at hand. Moreover, they require a long training time to learn the input-output relation of the given data. These drawbacks prevent neural networks being the base classifier of the MCS for practical applications.

Self-generating neural tree (SGNT) [8] have simple network design and high speed learning. SGNT are an extension of the self-organizing maps (SOM) of Kohonen [9] and utilize the competitive learning. The abilities of SGNT make it suitable for the base classifier of the MCS. In order to improve in the accuracy of SGNN, we proposed ensemble self-generating neural networks (ESGNN) for classification [10] as one of the MCS. Although the accuracy of ESGNN improves by using various SGNT, the computation cost, that is, the computation time and the memory capacity increases in proportion to the increase in number of SGNN in the MCS.

In an earlier paper [11], we proposed a pruning method for the structure of the SGNN in the MCS to reduce the computation cost. In this paper, we propose a novel MCS pruning method for more effective processing and we call this model as self-organizing neural grove (SONG). This pruning method is constructed from two stages. At the first stage, we introduce an on-line pruning method to reduce the computation cost by using class labels in learning. At the second stage, we optimize the structure of the SGNT in the MCS to improve the generalization capability by pruning the redundant leaves after learning. In the optimization stage, we introduce a threshold value as a pruning parameter to decide which subtree's leaves to prune and estimate with 10-fold cross-validation [12]. After the optimization, the SONG can improve its classification accuracy as well as reducing the computation cost. We use bagging [2] as a resampling technique for the SONG.

We investigate the improvement performance of the SONG by comparing it with an MCS based on C4.5 [13] using ten problems in UCI machine learning repository [14]. Moreover, we compare the SONG with k-nearest neighbor (k-NN) [15] to investigate the computational cost and the classification accuracy. The SONG demonstrates higher classification accuracy and faster processing speed than k-NN on average.

2 Constructing Self-organizing Neural Grove

In this section, we describe how to prune redundant leaves in the SONG. First, we mention the on-line pruning method in learning of the SGNT. Second, we show the optimization method in constructing the SONG. Finally, we show a simple example of the pruning method for a two dimensional classification problem.

2.1 On-Line Pruning of Self-generating Neural Tree

SGNT is based on SOM and implemented as a competitive learning. The SGNT can be constructed directly from the given training data without any intervening human effort. The SGNT algorithm is defined as a tree construction problem of how to construct a tree structure from the given data which consist of multiple attributes under the condition that the final leaves correspond to the given data.

```
Input:
  A set of training examples E = {e_i}, i = 1, ... , N.
  A distance measure d(e_i,w_j).
Program Code:
  copy(n_1,e_1);
  for (i = 2, j = 2; i <= N; i++) {
    n_win = choose(e_i, n_1);
    if (leaf(n_win)) {
      copy(n_j, w_win);
      connect(n_j, n_win);
      j++;
    }
    copy(n_j, e_i);
    connect(n_j, n_win);
    j++;
    prune(n_win);
  }
Output:
  Constructed SGNT by E.
```

Fig. 1. SGNT algorithm.

Table 1. Sub procedures of the SGNT algorithm.

Sub procedure	Specification
$copy(n_j, e_i/w_{win})$	Create n_j, copy e_i/w_{win} as w_j in n_j.
$choose(e_i, n_1)$	Decide n_{win} for e_i.
$leaf(n_{win})$	Check n_{win} whether n_{win} is a leaf.
$connect(n_j, n_{win})$	Connect n_j as a child leaf of n_{win}.
$prune(n_{win})$	Prune leaves if they have the same class.

Before we describe the SGNT algorithm, we denote some notations.

- input data vector: $e_i \in \mathbb{R}^m$.
- root, leaf, and node in the SGNT: n_j.
- weight vector of n_j: $w_j \in \mathbb{R}^m$.
- the number of the leaves in n_j: c_j.
- distance measure: $d(e_i, w_j)$.
- winner leaf for e_i in the SGNT: n_{win}.

The SGNT algorithm is a hierarchical clustering algorithm. The pseudo C code of the SGNT algorithm is given in Figure 1. In Figure 1, several sub procedures are used. Table 1 shows the sub procedures of the SGNT algorithm and their specifications.

In order to decide the winner leaf n_{win} in the sub procedure choose(e_i,n_1), the competitive learning is used. If an n_j includes the n_{win} as its descendant in the SGNT, the weight w_{jk} ($k = 1, 2, \ldots, m$) of the n_j is updated as follows:

$$w_{jk} \leftarrow w_{jk} + \frac{1}{c_j} \cdot (e_{ik} - w_{jk}), \quad 1 \leq k \leq m. \qquad (1)$$

After all training data are inserted into the SGNT as the leaves, the leaves have each class label as the outputs and the weights of each node are the averages of the corresponding weights of all its leaves. The whole network of the SGNT reflects the given feature space by its topology. For more details concerning how to construct and perform the SGNT, see [8]. Note, to optimize the structure of the SGNT effectively, we remove the threshold value of the original SGNT algorithm in [8] to control the number of leaves based on the distance because of the trade-off between the memory capacity and the classification accuracy. In order to avoid the above problem, we introduce a new pruning method in the sub procedure prune(n_win). We use the class label to prune leaves. For leaves that have the n_{win}'s parent node, if all leaves belong to the same class, then these leaves are pruned and the parent node is given the class.

2.2 Optimization of the SONG

The SGNT has the capability of high speed processing. However, the accuracy of the SGNT is inferior to the conventional approaches, such as nearest neighbor, because the SGNT has no guarantee to reach the nearest leaf for unknown data. Hence, we construct the SONG by taking the majority of plural SGNT's outputs to improve the accuracy.

Although the accuracy of the SONG is superior or comparable to the accuracy of conventional approaches, the computational cost increases in proportion to the increase in the number of SGNTs in the SONG. In particular, the huge memory requirement prevents the use of the SONG for large datasets even with latest computers.

In order to improve the classification accuracy, we propose an optimization method of the SONG for classification. This method has two parts, the merge phase and the evaluation phase. The merge phase is performed as a pruning algorithm to reduce dense leaves (Figure 2). This phase uses the class information and a threshold value α to decide which subtree's leaves to prune or not. For leaves that have the same parent node, if the proportion of the most common class is greater than or equal to the threshold value α, then these leaves are pruned and the parent node is given the most common class.

```
1 begin    initialize j = the height of the SGNT
2    do for each subtree's leaves in the height j
3       if the ratio of the most class ≥ the threshold value α,
4       then merge all leaves to parent node
5    if all subtrees are traversed in the height j,
6    then j ← j − 1
7    until j = 0
8 end.
```

Fig. 2. The merge phase.

```
1 begin initialize α = 0.5
2   do for each α
3     evaluate the merge phase with 10-fold cross validation
4     if the best classification accuracy is obtained,
5     then record the α as the optimal threshold value
6     α ← α + 0.05
7   until α = 1
8 end
```

Fig. 3. The evaluation phase.

The optimum threshold values α of the given problems are different from each other. The evaluation phase is performed to choose the best threshold value by introducing 10-fold cross validation (Figure 3).

2.3 An Example of the Pruning Method for the SONG

We show an example of the pruning method for the SONG in Figure 4. This is a two-dimensional classification problem with two equal circular Gaussian distributions that have an overlap. The shaded plane is the decision region of class 0 and the other plane is the decision region of class 1 by the SGNT. The dotted line is the ideal decision boundary. The number of training samples is 200 (class0: 100,class1: 100) (Figure 4(a)).

The unpruned SGNT is given in Figure 4(b). In this case, 200 leaves and 120 nodes are automatically generated by the SGNT algorithm. In this unpruned SGNT, the height is 7 and the number of units is 320. In this, we define the unit to count the sum of the root, nodes, and leaves of the SGNT. The root is the node which is of height 0. The unit is used as a measure of the memory requirement in the next section. Figure 4(c) shows the pruned SGNT after the optimization stage in $\alpha = 1$. In this case, 159 leaves and 107 nodes are pruned away and 48 units remain. The decision boundary is the same as the unpruned SGNT. Figure 4(d) shows the pruned SGNT after the optimization stage in $\alpha = 0.6$. In this case, 182 leaves and 115 nodes are pruned away and only 21 units remain. Moreover, the decision boundary is improved more than the unpruned SGNT because this case can reduce the effect of the overlapping class by pruning the SGNT.

In the above example, we use all training data to construct the SGNT. The structure of the SGNT is changed by the order of the training data. Hence, we can construct the SONG from the same training data by changing the input order.

To show how well the SONG is optimized by the pruning algorithm, we show an example of the SONG in the same problem used above. Figure 5(a) and Figure 5(b) show the decision region of the SONG in $\alpha = 1$ and $\alpha = 0.6$, respectively. We set the number of SGNTs K as 25. The result of Figure 5(b) is a better estimation of the ideal decision region than the result of Figure 5(a). We investigate the pruning method for more complex problems in the next section.

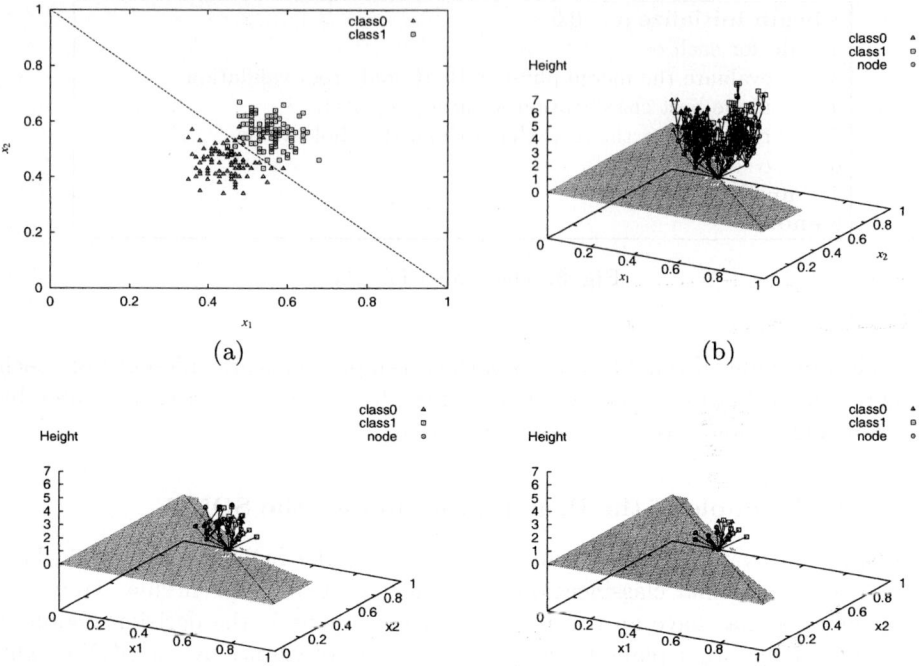

Fig. 4. An example of the SONG's pruning algorithm, (a) a two dimensional classification problem with two equal circular Gaussian distribution, (b) the structure of the unpruned SGNT, (c) the structure of the pruned SGNT ($\alpha = 1$), and (d) the structure of the pruned SGNT ($\alpha = 0.6$). The shaded plane is the decision region of class 0 by the SGNT and the doted line shows the ideal decision boundary.

3 Experimental Results

We investigate the computational cost (the memory capacity and the computation time) and the classification accuracy of the SONG with bagging for ten benchmark problems in UCI machine learning repository [14]. We evaluate how the SONG is pruned using 10-fold cross-validation for the ten benchmark problems. In this experiment, we use a modified Euclidean distance measure for the SONG and k-NN. Since the performance of the SONG is not sensitive in the threshold value α, we set the different threshold values α which are moved from 0.5 to 1; $\alpha = [0.5, 0.55, 0.6, \ldots, 1]$. We set the number of SGNT K in the SONG as 25 and execute 100 trials by changing the sampling order of each training set. All experiments in this section were performed on an UltraSPARC workstation with a 900MHz CPU, 1GB RAM, and Solaris 8.

Table 2 shows the average memory requirement and classification accuracy of 100 trials for the SONG. As the memory requirement, we count the number of units which is the sum of the root, nodes, and leaves of the SGNT. The average memory requirement is reduced from 65% to 96.6% and the classification

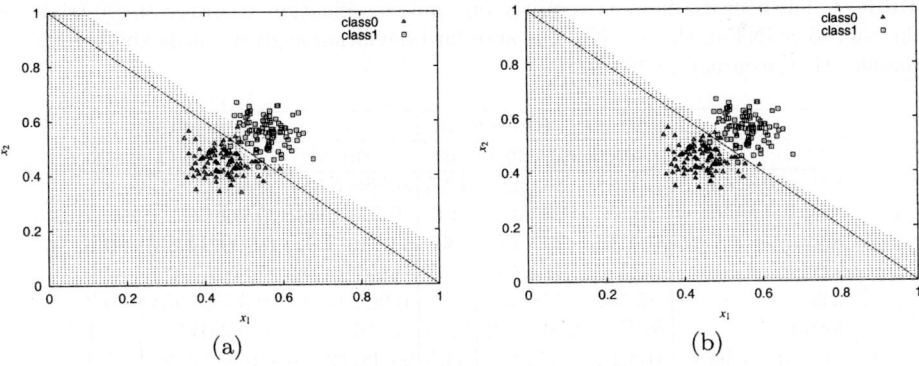

Fig. 5. An example of the SONG's decision boundary ($K = 25$), (a) $\alpha = 1$, and (b) $\alpha = 0.6$. The shaded plane is the decision region of class 0 by the SONG and the doted line shows the ideal decision boundary.

accuracy is improved 0.1% to 2.9% by optimizing the SONG. This supports that the SONG can be effectively used for all datasets with regard to both the computation cost and the classification accuracy.

To evaluate the SONG's performance, we compare the SONG with an MCS based on C4.5. We set the number of classifiers K in the MCS as 25 and we construct both MCS by bagging. Table 3 shows the improved performance of the SONG and the MCS based on C4.5. The results of the SGNT and the SONG are the average of 100 trials. The SONG has a better performance than the MCS based on C4.5 for 6 of the 10 datasets. Although the MCS based on C4.5 degrades the classification accuracy for iris, the SONG can improve the classification accuracy for all problems. Therefore, the SONG is an efficient MCS on the basis of both the scalability for large scale datasets and the robust improving generalization capability for the noisy datasets comparable to the MCS with C4.5.

To show the advantages of the SONG, we compare it with k-NN on the same problems. In the SONG, we choose the best classification accuracy of 100 trials with bagging. In k-NN, we choose the best accuracy where k is 1,3,5,7,9,11,13,15, and 25 with 10-fold cross-validation. All methods are compiled by using gcc with the optimization level -O2 on the same workstation.

Table 4 shows the classification accuracy, the memory requirement, and the computation time achieved by the SONG and k-NN. Although there are compression methods available for k-NN [16], they take enormous computation time to construct an effective model. We use the exhaustive k-NN in this experiment. Since k-NN does not discard any training sample, the size of this classifier corresponds to the training set size. The results of k-NN correspond to the average measures obtained by 10-fold cross-validation that is the same experimental procedure of the SONG. Next, we show the results for each category.

Table 2. The average memory requirement and classification accuracy of 100 trials for the bagged SGNT in the SONG. The standard deviation is given inside the bracket on classification accuracy ($\times 10^{-3}$).

	memory requirement			classification accuracy		
Dataset	pruned	unpruned	ratio	pruned	unpruned	ratio
balance-scale	107.68	861.18	12.5	0.866(6.36)	0.837(7.83)	+2.9
breast-cancer-w	30.88	897.37	3.4	0.97(2.41)	0.966(2.71)	+0.4
glass	104.33	297.75	35	0.714(13.01)	0.709(14.86)	+0.5
ionosphere	50.75	472.39	10.7	0.891(6.75)	0.862(7.33)	+2.9
iris	15.64	208.56	7.4	0.962(6.04)	0.955(5.45)	+0.7
letter	6197.5	27028.56	22.9	0.956(0.77)	0.955(0.72)	+0.1
liver-disorders	163.12	471.6	34.5	0.648(12.89)	0.636(13.36)	+1.2
new-thyroid	49.45	298.21	16.5	0.958(7.5)	0.957(7.49)	+0.1
pima-diabetes	204.4	1045.03	19.5	0.749(7.05)	0.728(7.83)	+2.1
wine	15	238.95	6.2	0.976(4.41)	0.972(5.57)	+0.4
Average	693.88	3181.96	16.9	0.869	0.858	+1.1

Table 3. The improved performance of the pruned MCS and the MCS based on C4.5 with bagging.

	MCS based on SGNT			MCS based on C4.5		
Dataset	SGNT	MCS	ratio	C4.5	MCS	ratio
balance-scale	0.779	**0.866**	+8.7	0.795	0.827	+3.2
breast-cancer-w	0.956	**0.97**	+1.4	0.946	0.963	+1.7
glass	0.642	0.714	+7.2	0.664	**0.757**	+9.3
ionosphere	0.852	0.891	+3.9	0.897	**0.92**	+2.3
iris	0.943	**0.962**	+1.9	0.953	0.947	−0.6
letter	0.879	**0.956**	+7.7	0.880	0.938	+5.8
liver-disorders	0.59	0.648	+5.8	0.635	**0.736**	+10.1
new-thyroid	0.939	**0.958**	+1.9	0.93	0.94	+1
pima-diabetes	0.695	0.749	+5.4	0.749	**0.767**	+1.8
wine	0.955	**0.976**	+2.1	0.927	0.949	+2.2
Average	0.823	0.869	+4.6	0.837	**0.874**	+3

First, with regard to the classification accuracy, the SONG is superior to k-NN for 8 of the 10 datasets and gives 1.6% improvement on average. Second, in terms of the memory requirement, even though the SONG includes the root and the nodes which are generated by the SGNT generation algorithm, this is less than k-NN for all problems. Although the memory requirement of the SONG is totally used K times in Table 4, we release the memory of SGNT for each trial and reuse the memory for effective computation. Therefore, the memory requirement is suppressed by the size of the single SGNT. Finally, in view of the computation time, although the SONG consumes the cost of K times of the SGNT to construct the model and test for the unknown dataset, the average computation time is faster than k-NN. The SONG is slower than k-NN for small

Table 4. The classification accuracy, the memory requirement, and the computation time of ten trials for the best pruned SONG and k-NN.

Dataset	classification acc.		memory requirement		computation time (s)	
	SONG	k-NN	SONG	k-NN	SONG	k-NN
balance-scale	0.878	**0.888**	**109.93**	562.5	**0.82**	1.14
breast-cancer-w	**0.974**	0.969	**26.8**	629.1	**1.18**	1.25
glass	**0.758**	0.701	**91.33**	192.6	0.36	**0.08**
ionosphere	**0.912**	0.866	**51.38**	315.9	1.93	**0.2**
iris	**0.973**	0.96	**11.34**	135	0.13	**0.05**
letter	0.958	**0.96**	**6208.03**	18000	**208.52**	503.14
liver-disorders	**0.685**	0.653	**134.17**	310.5	**0.54**	0.56
new-thyroid	**0.972**	**0.972**	**45.74**	193.5	0.23	**0.05**
pima-diabetes	**0.764**	0.751	**183.57**	691.2	**1.72**	2.49
wine	**0.983**	0.977	**11.8**	160.2	0.31	**0.15**
Average	**0.885**	0.869	**687.41**	2119.1	**21.57**	50.91

datasets such as glass, ionosphere, and iris. However, the SONG is faster than k-NN for large datasets such as balance-scale, letter, and pima-diabetes. In the case of letter, in particular, the computation time of the SONG is faster than k-NN by about 2.4 times. We need to repeat 10-fold cross validation many times to select the optimum parameters for α and k. This evaluation consumes much computation time for large datasets such as letter. Therefore, the SONG based on the fast and compact SGNT is useful and practical for large datasets. Moreover, the SONG has the ability of parallel computation because each classifier behaves independently. In conclusion, the SONG is a practical method for large-scale data mining compared with k-NN.

4 Conclusions

In this paper, we proposed a new pruning method for the MCS based on SGNT, which is called SONG, and evaluated the computation cost and the accuracy. We introduced an on-line and off-line pruning method and evaluated the SONG by 10-fold cross-validation. Experimental results showed that the memory requirement reduces remarkably, and the accuracy increases by using the pruned SGNT as the base classifier of the SONG. The SONG is a useful and practical MCS to classify large datasets. In future work, we will study an incremental learning and a parallel and distributed processing of the SONG for large scale data mining.

Acknowledgment

The authors are grateful to anonymous referees for their constructive comments and criticism that have helped to improve the paper. This research was partially supported by the Ministry of Education, Science, Sports and Culture, Grant in-Aid for Young Scientists (B), 15700206, 2004.

References

1. J. Han and M. Kamber. *Data Mining: Concepts and Techniques*. Morgan Kaufmann Publishers, San Francisco, CA, 2000.
2. L. Breiman. Bagging predictors. *Machine Learning*, 24:123–140, 1996.
3. R. E. Schapire. The strength of weak learnability. *Machine Learning*, 5(2):197–227, 1990.
4. J. R. Quinlan. Bagging, Boosting, and C4.5. In Proc. *the Thirteenth National Conference on Artificial Intelligence*, pages 725–730, Portland, OR, 1996.
5. G. Rätsch, T. Onoda, and K.-R. Müller. Soft margins for AdaBoost. *Machine Learning*, 42(3):287–320, March 2001.
6. C. M. Bishop. *Neural Networks for Pattern Recognition*. Oxford University Press, New York, 1995.
7. R. O. Duda, P. E. Hart, and D. G. Stork. *Pattern Classification*. John Wiley & Sons Inc., New York, 2nd ed., 2000.
8. W. X. Wen, A. Jennings, and H. Liu. Learning a neural tree. In Proc. *the International Joint Conference on Neural Networks*, volume 2, pages 751–756, Beijing, China, 1992. This paper is available at ftp://ftp.cis.ohio-state.edu/pub/neuroprose/wen.sgnt-learn.ps.Z.
9. T. Kohonen. *Self-Organizing Maps*. Springer-Verlag, Berlin, 1995.
10. H. Inoue and H. Narihisa. Improving generalization ability of self-generating neural networks through ensemble averaging. In T. Terano, H. Liu, and A. L P Chen, eds., *The Fourth Pacific-Asia Conference on Knowledge Discovery and Data Mining*, vol. 1805 of *LNAI*, pages 177–180, Springer-Verlag, Berlin, 2000.
11. H. Inoue and H. Narihisa. Optimizing a multiple classifier system. In M. Ishizuka and A. Sattar, eds., *PRICAI2002: Trends in Artificial Intelligence*, volume 2417 of *LNAI*, pages 285–294, Springer-Verlag, Berlin, 2002.
12. M. Stone. Cross-validation: A review. *Math. Operationsforsch. Statist., Ser. Statistics*, 9(1):127–139, 1978.
13. J. R. Quinlan. *C4.5: Programs for Machine Learning*. Morgan Kaufmann, San Mateo, CA, USA, 1993.
14. C.L. Blake and C.J. Merz. UCI repository of machine learning databases, University of California, Irvine, Dept of Information and Computer Science, 1998. Datasets is available at http://www.ics.uci.edu/~mlearn/MLRepository.html.
15. E. A. Patrick and F. P. Fischer. A generalized k-nearest neighbor rule. *Information and Control*, 16(2):128–152, 1970.
16. B. Zhang and S. N. Srihari. Fast k-nearest neighbor classification using cluster-based trees. *IEEE Trans. on Pattern and Machine Intelligence*, 26(4):525–528, 2004.

Evolutionary Multiobjective Knowledge Extraction for High-Dimensional Pattern Classification Problems

Hisao Ishibuchi and Satoshi Namba

Department of Industrial Engineering, Osaka Prefecture University,
1-1 Gakuen-cho, Sakai, Osaka 599-8531, Japan
{hisaoi,snamba}@ie.osakafu-u.ac.jp

Abstract. This paper proposes an evolutionary multiobjective optimization (EMO) approach to knowledge extraction from numerical data for high-dimensional pattern classification problems with many continuous attributes. The proposed approach is a three-stage rule extraction method. First each continuous attribute is discretized into several intervals using a class entropy measure. In this stage, multiple partitions with different granularity are specified. Next a prespecified number of candidate rules are generated from numerical data using a heuristic rule evaluation measure in a similar manner to data mining. Then a small number of candidate rules are selected by an EMO algorithm. The EMO algorithm tries to maximize the accuracy of selected rules. At the same time, it tries to minimize their complexity. Our rule selection problem has three objectives: to maximize the number of correctly classified training patterns, to minimize the number of selected rules and to minimize their total rule length. The length of each rule is defined by the number of its antecedent conditions. The main characteristic feature of the proposed EMO approach is that many rule sets with different accuracy and different complexity are simultaneously obtained from its single run. They are tradeoff solutions (i.e., non-dominated rule sets) with respect to the accuracy and the complexity. Through computational experiments, we demonstrate the applicability of the proposed EMO approach to high-dimensional pattern classification problems with many continuous attributes. We also demonstrate some advantages of the proposed EMO approach over single-objective ones.

1 Introduction

One advantage of evolutionary approaches to multiobjective optimization over classical ones is that many non-dominated solutions are simultaneously obtained from their single run [2]. This paper shows how this advantage of evolutionary multiobjective optimization (EMO) can be utilized in knowledge extraction from numerical data for high-dimensional pattern classification problems with many continuous attributes. One goal in knowledge extraction is to find a rule set that has high classification accuracy. Emphasis has usually been placed on the classification accuracy in the area of machine learning [10]-[12]. Another goal in knowledge extraction is to find a rule set that has high interpretability. This goal, which can be rephrased as finding understandable knowledge for human users, has been emphasized in the area of data mining [1], [5]. Simultaneous handling of these two goals is not straightforward because there exists a tradeoff between the accuracy of rule sets and their interpretability. That is, the accuracy is degraded by increasing the interpretability while the interpretability is degraded by increasing the accuracy.

We have already proposed an idea of utilizing EMO algorithms in the design of fuzzy rule-based classification systems [7]-[9] where the number of correctly classified training patterns is maximized, the number of fuzzy rules is minimized, and the total length of fuzzy rules is minimized. In those studies, we observed that EMO algorithms can find a large number of rule sets with different accuracy and different complexity. Human users can understand the tradeoff structure between the accuracy and the complexity from those rule sets. Without such understanding, it is very difficult for human users to choose a final rule set based on their preference.

The aim of this paper is to clearly demonstrate the usefulness of EMO approaches to knowledge extraction in more common situations (i.e., extraction of standard non-fuzzy rules). In our former studies on fuzzy rule extraction [7]-[9], each attribute was homogeneously divided into triangular fuzzy sets. Homogeneous fuzzy discretization works well because there are significant overlaps between adjacent fuzzy sets. Decision boundaries are adjustable over those overlapping regions using the certainty grade of each fuzzy rule. Homogeneous discretization into intervals with the equal width, however, does not work well because decision boundaries are directly specified by cutting points of continuous attributes into intervals. Thus we use a class entropy measure for the discretization of continuous attributes into intervals as in some approaches to the design of decision trees [4], [11]. Since an appropriate pre-specification of the number of intervals for each continuous attribute is very difficult, we simultaneously use multiple partitions with different granularity. Some are fine partitions into many intervals and others are coarse partitions into a few intervals.

In this paper, we propose a three-stage rule extraction method for finding multiple tradeoff solutions (i.e., non-dominated rule sets) with respect to the accuracy and the complexity. First each continuous attribute is discretized into several intervals using a class entropy measure. We generate multiple partitions with different granularity in this stage. For example, we generate five partitions in computational experiments where each continuous attribute is divided into one to five intervals (see Fig. 1 where K is the number of intervals). Thus we have 15 intervals for each continuous attribute. In the second stage, those intervals are used as antecedent conditions for generating candidate rules. A prespecified number of promising candidate rules are generated using a heuristic rule evaluation measure in a similar manner to data mining [1]. In the third stage, an EMO algorithm is used for finding non-dominated rule sets with different accuracy and different complexity from the generated candidate rules.

This paper is organized as follows. In Section 2, we briefly explain classification rules, a heuristic specification procedure of the consequent class and the certainty grade of each rule, a classification procedure based on a single winner rule, and a heuristic rule evaluation measure used for generating promising candidate rules in the second stage. In Section 3, we show a three-objective formulation of our rule extraction problem. In Section 4, we propose a three-stage rule extraction method based on an EMO algorithm. In Section 5, we demonstrate some advantages of the proposed EMO approach over single-objective ones through computational experiments on three benchmark data sets from the UC Irvine machine learning repository. Finally Section 6 concludes this paper.

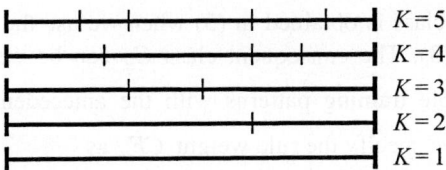

Fig. 1. Illustration of five partitions with different granularity in computational experiments.

2 Classification Rules

Let us assume that we have m training patterns $\mathbf{x}_p = (x_{p1}, ..., x_{pn})$, $p = 1, 2, ..., m$ from M classes where x_{pi} is the attribute value of the p-th training pattern for the i-th attribute ($i = 1, 2, ..., n$). We denote those training patterns by D (i.e., $D = \{\mathbf{x}_1, ..., \mathbf{x}_m\}$). We also denote training patterns from each class as $D(\text{Class } h)$ where $h = 1, 2, ..., M$.

For our n-dimensional M-class problem, we use the following classification rule:

Rule R_q: If x_1 is A_{q1} and ... and x_n is A_{qn} then Class C_q with CF_q, (1)

where R_q is the label of the q-th rule, $\mathbf{x} = (x_1, ..., x_n)$ is an n-dimensional pattern vector, A_{qi} is an antecedent interval, C_q is a class label, and CF_q is a rule weight (i.e., certainty grade). We denote the antecedent part of the classification rule R_q in (1) by $\mathbf{A}_q$ where $\mathbf{A}_q = (A_{q1}, ..., A_{qn})$. Thus R_q is denoted as "$\mathbf{A}_q \Rightarrow$ Class C_q".

For determining the consequent class C_q and the rule weight CF_q, we first calculate the confidence of the classification rule "$\mathbf{A}_q \Rightarrow$ Class h" for each class h according to its definition in the area of data mining [1]. Let $D(\mathbf{A}_q)$ be the set of compatible training patterns with the antecedent part $\mathbf{A}_q$:

$$D(\mathbf{A}_q) = \{\mathbf{x}_p \mid x_{p1} \in A_{q1}, ..., x_{pn} \in A_{qn}\}, \quad h = 1, 2, ..., M. \quad (2)$$

Then the confidence of the classification rule "$\mathbf{A}_q \Rightarrow$ Class h" is calculated as

$$c(\mathbf{A}_q \Rightarrow \text{Class } h) = |D(\mathbf{A}_q) \cap D(\text{Class } h)| \,/\, |D(\mathbf{A}_q)|, \quad h = 1, 2, ..., M. \quad (3)$$

The confidence is the ratio of compatible training patterns from Class h to all compatible training patterns. In the field of data mining [1], another measure called support is also used for rule evaluation. The support of the classification rule "$\mathbf{A}_q \Rightarrow$ Class h" is defined as

$$s(\mathbf{A}_q \Rightarrow \text{Class } h) = |D(\mathbf{A}_q) \cap D(\text{Class } h)| \,/\, |D|, \quad h = 1, 2, ..., M. \quad (4)$$

The consequent class C_q is specified as the class with the maximum confidence:

$$c(\mathbf{A}_q \Rightarrow \text{Class } C_q) = \max\{c(\mathbf{A}_q \Rightarrow \text{Class } h) \mid h = 1, 2, ..., M\}. \quad (5)$$

The same consequent class is obtained in (5) when we use the support in (4) instead of the confidence in (3). The consequent class C_q can be viewed as the dominant class among compatible training patterns with the antecedent part $\mathbf{A}_q$. Using the confidence measure, we specify the rule weight CF_q as

$$CF_q = c(\mathbf{A}_q \Rightarrow \text{Class } C_q) - \sum_{\substack{h=1 \\ h \neq C_q}}^{M} c(\mathbf{A}_q \Rightarrow \text{Class } h). \tag{6}$$

Let S be a set of classification rules in a single rule-based classifier. When an input pattern $\mathbf{x}_p$ is to be classified, a single winner rule R_w is identified as the compatible rule with the largest rule weight in the rule set S. The input pattern $\mathbf{x}_p$ is assigned to the consequent class C_w of the winner rule R_w.

In some computational experiments of this paper, we use multiple rule-based classifiers. An input pattern is classified by each individual classifier using the single winner-based method. Then the final classification is performed through the majority vote based on the classification result by each individual classifier.

3 Three-Objective Rule Selection Problem

As in our former studies on the design of fuzzy rule-based classifiers [7]-[9], we handle knowledge extraction as the following three-objective rule selection problem:

$$\text{Maximize } f_1(S), \text{ minimize } f_2(S), \text{ and minimize } f_3(S), \tag{7}$$

where S is a rule set, $f_1(S)$ is the number of correctly classified training patterns by the rule set S, $f_2(S)$ is the number of rules in S, and $f_3(S)$ is the total length of rules in S. The number of antecedent conditions of each rule is referred to as the rule length.

4 Proposed EMO Approach

We propose a three-stage approach based on evolutionary multiobjective optimization (EMO) for finding non-dominated rule sets of the three-objective rule selection problem in (7). First each continuous attribute is discretized into several intervals. One characteristic feature of the proposed approach is the simultaneous use of multiple partitions with different granularity. That is, we simultaneously use fine partitions into many intervals as well as coarse partitions into a few intervals.

In computational experiments, we simultaneously use five partitions with different granularity in Fig. 1 (including the whole domain interval itself). Let K be the number of intervals. That is, each continuous attribute is divided into K intervals ($K = 1,2,3,4,5$ in Fig. 1). For finding $(K-1)$ cutting points (i.e., for the discretization into K intervals), we use an optimal splitting method [4] based on the class entropy measure:

$$H(A_1, ..., A_K) = -\sum_{j=1}^{K} \frac{|D_j|}{|D|} \sum_{h=1}^{M} \left(\frac{|D_{jh}|}{|D_j|} \cdot \log_2 \frac{|D_{jh}|}{|D_j|} \right), \tag{8}$$

where $(A_1, ..., A_K)$ is K intervals generated by the discretization of a continuous attribute, D_j is training patterns in the interval A_j, and D_{jh} is training patterns from Class h in D_j. Using the optimal splitting method [4], we can find the optimal $(K-1)$ cutting points that minimize the class entropy measure in (8). In this manner, we have multiple optimal partitions corresponding to various specifications of K.

Next we generate a candidate rule by choosing an interval from those partitions for each attribute. The consequent class and the rule weight are determined by a heuristic manner in Section 2 after the antecedent part is specified. In the case of Fig. 1, the total number of possible combinations is 15^n for an n-dimensional problem. Of course, some rules are identical because 15 intervals in Fig.1 are not always different from one another. Among those combinations, we generate a prespecified number of candidate rules in a heuristic manner as in the field of data mining. In computational experiments, we use the following heuristic rule evaluation measure:

$$f_{\text{SLAVE}}(R_q) = s(\mathbf{A}_q \Rightarrow \text{Class } C_q) - \sum_{\substack{h=1 \\ h \neq C_q}}^{M} s(\mathbf{A}_q \Rightarrow \text{Class } h). \tag{9}$$

This is a modified version of a rule evaluation criterion used in an iterative fuzzy genetics-based machine learning algorithm called SLAVE [6]. Of course, we can use other criteria such as the product of the support and the confidence, the support with the minimum certainty level, and the certainty with the minimum support level.

In this paper, a prespecified number of candidate rules with the largest values of the SLAVE criterion are found for each class in a greedy manner. For designing rule-based classifiers with low complexity (i.e., high interpretability), only short rules are examined as candidate rules. This restriction on the rule length is consistent with the third objective (i.e., the total rule length) of the three-objective rule selection problem in (7).

Finally an EMO algorithm is applied to the generated candidate rules for finding non-dominated rule sets with respect to the three objectives in (7). Let us assume that N rules have been extracted as candidate rules using the SLAVE criterion. A subset S of the N candidate rules is handled as an individual in the EMO algorithm, which is represented by a binary string of length N as

$$S = s_1 s_2 \cdots s_N, \tag{10}$$

where $s_j = 1$ and $s_j = 0$ mean that the j-th candidate rule is included in S and excluded from S, respectively.

As in our former studies [7]-[9], we use two problem-specific heuristic tricks together with the NSGA-II [2]-[3], which is a well-known high-performance EMO algorithm, for efficiently finding non-dominated rule sets. One trick is the biased mutation where a larger probability is assigned to the mutation from 1 to 0 than that from 0 to 1. This is for efficiently decreasing the number of rules in each rule set. The other trick is the removal of unnecessary rules, which is a kind of local search. Since we use the single winner-based method for classifying each pattern by the rule set S, some rules in S may be chosen as winner rules for no training patterns. We can remove those rules without degrading the first objective (i.e., the number of correctly classified training patterns). At the same time, the removal of unnecessary rules leads to the improvement in the other objectives. Thus we remove all rules that are not selected as winner rules for any training patterns from the rule set S. The removal of unnecessary rules is performed after the first objective is calculated for each rule set and before the second and third objectives are calculated.

5 Computational Experiments

We use three data sets: Wisconsin breast cancer data with 9 attributes, Cleveland heart disease data with 13 attributes, and Sonar data with 60 attributes. These data sets, which have been frequently used in the literature, are available from the UC Irvine machine learning repository (http://www.ics.uci.edu/~mlearn/). All attributes in these data sets are handled as continuous attributes in our computational experiments. We evaluate the performance of the proposed approach in comparison with the reported results on the same data sets in Elomaa & Rousu [4] where six variants of the C4.5 algorithm [11] were examined. The performance of each variant was evaluated by ten independent iterations (with different data partitions) of the whole ten-fold cross-validation (10CV) procedure (i.e., 10×10CV) in [4]. We use the same performance evaluation procedure as [4].

In each run of the 10CV procedure, first each attribute is divided into intervals using training patterns (90% of the data set). As in Fig. 1, we simultaneously generate five optimal partitions for each attribute. Next we extract 300 candidate rules for each class in the heuristic greedy manner using the SLAVE criterion (i.e., $300M$ candidate rules in total where M is the number of classes). We examine candidate rules of the length three or less for Wisconsin breast cancer data and Cleveland heart disease data. Since Sonar data have a large number of attributes (i.e., they have a huge number of possible combinations of antecedent intervals), we only examine short rules of the length two or less as candidate rules for this data set. Then the NSGA-II is applied to the extracted $300M$ candidate rules for finding non-dominated rule sets. Each of the obtained rule sets is evaluated by test patterns (10% of the data set). We use the following parameter values in the NSGA-II for finding non-dominated rule sets:

Population size: 200 strings,
Crossover probability: 0.8,
Biased mutation probabilities: $p_m(0 \rightarrow 1) = 1/300M$ and $p_m(1 \rightarrow 0) = 0.1$,
Stopping condition: 5000 generations.

In ten iterations of the whole 10CV procedure, the NSGA-II is employed 100 times. Multiple rule sets are obtained from each run of the NSGA-II. We calculate error rates of each rule set on training patterns and test patterns. Those error rates are summarized by calculating their average values over rule sets with the same number of rules and the same average rule length obtained from 100 runs. We do not report the average error rates for rare combinations of the number of rules and the average rule length. More specifically, we report the average error rates only for combinations of the number of rules and the average rule length obtained from more than 30 (out of

100) runs. We also calculate the average error rates on training patterns and test patterns using the majority vote where all the obtained rule sets in each run except for too small ones are used for the classification of each pattern. We do not use small rule sets with less rules than the number of classes due to their poor performance.

For comparison, we also use a standard single-objective genetic algorithm with a single elite solution, the binary tournament selection, and the same genetic operations and the same parameter specifications as the NSGA-II. The single-objective genetic algorithm is applied to $300M$ candidate rules for finding a single optimal rule set with respect to the weighted scalar fitness function:

$$fitness(S) = w_1 f_1(S) - w_2 f_2(S) - w_3 f_3(S) . \qquad (11)$$

The weight values are specified as $w_1 = 10$, $w_2 = 1$ and $w_3 = 1$ since a larger weight has been usually assigned to the accuracy maximization than the complexity minimization in the literature. The average performance of the obtained rule sets by the single-objective genetic algorithm is evaluated by ten iterations of the whole 10CV procedure in the same manner as in the case of the NSGA-II.

In the following, we report experimental results on each data set.

Wisconsin Breast Cancer Data Set: Experimental results on training patterns and test patterns are summarized in Fig. 2 (a) and Fig. 2 (b), respectively. An open circle shows the average error rate for each combination of the number of rules and the average rule length. In each figure, we also show the results by the simple majority vote (solid line) and the single-objective genetic algorithm (black square). For comparison, we show in Fig. 2 (b) the best result (dashed line) and the worst result (dotted line) in Elomaa & Rousu [4] by the C4.5 algorithm.

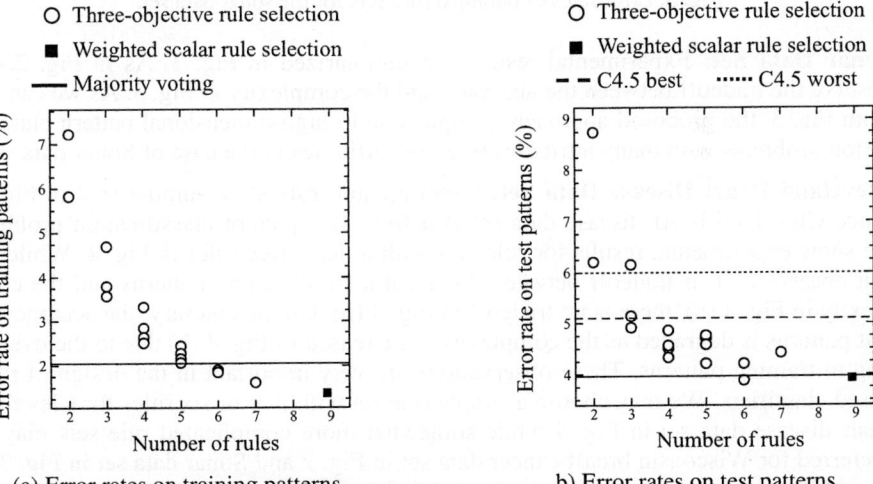

(a) Error rates on training patterns. b) Error rates on test patterns.

Fig. 2. Error rates of obtained rule sets for the Wisconsin breast cancer data set.

In Fig. 2 (a), we can observe a clear tradeoff between the accuracy on training patterns and the complexity. There also exists a similar tradeoff in Fig. 2 (b) between the accuracy on test patterns and the complexity. It should be noted that we can not observe such a tradeoff when we use the single-objective genetic algorithm for the weighted scalar fitness function. This is because only a single rule set is obtained from a single run of the single-objective genetic algorithm. From Fig. 2 (b), we can see that better results are obtained by the proposed approach and the alternative single-objective approach than the best result of the C4.5 algorithm in [4] for Wisconsin breast cancer data set. It should be noted that the best result on test patterns is obtained by the EMO approach in Fig. 2 (b) while the best result on training patterns is obtained by the single-objective approach in Fig. 2 (a).

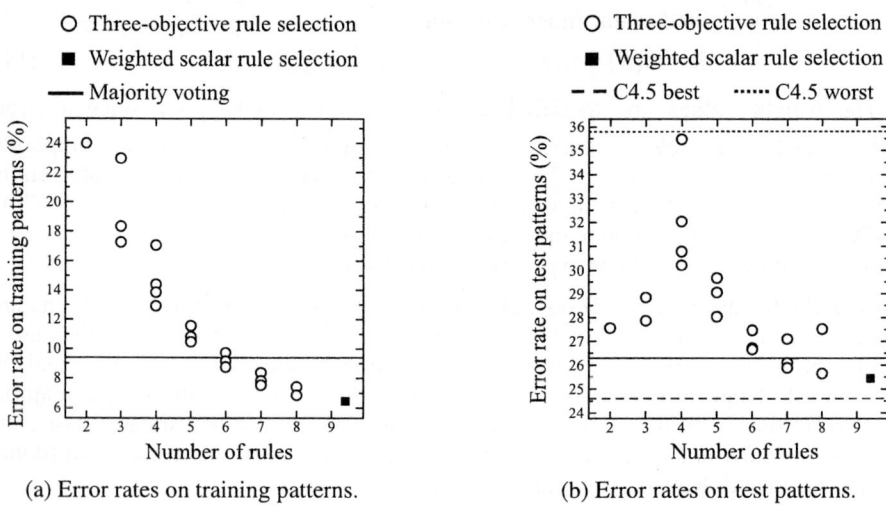

(a) Error rates on training patterns.   (b) Error rates on test patterns.

Fig. 3. Error rates of obtained rule sets for the sonar data set.

Sonar Data Set: Experimental results are summarized in Fig. 3. As in Fig. 2, we observe the tradeoff between the accuracy and the complexity in Fig. 3. As we can see from Fig. 3, the proposed approach is applicable to high-dimensional pattern classification problems with many attributes (e.g., 60 attributes in the case of Sonar data set).

Cleveland Heart Disease Data Set: Experimental results are summarized in Fig. 4. Since Cleveland heart disease data set is a five-class pattern classification problem, we show experimental results for rule sets with at least five rules in Fig. 4. While we can observe a clear tradeoff between the accuracy on training patterns and the complexity in Fig. 4 (a), there is no tradeoff in Fig. 4 (b). On the contrary, the accuracy on test patterns is degraded as the complexity is increased in Fig. 4 (b) due to the overfitting to training patterns. These observations are very important in the design of rule-based classifiers. We may choose a simple rule set with five or six rules for Cleveland heart disease data set in Fig. 4 while somewhat more complicated rule sets may be preferred for Wisconsin breast cancer data set in Fig. 2 and Sonar data set in Fig. 3. It should be noted that we cannot obtain such information for each data set with respect to the tradeoff structure when we use the single-objective genetic algorithm for the weighted scalar fitness function. From Fig. 4 (b), we can see that good results are not obtained for test patterns by the single-objective approach while very good results are obtained for training patterns.

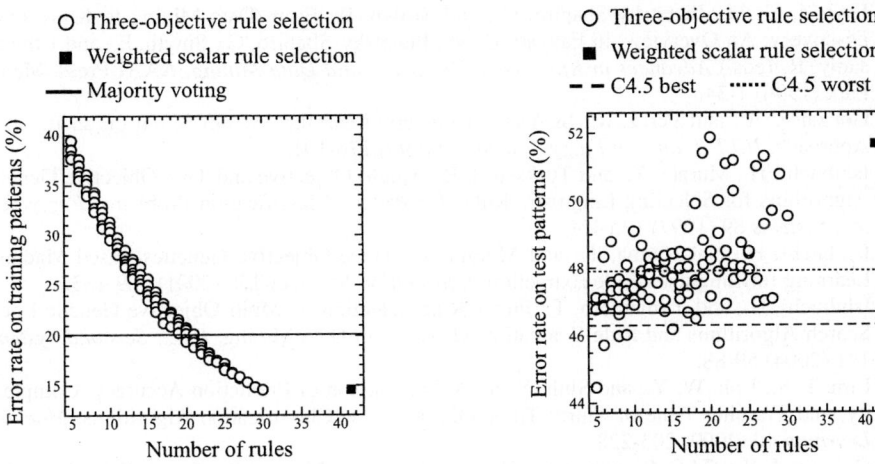

Fig. 4. Error rates of obtained rule sets for the Cleveland heart disease data set.

6 Concluding Remarks

We proposed an evolutionary multiobjective optimization (EMO) approach to knowledge extraction from numerical data for high-dimensional pattern classification problems with many continuous attributes. Many non-dominated rule sets can be simultaneously obtained from a single run of the EMO approach. From those rule sets, we can understand the tradeoff structure between the accuracy and the complexity. As shown in the computational experiments, the tradeoff structure is highly problem-dependent: Each problem has a different tradeoff structure. Thus the information on the tradeoff structure is very important in the design of rule-based classification systems. Such information is easily obtained by the EMO approach.

The authors would like to thank the financial support from Japan Society for the Promotion of Science (JSPS) through Grand-in-Aid for Scientific Research (B): KAKENHI (14380194).

References

1. Agrawal, R., Mannila, H., Srikant, R., Toivonen, H., and Verkamo, A. I.: Fast Discovery of Association Rules, in Fayyard, U. M., Piatetsky-Shapiro, G., Smyth, P., and Uthurusamy, R. (eds.) *Advances in Knowledge Discovery and Data Mining*, AAAI Press, Menlo Park (1996) 307-328.
2. Deb, K.: *Multi-Objective Optimization Using Evolutionary Algorithms*, John Wiley & Sons, Chichester (2001).
3. Deb, K., Pratap, A., Agarwal, S., and Meyarivan, T.: A Fast and Elitist Multiobjective Genetic Algorithm: NSGA-II, *IEEE Trans. on Evolutionary Computation* 6 (2002) 182-197.
4. Elomaa, T., and Rousu, J.: General and Efficient Multisplitting of Numerical Attributes, *Machine Learning* 36 (1999) 201-244.

5. Fayyad, U. M., Piatetsky-Shapiro, G., and Smyth, P.: From Data Mining to Knowledge Discovery: An Overview, in Fayyad, U. M., Piatetsky-Shapiro, G., Smyth, P., and Uthurusamy, R. (eds.) *Advances in Knowledge Discovery and Data Mining*, AAAI Press, Menlo Park (1996) 1-34.
6. Gonzalez, A., and Perez, R.: SLAVE: A Genetic Learning System Based on an Iterative Approach, *IEEE Trans. on Fuzzy Systems* 7 (1999) 176-191.
7. Ishibuchi, H., Murata, T., and Turksen, I. B.: Single-Objective and Two-Objective Genetic Algorithms for Selecting Linguistic Rules for Pattern Classification Problems, *Fuzzy Sets and Systems* 89 (1997) 135-150.
8. Ishibuchi, H., Nakashima, T., and Murata, T.: Three-Objective Genetics-Based Machine Learning for Linguistic Rule Extraction, *Information Sciences* 136 (2001) 109-133.
9. Ishibuchi, H., and Yamamoto, T.: Fuzzy Rule Selection by Multi-Objective Genetic Local Search Algorithms and Rule Evaluation Measures in Data Mining, *Fuzzy Sets and Systems* 141 (2004) 59-88.
10. Lim, T. S., Loh, W. Y., and Shih, Y. S.: A Comparison of Prediction Accuracy, Complexity, and Training Time of Thirty-Three Old and New Classification Algorithms, *Machine Learning* 40 (2000) 203-228.
11. Quinlan, J. R.: *C4.5: Programs for Machine Learning*, Morgan Kaufmann Publishers, San Mateo (1993).
12. Weiss, S. M., and Kulikowski, C. A.: *Computer Systems That Learn*, Morgan Kaufmann Publishers, San Mateo (1991).

Ensemble Learning with Evolutionary Computation: Application to Feature Ranking

Kees Jong[1], Elena Marchiori[1], and Michèle Sebag[2]

[1] Department of Mathematics and Computer Science
Vrije Universiteit Amsterdam, The Netherlands
{cjong,elena}@cs.vu.nl
[2] Laboratoire de Recherche en Informatique, CNRS-INRIA
Université Paris-Sud Orsay, France
sebag@lri.fr

Abstract. Exploiting the diversity of hypotheses produced by evolutionary learning, a new ensemble approach for Feature Selection is presented, aggregating the feature rankings extracted from the hypotheses. A statistical model is devised to enable the direct evaluation of the approach; comparative experimental results show its good behavior on non-linear concepts when the features outnumber the examples.

1 Introduction

Among the major advances of Machine Learning in the last decade is Ensemble Learning [6, 3, 5], based on the vote of hypotheses extracted from the dataset along independent (bagging [3]) or iterative (boosting [6]) learning procedures. The variance of the learning error is reduced through the vote mechanism, thereby increasing the predictive accuracy.

Indeed, stochastic algorithms and specifically evolutionary learners are natural candidates for ensemble learning approaches; they can provide collections of hypotheses, extracted using many runs or within a single run using diversity enforcing heuristics; see among many others [8, 12, 18].

In this paper, a new ensemble approach aimed at Feature Selection and Feature Ranking, referred to as Ensemble Feature Ranking, is presented, and implemented using evolutionary learning.

Feature Selection (FS) is commonly viewed as a major bottleneck of Supervised Machine Learning and Data Mining [13, 9]. For the sake of the learning performance, it is highly desirable to discard irrelevant features prior to learning, especially when the features significantly outnumber the examples. FS can be formalized as a combinatorial optimization problem, finding the feature set maximizing the quality of the hypothesis learned from these features. Global approaches to this optimization problem, referred to as wrapping methods, actually use an embedded learning algorithm to evaluate a feature set [20, 13]. For this reason, basic wrapping approaches hardly scale up to large size problems, though some progress has been done using ensemble-like evolutionary approaches [8, 18].

A relaxed formalization of FS is concerned with feature ranking (FR) [9]. In the FR approach, one selects the top ranked features, the number of which is either specified by the user [10] or analytically determined [19].

The proposed Ensemble Feature Ranking approach proceeds by exploiting a set of hypotheses independently learned from the dataset. Each hypothesis induces a ranking on the features, and EFR achieves the aggregation of these feature rankings. Based on the same principles as ensemble learning, the performance of an EFR increases with the ensemble size if it aggregates weakly competent feature rankings (misordering two features with probability $p < \frac{1}{2}$) [14].

EFR is implemented using an evolutionary learning algorithm termed *ROGER* for *ROC-based Genetic Learner*, first presented in [17]. *ROGER* extracts hypotheses optimizing the recently investigated AUC learning criterion, the area under the Receiver Operating Characteristics (ROC) curve [2,15,16].

The paper is organized as follows. Section 2 briefly reviews the state of the art in Feature Selection and Ranking. An overview of Ensemble Feature Ranking is given in Section 3, describing the *ROGER* algorithm for the sake of completeness. The experimental validation setting is described in Section 4; a statistical model is devised to enable a direct evaluation of FR algorithms, inspired from the phase transition paradigm developed in the CSP community [11] and imported in the ML community by [7]. Section 5 reports on the comparative empirical validation results, and the paper ends with a discussion and perspectives for further research.

2 State of the Art

This section introduces some Feature Ranking algorithms, referring to [9] for a more comprehensive discussion.

Notations used throughout the paper are first introduced. Only binary concept learning is considered in the following. The training set $\mathcal{E}$ includes n examples described from d continuous features, $\mathcal{E} = \{(\mathbf{x}_i, y_i), \mathbf{x}_i \in \mathbb{R}^d, y_i \in \{-1, 1\}, i = 1\ldots n\}$, where label y_i indicates whether the i-th example pertains to the target concept (positive example) or not (negative example).

2.1 Univariate Feature Ranking and Iterated Selection

In univariate approaches, a score is associated to each feature independently from the others. In counterpart for this simplicity, univariate approaches are adversely affected by disjunctive concepts and redundant features.

The feature score is computed after a statistical test, quantifying how well this feature discriminates positive and negative examples. For instance the Mann-Whitney test associates to the k-th feature the score $Pr(x_{i,k} > x_{j,k} \mid y_i > y_j)$, defined as the fraction of pairs of (positive, negative) examples such that feature k ranks the positive example higher than the negative one. This criterion coincides with the Wilcoxon rank sum test, which is equivalent to the AUC criterion [21].

A sophisticated extension of univariate approaches, based on an iterative selection process, is presented in [19]. The score associated to each feature is proportional to its cosine with the target concept according to the formula $score(k) = \sum_{i=1}^{n} x_{i,k} \cdot y_i / \sqrt{\sum_{i=1}^{n} x_{i,k}^2}$.

This two-step iterative process i) determines the current feature k maximizing the above score; ii) projects all remaining features and the target concept on the hyperplane perpendicular to feature k, thereby overcoming the limitations of univariate approaches with respect to redundant features.

2.2 ML-Based Feature Ranking

An alternative to univariate approaches is to exploit the output of a machine learning algorithm, which assumedly takes into account every feature in relation with the other ones [13].

Actually, a linear hypothesis ($h(\mathbf{x}) = \sum_{i=1}^{N} w_i x_i [+b]$) induces a feature ranking, associating to each feature k the absolute value of weight w_k; the higher the score, the more relevant the feature is *in combination with the other features*.

A two-step iterative process, termed SVM-Recursive Feature Elimination, is proposed by [10]. In each step, i) a linear SVM is learned, the features are ranked according to the square of the associated weight; ii) the worst features are filtered out.

Another approach, based on linear regression [1], uses a randomized approach for better robustness, extracting various hypotheses from subsamples of the dataset, and associating to each feature its average weight.

Another related work is concerned with learning an ensemble of GA-based hypotheses extracted along independent runs [8], where: i) the underlying GA-inducer looks for good feature subsets; and ii) the quality of a feature subset is measured from the accuracy of a k-nearest neighbor or euclidean decision table classification process, based on these features.

3 Ensemble Feature Ranking

This section introduces Ensemble Feature Ranking. EFR is implemented using the evolutionary learning algorithm *ROGER*, which is first described for the sake of completeness.

3.1 *ROGER*: ROc-Based GEnetic learneR

ROGER is an evolution strategy over a continuous hypothesis space, that maximizes the area under the ROC curve (AUC) associated to each hypothesis h. As mentioned already, the AUC is equivalent to the Wilcoxon statistics [21]:

$$AUC(h) = Pr(h(\mathbf{x}_i) > h(\mathbf{x}_j) \mid y_i > y_j)$$

The maximal fitness 1 is thus attained for a hypothesis h ranking all positive examples higher than negative examples (separating hypothesis).

Previous experiments using simple linear hypotheses ($h = \mathbf{w} \in \mathbb{R}^d$, $h(\mathbf{x})$ being set to the scalar product of $\mathbf{w}$ and $\mathbf{x}$) show good learning performances compared to state-of-art linear Support Vector Machines [4], *ROGER* reaching a similar predictive accuracy in a fraction of the SVM computational time [17].

Thanks to the flexibility of evolutionary search, *ROGER* can explore complex search spaces provided that they can be parameterized in a compact way. In this paper, *ROGER* considers hypotheses defined as the weighted L_1 distance to some point $\mathbf{c}$ of the instance space. Formally, $h \in \mathbb{R}^{2d}$ is characterized as $(w_1, \ldots, w_d, c_1, \ldots, c_d)$, with

$$h(\mathbf{x}) = \sum_{i=1}^{d} w_i \times |x_i - c_i|$$

This way, *ROGER* explores a limited kind of non linear hypotheses, while exploring search space $\mathbb{R}^{2d}$ with size linear in the number of features. In the meanwhile, such non-linear hypotheses still allow for feature ranking (in contrast with quadratic or Gaussian functions), again associating to feature k the absolute value of weight w_k.

3.2 Ensemble Feature Ranking

Let $h_1, \ldots h_T$ denote T hypotheses. At the moment, the h_t's are the best hypotheses extracted by *ROGER* along T independent runs; using diversity enforcing heuristics to extract several hypotheses from a single run is a perspective for further research. For the sake of simplicity and by abuse of notations, let us denote $h(k)$ the absolute value of the k-th weight in h. With no loss of generality, hypotheses h_t are normalized ($\sum_k h_t(k) = 1$).

The goal is to construct an ensemble feature ranking h^*, aggregating the feature rankings derived from the h_t's. The justification for such an aggregation, presented in [14], is based on the same principles as ensemble learning; assuming that an elementary feature ranking offers an advantage over random guessing (the probability p of misranking a pair of features being less than $\frac{1}{2}$), the aggregation mechanism allows for amplifying this advantage as the ensemble size T increases [5].

Several aggregation procedures have been considered. The first one defines $h^*(k)$ as the proportion of features ℓ that are ranked before k by a majority of h_ts ($h^*(k) = \#\{\ell \text{ s.t. } \#\{t \text{ / } h_t(\ell) < h_t(k)\} > \frac{T}{2}\}$, where $\#A$ stands for the size of set A). The convergence of this aggregation procedure wrt the ensemble size T has been analytically studied in [14].
The second (respectively the third) aggregation procedure associates to each feature k the median (resp. the maximal) value in $\{h_t(k), t = 1 \ldots T\}$.
A perspective for further research is concerned with a better exploitation of the order statistics of the $h_t(k)$ (e.g. setting $h^*(k)$ as some quantile of the set $\{h_t(k)\}$).

4 Statistical Validation Model

Before proceeding to experimental validation, it must be noted that the performance of a feature selection algorithm is commonly computed from the performance of a learning algorithm based on the selected features, which makes it difficult to compare standalone FS algorithms.

To sidestep this difficulty, a statistical model is devised, enabling the direct evaluation of the proposed FR approach. This model is inspired from the statistical complexity analysis paradigm developed in the Constraint Satisfaction community [11], and first imported in the Machine Learning community by Giordana and Saitta [7].

In this framework, the problem space is defined by a set of order parameters (e.g. the constraint density and tightness in CSPs [11]). The performance of a given algorithm is viewed as a random variable, observed in the problem space. To each point in the problem space (values of the order parameters), one associates the average behavior of the algorithm over all problem instances with same value of the order parameters.

4.1 Order Parameters

Seven order parameters are defined for Feature Selection: i) the number d of features; ii) the number n of examples; iii) the number r of relevant features, where a feature is said to be relevant iff it is involved in the definition of the target concept, see next; iv) the type l of target concept, linear ($l = 1$) or non-linear ($l = 2$), with

$$l = 1: \quad y(\mathbf{x}) = 1 \quad \text{iff} \quad (\sum_{i=1}^{r} x_i > s) \quad (1.1)$$
$$l = 2: \quad y(\mathbf{x}) = 1 \quad \text{iff} \quad (\sum_{i=1}^{r} (x_i - .5)^2 < s) \quad (1.2)$$

v) the redundancy $k = 0$ or 1 of the relevant features, where redundancy ($k = 1$) is implemented by replacing r of the irrelevant features, by linear random combinations of the r relevant ones; vi) the noise rate e in the class labels: the class associated to each example is flipped with probability e; vii) the noise rate σ in the feature values, where a Gaussian noise $\mathcal{N}(0, \sigma)$ is added to each feature value.

4.2 Artificial Problem Generator

For each point $(d, n, r, l, k, e, \sigma)$ in the problem space, independent instances of learning problems are generated after the following distribution.

All d features of all n examples are drawn uniformly in $[0, 1]$. The label of each example is computed as in equation (1.1) (for $l = 1$) or equation (1.2) (for $l = 2$)[1]. In case of redundancy ($k = 1$), r irrelevant features are selected

---
[1] The threshold s referred to in the target concept definition is set to $r/2$ in equation (1.1) (respectively $r/12$ in equation (1.2)), guaranteeing a balanced distribution of positive and negative examples. The additional difficulties due to skewed example distributions are not considered in this study.

and replaced by linear combinations of the r relevant ones. Last, the example labels are randomly flipped with probability e, and the features are perturbed by addition of a Gaussian noise with variance σ.

The above generator differs from the generator proposed in [9] in several respects. [9] only considers linear target concepts, defined from a linear combination of the relevant features; this way, the target concept differentially depends on relevant features, whilse all relevant features have the same relevance in our model. In contrast, the proposed model investigates linear as well as a (limited kind of) non-linear concepts.

4.3 Format of the Results

Feature rankings are evaluated and compared using a ROC-inspired setting. To each index $i \in \{1, d\}$ is associated the fraction of true relevant features (respectively, the fraction of irrelevant, or falsely relevant, features) with rank higher than i, denoted $TR(i)$ (resp. $FR(i)$). The curve $\{(FR(i), TR(i)), i = 1, \ldots, d\}$ is referred to as ROC-FS curve associated to the feature ranking.

The ROC-FS curve shows the trade-off achieved by the algorithm between the two objectives of setting high ranks (resp. low ranks) to relevant (resp. irrelevant) features. The ROC-FS curve associated to a perfect ranking (ranking all relevant features before irrelevant ones), reaches the global optimum $(0, 1)$.

The inspection of the ROC-FS curves shows whether a Feature Ranking algorithm consistently dominates over another one. The curve also gives a precise picture of the algorithm performance; the beginning of the curve shows whether the top ranked features are actually relevant, suggesting an iterative selection approach as in [19]; the end of the curve shows whether the low ranked features are actually irrelevant, suggesting a recursive elimination procedure as in [10].

Finally, three indicators of performance are defined on a feature ranking algorithm. The first indicator measures the probability for the best (top) ranked feature to be relevant, noted p_b, reflecting the FR potential for a selection procedure. The second indicator measures the worst rank of a relevant feature, divided by d, noted p_w, reflecting the FR potential for an elimination procedure. A third indicator is the area under the ROC-FS curve (AUC), taken as global indicator of performance (the optimal value 1 being obtained for a perfect ranking).

5 Experimental Analysis

This section reports on the experimental validation of the EFR algorithm described in section 3, compared to the baseline results provided by the cosine criterion [19].

5.1 Experimental Setting

A principled experimental validation has been conducted along the formal model defined in the previous section. The number d of features is set to 100, 200 and

500. The number r of relevant features is set to $d/20, d/10$ and $d/5$. The number n of examples is set to $d/2, d$ and $2d$. Linear and non-linear target concepts are considered ($l = 1$ or 2), with redundant ($k = 1$) and non-redundant ($k = 0$) feature sets. Last, the label noise e is set to 0, 5 and 10%, and the variance σ of the feature Gaussian noise is set to 0., .05 and .10.

In total 972 points $(d, r, m, l, k, e, \sigma)$ of the problem space are considered. For each point, 20 datasets are independently generated. For each dataset, 15 independent *ROGER* runs are executed to construct an ensemble feature ranking; the associated indicators p_b, p_w and the *AUC* are computed, and their median over all datasets with same order parameters is reported.

The reference results are obtained similarly from the cosine criterion [19]: for each point of the problem space, 30 datasets are independently generated, the cosine-based feature ranking is evaluated from indicators p_b, p_w and the *AUC*, and the indicator median over all 30 datasets is reported.

Computational runtimes are measured on PC Pentium-IV. *ROGER* is parameterized as a (20+200)-ES with self adaptive mutation, uniform crossover with rate .6, uniform initialization in [0, 1], and a maximum number of 50,000 fitness evaluations[2].

5.2 Reference Results

The performance of the cosine criterion for linear and non-linear concepts is illustrated on Fig. 1, for $d = 100, n = 50, r = 10, k = 0$.

The performance indicators summarized in Table 1.(a), show an outstanding behavior on linear concepts; complementary results, omitted due to space limitations, show similar trends for redundant problems $k = 1$ and higher values of d. With twice as many features as examples, the probability p_b of top ranking a relevant feature is around 90%. A graceful degradation of p_b is observed as the noise rate increases, more sensitive to the label noise than to the feature noise. The relevant features are in the top p_w features, where p_w varies from 1/3 to roughly 1/2. The performance steadily improves when the number of examples increases.

In contrast, the cosine criterion behaves no better than random ranking for non-linear concepts; this is visible as the ROC-FS curve is close to the diagonal, and the situation does not improve by doubling the number of examples.

5.3 Evolutionary Feature Ranking

The performance of EFR is measured under the same conditions (Fig. 2, Table 1.(b)). EFR is clearly outperformed by the cosine criterion in the linear case. With twice as many features as examples, the probability p_b of top ranking a relevant feature ranges between 35 and 50% (non redundant features), against

---

[2] All datasets and *ROGER* results are available at
http://www.lri.fr/~sebag/EFRDatasets
and http://www.lri.fr/~sebag/EFResults

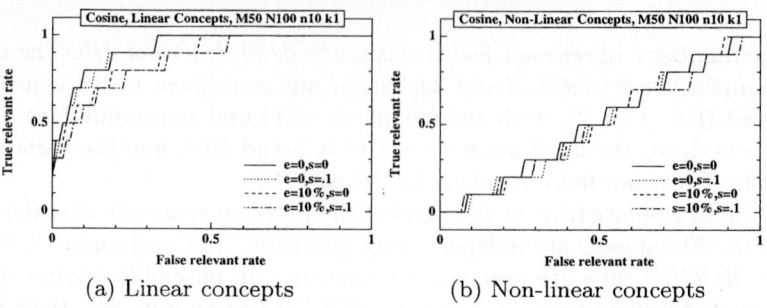

Fig. 1. Cosine criterion: Median ROC-FS curves over 30 training sets on Linear and Non-Linear concepts, with $d = 100$, $n = d/2$, $r = d/10$, Non redundant features.

Table 1. Comparative results of the cosine ranking criterion and EFR: Probability p_b of top ranking a relevant feature, Median relative rank p_w of the worst ranked relevant feature, Area under the ROC-FS curve.

n	d	r	e	σ	p_b p_w AUC	p_b p_w AUC	p_b p_w AUC	p_b p_w AUC
50	100	10	0	0	0.87 .33 0.920	0.03 .93 0.49	0.5 .92 0.67	0.20 .75 0.71
50	100	10	0	0.1	0.9 .33 0.916	0.03 .94 0.49	0.5 .80 0.63	0.45 .82 0.68
50	100	10	10%	0	0.87 .47 0.87	0.1 .93 0.49	0.35 .94 0.61	0.25 .81 0.68
50	100	10	10%	0.1	0.8 .56 0.848	0.03 .93 0.51	0.35 .89 0.62	0.25 .88 0.61
100	100	10	0	0	1 .18 0.97	0 .91 0.53	0.85 .79 0.79	0.55 .63 0.81
100	100	10	0	0.1	1 .22 0.966	0.03 .90 0.52	0.50 .74 0.77	0.60 .72 0.78
100	100	10	10%	0	0.93 .29 0.944	0.17 .92 0.52	0.55 .77 0.72	0.65 .78 0.77
100	100	10	10%	0.1	0.93 .36 0.934	0.1 .92 0.52	0.65 .82 0.75	0.40 .72 0.75
					Linear	Non-Linear	Linear	Non-Linear
					(a) Cosine criterion		(b) Ensemble Feature Ranking	

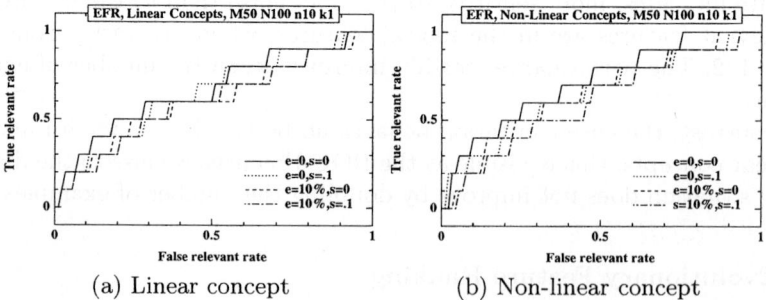

Fig. 2. EFR performance: Median ROC-FS curves over 20 training sets on Linear and Non-Linear concepts, with $d = 100$, $n = d/2$, $r = d/10$, Non redundant features.

80 and 90% for the reference results. When the number of examples increases, p_b increases as expected; but p_b reaches 55 to 85% against 93 to 100% for the reference results.

In opposition, EFR does significantly better than the reference criterion in the non-linear case. Probability p_b ranges around 30%, compared to 3% and 10% for the reference results with $n = 50$ and p_b increases up to circa 55% when n increases up to 100.

With respect to computational cost, the cosine criterion is linear in the number of examples and in $d \log d$ wrt the number of features; the runtime is negligible in the experiment range.

The computational complexity of EFR is likewise linear in the number of examples. The complexity wrt the number of features d is more difficult to assess as d governs the size of the $ROGER$ search space ($[0, 1]^{2d}$). The total cost is less than 6 minutes (for 20 data sets × 15 $ROGER$ runs) for $n = 50, d = 100$ and less than 12 minutes for $n = 100, d = 100$. The scalability is demonstrated in the experiment range as the cost for $n = 50, d = 500$ is less than 23 minutes.

6 Discussion and Perspectives

The contribution of this paper is based on the exploitation of the diverse hypotheses extracted along independent runs of evolutionary learning algorithms, here $ROGER$. This collection of hypotheses is exploited for ensemble-based feature ranking, extending the ensemble learning approach [3] to Feature Selection and Ranking [9].

As should have been expected, the performances of the Evolutionary Feature Ranker presented are not competitive with the state of the art for linear concepts. However, the flexibility of the hypothesis search space explored by $ROGER$ allows for a breakthrough in (a limited case of) non-linear concepts, even when the number of examples is a fraction of the number of features.

These results are based on experimental validation over 18,000 datasets, conducted after a statistical model of Feature Ranking problems. Experiments on real-world data are underway to better investigate the EFR performance, and the limitations of the simple model of non-linear concepts proposed.

Further research will take advantage of multi-modal evolutionary optimization heuristics to extract diverse hypotheses from each $ROGER$ run, hopefully reducing the overall computational cost of the approach and addressing more complex learning concepts (e.g. disjunctive concepts).

Acknowledgments

We thank the anonymous referees and Mary Felkin, LRI, for their help and suggestions. The third author is partially supported by the PASCAL Network of Excellence, IST-2002-506778.

References

1. J. Bi, K.P. Bennett, M. Embrechts, C.M. Breneman, and M. Song. Dimensionality reduction via sparse support vector machines. *J. of Machine Learning Research*, 3:1229–1243, 2003.

2. A.P. Bradley. The use of the area under the ROC curve in the evaluation of machine learning algorithms. *Pattern Recognition*, 1997.
3. L. Breiman. Arcing classifiers. *Annals of Statistics*, 26(3):801–845, 1998.
4. R. Collobert and S. Bengio. SVMtorch: Support vector machines for large-scale regression problems. *J. of Machine Learning Research*, 1:143–160, 2001.
5. R. Esposito and L. Saitta. Monte Carlo theory as an explanation of bagging and boosting. In *Proc. of IJCAI'03*, pp. 499–504. 2003.
6. Y. Freund and R.E. Shapire. Experiments with a new boosting algorithm. In L. Saitta, editor, *Proc. ICML'96*, pp. 148–156. Morgan Kaufmann, 1996.
7. A. Giordana and L. Saitta. Phase transitions in relational learning. *Machine Learning*, 41:217–251, 2000.
8. C. Guerra-Salcedo and D. Whitley. Genetic approach to feature selection for ensemble creation. In *Proc. GECCO'99*, pp. 236–243, 1999.
9. I. Guyon and A. Elisseeff. An introduction to variable and feature selection. *J. of Machine Learning Research*, 3:1157–1182, 2003.
10. I. Guyon, J. Weston, S. Barnhill, and V. Vapnik. Gene selection for cancer classification using support vector machines. *Machine Learning*, 46:389–422, 2002.
11. T. Hogg, B.A. Huberman, and C.P. Williams (Eds). *Artificial Intelligence: Special Issue on Frontiers in Problem Solving: Phase Transitions and Complexity*, volume 81(1-2). Elsevier, 1996.
12. K. Imamura, R.B. Heckendorn, T. Soule, and J.A. Foster. Abstention reduces errors; decision abstaining n-version genetic programming. In *Proc. GECCO'02*, pp. 796–803. Morgan Kaufmann, 2002.
13. G.H. John, R. Kohavi, and K. Pfleger. Irrelevant features and the subset selection problem. In *Proc. ICML'94*, pp. 121–129. Morgan Kaufmann, 1994.
14. K. Jong, J. Mary, A. Cornuéjols, E. Marchiori, and M. Sebag. Ensemble feature ranking. In *Proc. ECML-PKDD'04*, 2004. to appear.
15. C.X. Ling, J. Hunag, and H. Zhang. AUC: a better measure than accuracy in comparing learning algorithms. In *Proc. of IJCAI'03*, 2003.
16. S. Rosset. Model selection via the AUC. In *Proc. ICML'04*. Morgan Kaufmann, 2004, to appear.
17. M. Sebag, J. Azé, and N. Lucas. ROC-based evolutionary learning: Application to medical data mining. In *Artificial Evolution VI*, pp. 384–396. Springer Verlag LNCS 2936, 2004.
18. D. Song, M. I. Heywood, and A. Nur Zincir-Heywood. A linear genetic programming approach to intrusion detection. In *Proc. GECCO'02*, pp. 2325–2336. Springer-Verlag, 2003.
19. H. Stoppiglia, G. Dreyfus, R. Dubois, and Y. Oussar. Ranking a random feature for variable and feature selection. *J. of Machine Learning Research*, 3:1399–1414, 2003.
20. H. Vafaie and K. De Jong. Genetic algorithms as a tool for feature selection in machine learning. In *Proc. ICTAI'92*, pp. 200–204, 1992.
21. L. Yan, R. H. Dodier, M. Mozer, and R. H. Wolniewicz. Optimizing classifier performance via an approximation to the Wilcoxon-Mann-Whitney statistic. In *Proc. ICML'03*, pp. 848–855. Morgan Kaufmann, 2003.

Fast Unsupervised Clustering
with Artificial Ants

Nicolas Labroche[1], Christiane Guinot[2], and Gilles Venturini[1]

[1] Université de Tours, Laboratoire d'Informatique,
64 avenue J. Portalis 37200 Tours, France
{nicolas.labroche,venturini}@univ-tours.fr
http://www.antsearch.univ-tours.fr/
[2] CE.R.I.E.S,
20 rue Victor Noir, 92521 Neuilly sur Seine Cedex, France
christiane.guinot@ceries-lab.com

Abstract. AntClust is a clustering algorithm that is inspired by the chemical recognition system of real ants. It associates the genome of each artificial ant to an object of the initial data set and simulates meetings between ants to create nests of individuals that share a similar genome. Thus, the nests realize a partition of the original data set with no hypothesis concerning the output clusters (number, shape, size ...) and with minimum input parameters. Due to an internal mechanism of nest selection and finalization, AntClust runs in the worst case in quadratic time complexity with the number of ants. In this paper, we evaluate new heuristics for nest selection and finalization that allows AntClust to run on linear time complexity with the number of ants.

1 Introduction

The ant metaphor has often been used in the last years to imagine innovative solutions for hard computer sciences problems. One may cite the well-known Ant Colony Optimization (ACO) heuristic [1] that reproduces the ability of real ants to drop and follow pheromone trails. In particular, this approach has been recently applied to the problem of the dynamic reorganization of an e-learning Web site in [2].

Other studies focus on the ability of real ants to sort their cemetery or their brood and lead to the development of a clustering algorithm by Lumer and Faieta in [3]. This algorithm uses a discrete grid on which data and artificial ants are randomly placed. Each ant can move across the grid and pick up or drop objects according to the similarity between an object that may be already carried by the ant and the objects that may be in its neighbourhood. This method has some limitations: numerous parameters to set and a difficulty to find the expected number of clusters, therefore many researchers tried to improve this algorithm. In [4], the authors developed a hybrid approach named Antclass in which a variant of the algorithm of Lumer and Faieta is used to generate the clusters seeds for a k-means algorithm. In this approach, the grid is toroidal to avoid undesirable side effects and each ant can drop several objects in the same location of the grid to avoid the problem of heap aggregation. However, AntClass can only handle numeric data sets because of its hybridization with k-means algorithms. More recently other computer scientists have proposed new variants such as Handl in [5] or Ramos in [6] with the ACluster algorithm. In this approach the author defines the notion of bio-inspired spatial transition probabilities in which artificial ants move on the grid according to pheromone trails whose densities are proportional to the number of objects in the neighbourhood.

In our previous work [7], we propose a new clustering algorithm inspired by the chemical recognition system of real ants named AntClust. To achieve this goal we work in collaboration with biologists to develop a new model that describes and formalizes the chemical circuits that enable the emergence of a colonial odour that is recognized and updated by every nestmates. The resulting clustering algorithm, AntClust, allows manipulating any data type if a similarity measure is defined and does not need to be parameterized in term of number, shape or size of the expected clusters. However, due to an internal mechanism of nest selection and finalization, AntClust runs in the worst case in quadratic time complexity with the number of ants. In this paper, we describe and study the performances of a new heuristic for nests selection and propose a new heuristic for nests finalization (that aims at reassigning the ants with no nest to the best one), that allow AntClust to run on linear time complexity with the number of ants. This paper is organized as follows: the section 2 details the principles of AntClust (artificial ants and behavioural rules). The section 3 introduces the new heuristics for nest selection and nest finalization. The section 4 compares the results obtained with these new methods to those of the AntClass algorithm and finally the section 5 concludes and discusses the future evolutions of the algorithm.

2 AntClust Algorithm

2.1 General Principles

AntClust aims at solving the unsupervised clustering problem in an original way, by reproducing principles inspired by the chemical recognition system of ants. In this biological system, each ant possesses its own odour called label that is spread over its cuticle (its "skin"). This label acts as an identity card and is partially determined by the genome of the ant and by the substances extracted from its environment (mainly the nest materials and the food). During their youth, young ants learn to distinguish the labels of the colony members and learn a neuronal template of what should be the label of a nestmate. This template is continually updated and is used at each meeting between two ants, to decide if they should accept each others and exchange chemical cues (by trophallaxies, allo-grooming or simple social contacts). The continuous chemical exchanges between the nestmates lead to the establishment of a colonial odour that is shared and recognized by every nestmates, according to the "Gestalt theory" [8].

The main idea of AntClust is to associate an object of the data set to the genome of an artificial ant. It simulates meetings between artificial ants according to behavioural rules to allow each ant to find the label that best fits its genome and to therefore to belong to the best nest (or best cluster). AntClust is able to determine a partition, as close as possible to the natural partition of a data set, with no hypothesis concerning the definition of the objects (numeric, symbolic ...) or concerning the expected clusters (number, shape ...).

2.2 Artificial Ants

An artificial ant can be considered as an agent defined by a set of parameters that evolve according to bio-inspired behavioural rules that apply when two ants meet. Given an ant a, we define the parameters listed hereafter.

The label L_a reflects the nest membership of the ant and is simply coded by a number. Initially, the ant does not belong to a nest, so L_a is set to 0. During the meetings, the label evolves until the ant finds the nest that best fits its genome.

The genome G_a corresponds to an object of the data set and thus it does not evolve during the algorithm. When they meet, ants compare their genome to evaluate their similarity.

The template T_a is an acceptance threshold that is coded by a real value between 0 and 1. It is learned during an initialization period, comparable with the ontogenesis period of the real ants, in which each artificial ant a meets other ants, and each time evaluates the similarity between their genomes. The resulting acceptance threshold T_a is a function of the maximal $\max(Sim(a,\cdot))$ and mean $\overline{Sim}(a,\cdot)$ similarities observed during this period. T_a is dynamic and is updated after each meeting realized by the ant a, as the similarities observed may have changed. The following equation shows how this threshold is learned and then updated:

$$T_a \leftarrow \frac{\overline{Sim}(a,\cdot) + \max(Sim(a,\cdot))}{2} \quad (1)$$

Once artificial ants have learned their template, they use it during their meetings to decide if they should accept each others. The acceptance mechanism between two ants a and b is a symmetric relation $Acc(a,b)$ in which the similarity between genomes is compared to both templates as follows:

$$Acc(a,b) \Leftrightarrow (Sim(a,b) \geq T_a) \wedge (Sim(a,b) \geq T_b) \quad (2)$$

We state that there is "positive meeting" when there is acceptance between ants.

The estimators M_a and M_a^+ indicate respectively the proportion of meetings and the proportion of positive meetings realized with nestmates. These estimators are initially set to 0. M_a is increased (resp. decreased) each time the ant a meets another ant with the same label (resp. distinct label) and reset when the ant is ejected from its nest. M_a^+ is roughly similar to M_a but add the "acceptance notion". It is increased when the ant a meets and accepts a nestmate and decreased when there is no acceptance with the encountered nestmate. In fact,

M_a enables each ant to estimate the size of its nest whereas M_a^+ measures how well accepted is the ant a in its own nest.

The age A_a is set to 0 and is increased each time the ant a meets another ant. It is used to update the maximal and mean similarities values and thus the value of the acceptance threshold T_a.

The score S_a is a new parameter that reflects the mean similarity of the ant with the members of its own nest. At the beginning, S_a is set to 0 because a does not belong to any nest. At each meeting with a nestmate b, S_a is updated with the value of similarity $Sim(a, b)$ between the genomes of ant a and b, as the next equation shows:

$$S_a \leftarrow (1 - \alpha) \times S_a + \alpha \times Sim(a, b) \qquad (3)$$

where $\alpha \in]0, 1[$ has been set experimentally to 0.2 in order that S_a estimates the mean value of the similarity of the ant a with the other nestmates over all its meetings.

2.3 Behavioural Rules and Main Algorithm

At each iteration, AntClust randomly selects two ants, simulates meetings between them and applies a set of behavioural rules that enable the convergence of the method.

The 1st rule creates a new nest when two ants with no nest meet and accept each other. This rule initiates the gathering of similar ants in the very first clusters. These clusters "seeds" are then used to generate the final clusters according to the other rules.

The 2nd rule allows an ant that is alone to join the nest of another one that already belongs to a nest if they accept each others. This rule enlarges the existing clusters by adding similar ants.

The 3rd rule increments the estimators M and M^+ in case of acceptance between two ants that belong to the same nest. Each ant, as it meets a nestmate and tolerates it, imagines that its nest is bigger and, as there is acceptance, feels more integrated in its nest.

The 4th rule applies when two nestmates meet and do not accept each other. In this case, the worst integrated ant is ejected from the nest. This rule permits to remove non-optimally clustered ants to change their nest and try to find a more appropriate one.

The 5th rule applies when two ants that belong to a distinct nest meet and accept each other. This rule is very important because it allows the gathering of similar clusters, the small one being progressively absorbed by the big one.

We have shown experimentally in our previous work [7] that N_{App} could be set to 75 meetings per ant and that Nb_{Iter} could be intialized to $150 \times N$ where N is the number of objets in the data set.

The AntClust main algorithm can be summarized as follows:

Algorithm 1: ANTCLUST main algorithm.

ANTCLUST(Data set with N objects)

(1) Initialization of the ants:
(2) $\forall$ ants $a \in [1, N]$
(3) $\quad G_a \leftarrow a^{th}$ object of the data set
(4) $\quad L_a \leftarrow 0$
(5) $\quad T_a$ is learned during N_{App} iterations
(6) $\quad M_a \leftarrow 0, M_a^+ \leftarrow 0, A_a \leftarrow 0, S_a \leftarrow 0$
(7) Simulate Nb_{Iter} meetings between two randomly chosen ants
(8) Select the nests that will establish the final partition of the objects (see section 3.1)
(9) Finalize the nests by re-assigning the ants that have no more nest to the nest of the most similar ant (see section 3.2).

3 New Heuristics for Nest Selection and Finalization

3.1 The New Nest Selection Heuristic

With the end of the meeting period, ants generally create too many nests. Thus, a heuristic for nest selection may be applied to choose from the nests, those that are more likely to build a partition close to the natural partition of the data set. In this section, we describe a new heuristic H that decides which nests are conserved according to a two steps approach using successively a threshold selection method then a probabilistic method. H mainly relies on an integration value M_η^+ computed for each nest η as the following equation 4 shows:

$$M_\eta^+ \leftarrow \sum_{\forall a \in \eta} M_a^+ \qquad (4)$$

M_η^+ reflects the homogeneity of the nest (or cluster) η since the integration M_a^+ of each ant a in the nests (or each data in this cluster) indirectly depends on its similarity with the other nestmates (the other data of the cluster). The first step of the heuristic H aims at conserving only the nests that shows an integration value greater than a strictly positive threshold θ (defined in the equation 5) to ensure the selection of the best candidates for the nests.

$$\theta \leftarrow \frac{1}{1-\alpha} \qquad (5)$$

where $\alpha \in [0, 1[$ has been set experimentally on artificial and real data sets.

M_η^+ also estimates the size of the nest (cluster) η since its value equals the sum of the integration value for each nestmate (or each data in the cluster). As we want our algorithm to be able to conserve small clusters if they are homogeneous (and thus representative of a trend in the data set), we propose, in the second step of the heuristic H, to compute a probality threshold $P_{Keep}(\eta)$ (see eq. 6) to keep the nests that have not been selected in the first step.

$$P_{Keep}(\eta) \leftarrow \frac{M_\eta^+}{\theta} \tag{6}$$

where θ is the first step threshold value defined in the equation 5. For each nest η, the heuristic H draws a random value $R_d(\eta)$. If $R_d(\eta)$ is smaller than the value of $P_{Keep}(\eta)$ then the nest η is selected for the final partition.

3.2 New Heuristic for Nest Finalization

For the time being, our nest finalization method considers all the ants whose nest was destroyed, and for each of them it searches the most similar ant that belongs to a nest. This method, although accurate and simple, has a quadratic time complexity with the number of ants (or objects of the data set) which is not acceptable to treat large data sets.

In this paper, we propose a new method whose complexity is linear with the number of ants/objects. The idea is to search for each nest an ant representative and then to associate each ant that has no more nest to the nest of the most similar representative. The nest representative is the ant that has the best mean similarity with the other nestmates. To achieve our goal, we have introduced a new parameter to describe an artificial ant named "the score" (see section 2.2). This parameter estimates the mean similarity of the ant with its nestmates. This score is updated each time the ant realizes a meeting (positive or not) with a nestmate. Consequently, we update the ant representative for each nest after a meeting between two of its members.

4 Comparative Results

In this section, we evaluate the performances of our new heurisitics for nest selection and nest finalization on artificial and real data sets. Firstly, we quickly introduce the similarity measure, the main characteristics of the data sets and the clustering error measure used in our tests. Secondly, we study the influence of the α parameter (see section 3.1) on the quality of the final partition. Finally, we define two new AntClust versions: one with the classical nest finalization method and one with the new nest finalization heuristic and we compare their results to those of the AntClass algorithm.

4.1 Similarity Measure, Clustering Error and Data Sets

We condider that each of the N objects of the data set is described by a set of M attributes. The similarity $sim(o_a, o_b)$ between two object o_a and o_b is defined as the sum of the similarities between each of their attributes depending on their type t (numeric, symbolic, ...) as the next equations show:

$$sim(o_a, a_b) \leftarrow \frac{1}{M} \times \sum_{i \in [1,M]} sim_t(o_a(i), o_b(i)) \tag{7}$$

$$sim_{numeric}(o_a(i), o_b(i)) \leftarrow \frac{|o_a(i) - o_b(i)|}{|\max_{k \in [1,N]}(o_k(i)) - \min_{k \in [1,N]}(o_k(i))|} \quad (8)$$

We use a clustering error adapted from the measure developed by Fowlkes and Mallows as used in [9]. The measure evaluates the differences between two partitions by comparing each pair of objects and by verifying each time if they are similarly clustered or not. Let P_i be the expected partition and P_a the output partition of AntClust. The clustering error $C_e(P_i, Pa)$ can be defined as follows:

$$C_e(P_i, P_a) = \frac{2}{N(N-1)} \times \sum_{(m,n) \in [1,,N]^2, m<n} \epsilon_{mn} \quad (9)$$

where:

$$\epsilon_{mn} = \begin{cases} 0 & \text{if } (P_i(m) = P_i(n) \wedge P_a(m) = P_a(n)) \vee (P_i(m) \neq P_i(n) \wedge P_a(m) \neq P_a(n)) \\ 1 & \text{otherwise} \end{cases} \quad (10)$$

$P_i(o_b)$ (resp. $P_a(o_b)$) is the cluster number of the object o_b in the partition P_i (resp. P_a).

We use artificial and real data sets in our tests. The artificial data sets are named $Art_{1,2,3,4,5,6}$ and have been generated according to gaussian or uniform laws with distinct difficulties (irrelevant attributes, clusters overlap) (see [3]). The real data sets are extracted from the Machine Learning Repository and are named: $Iris$, $Glass$, $Pima$, $Soybean$ and $Thyroid$. We expect them to be more difficult to cluster as real data may be more unpredictable than artificial ones. The table 1 sums up the main characteristics of these data sets. The fields for each data set are: the number of objects (N), their associated number of attributes (M), and the number of clusters (K).

Table 1. Main characteristics of the data sets.

	Art_1	Art_2	Art_3	Art_4	Art_5	Art_6	Iris	Glass	Pima	Soybean	Thyroid
N	400	1000	1100	200	900	400	150	214	798	47	215
M	2	2	2	2	2	8	4	9	8	35	5
K	4	2	4	2	9	4	3	6	2	4	3

4.2 Influence of the α Parameter

We test several values for the α parameter between 0 and 0.9 to determine the best one over the artificial and real data sets. The figure 1 shows the clustering error and the mean number of cluster for each value of α and for each artificial data set over 10 runs (the results are similar with real data sets). The line entitled "theory" indicates the theoric number of clusters of the data sets. We generally observe on the figure 1 that the number of clusters that is found by the heuristic decreases when the value of α increases. This is an advantage for the data sets Art_1 and Art_4 for which our algorithm tends to find too many clusters but it is

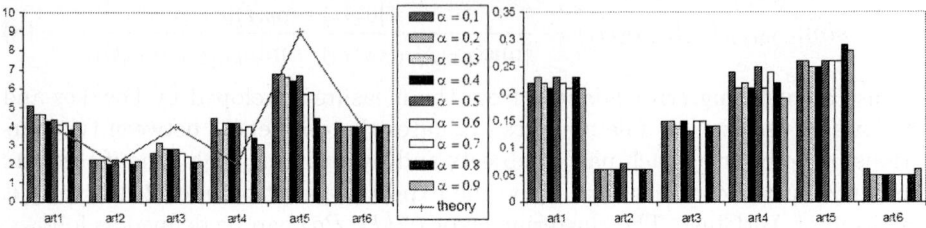

Fig. 1. Mean number of clusters (left) and mean clustering error (right) on artificial data sets for each value of $\alpha \in [0, 1[$ over 10 runs.

also a limitation for the data sets Art_3 and Art_5 for which the number of clusters discovered by the algorithm is insufficient. However, the discovery of too many clusters is not prejudiciable because as the figure 1 shows, the clustering error for these data sets seems to be independent from the value of α. Consequently, we state that $\alpha = 0.2$ in the next experiments of this paper.

4.3 Comparison of the New Versions of AntClust and the AntClass Algorithm

In this section, we define two versions of AntClust. The first, named $AntClust_1$, uses the new heuristic for nest selection and the previous nest finalization heuristic based on the assignment of the ants with no nest to the nest of the most similar ant. The second, named $AntClust_2$ combines the new heurisitics for nest selection and nest finalization. Both are compared with the AntClass algorithm that has been introduced in the section 1. We have conducted the tests on the artificial and real data sets presented previously over 10 runs. The table 2 presents the mean number of clusters ("# clusters") found by each method, the clustering error ("Clustering Error") and their standard-deviations ("[std]").

According to the table 2 we can observe that AntClass manages to find a better approximation of the number of expected clusters for the data sets Art_1, Art_4 and $Pima$. For all the other data sets AntClust (version 1 or 2) manages to have similar or better results. AntClass has a smaller clustering error than the AntClust algorithms only twice for Art_1 and Art_5. For Art_1, AntClass better approximates the number of clusters, and thus it may be helped by our clustering error measure that takes it into account. For Art_5, AntClass seems to produce clusters of better quality than AntClust as none of the algorithms is able to correctly estimate the number of clusters. However, the results of AntClust are pretty good since it manages to have similar clustering error results than AntClass for $Iris$, $Pima$ and $Glass$ data sets and performs very well on Art_2, Art_3, Art_6 and $Soybean$.

$AntClust_1$ and $AntClust_2$ have roughly the same results on our data sets. The real interest of $AntClust_2$ lies in its time complexity that becomes linear with the number of ants and the number of nests whereas $AntClust_1$ has a quadratic time complexity with the number of ants(because of its nest final-

Table 2. Mean number of clusters and mean clustering error on the artificial and real data sets for *AntClass*, *AntClust*$_1$ and *AntClust*$_2$.

	# clusters						Clustering Error					
	AntClass		AntClust$_1$		AntClust$_2$		AntClass		AntClust$_1$		AntClust$_2$	
Data sets	mean	[std]	mean	[std]	mean	[std]	mean	[std]	mean	[std]	mean	[std]
Art_1	4.22	[1.15]	4.6	[1.17]	4.6	[0.84]	0.15	[0.05]	0.23	[0.02]	0.22	[0.02]
Art_2	12.32	[2.01]	2.2	[0.42]	2.1	[0.32]	0.41	[0.01]	0.06	[0.01]	0.05	[0.01]
Art_3	14.66	[2.68]	3.1	[1.45]	3.2	[1.14]	0.35	[0.01]	0.15	[0.02]	0.14	[0.01]
Art_4	1.68	[0.84]	3.8	[0.63]	4.0	[1.05]	0.29	[0.23]	0.21	[0.04]	0.21	[0.06]
Art_5	11.36	[1.94]	6.8	[2.10]	5.7	[1.25]	0.08	[0.01]	0.26	[0.04]	0.25	[0.03]
Art_6	3.74	[1.38]	4.0	[0.00]	4.0	[0.00]	0.11	[0.13]	0.05	[0.02]	0.06	[0.01]
$Iris$	3.52	[1.39]	2.7	[0.67]	2.4	[0.52]	0.19	[0.08]	0.22	[0.01]	0.22	[0.01]
$Pima$	6.10	[1.84]	8.7	[1.49]	11.7	[2.91]	0.47	[0.02]	0.46	[0.01]	0.48	[0.01]
$Soybean$	1.60	[0.49]	4.0	[0.47]	3.9	[0.32]	0.54	[0.17]	0.09	[0.04]	0.08	[0.05]
$Thyroid$	5.84	[1.33]	4.5	[1.18]	5.0	[1.15]	0.22	[0.09]	0.16	[0.02]	0.16	[0.04]
$Glass$	5.60	[2.01]	5.4	[1.84]	6.1	[1.37]	0.40	[0.06]	0.38	[0.02]	0.35	[0.02]

Table 3. Mean running time over 10 runs for *AntClust*$_1$ and *AntClust*$_2$ in seconds and mean reassignment error ratio r.

Data sets	Art_1	Art_2	Art_3	Art_4	Art_5	Art_6	$Iris$	$Pima$	$Soybean$	$Thyroid$	$Glass$
$AntClust_1$	0.74	2.62	3.19	0.32	2.26	0.92	0.28	3.14	0.34	0.45	0.56
$AntClust_2$	0.56	1.36	1.5	0.28	1.23	0.78	0.24	1.51	0.33	0.36	0.45
Error ratio r	0.025	0.004	0.014	0.026	0.050	0.002	0.011	0.111	0.019	0.017	0.055

ization heuristic). The table 3 compares the running time (in seconds) of both versions of AntClust on a Centrino 1.4 GHz with 512 Mo Ram. It shows that *AntClust*$_2$ manages to be two times faster than *AntClust*$_1$ for some data sets where there is a large number of (reassigned) ants. This table also shows the reassignment error ratio $r = \frac{\text{\# badly reassigned ants}}{\text{\# total ants}}$, that may occur in *AntClust*$_2$ when the more similar ant and the most similar representative do not belong to the same nest.

5 Conclusion

In this paper, we have proposed two new heuristics for the AntClust algorithm. The nest selection heuristic allows AntClust to gain flexibility and the ability to adapt to many different data sets without any new parameter settings. The counterpart may be a worse estimation of the number of clusters for some data sets, but our results show that the clustering error is still good compared to the AntClass algorithm for example. The nest finalization heuristic decreases the time complexity of our method by introducing the notion of ant representative of the nest. This notion is very interesting since it may be used to solve the incrementality problem which is crucial when dealing with very large data sets.

We plan to work extensively in this direction in order to evaluate the ability of AntClust to treat extremely large data sets such as Web log files in the Web usage mining problem for example. In conclusion, AntClust is now a fast clustering algorithm that does not need to be parameterized by the user, that can handle every data types (numeric, symbolic, ...) and that may be parallelized and become incremental in future evolutions.

References

1. E. Bonabeau, M. Dorigo, and G. Theraulaz, *From natural to artificial swarm intelligence*. New York: Oxford University Press, 1999.
2. Y. Semet, E. Lutton, and P. Collet, "Ant colony optimisation for e-learning: Observing the emergence of pedagogic suggestions," in *IEEE Swarm Intelligence Symposium 2003*, (Indianapolis, Indiana), april 2003.
3. E. Lumer and B. Faieta, "Diversity and adaptation in populations of clustering ants," in *Proceedings of the Third International Conference on Simulation of Adaptive Behavior* (D. Cliff, P. Husbands, J. Meyer, and S. W., eds.), pp. 501–508, MIT Press, Cambridge, Massachusetts, 1994.
4. N. Monmarché, M. Slimane, and G. Venturini, "On improving clustering in numerical databases with artificial ants," in *Lecture Notes in Artificial Intelligence* (D. Floreano, J. Nicoud, and F. Mondala, eds.), (Swiss Federal Institute of Technology, Lausanne, Switzerland), pp. 626–635, Springer-Verlag, 13-17 September 1999.
5. J. Handl and B. Meyer, "Improved ant-based clustering and sorting in a document retrieval interface," in *Proc. of the 7th International Conference on Parallel Problem Solving from Nature (PPSN VII)* (J. M. G. et al. (Eds.), ed.), (Granada, Spain), Springer-Verlag, 7-11 September 2002.
6. V. Ramos and J. Merelo, "Self-organized stigmergic document maps: Environment as mechanism for context learning," in *Proceedings of the First Spanish Conference on Evolutionary and Bio-Inspired Algorithms (AEB' 2002)*, (Centro Univ. de Mérida, Mérida, Spain), E. Alba, F. Herrera, J.J. Merelo et al., 6-8 February 2002.
7. N. Labroche, N. Monmarché, and G. Venturini, "Antclust: Ant clustering and web usage mining," in *Proceedings of the Genetic and Evolutionary Computation Conference (Gecco 2003)*, (Chicago, USA), july 12-16 2003.
8. B. Hölldobler and E. Wilson, *The Ants*, ch. Colony odor and kin recognition, pp. 197–208. Springer Verlag, Berlin, Germany, 1990.
9. J. Heer and E. Chi, "Mining the structure of user activity using cluster stability," in *Proceedings of the Workshop on Web Analytics, SIAM Conference on Data Mining*, April 2002.

A Novel Method of Searching the Microarray Data for the Best Gene Subsets by Using a Genetic Algorithm*

Bin Ni[1] and Juan Liu[1,2]

[1] School of Computer, Wuhan University, Wuhan 430079, China
liujuan@whu.edu.cn
[2] The State Key Lab. of Soft. Eng., Wuhan University, Wuhan 430072, China

Abstract. Searching for a small subset of genes out of the thousands of genes in Microarray is a crucial problem for accurate cancer classification. In this paper, a novel gene selection method based on genetic algorithms (GAs) is proposed. In order to reduce the search space of GAs, a novel *pre-selection* procedure is also introduced. To evaluate the performance of the presented method, experiments on five open datasets are conducted, and the results show that it performs rather well.

1 Introduction

Recent studies on molecular level classification of cancer cells produced remarkable results, strongly indicating the usability of gene expression assays as diagnostic tools [1]-[5]. A central goal of the analysis of gene expression data is the identification of sets of genes that can serve, via expression profiling assays, as classification or diagnosis platforms.

The cancer classification process based on Microarray can be divided into two steps [1]. First of all, in order to alleviate the computational complexity and eliminate the noisy genes, a special gene selection method must be necessary [1][6][7]; secondly, in order to distinguish the tumor samples from the normal ones, a fine-work classifier, which can analyze the Microarray data, must be constructed [1][2]. Though the capability of the classifier is of great significance for the cancer classification, the gene selection method also plays an important role in improving the performance of the classifier, and more important, the selected gene subsets of unknown functions might suggest new research directions.

Generally speaking, the goal of the gene selection method is to find out as few genes as possible to achieve fine classification performance. However, for a dataset with m genes, there are $2^m - 1$ subsets, and the number of subsets is exponentially increasing as the number m is increasing, which makes the search space too large to find out optimal gene subsets accurately. Genetic algorithms

---

* Supported by the National Nature Science Foundation of China (60301009), Chenguang Project of Wuhan city (211121009), and the Open Foundation of State Key Laboratory of Software Engineering of Wuhan University (SKLSE03-09).

(GAs), as introduced by Holland, are randomized search and optimization techniques that derive their working principles by analogy to evolution and natural genetics. Because GAs are aided by large amounts of implicit parallelism, they are capable of searching for optimal or near-optimal solutions on very complex and large spaces of possible solutions. Because of these advantages, GAs may represent a wide use in gene selection researches based on gene expression data. However, too large search space might also delay the GAs' convergence.

In this paper, we propose a novel gene selection method based on GAs, in which, the GA searches a small space rather than the whole gene subset space. Furthermore, this method can also control the size of the final selected gene subset via a parameter. The method consists of two steps: in the pre-selection step, genes are ranked according to the *relative proximity degree* criterion, and the top genes are selected to construct the search space of the GA; and then in the gene subset selection step, a GA is used to find out the optimal gene subsets with small size.

The organization of the rest is as follows. In section 2, our GA-based gene subsets selection method is described in details; and then the evaluation experiments and the results are presented in section 3; finally, some discussions and conclusions are addressed in section 4.

2 The Proposed Method

The proposed method consists of two steps: in the first step, each gene is evaluated by a newly defined criterion, and the top-ranking genes are selected; and in the second step, a GA is used to choose the optimized gene subsets from the top-ranking genes.

2.1 Pre-selecting Top Genes by Relative Proximity Degree

In this paper, we mainly address the two-label tissue classification problem. Assuming that we are given a dataset consisting of n samples and m genes $D = \{P_i = <s_i, l_i>|s_i \in R^m, l_i \in \{0,1\}, i = 1, 2, \ldots, n\}$, where s_i is a vector in R^m that describes expression values of m genes. l_i is the label associated with s_i. Suppose for each gene $j(j = 1, 2, \ldots, m)$, the vector g_j denotes its expression values on all the n samples. Let $x_{i,j}$ represent the value of gene j on sample i, then $s_i = <x_{i,1}, x_{i,2}, \ldots, x_{i,m}>$ and $g_j = <x_{1,j}, x_{2,j}, \ldots, x_{n,j}>$.

Obviously, if there exists a gene j such that in g_j, all values $x_{i,j}$ associated with label 1 are less than (or greater than) all values $x_{i,j}$ associated with label 0, then this gene is powerful enough to distinguish the samples. However, the existence of such a gene is a perfect situation. In most cases, we can only find a gene j of which the variety of the value $x_{i,j}$ in g_j can *nearly* reflect the category of the tissue. So we need a criterion to evaluate the relative proximity of each gene to the perfect situation.

Definition 1 (Perfect label vector). *Suppose there are k of n samples labeled as 1(or 0) and the rest are labeled as 0(or 1), the perfect label vector is defined* as $\hat{L} = <\hat{l}_1, \ldots, \hat{l}_n>$ iff for each $i \in \{1, \ldots, k\}$, $\hat{l}_i = 1$ (or 0), and for each $i \in \{k+1, \ldots, n\}$, $\hat{l}_i = 0$ (or 1).

According to definition 1, if there are 15 samples in all, of which 9 are tumors (labeled as 1) and 6 are normal ones (labeled as 0), then <1, 1, 1, 1, 1, 1, 1, 1, 1, 0, 0, 0, 0, 0, 0> and <0, 0, 0, 0, 0, 0, 1, 1, 1, 1, 1, 1, 1, 1, 1> are the two perfect label vectors. In order to indicate whether 1s or 0s are the heading characters in the vector, we further introduce two denotations.

Definition 2 (Template α). *A perfect label vector with 1s as the heading characters is defined as Template α.*

Definition 3 (Template β). *A perfect label vector with 0s as the heading characters is defined as Template β.*

For each gene j, we sort the $x_{i,j}$ in g_j in descending order, along with the label l_i of tissue i changing its position accordingly, then we get a new vector L_j for gene j. Obviously, the difference between L_j and $\hat{L}$ reflects the correlation of gene j to the category of the tissue to some extent. But only the difference is not enough. For example, after sorting the values for all genes, we get two genes j_1 and j_2 with $L_{j1} = $ <1, 1, 1, 1, 1, 1, 1, 0, 0, 1, 1, 0, 0, 0, 0> and $L_{j2} = $ <1, 1, 0, 0, 1, 1, 1, 1, 1, 1, 1, 0, 0, 0, 0> respectively. Though the differences of the two to the perfect situation are equal, we still consider gene j_1 is better than gene j_2, because in L_{j1}, 1s and 0s are more tendentious to cluster together, which means that the values of the gene j_1 fluctuate less slightly than those of gene j_2.

Since there are two templates in the perfect situation, we should match L_j to each of them to see how close it is to the perfect situation.

Definition 4 (Position weight). *For each position i in $L_j = \{l'_i\}$, the position weight for template α is defined as:*

$$w(i, \alpha) = \begin{cases} i - 1 & \text{if } l'_i = 1 \\ n - i & \text{if } l'_i = 0 \end{cases} \quad (1)$$

the position weight for template β is defined as:

$$w(i, \beta) = \begin{cases} i - 1 & \text{if } l'_i = 0 \\ n - i & \text{if } l'_i = 1 \end{cases} \quad (2)$$

Definition 5 (Proximity degree). *The proximity degree of L_j is defined as the minimum of the sum of position weights for template α and the sum of position weights for template β:*

$$\rho(L_j) = \min\{\sum_{i=1}^{n} w(i, \alpha), \sum_{i=1}^{n} w(i, \beta)\} \quad (3)$$

Apparently, the smaller the *proximity degree*, the closer L_j is to the perfect situation, and $\rho(\alpha) = \rho(\beta) = \frac{k(k-1)}{2} + \frac{(n-k) \cdot (n-k-1)}{2}$, where n is the number of samples, k denotes the number of samples labeled as 1(or 0). Take above metioned L_{j1} and L_{j2} as examples, $\rho(L_{j1})= 59$, $\rho(L_{j2})= 79$, so L_{j1} is better than L_{j2}, which does agree with the fact.

However, there is another problem. Although L_1 is better than L_2, how can we know to what extent L_1 is close to the perfect vector? Thus, we introduce the *relative proximity degree*.

Definition 6 (Relative proximity degree). *The relative proximity degree of L_j is defined by the following formula:*

$$\rho'(L_j) = \min\{\sum_{i=1}^{n} w(i,\alpha) - \rho(\alpha), \sum_{i=1}^{n} w(i,\beta) - \rho(\beta)\} \quad (4)$$

According to definition 6, $\rho'(L_{j1})=8$ and $\rho'(L_{j2})=28$. Of course, $\rho'(\alpha)=\rho'(\beta)=0$. So we can pre-select the top genes with low *relative proximity degrees* for further evolution in the GA, therefore the search space of the GA is reduced sharply. How many top genes should be chosen depends upon the dimensions of the experiment datasets. The affect of the top gene number T on the experiment results will be shown in section 3.

2.2 Searching for Gene Subsets by Using a GA

In section 2.1, we consider each single gene's discriminating capability using *relative proximity degree*, however, as it has been known, the group of the best genes does not always show strong power of discriminability. So in this section, we use a GA to search for optimal gene subsets that in groups have the highest abilities to discriminate the tumors and normal tissues.

Initial Population and Terminate Condition. Assuming that in the former pre-selection process, T top genes are selected, the individual (gene subset) is represented by a binary array with T bits. If ith bit is set to 1, it means that the ith gene in the T top genes is included in the gene subset. For an instance, suppose T is equal to 10, then [1, 0, 0, 0, 0, 1, 0, 1, 0, 0] denotes that the *1st, 6th, 8th* genes in the top 10 genes are selected into the subset. When generating the initial population we use a threshold parameter $\Theta \in (0,1)$, called *size control probability*, to control the size of the gene subsets. If the ith random number is less than Θ, then the ith bit in the array is set to "1", otherwise, it is set to 0. By this way, the size of gene subset is controlled around $T * \Theta$.

In this paper, when the average fitness value of the population is nearly equal to the best fitness value, the iteration process terminates.

Fitness Function. The fitness function is critical to the performance of the GAs. In this paper, we use the classification capability of the gene subset as its fitness. The classifier is built by a very simple strategy. Let

T: the number of pre-selected genes;
t_j: the jth bit value of the individual, $t_j=0$ or 1;
n_k: the number of training samples of class $k(k=0,1)$;
$x_{ij}^{(k)}$: the jth gene's value in training sample i of class $k(k=0,1)$;
$x_j^{(*)}$: the jth gene's value in the test sample;

Firstly, we calculate each gene's average value in different classes by the following formula:

$$c_{k,j} = \frac{\sum_{i=1}^{n_k} x_{ij}^{(k)}}{n_k} \quad (k=0,1; j=1,2,\ldots,T) \tag{5}$$

Secondly, we calculate the "distances" between the test sample vector and two classes' average vectors separately.

$$d_k = \sum_{j=1}^{j=T} \left(x_j^{(*)} - c_{k,j}\right)^2 \cdot t_j \tag{6}$$

According to the distances, the test sample is labeled as follow:

$$l^{(*)} = \begin{cases} 1 & d_0 > d_1 \\ 0 & d_0 < d_1 \\ \text{uncertain} & d_0 = d_1 \end{cases} \tag{7}$$

After the classifier is constructed, the *fitness value* is defined as the accuracy of the *LOOCV*.

Selection, Crossover and Mutation. Basically, we adopt the simple *roulette-wheel* selection mechanism in our experiments, and we also use the elitism strategy to reserve the best individuals. Moreover, since the number of the genes used in the classifier is also a criterion of the classifier, the number of "1" in each individual must be considered, when several individuals have the same classification accuracy, we choose the ones with fewer number of "1"s.

Because the individual length T is much larger than the gene subset size, single point crossover may have few changes to the two parents. For an instance, suppose T is 20, and there are two gene subsets [0, 0, 0, 0, 0, 0, 0, 0, 0, 0, 1, 0, 0, 1, 1, 0, 1, 1, 0, 1] and [0, 0, 0, 0, 0, 0, 0, 0, 0, 0, 1, 0, 1, 1, 1, 1, 1, 0, 0], if we crossover them at bits 0 - 10, the offsprings are all the same as the parents. To increase the efficiency, we use the multiple-point crossover.

For the sake of achieving smaller size of gene subset, we use a simplified mutation strategy, which has been shown to be effective in our experiment, i.e. randomly generate a mutation point i in which the value is "1", and then randomly replace it with "0", which means removing the gene from the gene subset. Though adding certain gene to the gene subset may also be workable, the removal mechanism is only adopted to reduce the size of gene subset.

3 Evaluations and Results

3.1 Data Description and Preprocessing

AML/ALL: A collection of 72 expression measurements reported by Golub et al., which consists of 25 samples of Acute Myeloid Leukemia(AML) and 47 samples of Acute Lymphoblastic Leukemia(ALL). The expression levels of 7129 genes are reported in [1].

Colon: This is a collection of expression measurements from colon biopsy samples reported by Alon et al. The dataset consists of 62 samples, of which 22 is normal and 40 is colon caner tissues. 2000 genes were selected based on the confidence in the measured expression levels [3].

Lymph: Lymph dataset contains 58 patients with DLBCL, 32 with cured disease and 26 with fatal or refractory disease. The gene number of the dataset is 7129. This dataset is described in [4].

CNS-1, CNS-2: CNS-1 contains 34 medulloblastoma samples in which 25 are of classic and the remains are of desmoplastic. CNS-2 contains 60 samples of medulloblastoma treatment outcomes, 39 of them are treatment survivors and 21 are treatment failures. These two sets are described in [8].

All the data are pre-processed by two steps: first, following [9], we take logarithms of all values; then we normalize the values by the formula $x' = \frac{x-\bar{x}}{1/n*\sqrt{\sum_{i=1}^{n}(x-\bar{x})^2}}$, where x is the original input samples vector, $\bar{x}$ is the mean value vector of all the samples, x is the normalized vector; n is the number of the samples.

3.2 Methods and Results

In all GA runs, the population size $P=500$; the crossover ratio $Pc=1$; the mutation ratio $Pm=0.05$. In order to investigate the performances of the method on different parameter settings of the additional parameters Θ and T, we set Θ to 0.2, 0.4, 0.6, 0.8 respectively and set T to 10, 20, 30,..., and so on, then observe the classification accuracies of the classifiers built with the selected gene subsets.

The classification accuracies on the five datasets with different parameter values (T and Θ) are illustrated in Fig. 1-Fig. 5. Θ is set to 0.2, 0.4, 0.6 and 0.8 respectively. In Fig. 3, T ranges from 10 to 100 and in Fig. 4, T ranges from 10 to 130 because in the two cases, classification accuracies achieved 100% ultimately. In the other figures the T ranges from 10 to 140.

From Fig. 1-Fig. 5, we can see that, when T increases, the classification accuracies also increase up to a certain value, and then begin to fall; while parameter Θ does not act as T, even in some figures, for instance, in Fig. 2 and Fig. 3, the accuracies fall sharply. That is to say, although Θ is used to control the size of the gene subsets, it affects little on the classification accuracies. In fact, we can get the best classification accuracy when Θ is set to 0.2. Table 1 is a summary of the best results on the five datasets with Θ as 0.2 of several runs. From the table, we can see that, the proposed method can find a very compact gene subsets with high classification performances.

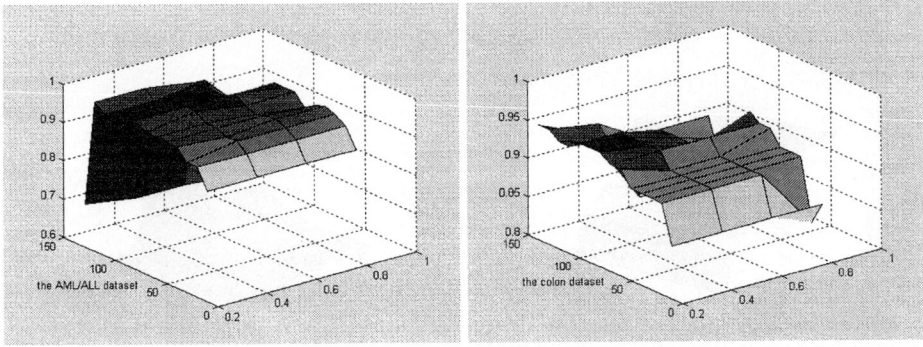

Fig. 1. The classification accuracy on the AML/ALL dataset.

Fig. 2. The classification accuracy on the Colon dataset.

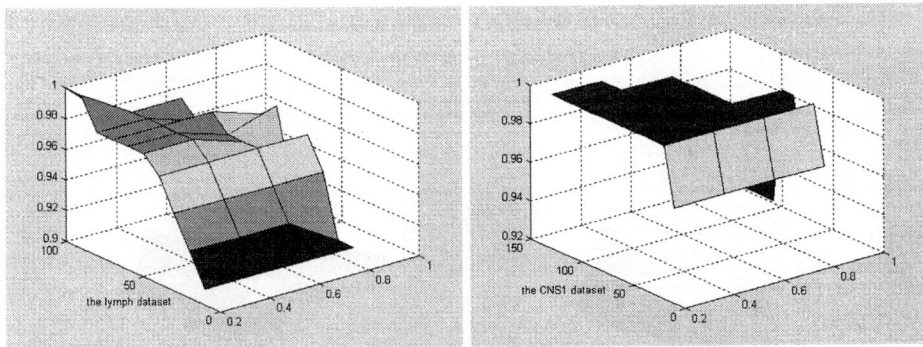

Fig. 3. The classification accuracy on the Lymph dataset.

Fig. 4. The classification accuracy on the CNS1 dataset.

There is also another phenomenon that when both of T and Θ become larger, the accuracies become lower. This is because that the initial populations in the GA are nearly all the same when Θ is great, which leads to the GA converging prematurely.

Fig. 6-Fig. 10 illustrate the affects of parameter T and Θ on the evolutionary generation number. From these figures, we can see that, when Θ equals to 0.2, the generation number is relative steady with different values of T. But when Θ goes up, the generation number increases accordingly. However, when the T and Θ are both set to larger values, the generation number becomes smaller, which is consistent with the low classification accuracies mentioned above.

To show how well our method is, we compare our classification accuracies against the resulsts listed in [10] on two benchmark datasets shown in Table 2, from which we can see that our method outweighs almost of the methods except for the JCFO with linear kernel method. Even though the LOOCV classification accuracies of our method are slightly lower, the needed genes are much more less than the later (8 for AML/ALL, 9 for Colon).

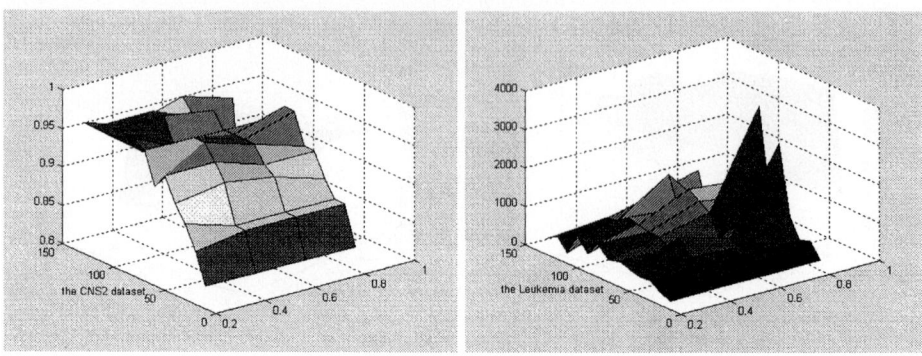

Fig. 5. The classification accuracy on the CNS2 dataset.

Fig. 6. The generation number on AML/ALL dataset with different T and Θ.

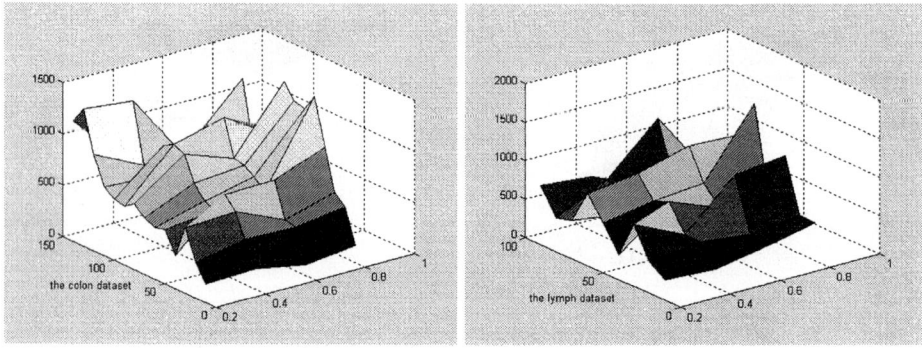

Fig. 7. The generation number on Colon dataset with different T and Θ.

Fig. 8. The generation number on Lymph dataset with different T and Θ.

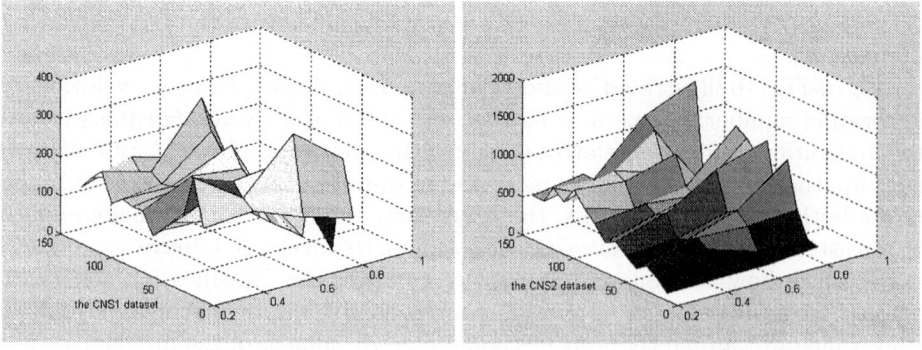

Fig. 9. The generation number on CNS1 dataset with different T and Θ.

Fig. 10. The generation number on CNS2 dataset with different T and Θ.

Table 1. The best accuracies on different datasets ($\Theta=0.2$).

Dataset	Accuracy	T	Gene number
AML/ALL	98.6	80	9
		90	10
		100	8
Colon	95.1	80	13
		90	9
		100	10
Lymph	100.0	90	12
		100	11
CNS1	100.0	30	3
		40	3
CNS2	98.3	80	12
		90	14
		100	11

Table 2. Classification accuracy of LOOCV: multiple classifiers.

Classifier	AML/ALL	Colon
Adaboosting (Decision stumps)	95.8	72.6
SVM (Linear kernel)	94.4	77.4
SVM (Quadratic kernel)	95.8	74.2
RVM (No Kernel)	97.2	88.7
Logistic regression (No kernel)	97.2	71.0
Sparse probit regression (Quadratic kernel)	95.8	84.6
Sparse probit regression (Linear kernel)	97.2	91.9
JCFO (Quadratic kernel)	98.6	88.7
JCFO (Linear kernel)	100.0	96.8
Proposed method	98.6	95.1

4 Conclusions and Discussions

In this paper, a gene selection method based on GAs was proposed, which consisted of two steps. Firstly, the top genes were pre-selected based on the newly defined *relative proximity degree* criterion; secondly, the optimized gene subsets were selected from the top genes using a GA. The experiments results show that the proposed method has wonderful performances.

From the experiment results shown in Fig. 1-Fig. 5, we can also conclude that using several top genes arbitrarily may not get fine classification accuracy, while after the recombination of the top genes using GAs, the accuracy is improved observably. This phenomenon interprets that though single gene may have high relativity to the cancer, optimized gene subsets are the key of the pathology.

The pre-selected top gene number T also has impact on the final results. If the T is too small, some informative genes may be omitted improperly, and if the T is too large, the search space is too large to find optimized gene subsets with a reasonable time cost. In our experiments, setting T to 80-100 has been proved to have fine results.

The size of the optimized gene subsets which are finally selected can be controlled in advance by setting the parameter $\Theta \in (0,1)$. In our experiments we find out that increasing Θ does not improve the classification accuracy but makes the generation number increase sharply. Therefore, setting Θ to 0.2 is adequate for high accuracy with low time cost.

The correlation of the genes was not specially considered in our experiments because the gene subsets found out by GAs are all small enough with the capability of high classification accuracies. Maybe there are also correlations between the genes in a certain subset, but high classification accuracy is the primary goal of the experiments.

Recently, we mainly addressed the two-class problem in the future, we will extend our work to multi-class problem.

References

1. Golub T.R., Slonim D.K. and Tamayo P., et al.: Molecular Classification of Cancer: Class Discovery and Class Prediction by Gene Expression Monitoring, Science **286** (1999) 531-537
2. Ben-Dor A., Bruhn L. and Friedman N., et al.: Tissue Classification with Gene Expression Profiles, Computational Biology **7** (2000) 559-584
3. Alon U.,Barkai N. and Notterman D., et al.: Broad Patterns of Gene Expression Revealed by Clustering Analysis of Tumor Colon Tissues Probed by Oligonucleotide Arrays, PNAS **96** (1999) 6745-6750
4. Shipp M.A, Ross K.N. and Tamayo P., et al.: Diffuse Large B-cell Lymphoma Outcome Prediction by Gene Expression Profiling and Supervised Machine Learning, Nature Machine **8** (2002) 68-74
5. Keller A.D., Schummer M., and Hood L., et al.: Bayesian Classification of DNA Array Expression Data, Technical Report UW-CSE-2000-08-01, Department of Computer Science & Engineering, University of Washington, Seattle (2000)
6. Chirs Ding and Hanchuan Peng: Minimum Redundancy Feature Selection from Microarray Gene Expression Data, CSB2003 (2003) 523-529
7. Xue-wen Chen: Gene Selection for Cancer Classification Using Bootstrapped Genetic Algorithms and Support Vector Machines, CSB2003 (2003) 504-505
8. Pomeroy S.L.,Tamayo P. and Gaasenbeek M., et al.: Prediction of Central Nervous System Embryonal Tumor Outcome Based on Gene Expression, Nature **415** (2002) 436-442
9. Yang Y.H., Dudoit S. and Lin D.M., et al.: Normalization for cDNA Microarray Data: a Robust Composite Method Addressing Single and Multiple Slide Systematic Variation, Nucleic Acids Res. **30** (2002) e15.1-e15.10
10. Krishnapuram B., Carin L. and Hartemink A.: Joint Classifier and Feature Optimizationi for Cancer Diagnosis Using Gene Expression Data, Journal of Computational Biology (to appear)

Using Genetic Programming for Feature Creation with a Genetic Algorithm Feature Selector

Matthew G. Smith and Larry Bull

Faculty of Computing, Engineering & Mathematical Sciences,
University of the West of England, Bristol BS16 1QY, UK
Matt@matt-smith.me.uk, Larry.Bull@uwe.ac.uk

Abstract. The use of machine learning techniques to automatically analyse data for information is becoming increasingly widespread. In this paper we primarily examine the use of Genetic Programming and a Genetic Algorithm to pre-process data before it is classified using the C4.5 decision tree learning algorithm. Genetic Programming is used to construct new features from those available in the data, a potentially significant process for data mining since it gives consideration to hidden relationships between features. A Genetic Algorithm is used to determine which such features are the most predictive. Using ten well-known datasets we show that our approach, in comparison to C4.5 alone, provides marked improvement in a number of cases. We then examine its use with other well-known machine learning techniques.

1 Introduction

Classification is one of the major tasks in data mining, involving the prediction of class value based on information about some other attributes. In this paper we examine the combination of Genetic Programming (GP) [8] and a Genetic Algorithm (GA) [5] to improve the performance of, initially, the decision tree learning algorithm C4.5 [12] through feature *construction* and feature *selection*. Feature construction is a process that aims to discover hidden relationships between features, inferring new composite features. In contrast, feature selection is a process that aims to refine the list of features used thereby removing potential sources of noise and ambiguity. We use GP individuals consisting of a number of separate trees/automatically defined functions (ADFs) [8] to construct features for C4.5. A GA is simultaneously used to select over the new set of constructed features for a final hybrid C4.5 classifier system. Results show that the system is able to outperform standard C4.5 on a number of datasets held at the UCI repository (http://www.ics.uci.edu/~mlearn/MLRepository.html). We then show how similar benefits are obtained for the k-nearest neighbour algorithm [18] and Naïve Bayes [19].

Raymer et al. [13] have used ADFs for feature *extraction* in conjunction with the k-nearest-neighbour algorithm. Feature extraction replaces an original feature with the result from passing it through a functional mapping. In Raymer et al.'s approach each feature is altered by an ADF, evolved for that feature only, with the aim of increasing the separation of pattern classes in the feature space; for problems with n features, individuals consist of n ADFs. Ahluwalia and Bull [1] extended Raymer et al.'s approach by coevolving the ADFs for each feature and adding an extra coevolving GA population of feature selectors; extraction and selection occurred simultaneously in $n+1$ populations. For other (early) examples of evolutionary computation approaches to data mining see [14] for a GA-based feature selection approach using k-nearest-neighbour and [6] for a similar GA-based approach also using k-nearest-neighbour. Since first undertaking the work presented here we have become aware of Vafaie and DeJong's [16] combination of GP and a GA for use with C4.5. They used the GA to perform feature selection for a face recognition dataset where feature subsets were evaluated through their use by C4.5. GP individuals were then evolved which contained a variable number of ADFs to construct new features from the selected subset, again using C4.5. Our approach is very similar to Vafaie and DeJong's but the feature operations are reversed such that feature construction occurs before selection. We find that our approach performs as well or better than Vafaie and DeJong's. Krawiec [9] has also presented a similar approach.

More recent work using GP to construct features for use by C4.5 includes that of Otero et al. [11]. They use a population of GP trees to evolve a single new feature using information gain as the fitness measure (this is the criteria used by C4.5 to select attributes to test at each node of the decision tree). This produces a single feature that attempts to cover as many instances as possible – a feature that aims to be generally useful and which is appended to the set of original features for use by C4.5. Ekárt and Márkus [4] use GP to evolve new features that are useful at specific points in the decision tree by working interactively with C4.5. They do this by invoking a GP algorithm when constructing a new node in the decision tree – e.g., when a leaf node incorrectly classifies some instances. Information gain is again used as the fitness criterion but the GP is trained only on those instances relevant at that node of the tree.

This paper is arranged as follows: the next section describes the algorithm; section 3 presents results from its use on a number of well-known datasets and discusses the results. This is followed by some amendments to the algorithm and further results; finally section 4 presents comparisons with other algorithms, some conclusions and future directions.

2 The GAP Algorithm

In this work we have used the WEKA [17] implementation of C4.5, known as J48, to examine the performance of our Genetic Algorithm and Programming (GAP) approach. This is a wrapper approach [7], in which the fitness of individuals is evaluated by performing 10-fold cross validation using the same inducer as used to create the final classifier: C4.5(J48). An early version of this algorithm was presented in [15] The algorithm is described below (see [15] for a more detailed description of the original algorithm, and some analysis of the feature sets created).

A population of 101 genotypes is created at random. Each genotype consists of n trees, where n is the number of numeric valued features in the dataset, subject to a minimum of 7. This minimum is chosen to ensure that, for datasets with a small number of numeric features, the initial population contains a large number of compound features. A tree can be either an original feature or an ADF. That is, a genotype consists of n GP trees, each of which may contain 1 or more nodes. The chance of a node being a leaf node (a primitive attribute) is determined by:

$$P_{leaf} = 1 - \frac{1}{(depth+1)}$$

Where *depth* is the depth of the tree at the current node. Hence a root node will have a depth of 1, and therefore a probability of 0.5 of being a leaf node, and so on. If a node is a leaf, it takes the value of one of the original features chosen at random. Otherwise, a function is randomly chosen from the set {*, /, +, -, %} and two child nodes are generated. In this manner there is no absolute limit placed on the depth any one tree may reach but the average depth is limited. During the initial creation no two trees in a single genotype are allowed to be alike and no two genotypes are allowed to be the same, though these restrictions are not enforced in later stages. Additionally, nodes with '−', '%' or '/' for functions cannot have child nodes that are equal to each other. In order to enforce this, child nodes within a function '*' or '+' are ordered lexicographically to enable comparison (e.g. [width + length] will become [length + width]). Each tree has an associated activity − a boolean switch set randomly in the initial population that determines if the feature created by the tree will be used.

An individual is evaluated by constructing a new dataset with one feature for each active tree in the genotype. This dataset is then passed to a C4.5(J48) classifier (using default parameters), whose performance on the dataset is evaluated using 10-fold cross validation. The percentage correct is then assigned to the individual and used as the fitness score.

Once the initial population has been evaluated, several generations of selection, crossover, mutation and evaluation are performed. After each evaluation, if the fittest individual in the current generation is fitter than the fittest so far (or is as fit and has fewer active trees), a copy of it is set aside and the generation noted. We use tournament selection to select the parents of the next generation, with tournament size 8 and a 0.3 probability of the fittest individual winning (otherwise a 'winner' is selected at random from the tournament group). There is a 0.6 probability of uniform crossover occurring between the ADFs of the two selected parents (whole trees are exchanged between genotypes). The activity switch remains associated with the tree.

There is an additional 0.6 probability that crossover will occur within two ADFs at a randomly chosen locus (sub-trees are exchanged between trees in the same position in the child genotypes). Mutation is used with probability 0.008 per node, whereby a randomly created subtree replaces the subtree under the selected node. The activity switch is flipped with a chance of 0.005. We also use a form of inversion with probability 0.2 whereby the order of the trees between two randomly chosen loci is reversed. Experimentation on varying these parameters with early versions of this algorithm has found it to be fairly robust to their setting (not shown). The fittest individual in each generation is copied unchanged to the next generation.

The evolutionary process continues until the following conditions are met: at least 20 generations have passed, and the fittest individual so far is at least 12 generations old. This is a lengthy process, as performing 10-fold cross validation for each member of the population is very processor intensive. The extra time required can justified by the improvement in the results over using, e.g., a single train and test set (results not shown). Information Gain, the fitness criterion employed by both Otero and Ekárt, is much faster but is only applicable to a single feature − it cannot provide the fitness criterion for a set of features.

Table 1. UCI dataset information.

Dataset	Features	Classes	Instances
BUPA Liver Disorder (Liver)	6	2	345
Glass Identification (Glass)	9	6	214
Ionosphere (Iono.)	34	2	351
New Thyroid (NT)	5	3	215
Pima Indians Diabetes (Diab.)	8	2	768
Sonar	60	2	208
Vehicle	18	4	846
Wine Recognition (Wine)	13	3	178
Wisconsin Breast Cancer – New (WBC New)	30	2	569
Wisconsin Breast Cancer – Original (WBC Orig.)	9	2	699

3 Experimentation

We have used ten well-known data sets from the UCI repository to examine the performance of the GAP algorithm. The UCI datasets were chosen because they consisted entirely of numeric attributes (though the algorithm can handle some nominal attributes, as long as there are two or more numeric attributes present). Table 1 shows the details of the ten datasets used here.

For performance comparisons the tests were performed using ten-fold cross-validation (in which 90% of the data was used for training and 10% for testing). An additional set of ten runs using ten-fold cross validation were made (a total of twenty runs - two sets of ten-fold cross-validation) to allow a paired t-test to establish the significance of any improvement over C4.5(J48).

3.1 Initial Results

The highest classification score for each dataset is shown in Table 2 in bold. The first two columns show the performance of the GAP algorithm on the test data and the last column shows the results of the paired t-test. Results that are significant at the 95% confidence level are shown in bold.

Table 2. Comparative performance of GAP algorithm and C4.5 (J48).

Dataset	GAP	S.D.	C4.5 (J48)	S.D.	Paired t-test
Liver	65.77	8.67	66.37	8.86	-0.35
Glass	69.55	10.04	68.28	8.86	0.58
Iono.	90.21	4.74	89.82	4.79	0.33
NT	96.56	4.17	92.31	4.14	**2.96**
Diab.	74.88	3.42	73.32	5.25	1.36
Sonar	75.63	14.71	73.86	10.92	0.55
Vehicle	73.23	5.06	72.22	3.33	1.07
Wine	95.29	5.64	93.27	5.70	1.71
(WBC New)	95.09	3.88	93.88	4.22	1.40
(WBC Orig.)	95.57	1.79	94.42	3.05	**2.32**
Overall	83.18		81.77		**2.84**

The GAP algorithm out-performs C4.5(J48) on nine of ten datasets, and provides a significant improvement on two (New Thyroid, and Wisconsin Breast Cancer Original). GAP never performs significantly worse than C4.5(J48) alone. On all datasets GAP reduces the number of features used on average, and further analysis shows repeated construction of useful features (see [15] for more details).

3.2 Applying GAP to Other Classification Algorithms

As the version of C4.5 used is part of the Weka package, it is a simple matter to replace C4.5(J48) with different classifiers and thus test the GAP algorithm with a number of different classification techniques. We replaced C4.5(J48) with the following classifiers: IBk (a k-nearest neighbour classifier [18] with k=1) and Naïve Bayes (a probability based classifier [19]).

Table 3. Results with Ibk.

Dataset	GAP	SD	IBk	SD	t-Test
Liver	60.05	11.23	62.62	8.68	-0.89
Glass	74.41	11.21	68.79	10.00	**1.96**
Iono.	90.50	3.57	86.95	4.53	**3.13**
NT	95.34	4.01	96.95	3.73	-1.45
Diab.	67.77	5.67	69.90	4.27	-1.81
Sonar	84.23	6.71	86.65	6.56	-1.39
Vehicle	75.47	5.40	70.03	4.10	**4.39**
Wine	96.55	4.75	95.44	5.81	0.85
(WBC New)	95.37	3.95	95.44	3.00	-0.13
(WBC Orig.)	94.99	2.16	95.42	2.16	-0.97
Overall	83.47		82.82		1.20

Table 3 shows that IBk on its own offers slightly better performance over the ten datasets than C4.5 (on average only – there are several individual datasets on which C4.5 performs better) and perhaps offers the GAP algorithm less scope for improvement. There is no significant overall improvement over IBk at the 95% level and no improvement at all on six of ten datasets, but there are three datasets on which GAP does offer a significant improvement (Glass, Ionosphere and Vehicle) and none where there is a significant drop in performance. Overall the result is competitive with GAP using C4.5.

By looking at the overall average of table 4 it can be quickly seen that, on its own, Naïve Bayes cannot compete with C4.5 or IBk over the ten datasets – it is approx. 6% worse on average (though again there are individual datasets where Naïve Bayes performs better than the other two – e.g., New Thyroid, Wine). This relatively poor performance gives the GAP algorithm much greater scope for improvement. In fact, the GAP algorithm brings the results very closely into line with those achieved using C4.5 and IBk – it beats them both, though only marginally.

While neither of the two new classifiers provide a dramatic improvement on GAP's overall result using C4.5 both results are competitive – regardless of the performance of the classifier on its own. It seems as if there is a ceiling on the average results achievable with any one classifier. When using any particular classifier GAP may perform well on some datasets and worse on others, while the average seems to settle out at somewhere over 83% no matter which classifier is employed. That is, GAP appears to provide robustness to the classifier techniques used.

Table 4. Results with Naïve Bayes.

Dataset	GAP	SD	N.B.	SD	t-test
Liver	70.44	6.33	54.19	9.61	**5.31**
Glass	65.32	9.33	48.50	14.03	**4.96**
Iono.	91.32	4.82	82.37	7.31	**4.97**
NT	96.05	3.47	97.20	3.83	-1.67
Diab.	76.69	4.48	75.13	5.00	1.74
Sonar	76.50	10.74	67.16	7.53	**3.52**
Vehicle	70.45	5.30	43.98	4.61	**20.5**
Wine	96.36	5.00	97.99	3.85	-1.96
(WBC New)	97.10	2.59	93.26	4.79	**4.07**
(WBC Orig.)	96.63	2.10	96.06	1.74	**2.31**
Overall Average	83.69		75.58		**9.95**

3.3 Allowing the Algorithm to Select the Type of Classifier

The GAP algorithm has been successfully applied to 3 different types of classifier, each of which performs relatively well on some datasets and poorly on others (both with and without pre-processing by the GAP algorithm). It seems plausible that we could improve the results of the algorithm by allowing it to select the most appropriate classifier for a particular dataset based on the fitness score. We amended the genotype to include the classifier type and set the classifier type at random in the initial population. In subsequent generations the likelihood of mutating the classifier type was set at 0.2 (this being the same as the chance of inverting sections of the genotype. Future work will involve determining the most appropriate setting for this value). In each new generation the fittest genotype for every classifier is copied unchanged to the next generation (so instead of just the single fittest genotype being carried forward in each generation, there are now 3 genotypes being carried forward).

As before, the algorithm was evaluated using two sets of 10-fold cross validation for each of 10 datasets, giving an average result of 84.01% - a slight improvement over the algorithm with any single classifier. This result was a surprise – we had been expecting more improvement than that. Looking in more detail at the results it emerged that J48 appears more prone to over-fitting than the other classifiers and J48 genotypes often overshadow other, ultimately more accurate, genotypes. The Liver Disorder dataset is a good example of this: the J48 genotype was selected in 16 of 20 runs and Naïve Bayes genotypes selected in the remaining 4 runs, giving an average result for the 20 runs of 65.7%. However if the Naïve Bayes genotype had been selected in every run the average result would have improved to 70.1%.

One simple method to try to compensate for this is to randomly re-order the dataset at the end of the breeding process and re-test the fittest genotype for each classifier, then choose the genotype based on this 'train' score rather than the original fitness. Using this method a different genotype/classifier is chosen in 43 of the 200 runs (20 of which result in an improvement against 11 that are worse) for a small improvement of the overall average to 84.26%[1] (table 5). Future work will look at changing the settings of J48 (e.g. the confidence value) during fitness evaluation to further reduce over-fitting.

Table 5. Selecting the classifier type:

Dataset	GAP	SD	Simple Meta	SD	t-test
Liver	**65.78**	8.03	64.76	8.98	0.61
Glass	**70.89**	11.02	68.77	11.46	0.71
Iono.	**89.90**	5.61	89.82	4.79	0.06
NT	94.87	4.48	**96.25**	4.19	-2.78
Diab.	75.72	5.20	**76.04**	4.86	-0.34
Sonar	85.57	7.63	**86.64**	6.56	-0.55
Vehicle	**72.99**	3.74	72.22	3.32	0.64
Wine	95.44	5.11	**97.99**	3.84	-2.38
(WBC New)	**96.14**	2.50	95.09	3.06	1.67
(WBC Orig.)	95.27	2.46	**95.99**	1.84	-1.32
Overall Average	84.26	5.58	84.36	5.29	-3.04

It is difficult to compare the performance of the modified algorithm to that of a single classifier (which classifier do you choose for the comparison?), so we created a simple meta-classifier for comparison purposes. This evaluated each of the 3 available classifiers on the training data and selected the fittest, based on 10-fold cross validation, for use on the test data. This comparison is very disappointing – the simple meta-classifier performs marginally better than the GAP algorithm (significantly better overall and on 2 datasets) with just a small fraction of the computational effort. However, our disappointment was offset by the results from the pragmatic use of such systems.

3.4 Looking at the Best-Of-Run Genotypes

The GAP algorithm is probabilistic in nature and, obviously, is likely produce a different set of features every time it is run – some of which will bet better than others. All the results shown so far have been obtained from 20 runs per dataset, every run providing a distinct set of features and the result an average over the 20 feature sets (or feature/classifier combinations) - each set tested on a single data fold.

In a practical situation we are not interested in the average utility of a number of feature sets, but in using the best available feature set. We therefore evaluated each of the 20 feature set/classifier combinations on *all* of the data folds, and discovered that the best set of features offers a marked improvement over the average performance, and over the performance of an unaided classifier. For 8 of the 10 datasets there were at least 2 (often 5 or more) feature sets with results more than a standard deviation better than the best unaided classifier. (There was one such feature set for Diabetes and none for New Thyroid). That is to say that run 20 times the GAP algorithm is highly likely to produce at least one, and often many more, sets of features that offer a marked and significant improvement over an unaided classifier (all results have t-test scores over 8 – a significance level of more than 99%).

---

[1] This figure is directly comparable to the 84.01% figure given above as both sets of results were collected on the same runs.

Table 6 shows results using the single best feature set/classifier combination found for each dataset and the comparison meta-classifier – "simple Meta" - compared with the best performing unaided classifier (chosen using results on test data).

Table 6. Performance of GAP and other algorithms on the UCI datasets.

Dataset	GAP (avg.)	Simple Meta	GAP (best of run)	C4.5	HIDER	XCS	O. F. A.	LVSM
Liver	65.78	64.76	**75.38**	65.27	64.29	67.85	57.01	68.68
Glass	70.89	68.77	**83.49**	67.27	70.59	72.53	69.56	
Iono.	89.90	89.82	**96.17**					87.75
NT	94.87	96.25	**98.86**					
Diab.	75.72	76.04	**79.62**	67.94	74.10	68.62	69.80	78.12
Sonar	85.57	86.64	**96.42**	69.69	56.93	53.41	79.96	
Vehicle	72.99	72.22	**80.97**					
Wine	95.44	97.99	**100.00**	93.29	96.05	92.74	98.27	
(WBC New)	96.14	95.09	**98.86**					
(WBC Orig.)	95.27	95.99	**97.85**	93.72	95.71	96.27	94.39	

4 Summary

We have presented an approach to the use of genetic programming and a genetic algorithm for feature creation and selection. Further, we have presented a mechanism by which the evolving feature pre-processor may select the most effective classifier. Table 6 also presents a number of published results we have found regarding the same ten UCI datasets using other machine learning algorithms. It should be noted that in the table the results for C4.5 were not obtained using J48. The GAP (avg.) column presents results for the multi-classifier version of the algorithm (from which the best-of-run feature sets were taken). Cells in the table are left blank where algorithms were not tested on the dataset in question. The highest classification score for each dataset is shown in bold.

The results for C4.5, HIDER and XCS were obtained from [3], those for O.F.A. ('Ordered Fuzzy ARTMAP', a neural network algorithm) from [2] and LVSM (Lagrangian Support Vector Machines) from [10].

The differences between the reported results for C4.5 and those for C4.5 as used in this paper (J48, the WEKA implementation of C4.5) are likely to arise from different data partitions used for the tests (the most notable being the 5.38% difference in results for Pima Indians Diabetes). This discrepancy highlights the dangers inherent in comparing results with published data – the comparison should be seen as purely informal. The only comparisons that can be relied upon are those between the GAP classifier, the simple meta classifier and C4.5(J48), IBK, Naïve Bayes (shown in previous tables) as these have been performed using exactly the same procedure and data partitions. The results are by no means an exhaustive list of current machine learning algorithms, nor are they guaranteed to be the best performing algorithms available, but they give some indication of the relative performance of our approach – which appears competitive when results are taken on average, and very good indeed when using the best-of-run feature sets.

References

1. Ahluwalia, M. & Bull, L. (1999) Co-Evolving Functions in Genetic Programming: Classification using k-nearest neighbour. In W. Banzhaf, J. Daida, G. Eiben, M-H. Garzon, J. Honavar, K. Jakeila, R. Smith (eds) *GECCO-99: Proceedings of the Genetic and Evolutionary Computation Conference*. Morgan Kaufmann, pp. 947–952.
2. Dagher, I., Georgiopoulos, M., Heileman, G.L., & Bebis, G. (1999). An Ordering Algorithm for Pattern Presentation in Fuzzy ARTMAP That Tends to Improve Generalization Performance. IEEE Transactions on Neural Networks, 10(4), 768-778.
3. Dixon, P. W., Corne, D. W., & Oates, M. J. (2001) A Preliminary Investigation of Modified XCS as a Generic Data Mining Tool. In P-L. Lanzi, W. Stolzmann, S. Wilson (eds) *Advances in Learning Classifier Systems*. Springer, pp.133-151.
4. Ekárt, A. & Márkus, A. (2003). Using Genetic Programming and Decision Trees for Generating Structural Descriptions of Four Bar Mechanisms. To appear in *Artificial Intelligence for Engineering Design, Analysis and Manufacturing*, volume 17, issue 3.
5. Holland, J.H. (1975) *Adaptation in Natural and Artificial Systems*. Univ. Michigan.
6. Kelly, J.D. & Davis, L. (1991) Hybridizing the Genetic Algorithm and the K Nearest Neighbors Classification Algorithm. In R. Belew & L. Booker (eds) *Proceedings of the Fourth International Conference on Genetic Algorithms*. Morgan Kaufmann, pp377-383.
7. Kohavi, R. & John, G. H. (1997). Wrappers for feature subset selection. Artificial Intelligence Journal vol. 1-2: 273-324.
8. Koza, J.R. (1992) *Genetic Programming*. MIT Press.
9. Krawiec, K. (2002). Genetic Programming-based Construction of Features for Machine Learning and Knowledge Discovery Tasks. *Genetic Programming and Evolvable Machines* vol. 3 no. 4: 329-343.
10. Mangasarian, O. L. & Musicant, D. R. (2001) Lagrangian support vector machines. *Journal of Machine Learning Research* 1:161-177.
11. Otero, F. E. B., Silva, M. M. S., Freitas, A. A. & Nievola J. C. (2003). Genetic Programming for Attribute Construction in Data Mining. In C. Ryan, T. Soule, M. Keijzer, E. Tsang, R. Poli, E. Costa (Eds.) *Genetic Programming: 6th European Conference, EuroGP 2003, Essex, UK, April 2003, Proceedings*. Springer, pp. 384-393.
12. Quinlan, J.R. (1993) *C4.5: Programs for Machine Learning*. Morgan Kaufmann.
13. Raymer, M.L., Punch, W., Goodman, E.D. & Kuhn, L. (1996) Genetic Programming for Improved Data Mining - Application to the Biochemistry of Protein Interactions. In J.R. Koza, K. Deb, M. Dorigo, D.B. Fogel, M.Garzon, H. Iba & R. Riolo (eds) *Proceedings of the Second Annual Conference on Genetic Programming*, Morgan Kaufmann, pp375-380.
14. Siedlecki, W. & Sklansky, J. (1988) On Automatic Feature Selection. *International Journal of Pattern Recognition and Artificial Intelligence* 2:197-220.
15. Smith, M. & Bull, L. (2003) Feature Construction and Selection using Genetic Programming and a Genetic Algorithm. In C. Ryan, T. Soule, E. Tsang, R. Poli & E. Costa (eds) *Genetic Programming: Proceedings of 6th European Conference, EuroGP 2003*. Springer, pp229-237.
16. Vafaie, H. & De Jong, K. (1995). Genetic Algorithms as a Tool for Restructuring Feature Space Representations. In *Proceedings of the International Conference on Tools with A.I.* IEEE Computer Society Press.
17. Witten, I.H. & Frank, E. (2000). *Data Mining: Practical Machine Learning Tools and Techniques with Java Implementations*. Morgan Kaufmann.
18. Aha, D., and D. Kibler (1991). Instance-based learning algorithms. *Machine Learning* vol.6, pp. 37-66.
19. John, G.H & Langley, P. (1995). Estimating Continuous Distributions in Bayesian Classifiers. *Proceedings of the Eleventh Conference on Uncertainty in Artificial Intelligence*. Morgan Kaufmann, San Mateo. pp. 338-345.

AgentP Model: Learning Classifier System with Associative Perception

Zhanna V. Zatuchna

University of East Anglia, Norwich, NR4 7TJ, England
z.zatuchna@uea.ac.uk

Abstract. Aliasing environments present the tasks of increased difficulty for Learning Classifier Systems. Aliasing squares look identical for an agent with limited perceptive power, but may demand a completely different optimal strategy. Thus, the presence of aliasing squares in a maze may lead to a non-optimal behaviour and decrease the agent's performance. As a possible approach to the problem we introduce a psychological model of associative perception learning and based on the model AgentP, an LCS with explicitly imprinted images of the environmental states. The system is tested on several aliasing environments to establish the learning effectiveness of the approach.

1 Introduction

Learning Classifier Systems (LCS) belong to the class of systems based on the principle of self-organization and evolution adopted from real nature. The commonly used problem to estimate LCS performance is a maze environment [23, 9, 2]. The agent does not have a model of the maze and has to learn based on a limited feedback from the environment. An LCS is an algorithm for processing the feedback and selecting an action based on a set of behavioural rules.

Mazes with aliasing squares, that look identical for an agent with limited perceptive power, but are different in fact, present a task of increased difficulty for LCS. As a possible approach to the problem we introduce the AgentP system, a Learning Classifier System with associative perception, that has inherited its name from the psychological learning model, also introduced in the paper.

The next section provides a summary of related work and is followed by the description of the associative perception learning model. Section 4 describes the structure and main operators of the AgentP system. The conducted experiments and the obtained results are discussed in Section 5. Next, the areas of future work are outlined. Finally, conclusions are provided.

2 Related Work

The original version of LCS was proposed by John Holland in 1978 [6]. Wilson [24] simplified the original framework and introduced ZCS with Q-learning like distribution of the reward, and XCS [23], where fitness of a classifier depended on the accuracy of the classifier's prediction instead of the prediction itself.

Tomlinson and Bull [19, 20] developed Corporate Classifier Systems, introducing ZCS and XCS with Michigan-style classifiers. Recently Bull [3] presented his new YCS, a Simple Accuracy-based Learning Classifier System, that kept much of Wilson's framework, but was simplified to increase understandability.

AgentP belongs to the class of predictive modelling trend in LCS. In 1990 Holland [7] presented a general framework for incorporating future state predictions into LCS using a tag system. In 1998 Stolzmann [17] combined the LCS framework with the anticipatory behaviour control mechanism [5] and introduced a learning system with the next state representation called Anticipatory Classifier System. Later Bull [2] incorporated lookahead in ZCS.

As an approach to the problem of perceptual aliasing, internal memory was added to ZCS [4] and XCS [8, 9]. Another approach in the form of classifiers with behavioural sequences was found by Stolzmann [16] and investigated by Metivier and Lattaud [13].

The main distinctions of the AgentP system from the other LCS are discussed in Section 4.

3 Associative Perception Learning Model

Reinforcement Learning is a part of the machine learning research that has inherited its ideas from the psychological theory of animal learning proposed by Thorndike [18]. According to the theory, learning is the result of the connections formed between stimuli and responses (S-R). The paradigm for S-R theory is trial-and-error learning in which certain responses come to dominate others because of rewards. The proposed *learning model of associative perception* is based on two further psychological principles: *laws of organization* and *imprinting*.

Laws of Organization. Early in the XX century Wertheimer and others created Gestalt theory [22], which emphasized higher-order cognitive processes. The focus of the theory was the idea of grouping, when characteristics of stimuli cause an individual to structure or interpret a visual field or problem as a global construct. The rules of interpretation may take several forms, such as grouping by proximity, similarity, closure, etc. These factors were called the laws of organization and were explained in the context of perception and problem-solving.

Imprinting. Imprinting is an especially rapid and relatively irreversible learning process first observed and described by Konrad Lorenz [11]. In the process of imprinting, distinctive attributes of external objects are imprinted in an individual's memory and become connected with behavioural reactions of the individual. The imprinted information becomes his reference point for both "individual-to-objects" and "objects-to-objects" interconnections. Thus, the imprinted relations define further behaviour of the individual.

Thus, the main concept of the learning model comprises two assumptions:
- during the early period of life an individual absorbs the environmental signals as he perceives them, without any changes or generalizations;
- environmental signals, received sequentially with or without any activity of the individual, are perceived as a single indecomposable image.

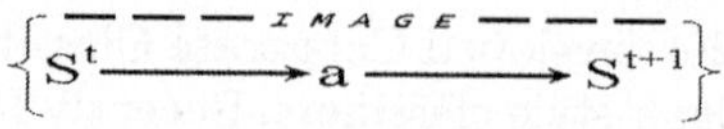

$$\left\{S^t \xrightarrow{\quad IMAGE \quad} a \longrightarrow S^{t+1}\right\}$$

Fig. 1. Image creation in the associative perception learning model.

Fig.1 shows an image creation scheme for the case of the presence of the individual's activity. S^t and S^{t+1} are explicitly imprinted representations of the perceived environmental signals at time t and $t+1$ accordingly, and a is an action conducted by the individual.

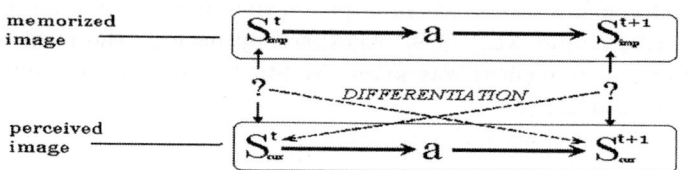

Fig. 2. Functional scheme of associative perception learning.

Fig.2 presents a functional scheme of the associative perception learning:

1. Currently perceived environmental information is grouped into a single integrated image that includes two images of consecutive environmental states S_{cur}^t and S_{cur}^{t+1} associated with a performed action a.
2. The newly created image is matched with memorized images step-by-step: for the performed action a the perceived initial state S_{cur}^t is compared with the imprinted initial state S_{imp}^t, and the perceived next state S_{cur}^{t+1} is compared with the imprinted next state S_{imp}^t.
3. If at least one state S_{cur}^t or S_{cur}^{t+1} differs from that one in the memorized image, the other state is considered to be distinctive as well, and the whole new image is believed to be a different one.
4. If there is not an exact match for the perceived image, it is memorized by imprinting it into the memory.

Having received a new environmental signal at time $t+1$, the associative perception mechanism is able to correctly differentiate both, the initial and the next environmental states, while the anticipatory behaviour control mechanism used in ACS [17] is meant to differentiate the initial state only.

The associative perception mechanism employs a *sliding image formation* principle (Fig.3). According to the laws of organization [22], the perceptive im-

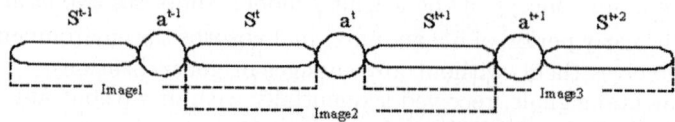

Fig. 3. Sliding image formation.

ages are perceived not separately, but in connection with each other. Each representation of an environmental state S^t is associated with two others, the previous S^{t-1} and the following S^{t+1}. Thus, the formation of images is performed under the "sliding" state-to-state attention and the individual is always able to recognize the "individual-to-objects" and "objects-to-objects" interconnections, at least for a quantum of time T, where $T >= [t-1, t+1]$.

4 AgentP Model: Learning Classifier System with Associative Perception

Detailed description of AgentP structure and performance can be found in [25]. The most significant distinctions of the AgentP system from the other LCS [24, 23, 17] are as follows:

1. AgentP operates only the classifiers with explicitly imprinted representations of the perceived environmental signals with no 'don't care' symbols.
2. There is no a super-creative mechanism, like the genetic algorithms [6], provided for the rule discovery process. The system performs on the "perceived-differentiated-memorized" principle.
3. The consecutive environmental states are perceived not only as a cause-effect time vector, but also as a single perceptive image that is compared with previously memorized images for differentiation purposes. Thus, AgentP is able to recognize aliasing in both, current and next environment states.
4. There is no reward-value based reinforcement, the distance-based learning coefficients are used for the reinforcement purposes.

4.1 Structural Elements of the AgentP System

Except input/ouput interfaces and the classifier sets that have been employed in other LCS research [23, 17], AgentP contains a *current perceptive image* I with the structure as shown on Fig.1 and a *state list* L containing all the states that the agent has perceived during a learning run. Each state in L has a *valency* parameter ν, reflecting the number of aliasing squares for that state.

The basic part of a single classifier is similar to the *condition* $\rightarrow$ *action* $\rightarrow$ *expectation* structure as used by Stolzmann for ACS [17]. It is supplemented with an ID system, that inherited its basic structure from Wilson's memory extension [24], but is extended with a verification mechanism and has deterministic character.

The parts of the classifier that represent an environmental state have an *identification mark ID* and a *verification sign F*. Identification mark is used for refined differentiation of aliasing states. If the verification sign of a state in a classifier is positive, the state is considered as having a *fixed* ID. Thus, in case of aliasing, the agent is "sure" about its position in the environment, if the perceptive image, it is guided by, has a matching classifier with a fixed ID in its corresponding part. Each classifier in AgentP is associated with a *prediction D*

$$S^t \text{---} ID^t_s \text{---} F^t_s \longrightarrow a \longrightarrow S^{t+1}_s \text{---} ID^{t+1}_s \text{---} F^{t+1}_s$$

Fig. 4. Classifier in AgentP.

that represents the classifier's d-coefficient (Section 4.4), related to the expected distance to food at time $t+1$.

Thus, a classifier in the AgentP model consists of the following parts (Fig.4):

initial state S^t with information about attributes of an environmental state at time t, where $S^t \in \{0,1\}^n$, and n is the number of the detectors,
identification mark ID^t_s for the initial state S^t, where $ID^t_s \in \{0,1,2\ldots\infty\}$,
verification sign F^t_s for the initial state S^t, where $F^t_s \in \{true, false\}$,
action a representing the action undertaken by the effectors at time t,
next state S^{t+1} with information about attributes of an environmental state at time $t+1$, where $S^{t+1} \in \{0,1\}^n$,
identification mark ID^{t+1}_s for the result state S^{t+1}, where $ID^{t+1}_s \in \{0,1,2\ldots\infty\}$,
verification sign F^{t+1}_s for the result state S^{t+1}, where $F^{t+1}_s \in \{true, false\}$.

4.2 Differentiation

The differentiation operator performs according to the associative perception learning scheme (Fig.2). All classifiers, that have S^t_{imp} corresponding to the environmental state $\sigma(t)$ and action a, are placed into $[A_{ini}]$; and those with the next state S^{t+1}_{imp} matching $\sigma(t+1)$ and action a are placed into $[A_{res}]$. Then S^{t+1}_{cur} from the perceived image I is compared to the corresponding part S^{t+1}_{imp} of each classifier within $[A_{ini}]$. If there is at least one classifier with a non-matching next-state condition, the state $\sigma(t)$ is considered to be an alias. If the valency of the initial state $\nu(\sigma(t))$ is equal to the number of classifiers in $[A_{ini}]$, which have a fixed initial ID, or if $\sigma(t)$ was believed to be a non-aliasing state before ($\nu = 1$), the value of the valency ν is increased by 1: $\nu' = \nu + 1$. The current classifier receives the new ID with positive verification sign (fixed ID). If new valency $\nu' = 2$, i.e. the aliasing state has just been recognized as an alias, the reference classifier from $[A_{ini}]$ has its initial ID fixed. The classifier that has increased the valency of a state becomes an *arrow*. Each cell may have only one arrow and its role is to spread the saved ID through the *associative correction* operator to all other classifiers that are related to the cell. The same procedure is then applied to the result action set $[A_{res}]$ to differentiate possible aliasing in $\sigma(t+1)$. If no new alias has been recognized, a new classifier is created if necessary, but no ID fixing is performed. Figure 5 presents the differentiation process. Remembering being in state $A-1$ (A is an alias) the agent compares previously memorized classifiers with the perceived image $A-5-B$. Classifier $A-0(F)-5-B-0(-)$ is similar, but has a different ID of state A. Thus, there are two different states, leading to B through action 1: $A-0$ and $A-1$. Hence, B is an alias. The classifiers $A-0(F)-5-B-0(F)$ and $A-1(F)-5-B-1(F)$ become arrows for the newly discovered alias.

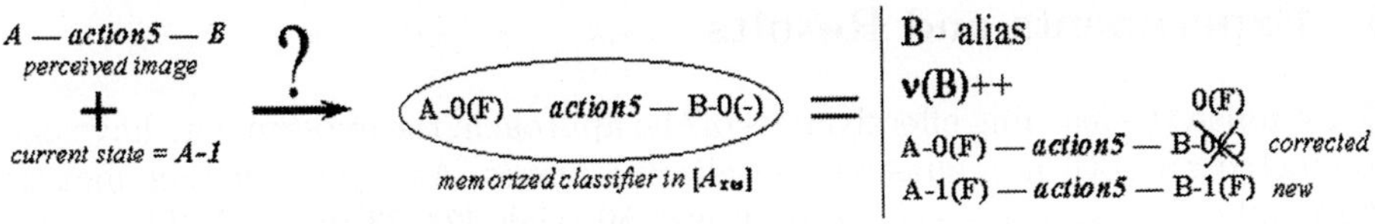

Fig. 5. Differentiation of an aliasing state.

4.3 Associative Correction

The associative correction operator performs according to the sliding image formation principle (Fig.3). If the previous action set $[A^{t-1}]$ contains a single classifier that has a fixed next-state ID, i.e. $cl(A^{t-1}).F_s^{t+1} = true$, the agent is able to recognize ID of the aliasing square precisely. In that case the previous state ID of the classifier in $[A]$ can be corrected and verified: $cl(A).ID_s^t = cl(A^{t-1}).ID_s^{t+1}$; $cl(A).F_s^t = true$. The same procedure may be applied conversely. Thus, the associative correction may be performed both ways, from the previous classifier to the following one and backwards. The scheme allows transferring the knowledge about an aliasing state in the classifier population.

4.4 Reinforcement Learning Process

The Q-reinforcement procedure [21] has been widely used in LCS [24, 23, 13]. Although, the way how Q-coefficients depend on the distance to food d may lead to some disadvantages. Considering that $\lim_{t \to \infty} Q = \gamma^d$, where γ is the discount factor, the expected difference between two successive Q-learning coefficients approaches zero: $\lim_{t,d \to \infty}(\gamma^d - \gamma^{d+1}) = 0$. The influence of some stochastic processes in the agent may lead to the situation when the actual coefficients Q^A may significantly fluctuate around their rated values Q^R, and upon increasing d the actual coefficients for non-optimal actions may become larger than the actual coefficients for the optimal actions: $|Q^R - Q^A| \geq \gamma^{d-1} - \gamma^d$.

Based on the aforesaid, the reinforcement procedure for the research has been modified so that with increasing the distance to food the difference between the learning coefficients remains the same. Thus, instead of Q-learning coefficients the distance-modified learning coefficients K_d are used, such that for any (S^t, a, S^{t+1}) with an expectance to be within d_{exp} steps to food, the d-learning coefficient is $K_d(S^t, a, S^t) = d_{exp}$.

For each performance cycle, when the previous action set $[A^{t-1}]$ contains a single classifier, and S^{t+1} of the classifier represents either a non-aliasing environmental state or has a fixed ID, the d-based reinforcement operator is applied. The new value of the prediction D for the classifier in $[A^{t-1}]$ is equal to the minimal prediction from the current match set $[M]$ increased by 1: $cl(A^{t-1}).D = min(K_d(S_t', a') \forall a) + 1$, where $(S_t', a') \in [M]$.

5 Experiments and Results

To establish the learning effectiveness of the approach, the experiments have been conducted on both non-aliasing and aliasing mazes. As a performance measure the number of average steps to food over 50 trials [24, 23] is used. There is no restriction on populations size, the reported figures are the actual number of classifiers for the mazes. ACS [17] omits all the classifiers for $\sigma(t) = \sigma(t+1)$, thus, we report both, the full population size N, and the number of classifiers with the distinctive initial and resulting states $N_{\neq}$ (ACS style) for comparison purposes. For each maze we list *average* steps-to-food (ϕ_m) and the *alias-expected average* (ϕ'_m) steps-to-food value (optimal performance for an agent with limited perceptive power).

The first tested maze is a non-aliasing maze Woods1 [24], used for verification purposes. The parameters of the maze are $\phi_m = 1.68$, $\phi'_m = 1.68$, with 128 possible state-action-state representations (16 available for the agent squares * 8 directions). According to the results, the system reaches the optimal performance (1.68) after 26 trials on average. AgentP develops a full internal model of the environment with $N = 128$ classifiers, 101 of which are the classifiers with the distinctive initial and resulting states ($N_{\neq} = 101$, compared to $N_{\neq} = 190$ classifiers produced by the ACS with behavioral sequences [13]).

MazeF4 [17] ($\phi_m = 4.3$, $\phi'_m = 4.5$, 80 representations) is an aliasing environment with two aliasing squares, that have a different distance and different directions to food. The system reaches 4.4 step-to-food value after 74 trials on average and develops a full internal model of the environment with $N = 80$ ($N_{\neq} = 25$) classifiers. Similar results were obtain on Maze7 environment, introduced by Lanzi [8] for XCSM. It is worth to mention although, that XCSM was not able to reach the optimum for the maze during the learning, and the final optimal solution was formed almost completely of the classifiers created by the covering operator with genetic algorithms turned off. AgentP reaches the optimal performance for the maze after 84 trials in average.

Woods100 [10] ($\phi_m = 2.0$, $\phi'_m = 2.33$, 48 representations) and Woods101 [12] ($\phi_m = 2.7$, $\phi'_m = 2.9$, 80 representations) are aliasing mazes with two aliasing states each. The aliasing states have different directions, but the same distance to food. The system converges to the performance 2.3 steps for Woods100 and 2.9 steps for Woods101. The classifier population for Woods100 consists of $N = 48$ ($N_{\neq} = 10$) classifiers (compared to the $N_{\neq}$ value up to 60 classifiers produced by the ACS with behavioral sequences [13]) For Woods101 the parameter values are $N = 80$ and $N_{\neq} = 27$ classifiers.

Woods101-1/2 [9] ($\phi_m = 2.8$, $\phi'_m = 3.1$, 160 representations) is an aliasing maze consisting of two non-communicating parts with four aliasing squares in total. All the squares have the same distance, but different directions to food. AgentP reaches the optimal performance near 3.1 after 86 trials with $N = 160, N_{\neq} = 42$ classifiers. Similar results were obtained on Woods102 [4], where the system shows performance 3.3 after 216 trials on average.

The table of performance (Fig. 6) represents the best available to our knowledge results on the mazes for learning agents in every LCS group. Population

Maze \ LCS	ϕ_m / ϕ'_m	ZCSM (N)	XCSM, XC-SMH (N)	ACS ($N_{\neq}$)	AgentP ($N_{\neq}/N$)
Woods100	2 / 2.33	—	—	2.3(60) [13]	2.3(10/48)
Woods101	2.7 / 2.9	5(400) [4] 2.9(400) [1]	3(800) [8] 2.9(800) [9]	—	2.9(27/80)
Woods101 1/2	2.8 / 3.1	—	3.1(2800) [9]	—	3.1(42/160)
Woods102	2.77 / 3.31	9(400) [4]	5(2400) [8] 3.3(6000) [9]	—	3.3(82/208)
MazeF4	4.3 / 4.5	—	—	4.5 [17]	4.4(25/80)
Maze7	4.11 / 4.33	—	10(1600) [8] 4.3(1600) [9]	—	4.3(21/72)

Fig. 6. Table of performance of different LCS agents on the aliasing mazes.

size is shown in parenthesis. Some figures are approximate because the precise average step-to-goal value is not always available from the original paper.

The obtained results should be considered as preliminary and further experiments on different kind of aliasing environments are required to draw final conclusions. Although, the performed tests have demonstrated some advantages of the developed system. First, the system learns faster that the other LCS. For example, AgentP needs 22 trials (440 steps) on average to reach the optimal performance on Woods100, while it takes 2000 steps to reach 100% knowledge for the maze by ACS [13]. Similar comparison can be made for MazeF4 (74 trials on average, while ACS [17] been reported to need more than 500 trials). Next, the system builds the internal model of the environments with a significantly less amount of classifiers compare to the other agents. Also, once reached, the optimal performance level remains stable and the number of classifiers keeps the same. The Fig.7(a) and 7(b) present the summary diagrams for the performance and population size on the mazes (all the curves are averages of 10 runs).

Thus, the system has showed the ability to reach the optimal performance level for the tested environments, achieving the same performance results as the other LCS agents and outperforming them in some learning parameters: speed, computation resources and stability.

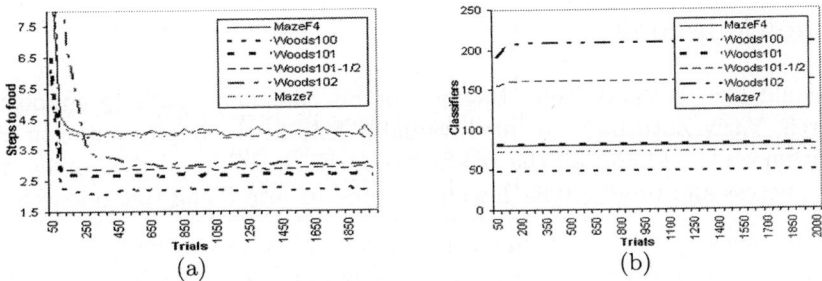

Fig. 7. (a) Average steps-to-food value; (b) Population size.

6 Future Research

Finding AgentP's learning capabilities and limitations by conducting further experiments on different aliasing mazes is the priority task for the research. Other research directions may include:

Generalization. The behavioral phenomenon termed *stimulus generalization* was first described and interpreted by Pavlov [14] and later extensively studied by Skinner [15]. According to their research, an individual that has learnt a certain behaviour, responds in a similar manner to stimuli that are similar to the one on which he was trained. In terms of maze learning, development of a post-learning generalization mechanism would allow the agent to extrapolate the knowledge obtained in a certain environment to other similar environments.

Hierarchical Motivation. In the real-life conditions many different stimuli, frequently confronting, are present. Incorporating into the system a hierarchical motivation mechanism could allow the agent to build its strategy subject to the presence of different motivating objects in the environment and will bring the system closer to the real-life problems.

7 Conclusion

The paper presented a new approach to learning in aliasing environments. The psychological model of associative perception learning and the AgentP system, a Learning Classifier System with associative perception, were introduced. AgentP employs explicitly imprinted images of the environmental states and uses the deterministic IDs system for the differentiation of aliasing squares. To establish the learning effectiveness of the approach, AgentP has been tested on several aliasing maze environments. The system has showed the ability to reach the optimal performance level for the mazes faster and with a smaller population of classifiers than the other LCS systems. Also the system has proved to be able to stably maintain the optimal performance level and to keep the constant population size during the rest of experiment. The obtained evidence allows a conclusion to be drawn that the developed AgentP system shows some reassuring results and is a perspective approach to the aliasing maze problem.

Acknowledgments

We would like to thank Tony Bagnall for his constant efforts to support the research, Yuriy Zatuchnyy for his invaluable help in the implementation of the algorithm on C++, and all the researches in XCS, ACS and ZCS areas whose work, success and productivity have prompted us into doing this research.

References

1. Bull, L., Hurst, J.: ZCS: Theory and Practice. UWELCSG01-001 UWE (2001)
2. Bull, L.: Lookahead And Latent Learning In ZCS. GECC (2002) 897–904
3. Bull, L.: A Simple Accuracy-based Learning Classifier System. UWELCSG03-005 UWE (2003)
4. Cliff, D., Ross, S.: Adding memory to ZCS. Adaptive Behavior **3**(2) (1994) 101-150
5. Hoffman, J.: Vorhersage und Erkenntnis. Gott. Hogr. (1993)
6. Holland, J.H., Reitman, J.S.: Cognitive systems based on adaptive algorithms. PDIS, Water. Hay.-Roth. N.Y. Acad. Pr. (1978)
7. Holland, J.H.: Concerning the Emergence of Tag-Mediated Lookahead in Classifier Systems. **42** Physica D (1990) 188–201
8. Lanzi, P.L.: Solving Problems in Partially Observable Environments with Classifier Systems. 97.45 Politecnico di Milano (1997)
9. Lanzi, P. L., Wilson S. W.: Optimal Classifier System Performance in Non-Markov Environments. 99.36 Politecnico di Milano (1999)
10. Lanzi, P.L.: Adaptive Agents with Reinforcement Learning and Internal Memory. SAB2000 MIT Press (2000) 333–342
11. Lorenz, K.: Der Kumpan in der Umwelt des Vogels. Jour.Ornit. **83** (1935) 137–215
12. McCallum, R. A.: Overcoming Incomplete Perception with Utile Distinction Memory. MLCA (1993)
13. Metivier, M., Lattaud, C.: Anticipatory Classifier System using Behavioral Sequences in Non-Markov Environments. IWLCS (2002)
14. Pavlov, I.P.: Conditioned Reflexes. Lon. Oxf. Un. Pr. (1927)
15. Skinner, B.F.: Science and Human Behavior. N.Y. Macm. (1953)
16. Stolzmann, W.: Latent Learning in Khepera Robots with Anticipatory Classifier Systems. IWLCS (1999) 290–297
17. Stolzmann, W.: An introduction to Anticipatory classifier system. Learning Classifier Systems, From Foundations to Applications. Springer (2000) 175–194
18. Thorndike, E. L.: Animal Intelligence. Hafner, Darien, Conn. (1911)
19. Tomlinson, A., Bull, L.: Corporate Classifier System. PPSN V. (1998) 550–559
20. Tomlinson, A., Bull, L.: A Corporate XCS. Learning Classifier Systems, From Foundations to Applications. Springer (1999) 195–208
21. Watkins, C.J.C.H., Dayan, P.: Q-Learning. Machine learning **8**(3) (1992) 272–292
22. Wertheimer, M.: Laws of organization in perceptual forms. (1938)
23. Wilson. S.W.: Classifier Fitness Based on Accuracy. Ev.Comp.**3**(2) (1995) 149–175
24. Wilson, S.W.: ZCS: A Zeroth Level Classifier System. Ev.Comp. **2**(1) (1994) 1–18
25. Zatuchna, Z.V.: AgentP model: Learning Classifier System with associative perception. CMP-C04-03 UEA (2004)

Author Index

Abbass, Hussein A.   712
Ahn, Byung-Ha   430
Aickelin, Uwe   581
Akama, Kiyoshi   322
Alves, Roberto T.   1011
Aoki, Takafumi   342
Asselin-Miller, Chris   732
Auger, Anne   182
Aupetit-Bélaidouni, Mériéma   101

Bacardit, Jaume   1021
Bakke, Jorgen W.   682
Banzhaf, Wolfgang   571
Barone, Luigi   862
Bell, Theo   732
Bentley, Peter J.   702
Beyer, Hans-Georg   1
Bianchi, Leonora   450
Birattari, Mauro   450
Boonlong, Kittipong   772
Borenstein, Yossi   11
Bosman, Peter A.N.   192
Branke, Jürgen   202, 722
Briest, Patrick   21, 31
Brockhoff, Dimo   21, 31
Bull, Larry   942, 1032, 1042, 1163
Butz, Martin V.   1021, 1051

Canright, Geoff   491
Cantú-Paz, Erik   272
Carse, Brian   1103
Castillo-Valdivieso, Pedro   602
Chaiyaratana, Nachol   772
Chang, Chun-Fan   511
Chen, Min-You   762
Chiang, Leo   522
Chiarandini, Marco   450
Cho, Dong-Yeon   212
Cho, Sung-Bae   440
Chu, Dominique   222
Chuang, Han-Yu   511
Claridge, Ela   902
Clarkson, John   732
Cordón, Oscar   471
Corne, David   430

Cotta, Carlos   481, 612

Damas, Sergio   471
Darabos, Christian   672
Deb, Kalyanmoy   722
Degener, Bastian   21, 31
Delgado, Myriam R.   1011
de Jong, Edwin D.   192, 232, 843, 872
De Jong, Kenneth   420
delaOssa, Luis   242
D'Eleuterio, Gabriele M.T.   991
Deutsch, Andreas   491
Di Caro, Gianni   461
Dierolf, Henning   722
Dorigo, Marco   852, 1001
Ducatelle, Frederick   461

Eggermont, Jeroen   1071
Eiben, A.E.   41
Enache, Razvan   253
Englert, Matthias   21, 31

Federici, Diego   391
Fernández, Antonio J.   481
Fernández de Vega, Francisco   263, 272, 622
Frayn, Colin   591
Freitas, Alex A.   1011, 1092

Gallagher, Marcus   172
Gambardella, Luca Maria   461
Gámez, José A.   242
Ganguly, Niloy   491
Garrell, Josep M.   1021
Giacobini, Mario   672
Gil, German Galeano   263
Godzik, Nicolas   932
Goldberg, David E.   1021, 1051
Gómez Pulido, Juan Antonio   263
Groß, Roderich   852
Guinot, Christiane   1143
Guisado, Jose Luis   263
Gunia, Christian   21, 31

Handl, Julia   1081
Hansen, Nikolaus   282, 352
Hao, Jin-Kao   652

Hasenjäger, Martina 253
Hasson, Yehudit 501
He, Jun 922
Heering, Oliver 21, 31
Hernández Castro, Julio César 1061
Higuchi, Tatsuo 342
Hingston, Philip 862
Hiroyasu, Tomoyuki 742
Holden, Nicholas 1092
Holley, Julian C. 1103
Homma, Naofumi 342
Hoos, Holger H. 51
Huang, Yu-Cheng 511
Hurst, Jacob 942

Inoue, Hirotaka 1113
Ishibuchi, Hisao 1123
Ishii, Shin 972

Jaeggi, Daniel 732
Jansen, Thomas 21, 31, 61
Jin, Yaochu 792
Jong, Kees 1133
Jordaan, Elsa 522
Joung, Je-Gun 532

Kang, Lishan 922
Kao, Cheng-Yan 511
Katada, Yoshiaki 952
Kavka, Carlos 541
Kern, Stefan 282, 352
Khare, Vineet R. 882
Khosroshahi, Habib G. 591
Kim, DaeEun 551, 962
Kim, Mifa 742
Kimbrough, Steven Orla 292
Kipouros, Timoleon 732
Knowles, Joshua 1081
Kok, Joost N. 1071
Koller, Gabriele 302
Koopman, Arne 561
Kordon, Arthur 522
Körner, Edgar 662
Kosters, Walter A. 1071
Koumoutsakos, Petros 352
Kukkonen, Saku 752
Künzli, Simon 832
Kuo, P. Dwight 571

Labib, Richard 803

Labroche, Nicolas 1143
Lampinen, Jouni 752
Lanzi, Pier Luca 1051
La Poutré, J.A. 692
Lasarczyk, Christian 91
Lecarpentier, Benoît 803
Leier, André 571
Leifhelm, Michael 21, 31
Li, Jin 591
Li, Jingpeng 581
Linkens, Derek Arthur 762
Liu, Jian-Qin 312
Liu, Juan 1153
Liu, Minzhong 922
Llorà, Xavier 1021, 1051
Lopes, Heitor S. 1011
López, J.I. 272
Lu, Ming 292
Luke, Sean 892
Luque del Arco-Calderón, Cristóbal 1061
Lutton, Evelyne 622

Mahfouf, Mahdi 762
Maneeratana, Kuntinee 772
Manfrin, Max 450
Manzano, T. 272
Marchiori, Elena 41, 1133
Mastrolilli, Monaldo 450
McCall, John 633
Merelo-Guervós, Juan Julián 602
Meyer-Nieberg, Silja 1
Miki, Mitsunori 742
Moey, Cheah C.J. 72
Mori, Takeshi 972
Munetomo, Masaharu 322
Murao, Naoya 322
Muruzábal, Jorge 612

Nagata, Yuichi 332
Nakamura, Yutaka 972
Namba, Satoshi 1123
Narihisa, Hiroyuki 1113
Natsui, Masanori 342
Neumann, Frank 81
Ni, Bin 1153

Ocenasek, Jiri 352
Oduguwa, Victor 782
Oh, Sok June 532
Ohkura, Kazuhiro 952
Okabe, Tatsuya 792

Olague, Gustavo 622
Olhofer, Markus 253, 792
Osswald, Matthias 722

Panait, Liviu 892
Pani, Danilo 362
Paquete, Luis 450
Parks, Geoff 732
Pérez, Cynthia B. 622
Petrovski, Andrei 633
Pipe, Anthony G. 1103
Plociennik, Kai 21, 31
Poli, Riccardo 11, 382
Pošík, Petr 372
Preuss, Mike 91
Price, Richard 982
Puchinger, Jakob 642
Puerta, José M. 242
Pujol, Joao C. F. 382

Raffo, Luigi 362
Raidl, Günther R. 302, 642
Ratle, Frédéric 803
Raychaudhury, Somak 591
Reeves, Colin R. 101
Richter, Hendrik 111
Riddle, Patricia 121
Roberts, Mark E. 902
Rodriguez-Tello, Eduardo 652
Roggen, Daniel 391, 561
Röglin, Heiko 21, 31
Rossi-Doria, Olivia 450
Rowe, Jonathan E. 72, 222
Roy, Rajkumar 782
Rudenko, Olga 812
Runarsson, Thomas Philip 401

Santamaría, José 471
Sarma, Jayshree 912
Schiavinotto, Tommaso 450
Schmidt, Christian 202
Schneider, Georg 662
Schoenauer, Marc 182, 541, 812, 932
Schweer, Andrea 21, 31
Sebag, Michèle 932, 1133
Sekaj, Ivan 411
Sekanina, Lukas 682
Sendhoff, Bernhard 253, 662, 792, 882
Shimohara, Katsunori 312
Sipper, Moshe 501
Skinner, Cameron 121
Skolicki, Zbigniew 420

Smith, Matthew G. 1163
Smits, Guido 522
Smyth, Kevin 51
Soak, Sang-Moon 430
Stützle, Thomas 51
Sudha, Bhavani 633
Sudholt, Dirk 21, 31

Tannenbaum, Stefan 21, 31
Thangavelautham, Jekanthan 991
Thierens, Dirk 141, 232
't Hoen, Pieter J. 872
Ting, Chuan-Kang 131
Tiwari, Ashutosh 782
Tiňo, Peter 982
Tomassini, Marco 672
Torresen, Jim 682
Torres-Jimenez, Jose 652
Trianni, Vito 1001
Trochu, François 803
Tsai, Huai-Kuang 511
Tuci, Elio 1001
Tyni, Tapio 822

Ueda, Kanji 952
Urquhart, Neil B. 151

Valkó, V.A. 41
van Dijk, Steven 141
Vanhaecke, Nicolas 182
van Hemert, Jano I. 151, 692
Venturini, Gilles 1143
Viñuela, Pedro Isasi 1061

Watanabe, Shinya 742
Watson, Richard A. 161, 232
Wegener, Ingo 21, 31
Wersing, Heiko 662
Wiegand, R. Paul 61, 892, 912
Wloch, Krzysztof 702
Wood, David Harlan 292

Yao, Xin 591, 882
Ylinen, Jari 822
Yoo, Si-Ho 440
Yuan, Bo 172

Zatuchna, Zhanna V. 1172
Zhang, Byoung-Tak 212, 532
Zitzler, Eckart 832
Zou, Xiufen 922

Lecture Notes in Computer Science

For information about Vols. 1–3130

please contact your bookseller or Springer

Vol. 3263: M. Weske, P. Liggesmeyer (Eds.), Object-Oriented and Internet-Based Technologies. XII, 239 pages. 2004.

Vol. 3260: I. Niemegeers, S.H. de Groot (Eds.), Personal Wireless Communications. XIV, 478 pages. 2004.

Vol. 3258: M. Wallace (Ed.), Principles and Practice of Constraint Programming – CP 2004. XVII, 822 pages. 2004.

Vol. 3256: H. Ehrig, G. Engels, F. Parisi-Presicce (Eds.), Graph Transformations. XII, 451 pages. 2004.

Vol. 3255: A. Benczúr, J. Demetrovics, G. Gottlob (Eds.), Advances in Databases and Information Systems. XI, 423 pages. 2004.

Vol. 3254: E. Macii, V. Paliouras, O. Koufopavlou (Eds.), Integrated Circuit and System Design. XVI, 910 pages. 2004.

Vol. 3253: Y. Lakhnech, S. Yovine (Eds.), Formal Techniques in Timed, Real-Time, and Fault-Tolerant Systems. X, 397 pages. 2004.

Vol. 3250: L.-J. (LJ) Zhang, M. Jeckle (Eds.), Web Services. X, 300 pages. 2004.

Vol. 3249: B. Buchberger, J.A. Campbell (Eds.), Artificial Intelligence and Symbolic Computation. X, 285 pages. 2004. (Subseries LNAI).

Vol. 3246: A. Apostolico, M. Melucci (Eds.), String Processing and Information Retrieval. XIV, 316 pages. 2004.

Vol. 3242: X. Yao, E. Burke, J.A. Lozano, J. Smith, J.J. Merelo-Guervós, J.A. Bullinaria, J. Rowe, P. Tiňo, A. Kabán, H.-P. Schwefel (Eds.), Parallel Problem Solving from Nature - PPSN VIII. XX, 1185 pages. 2004.

Vol. 3241: D. Kranzlmüller, P. Kacsuk, J.J. Dongarra (Eds.), Recent Advances in Parallel Virtual Machine and Message Passing Interface. XIII, 452 pages. 2004.

Vol. 3240: I. Jonassen, J. Kim (Eds.), Algorithms in Bioinformatics. IX, 476 pages. 2004. (Subseries LNBI).

Vol. 3239: G. Nicosia, V. Cutello, P.J. Bentley, J. Timmis (Eds.), Artificial Immune Systems. XII, 444 pages. 2004.

Vol. 3238: S. Biundo, T. Frühwirth, G. Palm (Eds.), KI 2004: Advances in Artificial Intelligence. XI, 467 pages. 2004. (Subseries LNAI).

Vol. 3232: R. Heery, L. Lyon (Eds.), Research and Advanced Technology for Digital Libraries. XV, 528 pages. 2004.

Vol. 3229: J.J. Alferes, J. Leite (Eds.), Logics in Artificial Intelligence. XIV, 744 pages. 2004. (Subseries LNAI).

Vol. 3224: E. Jonsson, A. Valdes, M. Almgren (Eds.), Recent Advances in Intrusion Detection. XII, 315 pages. 2004.

Vol. 3223: K. Slind, A. Bunker, G. Gopalakrishnan (Eds.), Theorem Proving in Higher Order Logics. VIII, 337 pages. 2004.

Vol. 3221: S. Albers, T. Radzik (Eds.), Algorithms – ESA 2004. XVIII, 836 pages. 2004.

Vol. 3220: J.C. Lester, R.M. Vicari, F. Paraguaçu (Eds.), Intelligent Tutoring Systems. XXI, 920 pages. 2004.

Vol. 3217: C. Barillot, D.R. Haynor, P. Hellier (Eds.), Medical Image Computing and Computer-Assisted Intervention – MICCAI 2004. XXXVIII, 1114 pages. 2004.

Vol. 3216: C. Barillot, D.R. Haynor, P. Hellier (Eds.), Medical Image Computing and Computer-Assisted Intervention – MICCAI 2004. XXXVIII, 930 pages. 2004.

Vol. 3210: J. Marcinkowski, A. Tarlecki (Eds.), Computer Science Logic. XI, 520 pages. 2004.

Vol. 3208: H.J. Ohlbach, S. Schaffert (Eds.), Principles and Practice of Semantic Web Reasoning. VII, 165 pages. 2004.

Vol. 3207: L.T. Yang, M. Guo, G.R. Gao, N.K. Jha (Eds.), Embedded and Ubiquitous Computing. XX, 1116 pages. 2004.

Vol. 3206: P. Sojka, I. Kopecek, K. Pala (Eds.), Text, Speech and Dialogue. XIII, 667 pages. 2004. (Subseries LNAI).

Vol. 3205: N. Davies, E. Mynatt, I. Siio (Eds.), UbiComp 2004: Ubiquitous Computing. XVI, 452 pages. 2004.

Vol. 3203: J. Becker, M. Platzner, S. Vernalde (Eds.), Field Programmable Logic and Application. XXX, 1198 pages. 2004.

Vol. 3202: J.-F. Boulicaut, F. Esposito, F. Giannotti, D. Pedreschi (Eds.), Knowledge Discovery in Databases: PKDD 2004. XIX, 560 pages. 2004. (Subseries LNAI).

Vol. 3201: J.-F. Boulicaut, F. Esposito, F. Giannotti, D. Pedreschi (Eds.), Machine Learning: ECML 2004. XVIII, 580 pages. 2004. (Subseries LNAI).

Vol. 3199: H. Schepers (Ed.), Software and Compilers for Embedded Systems. X, 259 pages. 2004.

Vol. 3198: G.-J. de Vreede, L.A. Guerrero, G. Marín Raventós (Eds.), Groupware: Design, Implementation and Use. XI, 378 pages. 2004.

Vol. 3194: R. Camacho, R. King, A. Srinivasan (Eds.), Inductive Logic Programming. XI, 361 pages. 2004. (Subseries LNAI).

Vol. 3193: P. Samarati, P. Ryan, D. Gollmann, R. Molva (Eds.), Computer Security – ESORICS 2004. X, 457 pages. 2004.

Vol. 3192: C. Bussler, D. Fensel (Eds.), Artificial Intelligence: Methodology, Systems, and Applications. XIII, 522 pages. 2004. (Subseries LNAI).

...o (Ed.), Cooperative Design, Visualiza-
...eering. IX, 248 pages. 2004.

...C. Yew, J. Xue (Eds.), Advances in Computer
...hitecture. XVII, 598 pages. 2004.

...Z. Bellahsène, T. Milo, M. Rys, D. Suciu, R.
...ds.), Database and XML Technologies. X, 235
...04.

...85: M. Bernardo, F. Corradini (Eds.), Formal Meth-
...r the Design of Real-Time Systems. VII, 295 pages.

Vol. 3184: S. Katsikas, J. Lopez, G. Pernul (Eds.), Trust
...d Privacy in Digital Business. XI, 299 pages. 2004.

Vol. 3183: R. Traunmüller (Ed.), Electronic Government. XIX, 583 pages. 2004.

Vol. 3182: K. Bauknecht, M. Bichler, B. Pröll (Eds.), E-Commerce and Web Technologies. XI, 370 pages. 2004.

Vol. 3181: Y. Kambayashi, M. Mohania, W. Wöß (Eds.), Data Warehousing and Knowledge Discovery. XIV, 412 pages. 2004.

Vol. 3180: F. Galindo, M. Takizawa, R. Traunmüller (Eds.), Database and Expert Systems Applications. XXI, 972 pages. 2004.

Vol. 3179: F.J. Perales, B.A. Draper (Eds.), Articulated Motion and Deformable Objects. XI, 270 pages. 2004.

Vol. 3178: W. Jonker, M. Petkovic (Eds.), Secure Data Management. VIII, 219 pages. 2004.

Vol. 3177: Z.R. Yang, H. Yin, R. Everson (Eds.), Intelligent Data Engineering and Automated Learning – IDEAL 2004. XVIII, 852 pages. 2004.

Vol. 3176: O. Bousquet, U. von Luxburg, G. Rätsch (Eds.), Advanced Lectures on Machine Learning. IX, 241 pages. 2004. (Subseries LNAI).

Vol. 3175: C.E. Rasmussen, H.H. Bülthoff, B. Schölkopf, M.A. Giese (Eds.), Pattern Recognition. XVIII, 581 pages. 2004.

Vol. 3174: F. Yin, J. Wang, C. Guo (Eds.), Advances in Neural Networks - ISNN 2004. XXXV, 1021 pages. 2004.

Vol. 3173: F. Yin, J. Wang, C. Guo (Eds.), Advances in Neural Networks – ISNN 2004. XXXV, 1041 pages. 2004.

Vol. 3172: M. Dorigo, M. Birattari, C. Blum, L. M. Gambardella, F. Mondada, T. Stützle (Eds.), Ant Colony, Optimization and Swarm Intelligence. XII, 434 pages. 2004.

Vol. 3170: P. Gardner, N. Yoshida (Eds.), CONCUR 2004 - Concurrency Theory. XIII, 529 pages. 2004.

Vol. 3166: M. Rauterberg (Ed.), Entertainment Computing – ICEC 2004. XXIII, 617 pages. 2004.

Vol. 3163: S. Marinai, A. Dengel (Eds.), Document Analysis Systems VI. XI, 564 pages. 2004.

Vol. 3162: R. Downey, M. Fellows, F. Dehne (Eds.), Parameterized and Exact Computation. X, 293 pages. 2004.

Vol. 3160: S. Brewster, M. Dunlop (Eds.), Mobile Human-Computer Interaction – MobileHCI 2004. XVII, 541 pages. 2004.

Vol. 3159: U. Visser, Intelligent Information Integration for the Semantic Web. XIV, 150 pages. 2004. (Subseries LNAI).

Vol. 3158: I. Nikolaidis, M. Barbeau, E. Kranakis (Eds.), Ad-Hoc, Mobile, and Wireless Networks. IX, 344 pages. 2004.

Vol. 3157: C. Zhang, H. W. Guesgen, W.K. Yeap (Eds.), PRICAI 2004: Trends in Artificial Intelligence. XX, 1023 pages. 2004. (Subseries LNAI).

Vol. 3156: M. Joye, J.-J. Quisquater (Eds.), Cryptographic Hardware and Embedded Systems - CHES 2004. XIII, 455 pages. 2004.

Vol. 3155: P. Funk, P.A. González Calero (Eds.), Advances in Case-Based Reasoning. XIII, 822 pages. 2004. (Subseries LNAI).

Vol. 3154: R.L. Nord (Ed.), Software Product Lines. XIV, 334 pages. 2004.

Vol. 3153: J. Fiala, V. Koubek, J. Kratochvíl (Eds.), Mathematical Foundations of Computer Science 2004. XIV, 902 pages. 2004.

Vol. 3152: M. Franklin (Ed.), Advances in Cryptology – CRYPTO 2004. XI, 579 pages. 2004.

Vol. 3150: G.-Z. Yang, T. Jiang (Eds.), Medical Imaging and Augmented Reality. XII, 378 pages. 2004.

Vol. 3149: M. Danelutto, M. Vanneschi, D. Laforenza (Eds.), Euro-Par 2004 Parallel Processing. XXXIV, 1081 pages. 2004.

Vol. 3148: R. Giacobazzi (Ed.), Static Analysis. XI, 393 pages. 2004.

Vol. 3147: H. Ehrig, W. Damm, J. Desel, M. Große-Rhode, W. Reif, E. Schnieder, E. Westkämper (Eds.), Integration of Software Specification Techniques for Applications in Engineering. X, 628 pages. 2004.

Vol. 3146: P. Érdi, A. Esposito, M. Marinaro, S. Scarpetta (Eds.), Computational Neuroscience: Cortical Dynamics. XI, 161 pages. 2004.

Vol. 3144: M. Papatriantafilou, P. Hunel (Eds.), Principles of Distributed Systems. XI, 246 pages. 2004.

Vol. 3143: W. Liu, Y. Shi, Q. Li (Eds.), Advances in Web-Based Learning – ICWL 2004. XIV, 459 pages. 2004.

Vol. 3142: J. Diaz, J. Karhumäki, A. Lepistö, D. Sannella (Eds.), Automata, Languages and Programming. XIX, 1253 pages. 2004.

Vol. 3140: N. Koch, P. Fraternali, M. Wirsing (Eds.), Web Engineering. XXI, 623 pages. 2004.

Vol. 3139: F. Iida, R. Pfeifer, L. Steels, Y. Kuniyoshi (Eds.), Embodied Artificial Intelligence. IX, 331 pages. 2004. (Subseries LNAI).

Vol. 3138: A. Fred, T. Caelli, R.P.W. Duin, A. Campilho, D.d. Ridder (Eds.), Structural, Syntactic, and Statistical Pattern Recognition. XXII, 1168 pages. 2004.

Vol. 3137: P. De Bra, W. Nejdl (Eds.), Adaptive Hypermedia and Adaptive Web-Based Systems. XIV, 442 pages. 2004.

Vol. 3136: F. Meziane, E. Métais (Eds.), Natural Language Processing and Information Systems. XII, 436 pages. 2004.

Vol. 3134: C. Zannier, H. Erdogmus, L. Lindstrom (Eds.), Extreme Programming and Agile Methods - XP/Agile Universe 2004. XIV, 233 pages. 2004.